Speer Handloading Manual #15

Lewiston, Idaho U.S.A.

DISCLAIMER

These loads are for the listed Speer® bullets only. Other bullets may not produce the same pressures and velocities and can create an unsafe condition if used with loads shown here.

While handloading is a safe and enjoyable hobby, Speer has no control over individual loading practices, handloading equipment used, other ammunition components used, or the quality of the firearms in which the resulting ammunition may be used. Accordingly, all handloading activities are at your own risk, and Speer and its affiliates makes no warranty—express or implied—and assumes no liability or responsibility for the use of this load data or instructions herein. The safety information and instruction in this manual is intended only to increase general knowledge of handloading safety practices, and is not intended to be comprehensive or complete. Read and follow all instructions and safety information accompanying your handloading equipment, components and firearm.

Copyright © 2018 Vista Outdoor

All Rights Reserved

ISBN 10 : 1-936120-70-4
ISBN 13 : 978-1-936120-70-3

Speer Bullets
P.O. Box 856
Lewiston, ID 83501

Printed in China

Published by

Blue Book Publications, Inc.
8009 34th Ave. South, Suite 250
Minneapolis, MN 55425

Table Of Contents

Table Of Contents iii
Acknowledgements viii
From The Editor's Desk ix
How To Use The Cartridge Case Drawings xi

Chapter 1
    A Proud Heritage 1

Chapter 2
    A Parting Thought 7

Chapter 3
    Ammunition Basics 11

Chapter 4
    Component Parts Of A Cartridge 17
    Bullets 17
    Cartridge Case 20
    Primers 24
    Propellant 27
    Propellant Relative Burn Rate Chart - Shotshell And Pistol Powders 29
    Propellant Relative Burn Rate Chart - Rifle Powders 30
    Primer Reference Chart 31

Chapter 5
    Handloading Safety: Basic Safety Practices And Procedures 33

Chapter 6
    Guide To Handloading Rifle Cartridges 45

Chapter 7
    Fine-Tuning 67

Chapter 8
    Automating The Loading Process 75

Chapter 9
    When All Else Fails: Troubleshooting Techniques 81

Chapter 10
    Our Youth: The Future Of Our Shooting And Hunting Heritage 91

Chapter 11
    Increasing Hit Probability 95

Introduction To Rifle Data 99
Rifle Data
    204 Ruger 102
    22 Hornet 105

Rifle Data, Cont.

- 218 Bee 111
- 222 Remington 114
- 223 Remington 123
- 5.56mm NATO 137
- 222 Remington Magnum 145
- 225 Winchester 153
- 22-250 Remington 158
- 220 Swift 168
- 223 Winchester Super Short Magnum 178
- 6mm PPC 183
- 6mm Creedmoor 187
- 243 Winchester 191
- 6mm Remington 198
- 243 Winchester Super Short Magnum 205
- 240 Weatherby Magnum 211
- 25-20 Winchester 215
- 250 Savage 218
- 257 Roberts +P 223
- 25-06 Remington 228
- 25 Winchester Super Short Magnum 233
- 257 Weatherby Magnum 238
- 6.5 Grendel 243
- 260 Remington 249
- 6.5 Creedmoor 253
- 6.5x55 Swedish 259
- 6.5x55 Swedish (Military Actions) 262
- 6.5x55 Swedish (Strong Commercial Actions) 264
- 6.5 Remington Magnum 266
- 264 Winchester Magnum 269
- 6.8mm Remington SPC 272
- 270 Winchester Short Magnum 279
- 270 Winchester 284
- 270 Weatherby Magnum 290
- 7-30 Waters 296
- 7mm-08 Remington 301
- 7mm Mauser (7x57) 308
- 280 Remington 316
- 284 Winchester 324
- 7mm Remington Short Action Ultra Magnum 331

Rifle Data, Cont.

Cartridge	Page
7mm Winchester Short Magnum	337
7mm Remington Magnum	343
7mm Weatherby Magnum	350
7mm Shooting Times Westerner	357
7mm Remington Ultra Magnum	363
30 Carbine	368
30-30 Winchester	372
300 AAC Blackout	379
300 Savage	388
300 Ruger Compact Magnum	398
308 Winchester	405
30-40 Krag	420
30-06 Springfield	428
300 Remington Short Action Ultra Magnum	440
300 Winchester Short Magnum	446
300 Holland & Holland Magnum	452
308 Norma Magnum	461
300 Winchester Magnum	469
300 Weatherby Magnum	480
300 Remington Ultra Magnum	489
30-378 Weatherby Magnum	497
7.62x39	505
303 British	509
32 Winchester Special	513
8mm Mauser	516
325 Winchester Short Magnum	522
8mm Remington Magnum	527
338 Federal	532
338 Ruger Compact Magnum	536
338 Winchester Magnum	542
340 Weatherby Magnum	548
338 Remington Ultra Magnum	554
338 Lapua Magnum	560
357 Magnum (Rifle)	566
35 Remington	570
350 Remington Magnum	575
356 Winchester	581
358 Winchester	586
35 Whelen	592

Rifle Data, Cont.

358 Norma Magnum	598
9.3x62	603
9.3x74R	606
375 Holland & Holland Magnum	609
375 Ruger	615
375 Remington Ultra Magnum	619
378 Weatherby Magnum	624
416 Ruger	628
416 Remington Magnum	631
416 Rigby	635
44 Remington Magnum (Rifle)	638
444 Marlin	643
45-70 Government	647
45-70 Government (Trap-Door Actions)	650
45-70 Government (Lever-Actions)	653
45-70 Government (Strong Actions)	655
450 Marlin	658
458 Winchester Magnum	663
458 Lott	668

Chapter 12
A Reloader's Journey; From Junior Shooter To Champion ... 673

Chapter 13
Speer Handgun Bullets ... 677

Chapter 14
Reloading Handgun Cartridges ... 679

Chapter 15
Speer® Shotshell Capsules ... 693

Chapter 16
Speer® Plastic Training Ammunition Effective, Low-Cost Training ... 697

Introduction To Handgun Data ... 700

Handgun Data

22 Hornet	703
221 Remington Fireball	708
223 Remington	712
25 Automatic	719
7-30 Waters	723
30 Carbine	728

Handgun Data, Cont.

- 30-30 Winchester 732
- 32 Smith & Wesson Long 739
- 32 H&R Magnum 743
- 327 Federal Magnum 746
- 32-20 Winchester (Contender Only) 749
- 380 Automatic 754
- 9mm Luger 759
- 9mm Largo 767
- 357 Sig 772
- 38 Super Automatic +P 776
- 38 Special 783
- 38 Special +P 791
- 357 Magnum 800
- 35 Remington 810
- 9x18 Makarov 815
- 40 Smith & Wesson 819
- 10mm Automatic 825
- 41 Remington Magnum 831
- 44 S&W Special 834
- 44 Remington Magnum 839
- 45 Glock Automatic Pistol 847
- 45 Automatic 853
- 45 Colt 863
- 45 Colt (Ruger & Contender Only) 872
- 454 Casull 876
- 460 S&W Magnum 883
- 480 Ruger 890
- 475 Linebaugh 894
- 50 Action Express 898
- 500 S&W Magnum 903

Reference Material 908
Common Headstamps 918
Glossary 919

Acknowledgements

Along the way, numerous people have provided support in the form of images, specifications, technical data, advice and valuable calendar time. We thank you. This book could not have been done without you.

Jeff Williams – Content and Resource Direction

Anne Beihoffer – Project Management

Dave Imthurn – Point Man; from proofing data to testing rounds

Paul Furrier and Bruce Young – Ballistic Supervision and Analysis

Paul Westlund, Dave Dellapaolera, and Brian Talbert – Ballistic Data Collection, Anoka

Kelly Baldwin – Ballistic Data Collection, Lewiston

Coy Getman and Kent Sakamoto – Technical Proofing and Guidance

Allan Jones, Lane Pearce, and Steve Rodgers – Editorial Composition

Megan Robertson – Data Composition

Matt Schroeder, Penney Rudd, and Michael Albrecht – Graphic Design

Paul Rowe – Model Design

Justin Mortensen, Duane VonBargen, and Cody Barker – Speer Tech Services

Steve Moore and Joel Foley – Speer Development Engineering

Jared Kutney, Larry Head, and Drew Goodlin – Federal Cartridge Development Engineering

Mike Holm, Justin Johnson, Brian Anderson, and Jenna Selchow – Federal Cartridge Creative Direction

Also, the folks at Blue Book Publications, Inc. for all their expertise and support during the publishing process:

S.P. Fjestad – Publisher

Clint Schmidt – Layout and Design

Lisa Beuning – Proofing

From The Editor's Desk

We recognize that you rely on the Speer Handloading Manual to provide safe, tested loading data and information that is accurate and up-to-date. Rest assured that all loading recommendations and data in this manual are based on the industry's most rigorous development process.

Pressure and velocity tests for every load listed are collected in our in-house ballistic laboratory by technicians with decades of experience, using state-of-the-art pressure and velocity equipment. All test data is statistically analyzed for accuracy and conformity with industry standards.

Industry expert and Editor Mike Bussard

In addition, the Speer Handloading Manual must serve as a reference source that explains both the fundamentals and the advanced techniques of handloading, as well as how to choose the right components for your application.

It is precisely for this reason that we have revised the format and content of the 15th Edition of the Speer Handloading Manual with the following goals in mind:

- Present information and data in a clear and focused format that allows you to quickly find what you are looking for.
- We have added many new cartridges, including the popular 204 Ruger, 6.5 Creedmoor, 300 AAC Blackout, 338 Lapua Magnum, and 416 Ruger.
- We have added Safety Data with maximum ranges and cartridge-specific tips and notes.
- We have added information on factory loaded ammunition, bullet weights, and muzzle velocities for comparison purposes.
- The Glossary chapter has been expanded into the most comprehensive in the industry.
- We have added practical advice from industry experts and simplified the ballistic science to be useful for a shooter rather than a hobby mathematician.
- We have refined and updated Historical Notes for each cartridge.
- We have updated load data with hundreds of new load combinations, incorporating new propellants across industry brands.

Our new format presents the technical characteristics of each cartridge in three compact sections organized for quick reference—Cartridge/Bullet Data, Notes, and Handloading Data.

CARTRIDGE DATA
- Nomenclature: related cartridges, origin, status, and governing bodies.
- Cartridge Case Data: specifications, sources, and a detailed drawing.
- Bullet Data: diameter, weights, types, and rifling twist rates.
- Ballistic Data: muzzle velocity of typical factory ammunition, changes with barrel length, and maximum allowable pressures.

NOTES
- Historical Notes: background, purpose, variations.
- Ballistic Notes: ballistics, applications, bullet recommendations.

- Technical Notes: cartridge characteristics.
- Handloading Notes: recommendations, loading techniques.
- Safety Notes: maximum range, unique considerations.

HANDLOADING DATA

- Starting and maximum loads for appropriate Speer bullets.
- Data on new propellants.
- Data on new bullets including Gold Dot® Rifle and TNT Green®.

At this point, I would like to invoke Editor's Prerogative to remind ourselves that we stand on the shoulders of giants who have guided us. These include:

- Vernon Speer (Speer Bullets)
- Ray Speer (Speer Bullets)
- Dick Speer (CCI)
- Fred Huntington (RCBS)
- Charles "Buzz" Huntington (RCBS)
- Charles L. Horn (Federal)
- William B. Horn (Federal)
- Elmer Keith (357 Magnum, 44 Magnum)
- Mike Walker (222 Remington)
- Jim Sullivan (5.56x45mm)
- Dr. Louis Palmisano (22 PPC, 6mm PPC)
- Ferris Pindell (22 PPC, 6mm PPC)
- Warren Page (243 Winchester)
- Jim Carmichel (various cartridges)
- Roy Weatherby (Weatherby guns and ammunition)
- Layne Simpson (7mm STW)
- Messrs. Dornaus and Dixon (10mm Auto)
- Dick Casull (454 Casull)
- Evan Whildin (50 AE)

I am privileged to call each of these my friend and to work with many of them. Without them, the shooting sports would not be what it is today. We owe them a great debt.

I would also like to recognize the contributions that Allan Jones, Elmer Imthurn, Dave Andrews, and Arlen Chaney have made to previous Speer Bullet Reloading Manuals. The present Speer Manual would not be what it is today without them.

We thank you for your interest in and support of Speer Bullets. We hope to continue to earn your business in the future. Meanwhile, please make safety your first priority.

Michael Bussard

October 2017

How To Use
The Cartridge Case Drawings

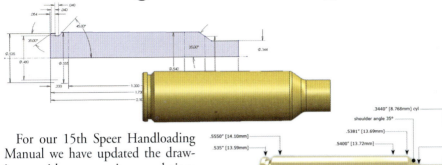

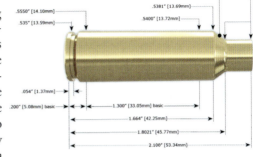

For our 15th Speer Handloading Manual we have updated the drawings with composite renderings that closely represent each cartridge shown. These are printed in true-to-life-size to give you an accurate visual reference. Combined with the dimensions shown, this allows you to compare cartridge cases that you may not have seen firsthand or help size a cartridge or chamber from an old hand-me-down that you may be curious to identify.

Dimensions for most cartridge cases are defined by either the Sporting Arms and Ammunition Manufacturers' Institute (SAAMI) or, in the case of non-U.S. standardization, the Commission Internationale Permanente (CIP) and are labeled to follow their respective conventions. These are generally "maximum cartridge dimensions," meaning they set an upper boundary for component manufacturers to ensure they will always fit in a firearm with minimum chamber dimensions.

Most cartridge cases are designed with some taper from head to mouth to aid extraction. Consequently, for a diameter to be meaningful, you must also define a datum and a distance from that datum to measure the diameter. When you see the term "basic" on these dimensions, this is the intent.

Also, if you reload the same case a few times, it is common to have it 'grow' in length to greater than the permissible "maximum case length" as the sidewalls stretch and become thinner. Semi-automatic or full-automatic fired cases can grow substantially on the first firing. This information allows you to verify the case length prior to loading and 'reset', if needed, by trimming the mouth back into specification.

Cartridge Case Drawing Copyright Information
© 2017 Vista Outdoor Operations LLC

All cartridge case drawings contained in this book are the intellectual property of Vista Outdoor. All rights are reserved. Reproduction of these images by any means without express written permission of Vista Outdoor is prohibited. The sole exception is the portrayal of book pages for journalistic review purposes.

CHAPTER 1

A PROUD HERITAGE

Vista Outdoor offers products from five premier manufacturers of reloading components and equipment: Speer®, CCI®, Federal Premium®, RCBS® and Alliant Powder®. Each of these brands earned its reputation by making a long-term commitment to develop, manufacture, and sell only the finest components and equipment. The employees behind each of these brands are passionate about the shooting sports, listen to their customers, and introduce products based on that interaction. Their success can be measured by the fact that, collectively, they have accumulated more than 435 years of experience in the reloading business!

WORLD CLASS COMPONENT BULLETS AND AMMUNITION

Things were not good for shooters in the early 1940s. With the advent of World War II, copper became a strategic metal reserved for production of military ammunition. Production and sales of sporting centerfire rifle and handgun ammunition was suspended for the duration. This included reloading components, which quickly became scarce.

Vernon Speer was an avid shooter and reloader and recognized the growing shortage of jacketed bullets for reloading. Demonstrating his inventiveness, Vernon devised an ingenious solution to the problem. He designed and built a machine to iron out the rims of spent 22 rimfire cartridge cases so they could be used as jackets for 22 caliber rifle bullets. The supply of raw materials was no longer a problem. Shooting ranges were covered with spent 22 rimfire cartridge cases.

In 1944, Speer moved to Lewiston, Idaho where he set up his bullet-making operation in the basement of a grocery store. His business prospered and the Speer Bullet Company was born.

Copper and gilding metal for bullet jackets became available again following World War II, allowing Speer to expand his product line. In 1952, Vernon's son, Ray Speer, joined the company and took on the sales and marketing functions. This left Vernon more time to develop new products. These included the line of Speer Hot-Cor® rifle bullets still in production today. In the 1970s, Speer Bullets pioneered the development of high-performance jacketed handgun bullets.

Speer Bullets, Inc. remained a family-owned and operated business until 1975 when it was sold to Omark Industries. Today, Speer Bullets is a member of Vista Outdoor, a leading provider of innovative outdoor products, including several top brands in the shooting sports market.

CCI

WORLD LEADER IN COMPONENT PRIMERS AND RIMFIRE AMMUNITION

Dick Speer shared a talent for things technical with his older brother Vernon. When Dick saw there was a niche in the marketplace for cartridge cases in hard-to-find calibers, Dick quit his job at Boeing and moved to Lewiston, where he set up his cartridge-case production in the Speer Bullet plant.

However, it soon became clear that production of centerfire cartridge cases could not support a successful business.

With ammunition manufacturers reluctant to provide component primers for reloading, Dick identified another attractive market niche. Speer did not have primer chemistry technology, so Dick hired Dr. Victor Jasaitis in 1951 to develop the chemistry needed for non-corrosive, Boxer primers.

Primer production operations quickly outgrew available space at the Speer Bullets plant, so Dick built a dedicated, new facility on Snake River Avenue in Lewiston. Initial production focused on centerfire rifle and handgun primers. In 1957, the 209 shotshell primer was added. In 1963, rimfire ammunition manufacturing began.

To avoid consumer confusion with Speer Bullets, Dick changed the name of his company to Cascade Cartridge, Inc., a title that became abbreviated as CCI®. In 1967, Dick sold CCI to Omark Industries. Under Omark ownership, growth continued.

In 1980, CCI introduced Blazer® handgun ammunition with an industry first aluminum alloy cartridge case. Primer production moved into a new, state-of-the-art production facility in 1991. The following year, CCI become the first domestic ammunition manufacturer to receive the ISO 9001 certification for its quality control systems.

CCI's success in the shooting sports marketplace has continued to grow. Today, CCI is a core brand of Vista Outdoor.

PREMIUM QUALITY BRASS AND COMPONENT PRIMERS

In 1916, Harry and Lewis Sherman incorporated the Federal Cartridge and Machine Company in Anoka, Minnesota to make shotshells. The following year, the company was reorganized as the Federal Cartridge Corporation and the first orders of loaded shotshells were shipped. However, the company did not prosper, and the factory ceased production.

In 1922, Charles L. Horn, an entrepreneur from Minneapolis, took over the leadership of the company. Horn developed a new distribution system based on non-traditional outlets such as grocery stores, hardware stores, filling stations and even barbershops. The strategy worked so well that Federal introduced 22 rimfire ammunition and air rifle shot (BBs) in 1924.

The Depression years of the 1930s were difficult times for ammunition manufacturers, and Federal was no exception. Federal survived thanks to Horn's creative distribution system and sales to "private label" accounts such as Sears, Roebuck & Co., Montgomery Wards and Western Auto. Production capacity at Federal was increased by purchasing the equipment from small, bankrupt ammunition makers.

In late 1941, the U.S. Government awarded Federal an $87-million contract to build and operate the new Twin Cities Army Ammunition Plant in nearby New Brighton, Minnesota. By August 1942, the new plant employed 25,000 people working in three shifts who made tens of millions of rounds of 30 and 50 caliber ammunition during World War II, the Korean Conflict and Vietnam.

In 1951, Federal began manufacturing centerfire rifle and pistol primers for reloading. Federal entered the centerfire sporting ammunition market in 1963.

William B. Horn (Charles' son) joined Federal in 1965. He began a series of marketing and advertising programs to build Federal's brand recognition and market share. When the private label market declined in the early 1970s, Federal developed the Premium® line of ammunition for distribution through classic firearm wholesalers.

On December 31, 1977, Charles Horn retired. He passed away in June, 1978. In 1985, Federal was acquired by a group of investors and members of the Federal management team. Three years later, the company was sold to Pentair, Inc. and in 1997 to Blount International who already held CCI and Speer. In 2001 these brands and others in Blount's "Sporting Equipment Group" were sold to Alliant Techsystems Inc. (ATK). In 2015, Federal became a leading brand in the Vista Outdoor portfolio.

THE FINEST RELOADING EQUIPMENT IN THE WORLD

In 1943, wartime priorities for the production of military ammunition meant that component bullets for reloading were no longer available. Fred Huntington, an avid hunter of Western rock chucks, would not be thwarted. Using scrap steel automobile axles, he designed and made a set of dies to swage lead rifle bullets.

As word spread, and demand for Fred's dies increased, he quickly outgrew his shop in the back of his father's laundry. He soon outgrew his garage as well and built a permanent facility in Oroville, California.

Die sets, a complete line of reloading tools and accessories soon followed. A general purpose "A" model reloading press was introduced in 1949, followed by the massive "A-2" compound leverage press in 1954. These two models established

RCBS's reputation for strength, reliability and quality. The economical "Rock Chucker" (1960s) and "Rock Chucker Supreme" (2003) followed. Both remain cornerstone products of RCBS to this day.

Reloading requires various types of die sets. Fred did not like existing designs of dies, so he "Precisioneered" better ones and put them into production. Next, Fred introduced a service that would earn him the admiration and gratitude of every reloader—he established a custom die service. Consumers with a special reloading problem, or those who wanted to design a wildcat cartridge of their own, could provide the specifications, and the RCBS Custom Die Service built a set of precision dies at a reasonable price.

Many reloaders ask what the acronym RCBS stands for. The answer is: Rock Chuck Bullet Swage. Today, RCBS offers more dies, presses and accessories for reloaders than any other company.

In 1976, Fred sold RCBS to Omark Industries. Today RCBS is an essential brand of Vista Outdoor.

Alliant Powder is the oldest company in the Vista Outdoor brand portfolio. It was organized as the Hercules Powder Co. at the dawn of the smokeless powder age in 1882. As a wholly owned subsidiary, it joined the DuPont business empire. In that era, DuPont and friendly rival Laflin & Rand controlled two-thirds of the propellant and explosives manufacturing industry in the U.S. When DuPont took over rival Laflin & Rand in 1902, the acquisition attracted the attention of government anti-trust officials.

In 1912, DuPont was forced to divest itself of the Hercules Powder Co. which then became an independent company. As part of the divestiture agreement, Hercules Powder Co. was granted the smokeless powder propellant patents formerly owned by Laflin & Rand.

For the next 50 years, the Hercules Powder Co. faced an uphill struggle in the North American propellant market against the entrenched and rival DuPont Powder Co. By the mid-1960s, Hercules powders had become a staple product of handloaders as well as commercial and military ammunition manufacturers such as Federal Cartridge. When Hercules entered the rocket propulsion market, the name was changed to Hercules Aerospace.

In 1996, ATK purchased Hercules Aerospace as part of its growing space and defense portfolio. The reloading powder segment of Hercules was renamed Alliant Powder and moved to Radford, Virginia after the original Hercules plant at Carney's Point in New Jersey was closed.

In 2015, Alliant Powder became another key brand of Vista Outdoor.

In 1967, Omark Industries purchased CCI, followed by Speer in 1975, and RCBS along with other consumer-product companies in the shooting sports market in 1976 to create the Sporting Equipment Group. This group was purchased by Blount International in 1985. However, by 2000, Blount's business focus changed and they decided to sell their Sporting Equipment Group.

In the mid-1990s, ATK expanded into the commercial ammunition business and formed the Security and Sporting Group. ATK purchased Alliant Powder in 1996. In 2001, ATK purchased the entire Sporting Equipment Group from Blount International. The group of five companies formed the foundation of ATK's Security and Sporting Group.

Other acquisitions followed, adding to what became ATK's Sporting Group. In 2008, the repurchase of Weaver Optics; in 2009, the acquisition of Eagle Industries; in 2010, the acquisition of BLACKHAWK!; in 2013, the acquisition of Caliber Company, the parent company of Savage Sports Corporation; and in 2014, the acquisition of Bushnell Group Holdings, Inc.

In 2015, ATK spun-off its Sporting Group to become Vista Outdoor Inc., an independent, publicly traded company.

Vista Outdoor is a leading global designer, manufacturer, and marketer of consumer products in the growing outdoor sports and recreation markets. We serve these markets through our diverse portfolio of well-recognized brands that provide consumers with a range of performance-driven, high-quality and innovative products. These include sporting ammunition and firearms, outdoor products, outdoor cooking solutions, outdoor sports optics, hydration systems, golf rangefinders, performance eyewear, sport protection helmets and goggles, footwear and a variety of cycling accessories, and stand up paddle boards and accessories. We serve a broad range of end consumers, including outdoor enthusiasts, hunters and recreational shooters, professional athletes, as well as law enforcement and military professionals. Vista Outdoor's headquarters are in Farmington, Utah, with facilities in 13 states, Canada, Mexico, Europe, Australia and Asia.

CHAPTER 2

A PARTING THOUGHT
Allan Jones
Ballistics Editor, Shooting Times Magazine
Retired Editor, Speer Reloading Manuals 12, 13, and 14.

I retired as reloading manual editor and developer ten years ago, shortly before my last manual (*Speer Number 14*) went to press. Now I'm back as a guest. In the intervening time I've stayed busy as Ballistics Editor for *Shooting Times* magazine and volunteering in my community.

When Speer asked me to write an article for *Speer Handloading Manual #15*, one idea stood out:

What is the single and most basic thing that will make us better handloaders and shooters?

I found that question in looking back 50 years to my early struggles in reloading metallic ammo. Today I clearly see misinformation and errors that cost me time, components, and frustration.

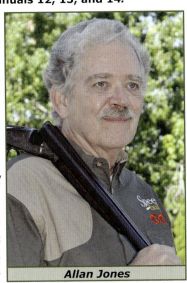

Allan Jones

In 1968 little information on ammo addressed effective accuracy testing. I adopted a published system for testing one propellant under one bullet style/weight based on five-shot groups. The published start load weight was the first test increment. After loading five rounds at that weight, you increased that by one-half to one grain and loaded five more. Reaching the published maximum charge weight was "STOP!"

At the range you were to start with the lowest weight, fire the five rounds into one group, then change point of aim and shoot the next higher weight sample into another group. The tightest group was your "accuracy load."

I used this system for years but today I realize it was a waste of time. The clue I either missed or ignored was a *lack of repeatability*. I could "work up" a load for my rifle that shot well but, a week later, the same rifle and ammo batch could not do it again. This pattern kept repeating with that rifle and others, so it wasn't the rifle.

It took a long time to finally discover my problem. In simple terms it was *sample size*. In more complete terms, I failed to understand and respect *statistics*.

Statistics is often considered a dirty word. Yes, misused, statistics can make almost any position sound practical but rejecting the science is like wanting to ban automobiles because bank robbers drive them. For our purposes, statistics' contribution is its ability to reasonably predict the performance of a larger group of items through testing of a smaller subset.

A major ammunition manufacturer can easily load 1,000,000 cartridges in a shift. It's impossible to test every cartridge for pressure, velocity or accuracy and still have something left to ship. Fortunately standard statistical practices and methods allow Quality Assurance engineers to test a smaller segment and have a very high confidence level that the rest of the ammo will shoot within specified limits. Statistics determine a sample size that is large enough to be representative yet small enough to be cost-effective in lab time and having remaining ammo to ship.

You can do a simple test to experience how sample size predicts a larger truth. Get a coin and something to write on. Make two columns labeled "heads" and "tails" for recording results. Flip the coin in a consistent manner onto a hard surface. Record which side is up.

It is very possible that in the first five flips you could have four "heads" and one "tails." Does that mean that in every case a flip will show "heads" 80 percent of the time? No, you know better; something with only two sides can land either way equally. Add five more flips and look at the results of ten. Usually the ratio will shift toward 50/50. By the time you get to a total of 100 flips your little data set should be close to 50 heads and 50 tails. Why? Sample size was finally sufficient to predict results.

Here the hobbyist handloader faces the same quandary as a major manufacturer. You have to balance how much you test against component costs and how much is left for the hunt. You can't really claim an "accuracy load" after only five shots. Here I can provide tips based on statistics that may guide you.

First find a number. Years ago a PhD statistician at CCI-Speer was asked, "What is the minimum number of rounds from an ammo batch you can fire into a single group and still achieve acceptable confidence in the entire batch's accuracy?" He applied standard methods of his science and came up with seven (7). A seven-shot group was the balance between the number of rounds expended in testing and confidently detecting variations in accuracy. The next best confidence level meant adding a group: two five-shot groups of the same ammo averaged. Unlike a big manufacturer that may shoot millions of rounds a year just in testing, this means the average handloader can get a better picture of the results of his effort with a modest increase in component costs.

Sample size will vary with the amount of difference between groups you need to detect. If you are trying to sort one-inch groups from six-inch groups, shooting one five-shot group of each sample is more than adequate to be confident that any accuracy difference is real. As the difference you wish to detect gets smaller, you need a larger number of groups from each batch. Most of us will be sorting the one-inch groups from the two-inch ones; this is certainly doable without shooting up an entire ammo batch in testing.

A sufficiently large sample assaults one of the sacred cows of handloading—the search for the "most accurate charge weight." If you use the old incremental method I described at the beginning of this article, but shoot a seven- or ten-round sample instead of five, you will start to see the differences between charge weights reduce to the point that I must question the expense of testing so many weight levels.

It is not my goal to make you a degreed statistician. Rather I want you to think *sample size* when you load and test. Whether you need to find if a rifle is accurate or if that last batch of handloads is accurate, sample size needs to be your new best friend.

One more thing—this is something that causes many shooters grief yet they blindly cling to the wrong view. The fact is:

There is a huge difference between determining accuracy and determining point of impact.

People say they only need three rounds for accuracy testing because they've never needed more than three shots to take down a critter. When I hear this my eyes start rolling like the wheels on a slot machine! Accuracy is the ability of a sample set to repeat performance. For shooting it is having bullets land in the same spot.

Point of impact (POI) is the place a group of bullets prints relative to where the firearm's sights are looking. So what if it prints a foot from the point of aim while testing accuracy? Once you shoot enough to know a batch of ammo is accurate, you then adjust the sights to make the point of aim and point of impact coincide.

Adjusting POI can be done with fewer shots if you already know that the ammo batch is accurate. Here, those three-shot groups are useful. I "rough in" the POI with three-shot groups and, as the groups get very close to the desired POI, and the barrel has cooled, I'll shoot one five-shot group to verify.

Yes, effective accuracy testing will use more components than you probably use for testing today. However, the payoff, especially on an expensive big game hunt, can be huge. It seems false economy to make shaky assumptions because you scrimped on accuracy testing; you may ultimately suffer a failure afield as a result.

That is what I want to leave with you. You don't have to change anything if you don't want to. However, the importance of proper testing is something I've grown to embrace over almost 50 years of handloading, and with the help of the amazing technical minds in Engineering and Quality Assurance at CCI and Speer.

CHAPTER 3

AMMUNITION BASICS

Like any new endeavor, before you begin handloading, it is important to learn the basics of centerfire rifle and handgun ammunition. The nomenclature, in particular, can be difficult to grasp as it was developed by varied cultures and across hundreds of years. With a little background study, however, and you can skip the trial and error and take advantage of the vast knowledge of the past. Handloading offers endless possibilities to experiment with different combinations of components and to use your skills in various laboratory and fabrication disciplines. We'll help guide you.

BASIC DEFINITIONS
WHAT IS A CARTRIDGE?

A cartridge is a complete assembly of self-contained ammunition with four primary component parts: case, primer, propellant, and bullet.

When a cartridge is fired, the primer energetics and propellant are consumed in the process of producing hot gases that expand rapidly, accelerating the bullet down the barrel, and leaving the empty cartridge case and primer cup behind.

The terms reloading and handloading, for the most part can be used interchangeably.

RELOADING is the process in which a *fired*, empty, centerfire cartridge case is remanufactured by replacing the primer, propellant charge, and bullet to make a complete round of ammunition that can be fired again. Often the term reloading is also used when describing the repetitive assembly of hundreds of rounds of ammunition using the same components and the same recipe.

HANDLOADING is the process in which a new or previously fired empty cartridge case is loaded with a primer, propellant charge, and bullet to create a complete round of ammunition on a personal scale. The term often encompasses the research and observation needed to improve your product and tailor it to your specific use.

WHY DO SHOOTERS HANDLOAD?

Shooters handload for a variety of reasons, all directly related to their interests in various shooting disciplines and cartridges. As most shooters participate in more than one area, so do they practice their handloading craft for various reasons. These include:

- The personal satisfaction of an instructive, practical and enjoyable hobby with a long, colorful history.
- Economics—Handloading can save money or you can shoot more for the same cost.
- Fine tuning the ammunition to a rifle or handgun for maximum performance.
- Keep a rifle or handgun chambered in a "classic" caliber in service long after factory loaded ammunition is no longer available.
- Experiment with load combinations not offered by ammunition manufacturers.
- Increase the flexibility of rifles and handguns using various combinations of components.
- Keep shooting during times when factory ammunition may be scarce or not available.
- Develop interesting wildcat cartridges.

From the above list, it is obvious that the reasons shooters reload or handload change with the times. For example, when ammunition is scarce, shooters reload to keep shooting. When prices of loaded ammunition increase, the interest in reloading to save money increases.

HANDLOADERS AND FACTORY AMMUNITION

There is an enduring truth in the ammunition business: Ammunition factories can do things that handloaders cannot, and handloaders can do things that ammunition factories cannot. This means that ammunition manufacturers must load their products to suit a broad range of applications. On the other hand, handloaders can load ammunition specifically tailored to a narrow set of requirements, even including a firearm.

SAMPLING HISTORY

The historical aspects of reloading and handloading can be most instructive and enjoyable.

Want to find out what it felt like to shoot the guns of the Old West? You can try on their boots when you load the 44-40 Winchester (yes, the one that "killed more men, good and bad, than any other cartridge in the Old West"), the 45 Colt, the 45-70 Government or the 50-90 Sharps (the "poison slinger") of the buffalo hunters.

Want to go on safari to find out what it is like to fire a large caliber rifle for dangerous game? You can load the classic African calibers such as the 375 H&H Magnum, the 416 Rigby or the 458 Winchester Magnum.

How about honing your long-range marksmanship skills? For that purpose, select the 6.5 Creedmoor, the 300 Winchester Magnum, or the 338 Lapua Magnum.

Maybe you want to find out what it felt like to shoot the military cartridges used in World Wars I or II? Start loading the classic 30 M1 (aka the 30-06 Springfield), the 8x57mm Mauser, or the 6.5x50mm Japanese Arisaka.

THE BOTTOM LINE

Perhaps most important, on a personal level, the satisfaction of an instructive, practical, and enjoyable hobby will always remain the primary reason for handloading.

BASIC NOMENCLATURE OF CENTERFIRE CARTRIDGES

A centerfire cartridge is an assembly of four parts:

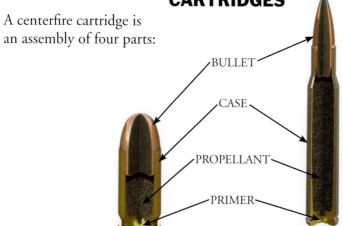

BULLET
CASE
PROPELLANT
PRIMER

Typical Handgun Cartridge   Typical Rifle Cartridge

CARTRIDGE NAMING CONVENTIONS

There are hundreds of different cartridges in a wide variety of sizes, shapes, and applications. Many cartridges are visually similar and use the same diameter of bullet. It can be difficult but is equally important to be able to identify a specific cartridge using other techniques. When available, this is exactly what cartridge naming nomenclature is intended to do. It is beneficial for you to become familiar with these designation systems for reasons of convenience, inspection, and safety.

While various nomenclature schemes for cartridge naming do exist, it is important to point out that there is no legal requirement mandating that a cartridge designer or manufacturer follow any specific system. Many are simply trade names. For this reason, there are many creative cartridge designations that owe their existence to hubris, merchandising, nostalgia, or technology.

There is one constant in all this: each cartridge has a unique name with which to identify it.

CALIBER DEFINED

Cartridge names are broadly based on the concept of "caliber" which is normally expressed in two or more parts:

1. The first part is a number which is the *approximate* bore diameter of the barrel as expressed in English (inches) or metric (millimeters) units of measurement.
2. The second is a name or names indicating the originator, application or purpose which may be followed by a second name denoting the type or nature of a cartridge, for example; Express, Magnum, Short Magnum, Ultra Magnum, or BR (benchrest).

DECIPHERING CARTRIDGE NAMES

There are three common, modern naming conventions: two are associated with industry standards groups in Europe and the U.S. The third are military systems.

The three modern naming conventions are:

- Sporting Arms and Ammunition Manufacturers' Institute (SAAMI)

  The SAAMI convention is used by U.S. ammunition manufacturers. It constitutes a two-part naming system of a two or three digit number indicating the approximate land diameter of the barrel followed by the name, which may be the name(s) of the originator(s). An additional word is sometimes added to indicate the intended purpose. Examples include: 220 Swift, 300 Holland & Holland Magnum, 300 Winchester Short Magnum, 338 Ruger Compact Magnum.

- Commission Internationale Permanente (CIP)

  The CIP cartridge designation system is used by European ammunition makers as well as those in many other countries. It consists of a four-part system beginning with the approximate bore diameter of the barrel expressed by a one, two or three digit number in millimeters, an "x", followed by the cartridge case length in millimeters. Next, a letter indicating the bullet diameter and/or the rim configuration of the cartridge is *sometimes* included. If no letter is used, the cartridge is assumed to be rimless. Last are the name(s) of the originator(s). Examples include: 6x62Rmm Freres, 6.5x50mmSR Japanese, 7x61mm Sharp & Hart Super, 8x57mmJ Mauser, 8x57mmR Mauser, 8x57mmJR Mauser, and 9.3x66mm Sako.

- Military systems (MILSPEC)

  Modern military cartridge designation systems vary from country to country.

That said, most European, North American and many Asian and Middle Eastern countries use the NATO system that employs some parts of the CIP system followed by model numbers and nature designations. Examples include: 5.56x45mm NATO Ball M855A1, 7.62x51mm NATO Ball M80, and 9mm NATO Ball M882. Here it must be pointed out that although some military cartridges appear similar to sporting cartridges, the two are not the same. In some cases, there is compatibility one way but not the other. Similar but not identical cartridge examples include: the 223 Remington and 5.56x45mm NATO. Also, the 308 Winchester and 7.62x51mm NATO.

Two obsolete cartridge naming systems remain in limited use:

- U.S. black powder cartridge designation system

  This system used a three-part cartridge naming system. First was a two digit number indicating the approximate bore diameter of the barrel in inches followed by a two or three digit number indicating the powder charge weight in grains of black powder. Lastly, was the name of the originator. Examples include: 32-40 Ballard, 44-40 Winchester, 45-70 Government, and 45-110 Sharps. This system became obsolete when smokeless powder was introduced in the later 1800s. However, it is still used to designate cartridges from that era that remain in production.

- British cartridge designation system

  The British used a complex three or four-part system to name cartridges of domestic origin. The first entry was a three digit number indicating the parent cartridge. In some cases, a set of two or three digit numbers indicating the approximate bore diameter followed. Next was the name of the originator sometimes followed by one or more words indicating the type of load. Lastly, the cartridge case length in inches was sometimes added.

  Examples include: 30 Super Flanged Holland & Holland, 577/450 Martini-Henry, 475 No. 2 Jeffery 3 ½ inch, 500 Black Powder Express 3 ¼ inch, 500 Nitro Express 3 ¼ inch, 577 Snider and 600 Nitro Express.

BORDERLINE CHAOS

Recently, some European ammunition makers have used the U.S. designation system in English units to describe the caliber of new cartridges. Examples include: 220 Russian, 30R Blaser, 338 Blaser Magnum, 375 Blaser Magnum, 376 Steyr, and 460 Steyr.

On the U.S. side, cartridges with European designations have appeared such as: 6x45mm, 6mm Remington BR, 6.8mm Remington SPC, 7mm Remington Magnum, and the 8mm Remington Magnum. In addition, U.S. ammunition companies now manufacture many European cartridges.

As if that were not enough, Sharps recently revived the old U.S. system of cartridge designation with their new 25-45 Sharps cartridge (although the "45" does not indicate the black powder charge weight but rather the length of the cartridge case in millimeters). Cowboy action shooters have injected new life into near-death calibers such as the 32-20 Winchester, 32-40 Ballard, 38-40 Winchester, and 44-40 Winchester.

In addition, many of the old British calibers have come back to life such as the 450/400 Nitro Express 3 in. and 3 ¼ in., 470 Nitro Express, 500 Nitro Express 3 in. and 3 ¼ in., 416 Rigby and 500 Jeffery.

Then there are the mavericks that fit no designation system at all such as: 7-30 Waters, 7mm-08 Remington, 30-40 Krag and, yes, the 30-06 Springfield (1906 being the year of adoption by the U.S. Army).

Are you confused yet? While all this may seem like borderline chaos, once you get started loading, these cartridges will become familiar and, after a short time, seem like old friends.

HOW TO IDENTIFY AN UNKNOWN CARTRIDGE

Perhaps the easiest way to identify a cartridge is to look at the label on the box they came in. If the box is not available, your next source of information is the headstamp on the base of the cartridge. On most sporting cartridges, the headstamp will indicate the manufacturer and the caliber. Typically, the manufacturer's name is located at the 12 o'clock position and the caliber at the 6 o'clock position. Both the manufacturer and the caliber can be abbreviated due to space limitations. If the vagaries of the various headstamp naming configurations still have you scratching your head, we have included a detailed dimensioned drawing for each cartridge in this book. A micrometer and set of Vernier calipers will help you narrow down and distinguish between some of the subtle variations in geometries.

See a list of common manufacturer's headstamps in the Reference Section at the end of this book.

Streamline analysis illustrating flow and pressure across bullet features

CHAPTER 4

COMPONENT PARTS OF A CARTRIDGE
Speer® Rifle Bullets

In this chapter we will cover the four component parts of a centerfire cartridge, as well as the nomenclature of bullets, primers, cartridge cases, and propellants. These sections include tips on how to select the proper bullet, primer, and the right assembly techniques for your requirements.

BULLETS
WHAT DOES A BULLET DO?

The bullet is the means of converting the stored chemical energy in the primer and propellant into kinetic energy which it then transfers to the target. As the hot, rapidly expanding propellant gases accelerate the bullet down the barrel, the stored chemical energy is converted into kinetic energy in the form of bullet velocity.

When the bullet exits the barrel, it follows a semi-parabolic flight path through the air toward the intended target. During flight the rotation imparted by the rifling in the barrel keeps the bullet in a stable, nose-first attitude. When the bullet strikes the target, the kinetic energy it possesses is transferred to the target as it penetrates.

To get the best performance from their bullet, the handloader should consider configuration, weight, caliber and construction for the intended application. Here we must point out that ammunition manufacturers use bullets designed to perform reasonably well over a wide range of *average* shooting/hunting activities. The ability to select a specific bullet for the exact ballistic requirements needed is a significant advantage for the handloader. However, this can be a daunting task. For example, Speer offers approximately 97 different rifle bullets in all popular calibers. How do you find the ones that fit your needs?

Speer offers three types of bullet:

1. Monolithic lead or other material

    This type of bullet is a popular choice for low cost shooting with revolvers. Speer offers a wide range of this type of bullet including round nose, hollow point, wadcutters and round balls. Speer also offers plastic bullet training ammunition.

2. A two-piece bullet consisting of a jacket of copper or copper/zinc alloy and a lead alloy core.

    This is the most common type of bullet in use today for rifles and pistols. Outstanding examples of this type of bullet include the Speer Hot-Cor®, Gold Dot® and Grand Slam® bullets.

3. A two-piece, lead-free bullet having a copper alloy jacket and a core of compressed copper powder.

    This ultra-modern design is for hunting or shooting in areas where lead bullets may be restricted. Speer TNT Green® bullets are examples of this type.

A typical bullet design consists of four parts that can profoundly influence both in-flight and on-target performance. These are:

1. Meplat (tip)
   - Soft point
   - Hollow point
   - Full metal jacket
   - Polymer/metal tipped
2. Ogive (pronounced "OH-jive", the radius between the meplat and bearing surface)
   - Spitzer (usually a tangent transition)
   - Spire Point (often a secant transition)
   - Combinations (ending in a pointed, rounded, or flat nose shape)
3. Bearing surface (parallel body surface that is engraved by the rifling)
   - Plain
   - With crimping cannelure or friction reducing grooves
4. Base
   - Hollow or concave
   - Flat
   - Boat tail (tapered)

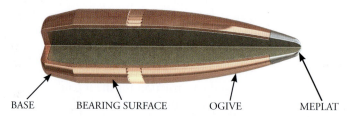

BASE   BEARING SURFACE   OGIVE   MEPLAT

FEATURES OF SPEER RIFLE BULLETS
GOLD DOT® RIFLE

Over twenty years ago, Gold Dot handgun bullets set new standards for critical terminal performance that still stand today. Now Speer brings that well-honed technology to rifle reloading.

Gold Dot Rifle bullets start with an alloyed lead core chosen for the caliber and the game capabilities of that caliber. It is then electroplated with a purified copper. Electroplating is used for many products from kitchen pans to pennies but this process has been highly refined by Speer and the resulting technology creates a true bond with the core and nearly perfect concentricity. These are real jackets, not some thin copper wash. In larger calibers, they are up to .038 inches thick. Consistency is inherent to the process and not subject to traditional machine tolerances. As such, accuracy-robbing jacket runout is virtually eliminated.

The plated core then undergoes a two-stage, ogive-forming operation that creates a cavity with "memory planes" in the lead. These planes uniformly "program" the core for consistent, reliable expansion, high retained bullet weight, and appropriate penetration on impact. The cavity is then reformed to a protected point profile to resist in-magazine damage from recoil.

Most Speer Gold Dot rifle bullets incorporate a boat tail base for a high ballistic coefficient designed to provide higher down-range velocity, increased striking energy, flatter trajectory and less wind drift at all ranges.

Testing in both the laboratory and in the field confirm reliable expansion and consistent core/jacket retention. You will see Gold Dot Rifle data presented here for some of the latest popular chamberings and for many of the multi-sport rifle cartridges.

GRAND SLAM® Soft Point Bullets

A popular choice among experienced hunters, Speer Grand Slam rifle bullets offer the premium features you need for that trophy shot you cannot afford to miss. Grand Slam starts with proven Speer Hot-Cor technology and adds cutting edge features including a precision drawn, copper alloy jacket with a profiled internal taper and flutes to reliably control expansion, retained weight and penetration. Grand Slam is Speer's best large game rifle bullet. Magnum velocities will typically benefit from the additional jacket thickness found in the Grand Slam designs.

HOT-COR® Soft Point Bullets

Speer Hot-Cor bullets have remained a favorite of American hunters for over 65 years now. The Hot-Cor design is unique. It features a precision drawn, copper alloy jacket into which a molten lead alloy is poured after which the bullet is formed and sized. This process eliminates the lubricant layer that is needed when inserting a swaged, preformed core into a jacket. It also eliminates oxide layers and air pockets in the core which can have a detrimental effect on core-jacket adhesion and accuracy. For standard hunting conditions, few bullets can match the consistent ballistic performance of the Speer Hot-Cor design.

Boat Tail Soft Point Bullets

The long, tapered base of Speer boat tail bullets substantially reduce drag. This offers the hunter higher retained velocity, greater striking energy, flatter trajectory, and less wind drift. With such advantages, boat tail bullets are the obvious choice for long range shots.

Target Match Hollow Point Boat Tail Bullets

Perhaps you are not a target shooter, but would like to find out how accurate your rifle is. Or, maybe you <u>are</u> a target shooter. Either way, these match hollow point bullets are held to the tightest tolerances for all types of competitive shooting. The precision jackets, small hollow point cavity, and internal construction of Speer Target Match bullets are designed for enhanced in-flight ballistics, not terminal performance. These bullets are not intended for hunting game.

TNT® Hollow Point Bullets

Varmint bullets must combine "explosive" expansion with accuracy to hit small, fleeting targets. The Speer TNT bullet has been designed specifically for this purpose, with dead-soft lead cores and a precision-drawn jacket with flutes for maximum expansion. Its ultra-thin jacket and large hollow point produce immediate fragmentation on impact. When loaded with care, Speer TNT bullets can produce ½ MOA accuracy in many rifles.

TNT bullets are not designed as a general purpose bullet. Do not use them for hunting large game as they will not reliably penetrate deep enough to engage the vitals.

TNT GREEN® Hollow Point Bullets

In some areas, lead-free hunting bullets are required by law or desirable for environmental compliance. Speer's TNT Green bullet checks all the boxes in this regard. These bullets use the same fluted, highly concentric jackets as their lead-core counterpart but utilize a compressed powdered copper core to maintain sectional density and yet still disintegrate on impact.

TNT Green bullets are not designed for general purpose hunting. Do not use them for hunting large game as they will not reliably penetrate deep enough to engage the vitals.

CARTRIDGE CASE

What is a Cartridge Case?

A cartridge case (often referred to as simply a "case") is the container that holds the bullet, primer, and propellant powder. Most commonly it is made of brass, steel, or aluminum. While there has been much development and some successful use of polymer or hybrid metal/polymer cases, most of these designs cannot be reloaded. For this reason, we have not included reloading data for these in this manual.

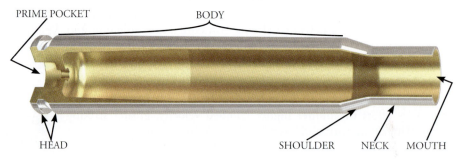

Brass cartridge cases are typically drawn from preformed cups made from an alloy of approximately 70% copper, 30% zinc. To form sporting cartridge cases, the preform cups may be drawn up to four times. In most instances, the preformed cup is designed specifically for a particular caliber of case to reduce waste.

Brass cartridge cases are sometimes coated with nickel to prevent corrosion and aid extraction. Steel cartridge cases must be coated with polymer, lacquer or phosphate to prevent corrosion. Aluminum cartridge cases are often given an anodized finish.

Centerfire rifle and handgun cartridges are made in four basic head configurations:
1. Rimless
   - The rim is approximately the same diameter as the case body.
   - There is an undercut in front of the rim for extraction.
   - Rimless cases typically headspace on the shoulder.
   - Examples include: 223 Remington, 30-06 Springfield, and 416 Rigby.

2. Rimmed
   - The rim diameter is considerably greater than that of the case body.
   - There is no undercut for extraction.
   - Rimmed cases typically headspace on the rim or the case mouth.
   - Examples include: 22 Hornet, 30-30 Winchester, and 45-70 Government.

   Semi-rimmed (A sub-type of Rimmed case)
   - The rim diameter is appreciably greater in diameter than the case body.
   - There is an undercut in front of the rim for extraction.
   - Semi-rimmed cases typically headspace on the rim.
   - Examples include: 6.5x50mm Japanese.

3. Belted
   - There is a conspicuous belt in the case body in front of the rim and approximately the same diameter.
   - There is an undercut for extraction.
   - Belted cases typically headspace on the belt, sometimes the shoulder.
   - Examples include: 300 Weatherby Magnum, 375 Holland & Holland Magnum, and 458 Winchester Magnum.

4. Rebated
   - The rim is conspicuously smaller in diameter than the case body.
   - There is an undercut for extraction.
   - Rebated cartridge cases typically headspace on the shoulder.
   - Examples include: 284 Winchester.

Belted ex: 6.5 Rem. Mag.

Rimless ex: 308 Winchester

Rebated Rim ex: 458 SOCOM

Rimmed ex: 7-30 Waters

HOW DOES A CARTRIDGE CASE WORK?

When a cartridge is fired, the pressure from the hot, expanding propellant gases cause the cartridge case to expand against the chamber walls and the bolt face. This acts as a seal preventing the gas from leaking rearward into the gun's action. As the chamber pressure drops, the cartridge case springs back to near its original dimensions to facilitate extraction. Most types of fired, empty, centerfire cartridge cases can be reloaded.

CCI, Blazer Brass, Speer, and Federal manufacture brass cartridge cases in a number of popular rifle and handgun calibers; some are nickel-plated, all are reloadable. An exception is the Blazer aluminum case handgun ammunition which cannot be reloaded.

WHY ARE SOME BRASS CARTRIDGE CASES NICKEL-PLATED?

The nickel-plating on cartridge cases serves to slightly reduce the friction between it and the chamber sidewall. This is especially helpful in reducing the extraction effort in revolver and long, straight-walled rifle cartridges. The nickel is also quite corrosion resistant; much more so than brass. This helps maintain feed and function ability over time and in exposed environments. Often nickel-plating is applied to create a visual distinction between premium hunting or self-defense ammunition and low-cost or training ammunition.

WHAT IS THE RELOADING LIFE OF BRASS CARTRIDGE CASES?

The reloading life of a cartridge case depends on several factors:

1. The type of gun it is fired in.
   - Most rifle cartridges loaded to moderate pressures and fired in single-shot, or bolt-action rifles can be reloaded ten or more times.
   - Semi-automatic rifles treat cases to a good thrashing. Large dents in case bodies and mouths caused by the violent extraction and ejection forces are common which increases the number of unserviceable cases substantially. In addition, the case heads become "bloated" making it necessary to use plenty of lubrication and small-base dies to resize them followed by a major cleaning job before they can be reloaded. Sometimes, cases fired in semi-automatic rifles are coated with soot and grit from unburned propellant. Cartridge cases subjected to such abuse do not last long—often for three or four reloads.

2. The chamber pressure of the load used.
   - Reloading life of rifle cases is normally extended if moderate pressure loads are used and reduced if high pressure loads are used.
   - Modest-pressure cartridges like 7mm Mauser can often be reloaded 10 or more times.
   - High-pressure +P, Express or Magnum cartridges normally give fewer loadings.

3. The reloading procedure used.
   - A reloading technique that improves case life is to neck size only. A disadvantage of this procedure is that the so-called "fire-formed" case must now be used in the same bolt-action chamber it was previously fired in. This may be a way for you to extend case life at the range, but we recommend full length resizing for in-field applications due to enhanced feed reliability and compatibility should you need to switch firearms.

4. The type of cartridge case.
   - High pressure, belted magnum rifle cartridges often show acute case stretching between the belt and the case body after four or five reloads, resulting in case-head separation. As a result, reloading life for many of these cartridges is reduced.
   - Military cartridge cases are hard to reload due to crimped primers, Berdan primers, residue from waterproofing, dirt, or damage from being fired in semi-automatic or fully automatic guns.

There are four primary causes for fired cartridge cases becoming unserviceable:
1. A split case mouth that will not hold the bullet securely in place.
2. Case wall stretching or splitting in front of the case head which will leak high pressure propellant gases.
3. An expanded primer pocket that will no longer hold a primer securely in place.
4. Crushing from misfeeds, large dents from impacts, or perforations that compromise case integrity.

CAN STEEL CARTRIDGE CASES BE RELOADED?

While it is technically possible to reload steel cartridge cases, attempting to do so is not recommended. Essentially, steel cartridge cases are not designed for reloading.
- Steel is highly susceptible to corrosion and must be coated to prevent rusting. Such coatings are designed to protect the case from corrosion only thru the first firing. The inevitable scratches and dings caused by firing expose the base metal to corrosion that will rapidly compromise the integrity of the case.
- Some popular military calibers with steel cartridge cases are still loaded with corrosive primers. Corrosive primers leave a residue inside the cartridge case that quickly attacks the steel, weakening the case walls and case head inside where it cannot be seen.
- Many steel cartridge cases are loaded with Berdan primers. Berdan primers are difficult to remove and replacements are unavailable.
- Most all reloading dies are dimensioned for the spring-back properties of brass.

Badly corroded steel-cased 9mm

CAN RIMFIRE CARTRIDGE CASES BE RELOADED?

In a word, no.

Rimfire cartridges are designed for one time use only. When a rimfire cartridge is fired, the striker or firing pin initiates the priming compound in the hollow rim by crushing a small section of the rim. This creates a weak spot in the rim which compromises case integrity for any future use.

Attempting to reload rimfire ammunition at home requires making and handling dangerous components and procedures that can result in serious personal injury and/or property damage.

If these problems do not serve to deter one from such a project, the low retail price of a box of 22 rimfire ammunition should do the trick.

PRIMERS

A primer is a percussion-initiated ignition device located in the case head of a self-contained round of centerfire ammunition.

There are two major types of centerfire rifle and handgun primers: Boxer and Berdan.

Boxer Primers

Most modern primers for use by handloaders are the Boxer type named after Col. Edward Boxer who invented them in 1866 when he was superintendent of the Royal Arsenal in England. Boxer primers consist of four component parts:

- A U-shaped metal primer cup.
- A precisely measured pellet of priming compound (an energy-dense high explosive) in the bottom of the cup.
- A metal anvil having two or three legs mounted in the open end of the cup.
- A foil cover sealed with a drop of lacquer between the priming compound and the anvil to prevent contamination.

Cross-section of a Boxer primer

The priming pellet used in modern primers is a non-mercuric, non-corrosive mixture of normal or basic lead styphnate.

Boxer primer pockets normally have a single flash hole on their center through the web of the cartridge case.

Berdan Primers

Some centerfire rifle and handgun military ammunition manufactured overseas is made with Berdan primers. This type of primer was invented in 1866 by American Gen. Hiram Berdan of Civil War fame. The Berdan primer is a three piece design consisting of:

- A shallow metal primer cup.
- A precisely measured pellet of priming compound (an energy-dense high explosive) in the bottom of the cup.
- A foil cover over the primer pellet sealed with a drop of lacquer to prevent contamination.

The anvil, however, is integral to the case head rather than seated into the primer itself. You can identify a Berdan primed case by looking into the spent case mouth. There you will see one or two off-center flash holes.

While it is possible to reload Berdan primed cartridge cases, doing so requires special equipment not normally available. In addition, Berdan primers are not manufactured in the U.S. or imported from overseas manufacturers.

PRIMER NOMENCLATURE
Left side is showing Berdan-type priming; note the anvil built into the head of the case and the dual flash holes. On the right is the more typical configuration used with modern Boxer-type primers.

WHAT DOES A PRIMER DO?

The primer serves as the ignition source to ignite the propellant in a self-contained round of ammunition. When an empty cartridge case is reloaded, the spent primer must be replaced with a fresh one.

HOW DO PRIMERS WORK?

When the firing pin of the gun strikes the primer, the impact creates an indentation in the surface of the cup. The indent crushes the explosive priming compound between the cup and the tip of the anvil, causing it to explode. The explosion sends high-temperature gas and burning particles through the flash hole in the case head where they ignite the propellant. The metal cup is seated tightly in the primer pocket of the case head to prevent hot gas from leaking into the gun's mechanism.

High-speed image of a primer detonation showing the hot metal particles used to initiate combustion of the propellant.

WHAT TO DO IN THE EVENT A PRIMER FAILS TO FUNCTION

MISFIRE: A primer that fails to initiate given a fair hit is called a misfire. This can be caused by a problem with the striker (or firing pin) in the firearm or by failure of the round to headspace properly in the chamber. Should this happen, keep the gun pointed in a safe direction and wait one minute. Then, carefully unload the gun while holding the breech away from your face.

If your firearm has been shooting properly with factory ammo but you experience misfires with your handloads, the most likely culprit is a "high primer." The striker uses too much energy seating the primer cup hard against the pocket in the case head. A shallow dent in the primer cup is usually symptomatic of this. The case's primer pocket is typically designed to seat the primer about .005 inches below flush with the case head.

HANGFIRE: A primer that hesitates for a short period after a fair hit from the firing pin, then functions normally is called a hangfire (a "click---bang".) Should this occur, remove the fired case from the gun, then carefully inspect the chamber and bore for unburned propellant and a lodged bullet. A hangfire can be caused by contamination of either the primer or the propellant. As a result, full chamber pressure was likely not produced. The initial bullet in bore itself poses little risk but a second round fired into it could be disastrous.

For this reason, we strongly recommend discarding any remaining supplies of ammunition from which the hangfire came.

SLAMFIRE: A slamfire is caused when a protruding firing pin in the bolt hits the primer cup with sufficient force to ignite the primer before the action is locked. Normally, this causes a catastrophic explosion that damages the rifle and may cause personal injury.

Slamfires are usually associated with military style automatic and semi-automatic rifles that do not have retracting firing pins. Popular examples include the M1 Garand and M1A rifles.

When shooting such rifles, we recommend double checking your handloads for proper primer seating depth. However, a slamfire can happen even with properly seated primers. Fortunately, CCI has a solution for this problem in the form of CCI No. 34, No. 35, and No. 41 primers that have thicker cups and are less sensitive than standard primers.

PRIMER TYPES AND SIZES

Primers come in different sizes and ignition capabilities according to their intended application. There are four sizes of Boxer primers:

- Small Pistol
- Small Rifle
- Large Pistol
- Large Rifle

Each is available in standard, benchrest, and magnum versions. These are summarized and compared on page 31 of this manual. All CCI and Federal component primers for reloading are non-mercuric and non-corrosive.

PROPELLANT

The propellant is the fuel of a cartridge.

There are two basic types of propellant:
- Smokeless propellants which are a <u>chemical</u> mixture based on nitrated cellulose.
- Black powder which is a <u>physical</u> mixture of potassium nitrate, sulphur, and charcoal.

HOW DO PROPELLANTS WORK?

When the primer explodes, it sends hot gases and particles through the flash hole into the cartridge case. The hot gasses raise the temperature and pressure inside the cartridge, igniting the propellant. The propellant then begins to deflagrate (burn very quickly) releasing large amounts of energy in the form of hot, rapidly expanding gasses that accelerate the bullet down the barrel to high velocities.

TYPES OF SMOKELESS PROPELLANTS

There are three types of smokeless propellants:

1. Single-base
    - Single-base propellants are made of nitrocellulose.
    - The burning temperature of single-base propellants is approximately 4,600° F.
    - Most single-base propellants are in the form of perforated sticks of various lengths.
    - Single-base propellants with long sticks are the most difficult to meter through powder measures as some of the long grains must be cut on every cycle. Short sticks are no problem.

2. Double-base
    - Double-base propellants are made of nitrocellulose with the addition of nitroglycerine to provide additional energy.
    - Double-base propellants contain 15-20% more stored chemical energy than single-base propellants.
    - The burning temperature of double-base propellants is approximately 5,300° F.
    - Most double-base propellants are in the form of flakes or spheres.
    - Spherical propellants are the best choice for smooth metering through powder droppers.

3. Triple-base (rare)
    - Triple-base propellants are double-base propellants with nitroguanidine added.
    - The burning temperature of triple-base propellants is approximately 4,000° F.

Propellant granules are made in different shapes and sizes to control their burning rate. In this manner, the time-pressure curve of the propellant as it burns can be matched to the interior ballistic requirements of a given bullet and muzzle velocity.

The art of interior ballistics is balancing these factors to obtain the best possible performance.

Canister propellants for reloading normally contain:
- Solvents such as alcohol, ether, or acetone
- Stabilizers such as diphenylamine
- Deterrent coating in the form of DNT or centralite
- Anti-static coatings, graphite is a popular choice

In addition, canister powders may contain:
- Flash inhibitors such as potassium sulphate
- Decoppering agents; tin or bismuth is a popular choice
- Wear inhibitors like titanium dioxide, polymer, or centralites

PROPELLANT RELATIVE BURN RATE CHART - SHOTSHELL AND PISTOL POWDERS

ALLIANT	ACCURATE	RAMSHOT	HODGDON	IMR	WINCHESTER	VIHTAVOURI	NORMA	
Extra-Lite							R1	*faster* ↑
	Nitro 100 NF					N310		
	Nitro 100	Competition	Titewad		WST			
	A - No.2	ZIP				N312		
e3	Solo - 1000		HP-38	"Hi-Skor" 700-X	231			
Red Dot, Promo, Clay Dot			Clays					
			TITEGROUP	Trail Boss				
Bullseye								
American Select, Sport Pistol			International		WSL	N320		
Green Dot								
	A - No.5			PB	WAP	N330		
20/28						N32C		
Unique		Silhouette	Universal	SR 7625		N340		
BE-86		True Blue	CFE Pistol		AutoComp			
Power Pistol			HS -6		540			
						3N37		
Herco				SR 4756	WSF	N350		
				"Hi-Skor" 800-X				
Pro Reach			Longshot					
Blue Dot	A - No.7					3N38		
						N105		
Steel			HS - 7		571		123	
2400	A - No.9				630			
						N110		
410			H4227	IMR 4227				
	A - 4100	Enforcer	Lil' Gun	SR 4759				
			H110		296			
Power Pro 300-MP								*slower* ↓

← *similar burn speeds* →

The burn rate chart is a general reference that can be used to view propellants that have similar burn speed characteristics to one another. Measuring burn speed is not an absolute or exact science as many variables impact a propellant's burn rate, such as the individual lot of propellant, the cartridge it is loaded in, and when it was manufactured. The information shown here is general information only and must never be used as load data or to substitute one propellant for another. Always use the propellant as stated in the cartridge load data provided in the Rifle Data and Handgun Data sections of this manual.

PROPELLANT RELATIVE BURN RATE CHART - RIFLE POWDERS

faster → *slower* (similar burn speeds)

ALLIANT	ACCURATE	RAMSHOT	HODGDON	IMR	WINCHESTER	VIHTAVOURI	NORMA
	A - 5744						
	A - 1680				680		
						N120	
			H4198	IMR 4198			200
		LT-32					
Reloder 7	A - 2200						
						N130	
	A - 2015						
Power Pro 1200-R			H322	IMR 3031			
Reloder 10x	A - 2230	X-Terminator	Benchmark			N133	201
	A - 2460					N530	
			BL-C(2)			N135	
	A - 2495	TAC	H335				202
Reloder 12				IMR 8208 XBR		N140	
AR-Comp	A - 2520			IMR 4895			
Power Pro Varmint			H4895	IMR 4064	748	N540	
			Varget	IMR 4166			
Reloder 15	A - 4064		CFE 223	IMR 4320			203-B
			H380			N150	
Power Pro 2000-MR		Big Game					
	A - 2700						
			H414		760	N550	
			H4350	IMR 4350			
Reloder 16	A - 4350		Hybrid 100V	IMR 4451			
Reloder 17							204
			Hunter				
			Superformance				
Reloder 19	A - 3100		H4831SC	IMR 4831	WMR	N160	205
Power Pro 4000-MR			H4831	IMR 4955			
					WXR	N560	MRP
Reloder 22				IMR 7977		N165	
Reloder 23				IMR 7828			MRP2
		MagPro					
			H1000			N170	
Reloder 25							
Reloder 26		Magnum					
			Retumbo				
Reloder 33						N570	
			H870		870		
			H50BMG				
Reloder 50						24N41	
						20N29	

PRIMER REFERENCE CHART

	CCI Type	Federal Type	USE
"Shotshell (0.243 dia)"	209		All shotshell gauges: 10, 12, 20, 28, and .410 bore
	209M		Magnum shotshell primer for heavy waterfowl and turkey loads
		209A	All shotshell gauges (may require a reduced powder charge)
"Small Rifle (0.175 dia)"	400	205	Std. case volume small rifle cartridges
	450 Mag		Large case volume or hard to ignite propellants in small rifle cartridges
	No. 41/5.56	GM205MAR (AR Match)	Thicker cup bottom to minimize 'slamfire' in military style firearms
	BR4	GM205M Match	Tightly controlled pellet weight for improved ignition consistency in small rifle
"Large Rifle (0.210 dia)"	200	210	Std. case volume large rifle cartridges
	200 Mag	215 Mag	Large case volume or hard to ignite propellants in large rifle cartridges
	No. 34/7.62		Thicker cup bottom to minimize 'slamfire' in military style firearms
	BR2	GM210M Match	Tightly controlled pellet weight for improved ignition consistency in large rifle
		GM215M Match	Tightly controlled pellet weight in a magnum large rifle
"Small Pistol (0.175 dia)"	500	100	Std. case volume small pistol and revolver cartridges
	550 Mag	200 Mag	Large case volume magnum pistol and revolver cartridges
		GM100M Match	Tightly controlled pellet weight for improved ignition consistency in std. case volume small pistols and revolvers
		GM200M Match	Tightly controlled pellet weight for improved ignition consistency in small pistols and revolvers
"Large Pistol (0.210 dia)"	300	150	Std. case volume large pistol and revolver cartridges
	350 Mag	155 Mag	Large magnum revolver cartridges
		GM150M Match	Tightly controlled pellet weight for improved ignition consistency in std. case volume large pistols and revolvers
		GM155M Match	Tightly controlled pellet weight for improved ignition consistency in large revolvers
"Muzzle loading (0.245 dia)"	209		For In-line muzzle loader configurations. Designed to ignite in humid conditions
Percussion Caps	10		Non-corrosive priming cap for small nipple revolvers
	11		Non-corrosive priming cap for std. diameter nipples
	11 Mag		Increased energy for ignition of black powder substitutes using std. dia. nipples
	Four Wing Musket Caps		Lighter explosive charge. Custom designed for reenactment using musket sized nipples
"50 BMG (0.312 dia)"	35		Aresenal primers to ignite the massive charges found in the 50 BMG

CHAPTER 5

HANDLOADING SAFETY: BASIC SAFETY PRACTICES AND PROCEDURES

Introduction

At Speer® Bullets, we take safety seriously. While reloading is a safe and enjoyable hobby, certain safety practices and procedures must be followed. Always put safety first in your personal reloading and shooting activities. By understanding the potential hazards and following well-established guidelines and procedures, the average shooter can satisfy their lifetime need for quality ammunition and avoid significant injury or property damage.

WARNING

Failure to read, understand, and follow these safety rules and guidelines in your reloading practices and procedures can result in serious personal injury and/or property damage. It is **your** responsibility to assure the safe operating condition and function of your reloading equipment and firearms. Know the required components and correct cartridge for which your firearm is chambered. Always place safety first among your daily reloading and shooting habits.

This chapter will provide both the novice and the advanced handloader with important safety information on the properties, handling, and storing of reloading components. If you have any questions regarding these guidelines or recommendations, call the Speer Bullets Technical Staff at (800) 379-1732 for more information.

In the interest of promoting safe and consistent guidelines for the shooter and handloader, the information contained within Sections 1, 2 and 3 of this chapter have been prepared and reprinted with the permission of the Sporting Arms and Ammunition Manufacturers' Institute, Inc. (SAAMI). SAAMI was created in 1926 at the request of the United States government to create standards for safety and reliability in the design, manufacture, transportation, storage, and use of firearms, ammunition and components. Note: In order to provide the reader with more relevant content and context related to reloading, portions of the information provided by SAAMI have been deleted or condensed from their original format.

The following guidelines and recommendations do not supersede any applicable state or local regulations. Before you begin reloading, contact your local fire chief or fire marshal for more information regarding regulations which may apply to the transport, storage, ownership and use of reloading components.

SECTION 1: Safe Ammunition Storage and Handling

Properties of Sporting Ammunition

All sporting and law-enforcement ammunition manufactured by SAAMI-member companies is carefully engineered and manufactured as an article of commerce. It has a specific use. Ammunition should always be stored and handled in a proper manner, and used as intended in firearms in good condition and designed for the specific cartridge.

Manufacturers package ammunition in cartons and boxes to meet criteria as specified by the U.S. Department of Transportation and The United Nations Model Regulations.

Smokeless powder is a unique product. For example, powder in consumer packaging will burn but not explode. However, even a small amount ignited in the confined space of the chamber of a firearm will result in a significant but managed increase in pressure, which drives the projectile down the bore of the firearm at highly repeatable pressures and velocities. Individual cartridges and shotshells should only be used for their intended purpose. Individual cartridges and shotshells will burst if ignited outside the chamber of a firearm. A burst cartridge or shotshell may project the primer and possibly the projectile and/or fragments of case material. It is also important to remember that cartridges may ignite if the primer is struck when the cartridge is dropped, struck, or otherwise mishandled. However, it is important to note that if one cartridge ignites and bursts, it will not cause surrounding cartridges to ignite.

In the event of a fire in an area where sporting ammunition is stored, firefighter turnout gear will offer protection but should be kept on until a fire is fully extinguished. It is important to note, however, that if a cartridge is chambered in a firearm and ignited by the heat of a fire, it will send the projectile down the barrel with the same velocity and energy as if the trigger were pulled.

Visit saami.org/videos/sporting_ammunition_and_the_firefighter.com for a video that more fully discusses and demonstrates the properties of ammunition in different fire situations.

Temperature and humidity may affect the performance of ammunition. Factory fresh ammunition will function properly in conditions ranging from dry arctic regions to tropical rainforests; however, extended exposure to high temperatures and/or high humidity may damage ammunition. Often the degradation will result in lower pressures, incomplete burning, or failure to fire, but sometimes the degradation may result in increased pressures.

Contact with water, solvents, petroleum products, ammonia, and similar chemicals may render the primer and/or the powder non-functional. These chemicals can find their way into the cartridge to contaminate the powder and/or primer mixture. External contact with the cartridge can also cause corrosion to the cartridge case and make it unsafe to fire by either preventing proper chambering, weakening the case wall, or both.

Repeated exposure to heavy recoil can also damage cartridges and shotshells.

Storage Guidelines

- Ammunition should be stored in its original packaging or other packaging designed for the purpose.
- Ammunition should be stored in a cool, dry location away from solvents and other chemicals, heat sources, or open flames.
- It is not advisable to leave ammunition inside a vehicle or in a trunk on a hot day.
- Ammunition should be stored separately from firearms and made inaccessible to unauthorized users such as children and other uninformed or incompetent persons. Firearms should be securely stored to prevent unauthorized access by unauthorized

individuals such as children and others who are not physically or mentally capable of giving them correct, proper use and respect.

Handling Guidelines

- Always make sure the cartridge designation on the ammunition's headstamp matches the cartridge designation marked on the firearm's barrel.

- Ammunition should chamber easily and allow the bolt or breech face to close without the use of unusual force. NEVER fire a cartridge that requires force to close the bolt or breech of any firearm.

- Inspect ammunition prior to use and properly dispose of cartridges or shotshells that show signs of physical damage, such as corrosion, deep dents and/or scratches, etc. If in doubt, do not chamber or fire the ammunition.

- The repeated rechambering of a cartridge or shotshell in repeating firearms may cause physical damage to the case or hull, which could prevent the cartridge or shotshell from firing. It can also damage the primer pellet, resulting in a misfire. Repeated rechambering of a cartridge can push the projectile deeper into the case and thereby reduce internal case volume and increase chamber pressure. Do not repeatedly rechamber the same cartridge.

- When loading a magazine, do not insert fresh ammunition on top of existing ammunition. Empty the magazine and inspect the cartridges or shotshells that were removed. Reload the magazine ensuring the older ammunition is fired first.

SECTION 2: Smokeless Powder Properties and Storage

Properties of Smokeless Powder

Smokeless powders, or propellants, are essentially mixtures of chemicals designed to burn under controlled conditions at the proper rate to propel a projectile from a gun.

Smokeless powders are made in three forms:
1. Thin, circular flakes or wafers.
2. Small cylinders, both perforated and unperforated.
3. Small spheres or flattened spheres.

Single-base smokeless powders derive their main source of energy from nitrocellulose.

The energy released from double-base smokeless powder is derived from both nitrocellulose and nitroglycerin.

All smokeless powders are extremely flammable; by design, they are intended to burn rapidly and vigorously when ignited.

Oxygen from the air is not necessary for the combustion of smokeless powders since they contain sufficient built-in oxygen to burn completely, even in an enclosed space such as the chamber of a firearm.

Ignition occurs when the powder granules are heated above their ignition temperature. This can occur by exposing the powder to:
1. A flame such as a match or a primer flash.
2. An electrical spark or the sparks from welding, grinding, etc.
3. Heat from an electric hot plate or a fire directed against or near a closed container even if the powder itself is not exposed to the flame.

When smokeless powder burns, a great deal of gas at high temperature is formed. If the powder is confined, this gas will create pressure in the surrounding structure. The rate of gas generation is such, however, that the pressure can be kept at a low level if sufficient space is available or if the gas can escape.

In this respect smokeless powder differs from blasting agents or high explosives such as dynamite or blasting gelatin, although powder may contain chemical ingredients common to both of these products.

Smokeless powder does not detonate like high explosives as it has a controlled rate of burn and differs considerably in its burning characteristics from common "black powder." Black powder burns at essentially the same rate out in the open (unconfined) as when in a gun.

When ignited in an unconfined state, smokeless powder burns inefficiently with an orange-colored flame. It may produce a considerable amount of light brown, noxious smelling smoke. It leaves a residue of ash and partially burned powder. The flame is hot enough to cause severe burns.

When it burns under pressure, as in a cartridge fired in a gun, smokeless powder produces very little smoke, a small glow and leaves very little or no residue. The burning rate of smokeless powder increases with increased pressure.

If burning smokeless powder is confined, gas pressure will rise and eventually can cause the container to burst. Under such circumstances, the bursting of a strong container creates effects similar to an explosion.

For this reason, the U.S. Department of Transportation (formerly Interstate Commerce Commission) sets requirements for shipping containers for propellants and requires tests of loaded containers under actual fire conditions before approving them for use.

When smokeless powder in DOT-approved containers is ignited during such tests, the container seams split open or lids pop off to release gasses and powder from confinement at low pressure. Additional details are available in a SAAMI video "Smokeless Powder and the Fire Service."

How To Check Smokeless Powder For Deterioration

Although modern smokeless powders contain stabilizers and are basically free from deterioration under proper storage conditions, safe practices require a recognition of the signs of deterioration and its possible effects.

Deteriorating smokeless powders produce an acidic odor and may produce a reddish brown fume. (Don't confuse this with common solvent odors such as alcohol, ether and acetone). Dispose of deteriorating smokeless powders immediately.

Check to make certain that smokeless powder is not exposed to extreme heat as this may cause deterioration. Such exposure produces an acidity which accelerates further reaction and has been known, because of heat generated by the reaction, to cause spontaneous combustion.

Never salvage powder from old cartridges and do not attempt to blend salvaged powder with new powder or attempt to blend two types of powder to make a "custom" blend. Don't accumulate old powder stocks.

Considerations For Storage of Smokeless Powder

Smokeless powder is intended to function by burning, so it must be protected against accidental exposure to flame, sparks or high temperatures.

For these reasons, storage enclosures should be made of insulating materials to protect the powder from external heat sources.

Once smokeless powder begins to burn, it will continue to burn (and generate gas pressure) until it is consumed.

DOT-approved containers are constructed to open up at low internal pressures to avoid the effects normally produced by the rupture or bursting of strong containers.

Storage enclosures for smokeless powder should be constructed in a similar manner:

- Of fire-resistant and heat-insulating materials to protect contents from external heat.
- Sufficiently loose to vent the gaseous products of combustion satisfactorily which would result if the quantity of smokeless powder within the enclosure accidentally ignited.

If a small, tightly enclosed storage enclosure is loaded to capacity with containers of smokeless powder, the walls of the enclosure will expand or move outwards to release the gas pressure — if the smokeless powder in storage is accidentally ignited.

Under such conditions, the effects of the release of gas pressure are similar or identical to the effects produced by an explosion. Therefore, storage of smokeless powder should be in strict compliance with all applicable regulations and recommendations of the National Fire Protection Association.

Recommendations For Storage of Smokeless Powder

Store in a cool, dry place. Be sure the storage area selected is free from any possible sources of excess heat and is isolated from open flame, furnaces, hot water heaters, etc. Do not store smokeless powder where it will be exposed to the sun's rays. Avoid storage in areas where mechanical or electrical equipment is in operation. Restrict from the storage areas heat or sparks which may result from improper, defective or overloaded electrical circuits.

Do not store smokeless powder in the same area with solvents, flammable gasses or highly combustible materials. Store only in Department of Transportation approved containers.

Do not transfer the smokeless powder from an approved container into one which is not approved.

Do not smoke in areas where smokeless powder is stored or used. Place appropriate "No Smoking" signs in these areas.

Do not subject the storage cabinets to close confinement.

Storage cabinets should be constructed of insulating materials and with a weak wall, seams or joints to provide an easy means of self-venting.

Do not keep old or salvaged powders. Check old powders for deterioration regularly. Destroy deteriorated powders immediately.

Obey all regulations regarding quantity and methods of storing. Do not store all your smokeless powders in one place. If you can, maintain separate storage locations. Many small containers are safer than one large container.

Keep your storage and use area clean. Clean up spilled smokeless powder promptly. Make sure the surrounding area is free of trash or other readily combustible materials.

SECTION 3: Sporting Ammunition Primers Properties, Handling and Storage

Properties of Primers

Sporting ammunition primers contain carefully engineered mixtures of chemical ingredients. Primers are designed to explode and produce the heat, gas and hot particles necessary to ignite the propellant powders in sporting ammunition when the firing pin of a firearm strikes them properly.

Properties of particular importance to the dealer and user of primers are as follows:

1. Primers may explode if subjected to mishandling. Explosions may be caused by friction and by percussion, such as hammering, pounding, dropping or bullet impact. Heating by fire, static electricity, sparks, hot tobacco ashes, or other unspecified abuses may also cause primers to explode.

2. If primers are loose or in bulk, having contact with one another, one primer exploding can, and usually will, cause a violent, sympathetic explosion of all primers so situated. In other words, one primer exploding for any reason under these circumstances will normally cause all of the primers to explode in one violent blast.

3. Primers may "dust." Small particles of priming compound may separate from the primers in the form of dust, especially when they are subjected to shaking or jolting. Accumulation of this dust in primer feed tubes, loading machines, and loading areas is extremely hazardous as it might cause explosions or fires.

4. Primers exposed to water or any organic solvent, such as paint thinner, gasoline, kerosene, oil, grease, etc. may deteriorate, resulting in misfires or poor ignition.

5. Modern sporting ammunition primers will not absorb moisture under normal or even severe conditions of atmospheric humidity. There is no advantage to be gained from airtight containers. The factory containers in which they are packaged need only normal conditions of storage. They should be kept dry and not exposed to high temperatures (in excess of 150° F). If exposed to wet conditions or high temperatures, they may deteriorate, yielding misfires or poor ignition of the propellant powder.

Handling of Primers

Primers do explode. This is the purpose for which they have been designed. They demand the respect and careful handling due any device containing explosives.

Primers should never be handled, used, or stored in bulk, since primers in bulk can explode simultaneously. The placing of primers in tubes or columns, or using other bulk systems in which the explosion of any one primer may cause the explosion of all others, is a potentially hazardous condition. The manufacturers of primers do not recommend the use of primer feeds for reloading unless adequate protection from the hazard of explosion is provided. It is the responsibility of the manufacturers of primer handling systems to provide safety and protective features for their equipment. It is recommended that primers be handled individually unless adequate safeguards are provided and used.

Care must always be exercised in any handloading operation to avoid rough handling and undue force where a primer is involved, since the primer may fire. Any malfunction of equipment must be cleared with extreme caution. The decapping of shells or cases containing live primers is to be avoided.

Precautions should be taken to avoid buildup of static electricity on the person when handling primers or conducting handloading procedures. Loading equipment should be electrically grounded.

All loading equipment and adjacent areas must be kept scrupulously clean and free of primer dust and powder accumulations. Work areas and loading equipment must be cleaned by wiping with a damp cloth or sponge which should be thoroughly rinsed after each use. Fired primers, primer cups, anvils, or other bits of hard, abrasive material are a hazard during loading operation as contact with them may cause primers to fire.

Accidentally spilled primers should be picked up immediately as they may explode when stepped upon.

An absolute minimum of primers should be maintained at the loading operation. Only one tray at a time should be removed from the primer storage.

When a priming operation is completed, any remaining primers should be returned to the package in which they were originally contained. These packages have been specifically designed to protect primers during shipment and storage and also to protect the consumer.

Primers available to children, household pets, or persons not recognizing them as potentially hazardous, are an unnecessary risk to all concerned.

Never have an open flame, source of sparks, or hot particles in the vicinity of primers or any ammunition loading operation.

Do not smoke near primers.

Safety glasses must be worn when performing any and all handloading operations. Additional protection such as face shields or machine guards are strongly recommended.

Recommended Storage of Primers

Storage cabinets containing only primers are recommended. These cabinets should be ruggedly constructed of lumber at least 1" nominal thickness to delay or minimize the transmission of heat in the event of fire. SAAMI recommends against storing primers in sealed or pressurized containers.

Keep your storage and use area clean. Make sure the surrounding area is free of trash or other readily combustible materials.

Be sure your storage area is free from any possible sources of excessive heat and is isolated from open flame, furnaces, water heaters, etc. Do not store primers where they can be exposed to direct sunlight. Avoid storage in areas where mechanical or electrical equipment is in operation.

Do not store primers in the same area with solvents, flammable gases, or highly combustible materials. Store primers only in their original factory containers. Do not transfer the primers from this approved container into one which is not approved. The use of glass bottles, fruit jars, plastic or metal containers, or other bulk containers for primer storage is extremely hazardous.

Do not smoke in areas where primers are stored. Place appropriate "No Smoking" signs in these areas.

Do not store primers in any area where they might be exposed to gun fire, bullet impact, or ricochets.

Do not store primers with propellant powders or any other highly combustible materials so as to avoid involving primers in a fire as much as possible.

Observe all regulations regarding quantity and methods of storing primers.

SECTION 4: Reloading Safety

General Safety

1. Reload ammunition only when you can give your full and undivided attention. Allow sufficient time to load ammunition so that you don't rush. Loading at a consistent and leisurely pace is a key part of safe reloading. Never reload while watching television, YouTube, or engaged in conversation. Distraction can lead to serious accidents. Limit your visitors; if they want to talk, stop loading.

2. Set up your reloading operations in a quiet area where you will not be interrupted. Keep small children out of the loading area, locking the room if necessary. Use your parental discretion when allowing older children to observe and learn.

3. Never attempt to reload while under the influence of alcohol or medications. Do not reload when fatigued or ill.

4. Thoroughly read and understand equipment instructions before using the equipment. All manufacturers of reloading equipment furnish thorough instructions covering the safe operation of their equipment. If you do not have instructions, contact the equipment manufacturer to request a copy before attempting to load ammunition. In addition, if there is something you don't understand, contact the manufacturer.

5. Wear approved safety glasses during all reloading operations and while shooting. This is standard practice for any shop, not just reloading rooms. Eye protection reduces the risk of eye injury from flying particles should a reloading mishap occur. Provide safety glasses to others you authorize to be in the loading area.

6. Keep your loading area clean and organized. Store all components in their proper places and keep tools clean. Clean up any spilled propellants or primers promptly and completely. Limit the components on your loading bench to just those needed for assembling one load type.

7. Keep complete records of your reloading activities and load information. Don't trust your memory. Use a logbook to track which loads were assembled on a particular day and the inventory of your components.

8. Accurately and properly label all ammunition containers. Never guess at the identity of reloads. Each box of Speer bullets comes with adhesive labels that can be attached to ammo boxes for positive load identification.

Safety With Inertial Bullet Pullers

1. These devices are basically hollow hammers that allow the handloader to disassemble and potentially salvage components from any mistakes made during the reloading process. The cartridge requiring disassembly is locked inside the hammers

hollow cavity. The hammer is then struck against a sturdy surface and inertial forces cause the heavy bullet to move forward and eventually exit the case. The bullet and propellant are then captured within the hollow cavity for recovery.

2. Heed these safety rules for inertial bullet pullers:
   a. Always use short, light blows rather than one massive one. Several light blows do the job better and significantly lower the potential of damaging components, the tool, and yourself.
   b. Never use excessive force to pull bullets.
   c. Never put a rimfire case in an inertial puller. The case holder used on most pullers can pinch the rim and discharge the cartridge.
   d. Never attempt to disassemble a black powder cartridge with an inertial tool.
   e. Never use an inertial tool to pull bullets with high primers. Under certain conditions, the primer cup can suddenly shift to the bottom of the primer pocket and ignite the cartridge.
   f. Never attempt to pull bullets you cannot positively identify. This is especially important with military surplus ammo, where explosive or incendiary bullets may exist.
   g. Always wear safety glasses when pulling bullets, just as in any other stage of reloading.

Static Electricity and the Reloader

1. Static electricity is a high-voltage, low-current form of energy that builds on surfaces due to friction and can be highly hazardous for the reloader.
2. Of the components we use, primers are most sensitive to static charges. The energy is enough to ignite primer dust in and around priming tools. If you scuff your feet on carpet and then touch a priming tube, the dust can ignite and propagate to all the primers in the tube. The result is a serious explosion. This is the reason to keep those tubes clean!
3. Static charges prefer low-humidity environments. If you live in an area where low humidity is a common condition, you have probably experienced static effect in other areas. Your heating/cooling system probably dries the air so much that you notice a "shock" when you touch a doorknob. If so, you should take some simple precautions:
   a. Use a humidifier. This raises the relative humidity, reducing static build up. A humidifier can either be a portable unit that you place in your shop or a house wide system incorporated into the heating/cooling system.
   b. Avoid or remove carpet from reloading areas. This is the prime cause of static energy accidents. In addition to static charges, carpet can hold spilled powder. That alone can cause a fire if some ignition source comes in contact with the carpet.
   c. Clean the reloading area on a schedule. Good housekeeping is a safety measure. Routine cleaning removes residues of primers and propellants that can react to static energy. Clean hard surface counters and floors with a damp rag or mop.
   d. Use an anti-static product. Hard smooth surfaces like laminate bench tops can be wiped with a laundry product called an anti-static dryer sheet. The sheets also reduce static on plastic powder measure hoppers, scale pans, and powder funnels. If you are unable to eliminate carpeting from the area, use an approved spray anti-static product on the carpet to reduce static charge buildup.

Lead Exposure

1. Lead is a toxic metal that may be released during the firing of primers and certain types of lead bullets. Care should be taken to minimize exposure potential. At high exposure levels, lead can cause serious physical impairment. Some individuals are more susceptible than others. One person may not discover they have lead poisoning until they have a routine blood test; another may become ill before tests find the problem.

2. It is possible to be exposed to lead during reloading as certain reloading components contain lead or lead residue; i.e. bullets, primers and fired cartridge cases. Lead can enter the body in several ways, but the most common avenues are through the nose and mouth.

3. The reloader can lower their exposure to lead with these simple precautions;
   - Observe good hygiene. Wash hands thoroughly with soap as soon as you finish loading or shooting.
   - Never eat or drink while reloading or shooting.
   - Keep your hands away from your nose and mouth while loading.
   - Avoid breathing dust in the reloading area. Wear a dust mask when working with dry case cleaning media. Lead residue from fired cases builds up in the media with use. When pouring the media in and out of a case cleaner, use a mask to avoid any dust that might escape. Change out your media often to reduce lead accumulation.
   - Keep the loading area clean. Regular cleaning will prevent the buildup of residues including those containing lead. Clean bench surfaces with a damp cloth. If the area has a hard-surface floor (which it should be), damp mopping is preferable to vacuuming.

Load Data

1. NOTICE: The reloading information in this manual is for SPEER bullets. Substituting bullets of other makes may cause excessive pressures. These loads were developed using current standards, equipment and components. They supersede, replace, and make obsolete any reloading data previously published by Speer, Omark Industries, Blount International, Inc, or ATK. Speer makes hundreds of different bullets. We do not have the time to test all the other makes of bullets on the market. The loads published here were developed with SPEER bullets. Bullets of other makes may not produce the same pressures and velocities. Yes, in the past, bullets were all quite similar, but today's hi-tech designs differ considerably by make.

2. Most of the loads shown in this manual were developed using industry standard pressure testing equipment and techniques. Maximum loads shown do not exceed published industry pressures unless noted otherwise. Certain older cartridges whose pressure limits were originally set relatively low have seen a new popularity because of their reintroduction in modern, strong firearms. Examples are the 6.5x55mm Mauser, 7mm Mauser, 32-20 Winchester, 45-70 and 45 Colt. In these cases, the reloading data is clearly identified as being only for modern firearms and the acceptable loading practices for older firearms are specifically discussed.

3. Because no industry pressure standards exist for wildcat and proprietary cartridges, recommended loads were developed using the technique of monitoring case head expansion. It is especially important to begin with the start load when preparing ammunition for non-standard cartridges.

4. Never start with a maximum load. Always begin with the minimum charge shown for a bullet/propellant combination. Work up in small increments but do not exceed the listed maximum, carefully watching for any signs of excessive pressure at

each step. Even though our maximum loads are within industry specifications, they may function improperly or exhibit pressure signs in a particular firearm, especially a custom or foreign model having non-standard chamber or bore dimensions.

5. Manufacturers of propellants strive to make every lot uniform when compared with prior lots of the same powder. However, some minor differences do occur. This is another reason to start low and work up toward the maximum. The powder lot that Speer used to develop the data shown is unlikely the same as your lot.

6. Use only light to moderate loads until your experience increases. New reloaders need a little time to grow accustomed to their equipment and reloading operations. Avoiding maximum loads during this learning period insures an extra safety margin.

7. Only use lab-tested load data. Reloading manuals like this one are basically "recipe books" for handloaders. However, unlike a cookbook, a reloading manual is not intended to be a "jumping-off point" for wild experimentation. The component combinations shown in loading manuals have been carefully selected and tested for compatibility with the cartridge being reloaded. Going outside these recommendations is an invitation to disaster!

8. We receive calls and letters asking, "Isn't this data really conservative? Can't I go higher?" The answer to both is emphatically "NO!" The maximum loads are just that—maximum! Do not exceed these levels under any circumstance. Never mix propellants. To do so is the height of folly! Blending powders to get a particular performance level is extremely hazardous. Stick with standard commercial propellants.

9. Always reduce loads when changing components. Changing components can affect pressure. First try to match our recipes as closely as possible. If that is not possible and you need to change part of the combination—a different brand of cartridge case, for example—reduce the load to our start load and work back up in steps.

10. Avoid excessive load reduction with slow-burning rifle powders. Over the years, reports have circulated that severely reduced charges of slow-burning rifle powders have caused pressures high enough to damage or even destroy a rifle. Do not load lighter than the start load shown.

CHAPTER 6
GUIDE TO HANDLOADING RIFLE CARTRIDGES
From the Loading Bench to the Range:
A Step-by-Step Guide to Handloading Rifle Cartridges

In this chapter, we look at the basic and optional equipment needed for handloading. Then we will explore the steps of loading rifle ammo, starting at the loading bench and ending at the range.

Even if you plan to only load handgun cartridges, read this rifle information first. There are more similarities than differences, and most of the handloading basics are here. Chapter 14 deals with specific techniques and equipment used for loading handgun cartridges.

• • • • •

Handloading requires an initial investment in the tools and related equipment needed to safely assemble ammunition. The *minimum* equipment you should have includes:

A quality handloading manual—if you're reading this, you've already made the most important purchase. Safe handloading can be accomplished only after reading and understanding appropriate instructional materials and then using loading data developed in laboratories employing standardized test methods. Never guess at a powder charge. Use only published load data from a reputable reloading component or equipment manufacturer.

A place to load—set up your handloading equipment in a reasonably quiet area that's well-lit, comfortable, and where you can give your undivided attention. An unheated garage workshop can get very cold in winter and, in humid climates, tools and equipment can rust. For safety, choose a place that can be secured to prevent others—especially children—from tampering with your equipment and components.

A reloading press—the press provides the mechanical advantage required to recondition the cartridge case. The press also holds the next two equipment items—the reloading dies and shell holder—in perfect alignment. RCBS® makes several single-stage presses from the compact Partner™ press to the powerful Rock Chucker™ Supreme. All RCBS presses include the hardware needed to prime cases. Reloading presses are designed expressly for handloading ammunition, and you should never attempt to cut corners by using other tools such as an arbor press or a bench vise as substitutes.

A place to mount the reloading press—although there are some handheld loading tools on the market, the bench press provides maximum power and precision for full-length resizing and must be firmly mounted for safe and easy use.

Clamping a press directly to a tabletop is an unsafe and unacceptable mounting technique. Clamps can work loose and allow the press to move under pressure. Worse yet, the heavy press can fall to the floor and severely injure your feet and legs.

A sturdy workbench is best. It need not be elaborate, and lighter benches can be weighted with bullets or other heavy objects to steady them.

RCBS® offers the Accessory Base Plate 3 that is predrilled to accept most RCBS presses

CHAPTER 6

A dedicated, organized place to load

and accessories. These heavy metal plates attach to the bench top and allow quick changing of tools. They are especially useful where bench top space is tight. If you don't use these base plates, presses should be attached to the bench top with bolts, not wood screws. Wood screws can pull out under heavy loads. Large presses like the RCBS Rock Chucker™ Supreme can be attached with 5/16 inch carriage bolts.

Accessory Base Plate

If a permanent setup is not possible due to space limitations, portable loading benches are a good alternative. Typically, they include a built-in seat, so your weight steadies the workstation. Ready-made portable benches are available from several sources, or you can build one from remnant lumber. Most designs can be folded or taken apart for storage in a closet or under a bed.

Reloading dies—normally, you will need only one press to reload metallic ammunition. However, you will need a different set of loading dies for each cartridge that you wish to load. Don't cut corners by trying to load a cartridge in a set of dies intended for another cartridge. Doing so can produce poor-quality ammunition and create a serious safety hazard.

Die sets for bottleneck rifle cartridges like the 30-06 Springfield consist of two dies. The sizing die reshapes the brass case to permit easy chambering in standard rifles and ensures the case neck is the proper diameter to grip the bullet. The sizing die also ejects the spent primer. The seater die aligns the bullet with the case and pushes it to the desired depth in the case neck. If required, the seater die will crimp the case mouth into the bullet's crimp groove for a firmer grip.

Die sets for straight or straight-taper cases (e.g., the 45-70 and most handgun cartridges) have three dies. The sizing die returns the case body to its proper dimensions. The expander die forms the case mouth to proper size and flares it slightly to make bullet seating easier.

The seater die functions just as it does in a bottleneck set with the option of crimping the case mouth if needed.

Like presses, die sets are available with a range of features. RCBS standard dies are available in a wide selection of calibers and provide very high quality at a reasonable price. RCBS Gold Medal Match Series dies offer interchangeable neck sizing inserts to allow fine-tuning of the case neck grip for precision shooting. The seater die has a free-floating bullet guide with micrometer-type seating depth adjustment. RCBS Competition Dies are premium dies with special features including a precision-alignment bullet seater with a micrometer-type depth adjustment. Cowboy Dies are specially dimensioned to precisely prepare the cases for loading lead bullets required in Cowboy Action Shooting.

Reloading dies, regardless of make or model, are the precision tools that can make your handloaded ammunition perform better than factory ammunition. They should be treated with the same care you would give a fine firearm.

Most modern rifle/pistol dies have the standard 7/8-14 thread used by the reloading industry. Larger die diameters up to 1½ inch may be required in special applications like the 50-caliber BMG cartridge and some large English cartridges. If you plan to load one of these, make sure your press has the ability to handle larger diameter dies as well as enough opening to allow both sizing and seating. Several RCBS presses have removable die bushings for larger specialty dies.

Shell holder—the shell holder attaches to the ram of the loading press and holds the rim of the cartridge to accurately align the case with the reloading die. Most modern loading presses accept interchangeable shell holders. RCBS shell holders are available in standard rim configurations for all popular cartridges. Many shell holders can be used for more than one cartridge. The data pages in this manual list the RCBS shell holder needed for each cartridge.

Industry standards control the dimensional relation of the shell holder to the sizer die. Even so, the best way to get a uniform and safe headspace with bottleneck cartridges is to use dies and shell holders of the same make.

Powder scale—a reliable and accurate scale is absolutely *mandatory* for safe handloading. A reloading scale must be calibrated in grains (1 ounce = 437.5 grains) and be accurate to ± 0.1 grain. Reloading scales are furnished with a special pan to facilitate pouring propellant

A scale made for weighing propellant is mandatory to ensure you are loading the correct charge

into the case. To avoid any confusion, buy a scale sold by one of the reloading companies.

Some novice reloaders have suffered accidents when trying to use a scale intended for another purpose that is calibrated for grams or ounces. Read and fully understand the operating instructions for your reloading scale, especially those pertaining to reading and adjusting the poises on mechanical scales. Misreading a scale setting can cause accidents. RCBS markets both mechanical scales and electronic scales specifically designed for handloading.

Case lube and pad—rifle cases must be lubricated before resizing. If not, they will stick in the die. A lube pad is similar to an ink pad. When a case is rolled on the pad's porous surface, the proper amount of lubricant is applied. Case lube can be applied by hand but may not be uniform. A lube pad is among the least expensive handloading gadgets so why not make things easy on yourself?

There are many materials used as lubricants. Use only those formulated for handloading when preparing cases for sizing. RCBS sells the Case Lube Kit that includes lubricant, pad, and brushes for cleaning and lubricating the inside of the case neck. RCBS Case Lube 2 is water-soluble for easy cleanup. For ease of application, there is RCBS Case Slick®, a spray lubricant that delivers very low sizing effort. Owners of progressive presses should consider the excellent RCBS Lube Die that makes automated loading a cleaner experience.

Powder funnel—a powder funnel will save a lot of time and aggravation when pouring propellant from the scale pan to the cartridge case. Funnels designed especially for handloading are available from RCBS and other reloading

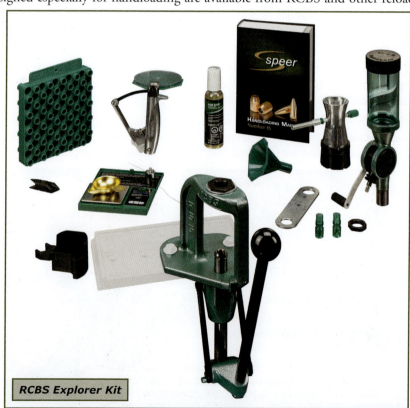

RCBS Explorer Kit

manufacturers. A key feature of powder funnels is a cupped spout that centers the funnel on the case mouth to eliminate spillage. The RCBS Quick Change Powder Funnel includes inserts for various neck diameters plus a long drop tube to facilitate loading large propellant charges.

Loading block—this item holds cases neatly in rows for easier processing. Proper use of a loading block minimizes the chance of a double charge, minimizes powder spillage and makes inspection easier. The RCBS Universal Case Loading Block handles the new, larger diameter rifle cases as well as short handgun cases.

Case length gauge—this tool measures the various dimensions of a cartridge. It helps you more accurately adjust your loading dies, determine correct cartridge case length, check bullet diameter, and measure cartridge overall length.

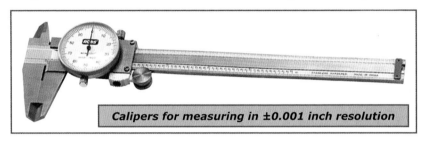

Calipers for measuring in ±0.001 inch resolution

The most convenient case length tool is a caliper, either a digital or dial type. Calipers for reloading should be calibrated in inches and be accurate to at least ±0.001 inch. RCBS sells a mechanical Stainless Steel Dial Caliper and an electronic Digital Caliber. Both are precision measuring devices with six inch capacities. Both digital and dial calipers are superior to older Vernier models because they reduce the chance of misreading the results.

• • • • •

With this basic equipment, you are ready to load quality ammunition. However, there are other accessories that can speed up the operation and add convenience.

Powder Measure—a powder measure meters the same volume of propellant time after time, speeding up the propellant charging operation. Measures are available in both fixed cavity and adjustable cavity designs. The RCBS Little Dandy® is a fixed-cavity design primarily intended for handgun use. Little Dandy rotors come predrilled to dispense different volumes of propellant. To change the charge weight, a different rotor is selected. It comes with a chart showing the nominal powder charge for each rotor for a variety of popular propellants. They are very accurate but it is recommended that you weigh the charge for the first few drops to verify your setup is correct and your method is consistent.

Adjustable-cavity powder measures are more versatile. The RCBS Quick Change™ and Uniflow® powder measures have adjustable chambers that will consistently meter small propellant charges for handguns to heavy charge weights for rifles. The repeatability of any powder measure is equally dependent on the type of propellant and the operator's technique. Fine-grained ball powders dispense from adjustable powder measures with little or no variation in weight. Large-grained, cylindrical powders may meter less uniformly depending on the shape of the metering cavity in the measure. All RCBS powder measures use a steel-on-steel contact surface and are precision-machined ensuring uniform charges, smooth operation, and long life expectancy.

Any mechanical powder measure requires the human factor to be consistent. We strongly encourage new reloaders to do some "dry runs" before using their new measure to charge ammunition. Dispensing and weighing charges will help you develop a style that delivers consistent charges.

For the advanced reloader, an electronic powder measure is a must-have upgrade. The RCBS ChargeMaster Combo and ChargeMaster Lite combine an electronic dispenser with an electronic scale. All you need to do is to calibrate the unit, enter the desired charge weight on the keypad, and press a button. The unit automatically dispenses and weighs the correct charge.

RCBS Chargemaster Combo

NOTE: A mechanical powder measure must be ADJUSTED and the charges verified using an accurate reloading scale. The measure does not replace the scale; it simply makes case charging faster.

Case trimmer—a case trimmer is a miniature lathe-like device used to accurately trim your cases to a uniform length. Trimming the mouth reduces the overall case length to the proper dimension. New cases from the same lot can vary in length, and the wise reloader will trim all new cases to a consistent length. If you are shooting a high-capacity bottleneck rifle cartridge, consider buying a trimmer sooner rather than later. The cases can lengthen quickly and exceed the length of your rifle's chamber causing hard chambering and high pressures.

The RCBS Trim Pro-2® and RCBS Universal Case Prep Center system represent the ultimate in trimmer evolution. Cases can be quickly moved in and out because of the special quick-change case holder system that replaces the awkward collet holders employed by other trimmers. Both coarse and fine adjustment collars ensure precise length control that's accurate case after case. Trim Pro comes in a standard, manually-driven model and a powered version for high-volume trimming.

RCBS Trim Pro-2 Power Case Trimmer

Proper case length can also be obtained with a trim die. Install the trim die in the press and adjust it like a sizer die. Run a lubed case into the die; if it is too long the mouth will protrude above the top of the die. The excess is removed with a fine-cut file. The top surface of the die is hardened to prevent the file from damaging it. Like most reloading dies, trim dies are cartridge-specific.

Off-press priming—although you can prime cases on the reloading press, some reloaders choose to perform this operation with separate equipment. The reasons can vary from wanting a better "feel" of the primer entering the case to simply speeding up the process. RCBS offers several off-press priming accessories. The

RCBS Universal Hand Priming Tool is a tray-fed, handheld unit that can be used almost anywhere you want to prime cases. The universal shell holder accepts cases from 32 Auto to 45-70 Government. It also has an important safety feature: an integral gate that separates the primer supply from the insertion operation.

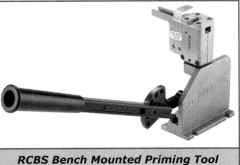

RCBS Bench Mounted Priming Tool

APS® priming is a unique RCBS priming development. CCI® APS primers are packaged in plastic strips that feed into the APS priming tool that makes spilled and contaminated primers a thing of the past. Strips can be linked together for continuous feeding. The RCBS Pro 2000® progressive press is configured for APS priming. Two stand-alone priming tools are also APS-compatible, including the popular APS Hand Priming Tool with a universal shell holder. Check out www.rcbs.com for additional information on this and other off-press priming systems.

Starting the Handloading Process

Go to your local gun shop knowing the components you will need. That is to say, go from the Handloading Manual to the gun shop, not the reverse. You've been to your local gun shop and now have all the components, tools and equipment you need to start loading for that favorite rifle. It's time to look at the steps that will produce your handloaded ammunition. Note that some steps are labeled "optional." Everything else is a "MUST DO!" operation.

Step One—Read the Instructions

Read the equipment instructions and load data manuals carefully and completely. It is important to understand how your hardware works. Time invested in study now will help avoid headaches and safety hazards later. If you fail to understand the instructions, get help. Most equipment makers have toll-free phone numbers or useful tutorials on their websites. RCBS tech support is at (800) 379-1732 and on the Internet at www.rcbs.com. Use these resources to ensure that you fully understand your equipment before attempting to load.

Understanding your firearm is as critical as understanding the reloading equipment and processes. It is your responsibility, and yours alone, to know your firearm and its characteristics. It is vitally important to know what is "normal" based on firing factory ammunition in order to recognize something abnormal if you have a problem with your handloads.

Step Two—Case Cleaning (optional)

Fired cases can get very dirty. In addition to powder and primer residues, the case can pick up residual oils left in the firearm. When the case falls to the ground it picks up dirt. Cases can become stained or darken with age. Stains won't keep a cartridge from shooting accurately. However, most reloaders take pride in their hobby and usually want the product of their labors to look good. On the other hand, extremely dirty cases will eventually damage loading dies and firearms and should be cleaned before proceeding. Clean cases are also easier to inspect than dirty ones. Cases can be cleaned in two ways—wet or dry.

Wet cleaning involves giving the cases a bath. Cases should be deprimed before wet cleaning to ensure thorough drying. The RCBS Universal Decapping Die removes primers without performing any other operations on the case. If cases are washed with primers still in place, trapped moisture can cause spent primers to corrode with the potential for serious decapping problems later.

Washing can be as simple as placing deprimed cases in a bucket and rinsing them with clear, hot water. Dirtier cases may require adding soap. A small quantity of liquid dish washing detergent will help speed cleaning. RCBS sells an excellent Liquid Case Cleaner that removes most stains and rinses cleanly.

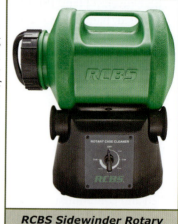

RCBS Sidewinder Rotary Case Cleaner

For more aggressive washing and stain removal check out one of many case cleaning tools from RCBS, from Ultrasonic to mechanical.

Washed cases must be completely dry before handloading. Cases can be placed in the sun or on a stationary rack available for many brands of clothes dryers. About 45 minutes with the dryer set on high heat will dry them nicely. Cases should never be dried in a kitchen oven. Even at the lowest settings, the temperature may reach levels that could dangerously weaken brass.

Dry cleaning of cases is accomplished by the action of mild polishing media that is vibrated or tumbled against the cases. Vibratory cleaners consist of a large bowl attached to a motor-driven base and are available from RCBS. The cases and cleaning media are placed in the bowl, and the unit is allowed to run for several hours. Vibratory case cleaners should never be used for wet cleaning unless so specified by the manufacturer.

Tumbling cases means they are placed in a rotating drum that causes the cases and media to fall against and rub each other, providing the friction needed to remove stains and dirt. Tumbling can be performed in the RCBS Sidewinder.

RCBS offers two different types of dry media for case cleaning. Ground walnut hull media charged with a red oxide cleaning agent is best for heavily stained cases. Ground corn cob media is excellent for cleaning less dirty cases and gives a higher degree of polish. Corn cob media comes with white oxide compound in a separate packet so you can add as much as you need. Plain (untreated) cob is an excellent light cleaning agent for cases that are not very dirty, and will remove case lubricants that are not water-soluble.

Regardless of how you choose to clean cases, the time and effort expended will ensure longer case and die life. See the RCBS website for an excellent array of case preparation accessories.

RCBS Vibratory Case Cleaner

Step Three—Case Inspection

First, individually inspect the cases for obvious defects. If using military surplus cases, this is a good time to run a magnet through them to sort out any steel cases. If you are uncertain of the "pedigree" of the cases, make sure they are Boxer—not Berdan—primed. Shine a strong light into the case mouth and look at the web area. Boxer-primed cases have a single, centered flash hole. Berdan-primed cases normally have two very small flash holes located on either side of center. Unless you have the special depriming equipment to handle Berdan cases, you are better off to discard them.

Any cases with the following defects should be segregated or discarded:

- **Mixed calibers**—it is quite easy to get a 270 Winchester case mixed in with 30-06 Springfield cases as they are very similar in size and shape. Having the wrong case on the bench will disrupt the loading process and could result in an unsafe cartridge if it were somehow reloaded.

- **Split case mouths**.

- **Cracks, splits or holes**.

- **Crushed cases**—even though some may look salvageable, the damage may have weakened the case internally and the flaws may not show until the case is fired. Discard any crushed cases.

Mouth splits and folds

- **Pitted or corroded cases**—cases that have been stored in leather belt loops or exposed to a corrosive environment will be weakened and should never be reloaded.

Body split in 300 Winchester case

- **Excessive case bulges**—some bulging is normal in fired cases, but you will occasionally find one that seems out of the ordinary. Excessive bulging, especially just above the case head, indicates potential weakening of the case. When resized, the case may be too thin in this critical area and could fail on the next firing. Watch for narrow bright rings close to the web of the case. A certain amount of swelling is normal at this point. However, bright rings associated with normal expansion are generally wider than the narrow bands that indicate excessive stretching. Excessive headspace, excessive resizing and high-pressure loads can cause cases to fail at this point.

If you are unsure of the condition of a case, make a probe from a short length of stiff wire with the tip bent about 45 degrees and use it to "feel" the inside of the case above the web. A shallow depression of ridge indicates thinning and a potential for failure. Better yet, use the case probe on the RCBS Case Master® gauging tool to examine for thinning. If this condition is detected in once-fired factory cases, you should have the rifle's headspace checked by a competent gunsmith. See the next chapter, "Advanced Techniques" for additional information.

- **Cases with damaged rims**—damaged rims can cause a case to stick in the shell holder, or the cartridge may fail to chamber or extract properly in your rifle. Minor rim burrs can be removed using a fine-cut file.

Note: Some prefer to deform any defect cases (pliers work well) beyond repair to ensure they don't inadvertently end up in your inspection process again.

Step Four—Case Lubrication

Cartridge cases must be lubricated before resizing to prevent sticking in the sizing die. The only exception is when you size straight-wall or straight-taper handgun cartridges with a carbide sizer die.

For single-stage loading, use a case lube pad with a good reloading lubricant like RCBS Case Lube-2®. Other shop lubricants may not work properly under the heavy contact

A case lube pad is convenient to ensure a thin, even coating of case lube is applied only where it is needed.

stresses of sizing. Place about a half teaspoon of lube on the pad and rub it in evenly over the surface of the pad. Allow a few minutes for the lube to soak in.

Tech Tip: Just bought a new case lube pad? Charge it with lube as soon as you get home, not five minutes before you need it for loading. New pads take longer for the lube to distribute evenly. Overnight is about the right amount of time to condition a new pad.

Place about five inspected cases on the pad and lightly roll them so each case has a thin film of lube completely around the body. Avoid getting lube on the shoulder or neck of bottleneck cases. Excess lube trapped at this point can cause hydraulic dents in the case shoulder.

The inside of the case neck can accumulate propellant residue that can make neck expansion and bullet seating more difficult. The inside of the case necks can be lubricated by either lightly dragging the open end of the case across the pad or by rolling a case neck brush on the pad and brushing the inside of the neck. Avoid excessive lube in the neck area. Too much lube can contaminate the propellant powder later. Often, simply dry-brushing the neck is sufficient to let them pass easily over the expander ball.

RCBS also makes Case Slick®, a spray lubricant that greatly reduces sizing forces yet can be applied sparingly. A little Case Slick will go a long way. One of the best ways to apply a spray lube is to place the cases in a large plastic bag. Puff a small amount of spray lube into the bag, aiming at the bag's walls, and roll the bag between your hands. Each case gets just the right amount.

Case lube must be removed before firing the cartridges. Cleaning the lube from the cases immediately after sizing is excellent insurance against getting oil in primers and propellants later in the loading operation. This is also a great time to reinspect cases, post-sizing. Water-soluble lubes can be removed with a damp cloth. Wiping with a dry cloth can remove other lubes, but tumbling the cases in plain corn cob media will remove the lubricant plus gives the cases a nice finish.

Step Five—Full-length Case Sizing and Neck Expansion

Resizing returns the case to the proper dimensions to insure reliable chambering and proper grip of the bullet. Sizing dies for bottleneck cartridges are designed to reduce the neck's internal diameter, so it is slightly smaller than the bullet diameter. When the case is withdrawn from the die, an expander ball mounted on the decapping spindle is pulled through the case neck, setting the correct diameter for bullet seating. Proper adjustment of the sizing die is critical for handloading accurate and safe ammunition.

Tech Tip: Clean new dies with solvent before using them to remove preservative oils. If the die has a vent hole in the shoulder area, clear it with a wire or small punch. The first case sized in a new die may require more lubricant than used for normal handloading.

Install the proper shell holder in the press ram and screw the sizing die into the threaded hole in the top of the press. With the ram at the top of its stroke, turn the die until it touches the shell holder. Release the ram slightly and tighten the die one-quarter turn more, then bring the ram back up. You should feel a slight springing when the ram is fully raised against the die. The die is now properly adjusted for full-length resizing. To prevent the setting from changing while handloading, screw the lock ring down until it touches the press body, and tighten the lock ring's setscrew. *NOTE: Carbide sizing dies for handgun cartridges must be adjusted differently—see the section on loading handgun ammunition.*

Cutaway of a size die and a bullet seating die

Remember that most bottleneck cases headspace on the shoulder. With the proper die setting, the shoulder will not be pushed back past its original position. Pushing the shoulder beyond this point will create excessive headspace. Excessive headspace may degrade accuracy and can cause a case failure when the cartridge is fired. Modern dies and shell holders are engineered to prevent this from happening. However, some people insist on modifying the die or shell holder. This creates a dangerous condition. Never attempt to remove metal from either the sizing die or shell holder. For best results, use dies and shell holders made by the same manufacturer.

Sizing die set for full-length case resize

Most sizing dies have a decapping pin that ejects the spent primer during the sizing operation. The pin should be adjusted so that it protrudes beyond the bottom of the sizing die about one-quarter inch.

Once the die is adjusted, place a lubricated case in the shell holder and lower the press handle. The leverage of the press forces the fired case into the die and performs the necessary dimensional changes. The fired primer is ejected at the same time. Keep some extra decapping pins on-hand.

Partial neck size setting using a full-length sizing die

As you raise the press handle to remove a bottleneck rifle case from the die, you will notice a slight resistance. This is normal; the case neck is passing over the expander ball. After fully lowering the ram, remove the case from the shell holder. Inspect the case to make sure it is free from dents or mouth damage. Set the case aside in a loading block and size the next lubed case. Before going to the next operation, be sure to remove the case lube from the cases.

Check the Case Length Now

Resizing affects case length. The best time to check the case length is after sizing. Measure the cases with a caliper and trim any that are over the maximum length to about .010 inches under the maximum. The maximum case length is noted on the drawing for each cartridge in this manual. Case neck growth is common with high-pressure rifle cartridges. Some cases may never grow; in fact, those that headspace on the case mouth may actually become shorter after repeated firings.

Neck Expansion for Straight-Wall Cases

Sizing straight-wall rifle cases requires the same procedure noted above except that neck expansion is not performed in the sizer die. Neck expansion for these cases requires a separate step and an extra die that comes with the die set. This operation also flares the case mouth in straight-wall cases.

Lower the press handle and screw the expander die into the press until the die body lightly touches the shell holder. Adjust the expander plug until a sized case just touches the plug when the ram is fully raised. Lift the handle to lower the ram slightly and screw the plug down one-quarter turn at a time until the case mouth is slightly flared. Avoid excessive flare to avoid premature mouth splits. Using a bullet you intend to load, check that there is just enough flare to keep it from catching on the edge of the case, yet allow it to freely enter the case about one-sixteenth of an inch.

Step Six—Priming

Before handling primers, make sure your hands are free of case lube and other oils. Contaminated primers can cause misfires or erratic ignition.

How primers are inserted depends on the type of press. Some presses like the Rock Chucker have an attached priming arm that swings under the shell holder. Others like the RCBS AmmoMaster® single-stage use a special ram priming device mounted in the die station. Primers can also be seated in an off-press unit, either bench-mounted or handheld.

A primer tray is a simple device for orienting primers anvil up

Because priming methods vary with the type of equipment used, carefully read the instructions for your handloading equipment before priming. Regardless of equipment make, there are several universal rules for priming safely and successfully:

- Primers must be correctly seated to avoid misfires. "High" primers—those whose anvil legs do not touch the bottom of the pocket—cause about 95 percent of all misfires. CCI primers provide optimum sensitivity when seated .003 to .005 inches below flush with the anvil legs in contact with the bottom of the pocket. With practice, you will soon recognize how a properly seated primer feels as it is pressed into the pocket.

- Use a slow, even pressure to seat primers. Never use a sharp blow. If you feel unexpected resistance, STOP! Carefully remove the case from the shell holder and identify and correct the cause of the problem before proceeding.

- Fired cases will have a buildup of primer residue in the bottom of the primer pocket. Excessive residue can make seating the new primer difficult and can cause high primers. This residue can be quickly removed with an RCBS Primer Pocket Brush of the appropriate size.

- Military surplus cases commonly have crimped-in primers. Before priming them, be sure that the original crimp is removed completely. The RCBS Primer Pocket Swaging Combo will reform the military primer pocket to one with a smooth, commercial type profile. Failure to remove military primer crimps increases the risk of igniting a primer inadvertently.

- Almost all priming devices have a spring-loaded sleeve around the punch to hold and align the primer. Before priming, make certain that the proper size sleeve and punch are selected. Visually check the punch and sleeve area for debris. Older reloading equipment may have a cup-shaped primer punch. This type of punch is intended for an obsolete style of primer with a domed base. Unless you have a supply of these older primers, make sure to use a flat primer punch. A punch contoured for domed primers will deform current production primers and increase the risk of an accident.

IMPORTANT Safety Warning!

If you discover a high primer after the cartridge is fully loaded, do not attempt to reseat it. It can ignite and the cartridge will rupture with potentially dangerous results. There is only one way to safely deal with this: pull the bullet (do not use a kinetic bullet puller) and remove the powder charge. Then—and ONLY then—is it safe to reseat the primer.

Step Seven—Charging the Case with Propellant

Proper propellant charging is critical to safe handloading. Never guess at the correct charge weight. Refer to the loading data furnished by a reputable handloading component or equipment supplier. The loads contained in this manual were developed under laboratory conditions and conform to established pressure limits.

Never start with the maximum listed charge levels. Begin with the listed start load and work the load up in your firearm in small increments. Chances are that you will find an accurate load before reaching the maximum load shown.

Charging cases in a loading block keeps things in line and decreases the chance of making a mistake.

Charging must be done only with a reliable and accurate reloading scale. Place the cases to be charged into a loading block. Weigh the desired amount of propellant on the scale and transfer it to a case using a powder funnel. Repeat until all the cases are charged. Before seating bullets, shine a flashlight into every case in the loading block to verify the desired powder charge is in each case. All cases should appear to have the same amount of propellant. If you have the slightest doubt about a charge, pour it back into the scale pan and verify the weight. It is critical to charge and inspect all cases before *seating bullets*.

Powder Measures

Many reloaders use a powder measure to speed the charging process after a favorite load has been carefully developed and recorded. Most quality measures will meter charges as consistently as you can weigh them. All factory ammunition has metered propellant charges with remarkable charge-to-charge uniformity. Because a powder measure works by volume, it is mandatory that you use a reloading scale to set the measure to throw the desired weight of propellant. Pour the proper propellant into the measure's hopper, so the hopper is at least half-full. Place the scale pan under the powder measure and operate the handle a dozen times to settle the powder. Weigh the powder charge and adjust the measure until you reach the proper charge weight. Meter five additional charges to settle the powder and then recheck the weight. Adjust as needed to reach the proper charge weight. Remember that the meter must be reset when you change propellant types. Fifty grains of Reloder 19 will not occupy the same volume as a 50-grain charge of Winchester 760.

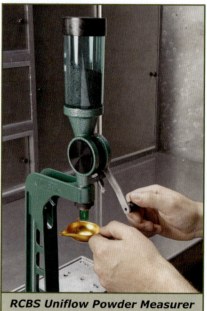

RCBS Uniflow Powder Measurer

It is a good idea to pour more propellant into the hopper than you will need. Many powder measures begin to throw lighter charges if the hopper runs low. For most measures, keeping the level above 1/2 full will ensure consistent weights.

Take a primed case from the loading block, place the mouth in contact with the measure's drop tube and operate the handle. After charging the first case, return it to the loading block at the opposite end from the uncharged cases or, better yet, place the charged case in a second block. Pick up the next empty case and repeat the sequence. Operating the handle with a consistent stroke will insure uniform charge weights. After charging the tenth case, pour the powder back into the scale pan to verify the weight. Continue until all cases are charged.

Large Case Precaution: The greater the charge weight, the longer it takes to flow from the powder hopper into the metering unit, and from the metering unit to the case. Cycling the handle too fast will stop the powder flow prematurely, resulting in inconsistent and even dangerously low charge weights. A small charge for the tiny 22 Hornet cartridge will drop almost instantaneously while the charge for a 378 Weatherby can take one to two seconds. Allow extra time for a large propellant charge to flow into the case. Develop a rhythm for operating the handle and stick with it.

Propellant Bridging

Bridging is the "log-jamming" of large propellant granules in the neck of a powder measure and is always a result of inconsistent operation of the measure combined with coarsely granulated propellants. Part of the charge falls into the case, but a portion of it remains stuck below the metering unit. When the next case is charged, it receives the remainder of the previous charge plus all of another, and you have two dangerous cartridges, one with too little powder and another with too much.

You can eliminate bridging by sharply "clicking" the measure handle as you operate it. When you raise the handle, click it against the upper stop. When you lower it, click it against the lower stop. Do this consistently and with a set rhythm.

Bridging can occur in measures with interchangeable spout tips if you leave the 22 caliber tip in place when you start to load a larger case. Be sure that the proper tip is installed before metering charges.

Powder Measures and Maximum Loads

Near-maximum loads should always be weighed. However, you can use a modified procedure combining both metering and weighing that is not as slow as using the scale alone. For near-maximum loads, set the measure to meter about 0.5 grains under the desired charge. Throw the charge directly from the powder measure into the scale pan and put the pan on the scale. Use an RCBS Powder Trickler or a small spoon to add a few kernels of powder at a time until the scale shows you have reached the desired charge weight. Using this technique, you have the confidence of knowing each charge is individually weighed yet the charging goes much faster than when using the scale alone.

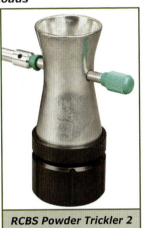

RCBS Powder Trickler 2

Inspect, Inspect, Inspect!

As with any powder charging operation, look into every case before seating bullets. Some handloaders have developed the habit of metering a charge into one case and then seating the bullet before going to the next case. This technique is extremely hazardous because it is possible to incorrectly charge and seat a bullet without recognizing that a problem exists. Inspecting all the charged cases in a loading block before seating the bullets ensures they are uniform and correct.

When using a powder charge that does not fill the case, take extra time in the inspection stage to look for double charges. A strong light source like a pen light will make inspection easier. A double-charge of a fast-burning powder can destroy a fine rifle and injure the shooter or bystanders.

Compressed Powder Charges

Some combinations of powder charges and cases may result in compressing the powder charge when the bullet is seated. This is normal with small, high-pressure cartridges like the 308 Winchester and with many of the larger cases when slow-burning propellants are loaded. Compressed loads in this manual are indicated with the letter "C" next to the charge weight.

The new handloader may wonder how they can get so much powder in the case. Slight modifications to the charging technique will help you accomplish this task with minimum effort. Don't dump the entire scale pan at once. Pour the charge slowly onto the upper portion of the funnel while tipping the funnel slightly to one side. This causes the powder to swirl down the funnel, allowing extra time for the charge to settle. This will usually give enough room to easily start the bullet into the case.

You can also facilitate loading compressed charges by using a funnel with a long drop tube. Combined with slow pouring, a drop tube allows even more time for the charge to settle. We used long drop tube funnels when developing load data for this manual. The RCBS Quick Change Powder Funnel Kit includes a 4-inch drop tube accessory.

Slow, even pressure on the press handle when seating bullets on compressed charges will prevent damage to the case or bullet. Heavily-compressed charges of fine-grained powders with a boat tail bullet can create problems. A few of the granules can wedge between the tapered bullet heel and the case neck, creating a tiny bulge. In some rifles, this bulge can prevent the cartridge from chambering. If this happens, you must use a different propellant or switch to a flat-base bullet.

Step Eight—Bullet Seating

Before seating a bullet, you need to determine the proper seating depth. The loads listed in this manual show the cartridge overall length (COAL) used by Speer for load development. In most cases, this is under the maximum SAAMI cartridge length specified in industry standards.

Although the SAAMI maximum COAL should function properly in any factory rifle having the shortest action, your rifle's throat will also affect the maximum COAL. One rifle may have less freebore in the throat than another. Magazine length can also affect the required cartridge length. The bullet itself is also a factor. The ogive (the curvature of the bullet nose) will vary between styles of bullets and affect where the bullet contacts the rifling. A round nose bullet often must be loaded shorter than a spitzer.

For reliable function, ammunition for semi-automatic, slide-action and lever-action rifles should be loaded very close to factory dimensions. Rifles with tubular magazines are often the most sensitive to cartridge length. Bullets intended for tubular magazine rifles have a flat tip for safety. A crimping cannelure ("crimp groove") sets the proper length for that cartridge. COAL for a falling block single-shot rifle such as the Ruger No. 1 is not so critical, and need only to clear the rifling.

Often, best accuracy is obtained when the bullet almost touches the rifling in the chamber throat. However, under no condition should a jacketed bullet contact the rifling before firing. This condition may cause high pressures in an otherwise safe load.

Seating a bullet without crimping: place a charged case (sized and, if needed, trimmed) in the shell holder and raise the ram fully. Screw the seater die into the press until you feel a slight resistance. The case mouth is now lightly touching the crimp shoulder in the die.

We do not want to crimp this load, so back the die out (up) one turn and tighten the lock ring. Loosen the lock nut on the seating stem and unscrew the stem as far as possible. Remove the empty case. Place a bullet on the mouth of a charged case. If the bullet does not readily stay on the case mouth, support it between your thumb and forefinger. Insert the case head into the shell holder and raise the ram. As the case neck enters the die, let go of the case and give the press handle a full stroke. Slight resistance means the bullet has started into the case. If the bullet has not started to seat, screw the seating stem in and repeat the steps until you feel the bullet start to seat. Lower the ram and measure the cartridge with a caliper. If the bullet needs to go deeper, screw in the stem and repeat. Continue until the proper COAL is obtained. Securing the lock nut on the seating stem will preserve the COAL setting.

Sometimes, a factory cartridge or published loading length is not available. A good way to determine proper seating depth for your rifle is to make a dummy round (no primer or powder) with the bullet you plan to use. Start a bullet into the sized case but leave it long. Try gently chambering the dummy round in your rifle. If you feel resistance, remove the dummy round and screw the seater stem in (down) one full turn and seat the bullet deeper. Try the round again in your rifle.

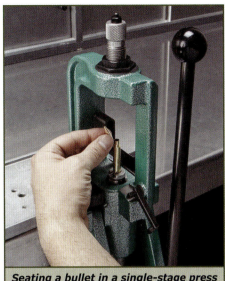

Seating a bullet in a single-stage press

As soon as the action can fully close with only a slight effort, remove the cartridge and rub a dark-colored "whiteboard" marker over the bullet or soot the bullet with a match/candle (dummy rounds only!). Chamber the round and see if the ink or soot has rubbed off at evenly spaced points. If so, this shows that the origin of the rifling is contacting the bullet and the bullet must be seated slightly deeper. Usually, one more full turn of the stem will position the bullet off the rifling yet be close enough for excellent accuracy.

Once the bullet is properly seated, keep this dummy round with your loading dies as a gauge for quickly setting your dies in the future. Mark it to clearly show the bullet weight and style, and for which gun it's for if you have more than one rifle chambered for that cartridge. Different rifles can have different chamber throat dimensions although chambered for the same cartridge. The RCBS Precision Mic™ can also be used to set the seater die. Refer to the instruction sheet for details.

By popular request, we have included the COAL we used for testing each load. Remember—this length is presented as a guideline, not gospel. It may not be right for your rifle. You alone bear the responsibility to determine and apply the correct COAL for your rifle.

Step Nine—Crimping (optional)

For certain applications, it may be necessary to crimp the bullet after seating. Crimping rolls the edge of the case mouth into a recessed groove in the bullet—the *crimping cannelure*. The groove provides the needed clearance to allow the crimp to form properly without damaging the bullet or the case. Crimping is not needed for most cartridges or firearms but, when appropriate, helps prevent the bullet from moving.

Important: Bullets to be crimped must have a crimping groove. Crimping a bullet that does not have a crimping groove deforms the jacket, and poor accuracy can result. Any gains in interior ballistic uniformity are meaningless if the load is not accurate.

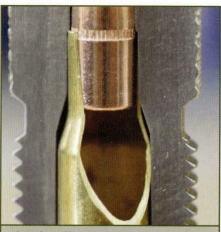
Seating die showing proper setup to crimp into the bullet cannelure

Seating die as set for no bullet crimp

Crimping is recommended for the following applications:

- Ammunition intended for semi-automatic rifles, particularly the military style firearms. The normal loading and firing cycle is rather violent and uncrimped bullets may dislodge.

- Ammunition for rifles with tubular magazines. With the cartridges stacked end-to-end, recoil can push the bullets into the cases, causing feeding problems and potentially raising pressures.

- Ammunition for magazine rifles that produce very heavy recoil. Depending on the design of the box magazine, the bullets can unseat when the rifle recoils making the cartridge too long to properly chamber. As you can imagine, this is a very hazardous condition when hunting dangerous game.

Most standard seating dies have the capability to crimp bullets. The die has a tapered shoulder in the neck area of the die that forms the crimp when properly set.

Handy Crimping Tips: When seating cannelured bullets that will be crimped, seat the bullet gradually into the case until you can see only the upper edge of the cannelure above the case mouth. This provides the maximum surface area into which the crimp can form to avoid case bulging. You will get the best crimps in case batches that have been trimmed to uniform length.

To set the die for crimping, seat a cannelured bullet as described above. Then unscrew the seating stem several full turns. Loosen the lock ring on the die body and make sure the seating die is "backed off" a little, too. With the cartridge in the shell holder and the ram up, screw the die body in until you feel it touch the case. Lower the ram slightly and screw in the die one-quarter to one-half turn. Slowly raise the ram again. You should feel a small resistance as the crimp forms.

Inspect the cartridge. If more crimp is needed, screw in the die body one-eighth to one-quarter turn at a time until you are satisfied with the crimp. Don't adjust in big steps—a little crimp goes a long way! When the crimp is sufficient, set the lock ring on the die body. If you wish to seat and crimp at the same time, replace the cartridge in the press and raise the ram fully. Screw in the seater stem until it stops and secure the lock nut. The die is now correctly set to seat the bullet and apply the desired amount of crimp. Seat bullets as before; the crimp is formed just as the bullet finishes seating. Use care—excessive crimp will bulge the case neck and shoulder. A cartridge with a bulged neck may not chamber and surely looks bad. Now is the time to test a few of the first rounds in the firearm, ensuring they will chamber.

Cartridges with very thin case mouths (e.g., 32-20 Winchester; 375 H&H) may be difficult to seat and crimp in one operation without bulging. If this is the case, crimp in a separate step. Seat bullets in all the cases and then unscrew the seater stem fully. Set the crimp as before, but do not lower the seating stem after the crimp is set. Even if the cartridge case is not one of the thin-neck varieties, separating the seating and crimping operations often produces the best-looking crimp.

Too much crimp can cause the case neck to collapse

Step Ten—Another Inspection

Now you have finished cartridges ready for firing. There is one more step you must do before boxing up the ammunition—inspect your work.

Remove any residual lubricant and metal chips at this time. Lay the cartridges on a light colored cloth or towel and look them over while rolling them with your hand.

Check for:
- consistent bullet seating depth
- damaged case mouths
- high or deformed primers
- bulged or split necks
- damaged bullets, especially on the tip
- missing crimps (if you planned to crimp)

As you box the ammunition, run your finger across the case head to check once more for high primers. Remember that you must never attempt to reseat a high primer in a loaded cartridge. Set them aside for later disassembly and reprocessing.

Hunting ammunition should be checked to see if it feeds and chambers easily in the rifle you plan to use. However, you must follow standard safety procedures. If you must test ammo fit in the shop, disassemble the bolt and remove the firing pin and its spring. If you cannot disassemble the firing mechanism, test the ammunition only at an approved shooting facility with the muzzle pointed downrange.

Inspection and testing of your handloads before the big hunt can save you much disappointment, frustration and missed game.

The Final Step—Proper Identification

After the ammo is boxed, record the exact loading information and the date on a label and attach it to the box. Speer bullets come with stick-on labels for this purpose. If you are keeping a logbook, this is the right time to bring it up to date. Proper identification of your handloads is an important step in safe handloading.

You've Now Loaded Your Own Ammo!

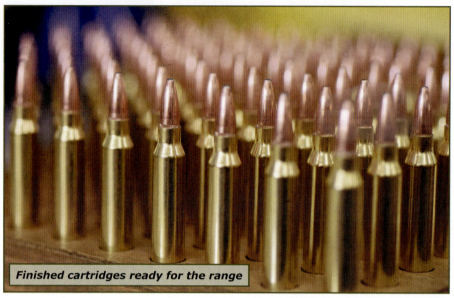

Finished cartridges ready for the range

The steps listed above sound lengthy when reading them. However, you will find that, as your experience increases, handloading is neither complicated nor time-consuming. This text is written so that the beginning handloader can fully understand the operations. Hopefully, some of you experienced reloaders will pick up a few pointers, too. Now it's time to shoot those custom loads.

At the Range

The proof of quality handloads is whether they shoot safely and perform well. Range testing for accuracy and function is required to assess the loads and make sure that they meet your requirements.

Safety at the Range

Always wear safety glasses to protect your eyes. Wear approved hearing protectors to prevent hearing loss. Make sure of your backstop. Understand and follow all of the commandments of gun safety!

Getting Started

While loading, you should have observed the "working up" method. Begin with the starting load shown in this Manual and load seven to ten rounds. Without changing the seater die settings, increase the charge weight in the next set of cartridges by one-half to one grain depending on the size of the case. Repeat this loading process until you reach the maximum load listed. Mark each batch of cartridges with the powder weight used and place them in separate boxes or, better yet, use a marker to code each group by coloring the primers (just remember to record your color code system).

A single, five-shot group is seldom adequate to give you an accurate picture of the quality of your ammunition. Even though a load produces a five-shot group of 0.75 inches, you don't know if the next group will be 0.55 inches or 1.75 inches.

For an industrial level of statistical confidence, four groups of five shots each is considered the minimum. However, the cost of components mounts up quickly. A statistical analysis performed by CCI-Speer Quality Assurance, showed that seven-shot groups gave the highest degree of statistical confidence with the fewest shots.

At the range, start with the lowest charge weight and shoot one seven-shot group or two five-shot groups. You are looking for the load that gives the smallest group size—not the one closest to the bull! Once an accurate load is developed, it is easy to adjust the sights to correct the point of impact relative to the aiming point.

Fire each group on a separate target, or use targets with multiple bullseyes. After completing the series, compare the group sizes to determine which powder charge gave the best accuracy in your rifle. Inspect each case as you remove it from the rifle. If you encounter any pressure signs while shooting a particular load, stop!

Pressure signs indicating you are in the "yellow zone" are sticky bolt opening or bright raised marks on the case head corresponding to extractor and/or ejector cuts in the bolt. You are well into the dangerous "red zone" if headstamp markings are deformed or the primer falls out. If you encounter any of these don't shoot any more of that batch—and surely none from the next higher increment. For whatever reason, your rifle has reached its own maximum.

From these tests, you should be able to find a safe and accurate load. If no groups in the series meet your needs, the next step is to adjust the bullet seating depth. If that doesn't improve accuracy, try a different powder and repeat the process until you are satisfied you have found the "right" load. Eventually, you will find a combination of components that delivers the accuracy and performance you seek.

Accuracy of Ammunition

New reloaders often ask, "What kind of accuracy should I get?" Well, that's a difficult question to answer because there are so many variables. Shooters often find their carefully developed handloads shoot better than factory ammunition in their rifles.

In a bolt-action, sporter-weight deer rifle with typical hunting bullets, 100-yard groups less than 1½ inches are typical with good handloads. Many semi-automatic, slide-action, and lever-action rifles will produce larger groups in the range of two to three inches. This accuracy is still quite adequate for most large game at normal ranges. Heavy varmint rifles with hollow point bullets will commonly shoot groups between three-eighths and three-quarters of an inch. With the right combination of rifle, components and shooting technique, even smaller groups are quite common.

Shooters' Tips for Effective Testing
- Use a shooting bench that allows you to sit comfortably. Many ranges have benches; if not, a portable bench kit can be purchased or you can build one yourself. Kits and plans are advertised in most of the popular shooting magazines.
- Support the rifle firmly on sandbags or a shooting rest such as the Blackhawk® Sportster™ Titan™ FX Rifle Rest. If you use a rest, support the forend—not the barrel. For minor elevation adjustments turn the micro windage adjustment knob under the front sand bag with your non-shooting hand. Proper support removes most of the human factor and lets you shoot better groups and enjoy longer test sessions because you are more comfortable.

- Don't get kicked! Heavy caliber rifles can be painful when fired on the bench. Several firms offer recoil-absorbing shoulder pads that slip over your shirt or jacket. High-recoil sandbags are also available that transmit a portion of the recoil to the shooting bench. You can shoot better and longer if your rifle isn't abusing you. Wearing an extra recoil pad doesn't make you look like a novice. It simply indicates that you're more interested in serious shooting than in trying to impress someone!
- Position the rifle consistently for each shot. Pull the rifle butt firmly into your shoulder. Varying your grip can affect group size.
- Press the trigger consistently. Pace your breathing so you let out your breath just before each shot.
- Pace your shots and shoot slowly. Rapid firing heats up the barrel resulting in unpredictable groups.
- Take your time. Plan your shooting sessions and allow sufficient time to shoot at a leisurely rate.
- Most importantly—have fun!

CHAPTER 7

FINE-TUNING

Advanced Techniques and Time Saving Tips from the Experts' Notebooks

This chapter covers techniques for accuracy improvement and more efficient reloading. These tips have been gathered from the years of reloading experience at Speer® and RCBS®, and from the comments and suggestions of involved shooters willing to share their knowledge.

Loading New Cases

In recent years, the reloader can buy bulk quantities of new, unprimed cases at substantial savings. Even though the loading techniques (other than resizing) are essentially the same, a few simple steps can make loading new brass easier.

Normal case manufacturing and bulk shipping can cause dents in the case mouths. Some dents are deep enough to catch a bullet during seating and damage the case. Denting is more prevalent in cases bought in bulk than those that come in 20-count boxes because cases bang together during shipping.

With new bottleneck cases, you should condition the necks by adjusting the proper sizing die so that it will only size about half of the length of the case neck. When the case is withdrawn from the die, the expander ball will ensure that the neck is both the proper diameter and round. Because only a small portion of the case touches the die, lubrication is seldom required, and the operation can be done quickly. If you find a case with a severe mouth dent, you may need to straighten it manually with a wooden dowel before running it into the die. Cases with sharp mouth folds should be discarded. A severe fold can weaken the case mouth even if it can be fixed.

For straight-wall cases, whether rifle or handgun, usually running the case into the expander die set for normal flaring will ensure round case mouths. However, the case neck tension must be sufficient to hold the bullet you plan to load, especially a jacketed bullet in cartridges usually factory-loaded with lead bullets, e.g., 44 Special and 45 Colt. If the bullets seat too easily, partially size the new cases before flaring. Running the case about halfway into the die usually is enough. Straight cases must be lubricated unless you have a carbide sizer die.

With the case mouths now uniformly round, it's a good time to check the case length. You will probably find that they vary. If you have a Rotary Case Trimmer, set it to the "trim-to" length for the cartridge and trim the cases. This sets a consistent length that can improve accuracy and, if needed, ensure uniform crimping. Remember to use a deburring tool on the case mouths after trimming to give a finished edge inside and out. Deburring makes bullet seating easier and should be performed on all new cases, even if trimming is not required.

While you have everything set up for neck conditioning and trimming, perform this operation on all the cartridges in the batch. Let's say you bought 500 cases. Go ahead and invest the time to trim all the cases even though you don't plan to load all of them right now. The remainder can be stored, and you have one less thing to deal with later.

Resizing for Maximum Accuracy and Case Life

Most bottleneck cases headspace on the case shoulder. When fired, the shoulder can change position relative to the base of the case as pressure expands the case to fill the chamber.

Sizing dies for each cartridge are designed to reset the shoulder to near the minimum dimension specified by the U.S. industry association, SAAMI. This ensures that the reloaded ammunition will fit any standard factory chamber. However, it is possible to have a rifle with a "long" chamber. Cases fired in this rifle will have the shoulder pushed back too much if the dies are set in the normal manner. Cartridges that fit the chamber closely are usually more accurate than those that don't. Another advantage to fitting the fired case to your chamber is that cases will last longer if the shoulder is not constantly pushed back during sizing and shoved forward at the next firing.

For precise measurement of the relative headspace of your rifle, RCBS offers a device called the Precision Mic™. These tools are individually calibrated for the industry base-to-shoulder length of many standard rifle cartridges. To use the tool, place a factory round or a new, unfired case in the gauge and screw the thimble down until it lightly touches the case. Record this reading and then take a case that has been fired in your rifle and gauge it in the same manner. Compare the two readings. A "zero" reading in the gauge is the minimum length for that particular cartridge. If the new case reads

RCBS Precision Mic™

.002 inches and the fired case reads .008 inches, then the case shoulder moved forward .006 inches. If resizing returns the shoulder to its original position, the next firing will again stretch the case to fill the chamber, reducing the life of the case. Instead, you can use the Precision Mic reading to set the sizer die to move the shoulder back only .002 inches to get a custom fit for that rifle.

This technique is best suited to target or varmint loads in bolt-action and single-shot rifles. A case sized in this manner will fill the chamber better, last longer and often give better accuracy. For hunting ammunition where reliable function is vitally important, this method of fitting the case to the chamber might cause problems. If dirt or other foreign material gets into the chamber, a tight-fitting cartridge may fail to fully chamber and cause a jam. Cases for semi-automatic, pump-action and lever-action rifles should always be full-length resized for reliable function.

Sizing Belted Cases

The belted case has become synonymous with the word "magnum." The original purpose of the belt was to provide positive headspace control on cartridges like the 300 H&H and 375 H&H Magnums that have very little shoulder. Modern belted magnums like the 7mm Remington Magnum, and the 300 Winchester are also bottlenecked but have adequate shoulders for headspace control. As such, these cartridges can be sized to headspace off either the belt or the shoulder.

To get top accuracy from your belted magnum, use the method described above to assure that the case headspaces on its shoulder instead of the belt. Many rifles will also shoot better when this technique is used, and the cases will last longer.

Tip: Clean the lubricant off sized cases before storing them. The lubricant can dry out making it harder to remove later.

Flash Hole Conditioning

The flash holes in most modern cartridge cases are punched into the case web, not drilled. Excess metal can be pushed up around the inside edge of the hole. In medium to large volume cartridges, the presence of this burr usually has little effect on the performance of hunting ammunition. However, for critical applications like match or varmint ammunition, or in small cases like the 22 Hornet or 222 Remington, an uneven flash hole burr can cause inconsistent ignition from shot to shot.

To provide a uniform flash hole, you can remove the burr with the RCBS Flash Hole Deburring tool and leave a neat beveled edge around the flash hole. The RCBS unit has a caliber-specific pilot that aligns with the neck and centers the trimmer in the case without the need to "fish" for the flash hole. The pilot also features a positive stop so that all flash holes are uniformly trimmed. The deburring tool shaft can be removed from its handle and mounted on the powered Trim Mate™ or Universal Case Prep Center. Pilots are available in popular sizes from 22 through 50-caliber.

Loading for Semi-Auto and Pump-Action Rifles

Rifle cartridges originally designed for bolt-action or single-shot rifles may be fired in semi-automatic and pump-action rifles. The case heads of cartridges fired in these rifles are often enlarged or bloated to a point that a standard resizing die will not reduce the case head enough to allow smooth chambering. RCBS offers Small Base sizing dies (in both complete sets and the sizer die only) that are designed to reduce the base of the case slightly more than a standard sizer die. Full-length resizing with a small base die is recommended for any reloaded ammunition used in semi-automatic and pump-action rifles.

Standard dies for cartridges such as the 7.62x39mm and the 30 Carbine originally designed for semi-auto rifles are already a small base design, so no special dies are normally required for resizing.

Chapter 9 has additional information about loading for semi-automatic rifles.

Case Neck Turning

Cartridge case manufacturers take great pains to hold case neck walls to a uniform thickness. Although most modern cases are manufactured to tight tolerances, you may occasionally find a case lot where neck wall thickness varies on the high side of the tolerance. Handloaders making one case out of another will more commonly encounter this especially if they have to shorten the parent case. Normal case resizing will not correct this condition. Case neck turning is the key to uniform neck thickness.

The RCBS Hand Case Neck Turner lets you obtain uniform neck thickness with ease. The cutter features a micrometer adjustment that permits .0005 inch increments; you can "zero" the cutter tip against the pilot and then use the micrometer settings to set a precise neck wall dimension. The Hand Case Neck Turner can be easily configured for either right- or left-hand operation. Interchangeable pilots/mandrels are available in 23 different diameters for most popular cartridges.

RCBS Hand Case Neck Turner

Owners of the RCBS Trim Pro® manual case trimmer can buy the Case Neck Turner Kit from RCBS. This accessory attaches to the trimmer and turns the inside and outside of the neck simultaneously. An optional automatic feed mechanism advances the cutter at a constant rate for clean and even cutting.

RCBS Trim Pro-2 Power Case Trimmer

By setting the adjustable cutter to lightly contact the highest point of the case neck, any variation in the thickness should be readily apparent. A properly turned case neck should have the cutting action visible only on the high side.

Except for cases you form from another cartridge, neck wall thickness variation will seldom have an adverse effect on hunting ammunition accuracy. Target and varmint shooters are more likely to benefit from case neck conditioning.

Case Forming

Many cartridge cases share similar dimensions. Because of this, a case of one caliber can be used to form a case of another caliber. The case you start with is called the *parent case*. Handloaders normally reform cases for three reasons:

- They wish to reload a cartridge for which factory cases are either hard to find or discontinued. As an example, there are a number of Mauser rifles in circulation chambered for the 7.65mm Argentine Mauser cartridge but only one make of imported brass is available in this country. The Argentine case has a head and body diameter very similar to the 30-06 Springfield. The longer '06 case can be reformed to make excellent 7.65 Mauser cases with a minimum of special equipment.

- The handloader owns a rifle chambered for a "wildcat" cartridge. A wildcat is a custom cartridge derived by modifying a standard case. Many popular commercial cartridges we shoot today started life as wildcats.

- The handloader has a surplus of one cartridge case but needs cases for another. As long as the two cartridges share certain common dimensions, the desired case dimensions can be achieved with case forming.

Reforming operations are similar to case sizing in most respects, including the need to lubricate the case. For a simple conversion, it is often possible to use standard sizing dies. The 257 Roberts case can be formed from 7mm Mauser brass by running the Mauser cases into a properly adjusted 257 Roberts sizer die.

Because the cases are nearly identical except for neck diameter, no other forming is necessary except checking case length and, if necessary, trimming. Often, an existing sizer die for another cartridge can be used as an intermediate step. For example, in forming the 6.5-08 A-Square from 308 Winchester cases, a 7mm-08 Remington full-length sizing die can provide an intermediate step between the parent case and the wildcat.

Other case conversions are more complex. If the new case is significantly shorter than the parent case, metal in the newly formed neck may be too thick and neck reaming dies are required. When the neck diameter or case length needs to be changed significantly, it is often necessary to perform the conversion in steps.

Some conversions require *fire-forming*, using the pressure of firing to contour a case to the dimensions of the rifle's chamber. In some wildcats, referred to as "Improved" cartridges, the only difference between the wildcat and the parent case is the body taper and the shoulder angle. For these, simply firing a standard cartridge in the custom rifle often makes the new case. In more complex conversions, fire-forming is usually the last step.

Easier Neck Expansion for Bottleneck Cartridges

When set up in the normal manner, the sizer die also expands the case neck just before the case exits the die body. Because the expander ball is near the mouth of the die, you feel the normal resistance of the ball when the press stroke leverage is relatively low. This resistance can be nearly eliminated if you are sizing cases that have already been deprimed in a separate operation (for example, if you deprime cases prior to cleaning).

To do so, loosen the lock nut that holds the expander rod in the guide bushing. Screw the expander rod counterclockwise until the top of the expander ball is roughly even with the shoulder section of the die. Make sure that the ball is not close to the neck of the die or the cases will be damaged. Tighten the lock nut and continue with sizing. With the expander ball in this higher position, the case neck is expanded when press stroke leverage is fairly high, and you will hardly feel the expander ball pass through the neck.

RCBS Summit, Single-stage press

Remember that this technique works only with bottleneck cases that have already been deprimed. If you plan to deprime when you size, leave the expander in its normal position. This technique is not necessary if you are using RCBS Competition dies. The expander ball is already at the higher position when the sizer die is adjusted to deprime.

Chamber Casting

Most sporting rifles are built to very consistent tolerances; however, it is sometimes useful to know the exact chamber and throat dimensions of your rifle. Although chamber dimensions are relatively uniform in production rifles, throats can vary. Chamber casting is an alternative to buying an expensive bore scope to examine your rifle's throat.

A good chamber cast gives you a "snapshot" of the throat. This part of the barrel is the most stressed during shooting. A rifle with a badly worn throat will usually shoot poorly even though the rest of the barrel looks good. A chamber cast can help you evaluate this hard-to-see area of the barrel.

A chamber cast is made by plugging the bore about an inch ahead of the throat with a cotton patch and pouring a low melting point metal such as Cerrosafe® or a polymer material into the chamber. Chamber casting kits are available from gunsmith supply catalogs. Follow the instructions supplied with the casting material to obtain the most accurate measurement.

Measuring Bore Diameter

It's often helpful to know the exact diameter of your barrel, especially when reloading for military surplus firearms. Measuring just inside the muzzle with a caliper seldom gives the true diameter. The most common method is called "slugging" the bore and is most accurate with barrels having an even number of grooves.

To slug the bore, clean the barrel thoroughly and apply a very thin coat of light machine oil. Select a piece of soft lead such as a buckshot pellet or a cast bullet that is just large enough that it cannot be pushed into the bore by hand. Place the lead slug on the muzzle and drive it flush with a non-metal mallet. Then use a short section of hardwood dowel that measures just under bore diameter to drive the bullet in a few inches. This step will usually cause a ring of excess lead to be cut off. This indicates you have a proper fit. Remove the dowel and continue driving the slug with a longer dowel until the slug falls from the chamber. The slug will be engraved by the rifling and can be measured with calipers or a micrometer. Be sure to measure the slug at several places and use the maximum dimension as the effective bore diameter. *NOTE*: Never attempt to drive a jacketed bullet through the bore in this manner. As you drive the slug through the barrel, "feel" the resistance and you will find areas where the bore is larger and smaller. Or not. Or not is good!

Some barrels have an odd number of rifling grooves. Their diameters are difficult to accurately measure without special gauging equipment.

IT IS CRITICALLY IMPORTANT that you remove the lead slug before firing live ammunition. Do not leave the slug in the barrel to be worked on at a later time lest you forget that it is there! NEVER try to 'shoot out' a stuck slug!"

Determining Twist Rate

In this manual, you will see reference to the rate of rifling twist. All rifled barrels have spiral grooves in the barrel to rotate the bullet at a predetermined rate. You can measure this rate using simple tools. You will need the following items:
- a metal cleaning rod appropriate for your rifle's bore, preferably light-colored and fitted with a rotating handle
- jag tip and patches of the correct size

- a long straightedge, such as a yardstick
- a dark-colored, fine-point felt-tip marker that will write on metal

Lay the cleaning rod on the bench and, using the straightedge and marker, draw a long line the full length of the rod parallel to its axis. If you find the long, straight line difficult to accomplish on small cleaning rods, a "flag" of masking tape can provide the reference. Place the jag and patch on the rod and start the rod into the barrel from the muzzle. If the patch fits properly, the rod should rotate smoothly. Make sure you see uniform rotation before proceeding. It may be necessary to adjust the position of the patch or change its size to achieve the proper fit.

Stop the rod so that the line you drew is facing up. If the rifle has a front sight, use it as a reference point. In the absence of an existing reference point, you can make a temporary one by placing a bit of masking tape adjacent to the muzzle and making a pencil mark on it. Make a cross mark on the rod with the marker even with the muzzle. Push the rod slowly through the bore while making sure it is rotating smoothly. When the long line returns to the reference point, make another cross mark even with the muzzle, then remove the rod. The distance between the two cross marks is the approximate rate of twist. One turn in (your measured distance in inches).

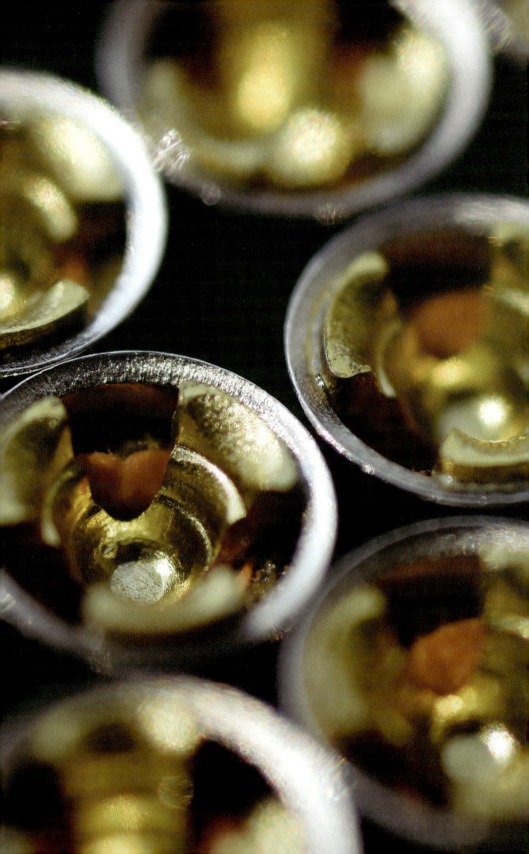

CHAPTER 8
AUTOMATING THE LOADING PROCESS
Progressive Equipment

Shooters who require large quantities of ammunition eventually reach the point where single-stage reloading can no longer satisfy their needs. The need to maximize practice time and reduce the time spent loading has sparked the development of faster ways to reload ammunition.

Progressive reloading presses accomplish all of the steps performed on a single-stage press. However, the steps are performed on several different cases at the same time. This is possible by providing multiple die stations and a moving shell carrier or shellplate. With each stroke of the handle, a typical progressive press will resize and deprime one case, expand the case neck and seat a new primer in another, charge yet another case with powder and seat the bullet in still another.

This saves time because the tool performs several operations with every stroke of the press handle. Some tools are more automated than others. For example, one tool may advance the cartridges to the next station automatically while others require the operator to manually rotate the shell carrier. There are two basic types of progressive, multi-station loading machines: rotary and linear.

Most current progressive loaders for the consumer market are rotary designs. RCBS®, Dillon, and Hornady fall into this category. Other progressive tools employ a linear design. The cases move in a straight line from left to right under a rack of dies.

There are many progressive tools on the market today at prices most shooters can afford. Some models can load selected rifle cartridges as well as handgun cartridges. Die stations range from three to eight.

RCBS's leading progressive presses are the rotary Pro Chucker 5 and the Pro Chucker 7. The Pro Chuckers will load rifle cartridges with CCI APS® strip-priming technology for safety and reliability.

Regardless of the type of progressive press you choose, we strongly recommend that you master the basics of reloading on single-stage equipment before automating the process. In other words, it's smarter to learn to walk before you try to run when loading ammunition. If you understand what's happening in the progressive tool, troubleshooting loading problems will be easier.

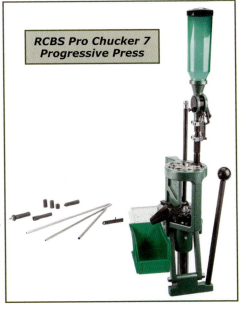

RCBS Pro Chucker 7 Progressive Press

Turret Presses

Turret reloading presses, often grouped with true progressive tools, are really enhanced single-stage presses. The lower unit of the typical turret press is much like a single-stage unit with a ram that holds one cartridge at a time. The difference is at the top. Instead of a single die station, the press features a large rotating disk or turret with from three to seven die stations.

The reason that turret presses get included with progressive presses is that they can be used to perform semi-progressive loading. If you have all the dies for one cartridge installed and adjusted, you can perform one operation, index the turret to the next die, perform that operation and continue the sequence until you have a loaded cartridge. It's slower than a true progressive but faster than single-stage loading.

The turret press has other benefits. Because a complete die set can be left installed and ready to use, you lose no time in changing or adjusting dies. This is very useful when one or two cartridges make up the majority of your

RCBS Turret Press

reloading. Let's consider the handgun reloader who loads more 38 Special and 45 Auto than anything else. The reloader can set up a six-station turret press with a full set of dies preset for each cartridge and quickly begin loading without having to do anything other than changing the shell holder. In this situation, the user can use the turret press as a single-stage, only rotating the turret to the next die after all cases have been through the previous stage. If you are loading bottleneck rifle cartridges, a six-station turret will let you preset dies for three cartridges, saving much setup time.

RCBS makes an excellent six-station turret press with 21st Century features. It has a heavy-duty, interchangeable turret mounted on a large pivot, a robust cast frame and convenient primer feeding from a protected magazine. It uses standard RCBS dies and shell holders. A heavy pedestal rising from the base snugly supports the turret head under load so the plate remains flat when full-length sizing. Install the optional Case Activated Linkage Kit and a Uniflow powder measure, and you have a dedicated and convenient charging station.

Extra turret heads are available to let you keep even more dies set up and ready to load. Switching heads is easy. You can quickly remove the heavy-duty turret nut with the same handle that turns the plate while loading, so there is no time lost looking for tools.

The RCBS Turret Press is a very useful tool and is the highest evolutionary step of this loading tool system that's been with reloaders for decades.

Progressive Loading—Pros and Cons

Progressive reloading tools have their strong points and weak points. The most obvious benefit is capacity—the number of cartridges that can be loaded in a specific period of time. Most progressive reloaders can yield 200 to 400 rounds per hour at a safe and steady pace. A steady pace minimizes the chance for error and will produce reliable and accurate ammunition. Regardless of make and model, trying to load too fast will result in unsafe loading practices and poor or unsafe ammunition.

With care, ammunition loaded on a progressive tool can be every bit as accurate as ammo loaded on single-stage equipment. Because quite a bit of hardware is often linked to the powder measure, progressive presses often damp out slight variations in operator technique resulting in very uniform charge weights with many propellants.

The only real drawback to a properly operated progressive loader is that you have little chance to perform "right now" inspections as you load. A high primer won't be found until the cartridge is fully loaded. You may not be able to inspect each case for a powder charge before seating bullets. With reasonable loading techniques and a couple of handy RCBS accessories, charge inspection is readily available.

The best insurance against a missing or incorrect powder charge is a powder level detector. RCBS makes two such items—the Powder Checker™ and the Lock Out Die™. The Powder Checker is a visual powder level indicator that is installed in the die station just past the powder measure. When the press ram reaches the top of its stroke, glance at the Checker. The alignment of a sensor rod with a reference marker tells you if the charge is correct, over, under, or missing. The Powder Checker works with any metallic cartridge.

The Lock Out Die performs a similar function for straight-wall pistol cases but with a twist. When it detects a charge that is too heavy or light or missing, the Lock Out Die halts the ram travel abruptly. The operator is instantly alerted to the problem even if they're not paying attention. Both of these safety devices are best suited to presses with at least five stations—they have the necessary extra die position.

Progressive presses need more maintenance than single-stage presses. As you deprime on a progressive press, primer residue will eventually accumulate under the rotary shellplate and in the primer transport mechanism. You must keep these areas clean to avoid erratic shellplate rotation or priming difficulties. Clean under the plate thoroughly with a brush every time you change plates or at 1000-round intervals. Clean up any spilled propellant immediately to eliminate a fire hazard and avoid interruption of normal press operation.

High or tipped primers can also result from a buildup of residue in the primer pocket after several firings. Avoid this problem by periodically depriming the cases off-press with an RCBS Universal Decapping Die. Remove any primer pocket residue before putting the cases back through the progressive press. This is also a good time to clean and inspect the cases.

Speed—Claims vs. Reality

Progressive presses all have the same guarantee: if you make a mistake in set-up or operation they will build ammunition faster than you can disassemble the rounds to recover your components.

Don't become a "speed addict" just because you are loading with progressive equipment. Never try to match "advertised" production rates. In normal usage, you will not safely achieve such rates. Powder hoppers and primer tubes eventually run low, and you must stop to refill them. Sometimes you drop a case or bullet that has to be retrieved. Load at a comfortable pace and you will still be far ahead compared to single-stage loading. Speed means nothing if you produce inferior or dangerous ammo.

Operate the equipment so that you complete a cartridge every 10 or 15 seconds. This rate will produce plenty of ammo, and gives you adequate time to handle the components and verify that the equipment is working correctly. The equipment must always be operated smoothly. Avoid a "jerking" motion that can cause irregular powder charges or tipped primers. Cases snap too fast from one station to the next and may lose part of their powder charge. If you're operating the tool too fast, you may not notice some unusual resistance to normal operation that would otherwise alert you to a problem. Poor ammunition or equipment damage may result.

Securely mounting the progressive press to a stable and level surface is mandatory. Movement and vibration that would go unnoticed on a single-stage press can cause malfunctions with a progressive. Mount it on a heavy bench and secure with carriage bolts whenever possible.

Sizing Dies in Progressive Loaders

A carbide sizer die is recommended—almost mandatory—to eliminate the need to lube cases when reloading straight-wall handgun cartridges on a progressive press. In addition to greatly speeding up the process, you will avoid handling greasy cases with the same hand that handles bullets. Getting case lube on bullets can cause irregular bullet pulls or contaminate the powder and cause a misfire.

Few hobbyists can afford carbide dies for bottleneck cartridges. The best way to avoid lubrication problems is to use the RCBS Lube Die. It has a reservoir for liquid case lube and automatically meters it onto a felt ring at the mouth of the die. The die, installed in station one, also deprimes the case. The case sizing die with the decapping pin removed is installed in station two. RCBS Lube Dies are available in four sizes to handle most bottleneck rifle cartridges.

Of course, you can spray the cases with RCBS Case Slick® before putting them into the press. With either method, remember to remove the lube from finished cartridges.

"Interrupted" Progressive Loading

You can interrupt the progressive sequence when loading bottleneck rifle cases to allow lube removal and ensure clean, reliable ammunition. Install a Lube Die in station 1 and the sizer die in station 2. No other dies are used nor are any primers or propellant. Insert the cases normally and start the cycle. Cases are lubed and decapped in the first station and sized in the second. Continue until all cases are processed and ejected.

To remove the lubricant from the cases, use plain corn cob media in a tumbler or vibratory cleaner to have a clean, dry case. The cases aren't primed so you can even wash off the lube if it is water-soluble like RCBS Case Lube-2. Be sure cases are completely dry before proceeding. Dry cleaning with cob is preferable because it takes only about 10-15 minutes. Washing and drying take longer.

With the cases clean and dry, install a Universal Decapping Die™ in the first station to knock out any cob residue that's lodged in the flash hole. Install and fill the primer feeder device, fill the powder measure and remember to put an RCBS powder level detector behind it. Finish with the bullet seater die and start loading. Cases get their flash holes cleared, are primed, charged, the charge verified, and the bullets seated. Each cartridge ejected into the catch bin is clean and ready to inspect.

Picking the Right Propellant for a Progressive Press

Progressive presses mechanically move the cartridge cases from station to station and some vibration is bound to occur. Cases filled close to the top with propellant may shake out part of the charge before the bullet is seated. Select a propellant and charge weight that keeps the powder level well below the case mouth.

A number of loads in this and other reloading manuals call for compressed propellant charges. Most progressive tools can handle a little compression without a problem. We recommend you avoid heavily compressed loads when using rotary progressive loaders. Because the case is not directly over the centerline of the ram during bullet seating, abnormal flexing of the shellplate carrier and/or die plate may lead to inconsistent bullet seating depths or upset other operations happening at the same time. Over a long time, the shellplate carrier could be permanently damaged. It's best to assemble heavily compressed loads on single-stage equipment.

When loading large-capacity rifle cases, you must always pause a second or two with the ram at the top of its stroke. This ensures that the propellant charge will have adequate time to pass through the powder measure into the case. You will likely need to modify your pacing from one used when loading small-capacity cartridges. The best way to gauge how much time you must allow is to test flow time during set-up. You can use the measure on the progressive press to test in single-stage mode, or use a similar model measure off-press. Operating the press too fast will produce defective ammo with light charges and cause propellant spills.

Safety with the Progressives

Although each manufacturer's design and operation vary, progressive presses share several universal safety guidelines:

- **Read and understand** all instructions furnished with the equipment. Progressive presses are quite complex compared to single-stage equipment. If you don't understand how it works, call the equipment manufacturer for help. Most have a toll-free number and websites for technical assistance. Use them!

- Electrically ground your progressive press.

- **Always** wear eye protection when reloading, regardless of the type of equipment being used.

- **Avoid** anything that may distract you when loading. Progressive presses have many things happening at once and require your full attention.

- **Develop the habit** of routinely checking all parts and connections for tightness, alignment and fit. Keep the press clean and lubricate it only according to the manufacturer's recommendations. Excessive lubrication is often worse than no lubrication.

- **Never** attempt to modify built-in safety features of any reloading tool.

- **Never** attempt to increase the capacity of primer feeders and powder hoppers beyond their original design.
- **Make certain** that replacement primer tubes are the correct ones for the make and model of your tool. The wrong tube can lead to big problems including a dangerous primer tube detonation. Replace—don't repair—any damaged primer tubes.
- **Don't rush!** Operate the press with a smooth, even stroke of the handle and maintain a steady pace of one finished round every ten or fifteen seconds. Never attempt to load so fast that you cannot keep an eye on all equipment functions. When operating the press for the first time, pay close attention to the feel and sound of the equipment. Knowing what feels and sounds "normal" makes it easier to detect malfunctions that may happen later.
- **Take a break** if you get tired. Extended progressive loading sessions can be physically exerting and operator fatigue can lead to inattentiveness and dangerous mistakes.
- **Never use excessive force.** If you feel something out of the ordinary, *stop loading immediately*! Do not resume until the problem is found, understood and corrected.
- **Develop** a consistent routine for picking up cases and bullets and smoothly coordinate these motions with the stroke of the press handle.
- **Case preparation** is still important when loading on progressive equipment. You still must check cases for defects and proper length before loading them.

• • • • •

Observe these guidelines, and you and your progressive reloader will soon be producing an impressive amount of quality ammunition with complete safety.

CHAPTER 9

WHEN ALL ELSE FAILS: TROUBLESHOOTING TECHNIQUES

This section should help you diagnose and fix problems that may occur during the loading process or at the range.

Sizing Problems—Stuck Cases

The most common sizing problem is sticking a case in the sizer die. When you lower the ram, the shell holder pulls the rim off the case, leaving it stuck in the die. The usual cause for this problem—little or no lube on the case. Frictional forces during sizing are very high, and without adequate lubrication, the case may seize in the die. Removing a stuck case from the die must be done with care and special equipment to avoid ruining the die. The stuck case seldom harms the die; improper removal techniques do the damage.

RCBS® makes two tools to handle this problem: the Stuck Case Remover™ and the Stuck Case Remover-2™ kits. The former is used with standard dies and the latter with dies having a removable guide bushing or elevated expander balls. Both units are designed to gently ease a case from the die. The case is lost, but not your precision die. If you do not have one of these tools, you can send your die to the RCBS Customer Service department to have a stuck case removed.

Ensuring the case has adequate lube will usually eliminate this problem. The first case sized in a new die usually requires slightly more lube than subsequent cases. After the first few cases are sized, less lubricant can be used. If you feel a case hesitate as it enters or exits the die, make sure the next case has enough lubricant before sizing. When using a new die for the first time, flush it with an aerosol solvent such as Gun-Flush® from Gunslick to remove the shipping preservatives. For bottleneck cartridges, clear any material from the small vent hole in the side of the die with a small wire or punch. They do their best to hide the hole; look in the threads as it is often found there.

A die that has been damaged by sizing too many gritty cases will become rough enough to increase resizing forces. Stop using the die until it can be repaired or replaced. To avoid this problem, thoroughly clean cases before sizing.

Dents in the Case Shoulder

You can have too much of a good thing. Only the case body—not the shoulder and neck—needs lubrication. Although lubrication is necessary, excessive lube will collect in the shoulder area of the die. When a case is sized, the trapped lubricant can create hydraulic dents in the shoulder. The vent hole normally allows excess lubricant to escape. However, if force is applied rapidly, the excess lube may not vent fast enough. If you find hydraulic dents, first check to see that the vent hole is clear and clean the die. Excess lube on the pad can be removed with a clean shop rag or paper towel.

An oil-dented case will usually fire without failing, but it may be weakened. Discard the case rather than risk a case failure.

Difficult Sizing

If you notice that you need to exert more force than usual when sizing (even though the case is clean and properly lubed and the die is clean), stop and do the following:

- Make sure that you have the correct die installed.
- See if the case is the correct one. A 358 Winchester case is similar in appearance to the 35 Remington but is larger in diameter.
- See if the case was excessively bulged from previous firings. Some surplus military cases that have been fired in machine guns will have more bulge than cases fired in a sporting rifle.
- Check the case for major dents or other damage.

Special Sizing Dies for Semi-Automatic Rifles

Difficult chambering or extraction can occur in some makes of semi-automatic rifles. Reloading with RCBS Small Base™ sizing dies usually corrects the problem because the SB die reduces the case diameter slightly more than a standard sizing die.

Headspace Problems—Bottleneck Cases

Headspace for a bottleneck cartridge is controlled by the position of the shoulder. If the case shoulder is pushed back too far during sizing, excessive headspace will result and cause poor accuracy or misfires. In the worst case, a case may rupture and ruin a rifle and/or injure the shooter or bystanders.

Shoulder position can be accurately measured to ±.001 inches with the RCBS Precision Mic™. See Chapter 7 for more information on this tool. Due to the quality of most current reloading dies, oversizing is rare. However, three factors can cause this:

- The die or shell holder has been modified by removing metal where they meet. Either alteration puts the shoulder of the die too close to the shell holder resulting in excess headspace. Never modify a sizer die or shell holder.
- The sizer die and shell holder are different makes. Although most manufacturers of dies and shell holders use the same reference dimensions, a mismatch can occur. Usually it is small and does not create a safety hazard. Avoid homemade shell holders or mixing different brands of dies and holders—you have no guarantee that they are dimensionally compatible.
- A rifle has a "long" chamber due to excessive headspace. Even though the dies are properly adjusted, the case will fire-form to the chamber's longer base-to-shoulder length. Normal sizing pushes the stretched shoulder back, reducing accuracy potential and case life. The Precision Mic will tell you if your rifle has this condition and how much to adjust the die to avoid recreating an excessive headspace condition.

Neck Expansion Problems

If neck expanding seems unusually difficult, remove the spindle assembly and inspect the expander ball. Grit accumulating on top of the ball increases the force needed to expand the neck. Clean it while it's out and verify that the rod is not bent.

Normally, expander balls will process tens of thousands of cartridge cases without showing wear. However, really dirty cases can scratch the working surfaces of the ball. If so, polish the ball lightly or replace it.

It's normal for fired cases to have powder residue on the interior. If the residue is unusually heavy, it can cause hard neck expansion even with a properly adjusted and maintained expander. Case necks should be cleaned thoroughly with an RCBS Case Neck Brush after lightly rolling the brush across your case lube pad. Don't dip the brush in lube—too much lube will contaminate the powder.

Priming Difficulties—"Hard" Primer Seating

Difficult primer seating is a fairly common problem. If you encounter this, STOP LOADING UNTIL THE PROBLEM IS CORRECTED. Never force a primer or use sharp blows during any priming operation. Slow, even pressure is mandatory for safety. Here are some things to check:

- Is the primer the correct size?
- Is the primer punch the correct size and shape?
- Is the primer punch bent?
- **On swing-arm primer punches, is the arm free to move fully into position?** A buildup of primer residue on and around the arm and its spring can prevent it from centering under the case. The effect is similar to that of a bent punch—the primer is misaligned and cannot smoothly slip into the case. Clean excess residue from the press regularly.
- Is the primer pocket clean and undamaged?
- **Does the case have a crimped pocket?** Completely remove the crimp with an RCBS Primer Pocket Swager.

Primer pocket shape can vary with the brand of case, and even within one brand. If the radius between the sidewall and the bottom of the pocket is too large, it will stop the primer anvil prematurely causing a high primer and misfires. RCBS makes three sizes of its Primer Pocket Uniformer to remove this excess metal leaving a square pocket bottom that greatly improves seating and ignition. The Uniformer fits in the electric Trim Mate™ or Universal Case Prep Center but may also be used manually.

RCBS Primer Pocket Brush

You will eventually encounter some combination of primer and cartridge case that causes excessive priming force. A different combination is the only solution to this problem.

Primer Feeding in Progressive Reloading Equipment

Progressive reloading presses feed primers through automated devices. A buildup of dirt and residue causes most malfunctions in these priming systems. Progressive equipment must be cleaned regularly to ensure safe and smooth operation. Remove the shellplate in rotary-type loaders to clean under it. Keep the primer shuttle and the surrounding area clean. DO NOT USE OIL except as directed by the tool manufacturer.

Check primer feed tubes for residue and damage. Replace any bent or damaged tubes; never attempt to repair them. If the tubes are dirty inside, clean them with hot, soapy water and thoroughly dry before use.

If the priming mechanism is clean and still doesn't work properly, go back to your instruction manual to learn the procedure for proper adjustment. If in doubt, contact the equipment manufacturer.

Powder Charging

This critical area of handloading is, fortunately, one where few problems occur. However, two potential problems can occur that can lead to significant safety problems.

Missing Powder Charge

A missing powder charge will cause a misfire. In small-capacity cases, it is also possible for the primer's output to drive the bullet out of the case and stick it in the bore—a dangerous condition if another cartridge is fired! Careful process control and simply paying attention when handloading will assure you avoid this situation.

If after you have seated the bullet, you suspect that you failed to charge a case, a simple test will help you find out. Place a primed, uncharged case (same brand) and a bullet of the same weight you loaded in the scale pan and record the weight. Then weigh the suspect cartridge. If the suspect cartridge weighs within a few grains of the weight of the bullet and primed case alone, then the charge is missing.

Proper charging practices and inspection will eliminate missing powder charges. Review Chapter 5 for the recommended procedures.

Progressive loading equipment reduces the opportunity for inspection compared to single-stage equipment. Review Chapter 8 for more information on these tools.

Variable Powder Charges

A charge variation of a few tenths of a grain in a large rifle case may have little effect on accuracy or performance. However, variations of several grains can cause problems.

Accuracy can suffer and charges falling on the high side may cause excessive pressures. These large variations are usually caused by improper powder measure techniques.

Operate the handle in a consistent manner. When throwing large charges of rifle powder, allow enough time for the entire charge to flow through the measure. Check the powder measure routinely to see that all lock screws and fittings are tight. Routinely check a charged case on your scale to ensure the charge weight hasn't changed.

If you are not using a powder measure and get large variations in hand-weighed charges, make certain that your scale is clean. Dust in the pivots (mechanical scales) can cause erroneous readings. Is the scale level? If you move the scale to another location in the shop, always rezero it with the leveling screw. Check the scale with calibrated weights available from RCBS and other manufacturers.

Is the scale affected by drafts? A cardboard deflector placed over a vent or around the scale will eliminate the problem. Mechanical scales must be located at least three feet from fluorescent light fixtures to avoid interference from electromagnetic fields.

Bullet Seating Problems—Hard Bullet Seating

Hard bullet seating can ruin cases for further reloading. Here's a checklist:

- **Are you using the proper diameter bullet?** A 7mm bullet is .007 inches larger than a 270 Winchester bullet and will also cause dangerous pressures if the cartridge is chambered and fired.

- **Has the case neck been properly sized and expanded?** If you fail to adjust the expander ball properly, the bullet can collapse the case. Expander rods held by collets in some makes of dies can loosen, slide up, and not expand the case neck at all.

- **On straight-wall cases, is there enough flare on the case mouth?** Variable flare is often due to non-uniform case lengths.
- **Is the case mouth too sharp?** If loading new cases, you must chamfer the inside of the case mouth to remove burrs, but only after you have made sure the case mouth is round; otherwise, it will be uneven or incomplete.
- **Is the seater die adjusted properly?** If the die is too low it will deform the area below the shoulder on bottleneck cases. A very small bulge can result (often nearly invisible) but feeling the case may let you know if there's a problem. If the case will not chamber, this could be the reason.

Bullets Fall into the Case

This is an easy problem to spot and fix. Check the following items:
- Are you using a bullet of the correct diameter?
- Did you fail to properly size the case?

Lead Bullets that Seat Deeper as Loading Progresses

This is caused by bullet lubricant gradually building up on the seater plug or the crimp shoulder. The buildup pushes each bullet slightly deeper into the case until the seating depth is excessive. In some cartridges this can cause excessive pressure. Remove the seater die and disassemble and clean it thoroughly. A very light coat of oil or release compound will slow future buildup. Remember that too much oil is worse than none at all!

All Speer® lead handgun bullets now feature an improved lubricant that virtually eliminates lube accumulating in the seater die.

Crimping Problems

Never attempt to roll-crimp jacketed bullets that do not have a crimping groove. Doing so will only damage the bullet and degrade accuracy.

If you have trouble crimping bullets that have a crimping groove, look for the following:
- **Is the proper die installed in the press?**
- **Is the seater plug adjusted so that the crimp groove meets the crimp shoulder in the die?** If not, adjust the seating depth accordingly. Attempting to crimp above or below the groove will probably damage both case and bullet.
- **Are the cases trimmed to uniform length?** Variable lengths will cause some cases to be crimped too much and others very little. If cases are trimmed too short, you may not be able to crimp them at all.
- **Are you collapsing the case mouths or shoulders during crimping?** If so, you are applying too much crimp. Adjust the die to apply less crimp. When crimping bullets in cases with thin mouths (32-20, 44-40, 375 H&H, etc.), you will find that seating and crimping in separate operations will minimize this.

"Erasers" for Reloaders

If you discover that you have made a mistake, you will need to take the defective cartridge apart to salvage the components. Just as pencils have erasers to correct mistakes, the reloader has access to a couple of different ways to "erase" their errors. Bullet pullers come in both collet and inertial types.

Collet Bullet Pullers

RCBS sells a collet-type bullet puller that mounts in the die station of a single-stage press. The puller unit usually consists of three parts: the body, a threaded shaft with a handle and a collet. Collets are caliber-specific—you will need a collet for each diameter bullet you need to pull. A 30-caliber collet will work with most standard .308 inch diameter rifle bullets.

The puller body is screwed into the die station and the collet attached to the handle assembly. Insert the cartridge into the proper shell holder and raise the ram so that the bullet (but not the case mouth) fully enters the collet. Turn the puller handle clockwise until the bullet is firmly gripped. Give the press handle a sharp upward blow to lower the ram and extract the bullet. Turning the handle counterclockwise releases the pulled bullet from the collet.

The pulled bullet will likely have shallow marks from the collet jaws. Most bullets' performance will not be affected by these marks and can be reused. However, thin-jacketed varmint bullets may be crushed in the process and should be discarded.

Inertial Bullet Pullers

The collet-type puller cannot be used to pull lead bullets or most jacketed handgun bullets and can damage thin-jacketed varmint bullets. In these situations, an inertial puller is the answer.

Inertial pullers look like hammers with hollow heads. The cartridge is placed in a chuck assembly that grips the rim or extractor groove with the cartridge inside the puller body. The assembled unit is struck against a hard surface. The puller and the cartridge case stop but the inertia of the bullet causes it to move forward out of the case.

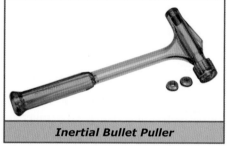

Inertial Bullet Puller

Bullets removed with the inertial puller are seldom damaged unless excess force is used. The bullet and powder charge are caught in the puller body for reclaiming.

Do not try to pull the bullet with one hard blow. Several light taps will pull the bullet safely and effectively. Heavy blows can break the puller or deform the bullet and may cause the cartridge to discharge.

Here are some safety precautions to follow when using an inertial puller, regardless of make:

- **NEVER** put a rimfire case in an inertial puller.
- **NEVER** attempt to disassemble a black powder cartridge with an inertial puller.
- **NEVER** use an inertial puller to pull bullets from cartridges with high primers. Under certain conditions, the primer can snap hard against the bottom of the pocket and ignite. Use a collet-type puller if possible.
- **NEVER** attempt to disassemble any cartridge whose projectile type cannot be positively identified. Accidents have occurred when someone attempted to pull an explosive military projectile.
- **ALWAYS** use short, light taps instead of one heavy blow to remove the bullet.

- **ALWAYS** wear safety/shooting glasses when pulling bullets, just as in any other stage of reloading.

Tech Tip: Some factory ammunition, particularly military ammo, has a mouth sealant that effectively "glues" the bullet in place. When disassembling ammunition that may have this seal, run the cartridge into a bullet seating die of the proper size and seat the bullet about .005 to .015 inches deeper. This normally breaks the seal and makes extraction much easier.

At the Range

Sometimes problems with handloaded ammunition does not show up until you get to the range. They may be functional problems but can also be accuracy problems.

Misfires

Misfires have been discussed in Chapter 4, but this problem is common enough to warrant additional discussion. By far, the majority of misfire problems are due to a handloading error or a gun problem—not a primer defect.

Handloading Problems

- **Is the cartridge the correct one for the firearm?**
- **Is there propellant in the case?** Weighing the cartridge and comparing it to a primed case and loose bullet of the same type will usually tell you if the charge is missing.
- **Did you fail to remove the old primer from the case?**
- **Is the primer seated below flush with the case head?** Incorrect primer seating depth is the most common cause of misfires in handloaded ammunition. The anvil legs must make contact with the bottom of the cup. CCI and Federal primers should be seated between .003 and .005 inches below flush for optimum sensitivity.
- **Has the primer or ammunition become contaminated with oil or water?**
- **In a bottleneck case, has the shoulder been pushed back too far?** This creates excessive headspace, and the firing pin has to reach too far to make solid contact with the primer. Shoulder position can be checked with the RCBS Precision Mic.
- **In a straight-wall rimless case, is the case short?** This also increases headspace. Measure the case length with calipers and check against the minimum case length in the reloading data.

Gun Problems

Gun problems also cause misfires. Firearms-related items to check are:
- **Is the firing pin broken or damaged?** Check to see if the firing pin marked the primer.
- **Is the firing pin spring adequate?** Some after-market spring kits may not have the same energy as the original spring. Original springs may be altered or weaken with age. See that the firing mechanism is properly assembled. Some revolvers have a screw that controls the position and tension of the mainspring. Make sure this screw is fully seated.
- **Is the firing mechanism coated with grease or dirt that can slow the firing pin fall?** This problem will most likely show up in cold weather. A spray solvent like Gun-Flush® from Gunslick is useful for cleaning grease buildup.

- Is there a buildup of powder residue or grease in the area of the chamber and breech face? Residue here can cushion the firing pin blow, especially with rimmed cartridges. Thorough cleaning will usually correct the problem.
- **In rifles and semi-auto pistols, is there excessive headspace?** In revolvers, is there excessive front-to-rear play in the cylinder? This condition, *endshake*, is due to normal wear. Excessive headspace or endshake puts the cartridge too far from the firing pin, weakening its blow. Consult a qualified gunsmith to determine if excessive headspace or endshake is present and have it corrected.

The Bolt is Hard to Open

With any ammunition, a "sticky" bolt lift is a BIG DANGER SIGN. The cartridge may have produced excessive pressure causing the brass case to deform and wedge in the chamber. When you get the action open, examine the case for signs of high-pressure. DO NOT fire any more loads from that batch.

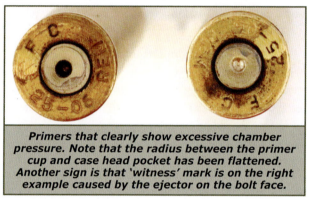

Primers that clearly show excessive chamber pressure. Note that the radius between the primer cup and case head pocket has been flattened. Another sign is that 'witness' mark is on the right example caused by the ejector on the bolt face.

For safety's sake, always assume the hard bolt opening is signaling excessive pressure. However, having difficulty opening the bolt could also be due to a mechanical problem with the rifle such as a rough or dirty chamber.

Clean and dry the bore and chamber to completely remove grease or oil before each range trip. Cartridge cases are designed to grip the chamber walls at peak pressure and then release when the pressure drops. Oil in the chamber or on the cartridge will cause the case to slip in the chamber at peak pressure and increase the thrust on the bolt. This may cause hard opening at normal pressures. In addition, excessive lubricant can attract and accumulate dirt.

Again, hard opening can be due to several factors; but your first reaction must be to think "DANGER!" and cease firing until the cause is understood and corrected.

Unusual Sounds and/or Recoil

Firearms producing supersonic velocities (over about 1100 fps) make a sharp crack when fired. You probably have a good idea of how your firearm sounds and feels when firing factory ammunition. A soft report or unusually light recoil could indicate a squib load and the danger of a bullet being lodged in the barrel. Before firing any more ammunition, check for a bore obstruction.

If you hear a faint hissing sound following a shot or hear a sound like the opening of a beverage can when you open the bolt, you almost certainly have a bullet stuck in the bore! The bullet has plugged the bore, and the residual gases are slowly escaping.

Luckily this revolver was strong enough to hold together for 14 bullet-in-bore shots! This shooter failed to recognize not only the lack of recoil, or the odd report, but also that their gun was nearly half a pound heavier by the time the cylinder locked up!

Wait until the hissing noise stops then check the bore and clear any obstructions before taking another shot.

Variable reports are a sign of inconsistent propellant charge weights or ignition. These variations usually occur when using a hard-to-ignite propellant with a standard primer or when trying to develop reduced velocity loads in a large case. Either switch to a magnum primer or choose a different propellant from the load data.

Double sounds such as a "ker-WHUMP" or a detectable delay after pulling the trigger are also signs of poor ignition. They are relatively common when working up reduced loads in large cases. Normally, switching to a quicker burning propellant will eliminate this problem. We have provided lab-tested reduced loads for many of the rifle cartridges in this manual.

Semi-Automatic Rifles

For best performance in most gas-operated semi-autos, use propellants having a medium burning rate. Slow-burning propellants may create too much gas for the gas system to handle. On the other hand, quick-burning powders may not generate enough gas to operate the action. Reloads should be kept close to factory velocity specifications for reliable functioning.

Light loads or a dirty chamber can cause poor extraction. If you discover that fired cases are covered with tiny dents, powder residue has built up in the chamber. Clean the chamber with a brush. Light loads can also cause poor feeding and extraction because they do not generate enough gas to fully cycle the action. The first round fired may have enough power to eject the fired case but not enough to move the bolt far enough to pick up the next cartridge in the magazine.

Some rifles function best with crimped bullets; others require no crimping. Several Speer bullets feature cannelures so that secure crimping can be performed. If a handloader wants to shoot 150-grain bullets in a 30-caliber semi-auto, they can choose the 150-grain Grand Slam which has a crimping cannelure. The crimp has two advantages in this class of rifle. It smoothes the sharp edge at the case mouth and also prevents the bullet from being shoved into the case when it strikes the feed ramp.

Many semi-auto sporters have very light barrels. To effectively evaluate accuracy, allow sufficient time between shots for the barrel to cool. This recommendation also applies to any rifle with a slim barrel profile.

Poor Accuracy

There are many factors that can affect accuracy. We will assume you are shooting from a solid rest and using a firearm that has already demonstrated its ability to produce good groups. Before troubleshooting the ammo, it is a good idea to troubleshoot the gun as follows:

- **Is the rifle chambered for the ammunition you're shooting?** Some cartridges will chamber and fire in firearms intended for a different cartridge. If you shoot a 257 Roberts cartridge in a 7mm Mauser rifle, the bullets would not properly contact the rifling and you will see "keyholes" in the target—if they even hit the target! Keyholes are elongated bullet holes caused by a tumbling bullet.
- **Are you positioning the firearm on the rest consistently?** Try to make each setup the same.
- **Is the barrel touching the rest?** Bench testing requires that the rest contact the rifle's forearm, not the barrel.
- **Are the sights firmly attached to the firearm?** Screws can work loose from recoil, allowing the sights to move with each shot.
- **Are the screws holding the action in the stock secure?** A loose action screw in a bolt-action rifle can open groups significantly. Front screw should be tight, rear screw snug.
- **Is the bore fouled with lead or jacket material?** This problem will usually show up later in the shooting session as more residue builds up in the bore.
- **Has a wood stock warped due to moisture absorption?** If your rifle and ammo shot well last season but refuse to perform now, a warped stock should be a prime suspect. If this happens, consult a gunsmith to have the situation corrected.

If these factors do not seem to be the problem, then review the things that can directly affect the ammunition:

- **Under-ignition**—This is usually caused by using a standard primer when a magnum primer is recommended. The lower energy output of a standard primer may result in widely varying velocities. On the target, this usually takes the form of vertical stringing of the shots. This condition is more prevalent in cold weather.
- **Excessive headspace**—A bottleneck case with the shoulder pushed back too far or a rimless straight case trimmed too short can degrade accuracy.
- **Unnecessary crimp**—Have you attempted to crimp a rifle bullet that doesn't have a crimping groove? Group sizes can increase as much as 40 percent because this damages the jacket.
- **Mixed cartridge cases**—Your cases should have the same headstamp and preferably be from the same lot. Some folks weigh their cases and sort into groups. Near-equal weights can mean near-equal capacity. You will have to do your own research as to whether or not this has an effect on group size.
- **Excessive lubricant**—Have you removed all traces of sizing lubricant from the cases? If not, they will be inconsistent in the way they grip the chamber at peak pressure.
- **Wind conditions**—A strong, gusting crosswind will cause horizontal dispersion of the groups. Light, high-velocity bullets are more subject to wind conditions than heavier, slower bullets. There's not much you can do about this problem. You may have to pack up and try again on a calmer day.

• • • • •

Ammunition loaded with care and attention will give fine results. Handloading is a more rewarding hobby if you relax and take the time to enjoy it.

CHAPTER 10

OUR YOUTH: THE FUTURE OF OUR SHOOTING AND HUNTING HERITAGE
Tom Saleen
Vice President of International Sales (Retired), ATK

My father survived a major wound in the European theatre of WWII, but passed away in 1959 leaving our 29-year-old mother and seven children. At age nine, a few months before Dad died, I went on my one and only hunt with him. He took the buck offhand with the 270 Winchester as it raced across the hillside; it turned out to be my favorite memory of time with my father.

I was the second oldest in a family of five boys and two girls. Within a few years, my four brothers and I had access to Dad's rimfire and centerfire rifles just about any time we wanted to use them. Living in back country Yellow Pine, Idaho in the early 60s, we could go shooting as frequently as we wanted if we could come up with ammunition. Our biggest problem was always access to ammunition. In fact, early deer and elk hunting trips found us borrowing a few rounds from more than one friend. At the time, all we really cared about was if we had the right cartridge. One sight-in shot was usually deemed adequate. Little did we know and understand the need to properly sight in a rifle or what it took to be truly efficient and competent with a firearm.

Later, I became a Lewiston, Idaho policeman and was soon initiated to the thorough and constructive shooting disciplines taught at the police academy and in recurring training exercises. Fifteen years in law enforcement, many of those with emphasis on practical training, shooting on the pistol team, and range exposure nearly every day during a three month course at the FBI Academy in Quantico, solidified a respect for the fairly comprehensive shooting resume I had built. It also heightened my awareness of the absolute need for a significantly broader and stronger firearms training program for future shooters and for our youth.

In some capacity, I've spent much of my life around firearms and ammunition.

CHAPTER 10

After a bombing incident during a robbery killed a colleague and prematurely ended my law enforcement profession, I transitioned to what became a three decade long career with CCI/Speer and worked to initiate the company's first law enforcement sales program. Working in this capacity, I was often away from home on business travel and had yet to spend as much time as I hoped teaching the youth in my own family the skills I now considered essential. As those of you with young sons and daughters interested in hunting might appreciate, there was a lot of anxiety when at age 12 my son, Travis, passed his Hunters Safety Course and wanted to go on his first deer hunt.

I also clearly realized the lack of disciplined firearms and safety training I had received as a youngster. What's more, as a former police officer, I had observed first-hand many and varied tragedies associated with the improper use of firearms. Beyond any doubt, I was strongly motivated to make certain Travis went to the field with the training he needed to make him competent and safe. Accordingly, before the opening of deer season and over the next few months, we organized and executed a detailed firearms training program for Travis.

I grew up reading Jack O'Connor and it was Dad's 270 Winchester with a shortened stock that was going to be Travis' first rifle. Together, we set up the RCBS Rock Chucker press and with the oversight of his little sister, Tami, we loaded up 200 rounds of light 270 practice loads. We then went to the range over several days where Travis shot at various targets and distances to gain knowledge of the rifle and to understand what it took to be proficient, safe, and accurate. Next, we loaded up the spent cases a little hotter and repeated the process.

Later we loaded up the cases for a third time, now with the 150-grain Grand Slam bullets that would be his hunting loads. When he started shooting the hunting loads, I can recall being astounded at the results. There is a lot of difference between a lad that fires a few rounds with his hunting rifle and one who has fired a few hundred rounds. It was rewarding to see Travis could shoot well on the bench, shoot well in a prone position and shoot competently in a sitting position. He was starting to understand too how to shoot offhand; but realized right away that a rest for the rifle worked a lot better for him. Most important to me though, was that he understood clearly the safety aspects of gun handling and knew the rifle, the optics, the safety, and how to load and unload his rifle like a pro.

The time to put this practice into action had arrived. I took Travis to my old hunting area in Idaho's Salmon River Mountains where he harvested a very nice mule deer buck shortly after daylight on his first hunting trip. To this day that remains the best hunting trip of my life. That has been close to 28 years ago, and I am happy to report that Travis continues to climb up and down the Idaho mountains on every occasion that presents itself. It is also rewarding to see that where I used to plan the trip and lead the way, the torch has passed and he is now the undisputable master guide of our annual hunting adventures.

Travis has also developed an enviable harvest record on fair chase wilderness land. A few years ago I was with him when he used his custom built 270 he received as a high school graduation present and firing a 150-grain Grand Slam bullet, that he handloaded, to take a Royal bull elk at 320 yards. But the most satisfying result of Travis' experience is to see this legacy passed down to his 12 year-old son, Ross. Ross too fired hundreds of rounds before his first hunt. He knows not to shoot at noise coming from the brush and how excitement and adrenaline can lead to poor judgment calls. On his initial hunt, Ross harvested a nice mule deer his first day out. Considering all the aspects of handling, loading, unloading, and shooting his rifle, he knows that 270 backward and forward. And just like Travis, he keeps shooting to maintain proficiency.

Over the years I have told many family members, friends and acquaintances about the way we initiated Travis to hunting and shooting. It was the right thing to do and I firmly believe that training of this nature and extent is mandatory for the new generations of hunters growing up. For the future of the shooting sports, both parents and the hunting public need to be assured that youngsters taking to the field have gone the extra miles to develop their firearms safety skills and are competent marksmen. Hunter Safety courses are the right start, but shooting hundreds of rounds in your personal hunting rifle goes a long way to improve levels of safety and hone shooting skills.

A lot of seasons have come and gone, and I have enjoyed and appreciated the fall hunting trips about as much as anything in my life. Hopefully, many parents and grandparents will think about the way Travis was initiated to hunting and will understand the importance of a broad, realistic, and extensive firearms training program for their children and grandchildren. We have more big game hunting and shooting opportunities than at any time in our history. Now more than ever, the future of the shooting sports depends on new shooters going to the field with higher safety awareness and better shooting competencies than has ever been necessary.

The author, Tom Saleen and his grandson Ross

CHAPTER 11

INCREASING HIT PROBABILITY
Jim Gilliland
Shadow 6 Consulting

In recent years, long-range shooting has really come into its own. Information, equipment, and ammunition technology has become – well - more technical. Over the last twenty years of true long-range shooting, I've had the advantage of learning things the way they were first taught many years ago to just yesterday; from traditional positions with iron sights, slings and a standard rifle to the latest support bag, gadgets, and custom hand-built rifle, ammo, and optics.

One thing keeps coming back to the top of my shooting lessons and learning curve:

You Have To Shoot Correctly To Hit Correctly

That's it, plain and simple. There are several things I will not go to the range without anymore and don't think any shooter who is somewhat serious should avoid. Technology can make an average shooter a great shooter, but that can be sidetracked by weak batteries. I'm going to share what I feel is essential to actually increasing your true "hit probability" and not just the gadgetry in your range bag.

First, you have to **actually shoot**—a LOT. This should not come as a surprise, as usually the more often you do something, the better you get at doing it. In fact, to be a *great* shot, you only have to do two things consistently.

- Point the rifle at the exact place you want the projectile to hit
- Fire the rifle without moving it

That's it — the secret is out. You can now become the greatest marksman in the history of mankind. Well, except for all the other things you do that make accomplishing those two simple tasks hard. Things like poor mental preparation, not lining the sights up consistently, not being perfectly still, improper trigger control, etc., etc. It's true that if you can precisely aim and fire a rifle without moving it, you will make a perfect shot. But it's also true that you have to *isolate all the other variables.*

We have all heard the four fundamentals of marksmanship. They are likely the second thing young shooters learn by heart, just after the rules of gun safety. Well, what if I told you the long revered fundamentals of marksmanship were bologna. Now that many capable shooters have closed the book and cussed me, the rest of you can continue reading.

Here's the low down: *"Perfect"* is the enemy of *"good enough."* Suppose you were hanging from a rope tied to a helicopter with a 30MPH crosswind trying to hit the "X" on the side of a boat in 5-foot seas. The only way you could be successful is to make sure the rifle was pointed where the "X" will be when the bullet arrives. Could that happen? The law of probability says it can. All the dramatic lead-in aside, hitting any given shot means you have to get as steady as possible given your particular position. Align the sights and place them on the target correctly, concentrate solely on the sight picture and press the trigger straight to the rear, without moving until the recoil stops.

Now, notice I omitted one of the four *sacred fundamentals*. If you can solely concentrate on your sight picture, your body will naturally control your breathing and heartbeat; there's no need to waste brainpower on something your body will do subconsciously. Please pass the smelling salts to half of the remaining readers who just passed out from reading such heresy.

Think about this. Did you do this crazy breathing ritual the last time you lined up a needle and thread? Did you pray to the Coffee God to control your heartbeat and slow your breathing? Or were you so concentrated on the act of "pressing" the thread through the "X" in the needle you magically didn't breathe or thump in rhythm? In fact, you lined the two objects up, concentrating on the single task, your body regulated itself to control movement, and you were successful. Sounds like a good shot to me. You must practice this over and over to get proficient at it to increase the "probability" of doing it correctly. You have to get out and **actually shoot**.

Mechanical Technology

No one doubts that today's manufacturing techniques and technologies are vastly better than ever before. The quality of metals, computerized machining, and precision tooling allow even the mediocre to make great gun parts. From the components of a loaded round, to wire EDM cutting of raceways, today's dispersion standards are a third of what they were when I was growing up. The average gunsmith can make a rifle shoot half-MOA where just twenty years ago one-MOA was the benchmark. Today shooters of all experience levels have access to much higher quality production rifles and optics than were available just a few decades ago. Today's rifleman is better outfitted than ever in history — yet we still want more.

I've noticed this in most of my classes. We expect more because we have adopted a mindset that a material solution will remedy any training deficiency. The common thread is that shooters can tell you every intimate detail of their rifle: the make and model of the stock, what it is made of, and the process used to make it. They can tell you who made the action, and of what type metal, how the raceways were cut and why it's unique. They know every barrel detail including the contour, its metallurgy, the target crown specs, the twist rate and style of rifling.

They quote every tiny detail until you ask what kind of scope they have. You get a very short "It's a Swarovski with X reticle." They have no clue as to how many lenses are in it, or any other technical detail. Most of us have a mental disconnect because we only wish to talk about the things we can grasp and not what is voodoo to us.

Actually, how your rifle and optics are made don't matter if you can't use them properly. The probability of hitting your target is poor. Even if you have the best quality products, you still have to get out and **actually shoot**.

Caliber selection is one of the most overlooked aspects of the whole shooting program. Too many shooters select a firearm *before* deciding what they want to shoot. Remember, *the bullet is what matters most*. You cannot expect a typical, precision-made match round to have the proper lethality on game just as an expanding hunting bullet will not be as accurate as a match projectile. Match bullet design is focused primarily on achieving optimum external ballistic performance, while the hunting bullet emphasizes reliable terminal results. That simply means one is meant to fly good and the other hit good.

A shooter must decide what they want to do: hunt elk at 400 yards, deer at 150, prairie dogs at 800 or paper at 1000. Once you have decided *what* you want to do, then you must select a bullet designed to do just that. The next step is to decide what propellant and charge weight you need to launch that bullet to achieve a desired velocity. WABAM! You have your cartridge. Now you can figure out what rifle action you need to fit that cartridge.

Of course, I've over-simplified the process quite a bit. However, this is one path and there are some shortcuts. Today's market makes it easy to find a factory cartridge to accomplish just about anything, e.g., shooting as far and as fast as possible; but, alas, we often want even more. No need to worry. With just a few drawings and some brainpower you can design your own wildcat and contact one of several companies to have dies, brass, or even cartridges made to your custom specs. Still however, you'll have to take the cartridge, rifle, and scope to the range and **actually shoot**.

Properly ranging and calling wind conditions are two basic attributes you must master to begin your successful shot process. No matter the cartridge, you have to be able to accurately set the elevation and know just how much to hold off to increase your "hit probability." Sadly, we apparently have declined in core knowledge tremendously since I was a kid because now a 30-06 Springfield zeroed 1.5 inches high at 100 yards can kill any animal -- at any distance -- when you "hold just over its back?" I swear if another childhood friend of mine tells me they killed their monster buck at 783 yards and all they did was hold just over its back, I'm going to punch them in the throat.

Now, threats of violence aside, let's discuss both topics further. First, knowing the true range to your target is one surefire way of setting yourself up for success. Gravity's pull is constant so the flight of the bullet from muzzle to target can be mathematically determined using the bullet muzzle velocity, weight, BC, sight height over the bore, and rifling twist rate. Today we can use our computers and even our phones for this.

Actually, there are two different ranges you must consider. The first is the *actual range* from the muzzle to the target. The second is the *ballistic range*. The actual range, is simply the distance from you to the target in a straight line. When shots are relatively flat, all you need to know is the actual range. The ballistic range becomes important if you are shooting at a noticeable angle – uphill or down. Without getting into a physics lesson, if you do not compensate for this, you will always shoot over your target (compared to a flat distance condition) because the bullets trajectory is affected by gravity over a shorter distance. There are lots of articles about this topic as well as instructors who offer shooting classes.

The second factor to be considered is the effect of wind on the projectile. Again, without enrolling you in an external ballistics class, let's discuss how wind affect's the bullet's horizontal trajectory. To accommodate wind conditions, you have to know the direction, speed, and what terrain the wind is rolling over. For typical hunting shots up to 200 yards there's little need to bother unless the wind is very strong and running directly across the bullet's flight path. However, to increase the "hit probability" you really must get out in the areas where you are going to be hunting or shooting in the conditions you will encounter and spend plenty of time training with your equipment.

Recent technology gains have no doubt allowed the enthusiast long-range shooter to do things easier; but, all too often they have little understanding of what is actually making them successful. I've become more reliant on technology. I could not imagine going to a match or on a hunting trip without a compact range finder or having my rifle info in my Kestrel wind meter. While these new masterpieces of technology provide valuable information, they have in some ways made shooters too lazy to gain the information manually, thus giving some a false sense of ability.

Now don't get me wrong. As I said, I use technology. I use a MagnetoSpeed V3 chronograph to get my bullet velocity, type this into my Kestrel with the rest of my information and, *poof*, I have data to shoot to my rifle's ability at distance. However, I know how to do that *without the technology* and that is why I feel that one should acquire the basic knowledge before applying technology. I want my children to learn to shoot with iron sights before I give them a scope.

Training on your equipment should start with the basic mechanical aspects and work to the sophisticated technical ones. Honestly, technology and new waves of information available to the end user have raised our awareness and given the shooter greater power when it comes to what kind of accuracy they demand. Today's typical shooter knows more about ammo, components, manufacturing techniques and processes than ever before. But all that knowledge will not help if you do not put it into practice. You will never be able to obtain your end goal without practice. Once again, you have to **actually shoot.**

In closing, training—be it on your own or, better yet, with a qualified and vetted instructor—will get you out of your comfort zone and teach you what you don't know and need to learn. If you are going to take that once-in-a-lifetime shot at a living animal, you have to put some rounds down range first and learn how to successfully improve your "hit probability." You don't need a computer program, or a book. You just have to get out there and **actually shoot.**

INTRODUCTION TO RIFLE DATA

The following section contains data for use with Speer® bullets in today's popular rifle calibers and for many legacy cartridges that are still widely handloaded.

We do not guess at these numbers. Charge weights and velocities published here are the result of thousands of ballistician-hours spent in loading, experimenting, collecting and vetting data. Speer's load recommendations are more robust than any in the industry and one of the most comprehensive offerings. All charge weights and velocities have been developed from meticulously collected laboratory pressure correlations using state-of-the-art equipment and techniques. There may be subjectivity in the 'kill power' of a bullet design or the distance to zero-sight your rifle, but when it comes to the handloading data presented here, this is the best ballistic science on the market.

You will notice some differences in how the numbers are presented compared to previous load manuals. The number of propellants available to the handloader grows each year. Many of these are formulated for specific case volumes and operating pressures with their sweet spot in only a small family of cartridge designs. Finding charge recommendations for new propellants (and for new bullets using old propellants) is a continual process and you will see some cartridges have well over a dozen offerings. Classic loads in legacy cartridges are presented alongside the latest and greatest. We think you will find the comparisons interesting. Many still rank in the top five highest posted velocities.

The newest powders, in most cases however, are phenomenal products. We are proud to collaborate with our sister company, Alliant Powder, using many of their current selection of cutting edge propellants that are two steps ahead of the double-based propellants of decades past. They are much cleaner burning, with wide-ranging temperature stability, de-coppering agents, and low flash – all while generating some of the highest velocities at safe pressure. Our competitors are producing some top-notch offerings as well and we don't discriminate when it comes to loading data collection.

Powders are listed in descending order by maximum charge velocity. Charge weights are determined with the specific components listed for each data set. This does not mean that you will get the same velocity even if you use all of the same components shown. There is inherent variation in case volume, primer and powder chemistry, and barrel geometries. That said, you will get much closer to our results than you will by substituting components. Regardless of whose components you load with, this is why it's important to begin with the start charge anytime you make a change and work up from there.

Contrary to popular Internet 'wisdom', we do not drastically limit maximum charge weights and pressures but rather apply the same industry-accepted practices that are used to produce high-performance factory ammunition. Our goal is to help handloaders duplicate that same top performance while keeping loads safe. Remember, maximum charges put you near the upper limit of acceptable pressures established by the industry and it will not benefit you or your rifle to exceed them. Starting charges on newly acquired data generally fall between 70 and 90 percent of the maximum pressure allowed for the cartridge. They are reduced enough to allow for component variation. In cases where unsafe conditions could result from too low of a charge weight, we have indicated "DNR" – Do Not Reduce. Bullet in bore, delayed ignition, and other phenomena can cause high pressure events with too little powder in these rare cases.

A significant change in Speer #15 to note is that we have published rifle velocities (with a few exceptions) from a 24" barrel. In the past we have picked cartridge-specific barrel lengths in an attempt to provide a representative velocity for popular models. For instance, how many 30 M1 Carbines are shot thru 24" barrels? This has always been a subject of "enthusiastic discussion" among handloaders. For this edition we decided that adopting a consistent barrel length across all cartridges is more appropriate than our guessing at what model rifle you are likely to be shooting.

Cartridge overall lengths (COAL) used in testing are shown for each bullet as has been standard in most recent load manuals. Note that these are provided only as a guideline. For some bullets, COAL is determined by a crimping feature. In those instances, it will be necessary to tweak to match your specific case length, ensuring a good crimp and smooth chambering. For compressed charges (denoted with the letter 'C' following the charge weight), the tested COAL shown gave us 'substantial' compression. We didn't list this just because the bullet heel may have touched the top of the powder charge. Consequently, you may find variations in case volume between manufacturers preventing you from putting this much powder in the case depending on your charging technique. If your chamber allows the bullet to be seated out farther in the case mouth you should have no issues and, for most cartridges, accuracy may improve.

We are also excited to offer Gold Dot® Rifle bullets for the first time to handloaders. These bullets have in-bore characteristics different from traditional jacketed projectiles and may produce different pressures. That is why you will see their load data listed separately.

Gold Dot Rifle bullets are coated with boron nitride (BN) to reduce pressure variation and allow them to be loaded with a wider variety of propellants. This coating is a synthetically produced crystalline powder composed of the two elements, boron and nitrogen. It is non-toxic and chemically inert. BN is widely used in products ranging from cosmetics to dental inserts. When properly applied, we've found this coating to significantly reduce bore friction that has the effect, in many cases, of lowering measured peak pressures. This often allows us to post higher velocities while remaining within pressure limits for a given cartridge. Even in examples where we do not see significant velocity increases, shot-to-shot pressure and velocity variations are drastically reduced: meaning a more consistent product for the handloader.

Perhaps the largest benefit is to our customers who load for notoriously rangy cartridges. Our testing with BN coated products has demonstrated drastic reductions or elimination of pressure "flyers" in some cartridges. It should go without saying that the coating must be present on these bullets when you load them. It's a very durable treatment, embedded into the surface of the copper jacket and, though you may wipe off some loose residual BN, the coating will stand up to normal handling. Do not tumble or wash these bullets in media however as you will reduce the coatings' effect and higher pressures could result. Clean your firearms as you normally would with powder solvents or foaming bore cleaners. No special methods or chemicals are required.

SAFETY INFORMATION

All reloading data contained herein is intended for use only by persons familiar with handloading practices, their own firearms and reloading equipment. Before using this data to assemble any ammunition, you must read and understand the reloading safety guidelines in Chapter Five and all safety related cautions in the individual cartridge sections. We strongly urge new reloaders to read and understand the text of this manual. It has been written to give clear instruction in the principles and processes of reloading. Use the most current data. Components and cartridge standards change over time and these changes will affect load recommendations in the Speer Manual. It is fruitless to compare modern data to that published decades ago. Using old data with current components can create unsafe ammunition. If you are uncertain of the operation of your reloading equipment or the properties of any components, contact the manufacturer for additional assistance. Never be afraid to ask for help.

DISCLAIMER

These loads are for Speer bullets. Bullets of other makes will not produce the same pressures and velocities and can create an unsafe condition if used with loads shown here. Because Vista Outdoor has no control over individual loading practices or the quality of the firearms in which the resulting ammunition may be used, we assume no liability—either expressed or implied—for the use of this load data information and instructional materials. The data contained herein replaces, supersedes and obsoletes all data previously published by Speer, Omark Industries, Blount International, Inc., and ATK.

204 RUGER

Parent Cartridge:	222 Remington Magnum
Country of Origin:	USA
Year of Introduction:	2004
Designer(s):	Remington & Ruger
Governing Body:	SAAMI/CIP

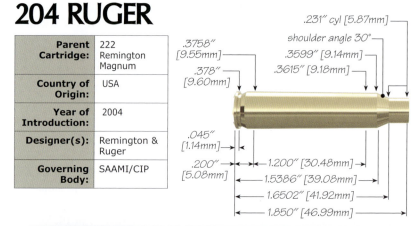

CARTRIDGE CASE DATA

Case Type:	Rimless, bottleneck		
Average Case Capacity:	33.0 grains H$_2$O	Max. Cartridge OAL	2.260 inch
Max. Case Length:	1.850 inch	Primer:	Small Rifle
Case Trim to Length:	1.840 inch	RCBS Shell holder:	# 10
Current Manufacturers:	Hornady, Federal, Remington, Winchester		

BALLISTIC DATA

Max. Average Pressure (MAP):	57,500 psi, CUP not established for this cartridge - SAAMI	Test Barrel Length:	24 inch
Rifling Twist Rate:	1 turn in 12 inch		
Muzzle velocities of factory loaded ammunition	Bullet Wgt.		Muzzle velocity
	32-grain		4,225 fps
	34-grain		4,025 fps
	40-grain		3,900 fps

Muzzle velocity will decrease approximately 40 fps per inch for barrels less than 24 inches.

HISTORICAL NOTES

- Although he was one of the revered modern American gun designers, William B. Ruger, Sr. never had a cartridge named in his honor until after his death.
- The 204 Ruger is the first rifle cartridge to honor his name.
- Yes, you read that right. The 204 Ruger cartridge fires a .204 inch/5mm diameter bullet, not a .224 inch diameter bullet. In this, it is unique in the industry.

- Previously, this diameter was pioneered in the 20 caliber Sheridan air rifle. Since then, 20-cailber bores have become popular in air rifles but remain limited in firearms.
- Not to worry, several bullet makers including Speer, now offer bullets in 20 caliber for reloading.

BALLISTIC NOTES

- Introduction of the 204 Ruger with its unique diameter bullet invites comparison with the many existing 17 and 22 caliber cartridges.
- However, there is no ballistic magic in .204 inch diameter bullets. Bullet weights in 20 caliber (26-45 grains) do occupy the gap between the 17 (15.5-25 grains) and the 22 caliber (40-60+ grains), but this does not confer any specific ballistic advantage.
- The 204 Ruger does offer excellent ballistic performance for hunting varmints, pests, rodents, small game and fur bearers. It is not suitable for larger game such as deer.

TECHNICAL NOTES

- The 204 Ruger is derived from the 222 Remington Magnum case which yields approximately 5% more case volume than the 223 Remington case. The shoulder of the 204 Ruger is moved forward with a sharper angle.
- 204 Ruger cartridge cases can be made by necking down 222 Remington Magnum cases and trimming them to the correct length. It should not be necessary to anneal the necks.

HANDLOADING NOTES

- Speer has developed a 39-grain TNT Hollow Point (TNT HP) bullet specifically for the 204 Ruger cartridge. The TNT bullets are well known for their outstanding performance for hunting varmints, pests and rodents.
- Some rifle manufacturers now offer AR15 rifles chambered in 204 Ruger. Cartridge cases fired in these rifles must be full length resized using a small base die. Thoroughly clean and lubricate your cases before sizing them.
- Cartridge cases fired in bolt-action and single shot rifles and handguns can be neck sized.
- With its small diameter case neck and high MAP levels, you may have to trim your cases to the correct length often.
- The commercial or production powder used in factory loaded 204 Ruger ammunition is not available to handloaders. However with currently available canister powders, you can handload the Speer 39-grain bullet to just over 3,800 fps.
- Powders of medium burn rate yield the best ballistics for this round.

SAFETY NOTES

SPEER 39-grain TNT HP bullet @ a muzzle velocity of 3,900 fps:
- Maximum vertical altitude @ 90° elevation is 7,218 feet.
- Maximum horizontal distance to first impact with ground @ 31° elevation is 3,153 yards.

39 GRAINS

DIAMETER	SECTIONAL DENSITY
0.204"	0.134

20 TNT® HP

Ballistic Coefficient	0.202
COAL Tested	2.260"
Speer Part No.	1015

			Starting Charge		Maximum Charge	
Propellant	Case	Primer	Weight (grains)	Muzzle Velocity (feet/sec)	Weight (grains)	Muzzle Velocity (feet/sec)
Alliant Power Pro 2000-MR	Federal	CCI 400	26.9	3495	29.9	3804
Alliant AR-Comp	Federal	CCI 400	24.0	3559	26.2	3764
Alliant Reloder 15	Federal	CCI 400	25.6	3466	28.2	3756
Hodgdon CFE 223	Federal	CCI 400	24.9	3443	27.5	3745
IMR 8208 XBR	Federal	CCI 400	23.8	3463	26.2	3735
Alliant Power Pro Varmint	Federal	CCI 400	23.7	3393	26.4	3718
Ramshot X-Terminator	Federal	CCI 400	23.5	3424	25.8	3710
Vihtavuori N140	Federal	CCI 400	24.8	3435	27.4	3688
Accurate 2230	Federal	CCI 400	22.8	3421	24.9	3676
Vihtavuori N530	Federal	CCI 400	22.5	3435	24.3	3668
Alliant Power Pro 1200-R	Federal	CCI 400	21.5	3425	23.7	3665

WARNING! *Maximum loads should be used with CAUTION • C = Compressed Load*

22 HORNET

Alternate Names:	5.56x36R, 5.56x36mm Rimmed
Parent Cartridge:	22 W.C.F.
Country of Origin:	USA
Year of Introduction:	1932
Designer(s):	G.L. Wotkyns, T. Whelen
Governing Body:	SAAMI/CIP

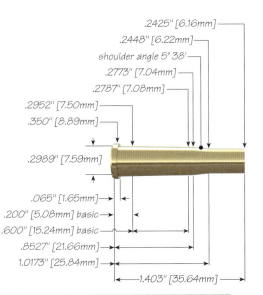

CARTRIDGE CASE DATA

Case Type:	Rimmed, necked
Average Case Capacity:	15.3 grains H$_2$O
Max. Cartridge OAL	1.723 inch
Max. Case Length:	1.403 inch
Primer:	Small Rifle
Case Trim to Length:	1.393 inch
RCBS Shell holder:	# 12
Current Manufacturers:	Federal, Remington, Winchester, Hornady, Nosler, RUAG (RWS), Prvi Partizan, Sellier & Bellot

BALLISTIC DATA

Max. Average Pressure (MAP):	49,000 psi, 43,000 CUP
Test Barrel Length:	24 inch
Rifling Twist Rate:	1 turn in 16 inch

Muzzle velocities of factory loaded ammunition	Bullet Wgt.	Muzzle velocity
	35-grain	3,000 fps
	40-grain	2,800 fps
	45-grain	2,650 fps

Muzzle velocity will decrease approximately 20 fps per inch for barrels less than 24 inches

HISTORICAL NOTES

- The 22 Hornet is a cartridge of opposites. It was the first varmint cartridge designed for smokeless propellants, however its parent cartridge was the obsolete, black powder 22 Winchester Center Fire (WCF).

- It began life as a wildcat designed by two Army officers at Springfield Armory, yet it was standardized and introduced to the commercial trade by Winchester and Savage in 1932.
- By modern standards, the ballistics of the 22 Hornet are the measure of a bygone era. However, its limited ballistic capabilities occupy a market niche no other cartridge has successfully challenged.
- One would expect technology to have advanced far enough for the 22 Hornet to fossilize into history by now. But you would be wrong. The 22 Hornet recently celebrated its 85th year in the field where it remains firmly rooted in the product lines of no less than eight major ammunition companies!

22 Hornet Factoid

The 22 Hornet is the hands down favorite cartridge of the Australian kangaroo market hunters ("cullers"). These thin-skinned animals are culled at close range at night where low noise levels and light recoil are needed. As both the hides and meat are harvested, a clean kill with minimal damage from the bullet impact is very important. The cullers reload ammunition to reduce costs. Perfect conditions for the Hornet.

TECHNICAL NOTES

- The 22 Hornet is a cartridge of limited case capacity, modest pressure levels, leisurely muzzle velocities, and round nose bullets combined to offer a maximum effective range of around 150 yards.
- The slow 1 turn in 16 inch rifling twist of the Hornet limits bullet weights to 52 grains or less.
- The "traditional" 22 Hornet factory load was (and still is) a 45-grain SP bullet at a muzzle velocity of about 2,650 fps.
- Due to its case size, moderate MAP, 22 caliber bullet, and 16 inch rifling twist rate (conveniently the same as the 22 Long Rifle), many rifles are built on modified rimfire actions. These ex-rimfire actions will not withstand high pressure handloads exceeding the MAP lists above.
- 22 Hornet cases are numerical orphans in the sense that they share dimensions with no other modern cartridge case. Now you know why ammunition makers are not keen on the Hornet.
- Many old rifles chambered for the 22 Hornet have a .223 inch bore diameter.
- Ammunition manufacturers have recently injected new life into the Hornet by introducing the new 17 Hornet cartridge.
- Today, American hunters are rediscovering the many advantages of the 22 Hornet—capable ballistic performance to 150 yards combined with low cost, reduced noise signature, excellent accuracy, and long barrel life.

HANDLOADING NOTES

- Due to its small case capacity and modest pressures, the 22 Hornet prefers fast burning propellants.
- The standard 22 Hornet chamber has little or no free-bore between the end of the chamber and the origin of the rifling. Some recent rifles in this caliber have chambers with a small amount of free-bore which may adversely affect accuracy with ammunition loaded to factory OAL.

- Note that 22 Hornet ammunition loaded to an OAL exceeding 1.723 inches may not fit in or feed from box magazines.
- Although the 22 Hornet was designed to fire round nose bullets, spitzer bullets can be handloaded that will significantly improve down range ballistics. Note the overall loaded cartridge length specified in the loading data when doing so.

SAFETY NOTES

SPEER 52-grain HP @ 2,515 fps muzzle velocity:
- Maximum vertical altitude @ 90° elevation is 6,800 feet.
- Maximum horizontal distance to first impact with ground @ 33° elevation is 3,080 yards.
- For the heavier bullets in 22 Hornet, the data was generated using Small Pistol primers in place of Small Rifle primers. The Small pistol primers improved uniformity for this small volume case.
- Never fire 22 Hornet ammunition in European multi-barrel combination rifles chambered for the 5.6x35Rmm Vierling cartridge which is loaded to a much lower Maximum Average Pressure!

30 GRAINS

DIAMETER	SECTIONAL DENSITY
0.224"	0.085

22 TNT Green®	
Ballistic Coefficient	0.091
COAL Tested	1.675"
Speer Part No.	1021

			Starting Charge		Maximum Charge	
Propellant	Case	Primer	Weight (grains)	Muzzle Velocity (feet/sec)	Weight (grains)	Muzzle Velocity (feet/sec)
Winchester 296	Winchester	Federal 205	12.0	3086	13.0 C	3279
Hodgdon H110	Winchester	Federal 205	11.5	3042	12.5	3239
Alliant 2400	Winchester	Federal 205	10.5	2948	11.5 C	3107
Vihtavuori N110	Winchester	Federal 205	9.5	2741	10.5 C	2888
Accurate 1680	Winchester	Federal 205	12.5	2623	13.5 C	2826
IMR 4227	Winchester	Federal 205	10.5	2649	11.5 C	2814

WARNING! Maximum loads should be used with CAUTION • C = Compressed Load

33 GRAINS

DIAMETER	SECTIONAL DENSITY
0.224"	0.094

22 Hornet HP

Ballistic Coefficient	0.080
COAL Tested	1.680"
Speer Part No.	1014

			Starting Charge		Maximum Charge	
Propellant	Case	Primer	Weight (grains)	Muzzle Velocity (feet/sec)	Weight (grains)	Muzzle Velocity (feet/sec)
Hodgdon H110	Winchester	CCI 500	12.4	3198	12.8	3229
Winchester 296	Winchester	CCI 500	12.4	3054	12.8	3217
Accurate No. 9	Winchester	CCI 500	10.2	2944	10.8	3106
Hodgdon Lil' Gun	Winchester	CCI 500	13.5 C	3068	14.0 C	3093
Alliant 2400	Winchester	CCI 500	11.0	2953	11.5 C	2985
Vihtavuori N110	Winchester	CCI 500	10.0	2879	10.6 C	2947

40 GRAINS

DIAMETER	SECTIONAL DENSITY
0.224"	0.114

22 Spire SP

Ballistic Coefficient	0.144
COAL Tested	1.723"
Speer Part No.	1017

			Starting Charge		Maximum Charge	
Propellant	Case	Primer	Weight (grains)	Muzzle Velocity (feet/sec)	Weight (grains)	Muzzle Velocity (feet/sec)
Hodgdon Lil' Gun	Winchester	CCI 500	12.0	2936	13.0 C	3020
Winchester 296	Winchester	CCI 500	9.2	2639	10.2	2782
Accurate 1680	Winchester	CCI 500	12.4	2574	13.4 C	2757
Hodgdon H110	Winchester	CCI 500	9.2	2589	10.2	2730
IMR 4227	Winchester	CCI 500	10.5	2436	11.3 C	2619
Vihtavuori N110	Winchester	CCI 500	8.1	2407	9.1	2587
Alliant 2400	Winchester	CCI 500	8.1	2278	9.1	2557

WARNING! Maximum loads should be used with CAUTION • C = Compressed Load

45 GRAINS

DIAMETER	SECTIONAL DENSITY
0.224"	0.128

22 Spitzer SP	
Ballistic Coefficient	0.143
COAL Tested	1.723"
Speer Part No.	1023

			Starting Charge		Maximum Charge	
Propellant	Case	Primer	Weight (grains)	Muzzle Velocity (feet/sec)	Weight (grains)	Muzzle Velocity (feet/sec)
Hodgdon Lil' Gun	Winchester	CCI 500	12.0	2750	13.0 C	2913
Winchester 296	Winchester	CCI 500	9.0	2441	10.0	2619
Hodgdon H110	Winchester	CCI 500	9.0	2458	10.0	2599
Accurate 1680	Winchester	CCI 500	12.0	2442	13.0 C	2565
IMR 4227	Winchester	CCI 500	10.1	2300	11.1	2511
Alliant 2400	Winchester	CCI 500	8.0	2220	9.0	2506
Vihtavuori N110	Winchester	CCI 500	8.2	2349	9.0	2450

50 GRAINS

DIAMETER	SECTIONAL DENSITY
0.224"	0.142

22 Spitzer SP	
Ballistic Coefficient	0.207
COAL Tested	1.723"
Speer Part No.	1029

			Starting Charge		Maximum Charge	
Propellant	Case	Primer	Weight (grains)	Muzzle Velocity (feet/sec)	Weight (grains)	Muzzle Velocity (feet/sec)
Hodgdon Lil' Gun	Winchester	CCI 500	11.0 C	2655	12.0 C	2712
Winchester 296	Winchester	CCI 500	9.0	2358	9.7	2503
Hodgdon H110	Winchester	CCI 500	9.0	2382	9.7	2499
Accurate 1680	Winchester	CCI 500	10.9	2243	11.8	2381
Vihtavuori N110	Winchester	CCI 500	7.9	2201	8.6	2306
Accurate 2015	Winchester	CCI 500	11.5 C	2035	12.0 C	2071

WARNING! Maximum loads should be used with CAUTION • C = Compressed Load

52 GRAINS

	DIAMETER	SECTIONAL DENSITY
	0.224"	0.148

22 HP
Ballistic Coefficient	0.168
COAL Tested	1.723"
Speer Part No.	1035

22 Match BTHP
Ballistic Coefficient	0.230
COAL Tested	1.723"
Speer Part No.	1036

			Starting Charge		Maximum Charge	
Propellant	Case	Primer	Weight (grains)	Muzzle Velocity (feet/sec)	Weight (grains)	Muzzle Velocity (feet/sec)
Hodgdon Lil' Gun	Winchester	CCI 500	9.0	2401	9.7	2515
Hodgdon H110	Winchester	CCI 500	7.9	2123	8.9	2315
Winchester 296	Winchester	CCI 500	7.9	2118	8.9	2311
IMR 4227	Winchester	CCI 500	8.6	1863	9.6	2261
Accurate 1680	Winchester	CCI 500	10.1	2054	10.8	2257
IMR 4198	Winchester	CCI 500	9.7	2069	10.5 C	2216
Vihtavuori N110	Winchester	CCI 500	7.4	2071	8.0	2194
Alliant 2400	Winchester	CCI 500	6.7	1853	7.7	2128

218 BEE

Parent Cartridge:	25-20 Winchester
Country of Origin:	USA
Year of Introduction:	1938
Designer(s):	Winchester
Governing Body:	SAAMI

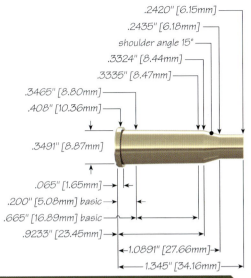

CARTRIDGE CASE DATA

Case Type:	Rimmed, bottleneck		
Average Case Capacity:	20.0 grains H₂O	Max. Cartridge OAL	1.680 inch
Max. Case Length:	1.345 inch	Primer:	Small Rifle
Case Trim to Length:	1.335 inch	RCBS Shell holder:	# 1
Current Manufacturers:	Winchester, Hornady		

BALLISTIC DATA

Max. Average Pressure (MAP):	40,000 CUP, Piezo not established for this round - SAAMI	Test Barrel Length:	24 inch
Rifling Twist Rate:	1 turn in 16 inch		
Muzzle velocities of factory loaded ammunition	Bullet Wgt.		Muzzle velocity
	46-grain		2,760 fps
	Muzzle velocity will decrease approximately 20 fps per inch for barrels less than 24 inches.		

HISTORICAL NOTES

- The 218 Bee was the first, modern, American varmint cartridge designed specifically for lever-action rifles.
- The parent cartridge case of the 218 Bee is the 25-20 Winchester- a dated cartridge still manufactured by Winchester today.
- The 218 Bee was designed by Winchester in 1938 as a follow on to their sales success with the 22 Hornet.

- Winchester's Model 65 was the first rifle chambered for this cartridge; in 1989 Marlin and Browning introduced lever-action rifles in 218 Bee and Ruger offered it in their No. 1 model single-shot rifle.
- The enduring popularity of the 22 Hornet has eluded the 218 Bee which has remained a semi-obscure competitor.
- The future of the 218 Bee remains cloudy. As time passes and trends continue to change, the 218 Bee may soon fall victim to the cost accountant's pencil.

BALLISTIC NOTES

- Although the 218 Bee is a cartridge of limited case capacity and modest pressure levels, it offers 30% more volume than the Hornet. The 218 Bee cannot take full advantage of the additional case volume as its MAP is lower than the Hornet, however, the muzzle velocity of factory ammunition is 110 fps higher than the 22 Hornet with the same bullet weight.
- Unfortunately, the 218 Bee cannot exploit its advantage in muzzle velocity. In order to prevent magazine tube explosions in lever-action rifles, the 218 Bee must be loaded with a blunt 46-grain bullet having a ballistic coefficient approximately that of a brick. This severely limits the maximum effective range of the 218 Bee.
- The slow rifling twist rate of 1 turn in 16 inches limits the 218 Bee to bullets of 52-grain or less.

SAFETY NOTES

SPEER 46-grain SPFN @ 2,738 fps muzzle velocity:
- Maximum vertical altitude @ 90° elevation is 4,715 feet.
- Maximum horizontal distance to first impact with ground @ 28° elevation is 2,100 yards.
- Never use Magnum primers of any brand for loading or reloading 218 Bee ammunition!
- The 218 Bee cartridge requires a unique flat nose bullet for use in lever-action tubular magazines to prevent magazine tube explosions. Crimp the bullet firmly in the cannelure. Never load 218 Bee ammunition with a spitzer bullet in a tubular magazine!

46 GRAINS

DIAMETER	SECTIONAL DENSITY
0.224"	0.131

22 FNSP	
Ballistic Coefficient	0.087
COAL Tested	1.655"
Speer Part No.	1024

			Starting Charge		Maximum Charge	
Propellant	Case	Primer	Weight (grains)	Muzzle Velocity (feet/sec)	Weight (grains)	Muzzle Velocity (feet/sec)
IMR 4198	Winchester	CCI 400	12.8	2466	14.2 C	2738
Hodgdon Lil' Gun	Winchester	CCI 400	9.5	2441	10.5	2662
Accurate 2460	Winchester	CCI 400	15.3	2365	17.0 C	2551
Accurate 1680	Winchester	CCI 400	10.8	2329	12.0	2517
Vihtavuori N110	Winchester	CCI 400	8.3	2224	9.2	2379
Ramshot Enforcer	Winchester	CCI 400	8.7	2234	9.4	2376
Winchester 296	Winchester	CCI 400	8.1	2161	9.0	2325
Accurate No. 9	Winchester	CCI 400	7.8	2082	8.7	2290
Hodgdon H110	Winchester	CCI 400	8.1	1959	9.0	2215
Alliant 2400	Winchester	CCI 400	7.5	1997	8.3	2151
IMR 4227	Winchester	CCI 400	8.9	1914	9.8	2127

WARNING! *Maximum loads should be used with CAUTION • C = Compressed Load*

222 REMINGTON

Alternate Names:	"Triple Deuce"
Country of Origin:	USA
Year of Introduction:	1950
Designer(s):	Mike Walker, Remington
Governing Body:	SAAMI/CIP

Dimensions:
- .253" [6.43mm] cyl
- shoulder angle 23°
- .3759" [9.55mm]
- .3573" [9.08mm]
- .378" [9.60mm]
- .3584" [9.10mm]
- .045" [1.14mm]
- 1.000" [25.40mm] basic
- .200" [5.08mm] basic
- 1.2645" [32.12mm]
- 1.3873" [35.24mm]
- 1.700" [43.18mm]

CARTRIDGE CASE DATA			
Case Type:	Rimless, bottleneck		
Average Case Capacity:	29.5 grains H_2O	Max. Cartridge OAL	2.130 inch
Max. Case Length:	1.700 inch	Primer:	Small Rifle
Case Trim to Length:	1.690 inch	RCBS Shell holder:	# 10
Current Manufacturers:	Federal, Remington, Winchester, Hornady, Nosler, RUAG (RWS), Prvi Partizan, Sellier & Bellot, Sako, Lapua		

BALLISTIC DATA			
Max. Average Pressure (MAP):	50,000 psi, 46,000 CUP - SAAMI	Test Barrel Length:	24 inch
Rifling Twist Rate:	1 turn in 14 inch		
Muzzle velocities of factory loaded ammunition	Bullet Wgt.		Muzzle velocity
	35-grain		3,760 fps
	40-grain		3,450 fps
	45-grain		3,400 fps
	50-grain		3,140 fps

Muzzle velocity will decrease approximately 30 fps per inch for barrels less than 24 inches.

HISTORICAL NOTES

- The 222 Remington cartridge was the first modern, rimless, high pressure cartridge designed from the ground up for varmint hunting.
- In 1950, Remington introduced the new 222 Remington cartridge along with Model 722 bolt-action rifles in this caliber.

- The 222 Remington quickly became known for its accuracy. As a result, it became a popular choice for both varmint hunting and benchrest competition.
- Today, the 222 Remington has become a staple item in nearly every ammunition maker's catalog.
- At the ripe old age of 68 years, the 222 Remington has been eclipsed by the improved ballistic performance of the 223 Remington for varmint hunting and many benchrest competitors have moved on to 6mm calibers.
- Today, American shooters are rediscovering the many advantages of the 222 Remington: capable ballistic performance to 200+ yards combined with low cost, reduced noise signature, excellent accuracy, and long barrel life.

222 Remington Factoid

The 222 Remington is the father of a surprising number of offspring calibers (10 at last count). These include: 17 Fireball, 17 Remington, 204 Ruger, 221 Fireball, 222 Remington Magnum, 223 Remington, 5.56x50mm Magnum, 25-45 Sharps, 300 Blackout and 5.56x45mm NATO.

BALLISTIC NOTES

- The classic 222 Remington factory load was (and still is) a 50-grain SP bullet at a muzzle velocity of 3,140 fps.
- Recently, the 222 Remington has entered the 21st century updated with lightweight, 35-grain bullets at muzzle velocities exceeding 3,600 fps.
- The 222 Remington offers improved ballistics and flatter trajectory than the 22 Hornet or 218 Bee. The 222 Remington enjoys four major advantages over its 22 Hornet and 218 Bee predecessors:
  - The rimless case design is more compatible with bolt-action and semi-automatic rifles.
  - There is an adequate free-bore throat between the end of the chamber and the origin of the rifling.
  - The 222 Remington is loaded to higher maximum average pressures (MAP) that enable higher factory muzzle velocities across the board.
  - It does not suffer from a slow 1 turn in 16 inch rifling twist. The 1 turn in 14 inch twist of the 222 Remington allows it to stabilize bullets up to 55 grains.

HANDLOADING NOTES

- Due to its small case capacity, the 222 Remington cartridge prefers fast burning propellants.
- The 222 Remington cartridge gives best results with 50-grain bullets, however it can be handloaded with bullets from 33-grain to 55 grains.
- Bullets weighing more than 55-grain should not be used to handload 222 Remington ammunition as they may not stabilize.
- Neck sizing can extend case life dramatically. The author has personally reloaded many 222 Remington cases more than 80 times!

SAFETY NOTES

SPEER 55-grain Spitzer SP @ 3,235 fps:
- Maximum vertical altitude @ 90° elevation is 8,380 feet.
- Maximum horizontal distance to first impact with ground @ 33° elevation is 3,752 yards.

40 GRAINS

DIAMETER	SECTIONAL DENSITY
0.224"	0.114

22 Spire SP

Ballistic Coefficient	0.144
COAL Tested	2.130"
Speer Part No.	1017

			Starting Charge		Maximum Charge	
Propellant	Case	Primer	Weight (grains)	Muzzle Velocity (feet/sec)	Weight (grains)	Muzzle Velocity (feet/sec)
Alliant Reloder 7	Remington	CCI 400	20.0	3382	22.0	3617
Accurate 2015	Remington	CCI 400	22.0	3301	24.0	3608
Accurate 2460	Remington	CCI 450	23.5	3212	25.5 C	3581
Hodgdon H322	Remington	CCI 400	22.5	3273	24.5	3538
Alliant Power Pro 1200-R	Federal	Federal 205	21.3	3189	23.6	3505
Hodgdon BL-C(2)	Remington	CCI 450	24.5	3236	26.5 C	3502
Hodgdon H4198	Remington	CCI 400	19.5	3306	21.5	3498
Alliant Power Pro Varmint	Federal	Federal 205	24.0	3137	26.6	3486
Accurate 2230	Remington	CCI 450	22.5	3143	24.5	3465
Accurate 2520	Remington	CCI 450	24.0	3299	26.0 C	3447
IMR 4198	Remington	CCI 400	19.0	3237	21.0	3444
Accurate LT-30	Federal	Federal 205	20.0	3117	22.1	3441
Alliant Reloder 10X	Federal	Federal 205	21.1	3111	23.4	3439
IMR 4895	Remington	CCI 400	23.0	3157	25.0 C	3432
Winchester 748	Remington	CCI 450	23.0	3079	25.0	3402
Vihtavuori N120	Remington	CCI 400	18.0	3049	20.0	3395
Hodgdon H335	Remington	CCI 450	23.0	3078	25.0	3382
Hodgdon H4895	Remington	CCI 400	22.0	3000	24.0 C	3333
IMR 3031	Remington	CCI 400	22.0	3080	24.0 C	3312
Alliant AR-Comp	Federal	Federal 205	23.1	3167	24.0 C	3281

WARNING! Maximum loads should be used with CAUTION • C = Compressed Load

43 GRAINS

DIAMETER	SECTIONAL DENSITY
0.224"	0.122

22 TNT Green®

Ballistic Coefficient	0.150
COAL Tested	2.100"
Speer Part No.	1022

			Starting Charge		Maximum Charge	
Propellant	Case	Primer	Weight (grains)	Muzzle Velocity (feet/sec)	Weight (grains)	Muzzle Velocity (feet/sec)
Hodgdon BENCHMARK	Federal	Federal 205	21.5	3073	23.5	3330
Vihtavuori N133	Federal	Federal 205	19.5	3050	21.5	3305
Ramshot X-Terminator	Federal	Federal 205	21.5	3040	23.5	3276
Alliant Reloder 10X	Federal	Federal 205	19.0	2973	21.0	3267
Winchester 748	Federal	Federal 205	23.0	3087	25.0 C	3262
IMR 3031	Federal	Federal 205	20.0	2914	22.0 C	3227

WARNING! Maximum loads should be used with CAUTION • C = Compressed Load

45 GRAINS

DIAMETER	SECTIONAL DENSITY
0.224"	0.128

22 Spitzer SP	
Ballistic Coefficient	0.143
COAL Tested	2.130"
Speer Part No.	1023

Propellant	Case	Primer	Starting Charge Weight (grains)	Starting Charge Muzzle Velocity (feet/sec)	Maximum Charge Weight (grains)	Maximum Charge Muzzle Velocity (feet/sec)
Hodgdon BL-C(2)	Remington	CCI 450	24.5	3148	26.5 C	3498
Accurate 2460	Remington	CCI 450	23.0	3071	25.0 C	3431
Alliant Reloder 7	Remington	CCI 400	19.5	3150	21.5	3424
Accurate 2015	Remington	CCI 400	21.0	3160	23.0	3398
Alliant Power Pro Varmint	Federal	Federal 205	23.8	3056	26.3	3376
Alliant Power Pro 1200-R	Federal	Federal 205	20.6	3040	22.9	3356
Hodgdon H322	Remington	CCI 400	21.5	3154	23.5	3338
Accurate LT-30	Federal	Federal 205	19.7	3009	21.9	3327
Alliant Reloder 10X	Federal	Federal 205	21.0	3049	23.1	3307
Accurate 2520	Remington	CCI 450	24.0	3037	26.0 C	3301
IMR 4198	Remington	CCI 400	18.5	3032	20.5	3278
Hodgdon H4198	Remington	CCI 400	18.5	3038	20.5	3267
IMR 4895	Remington	CCI 400	22.5	3064	24.5 C	3260
Winchester 748	Remington	CCI 450	23.0	3008	25.0	3234
Vihtavuori N120	Remington	CCI 400	17.5	2910	19.5	3216
Hodgdon H4895	Remington	CCI 400	22.0	2942	24.0 C	3215
Hodgdon H335	Remington	CCI 450	22.5	3002	24.5	3211
Accurate 2230	Remington	CCI 450	21.0	2891	23.0	3177

WARNING! Maximum loads should be used with CAUTION • C = Compressed Load

50 GRAINS

DIAMETER	SECTIONAL DENSITY
0.224"	0.142

22 Spitzer SP	
Ballistic Coefficient	0.207
COAL Tested	2.110"
Speer Part No.	1029

22 TNT® HP	
Ballistic Coefficient	0.228
COAL Tested	2.130"
Speer Part No.	1030

			Starting Charge		Maximum Charge	
Propellant	Case	Primer	Weight (grains)	Muzzle Velocity (feet/sec)	Weight (grains)	Muzzle Velocity (feet/sec)
Accurate 2015	Remington	CCI 400	21.0	3161	23.0	3345
Accurate 2520	Remington	CCI 450	24.0	3130	26.0 C	3270
Hodgdon BL-C(2)	Remington	CCI 450	24.0	2992	26.0	3238
Alliant Reloder 7	Remington	CCI 400	19.0	3010	21.0	3237
Hodgdon H322	Remington	CCI 400	21.0	2967	23.0	3225
Accurate 2460	Remington	CCI 450	22.0	2892	24.0	3224
IMR 3031	Remington	CCI 400	21.0	2959	23.0 C	3199
Accurate 2230	Remington	CCI 450	21.5	2890	23.5	3178
IMR 4895	Remington	CCI 400	22.0	2874	24.0 C	3158
Hodgdon H4895	Remington	CCI 400	22.0	2825	24.0 C	3156
IMR 4198	Remington	CCI 400	18.0	2931	20.0	3135
IMR 4320	Remington	CCI 400	24.0	2945	26.0 C	3134
Vihtavuori N120	Remington	CCI 400	17.0	2808	19.0	3126
Hodgdon H4198	Remington	CCI 400	18.0	2922	20.0	3109
Hodgdon H335	Remington	CCI 450	22.0	2800	24.0	3094
Alliant AR-Comp	Federal	Federal 205	20.3	2896	22.2 C	3094
Alliant Power Pro Varmint	Federal	Federal 205	22.0	2915	23.8	3087
Alliant Power Pro 1200-R	Federal	Federal 205	19.1	2827	21.1	3078
Hodgdon CFE 223	Federal	Federal 205	22.4	2845	24.4	3038
Alliant Reloder 10X	Federal	Federal 205	18.5	2722	20.4	2980
Accurate LT-30	Federal	Federal 205	17.2	2698	19.0	2940

WARNING! Maximum loads should be used with CAUTION • C = Compressed Load

50 GRAINS

DIAMETER	SECTIONAL DENSITY
0.224"	0.142

22 TNT Green®

Ballistic Coefficient	0.190
COAL Tested	2.100"
Speer Part No.	1028

Propellant	Case	Primer	Starting Charge		Maximum Charge	
			Weight (grains)	Muzzle Velocity (feet/sec)	Weight (grains)	Muzzle Velocity (feet/sec)
Alliant AR-Comp	Federal	Federal 205	20.3	2896	22.2 C	3094
Alliant Power Pro Varmint	Federal	Federal 205	22.0	2915	23.8	3087
Alliant Power Pro 1200-R	Federal	Federal 205	19.1	2827	21.1	3078
Winchester 748	Federal	Federal 205	21.5	2849	23.5	3066
Vihtavuori N133	Federal	Federal 205	18.0	2831	20.0	3063
Hodgdon BENCHMARK	Federal	Federal 205	19.5	2796	21.5	3062
IMR 3031	Federal	Federal 205	19.0	2782	21.0 C	3053
Ramshot X-Terminator	Federal	Federal 205	20.0	2818	22.0	3044
Hodgdon CFE 223	Federal	Federal 205	22.4	2845	24.4	3038
Alliant Reloder 10X	Federal	Federal 205	18.5	2722	20.4	2980
Accurate LT-30	Federal	Federal 205	17.2	2698	19.0	2940

WARNING! Maximum loads should be used with CAUTION • C = Compressed Load

52 GRAINS

DIAMETER	SECTIONAL DENSITY
0.224"	0.148

22 HP
Ballistic Coefficient	0.168
COAL Tested	2.130"
Speer Part No.	1035

22 Match BTHP
Ballistic Coefficient	0.230
COAL Tested	2.130"
Speer Part No.	1036

Propellant	Case	Primer	Starting Charge Weight (grains)	Starting Charge Muzzle Velocity (feet/sec)	Maximum Charge Weight (grains)	Maximum Charge Muzzle Velocity (feet/sec)
Accurate 2520	Remington	CCI 450	24.0	3003	26.0 C	3337
Vihtavuori N133	Remington	CCI 400	20.5	3077	22.5 C	3326
IMR 4895	Remington	CCI 400	22.5	3049	24.5 C	3279
Hodgdon H4895	Remington	CCI 400	22.0	3048	24.0	3277
Hodgdon H322	Remington	CCI 400	20.5	2979	22.5	3256
IMR 3031	Remington	CCI 400	21.5	3035	23.5 C	3246
Hodgdon BL-C(2)	Remington	CCI 450	23.5	2926	25.5	3233
Accurate 2460	Remington	CCI 450	21.5	2930	23.5	3185
Alliant Power Pro Varmint	Federal	Federal 205	22.2	2846	24.7	3163
Alliant Power Pro 1200-R	Federal	Federal 205	19.5	2860	21.5	3131
Alliant Reloder 7	Remington	CCI 400	18.0	2835	20.0	3115
Hodgdon CFE 223	Federal	Federal 205	22.7	2842	25.2	3114
Accurate 2230	Remington	CCI 450	21.0	2922	23.0	3109
Winchester 748	Remington	CCI 450	22.5	2904	24.5	3106
Alliant Reloder 10X	Federal	Federal 205	19.6	2820	21.6	3088
Hodgdon H4198	Remington	CCI 400	17.5	2917	19.5	3087
Accurate LT-30	Federal	Federal 205	18.6	2790	20.7	3079
Hodgdon H335	Remington	CCI 450	21.5	2880	23.5	3064
IMR 4198	Remington	CCI 400	17.5	2821	19.5	3050

WARNING! *Maximum loads should be used with CAUTION • C = Compressed Load*

55 GRAINS

DIAMETER	SECTIONAL DENSITY
0.224"	0.157

22 Spitzer SP
Ballistic Coefficient	0.212
COAL Tested	2.130"
Speer Part No.	1047

22 TNT® HP
Ballistic Coefficient	0.233
COAL Tested	2.130"
Speer Part No.	1032

Propellant	Case	Primer	Starting Charge Weight (grains)	Starting Charge Muzzle Velocity (feet/sec)	Maximum Charge Weight (grains)	Maximum Charge Muzzle Velocity (feet/sec)
Accurate 2520	Remington	CCI 450	24.0	2912	26.0 C	3235
Hodgdon H4895	Remington	CCI 400	22.0	2906	24.0 C	3159
Alliant AR-Comp	Federal	Federal 205	21.5	2893	23.8 C	3155
Hodgdon H322	Remington	CCI 400	20.5	2909	22.5	3145
IMR 4895	Remington	CCI 400	22.0	2969	24.0 C	3142
Vihtavuori N133	Remington	CCI 400	20.0	2866	22.0	3132
Accurate 2460	Remington	CCI 450	21.5	2826	23.5	3106
Alliant Power Pro Varmint	Federal	Federal 205	21.8	2766	24.2	3095
IMR 3031	Remington	CCI 400	21.0	2836	23.0 C	3083
Hodgdon BL-C(2)	Remington	CCI 450	23.0	2780	25.0	3072
Hodgdon CFE 223	Federal	Federal 205	22.5	2788	24.8	3065
Alliant Power Pro 1200-R	Federal	Federal 205	19.4	2820	21.5	3058
Alliant Reloder 7	Remington	CCI 400	18.0	2832	20.0	3045
Winchester 748	Remington	CCI 450	22.5	2838	24.5	3035
IMR 4064	Remington	CCI 400	21.5	2775	23.5 C	3033
Alliant Reloder 10X	Federal	Federal 205	19.3	2783	21.3	3024
IMR 4320	Remington	CCI 400	23.0	2794	25.0 C	3020
IMR 4198	Remington	CCI 400	17.5	2804	19.5	2999
Accurate LT-30	Federal	Federal 205	18.5	2729	20.4	2992
Alliant Reloder 15	Remington	CCI 400	22.0	2781	24.0 C	2990
Hodgdon H4198	Remington	CCI 400	17.5	2794	19.5	2974
IMR SR 4759 (reduced load)	Remington	CCI 400	9.0	1866	10.0	2070

WARNING! Maximum loads should be used with CAUTION • C = Compressed Load

223 REMINGTON

Parent Cartridge:	222 Remington
Country of Origin:	USA
Year of Introduction:	1964
Designer(s):	Remington
Governing Body:	SAAMI/CIP

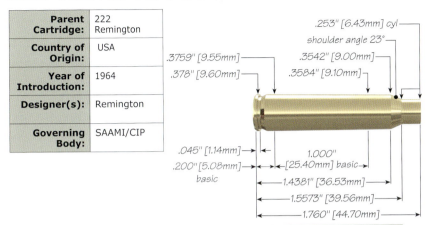

CARTRIDGE CASE DATA

Case Type:	Rimless, bottleneck
Average Case Capacity:	31.9 grains H_2O
Max. Cartridge OAL	2.260 inch
Max. Case Length:	1.760 inch
Primer:	Small Rifle
Case Trim to Length:	1.750 inch
RCBS Shell holder:	# 10
Current Manufacturers:	Federal, Remington, Winchester, Black Hills, IMI, PMC, Hornady, Nosler, Prvi Partizan, Lapua, Norma, Fiocchi, Aguila, Armscor, MEN, Sellier & Bellot, Sako

BALLISTIC DATA

Max. Average Pressure (MAP):	55,000 psi, 52,000 CUP - SAAMI
Test Barrel Length:	24 inch
Rifling Twist Rate:	1 turn in 12 inch, Alternates: 1/14, 1/10, 1/9, 1/8, 1/7

Muzzle velocities of factory loaded ammunition

Bullet Wgt.	Muzzle velocity
35-grain	4,000 fps
40-grain	3,800 fps
50-grain	3,325 fps
52-grain	3,440 fps
55-grain	3,240 fps
62-grain	3,000 fps
77-grain	2,720 fps

Muzzle velocity will decrease approximately 30 fps per inch for barrels less than 24 inches.

HISTORICAL NOTES

- Currently, the 223 Remington is the most popular and versatile 22-caliber centerfire cartridge on the world market.

- The 223 Remington is an offspring of the 222 Remington (1950) and the 222 Remington Magnum (1958).
- The 223 Remington sporting cartridge is based on the U.S. military 5.56x45mm cartridge used in the M16 rifle.
- Following its introduction in 1964, the ballistic performance and versatility of the new 223 Rem. cartridge quickly won over American sportsmen.
- At first, the 223 Remington cartridge gained acceptance in the European market slowly. This changed in 1980 when the 5.56x45mm cartridge was adopted by NATO.
- Today, there is virtually no major ammunition manufacturer that does not offer 223 Remington ammunition.
- The 223 Rem. has grown beyond its military and varmint hunting heritage to become a popular choice for match competition as well as for hunting some types of medium game.

BALLISTIC NOTES

- The 223 Remington entered early on in the 21st century with lightweight, lead-free bullets at muzzle velocities as high as 4,000 fps.
- Do not be fooled by the small size of the 223 Rem. cartridge case. Its Maximum Average Pressure is 10% greater than the 222 Remington. The 223 Remington's standard rifling twist rate is 1 turn in 12 inch. Some barrel/gun makers are using fast twist rates seldom seen in sporting rifles previously.
- Some rifle manufacturers build 223 Remington sporting rifles with rifling twist rates of 1 turn in 10 inch or faster to stabilize heavy bullets. Such fast twist rates are not compatible with most bullets of 50-grain or less and may cause poor accuracy and/or bullet disintegration in mid-air. Mid-air failure is due to excessive rotational speed of the bullet, and bullet integrity can be compromised as a result.

HANDLOADING NOTES

- Due to its small case capacity, the 223 Remington cartridge prefers fast burning propellants.
- Many handloaders report increased case life with less stretching and fewer head separations when neck sizing only. NOTE: this will work only with cases fired in the same bolt-action or single-shot chamber. All cases fired in semi-auto rifles must be full length resized with a small base die.

MAKING SENSE OF 223 REM. RIFLING TWIST RATES

The standard rifling twist rate for 22 caliber sporting cartridges is one turn in 14 inch. Both the military 5.56x45mm cartridge and the sporting 223 Rem. cartridge began life with this twist rate.

- After tests showed that the M16 rifle would not stabilize the 55-grain FMJ BT M193 military bullet at very low temperatures, the rifling twist rate of the M16 was changed to one turn in 12 inch.
- In 1980, the 5.56x45mm cartridge was adopted by NATO. In the process, the SS109 62-grain FMJ BT military bullet was standardized to improve long range ballistic performance. The new cartridge, called the M855 in U.S. military service, is identified by a green tip.

- As the SS109 bullet was longer and heavier than the M193 bullet, the rifling twist rate had to be increased to stabilize it. However, the deciding factor was the new tracer bullet (M856) which required a very fast one turn in 7 inch rifling twist to stabilize in Arctic weather.
- Countries who did not adopt a tracer bullet for their 5.56x45mm military rifles, found a one turn in 9 inch or one turn in 10 inch perfectly adequate to stabilize a 62-grain Ball bullet. Some commercial firearm manufacturers followed suit, such as Ruger with their Mini-14 carbine.
- Following the NATO adoption of the 5.56x45mm cartridge, the rifling twist rate of 223 Remington sporting rifles was changed to one turn in 12 inches.
- Today, manufacturers of the AR-15 Modern Sporting Rifle (MSR) and others offer 5.56x45mm and 223 Rem. barrels with a choice of twist rate and chamber type. See listing for 5.56x45mm caliber in the following pages.

SAFETY NOTES

SPEER 55-grain TNT HP @ a muzzle velocity of 3,313 fps:
- Maximum vertical altitude @ 90° elevation is 8,445 feet.
- Maximum horizontal distance to first impact with ground @ 33° elevation is 3,776 yards.
- Most often you will see that the spherical powders were tested with Magnum Small Rifle primers (the No. 41 can be substituted), other powders performed well with Standard Small Rifle primers.
- The 223 Remington and the 5.56x45mm NATO military cartridges are NOT the same and reloading data is NOT interchangeable!

40 GRAINS

DIAMETER	SECTIONAL DENSITY
0.224"	0.114

22 Spire SP	
Ballistic Coefficient	0.144
COAL Tested	2.060"
Speer Part No.	1017

Propellant	Case	Primer	Starting Charge Weight (grains)	Starting Charge Muzzle Velocity (feet/sec)	Maximum Charge Weight (grains)	Maximum Charge Muzzle Velocity (feet/sec)
Alliant AR-Comp	Federal	Federal 205	26.0	3495	28.5 C	3751
Alliant Power Pro Varmint	Federal	Federal 205	26.1	3400	28.9	3704
Ramshot X-Terminator	Federal	Federal 205	25.6	3487	27.7	3687
Alliant Power Pro 1200-R	Federal	Federal 205	23.1	3404	25.5	3680
Winchester 748	IMI	CCI 450	28.0	3396	30.0 C	3623
Vihtavuori N130	Federal	Federal 205	21.2	3280	23.6	3568
Vihtavuori N133	IMI	CCI 400	23.0	3188	25.0 C	3549
Alliant Reloder 10X	IMI	CCI 400	22.5	3250	24.5	3544
Accurate 2015	IMI	CCI 400	23.5	3115	25.5	3523
Hodgdon Varget	IMI	CCI 400	26.0	3198	28.0 C	3523
Accurate 2460	IMI	CCI 450	24.5	3133	26.5	3507
IMR 3031	IMI	CCI 400	25.0	3077	27.0 C	3470
Hodgdon H322	IMI	CCI 400	24.0	3072	26.0	3447
Accurate 2230	IMI	CCI 400	24.0	3108	26.0	3419
Hodgdon H4198	IMI	CCI 400	20.5	3024	22.5	3400
Hodgdon BL-C(2)	IMI	CCI 450	26.0	3111	28.0	3371
Hodgdon H4895	IMI	CCI 400	23.5	2996	25.5 C	3353
Hodgdon H335	IMI	CCI 450	26.5	2943	28.5	3182
Alliant Reloder 7	IMI	CCI 400	18.5	2727	20.5	3055
Accurate 5744 (reduced load)	IMI	CCI 400	11.0	2000	12.0	2148

WARNING! *Maximum loads should be used with CAUTION • C = Compressed Load*

43 GRAINS

DIAMETER	SECTIONAL DENSITY
0.224"	0.122

22 TNT Green®	
Ballistic Coefficient	0.150
COAL Tested	2.150"
Speer Part No.	1022

			Starting Charge		Maximum Charge	
Propellant	Case	Primer	Weight (grains)	Muzzle Velocity (feet/sec)	Weight (grains)	Muzzle Velocity (feet/sec)
Alliant AR-Comp	Federal	Federal 205	23.0	3310	25.6	3561
Accurate 2230	Federal	Federal 205	23.1	3287	25.5	3545
Winchester 748	Federal	Federal 205	25.5	3334	27.5 C	3538
Alliant Power Pro Varmint	Federal	Federal 205	24.6	3338	26.8	3531
Hodgdon Varget	Federal	Federal 205	24.7	3232	27.3 C	3531
Hodgdon H335	Federal	Federal 205	23.1	3291	25.4	3511
Ramshot TAC	Federal	Federal 205	24.0	3291	26.0	3505
Alliant Power Pro 1200-R	Federal	Federal 205	21.5	3214	23.9	3490
Vihtavuori N540	Federal	Federal 205	25.5	3246	27.5 C	3481
Hodgdon H322	Federal	Federal 205	21.9	3231	24.3	3476
Alliant Reloder 10X	Federal	Federal 205	21.0	3179	23.0	3468
IMR 4895	Federal	Federal 205	23.7	3120	26.3 C	3433
Alliant Reloder 7	Federal	Federal 205	19.4	3115	21.5	3397
IMR 4198	Federal	Federal 205	17.9	3069	19.9	3381
Vihtavuori N130	Federal	Federal 205	19.4	3164	21.1	3353
Accurate 2015	Federal	Federal 205	21.2	3089	23.4	3340

WARNING! *Maximum loads should be used with CAUTION • C = Compressed Load*

45 GRAINS

DIAMETER	SECTIONAL DENSITY
0.224"	0.128

22 Spitzer SP	
Ballistic Coefficient	0.143
COAL Tested	2.155"
Speer Part No.	1023

			Starting Charge		Maximum Charge	
Propellant	Case	Primer	Weight (grains)	Muzzle Velocity (feet/sec)	Weight (grains)	Muzzle Velocity (feet/sec)
Ramshot X-Terminator	Federal	Federal 205	26.1	3368	28.9 C	3659
Alliant Power Pro Varmint	Federal	Federal 205	26.0	3321	28.8	3634
IMR 8208 XBR	Federal	Federal 205	25.0	3293	27.6 C	3592
Alliant Power Pro 1200-R	Federal	Federal 205	22.8	3284	25.2	3569
IMR 4895	IMI	CCI 400	25.0	3146	27.0 C	3464
Winchester 748	IMI	CCI 450	27.0	3032	29.0 C	3456
Hodgdon Varget	IMI	CCI 400	26.0	3157	28.0 C	3446
IMR 4198	IMI	CCI 400	21.0	3050	23.0	3436
Hodgdon H322	IMI	CCI 400	24.0	3002	26.0	3420
IMR 3031	IMI	CCI 400	25.0	3117	27.0 C	3394
Alliant Reloder 10X	IMI	CCI 400	22.0	3085	24.0	3348
Accurate 2460	IMI	CCI 450	24.0	2990	26.0	3330
Vihtavuori N133	IMI	CCI 400	22.5	3012	24.5 C	3317
Accurate 2015	IMI	CCI 400	23.0	2941	25.0	3314
Hodgdon BL-C(2)	IMI	CCI 450	26.0	2937	28.0 C	3272
Accurate 2230	IMI	CCI 400	23.5	2813	25.5	3206
Alliant Reloder 7	IMI	CCI 400	18.0	2851	20.0	3105
Hodgdon H335	IMI	CCI 450	25.0	2721	27.0 C	3065
Accurate 5744 (reduced load)	IMI	CCI 400	11.0	1958	12.0	2104

WARNING! Maximum loads should be used with CAUTION • C = Compressed Load

50 GRAINS

DIAMETER	SECTIONAL DENSITY
0.224"	0.142

22 Spitzer SP
Ballistic Coefficient	0.207
COAL Tested	2.185"
Speer Part No.	1029

22 TNT® HP
Ballistic Coefficient	0.228
COAL Tested	2.235"
Speer Part No.	1030

Propellant	Case	Primer	Starting Charge Weight (grains)	Starting Charge Muzzle Velocity (feet/sec)	Maximum Charge Weight (grains)	Maximum Charge Muzzle Velocity (feet/sec)
Alliant AR-Comp	Federal	Federal 205	25.1	3256	27.8 C	3523
IMR 8208 XBR	Federal	Federal 205	24.7	3142	27.3	3471
Alliant Power Pro Varmint	Federal	Federal 205	25.1	3167	27.7	3467
Winchester 748	IMI	CCI 450	26.5	3130	28.5 C	3458
Alliant Reloder 15	Federal	Federal 205	26.2	3117	29.0 C	3437
Vihtavuori N135	Federal	Federal 205	24.2	3209	26.1	3398
Alliant Power Pro 1200-R	Federal	Federal 205	21.9	3132	24.2	3390
Accurate 2520	IMI	CCI 450	26.0	3229	28.0 C	3385
Hodgdon Varget	IMI	CCI 400	25.5	3079	27.5 C	3372
IMR 4895	IMI	CCI 400	25.0	3073	27.0 C	3369
Hodgdon H322	IMI	CCI 400	24.0	3045	26.0	3356
IMR 3031	IMI	CCI 400	24.0	3012	26.0 C	3339
Alliant Reloder 10X	IMI	CCI 400	21.5	3041	23.5	3322
Accurate 2015	IMI	CCI 400	22.5	2993	24.5	3320
Hodgdon H335	IMI	CCI 450	25.0	3018	27.0	3316
Vihtavuori N133	IMI	CCI 400	22.0	2939	24.0	3290
Hodgdon H4895	IMI	CCI 400	23.5	2910	25.5 C	3255
Hodgdon BL-C(2)	IMI	CCI 450	25.5	3004	27.5	3252
Hodgdon H4198	IMI	CCI 400	20.0	2888	22.0	3229
Accurate 2230	IMI	CCI 400	23.0	2885	25.0	3187
Accurate 5744 (reduced load)	IMI	CCI 400	11.0	1912	12.0	2058

WARNING! *Maximum loads should be used with CAUTION • C = Compressed Load*

50 GRAINS

DIAMETER	SECTIONAL DENSITY
0.224"	0.142

22 TNT Green®

Ballistic Coefficient	0.190
COAL Tested	2.150"
Speer Part No.	1028

			Starting Charge		Maximum Charge	
Propellant	Case	Primer	Weight (grains)	Muzzle Velocity (feet/sec)	Weight (grains)	Muzzle Velocity (feet/sec)
Hodgdon Varget	Federal	Federal 205	24.5	3115	26.5 C	3322
Winchester 748	Federal	Federal 205	24.0	3114	26.0 C	3308
Ramshot TAC	Federal	Federal 205	23.0	3070	25.0	3295
Alliant Reloder 10X	Federal	Federal 205	20.0	3002	22.0	3245
Vihtavuori N540	Federal	Federal 205	23.5	2970	25.5	3218
IMR 4895	Federal	Federal 205	23.5	2908	25.5 C	3169

WARNING! *Maximum loads should be used with CAUTION • C = Compressed Load*

52 GRAINS

DIAMETER	SECTIONAL DENSITY
0.224"	0.148

22 HP
Ballistic Coefficient	0.168
COAL Tested	2.200"
Speer Part No.	1035

22 MATCH BTHP
Ballistic Coefficient	0.230
COAL Tested	2.200"
Speer Part No.	1036

			Starting Charge		Maximum Charge	
Propellant	Case	Primer	Weight (grains)	Muzzle Velocity (feet/sec)	Weight (grains)	Muzzle Velocity (feet/sec)
Winchester 748	IMI	CCI 450	26.0	3187	28.0 C	3510
Alliant AR-Comp	Federal	Federal 205	24.0	3179	26.3 C	3394
IMR 8208 XBR	Federal	Federal 205	23.5	3081	26.1	3353
Alliant Power Pro Varmint	Federal	Federal 205	24.0	3032	26.5	3344
Hodgdon Varget	IMI	CCI 400	25.0	3039	27.0 C	3331
Alliant Reloder 15	Federal	Federal 205	24.9	3032	27.6 C	3322
Vihtavuori N135	Federal	Federal 205	22.8	3054	24.9 C	3277
Alliant Power Pro 1200-R	Federal	Federal 205	21.0	3020	23.1	3267
IMR 4895	IMI	CCI 400	24.5	2888	26.5 C	3254
IMR 3031	IMI	CCI 400	24.0	2915	26.0 C	3247
Alliant Reloder 10X	IMI	CCI 400	20.5	2955	22.5	3230
Vihtavuori N133	IMI	CCI 400	22.0	2864	24.0	3226
Hodgdon H4895	IMI	CCI 400	23.5	2902	25.5 C	3196
Hodgdon H335	IMI	CCI 450	24.5	2919	26.5	3178
Hodgdon H322	IMI	CCI 400	22.5	2859	24.5	3149
IMR 4064	IMI	CCI 400	24.0	2878	26.0 C	3134
Hodgdon BL-C(2)	IMI	CCI 450	25.0	2728	27.0	3108
Accurate 2460	IMI	CCI 450	23.0	2785	25.0	3102
Alliant Reloder 7	IMI	CCI 400	18.5	2639	20.5	2972
Accurate 5744 (reduced load)	IMI	CCI 400	11.0	1906	12.0	2047

WARNING! Maximum loads should be used with CAUTION • C = Compressed Load

55 GRAINS

DIAMETER	SECTIONAL DENSITY
0.224"	0.157

22 TNT® HP
Ballistic Coefficient	0.233
COAL Tested	2.235"
Speer Part No.	1032

22 Spitzer SP
Ballistic Coefficient	0.212
COAL Tested	2.175"
Speer Part No.	1047

			Starting Charge		Maximum Charge	
Propellant	Case	Primer	Weight (grains)	Muzzle Velocity (feet/sec)	Weight (grains)	Muzzle Velocity (feet/sec)
Winchester 748	IMI	CCI 450	26.0	3008	28.0 C	3369
IMR 8208 XBR	Federal	Federal 205	23.7	3045	26.0	3305
Hodgdon CFE 223	Federal	Federal 205	24.6	3004	27.2	3291
Accurate 2230	IMI	CCI 400	24.0	3062	26.0	3286
IMR 3031	IMI	CCI 400	24.0	3019	26.0 C	3276
Alliant Power Pro Varmint	Federal	Federal 205	23.7	3014	25.9	3270
Hodgdon Varget	IMI	CCI 400	25.0	3012	27.0	3268
Hodgdon H4895	IMI	CCI 400	23.5	2949	25.5 C	3246
Alliant AR-Comp	Federal	Federal 205	22.2	3021	24.6 C	3245
Accurate 2520	IMI	CCI 450	25.0	3066	27.0 C	3238
Alliant Power Pro 1200-R	Federal	Federal 205	21.0	2972	23.1	3210
Alliant Reloder 10X	IMI	CCI 400	21.0	2976	23.0	3209
Hodgdon H322	IMI	CCI 400	22.5	2860	24.5	3208
IMR 4064	IMI	CCI 400	24.5	2881	26.5	3193
Hodgdon BL-C(2)	IMI	CCI 450	25.0	2907	27.0	3187
Hodgdon H335	IMI	CCI 450	24.0	2842	26.0	3140
Vihtavuori N133	IMI	CCI 400	21.5	2811	23.5	3139
Accurate 2015	IMI	CCI 400	21.5	2788	23.5	3071
Hodgdon H4198	IMI	CCI 400	19.0	2726	21.0	3021
Accurate 5744 (reduced load)	IMI	CCI 400	11.0	1892	12.0	2033

WARNING! Maximum loads should be used with CAUTION • C = Compressed Load

GOLD DOT RIFLE

55 GRAINS

DIAMETER	SECTIONAL DENSITY	DIAMETER	SECTIONAL DENSITY
0.224"	0.157	0.224"	0.157

22 GD	
Ballistic Coefficient	0.250
COAL Tested	2.230"
Speer Part No.	22455GDB

22 TMJ®	
Ballistic Coefficient	0.250
COAL Tested	2.230"
Speer Part No.	22455TMJ

			Starting Charge		Maximum Charge	
Propellant	Case	Primer	Weight (grains)	Muzzle Velocity (feet/sec)	Weight (grains)	Muzzle Velocity (feet/sec)
Alliant Power Pro 2000-MR	Federal	Federal 205	26.1	3134	29.0 C	3392
Hodgdon CFE 223	Federal	Federal 205	24.7	3069	27.2	3328
Ramshot X-Terminator	Federal	Federal 205	22.5	2992	24.9	3262
Hodgdon Varget	Federal	Federal 205	24.0	2994	26.5 C	3259
Alliant Power Pro Varmint	Federal	Federal 205	22.6	2977	25.1	3259
IMR 8208 XBR	Federal	Federal 205	22.3	2964	24.8	3259
Alliant Reloder 15	Federal	Federal 205	23.7	2989	26.3 C	3242
Alliant AR-Comp	Federal	Federal 205	21.8	3000	24.2	3230
IMR 4895	Federal	Federal 205	23.3	2892	25.8 C	3224
Alliant Power Pro 1200-R	Federal	Federal 205	20.4	2935	22.6	3192
Alliant Reloder 10X	Federal	Federal 205	20.4	2909	22.6	3163
Hodgdon H335	Federal	Federal 205	21.3	2955	23.5	3160
Vihtavuori N135	Federal	Federal 205	20.8	2906	23.0	3143
Accurate LT-32	Federal	Federal 205	19.8	2942	20.9	3060

WARNING! *Maximum loads should be used with CAUTION • C = Compressed Load*

GOLD DOT RIFLE

62 GRAINS	DIAMETER	SECTIONAL DENSITY
	0.224"	0.177

22 GD	
Ballistic Coefficient	0.310
COAL Tested	2.230"
Speer Part No.	22462GDB

			Starting Charge		Maximum Charge	
Propellant	Case	Primer	Weight (grains)	Muzzle Velocity (feet/sec)	Weight (grains)	Muzzle Velocity (feet/sec)
Alliant Power Pro 2000-MR	Federal	Federal 205	25.0	2969	27.7 C	3217
Hodgdon CFE 223	Federal	Federal 205	23.4	2889	26.0	3141
Alliant Power Pro Varmint	Federal	Federal 205	22.0	2864	24.3	3076
Ramshot X-Terminator	Federal	Federal 205	21.7	2838	23.9	3071
Accurate 2460	Federal	Federal 205	22.3	2815	24.8	3069
Hodgdon Varget	Federal	Federal 205	22.4	2802	24.9 C	3064
IMR 8208 XBR	Federal	Federal 205	21.4	2822	23.7	3064
IMR 4895	Federal	Federal 205	22.3	2759	24.8 C	3064
Alliant Reloder 15	Federal	Federal 205	22.7	2808	25.1 C	3056
Alliant AR-Comp	Federal	Federal 205	20.8	2826	23.0	3030
Vihtavuori N540	Federal	Federal 205	22.4	2746	24.8	3009
Hodgdon H335	Federal	Federal 205	20.3	2770	22.4	2971

WARNING! Maximum loads should be used with CAUTION • C = Compressed Load

70 GRAINS

DIAMETER	SECTIONAL DENSITY
0.224"	0.199

22 Semi-Spitzer SP

Ballistic Coefficient	0.219
COAL Tested	2.140"
Speer Part No.	1053

			Starting Charge		Maximum Charge	
Propellant	Case	Primer	Weight (grains)	Muzzle Velocity (feet/sec)	Weight (grains)	Muzzle Velocity (feet/sec)
Winchester 748	IMI	CCI 450	25.0	2862	27.0	3115
Alliant Power Pro 2000-MR	Federal	Federal 205	25.0	2775	27.1	2982
Hodgdon H414	IMI	CCI 450	26.0	2690	28.0	2923
Hodgdon Varget	Federal	Federal 205	22.4	2659	24.8 C	2901
Alliant Power Pro Varmint	Federal	Federal 205	21.0	2632	23.2	2872
Alliant Reloder 15	Federal	Federal 205	22.5	2708	24.1 C	2871
IMR 4895	IMI	CCI 400	22.5	2658	24.5 C	2864
Hodgdon H335	IMI	CCI 450	22.5	2621	24.5	2849
Alliant AR-Comp	Federal	Federal 205	20.0	2679	21.9	2834
Accurate 2460	IMI	CCI 450	21.5	2526	23.5	2814
Accurate 2230	IMI	CCI 400	21.0	2489	23.0	2749
Hodgdon H380	IMI	CCI 450	26.0	2560	28.0	2733
Vihtavuori N135	IMI	CCI 400	20.5	2449	22.5	2693
IMR 4320	IMI	CCI 400	22.5	2474	24.5	2675
Hodgdon BL-C(2)	IMI	CCI 450	21.5	2474	23.5	2648
Accurate 2015	IMI	CCI 400	18.0	2348	20.0	2583

NOTE: Be sure to watch the overall length of the 70-grain Semi-Spitzer when loading as the long bullet can stick in the throat if seated too long. Also, as most loads for this bullet are under 3,000 fps, barrels used should have twist rates faster than 1-in-12 inches.

WARNING! Maximum loads should be used with CAUTION • C = Compressed Load

GOLD DOT RIFLE

75 GRAINS

DIAMETER	SECTIONAL DENSITY	DIAMETER	SECTIONAL DENSITY
0.224"	0.214	0.224"	0.213

22 GD

Ballistic Coefficient	0.411
COAL Tested	2.230"
Speer Part No.	22475GDB

22 TMJ®

Ballistic Coefficient	0.411
COAL Tested	2.230"
Speer Part No.	22475TMJ

			Starting Charge		Maximum Charge	
Propellant	Case	Primer	Weight (grains)	Muzzle Velocity (feet/sec)	Weight (grains)	Muzzle Velocity (feet/sec)
Alliant Power Pro 2000-MR	Federal	Federal 205	23.5	2655	26.1 C	2897
Hodgdon CFE 223	Federal	Federal 205	22.0	2583	24.0	2782
IMR 4895	Federal	Federal 205	21.2	2508	23.5 C	2767
Alliant Reloder 15	Federal	Federal 205	21.2	2514	23.6 C	2761
Ramshot X-Terminator	Federal	Federal 205	20.7	2544	22.9	2757
Alliant Power Pro Varmint	Federal	Federal 205	20.8	2533	23.0	2756
Accurate 2460	Federal	Federal 205	21.0	2524	23.2	2746
Hodgdon Varget	Federal	Federal 205	20.9	2515	23.2 C	2740
Vihtavuori N540	Federal	Federal 205	21.2	2462	23.5 C	2725
IMR 8208 XBR	Federal	Federal 205	20.0	2508	22.1	2723
Alliant AR-Comp	Federal	Federal 205	18.9	2480	20.9	2669
Hodgdon H335	Federal	Federal 205	19.0	2470	21.0	2638

NOTE: Rifling twist rate of 1-in-7 or 1-in-8 inches is recommended.

WARNING! Maximum loads should be used with CAUTION • C = Compressed Load

5.56mm NATO

Alternate Names:	5.56x45mm, 5.56
Parent Cartridge:	223 Remington
Country of Origin:	USA
Year of Introduction:	1964 (U.S), 1980 (NATO)
Designer(s):	U.S. Military (CONARC), Fairchild Industries, Armalite Division (Jim Sullivan) & Remington Arms
Governing Body:	NATO (STANAG 4172), SAAMI/CIP

.253" cyl [6.43mm]
shoulder angle 23°
.354" [8.99mm]
.376" [9.55mm]
.378" [9.60mm]
.045" [1.14mm]
.200" [5.08mm]
1.238" [31.45mm]
1.557" [39.55mm]
1.760" [44.70mm]

CARTRIDGE CASE DATA

Case Type:	Rimless, bottleneck		
Average Case Capacity:	31.0 grains H$_2$O	Max. Cartridge OAL	2.250 inch
Max. Case Length:	1.760 inch	Primer:	Small Rifle-military
Case Trim to Length:	1.750 inch	RCBS Shell holder:	# 10
Current Manufacturers:	Lake City Army Ammunition Plant, Federal, Winchester, Remington, MEN, RUAG, NAMMO, IMI, Greenwood & Battley, PMC, ADI, PMP, etc.		

BALLISTIC DATA

Max. Average Pressure (MAP):	62,366 psi EPVAT (Military Test Barrel); 62,366 psi - CIP	Test Barrel Length:	20 inch
Rifling Twist Rate:	1 turn in 7 inch Alternate: 1/14, 1/12, 1/10, 1/9, 1/8 inch		

Muzzle velocities of factory loaded ammunition	Bullet Wgt.	Muzzle velocity
	M193 – 55-grain	3,260 fps
	M855 – 62-grain	3,100 fps
	M855A1 – 62-grain	3,100 fps

Muzzle velocity will decrease approximately 30 fps per inch for barrels less than 20 inches.

HISTORICAL NOTES

- U.S. Continental Army Command (CONARC) requested bids for a Light Combat Rifle. The military requirements as outlined in the CONARC RFQ were as follows:

    1. 22-caliber
    2. A rifle weight of 6 pounds
    3. Magazine capacity of 20 rounds
    4. Selective fire: semi and full automatic
    5. Penetration on one side of a U.S. steel helmet at 500 yards
    6. Penetration of .135 inch steel plate at 500 yards
    7. Accuracy and ballistics equal to M2 ball ammunition (30-06)
    8. Wounding ability equal to M1 carbine

- The new rifle and cartridge were developed by Armalite, a division of Fairchild Industries, and Remington.

- The rifle was designed by Eugene Stoner and the cartridge by Jim Sullivan, both of whom were employed by Armalite.

- The M-16 was submitted for Air Force trials in 1959. General Curtis LeMay, Chief of Staff of the Air Force ordered 80,000 rifles in 1961.

- The rights to the rifle were later sold to Colt.

- The new cartridge was taken into U.S. military service in 1963 as the: Cartridge, 5.56mm Ball, M193.

- In 1962, Remington standardized the new cartridge with SAAMI and introduced it on the civil market as the 223 Remington.

- In 1980, NATO members adopted STANAG 4172 (STAndard Nato AGreement) to standardize the 5.56x45mm cartridge with the SS109 bullet designed by Browning in Belgium.

- The new 5.56x45mm NATO cartridge did not replace the 7.62x51mm NATO cartridge. Rather, it was adopted as an alternate to be used by the member countries as they saw fit.

- The SS109 offered substantially improved ballistic performance over the M193 and was adopted by the U.S. military in 1980 as the M855.

- The longer bullet of the SS109, and the longer tracer bullet in particular, required a change of rifle twist rate from 1-in-12 to 1-in-7 inches in the rifles, to stabilize the bullets.

TECHNICAL NOTES

- Although the 223 Remington and the 5.56x45mm NATO cartridges may look the same, they are in fact different. This is especially true of the freebore (throat) between the mouth of the case and the origin of the rifling.

- While the 223 Remington chamber has a very short freebore to improve accuracy, the 5.56x45mm NATO cartridge has a longer freebore to reduce pressure.

- If 5.56x45mm NATO ammunition is fired in rifles chambered for 223 Remington, the bullet will contact the rifling which will increase pressure beyond acceptable MAP limits when fired.

- **As a result, 223 Remington ammunition can be safely fired in SAAMI 223 Remington chambers or in NATO 5.56x45mm chambers.**

- However, 5.56x45mm NATO ammunition must not be fired in 223 Remington chambers.
- Some domestic rifle manufacturers have developed alternate chamber and leade dimensions designed to handle both the 5.56x45mm NATO or the 223 Remington safely.
- The C.I.P. specifications for the civilian 223 Remington chambers are much closer to the military 5.56x45mm NATO chambers than SAAMI 223 Remington chambers.

HANDLOADING NOTES

- All 5.56x45mm NATO ammunition has crimped primer pockets. The crimp must be removed to safely seat new primers when reloading. Many commercial manufacturers of 223 Rem. ammunition are crimping primers on selected loads as well. So the crimp removal task is going to be one of your first steps in reloading with both case types.
- The bullets of reloaded 223 Remington or 5.56x45mm NATO ammunition should be crimped; either with a roll crimp if a cannelure is present on the bullet, or a taper crimp if one is not.

SAFETY NOTES

SPEER 75-grain Gold Dot @ a muzzle velocity of 2,849 fps:
- Maximum vertical altitude @ 90° elevation is 10,695 feet.
- Maximum horizontal distance to first impact with ground @ 32° elevation is 4,945 yards.
- With different AR type rifles being made by so many different manufacturers with different chambers, check the chamber designation on the barrel as the cartridge designation on the upper and/or lower receiver may be different.
- Do not fire 5.56x45mm NATO ammunition in rifles chambered for the 223 Remington.

55 GRAINS

DIAMETER	SECTIONAL DENSITY
0.224"	0.157

22 Spitzer SP	
Ballistic Coefficient	0.212
COAL Tested	2.260"
Speer Part No.	1047

			Starting Charge		Maximum Charge	
Propellant	Case	Primer	Weight (grains)	Muzzle Velocity (feet/sec)	Weight (grains)	Muzzle Velocity (feet/sec)
Alliant Power Pro 2000-MR	Federal	CCI 41	27.2	2951	29.3	3177
Hodgdon CFE 223	Federal	CCI 41	24.9	3005	26.7	3119
Alliant Power Pro Varmint	Federal	CCI 41	24.1	2935	25.7	3090
Ramshot X-Terminator	Federal	CCI 41	23.3	2926	25.1	3087
Hodgdon Varget	Federal	CCI 41	25.1	2950	26.5	3077
IMR 4895	Federal	CCI 41	24.5	2883	26.5	3077
Alliant Reloder 15	Federal	CCI 41	24.7	2855	26.4	3066
IMR 8208 XBR	Federal	CCI 41	23.4	2956	25.2	3061
Alliant AR-Comp	Federal	CCI 41	22.8	2907	24.3	3058
Hodgdon H335	Federal	CCI 41	23.7	2959	24.9	3051
Vihtavuori N135	Federal	CCI 41	22.5	2876	23.7	2994
Alliant Reloder10X	Federal	CCI 41	20.9	2847	22.7	2985
Accurate LT-32	Federal	CCI 41	20.8	2889	21.7	2966
Alliant Power Pro 1200-R	Federal	CCI 41	18.4	2640	20.1	2885

WARNING! Maximum loads should be used with CAUTION • C = Compressed Load

GOLD DOT RIFLE

55 GRAINS

DIAMETER	SECTIONAL DENSITY	DIAMETER	SECTIONAL DENSITY
0.224"	0.157	0.224"	0.157

22 GD		22 TMJ®	
Ballistic Coefficient	0.250	Ballistic Coefficient	0.250
COAL Tested	2.260"	COAL Tested	2.260"
Speer Part No.	22455GDB	Speer Part No.	22455TMJ

			Starting Charge		Maximum Charge	
Propellant	Case	Primer	Weight (grains)	Muzzle Velocity (feet/sec)	Weight (grains)	Muzzle Velocity (feet/sec)
Alliant Power Pro 2000-MR	Federal	CCI 41	27.5	2942	30.5 C	3227
Alliant Power Pro Varmint	Federal	CCI 41	24.7	2916	27.3	3193
IMR 8208 XBR	Federal	CCI 41	24.8	2992	26.2	3130
Ramshot X-Terminator	Federal	CCI 41	23.9	2893	25.9	3129
Hodgdon H335	Federal	CCI 41	24.0	2932	26.0	3117
Alliant Reloder 15	Federal	CCI 41	24.7	2787	27.4 C	3111
Alliant AR-Comp	Federal	CCI 41	23.0	2908	25.1 C	3096
Alliant Power Pro 1200-R	Federal	CCI 41	22.3	2956	23.7	3084
Vihtavuori N135	Federal	CCI 41	22.6	2804	25.0	3064
Hodgdon Varget	Federal	CCI 41	25.0	2880	27.0 C	3062
Alliant Reloder 10X	Federal	CCI 41	21.7	2859	23.7	3041
IMR 4895	Federal	CCI 41	24.1	2763	26.5 C	3026
Accurate LT-32	Federal	CCI 41	20.6	2749	22.6	2997

WARNING! Maximum loads should be used with CAUTION • C = Compressed Load

GOLD DOT RIFLE

62 GRAINS

DIAMETER	SECTIONAL DENSITY
0.224"	0.177

22 GD

Ballistic Coefficient	0.310
COAL Tested	2.260"
Speer Part No.	22462GDB

			Starting Charge		Maximum Charge	
Propellant	Case	Primer	Weight (grains)	Muzzle Velocity (feet/sec)	Weight (grains)	Muzzle Velocity (feet/sec)
Alliant Power Pro 2000-MR	Federal	CCI 41	27.3	2937	30.2 C	3180
Hodgdon CFE 223	Federal	CCI 41	25.1	2848	27.8	3089
Alliant Varmint	Federal	CCI 41	23.6	2794	26.2	3063
Ramshot X-Terminator	Federal	CCI 41	22.8	2780	25.3	3034
Hodgdon Varget	Federal	CCI 41	24.0	2794	26.6 C	3029
Accurate 2460	Federal	CCI 41	23.7	2789	26.2	3026
IMR 8208 XBR	Federal	CCI 41	23.0	2822	25.4	3024
Alliant Reloder 15	Federal	CCI 41	24.0	2731	26.6 C	3019
Alliant AR-Comp	Federal	CCI 41	22.3	2752	24.8	3013
IMR 4895	Federal	CCI 41	23.4	2695	25.9 C	2985
Hodgdon H335	Federal	CCI 41	22.5	2731	25.0	2975
Vihtavuori N540	Federal	CCI 41	24.1	2680	26.6	2971

WARNING! *Maximum loads should be used with CAUTION • C = Compressed Load*

70 GRAINS

DIAMETER	SECTIONAL DENSITY
0.224"	0.199

22 Semi-Spitzer SP

Ballistic Coefficient	0.219
COAL Tested	2.230"
Speer Part No.	1053

			Starting Charge		Maximum Charge	
Propellant	Case	Primer	Weight (grains)	Muzzle Velocity (feet/sec)	Weight (grains)	Muzzle Velocity (feet/sec)
Alliant Power Pro 2000-MR	Federal	CCI 41	23.7	2580	26.3	2816
Alliant Power Pro Varmint	Federal	CCI 41	21.8	2525	24.2	2788
Alliant Reloder 15	Federal	CCI 41	22.1	2503	24.6	2769
IMR 4895	Federal	CCI 41	22.0	2554	24.4	2768
Ramshot X-Terminator	Federal	CCI 41	21.0	2512	23.4	2757
Hodgdon CFE 223	Federal	CCI 41	21.9	2530	24.3	2757
Hodgdon Varget	Federal	CCI 41	22.1	2588	24.2	2751
Accurate 2460	Federal	CCI 41	20.4	2533	22.7	2746
IMR 8208 XBR	Federal	CCI 41	20.7	2553	22.9	2732
Vihtavuori N540	Federal	CCI 41	22.1	2468	24.4	2715
Alliant AR-Comp	Federal	CCI 41	20.2	2501	22.4	2710
Hodgdon H335	Federal	CCI 41	20.2	2421	22.4	2664

WARNING! *Maximum loads should be used with CAUTION • C = Compressed Load*

GOLD DOT RIFLE

75 GRAINS

DIAMETER	SECTIONAL DENSITY	DIAMETER	SECTIONAL DENSITY
0.224"	0.214	0.224"	0.214

 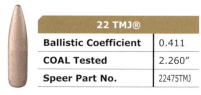

22 GD	
Ballistic Coefficient	0.411
COAL Tested	2.260"
Speer Part No.	22475GDB

22 TMJ®	
Ballistic Coefficient	0.411
COAL Tested	2.260"
Speer Part No.	22475TMJ

			Starting Charge		Maximum Charge	
Propellant	Case	Primer	Weight (grains)	Muzzle Velocity (feet/sec)	Weight (grains)	Muzzle Velocity (feet/sec)
Alliant Power Pro 2000-MR	Federal	CCI 41	24.4	2541	27.1 C	2849
Alliant Power Pro Varmint	Federal	CCI 41	22.0	2485	24.5	2744
Alliant Reloder 15	Federal	CCI 41	22.3	2456	24.8 C	2721
IMR 4895	Federal	CCI 41	22.1	2498	24.4 C	2705
Ramshot X-Terminator	Federal	CCI 41	21.2	2484	23.6	2701
Accurate 2460	Federal	CCI 41	22.1	2515	24.4	2701
Hodgdon Varget	Federal	CCI 41	22.3	2562	23.6 C	2667
Vihtavuori N540	Federal	CCI 41	22.0	2372	24.5	2658
Alliant AR-Comp	Federal	CCI 41	20.3	2437	22.6 C	2655
Hodgdon H335	Federal	CCI 41	21.1	2423	23.3	2634

NOTE: *Rifling twist rate of 1-in-7 or 1-in-8 inches is recommended.*

WARNING! Maximum loads should be used with CAUTION • C = Compressed Load

222 REMINGTON MAGNUM

Parent Cartridge:	222 Remington
Country of Origin:	USA
Year of Introduction:	1958
Designer(s):	Remington
Governing Body:	SAAMI/CIP

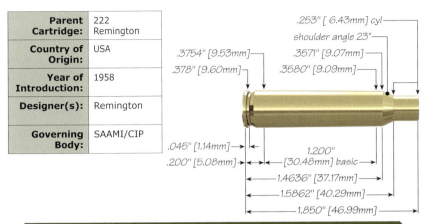

CARTRIDGE CASE DATA

Case Type:	Rimless, bottleneck
Average Case Capacity:	33.3 grains H_2O
Max. Cartridge OAL:	2.280 inch
Max. Case Length:	1.850 inch
Primer:	Small Rifle
Case Trim to Length:	1.840 inch
RCBS Shell holder:	# 10
Current Manufacturers:	Nosler, Sako

BALLISTIC DATA

Max. Average Pressure (MAP):	55,000 psi, 50,000 CUP - SAAMI
Test Barrel Length:	24 inch
Rifling Twist Rate:	1 turn in 14 inch

Muzzle velocities of factory loaded ammunition

Bullet Wgt.	Muzzle velocity
50-grain	3,340 fps
50-grain	3,200 fps
55-grain	3,215 fps

Muzzle velocity will decrease approximately 30 fps per inch for barrels less than 24 inches.

HISTORICAL NOTES

- The 222 Remington Magnum is the largest member of the 222 Remington family of cartridges. It was designed at Remington under a U.S. government contract as the cartridge for the new M16 military rifle.

- When the new cartridge design was found to be more powerful than the military wanted, it was modified by reducing the case length and capacity to make it more compact. In an effort to salvage something from their efforts,

- Remington introduced their original design as the 222 Remington Magnum cartridge in 1958.
- When the new case design was eventually adopted by the U.S. Army as the 5.56x45mm in 1964, Remington bowed to the inevitable and introduced a version of it on the commercial market as the 223 Remington.
- This sealed the fate of the 222 Remington Magnum cartridge. Today, the 223 Rem. cartridge has become the accepted standard for varmint hunting, a benchrest favorite, and a law enforcement staple while the 222 Remington Magnum has become a rapidly fading anachronism.
- Nosler and Sako still offer loaded ammunition in 222 Remington Magnum. New rifles have not been offered for many years now.

BALLISTIC NOTES

- Both the 222 Remington Magnum and the 223 Remington share the same MAP of 55,000 psi. The 222 enjoys slightly greater case capacity than the 223 Remington.
- The result of the trade-offs above mean that both cartridges are factory loaded to the same muzzle velocity leaving the 222 Remington Magnum with no advantage over the 223 Rem.
- In SAAMI, the 222 Rem. Magnum cartridge is considered obsolete but is still listed. It remains active in CIP, but only just barely.
- While the 222 Rem. Magnum is a fine cartridge, it has no ballistic niche to fill, and factory ammunition is not loaded to the cartridge's full potential.

HANDLOADING NOTES

- The 222 Remington Magnum cartridge prefers fast burning propellants and can be handloaded with bullet weights from 40-70 grains.
- Be careful with your cases, they may prove hard to find some day.

SAFETY NOTES

SPEER 55-grain TNT® HP @ 3,480 fps muzzle velocity:

- Maximum vertical altitude @ 90° elevation is 8,586 feet.
- Maximum horizontal distance to first impact with ground @ 33° elevation is 3,825 yards.

40 GRAINS

DIAMETER	SECTIONAL DENSITY
0.224"	0.114

22 Spire SP	
Ballistic Coefficient	0.144
COAL Tested	2.200"
Speer Part No.	1017

			Starting Charge		Maximum Charge	
Propellant	Case	Primer	Weight (grains)	Muzzle Velocity (feet/sec)	Weight (grains)	Muzzle Velocity (feet/sec)
Hodgdon H335	Remington	CCI 450	27.0	3437	29.0	3739
IMR 4320	Remington	CCI 400	27.0	3458	29.0	3701
Winchester 748	Remington	CCI 450	29.0	3412	31.0	3669
IMR 3031	Remington	CCI 400	25.0	3377	27.0	3631
Hodgdon BL-C(2)	Remington	CCI 450	26.0	3316	28.0	3595
IMR 4198	Remington	CCI 400	21.5	3258	23.5	3548
IMR 4064	Remington	CCI 400	26.0	3262	28.0	3497
IMR SR 4759 (reduced load)	Remington	CCI 400	8.0	1541	10.0	1913

WARNING! Maximum loads should be used with CAUTION • C = Compressed Load

222 REMINGTON MAGNUM

45 GRAINS

DIAMETER	SECTIONAL DENSITY
0.224"	0.128

22 Spitzer SP	
Ballistic Coefficient	0.143
COAL Tested	2.220"
Speer Part No.	1023

			Starting Charge		Maximum Charge	
Propellant	Case	Primer	Weight (grains)	Muzzle Velocity (feet/sec)	Weight (grains)	Muzzle Velocity (feet/sec)
Hodgdon H335	Remington	CCI 450	27.0	3397	29.0	3670
Winchester 748	Remington	CCI 450	28.0	3396	30.0	3662
IMR 4320	Remington	CCI 400	27.0	3339	29.0	3569
IMR 3031	Remington	CCI 400	25.0	3276	27.0	3532
IMR 4198	Remington	CCI 400	21.5	3203	23.5	3496
IMR 4895	Remington	CCI 400	25.0	3167	27.0	3403
Alliant Reloder 7	Remington	CCI 400	21.5	3083	23.5	3355
IMR SR 4759 (reduced load)	Remington	CCI 400	8.5	1607	10.5	1987

WARNING! *Maximum loads should be used with* **CAUTION** *• C = Compressed Load*

50 GRAINS

DIAMETER	SECTIONAL DENSITY
0.224"	0.142

22 Spitzer SP
Ballistic Coefficient	0.207
COAL Tested	2.250"
Speer Part No.	1029

22 TNT® HP
Ballistic Coefficient	0.228
COAL Tested	2.250"
Speer Part No.	1030

			Starting Charge		Maximum Charge	
Propellant	Case	Primer	Weight (grains)	Muzzle Velocity (feet/sec)	Weight (grains)	Muzzle Velocity (feet/sec)
Hodgdon H335	Remington	CCI 450	26.5	3250	28.5	3522
IMR 4320	Remington	CCI 400	27.0	3262	29.0	3490
IMR 4198	Remington	CCI 400	21.0	3138	23.0	3423
IMR 4064	Remington	CCI 400	26.0	3196	28.0	3422
Hodgdon BL-C(2)	Remington	CCI 450	25.0	3196	27.0	3405
IMR 3031	Remington	CCI 400	24.5	3155	26.5	3403
Hodgdon H414	Remington	CCI 450	29.0	3139	31.0	3388
IMR SR 4759 (reduced load)	Remington	CCI 400	9.0	1690	11.0	2077

WARNING! *Maximum loads should be used with CAUTION • C = Compressed Load*

52 GRAINS

DIAMETER	SECTIONAL DENSITY
0.224"	0.148

22 HP	
Ballistic Coefficient	0.168
COAL Tested	2.250"
Speer Part No.	1035

22 Match BTHP	
Ballistic Coefficient	0.230
COAL Tested	2.250"
Speer Part No.	1036

Propellant	Case	Primer	Starting Charge		Maximum Charge	
			Weight (grains)	Muzzle Velocity (feet/sec)	Weight (grains)	Muzzle Velocity (feet/sec)
Hodgdon H335	Remington	CCI 450	26.0	3232	28.0	3488
Hodgdon BL-C(2)	Remington	CCI 450	24.5	3187	26.5	3466
IMR 4320	Remington	CCI 400	27.0	3229	29.0	3454
IMR 3031	Remington	CCI 400	24.5	3177	26.5	3429
IMR 4064	Remington	CCI 400	26.0	3195	28.0	3423
IMR 4895	Remington	CCI 400	25.0	3104	27.0	3337
Hodgdon H414	Remington	CCI 450	29.0	3066	31.0 C	3301
Alliant Reloder 7	Remington	CCI 400	20.0	2935	22.0	3227

WARNING! Maximum loads should be used with CAUTION • C = Compressed Load

55 GRAINS

DIAMETER	SECTIONAL DENSITY
0.224"	0.157

22 TNT® HP
Ballistic Coefficient	0.233
COAL Tested	2.250"
Speer Part No.	1032

22 Spitzer SP
Ballistic Coefficient	0.212
COAL Tested	2.250"
Speer Part No.	1047

			Starting Charge		Maximum Charge	
Propellant	Case	Primer	Weight (grains)	Muzzle Velocity (feet/sec)	Weight (grains)	Muzzle Velocity (feet/sec)
Hodgdon H335	Remington	CCI 450	25.5	3090	27.5	3350
IMR 4320	Remington	CCI 400	26.0	3091	28.0	3318
Hodgdon BL-C(2)	Remington	CCI 450	24.5	3044	26.5	3302
IMR 4064	Remington	CCI 400	25.5	3083	27.5	3301
IMR 3031	Remington	CCI 400	24.0	3059	26.0	3297
IMR 4895	Remington	CCI 400	24.5	3046	26.5	3282
Hodgdon H414	Remington	CCI 450	29.0	2988	31.0	3230
IMR SR 4759 (reduced load)	Remington	CCI 400	9.0	1694	11.0	2068

WARNING! *Maximum loads should be used with CAUTION • C = Compressed Load*

70 GRAINS

DIAMETER	SECTIONAL DENSITY
0.224"	0.199

22 Semi-Spitzer SP	
Ballistic Coefficient	0.219
COAL Tested	2.260"
Speer Part No.	1053

			Starting Charge		Maximum Charge	
Propellant	Case	Primer	Weight (grains)	Muzzle Velocity (feet/sec)	Weight (grains)	Muzzle Velocity (feet/sec)
IMR 4064	Remington	CCI 400	24.5	2825	26.5	3049
IMR 4320	Remington	CCI 400	24.5	2781	26.5	2988
IMR 4895	Remington	CCI 400	23.0	2727	25.0	2943
Hodgdon H335	Remington	CCI 450	23.0	2685	25.0	2943
IMR 3031	Remington	CCI 400	22.0	2659	24.0	2885
Hodgdon H414	Remington	CCI 450	26.0	2655	28.0	2878
Hodgdon H380	Remington	CCI 450	27.0	2621	29.0	2855
IMR SR 4759 (reduced load)	Remington	CCI 400	10.0	1615	12.0	1926

WARNING! *Maximum loads should be used with CAUTION • C = Compressed Load*

225 WINCHESTER

Alternate Names:	5.6x49R, 5.6x49mm Rimmed
Parent Cartridge:	Modified 30-30 Winchester
Country of Origin:	USA
Year of Introduction:	1964
Designer(s):	Winchester
Governing Body:	SAAMI

Case diagram dimensions:
- .260" [6.60mm] cyl
- shoulder angle 25°
- .4060" [10.31mm]
- .4068" [10.33mm]
- .4220" [10.72mm]
- .473" [12.01mm]
- .4238" [10.76mm]
- .049" [1.24mm]
- .200" [5.08mm] basic
- 1.260" [32.00mm] basic
- 1.530" [38.86mm]
- 1.6865" [42.84mm]
- 1.930" [49.02mm]

CARTRIDGE CASE DATA

Case Type:	Semi-rimmed, bottleneck		
Average Case Capacity:	44.3 grains H$_2$O	Max. Cartridge OAL	2.500 inch
Max. Case Length:	1.930 inch	Primer:	Large Rifle
Case Trim to Length:	1.920 inch	RCBS Shell holder:	# 11
Current Manufacturers:	Winchester		

BALLISTIC DATA

Max. Average Pressure (MAP):	50,000 CUP, Piezo not established for this cartridge - SAAMI	Test Barrel Length:	24 inch
Rifling Twist Rate:	1 turn in 14 inch		

Muzzle velocities of factory loaded ammunition	Bullet Wgt.	Muzzle velocity
	55-grain	3,570 fps
	Muzzle velocity will decrease approximately 30 fps per inch for barrels less than 24 inches.	

HISTORICAL NOTES

- Winchester is the only manufacturer to offer ammunition in 225 Winchester. Although factory-loaded ammunition is still listed in their catalog, rifles in this caliber have not been made since 1974.

- Winchester introduced the 225 Win. cartridge in 1964 as a modern replacement for the 220 Swift cartridge which they pioneered in 1935.

- Just one year after Winchester introduced the 225 Win. cartridge, Remington introduced their new 22-250 Remington cartridge.

- Remington's new cartridge quickly became a popular choice among American sportsmen; the 225 Winchester cartridge did not, despite it being chambered in Winchester's Model 70 rifle.

- The current status of the 225 Win. cartridge must be rated as "semi-obsolete". It is unknown to European sportsmen.

- Perhaps the most important shortcoming of the 225 Win. is that it did not replace the 220 Swift in ballistics or in the hearts of American sportsmen.

BALLISTIC NOTES

- Unlike other .224 inch centerfire cartridges, factory 225 Win. ammunition has not undergone the ballistic improvements and additional bullet weights made possible by new propellants. However, some improvements can be achieved by handloading.

FACTOID "Say it ain't so"

Do not be fooled by the appearance of the 225 Winchester cartridge case. While most shooters would call it a "rimmed" design, it is rated as being "semi-rimless". Undoubtedly, this is because the 225 Winchester case head lacks the deep undercut extractor groove of rimless cases. However, the rim diameter of the 225 Win. is identical to the 30-06 Springfield and 308 Winchester. This is intentional so it will feed and fit in bolt-faces of rifles designed for 30-06 head dimensions. Surely this is a unique case design concept!

HANDLOADING NOTES

- In terms of ballistic capabilities, the 225 Winchester ranks above the 223 Rem. and the 222 Rem. Magnum.

- Handloaders have the advantage of being able to load the 225 Win. with bullet weights and styles the factory does not offer. As the factory load is a conventional, 55-grain soft point, such a task is not difficult.

- As 225 Winchester ammunition will be fired in bolt-action rifles, neck sizing is a good idea to control case length growth and head separations and extend the life of the brass, as supplies are rapidly diminishing.

SAFETY NOTES

SPEER 55-grain TNT® HP @ a muzzle velocity of 3,503 fps:
- Maximum vertical altitude @ 90° elevation is 8,607 feet.
- Maximum horizontal distance to first impact with ground @ 33° elevation is 3,832 yards.

40 GRAINS

DIAMETER	SECTIONAL DENSITY
0.224"	0.114

22 Spire SP
Ballistic Coefficient	0.144
COAL Tested	2.370"
Speer Part No.	1017

			Starting Charge		Maximum Charge	
Propellant	Case	Primer	Weight (grains)	Muzzle Velocity (feet/sec)	Weight (grains)	Muzzle Velocity (feet/sec)
IMR 3031	Winchester	CCI 200	28.5	3391	32.5	3815
IMR 4064	Winchester	CCI 200	30.5	3344	34.5	3791
Hodgdon H380	Winchester	CCI 250	34.0	3351	38.0 C	3717
Winchester 748	Winchester	CCI 250	31.0	3310	35.0	3711
Hodgdon H322	Winchester	CCI 200	27.5	3214	31.5	3683
Winchester 760	Winchester	CCI 250	34.0	3331	38.0 C	3682
IMR 4350	Winchester	CCI 200	33.0	3273	37.0 C	3614
Hodgdon H335	Winchester	CCI 250	27.5	3078	31.5	3496
IMR SR 4759 (reduced load)	Winchester	CCI 200	8.0	1560	10.0	1967

45 GRAINS

DIAMETER	SECTIONAL DENSITY
0.224"	0.128

22 Spitzer SP
Ballistic Coefficient	0.143
COAL Tested	2.240"
Speer Part No.	1023

			Starting Charge		Maximum Charge	
Propellant	Case	Primer	Weight (grains)	Muzzle Velocity (feet/sec)	Weight (grains)	Muzzle Velocity (feet/sec)
IMR 4064	Winchester	CCI 200	30.0	3284	34.0	3737
Winchester 748	Winchester	CCI 250	31.0	3237	35.0	3666
IMR 3031	Winchester	CCI 200	28.0	3176	32.0	3650
Winchester 760	Winchester	CCI 200	34.0	3244	38.0 C	3639
Hodgdon H322	Winchester	CCI 200	27.0	3163	31.0	3609
Hodgdon H380	Winchester	CCI 250	34.0	3181	38.0 C	3588
IMR 4350	Winchester	CCI 200	33.0	3164	37.0 C	3535
Hodgdon H335	Winchester	CCI 250	27.0	3011	31.0	3452
IMR SR 4759 (reduced load)	Winchester	CCI 200	9.0	1659	11.0	2039

WARNING! Maximum loads should be used with CAUTION • C = Compressed Load

225 WINCHESTER

50 GRAINS

DIAMETER	SECTIONAL DENSITY
0.224"	0.142

22 Spitzer SP
Ballistic Coefficient	0.207
COAL Tested	2.460"
Speer Part No.	1029

22 TNT® HP
Ballistic Coefficient	0.228
COAL Tested	2.480"
Speer Part No.	1030

Propellant	Case	Primer	Starting Charge Weight (grains)	Starting Charge Muzzle Velocity (feet/sec)	Maximum Charge Weight (grains)	Maximum Charge Muzzle Velocity (feet/sec)
IMR 4064	Winchester	CCI 200	29.5	3202	33.5	3641
Winchester 748	Winchester	CCI 250	30.5	3224	34.5	3615
Winchester 760	Winchester	CCI 250	33.0	3183	37.0	3557
Hodgdon H414	Winchester	CCI 250	33.0	3159	37.0	3545
IMR 4350	Winchester	CCI 200	32.5	3150	36.5 C	3526
Hodgdon H322	Winchester	CCI 200	26.5	3138	30.5	3507
IMR 3031	Winchester	CCI 200	27.5	3030	31.5	3446
Hodgdon H380	Winchester	CCI 250	32.0	3093	36.0	3440
IMR SR 4759 (reduced load)	Winchester	CCI 200	9.5	1679	11.5	2027

52 GRAINS

DIAMETER	SECTIONAL DENSITY
0.224"	0.148

22 HP
Ballistic Coefficient	0.168
COAL Tested	2.500"
Speer Part No.	1035

22 Match BTHP
Ballistic Coefficient	0.230
COAL Tested	2.500"
Speer Part No.	1036

Propellant	Case	Primer	Starting Charge Weight (grains)	Starting Charge Muzzle Velocity (feet/sec)	Maximum Charge Weight (grains)	Maximum Charge Muzzle Velocity (feet/sec)
Winchester 760	Winchester	CCI 250	33.0	3170	37.0 C	3571
IMR 4064	Winchester	CCI 200	29.0	3134	33.0	3551
Winchester 748	Winchester	CCI 250	30.0	3075	34.0	3533
IMR 3031	Winchester	CCI 200	27.0	3059	31.0	3524
IMR 4350	Winchester	CCI 200	32.5	3122	36.5 C	3519
Hodgdon H380	Winchester	CCI 250	31.5	3096	35.5	3502
Hodgdon H322	Winchester	CCI 200	26.5	3018	30.5	3445
Hodgdon H414	Winchester	CCI 250	32.0	3047	36.0	3410
IMR 4895	Winchester	CCI 200	27.0	2915	31.0	3362

WARNING! Maximum loads should be used with CAUTION • C = Compressed Load

55 GRAINS

DIAMETER	SECTIONAL DENSITY
0.224"	0.157

22 TNT® HP
Ballistic Coefficient	0.233
COAL Tested	2.500"
Speer Part No.	1032

22 Spitzer SP
Ballistic Coefficient	0.212
COAL Tested	2.500"
Speer Part No.	1047

			Starting Charge		Maximum Charge	
Propellant	Case	Primer	Weight (grains)	Muzzle Velocity (feet/sec)	Weight (grains)	Muzzle Velocity (feet/sec)
IMR 4064	Winchester	CCI 200	28.5	3095	32.5	3503
Winchester 748	Winchester	CCI 250	29.5	3036	33.5	3424
Hodgdon H380	Winchester	CCI 250	31.0	3023	35.0	3414
IMR 4350	Winchester	CCI 200	32.0	3027	36.0 C	3397
Winchester 760	Winchester	CCI 250	32.0	3003	36.0	3359
Hodgdon H322	Winchester	CCI 200	26.0	2888	30.0	3318
Hodgdon H414	Winchester	CCI 250	31.0	2926	35.0	3279
IMR 4895	Winchester	CCI 200	26.5	2833	30.5	3251
IMR SR 4759 (reduced load)	Winchester	CCI 200	10.0	1679	12.0	2009

70 GRAINS

DIAMETER	SECTIONAL DENSITY
0.224"	0.199

22 Semi-Spitzer SP
Ballistic Coefficient	0.219
COAL Tested	2.310"
Speer Part No.	1053

			Starting Charge		Maximum Charge	
Propellant	Case	Primer	Weight (grains)	Muzzle Velocity (feet/sec)	Weight (grains)	Muzzle Velocity (feet/sec)
Winchester 760	Winchester	CCI 250	32.0	2740	36.0	3162
IMR 4831	Winchester	CCI 200	32.0	2772	36.0 C	3094
Hodgdon H414	Winchester	CCI 250	30.0	2740	34.0	3092
IMR 4350	Winchester	CCI 200	30.5	2743	34.5	3064
IMR 4895	Winchester	CCI 200	24.5	2543	28.5	2988
Hodgdon H380	Winchester	CCI 250	28.0	2590	32.0	2983
IMR 4064	Winchester	CCI 200	26.0	2585	30.0	2980
IMR 3031	Winchester	CCI 200	24.0	2596	28.0	2938
IMR SR 4759 (reduced load)	Winchester	CCI 200	12.0	1719	14.0	1988

WARNING! Maximum loads should be used with CAUTION • C = Compressed Load

22-250 REMINGTON

Alternate Names:	22 Varminter
Parent Cartridge:	250-3000 Savage
Country of Origin:	USA
Year of Introduction:	1965
Designer(s):	J.E. Gebby (wildcat) & Remington
Governing Body:	SAAMI/CIP

CARTRIDGE CASE DATA

Case Type:	Rimless, bottleneck		
Average Case Capacity:	49.9 grains H$_2$O	Max. Cartridge OAL	2.350 inch
Max. Case Length:	1.912 inch	Primer:	Large Rifle
Case Trim to Length:	1.902 inch	RCBS Shell holder:	# 3
Current Manufacturers:	Federal, Remington, Winchester, Black Hills, Sako, Hornady, Sellier & Bellot, Nosler, PPU, Lapua, Norma, Fiocchi		

BALLISTIC DATA

Max. Average Pressure (MAP):	65,000 psi, 53,000 CUP - SAAMI	Test Barrel Length:	24 inch
Rifling Twist Rate:	1 turn in 14 inch		
Muzzle velocities of factory loaded ammunition	Bullet Wgt.	Muzzle velocity	
	35-grain	4,450 fps	
	40-grain	4,150 fps	
	45-grain	3,950 fps	
	50-grain	3,850 fps	
	55-grain	3,680 fps	
	60-grain	3,500 fps	

Muzzle velocity will decrease approximately 40 fps per inch for barrels less than 24 inches.

HISTORICAL NOTES

- Currently, the 22-250 Remington is the most popular high velocity, long range, 22 centerfire rifle cartridge on the market.

- The 22-250 Remington can trace its ancestry all the way back to 1915 when Charles Newton introduced his 250-3000 Savage cartridge to popular acclaim.
- For many years, the 250-3000 Savage was a favorite of wildcatters who necked it down to 224 caliber in a wide variety of case configurations. One of the most well-known was J.E. Gebby who trademarked the name "22 Varminter" for his creation.
- The ballistic performance and versatility of Gebby's 22 Varminter gradually won over American sportsmen who found it COULD match the exterior performance of the legendary 220 Swift, but with longer barrel life.
- When the 22-250 Remington cartridge was introduced in 1965, it quickly overshadowed its competitor, the then-new 225 Winchester cartridge.
- Today, virtually all major ammunition manufacturers offer 22-250 Remington ammunition.

BALLISTIC NOTES

- The 22-250 Rem. makes good use of 60% more case volume and an 18% MAP increase over the 223 Remington. In short, the 22-250 Rem. cartridge is one quantum level of ballistic performance over the 223 Rem.
- The 22-250 Rem. can handle bullet weights from 40-grain to 70-grain with aplomb. Few other cartridges can match this.
- Muzzle velocities range from 3,400 fps to an industry topping 4,450 fps, a record even the legendary 220 Swift cannot match!
- Competitors such as the 223 Rem. are handicapped by a deficit of 440+ fps of muzzle velocity with similar bullet weights which places the 22-250 Rem. cartridge in a league of its own.
- The high muzzle velocity and wide variety of bullet weights and styles have combined to make the 22-250 Rem. one of the most versatile varmint cartridges on the market.
- Although the 22-250 Remington's standard rifling twist rate is 1 turn in 14 inches, it will stabilize bullets up to 70-grain in weight but the velocity must exceed 3,000 fps. Try a few to see if they stabilize in your gun. As a general rule, Speer recommends a minimum twist rate of 1-in-10 inch for use with this bullet.

HANDLOADING NOTES

- Handloaders have found the 22-250 Rem. friendly to their hobby due to its versatility, high performance, and the large number of component manufacturers.
- These handloaders will find their requirements for the 22-250 Rem. well-met with over 11 different 22-caliber Speer bullets to choose from, ranging between 40 and 70 grains. Due to its large case capacity in comparison to other varmint cartridges, the 22-250 Remington cartridge can use slower burning propellants to increase barrel life.

SAFETY NOTES

SPEER 55-grain TNT®HP @ 3,663 fps muzzle velocity:
- Maximum vertical altitude @ 90° elevation is 7,879 feet.
- Maximum horizontal distance to first impact with ground @ 32° elevation is 3,471 yards.

22-250 REMINGTON

40 GRAINS

DIAMETER	SECTIONAL DENSITY
0.224"	0.114

22 Spire SP

Ballistic Coefficient	0.144
COAL Tested	2.235"
Speer Part No.	1017

			Starting Charge		Maximum Charge	
Propellant	Case	Primer	Weight (grains)	Muzzle Velocity (feet/sec)	Weight (grains)	Muzzle Velocity (feet/sec)
Alliant AR-Comp	Federal	Federal 210	33.1	3880	36.7	4228
IMR 8208 XBR	Federal	Federal 210	32.5	3873	36.1	4182
Alliant Reloder 10X	Remington	CCI 200	31.5	3780	35.5	4164
Ramshot X-Terminator	Federal	Federal 210	31.3	3805	34.8	4142
Alliant Power Pro 1200-R	Federal	Federal 210	29.5	3881	32.2	4108
Hodgdon Varget	Remington	CCI 200	35.0	3582	39.0	4090
Accurate 2460	Remington	CCI 250	34.0	3468	38.0	4033
Vihtavuori N130	Federal	Federal 210	28.5	3771	31.7	4033
Alliant Reloder 15	Remington	CCI 200	36.0	3443	40.0	4027
Hodgdon H4895	Remington	CCI 200	34.0	3542	38.0	4025
Vihtavuori N135	Remington	CCI 200	33.0	3463	37.0	3958
IMR 4320	Remington	CCI 200	36.0	3360	40.0	3930
Accurate 2520	Remington	CCI 250	33.0	3382	37.0	3910
Winchester 748	Remington	CCI 250	35.5	3403	39.5	3867
Winchester 760	Remington	CCI 250	38.0	3342	42.0	3841
IMR 4064	Remington	CCI 200	34.0	3390	38.0	3830
Hodgdon H380	Remington	CCI 250	39.0	3284	43.0 C	3796
Hodgdon H335	Remington	CCI 250	33.0	3280	37.0	3748
IMR 3031	Remington	CCI 200	32.0	3315	36.0	3746
IMR SR 4759 (reduced load)	Remington	CCI 200	9.0	1641	11.0	1979

WARNING! Maximum loads should be used with CAUTION • C = Compressed Load

43 GRAINS

DIAMETER	SECTIONAL DENSITY
0.224"	0.122

22 TNT Green®	
Ballistic Coefficient	0.150
COAL Tested	2.320"
Speer Part No.	1022

			Starting Charge		Maximum Charge	
Propellant	Case	Primer	Weight (grains)	Muzzle Velocity (feet/sec)	Weight (grains)	Muzzle Velocity (feet/sec)
Vihtavuori N540	Federal	Federal 210	38.5	3976	40.5	4175
IMR 4895	Federal	Federal 210	38.0	3925	40.0 C	4154
Alliant Reloder 15	Federal	Federal 210	36.5	3909	38.5	4125
Hodgdon Varget	Federal	Federal 210	38.0	3951	40.0 C	4121
Ramshot TAC	Federal	Federal 210	33.0	3809	37.0	4107
Alliant Reloder 10X	Federal	Federal 210	32.0	3919	34.0	4077

WARNING! *Maximum loads should be used with CAUTION • C = Compressed Load*

45 GRAINS

DIAMETER	SECTIONAL DENSITY
0.224"	0.128

22 Spitzer SP

Ballistic Coefficient	0.143
COAL Tested	2.240"
Speer Part No.	1023

			Starting Charge		Maximum Charge	
Propellant	Case	Primer	Weight (grains)	Muzzle Velocity (feet/sec)	Weight (grains)	Muzzle Velocity (feet/sec)
Alliant AR-Comp	Federal	Federal 210	32.3	3758	35.3	4038
IMR 8208 XBR	Federal	Federal 210	31.2	3753	34.6	3995
Alliant Reloder 10X	Remington	CCI 200	30.5	3569	34.5	3974
Ramshot X-Terminator	Federal	Federal 210	30.2	3653	33.5	3953
Accurate 2460	Remington	CCI 250	33.5	3333	37.5	3898
Alliant Reloder 15	Remington	CCI 200	35.0	3351	39.0	3897
Alliant Power Pro 1200-R	Federal	Federal 210	28.0	3678	30.5	3896
Hodgdon Varget	Remington	CCI 200	33.5	3345	37.5	3881
IMR 4320	Remington	CCI 200	35.5	3364	39.5	3867
Vihtavuori N130	Federal	Federal 210	27.8	3624	30.6	3843
Vihtavuori N135	Remington	CCI 200	32.5	3372	36.5	3832
Hodgdon H380	Remington	CCI 250	38.5	3317	42.5 C	3748
Winchester 748	Remington	CCI 250	34.5	3170	38.5	3708
Winchester 760	Remington	CCI 250	37.5	3194	41.5 C	3693
IMR 4064	Remington	CCI 200	33.5	3207	37.5	3665
Winchester H414	Remington	CCI 250	37.5	3183	41.5 C	3659
IMR 4895	Remington	CCI 200	32.0	3209	36.0	3647
Hodgdon BL-C(2)	Remington	CCI 250	33.5	3179	37.5	3633
IMR 3031	Remington	CCI 200	31.5	3211	35.5	3628
IMR SR 4759 (reduced load)	Remington	CCI 200	9.5	1656	11.5	1984

WARNING! Maximum loads should be used with CAUTION • C = Compressed Load

50 GRAINS

DIAMETER	SECTIONAL DENSITY
0.224"	0.142

22 Spitzer SP	
Ballistic Coefficient	0.207
COAL Tested	2.350"
Speer Part No.	1029

			Starting Charge		Maximum Charge	
Propellant	Case	Primer	Weight (grains)	Muzzle Velocity (feet/sec)	Weight (grains)	Muzzle Velocity (feet/sec)
IMR 8208 XBR	Federal	Federal 210	31.8	3635	35.3	3875
Alliant AR-Comp	Federal	Federal 210	31.8	3570	35.2	3862
Alliant Reloder 10X	Remington	CCI 200	30.0	3491	34.0	3837
Accurate 2460	Remington	CCI 250	33.0	3355	37.0	3804
Hodgdon Varget	Remington	CCI 200	32.5	3283	36.5	3796
Alliant Reloder 15	Remington	CCI 200	34.0	3209	38.0	3736
Vihtavuori N135	Remington	CCI 200	32.0	3231	36.0	3693
Hodgdon H380	Remington	CCI 250	38.0	3229	42.0 C	3693
Alliant Power Pro 1200-R	Federal	Federal 210	26.6	3353	29.4	3686
Accurate 2230	Remington	CCI 250	31.0	3188	35.0	3685
Winchester 760	Remington	CCI 200	37.0	3218	41.0	3636
IMR 4064	Remington	CCI 200	33.0	3136	37.0	3625
Hodgdon H414	Remington	CCI 200	37.0	3081	41.0	3604
IMR 4320	Remington	CCI 200	34.0	3117	38.0	3603
Winchester 748	Remington	CCI 250	34.0	3079	38.0	3601
IMR 4895	Remington	CCI 200	31.5	3116	35.5	3561
Hodgdon BL-C(2)	Remington	CCI 250	33.0	3149	37.0	3558
IMR SR 4759 (reduced load)	Remington	CCI 200	10.0	1650	12.0	1982

WARNING! *Maximum loads should be used with* CAUTION • *C = Compressed Load*

50 GRAINS

DIAMETER	SECTIONAL DENSITY
0.224"	0.142

22 TNT Green®

Ballistic Coefficient	0.190
COAL Tested	2.320"
Speer Part No.	1028

Propellant	Case	Primer	Starting Charge		Maximum Charge	
			Weight (grains)	Muzzle Velocity (feet/sec)	Weight (grains)	Muzzle Velocity (feet/sec)
Ramshot Big Game	Federal	Federal 210	39.0	3765	41.0	3901
IMR 4064	Federal	Federal 210	34.0	3665	36.0 C	3869
Alliant Reloder 15	Federal	Federal 210	34.5	3687	36.5	3868
Vihtavuori N540	Federal	Federal 210	36.0	3664	38.0	3856
Hodgdon Varget	Federal	Federal 210	35.0	3651	37.0	3836
Alliant Reloder 10X	Federal	Federal 210	30.0	3605	32.0	3774

WARNING! *Maximum loads should be used with* **CAUTION** • C = Compressed Load

52 GRAINS

DIAMETER	SECTIONAL DENSITY
0.224"	0.148

22 HP	
Ballistic Coefficient	0.168
COAL Tested	2.350"
Speer Part No.	1035

22 Match BTHP	
Ballistic Coefficient	0.230
COAL Tested	2.350"
Speer Part No.	1036

			Starting Charge		Maximum Charge	
Propellant	Case	Primer	Weight (grains)	Muzzle Velocity (feet/sec)	Weight (grains)	Muzzle Velocity (feet/sec)
Alliant AR-Comp	Federal	Federal 210	30.6	3498	33.9	3755
Alliant Reloder 10X	Remington	CCI 200	29.0	3406	33.0	3744
IMR 3031	Remington	CCI 200	32.0	3251	36.0	3715
Winchester 748	Remington	CCI 250	34.0	3231	38.0	3714
Hodgdon H4895	Remington	CCI 200	32.5	3230	36.5	3713
Accurate 2460	Remington	CCI 250	32.5	3173	36.5	3711
Hodgdon Varget	Remington	CCI 200	32.0	3338	36.0	3706
Hodgdon H380	Remington	CCI 250	38.0	3164	42.0 C	3700
IMR 8208 XBR	Federal	Federal 210	29.5	3483	32.2	3680
Vihtavuori N140	Remington	CCI 200	33.5	3233	37.5	3674
Alliant Reloder 15	Remington	CCI 200	33.5	3204	37.5	3662
Vihtavuori N135	Remington	CCI 200	31.5	3177	35.5	3610
Winchester 760	Remington	CCI 250	36.5	3120	40.5	3607
Hodgdon H414	Remington	CCI 250	36.5	3093	40.5	3597
IMR 4064	Remington	CCI 200	32.5	3064	36.5	3563
IMR 4320	Remington	CCI 200	33.5	3150	37.5	3559
IMR 4895	Remington	CCI 200	31.0	3121	35.0	3526
Alliant Power Pro 1200-R	Federal	Federal 210	24.9	3174	27.6	3525

WARNING! *Maximum loads should be used with CAUTION • C = Compressed Load*

55 GRAINS

DIAMETER	SECTIONAL DENSITY
0.224"	0.157

22 Spitzer SP	
Ballistic Coefficient	0.212
COAL Tested	2.350"
Speer Part No.	1047

22 TNT® HP	
Ballistic Coefficient	0.233
COAL Tested	2.350"
Speer Part No.	1032

Propellant	Case	Primer	Starting Charge		Maximum Charge	
			Weight (grains)	Muzzle Velocity (feet/sec)	Weight (grains)	Muzzle Velocity (feet/sec)
Alliant Reloder 15	Federal	Federal 210	32.9	3379	36.5	3712
Alliant AR-Comp	Federal	Federal 210	30.7	3432	34.0	3689
IMR 3031	Remington	CCI 200	32.0	3132	36.0	3663
Accurate 2460	Remington	CCI 250	32.0	3168	36.0	3662
Winchester 748	Remington	CCI 250	34.0	3237	38.0	3658
Hodgdon Varget	Remington	CCI 200	32.0	3260	36.0	3655
Hodgdon H380	Remington	CCI 250	38.0	3143	42.0 C	3633
Hodgdon H4895	Remington	CCI 200	32.0	3104	36.0	3630
IMR 8208 XBR	Federal	Federal 210	28.5	3301	31.6	3584
Vihtavuori N140	Remington	CCI 200	33.0	3134	37.0	3582
Hodgdon H335	Remington	CCI 250	32.0	3091	36.0	3532
Accurate 2520	Remington	CCI 250	30.0	2972	34.0	3476
IMR 4064	Remington	CCI 200	32.0	2999	36.0	3467
Winchester 760	Remington	CCI 250	35.5	2949	39.5	3449
IMR 4895	Remington	CCI 200	31.0	2993	35.0	3421
IMR 4350	Remington	CCI 200	36.0	3012	40.0 C	3403
IMR SR 4759 (reduced load)	Remington	CCI 200	11.0	1688	13.0	2002

WARNING! *Maximum loads should be used with CAUTION • C = Compressed Load*

70 GRAINS

DIAMETER	SECTIONAL DENSITY
0.224"	0.199

22 Semi-Spitzer SP

Ballistic Coefficient	0.219
COAL Tested	2.330"
Speer Part No.	1053

			Starting Charge		Maximum Charge	
Propellant	Case	Primer	Weight (grains)	Muzzle Velocity (feet/sec)	Weight (grains)	Muzzle Velocity (feet/sec)
Alliant Reloder 16	Federal	Federal 210	33.1	3109	36.6 C	3368
Alliant Reloder 17	Federal	Federal 210	33.2	3075	36.8	3364
Hodgdon H414	Remington	CCI 250	35.0	2888	39.0	3300
Alliant Reloder 15	Federal	Federal 210	30.2	3043	33.4	3294
Alliant Power Pro 2000-MR	Federal	Federal 210	30.3	2970	33.6	3262
Hodgdon CFE 223	Federal	Federal 210	29.0	2937	32.2	3221
Alliant Power Pro Varmint	Federal	Federal 210	28.1	2961	31.1	3216
Alliant AR-Comp	Federal	Federal 210	27.8	3009	30.5	3205
IMR 4320	Remington	CCI 200	31.0	2701	35.0	3158
IMR 4831	Remington	CCI 200	35.0	2727	39.0	3135
IMR 4350	Remington	CCI 200	34.0	2751	38.0 C	3126
Hodgdon H380	Remington	CCI 250	33.0	2651	37.0	3083
IMR 4064	Remington	CCI 200	29.5	2725	33.5	3079
Vihtavuori N140	Remington	CCI 200	29.0	2666	33.0	3064
IMR 4895	Remington	CCI 200	28.0	2671	32.0	3052
IMR 3031	Remington	CCI 200	28.0	2611	32.0	3018
Winchester 748	Remington	CCI 250	29.5	2665	33.5	3011
Accurate 2460	Remington	CCI 250	27.0	2623	31.0	2964
Hodgdon H335	Remington	CCI 250	27.0	2486	31.0	2908
Accurate 2520	Remington	CCI 250	26.0	2441	30.0	2838
Alliant Reloder 7	Remington	CCI 200	21.0	2381	25.0	2753
IMR SR 4759 (reduced load)	Remington	CCI 200	13.0	1711	15.0	1939

WARNING! *Maximum loads should be used with CAUTION • C = Compressed Load*

220 SWIFT

Parent Cartridge:	6mm Lee Navy
Country of Origin:	USA
Year of Introduction:	1935
Designer(s):	Winchester
Governing Body:	SAAMI/CIP

Case diagram dimensions:
- .2600" [6.60mm]
- .2615" [6.64mm]
- shoulder angle 21°
- .4020" [10.21mm]
- .4055" [10.30mm]
- .4449" [11.30mm]
- .473" [12.01mm]
- .049" [1.24mm]
- .200" [5.08mm] basic
- 1.400" [35.56mm] basic
- 1.7227" [43.76mm]
- 1.9057" [48.41mm]
- 2.205mm [56.01mm]

CARTRIDGE CASE DATA

Case Type:	Semi-rimmed, bottleneck		
Average Case Capacity:	52.5 grains H₂O	Max. Cartridge OAL	2.680 inch
Max. Case Length:	2.205 inch	Primer:	Large Rifle
Case Trim to Length:	2.195 inch	RCBS Shell holder:	# 11
Current Manufacturers:	Remington, Winchester, Hornady, Nosler, Norma		

BALLISTIC DATA

Max. Average Pressure (MAP):	62,000 psi, 54,000 CUP - SAAMI	Test Barrel Length:	24 inch
Rifling Twist Rate:	1 turn in 14 inch		

Muzzle velocities of factory loaded ammunition	Bullet Wgt.	Muzzle velocity
	50-grain	3,870 fps
	55-grain	3,680 fps
	60-grain	3,550 fps

Muzzle velocity will decrease approximately 40 fps per inch for barrels less than 24 inches.

HISTORICAL NOTES

- From its introduction in 1935, the 220 Swift cartridge with its muzzle velocity of 4,000+ fps entered the mystical world of ballistic legend.
- Varmint hunters praised its high muzzle velocity, flat trajectory and incredible bullet expansion while damning its short barrel life, muzzle blast and cost.
- In the European market, the 220 Swift never caught on. In the years since its introduction, the demise of the 220 Swift has been predicted many times. This was especially true following the introduction of the 22-250 Remington cartridge in 1965. All of them proved wrong.

BALLISTIC NOTES

- The 220 Swift's impressive muzzle velocity of 4,000+ fps was achieved using the simple expedient of a lightweight bullet with a stout charge of propellant. While this may seem obvious today, in the 1930s this was astounding news in factory loaded ammunition.
- In its present form, 220 Swift factory ammunition loaded with 50 to 55 grain bullets offers near identical ballistic performance to the 22-250 Remington. The ultra-high muzzle velocity 4,000+ fps loads on which the Swift's reputation is based have been dropped, but you can load them.
- Beginning in the early 2000s, the 22-250 Remington was updated using new propellants and ultra-lightweight bullets at muzzle velocities as high as 4,450 fps! Sadly, the 220 Swift was not upgraded in a similar manner allowing the 22-250 Remington to usurp it on the muzzle velocity throne.

HANDLOADING NOTES

- Although the 220 Swift's normal rifling twist rate is 1 turn in 14 inch, it will stabilize bullets up to 55-grain in weight. Speer recommends a 1:10 inch twist rate for the 70-grain bullet.
- The 220 Swift cartridge case is a semi-rimmed, dimensional orphan completely different from other modern cartridge cases. (Now you know why ammunition makers would love to see the Swift quickly disappear.)
- With its large case capacity, the 220 Swift cartridge can use slower burning propellants to increase barrel life.
- The 220 Swift can be handloaded to "traditional" 4,000+ fps muzzle velocities using lightweight bullets from 40-grain to 50-grain. Few other 22-caliber varmint cartridges can match this.
- Neck sizing is recommended to reduce case stretching and head separations.
- Note the 220 Swift uses a Large Rifle size primer while the smaller capacity 22-caliber varmint cartridges including the 223 Remington use a Small Rifle primer.

SAFETY NOTES

SPEER 55-grain TNT®HP @ 3,807 fps muzzle velocity:
- Maximum vertical altitude @ 90° elevation is 7,970 feet.
- Maximum horizontal distance to first impact with ground @ 32° elevation is 3,504 yards.

40 GRAINS	DIAMETER	SECTIONAL DENSITY
	0.224"	0.114

22 Spire SP	
Ballistic Coefficient	0.144
COAL Tested	2.625"
Speer Part No.	1017

			Starting Charge		Maximum Charge	
Propellant	Case	Primer	Weight (grains)	Muzzle Velocity (feet/sec)	Weight (grains)	Muzzle Velocity (feet/sec)
Alliant Power Pro 2000-MR	Hornady	CCI 200	39.1	3879	43.4	4253
Hodgdon Varget	Hornady	CCI 200	37.8	3866	41.8	4221
Alliant Reloder 17	Hornady	CCI 200	41.0	3830	44.4	4214
Alliant AR-Comp	Hornady	CCI 200	34.9	3867	38.6	4197
IMR 4451	Hornady	CCI 200	41.5	3705	44.5 C	3973
Alliant Reloder 16	Hornady	CCI 200	41.5	3769	43.5 C	3942
Hodgdon H380	Winchester	CCI 250	41.0	3588	45.0 C	3922
Alliant Reloder 15	Winchester	CCI 200	37.0	3513	41.0	3910
Vihtavuori N140	Winchester	CCI 200	36.0	3471	40.0	3860
Vihtavuori N160	Winchester	CCI 200	42.0	3440	46.0 C	3841
Winchester 760	Winchester	CCI 250	39.0	3433	43.0	3821
IMR 4350	Winchester	CCI 200	41.0	3363	45.0 C	3802
IMR 3031	Winchester	CCI 200	34.5	3445	38.5	3797
Accurate 4350	Winchester	CCI 200	41.0	3265	45.0 C	3691
Alliant Reloder 19	Winchester	CCI 200	42.0	3287	46.0 C	3671
IMR 4064	Winchester	CCI 200	35.0	3321	39.0	3642
IMR SR 4759 (reduced load)	Winchester	CCI 200	10.5	1662	12.5	1964

WARNING! *Maximum loads should be used with CAUTION • C = Compressed Load*

43 GRAINS

DIAMETER	SECTIONAL DENSITY
0.224"	0.122

22 TNT Green®

Ballistic Coefficient	0.150
COAL Tested	2.650"
Speer Part No.	1022

Propellant	Case	Primer	Starting Charge Weight (grains)	Starting Charge Muzzle Velocity (feet/sec)	Maximum Charge Weight (grains)	Maximum Charge Muzzle Velocity (feet/sec)
Alliant Power Pro 2000-MR	Hornady	CCI 200	38.5	3877	42.7	4197
Alliant Reloder 17	Hornady	CCI 200	40.1	3774	44.3	4196
Ramshot Big Game	Hornady	CCI 200	40.0	3855	44.5	4179
IMR 3031	Federal	Federal 210	35.5	3995	37.5	4165
Vihtavuori N540	Federal	Federal 210	40.5	3990	42.5	4162
Hodgdon Varget	Hornady	CCI 200	36.4	3814	40.4	4146
Alliant AR-Comp	Hornady	CCI 200	34.2	3848	37.8	4143
Hodgdon H380	Hornady	CCI 200	39.5	3848	43.7	4128
Hodgdon H414	Federal	Federal 215	42.0	3960	44.0	4127
Alliant Reloder 15	Federal	Federal 210	40.0	3922	42.0	4124
Winchester 760	Hornady	CCI 200	39.3	3794	43.5	4121
Vihtavuori N140	Hornady	CCI 200	35.4	3775	39.2	4087
Accurate 2015	Federal	Federal 210	35.0	3832	37.0	4065
IMR 4451	Hornady	CCI 200	41.5	3793	44.5 C	4037
Vihtavuori N160	Hornady	CCI 200	41.7	3694	46.0 C	4026
Alliant Reloder 16	Hornady	CCI 200	41.4	3817	43.5 C	4004

WARNING! Maximum loads should be used with CAUTION • C = Compressed Load

45 GRAINS

DIAMETER	SECTIONAL DENSITY
0.224"	0.128

22 Spitzer SP

Ballistic Coefficient	0.143
COAL Tested	2.650"
Speer Part No.	1023

Propellant	Case	Primer	Starting Charge Weight (grains)	Starting Charge Muzzle Velocity (feet/sec)	Maximum Charge Weight (grains)	Maximum Charge Muzzle Velocity (feet/sec)
Alliant Power Pro 2000-MR	Hornady	CCI 200	37.4	3717	41.6	4069
Alliant Reloder 17	Hornady	CCI 200	40.0	3699	43.3	4060
Alliant Power Pro Varmint	Hornady	CCI 200	34.9	3698	38.7	4024
Alliant AR-Comp	Hornady	CCI 200	33.5	3709	37.2	4006
IMR 4451	Hornady	CCI 200	40.5	3615	45.0 C	3995
Alliant Reloder 16	Hornady	CCI 200	40.5	3691	43.5 C	3944
Alliant Reloder 15	Winchester	CCI 200	37.5	3471	41.5	3923
Vihtavuori N160	Winchester	CCI 200	42.0	3421	46.0 C	3819
Hodgdon H380	Winchester	CCI 250	40.5	3482	44.5 C	3806
Vihtavuori N140	Winchester	CCI 200	35.5	3360	39.5	3740
Winchester 760	Winchester	CCI 250	38.5	2282	42.5	3712
Accurate 4350	Winchester	CCI 200	41.0	3273	45.0 C	3700
Alliant Reloder 19	Winchester	CCI 200	42.0	3281	46.0 C	3658
IMR 3031	Winchester	CCI 200	33.5	3275	37.5	3649
IMR 4064	Winchester	CCI 200	33.5	3229	37.5	3582
IMR 4350	Winchester	CCI 200	40.5	3019	44.5 C	3413
IMR SR 4759 (reduced load)	Winchester	CCI 200	10.5	1631	12.5	1930

WARNING! *Maximum loads should be used with CAUTION • C = Compressed Load*

50 GRAINS

DIAMETER	SECTIONAL DENSITY
0.224"	0.142

22 Spitzer SP
Ballistic Coefficient	0.207
COAL Tested	2.650"
Speer Part No.	1029

22 TNT® HP
Ballistic Coefficient	0.228
COAL Tested	2.650"
Speer Part No.	1030

			Starting Charge		Maximum Charge	
Propellant	Case	Primer	Weight (grains)	Muzzle Velocity (feet/sec)	Weight (grains)	Muzzle Velocity (feet/sec)
Alliant Reloder 17	Hornady	CCI 200	39.5	3561	43.1	3952
Alliant Power Pro 4000-MR	Hornady	CCI 200	41.5	3561	45.6 C	3942
Alliant Power Pro 2000-MR	Hornady	CCI 200	37.5	3570	41.6	3930
IMR 4451	Hornady	CCI 200	40.6	3544	44.5 C	3890
Alliant AR-Comp	Hornady	CCI 200	33.5	3560	37.1	3863
Alliant Reloder 16	Hornady	CCI 200	40.5	3589	43.5 C	3858
Vihtavuori N160	Winchester	CCI 200	42.0	3391	46.0 C	3788
Hodgdon H380	Winchester	CCI 250	40.0	3450	44	3772
Alliant Reloder 15	Winchester	CCI 200	36.0	3329	40	3706
Hodgdon H414	Winchester	CCI 250	38.5	3370	42.5	3694
Accurate 4350	Winchester	CCI 200	41.0	3288	45.0 C	3685
Winchester 760	Winchester	CCI 250	38.5	3310	42.5	3668
Vihtavuori N140	Winchester	CCI 200	35.0	3342	39.0	3665
Alliant Reloder 19	Winchester	CCI 200	42.0	3219	46.0 C	3647
IMR 4350	Winchester	CCI 200	40.0	3211	44.0 C	3630
IMR 3031	Winchester	CCI 200	33.0	3227	37.0	3538
IMR 4831	Winchester	CCI 200	40.0	3064	44.0 C	3531
IMR 4064	Winchester	CCI 200	34.0	3156	38.0	3497
Accurate 2700	Winchester	CCI 250	36.0	3117	40.0	3455
IMR SR 4759 (reduced load)	Winchester	CCI 200	11.0	1668	13.0	1968

WARNING! Maximum loads should be used with CAUTION • C = Compressed Load

50 GRAINS

DIAMETER	SECTIONAL DENSITY
0.224"	0.142

22 TNT Green®

Ballistic Coefficient	0.190
COAL Tested	2.630"
Speer Part No.	1028

Propellant	Case	Primer	Starting Charge Weight (grains)	Starting Charge Muzzle Velocity (feet/sec)	Maximum Charge Weight (grains)	Maximum Charge Muzzle Velocity (feet/sec)
Alliant Reloder 17	Hornady	CCI 200	38.2	3472	42.3	3927
Alliant Power Pro 4000-MR	Hornady	CCI 200	41.5	3599	46.0 C	3911
Alliant Reloder 19	Hornady	CCI 200	42.0	3520	46.5 C	3903
Alliant Reloder 16	Hornady	CCI 200	39.3	3553	43.5 C	3894
Hodgdon H4350	Hornady	CCI 200	40.4	3577	44.9 C	3891
Vihtavuori N540	Federal	Federal 210	38.0	3733	40.0	3890
Ramshot Big Game	Federal	Federal 215	40.0	3734	42.0	3881
Winchester 760	Hornady	CCI 200	38.1	3553	42.3	3877
Hodgdon H4895	Federal	Federal 210	34.0	3712	36.0	3866
Hodgdon H380	Hornady	CCI 200	39.2	3656	42.1	3849
Alliant Reloder 15	Federal	Federal 210	35.5	3656	37.5	3841
IMR 3031	Federal	Federal 210	33.0	3692	35.0	3831
Accurate 4350	Hornady	CCI 200	40.6	3499	44.5 C	3812
Accurate 2015	Federal	Federal 210	33.5	3566	35.5	3779
Hodgdon H4831SC	Hornady	CCI 200	42.1	3447	46.0 C	3718
Alliant Reloder 23	Hornady	CCI 200	42.0 C	3490	44.0 C	3652
IMR 7828	Hornady	CCI 200	42.5	3351	44.5 C	3513

WARNING! *Maximum loads should be used with CAUTION • C = Compressed Load*

52 GRAINS

DIAMETER	SECTIONAL DENSITY
0.224"	0.148

22 HP
Ballistic Coefficient	0.168
COAL Tested	2.680"
Speer Part No.	1035

22 Match BTHP
Ballistic Coefficient	0.230
COAL Tested	2.680"
Speer Part No.	1036

			Starting Charge		Maximum Charge	
Propellant	Case	Primer	Weight (grains)	Muzzle Velocity (feet/sec)	Weight (grains)	Muzzle Velocity (feet/sec)
Alliant Reloder 17	Hornady	CCI 200	37.9	3473	42.1	3886
Alliant Reloder 16	Hornady	CCI 200	39.6	3571	43.5 C	3881
Alliant Power Pro 4000-MR	Hornady	CCI 200	40.4	3499	44.4 C	3863
Alliant Power Pro 2000-MR	Hornady	CCI 200	35.6	3557	39.6	3816
IMR 4451	Hornady	CCI 200	38.6	3401	42.7	3772
Vihtavuori N160	Winchester	CCI 200	42.0	3372	46.0 C	3765
Alliant AR-Comp	Hornady	CCI 200	32.1	3492	35.6	3743
Alliant Reloder 15	Winchester	CCI 200	35.5	3295	39.5	3668
Accurate 4350	Winchester	CCI 200	41.0	3240	45.0 C	3663
Alliant Reloder 19	Winchester	CCI 200	42.0	3267	46.0 C	3642
Vihtavuori N140	Winchester	CCI 200	35.0	3268	39.0	3639
Hodgdon H380	Winchester	CCI 250	39.5	3328	43.5	3637
IMR 4350	Winchester	CCI 200	39.0	3199	43.0	3616
Winchester 760	Winchester	CCI 250	37.5	3212	41.5	3577
IMR 4831	Winchester	CCI 200	40.0	3028	44.0 C	3509
IMR 3031	Winchester	CCI 200	32.5	3200	36.5	3509
Hodgdon H4831	Winchester	CCI 200	41.0	3086	45.0 C	3492
IMR SR 4759 (reduced load)	Winchester	CCI 200	11.0	1679	13.0	1991

WARNING! Maximum loads should be used with CAUTION • C = Compressed Load

55 GRAINS

DIAMETER	SECTIONAL DENSITY
0.224"	0.157

22 TNT® HP
Ballistic Coefficient	0.233
COAL Tested	2.680"
Speer Part No.	1032

22 Spitzer SP
Ballistic Coefficient	0.212
COAL Tested	2.650"
Speer Part No.	1047

			Starting Charge		Maximum Charge	
Propellant	Case	Primer	Weight (grains)	Muzzle Velocity (feet/sec)	Weight (grains)	Muzzle Velocity (feet/sec)
Alliant Reloder 16	Hornady	CCI 200	39.3	3484	43.5 C	3846
Alliant Reloder 17	Hornady	CCI 200	37.7	3418	41.6	3793
Alliant Power Pro 4000-MR	Hornady	CCI 200	39.6	3372	43.8	3769
Alliant Power Pro 2000-MR	Hornady	CCI 200	35.6	3501	39.4	3730
Vihtavuori N160	Winchester	CCI 200	42.0	3340	46.0 C	3730
Accurate 4350	Winchester	CCI 200	41.0	3280	45.0 C	3708
IMR 4451	Hornady	CCI 200	38.1	3342	42.3	3692
Alliant AR-Comp	Hornady	CCI 200	32.3	3442	35.8	3670
Alliant Reloder 19	Winchester	CCI 200	42.0	3174	46.0 C	3637
Vihtavuori N140	Winchester	CCI 200	35.0	3256	39.0	3624
Hodgdon H380	Winchester	CCI 250	39.0	3304	43.0	3610
Alliant Reloder 15	Winchester	CCI 200	35.0	3221	39.0	3585
IMR 4320	Winchester	CCI 200	35.0	3225	39.0	3536
IMR 4350	Winchester	CCI 200	39.0	3116	43.0	3523
Hodgdon H4831SC	Winchester	CCI 200	41.0	3053	45.0 C	3516
Accurate 2700	Winchester	CCI 250	37.0	3203	41.0	3500
Winchester 760	Winchester	CCI 250	36.5	3116	40.5	3468
IMR 3031	Winchester	CCI 200	32.0	3149	36.0	3442
IMR SR 4759 (reduced load)	Winchester	CCI 200	11.5	1707	13.5	1990

WARNING! *Maximum loads should be used with CAUTION • C = Compressed Load*

70 GRAINS

DIAMETER	SECTIONAL DENSITY
0.224"	0.199

22 Semi-Spitzer SP	
Ballistic Coefficient	0.219
COAL Tested	2.570"
Speer Part No.	1053

			Starting Charge		Maximum Charge	
Propellant	Case	Primer	Weight (grains)	Muzzle Velocity (feet/sec)	Weight (grains)	Muzzle Velocity (feet/sec)
Alliant Reloder 26	Hornady	CCI 200	40.0	3130	44.5 C	3487
Alliant Reloder 17	Hornady	CCI 200	35.0	3075	38.9	3426
Alliant Power Pro 4000-MR	Hornady	CCI 200	37.3	3114	41.2	3416
Alliant Reloder 16	Hornady	CCI 200	35.6	3139	39.4	3416
Vihtavuori N160	Winchester	CCI 200	38.0	2902	42.0 C	3306
Alliant Power Pro 2000-MR	Hornady	CCI 200	32.7	3035	36.2	3302
IMR 4451	Hornady	CCI 200	35.1	2981	39.0	3295
Accurate 3100	Winchester	CCI 200	39.0	2846	43.0 C	3214
Alliant Reloder 15	Winchester	CCI 200	32.0	2855	36.0	3178
Alliant Reloder 19	Winchester	CCI 200	38.0	2836	42.0 C	3166
IMR 4320	Winchester	CCI 200	32.0	2781	36.0	3106
Hodgdon H380	Winchester	CCI 250	34.0	2834	38.0	3097
Accurate 2700	Winchester	CCI 250	34.0	2813	38.0	3068
Winchester 760	Winchester	CCI 250	33.0	2776	37.0	3038
IMR 4831	Winchester	CCI 200	36.0	2604	40.0	3000
Hodgdon H414	Winchester	CCI 250	33.0	2707	37.0	2972
IMR 4350	Winchester	CCI 200	34.0	2608	38.0	2948
IMR SR 4759 (reduced load)	Winchester	CCI 200	12.0	1642	14.0	1899

WARNING! Maximum loads should be used with CAUTION • C = Compressed Load

223 WINCHESTER SUPER SHORT MAGNUM

Alternate Names:	223 WSSM
Country of Origin:	USA
Year of Introduction:	2003
Designer(s):	Winchester
Governing Body:	SAAMI

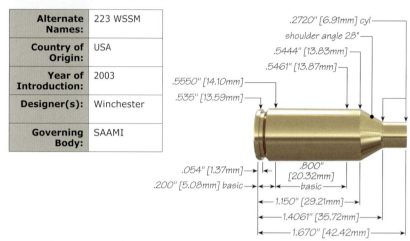

CARTRIDGE CASE DATA

Case Type:	Rimless, bottleneck		
Average Case Capacity:	56.3 grains H$_2$O	Max. Cartridge OAL	2.360 inch
Max. Case Length:	1.670 inch	Primer:	Large Rifle
Case Trim to Length:	1.660 inch	RCBS Shell holder:	# 43
Current Manufacturers:	Winchester		

BALLISTIC DATA

Max. Average Pressure (MAP):	65,000 psi, CUP not established for this cartridge - SAAMI	Test Barrel Length:	24 inch
Rifling Twist Rate:	1 turn in 10 inch		
Muzzle velocities of factory loaded ammunition	Bullet Wgt.		Muzzle velocity
	55-grain		3,850 fps
	64-grain		3,600 fps

Muzzle velocity will decrease approximately 40 fps per inch for barrels less than 24 inches.

HISTORICAL NOTES

- The 223 Winchester Super Short Magnum cartridge has no parent case. It is a progenitor of a completely new design.
- It was designed by Winchester and introduced in 2003 followed by similar cartridges in .243 inch and .257 inch diameters.

- Shortly after the 223 WSSM cartridge was introduced, problems with excessive chamber pressures were discovered with lightweight bullets. Winchester settled on the most popular weight, the 55-grain, as their factory load. They are the sole manufacturer of 223 WSSM ammunition.

BALLISTIC NOTES

- On paper, the 223 WSSM cartridge with a 55-grain bullet has more than a 200 fps ballistic edge over the 22-250 Remington.
- Also, with its 10 inch rifling twist rate, the 223 WSSM is more comfortable with heavier bullets than the 22-250 Rem. cartridge.
- Factory ammunition in 223 WSSM caliber is offered only in 55-grain and 64-grain bullet weights.

INTERESTING FACTOID

A major technical design point of the WSSM cartridge family is to allow a high velocity, beltless magnum cartridge to fit into a short rifle action. This is accomplished partly by lowering the length/diameter ratio. (See chart below)

Cartridge	L/D ratio
220 Swift	4.955
223 Rem.	4.682
222 Rem.	4.523
22-250 Rem.	4.096
223 WSM	3.009

The second design element of the 223 WSSM is to use the .535 inch rim diameter of belted magnum cartridges (albeit without the belt) to increase the case diameter while reducing its length. For interior ballistic purposes, this means a shorter, fatter powder column. As it turns out, the claimed advantages of a super short cartridge in a short rifle action have proven illusory for sales.

HANDLOADING NOTES

- Due to its large case capacity, the 223 WSSM cartridge prefers slower burning propellants.
- Use of bullets lighter than 50-grain is not recommended.
- As rifles chambered for the 223 WSSM cartridge are bolt-action types, neck sizing should be considered to reduce length growth and head separations. Another factor is prolonging case life.

SAFETY NOTES

SPEER 55-grain TNT®HP @ a muzzle velocity of 3,900 fps:

- Maximum vertical altitude @ 90° elevation is 8,030 feet.
- Maximum horizontal distance to first impact with ground @ 32° elevation is 3,525 yards.

50 GRAINS

DIAMETER	SECTIONAL DENSITY
0.224"	0.142

22 Spitzer SP	
Ballistic Coefficient	0.207
COAL Tested	2.100"
Speer Part No.	1029

Propellant	Case	Primer	Starting Charge Weight (grains)	Starting Charge Muzzle Velocity (feet/sec)	Maximum Charge Weight (grains)	Maximum Charge Muzzle Velocity (feet/sec)
Alliant Power Pro 2000-MR	Winchester	Federal 210	42.7	3799	47.4	4080
IMR 8208 XBR	Winchester	Federal 210	37.4	3772	41.6	4050
Alliant Reloder 15	Winchester	Federal 210	42.5	3846	44.5	4036
Alliant Power Pro Varmint	Winchester	Federal 210	39.1	3762	43.2	4034
Hodgdon Varget	Winchester	Federal 210	43.0	3890	45.0	4033
Hodgdon H414	Winchester	Federal 215	47.0	3866	49.0	4027
Winchester 760	Winchester	Federal 215	47.5	3834	49.5	4009
IMR 4166	Winchester	Federal 210	39.3	3683	43.5	4005
Vihtavuori N540	Winchester	Federal 210	43.5	3816	45.5	3995
Alliant AR-Comp	Winchester	Federal 210	36.9	3694	41.0	3995
IMR 4895	Winchester	Federal 210	42.0	3820	44.0	3993
IMR 4064	Winchester	Federal 210	41.5	3807	43.5	3988
Ramshot Big Game	Winchester	Federal 215	45.5	3780	47.5	3971
Accurate 4064	Winchester	Federal 210	42.0	3765	44.0	3952
Alliant Reloder 10X	Winchester	Federal 210	36.5	3795	38.5	3929

WARNING! Maximum loads should be used with CAUTION • C = Compressed Load

55 GRAINS

DIAMETER	SECTIONAL DENSITY
0.224"	0.157

22 TNT® HP
Ballistic Coefficient	0.233
COAL Tested	2.210"
Speer Part No.	1032

22 Spitzer SP
Ballistic Coefficient	0.212
COAL Tested	2.210"
Speer Part No.	1047

			Starting Charge		Maximum Charge	
Propellant	Case	Primer	Weight (grains)	Muzzle Velocity (feet/sec)	Weight (grains)	Muzzle Velocity (feet/sec)
Hodgdon H414	Winchester	Federal 215	45.5	3724	47.5	3900
Winchester 760	Winchester	Federal 215	46.0	3727	48.0	3894
IMR 4895	Winchester	Federal 210	41.0	3706	43.0	3873
Alliant Reloder 15	Winchester	Federal 210	40.5	3703	42.5	3867
Hodgdon Varget	Winchester	Federal 210	41.5	3712	43.5	3867
Ramshot Big Game	Winchester	Federal 215	45.0	3722	47.0	3860
Alliant Power Pro 2000-MR	Winchester	Federal 210	39.8	3654	43.8	3859
IMR 4350	Winchester	Federal 210	46.0	3671	48.0 C	3837
IMR 8208 XBR	Winchester	Federal 210	35.7	3572	39.4	3825
IMR 4166	Winchester	Federal 210	37.5	3518	41.4	3820
Alliant Power Pro Varmint	Winchester	Federal 210	36.5	3559	40.4	3805
Alliant Reloder 19	Winchester	Federal 210	47.5	3566	49.5 C	3746
Accurate 4350	Winchester	Federal 210	46.0	3567	48.0 C	3733
Alliant AR-Comp	Winchester	Federal 210	34.2	3480	37.9	3731
Vihtavuori N560	Winchester	Federal 210	49.0	3558	51.0 C	3717

WARNING! Maximum loads should be used with CAUTION • C = Compressed Load

70 GRAINS

DIAMETER	SECTIONAL DENSITY
0.224"	0.199

22 Semi-Spitzer SP
Ballistic Coefficient	0.219
COAL Tested	2.080"
Speer Part No.	1053

Propellant	Case	Primer	Starting Charge Weight (grains)	Starting Charge Muzzle Velocity (feet/sec)	Maximum Charge Weight (grains)	Maximum Charge Muzzle Velocity (feet/sec)
Alliant Power Pro 4000-MR	Winchester	Federal 210	41.0	3313	45.3	3574
Alliant Reloder 23	Winchester	Federal 210	42.0	3282	46.4 C	3566
Alliant Reloder 16	Winchester	Federal 210	38.5	3261	42.7	3539
Alliant Reloder 17	Winchester	Federal 210	37.3	3245	41.5	3527
Alliant Reloder 22	Winchester	Federal 210	45.5	3407	47.5	3523
Vihtavuori N560	Winchester	Federal 210	45.0	3358	47.0	3495
Accurate MagPro	Winchester	Federal 215	48.0	3329	50.0	3489
Alliant Reloder 19	Winchester	Federal 210	43.5	3361	45.5	3478
Hodgdon H4831SC	Winchester	Federal 210	41.0	3332	43.1	3440
Hodgdon H414	Winchester	Federal 215	40.0	3308	42.0	3432
Winchester 760	Winchester	Federal 215	40.5	3307	42.5	3424
IMR 4350	Winchester	Federal 210	40.0	3282	42.0	3412
Hodgdon H4350	Winchester	Federal 210	39.0	3282	41.0	3397
Ramshot Big Game	Winchester	Federal 215	39.0	3252	41.0	3383
Accurate 4350	Winchester	Federal 210	40.5	3260	42.5	3382

WARNING! Maximum loads should be used with CAUTION • C = Compressed Load

6mm PPC

Parent Cartridge:	220 Russian
Country of Origin:	USA
Year of Introduction:	1987
Designer(s):	Ferris Pindell, Dr. Louis Palmisano
Governing Body:	CIP

CARTRIDGE CASE DATA

Case Type:	Rimless, bottleneck			
Average Case Capacity:	34.1 grains H$_2$O	Max. Cartridge OAL:	2.193 inch	
Max. Case Length:	1.515 inch	Primer:	Small Rifle	
Case Trim to Length:	1.505 inch	RCBS Shell holder:	# 32	
Current Manufacturers:	none			

BALLISTIC DATA

Max. Average Pressure (MAP):	58,740 psi – CIP	Test Barrel Length:	24 inch	
Rifling Twist Rate:	1 turn in 12 inches. Also 1/13, 1/14 and 1/15 inch			
	Muzzle velocity will decrease approximately 30 fps per inch for barrels less than 24 inches.			

HISTORICAL NOTES

- The 6mm PPC-USA cartridge was designed by Dr. Louis Palmisano, a noted heart surgeon, and Ferris Pindell, a master tool and die maker. Both were avid benchrest competitors.
- The 22 PPC was introduced in 1975 followed by the 6mm PPC in 1987. Both are now obsolete and out of production.
- Although both cartridges were designed for benchrest competition, they found a limited following for hunting, especially in Finland.
- Both cartridges were standardized by CIP, but not SAAMI.
- Sako of Finland was the primary manufacturer of the 6mm PPC cartridge case. New, unprimed, empty brass from Sako was imported and distributed to U.S. customers for many years.
- The success of the 22 PPC and 6mm PPC cartridges spawned a number of competitors, namely the 6mm Remington BR cartridge and the 6mm Norma BR. Both of these currently are in production.

- As a benchrest caliber, the 6mm PPC-USA was popular mainly as a new, unprimed, empty case. Sporadic efforts to introduce loaded ammunition in 6mm PPC caliber for hunting were not successful, no ballistics for factory ammunition is available.
- Sako at one time offered loaded ammunition with a 70-grain bullet of their manufacture but it is no longer available.

BALLISTIC NOTES

- CIP lists two 6mm PPC cartridges: one called the 6mm PPC-USA (as shown here) sponsored by Sako, and the other called simply the 6mm PPC. The two cartridges differ in minor detail only, but may not be interchangeable in tight benchrest chambers.
- CIP data lists the rifling twist rate of the 6mm PPC-USA as being one turn in 12 inches. This twist rate works well for loads with bullets up to 90-grain. However, many bench rest shooters prefer a slower rifle twist rate of one turn in 14 inch as they use lightweight match bullets.

HANDLOADING NOTES

- Note that the 6mm PPC-USA uses a Small Rifle primer as benchrest shooters prefer it for accuracy while larger 6mm cartridges such as the 243 Winchester use Large Rifle primers.
- Although it was not designed for hunting, with suitable bullets, the 6mm PPC-USA makes a satisfactory varmint and light deer caliber. For this application, consider the Speer 85-grain Spitzer BTSP.
- Bullets weighing over 90-grain will not stabilize if fired from the 1/14 inch twist 6mm PPC as its slow rifling twist rate is optimized for lighter bullets.
- Due to its modest case capacity, the 6mm PPC-USA cartridge prefers faster burning propellants.
- New, unprimed brass in this caliber is no longer being made.

SAFETY NOTES

SPEER 85-grain Spitzer BTSP @ a muzzle velocity of 3,156 fps:

- Maximum vertical altitude @ 90° elevation is 10,566 feet.
- Maximum horizontal distance to first impact with ground @ 35° elevation is 4,819 yards.

75 GRAINS

DIAMETER	SECTIONAL DENSITY
0.243"	0.181

6mm HP

Ballistic Coefficient	0.192
COAL Tested	2.115"
Speer Part No.	1205

			Starting Charge		Maximum Charge	
Propellant	Case	Primer	Weight (grains)	Muzzle Velocity (feet/sec)	Weight (grains)	Muzzle Velocity (feet/sec)
Hodgdon H335	Sako	CCI BR4	26.0	2790	30.0 C	3257
Hodgdon BL-C(2)	Sako	CCI BR4	27.0	2931	29.0 C	3169
Hodgdon H322	Sako	CCI BR4	26.5	2910	28.5 C	3127
Alliant Reloder 7	Sako	CCI BR4	23.0	2791	25.0	3011
IMR 4198	Sako	CCI BR4	24.0	2620	26.0	2910
Winchester 748	Sako	CCI BR4	27.0	2634	29.0 C	2904
IMR 4895	Sako	CCI BR4	24.0	2508	26.0 C	2705

85 GRAINS

DIAMETER	SECTIONAL DENSITY
0.243"	0.206

6mm Spitzer BTSP

Ballistic Coefficient	0.380
COAL Tested	2.115"
Speer Part No.	1213

			Starting Charge		Maximum Charge	
Propellant	Case	Primer	Weight (grains)	Muzzle Velocity (feet/sec)	Weight (grains)	Muzzle Velocity (feet/sec)
Hodgdon H335	Sako	CCI BR4	25.5	2703	29.5 C	3156
Hodgdon BL-C(2)	Sako	CCI BR4	26.5	2858	28.5 C	3098
Hodgdon H322	Sako	CCI BR4	26.0	2878	28.0 C	3083
IMR 4198	Sako	CCI BR4	23.5	2838	25.5 C	3068
Alliant Reloder 7	Sako	CCI BR4	22.0	2633	24.0	2863
Winchester 748	Sako	CCI BR4	27.0	2625	29.0 C	2838
IMR 4320	Sako	CCI BR4	25.0	2623	27.0 C	2815

WARNING! *Maximum loads should be used with CAUTION • C = Compressed Load*

90 GRAINS

DIAMETER	SECTIONAL DENSITY
0.243"	0.218

6mm Spitzer SP Hot-Cor®

Ballistic Coefficient	0.365
COAL Tested	2.115"
Speer Part No.	1217

			Starting Charge		Maximum Charge	
Propellant	Case	Primer	Weight (grains)	Muzzle Velocity (feet/sec)	Weight (grains)	Muzzle Velocity (feet/sec)
Hodgdon H335	Sako	CCI BR4	25.0	2601	29.0 C	3031
Hodgdon H322	Sako	CCI BR4	25.5	2718	27.5 C	2958
Hodgdon BL-C(2)	Sako	CCI BR4	26.0	2714	28.0 C	2945
IMR 4198	Sako	CCI BR4	23.0	2699	25.0 C	2916
Winchester 748	Sako	CCI BR4	26.5	2505	28.5 C	2712
IMR 4320	Sako	CCI BR4	24.5	2463	26.5 C	2678
IMR 4895	Sako	CCI BR4	23.5	2412	25.5 C	2603
IMR 4064	Sako	CCI BR4	23.5	2308	25.5 C	2510

WARNING! *Maximum loads should be used with CAUTION • C = Compressed Load*

6mm CREEDMOOR

Alternate Names:	6mm CM
Parent Cartridge:	6.5 Creedmoor
Country of Origin:	USA
Year of Introduction:	2017
Designer(s):	John Snow & George Gardner; introduced by Hornady
Governing Body:	SAAMI

Case dimensions: .275" cyl [6.99mm]; shoulder angle 30°; .4703" [11.95mm]; .462" [11.73mm]; .473" [12.01mm]; .4639" [11.76mm]; .054" [1.38mm]; .200" [5.08mm]; 1.150" [29.21mm]; 1.490" [37.85mm]; 1.651" [41.94mm]; 1.920" [48.77mm]

CARTRIDGE CASE DATA

Case Type:	Rimless, bottleneck		
Average Case Capacity:	53.7 grains H₂O	Max. Cartridge OAL	2.193 inch
Max. Case Length:	1.920 inch	Primer:	Large Rifle and Small Rifle
Case Trim to Length:	1.910 inch	RCBS Shell holder:	# 3
Current Manufacturers:	Hornady, Lapua		

BALLISTIC DATA

Max. Average Pressure (MAP):	62,000 psi, CUP not established for this cartridge - SAAMI	Test Barrel Length:	24 inch
Rifling Twist Rate:	1 turn in 8 inch, 1/7.7 inch alternative		

Muzzle velocities of factory loaded ammunition	Bullet Wgt.	Muzzle velocity
	108-grain	2,950 fps
	Muzzle velocity will decrease approximately 20 fps per inch for barrels less than 24 inches.	

HISTORICAL NOTES

- The 6mm Creedmoor was derived from the 6.5 Creedmoor by necking it down. It was a wildcat that was accepted by SAAMI in 2017.
- Custom rifles were made for the 6mm Creedmoor as a wildcat cartridge soon after the 6.5 Creedmoor was on the commercial market in 2008.
- Ruger is currently chambering their Precision Rifle and their American Rifle Predator model in 6mm Creedmoor.

HANDLOADING NOTES

- Brass is easily reformed from available 6.5 Creedmoor by sizing and trimming.

SAFETY NOTES

Speer 100-grain Spitzer BTSP @ a muzzle velocity of 3,250 fps:

- Maximum vertical altitude @ 90° elevation is 16,068 feet.
- Maximum horizontal distance to first impact with ground @ 37° elevation is 7,309 yards.

75 GRAINS

DIAMETER	SECTIONAL DENSITY
0.243"	0.181

6mm HP	
Ballistic Coefficient	0.192
COAL Tested	2.550"
Speer Part No.	1205

			Starting Charge		Maximum Charge	
Propellant	Case	Primer	Weight (grains)	Muzzle Velocity (feet/sec)	Weight (grains)	Muzzle Velocity (feet/sec)
Alliant Reloder 17	Hornady	CCI 200	42.1	3297	46.8	3656
Alliant Power Pro 2000-MR	Hornady	CCI 200	40.8	3349	45.3	3639
Ramshot Hunter	Hornady	CCI 200	46.7	3404	50.3 C	3620
Vihtavuori N550	Hornady	CCI 200	41.1	3300	45.6	3618
Winchester 760	Hornady	CCI 200	41.9	3293	46.5	3587
Hodgdon H4350	Hornady	CCI 200	43.4	3293	48.2 C	3578
Alliant Power Pro 4000-MR	Hornady	CCI 200	45.0	3303	48.5 C	3559
IMR 4451	Hornady	CCI 200	42.7	3225	46.8 C	3508
Alliant Reloder 16	Hornady	CCI 200	44.2	3361	45.4 C	3452
Accurate 4350	Hornady	CCI 200	44.5	3270	46.0 C	3377

WARNING! Maximum loads should be used with CAUTION • C = Compressed Load

90 GRAINS

DIAMETER	SECTIONAL DENSITY
0.243"	0.218

6mm Spitzer SP Hot-Cor®	
Ballistic Coefficient	0.365
COAL Tested	2.700"
Speer Part No.	1217

			Starting Charge		Maximum Charge	
Propellant	Case	Primer	Weight (grains)	Muzzle Velocity (feet/sec)	Weight (grains)	Muzzle Velocity (feet/sec)
Alliant Reloder 26	Hornady	CCI 200	44.2	3142	49.0	3418
Alliant Power Pro 4000-MR	Hornady	CCI 200	41.9	3071	46.7	3362
Alliant Reloder 19	Hornady	CCI 200	43.2	3070	48.2	3361
Alliant Reloder 22	Hornady	CCI 200	42.7	3104	47.2	3356
Alliant Reloder 16	Hornady	CCI 200	40.6	3115	45.2	3348
Alliant Reloder 17	Hornady	CCI 200	39.2	3066	43.6	3341
Alliant Reloder 23	Hornady	CCI 200	42.9	3067	47.7 C	3318
Hodgdon H4350	Hornady	CCI 200	39.3	3044	43.3	3251
IMR 4831	Hornady	CCI 200	41.1	2950	45.6	3225
Winchester 760	Hornady	CCI 200	37.9	2999	42.1	3220
IMR 4451	Hornady	CCI 200	39.0	2962	43.2	3211
Accurate 4350	Hornady	CCI 200	36.0	2929	40.3	3167

WARNING! *Maximum loads should be used with CAUTION • C = Compressed Load*

100 GRAINS

DIAMETER	SECTIONAL DENSITY
0.243"	0.242

6mm Spitzer BTSP	
Ballistic Coefficient	0.446
COAL Tested	2.700"
Speer Part No.	1220

			Starting Charge		Maximum Charge	
Propellant	Case	Primer	Weight (grains)	Muzzle Velocity (feet/sec)	Weight (grains)	Muzzle Velocity (feet/sec)
Alliant Reloder 26	Hornady	CCI 200	43.8	2953	48.7 C	3293
Alliant Power Pro 4000-MR	Hornady	CCI 200	40.9	2918	45.4	3221
Alliant Reloder 23	Hornady	CCI 200	42.6	2917	47.5 C	3219
Alliant Reloder 22	Hornady	CCI 200	41.1	2962	45.7	3212
Alliant Reloder 19	Hornady	CCI 200	41.6	2922	46.7	3206
IMR 7828	Hornady	CCI 200	42.3	2877	47.1 C	3199
Alliant Reloder 17	Hornady	CCI 200	38.3	2906	42.5	3192
Alliant Reloder 16	Hornady	CCI 200	38.7	2919	43.5	3191
Hodgdon 4350	Hornady	CCI 200	38.1	2880	42.3	3119
Accurate 4350	Hornady	CCI 200	38.2	2913	42.2	3111
IMR 7977	Hornady	CCI 200	44.3	2790	49.1 C	3101
IMR 4831	Hornady	CCI 200	39.7	2806	44.1	3082

WARNING! *Maximum loads should be used with CAUTION • C = Compressed Load*

243 WINCHESTER

Parent Cartridge:	308 Winchester
Country of Origin:	USA
Year of Introduction:	1955
Designer(s):	Winchester
Governing Body:	SAAMI/CIP

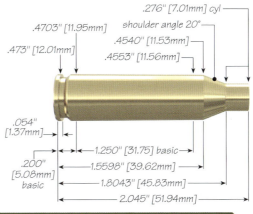

CARTRIDGE CASE DATA

Case Type:	Rimless, bottleneck
Average Case Capacity:	56.0 grains H_2O
Max. Case Length:	2.045 inch
Case Trim to Length:	2.035 inch
Max. Cartridge OAL:	2.710 inch
Primer:	Large Rifle
RCBS Shell holder:	# 3
Current Manufacturers:	Winchester, Federal, Remington, Norma, RUAG (RWS), Fiocchi, Hornady, Nosler, Lapua, Sako, Prvi Partizan, Black Hills, Sellier & Bellot

BALLISTIC DATA

Max. Average Pressure (MAP):	60,000 psi, 52,000 CUP - SAAMI
Test Barrel Length:	24 inch
Rifling Twist Rate:	1 turn in 10 inch

Muzzle velocities of factory loaded ammunition

Bullet Wgt.	Muzzle velocity
55-grain	3,850 fps
75-grain	3,580 fps
80-grain	3,350 fps
85-grain	3,200 fps
95-grain	3,025 fps
100-grain	2,960 fps

Muzzle velocity will decrease approximately 30 fps per inch for barrels less than 24 inches.

HISTORICAL NOTES

- When Winchester designed the 243 Winchester in 1955, their goal was to create a new 6mm cartridge with light recoil for deer hunting using 100-grain bullets. Accordingly, they set the rifling twist rate for their new cartridge at one turn in 10 inch to stabilize such bullets. They were proved right.

- In the same year, Remington introduced their new 244 Remington cartridge which they saw as a varmint cartridge using lightweight bullets. Accordingly, they set the rifling twist rate at one turn in 12 inch to stabilize such bullets. The 244 Remington cartridge would not stabilize the 100-grain bullets suitable for hunting deer.
- The 243 Winchester quickly became a best-seller and remains so to this day.
- In 1963, Remington threw in the towel, put the 244 Remington to rest, and introduced their new 6mm Remington cartridge having a rifling twist rate of one turn in 9 inch which will stabilize the heavy 6mm bullets suitable for deer hunting. While the 6mm Remington cartridge is an excellent one, it was too late to compete on equal terms with the 243 Winchester.
- Lately, the tastes of North American hunters have changed. Interest in both cartridges as versatile deer/varmint calibers has grown. In response, lightweight bullets of 55-grain have been introduced in both calibers by several ammunition manufacturers. Today, there are few major ammunition makers that do NOT offer the 243 Winchester.

BALLISTIC NOTES

- A lightweight, short-action, sporter rifle and the light recoil of the 243 Winchester are an excellent combination for new shooters.
- One-gun hunters appreciate the versatility of the 243 Win. for game animals up to and including deer. However, it is underpowered for larger game.
- Use the lighter bullets for small game, varmints, pests, and rodents. We recommend the heavier bullets from 90 to 100 grains for deer.

TECHNICAL NOTES

- The 243 Winchester is essentially a 308 Winchester cartridge necked down to accept .243 inch / 6mm diameter bullets.
- Be aware that the 243 Winchester is a high intensity cartridge that can accelerate wear in the throat of the chamber.

HANDLOADING NOTES

- The case capacity of the 243 Winchester allows the use of slower burning propellants with most bullet weights.
- Because of the large number of manufacturers of 243 Winchester ammunition, there is a wide variety in case interior dimensions which can cause problems for the handloader. For this reason, you should not mix cases from various manufacturers when reloading.
- When fired in a bolt-action rifle, the 243 Winchester cartridge case can be neck-sized to reduce growth and head separations. We suggest hunting with full length sized rounds.
- The Speer 100-grain Spitzer BTSP is an excellent choice for hunting deer.

SAFETY NOTES

SPEER 100-grain Spitzer BTSP @ a muzzle velocity of 3,140 fps:
- Maximum vertical altitude @ 90° elevation is 11,487 feet.
- Maximum horizontal distance to first impact with ground @ 36° elevation is 5,310 yards.

70 GRAINS

DIAMETER	SECTIONAL DENSITY
0.243"	0.169

6mm TNT® HP	
Ballistic Coefficient	0.279
COAL Tested	2.625"
Speer Part No.	1206

			Starting Charge		Maximum Charge	
Propellant	Case	Primer	Weight (grains)	Muzzle Velocity (feet/sec)	Weight (grains)	Muzzle Velocity (feet/sec)
Alliant Reloder 16	Federal	Federal 210	42.0	3338	46.4 C	3623
Vihtavuori N540	Winchester	Federal 210	41.0	3237	45.0	3552
Alliant Reloder 17	Federal	Federal 210	40.7	3218	45.3	3552
IMR 4895	Winchester	Federal 210	39.0	3303	43.0	3540
Hodgdon H414	Winchester	Federal 215	45.0	3332	47.0	3520
Hodgdon Varget	Winchester	Federal 210	39.0	3236	43.0	3515
Winchester 760	Winchester	Federal 215	44.0	3195	48.0	3514
Ramshot Big Game	Winchester	Federal 215	42.0	3303	46.0	3508
Alliant Reloder 15	Winchester	Federal 210	39.5	3189	43.5	3506
Alliant Power Pro 2000-MR	Federal	Federal 210	37.7	3295	41.5	3492
IMR 4350	Winchester	Federal 210	44.5	3135	48.5	3461
Alliant AR-Comp	Federal	Federal 210	33.5	3242	37.1	3456
Hodgdon CFE 223	Federal	Federal 210	35.1	3216	38.8	3449
Alliant Reloder 10X	Winchester	Federal 210	32.5	3189	36.5	3421
Accurate 4064	Winchester	Federal 210	39.0	3089	43.0	3419
Alliant Power Pro Varmint	Federal	Federal 210	32.5	3137	36.1	3394

Warning: *Do not substitute other brands of cartridge case. Excessive pressure may result.*

WARNING! *Maximum loads should be used with CAUTION • C = Compressed Load*

75 GRAINS

DIAMETER	SECTIONAL DENSITY
0.243"	0.181

6mm HP

Ballistic Coefficient	0.192
COAL Tested	2.590"
Speer Part No.	1205

			Starting Charge		Maximum Charge	
Propellant	Case	Primer	Weight (grains)	Muzzle Velocity (feet/sec)	Weight (grains)	Muzzle Velocity (feet/sec)
Alliant Reloder 16	Federal	Federal 210	40.4	3252	44.0	3454
Vihtavuori N540	Winchester	Federal 210	40.5	3099	44.5	3447
IMR 4895	Winchester	Federal 210	38.5	3183	42.5	3407
Alliant Reloder 15	Winchester	Federal 210	39.0	3077	43.0	3400
Alliant Reloder 17	Federal	Federal 210	39.0	3142	43.1	3395
Ramshot Big Game	Winchester	Federal 215	41.0	3185	45.0	3390
Hodgdon Varget	Winchester	Federal 210	38.0	3186	42.0	3388
Winchester 760	Winchester	Federal 215	43.5	3114	47.5	3387
IMR 4350	Winchester	Federal 210	44.0	3043	48.0 C	3384
Hodgdon H414	Winchester	Federal 215	42.0	3087	46.0	3376
Accurate 4064	Winchester	Federal 210	38.5	2930	42.5	3301
Alliant AR-Comp	Federal	Federal 210	32.1	3073	35.3	3271
Alliant Reloder 10X	Winchester	Federal 210	32.0	3023	36.0	3240
Accurate 4350	Winchester	Federal 210	44.0	2916	48.0 C	3238

Warning: *Do not substitute other brands of cartridge case. Excessive pressure may result.*

WARNING! *Maximum loads should be used with CAUTION • C = Compressed Load*

85 GRAINS

DIAMETER	SECTIONAL DENSITY
0.243"	0.206

6mm Spitzer BTSP	
Ballistic Coefficient	0.380
COAL Tested	2.625"
Speer Part No.	1213

			Starting Charge		Maximum Charge	
Propellant	Case	Primer	Weight (grains)	Muzzle Velocity (feet/sec)	Weight (grains)	Muzzle Velocity (feet/sec)
Alliant Reloder 17	Federal	Federal 210	39.2	3006	43.2	3293
Hodgdon Varget	Winchester	Federal 210	37.5	3023	41.5	3268
Winchester 760	Winchester	Federal 215	41.0	2991	45.0	3265
Alliant Reloder 16	Federal	Federal 210	37.8	2975	41.8	3261
Hodgdon H4350	Federal	Federal 210	38.7	3023	42.7	3254
IMR 4895	Winchester	Federal 210	37.5	2910	41.5	3249
Alliant Power Pro 2000-MR	Federal	Federal 210	36.2	2988	40.2	3247
Vihtavuori N550	Federal	Federal 210	36.4	2932	40.4	3245
Ramshot Big Game	Winchester	Federal 215	39.5	2999	43.5	3240
Hodgdon H414	Winchester	Federal 215	40.5	2904	44.5	3236
IMR 4350	Winchester	Federal 210	42.0	2873	46.0	3231
Alliant Reloder 15	Winchester	Federal 210	37.0	2902	41.0	3218
Vihtavuori N560	Winchester	Federal 210	46.0	2890	50.0 C	3216
Alliant Power Pro Varmint	Federal	Federal 210	34.0	2988	37.6	3196
Alliant Reloder 19	Winchester	Federal 210	46.0	3016	48.0 C	3182
Accurate 4350	Winchester	Federal 210	43.0	2858	47.0 C	3172
Alliant AR-Comp	Federal	Federal 210	31.5	2928	35.5	3165
Alliant Reloder 10X	Winchester	Federal 210	31.0	2910	35.0	3122

Warning: *Do not substitute other brands of cartridge case. Excessive pressure may result.*

WARNING! *Maximum loads should be used with CAUTION • C = Compressed Load*

90 GRAINS

DIAMETER	SECTIONAL DENSITY
0.243"	0.218

6mm Spitzer SP Hot-Cor®

Ballistic Coefficient	0.365
COAL Tested	2.625"
Speer Part No.	1217

Propellant	Case	Primer	Starting Charge Weight (grains)	Starting Charge Muzzle Velocity (feet/sec)	Maximum Charge Weight (grains)	Maximum Charge Muzzle Velocity (feet/sec)
Alliant Power Pro 4000-MR	Federal	Federal 210	39.6	2947	43.8	3203
Vihtavuori N560	Winchester	Federal 210	45.0	2880	49.0 C	3175
Alliant Reloder 17	Federal	Federal 210	37.3	2914	41.3	3170
Alliant Reloder 16	Federal	Federal 210	37.4	2934	41.5	3163
IMR 4350	Winchester	Federal 210	41.0	2877	45.0	3149
Hodgdon H4350	Winchester	Federal 210	40.0	2853	44.0	3132
Hodgdon H414	Winchester	Federal 215	39.5	2830	43.5	3126
Ramshot Big Game	Winchester	Federal 215	37.5	2856	41.5	3084
Accurate 4350	Winchester	Federal 210	41.5	2805	45.5 C	3080
Alliant Reloder 19	Winchester	Federal 210	43.0	2879	47.0 C	3079
IMR 4895	Winchester	Federal 210	35.0	2826	39.0	3071
Hodgdon H4831Sc	Federal	Federal 210	37.5	2861	41.1	3070
Alliant Power Pro 2000-MR	Federal	Federal 210	34.5	2837	38.2	3063
Hodgdon 760	Winchester	Federal 215	39.0	2749	43.0	3056
Alliant Reloder 22	Winchester	Federal 210	44.0	2837	48.0 C	3053
Alliant Reloder 15	Winchester	Federal 210	34.0	2767	38.0	3020
Accurate 5744 (reduced load)	Winchester	Federal 210	21.0	2105	23.0	2273

Warning: *Do not substitute other brands of cartridge case. Excessive pressure may result.*

WARNING! *Maximum loads should be used with CAUTION • C = Compressed Load*

100 GRAINS

DIAMETER	SECTIONAL DENSITY
0.243"	0.242

6mm Spitzer BTSP	
Ballistic Coefficient	0.446
COAL Tested	2.625"
Speer Part No.	1220

6mm GrandSlam® SP	
Ballistic Coefficient	0.327
COAL Tested	2.580"
Speer Part No.	1222

			Starting Charge		Maximum Charge	
Propellant	Case	Primer	Weight (grains)	Muzzle Velocity (feet/sec)	Weight (grains)	Muzzle Velocity (feet/sec)
Alliant Reloder 26	Federal	Federal 210	42.3	2847	46.8 C	3143
Alliant Power Pro 4000-MR	Federal	Federal 210	38.2	2789	42.4	3045
Alliant Reloder 17	Federal	Federal 210	36.3	2764	40.6	3030
Alliant Reloder 23	Federal	Federal 210	40.2	2850	43.7 C	3028
Alliant Reloder 16	Federal	Federal 210	35.1	2775	39.0	2986
Ramshot Hunter	Federal	Federal 210	38.0	2770	41.7	2982
Vihtavuori N560	Winchester	Federal 210	41.5	2736	45.5	2966
Alliant Reloder 22	Winchester	Federal 210	42.0	2773	46.0	2960
IMR 4831	Winchester	Federal 210	38.0	2659	42.0	2913
Alliant Reloder 19	Winchester	Federal 210	39.5	2731	43.5	2903
IMR 4350	Winchester	Federal 210	37.5	2643	41.5	2880
Hodgdon H4831SC	Winchester	Federal 210	40.0	2639	44.0	2874
Ramshot Magnum	Winchester	Federal 215	45.0	2673	49.0 C	2868
Hodgdon H414	Winchester	Federal 215	36.5	2602	40.5	2862
Winchester 760	Winchester	Federal 215	36.5	2558	40.5	2828
Accurate 4350	Winchester	Federal 210	37.0	2581	41.0	2802
Alliant Reloder 15	Winchester	Federal 210	30.0	2443	34.0	2691

Warning: *Do not substitute other brands of cartridge case. Excessive pressure may result.*

WARNING! Maximum loads should be used with CAUTION • C = Compressed Load

6mm REMINGTON

Alternate Names:	244 Remington
Parent Cartridge:	7x57mm
Country of Origin:	USA
Year of Introduction:	1963
Designer(s):	Remington
Governing Body:	SAAMI

CARTRIDGE CASE DATA

Case Type:	Rimless, necked		
Average Case Capacity:	57.9 grains H$_2$O	Max. Cartridge OAL	2.825 inch
Max. Case Length:	2.233 inch	Primer:	Large Rifle
Case Trim to Length:	2.223 inch	RCBS Shell holder:	# 3
Current Manufacturers:	Remington, Federal, Winchester, Hornady		

BALLISTIC DATA

Max. Average Pressure (MAP):	65,000 psi, 52,000 CUP - SAAMI	Test Barrel Length:	24 inch
Rifling Twist Rate:	1 turn in 9 inch for the 6mm Remington, 1 turn in 12 inch for the 244 Remington.		
Muzzle velocities of factory loaded ammunition	Bullet Wgt.		Muzzle velocity
	55-grain		3,860 fps
	95-grain		3, 235 fps
	100-grain		3,100 fps
	Muzzle velocity will decrease approximately 30 fps per inch for barrels less than 24 inches.		

HISTORICAL NOTES

- When Winchester designed the 243 Winchester cartridge in 1955, they viewed their creation as an excellent choice for deer using 100-grain bullets. Accordingly, they set the rifling twist rate for their new cartridge at one turn in 10 inches. In the same year, Remington introduced their 244 Remington cartridge which they saw as a varmint cartridge using lightweight bullets. Accordingly, they set the rifling twist rate at one turn in 12 inches, limiting its use with heavier bullets.

- The 243 Winchester cartridge quickly became a best-seller and remains so to this day. In 1963, Remington put the 244 Remington cartridge to rest and introduced their new 6mm Remington having a considerably steeper one turn in 9 inch rifling twist which will stabilize the heavy 6mm bullets suitable for deer hunting. As a result, the 6mm Remington cartridge got a very late start and never caught up with the 243 Winchester.
- Today, four ammunition makers offer the 6mm Remington cartridge. Most offer only one bullet weight around 100 grains.

BALLISTIC NOTES

- There is nothing wrong, ballistically, with the 6mm Remington cartridge. It will do anything the 243 Winchester will do and just a bit more. For example, in typical factory loads, the 6mm Remington has about 140 fps muzzle velocity advantage over the 243 Winchester with 100-grain bullets.
- In a head-to-head comparison, the 6mm Remington and the 243 Winchester cartridges look like two peas in a pod. For example, their case volumes differ by only about 3%. Two cartridges could hardly be more alike, however they are not interchangeable.
- Ammunition in 244 Remington can be fired in rifles chambered for the 6mm Remington cartridge and vice versa. The difference in twist rates will dictate proper bullet use.

SAFETY NOTES

SPEER 100-grain Spitzer BTSP @ a muzzle velocity of 3,145 fps:
- Maximum vertical altitude @ 90° elevation is 11,778 feet.
- Maximum horizontal distance to first impact with ground @ 36° elevation is 5,410 yards.
- Note that 244 Remington rifles will not stabilize bullets over 90 grains.

70 GRAINS

DIAMETER	SECTIONAL DENSITY
0.243"	0.169

6mm TNT® HP

Ballistic Coefficient	0.279
COAL Tested	2.775"
Speer Part No.	1206

			Starting Charge		Maximum Charge	
Propellant	Case	Primer	Weight (grains)	Muzzle Velocity (feet/sec)	Weight (grains)	Muzzle Velocity (feet/sec)
Alliant Reloder 17	Federal	Federal 210	43.9	3252	48.7 C	3644
Hodgdon H4350	Remington	CCI 200	47.0	3198	51.0 C	3593
Accurate 4350	Remington	CCI 200	48.0	3106	52.0 C	3531
Alliant Reloder 16	Federal	Federal 210	44.0	3313	47.0 C	3525
Alliant Power Pro 4000-MR	Federal	Federal 210	45.1	3269	49.0 C	3522
IMR 4451	Federal	Federal 210	44.0	3215	48.2 C	3516
Alliant Reloder 19	Remington	CCI 200	49.0	3262	53.0 C	3507
Alliant Reloder 22	Remington	CCI 200	50.0	3287	54.0 C	3497
IMR 4831	Remington	CCI 200	48.0	3171	52.0 C	3485
Hodgdon H380	Remington	CCI 250	42.0	3132	47.0	3442
IMR 4064	Remington	CCI 200	40.0	3119	44.0	3427
Winchester 760	Remington	CCI 250	44.0	3078	48.0	3420
IMR 4350	Remington	CCI 200	45.0	3040	49.0	3416
IMR 4895	Remington	CCI 200	38.0	3111	42.0	3381
Hodgdon H414	Remington	CCI 250	44.0	3100	48.0	3370
Vihtavuori N140	Remington	CCI 200	39.0	3023	43.0	3322
Hodgdon H4831	Remington	CCI 250	48.0	3104	52.0 C	3302

WARNING! *Maximum loads should be used with CAUTION • C = Compressed Load*

75 GRAINS

DIAMETER	SECTIONAL DENSITY
0.243"	0.181

6mm HP	
Ballistic Coefficient	0.192
COAL Tested	2.775"
Speer Part No.	1205

			Starting Charge		Maximum Charge	
Propellant	Case	Primer	Weight (grains)	Muzzle Velocity (feet/sec)	Weight (grains)	Muzzle Velocity (feet/sec)
Alliant Power Pro 4000-MR	Federal	Federal 210	45.0	3198	49.8 C	3521
Hodgdon H4350	Remington	CCI 200	46.0	3157	50.0 C	3515
Alliant Reloder 17	Federal	Federal 210	43.3	3198	48.1	3504
Accurate 4350	Remington	CCI 200	47.0	3083	51.0 C	3495
Alliant Reloder 16	Federal	Federal 210	42.7	3179	47.2 C	3494
Alliant Reloder 22	Remington	CCI 200	49.0	3262	53.0 C	3474
Accurate 2700	Remington	CCI 250	43.0	3147	47.0	3458
IMR 4451	Federal	Federal 210	42.9	3184	47.4 C	3446
Alliant Reloder 19	Remington	CCI 200	48.0	3165	52.0 C	3440
IMR 4350	Remington	CCI 200	44.0	3064	48.0 C	3367
Winchester 760	Remington	CCI 250	43.0	3018	47.0	3318
Hodgdon H4831	Remington	CCI 250	47.0	3045	51.0 C	3310
Hodgdon H380	Remington	CCI 250	42.0	3012	46.0	3310
IMR 4831	Remington	CCI 200	45.0	3001	49.0 C	3298
Vihtavuori N140	Remington	CCI 200	39.0	2999	43.0	3293
IMR 4064	Remington	CCI 200	38.5	3010	42.5	3272
IMR 4895	Remington	CCI 200	37.0	2969	41.0	3248
Hodgdon H414	Remington	CCI 250	42.0	2959	46.0	3216

WARNING! Maximum loads should be used with CAUTION • C = Compressed Load

85 GRAINS

DIAMETER	SECTIONAL DENSITY
0.243"	0.206

6mm Spitzer BTSP	
Ballistic Coefficient	0.380
COAL Tested	2.775"
Speer Part No.	1213

			Starting Charge		Maximum Charge	
Propellant	Case	Primer	Weight (grains)	Muzzle Velocity (feet/sec)	Weight (grains)	Muzzle Velocity (feet/sec)
Alliant Power Pro 4000-MR	Federal	Federal 210	46.4	3284	48.5 C	3411
Vihtavuori N550	Federal	Federal 210	42.0	3271	43.5	3372
Hodgdon H4350	Federal	Federal 210	44.0	3215	46.4	3371
Alliant Reloder 23	Federal	Federal 210	45.0	3175	48.0 C	3368
Alliant Reloder 16	Federal	Federal 210	41.9	3221	43.9	3354
Alliant Power Pro 2000-MR	Federal	Federal 210	40.5	3219	42.1	3334
Alliant Reloder 22	Remington	CCI 200	48.0	3048	52.0 C	3285
Alliant Reloder 19	Remington	CCI 200	46.5	3007	50.5 C	3269
Accurate 4350	Remington	CCI 200	45.0	2878	49.0	3264
Hodgdon H4831	Remington	CCI 250	47.0	2968	51.0 C	3226
Winchester 760	Remington	CCI 250	41.0	2859	46.0	3152
IMR 4350	Remington	CCI 200	41.0	2881	46.0	3138
Accurate 2700	Remington	CCI 250	40.5	2846	44.5	3128
IMR 4831	Remington	CCI 200	43.0	2838	47.0	3085
Accurate 2520	Remington	CCI 250	36.0	2786	40.0	3061
Hodgdon H380	Remington	CCI 250	39.0	2777	43.0	3052
IMR 4895	Remington	CCI 200	35.0	2742	39.0	3000
IMR 4064	Remington	CCI 200	36.0	2704	40.0	2965
Vihtavuori N140	Remington	CCI 200	35.5	2723	39.5	2960
Hodgdon H414	Remington	CCI 250	40.0	2685	44.0	2921

WARNING! Maximum loads should be used with CAUTION • C = Compressed Load

90 GRAINS

DIAMETER	SECTIONAL DENSITY
0.243"	0.218

6mm Spitzer SP Hot-Cor®	
Ballistic Coefficient	0.365
COAL Tested	2.775"
Speer Part No.	1217

			Starting Charge		Maximum Charge	
Propellant	Case	Primer	Weight (grains)	Muzzle Velocity (feet/sec)	Weight (grains)	Muzzle Velocity (feet/sec)
Alliant Reloder 26	Federal	Federal 210	45.2	2961	50.0 C	3334
Alliant Power Pro 4000-MR	Federal	Federal 210	42.4	2973	46.9	3281
Alliant Reloder 16	Federal	Federal 210	40.8	2968	45.2 C	3281
Alliant Reloder 17	Federal	Federal 210	40.7	2924	45.2	3261
Alliant Reloder 22	Remington	CCI 200	47.0	3063	51.0 C	3258
Alliant Reloder 19	Remington	CCI 200	46.0	2976	50.0	3256
Accurate 4350	Remington	CCI 200	44.0	2852	48.0 C	3205
IMR 4451	Federal	Federal 210	40.4	2889	44.9	3191
Hodgdon H4350	Remington	CCI 200	43.0	2821	47.0	3170
Accurate 3100	Remington	CCI 200	45.0	2870	49.0 C	3154
Alliant Reloder 23	Federal	Federal 210	44.1	2981	46.5 C	3146
IMR 4350	Remington	CCI 200	42.0	2858	46.0	3107
Winchester 760	Remington	CCI 250	41.0	2811	45.0	3055
IMR 4831	Remington	CCI 200	43.0	2755	47.0	3026
Hodgdon H414	Remington	CCI 250	40.0	2759	44.0	2999
IMR 4064	Remington	CCI 200	35.0	2685	39.0	2982
Accurate 2700	Remington	CCI 250	39.0	2706	43.0	2974
IMR 4895	Remington	CCI 200	34.0	2711	38.0	2967
Vihtavuori N140	Remington	CCI 200	35.0	2675	39.0	2908
IMR 4198 (reduced load)	Remington	CCI 200	17.0	1770	19.0	1987

WARNING! Maximum loads should be used with CAUTION • C = Compressed Load

100 GRAINS

DIAMETER	SECTIONAL DENSITY
0.243"	0.242

6mm Spitzer BTSP

Ballistic Coefficient	0.446
COAL Tested	2.800"
Speer Part No.	1220

Propellant	Case	Primer	Starting Charge Weight (grains)	Starting Charge Muzzle Velocity (feet/sec)	Maximum Charge Weight (grains)	Maximum Charge Muzzle Velocity (feet/sec)
Alliant Reloder 26	Federal	Federal 210	43.8	2883	48.6 C	3230
Alliant Reloder 16	Federal	Federal 210	39.4	2864	43.5	3147
IMR 4831	Remington	CCI 200	41.0	2831	45.0	3145
Alliant Reloder 17	Federal	Federal 210	39.1	2858	43.2	3139
Alliant Power Pro 4000-MR	Federal	Federal 210	40.0	2836	44.5 C	3145
IMR 7828	Remington	CCI 250	46.0	2814	50.0	3059
Accurate 4350	Remington	CCI 200	41.5	2622	45.5	2979
Alliant Reloder 22	Remington	CCI 200	43.0	2763	47.0	2971
Accurate 3100	Remington	CCI 200	43.0	2716	47.0	2952
IMR 7977	Federal	Federal 210	45.2	2744	48.2 C	2939
Hodgdon H4350	Remington	CCI 200	40.0	2570	44.0	2888
IMR 4350	Remington	CCI 200	39.0	2533	43.0	2846
Alliant Reloder 19	Remington	CCI 200	41.0	2608	45.0	2835
Winchester 760	Remington	CCI 250	37.0	2506	41.0	2754
Accurate 2700	Remington	CCI 250	36.0	2466	40.0	2710
IMR 4064	Remington	CCI 200	33.0	2478	37.0	2694
Hodgdon H380	Remington	CCI 250	35.0	2381	39.0	2616
Hodgdon H414	Remington	CCI 250	36.0	2353	40.0	2614
IMR 4198 (reduced load)	Remington	CCI 200	18.0	1725	20.0	1924

WARNING! Maximum loads should be used with CAUTION • C = Compressed Load

243 WINCHESTER SUPER SHORT MAGNUM

Alternate Names:	243 WSSM
Country of Origin:	USA
Year of Introduction:	2003
Designer(s):	Winchester
Governing Body:	SAAMI/CIP

CARTRIDGE CASE DATA

Case Type:	Rimless, bottleneck		
Average Case Capacity:	57.2 grains H$_2$O	Max. Cartridge OAL	2.360 inch
Max. Case Length:	1.670 inch	Primer:	Large Rifle
Case Trim to Length:	1.660 inch	RCBS Shell holder:	# 43
Current Manufacturers:	Winchester		

BALLISTIC DATA

Max. Average Pressure (MAP):	65,000 psi, CUP not established for this cartridge - SAAMI	Test Barrel Length:	24 inch
Rifling Twist Rate:	1 turn in 10 inch		

Muzzle velocities of factory loaded ammunition	Bullet Wgt.	Muzzle velocity
	95-grain	3,150 fps
	100-grain	2,990 fps
	Muzzle velocity will decrease approximately 30 fps per inch for barrels less than 24 inches.	

HISTORICAL NOTES

- In 2003, Winchester announced an innovative new line of Winchester Super Short Magnum (WSSM) cartridges designed to fit in short action rifles. The first cartridges of this type was the 223 WSSM and 243 WSSM.
- The 223 & 243 WSSM were introduced in 2003, the 25 WSSM in 2004.

- These three cartridges form a subset of small caliber WSSM cartridges. Other Winchester "Short Magnum" cartridges of larger caliber and case dimensions have been released as well.

BALLISTIC NOTES

- As Winchester markets the 243 WSSM cartridge to deer hunters, the company loads only heavy bullets in this caliber. (2017: Winchester lists 95 & 100-grain bullets in loaded ammunition).

- Maximum Average Pressure limits for the 243 WSSM are higher than those for the 243 Winchester cartridge (65,000 psi vs. 60,000 psi). Despite this, the 243 WSSM offers only a modest ballistic advantage over the 243 Winchester. With a 100-grain bullet, the 243 WSSM offers a 150 fps advantage in muzzle velocity over the 243 Winchester with a similar bullet. The advantage is negligible with 95-grain bullets.

TECHNICAL NOTES

A major technical design point of the WSSM cartridge family is to allow a high velocity, beltless magnum cartridge to fit into a short rifle action. This is accomplished partly by lowering the length/diameter ratio. (See chart below)

Cartridge	L/D ratio
243 WSSM	3.009
243 Winchester	4.348
6mm PPC	3.418
6mm Remington	4.740
240 Weatherby Magnum	5.524

- The second design element of the 243 WSSM is the .535 inch rim diameter from the beltless Winchester Short Magnum cartridges to increase the case diameter while reducing its length. For interior ballistic purposes, this means a shorter, fatter powder column.

- In theory, the WSSM short/fat concept avoids the problem of overbore capacity.

HANDLOADING NOTES

- The 243 WSSM cartridge lends itself well to handloading bullets lighter than 95 grains.

- The 243 WSSM cartridge case is significantly heavier and stronger than the 243 Winchester. Neck sizing is recommended for the 243 WSSM due to the heavy case construction.

- The 243 WSSM prefers slow burning propellants.

SAFETY NOTES

SPEER 100-grain Spitzer BTSP @ a muzzle velocity of 3,005 fps:
- Maximum vertical altitude @ 90° elevation is 11,553 feet.
- Maximum horizontal distance to first impact with ground @ 36° elevation is 5,332 yards.

70 GRAINS

DIAMETER	SECTIONAL DENSITY
.243"	0.169

6mm TNT® HP	
Ballistic Coefficient	0.279
COAL Tested	2.250"
Speer Part No.	1206

75 GRAINS

DIAMETER	SECTIONAL DENSITY
.243"	0.181

6mm HP	
Ballistic Coefficient	0.192
COAL Tested	2.185"
Speer Part No.	1205

			Starting Charge		Maximum Charge	
Propellant	Case	Primer	Weight (grains)	Muzzle Velocity (feet/sec)	Weight (grains)	Muzzle Velocity (feet/sec)
Hodgdon H414	Winchester	Federal 215	45.0	3417	47.0	3547
Winchester 760	Winchester	Federal 215	45.5	3409	47.5	3531
Vihtavuori N540	Winchester	Federal 210	40.0	3367	42.0	3484
IMR 4350	Winchester	Federal 210	44.5	3358	46.5	3483
Alliant Reloder 15	Winchester	Federal 210	39.0	3350	41.0	3478
Alliant Reloder 19	Winchester	Federal 210	47.5	3337	49.5 C	3464
IMR 4895	Winchester	Federal 210	38.5	3333	40.5	3461
Hodgdon Varget	Winchester	Federal 210	39.0	3347	41.0	3456
Ramshot Big Game	Winchester	Federal 215	43.0	3339	45.0	3454
Accurate 4350	Winchester	Federal 210	45.0	3262	47.0 C	3404
Accurate 4064	Winchester	Federal 210	37.5	3214	39.5	3341

WARNING! Maximum loads should be used with CAUTION • C = Compressed Load

85 GRAINS

DIAMETER	SECTIONAL DENSITY
0.243"	0.206

6mm Spitzer BTSP	
Ballistic Coefficient	0.380
COAL Tested	2.255"
Speer Part No.	1213

Propellant	Case	Primer	Starting Charge		Maximum Charge	
			Weight (grains)	Muzzle Velocity (feet/sec)	Weight (grains)	Muzzle Velocity (feet/sec)
Hodgdon H414	Winchester	Federal 215	41.5	3169	43.5	3274
Alliant Reloder 19	Winchester	Federal 210	45.0	3131	47.0 C	3272
Winchester 760	Winchester	Federal 215	41.5	3162	43.5	3271
Alliant Reloder 15	Winchester	Federal 210	37.0	3146	39.0	3260
IMR 4350	Winchester	Federal 210	41.0	3145	43.0	3252
Ramshot Big Game	Winchester	Federal 215	39.5	3113	41.5	3222
Accurate 4350	Winchester	Federal 210	41.5	3086	43.5	3201
Vihtavuori N540	Winchester	Federal 210	36.0	3076	38.0	3191
IMR 4895	Winchester	Federal 210	35.0	3066	37.5	3184

WARNING! Maximum loads should be used with CAUTION • C = Compressed Load

90 GRAINS

DIAMETER	SECTIONAL DENSITY
0.243"	0.218

6mm Spitzer SP Hot-Cor®

Ballistic Coefficient	0.365
COAL Tested	2.360"
Speer Part No.	1217

			Starting Charge		Maximum Charge	
Propellant	Case	Primer	Weight (grains)	Muzzle Velocity (feet/sec)	Weight (grains)	Muzzle Velocity (feet/sec)
Alliant Reloder 22	Winchester	Federal 210	44.5	3149	46.5	3250
Alliant Reloder 19	Winchester	Federal 210	43.0	3114	45.0	3218
IMR 4350	Winchester	Federal 210	40.5	3088	42.5	3208
Hodgdon H414	Winchester	Federal 215	41.0	3095	43.0	3205
Winchester 760	Winchester	Federal 215	40.5	3080	42.5	3182
Accurate 4350	Winchester	Federal 210	41.0	3023	43.0	3140
Ramshot Magnum	Winchester	Federal 215	50.0	3007	52.0 C	3122
Ramshot Big Game	Winchester	Federal 215	38.0	3010	40.0	3113
IMR 4895	Winchester	Federal 210	34.5	2960	36.5	3079

WARNING! *Maximum loads should be used with* **CAUTION** • *C = Compressed Load*

100 GRAINS

DIAMETER	SECTIONAL DENSITY
0.243"	0.242

6mm Spitzer BTSP

Ballistic Coefficient	0.446
COAL Tested	2.360"
Speer Part No.	1220

Propellant	Case	Primer	Starting Charge		Maximum Charge	
			Weight (grains)	Muzzle Velocity (feet/sec)	Weight (grains)	Muzzle Velocity (feet/sec)
Ramshot Magnum	Winchester	Federal 215	50.5	2993	52.5 C	3116
Alliant Reloder 22	Winchester	Federal 210	41.5	2920	43.5	3004
Vihtavuori N560	Winchester	Federal 210	40.0	2860	42.0	2948
Alliant Reloder 19	Winchester	Federal 210	38.5	2829	40.5	2915
Accurate 4350	Winchester	Federal 210	38.5	2785	40.5	2904
IMR 4350	Winchester	Federal 210	36.5	2792	38.5	2894
Hodgdon H4350	Winchester	Federal 210	35.5	2780	37.5	2881
Hodgdon H414	Winchester	Federal 215	36.0	2745	38.0	2856
Winchester 760	Winchester	Federal 215	35.5	2733	37.5	2835

WARNING! Maximum loads should be used with CAUTION • C = Compressed Load

240 WEATHERBY MAGNUM

Country of Origin:	USA
Year of Introduction:	1968
Designer(s):	Weatherby
Governing Body:	CIP (SAAMI does not list this cartridge in either 1998 or 2015 Editions)

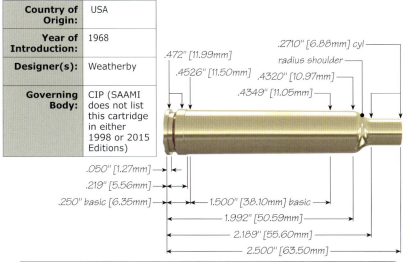

CARTRIDGE CASE DATA

Case Type:	Rimless, belted, bottleneck		
Average Case Capacity:	64.5 grains H$_2$O	Max. Cartridge OAL	3.100 inch
Max. Case Length:	2.500 inch	Primer:	Large Rifle
Case Trim to Length:	2.490 inch	RCBS Shell holder:	# 3
Current Manufacturers:	Weatherby (Norma), Nosler		

BALLISTIC DATA

Max. Average Pressure (MAP):	63,817 psi - CIP	Test Barrel Length:	24 inch (Weatherby uses a 26 inch test barrel)
Rifling Twist Rate:	1 turn in 10 inch		
Muzzle velocities of factory loaded ammunition	Bullet Wgt.		Muzzle velocity
	85-grain		3,500 fps
	100-grain		3,406 fps
	Muzzle velocity will decrease approximately 30 fps per inch for barrels less than 24 inches.		

HISTORICAL NOTES

- Currently, Weatherby offers 14 different proprietary calibers of their own design. The 240 Weatherby Magnum is one of the smallest.
- The 240 Weatherby Magnum is unique in that it is the only belted 6mm magnum cartridge on the market today.

- For many years now, all Weatherby ammunition has been manufactured by Norma in Sweden. It is for this reason that Weatherby cartridges were originally standardized by CIP.
- Weatherby ammunition is loaded with component bullets made by well-known manufacturers such as Nosler, Barnes, Swift and Norma. At Weatherby, the 240 Weatherby Magnum cartridge is clearly intended for hunting deer and antelope at long ranges.

BALLISTIC NOTES

- Weatherby cartridges are designed to use the hydraulic shock generated by bullets striking a target at high velocities as their main incapacitation mechanism.
- To achieve the required high striking velocity, Weatherby cartridges are proprietary, belted designs of sufficient volume to hold the large propellant charges needed to drive bullets to the high velocities needed. As with most cartridges of this type, the belt is strictly cosmetic.
- The very high muzzle velocity of the 240 Weatherby Magnum cartridge will extend the maximum effective range of handloaded lightweight bullets to well beyond 300 yards.
- Due to the heavy loads and high velocities, recoil of most Weatherby cartridges is heavy.
- Note that the muzzle velocities quoted in the Weatherby catalog are taken from a 26 inch rifle barrel, typical of Weatherby rifle barrel lengths.
- All muzzle velocities for Weatherby ammunition shown in this manual are taken from a 24 inch barrel. Use the correction factors to cross reference these quickly or see the load data.

HANDLOADING NOTES

- The 240 Weatherby Mag. cartridge lends itself well to handloading bullets lighter than 95-grain to reach even higher muzzle velocities.
- Neck sizing is recommended for practice and sight-in of the 240 Weatherby Magnum to control length growth and reduce head separations. Full length size for hunting loads.
- The 240 Weatherby Magnum prefers slow burning propellants due to the need for large propellant charges.

SAFETY NOTES

SPEER 100-grain Spitzer BTSP @ a muzzle velocity of 3,200 fps:
- Maximum vertical altitude @ 90° elevation is 15,837 feet.
- Maximum horizontal distance to first impact with ground @ 36° elevation is 5,332 yards.

75 GRAINS

DIAMETER	SECTIONAL DENSITY
0.243"	0.181

6mm HP	
Ballistic Coefficient	0.192
COAL Tested	3.060"
Speer Part No.	1205

			Starting Charge		Maximum Charge	
Propellant	Case	Primer	Weight (grains)	Muzzle Velocity (feet/sec)	Weight (grains)	Muzzle Velocity (feet/sec)
Hodgdon H414	Weatherby	CCI 250	52.0	3447	56.0	3734
IMR 4831	Weatherby	CCI 250	51.0	3322	55.0 C	3620
Winchester 760	Weatherby	CCI 250	47.5	3281	51.5	3602
IMR 4350	Weatherby	CCI 250	49.0	3334	53.0	3583
IMR 4064	Weatherby	CCI 250	42.0	3126	46.0	3481
Hodgdon H380	Weatherby	CCI 250	45.0	3094	49.0	3429

85 GRAINS

DIAMETER	SECTIONAL DENSITY
0.243"	0.206

6mm Spitzer BTSP	
Ballistic Coefficient	0.380
COAL Tested	3.060"
Speer Part No.	1213

			Starting Charge		Maximum Charge	
Propellant	Case	Primer	Weight (grains)	Muzzle Velocity (feet/sec)	Weight (grains)	Muzzle Velocity (feet/sec)
IMR 4831	Weatherby	CCI 250	49.0	3304	53.0 C	3473
Hodgdon H414	Weatherby	CCI 250	48.0	3161	52.0	3430
IMR 4350	Weatherby	CCI 250	47.5	3162	51.5	3417
Winchester 760	Weatherby	CCI 250	46.0	3071	50.0	3349
IMR 4064	Weatherby	CCI 250	40.0	2976	44.0	3242
Hodgdon H380	Weatherby	CCI 250	43.0	2949	47.0	3236

WARNING! Maximum loads should be used with CAUTION • C = Compressed Load

90 GRAINS

DIAMETER	SECTIONAL DENSITY
0.243"	0.218

6mm Spitzer SP Hot-Cor®
Ballistic Coefficient	0.365
COAL Tested	3.060"
Speer Part No.	1217

			Starting Charge		Maximum Charge	
Propellant	Case	Primer	Weight (grains)	Muzzle Velocity (feet/sec)	Weight (grains)	Muzzle Velocity (feet/sec)
IMR 4831	Weatherby	CCI 250	48.0	3176	52.0 C	3420
Hodgdon H414	Weatherby	CCI 250	48.0	3057	52.0	3367
IMR 4350	Weatherby	CCI 250	46.5	3059	50.5	3304
Winchester 760	Weatherby	CCI 250	46.0	2992	50.0	3302
Hodgdon H380	Weatherby	CCI 250	43.0	2813	47.0	3107
IMR 4064	Weatherby	CCI 250	40.0	2854	44.0	3098

100 GRAINS

DIAMETER	SECTIONAL DENSITY
0.243"	0.242

6mm Spitzer BTSP
Ballistic Coefficient	0.446
COAL Tested	3.060"
Speer Part No.	1220

			Starting Charge		Maximum Charge	
Propellant	Case	Primer	Weight (grains)	Muzzle Velocity (feet/sec)	Weight (grains)	Muzzle Velocity (feet/sec)
Winchester 760	Weatherby	CCI 250	45.0	2922	49.0	3209
Hodgdon H414	Weatherby	CCI 250	46.0	2897	50.0	3167
IMR 4831	Weatherby	CCI 250	45.5	2915	49.5 C	3154
IMR 4350	Weatherby	CCI 250	43.5	2768	47.5	3007
IMR 4064	Weatherby	CCI 250	38.0	2714	42.0	2977
Hodgdon H380	Weatherby	CCI 250	41.0	2601	45.0	2901

WARNING! *Maximum loads should be used with CAUTION • C = Compressed Load*

25-20 WINCHESTER

Alternate Names:	25-20 W.C.F. (Winchester Center Fire)
Parent Cartridge:	32-20 W.C.F.
Country of Origin:	USA
Year of Introduction:	1893
Designer(s):	Winchester
Governing Body:	SAAMI/CIP

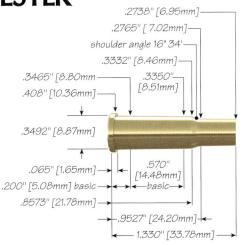

CARTRIDGE CASE DATA

Case Type:	Rimmed, bottleneck		
Average Case Capacity:	18.1 grains H$_2$O	Max. Cartridge OAL	1.592 inch
Max. Case Length:	1.330 inch	Primer:	Small Rifle
Case Trim to Length:	1.320 inch	RCBS Shell holder:	# 1
Current Manufacturers:	Winchester, Remington		

BALLISTIC DATA

Max. Average Pressure (MAP):	28,000 CUP, Piezo not established for this cartridge - SAAMI	Test Barrel Length:	24 inch
Rifling Twist Rate:	1 turn in 14 inch		

Muzzle velocities of factory loaded ammunition	Bullet Wgt.	Muzzle velocity
	60-grain	2,250 fps (obsolete)
	86-grain	1,460 fps (current)
	Muzzle velocity will decrease approximately 5 fps per inch for barrels less than 24 inches.	

HISTORICAL NOTES

- Not many varmint cartridges can claim to be over 125 years old. The 25-20 Winchester can. It was introduced by Winchester in 1895 for their Model 92 lever-action rifle.
- The 25-20 was the first true varmint cartridge developed for hunting predators, varmints, pests, and rodents.

- It is the offspring of the 32-20 W.C.F. cartridge introduced by Winchester in 1882. Although the parent 32-20 was a black powder cartridge, the 25-20 Winchester was loaded with smokeless powder from the start despite its black powder nomenclature.
- The 22 Hornet was developed to replace the 25-20 Winchester in the 1930s.
- By the late 1980s, the 25-20 Winchester cartridge was fast becoming a fond memory. Then, in 1989, Marlin offered it in the Model 1894CL lever-action rifle and the old caliber received a new lease on life.
- Consider the 25-20 Winchester as a 19th century hold over that cannot be saved from obsolescence much longer. Winchester and Remington remain the sole manufacturers of this cartridge.

BALLISTIC NOTES

- Ballistics of the 25-20 WCF cartridge is poor, even by 19th century standards.
- The blunt nose bullet required by lever-action rifles, the relatively low maximum average chamber pressures, and limited case capacity conspire to keep muzzle velocity low.
- Handloading with modern propellants, primers and bullets cannot overcome the poor ballistics of the 25-20 Winchester.
- Although mention was made in the early 1900s of using the 25-20 for deer hunting, this caliber is completely outclassed for such purposes by modern standards. In many states it will not meet the regulations for deer hunting.

TECHNICAL NOTES

- The 25-20 Winchester is essentially a 32-20 Winchester cartridge necked down to accept 0.257 inch diameter bullets.
- Original factory loads offered the shooter a choice of 60 and 86-grain bullets. Arguably the 60-grain bullet at a muzzle velocity of 2,250 fps was the most useful for varmint hunting. However, it has not survived and the 86-grain bullet is the sole load on offer today by Winchester and Remington.

HANDLOADING NOTES

- The limited case capacity of the 25-20 Winchester dictates the use of fast burning propellants.
- Cases in this caliber are scarce and expensive. As a result, most handloaders are forced to purchase factory ammunition and reload the empty cases.
- The Speer 75-grain SPFN is a good compromise between the current 86-grain factory load and the obsolete 60-grain load. This Speer bullet has a cannelure for crimping as the 25-20 is mainly fired in lever-action rifles with tubular magazines.

SAFETY NOTES

SPEER 75-grain SPFN @ a muzzle velocity of 2,000 fps:
- Maximum vertical altitude @ 90° elevation is 4,446 feet.
- Maximum horizontal distance to first impact with ground @ 36° elevation is 1,992 yards.
- Do not load spitzer bullets in the 25-20 Winchester as they can cause magazine tube explosions.

- Do not confuse the 25-20 Winchester cartridge with the obsolete 25-20 Single Shot cartridge. The two cartridges are quite different and NOT interchangeable despite their somewhat similar nomenclature.

75 GRAINS

DIAMETER	SECTIONAL DENSITY
.257"	0.162

25 SPFN

Ballistic Coefficient	0.135
COAL Tested	1.545"
Speer Part No.	1237

			Starting Charge		Maximum Charge	
Propellant	Case	Primer	Weight (grains)	Muzzle Velocity (feet/sec)	Weight (grains)	Muzzle Velocity (feet/sec)
Accurate 1680	Winchester	CCI 450	11.5	1782	12.5	2018
IMR 4198	Winchester	CCI 400	11.6	1747	12.6 C	1908
Accurate 2015	Winchester	CCI 400	13.5	1771	14.5 C	1897
Vihtavuori N110	Winchester	CCI 400	7.8	1658	8.8	1843
Winchester 296	Winchester	CCI 450	7.6	1643	8.6	1794
Hodgdon H110	Winchester	CCI 450	7.4	1547	8.4	1746
IMR 4227	Winchester	CCI 400	9.0	1547	10.0	1702
Accurate No. 9	Winchester	CCI 400	6.8	1488	7.8	1693
Alliant 2400	Winchester	CCI 400	7.0	1547	8.0	1686

WARNING! Maximum loads should be used with CAUTION • C = Compressed Load

250 SAVAGE

Alternate Names:	250-3000 Savage, 250 Hi-Power
Parent Cartridge:	30-06 Springfield
Country of Origin:	USA
Year of Introduction:	1915
Designer(s):	Charles Newton
Governing Body:	SAAMI/CIP

CARTRIDGE CASE DATA

Case Type:	Rimless, bottleneck		
Average Case Capacity:	48.0 grains H_2O	Max. Cartridge OAL	2.515 inch
Max. Case Length:	1.912 inch	Primer:	Large Rifle
Case Trim to Length:	1.902 inch	RCBS Shell holder:	# 3
Current Manufacturers:	Hornady, Remington		

BALLISTIC DATA

Max. Average Pressure (MAP):	45,000 CUP, Piezo not established for this cartridge - SAAMI		Test Barrel Length:	24 inch
Rifling Twist Rate:	1 turn in 12 inch or 1 turn in 14 inch (both in older rifles); 1 turn in 10 inch (newer rifles).			
Muzzle velocities of factory loaded ammunition	**Bullet Wgt.**		**Muzzle velocity**	
	87-grain		3,030 fps (obsolete)	
	100-grain		2,820 fps	
	120-grain		2,645 fps (obsolete)	
	Muzzle velocity will decrease approximately 10 fps per inch for barrels less than 24 inches.			

HISTORICAL NOTES

- The 250 Savage was designed by Charles Newton for the Savage Arms Co.
- As Newton saw his new 250 Savage cartridge as a deer cartridge, he proposed a 100-grain soft point bullet at a muzzle velocity of 2,820 fps.
- Savage disagreed for marketing and sales reasons. The company wanted a

cartridge with a muzzle velocity over 3,000 fps. Newton developed such a load using an 87-grain bullet, the heaviest weight that allowed the desired muzzle velocity.

- Savage introduced the new cartridge in 1915 for their Model 99 lever-action rifle.
- Newton's creation was the first high velocity varmint hunting rifle cartridge and revolutionized the role of lever-action rifles by giving the Model 99 and other lever-actions a modern, high pressure cartridge offering ballistic performance on par with bolt-action rifles.
- Subsequently, bolt-action rifles were offered in 250 Savage by Remington, Ruger, and Weatherby (in the Vanguard) up to 1971. Currently, no new rifles are being offered in 250 Savage. Today, it is near extinction in the marketplace—that is unless a firearm manufacturer (re)introduces a rifle in this fine old caliber.
- Contrary to popular perception, the 250 Savage is not an offspring of the 300 Savage cartridge. Rather the opposite is true: the 300 Savage was introduced in 1920 some five years *after* the 250 Savage.

BALLISTIC NOTES

- The 250 Savage was the first commercial cartridge to achieve a muzzle velocity of 3,000 fps. It created a sensation when it was introduced that carried it into the late 1950s.
- To emphasize the muzzle velocity, Savage renamed their new cartridge the 250-3000 Savage.
- After Western Cartridge Company introduced a 100-grain bullet for the 250 Savage in 1920, it became a true dual purpose varmint/deer cartridge.
- Today, the 87-grain bullet at 3,000 fps muzzle velocity that created the 250-3000 Savage's reputation has been surpassed by new cartridges with higher performance. As a result, the 100-grain bullet is the only factory load today and the 250 Savage is no longer a dual purpose cartridge.
- The low recoil of the 250 Savage makes it an ideal caliber for novice hunters.

HANDLOADING NOTES

- Hornady and Remington still offer loaded ammunition in 250 Savage, but they do not sell component brass. Handloading brass is available from Captech Int. (Jamison Brass) and Quality Cartridge. Winchester also sells 250 Savage brass as a component, but does not offer loaded ammunition.
- Long heavy bullets such as the 120-grain take up a lot of space in the 250 Savage case reducing powder capacity and limiting muzzle velocities to approximately 2,500 fps. These bullets will stabilize in rifles with 10 or 12 inch rifling twists.
- 100-grain bullets will stabilize from any of the three rifling twist rates. As this bullet weight does not take up as much case capacity as the 120-grain bullets, a better balance between muzzle velocity and striking energy can be obtained.

SAFETY NOTES

SPEER 120-grain Spitzer BTSP @ a muzzle velocity of 2,610 fps:
- Maximum vertical altitude @ 90° elevation is 14,505 feet.
- Maximum horizontal distance to first impact with ground @ 36° elevation is 6,874 yards.

87 GRAINS

DIAMETER	SECTIONAL DENSITY
.257"	0.188

25 Spitzer SP Hot-Cor®

Ballistic Coefficient	0.300
COAL Tested	2.465"
Speer Part No.	1241

25 TNT® HP

Ballistic Coefficient	0.337
COAL Tested	2.500"
Speer Part No.	1246

			Starting Charge		Maximum Charge	
Propellant	Case	Primer	Weight (grains)	Muzzle Velocity (feet/sec)	Weight (grains)	Muzzle Velocity (feet/sec)
Hodgdon CFE 223	Hornady	CCI 200	37.5	3046	39.7	3207
Alliant Power Pro 2000-MR	Hornady	CCI 200	36.5	2937	40.1	3164
Alliant Power Pro Varmint	Hornady	CCI 200	34.0	2947	37.0	3148
Hodgdon H380	Winchester	CCI 250	38.0	2821	42.0 C	3097
Hodgdon Benchmark	Hornady	CCI 200	31.5	2929	33.9	3059
IMR 8208 XBR	Hornady	CCI 200	32.5	2891	34.9	3051
Alliant AR-Comp	Hornady	CCI 200	30.5	2868	33.8	3048
Hodgdon H414	Winchester	CCI 250	37.0	2749	41.0 C	3005
Winchester 760	Winchester	CCI 250	37.0	2733	41.0 C	2994
Alliant Reloder 15	Winchester	CCI 200	33.0	2642	37.0	2982
IMR 4350	Winchester	CCI 200	37.0	2589	41.0 C	2963
Accurate 2700	Winchester	CCI 200	37.0	2646	41.0	2901
IMR 4831	Winchester	CCI 200	38.0	2507	42.0 C	2866
IMR 4064	Winchester	CCI 200	31.0	2578	35.0	2849
Winchester 748	Winchester	CCI 250	31.0	2486	35.0	2793
Accurate 3100	Winchester	CCI 200	37.0	2451	41.0 C	2788
Hodgdon BL-C(2)	Winchester	CCI 250	31.0	2476	35.0	2767
SR 4759 (reduced load)	Winchester	CCI 200	12.5	1622	14.5	1928

WARNING! Maximum loads should be used with CAUTION • C = Compressed Load

100 GRAINS

DIAMETER	SECTIONAL DENSITY
.257"	0.216

25 Spitzer SP Hot-Cor®
Ballistic Coefficient	0.334
COAL Tested	2.450"
Speer Part No.	1405

25 HP
Ballistic Coefficient	0.263
COAL Tested	2.400"
Speer Part No.	1407

25 Spitzer BTSP
Ballistic Coefficient	0.393
COAL Tested	2.490"
Speer Part No.	1408

			Starting Charge		Maximum Charge	
Propellant	Case	Primer	Weight (grains)	Muzzle Velocity (feet/sec)	Weight (grains)	Muzzle Velocity (feet/sec)
Hodgdon CFE 223	Hornady	CCI 200	36.0	2877	38.2	3026
Alliant Power Pro Varmint	Hornady	CCI 200	33.0	2792	35.4	2954
IMR 4451	Hornady	CCI 200	36.0	2629	38.7	2791
IMR 4166	Hornady	CCI 200	30.5	2640	32.7	2783
Accurate 2520	Winchester	CCI 250	29.0	2392	33.0	2763
Hodgdon H414	Winchester	CCI 250	34.0	2504	38.0 C	2743
Winchester 760	Winchester	CCI 250	34.0	2480	38.0 C	2716
Hodgdon H4350	Winchester	CCI 200	34.0	2340	38.0 C	2674
Accurate 3100	Winchester	CCI 200	36.0	2340	40.0 C	2670
Winchester 748	Winchester	CCI 250	30.0	2294	34.0	2649
IMR 4350	Winchester	CCI 200	33.5	2313	37.5 C	2647
IMR 4831	Winchester	CCI 200	35.0	2301	39.0 C	2633
IMR 4064	Winchester	CCI 200	29.0	2346	33.0	2622
Hodgdon H380	Winchester	CCI 250	31.0	2256	35.0	2604
Alliant Reloder 15	Winchester	CCI 200	28.0	2244	32.0	2532
Hodgdon BL-C(2)	Winchester	CCI 250	28.0	2223	32.0	2509

WARNING! *Maximum loads should be used with CAUTION • C = Compressed Load*

250 SAVAGE — 120 GRAINS

DIAMETER	SECTIONAL DENSITY
.257"	0.260

25 Spitzer BTSP

Ballistic Coefficient	0.480
COAL Tested	2.450"
Speer Part No.	1410

			Starting Charge		Maximum Charge	
Propellant	**Case**	**Primer**	**Weight (grains)**	**Muzzle Velocity (feet/sec)**	**Weight (grains)**	**Muzzle Velocity (feet/sec)**
Alliant Reloder 17	Hornady	CCI 200	33.5	2452	35.9	2619
Alliant Power Pro Varmint	Hornady	CCI 200	29.0	2416	32.0	2597
Hodgdon H414	Winchester	CCI 250	32.0	2290	36.0	2511
Winchester 760	Winchester	CCI 250	32.0	2289	36.0	2507
Alliant Reloder 19	Winchester	CCI 200	34.0	2200	38.0	2497
IMR 4166	Hornady	CCI 200	27.0	2333	30.3	2488
IMR 4831	Winchester	CCI 200	33.0	2116	37.0	2421
Accurate 3100	Winchester	CCI 200	33.0	2163	37.0 C	2411
Alliant Reloder 15	Winchester	CCI 200	27.0	2123	31.0	2397
IMR 4320	Winchester	CCI 200	27.0	2084	31.0	2371
Hodgdon H380	Winchester	CCI 250	29.0	2159	33.0	2370
Hodgdon H4350	Winchester	CCI 200	31.0	2059	35.0 C	2354
IMR 4350	Winchester	CCI 200	30.0	2062	34.0	2344
IMR 4198 (reduced load)	Winchester	CCI 200	18.0	1644	20.0	1858

WARNING! Maximum loads should be used with CAUTION • C = Compressed Load

257 ROBERTS +P

Parent Cartridge:	7x57mm Mauser
Country of Origin:	USA
Year of Introduction:	1934 (standard cartridge), 1988 (+P cartridge)
Designer(s):	Ned Roberts/Remington (standard cartridge), Winchester (+P cartridge)
Governing Body:	SAAMI/CIP

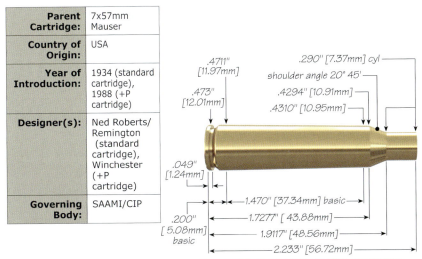

CARTRIDGE CASE DATA

Case Type:	Rimless, bottleneck		
Average Case Capacity:	59.2 grains H₂O (standard case), 58.6 (+P case)	Max. Cartridge OAL	2.780 inch
Max. Case Length:	2.233 inch	Primer:	Large Rifle
Case Trim to Length:	2.223 inch	RCBS Shell holder:	# 3
Current Manufacturers:	Winchester, Remington, Nosler, Federal, Hornady		

BALLISTIC DATA

Max. Average Pressure (MAP):	54,000 psi, 45,000 CUP (Non +P); 58,000 psi, 50,000 CUP (+P) - SAAMI	Test Barrel Length:	24 inch
Rifling Twist Rate:	1 turn in 10 inch		
Muzzle velocities of factory loaded ammunition			

Bullet Wgt.	Muzzle velocity
87-grain	3,030 fps (obsolete)
100-grain	2,650 fps (non +P)
115-grain	2,780 fps (+P)
120-grain	2,800 fps (+P)

Muzzle velocity will decrease approximately 20 fps per inch for barrels less than 24 inches.

HISTORICAL NOTES

- The 257 Roberts cartridge began life as a wildcat designed by Ned Roberts in the early 1930s. The popularity of Ned's new wildcat grew quickly.
- In 1934, Remington decided to introduce the 257 Roberts as a standard cartridge in their product line, changing the shoulder angle slightly in the process. To avoid confusion with the existing 25 Remington cartridge, Remington named their new offering the 257 Roberts.
- When the 257 Roberts was introduced, it became one of the few wildcat cartridges to be standardized for industry production. Others eventually included the 22 Hornet, 22-250 Remington, 25-06 Remington and 35 Whelen.
- The original factory load was listed with an 87-grain at a muzzle velocity of 3,030 fps.
- For the next 21 years, the 257 Roberts had few rivals. Then, in 1955 Winchester introduced their new 243 Winchester cartridge and everything changed. Hunters switched to the new cartridge in droves — many at the expense of the 257 Roberts.

BALLISTIC NOTES

- In the late 1980s, Winchester made an effort to update the 257 Roberts with a stronger, heavier cartridge case and an increase in MAP from 45,000 CUP to 50,000 CUP. These updates allowed muzzle velocity with the 117-grain bullet to be increased by 130 fps. The updated cartridge was called the 257 Roberts +P.
- Winchester's effort had little effect on the 257 Roberts declining sales.
- Today, five manufacturers offer 257 Roberts factory-loaded ammunition. Each lists only a single load with between 117 and 120 grain bullet weight. Winchester, Federal, Hornady, and Nosler offer the +P load while Remington offers the standard load.
- The light recoil and 115 to 120-grain bullet of the 257 Roberts make an excellent combination for deer hunting and for novice shooters.

TECHNICAL NOTES

- The 257 Roberts is unashamedly a single-purpose deer cartridge with little or no secondary application for predator and varmint hunting. The 115 to 120-grain bullets of the 257 Roberts are a better choice for deer than the 100-grain bullets used in the 243 Winchester.
- Maximum effective range of the heavier bullets used in the 257 Roberts is longer than those of the 243 Winchester.

HANDLOADING NOTES

- In addition to the ammunition manufacturers above, Winchester and Remington offer new, unprimed brass in 257 Roberts. Winchester cases are +P and Remington cases are standard. In either instance, brass in 257 Roberts can be hard to find and expensive.
- The 1 turn in 10 inch rifling twist and large case capacity of the 257 Roberts is designed for long heavy bullets such as the 120-grain. The 257 Roberts will also stabilize lighter bullets well.
- As most 257 Roberts' cartridges will be fired in bolt-action rifles, neck sizing will extend case life.
- Due to its large case capacity, the 257 Roberts cartridge prefers slower burning propellants.

- To load non +P ammunition for older rifles, reduce maximum powder charges by at least two grains.

SAFETY NOTES

SPEER 120-grain Spitzer BTSP @ a muzzle velocity of 2,795 fps:
- Maximum vertical altitude @ 90° elevation is 15,390 feet.
- Maximum horizontal distance to first impact with ground @ 36° elevation is 7,188 yards.

87 GRAINS

DIAMETER	SECTIONAL DENSITY
.257"	0.188

25 Spitzer SP Hot-Cor®	
Ballistic Coefficient	0.300
COAL Tested	2.760"
Speer Part No.	1241

25 TNT® HP	
Ballistic Coefficient	0.337
COAL Tested	2.780"
Speer Part No.	1246

			Starting Charge		Maximum Charge	
Propellant	Case	Primer	Weight (grains)	Muzzle Velocity (feet/sec)	Weight (grains)	Muzzle Velocity (feet/sec)
Alliant Reloder 16	Federal	Federal 210	44.9	3064	49.6 C	3386
Hodgdon H4350	Winchester	CCI 200	47.0	3161	51.0 C	3381
Ramshot Hunter	Federal	Federal 210	46.7	3121	51.6	3367
Alliant Power Pro 2000-MR	Federal	Federal 210	41.6	2993	46.2	3295
Alliant Power Pro 4000-MR	Federal	Federal 210	44.8	2994	49.6 C	3294
Alliant Reloder 17	Federal	Federal 210	43.6	2940	48.4	3290
IMR 4831	Winchester	CCI 200	47.0	2993	51.0	3226
Alliant Reloder 19	Winchester	CCI 200	47.0	2947	51.0 C	3187
IMR 7828	Winchester	CCI 200	50.0	2955	54.0	3184
Hodgdon H380	Winchester	CCI 250	42.0	2884	46.0	3170
Winchester 760	Winchester	CCI 250	43.0	2868	47.0	3163
Accurate 3100	Winchester	CCI 200	48.0	2925	52.0 C	3153
Alliant Reloder 15	Winchester	CCI 200	39.0	2804	43.0	3129
IMR 4350	Winchester	CCI 200	43.0	2876	47.0	3069
Winchester 748	Winchester	CCI 250	39.0	2735	43.0	3056
Hodgdon H414	Winchester	CCI 250	42.0	2726	46.0	3009
IMR SR 4759 (reduced load)	Winchester	CCI 200	15.0	1762	17.0	2008

WARNING! Maximum loads should be used with CAUTION • C = Compressed Load

100 GRAINS

DIAMETER	SECTIONAL DENSITY
.257"	0.216

25 Spitzer SP Hot-Cor®	
Ballistic Coefficient	0.334
COAL Tested	2.770"
Speer Part No.	1405

25 HP	
Ballistic Coefficient	0.263
COAL Tested	2.760"
Speer Part No.	1407

25 Spitzer BTSP	
Ballistic Coefficient	0.393
COAL Tested	2.770"
Speer Part No.	1408

			Starting Charge		Maximum Charge	
Propellant	Case	Primer	Weight (grains)	Muzzle Velocity (feet/sec)	Weight (grains)	Muzzle Velocity (feet/sec)
Winchester 760	Winchester	CCI 250	41.0	2804	45.0	3113
Alliant Reloder 16	Federal	Federal 210	41.3	2822	45.8 C	3110
Alliant Reloder 19	Winchester	CCI 200	45.0	2843	49.0	3094
Ramshot Hunter	Federal	Federal 210	45.2	2946	48.0	3091
Alliant Power Pro 4000-MR	Federal	Federal 210	42.2	2775	46.8 C	3069
Alliant Reloder 23	Federal	Federal 210	44.0	2773	48.8 C	3064
Hodgdon H4350	Winchester	CCI 200	43.0	2795	47.0 C	3055
IMR 4831	Winchester	CCI 200	44.0	2805	48.0	3053
Alliant Reloder 17	Federal	Federal 210	42.0	2843	45.1	3050
Hodgdon H4831	Winchester	CCI 200	46.0	2774	50.0 C	3030
IMR 7828	Winchester	CCI 200	47.0	2711	51.0 C	3023
IMR 4350	Winchester	CCI 200	41.0	2694	45.0	2944
Hodgdon H414	Winchester	CCI 250	40.0	2657	44.0	2878
IMR 4064	Winchester	CCI 200	35.0	2584	39.0	2871
Hodgdon H380	Winchester	CCI 250	38.0	2566	42.0	2842
Accurate 2700	Winchester	CCI 250	37.0	2529	41.0	2807
Alliant Reloder 15	Winchester	CCI 200	33.0	2509	37.0	2785
IMR 4320	Winchester	CCI 200	35.0	2505	39.0	2768
IMR SR 4759 (reduced load)	Winchester	CCI 200	15.0	1728	17.0	1945

WARNING! *Maximum loads should be used with CAUTION • C = Compressed Load*

120 GRAINS

DIAMETER	SECTIONAL DENSITY
.257"	0.260

25 Spitzer BTSP	
Ballistic Coefficient	0.480
COAL Tested	2.770"
Speer Part No.	1410

			Starting Charge		Maximum Charge	
Propellant	Case	Primer	Weight (grains)	Muzzle Velocity (feet/sec)	Weight (grains)	Muzzle Velocity (feet/sec)
Alliant Power Pro 4000-MR	Federal	Federal 210	40.2	2589	44.7	2858
Alliant Reloder 23	Federal	Federal 210	41.2	2608	45.8 C	2852
Alliant Reloder 16	Federal	Federal 210	38.6	2590	42.8	2836
Alliant Reloder 17	Federal	Federal 210	38.5	2586	42.5	2826
Ramshot Hunter	Federal	Federal 210	39.8	2631	43.6	2817
IMR 4831	Winchester	CCI 200	41.0	2552	45.0	2793
Winchester 760	Winchester	CCI 250	39.0	2496	43.0	2770
Hodgdon H414	Winchester	CCI 250	39.0	2507	43.0	2767
IMR 4350	Winchester	CCI 200	39.0	2512	43.0	2758
Alliant Reloder 19	Winchester	CCI 200	39.0	2476	43.0	2709
IMR 4064	Winchester	CCI 200	34.0	2423	38.0	2705
Alliant Reloder 22	Winchester	CCI 200	39.0	2399	43.0	2635
IMR 7828	Winchester	CCI 200	40.0	2304	44.0	2583
IMR 4320	Winchester	CCI 200	32.0	2316	36.0	2545
Alliant Reloder 15	Winchester	CCI 200	30.0	2322	34.0	2541
IMR 4895	Winchester	CCI 200	30.0	2249	34.0	2527
Accurate XMR 3100	Winchester	CCI 200	38.0	2301	42.0	2507
Hodgdon H380	Winchester	CCI 250	33.0	2275	37.0	2482
IMR SR 4759 (reduced load)	Winchester	CCI 200	17.0	1776	19.0	2003

WARNING! *Maximum loads should be used with CAUTION • C = Compressed Load*

25-06 REMINGTON

Parent Cartridge:	30-06 Springfield
Country of Origin:	USA
Year of Introduction:	1969
Designer(s):	A.O. Niedner (1920)
Governing Body:	SAAMI/CIP

Case dimensions:
- .2900" [7.37mm]
- .2910" [7.39mm]
- shoulder angle 17° 30'
- .4410" [11.20mm]
- .4426" [11.24mm]
- .4698" [11.93mm]
- .473" [12.01mm]
- .049" [1.24mm]
- .200" [5.08mm] basic
- 1.650" [41.91mm] basic
- 1.9480" [49.48mm]
- 2.1858" [55.52mm]
- 2.494" [63.36mm]

CARTRIDGE CASE DATA

Case Type:	Rimless, Bottleneck		
Average Case Capacity:	68.6 grains H₂O	Max. Cartridge OAL	3.250 inch
Max. Case Length:	2.494 inch	Primer:	Large Rifle
Case Trim to Length:	2.484 inch	RCBS Shell holder:	# 3
Current Manufacturers:	Remington, Winchester, Federal, Hornady, Nosler, Black Hills, Prvi Partizan, Norma, Fiocchi, Sako		

BALLISTIC DATA

Max. Average Pressure (MAP):	63,000 psi, 53,000 CUP - SAAMI	Test Barrel Length:	24 inch
Rifling Twist Rate:	1 turn in 10 inch		

Muzzle velocities of factory loaded ammunition:

Bullet Wgt.	Muzzle velocity
85-grain	3,470 fps
100-grain	3,230 fps
115-grain	3,220 fps
120-grain	2,990 fps

Muzzle velocity will decrease approximately 30 fps per inch for barrels less than 24 inches.

HISTORICAL NOTES

- The 25-06 Remington cartridge began life as a wildcat designed by A.O. Niedner in 1920. It remained a wildcat until 1969 when it was standardized and introduced by Remington.
- Today, the 25-06 Remington cartridge is a staple item in the product lines of ten large ammunition manufacturers.
- While the 25-06 Rem. cartridge has been well received by North American sportsmen, it has failed to find popularity in Europe.

BALLISTIC NOTES

- Although the 25-06 Remington is not classified as a magnum cartridge, it offers magnum-level high velocity and striking energy, flat trajectory, and low wind drift.
- These ballistic characteristics make the 25-06 Remington an ideal choice for hunting at the longer ranges prevalent in the western states.
- When loaded with lightweight bullets of less than 85 grains, the 25-06 Remington is a very good varmint cartridge indeed. However, factory ammunition is not offered with the lightweight bullets suitable for this type of hunting.

TECHNICAL NOTES

- The 25-06 Remington is a 30-06 Springfield case necked down to 25 caliber.
- Some idea of what places the 25-06 in a ballistic category well above its competitors can be gauged from the following data:
  - Case capacity of the 25-06 Rem. is 16% greater than the 257 Roberts and 43% greater than the 250 Savage.
  - Maximum average pressure of the 25-06 Rem. cartridge is 6% higher than the 257 Roberts +P and 18% higher than the 250 Savage.
- Combined, these features enable the 25-06 Remington to fire a 100-grain bullet with 6% greater muzzle velocity than the 257 Roberts +P and about 20% greater muzzle velocity than the 250 Savage.

HANDLOADING NOTES

- The 1 turn in 10 inch rifling twist combined with the high muzzle velocity easily stabilize long, heavy bullets up to 120 grains.
- With its large case capacity, the 25-06 Rem. can use slow burning propellants.
- Neck sizing is recommended to prolong case life and prevent head separations.

SAFETY NOTES

SPEER 120-grain Spitzer BTSP @ a muzzle velocity of 3,070 fps:

- Maximum vertical altitude @ 90° elevation is 16,233 feet.
- Maximum horizontal distance to first impact with ground @ 36° elevation is 7,483 yards.

25-06 REMINGTON

87 GRAINS

DIAMETER	SECTIONAL DENSITY
.257"	0.188

25 Spitzer SP Hot-Cor®

Ballistic Coefficient	0.300
COAL Tested	3.115"
Speer Part No.	1241

25 TNT® HP

Ballistic Coefficient	0.337
COAL Tested	3.115"
Speer Part No.	1246

			Starting Charge		Maximum Charge	
Propellant	Case	Primer	Weight (grains)	Muzzle Velocity (feet/sec)	Weight (grains)	Muzzle Velocity (feet/sec)
Vihtavuori N560	Winchester	CCI 200	53.0	3353	57.0	3552
Alliant Reloder 19	Winchester	CCI 200	56.0	3089	60.0 C	3452
Alliant Power Pro 4000-MR	Federal	Federal 210	51.0	3166	55.5	3434
Hodgdon H4350	Winchester	CCI 200	54.0	3157	58.0	3431
IMR 4831	Winchester	CCI 200	55.0	3102	59.0	3428
IMR 7828	Winchester	CCI 200	59.0	3076	63.0 C	3419
Hodgdon H4831SC	Winchester	CCI 200	55.5	3298	57.5	3410
IMR 4350	Winchester	CCI 200	52.0	3075	56.0	3380
Hodgdon H414	Winchester	CCI 250	47.0	3077	51.0	3359
Accurate 3100	Winchester	CCI 200	57.0	3021	61.0 C	3357
IMR 4064	Winchester	CCI 200	45.0	3083	49.0	3352
Alliant AR-Comp	Federal	Federal 210	39.5	3055	43.4	3278
Hodgdon H380	Winchester	CCI 250	48.0	2940	52.0	3268
Alliant Reloder 15	Winchester	CCI 200	43.0	2983	47.0	3268
Alliant Power Pro Varmint	Federal	Federal 210	33.5	2846	36.9	3078
IMR SR 4759 (reduced load)	Winchester	CCI 200	13.0	1502	17.0	1933

WARNING! Maximum loads should be used with CAUTION • C = Compressed Load

100 GRAINS

DIAMETER	SECTIONAL DENSITY
.257"	0.216

25 Spitzer SP Hot-Cor®
Ballistic Coefficient	0.334
COAL Tested	3.095"
Speer Part No.	1405

25 HP
Ballistic Coefficient	0.263
COAL Tested	3.095"
Speer Part No.	1407

25 Spitzer BTSP
Ballistic Coefficient	0.393
COAL Tested	3.095"
Speer Part No.	1408

			Starting Charge		Maximum Charge	
Propellant	Case	Primer	Weight (grains)	Muzzle Velocity (feet/sec)	Weight (grains)	Muzzle Velocity (feet/sec)
Alliant Reloder 23	Federal	Federal 210	50.5	3000	55.0	3323
Alliant Reloder 17	Federal	Federal 210	46.5	2956	51.3	3301
IMR 4350	Winchester	CCI 200	49.0	3067	53.0	3298
IMR 4831	Winchester	CCI 200	52.0	2997	56.0	3287
Alliant Power Pro 4000-MR	Federal	Federal 210	48.0	2947	52.8	3235
Alliant Reloder 19	Winchester	CCI 200	53.0	2903	57.0	3226
Alliant Reloder 25	Winchester	CCI 200	57.0	3123	59.0 C	3224
IMR 7828	Winchester	CCI 200	56.0	2892	60.0 C	3222
Hodgdon H4831SC	Winchester	CCI 200	51.0	2999	55.0	3215
Hodgdon H1000	Winchester	CCI 200	57.0	2933	61.0 C	3151
Vihtavuori N160	Winchester	CCI 200	49.0	2828	53.0	3129
Accurate 3100	Winchester	CCI 200	52.0	2845	56.0	3120
Hodgdon H414	Winchester	CCI 250	46.0	2783	50.0	3111
IMR SR 4759 (reduced load)	Winchester	CCI 200	15.0	1524	19.0	1892

WARNING! Maximum loads should be used with CAUTION • C = Compressed Load

120 GRAINS

DIAMETER	SECTIONAL DENSITY
.257"	0.260

25 Spitzer BTSP	
Ballistic Coefficient	0.480
COAL Tested	3.200"
Speer Part No.	1410

			Starting Charge		Maximum Charge	
Propellant	Case	Primer	Weight (grains)	Muzzle Velocity (feet/sec)	Weight (grains)	Muzzle Velocity (feet/sec)
Alliant Reloder 25	Winchester	CCI 200	56.0	2971	58.0 C	3071
Alliant Reloder 26	Federal	Federal 210	49.0	2770	53.2	3024
Alliant Reloder 23	Federal	Federal 210	46.5	2718	51.0	3010
IMR 4350	Winchester	CCI 200	44.5	2773	48.5	2990
IMR 4831	Winchester	CCI 200	46.0	2769	50.0	2980
Alliant Reloder 17	Federal	Federal 210	43.0	2708	47.2	2972
Hodgdon H4831SC	Winchester	CCI 200	48.0	2769	52.0	2958
Alliant Power Pro 4000-MR	Federal	Federal 210	44.5	2682	48.7	2929
Hodgdon H1000	Winchester	CCI 200	51.0	2644	55.0	2922
IMR 7828	Winchester	CCI 200	51.0	2644	55.0	2885
Accurate 4350	Winchester	CCI 200	45.0	2655	49.0	2843
Accurate 3100	Winchester	CCI 200	47.0	2567	51.0	2818
Hodgdon H4350	Winchester	CCI 200	44.0	2577	48.0	2792
IMR SR 4759 (reduced load)	Winchester	CCI 200	17.0	1501	21.0	1861

WARNING! Maximum loads should be used with CAUTION • C = Compressed Load

25 WINCHESTER SUPER SHORT MAGNUM

Alternate Names:	25 WSSM
Parent Cartridge:	243 WSSM
Country of Origin:	USA
Year of Introduction:	2004
Designer(s):	Winchester
Governing Body:	SAAMI/CIP

CARTRIDGE CASE DATA

Case Type:	Rimless, bottleneck		
Average Case Capacity:	56.6 grains H_2O	Max. Cartridge OAL	2.360 inch
Max. Case Length:	1.670 inch	Primer:	Large Rifle
Case Trim to Length:	1.660 inch	RCBS Shell holder:	# 43
Current Manufacturers:	Winchester		

BALLISTIC DATA

Max. Average Pressure (MAP):	65,000 psi, CUP not established for this cartridge - SAAMI	Test Barrel Length:	24 inch
Rifling Twist Rate:	1 turn in 10 inch		
Muzzle velocities of factory loaded ammunition	Bullet Wgt.		Muzzle velocity
	85-grain		3,470 fps
	120-grain		2,990 fps
	Muzzle velocity will decrease approximately 20 fps per inch for barrels less than 24 inches.		

HISTORICAL NOTES

- The 25 WSSM cartridge was designed by Winchester and introduced along with its sibling, the 243 WSSM, in 2004.

- The 25 WSSM is the largest caliber in the WSSM series of cartridges, all of which are below 270 caliber.
- All three WSSM cartridges have an unusually short length-to-diameter ratio allowing them to fit into short length, bolt-action rifles.

BALLISTIC NOTES

- Case capacity of the 25 WSSM is a significant 20% less than the 25-06 Remington. The smaller case capacity means smaller maximum propellant charges can be loaded.
- Normally, this would be a handicap, however the 25 WSSM offsets this with a higher MAP and a more heavily constructed case.
- Both cartridges offer nearly identical muzzle velocities using the same bullet weights.

TECHNICAL NOTES

- The 25 WSSM cartridge and its siblings share case head dimensions with the 300 Winchester Short Magnum cartridge, but with a case shortened from 2.100 inch to 1.670 inch.
- Although the 25 WSSM is intended to be a deer cartridge, by handloading lightweight bullets it can serve as a very good varmint cartridge.
- The one turn in 10 inch rifling twist rate is optimized for long heavy bullets over 100 grains. However, it will work well with lighter bullets also.

HANDLOADING NOTES

- Winchester is the sole manufacturer of 25 WSSM ammunition and brass cartridge cases for reloading.
- The heavy construction of 25 WSSM cartridge cases can cause problems with neck expander balls and full length resizing. Extra effort may be required for both neck and case body resizing.
- You can reduce sizing effort by thoroughly cleaning and lubricating cases before sizing. Reduce neck sizing ball effort caused by the thick case necks by polishing the necks inside with a bore brush held in an electric drill.
- The 25 WSSM cartridge prefers slow burning propellants for heavy bullets.

SAFETY NOTES

SPEER 120-grain Spitzer BTSP @ a muzzle velocity of 2,920 fps:
- Maximum vertical altitude @ 90° elevation is 15,804 feet.
- Maximum horizontal distance to first impact with ground @ 36° elevation is 7,334 yards.

87 GRAINS

DIAMETER	SECTIONAL DENSITY
.257"	0.188

25 Spitzer SP Hot-Cor®
Ballistic Coefficient	0.300
COAL Tested	2.270"
Speer Part No.	1241

25 TNT® HP
Ballistic Coefficient	0.337
COAL Tested	2.350"
Speer Part No.	1246

			Starting Charge		Maximum Charge	
Propellant	Case	Primer	Weight (grains)	Muzzle Velocity (feet/sec)	Weight (grains)	Muzzle Velocity (feet/sec)
Ramshot Big Game	Winchester	CCI 250	46.0	3159	50.0	3445
Alliant Reloder 15	Winchester	CCI 200	41.5	3176	45.5	3428
Hodgdon H414	Winchester	CCI 250	47.0	3183	51.0 C	3428
Hodgdon H380	Winchester	CCI 250	46.0	3177	50.0 C	3417
IMR 4895	Winchester	CCI 200	40.0	3153	44.0	3411
Winchester 760	Winchester	CCI 250	49.0	3258	51.0 C	3392
Hodgdon Varget	Winchester	CCI 200	39.0	3095	43.0	3358
IMR 4350	Winchester	CCI 200	46.0	3073	50.0 C	3354
Alliant Reloder 19	Winchester	CCI 200	48.0	3066	52.0 C	3333
Alliant Reloder 10X	Winchester	CCI 200	35.0	3056	39.0	3313
Accurate 4350	Winchester	CCI 200	48.0	3170	50.0 C	3294
Vihtavuori N560	Winchester	CCI 200	48.0	3041	52.0 C	3271
Accurate 5744 (reduced load)	Winchester	CCI 200	19.0	1989	21.0	2141

WARNING! Maximum loads should be used with CAUTION • C = Compressed Load

100 GRAINS

DIAMETER	SECTIONAL DENSITY
.257"	0.216

25 Spitzer SP Hot-Cor®
Ballistic Coefficient	0.334
COAL Tested	2.270"
Speer Part No.	1405

25 HP
Ballistic Coefficient	0.263
COAL Tested	2.280"
Speer Part No.	1407

25 Spitzer BTSP
Ballistic Coefficient	0.393
COAL Tested	2.270"
Speer Part No.	1408

			Starting Charge		Maximum Charge	
Propellant	Case	Primer	Weight (grains)	Muzzle Velocity (feet/sec)	Weight (grains)	Muzzle Velocity (feet/sec)
Winchester 760	Winchester	CCI 250	45.5	2995	49.5	3254
Hodgdon H414	Winchester	CCI 250	44.5	2991	48.5	3222
Accurate 4350	Winchester	CCI 200	44.0	2954	48.0 C	3200
Alliant Reloder 19	Winchester	CCI 200	45.5	2927	49.5 C	3180
Vihtavuori N560	Winchester	CCI 200	46.0	2891	50.0 C	3154
Ramshot Big Game	Winchester	CCI 250	42.0	2924	46.0	3141
IMR 4350	Winchester	CCI 200	43.0	2909	47.0 C	3137
Hodgdon H380	Winchester	CCI 250	41.5	2890	45.5	3135
Alliant Reloder 15	Winchester	CCI 200	37.5	2890	41.5	3110
Hodgdon Varget	Winchester	CCI 200	36.0	2886	40.0	3099
IMR 4895	Winchester	CCI 200	36.0	2845	40.0	3084
Alliant Reloder 10X	Winchester	CCI 200	31.0	2751	35.0	2984
Accurate 5744 (reduced load)	Winchester	CCI 200	20.0	1996	22.0	2136

WARNING! *Maximum loads should be used with CAUTION • C = Compressed Load*

120 GRAINS

DIAMETER	SECTIONAL DENSITY
.257"	0.260

25 Spitzer BTSP	
Ballistic Coefficient	0.480
COAL Tested	2.270"
Speer Part No.	1410

			Starting Charge		Maximum Charge	
Propellant	Case	Primer	Weight (grains)	Muzzle Velocity (feet/sec)	Weight (grains)	Muzzle Velocity (feet/sec)
Hodgdon H414	Winchester	CCI 250	41.0	2709	45.0	2929
Winchester 760	Winchester	CCI 250	41.0	2713	45.0	2921
Alliant Reloder 19	Winchester	CCI 200	42.0	2685	46.0 C	2914
Vihtavuori N560	Winchester	CCI 200	42.0	2662	46.0	2901
IMR 4350	Winchester	CCI 200	39.0	2624	43.0	2881
Accurate 4350	Winchester	CCI 200	39.0	2649	43.0	2861
Hodgdon H380	Winchester	CCI 250	38.5	2624	42.5	2846
Ramshot Big Game	Winchester	CCI 250	38.0	2622	42.0	2840
Alliant Reloder 15	Winchester	CCI 200	34.0	2551	38.0	2792
IMR 4895	Winchester	CCI 200	33.0	2528	37.0	2776
Hodgdon Varget	Winchester	CCI 200	32.5	2522	36.5	2744
Alliant Reloder 10X	Winchester	CCI 200	27.5	2368	31.5	2607

WARNING! Maximum loads should be used with CAUTION • C = Compressed Load

257 WEATHERBY MAGNUM

Parent Cartridge:	300 H&H Magnum
Country of Origin:	USA
Year of Introduction:	Designed 1944, Introduced 1948
Designer(s):	Roy Weatherby
Governing Body:	SAAMI/CIP

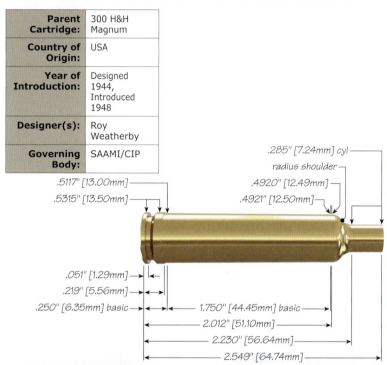

CARTRIDGE CASE DATA

Case Type:	Rimless, belted, bottleneck		
Average Case Capacity:	86.3 grains H_2O	Max. Cartridge OAL	3.170 inch
Max. Case Length:	2.549 inch	Primer:	Large Rifle
Case Trim to Length:	2.539 inch	RCBS Shell holder:	# 4
Current Manufacturers:	Weatherby, Hornady, Nosler, Norma (brass only)		

BALLISTIC DATA

Max. Average Pressure (MAP):	62,500 psi, 53,500 CUP - SAAMI	Test Barrel Length:	24 inch
Rifling Twist Rate:	1 turn in 10 inch		
Muzzle velocities of factory loaded ammunition	Bullet Wgt.		Muzzle velocity
	80-grain		3,870 fps
	100-grain		3,600 fps
	115-grain		3,400 fps
	120-grain		3,305 fps
	Muzzle velocity will decrease approximately 40 fps per inch for barrels less than 26 inches.		

HISTORICAL NOTES

- The 257 Weatherby Magnum is the smallest of the four Weatherby' cartridges based on the 300 H&H Magnum cartridge. It is consistently one of Weatherby's best sellers. It may be the most versatile cartridge in the Weatherby line of ammunition.
- This is due to its proven capability for taking most species of North American big game as well as its outstanding performance for hunting predators and varmints. Light African plains game are also on its ballistic menu.
- An interesting point about the 257 Weatherby Magnum cartridge is that Weatherby rifles in this caliber are not "showcase queens". Rather, the 257 Weatherby Mag. is the one that owners of multiple Weatherby rifles reach for when they go hunting for North American game.

BALLISTIC NOTES

- The versatility of the 257 Weatherby Magnum can be attributed to its wide range of bullet weights, all of which are launched at industry topping velocities that provide long range, high striking energy, and a flat trajectory.
- The long effective range of the 257 Weatherby Magnum places a premium on the shooter's marksmanship skills. However, the outstanding exterior ballistics and relatively light (for a Weatherby Magnum) recoil work to the shooter's advantage.
- There is no ballistic secret to the 257 Weatherby Magnum cartridge. Its high muzzle velocity is achieved by loading to industry high MAP levels and burning heavy propellant charges.
- Weatherby ammunition ballistics listed in the company catalog are taken from 26-inch barrels (most other SAAMI standard cartridge of this size use 24-inch barrels). To determine Weatherby ballistics in 24 inch barrels, subtract about 80 fps from Weatherby catalog muzzle velocities.
- For handloading the 257 Weatherby Magnum cartridge, Speer offers six bullets to take full advantage of this cartridge's versatility.
  - There are two 87-grain bullets that can be loaded to a muzzle velocity of up to 3,730 fps!
  - To take maximum advantage of the ballistic performance of the 257 Weatherby Magnum, Speer offers two outstanding boat tail bullets: A 100-grain Spitzer Boat tail SP and 120-grain Spitzer Boat tail SP. For hunting at longer ranges up to 500 yards, these bullets offer the advantages of higher striking velocity and energy with a flatter trajectory and less wind drift.

TECHNICAL NOTES

- The 257 Weatherby Magnum shares its basic case configuration with its 300 H&H Magnum based brethren. Namely, it is a rimless, belted, necked magnum of heavy construction designed for high pressures.
- Most shooters of the 257 Weatherby Magnum would agree that one secret of its accuracy is the long case neck which provides better alignment with the bore axis.

HANDLOADING NOTES

- We recommend using new or once fired cases for all maximum loads.
- We recommend that you set your sizing dies to headspace this cartridge case on the shoulder instead of the belt.

- As with other Weatherby Magnum calibers, 257 Wby. Mag. cases tend to stretch just in front of the belt. After four to six firings, these cases often separate at the stretch point.
- The heavy construction of the 257 Weatherby Magnum cartridge case can cause problems with full length resizing such as excessive effort, case stretching, brass hardening and head separations, all leading to short case life. For this reason, neck sizing only is recommended as all rifles in 257 Weatherby Magnum caliber are bolt-action types.
- Do not use lighter propellant charges than those listed in the data as the bullet may fail to clear the barrel.

SAFETY NOTES

SPEER 120-grain Spitzer BTSP @ a muzzle velocity of 3,235 fps:
- Maximum vertical altitude @ 90° elevation is 16,734 feet.
- Maximum horizontal distance to first impact with ground @ 36° elevation is 7,656 yards.

87 GRAINS

DIAMETER	SECTIONAL DENSITY
.257"	0.188

25 Spitzer SP Hot-Cor®	
Ballistic Coefficient	0.300
COAL Tested	3.150"
Speer Part No.	1241

25 TNT® HP	
Ballistic Coefficient	0.337
COAL Tested	3.170"
Speer Part No.	1246

			Starting Charge		Maximum Charge	
Propellant	Case	Primer	Weight (grains)	Muzzle Velocity (feet/sec)	Weight (grains)	Muzzle Velocity (feet/sec)
Ramshot Magnum	Federal	CCI 250	74.0	3570	78.0	3731
Hodgdon Retumbo	Federal	CCI 250	74.0	3462	78.0 C	3672
Alliant Reloder 25	Federal	CCI 250	69.0	3427	73.0 C	3670
Alliant Reloder 22	Federal	CCI 250	67.0	3429	71.0	3661
Vihtavuori N560	Federal	CCI 250	68.0	3507	70.0	3651
Alliant Reloder 19	Federal	CCI 250	64.0	3372	68.0	3637
IMR 7828	Federal	CCI 250	67.0	3334	71.0	3604
IMR 4831	Federal	CCI 250	63.0	3433	65.0	3564
Accurate MagPro	Federal	CCI 250	68.0	3400	70.0	3504

WARNING! Maximum loads should be used with CAUTION • C = Compressed Load

100 GRAINS

DIAMETER	SECTIONAL DENSITY
.257"	0.216

25 Spitzer SP Hot-Cor®
Ballistic Coefficient	0.334
COAL Tested	3.150"
Speer Part No.	1405

25 HP
Ballistic Coefficient	0.263
COAL Tested	3.140"
Speer Part No.	1407

25 Spitzer BTSP
Ballistic Coefficient	0.393
COAL Tested	3.150"
Speer Part No.	1408

			Starting Charge		Maximum Charge	
Propellant	Case	Primer	Weight (grains)	Muzzle Velocity (feet/sec)	Weight (grains)	Muzzle Velocity (feet/sec)
Alliant Reloder 25	Federal	CCI 250	69.0	3395	73.0	3545
Ramshot Magnum	Federal	CCI 250	70.0	3339	74.0	3494
Alliant Reloder 33	Weatherby	CCI 250	75.0	3092	82.9 C	3483
Alliant Reloder 26	Weatherby	CCI 250	63.6	3116	70.7	3483
Alliant Reloder 22	Federal	CCI 250	64.0	3225	68.0	3450
Alliant Reloder 23	Weatherby	CCI 250	62.5	3104	69.6	3450
IMR 7828	Federal	CCI 250	67.0	3306	69.0	3447
Alliant Power Pro 4000-MR	Weatherby	CCI 250	59.4	3111	66.0	3428
Vihtavuori N560	Federal	CCI 250	65.0	3290	67.0	3413
Hodgdon Retumbo	Federal	CCI 250	71.0	3283	73.0	3411
Hodgdon H1000	Federal	CCI 250	69.0	3302	71.0	3405
Alliant Reloder 19	Federal	CCI 250	61.0	3188	65.0	3405
IMR 7977	Weatherby	CCI 250	66.7	3065	73.9	3399
Accurate MagPro	Federal	CCI 250	65.0	3197	67.0	3292

WARNING! *Maximum loads should be used with CAUTION • C = Compressed Load*

120 GRAINS

DIAMETER	SECTIONAL DENSITY
.257"	0.260

25 Spitzer BTSP	
Ballistic Coefficient	0.480
COAL Tested	3.170"
Speer Part No.	1410

			Starting Charge		Maximum Charge	
Propellant	Case	Primer	Weight (grains)	Muzzle Velocity (feet/sec)	Weight (grains)	Muzzle Velocity (feet/sec)
Alliant Reloder 33	Weatherby	CCI 250	69.7	2953	77.4	3242
Alliant Reloder 25	Federal	CCI 250	63.0	3024	67.0	3236
Ramshot Magnum	Federal	CCI 250	66.0	3046	70.0	3211
Alliant Reloder 26	Weatherby	CCI 250	59.3	2901	65.9	3197
Vihtavuori N560	Federal	CCI 250	60.0	2963	64.0	3181
Alliant Reloder 23	Weatherby	CCI 250	60.8	3031	64.2	3164
Hodgdon Retumbo	Federal	CCI 250	65.0	2948	69.0	3159
Alliant Power Pro 4000-MR	Weatherby	CCI 250	56.9	2920	61.9	3148
IMR 7977	Weatherby	CCI 250	62.1	2875	68.9	3146
Alliant Reloder 22	Federal	CCI 250	59.0	2904	63.0	3120
Hodgdon H1000	Federal	CCI 250	64.5	3006	66.5	3108
IMR 7828	Federal	CCI 250	62.0	2988	64.0	3106
Hodgdon H4831SC	Federal	CCI 250	61.0	3000	63.0	3103
Accurate MagPro	Federal	CCI 250	62.0	2927	64.0	3027

WARNING! Maximum loads should be used with CAUTION • C = Compressed Load

6.5 GRENDEL

Alternate Names:	6.5x39mm
Parent Cartridge:	7.62x39mm Soviet
Related Cartridges:	6mm PPC
Country of Origin:	USA
Year of Introduction:	2003
Designer(s):	Bill Alexander, Alexander Arms
Governing Body:	SAAMI

Case dimensions: .293" cyl [7.44mm], shoulder angle 30°, .441" [11.20mm], .441" [11.20mm], .4301" [10.92mm], .4318" [10.97mm], .050" [1.27mm], .200" [5.08mm], .800" [20.32mm], 1.1507" [29.23mm], 1.2694" [32.24mm], 1.520" [38.61mm]

CARTRIDGE CASE DATA

Case Type:	Rimless, bottleneck		
Average Case Capacity:	35.6 grains H₂O	Max. Cartridge OAL	2.260 inch
Max. Case Length:	1.520 inch	Primer:	Small Rifle
Case Trim to Length:	1.510 inch	RCBS Shell holder:	# 32
Current Manufacturers:	Hornady, Federal, Wolf		

BALLISTIC DATA

Max. Average Pressure (MAP):	52,000 psi, CUP not established for this cartridge - SAAMI	Test Barrel Length:	24 inch
Rifling Twist Rate:	1 turn in 8 inch		
Muzzle velocities of factory loaded ammunition	**Bullet Wgt.**	**Muzzle velocity**	
	90-grain	3,000 fps	
	108-grain	2,700 fps	
	123-grain	2,620 fps	
	130-grain	2,400 fps	
	144-grain	2,450 fps	
	Muzzle velocity will decrease approximately 20 fps per inch for barrels less than 24 inches.		

HISTORICAL NOTES

- Bill Alexander developed the 6.5 Grendel cartridge in 2002 to improve down range ballistic performance of the 5.56 NATO and 223 Remington caliber rifles based on the AR15 platform.

- To meet these requirements, the omnipresent Soviet 7.62x39mm cartridge was necked down to 6.5mm (or, if you prefer, the Soviet 5.45x39mm cartridge was necked up to 6.5mm).
- The 6.5 Grendel cartridge was commercialized and is now offered by Hornady, Federal and Wolf.
- This cartridge is an example of the new breed of "semi-military" cartridges that enjoy limited production by commercial manufacturers (NOT government manufacturing facilities), but were never standardized or adopted for military use. Examples include: 4.6x30mm H&K, 5.7x28mm FN, 300 AAC Blackout, 6.8mm SPC, and 458 SOCOM.

Interesting Fact

The superior down range ballistics of .264 inch bullets has been apparent for decades. Witness the down range ballistics of the 6.5x55mm Swedish Mauser cartridge of 1894 as an example. The 6.5 Grendel builds on this.

BALLISTIC NOTES

- For many years, the armies of other NATO nations have complained about the inadequate down range performance of the 5.56x45mm cartridge. Adoption of the Belgian designed SS109 bullet (aka M855) helped matters, but did not resolve the dispute.
- Recent developments in Russian and Chinese small arms ammunition have resulted in an overmatch condition with the 5.56x45mm NATO cartridge. This means "they" can shoot at us from distances at which we cannot adequately respond. Belatedly, the U.S. Army has realized this and changes may be coming.
- Some idea of the down range ballistic potential of the 6.5 Grendel can be gauged from the following comparison:

  - 6.5 Grendel with 123-grain Spitzer boat tail bullet
    Muzzle velocity: 2,590 fps; muzzle energy 1,832 ft-lbs
    Velocity @ 500 yards: 1,804 fps; striking energy 889 ft-lbs

  - 223 Rem. with 62-grain FMJBT bullet
    Muzzle velocity: 3,020 fps; muzzle energy 1,255 ft-lbs
    Velocity @ 500 yards: 1,674 fps; striking energy 386 ft-lbs

- Which one would you rather have in a combat situation?
- For civilian hunting applications, the 6.5 Grendel is factory loaded with 120 to 123-grain soft point bullets suitable for predators and small deer at ranges of approximately 200 yards.
- For hunting, we recommend the Speer 140-grain Spitzer SP Hot-Cor®. The additional weight of this bullet over the factory 120-grain bullets will offer more striking energy and penetration.

TECHNICAL NOTES

- A crucial requirement for the 6.5 Grendel is it must be compatible with all M16/AR15 rifle upper and lower assemblies with a minimum number of changes.
- To accomplish this, the 6.5 Grendel is based on a shortened 7.62x39mm Soviet cartridge case necked down to accept 6.5mm diameter bullets.
- Maximum overall loaded length of the 6.5 Grendel cartridge is 2.260 inch which is the same as the 223 Remington cartridge. This allows the 6.5 Grendel to fit in and feed from existing AR15/M16 magazines and platforms.

- The 6.5 Grendel cartridge has the same MAP as the 5.56x45mm NATO military cartridge, allowing it to maintain port pressure levels needed to operate AR15/M16 Rifles.
- The rim diameter of the 7.62x39mm cartridge is .069 inch larger than the rim diameter of the 223 Remington cartridge, allowing it to fit the bolt face of AR15/M16 rifles with only minor modifications.

HANDLOADING NOTES

- Note that American-made 6.5 Grendel cases are designed for Small Rifle primers and 6.5mm/.264 inch diameter bullets.
- As most 6.5 Grendel ammunition will be fired in semi-automatic rifles, it will be necessary to full length resize fired cases with a small base die.
- Expect to discard a high number of fired cases damaged by the ejectors in MSR's.
- In addition to the manufacturers of loaded ammunition listed above, new, empty brass for reloading is offered by Hornady.
- The small case capacity of the 6.5 Grendel cartridge works best with medium burning powders due to the bullet weights used.

SAFETY NOTES

SPEER 140-grain Spitzer SP @ a muzzle velocity of 2,338 fps:
- Maximum vertical altitude @ 90° elevation is 11,373 feet.
- Maximum horizontal distance to first impact with ground @ 37° elevation is 5,391 yards.

90 GRAINS

DIAMETER	SECTIONAL DENSITY
.264"	0.184

6.5mm TNT® HP

Ballistic Coefficient	0.281
COAL Tested	2.190"
Speer Part No.	1445

			Starting Charge		Maximum Charge	
Propellant	Case	Primer	Weight (grains)	Muzzle Velocity (feet/sec)	Weight (grains)	Muzzle Velocity (feet/sec)
IMR 8208 XBR	Federal	Federal 205	28.7	2721	31.7 C	3013
Alliant Power Pro Varmint	Federal	Federal 205	30.1	2723	33.2	3009
Hodgdon H335	Federal	Federal 205	29.0	2745	32.0	3009
Accurate 2200	Federal	Federal 205	26.4	2732	29.2	2992
Accurate 2230	Federal	Federal 205	27.8	2731	30.7	2965
Alliant Power Pro 1200-R	Federal	Federal 205	26.5	2734	29.2	2964
Hodgdon Benchmark	Federal	Federal 205	28.2	2667	31.2	2952
Alliant Reloder 10X	Federal	Federal 205	25.9	2640	28.6	2916
Vihtavuori N135	Federal	Federal 205	27.7	2673	30.4 C	2910
Winchester 748	Federal	Federal 205	30.2	2670	33.2 C	2907
Alliant AR-Comp	Federal	Federal 205	28.8	2774	30.3 C	2898
IMR 3031	Federal	Federal 205	27.2	2621	29.4 C	2848

WARNING! Maximum loads should be used with CAUTION • C = Compressed Load

GOLD DOT RIFLE

120 GRAINS	DIAMETER	SECTIONAL DENSITY
	.264"	0.246

6.5mm GD	
Ballistic Coefficient	0.457
COAL Tested	2.260"
Speer Part No.	264120GDB

			Starting Charge		Maximum Charge	
Propellant	Case	Primer	Weight (grains)	Muzzle Velocity (feet/sec)	Weight (grains)	Muzzle Velocity (feet/sec)
Alliant Power Pro 2000-MR	Federal	Federal 205 AR	28.4	2390	31.4	2620
Alliant Power Pro Varmint	Federal	Federal 205 AR	24.5	2264	27.3	2483
Winchester 748	Federal	Federal 205 AR	25.7	2268	28.6	2481
Alliant Reloder 15	Federal	Federal 205 AR	25.1	2246	27.9 C	2469
Ramshot TAC	Federal	Federal 205 AR	25.1	2267	27.9	2469
Hodgdon Varget	Federal	Federal 205 AR	24.1	2202	26.8	2420
Alliant AR-Comp	Federal	Federal 205 AR	22.7	2228	25.3	2418
IMR 4895	Federal	Federal 205 AR	24.0	2191	26.6	2413
Accurate 4064	Federal	Federal 205 AR	24.8	2215	27.4 C	2408
IMR 8208 XBR	Federal	Federal 205 AR	22.9	2210	25.4	2405
Vihtavuori N135	Federal	Federal 205 AR	21.7	2162	24.1	2326

WARNING! Maximum loads should be used with CAUTION • C = Compressed Load

140 GRAINS

DIAMETER	SECTIONAL DENSITY
.264"	0.287

6.5mm Spitzer SP Hot-Cor®

Ballistic Coefficient	0.498
COAL Tested	2.140"
Speer Part No.	1441

			Starting Charge		Maximum Charge	
Propellant	Case	Primer	Weight (grains)	Muzzle Velocity (feet/sec)	Weight (grains)	Muzzle Velocity (feet/sec)
Winchester 748	Federal	Federal 205	25.4 C	2064	28.6 C	2338
Alliant Power Pro Varmint	Federal	Federal 205	25.1 C	2111	27.7 C	2323
Hodgdon CFE 223	Federal	Federal 205	25.4	2090	28.2 C	2315
Ramshot TAC	Federal	Federal 205	24.0	2070	26.5	2250
IMR 8208 XBR	Federal	Federal 205	22.9	2018	25.4 C	2230
Alliant AR-Comp	Federal	Federal 205	22.2	2025	24.4 C	2186
Vihtavuori N135	Federal	Federal 205	21.6 C	1972	23.9 C	2128
Accurate 4064	Federal	Federal 205	23.6	1943	24.5 C	2039

WARNING! Maximum loads should be used with CAUTION • C = Compressed Load

260 REMINGTON

Parent Cartridge:	308 Winchester
Country of Origin:	USA
Year of Introduction:	1997
Designer(s):	Jim Carmichael
Governing Body:	SAAMI/CIP

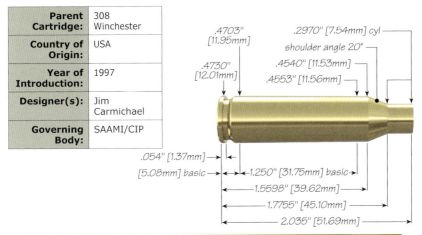

CARTRIDGE CASE DATA

Case Type:	Rimless, bottleneck		
Average Case Capacity:	56.5 grains H$_2$O	Max. Cartridge OAL	2.800 inch
Max. Case Length:	2.035 inch	Primer:	Large Rifle
Case Trim to Length:	2.025 inch	RCBS Shell holder:	# 3
Current Manufacturers:	Remington, Nosler, Federal, Hornady, Sako		

BALLISTIC DATA

Max. Average Pressure (MAP):	60,000 psi, CUP not established for this round - SAAMI	Test Barrel Length:	24 inch
Rifling Twist Rate:	1 turn in 9 inch		
Muzzle velocities of factory loaded ammunition	Bullet Wgt.		Muzzle velocity
	100-grain		3,200 fps
	120-grain		2,890 fps
	140-grain		2,750 fps
	Muzzle velocity will decrease approximately 20 fps per inch for barrels less than 24 inches.		

HISTORICAL NOTES

- Among European hunters, 6.5mm cartridges are very popular. On the other hand, they have been slow to gain popularity with North American sportsmen. When Remington introduced this cartridge in 1997, the company made an effort to change this.

- Whether or not the 260 Remington cartridge will succeed where others have failed remains to be seen.

- In any case, the 260 Remington is a modern, high pressure cartridge designed for hunting.

BALLISTIC NOTES

- Ballistically speaking, the 260 Remington is a step up from the 257 Roberts +P.
- With 117-120-grain bullets, the 260 Rem. offers a 150 fps increase in muzzle velocity and a 230 ft-lb increase in muzzle energy over the 257 Roberts +P.
- In addition, the 260 Remington can stabilize 140 and 160-grain bullets.
- The mild recoil in short, light rifles makes the 260 Remington an excellent choice for novice hunters and those sensitive to recoil.

HANDLOADING NOTES

- Although the 260 Remington is not considered a varmint cartridge, the Speer 90-grain TNT®HP will amaze with its spectacular performance anchoring varmints.
- With 140-grain Spitzer SP Hot-Cor®, the 260 Remington cartridge really comes into its own for deer hunting.
- The 260 Rem. works best with medium to slow burning powders.

SAFETY NOTES

SPEER 140-grain Spitzer SP Hot-Cor @ a muzzle velocity of 2,730 fps:
- Maximum vertical altitude @ 90° elevation is 11,922 feet.
- Maximum horizontal distance to first impact with ground @ 37° elevation is 5,588 yards.

90 GRAINS

DIAMETER	SECTIONAL DENSITY
.264"	0.184

6.5mm TNT® HP

Ballistic Coefficient	0.281
COAL Tested	2.650"
Speer Part No.	1445

| Propellant | Case | Primer | Starting Charge | | Maximum Charge | |
			Weight (grains)	Muzzle Velocity (feet/sec)	Weight (grains)	Muzzle Velocity (feet/sec)
Alliant Reloder 16	Federal	Federal 210	43.7	3086	48.4 C	3392
Hodgdon H380	Remington	CCI 250	45.0	3125	49.0	3367
Alliant AR-Comp	Federal	Federal 210	37.1	3127	41.1	3365
Hodgdon H414	Remington	CCI 250	46.0	3046	50.0	3348
Hodgdon CFE 223	Federal	Federal 210	37.8	3051	42.0	3328
Vihtavuori N160	Remington	CCI 200	47.0	3008	51.0 C	3315
Alliant Reloder 15	Remington	CCI 200	41.5	2970	45.5	3311
IMR 8208 XBR	Federal	Federal 210	36.3	3152	39.4	3309
IMR 4064	Remington	CCI 200	40.0	2910	44.0	3297
IMR 4350	Remington	CCI 200	46.0	2947	50.0 C	3268
Hodgdon Varget	Remington	CCI 200	40.5	2959	44.5	3261
Winchester 760	Remington	CCI 250	46.5	3096	48.5	3253
Winchester 748	Remington	CCI 250	40.0	2904	44.0	3250
Accurate 2700	Remington	CCI 250	46.0	3071	48.0	3247
IMR 4895	Remington	CCI 200	39.0	2841	43.0	3205
Accurate 4350	Remington	CCI 200	46.0	2852	48.0 C	3000
Alliant Reloder 19	Remington	CCI 200	48.0	2855	50.0 C	2985
Accurate 5744 (reduced load)	Remington	CCI 200	20.0	1981	24.0	2294

WARNING! *Maximum loads should be used with CAUTION • C = Compressed Load*

140 GRAINS

DIAMETER	SECTIONAL DENSITY
.264"	0.287

6.5mm Spitzer SP Hot-Cor®

Ballistic Coefficient	0.498
COAL Tested	2.745"
Speer Part No.	1441

			Starting Charge		Maximum Charge	
Propellant	Case	Primer	Weight (grains)	Muzzle Velocity (feet/sec)	Weight (grains)	Muzzle Velocity (feet/sec)
Alliant Reloder 19	Remington	CCI 200	43.5	2603	45.5 C	2731
IMR 4831	Remington	CCI 200	42.0	2587	44.0 C	2722
Alliant Reloder 22	Remington	CCI 200	44.0	2554	46.0 C	2701
Alliant Reloder 23	Federal	Federal 210	38.7	2514	42.7	2696
Alliant Power Pro 4000-MR	Federal	Federal 210	37.0	2509	40.4	2696
Accurate 4350	Remington	CCI 200	41.0	2540	43.0 C	2695
Vihtavuori N165	Remington	CCI 200	45.0	2568	47.0 C	2687
IMR 4350	Remington	CCI 200	41.0	2522	43.0 C	2687
Alliant Reloder 17	Federal	Federal 210	36.0	2506	39.0	2678
Hodgdon H4831SC	Remington	CCI 200	43.5	2531	45.5 C	2635
Alliant Reloder 16	Federal	Federal 210	34.8	2443	38.4	2635
Winchester 760	Remington	CCI 250	39.5	2528	41.5	2623
Accurate 3100	Remington	CCI 200	43.0	2542	45.0 C	2614
Hodgdon H4350	Federal	Federal 210	34.7	2413	38.4	2614
Hodgdon H414	Remington	CCI 250	39.5	2519	41.5	2596
IMR 4064	Remington	CCI 200	35.0	2460	37.0	2572
Accurate 5744 (reduced load)	Remington	CCI 200	22.0	1894	24.0	2021

WARNING! Maximum loads should be used with CAUTION • C = Compressed Load

6.5 CREEDMOOR

Parent Cartridge:	30 Thompson-Center
Country of Origin:	USA
Year of Introduction:	2008
Designer(s):	Hornady
Governing Body:	SAAMI/CIP

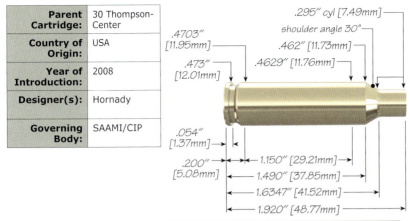

CARTRIDGE CASE DATA			
Case Type:	Rimless, bottleneck		
Average Case Capacity:	51.7 grains H$_2$O	Max. Cartridge OAL	2.825 inch
Max. Case Length:	1.920 inch	Primer:	Large Rifle, Small Rifle – Lapua
Case Trim to Length:	1.910 inch	RCBS Shell holder:	# 32
Current Manufacturers:	Hornady, Lapua, Federal, Nosler, Winchester		

BALLISTIC DATA			
Max. Average Pressure (MAP):	62,000 psi, CUP not assigned for this cartridge - SAAMI	Test Barrel Length:	24 inch
Rifling Twist Rate:	1 turn in 9 inch, 1 turn in 8 inch		
Muzzle velocities of factory loaded ammunition	Bullet Wgt.	Muzzle velocity	
	120-grain	2,800 fps	
	125-grain	2,850 fps	
	129-grain	2,940 fps	
	130-grain	2,875 fps	
	140-grain	2,690 fps	
	142-grain	2,700 fps	
	Muzzle velocity will decrease approximately 20 fps per inch for barrels less than 24 inches.		

HISTORICAL NOTES

- In the late 1880s, a few black powder cartridges were designed exclusively for long range target shooting. These included the 44-60 Peabody "Creedmoor" and the massive 44-100 Remington "Creedmoor" (550-grain lead RN bullet at a muzzle velocity of 1,380 fps). However, these were the exception rather than the norm even back then.

- Most modern rifle cartridges are designed for hunting or military purposes. A few can also serve for competition, usually due to need rather than design.
- While few modern cartridges begin life for target shooting, the 6.5 Creedmoor is one of the rare exceptions.
- For decades, American high power rifle competitors remained loyal to the 30-06 Springfield cartridge. Their loyalty transferred to the 308 Winchester/7.62x51mm NATO after the 30-06 Springfield left military service in the mid-1950s.
- Introduction of the 5.56x45mm NATO cartridge into U.S. military service in the early 1960s created a dilemma for high power shooters. While the light recoil of the new cartridge was an asset, the poor down range ballistics of the light bullets remained a severe handicap.
- Numerous efforts to improve the down range ballistics of the 5.56x45mm NATO cartridge for match competition proved only partially successful.
- It was for this reason that high power shooters clung to the 7.62x51mm cartridge for so long.
- Clearly, a new cartridge designed specifically for high power rifle match competition was needed.
- Messrs. Emery and DeMille were up to the task. They designed the 6.5 Creedmoor cartridge for high power rifle competition such as the NRA National Match course. It was a difficult task; many factors had to be considered for each aspect of the design and difficult compromises made.
- Hornady was one of the first ammunition makers to add this new cartridge to their product line in 2008. Since then, the 6.5 Creedmoor has joined the product lines of several other major manufacturers such as Federal, Winchester, and Nosler.

Interesting Fact

The name "Creedmoor" has a long and honorable history for high power rifle competition. The Creedmoor shooting range was located on Long Island, NY. Many national and international shooting competitions were held there from 1873 until 1910.

BALLISTIC NOTES

- The high ballistic coefficient of the 6.5mm spitzer boat tail bullets made the caliber selection for the new cartridge an easy one.
- Why 6.5mm? Some idea of the down range ballistic potential of the 6.5 Creedmoor can be gauged from the following comparison:

    - 6.5 Creedmoor with 120-grain SBT bullet B.C.: 0.486
        Muzzle velocity   3,050 fps
        Velocity @ 500 yards   2,132 fps

    - 308 Winchester with 168-grain HPBT bullet B.C.: 0.453
        Muzzle velocity: 2,680 fps
        Velocity @500 yards   1,786 fps

- In addition, a major advantage of the 6.5 Creedmoor is lighter recoil.
- For civilian hunting applications, the 6.5 Creedmoor is factory loaded with 120 to 140-grain soft point bullets suitable for predators and deer.

- For building a hunting load, we recommend the Speer 140-grain SP Spitzer Hot-Cor®. The additional weight of this bullet over the factory 120-grain bullets will offer more striking energy and penetration.
- For hunting pests and predators, you can do no better than the Speer 90-grain TNT®.

TECHNICAL NOTES

- As the vast majority of high power competitors used the 7.62x51mm NATO cartridge, this seemed the logical place to start designing the 6.5 Creedmoor.
  - Case head dimensions of the 7.62x51mm cartridge were retained.
  - Case length was shortened to 1.920 inches and body taper decreased to maintain case capacity.
  - A long 30° shoulder was used to provide a firm surface on which to maintain headspace.
  - A long 1.57 caliber case neck would hold the long, slender bullets securely to maintain bullet alignment with the bore axis.
- With these dimensions, the 6.5 Creedmoor is compatible with all short action rifles with a minimum number of changes.
- The 6.5 Creedmoor cartridge has a comparable MAP level to the 308 Winchester cartridge.

HANDLOADING NOTES

- Note that American-made 6.5 Creedmoor cases are designed for Large Rifle primers such as the CCI No. 200 and .264 inch diameter bullets.
- As most 6.5 Creedmoor ammunition will be fired in bolt-action rifles, neck sizing only is recommended to extend case life and reduce trimming chores for the target shooter. Full length resize for hunting applications.
- For high power rifle competition, we recommend that you use Large Rifle Match primers such as the CCI BR 2 which can be substituted for the CCI 200s used in testing.
- In addition to the manufacturers of loaded ammunition listed above, new, empty brass for reloading is offered by Hornady, Nosler, and Winchester.
- The 6.5 Creedmoor cartridge works best with medium burning powders due to the bullet weights used.
- If need be, 6.5 Creedmoor cases can be made by resizing and trimming 260 Remington cases.

SAFETY NOTES

SPEER 140-grain SP Spitzer Hot-Cor @ a muzzle velocity of 2,700 fps:

- Maximum vertical altitude @ 90° elevation is 11,865 feet.
- Maximum horizontal distance to first impact with ground @ 37° elevation is 5,567 yards.

90 GRAINS

DIAMETER	SECTIONAL DENSITY
.264"	0.184

6.5mm TNT® HP	
Ballistic Coefficient	0.281
COAL Tested	2.700"
Speer Part No.	1445

			Starting Charge		Maximum Charge	
Propellant	Case	Primer	Weight (grains)	Muzzle Velocity (feet/sec)	Weight (grains)	Muzzle Velocity (feet/sec)
Alliant Reloder 17	Hornady	CCI 200	45.2	3120	50.0 C	3499
Alliant Power Pro 2000-MR	Hornady	CCI 200	44.6	3112	49.5	3491
Accurate 2700	Hornady	CCI 200	46.2	3184	49.8	3474
Hodgdon H414	Hornady	CCI 200	45.7	3125	49.7	3437
Alliant Power Pro Varmint	Hornady	CCI 200	40.9	3097	45.3	3433
Alliant Reloder 15	Hornady	CCI 200	42.9	3195	46.1	3430
IMR 4064	Hornady	CCI 200	40.2	3111	44.1	3420
Hodgdon Varget	Hornady	CCI 200	41.1	3141	44.7	3415
Hodgdon H380	Hornady	CCI 200	45.1	3109	49.0 C	3382
Alliant AR-Comp	Hornady	CCI 200	38.3	3010	42.6	3372
Vihtavuori N140	Hornady	CCI 200	39.8	3008	44.1	3343

WARNING! *Maximum loads should be used with CAUTION • C = Compressed Load*

140 GRAINS

DIAMETER	SECTIONAL DENSITY
.264"	0.287

6.5mm Spitzer SP Hot-Cor®

Ballistic Coefficient	0.498
COAL Tested	2.760"
Speer Part No.	1441

			Starting Charge		Maximum Charge	
Propellant	Case	Primer	Weight (grains)	Muzzle Velocity (feet/sec)	Weight (grains)	Muzzle Velocity (feet/sec)
Alliant Reloder 23	Hornady	CCI 200	40.9	2553	45.4 C	2779
Alliant Reloder 19	Hornady	CCI 200	40.1	2537	44.5	2775
Alliant Power Pro 4000-MR	Hornady	CCI 200	40.2	2534	44.6	2771
Alliant Reloder 17	Hornady	CCI 200	37.4	2494	41.5	2747
Alliant Reloder 16	Hornady	CCI 200	38.0	2546	42.0	2746
IMR 4831	Hornady	CCI 200	38.9	2523	42.7	2731
Hodgdon Hybrid 100V	Hornady	CCI 200	37.2	2492	41.2	2719
Hodgdon H414	Hornady	CCI 200	37.2	2487	41.3	2710
Accurate 4350	Hornady	CCI 200	39.5	2550	42.5	2697
Hodgdon 4350	Hornady	CCI 200	36.7	2488	40.5	2678
Alliant Reloder 15	Hornady	CCI 200	34.6	2456	38.1	2651
IMR 4451	Hornady	CCI 200	37.4	2398	41.4	2638
Alliant Power Pro 2000-MR	Hornady	CCI 200	34.5	2458	37.9	2629
Hodgdon Varget	Hornady	CCI 200	33.4	2425	37.0	2615
IMR 4064	Hornady	CCI 200	33.0	2397	36.5	2602
Alliant Power Pro Varmint	Hornady	CCI 200	32.7	2388	36.2	2595
Vihtavuori N150	Hornady	CCI 200	32.0	2326	35.6	2529
Alliant AR-Comp	Hornady	CCI 200	30.9	2358	33.6	2500

WARNING! *Maximum loads should be used with CAUTION • C = Compressed Load*

GOLD DOT RIFLE

140 GRAINS

DIAMETER	SECTIONAL DENSITY
.264"	0.287

6.5mm GD

Ballistic Coefficient	0.571
COAL Tested	2.700"
Speer Part No.	264140GDB

Propellant	Case	Primer	Starting Charge		Maximum Charge	
			Weight (grains)	Muzzle Velocity (feet/sec)	Weight (grains)	Muzzle Velocity (feet/sec)
Alliant Reloder 26	Hornady	CCI 200	42.4	2582	46.9 C	2855
Alliant Power Pro 4000-MR	Hornady	CCI 200	40.1	2555	44.6 C	2804
Alliant Reloder 19	Hornady	CCI 200	42.1	2538	46.5 C	2801
Alliant Reloder 23	Hornady	CCI 200	41.3	2570	45.7 C	2794
Alliant Reloder 16	Hornady	CCI 200	38.6	2543	42.9 C	2790
Alliant Reloder 17	Hornady	CCI 200	37.2	2487	41.3	2769
Accurate 4350	Hornady	CCI 200	39.0	2505	43.3 C	2754
Hodgdon H4350	Hornady	CCI 200	37.9	2497	42.0	2737
Hodgdon Hybrid 100V	Hornady	CCI 200	36.9	2491	40.8	2726
Hodgdon H414	Hornady	CCI 200	37.3	2504	41.4	2724
Alliant Power Pro 2000-MR	Hornady	CCI 200	36.3	2483	40.3	2720
Vihtavuori N550	Hornady	CCI 200	35.9	2458	39.9	2716
IMR 4831	Hornady	CCI 200	38.9	2414	43.1 C	2679
IMR 4451	Hornady	CCI 200	37.1	2420	41.2	2658

WARNING! Maximum loads should be used with CAUTION • C = Compressed Load

6.5x55 SWEDISH

Alternate Names:	6.5 Swedish Mauser, 6.5 Swede, 6.5x55mm Swedish
Parent Cartridge:	8x57mm Mauser
Country of Origin:	Sweden
Year of Introduction:	1894
Designer(s):	Swedish/Norwegian Joint Military Commission
Governing Body:	SAAMI/CIP

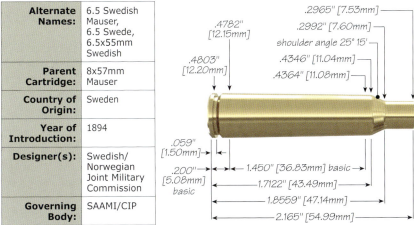

CARTRIDGE CASE DATA

Case Type:	Rimless, bottleneck		
Average Case Capacity:	58.6 grains H₂O	**Max. Cartridge OAL**	3.150 inch
Max. Case Length:	2.165 inch	**Primer:**	Large Rifle
Case Trim to Length:	2.155 inch	**RCBS Shell holder:**	# 2
Current Manufacturers:	Norma, Remington, Nosler, Winchester, Hornady, Federal, Sako, Lapua, Sellier & Bellot, RUAG (RWS)		

BALLISTIC DATA

Max. Average Pressure (MAP):	51,000 psi, 46,000 CUP - SAAMI (military actions only)	**Test Barrel Length:**	24 inch
Rifling Twist Rate:	1 turn in 8 inch (SAAMI), or 1/8.66 inch (military)		
Muzzle velocities of factory loaded ammunition	**Bullet Wgt.**		**Muzzle velocity**
	140-grain		2,650 fps
	Muzzle velocity will decrease approximately 20 fps per inch for barrels less than 24 inches.		

HISTORICAL NOTES

- The 6.5x55mm Swedish Mauser cartridge was adopted as the military service cartridge for both Sweden and Norway in 1894. This cartridge remained in front line Swedish military service until the early 1970s when it was replaced by the 7.62x51mm NATO cartridge. Military ammunition was loaded in both countries for their respective military organizations.

- The original full metal jacket round nose 156-grain bullet was updated in the late 1930s with a 139-grain sharply pointed boat tail design called the M41.

- Chamber pressure of the 6.5x55mm Swedish Mauser cartridge is higher than other

6.5mm military cartridges, but still modest by present standards.

- The 6.5x55mm Swedish Mauser cartridge was one of the first sporting cartridges for smokeless propellants. It became very popular for both hunting and competitive shooting in both countries.

- For North American hunters, the 6.5x55mm Swedish Mauser cartridge was virtually unknown until the late 1950s when thousands of surplus Swedish Mauser rifles were sold on the commercial market.

- Although 6.5mm cartridges have never found great favor with North American sportsmen, the 6.5x55mm Swedish is an exception. Although supplies of surplus Swedish military rifles have not been on the market for several decades now, demand for 6.5x55mm Swedish ammunition has remained strong.

Interesting fact

The Swedish M41 FMJBT military Ball bullet weighs 139 grains while the Norwegian version of the bullet weighs 144 grains. Muzzle velocity is the same at 2,600 fps. While this small weight difference may seem trivial, it is a major problem for shooting clubs in both countries. For Swedish government-sponsored club matches, the heavier 144-grain Norwegian bullet is not allowed. So the Norwegian shooting teams must fire 139-grain bullets when competing in Sweden.

BALLISTIC NOTES

- The 6.5x55mm Swedish Mauser cartridge is well known for its accuracy and excellent ballistic performance. For this reason, many shooters regard this cartridge as the best 6.5mm cartridge ever designed.

- Armchair ballisticians have often dismissed the 6.5x55mm Swedish with its 139 to 156-grain bullets as being too light for hunting large game such as moose. However, in the field, hunters have found the long, sleek 6.5mm bullets can be relied on to penetrate deeply for clean kills on most North American game.

- The low recoil of the 6.5x55mm Swedish makes it an ideal caliber for novice hunters.

TECHNICAL NOTES

- Chamber pressures of military rifles designed in the late 1890s were modest. In the case of the 6.5x55mm Swedish Mauser, MAP was limited to 51,000 psi which was normal for that time. SAAMI has adopted this MAP limit in deference to the large number of surplus military rifles in this caliber in use by American sportsmen.

- Loading data listed first is for military rifles (M94 & M96 Mauser) or sporting rifles with military actions.

- European ammunition makers have developed "sporting" 6.5x55mm SE loads with 27% higher maximum average pressures for improved ballistic performance. These loads are designed for use only in strong (M98 Mauser), commercial actions. These loads are listed in the next section.

HANDLOADING NOTES

- Swedish Mauser rifles have long throats to accommodate the original 156-grain round nose bullet.

- Lighter, pointed bullets may be seated out to take advantage of the maximum overall loaded length of 3.150 inches. However, test to make sure the seated bullet does not contact the rifling.

- We recommend neck sizing to reduce trimming chores and potential head separations.

- With its large case volume, the 6.5x55mm Swedish can be loaded with medium and slow burning propellants.
- The Speer 140-grain Spitzer SP Hot-Cor® will duplicate factory ballistics of American made 6.5x55mm ammunition.

SAFETY NOTES

SPEER 140-grain Spitzer SP Hot-Cor @ a muzzle velocity of 2,534 fps:
- Maximum vertical altitude @ 90° elevation is 11,781 feet.
- Maximum horizontal distance to first impact with ground @ 36° elevation is 5,536 yards.

6.5x55 SWEDISH (MILITARY ACTIONS)

90 GRAINS

DIAMETER	SECTIONAL DENSITY
.264"	0.184

6.5mm TNT® HP

Ballistic Coefficient	0.281
COAL Tested	2.850"
Speer Part No.	1445

			Starting Charge		Maximum Charge	
Propellant	Case	Primer	Weight (grains)	Muzzle Velocity (feet/sec)	Weight (grains)	Muzzle Velocity (feet/sec)
Hodgdon H414	Remington	CCI 250	48.0	3155	50.0	3278
Accurate 2700	Remington	CCI 250	47.0	3121	49.0	3244
Alliant Reloder 16	Federal	Federal 210	47.2	3152	49.0 C	3243
Alliant Reloder 17	Federal	Federal 210	45.1	2986	49.1	3240
IMR 4064	Remington	CCI 200	42.0	3105	44.0	3238
Hodgdon H4350	Remington	CCI 200	48.0	3098	50.0	3223
Alliant Reloder 15	Federal	Federal 210	40.1	2965	44.1	3215
Hodgdon Varget	Remington	CCI 200	41.0	3084	43.0	3193
IMR 4895	Remington	CCI 200	41.0	3051	43.0	3185
IMR 4350	Remington	CCI 200	48.0	3048	50.0	3178
IMR 3031	Remington	CCI 200	39.5	3038	41.5	3169
Accurate 4350	Remington	CCI 200	49.0	3029	51.0 C	3149
Alliant AR-Comp	Federal	Federal 210	36.0	2931	39.9	3143
Accurate 5744 (reduced load)	Remington	CCI 200	19.0	1841	21.0	2018

WARNING! *Maximum loads should be used with CAUTION • C = Compressed Load*

140 GRAINS

DIAMETER	SECTIONAL DENSITY
.264"	0.287

6.5mm Spitzer SP Hot-Cor®

Ballistic Coefficient	0.498
COAL Tested	3.000"
Speer Part No.	1441

			Starting Charge		Maximum Charge	
Propellant	Case	Primer	Weight (grains)	Muzzle Velocity (feet/sec)	Weight (grains)	Muzzle Velocity (feet/sec)
Alliant Reloder 26	Federal	Federal 210	37.7	2371	41.5	2534
Alliant Reloder 17	Federal	Federal 210	35.0	2309	38.6	2490
Alliant Power Pro 4000-MR	Federal	Federal 210	36.6	2368	38.7	2462
Alliant Reloder 22	Remington	CCI 200	38.0	2382	40.0	2461
Alliant Reloder 23	Federal	Federal 210	35.6	2293	39.3	2450
Alliant Reloder 19	Remington	CCI 200	38.0	2312	40.0	2399
Hodgdon H4831SC	Remington	CCI 200	37.0	2288	39.0	2379
Hodgdon H4350	Remington	CCI 200	34.0	2257	36.0	2350
IMR 4831	Remington	CCI 200	34.0	2254	36.0	2339
IMR 4350	Remington	CCI 200	34.0	2254	36.0	2337
IMR 4064	Remington	CCI 200	31.0	3193	33.0	2300
Hodgdon Varget	Remington	CCI 200	31.0	2165	33.0	2276

WARNING! *Maximum loads should be used with* CAUTION • C = Compressed Load

6.5x55 SWEDISH (STRONG COMMERCIAL ACTIONS)

Increased pressure load data below for use ONLY in strong, commercial actions.

90 GRAINS	DIAMETER	SECTIONAL DENSITY
	.264"	0.184

6.5mm TNT® HP	
Ballistic Coefficient	0.281
COAL Tested	2.850"
Speer Part No.	1445

			Starting Charge		Maximum Charge	
Propellant	Case	Primer	Weight (grains)	Muzzle Velocity (feet/sec)	Weight (grains)	Muzzle Velocity (feet/sec)
Alliant Reloder 17	Federal	Federal 210	45.1	2986	52.3 C	3443
Hodgdon Varget	Remington	CCI 200	45.0	3193	47.0	3410
Alliant Reloder 15	Federal	Federal 210	40.1	2965	47.2	3409
Hodgdon H414	Remington	CCI 250	50.0	3278	52.0	3401
Accurate 2700	Remington	CCI 250	49.0	3244	51.0	3385
IMR 4350	Remington	CCI 200	51.0	3243	53.0 C	3373
IMR 4064	Remington	CCI 200	44.0	3238	46.0	3371
Hodgdon H4350	Remington	CCI 200	50.0	3223	52.0 C	3348
Alliant AR-Comp	Federal	Federal 210	36.0	2931	43.5	3339
IMR 4895	Remington	CCI 200	43.0	3185	45.0	3320
IMR 3031	Remington	CCI 200	41.5	3169	43.5	3301
Alliant Reloder 16	Federal	Federal 210	47.2	3152	49.0 C	3243

WARNING! *Maximum loads should be used with CAUTION • C = Compressed Load*

Increased pressure load data below for use ONLY in strong, commercial actions.

140 GRAINS

DIAMETER	SECTIONAL DENSITY
.264"	0.287

6.5mm Spitzer SP Hot-Cor®

Ballistic Coefficient	0.498
COAL Tested	3.000"
Speer Part No.	1441

			Starting Charge		Maximum Charge	
Propellant	Case	Primer	Weight (grains)	Muzzle Velocity (feet/sec)	Weight (grains)	Muzzle Velocity (feet/sec)
Alliant Reloder 26	Federal	Federal 210	37.7	2371	46.4	2744
Alliant Reloder 17	Federal	Federal 210	35.0	2309	42.1	2666
Alliant Power Pro 4000-MR	Federal	Federal 210	36.6	2368	43.2	2664
Alliant Reloder 23	Federal	Federal 210	35.6	2293	44.2	2658
Alliant Reloder 22	Remington	CCI 200	43.0	2579	45.0	2655
Alliant Reloder 19	Remington	CCI 200	43.0	2529	45.0	2616
Hodgdon H4831SC	Remington	CCI 200	41.0	2464	43.0	2558
IMR 4831	Remington	CCI 200	39.0	2467	41.0	2551
IMR 4350	Remington	CCI 200	39.0	2462	41.0	2545
Hodgdon H4350	Remington	CCI 200	38.0	2444	40.0	2531
Alliant Reloder 16	Federal	Federal 210	34.0	2330	38.4	2528
Hodgdon Varget	Remington	CCI 200	35.0	2390	37.0	2498
IMR 4064	Remington	CCI 200	34.0	2351	36.0	2462

WARNING! *Maximum loads should be used with CAUTION • C = Compressed Load*

6.5 REMINGTON MAGNUM

Parent Cartridge:	6.5mm Remington Magnum, 350 Remington Magnum
Country of Origin:	USA
Year of Introduction:	1966
Designer(s):	Remington
Governing Body:	SAAMI/CIP

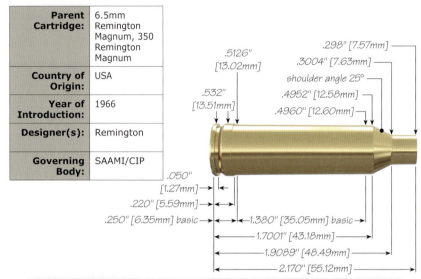

CARTRIDGE CASE DATA

Case Type:	Rimless, belted, bottleneck		
Average Case Capacity:	85.7 grains H$_2$O	Max. Cartridge OAL	2.800 inch
Max. Case Length:	2.170 inch	Primer:	Large Rifle
Case Trim to Length:	2.160 inch	RCBS Shell holder:	# 4
Current Manufacturers:	Remington, Nosler		

BALLISTIC DATA

Max. Average Pressure (MAP):	53,000 CUP, Piezo not listed for this cartridge - SAAMI	Test Barrel Length:	24 inch
Rifling Twist Rate:	1 turn in 9 inch		
Muzzle velocities of factory loaded ammunition	Bullet Wgt.		Muzzle velocity
	120-grain		3,210 fps

Muzzle velocity will decrease approximately 30 fps per inch for barrels less than 24 inches.

HISTORICAL NOTES

- In 1965-66 Remington introduced two innovative, new magnum rifle cartridges: the 350 Remington Magnum and the 6.5mm Remington Magnum. Both cartridges had case lengths reduced to 2.170 inch to allow them to fit in Remington's new Models 600 & 660 short action carbines.

- It was a good idea spoiled by a bad choice of calibers. American sportsmen had not taken to the 6.5mm caliber and Remington's new 6.5 Remington Magnum proved no exception. In addition, the short barrel of the Models 600 & 660 carbines did not allow the full benefit of the 6.5 Magnum cartridge.
- After a slow start, the 6.5mm Remington Magnum quickly faded away. Today, no new firearms are being made in this caliber. Remington and Nosler are the only two manufacturers of loaded ammunition in 6.5mm Remington Magnum.

BALLISTIC NOTES

- The 6.5mm Remington Magnum cartridge is capable of driving a 120-grain bullet at muzzle velocities of 100-200 fps higher than either the 6.5x55mm SE or 260 Remington cartridges.
- That said, the 6.5mm Remington Magnum's short case with its reduced volume is no match for the 264 Winchester Magnum with its long, large volume case.
- To gain the full ballistic performance of the 6.5mm Remington Magnum, it should be fired from barrels of 24 inches or longer.

HANDLOADING NOTES

- Although Remington and Nosler load only the 120-grain bullet, the 6.5mm Rem. Mag. can be handloaded to very good effect with Speer 140-grain Spitzer SP Hot-Cor® bullets.
- Speer TNT® bullets are not designed to be used at the high muzzle velocities of this cartridge.
- As a magnum cartridge, the 6.5mm Remington Magnum works best with slow burning propellants.
- After 3-4 reloads, inspect belted magnum case heads for evidence of separation due to case stretching. Discard any that show evidence of insipient cracking.

SAFETY NOTES

SPEER 140-grain Spitzer SP Hot-Cor @ a muzzle velocity of 2,765 fps:
- Maximum vertical altitude @ 90° elevation is 11,988 feet.
- Maximum horizontal distance to first impact with ground @ 36° elevation is 5,611 yards.

140 GRAINS

DIAMETER	SECTIONAL DENSITY
.264"	0.287

6.5mm Spitzer SP Hot-Cor®	
Ballistic Coefficient	0.498
COAL Tested	2.790"
Speer Part No.	1441

			Starting Charge		Maximum Charge	
Propellant	Case	Primer	Weight (grains)	Muzzle Velocity (feet/sec)	Weight (grains)	Muzzle Velocity (feet/sec)
Accurate 3100	Remington	CCI 250	48.0	2587	52.0 C	2765
IMR 4831	Remington	CCI 250	48.0	2547	52.0 C	2755
IMR 4350	Remington	CCI 250	46.0	2543	50.0 C	2750
Hodgdon H380	Remington	CCI 250	42.0	2396	46.0	2634
Hodgdon H414	Remington	CCI 250	43.0	2373	47.0	2628
IMR 4320	Remington	CCI 250	39.0	2324	43.0	2580
IMR 4895	Remington	CCI 250	41.0	2321	45.0	2562
IMR 4198 (reduced load)	Remington	CCI 250	20.5	1617	22.5	1792

WARNING! *Maximum loads should be used with CAUTION • C = Compressed Load*

264 WINCHESTER MAGNUM

Parent Cartridge:	375 H&H Magnum
Country of Origin:	USA
Year of Introduction:	1959
Designer(s):	Winchester
Governing Body:	SAAMI/CIP

CARTRIDGE CASE DATA

Case Type:	Rimless, belted, bottleneck		
Average Case Capacity:	72.1 grains H$_2$O	Max. Cartridge OAL	3.340 inch
Max. Case Length:	2.500 inch	Primer:	Large Rifle
Case Trim to Length:	2.490 inch	RCBS Shell holder:	# 4
Current Manufacturers:	Winchester, Remington, Hornady, Nosler, Prvi Partizan		

BALLISTIC DATA

Max. Average Pressure (MAP):	64,000 psi, 54,000 CUP - SAAMI	Test Barrel Length:	24 inch
Rifling Twist Rate:	1 turn in 9 inch		
Muzzle velocities of factory loaded ammunition	Bullet Wgt.		Muzzle velocity
	120-grain		3,250 fps
	140-grain		3,030 fps
	Muzzle velocity will decrease approximately 30 fps per inch for barrels less than 24 inches.		

HISTORICAL NOTES

- In 1956, Winchester introduced their new 458 Winchester Magnum cartridge. It was the first in a new line of short, belted magnum cartridges that would fit in standard actions.

- The 264 Win. Magnum and 338 Win. Magnum followed in 1958, and the 300 Win. Magnum completed the line in 1963. The 264 Winchester Magnum was the smallest of the group.

- American sportsmen have never taken to the 6.5mm caliber and the 264 Winchester Magnum proved no exception.
- In addition, the 264 Win. Mag. earned a bad reputation for quickly wearing out barrels, which did nothing to help sales.
- With these two strikes against it, the 264 Winchester Magnum never reached the popularity of its three brethren, all of which continue to be best sellers almost 60 years later.
- Today, no new guns are being made in 264 Win. Mag. caliber.
- Most ammunition manufacturers who still list this cartridge offer only a 140-grain bullet.
- By all odds, the 264 Winchester Magnum cartridge is well along on its way to fully obsolete status.

BALLISTIC NOTES

- The 264 Winchester Magnum cartridge is capable of driving a 120-grain bullet at muzzle velocities in the order of 3,235 fps which is almost 300 fps higher than both the 260 Remington and the 6.5mm Rem. Mag.
- To gain the full ballistic performance of the 264 Win. Mag. cartridge, it should be fired from barrels of 24 inches or longer.
- Due to the high muzzle velocities of the 264 Win. Mag., barrel wear can be a problem. Frequent cleaning and inspection is recommended. If the throat of the barrel is badly worn, the barrel should be replaced.

HANDLOADING NOTES

- New, unprimed brass for reloading in this caliber is offered by Winchester, Nosler, Hornady, and Prvi Partizan. Remington offers loaded ammunition, but not brass for reloading.
- Speer TNT® HP bullets are not designed to be used at the high muzzle velocities of this cartridge.
- The 264 Winchester Magnum works best with slow burning propellants.
- After 3 or 4 reloads, inspect belted magnum case heads for evidence of separation due to case stretching. Discard any that show evidence of cracking.

SAFETY NOTES

SPEER 140-grain Spitzer SP Hot-Cor® @ a muzzle velocity of 3,040 fps:
- Maximum vertical altitude @ 90° elevation is 12,504 feet.
- Maximum horizontal distance to first impact with ground @ 35° elevation is 5,794 yards.

140 GRAINS

DIAMETER	SECTIONAL DENSITY
.264"	0.287

264 WINCHESTER MAGNUM

6.5mm Spitzer SP Hot-Cor®	
Ballistic Coefficient	0.498
COAL Tested	3.320"
Speer Part No.	1441

			Starting Charge		Maximum Charge	
Propellant	Case	Primer	Weight (grains)	Muzzle Velocity (feet/sec)	Weight (grains)	Muzzle Velocity (feet/sec)
Hodgdon US 869	Hornady	CCI 250	67.6	2795	74.4	3050
Alliant Reloder 33	Hornady	CCI 250	61.7	2739	68.2	2989
Alliant Reloder 50	Hornady	CCI 250	62.8	2773	69.3	2986
Hodgdon Retumbo	Hornady	CCI 250	56.4	2735	62.7	2966
Alliant Reloder 25	Hornady	CCI 250	54.2	2709	60.1	2932
Ramshot Magnum	Hornady	CCI 250	56.8	2708	62.5	2929
IMR 7828	Hornady	CCI 250	52.4	2678	58.2	2916
Alliant Reloder 26	Hornady	CCI 250	52.5	2699	58.1	2912
Vihtavuori N560	Hornady	CCI 250	51.6	2680	57.3	2911
Alliant Reloder 22	Hornady	CCI 250	50.6	2695	55.8	2890
IMR 7977	Hornady	CCI 250	55.9	2628	62.1	2890
Alliant Reloder 23	Hornady	CCI 250	52.4	2698	56.9	2877
Alliant Reloder 19	Hornady	CCI 250	49.2	2655	54.6	2863
Alliant Power Pro 4000-MR	Hornady	CCI 250	49.6	2631	55.0	2857

WARNING! Maximum loads should be used with CAUTION • C = Compressed Load

6.8mm REMINGTON SPC

Alternate Names:	6.8 Special Purpose Cartridge, 6.8 x43mm
Parent Cartridge:	30 Remington
Country of Origin:	USA
Year of Introduction:	2004
Designer(s):	US SOCOM & Remington
Governing Body:	SAAMI/CIP

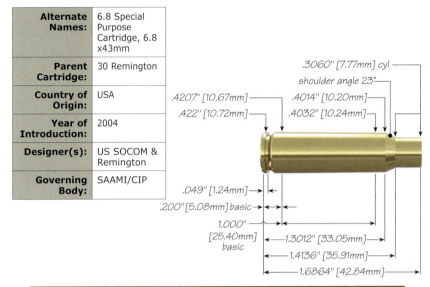

CARTRIDGE CASE DATA

Case Type:	Rimless, bottleneck		
Average Case Capacity:	34.8 grains H₂O	**Max. Cartridge OAL**	2.260 inch
Max. Case Length:	1.686 inch	**Primer:**	Large Rifle (Remington), all others Small Rifle
Case Trim to Length:	1.676 inch	**RCBS Shell holder:**	# 19
Current Manufacturers:	Remington, Hornady, Federal, Silver State Armory		

BALLISTIC DATA

Max. Average Pressure (MAP):	55,000 psi SAAMI	**Test Barrel Length:**	16 inches
Rifling Twist Rate:	1 turn in 11 inch (1/7, 1/9.5, 1/10, 1/12 alternate)		
Muzzle velocities of factory loaded ammunition	**Bullet Wgt.**		**Muzzle velocity**
	85-grain		2,950 fps
	90-grain		2,990 fps
	110-grain		2,570 fps
	115-grain		2,650 fps
	Muzzle velocity will decrease approximately 20 fps per inch for barrels less than 24 inches.		

HISTORICAL NOTES

- The 6.8 Special Purpose Cartridge (SPC) was developed by Remington in cooperation with the U.S. Special Operations Command (SOCOM) and the

U.S. Army Marksmanship Training Unit.

Interesting Fact

The 6.8mm Remington SPC is an example of the new breed of "semi-military" cartridges that enjoyed limited production by commercial manufacturers (NOT government manufacturing facilities) for specialized government agencies, but were never standardized or officially adopted for general U.S. military use. Examples include: 4.6x30mm H&K, 5.7x28mm FN, 300 AAC Blackout, 6.5 Grendel, and 458 SOCOM.

- The intent of the new cartridge was to improve the long range ballistic performance and lethality of the existing M4 military carbine with the fewest possible modifications to the firearm. The cartridge's performance met the expectations of specialized government agencies. The 6.8mm 115-grain FMJ bullet reached a muzzle velocity of 2,625 fps with a muzzle energy of 1,759 ft-lbs.
- To meet these requirements, Remington reached back in history to 1906 and the long-obsolete 30 Remington cartridge which was essentially a rimless version of the venerable 30-30 Winchester cartridge. This elderly cartridge served as the basis for development of the new 6.8mm SPC.
- The tentative designation for the new military cartridge was 6.8x43mm if it had been adopted for general U.S. military service. It was not.
- However, Remington recognized the advantages of such a cartridge for North American deer hunters using Modern Sporting Rifles (MSRs).
- Remington introduced the new 6.8mm Remington SPC cartridge to the commercial market where it has been a sales success.
- The 6.8mm Remington SPC is the first cartridge for Modern Sporting Rifles (MSRs-AR15 platform) that makes such rifles fully capable for hunting small deer species.

TECHNICAL NOTES

- To increase powder capacity, the 30 Remington case was blown out and the neck resized to hold .277 inch diameter bullets.
- Maximum overall loaded length of the 6.8 SPC cartridge is 2.260 inches which is very close to the current 5.56x45mm NATO military cartridge. This allows the 6.8mm SPC to fit in and feed from existing M16 magazines.
- The maximum case length of the 223 Remington cartridge is 1.760 inches. To accommodate the larger diameter bullet, the maximum case length of the 6.8mm SPC is .074 inches shorter.
- The head diameter of the obsolete 30 Remington cartridge is .045 inch larger than the head diameter of the 5.56x45mm NATO cartridge allowing it to fit the bolt face of M16 rifles with only minor modifications.

HANDLOADING NOTES

- Note that original 6.8mm SPC cases from Remington were made with Large Rifle primer pockets, they are now becoming less common. All commercial ammunition in 6.8mm SPC caliber is now made with Small Rifle primer pockets, some of the reloading data presented was developed with these cases. You will have to full length resize fired cases with a small base die if your handloads are fired in a semi-automatic MSR rifle.
- Expect to discard a high number of fired cases damaged during ejection in MSRs. New, empty brass for reloading is offered by Remington and Hornady.

- The small case capacity of the 6.8mm SPC cartridge works best with medium burning powders due to the bullet weights used.
- Forget trying to form 6.8mm SPC cartridge cases from 30 Remington cases. Cartridges/cases in 30 Remington are now expensive collector's items.

SAFETY NOTES

SPEER 130-grain Spitzer BTSP @ a muzzle velocity of 2,547 fps:
- Maximum vertical altitude @ 90° elevation is 13,275 feet.
- Maximum horizontal distance to first impact with ground @ 36° elevation is 6,219 yards.

90 GRAINS

DIAMETER	SECTIONAL DENSITY
.277"	0.168

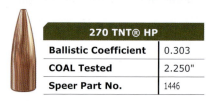

270 TNT® HP

Ballistic Coefficient	0.303
COAL Tested	2.250"
Speer Part No.	1446

			Starting Charge		Maximum Charge	
Propellant	Case	Primer	Weight (grains)	Muzzle Velocity (feet/sec)	Weight (grains)	Muzzle Velocity (feet/sec)
Alliant Power Pro 1200-R	Federal	CCI 400	30.3	3045	31.6	3170
Alliant Power Pro Varmint	Federal	CCI 400	33.9 C	3008	35.6 C	3170
Accurate 2230	Remington	CCI 200	31.5	2942	33.5 C	3067
Hodgdon H322	Remington	CCI 200	29.0	2824	31.0 C	2995
Hodgdon H335	Remington	CCI 200	33.0	2852	35.0 C	2995
Alliant Reloder 10X	Remington	CCI 200	27.5	2822	29.5	2991
Alliant Reloder 7	Remington	CCI 200	25.5	2782	27.5	2983
Ramshot X-Terminator	Remington	CCI 200	31.5	2833	33.5 C	2968
Accurate 2015	Remington	CCI 200	28.5	2746	30.5 C	2924
IMR 4198	Remington	CCI 200	23.5	2733	25.5	2915
Accurate 1680	Remington	CCI 200	25.0	2740	27.0	2906
Vihtavuori N120	Remington	CCI 200	23.5	2717	25.5	2905
Accurate 5744	Remington	CCI 200	21.5	2597	23.5	2787
IMR 4227	Remington	CCI 200	20.0	2579	22.0	2749

WARNING! *Maximum loads should be used with* CAUTION • C = Compressed Load

GOLD DOT RIFLE

90 GRAINS

DIAMETER	SECTIONAL DENSITY
.277"	0.168

270 GD	
Ballistic Coefficient	0.253
COAL Tested	2.260"
Speer Part No.	27790GDB

			Starting Charge		Maximum Charge	
Propellant	Case	Primer	Weight (grains)	Muzzle Velocity (feet/sec)	Weight (grains)	Muzzle Velocity (feet/sec)
Hodgdon CFE 223	Federal	GM205MAR	33.5	2873	37.2 C	3144
Accurate 2200	Federal	GM205MAR	27.3	2786	30.3	3053
Alliant Power Pro 1200-R	Federal	GM205MAR	27.4	2775	30.3	3025
Accurate 2230	Federal	GM205MAR	29.7	2822	32.6	3023
Hodgdon H335	Federal	GM205MAR	29.6	2767	32.8	3010
Alliant Reloder 10X	Federal	GM205MAR	26.4	2688	29.3	2976
Ramshot X-Terminator	Federal	GM205MAR	29.4	2777	32.6 C	2973
Hodgdon BENCHMARK	Federal	GM205MAR	28.5	2694	31.6	2972
Alliant Reloder 7	Federal	GM205MAR	25.2	2658	28.0	2899
Vihtavuori N120	Federal	GM205MAR	22.1	2599	24.7	2834

WARNING! *Maximum loads should be used with CAUTION* • *C = Compressed Load*

100 GRAINS

DIAMETER	SECTIONAL DENSITY
.277"	0.186

270 HP

Ballistic Coefficient	0.201
COAL Tested	2.250"
Speer Part No.	1447

			Starting Charge		Maximum Charge	
Propellant	Case	Primer	Weight (grains)	Muzzle Velocity (feet/sec)	Weight (grains)	Muzzle Velocity (feet/sec)
Alliant Power Pro Varmint	Federal	GM205MAR	30.6	2712	33.9 C	2982
Alliant Power Pro 1200-R	Federal	GM205MAR	27.1	2711	30.1	2947
Ramshot X-Terminator	Remington	CCI 200	31.0	2653	33.0	2815
Alliant Reloder 10X	Remington	CCI 200	26.5	2607	28.5 C	2791
Hodgdon H322	Remington	CCI 200	27.5	2592	29.5 C	2778
Hodgdon H335	Remington	CCI 200	31.0	2590	33.0 C	2739
Hodgdon BL-C(2)	Remington	CCI 200	32.0	2614	34.0 C	2727
IMR 4198	Remington	CCI 200	23.0	2566	25.0	2718
Alliant Reloder 7	Remington	CCI 200	24.0	2524	26.0	2715
Accurate 1680	Remington	CCI 200	24.0	2517	26.0	2702
Vihtavuori N120	Remington	CCI 200	22.5	2504	24.5	2680
Accurate 2015	Remington	CCI 200	27.0	2504	29.0 C	2677
Accurate 5744	Remington	CCI 200	21.0	2408	23.0	2582

WARNING! *Maximum loads should be used with CAUTION • C = Compressed Load*

GOLD DOT RIFLE

115 GRAINS	DIAMETER	SECTIONAL DENSITY
	.277"	0.214

270 GD	
Ballistic Coefficient	0.401
COAL Tested	2.260"
Speer Part No.	277115GDB

270 TMJ®	
Ballistic Coefficient	0.401
COAL Tested	2.260"
Speer Part No.	227115TMJ

Propellant	Case	Primer	Starting Charge		Maximum Charge	
			Weight (grains)	Muzzle Velocity (feet/sec)	Weight (grains)	Muzzle Velocity (feet/sec)
Hodgdon CFE 223	Federal	GM205MAR	30.3	2534	33.6 C	2771
Accurate 2230	Federal	GM205MAR	27.0	2493	30.0	2705
Alliant Power Pro Varmint	Federal	GM205MAR	28.0	2482	31.1 C	2699
Accurate 2200	Federal	GM205MAR	24.7	2441	27.4	2688
Hodgdon H335	Federal	GM205MAR	26.7	2429	29.7	2671
Alliant Power Pro 1200-R	Federal	GM205MAR	24.9	2444	27.6	2666
Ramshot X-Terminator	Federal	GM205MAR	26.4	2427	29.2	2637
Hodgdon BENCHMARK	Federal	GM205MAR	25.8	2380	28.7	2628
Alliant Reloder 10X	Federal	GM205MAR	24.0	2362	26.7	2626
Alliant Reloder 7	Federal	GM205MAR	22.9	2357	25.3	2573
Vihtavuori N130	Federal	GM205MAR	22.9	2353	25.3	2554

WARNING! *Maximum loads should be used with CAUTION • C = Compressed Load*

130 GRAINS

DIAMETER	SECTIONAL DENSITY
.277"	0.242

270 Spitzer BTSP	
Ballistic Coefficient	0.412
COAL Tested	2.250"
Speer Part No.	1458

270 Spitzer SP Hot-Cor®	
Ballistic Coefficient	0.383
COAL Tested	2.250"
Speer Part No.	1459

			Starting Charge		Maximum Charge	
Propellant	Case	Primer	Weight (grains)	Muzzle Velocity (feet/sec)	Weight (grains)	Muzzle Velocity (feet/sec)
Alliant AR-Comp	Federal	CCI 400	27.8	2466	29.8 C	2620
Alliant Power Pro Varmint	Federal	CCI 400	29.3	2483	31.0 C	2607
Winchester 748	Remington	CCI 200	29.0	2408	31.0 C	2547
Ramshot X-Terminator	Remington	CCI 200	27.0	2307	29.0 C	2450
Hodgdon H335	Remington	CCI 200	27.5	2261	29.5 C	2446
Alliant Reloder 10X	Remington	CCI 200	23.5	2276	25.5 C	2431
Hodgdon BL-C(2)	Remington	CCI 200	28.0	2245	30.0 C	2415
Ramshot TAC	Remington	CCI 200	26.5	2271	28.5	2399
Hodgdon Benchmark	Remington	CCI 200	25.0	2217	27.0 C	2391
Hodgdon H322	Remington	CCI 200	24.5	2223	26.5	2385
Accurate 2015	Remington	CCI 200	24.0	2165	26.0	2360
Vihtavuori N130	Remington	CCI 200	22.5	2185	24.5	2345
IMR 4198	Remington	CCI 200	20.0	2159	22.0	2317
Accurate 1680	Remington	CCI 200	20.5	2124	22.5	2262

WARNING! Maximum loads should be used with CAUTION • C = Compressed Load

270 WINCHESTER SHORT MAGNUM

Alternate Names:	270 WSM
Parent Cartridge:	300 Winchester Short Magnum
Country of Origin:	USA
Year of Introduction:	2002
Designer(s):	Winchester
Governing Body:	SAAMI

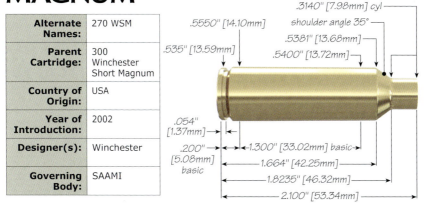

CARTRIDGE CASE DATA

Case Type:	Rimless, bottleneck
Average Case Capacity:	78.9 grains H₂O
Max. Cartridge OAL:	2.860 inch
Max. Case Length:	2.100 inch
Primer:	Large Rifle
Case Trim to Length:	2.090 inch
RCBS Shell holder:	# 43
Current Manufacturers:	Winchester, Federal, Nosler, Remington, Norma, Barnes

BALLISTIC DATA

Max. Average Pressure (MAP):	65,000 psi, CUP not established for this round - SAAMI
Test Barrel Length:	24 inch
Rifling Twist Rate:	1 turn in 10 inch

Muzzle velocities of factory loaded ammunition	Bullet Wgt.	Muzzle velocity
	130-grain	3,275 fps
	140-grain	3,200 fps
	150-grain	3,150 fps

Muzzle velocity will decrease approximately 30 fps per inch for barrels less than 24 inches.

HISTORICAL NOTES

- In 2001, Winchester introduced the new 300 Winchester Short Magnum (WSM) cartridge, the first in the company's series of short, beltless magnum cartridges designed for use in short-action rifles.
- The 270 WSM and the 7mm WSM followed in 2002 and the 325 WSM completed the series in 2004.

- Not wanting to be left behind in developing a trend, competing domestic and foreign ammunition manufacturers have added some of these new Winchester Short Magnum cartridges to their product lines. Copying is a compliment and availability is a key component of success in the marketplace.
- Remington introduced their own, competing line of "Short Action Ultra Magnum" cartridges of similar, but not identical or interchangeable dimensions, in 2002.
- Eager to ride a trending new market, many firearm manufacturers have recently introduced some WSM calibers to existing models of their short-action rifles.
- With their new 270 WSM, Winchester seeks to duplicate the market success of their venerable 270 Winchester cartridge.
- While the marketing battle of the short magnum cartridges continues to develop, it is too early to predict winners or losers.

BALLISTIC NOTES

- Case capacity and volume of the 270 WSM is a significant 15% greater than the venerable 270 Winchester, but about 7% less than the 270 Weatherby Magnum.
- However, with modern propellants and a 65,000 psi MAP, the 270 WSM cartridge can be handloaded to ballistic performance levels similar to and in some cases higher than the 270 Weatherby Magnum.
- Reloading data indicates the 270 WSM cartridge is a slightly more efficient design than the 270 Weatherby Magnum cartridge with some propellants.
  - For example, loading the 270 Weatherby Magnum with a Speer 150-grain bullet and 68 grains of Reloder® 22 yields a muzzle velocity of 3,215 fps.
  - Loading the 270 WSM with any of the same bullets and 66-grains of Reloder 22 yields a muzzle velocity of 3,230 fps.

TECHNICAL NOTES

- All Winchester Short Magnum cartridges share the same 2.100 inch case length, .555 inch head diameter and 35° shoulder angle.
- The one turn in 10 inch rifling twist rate is optimized for long, heavy bullets over 130-150 grains.

HANDLOADING NOTES

- In addition to the manufacturers of loaded ammunition listed above, Federal, Winchester, Remington, and Norma offer new, empty, unprimed brass cartridge cases for reloading.
- The heavy construction of 270 WSM cartridge cases can cause problems with full length resizing. For this reason neck sizing is recommended if you are using the reloaded cartridge in the same bolt-action rifle. Hunting loads should be full length sized to avoid issues in the field.
- You can reduce sizing effort by thoroughly cleaning and lubricating cases before sizing.
- Do not use bullets under 100-grains for hunting deer, even then expect major tissue damage at high velocities.
- The 270 WSM cartridge prefers slow burning propellants (except with 100-grain bullets).

SAFETY NOTES

SPEER 150-grain Spitzer BTSP @ a muzzle velocity of 3,060 fps:
- Maximum vertical altitude @ 90° elevation is 12,387 feet.
- Maximum horizontal distance to first impact with ground @ 37° elevation is 5,730 yards.

100 GRAINS

DIAMETER	SECTIONAL DENSITY
.277"	0.186

270 HP

Ballistic Coefficient	0.201
COAL Tested	2.730"
Speer Part No.	1447

Propellant	Case	Primer	Starting Charge		Maximum Charge	
			Weight (grains)	Muzzle Velocity (feet/sec)	Weight (grains)	Muzzle Velocity (feet/sec)
IMR 4064	Winchester	CCI 200	58.0	3451	62.0	3645
IMR 4350	Winchester	CCI 200	66.0	3426	70.0	3637
Alliant Reloder 16	Federal	Federal 215	60.4	3207	67.0	3614
Hodgdon Varget	Winchester	CCI 200	57.0	3433	61.0	3613
IMR 4320	Winchester	CCI 200	58.0	3381	62.0	3611
Alliant Reloder 17	Federal	Federal 215	59.8	3179	66.2	3606
IMR 4895	Winchester	CCI 200	57.0	3387	61.0	3600
Alliant Reloder 15	Winchester	CCI 200	58.0	3373	62.0	3564
Alliant Power Pro 2000-MR	Federal	Federal 215	56.0	3229	62.0	3517
Alliant Power Pro Varmint	Federal	Federal 215	52.2	3287	56.4	3457
Hodgdon CFE 223	Federal	Federal 215	52.9	3217	58.4	3455
Alliant AR-Comp	Federal	Federal 215	49.6	3264	54.2	3454
IMR 8208 XBR	Federal	Federal 215	47.3	3189	52.4	3432
Ramshot TAC	Federal	Federal 215	49.9	3260	53.9	3409
Accurate 5744 (reduced load)	Winchester	CCI 200	25.0	2010	26.0	2075

WARNING! *Maximum loads should be used with CAUTION • C = Compressed Load*

130 GRAINS

DIAMETER	SECTIONAL DENSITY
.277"	0.242

270 Spitzer BTSP	
Ballistic Coefficient	0.412
COAL Tested	2.250"
Speer Part No.	1458

270 Spitzer SP Hot-Cor®	
Ballistic Coefficient	0.383
COAL Tested	2.250"
Speer Part No.	1459

270 Grand Slam® SP	
Ballistic Coefficient	0.332
COAL Tested	2.670"
Speer Part No.	1465

Propellant	Case	Primer	Starting Charge Weight (grains)	Starting Charge Muzzle Velocity (feet/sec)	Maximum Charge Weight (grains)	Maximum Charge Muzzle Velocity (feet/sec)
Alliant Reloder 26	Federal	Federal 215	61.5	2928	68.1	3289
IMR 7828	Winchester	CCI 200	62.0	3105	66.0	3250
Alliant Reloder 19	Winchester	CCI 200	62.0	3097	66.0	3241
Alliant Reloder 23	Federal	Federal 215	60.1	2955	66.1 C	3235
Alliant Power Pro 4000-MR	Federal	Federal 215	57.9	2935	63.9	3233
Alliant Reloder 22	Winchester	CCI 200	62.0	3096	66.0	3228
IMR 4831	Winchester	CCI 200	58.0	3067	62.0	3226
Alliant Reloder 16	Federal	Federal 215	56.5	2949	62.5	3224
Alliant Reloder 17	Federal	Federal 215	55.4	2996	61.4	3223
Hodgdon H1000	Federal	Federal 215	65.0	2964	71.8 C	3219
Accurate 3100	Winchester	CCI 200	62.0	3039	66.0	3213
IMR 4350	Winchester	CCI 200	56.0	3026	60.0	3183
Hodgdon H4831SC	Winchester	CCI 200	59.0	3035	63.0	3173
Ramshot Hunter	Federal	Federal 215	57.3	2916	63.3	3168
Hodgdon H4350	Winchester	CCI 200	54.0	3013	58.0	3163
Vihtavuori N160	Federal	Federal 215	58.1	2781	64.1	3120
Accurate 5744 (reduced load)	Winchester	CCI 200	25.0	1940	27.0	2048

WARNING! Maximum loads should be used with CAUTION • C = Compressed Load

150 GRAINS

DIAMETER	SECTIONAL DENSITY
.277"	0.279

270 Spitzer BTSP
Ballistic Coefficient	0.489
COAL Tested	2.700"
Speer Part No.	1604

270 Spitzer SP Hot-Cor®
Ballistic Coefficient	0.455
COAL Tested	2.670"
Speer Part No.	1605

270 Grand Slam® SP
Ballistic Coefficient	0.378
COAL Tested	2.700"
Speer Part No.	1608

Propellant	Case	Primer	Starting Charge Weight (grains)	Starting Charge Muzzle Velocity (feet/sec)	Maximum Charge Weight (grains)	Maximum Charge Muzzle Velocity (feet/sec)
Alliant Reloder 26	Federal	Federal 215	58.3	2787	64.9 C	3093
Ramshot Magnum	Federal	Federal 215	63.6	2813	69.7 C	3093
Alliant Reloder 25	Winchester	CCI 200	60.0	2882	64.0	3058
Alliant Power Pro 4000-MR	Federal	Federal 215	55.1	2768	61.1 C	3041
Alliant Reloder 23	Federal	Federal 215	57.0	2773	63.1 C	3037
Hodgdon H1000	Federal	Federal 215	61.2	2824	67.8 C	3037
IMR 7828	Winchester	CCI 200	58.0	2796	62.0	3011
Alliant Reloder 22	Winchester	CCI 200	57.0	2839	61.0	3009
Vihtavuori N165	Federal	Federal 215	60.2	2682	66.9 C	3007
Alliant Reloder 17	Federal	Federal 215	51.1	2748	56.5	2994
Alliant Reloder 19	Winchester	CCI 200	56.0	2831	60.0	2990
IMR 4831	Winchester	CCI 200	54.0	2774	58.0	2959
Hodgdon H4831SC	Winchester	CCI 200	56.0	2776	60.0	2959
IMR 4350	Winchester	CCI 200	51.0	2757	55.0	2930
Accurate 3100	Winchester	CCI 200	56.0	2796	60.0	2848

WARNING! Maximum loads should be used with CAUTION • C = Compressed Load

270 WINCHESTER

Alternate Names:	6.8x64mm
Parent Cartridge:	30-06 Springfield
Country of Origin:	USA
Year of Introduction:	1925
Designer(s):	Winchester
Governing Body:	SAAMI/CIP

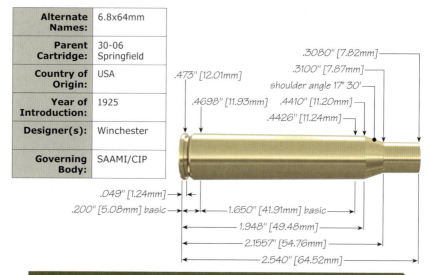

CARTRIDGE CASE DATA

Case Type:	Rimless, bottleneck
Average Case Capacity:	67.0 grains H$_2$O
Max. Cartridge OAL:	3.340 inch
Max. Case Length:	2.540 inch
Primer:	Large Rifle
Case Trim to Length:	2.530 inch
RCBS Shell holder:	# 3
Current Manufacturers:	Winchester, Federal, Remington, Hornady, Nosler, Sellier & Bellot, RUAG (RWS), Fiocci, Black Hills, Norma, and Sako

BALLISTIC DATA

Max. Average Pressure (MAP):	65,000 psi, 52,000 CUP - SAAMI
Test Barrel Length:	24 inch
Rifling Twist Rate:	1 turn in 10 inch

Muzzle velocities of factory loaded ammunition

Bullet Wgt.	Muzzle velocity
90-grain	3,603 fps
130-grain	2,702 fps
140-grain	2,916 fps
150-grain	2,850 fps

Muzzle velocity will decrease approximately 20 fps per inch for barrels less than 24 inches.

HISTORICAL NOTES

- In 1925, Winchester introduced a new, high velocity hunting cartridge based on the 30-06 Springfield cartridge case necked down to accept .277 inch diameter bullets. It was called the 270 Winchester.

- The new cartridge was loaded with a 130-grain bullet at a then amazing muzzle velocity of 3,060 fps.
- The 270 Winchester with its odd .277 inch diameter bullet caused a sensation, created a legend, and started an argument that continues to this day. Namely, which is better: lightweight bullets at high velocities or heavier bullets at "standard" velocities?
- The 270 Winchester quickly became a long range favorite of deer and antelope hunters for its flat trajectory, high striking energy and moderate recoil.
- For over 90 years, the 270 Winchester cartridge has remained in the top ten most popular sporting cartridges sold in the North American market.
- The 270 Winchester remained the ballistic king of the 27 caliber cartridges until the 270 Weatherby Magnum was developed in 1943.
- The 270 Winchester with its .277 inch diameter bullet never caught on with European hunters who did not see a yawning ballistic gap between the .264 inch/6.5mm and .284 inch/7mm calibers.
- Today, every major domestic and foreign manufacturer of sporting ammunition offers the 270 Winchester.

BALLISTIC NOTES

- Although the 270 Winchester cartridge is not a magnum, it is capable of delivering near-magnum ballistics using 130-grain bullets. The 270 Winchester is at its ballistic best in this weight.
- At 300 yards the 270 caliber 130-grain bullet strikes with 20% more energy than a 125-grain bullet fired from a 30-06 Springfield with the bonus of a flatter trajectory and shorter time of flight. These figures define the enduring popularity of the 270 Winchester cartridge.
- Although the new breed of 270 Short Magnum cartridges may challenge the venerable 270 Winchester for market share, they are not likely to unseat it in the hearts of American sportsmen in the foreseeable future.

TECHNICAL NOTES

- Case capacity of the 270 Winchester is the same as 30-06 Springfield. The 270 Winchester cartridge dimensions are designed to fit firearms originally designed for the 30-06 Springfield cartridge with a minimum number of changes.
- The 270 Winchester is intended to be a deer, antelope, and medium game cartridge. However, by handloading lightweight bullets the 270 Winchester can serve as a very good varmint and predator cartridge. If you read Jack O'Connor, years ago, he felt it was suitable for everything from butterflies to the largest North American game.
- The one in 10 inch rifling twist rate is optimized for long heavy bullets from 130-150 grains.

HANDLOADING NOTES

- In addition to the manufacturers of loaded ammunition listed above, Winchester, Remington, Federal, Norma, Hornady, Sako, Lapua, Prvi Partizan and Sellier & Bellot offer new, empty, unprimed brass cartridge cases in 270 Winchester caliber for reloading.
- As most 270 Winchester cartridges will be fired in bolt-action rifles, neck sizing is recommended to maximize case life. We recommend full length sizing for hunting loads.

- Do not use bullets under 130-grains for hunting deer.
- The 270 Winchester cartridge prefers slow burning propellants.
- Handloaders have the option of using lightweight bullets of 90-100 grains not offered by factories to develop high velocity loads for predator and varmint hunting.
- To improve long range ballistic performance or gain an extra edge at shorter ranges, handloaders have the option of using Speer spitzer boat tail soft point bullets in 130 or 150-grain. Boat tail bullets offer higher striking energy, flatter trajectory, and less wind drift than flat base bullets at all ranges.

SAFETY NOTES

SPEER 150-grain Spitzer BTSP @ a muzzle velocity of 2,907 fps:
- Maximum vertical altitude @ 90° elevation is 15,924 feet.
- Maximum horizontal distance to first impact with ground @ 38° elevation is 7,406 yards.

90 GRAINS

DIAMETER	SECTIONAL DENSITY
.277"	0.168

270 TNT® HP

Ballistic Coefficient	0.303
COAL Tested	3.170"
Speer Part No.	1446

			Starting Charge		Maximum Charge	
Propellant	Case	Primer	Weight (grains)	Muzzle Velocity (feet/sec)	Weight (grains)	Muzzle Velocity (feet/sec)
Alliant Reloder 16	Federal	Federal 210	56.8	3432	60.8 C	3656
Alliant Reloder 17	Federal	Federal 210	55.1	3330	61.0	3653
Alliant Power Pro 2000-MR	Federal	Federal 210	54.0	3515	56.6	3639
Alliant AR-Comp	Federal	Federal 210	47.8	3351	51.8	3603
Winchester 760	Winchester	CCI 250	53.0	3356	59.0	3579
Hodgdon Varget	Winchester	CCI 200	51.5	3302	55.5	3576
Alliant Reloder 15	Winchester	CCI 200	51.0	3230	55.0	3565
Hodgdon H380	Winchester	CCI 250	55.0	3277	59.0	3512
IMR 4064	Winchester	CCI 200	51.0	3155	55.0	3494
Vihtavuori N140	Winchester	CCI 200	50.0	3143	54.0	3451
Alliant Reloder 19	Winchester	CCI 200	60.0	3090	64.0 C	3398
IMR 4831	Winchester	CCI 250	58.0	3149	62.0 C	3329
Accurate 3100	Winchester	CCI 250	58.0	3039	62.0 C	3264

WARNING! Maximum loads should be used with CAUTION • C = Compressed Load

100 GRAINS

DIAMETER	SECTIONAL DENSITY
.277"	0.186

270 HP	
Ballistic Coefficient	0.201
COAL Tested	3.100"
Speer Part No.	1447

			Starting Charge		Maximum Charge	
Propellant	Case	Primer	Weight (grains)	Muzzle Velocity (feet/sec)	Weight (grains)	Muzzle Velocity (feet/sec)
Alliant Reloder 16	Federal	Federal 210	55.1	3289	60.8 C	3557
Hodgdon Varget	Winchester	CCI 200	51.0	3237	55.0	3497
Alliant Reloder 17	Federal	Federal 210	53.0	3152	58.6	3496
Accurate 4350	Winchester	CCI 200	57.0	3267	61.0 C	3474
Alliant Power Pro 2000-MR	Federal	Federal 210	49.9	3207	54.6	3438
IMR 4350	Winchester	CCI 200	57.0	3182	61.0 C	3414
Alliant AR-Comp	Federal	Federal 210	45.4	3153	50.2	3404
Hodgdon H414	Winchester	CCI 250	55.0	3203	59.0	3404
IMR 8208 XBR	Federal	Federal 210	44.1	3207	48.1	3356
Winchester 760	Winchester	CCI 250	54.0	3162	58.0	3345
IMR 4320	Winchester	CCI 200	49.0	3068	53.0	3343
Alliant Power Pro Varmint	Federal	Federal 210	44.8	3146	48.7	3330
Alliant Reloder 19	Winchester	CCI 200	58.0	3034	62.0 C	3273
Vihtavuori N140	Winchester	CCI 200	47.0	2993	51.0	3272
IMR 4064	Winchester	CCI 200	48.0	2994	52.0	3262
Hodgdon H380	Winchester	CCI 250	51.0	2998	55.0	3249
IMR 4895	Winchester	CCI 200	46.0	3126	50.0	3220
Accurate 3100	Winchester	CCI 250	58.0	2979	62.0 C	3214
IMR SR 4759 (reduced load)	Winchester	CCI 200	16.0	1545	20.0	1923

WARNING! *Maximum loads should be used with CAUTION • C = Compressed Load*

270 WINCHESTER

130 GRAINS

DIAMETER	SECTIONAL DENSITY
.277"	0.242

270 Spitzer BTSP
Ballistic Coefficient	0.412
COAL Tested	3.240"
Speer Part No.	1458

270 Spitzer SP Hot-Cor®
Ballistic Coefficient	0.383
COAL Tested	3.240"
Speer Part No.	1459

270 Grand Slam® SP
Ballistic Coefficient	0.332
COAL Tested	3.240"
Speer Part No.	1465

Propellant	Case	Primer	Starting Charge		Maximum Charge	
			Weight (grains)	Muzzle Velocity (feet/sec)	Weight (grains)	Muzzle Velocity (feet/sec)
Alliant Reloder 26	Federal	Federal 210	54.3	2878	60.3	3171
Hodgdon H1000	Winchester	CCI 250	60.0	2825	64.0	3166
Alliant Reloder 23	Federal	Federal 210	52.9	2854	58.6 C	3113
IMR 7828	Winchester	CCI 250	58.0	2858	62.0	3113
Alliant Reloder 17	Federal	Federal 210	48.7	2836	54.0	3102
Alliant Power Pro 4000-MR	Federal	Federal 210	50.4	2834	55.8	3092
Alliant Reloder 16	Federal	Federal 210	48.3	2843	53.5	3088
Winchester 760	Winchester	CCI 250	50.0	2838	54.0	3052
IMR 4831	Winchester	CCI 200	54.0	2731	58.0	3014
Hodgdon H4350	Winchester	CCI 200	52.0	2767	56.0	2991
Alliant Reloder 22	Winchester	CCI 200	54.0	2722	58.0	2989
Vihtavuori N160	Winchester	CCI 200	51.5	2750	55.5	2971
Hodgdon H414	Winchester	CCI 250	50.0	2753	54.0	2961
IMR 4350	Winchester	CCI 200	51.0	2912	55.0	2948
Alliant Reloder 19	Winchester	CCI 200	53.0	2732	57.0	2944
Accurate 3100	Winchester	CCI 250	52.0	2577	56.0	2860
IMR 4064	Winchester	CCI 200	43.0	2657	47.0	2838
Alliant Reloder 15	Winchester	CCI 200	41.0	2576	45.0	2777
IMR SR 4759 (reduced load)	Winchester	CCI 200	20.0	1651	24.0	2008

WARNING! Maximum loads should be used with CAUTION • C = Compressed Load

150 GRAINS

DIAMETER	SECTIONAL DENSITY
.277"	0.279

270 Spitzer BTSP
Ballistic Coefficient	0.489
COAL Tested	3.270"
Speer Part No.	1604

270 Spitzer SP Hot-Cor®
Ballistic Coefficient	0.455
COAL Tested	3.270"
Speer Part No.	1605

270 Grand Slam® SP
Ballistic Coefficient	0.378
COAL Tested	3.250"
Speer Part No.	1608

			Starting Charge		Maximum Charge	
Propellant	Case	Primer	Weight (grains)	Muzzle Velocity (feet/sec)	Weight (grains)	Muzzle Velocity (feet/sec)
IMR 7828	Winchester	CCI 250	54.0	2727	58.0 C	2948
Alliant Reloder 26	Federal	Federal 210	51.5	2701	56.8	2943
Winchester 760	Winchester	CCI 250	49.0	2665	53.0	2913
Accurate 3100	Winchester	CCI 200	53.0	2675	57.0	2906
Alliant Reloder 23	Federal	Federal 210	49.7	2670	54.7 C	2874
IMR 4831	Winchester	CCI 200	51.0	2636	55.0	2870
Alliant Power Pro 4000-MR	Federal	Federal 210	47.7	2647	52.9	2867
Alliant Reloder 17	Federal	Federal 210	45.9	2637	50.8	2867
Hodgdon H4831SC	Winchester	CCI 200	53.5	2669	57.5	2860
Alliant Reloder 16	Federal	Federal 210	45.5	2631	50.4	2844
Alliant Reloder 22	Winchester	CCI 200	50.0	2590	54.0	2805
Alliant Reloder 19	Winchester	CCI 200	49.0	2593	53.0	2780
IMR 4350	Winchester	CCI 200	48.0	2560	52.0	2761
Hodgdon H414	Winchester	CCI 250	46.0	2513	50.0	2712
Vihtavuori N160	Winchester	CCI 200	47.0	2490	51.0	2702
Hodgdon H4350	Winchester	CCI 200	47.0	2481	51.0	2675
IMR 4064	Winchester	CCI 200	41.0	2477	45.0	2666
IMR SR 4759 (reduced load)	Winchester	CCI 200	22.0	1655	26.0	1966

WARNING! *Maximum loads should be used with CAUTION • C = Compressed Load*

270 WEATHERBY MAGNUM

Parent Cartridge:	300 H&H Magnum
Country of Origin:	USA
Year of Introduction:	1945
Designer(s):	Roy Weatherby
Governing Body:	SAAMI

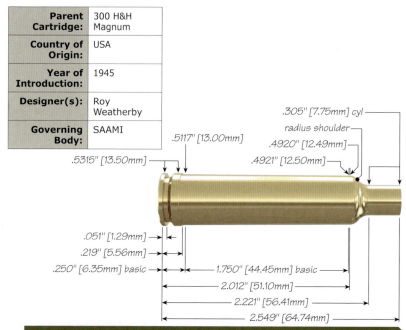

CARTRIDGE CASE DATA			
Case Type:	Rimless, belted, necked with double radii shoulder		
Average Case Capacity:	85.3 grains H$_2$O	Max. Cartridge OAL	3.295 inch
Max. Case Length:	2.549 inch	Primer:	Large Rifle
Case Trim to Length:	2.539 inch	RCBS Shell holder:	# 4
Current Manufacturers:	Weatherby, Norma, and Remington		

BALLISTIC DATA			
Max. Average Pressure (MAP):	62,500 psi, 53,500 CUP - SAAMI	Test Barrel Length:	24 inch
Rifling Twist Rate:	1 turn in 10 inch		
Muzzle velocities of factory loaded ammunition	Bullet Wgt.		Muzzle velocity
	130-grain		3,338 fps
	140-grain		3,242 fps
	150-grain		3,161 fps
	Muzzle velocity will decrease approximately 30 fps per inch for barrels less than 24 inches.		

HISTORICAL NOTES

- When it was introduced in 1943, the 270 Weatherby Magnum cartridge became the king of all 270 caliber ballistics, a throne it continues to occupy to this day.
- The 270 Weatherby Magnum cartridge was one of the first calibers designed by Roy Weatherby incorporating his ballistic concept of the hydraulic shock caused by bullets impacting at high velocities.
- The 270 Weatherby Magnum remains one of the most popular mainstays of the Weatherby Magnum ammunition product line.
- For many years now, all Weatherby magnum ammunition has been manufactured for them by Norma in Sweden.
- Weatherby became a victim of its own success when major domestic manufacturers began making 270 Weatherby Magnum ammunition in the late 1980s thus dividing a relatively small market. By 2000, most of the domestics had dropped the 270 Weatherby Magnum from their product line.
- In 2016, Weatherby announced plans to manufacture their ammunition in the U.S. for the first time.

Interesting Fact

The 270 Weatherby Magnum cartridge was one of the original Weatherby Magnum cartridges introduced when Roy Weatherby opened his commercial business in 1945. It was built as a proprietary Weatherby cartridge until standardized by SAAMI in 1994. The other founding calibers included the 7mm Weatherby Magnum and 300 Weatherby Magnum.

BALLISTIC NOTES

- There can be no doubt about it, the 270 Weatherby Magnum offers ballistic performance exceeding all other 270 caliber cartridges—even the new short magnums.
- Muzzle velocity of the 270 Weatherby Magnum loaded with a 130-grain bullet is 7% higher than the 270 Winchester and slightly higher than the 270 Winchester Short Magnum cartridge.
- To achieve such lofty performance levels, the 270 Weatherby Magnum cartridge has a whopping 30% greater case volume and capacity than the 270 Winchester cartridge.
- The new 270 Winchester Short Magnum also comes up short with 8% less case volume.
- All three cartridges have comparable (62,500 to 65,000 psi) MAP levels for an even comparison.
- The ballistic sweet spot of the 270 Weatherby Magnum cartridge is the 130-grain bullet weight evidenced by the wide variety of bullet types offered in this weight by ammunition manufacturers.

TECHNICAL NOTES

- Like its siblings, the parent cartridge of 270 Weatherby Magnum is based on the venerable 300 H&H Magnum with its body shortened and blown out to increase capacity then necked down to hold .277 inch diameter bullets.

- As with all Weatherby Magnum cartridges, the 270 Weatherby Magnum is a rimless, belted, necked design with radiused shoulder angles.
- As a key family member, the 270 Weatherby Magnum shares its head dimensions and case length with its 257 Weatherby Magnum and 7mm Weatherby Magnum brethren.
- The 270 Weatherby Magnum is intended for hunting medium and large North American game at long ranges under difficult conditions. For this reason, factory loaded ammunition is assembled with 130, 140, and 150-grain bullets only.
- The one in 10 inch rifling twist rate is optimized for long heavy bullets of 130-150 grains. This rifling twist rate is ideal for boat tail bullets for those long range shots.

HANDLOADING NOTES

- Weatherby and Nosler offer loaded ammunition in 270 Weatherby Magnum caliber. However, only Norma offers new, empty brass in this caliber for reloading.
- As with other Weatherby Magnum calibers, 270 Weatherby Magnum cases tend to stretch just in front of the belt. After four to six firings, these cases often separate at the stretch point.
- The heavy construction of 270 Weatherby Magnum cartridge cases can cause problems with full length resizing. For this reason neck sizing is recommended for all uses except hunting.
- If you prefer to full length resize your brass, you can reduce sizing effort by thoroughly cleaning and lubricating cases before sizing.
- The 270 Weatherby Magnum cartridge prefers slow burning propellants ignited by Large Rifle Magnum primers.

SAFETY NOTES

SPEER 150-grain Spitzer BTSP @ a muzzle velocity of 3,028 fps:
- Maximum vertical altitude @ 90° elevation is 16,305 feet.
- Maximum horizontal distance to first impact with ground @ 37° elevation is 7,539 yards.

100 GRAINS

DIAMETER	SECTIONAL DENSITY
.277"	0.186

270 HP	
Ballistic Coefficient	0.201
COAL Tested	3.250"
Speer Part No.	1447

			Starting Charge		Maximum Charge	
Propellant	Case	Primer	Weight (grains)	Muzzle Velocity (feet/sec)	Weight (grains)	Muzzle Velocity (feet/sec)
Alliant Reloder 26	Federal	Federal 215	68.5	3263	75.9	3680
Alliant Reloder 22	Federal	Federal 215	72.0	3423	76.0 C	3627
Alliant Power Pro 4000-MR	Federal	Federal 215	63.6	3296	70.4	3619
Accurate Magpro	Federal	Federal 215	76.0	3451	80.0 C	3618
Alliant Reloder 23	Federal	Federal 215	65.9	3266	72.9	3595
IMR 4831	Federal	Federal 215	67.0	3360	71.0	3575
Alliant Reloder 19	Federal	Federal 215	69.0	3359	73.0	3570
Ramshot Magnum	Federal	Federal 215	77.0	3386	81.0 C	3557
Hodgdon H4831SC	Federal	Federal 215	71.0	3371	75.0	3534
IMR 7828	Federal	Federal 215	72.0	3338	76.0	3531
IMR 7977	Federal	Federal 215	70.5	3201	77.5	3519
Alliant Reloder 25	Federal	Federal 215	73.0	3270	77.0 C	3478
Hodgdon Retumbo	Federal	Federal 215	75.0	3226	77.0 C	3329
Vihtavuori N560	Federal	Federal 215	72.0	3062	76.0	3294

WARNING! *Maximum loads should be used with CAUTION • C = Compressed Load*

130 GRAINS

DIAMETER	SECTIONAL DENSITY
.277"	0.242

270 Spitzer BTSP
Ballistic Coefficient	0.412
COAL Tested	3.250"
Speer Part No.	1458

270 Spitzer SP Hot-Cor®
Ballistic Coefficient	0.383
COAL Tested	3.250"
Speer Part No.	1459

270 Grand Slam® SP
Ballistic Coefficient	0.332
COAL Tested	3.250"
Speer Part No.	1465

Propellant	Case	Primer	Starting Charge		Maximum Charge	
			Weight (grains)	Muzzle Velocity (feet/sec)	Weight (grains)	Muzzle Velocity (feet/sec)
Alliant Reloder 26	Federal	Federal 215	62.8	2951	69.6	3292
Alliant Reloder 25	Federal	Federal 215	68.0	3080	72.0	3267
Ramshot Magnum	Federal	Federal 215	71.0	3079	75.0	3254
Alliant Reloder 23	Federal	Federal 215	60.4	2962	66.8	3241
Alliant Power Pro 4000-MR	Federal	Federal 215	58.0	2965	64.4	3237
Alliant Reloder 33	Federal	Federal 215	76.3	3044	80.0 C	3228
Vihtavuori N560	Federal	Federal 215	65.0	3030	69.0	3222
IMR 7828	Federal	Federal 215	65.0	3054	69.0	3217
Alliant Reloder 22	Federal	Federal 215	64.0	3048	68.0	3214
Hodgdon Retumbo	Federal	Federal 215	69.0	3026	73.0	3209
IMR 7977	Federal	Federal 215	66.6	2890	73.6	3202
Accurate Magpro	Federal	Federal 215	68.0	3014	72.0	3189
IMR 4831	Federal	Federal 215	60.0	3019	64.0	3181
Alliant Reloder 19	Federal	Federal 215	61.0	3040	65.0	3176
Hodgdon H4831SC	Federal	Federal 215	62.0	2980	66.0	3120

WARNING! Maximum loads should be used with CAUTION • C = Compressed Load

150 GRAINS

DIAMETER	SECTIONAL DENSITY
.277"	0.279

270 Spitzer BTSP
Ballistic Coefficient	0.489
COAL Tested	3.250"
Speer Part No.	1604

270 Spitzer SP Hot-Cor®
Ballistic Coefficient	0.455
COAL Tested	3.250"
Speer Part No.	1605

270 Grand Slam® SP
Ballistic Coefficient	0.378
COAL Tested	3.260"
Speer Part No.	1608

			Starting Charge		Maximum Charge	
Propellant	Case	Primer	Weight (grains)	Muzzle Velocity (feet/sec)	Weight (grains)	Muzzle Velocity (feet/sec)
Alliant Reloder 33	Federal	Federal 215	70.7	2772	78.3 C	3109
Alliant Reloder 26	Federal	Federal 215	60.0	2780	66.5	3067
Ramshot Magnum	Federal	Federal 215	68.0	2865	72.0	3028
Alliant Reloder 23	Federal	Federal 215	57.4	2778	63.8	3015
Alliant Reloder 50	Federal	Federal 215	72.7	2706	80.0 C	2998
IMR 7977	Federal	Federal 215	62.8	2706	69.6	2989
Hodgdon US 869	Federal	Federal 215	77.0	2862	81.0 C	2987
Hodgdon Retumbo	Federal	Federal 215	64.0	2862	68.0	2980
Alliant Reloder 25	Federal	Federal 215	62.0	2839	66.0	2966
Accurate 8700	Federal	Federal 215	77.0	2832	81.0 C	2957
IMR 7828	Federal	Federal 215	60.0	2803	64.0	2950
Alliant Reloder 22	Federal	Federal 215	59.0	2800	63.0	2942
IMR 4831	Federal	Federal 215	56.0	2759	60.0	2914
Alliant Reloder 19	Federal	Federal 215	56.0	2790	60.0	2903
Hodgdon H4831SC	Federal	Federal 215	58.0	2771	62.0	2903
Vihtavuori N560	Federal	Federal 215	58.0	2771	62.0	2902

WARNING! *Maximum loads should be used with CAUTION • C = Compressed Load*

7-30 WATERS

Parent Cartridge:	30-30 Winchester
Country of Origin:	USA
Year of Introduction:	1984
Designer(s):	Ken Waters
Governing Body:	SAAMI

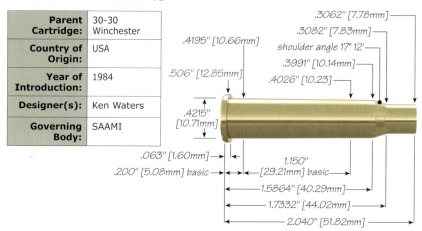

CARTRIDGE CASE DATA			
Case Type:	Rimmed, bottleneck		
Average Case Capacity:	45.0 grains H₂O	**Max. Cartridge OAL**	2.550 inch
Max. Case Length:	2.040 inch	**Primer:**	Large Rifle
Case Trim to Length:	2.030 inch	**RCBS Shell holder:**	# 2
Current Manufacturers:	Federal, Hornady		

BALLISTIC DATA			
Max. Average Pressure (MAP):	45,000 psi, 40,000 CUP - SAAMI	**Test Barrel Length:**	24 inch
Rifling Twist Rate:	1 turn in 9.5 inch		
Muzzle velocities of factory loaded ammunition		Bullet Wgt.	Muzzle velocity
		120-grain	2,700 fps
		139-grain	2,540 fps
		154-grain	2,347 fps
	Muzzle velocity will decrease approximately 15 fps per inch for barrels less than 24 inches.		

HISTORICAL NOTES

- Unhappy with the mediocre ballistics of the 30-30 Winchester cartridge, in 1976 experimenter and writer Ken Waters began working on a new, flatter shooting cartridge for lever-action rifles such as the Winchester Model 94.

- Waters' concept was to neck down the venerable 30-30 Winchester cartridge to 7mm which would allow the use of smaller diameter, lighter bullets at higher muzzle velocities without exceeding existing MAP levels of the parent cartridge.

- In 1984, U.S. Repeating Arms agreed to chamber their Model 94 lever-action rifle in the new caliber and Federal agreed to manufacture the ammunition for their Premium product line.
- The demise of U.S. Repeating Arms in 2005 has placed the future of the 7-30 Waters into question. Federal lists loaded ammunition in 7-30 Waters in their current catalog.
- The 7-30 Waters has become more popular as a pistol round.

BALLISTIC NOTES

- Waters' ballistic concept worked. Federal's 7-30 Waters factory load with a 120-grain bullet offers 17% higher muzzle velocity and 10% higher muzzle energy than the 150-grain bullet of the 30-30 Winchester.
- In a carbine with a 100 yard zero, the drop of the 120-grain bullet of the 7-30 Waters at 200 yards is just 5 inches compared to 8 inches in the 150-grain 30-30 Winchester bullet.

TECHNICAL NOTES

- All bullets must be crimped securely in the case mouth to prevent them from being pulled from the case mouth by recoil or pushed into the case by cartridges in the magazine tube.
- Do not try to "magnumize" the 7-30 Waters cartridge as the lightweight cartridge case is not designed for high pressures.

SAFETY NOTES

IF SPITZER BULLETS ARE HANDLOADED FOR USE IN TUBULAR MAGAZINE RIFLES: Load no more than one round in the magazine and one in the chamber.

SPEER 130-grain Spitzer SP Hot-Cor® @ a muzzle velocity of 2,600 fps:
- Maximum vertical altitude @ 90° elevation is 7,620 feet.
- Maximum horizontal distance to first impact with ground @ 36° elevation is 3,455 yards.
- Do not fill tubular-magazine rifles for the 7-30 Waters with spitzer bullets as doing so may result in a magazine tube explosion.

110 GRAINS

DIAMETER	SECTIONAL DENSITY
.284"	0.195

7mm TNT® HP

Ballistic Coefficient	0.384
COAL Tested	2.710"
Speer Part No.	1616

Propellant	Case	Primer	Starting Charge Weight (grains)	Starting Charge Muzzle Velocity (feet/sec)	Maximum Charge Weight (grains)	Maximum Charge Muzzle Velocity (feet/sec)
Alliant AR-Comp	Federal	Federal 210	34.4	2652	37.4 C	2863
Winchester 748	Federal	CCI 250	35.0	2503	39.0 C	2834
Alliant Power Pro Varmint	Federal	Federal 210	34.6	2662	37.2	2834
IMR 8208 XBR	Federal	Federal 210	33.2	2633	36.2	2828
Accurate 2015	Federal	CCI 200	29.0	2533	33.0	2767
Vihtavuori N530	Federal	Federal 210	31.7	2580	34.2	2763
Alliant Reloder 15	Federal	CCI 200	33.0	2354	37.0	2757
Hodgdon H4895	Federal	CCI 200	32.0	2425	36.0	2739
Vihtavuori N135	Federal	CCI 200	31.0	2354	35.0	2735
Hodgdon H335	Federal	CCI 250	32.0	2498	36.0	2716
Hodgdon BL-C(2)	Federal	CCI 250	31.0	2432	35.0	2665
IMR 4895	Federal	CCI 200	30.5	2325	34.5	2655
Accurate 2230	Federal	CCI 250	27.5	2226	31.5	2642
IMR 3031	Federal	CCI 200	30.0	2228	34.0	2615

WARNING! Maximum loads should be used with CAUTION • C = Compressed Load

130 GRAINS

DIAMETER	SECTIONAL DENSITY
.284"	0.230

7mm Spitzer SP Hot-Cor®

Ballistic Coefficient	0.368
COAL Tested	2.550"
Speer Part No.	1623

7mm Spitzer BTSP

Ballistic Coefficient	0.424
COAL Tested	2.710"
Speer Part No.	1624

			Starting Charge		Maximum Charge	
Propellant	Case	Primer	Weight (grains)	Muzzle Velocity (feet/sec)	Weight (grains)	Muzzle Velocity (feet/sec)
Alliant Power Pro 2000-MR	Federal	Federal 210	36.0	2457	40.0 C	2701
Alliant Reloder 15	Federal	CCI 200	31.5	2253	35.5	2609
Alliant AR-Comp	Federal	Federal 210	30.4	2369	33.7	2586
Hodgdon H335	Federal	CCI 250	29.0	2030	33.0	2583
Alliant Power Pro Varmint	Federal	Federal 210	30.2	2359	33.5	2570
Vihtavuori N135	Federal	CCI 200	28.5	2148	32.5	2532
Hodgdon H4895	Federal	CCI 200	30.0	2241	34.0	2514
Hodgdon BL-C(2)	Federal	CCI 250	32.0	2320	36.0	2510
IMR 3031	Federal	CCI 200	29.0	2320	33.0	2509
Winchester 748	Federal	CCI 250	31.0	2096	35.0	2487
Accurate 2015	Federal	CCI 200	26.0	2206	30.0	2480
IMR 4166	Federal	Federal 210	28.7	2198	31.7	2417
Accurate 2230	Federal	CCI 250	26.0	2039	30.0	2396

WARNING! *Maximum loads should be used with* CAUTION • *C = Compressed Load*

145 GRAINS

DIAMETER	SECTIONAL DENSITY
.284"	0.257

7mm Spitzer SP Hot-Cor®
Ballistic Coefficient	0.416
COAL Tested	2.710"
Speer Part No.	1629

7mm Spitzer BTSP
Ballistic Coefficient	0.416
COAL Tested	2.710"
Speer Part No.	1628

7mm Grand Slam® SP
Ballistic Coefficient	0.353
COAL Tested	2.780"
Speer Part No.	1632

			Starting Charge		Maximum Charge	
Propellant	Case	Primer	Weight (grains)	Muzzle Velocity (feet/sec)	Weight (grains)	Muzzle Velocity (feet/sec)
Alliant Power Pro 2000-MR	Federal	Federal 210	33.9	2259	36.9	2503
Alliant Reloder 15	Federal	CCI 200	31.0	2228	35.0	2480
IMR 4895	Federal	CCI 200	30.0	2130	34.0	2449
Winchester 748	Federal	CCI 250	30.0	2088	34.0	2435
Alliant Power Pro Varmint	Federal	Federal 210	31.1	2273	33.1	2434
Alliant AR-Comp	Federal	Federal 210	29.1	2187	32.1	2408
Hodgdon H4895	Federal	CCI 200	29.0	2103	33.0	2400
Hodgdon BL-C(2)	Federal	CCI 250	31.0	2164	35.0	2395
Accurate 2015	Federal	CCI 200	26.0	2086	30.0	2381
Vihtavuori N135	Federal	CCI 200	29.0	2130	33.0	2378
Hodgdon H335	Federal	CCI 250	28.0	2052	32.0	2360
IMR 3031	Federal	CCI 200	27.0	1979	31.0	2311
IMR 4166	Federal	Federal 210	28.7	2128	30.7	2280
Accurate 2230	Federal	CCI 250	24.0	1793	28.0	2201

WARNING! *Maximum loads should be used with CAUTION • C = Compressed Load*

7mm-08 REMINGTON

Parent Cartridge:	308 Winchester
Country of Origin:	USA
Year of Introduction:	1980
Designer(s):	Remington
Governing Body:	SAAMI

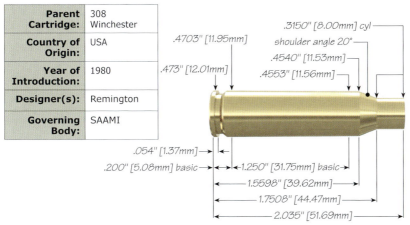

CARTRIDGE CASE DATA

Case Type:	Rimless, bottleneck
Average Case Capacity:	52.2 grains H_2O
Max. Cartridge OAL:	2.800 inch
Max. Case Length:	2.035 inch
Primer:	Large Rifle
Case Trim to Length:	2.025 inch
RCBS Shell holder:	# 3
Current Manufacturers:	Remington, Federal, Hornady, Nosler, Winchester

BALLISTIC DATA

Max. Average Pressure (MAP):	61,000 psi, 52,000 CUP - SAAMI
Test Barrel Length:	24 inch
Rifling Twist Rate:	1 turn in 9.5 inch

Muzzle velocities of factory loaded ammunition:

Bullet Wgt.	Muzzle velocity
140-grain	2,800 fps
150-grain	2,650 fps
175-grain	2,595 fps

Muzzle velocity will decrease approximately 20 fps per inch for barrels less than 24 inches.

HISTORICAL NOTES

- The 7mm-08 Remington began life as a wildcat for metallic silhouette competition.
- Recognizing the market demand for a new, short 7mm hunting cartridge, Remington standardized the 7mm-08 Remington cartridge in 1980.
- As deer hunters have come to appreciate the efficiency of the 7mm-08 Remington cartridge, its popularity has grown accordingly.

- Today it is a staple item in the product lines of most major domestic and many foreign ammunition manufacturers.
- Most firearm makers offer at least one model of centerfire rifle in this caliber.

INTERESTING FACT

The 7mm-08 Remington is one of the few cartridges designed for match competition that have successfully transitioned into the modern hunting cartridge market.

BALLISTIC NOTES

- The 7mm-08 Remington is a modern, high MAP centerfire rifle cartridge for short actions that can easily duplicate the ballistics of the much larger 7mm Mauser cartridge.
- For example, the muzzle velocity of the 7mm-08 Remington with a 140-grain bullet (2,800 fps) compares favorably with that of the same 140-grain bullet in the 7mm Mauser (2,660 fps). The same holds true for heavier bullets.
- This equivalence is made possible by the 61,000 psi MAP of the 7mm-08 Remington compared to the 7mm Mauser cartridge which is limited by its 51,000 psi MAP level.
- With its 1 turn in 9.5 inch rifling twist rate, the 7mm-08 Rem. cartridge can stabilize bullets weighing anywhere from 110 to 175 grains.

TECHNICAL NOTES

- Essentially, the 7mm-08 is a 308 Winchester case necked down to accept .284 inch diameter (7mm) bullets. As a result, it shares the basic dimensions with its parent cartridge.
- Without doubt, the ballistic sweet spot of the 7mm-08 Rem. cartridge is with the 140-grain bullets. In this, it is similar to its 7mm brethren.
- Case capacity of the 7mm-08 Rem. is about 13% less than the venerable 7x57mm Mauser and 25% less than the 280 Remington.
- The mild recoil in short, light rifles makes the 7mm-08 an excellent choice for novice hunters and those sensitive to recoil.

HANDLOADING NOTES

- In addition to the manufacturers of loaded ammunition listed above, Remington, Winchester, Prvi Partizan, Norma, Starline, and Hornady offer new, empty, unprimed brass in 7mm-08 Rem. caliber.
- Although the 7mm-08 Remington is not considered a varmint cartridge, the Speer 110-grain TNT® HP bullet will amaze with its spectacular performance anchoring varmints. For larger varmints and predators, the Speer 130-grain Spitzer BTSP is a good choice. Bullets of 130-grain weight such as the Speer Spitzer SP Hot-Cor® offers a good balance of muzzle velocity, striking energy, and light recoil. The factories ignore this niche.
- With 145-grain bullets such as the Speer Spitzer SP Hot-Cor and the Grand Slam® SP, handloaders can one-up the ballistic performance of factory loaded ammunition. This bullet weight is ideal for deer and medium game hunting.
- By handloading Speer 160-grain bullets such as the Spitzer and Grand Slam SPs, handloaders can move their 7mm-08 Remington rifles up a notch from deer to larger game – an option unavailable in factory loads.

- The 7mm-08 Remington works best with slow burning propellants.

SAFETY NOTES

SPEER 160-grain Spitzer BTSP @ a muzzle velocity of 2,735 fps:
- Maximum vertical altitude @ 90° elevation is 15,990 feet.
- Maximum horizontal distance to first impact with ground @ 38° elevation is 7,522 yards.

110 GRAINS

DIAMETER	SECTIONAL DENSITY
.284"	0.195

7mm TNT® HP

Ballistic Coefficient	0.384
COAL Tested	2.760"
Speer Part No.	1616

			Starting Charge		Maximum Charge	
Propellant	Case	Primer	Weight (grains)	Muzzle Velocity (feet/sec)	Weight (grains)	Muzzle Velocity (feet/sec)
IMR 3031	Remington	CCI 200	42.0	3023	46.0 C	3250
Alliant Reloder 15	Remington	CCI 200	44.0	2930	48.0	3238
Alliant Power Pro 2000-MR	Federal	Federal 210	45.4	3024	48.7	3228
Alliant AR-Comp	Federal	Federal 210	40.0	2950	44.3	3208
Winchester 760	Remington	CCI 250	47.0	2917	51.0 C	3206
Hodgdon Varget	Remington	CCI 200	43.0	2891	47.0	3194
Hodgdon H414	Remington	CCI 250	48.0	2858	52.0 C	3176
Hodgdon H380	Remington	CCI 250	49.0	2857	53.0 C	3174
IMR 4064	Remington	CCI 200	42.0	2890	46.0	3141
Vihtavuori N140	Remington	CCI 200	42.0	2855	46.0	3137
IMR 4895	Remington	CCI 200	40.0	2851	44.0	3066
Hodgdon H4350	Remington	CCI 200	47.0	2779	51.0 C	3044
IMR 4350	Remington	CCI 200	47.0	2777	51.0 C	3035
IMR 4320	Remington	CCI 200	41.0	2735	45.0	2973
Accurate 2460	Remington	CCI 250	39.0	2690	43.0	2908
Hodgdon H335	Remington	CCI 250	39.0	2659	43.0	2906

WARNING! *Maximum loads should be used with* **CAUTION** • **C = Compressed Load**

130 GRAINS

DIAMETER	SECTIONAL DENSITY
.284"	0.230

7mm Spitzer SP Hot-Cor®
Ballistic Coefficient	0.368
COAL Tested	2.730"
Speer Part No.	1623

7mm Spitzer BTSP
Ballistic Coefficient	0.424
COAL Tested	2.730"
Speer Part No.	1624

			Starting Charge		Maximum Charge	
Propellant	Case	Primer	Weight (grains)	Muzzle Velocity (feet/sec)	Weight (grains)	Muzzle Velocity (feet/sec)
IMR 4064	Remington	CCI 200	41.0	2835	45.0	3065
IMR 4350	Remington	CCI 200	46.0	2766	50.0	3006
Hodgdon H4350	Remington	CCI 200	46.0	2715	50.0 C	2984
Alliant Reloder 16	Federal	Federal 210	42.6	2708	47.3 C	2984
Winchester 760	Remington	CCI 250	45.0	2727	49.0	2980
Hodgdon H414	Remington	CCI 250	45.0	2673	49.0	2954
Ramshot Big Game	Federal	Federal 210	42.1	2764	45.9	2950
Alliant Power Pro 2000-MR	Federal	Federal 210	39.4	2690	43.5	2923
Accurate 4350	Federal	Federal 210	44.3	2644	49.0 C	2900
Hodgdon H380	Remington	CCI 250	44.0	2652	48.0	2898
Hodgdon Varget	Remington	CCI 200	39.0	2641	43.0	2888
IMR 3031	Remington	CCI 200	38.0	2684	42.0	2886
Alliant Power Pro Varmint	Federal	Federal 210	36.4	2648	40.5	2884
Alliant Reloder 17	Federal	Federal 210	41.7	2644	45.9	2882
IMR 4831	Remington	CCI 200	46.0	2678	50.0 C	2880
Hodgdon CFE 223	Federal	Federal 210	36.5	2570	41.1	2868
Alliant AR-Comp	Federal	Federal 210	35.8	2697	38.8	2857
Vihtavuori N140	Remington	CCI 200	38.0	2531	42.0	2812
Hodgdon H335	Remington	CCI 250	37.0	2607	41.0	2788
Alliant Reloder 15	Remington	CCI 200	38.0	2577	42.0	2786
Accurate 2520	Remington	CCI 250	34.0	2409	38.0	2662

WARNING! Maximum loads should be used with CAUTION • C = Compressed Load

145 GRAINS

DIAMETER	SECTIONAL DENSITY
.284"	0.257

7mm Spitzer BTSP
Ballistic Coefficient	0.472
COAL Tested	2.730"
Speer Part No.	1628

7mm Spitzer SP Hot-Cor®
Ballistic Coefficient	0.416
COAL Tested	2.730"
Speer Part No.	1629

7mm Grand Slam® SP
Ballistic Coefficient	0.353
COAL Tested	2.775"
Speer Part No.	1632

			Starting Charge		Maximum Charge	
Propellant	Case	Primer	Weight (grains)	Muzzle Velocity (feet/sec)	Weight (grains)	Muzzle Velocity (feet/sec)
Alliant Reloder 19	Remington	CCI 200	47.0	2692	51.0 C	2933
Winchester 760	Remington	CCI 250	45.0	2628	49.0	2920
Hodgdon H4350	Remington	CCI 200	44.0	2707	48.0 C	2911
Alliant Reloder 16	Federal	Federal 210	41.3	2615	45.9 C	2872
Accurate 4350	Remington	CCI 200	44.0	2644	48.0 C	2843
IMR 4350	Remington	CCI 200	44.0	2644	48.0	2841
Alliant Power Pro 4000-MR	Federal	Federal 210	43.1	2632	47.5 C	2833
Hodgdon H414	Remington	CCI 250	43.0	2560	47.0	2814
Ramshot Big Game	Federal	Federal 210	40.1	2584	44.1	2798
Alliant Reloder 17	Federal	Federal 210	40.5	2528	44.9	2787
Vihtavuori N165	Remington	CCI 200	47.0	2553	51.0 C	2781
Vihtavuori N550	Federal	Federal 210	38.5	2492	42.8	2780
Accurate 2520	Remington	CCI 250	38.0	2519	42.0	2772
Alliant Power Pro 2000-MR	Federal	Federal 210	37.5	2524	41.6	2769
Hodgdon H380	Remington	CCI 250	42.0	2520	46.0	2739
Accurate 3100	Remington	CCI 200	45.0	2480	49.0 C	2725
IMR 4895	Remington	CCI 200	37.0	2507	41.0	2724
Hodgdon Varget	Remington	CCI 200	37.0	2473	41.0	2707
Alliant Reloder 15	Remington	CCI 200	37.0	2458	41.0	2705

WARNING! Maximum loads should be used with CAUTION • C = Compressed Load

160 GRAINS

DIAMETER	SECTIONAL DENSITY
.284"	0.283

7mm Spitzer BTSP
Ballistic Coefficient	0.519
COAL Tested	2.800"
Speer Part No.	1634

7mm Spitzer SP Hot-Cor®
Ballistic Coefficient	0.504
COAL Tested	2.800"
Speer Part No.	1635

7mm Grand Slam® SP
Ballistic Coefficient	0.389
COAL Tested	2.760"
Speer Part No.	1638

Propellant	Case	Primer	Starting Charge Weight (grains)	Starting Charge Muzzle Velocity (feet/sec)	Maximum Charge Weight (grains)	Maximum Charge Muzzle Velocity (feet/sec)
Winchester 760	Remington	CCI 250	41.0	2475	45.0 C	2735
Alliant Reloder 19	Remington	CCI 200	43.0	2456	47.0 C	2710
Alliant Power Pro 4000-MR	Federal	Federal 210	44.0 C	2547	47.0 C	2706
Hodgdon H414	Remington	CCI 250	41.0	2474	45.0 C	2704
Alliant Reloder 17	Federal	Federal 210	40.0	2400	44.4 C	2682
Accurate 4350	Remington	CCI 200	42.0	2484	46.0 C	2671
Alliant Reloder 16	Federal	Federal 210	40.8 C	2462	45.0 C	2670
IMR 4350	Remington	CCI 200	41.0	2463	45.0 C	2666
Accurate 2520	Remington	CCI 250	36.0	2425	40.0	2659
Vihtavuori N165	Remington	CCI 200	45.0	2415	49.0 C	2654
Alliant Power Pro 2000-MR	Federal	Federal 210	37.9	2412	42.1	2652
Ramshot Big Game	Federal	Federal 210	38.6	2413	42.7	2632
IMR 4831	Remington	CCI 200	42.0	2406	46.0 C	2615
Hodgdon H4350	Remington	CCI 200	41.0	2423	45.0 C	2611
Hodgdon H4831SC	Remington	CCI 200	46.0	2512	48.0 C	2598
Alliant Reloder 15	Remington	CCI 200	34.0	2343	38.0	2506
Winchester 748	Remington	CCI 250	35.0	2315	39.0	2503
Hodgdon H380	Remington	CCI 250	38.0	2281	42.0	2502

WARNING! Maximum loads should be used with CAUTION • C = Compressed Load

175 GRAINS

DIAMETER	SECTIONAL DENSITY
.284"	0.310

7mm Grand Slam® SP

Ballistic Coefficient	0.436
COAL Tested	2.745"
Speer Part No.	1643

			Starting Charge		Maximum Charge	
Propellant	Case	Primer	Weight (grains)	Muzzle Velocity (feet/sec)	Weight (grains)	Muzzle Velocity (feet/sec)
Alliant Reloder 19	Remington	CCI 200	43.0	2396	47.0 C	2628
Alliant Power Pro 4000-MR	Federal	Federal 210	42.4 C	2407	46.2 C	2591
Alliant Reloder 16	Federal	Federal 210	40.3 C	2337	44.8 C	2576
Vihtavuori N165	Remington	CCI 200	43.0	2330	47.0 C	2575
Alliant Reloder 17	Federal	Federal 210	40.0	2297	44.2 C	2566
Alliant Power Pro 2000-MR	Federal	Federal 210	38.3	2298	42.4	2559
Ramshot Big Game	Federal	Federal 210	39.4	2366	43.6	2558
IMR 4350	Remington	CCI 200	40.0	2365	44.0	2542
Accurate 3100	Remington	CCI 200	43.0	2336	47.0 C	2536
Hodgdon H4350	Remington	CCI 200	40.0	2326	44.0 C	2507
Accurate 2520	Remington	CCI 250	35.0	2314	39.0	2502
IMR 4831	Remington	CCI 200	41.0	2240	45.0	2465
Hodgdon H4831SC	Remington	CCI 200	43.5	2355	45.5 C	2461
Winchester 760	Remington	CCI 250	41.0	2264	45.0	2461
Hodgdon H414	Remington	CCI 250	38.0	2208	42.0	2419
Hodgdon H380	Remington	CCI 250	38.0	2203	42.0	2408
Alliant Reloder 15	Remington	CCI 200	32.0	2153	36.0	2312

WARNING! Maximum loads should be used with CAUTION • C = Compressed Load

7mm MAUSER (7x57)

Alternate Names:	7x57mm, 7mm Spanish Mauser, 275 Rigby
Parent Cartridge:	8x57mm
Country of Origin:	Germany
Year of Introduction:	1892
Designer(s):	Paul Mauser
Governing Body:	SAAMI/CIP

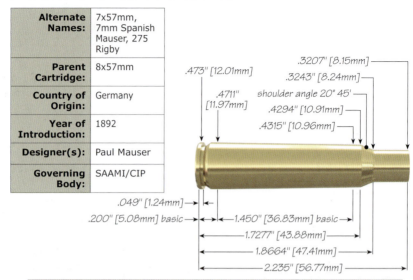

CARTRIDGE CASE DATA

Case Type:	Rimless, bottleneck		
Average Case Capacity:	60.2 grains H₂O	Max. Cartridge OAL	3.065 inch
Max. Case Length:	2.235 inch	Primer:	Large Rifle
Case Trim to Length:	2.225 inch	RCBS Shell holder:	# 3
Current Manufacturers:	Federal, Hornady, Remington, Nosler, Prvi Partizan, RUAG, Norma, Sellier & Bellot, Winchester		

BALLISTIC DATA

Max. Average Pressure (MAP):	51,000 psi, 46,000 CUP – SAAMI; 56,565 psi - CIP	Test Barrel Length:	24 inch
Rifling Twist Rate:	1 turn in 8.75 inch – SAAMI, (1/8.66, inch alternate)		
Muzzle velocities of factory loaded ammunition			
	Bullet Wgt.		Muzzle velocity
	140-grain		2,700 fps
	160-grain		2,600 fps
	175-grain		2,400 fps
	Muzzle velocity will decrease approximately 20 fps per inch for barrels less than 24 inches.		

HISTORICAL NOTES

- Now in its 125th year of production, the 7mm Mauser remains the grand old man of 7mm cartridges.
- Developed by Mauser in 1892 for their Model 1893 and 1895 bolt-action

military rifles, the 7mm Mauser soon became the standard military service cartridge of Spain, Mexico and many South American countries--a role in which it served until the mid-1950s.

- As its military use spread, the ballistic performance of the new cartridge soon attracted the attention of both European and North American sportsmen who adopted it for hunting all types of game.

- Unexpectedly, the 7mm Mauser became a favorite of African hunters who appreciated the deep penetration capability of the heavy, 175-grain bullets on dangerous game. Today, although the 7mm Mauser is no longer considered a wise choice for dangerous game, many resident African hunters continue to rely on the 7x57mm for taking plains game for the camp cooking pot.

- Most major ammunition manufacturers continue to list the 7mm Mauser cartridge in their regular product lines. Domestic manufacturers typically list only 139-grain bullets as changing tastes now favor lightweight bullets at high velocity. European manufacturers tend to list a wider variety of bullet weights.

- Sales of 7mm Mauser ammunition in the U.S. received a prolonged boost in the 1950s when thousands of surplus military rifles in this caliber were sold on the U.S. commercial market. At one time or another, most domestic firearm makers offered rifles chambered in 7mm Mauser. The energy of this marketing boost has long since dissipated.

- As sales volume of 7mm Mauser ammunition in the North American market has slowly declined, perennially solid sales levels of this cartridge in Canada have become increasingly important.

INTERESTING FACT

When Teddy Roosevelt and his Rough Riders charged up San Juan Hill during the Spanish-American War in 1898, the hill was defended by Spanish Army troops firing Model 1893 Mauser rifles chambered in 7mm Mauser. Many American veterans of this battle have frequently remarked on the accuracy, range and superior ballistics of the 7mm bullets fired at them.

BALLISTIC NOTES

- While the 7mm Mauser cartridge compares favorably in case capacity, volume and construction with many of the modern 7mm standard and short magnum cartridges, it is handicapped by MAP levels which are approximately 25% lower. As a result, muzzle velocity and energy is lower than its modern competitors when loaded with bullets of similar weight.

- As there are no weak, old Spanish Model 1893 or 1895 Mauser rifle actions to contend with in the European market, most European ammunition makers load 7mm Mauser ammunition to approximately 10% higher MAP levels than domestic ammunition makers.

- The 7mm Mauser cartridge does have one significant advantage over some of its modern competitors—it is fully capable of firing heavy weight bullets up to 175 grains as well as light weight bullets. Many modern 7mm cartridges are optimized for bullets of 150 grains or less.

TECHNICAL NOTES

- Many 7x57mm rifles are of the bolt-action type. Due to its maximum overall loaded length, the 7mm Mauser cartridge must be chambered in bolt-action rifles with a long or "standard" action length.

- The basic head configuration of the 7mm Mauser is similar to the classic 8x57mm Mauser cartridge as well as the 308 Winchester and 30-06 Springfield cartridges.
- If necessary, 7mm Mauser cases can be formed from 8x57mm Mauser brass.

HANDLOADING NOTES

- In addition to the manufacturers of loaded ammunition listed above, new, empty brass for reloading in this caliber is offered by Remington, Winchester, Norma, Prvi Partizan, Sellier & Bellot, and Hornady.
- As most military surplus 7mm Mauser ammunition was loaded with corrosive primers, we recommend scrapping brass from such ammunition regardless of condition.
- The 7mm Mauser is not a magnum and should not be expected to deliver magnum ballistics.
- For many years now, all commercial ammunition in 7mm Mauser has been loaded with non-corrosive, Large Rifle primers.
- Although the 7mm Mauser is not considered a varmint cartridge, the Speer 110-grain TNT® HP will amaze with its spectacular performance anchoring varmints. For larger varmints and predators, the Speer 130-grain Spitzer BTSP is a fine choice.
- Bullets of 130-grain weight such as the Spitzer SP Hot-Cor® offer a good balance of muzzle velocity, striking energy and light recoil in the 7mm Mauser. Ammunition makers have missed this market niche.
- With 145-grain soft point bullets such as the Spitzer SP Hot-Cor and Grand Slam® SP, handloaders can one-up the ballistic performance of factory loaded ammunition. This bullet weight is ideal for deer and medium game hunting.
- The 7mm Mauser is in its element with 160-grain bullets such as the Speer Spitzer BTSP and Spitzer SP Hot-Cor. This bullet weight combines the best elements of high muzzle velocity, high striking energy with moderate recoil.
- Neck sizing is recommended as the first option for reloading the 7mm Mauser cartridge as the low MAP levels and bolt-action rifles normally do not require full length resizing. We suggest full length sizing for hunting.
- If you plan to fire your reloaded 7mm Mauser ammunition in rifles having Spanish Model 1893 or 1895 Mauser actions, **DO NOT EXCEED STARTING LOADS LISTED IN THIS MANUAL!**
- The 7mm Mauser cartridge works best with slow burning powders.

SAFETY NOTES

SPEER 160-grain Spitzer BTSP @ a muzzle velocity of 2,605 fps:
- Maximum vertical altitude @ 90° elevation is 15,549 feet.
- Maximum horizontal distance to first impact with ground @ 37° elevation is 7,366 yards.

110 GRAINS

DIAMETER	SECTIONAL DENSITY
.284"	0.195

7mm TNT® HP	
Ballistic Coefficient	0.384
COAL Tested	2.985"
Speer Part No.	1616

			Starting Charge		Maximum Charge	
Propellant	Case	Primer	Weight (grains)	Muzzle Velocity (feet/sec)	Weight (grains)	Muzzle Velocity (feet/sec)
Winchester 760	Remington	CCI 250	50.0	2983	54.0 C	3304
Alliant Power Pro 2000-MR	Federal	Federal 210	46.9	2984	50.9	3197
Hodgdon H414	Remington	CCI 250	50.0	2881	54.0 C	3191
Hodgdon Varget	Federal	Federal 210	42.8	2944	46.9	3152
IMR 4064	Remington	CCI 200	44.0	2792	48.0	3146
Alliant Reloder 15	Remington	CCI 200	44.0	2820	48.0	3141
IMR 3031	Remington	CCI 200	42.0	2795	46.0	3131
Alliant Power Pro Varmint	Federal	Federal 210	41.9	2930	45.3	3124
Vihtavuori N140	Remington	CCI 200	43.5	2757	47.5	3088
Alliant AR-Comp	Federal	Federal 210	41.2	2906	44.4	3085
IMR 4166	Federal	Federal 210	41.6	2872	45.3	3085
Accurate 2700	Remington	CCI 250	47.0	2755	51.0 C	3068
Hodgdon H380	Remington	CCI 250	46.0	2685	50.0 C	2991
IMR 4320	Remington	CCI 200	43.0	2633	47.0	2983
Hodgdon BL-C(2)	Remington	CCI 250	41.0	2631	45.0	2964
Hodgdon H4895	Remington	CCI 200	40.5	2692	44.5	2948
IMR 4895	Remington	CCI 200	40.0	2614	44.0	2945

WARNING! Maximum loads should be used with CAUTION • C = Compressed Load

130 GRAINS

DIAMETER	SECTIONAL DENSITY
.284"	0.230

7mm Spitzer SP Hot-Cor®
Ballistic Coefficient	0.368
COAL Tested	2.800"
Speer Part No.	1623

7mm Spitzer BTSP
Ballistic Coefficient	0.424
COAL Tested	2.800"
Speer Part No.	1624

			Starting Charge		Maximum Charge	
Propellant	Case	Primer	Weight (grains)	Muzzle Velocity (feet/sec)	Weight (grains)	Muzzle Velocity (feet/sec)
Hodgdon H414	Remington	CCI 250	46.0	2680	50.0 C	3003
Winchester 760	Remington	CCI 250	46.0	2657	50.0 C	2994
Alliant Reloder 17	Federal	Federal 210	44.5	2754	48.1 C	2961
Alliant Power Pro 2000-MR	Federal	Federal 210	44.0	2768	47.5	2957
Alliant Reloder 15	Remington	CCI 200	41.0	2654	45.0	2954
Accurate XMR 4350	Remington	CCI 200	47.0	2624	51.0 C	2939
Hodgdon H4350	Remington	CCI 200	46.0	2661	50.0 C	2930
IMR 4064	Remington	CCI 200	42.0	2583	46.0	2910
Alliant Reloder 22	Remington	CCI 200	49.0	2633	53.0 C	2899
IMR 4350	Remington	CCI 200	46.0	2614	50.0 C	2895
Alliant Reloder 19	Remington	CCI 200	48.0	2642	52.0 C	2894
IMR 4320	Remington	CCI 200	41.0	2593	45.0	2888
Alliant Power Pro Varmint	Federal	Federal 210	39.5	2707	42.3	2865
IMR 4166	Federal	Federal 210	38.5	2651	41.4	2830
Alliant AR-Comp	Federal	Federal 210	38.0	2659	40.9	2826
IMR 3031	Remington	CCI 200	39.0	2521	43.0	2824
IMR 4895	Remington	CCI 200	38.0	2506	42.0	2808
Vihtavuori N140	Remington	CCI 200	38.0	2515	42.0	2785
IMR SR 4759 (reduced load)	Remington	CCI 200	18.0	1658	22.0	2014

WARNING! Maximum loads should be used with CAUTION • C = Compressed Load

145 GRAINS

DIAMETER	SECTIONAL DENSITY
.284"	0.257

7mm Spitzer BTSP
Ballistic Coefficient	0.472
COAL Tested	2.800"
Speer Part No.	1628

7mm Spitzer SP Hot-Cor®
Ballistic Coefficient	0.416
COAL Tested	2.800"
Speer Part No.	1629

7mm Grand Slam® SP
Ballistic Coefficient	0.353
COAL Tested	2.970"
Speer Part No.	1632

			Starting Charge		Maximum Charge	
Propellant	Case	Primer	Weight (grains)	Muzzle Velocity (feet/sec)	Weight (grains)	Muzzle Velocity (feet/sec)
Alliant Reloder 19	Remington	CCI 200	48.0	2571	52.0 C	2831
Hodgdon H4350	Remington	CCI 200	46.0	2547	50.0 C	2820
Alliant Power Pro 4000-MR	Federal	Federal 210	46.2	2610	50.2 C	2807
Alliant Reloder 16	Federal	Federal 210	43.7	2620	47.3 C	2799
Accurate 4350	Remington	CCI 200	47.0	2506	51.0 C	2792
Hodgdon H414	Remington	CCI 250	44.0	2527	48.0 C	2783
IMR 4831	Remington	CCI 200	47.0	2538	51.0 C	2780
Winchester 760	Remington	CCI 250	44.0	2507	48.0 C	2778
IMR 4350	Remington	CCI 200	45.0	2494	49.0 C	2761
Alliant Reloder 17	Federal	Federal 210	42.3	2559	46.1 C	2761
Alliant Power Pro 2000-MR	Federal	Federal 210	40.9	2538	44.4	2734
Alliant Reloder 22	Remington	CCI 200	47.0	2466	51.0 C	2716
IMR 4064	Remington	CCI 200	39.0	2421	43.0	2711
Vihtavuori N160	Remington	CCI 200	44.0	2449	48.0 C	2697
IMR 4451	Federal	Federal 210	42.4	2474	46.1 C	2652
Alliant Reloder 15	Remington	CCI 200	38.0	2345	42.0	2627
IMR 4895	Remington	CCI 200	36.0	2357	40.0	2593
IMR SR 4759 (reduced load)	Remington	CCI 200	18.0	1514	22.0	1847

WARNING! Maximum loads should be used with CAUTION • C = Compressed Load

160 GRAINS

DIAMETER	SECTIONAL DENSITY
.284"	0.283

7mm Spitzer BTSP

Ballistic Coefficient	0.519
COAL Tested	3.000"
Speer Part No.	1634

7mm Spitzer SP Hot-Cor®

Ballistic Coefficient	0.504
COAL Tested	3.000"
Speer Part No.	1635

7mm Grand Slam® SP

Ballistic Coefficient	0.389
COAL Tested	2.960"
Speer Part No.	1638

			Starting Charge		Maximum Charge	
Propellant	Case	Primer	Weight (grains)	Muzzle Velocity (feet/sec)	Weight (grains)	Muzzle Velocity (feet/sec)
Alliant Power Pro 4000-MR	Federal	Federal 210	43.4	2471	47.4	2669
Alliant Reloder 16	Federal	Federal 210	41.2	2482	44.9	2659
Alliant Reloder 17	Federal	Federal 210	40.4	2460	44.0	2646
Winchester 760	Remington	CCI 250	42.0	2393	46.0	2635
Hodgdon H414	Remington	CCI 250	42.0	2384	46.0	2611
IMR 4064	Remington	CCI 200	38.0	2281	42.0	2602
Alliant Reloder 19	Remington	CCI 200	45.0	2331	49.0 C	2598
IMR 4831	Remington	CCI 200	44.0	2300	48.0 C	2576
Accurate 4350	Remington	CCI 200	43.0	2273	47.0 C	2547
IMR 4350	Remington	CCI 200	42.0	2280	46.0 C	2542
Alliant Reloder 22	Remington	CCI 200	45.0	2254	49.0 C	2541
IMR 4451	Federal	Federal 210	40.4	2358	43.8	2529
Hodgdon H4350	Remington	CCI 200	42.0	2270	46.0 C	2528
IMR 4895	Remington	CCI 200	35.0	2212	39.0	2492
IMR 4320	Remington	CCI 200	36.0	2156	40.0	2443
Accurate 3100	Remington	CCI 200	42.0	2160	47.0 C	2420
IMR 4198 (reduced load)	Remington	CCI 200	21.0	1651	25.0	1950

WARNING! Maximum loads should be used with CAUTION • C = Compressed Load

175 GRAINS

DIAMETER	SECTIONAL DENSITY
.284"	0.310

7mm Grand Slam® SP	
Ballistic Coefficient	0.436
COAL Tested	2.995"
Speer Part No.	1643

			Starting Charge		Maximum Charge	
Propellant	Case	Primer	Weight (grains)	Muzzle Velocity (feet/sec)	Weight (grains)	Muzzle Velocity (feet/sec)
Alliant Reloder 26	Federal	Federal 210	46.7 C	2454	50.5 C	2633
Alliant Reloder 22	Remington	CCI 200	47.0	2383	51.0 C	2625
Alliant Power Pro 4000-MR	Federal	Federal 210	42.9	2385	46.4 C	2564
IMR 7828	Remington	CCI 250	46.0	2284	50.0 C	2545
Alliant Reloder 17	Federal	Federal 210	40.4	2371	43.7	2545
Alliant Reloder 19	Remington	CCI 200	44.0	2283	48.0 C	2529
Alliant Reloder 16	Federal	Federal 210	41.0	2362	44.2 C	2527
Alliant Reloder 23	Federal	Federal 210	44.9 C	2414	46.9 C	2512
IMR 4831	Remington	CCI 200	43.0	2228	47.0	2467
Winchester 760	Remington	CCI 250	40.0	2251	44.0	2466
IMR 4350	Remington	CCI 200	41.0	2231	45.0	2457
Hodgdon H4350	Remington	CCI 200	41.0	2204	45.0	2441
Hodgdon H414	Remington	CCI 250	40.0	2178	44.0	2426
Accurate 3100	Remington	CCI 200	44.0	2211	48.0 C	2422
IMR 4064	Remington	CCI 200	36.0	2142	40.0	2400
Accurate 4350	Remington	CCI 200	41.0	2152	45.0 C	2360
IMR 7977	Federal	Federal 210	45.8 C	2246	47.8 C	2336
Alliant Reloder 15	Remington	CCI 200	34.0	2053	38.0	2301
IMR 4198 (reduced load)	Remington	CCI 200	22.0	1633	26.0	1923

WARNING! Maximum loads should be used with CAUTION • C = Compressed Load

280 REMINGTON

Alternate Names:	7mm Remington Express, 7x64 Brenneke
Parent Cartridge:	30-06 Springfield
Country of Origin:	USA
Year of Introduction:	1957
Designer(s):	Remington
Governing Body:	SAAMI

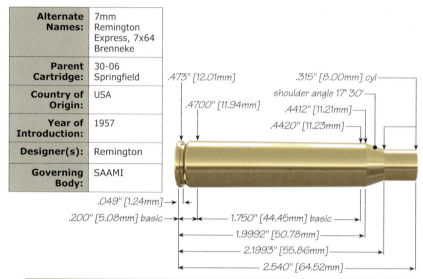

CARTRIDGE CASE DATA

Case Type:	Rimless, bottleneck		
Average Case Capacity:	68.6 grains H$_2$O	Max. Cartridge OAL	3.330 inch
Max. Case Length:	2.540 inch	Primer:	Large Rifle
Case Trim to Length:	2.530 inch	RCBS Shell holder:	# 3
Current Manufacturers:	Remington, Barnes, Federal, Hornady, Nosler, Norma		

BALLISTIC DATA

Max. Average Pressure (MAP):	60,000 psi, 50,000 CUP - SAAMI	Test Barrel Length:	24 inch
Rifling Twist Rate:	1 turn in 10 inch		
Muzzle velocities of factory loaded ammunition	Bullet Wgt.	Muzzle velocity	
	120-grain	3,112 fps	
	140-grain	2,839 fps	
	154-grain	2,825 fps	
	168-grain	2,723 fps	
	175-grain	2,681 fps	

Muzzle velocity will decrease approximately 20 fps per inch for barrels less than 24 inches.

HISTORICAL NOTES

- Most 7mm cartridges have been introduced in bolt-action rifles. The new 280

Remington cartridge proved an exception when, in 1957, Remington introduced it in their Model 740 semi-automatic and Model 760 pump-action rifles.

- Remington marketed the new 280 Remington creation against the well-established 270 Winchester cartridge. Bad choice.
- Although the newcomer delivered all the ballistic performance of the 270 Winchester with the added flexibility of handling a wider range of bullet weights, it could not displace the established occupant of this market segment.
- The 280 Remington began a slow back slide toward oblivion until, in 1979, Remington salvaged their creation by reintroducing it as the 7mm Remington Express in their venerable Model 700 bolt-action rifle. Another bad idea. Confusion reigned regarding the two designations for the same cartridge, forcing Remington to revert to the old 280 Remington designation.
- Today, the market segment occupied by the 280 Remington cartridge is properly considered against rival 7mm cartridges rather than the 270 Winchester.
- A sign that Remington has finally got it right can be gauged by the fact that most of Remington's competitors have added the 280 Remington cartridge to their regular ammunition product line.

BALLISTIC NOTES

- The 280 Remington is a modern cartridge designed to exploit high MAPs using the latest propellants.
- Although the 280 Remington is not considered a "magnum" cartridge, its ballistic capabilities are not far from many 7mm magnum cartridges. And, it uses significantly less propellant to achieve it.
- A key advantage of the 280 Remington is flexibility in handling a wide range of bullet weights from 110 to 175-grains. As a result, the 280 Remington is considered by many sportsmen to be an ideal "all-around" cartridge. This viewpoint is best summed up by quoting an anonymous source who stated; "If you could have only one cartridge for hunting, this would be it!"

TECHNICAL NOTES

- The 280 Remington is nearly identical to long-time European favorite: the 7x64mm Brenneke cartridge. However, the two are not interchangeable.
- From a wildcatting standpoint, the 280 Remington is the father of the 280 Ackley Improved.
- From a domestic standpoint, the 280 Remington is a 30-06 Springfield case necked down to hold .284 inch diameter bullets. As such, any rifle originally designed around the 30-06 Springfield cartridge can be converted to 280 Remington caliber with only minor modifications.
- Due to its 3.330 inch maximum overall loaded length, the 280 Remington cartridge is suitable only for rifles having a long or "standard" action length.
- If necessary, 280 Remington cases can be formed from (ironically) 270 Winchester brass.

HANDLOADING NOTES

- In addition to the manufacturers of loaded ammunition listed above, new, empty brass for reloading in this caliber is offered by Remington, Winchester, Norma, Prvi Partizan, RUAG, Nosler, and Hornady.

- Although capable of outstanding ballistic performance, the 280 Remington is not a magnum and should not be expected to deliver magnum ballistics.
- When reloading the 280 Remington cartridge cases fired in semi-automatic or slide-action rifles, full length resizing of the cases will be necessary to avoid feeding and extraction problems.
- Neck sizing can be used for cases fired in bolt-action rifles to extend case life.
- Although the 280 Remington is not considered a varmint cartridge, the Speer 110-grain TNT® HP is a popular choice for varmints and predators.
- The 280 Remington is in its element with a 160-grain bullet such as the Speer Spitzer soft point. It combines the best elements of high muzzle velocity, high striking energy with moderate recoil for hunting medium and some types of large North American game.
- Handloaders can expand the capabilities of the 280 Remington into the large game category using either the 160 or the 175-grain Grand Slam bullets.
- If you plan to fire your reloaded 280 Remington ammunition in semi-automatic or slide-action rifles, use the starting loads listed in the reloading data to avoid extraction issues.
- The 280 Remington cartridge works best with slow burning powders.

SAFETY NOTES

SPEER 160-grain Spitzer BTSP @ a muzzle velocity of 2,854 fps:
- Maximum vertical altitude @ 90° elevation is 16,386 feet.
- Maximum horizontal distance to first impact with ground @ 37° elevation is 7,664 yards.

110 GRAINS

DIAMETER	SECTIONAL DENSITY
.284"	0.195

7mm TNT® HP

Ballistic Coefficient	0.384
COAL Tested	3.300"
Speer Part No.	1616

			Starting Charge		Maximum Charge	
Propellant	Case	Primer	Weight (grains)	Muzzle Velocity (feet/sec)	Weight (grains)	Muzzle Velocity (feet/sec)
Alliant Reloder 16	Federal	Federal 210	53.4	3050	59.3	3381
Alliant Power Pro 4000-MR	Federal	Federal 210	53.7	2981	58.6	3302
Alliant Reloder 19	Remington	CCI 200	59.0	2991	63.0 C	3286
Alliant Reloder 17	Federal	Federal 210	52.9	3054	56.7	3279
Hodgdon H4350	Remington	CCI 200	55.0	2963	59.0	3261
Alliant Reloder 15	Federal	Federal 210	47.6	2988	52.5	3257
IMR 4831	Remington	CCI 200	60.0	3117	62.0 C	3237
IMR 4350	Remington	CCI 200	55.0	2912	59.0	3215
Alliant AR-Comp	Federal	Federal 210	44.5	3025	48.6	3213
IMR 4064	Remington	CCI 200	47.0	2950	51.0	3196
Winchester 760	Remington	CCI 250	53.0	2971	57.0	3190
Accurate 4350	Remington	CCI 200	56.0	2872	60.0	3187
Accurate 3100	Remington	CCI 200	60.0	3043	62.0 C	3143
IMR 4895	Remington	CCI 200	45.0	2883	49.0	3133
IMR 3031	Remington	CCI 200	44.0	2814	48.0	3061
Hodgdon Varget	Remington	CCI 200	45.0	2773	49.0	3026

WARNING! Maximum loads should be used with CAUTION • C = Compressed Load

130 GRAINS

DIAMETER	SECTIONAL DENSITY
.284"	0.230

7mm Spitzer SP Hot-Cor®

Ballistic Coefficient	0.368
COAL Tested	3.205"
Speer Part No.	1623

7mm Spitzer BTSP

Ballistic Coefficient	0.424
COAL Tested	3.205"
Speer Part No.	1624

Propellant	Case	Primer	Starting Charge Weight (grains)	Starting Charge Muzzle Velocity (feet/sec)	Maximum Charge Weight (grains)	Maximum Charge Muzzle Velocity (feet/sec)
Alliant Reloder 16	Federal	Federal 210	51.3	2896	56.8	3139
Alliant Reloder 19	Remington	CCI 200	55.0	2835	59.0	3134
Alliant Power Pro 4000-MR	Federal	Federal 210	54.0	2937	57.8	3114
IMR 4831	Remington	CCI 200	53.0	2828	57.0	3108
IMR 4350	Remington	CCI 200	53.0	2773	57.0	3106
Alliant Reloder 17	Federal	Federal 210	50.4	2845	55.7	3102
Hodgdon H4350	Remington	CCI 200	50.0	2827	54.0	3073
Accurate 4350	Remington	CCI 200	53.0	2791	57.0	3066
Ramshot Big Game	Federal	Federal 210	47.2	2790	52.1	3014
Hodgdon H414	Remington	CCI 250	48.5	2844	52.5	2993
Hodgdon H4831SC	Remington	CCI 200	53.5	2783	57.5	2993
Alliant Power Pro 2000-MR	Federal	Federal 210	46.4	2783	50.6	2993
Vihtavuori N160	Remington	CCI 200	50.0	2794	54.0	2977
Winchester 760	Remington	CCI 250	48.5	2801	52.5	2975
Accurate 3100	Remington	CCI 200	54.0	2721	58.0	2972
IMR 4895	Remington	CCI 200	42.0	2790	46.0	2969
Alliant Reloder 15	Remington	CCI 200	43.0	2774	47.0	2967
IMR 4064	Remington	CCI 200	43.0	2729	47.0	2958
IMR 4320	Remington	CCI 200	43.0	2743	47.0	2946
IMR SR 4759 (reduced load)	Remington	CCI 200	20.0	1680	24.0	2024

WARNING! Maximum loads should be used with CAUTION • C = Compressed Load

145 GRAINS

DIAMETER	SECTIONAL DENSITY
.284"	0.257

7mm Spitzer BTSP
Ballistic Coefficient	0.472
COAL Tested	3.180"
Speer Part No.	1628

7mm Spitzer SP Hot-Cor®
Ballistic Coefficient	0.416
COAL Tested	3.160"
Speer Part No.	1629

7mm Grand Slam® SP
Ballistic Coefficient	0.353
COAL Tested	3.275"
Speer Part No.	1632

			Starting Charge		Maximum Charge	
Propellant	Case	Primer	Weight (grains)	Muzzle Velocity (feet/sec)	Weight (grains)	Muzzle Velocity (feet/sec)
IMR 4831	Remington	CCI 200	54.0	2815	56.0	2975
Alliant Reloder 19	Remington	CCI 200	55.0	2752	57.0	2973
Alliant Power Pro 4000-MR	Federal	Federal 210	50.0	2716	55.4	2972
Alliant Reloder 23	Federal	Federal 210	52.0	2719	57.6 C	2964
Alliant Reloder 16	Federal	Federal 210	48.2	2717	53.6	2958
Alliant Reloder 17	Federal	Federal 210	48.1	2702	53.3	2951
Hodgdon H4350	Remington	CCI 200	50.5	2779	52.5	2950
IMR 4350	Remington	CCI 200	51.0	2697	55.0	2949
Alliant Reloder 22	Remington	CCI 200	54.0	2621	58.0 C	2880
Accurate 4350	Remington	CCI 200	50.0	2650	54.0	2879
Hodgdon H4831SC	Remington	CCI 200	54.0	2798	56.0	2861
Alliant Power Pro 2000-MR	Federal	Federal 210	43.6	2590	48.4	2826
IMR 4064	Remington	CCI 200	42.0	2609	46.0	2818
Accurate 3100	Remington	CCI 200	54.0	2726	56.0	2806
Hodgdon H414	Remington	CCI 250	48.0	2681	50.0	2789
Vihtavuori N160	Remington	CCI 200	48.0	2573	52.0	2777
Winchester 760	Remington	CCI 250	47.5	2692	49.5	2776
IMR 7828	Remington	CCI 200	56.0	2621	58.0 C	2767
Hodgdon Varget	Remington	CCI 200	42.0	2517	46.0	2734
IMR SR 4759 (reduced load)	Remington	CCI 200	21.0	1689	25.0	2012

WARNING! *Maximum loads should be used with CAUTION • C = Compressed Load*

160 GRAINS

DIAMETER	SECTIONAL DENSITY
.284"	0.283

7mm Spitzer BTSP
Ballistic Coefficient	0.519
COAL Tested	3.200"
Speer Part No.	1634

7mm Spitzer SP Hot-Cor®
Ballistic Coefficient	0.504
COAL Tested	3.200"
Speer Part No.	1635

7mm Grand Slam® SP
Ballistic Coefficient	0.389
COAL Tested	3.265"
Speer Part No.	1638

			Starting Charge		Maximum Charge	
Propellant	Case	Primer	Weight (grains)	Muzzle Velocity (feet/sec)	Weight (grains)	Muzzle Velocity (feet/sec)
Accurate 4350	Remington	CCI 200	50.0	2691	52.0	2854
Alliant Reloder 26	Federal	Federal 210	49.9	2625	55.0 C	2841
Hodgdon H4350	Remington	CCI 200	47.0	2571	51.0	2828
Alliant Reloder 19	Remington	CCI 200	53.0	2658	55.0	2813
IMR 4831	Remington	CCI 200	52.0	2686	54.0	2808
Alliant Reloder 22	Remington	CCI 200	54.0	2707	56.0	2807
Alliant Reloder 23	Federal	Federal 210	48.8	2584	54.2 C	2795
IMR 4350	Remington	CCI 200	49.0	2522	53.0	2791
Hodgdon H4831SC	Remington	CCI 200	53.0	2697	55.0	2773
Alliant Reloder 17	Federal	Federal 210	45.7	2538	50.6	2773
Alliant Power Pro 4000-MR	Federal	Federal 210	46.3	2530	51.4	2769
Alliant Reloder 16	Federal	Federal 210	45.2	2564	50.0	2758
IMR 7828	Remington	CCI 200	55.0	2654	57.0	2743
Accurate 3100	Remington	CCI 200	53.0	2637	55.0 C	2725
Ramshot Hunter	Federal	Federal 210	45.9	2491	50.7	2711
IMR 4064	Remington	CCI 200	41.0	2492	45.0	2677
Hodgdon H414	Remington	CCI 250	44.0	2468	48.0	2631
IMR 4895	Remington	CCI 200	39.0	2412	43.0	2624
IMR SR 4759 (reduced load)	Remington	CCI 200	22.0	1711	26.0	2008

WARNING! Maximum loads should be used with CAUTION • C = Compressed Load

175 GRAINS

DIAMETER	SECTIONAL DENSITY
.284"	0.310

7mm Grand Slam® SP

Ballistic Coefficient	0.436
COAL Tested	3.330"
Speer Part No.	1643

			Starting Charge		Maximum Charge	
Propellant	Case	Primer	Weight (grains)	Muzzle Velocity (feet/sec)	Weight (grains)	Muzzle Velocity (feet/sec)
Ramshot Magnum	Federal	Federal 210	55.5	2485	61.5 C	2729
Alliant Reloder 26	Federal	Federal 210	50.4	2477	55.5	2723
Alliant Reloder 23	Federal	Federal 210	49.1	2450	54.2 C	2671
Vihtavuori N560	Remington	CCI 200	50.0	2567	52.0	2644
Alliant Power Pro 4000-MR	Federal	Federal 210	46.4	2384	51.4	2639
Alliant Reloder 17	Federal	Federal 210	45.2	2363	50.2	2638
Alliant Reloder 16	Federal	Federal 210	45.6	2417	50.4	2627
Alliant Reloder 22	Remington	CCI 200	51.0	2520	53.0	2616
Hodgdon H1000	Remington	CCI 200	53.0	2434	57.0 C	2615
Alliant Reloder 19	Remington	CCI 200	48.0	2420	52.0	2597
IMR 4350	Remington	CCI 200	45.0	2338	49.0	2578
IMR 4831	Remington	CCI 200	48.0	2479	50.0	2570
IMR 7828	Remington	CCI 200	51.0	2465	53.0	2568
Hodgdon H4831SC	Remington	CCI 200	50.0	2454	52.0	2558
Hodgdon H4350	Remington	CCI 200	43.0	2388	47.0	2555
Accurate 3100	Remington	CCI 200	49.0	2416	51.0	2520
Hodgdon H414	Remington	CCI 250	44.0	2401	46.0	2461
Winchester 760	Remington	CCI 250	44.0	2370	46.0	2452
IMR SR 4759 (reduced load)	Remington	CCI 200	21.0	1490	25.0	1753

WARNING! Maximum loads should be used with CAUTION • C = Compressed Load

284 WINCHESTER

Parent Cartridge:	Hybrid
Related Cartridges:	6.5x284 Norma
Country of Origin:	USA
Year of Introduction:	1963
Designer(s):	Winchester
Governing Body:	SAAMI/CIP

Case dimensions:
- .473" [12.01mm]
- .500" [12.70mm]
- .320" [8.13mm] cyl
- shoulder angle 35°
- .4748" [12.06mm]
- .4776" [12.13mm]
- .054" [1.37mm]
- .200" [5.08mm]
- 1.400" [35.56mm] basic
- 1.7749" [45.08mm]
- 1.8854" [47.89mm]
- 2.170" [55.12mm]

CARTRIDGE CASE DATA

Case Type:	Rebated, rimless, bottleneck		
Average Case Capacity:	60.0 grains H_2O	Max. Cartridge OAL	2.800 inch
Max. Case Length:	2.170 inch	Primer:	Large Rifle
Case Trim to Length:	2.160 inch	RCBS Shell holder:	# 3
Current Manufacturers:	Winchester		

BALLISTIC DATA

Max. Average Pressure (MAP):	56,000 psi, 54,000 CUP – SAAMI; 63,817 psi CIP	Test Barrel Length:	24 inch
Rifling Twist Rate:	1 turn in 10 inch		

Muzzle velocities of factory loaded ammunition	Bullet Wgt.	Muzzle velocity
	100-grain	3,175 fps
	120-grain	2,968 fps
	139-grain	2,845 fps
	150-grain	2,860 fps

Muzzle velocity will decrease approximately 20 fps per inch for barrels less than 24 inches.

HISTORICAL NOTES

- Since its introduction in 1963, the 284 Winchester cartridge has been considered unusual as it is one of the very few sporting rifle cartridges with a rebated, rimless case.
- In order for the 284 Winchester cartridge to fit in the short actions of their Model 88

and Model 100 rifles, Winchester was forced to use a short 2.170 inch maximum case length. However, by combining a magnum diameter case head, a 35° shoulder angle, and the rim diameter of the 30-06 Springfield, sufficient case capacity was maintained to achieve the required ballistic goals. The result was the first rebated, rimless cartridge from a domestic ammunition maker.

- The 284 Winchester was conceived as a compact, high capacity, powerful new cartridge for the Winchester Model 88 lever-action and Model 100 semi-automatic rifles.
- Today, the 284 Winchester would have the suffix "Short Magnum" after its name.
- Savage offered the 284 Winchester in their Model 99 lever gun and Ruger offered it in their M77 bolt-action rifle as well, for a short time.
- When Winchester ended production of Model 88 and Model 100 rifles after they failed to reach profitable sales levels, the 284 Winchester cartridge became an orphan—a situation that continues to this day.
- To its credit, the 284 Winchester has been used as the basis for a number of excellent wildcat cartridges such as the 6.5x284 Norma which remains in production.
- The growing number of more efficient, short 7mm magnum cartridges has all but eliminated the market niche of the 284 Winchester and at this time it seems headed for retirement.

HANDLOADING NOTES

- In addition to building loaded ammunition, new, empty brass for reloading in this caliber is offered by Winchester.
- When reloading the 284 Winchester cartridge cases fired in semi-automatic or lever-action rifles, full length resizing (using small base dies) of the cases will be necessary to avoid feeding and extraction problems.
- To extend case life, neck sizing can be used for 284 Winchester brass fired in bolt-action rifles.
- Although the 284 Remington is not generally considered a varmint cartridge, the Speer 110-grain TNT® HP is a popular choice for varmints and predators.
- The 284 Winchester is in its element with 160-grain bullets. This combines the best elements of high muzzle velocity, high striking energy with moderate recoil for hunting medium and some types of large North American game.
- For hunting big game, we recommend the exceptional capabilities of the Speer 175-grain Grand Slam® SP when loaded to 2,600+ fps. If you plan to fire your reloaded 284 Winchester ammunition in semi-automatic or lever-action rifles, reduce the maximum loads listed in the reloading data by at least 2 grains to avoid extraction problems.
- The 284 Winchester cartridge works best with slow burning powders.

SAFETY NOTES

SPEER 160-grain Spitzer BTSP @ a muzzle velocity of 2,808 fps:
- Maximum vertical altitude @ 90° elevation is 16,233 feet.
- Maximum horizontal distance to first impact with ground @ 37° elevation is 7,609 yards.

110 GRAINS

DIAMETER	SECTIONAL DENSITY
.284"	0.195

7mm TNT® HP	
Ballistic Coefficient	0.384
COAL Tested	2.780"
Speer Part No.	1616

			Starting Charge		Maximum Charge	
Propellant	Case	Primer	Weight (grains)	Muzzle Velocity (feet/sec)	Weight (grains)	Muzzle Velocity (feet/sec)
Winchester 760	Winchester	CCI 250	58.0	3259	62.0 C	3499
Alliant Reloder 15	Winchester	CCI 200	53.0	3185	57.0	3443
Accurate 2460	Winchester	CCI 250	48.0	3122	52.0	3412
Winchester 748	Winchester	CCI 250	53.0	3134	57.0	3410
Hodgdon BL-C(2)	Winchester	CCI 250	52.0	3121	56.0	3403
Hodgdon H414	Winchester	CCI 250	57.0	3155	61.0 C	3398
Vihtavuori N135	Winchester	CCI 200	48.0	3047	52.0	3337
IMR 4350	Winchester	CCI 200	56.0	3045	60.0 C	3273
IMR 4831	Winchester	CCI 200	58.0	3016	62.0 C	3252
Alliant Reloder 19	Winchester	CCI 200	58.0	2976	62.0 C	3209
Hodgdon H4350	Winchester	CCI 200	55.0	2919	59.0 C	3138
Accurate 4350	Winchester	CCI 200	55.0	2899	59.0 C	3116

WARNING! *Maximum loads should be used with* **CAUTION** • *C = Compressed Load*

130 GRAINS

DIAMETER	SECTIONAL DENSITY
.284"	0.230

7mm Spitzer SP Hot-Cor®

Ballistic Coefficient	0.368
COAL Tested	2.800"
Speer Part No.	1623

7mm Spitzer BTSP

Ballistic Coefficient	0.424
COAL Tested	2.800"
Speer Part No.	1624

			Starting Charge		Maximum Charge	
Propellant	Case	Primer	Weight (grains)	Muzzle Velocity (feet/sec)	Weight (grains)	Muzzle Velocity (feet/sec)
IMR 4350	Winchester	CCI 200	54.0	2933	58.0	3148
IMR 4831	Winchester	CCI 200	55.0	2884	59.0	3085
Winchester 760	Winchester	CCI 250	52.0	2815	56.0	3047
Winchester 748	Winchester	CCI 250	46.0	2693	50.0	2935
IMR 4064	Winchester	CCI 200	45.0	2636	49.0	2879
IMR SR 4759 (reduced load)	Winchester	CCI 200	20.0	1695	24.0	2040

WARNING! Maximum loads should be used with CAUTION • C = Compressed Load

284 WINCHESTER

145 GRAINS

DIAMETER	SECTIONAL DENSITY
.284"	0.257

7mm Spitzer BTSP
Ballistic Coefficient	0.472
COAL Tested	2.800"
Speer Part No.	1628

7mm Spitzer SP Hot-Cor®
Ballistic Coefficient	0.416
COAL Tested	2.800"
Speer Part No.	1629

7mm Grand Slam® SP
Ballistic Coefficient	0.353
COAL Tested	2.800"
Speer Part No.	1632

			Starting Charge		Maximum Charge	
Propellant	Case	Primer	Weight (grains)	Muzzle Velocity (feet/sec)	Weight (grains)	Muzzle Velocity (feet/sec)
IMR 4350	Winchester	CCI 200	52.0	2779	56.0	2982
IMR 4831	Winchester	CCI 200	53.0	2754	57.0	2948
IMR 4895	Winchester	CCI 200	44.0	2631	48.0	2901
Winchester 760	Winchester	CCI 250	50.0	2660	54.0	2884
IMR 4064	Winchester	CCI 200	43.0	2514	47.0	2745
IMR SR 4759 (reduced load)	Winchester	CCI 200	21.0	1666	25.0	1989

WARNING! Maximum loads should be used with CAUTION • C = Compressed Load

160 GRAINS

DIAMETER	SECTIONAL DENSITY
.284"	0.283

7mm Spitzer BTSP
Ballistic Coefficient	0.519
COAL Tested	2.800"
Speer Part No.	1634

7mm Spitzer SP Hot-Cor®
Ballistic Coefficient	0.504
COAL Tested	2.800"
Speer Part No.	1635

7mm Grand Slam® SP
Ballistic Coefficient	0.389
COAL Tested	2.800"
Speer Part No.	1638

			Starting Charge		Maximum Charge	
Propellant	Case	Primer	Weight (grains)	Muzzle Velocity (feet/sec)	Weight (grains)	Muzzle Velocity (feet/sec)
IMR 4350	Winchester	CCI 200	50.0	2616	54.0 C	2845
IMR 4831	Winchester	CCI 200	51.0	2609	55.0 C	2800
Winchester 760	Winchester	CCI 250	48.0	2504	52.0	2736
IMR 4064	Winchester	CCI 200	41.0	2394	45.0	2640
Winchester 748	Winchester	CCI 250	42.0	2410	46.0	2640
IMR 4198 (reduced load)	Winchester	CCI 200	23.0	1675	27.0	1977

WARNING! Maximum loads should be used with CAUTION • C = Compressed Load

175 GRAINS

DIAMETER	SECTIONAL DENSITY
.284"	0.310

7mm Grand Slam® SP

Ballistic Coefficient	0.436
COAL Tested	2.800"
Speer Part No.	1643

			Starting Charge		Maximum Charge	
Propellant	Case	Primer	Weight (grains)	Muzzle Velocity (feet/sec)	Weight (grains)	Muzzle Velocity (feet/sec)
IMR 4831	Winchester	CCI 200	49.0	2475	53.0 C	2669
IMR 4350	Winchester	CCI 200	48.0	2451	52.0 C	2648
Winchester 760	Winchester	CCI 250	45.0	2293	49.0	2519
IMR 4064	Winchester	CCI 200	38.5	2184	42.5	2414
IMR 4320	Winchester	CCI 200	38.0	2106	42.0	2334
IMR 4198 (reduced load)	Winchester	CCI 200	24.0	1669	28.0	1958

WARNING! Maximum loads should be used with CAUTION • C = Compressed Load

7mm REMINGTON SHORT ACTION ULTRA MAGNUM

Alternate Names:	7mm RSAUM
Parent Cartridge:	7mm Remington Ultra Magnum
Country of Origin:	USA
Year of Introduction:	2002
Designer(s):	Remington
Governing Body:	SAAMI

CARTRIDGE CASE DATA

Case Type:	Rebated, bottleneck
Average Case Capacity:	76.1 grains H$_2$O
Max. Cartridge OAL	2.825 inch
Max. Case Length:	2.035 inch
Primer:	Large Rifle
Case Trim to Length:	2.025 inch
RCBS Shell holder:	# 38
Current Manufacturers:	Remington

BALLISTIC DATA

Max. Average Pressure (MAP):	65,000 psi, CUP not established for this round - SAAMI
Test Barrel Length:	24 inch
Rifling Twist Rate:	1 turn in 9.25 inch

Muzzle velocities of factory loaded ammunition	Bullet Wgt.	Muzzle velocity
	140-grain	3,175 fps
	150-grain	3,110 fps
	160-grain	2,960 fps

Muzzle velocity will decrease approximately 30 fps per inch for barrels less than 24 inches.

HISTORICAL NOTES

- In 2002, Remington introduced a new short magnum cartridge of their own — the 7mm Remington Short Action Ultra Magnum (RSAUM). The 300 RSAUM was introduced the following year.

- Remington did not try to match short action magnum calibers with rival Winchester. For example, there is no 270 RSAUM or 325 RSAUM.

- Introduction dates, calibers, bullet weights and case dimensions indicate that the RSAUM cartridges were not developed in response to the WSM cartridges. Rather, they were a parallel development of their own.
- Both Winchester and Remington based their short action magnum cartridges on a magnum head diameter of about .552 inch without a belt, a case length slightly longer than two inches and a MAP level of 65,000 psi.
- Remington and Winchester marketing strategies for their short magnum cartridges differ. While Winchester aimed at a dual purpose deer/big game market for their WSM cartridges, Remington proposed their RSAUM cartridges squarely at big game hunting.
- The difference in marketing concepts is highlighted by the number of line items offered for 7mm short magnums (Winchester: 6, Remington: 2) and the bullet weights offered (Winchester: 140, 150 and 160-grain; Remington: 150 and 160-grain)
- As Remington also manufactures firearms, the company was able to simultaneously introduce the new 7mm RSAUM cartridge along with rifles chambered for it.
- The concept of a short magnum rifle cartridge in any caliber has not been accepted by European sportsmen. While the marketing battle of the short magnum cartridges continues to develop, it is too early to predict winners or losers.

Interesting Dilemma

In the present market, Remington's 7mm RSAUM cartridge is up against a dense field of 14 different 7mm cartridges spread over an estimated 100 ammunition line items from domestic and foreign ammunition manufacturers. This raises the question: "How many 7mm cartridges/loads are enough?"

BALLISTIC NOTES

- Despite its smaller size, the efficient design of the 7mm RSAUM cartridge allows it to match the muzzle velocities of the 7mm WSM.
- With its fast one turn in 9.25 inch rifling twist rate, the 7mm RSAUM is optimized to stabilize bullets up to 160 grains. This rifling twist rate also is ideal to stabilize boat tail bullets for those long range shots.
- While the 7mm RSAUM cartridge is capable of firing lightweight bullets, ammunition makers do not offer such loadings. Hint: you can handload these.

HANDLOADING NOTES

- In addition to building loaded ammunition, Remington is the source for new, empty, unprimed 7mm RSAUM brass for reloading.
- The heavy construction of the 7mm RSAUM cartridge case can cause problems with full length resizing. For this reason neck sizing is recommended as most rifles in 7mm RSAUM caliber are bolt-action types. We recommend full length sizing for hunting.
- Do not use bullets weighing less than 130 grains for hunting deer.
- The 7mm RSAUM cartridge prefers slow burning propellants.
- Long, heavy bullets weighing over 160 grains may take up too much volume inside the 7mm RSAUM case to build a successful load.

SAFETY NOTES

SPEER 160-grain Spitzer BTSP @ a muzzle velocity of 3,024 fps:
- Maximum vertical altitude @ 90° elevation is 16,962 feet.
- Maximum horizontal distance to first impact with ground @ 36° elevation is 7,864 yards.

110 GRAINS

DIAMETER	SECTIONAL DENSITY
.284"	0.195

7mm TNT® HP

Ballistic Coefficient	0.384
COAL Tested	2.710"
Speer Part No.	1616

			Starting Charge		Maximum Charge	
Propellant	Case	Primer	Weight (grains)	Muzzle Velocity (feet/sec)	Weight (grains)	Muzzle Velocity (feet/sec)
Accurate 4350	Remington	CCI 200	64.0	3283	68.0 C	3487
Winchester 760	Remington	CCI 250	62.0	3265	66.0	3458
IMR 4350	Remington	CCI 200	62.0	3223	66.0	3451
Alliant Reloder 19	Remington	CCI 200	66.0	3224	70.0 C	3419
Hodgdon H414	Remington	CCI 250	61.0	3188	65.0	3416
Ramshot Big Game	Remington	CCI 250	59.0	3230	63.0	3401
Alliant Reloder 15	Remington	CCI 200	55.0	3194	59.0	3387
Hodgdon Varget	Remington	CCI 200	54.0	3182	58.0	3384
IMR 4895	Remington	CCI 200	53.0	3153	57.0	3374

WARNING! Maximum loads should be used with CAUTION • C = Compressed Load

130 GRAINS

DIAMETER	SECTIONAL DENSITY
.284"	0.230

7mm Spitzer SP Hot-Cor®	
Ballistic Coefficient	0.368
COAL Tested	2.785"
Speer Part No.	1623

7mm Spitzer BTSP	
Ballistic Coefficient	0.424
COAL Tested	2.785"
Speer Part No.	1624

			Starting Charge		Maximum Charge	
Propellant	Case	Primer	Weight (grains)	Muzzle Velocity (feet/sec)	Weight (grains)	Muzzle Velocity (feet/sec)
IMR 4831	Remington	CCI 200	58.0	3042	62.0	3231
Alliant Reloder 19	Remington	CCI 200	61.0	3051	65.0	3229
Vihtavuori N165	Remington	CCI 200	62.0	3106	66.0 C	3229
Alliant Reloder 22	Remington	CCI 200	61.0	3051	65.0	3214
Winchester 760	Remington	CCI 250	56.0	3032	60.0	3186
IMR 4350	Remington	CCI 200	55.0	3003	59.0	3173
Hodgdon H4831SC	Remington	CCI 200	59.0	2952	63.0	3112
Alliant Reloder 15	Remington	CCI 200	48.0	2924	52.0	3085

WARNING! Maximum loads should be used with CAUTION • C = Compressed Load

145 GRAINS

DIAMETER	SECTIONAL DENSITY
.284"	0.257

7mm Spitzer BTSP
Ballistic Coefficient	0.472
COAL Tested	2.785"
Speer Part No.	1628

7mm Spitzer SP Hot-Cor®
Ballistic Coefficient	0.416
COAL Tested	2.785"
Speer Part No.	1629

7mm Grand Slam® SP
Ballistic Coefficient	0.353
COAL Tested	2.750"
Speer Part No.	1632

			Starting Charge		Maximum Charge	
Propellant	Case	Primer	Weight (grains)	Muzzle Velocity (feet/sec)	Weight (grains)	Muzzle Velocity (feet/sec)
Vihtavuori N560	Remington	CCI 200	59.0	2876	63.0	3085
Alliant Reloder 22	Remington	CCI 200	59.0	2901	63.0	3061
IMR 4831	Remington	CCI 200	56.0	2872	60.0	3051
Alliant Reloder 19	Remington	CCI 200	58.0	2869	62.0	3040
IMR 4350	Remington	CCI 200	53.0	2816	57.0	3006
Winchester 760	Remington	CCI 250	54.0	2831	58.0	3004
Hodgdon H4831SC	Remington	CCI 200	57.0	2830	61.0	2984
Hodgdon H4350	Remington	CCI 200	52.0	2806	56.0	2981
Accurate 5744 (reduced load)	Remington	CCI 200	26.0	1914	28.0	2045

WARNING! *Maximum loads should be used with CAUTION • C = Compressed Load*

160 GRAINS

DIAMETER	SECTIONAL DENSITY
.284"	0.283

7mm Spitzer BTSP
Ballistic Coefficient	0.519
COAL Tested	2.800"
Speer Part No.	1634

7mm Spitzer SP Hot-Cor®
Ballistic Coefficient	0.504
COAL Tested	2.800"
Speer Part No.	1635

7mm Grand Slam® SP
Ballistic Coefficient	0.389
COAL Tested	2.785"
Speer Part No.	1638

			Starting Charge		Maximum Charge	
Propellant	Case	Primer	Weight (grains)	Muzzle Velocity (feet/sec)	Weight (grains)	Muzzle Velocity (feet/sec)
Alliant Reloder 25	Remington	CCI 200	62.0	2836	66.0 C	3024
IMR 7828	Remington	CCI 200	59.0	2794	63.0	2990
Alliant Reloder 22	Remington	CCI 200	57.0	2783	61.0	2930
IMR 4350	Remington	CCI 200	53.0	2731	57.0	2922
IMR 4831	Remington	CCI 200	54.0	2706	58.0	2913
Alliant Reloder 19	Remington	CCI 200	56.0	2774	60.0	2913
Accurate 3100	Remington	CCI 200	57.0	2730	61.0	2908
Hodgdon H4831SC	Remington	CCI 200	57.0	2717	61.0	2900

WARNING! *Maximum loads should be used with CAUTION • C = Compressed Load*

7mm WINCHESTER SHORT MAGNUM

Alternate Names:	7mm WSM
Parent Cartridge:	300 Winchester Short Magnum
Country of Origin:	USA
Year of Introduction:	2002
Designer(s):	Winchester
Governing Body:	SAAMI

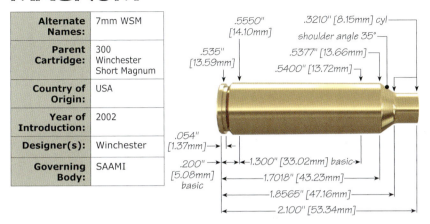

CARTRIDGE CASE DATA

Case Type:	Rimless, bottleneck
Average Case Capacity:	83.0 grains H$_2$O
Max. Cartridge OAL:	2.860 inch
Max. Case Length:	2.100 inch
Primer:	Large Rifle
Case Trim to Length:	2.090 inch
RCBS Shell holder:	# 43
Current Manufacturers:	Winchester, Federal, Hornady, Black Hills, Remington

BALLISTIC DATA

Max. Average Pressure (MAP):	65,000 psi, CUP not established for this round – SAAMI
Test Barrel Length:	24 inch
Rifling Twist Rate:	1 turn in 9.5 inch - SAAMI

Muzzle velocities of factory loaded ammunition	Bullet Wgt.	Muzzle velocity
	140-grain	3,225 fps
	150-grain	3,200 fps
	160-grain	2,990 fps

Muzzle velocity will decrease approximately 30 fps per inch for barrels less than 24 inches.

HISTORICAL NOTES

- In 2002, Winchester introduced the new 7mm Winchester Short Magnum (WSM) cartridge, the second entry in the company's new series of short, beltless magnum cartridges designed for use in short action rifles. The 270 Winchester Short Magnum (WSM) was introduced that same year.

- Both new cartridges (270 WSM & 7mm WSM) were developments of the 300 WSM, the first of the new calibers introduced in 2001. The 325 WSM completed the series in 2004.
- Not to be left behind in developing a trend, competing domestic and foreign ammunition manufacturers have added some of the new WSM cartridges to their product lines.
- While the marketing battle of the short magnum cartridges is on, it is too early to predict the winners or losers.
- Eager to share in a new market, many firearm manufacturers have recently introduced existing models of their rifles chambered for these new Winchester cartridges.

BALLISTIC NOTES

- Winchester offers 7mm WSM ammunition loaded with three different bullet weights: 140-grain, 150-grain and 160-grain.
- The two lighter weight bullets are aimed at deer hunters while the 160-grain bullet can be used on larger game. From this, it appears that Winchester views the 7mm WSM as a dual purpose cartridge.

TECHNICAL NOTES

- All Winchester Short Magnum cartridges share the same 2.100 inch case length, .535 inch beltless head diameter and 35° shoulder angle in order to fit in short rifle actions.
- Case capacity and volume of the 7mm WSM is 8% greater than its direct competitor in the short action magnum sweepstakes--the 7mm Remington Short Action Ultra Magnum.
- MAP levels similar to many of the larger magnums, combined with a more efficient case design, allow the 7mm WSM cartridge to compete with them on equal terms.
- With its one turn in 9.5 inch rifling twist rate, the 7mm WSM will stabilize long heavy bullets up to 160 grains, as well as lighter weight bullets.

HANDLOADING NOTES

- In addition to the manufacturers of loaded ammunition listed above, Winchester, Norma, and others offer new, empty, unprimed 7mm WSM brass cartridge cases for reloading.
- Do not use bullets weighing less than 130 grains for hunting deer with this cartridge.
- The 7mm WSM cartridge prefers slow burning propellants.
- Long, heavy bullets weighing 175 grains take up too much volume inside the 7mm WSM's short case to build a successful load.

SAFETY NOTES

SPEER 160-grain BTSP @ a muzzle velocity of 3,025 fps:
- Maximum vertical altitude @ 90° elevation is 16,956 feet.
- Maximum horizontal distance to first impact with ground @ 38° elevation is 7,863 yards.

110 GRAINS

DIAMETER	SECTIONAL DENSITY
.284"	0.195

7mm TNT® HP

Ballistic Coefficient	0.384
COAL Tested	2.800"
Speer Part No.	1616

			Starting Charge		Maximum Charge	
Propellant	Case	Primer	Weight (grains)	Muzzle Velocity (feet/sec)	Weight (grains)	Muzzle Velocity (feet/sec)
Alliant Reloder 16	Federal	Federal 215	62.1	3230	68.9	3587
Alliant Power Pro 4000-MR	Federal	Federal 215	64.1	3250	71.0	3581
Alliant Reloder 17	Federal	Federal 215	61.4	3258	68.2	3559
Accurate 4350	Federal	Federal 215	64.0	3182	71.2	3535
IMR 4451	Federal	Federal 215	61.9	3177	68.7	3492
Winchester 760	Winchester	CCI 250	65.0	3260	69.0	3425
Alliant Reloder 19	Winchester	CCI 200	68.0	3192	72.0	3392
IMR 4350	Winchester	CCI 200	64.0	3185	68.0	3391
IMR 4064	Winchester	CCI 200	56.0	3207	60.0	3385
Hodgdon H4831SC	Winchester	CCI 200	70.0	3201	74.0	3376
Hodgdon H4350	Winchester	CCI 200	63.0	3200	67.0	3363
Vihtavuori N540	Winchester	CCI 200	57.0	3167	61.0	3357
Alliant Reloder 15	Winchester	CCI 200	55.0	3144	59.0	3312
Accurate 5744 (reduced load)	Winchester	CCI 200	25.0	1975	27.0	2098

WARNING! Maximum loads should be used with CAUTION • C = Compressed Load

7mm WINCHESTER SHORT MAGNUM

130 GRAINS

DIAMETER	SECTIONAL DENSITY
.284"	0.230

7mm Spitzer SP Hot-Cor®
Ballistic Coefficient	0.368
COAL Tested	2.775"
Speer Part No.	1623

7mm Spitzer BTSP
Ballistic Coefficient	0.424
COAL Tested	2.775"
Speer Part No.	1624

			Starting Charge		Maximum Charge	
Propellant	Case	Primer	Weight (grains)	Muzzle Velocity (feet/sec)	Weight (grains)	Muzzle Velocity (feet/sec)
Alliant Reloder 26	Federal	Federal 215	64.4	3046	71.8	3387
Alliant Reloder 23	Federal	Federal 215	63.1	3035	69.9 C	3339
Alliant Power Pro 4000-MR	Federal	Federal 215	60.7	3034	67.3	3334
Alliant Reloder 17	Federal	Federal 215	58.7	3081	64.5	3320
Alliant Reloder 16	Federal	Federal 215	58.6	3025	65.0	3312
Alliant Reloder 19	Winchester	CCI 200	63.0	3077	67.0	3230
Alliant Reloder 22	Winchester	CCI 200	63.0	3064	67.0	3228
IMR 4831	Winchester	CCI 200	60.0	3062	64.0	3228
Accurate 3100	Winchester	CCI 200	64.0	3044	68.0	3216
IMR 4350	Winchester	CCI 200	58.0	3035	62.0	3204
Hodgdon H4350	Winchester	CCI 200	56.0	3011	60.0	3172
Hodgdon H4831SC	Winchester	CCI 200	61.0	3024	65.0	3151
Vihtavuori N160	Winchester	CCI 200	57.0	2995	61.0	3112
Accurate 5744 (reduced load)	Winchester	CCI 200	26.0	1990	28.0	2084

WARNING! *Maximum loads should be used with CAUTION • C = Compressed Load*

145 GRAINS

DIAMETER	SECTIONAL DENSITY
.284"	0.257

7mm Spitzer BTSP
Ballistic Coefficient	0.472
COAL Tested	2.780"
Speer Part No.	1628

7mm Spitzer SP Hot-Cor®
Ballistic Coefficient	0.416
COAL Tested	2.780"
Speer Part No.	1629

7mm Grand Slam® SP
Ballistic Coefficient	0.353
COAL Tested	2.745"
Speer Part No.	1632

			Starting Charge		Maximum Charge	
Propellant	Case	Primer	Weight (grains)	Muzzle Velocity (feet/sec)	Weight (grains)	Muzzle Velocity (feet/sec)
Alliant Reloder 26	Federal	Federal 215	60.9	2932	67.3	3185
Alliant Power Pro 4000-MR	Federal	Federal 215	58.4	2876	64.6	3143
Alliant Reloder 23	Federal	Federal 215	59.8	2886	66.4 C	3139
Alliant Reloder 17	Federal	Federal 215	56.0	2904	62.0	3139
Alliant Reloder 16	Federal	Federal 215	55.2	2852	61.1	3084
Alliant Reloder 22	Winchester	CCI 200	62.0	2927	66.0	3079
Alliant Reloder 19	Winchester	CCI 200	61.0	2893	65.0	3063
Accurate 3100	Winchester	CCI 200	62.0	2898	66.0	3052
IMR 4831	Winchester	CCI 200	58.0	2878	62.0	3047
IMR 4350	Winchester	CCI 200	56.0	2851	60.0	3027
Hodgdon H4350	Winchester	CCI 200	54.0	2818	58.0	2990
Hodgdon H4831SC	Winchester	CCI 200	59.0	2839	63.0	2986
Vihtavuori N160	Winchester	CCI 200	55.0	2814	59.0	2933
Accurate 5744 (reduced load)	Winchester	CCI 200	28.0	1959	30.0	2084

WARNING! Maximum loads should be used with CAUTION • C = Compressed Load

160 GRAINS

DIAMETER	SECTIONAL DENSITY
.284"	0.283

7mm Spitzer BTSP
Ballistic Coefficient	0.519
COAL Tested	2.820"
Speer Part No.	1634

7mm Spitzer SP Hot-Cor®
Ballistic Coefficient	0.504
COAL Tested	2.820"
Speer Part No.	1635

7mm Grand Slam® SP
Ballistic Coefficient	0.389
COAL Tested	2.800"
Speer Part No.	1638

			Starting Charge		Maximum Charge	
Propellant	Case	Primer	Weight (grains)	Muzzle Velocity (feet/sec)	Weight (grains)	Muzzle Velocity (feet/sec)
Alliant Reloder 25	Winchester	CCI 200	66.0	2963	70.0	3090
IMR 7828	Winchester	CCI 200	61.0	2881	65.0	2958
Alliant Reloder 19	Winchester	CCI 200	59.0	2797	63.0	2956
Alliant Reloder 26	Federal	Federal 215	54.9	2729	60.9	2949
IMR 7977	Federal	Federal 215	60.4	2688	66.7 C	2946
Alliant Reloder 22	Winchester	CCI 200	59.0	2780	63.0	2936
IMR 4831	Winchester	CCI 200	55.0	2677	59.0	2926
Alliant Reloder 17	Federal	Federal 215	51.4	2697	57.1	2916
Alliant Reloder 23	Federal	Federal 215	54.1	2693	60.2	2909
Alliant Power Pro 4000-MR	Federal	Federal 215	53.7	2713	58.9	2909
Accurate 3100	Winchester	CCI 200	60.0	2763	64.0	2893
Hodgdon H4831SC	Winchester	CCI 200	57.0	2692	61.0	2890
IMR 4350	Winchester	CCI 200	53.0	2630	57.0	2866
Alliant Reloder 16	Federal	Federal 215	48.8	2626	54.1	2812

WARNING! Maximum loads should be used with CAUTION • C = Compressed Load

7mm REMINGTON MAGNUM

Parent Cartridge:	375 Holland & Holland Magnum (1912), 300 Holland & Holland Magnum (1925)
Country of Origin:	USA
Year of Introduction:	1962
Designer(s):	Remington
Governing Body:	SAAMI/CIP

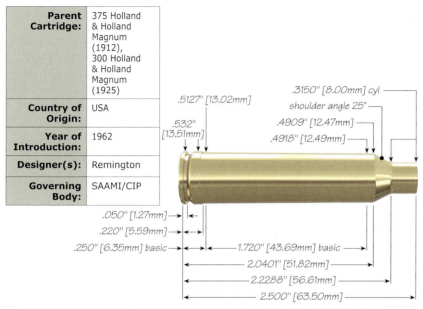

CARTRIDGE CASE DATA			
Case Type:	Belted, bottleneck		
Average Case Capacity:	87 grains H_2O	Max. Cartridge OAL	3.290 inch
Max. Case Length:	2.500 inch	Primer:	Large Rifle
Case Trim to Length:	2.490 inch	RCBS Shell holder:	# 4
Current Manufacturers:	All major ammunition manufacturers		

BALLISTIC DATA			
Max. Average Pressure (MAP):	61,000 psi, 52,000 CUP - SAAMI; 62,366 psi - CIP	Test Barrel Length:	24 inch
Rifling Twist Rate:	1 turn in 9.5 inch		
Muzzle velocities of factory loaded ammunition	Bullet Wgt.		Muzzle velocity
	110-grain		3,500 fps
	140-grain		3,110 fps
	150-grain		3,025 fps
	160-grain		2,950 fps
	175-grain		2,750 fps
	Muzzle velocity will decrease approximately 25 fps per inch for barrels less than 24 inches.		

HISTORICAL NOTES

- In the early 1960s, there was a growing interest in a 7mm magnum cartridge that would fit into a standard 30-06 Springfield length rifle action.
- To be sure, various wildcats and limited production cartridges of this type had been developed that served as "proof of concept", however, none made the transition into full commercial status.
- Remington correctly identified a marketing opportunity in this zone and began development of a new 7mm magnum cartridge based on a shortened 300 H&H Magnum case that would fit in standard-length action rifles.
- In 1962, Remington introduced the new 7mm Remington Magnum cartridge with a Model 700 rifle to fire it. Shooter acceptance was almost immediate and lasting.
- Today, the 7mm Remington Magnum cartridge is an integral part of every major ammunition manufacturer's product line and one of the most popular 7mm magnum cartridges on the market.

BALLISTIC NOTES

- The 7mm Remington Magnum is at its best when taking long shots. With heavy bullets, the 7mm Remington Magnum has proven its effectiveness on many species of African plains game as well.
- Long, heavy bullets fired at high velocities from barrels with fast rifling twist rates often require 100 yards or more to "settle down" and become fully stable. The 7mm Remington Magnum cartridge is no exception to this phenomenon.
- With its one turn in 9.5 inch rifling twist rate and large case capacity, the 7mm Remington Magnum will stabilize long, heavy bullets up to 175 grains.
- Published muzzle velocities of the 7mm Remington Magnum do not match those of the 7mm Weatherby Magnum. However, in the real world out in the field using various barrel lengths, the difference between the two is minimal.

TECHNICAL NOTES

- The 7mm Remington Magnum cartridge case shares its rim, belt, and head dimensions with its parent 300 H&H Magnum.
- In order to fit the 7mm Remington Magnum cartridge in a standard 30-06 Springfield length action, the 300 H&H case was shortened, necked down to 7mm, and blown out with a 25° shoulder angle so as to maintain maximum case capacity.
- Capacity of the 7mm Remington Magnum case is 87 grains of water which is nearly identical to the 7mm Weatherby Magnum.
- In concert with its relative magnum cartridges, the 7mm Remington Magnum achieves its muzzle velocities the traditional way—it burns heavy propellant charges. No short, efficient design concepts here!

HANDLOADING NOTES

- The ballistic sweet spot for loading the 7mm Remington Magnum cartridge is a Speer 160-grain bullet driven at 3,050 fps muzzle velocity using slow burning propellants and Large Rifle magnum primers.
- We recommend the 175-grain Grand Slam® SP bullet for large game.

SAFETY NOTES

SPEER 160-grain Spitzer BTSP @ a muzzle velocity of 3,012 fps:
- Maximum vertical altitude @ 90° elevation is 16,914 feet.
- Maximum horizontal distance to first impact with ground @ 38° elevation is 7,849 yards.

110 GRAINS

DIAMETER	SECTIONAL DENSITY
.284"	0.195

7mm TNT® HP

Ballistic Coefficient	0.384
COAL Tested	3.250"
Speer Part No.	1616

			Starting Charge		Maximum Charge	
Propellant	Case	Primer	Weight (grains)	Muzzle Velocity (feet/sec)	Weight (grains)	Muzzle Velocity (feet/sec)
Alliant Reloder 22	Remington	CCI 250	71.0	3265	75.0 C	3503
Alliant Reloder 19	Remington	CCI 250	70.0	3237	74.0 C	3489
Alliant Reloder 16	Federal	Federal 215	58.9	3180	65.2	3485
Vihtavuori N165	Remington	CCI 250	73.0	3275	77.0 C	3481
Hodgdon H4350	Remington	CCI 250	67.0	3227	71.0 C	3451
Accurate 4350	Remington	CCI 250	67.0	3255	71.0	3427
IMR 4831	Remington	CCI 250	67.0	3208	71.0	3412
IMR 4350	Remington	CCI 250	62.0	3211	66.0	3379
Accurate 3100	Remington	CCI 250	69.0	3160	73.0 C	3358
Hodgdon H4831SC	Remington	CCI 250	68.0	3174	72.0	3348
Winchester 760	Remington	CCI 250	61.0	3117	65.0	3323
Alliant Reloder 15	Remington	CCI 250	54.0	3034	58.0	3256

WARNING! *Maximum loads should be used with CAUTION • C = Compressed Load*

130 GRAINS

DIAMETER	SECTIONAL DENSITY
.284"	0.230

7mm Spitzer SP Hot-Cor®

Ballistic Coefficient	0.368
COAL Tested	3.170"
Speer Part No.	1623

7mm Spitzer BTSP

Ballistic Coefficient	0.424
COAL Tested	3.285"
Speer Part No.	1624

			Starting Charge		Maximum Charge	
Propellant	Case	Primer	Weight (grains)	Muzzle Velocity (feet/sec)	Weight (grains)	Muzzle Velocity (feet/sec)
Alliant Reloder 22	Remington	CCI 250	66.0	3118	70.0	3314
Alliant Reloder 26	Federal	Federal 215	65.3	2995	71.3	3304
Alliant Reloder 23	Federal	Federal 215	63.2	3021	69.2	3274
Alliant Power Pro 4000-MR	Federal	Federal 215	61.1	3007	67.1	3271
Alliant Reloder 19	Remington	CCI 250	65.0	3057	69.0	3270
Alliant Reloder 25	Federal	Federal 215	68.0	2960	75.2	3269
IMR 4831	Remington	CCI 250	61.0	3044	65.0	3243
IMR 7828	Federal	Federal 215	62.7	2990	68.7	3235
IMR 4350	Remington	CCI 250	59.0	3040	63.0	3234
Vihtavuori N165	Remington	CCI 250	68.0	3017	72.0	3231
Accurate 4350	Remington	CCI 250	60.0	3027	64.0	3227
Winchester 760	Remington	CCI 250	58.0	2989	62.0	3211
Alliant Reloder 17	Federal	Federal 215	54.8	2963	60.2	3196
Hodgdon H4350	Remington	CCI 250	60.0	3004	64.0	3189
Alliant Reloder 16	Federal	Federal 215	55.3	2959	60.9	3184
Hodgdon H414	Remington	CCI 250	58.0	2960	62.0	3164
Hodgdon H4831SC	Remington	CCI 250	62.0	3001	66.0	3141
Ramshot Hunter	Federal	Federal 215	56.2	2915	62.2	3133
Hodgdon H380	Remington	CCI 250	55.0	2841	59.0	3052
Alliant Reloder 15	Remington	CCI 250	51.0	2814	55.0	3049
IMR 4895	Remington	CCI 250	46.0	2737	50.0	2964
IMR SR 4759 (reduced load)	Remington	CCI 250	22.0	1768	26.0	2084

WARNING! Maximum loads should be used with CAUTION • C = Compressed Load

145 GRAINS

DIAMETER	SECTIONAL DENSITY
.284"	0.257

7mm Spitzer BTSP
Ballistic Coefficient	0.472
COAL Tested	3.280"
Speer Part No.	1628

7mm Spitzer SP Hot-Cor®
Ballistic Coefficient	0.416
COAL Tested	3.280"
Speer Part No.	1629

7mm Grand Slam® SP
Ballistic Coefficient	0.353
COAL Tested	3.235"
Speer Part No.	1632

			Starting Charge		Maximum Charge	
Propellant	Case	Primer	Weight (grains)	Muzzle Velocity (feet/sec)	Weight (grains)	Muzzle Velocity (feet/sec)
Alliant Reloder 26	Federal	Federal 215	63.2	2853	69.7	3167
Alliant Reloder 19	Remington	CCI 250	63.0	2948	67.0	3153
Alliant Reloder 22	Remington	CCI 250	64.0	2919	68.0	3136
Alliant Reloder 25	Federal	Federal 215	65.5	2805	72.5	3106
IMR 7828	Remington	CCI 250	65.0	2974	69.0	3103
Alliant Reloder 23	Federal	Federal 215	60.8	2861	66.8	3101
Hodgdon H1000	Remington	CCI 250	69.0	2910	73.0 C	3090
IMR 4831	Remington	CCI 250	59.0	2920	63.0	3081
IMR 4350	Remington	CCI 250	56.0	2881	60.0	3070
Alliant Reloder 17	Federal	Federal 215	54.0	2867	59.4	3060
Hodgdon H870	Remington	CCI 250	76.0	2860	80.0	3037
Vihtavuori N165	Remington	CCI 250	64.0	2828	68.0	3019
Accurate 4350	Remington	CCI 250	60.0	2837	64.0	3015
Winchester 760	Remington	CCI 250	54.0	2819	58.0	3012
Accurate 3100	Remington	CCI 250	62.0	2826	66.0	3008
Hodgdon H4350	Remington	CCI 250	59.0	2801	63.0	2987
Hodgdon H4831SC	Remington	CCI 250	59.5	2835	63.5	2981
IMR SR 4759 (reduced load)	Remington	CCI 250	24.0	1811	28.0	2112

WARNING! Maximum loads should be used with CAUTION • C = Compressed Load

160 GRAINS

DIAMETER	SECTIONAL DENSITY
.284"	0.283

7mm Spitzer BTSP
Ballistic Coefficient	0.519
COAL Tested	3.280"
Speer Part No.	1634

7mm Spitzer SP Hot-Cor®
Ballistic Coefficient	0.504
COAL Tested	3.280"
Speer Part No.	1635

7mm Grand Slam® SP
Ballistic Coefficient	0.389
COAL Tested	3.225"
Speer Part No.	1638

7mm REMINGTON MAGNUM

			Starting Charge		Maximum Charge	
Propellant	Case	Primer	Weight (grains)	Muzzle Velocity (feet/sec)	Weight (grains)	Muzzle Velocity (feet/sec)
Alliant Reloder 33	Federal	Federal 215	72.0	2742	79.2 C	3049
Alliant Reloder 25	Remington	CCI 250	66.0	2875	70.0	3012
Ramshot Magnum	Federal	Federal 215	64.3	2744	71.0	2999
Alliant Reloder 26	Federal	Federal 215	60.0	2698	66.3	2989
Alliant Reloder 22	Remington	CCI 250	61.0	2773	65.0	2976
Hodgdon H870	Remington	CCI 250	75.0	2819	79.0	2970
IMR 7828	Federal	Federal 215	59.2	2738	65.4	2961
Alliant Reloder 23	Federal	Federal 215	58.1	2705	64.2	2946
Alliant Reloder 19	Remington	CCI 250	60.0	2729	64.0	2941
Hodgdon H1000	Remington	CCI 250	65.0	2761	69.0	2936
IMR 4831	Remington	CCI 250	57.0	2784	61.0	2915
Hodgdon H4350	Remington	CCI 250	57.0	2735	61.0	2904
IMR 4350	Remington	CCI 250	54.0	2725	58.0	2901
Alliant Reloder 17	Federal	Federal 215	51.0	2667	56.7	2890
Accurate 8700	Remington	CCI 250	75.0	2736	79.0	2870
Accurate 3100	Remington	CCI 250	60.0	2691	64.0	2869
Vihtavuori N165	Remington	CCI 250	60.0	2692	64.0	2867
Hodgdon H4831SC	Remington	CCI 250	58.0	2711	62.0	2853
Accurate 4350	Remington	CCI 250	57.0	2680	61.0	2849
IMR SR 4759 (reduced load)	Remington	CCI 250	26.0	1770	30.0	2067

WARNING! Maximum loads should be used with CAUTION • C = Compressed Load

175 GRAINS

DIAMETER	SECTIONAL DENSITY
.284"	0.310

7mm Grand Slam® SP

Ballistic Coefficient	0.436
COAL Tested	3.220"
Speer Part No.	1643

			Starting Charge		Maximum Charge	
Propellant	Case	Primer	Weight (grains)	Muzzle Velocity (feet/sec)	Weight (grains)	Muzzle Velocity (feet/sec)
Hodgdon H870	Remington	CCI 250	74.0	2790	78.0	2954
Alliant Reloder 33	Federal	Federal 215	70.2	2728	75.0 C	2889
Alliant Reloder 25	Remington	CCI 250	65.0	2792	67.0	2888
Ramshot Magnum	Federal	Federal 215	65.8	2753	69.6	2884
Hodgdon Retumbo	Federal	Federal 215	63.4	2636	69.3 C	2865
Alliant Reloder 22	Remington	CCI 250	57.0	2618	61.0	2830
IMR 4831	Remington	CCI 250	55.0	2641	59.0	2827
Alliant Reloder 26	Federal	Federal 215	59.4	2660	63.4	2824
Alliant Reloder 19	Remington	CCI 250	58.0	2604	62.0	2812
Alliant Reloder 23	Federal	Federal 215	55.5	2565	61.8	2803
IMR 7828	Federal	Federal 215	56.5	2611	62.5	2802
Alliant Power Pro 4000-MR	Federal	Federal 215	54.3	2556	60.3	2796
IMR 4350	Remington	CCI 250	52.0	2630	56.0	2789
Hodgdon H1000	Remington	CCI 250	61.0	2620	65.0	2782
Vihtavuori N165	Remington	CCI 250	58.0	2565	62.0	2742
Alliant Reloder 17	Federal	Federal 215	48.7	2535	53.7	2741
Hodgdon H4831SC	Remington	CCI 250	56.0	2588	60.0	2733
Accurate 8700	Remington	CCI 250	71.0	2639	75.0	2722
Accurate 4350	Remington	CCI 250	55.0	2547	59.0	2713
Hodgdon H4350	Remington	CCI 250	55.0	2546	59.0	2703
IMR SR 4759 (reduced load)	Remington	CCI 250	28.0	1831	32.0	2085

WARNING! Maximum loads should be used with CAUTION • C = Compressed Load

7mm WEATHERBY MAGNUM

Parent Cartridge:	300 Holland & Holland Magnum
Country of Origin:	USA
Year of Introduction:	1940s
Designer(s):	Weatherby
Governing Body:	SAAMI/CIP

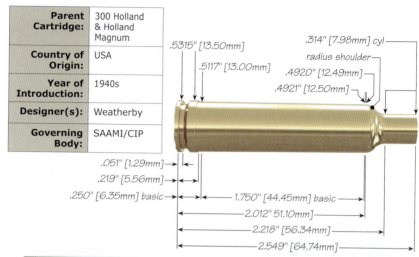

CARTRIDGE CASE DATA

Case Type:	Rimless, belted, necked with double radius shoulder
Average Case Capacity:	87.5 grains H₂O
Max. Cartridge OAL:	3.360 inch
Max. Case Length:	2.549 inch
Primer:	Large Rifle
Case Trim to Length:	2.539 inch
RCBS Shell holder:	# 4
Current Manufacturers:	Weatherby, Norma, Nosler, and Remington

BALLISTIC DATA

Max. Average Pressure (MAP):	65,000 psi, CUP not established for this round - SAAMI
Test Barrel Length:	24 inch
Rifling Twist Rate:	1 turn in 10 inch

Muzzle velocities of factory loaded ammunition	Bullet Wgt.	Muzzle velocity
	120-grain	3,430 fps
	139-grain	3,240 fps
	154-grain	3,123 fps
	175-grain	3,070 fps

Muzzle velocity will decrease approximately 30 fps per inch for barrels less than 24 inches.

HISTORICAL NOTES

- When it was developed in the early 1940s, the 7mm Weatherby Magnum cartridge set the bar for all 7mm cartridges, a throne it continued to occupy until the advent of the 7mm STW in the late 90s.

- The 7mm Weatherby Magnum cartridge was one of the first calibers designed by Roy Weatherby that incorporated his concept of the terminal ballistic benefits from the hydraulic shock caused by bullets impacting at high velocities.
- The 7mm Weatherby Magnum remains one of the most popular mainstays of the Weatherby Magnum ammunition product line. For many years now, all Weatherby Magnum ammunition has been manufactured for them by Norma, in Sweden.
- By the late 1980s, the 7mm Weatherby Magnum became a victim of its own success when major domestic manufacturers began making 7mm Weatherby Magnum ammunition, thus dividing a relatively small market.
- Fortunately for Weatherby, by 2000 most of the mainstream domestic ammunition manufacturers dropped the 7mm Weatherby Magnum from their product line when they began to focus on 7mm magnum cartridges of their own design.
- In 2016, Weatherby announced plans to manufacture their ammunition in the U.S. for the first time.

Interesting Fact

Roy Weatherby has been called, with justification: "The high priest of high velocity".

BALLISTIC NOTES

- The 7mm Weatherby Magnum set the bar for muzzle velocity of all cartridges in this caliber – a bar that remained unchallenged until 2001 when the 7mm RUM appeared.
- The 7mm Weatherby Magnum and the 7mm WSM share 65,000 psi MAP levels.

TECHNICAL NOTES

- Like its siblings, the parent cartridge of 7mm Weatherby Magnum is based on the venerable 300 H&H Magnum with its body shortened and blown out to increase capacity, then necked down to hold .284 inch diameter bullets.
- The 7mm Weatherby Magnum is intended for hunting medium and large North American game at long ranges under difficult conditions. For this reason, factory loaded ammunition is assembled with Spitzer bullets weighing from 120 to 175 grains.
- The one turn in 10 inch rifling twist rate is optimized for long heavy bullets of 140-175 grains. This rifling twist rate works well with boat tail bullets for those long range shots.

HANDLOADING NOTES

- In addition to those offering loaded ammunition listed above, Norma and Nosler offer new, empty brass in this cartridge for handloading.
- As with other Weatherby Magnum calibers, 7mm Weatherby Magnum cases tend to stretch just in front of the belt. After four to six firings, these cases can separate at the stretch point.
- A ballistic sweet spot for reloading the 7mm Weatherby Magnum cartridge is the Speer 160-grain Spitzer BTSP driven at 3,132 fps muzzle velocity using slow burning propellants and Large Rifle Magnum primers.
- Like all Weatherby Magnum cartridges, the 7mm Weatherby Magnum performs best when loaded with slow burning propellants.

SAFETY NOTES

SPEER 160-grain Spitzer BTSP @ a muzzle velocity of 3,132 fps:
- Maximum vertical altitude @ 90° elevation is 17,316 feet.
- Maximum horizontal distance to first impact with ground @ 37° elevation is 7,989 yards.

110 GRAINS

DIAMETER	SECTIONAL DENSITY
.284"	0.195

7mm TNT® HP

Ballistic Coefficient	0.384
COAL Tested	3.280"
Speer Part No.	1616

			Starting Charge		Maximum Charge	
Propellant	Case	Primer	Weight (grains)	Muzzle Velocity (feet/sec)	Weight (grains)	Muzzle Velocity (feet/sec)
Alliant Reloder 22	Federal	Federal 215	72.0	3301	76.0	3507
Alliant Reloder 19	Federal	Federal 215	70.0	3264	74.0	3485
IMR 4831	Federal	Federal 215	68.0	3266	72.0	3481
Vihtavuori N560	Federal	Federal 215	72.0	3276	76.0	3476
Ramshot Magnum	Federal	Federal 215	78.5	3242	82.5	3471
IMR 4350	Federal	Federal 215	67.0	3272	71.0	3459
Hodgdon H4350	Federal	Federal 215	66.0	3214	73.0	3455
Hodgdon H4831SC	Federal	Federal 215	72.0	3247	76.0	3433
Accurate 3100	Federal	Federal 215	69.0	3233	73.0	3425
Winchester 760	Federal	Federal 215	64.0	3227	68.0	3425
Alliant Reloder 15	Federal	Federal 215	59.0	3217	63.0	3405

WARNING! Maximum loads should be used with CAUTION • C = Compressed Load

130 GRAINS

DIAMETER	SECTIONAL DENSITY
.284"	0.230

7mm Spitzer SP Hot-Cor®
Ballistic Coefficient	0.368
COAL Tested	3.330"
Speer Part No.	1623

7mm Spitzer BTSP
Ballistic Coefficient	0.424
COAL Tested	3.330"
Speer Part No.	1624

			Starting Charge		Maximum Charge	
Propellant	Case	Primer	Weight (grains)	Muzzle Velocity (feet/sec)	Weight (grains)	Muzzle Velocity (feet/sec)
Alliant Reloder 26	Federal	Federal 215	67.3	3063	74.3	3406
Ramshot Magnum	Federal	Federal 215	78.0	3219	82.0	3374
Alliant Reloder 22	Federal	Federal 215	70.0	3153	74.0	3345
Alliant Reloder 23	Federal	Federal 215	65.3	3064	72.3	3344
Vihtavuori N560	Federal	Federal 215	70.0	3153	74.0	3338
Accurate 3100	Federal	Federal 215	68.0	3133	72.0	3328
IMR 4831	Federal	Federal 215	66.0	3121	70.0	3321
Alliant Reloder 19	Federal	Federal 215	68.0	3087	72.0	3317
Hodgdon H1000	Federal	Federal 215	70.6	3051	78.2 C	3316
IMR 7977	Federal	Federal 215	71.0	3007	78.7 C	3314
Hodgdon Retumbo	Federal	Federal 215	72.0	2995	79.0 C	3289
IMR 4350	Federal	Federal 215	64.0	3066	68.0	3269
Hodgdon H4350	Federal	Federal 215	63.0	3100	67.0	3261
Hodgdon H4831SC	Federal	Federal 215	69.0	3063	73.0	3251
Alliant Reloder 15	Federal	Federal 215	56.0	3053	60.0	3185
Alliant Reloder 33	Federal	Federal 215	78.9	2974	82.0 C	3123

WARNING! *Maximum loads should be used with CAUTION • C = Compressed Load*

7mm WEATHERBY MAGNUM

145 GRAINS

DIAMETER	SECTIONAL DENSITY
.284"	0.257

7mm Spitzer BTSP
Ballistic Coefficient	0.472
COAL Tested	3.350"
Speer Part No.	1628

7mm Spitzer SP Hot-Cor®
Ballistic Coefficient	0.416
COAL Tested	3.350"
Speer Part No.	1629

7mm Grand Slam® SP
Ballistic Coefficient	0.353
COAL Tested	3.290"
Speer Part No.	1632

Propellant	Case	Primer	Starting Charge		Maximum Charge	
			Weight (grains)	Muzzle Velocity (feet/sec)	Weight (grains)	Muzzle Velocity (feet/sec)
Alliant Reloder 22	Federal	Federal 215	67.0	2960	71.0	3177
Vihtavuori N560	Federal	Federal 215	67.5	2964	71.5	3167
Ramshot Magnum	Federal	Federal 215	73.0	2989	77.0	3139
IMR 4831	Federal	Federal 215	63.0	2948	67.0	3134
Alliant Reloder 19	Federal	Federal 215	65.0	2944	69.0	3133
IMR 4350	Federal	Federal 215	62.0	2913	66.0	3117
Accurate 3100	Federal	Federal 215	64.0	2927	68.0	3105
Hodgdon H4831SC	Federal	Federal 215	66.5	2931	70.5	3096
Alliant Reloder 15	Federal	Federal 215	52.0	2811	56.0	2940

WARNING! Maximum loads should be used with CAUTION • C = Compressed Load

160 GRAINS

DIAMETER	SECTIONAL DENSITY
.284"	0.283

7mm Spitzer BTSP
Ballistic Coefficient	0.519
COAL Tested	3.350"
Speer Part No.	1634

7mm Spitzer SP Hot-Cor®
Ballistic Coefficient	0.504
COAL Tested	3.350"
Speer Part No.	1635

7mm Grand Slam® SP
Ballistic Coefficient	0.389
COAL Tested	3.350"
Speer Part No.	1638

			Starting Charge		Maximum Charge	
Propellant	Case	Primer	Weight (grains)	Muzzle Velocity (feet/sec)	Weight (grains)	Muzzle Velocity (feet/sec)
Alliant Reloder 33	Federal	Federal 215	74.6	2781	82.0 C	3142
Alliant Reloder 25	Federal	Federal 215	71.0	2930	75.0 C	3132
Vihtavuori N560	Federal	Federal 215	67.0	2891	71.0	3095
Alliant Reloder 26	Federal	Federal 215	62.6	2763	69.4	3091
Ramshot Magnum	Federal	Federal 215	72.0	2926	76.0	3079
Alliant Reloder 22	Federal	Federal 215	66.0	2849	70.0	3065
Hodgdon Retumbo	Federal	Federal 215	67.3	2762	74.6 C	3063
IMR 7828	Federal	Federal 215	67.0	2859	71.0 C	3052
Alliant Reloder 23	Federal	Federal 215	61.3	2753	67.8	3040
Alliant Reloder 19	Federal	Federal 215	64.5	2837	68.5	3035
Hodgdon H1000	Federal	Federal 215	65.0	2754	72.2	3021
IMR 4350	Federal	Federal 215	61.0	2829	65.0	3019
IMR 4831	Federal	Federal 215	62.0	2856	66.0	3013
IMR 7977	Federal	Federal 215	65.4	2701	72.3	2996
Accurate 3100	Federal	Federal 215	63.5	2825	67.5	2992
Hodgdon H4831SC	Federal	Federal 215	66.0	2818	70.0	2989
Hodgdon H4350	Federal	Federal 215	60.0	2838	64.0	2988

WARNING! Maximum loads should be used with CAUTION • C = Compressed Load

175 GRAINS

DIAMETER	SECTIONAL DENSITY
.284"	0.310

7mm Grand Slam® SP

Ballistic Coefficient	0.436
COAL Tested	3.250"
Speer Part No.	1643

			Starting Charge		Maximum Charge	
Propellant	Case	Primer	Weight (grains)	Muzzle Velocity (feet/sec)	Weight (grains)	Muzzle Velocity (feet/sec)
Alliant Reloder 33	Federal	Federal 215	73.4	2629	81.6 C	3016
Alliant Reloder 25	Federal	Federal 215	70.0	2791	74.0 C	2982
Vihtavuori N560	Federal	Federal 215	65.0	2742	69.0	2942
IMR 7828	Federal	Federal 215	66.0	2752	70.0	2935
Ramshot Magnum	Federal	Federal 215	70.0	2761	74.0	2934
Alliant Reloder 26	Federal	Federal 215	61.8	2617	68.4	2929
Hodgdon Retumbo	Federal	Federal 215	66.1	2632	73.3 C	2910
Alliant Reloder 22	Federal	Federal 215	65.0	2731	69.0	2904
Alliant Reloder 19	Federal	Federal 215	63.0	2724	67.0	2885
Accurate 3100	Federal	Federal 215	63.0	2716	67.0	2882
Alliant Reloder 23	Federal	Federal 215	60.0	2609	66.3	2873
Hodgdon H1000	Federal	Federal 215	63.9	2634	70.7	2873
IMR 4831	Federal	Federal 215	60.0	2699	64.0	2864
IMR 4350	Federal	Federal 215	59.0	2693	63.0	2862
Hodgdon H4350	Federal	Federal 215	58.0	2711	62.0	2858
Hodgdon H4831SC	Federal	Federal 215	64.0	2702	68.0	2854
IMR 7977	Federal	Federal 215	64.4	2611	71.2 C	2850

7mm SHOOTING TIMES WESTERNER

Alternate Names:	7mm STW
Parent Cartridge:	8mm Remington Magnum
Country of Origin:	USA
Year of Introduction:	1998
Designer(s):	Layne Simpson
Governing Body:	SAAMI

Dimensions:
- .5126" [13.02mm]
- .532" [13.51mm]
- .3170" [8.05mm] cyl
- shoulder angle 25°
- .4870" [12.37mm]
- .4917" [12.49mm]
- .050" [1.27mm]
- .220" [5.59mm]
- .250" [6.35mm] basic
- 1.750" [44.45mm] basic
- 2.3890" [60.68mm]
- 2.5724" [65.34mm]
- 2.850" [72.39mm]

CARTRIDGE CASE DATA			
Case Type:	Belted, necked		
Average Case Capacity:	100.2 grains H₂O	Max. Cartridge OAL	3.600 inch
Max. Case Length:	2.850 inch	Primer:	Large Rifle
Case Trim to Length:	2.840 inch	RCBS Shell holder:	# 4
Current Manufacturers:	Nosler		

BALLISTIC DATA

Max. Average Pressure (MAP):	65,000 psi, 53,000 CUP - SAAMI	Test Barrel Length:	24 inch
Rifling Twist Rate:	1 turn in 9.5 inch, 1/8 and 1/10 inch are options		

Muzzle velocities of factory loaded ammunition	Bullet Wgt.	Muzzle velocity
	120-grain	3,384 fps
	140-grain	3,268 fps
	150-grain	3,233 fps
	160-grain	3,177 fps
	175-grain	3,047 fps

Muzzle velocity will decrease approximately 30 fps per inch for barrels less than 24 inches.

HISTORICAL NOTES

- When SAAMI standardized the 7mm Shooting Times Westerner (STW) cartridge it became one of the very few wildcats to make the transition to full commercial status.
- Designer of the new cartridge, writer Layne Simpson of *Shooting Times Magazine* named his creation after the magazine and the area of the U.S. where he felt the new cartridge would find the greatest acceptance.
- Simpson's goals for his new rifle cartridge were to improve on the muzzle velocity levels of the existing 7mm Remington Magnum and, hopefully, the 7mm Weatherby Magnum.
- Achieving the stated muzzle velocities proved difficult, but, in the end Simpson succeeded—if only just barely.
- Although Simpson's experiments registered success in reaching his goals, the industry standardization process watered down any real improvements to a narrower margin.
- A number of mainstream ammunition makers added the 7mm STW to their product lines following standardization. However, sales levels after the initial spurt of interest following introduction of this cartridge were disappointing.
- Currently, only Nosler lists this cartridge in their catalog.
- New rifles in 7mm STW caliber are no longer being made.

Interesting Fact

There was a 7mm Shooting Times Easterner and a Shooting Times Alaskan cartridge. Neither made the transition to full commercial production.

BALLISTIC NOTES

- The 7mm STW cartridge was designed for hunting big game at long ranges.
- Long, heavy bullets fired at high velocities from barrels with fast rifling twist rates often require 100 yards or more to "settle down" and become fully stable. The 7mm STW cartridge proves no exception to this phenomenon.
- With its one turn in 9.5 inch rifling twist rate and large case capacity, the 7mm STW will stabilize long, heavy, boat tail bullets up to 175 grains for those long range shots.

- While the 7mm STW cartridge is certainly capable of firing bullets weighing less than 140 grains, we recommend against such loadings for a good reason—this is not a varmint cartridge and such lightweight bullets are not suitable for deer.

TECHNICAL NOTES

- Essentially, the 7mm STW cartridge is an 8mm Remington Magnum case necked down to 7mm.
- The 7mm STW cartridge shares its rim, case head, case length, and overall loaded length dimensions with the 8mm Remington Magnum, making it suitable only for rifles with a long action.
- Capacity of the 7mm STW case is huge – approximately 15% more than either the 7mm Rem. Magnum or the 7mm Weatherby Magnum.
- Shoulder angle of the 7mm STW, the 7mm Rem. Mag., and the 8mm Rem. Mag. is 25°.
- The 7mm STW cartridge achieves its muzzle velocities the old fashioned way, it burns large amounts of powder.

HANDLOADING NOTES

- At this time the only sources for new, empty 7mm STW brass are Nosler and Quality Cartridge.
- Neck sizing is recommended for all reloading, except hunting rounds, as most rifles in 7mm STW caliber are bolt-action types.
- The ballistic sweet spot for reloading the 7mm STW cartridge is a 160-grain bullet driven at 3,133 fps muzzle velocity using slow burning propellants.

SAFETY NOTES

SPEER 160-grain Spitzer BTSP @ a muzzle velocity of 3,133 fps:
- Maximum vertical altitude @ 90° elevation is 17,316 feet.
- Maximum horizontal distance to first impact with ground @ 38° elevation is 7,989 yards.

WARNING!

All loading data in this manual is based on the industry standardized cartridge dimensions as shown on the drawing above. Some cartridge dimensions and associated reloading data from pre-standardized times when the 7mm STW was still a wildcat may produce MAPs as much as 20% over the current limit. These pressures can cause damage to your rifle and cause serious personal injury.

145 GRAINS

DIAMETER	SECTIONAL DENSITY
.284"	0.257

7mm Spitzer BTSP
Ballistic Coefficient	0.472
COAL Tested	3.600"
Speer Part No.	1628

7mm Spitzer SP Hot-Cor®
Ballistic Coefficient	0.416
COAL Tested	3.600"
Speer Part No.	1629

7mm Grand Slam® SP
Ballistic Coefficient	0.353
COAL Tested	3.550"
Speer Part No.	1632

			Starting Charge		Maximum Charge	
Propellant	Case	Primer	Weight (grains)	Muzzle Velocity (feet/sec)	Weight (grains)	Muzzle Velocity (feet/sec)
Alliant Reloder 33	Federal	Federal 215	80.5	2945	89.5	3289
Alliant Reloder 22	Remington	CCI 250	75.0	3184	77.0	3273
Alliant Reloder 25	Remington	CCI 250	76.0	3122	80.0	3273
Alliant Reloder 26	Federal	Federal 215	69.8	2912	77.4	3249
IMR 7977	Federal	Federal 215	74.2	2928	82.2	3239
IMR 7828	Remington	CCI 250	72.0	3079	76.0	3228
Hodgdon H1000	Federal	Federal 215	72.8	2929	80.8	3223
Alliant Reloder 23	Federal	Federal 215	67.8	2935	75.0	3215
Alliant Power Pro 4000-MR	Federal	Federal 215	65.5	2921	72.8	3212
Accurate 3100	Remington	CCI 250	76.0	3126	78.0	3201
Hodgdon H4350	Remington	CCI 250	66.0	3016	70.0	3159
IMR 4350	Remington	CCI 250	67.5	3073	69.5	3154
IMR 4831	Remington	CCI 250	69.0	3082	71.0	3149
Hodgdon H414	Remington	CCI 250	62.0	2940	66.0	3052

WARNING! *Maximum loads should be used with CAUTION • C = Compressed Load*

160 GRAINS

DIAMETER	SECTIONAL DENSITY
.284"	0.283

7mm Spitzer BTSP
Ballistic Coefficient	0.519
COAL Tested	3.580"
Speer Part No.	1634

7mm Spitzer SP Hot-Cor®
Ballistic Coefficient	0.504
COAL Tested	3.600"
Speer Part No.	1635

7mm Grand Slam® SP
Ballistic Coefficient	0.389
COAL Tested	3.550"
Speer Part No.	1638

			Starting Charge		Maximum Charge	
Propellant	Case	Primer	Weight (grains)	Muzzle Velocity (feet/sec)	Weight (grains)	Muzzle Velocity (feet/sec)
Accurate 8700	Remington	CCI 250	87.0	3001	91.0 C	3133
Alliant Reloder 33	Federal	Federal 215	79.6	2767	88.4 C	3125
Alliant Reloder 50	Federal	Federal 215	79.0	2846	87.6 C	3105
IMR 7828	Remington	CCI 250	72.0	2954	76.0	3097
Accurate 3100	Remington	CCI 250	74.0	3020	76.0	3093
IMR 7977	Federal	Federal 215	74.3	2773	82.4	3087
Alliant Reloder 26	Federal	Federal 215	69.2	2775	76.7	3086
Alliant Reloder 25	Remington	CCI 250	71.0	2952	75.0	3076
Alliant Reloder 22	Remington	CCI 250	69.0	2947	73.0	3074
Hodgdon Retumbo	Federal	Federal 215	72.4	2810	79.2	3072
Alliant Reloder 23	Federal	Federal 215	67.7	2782	74.9	3050
IMR 4831	Remington	CCI 250	69.0	2967	71.0	3040
IMR 4350	Remington	CCI 250	65.5	2895	69.5	3033
Alliant Power Pro 4000-MR	Federal	Federal 215	64.9	2771	71.7	3027
Hodgdon H4831SC	Remington	CCI 250	66.0	2884	70.0	3019
Hodgdon H1000	Remington	CCI 250	75.0	2890	79.0	3010
Vihtavuori N170	Remington	CCI 250	72.0	2827	76.0	2955

WARNING! Maximum loads should be used with CAUTION • C = Compressed Load

175 GRAINS

DIAMETER	SECTIONAL DENSITY
.284"	0.310

7mm Grand Slam® SP	
Ballistic Coefficient	0.436
COAL Tested	3.600"
Speer Part No.	1643

			Starting Charge		Maximum Charge	
Propellant	Case	Primer	Weight (grains)	Muzzle Velocity (feet/sec)	Weight (grains)	Muzzle Velocity (feet/sec)
Accurate 8700	Remington	CCI 250	85.0	2948	87.0	3009
Alliant Reloder 33	Federal	Federal 215	75.8	2704	83.9	2965
Alliant Reloder 50	Federal	Federal 215	76.3	2740	84.2	2957
Accurate 3100	Remington	CCI 250	71.0	2868	73.0	2951
Alliant Reloder 26	Federal	Federal 215	67.5	2664	74.8	2950
Alliant Reloder 25	Remington	CCI 250	72.0	2881	74.0	2947
IMR 7828	Remington	CCI 250	71.0	2874	73.0	2929
IMR 7977	Federal	Federal 215	69.7	2687	77.1	2915
Hodgdon Retumbo	Federal	Federal 215	69.3	2630	76.8	2912
Hodgdon H1000	Remington	CCI 250	73.0	2800	77.0	2909
IMR 4831	Remington	CCI 250	67.0	2830	69.0	2906
Alliant Reloder 23	Federal	Federal 215	64.9	2659	71.8	2893
Alliant Reloder 22	Remington	CCI 250	66.0	2746	70.0	2879

WARNING! *Maximum loads should be used with CAUTION • C = Compressed Load*

7mm REMINGTON ULTRA MAGNUM

Alternate Names:	7mm RUM
Parent Cartridge:	404 Jeffery
Country of Origin:	USA
Year of Introduction:	2001
Designer(s):	Remington
Governing Body:	SAAMI

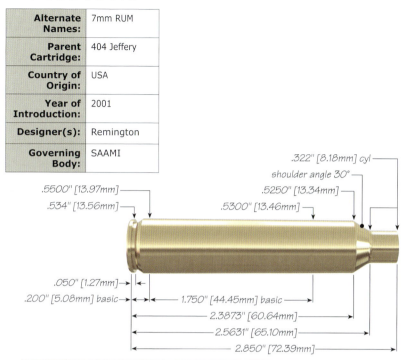

CARTRIDGE CASE DATA

Case Type:	Rimless, rebated, bottleneck		
Average Case Capacity:	112.7 grains H$_2$O	Max. Cartridge OAL	3.600 inch
Max. Case Length:	2.850 inch	Primer:	Large Rifle
Case Trim to Length:	2.840 inch	RCBS Shell holder:	# 38
Current Manufacturers:	Remington		

BALLISTIC DATA

Max. Average Pressure (MAP):	65,000 psi, 53,000 CUP - SAAMI	Test Barrel Length:	24 inch
Rifling Twist Rate:	1 turn in 9.5 inch		
Muzzle velocities of factory loaded ammunition			

Bullet Wgt.	Muzzle velocity
140-grain	3,425 fps
150-grain	3,325 fps
175-grain	3,025 fps

Muzzle velocity will decrease approximately 30 fps per inch for barrels less than 24 inches.

HISTORICAL NOTES

- In 2001, the magnum rifle cartridge market was stunned once again when Remington introduced the new 7mm Remington Ultra Magnum (RUM) cartridge.
- For the first time in over 55 years, a mainstream ammunition manufacturer offered a magnum rifle cartridge that could compete with the legendary 7mm Weatherby Magnum on its own terms.
- The new 7mm RUM cartridge incorporated the Remington Ultra Magnum design concept —it did not have the belted case head of other magnum rifle cartridges! Inspiration courtesy of the fatherly 404 Jeffrey cartridge.
- As the last of the series, the 7mm Remington Ultra Magnum consolidated the market impact of the 300 RUM, 338 RUM, and 375 RUM cartridges begun in 1999.
- As Remington also manufactured rifles, the 7mm RUM cartridge gained a considerable boost by entering the market simultaneously with rifles chambered for the new cartridge.
- The quartet of Remington Ultra Magnum cartridges firmly established the concept of beltless magnum cartridges in the world of modern sporting ammunition.

BALLISTIC NOTES

- Remington covered all the ballistic bases with the 7mm RUM cartridge. Bullet weights of 140, 150, and 160-grains are listed in the current Remington ammunition catalog. All of these loads can be duplicated using Speer bullets.
- With the 7mm Remington Ultra Magnum cartridge, Remington also introduced the concept of "power levels". For example, the 140-grain bullet is offered with a choice of two muzzle velocity levels, allowing the hunter to more closely match ballistic performance to the type of game hunted.
- The power level concept was not extended to the 338 RUM or 375 RUM cartridges.

TECHNICAL NOTES

- The Remington 7mm RUM case is slightly longer with a significantly larger head diameter than the 7mm Weatherby Magnum. As a result, case capacity of the 7mm RUM cartridge is 14% larger than its Weatherby rival.
- The 7mm RUM and the 300 RUM cartridges share a 2.850 inch maximum case length and an overall loaded length of 3.600 inch making them suitable only for rifles having long actions.
- Both the 7mm RUM and the 300 RUM cartridges achieve their exceptional muzzle velocities the old fashioned way - they burn a bunch of powder.

HANDLOADING NOTES

- Remington is the sole source of new, empty, unprimed 7mm RUM brass cartridge cases for reloading.
- Do not use bullets weighing less than 140 grains for hunting deer with the 7mm RUM. At 7mm RUM muzzle velocities, even bullets of this weight result in unnecessary meat damage. With this cartridge, we recommend the 160-grain bullets for deer as a good balance of ballistics and recoil.

SAFETY NOTES

SPEER 160-grain Spitzer BTSP @ a muzzle velocity of 3,311 fps:
- Maximum vertical altitude @ 90° elevation is 17,910 feet.
- Maximum horizontal distance to first impact with ground @ 38° elevation is 8,292 yards.

145 GRAINS

DIAMETER	SECTIONAL DENSITY
.284"	0.257

7mm Spitzer BTSP	
Ballistic Coefficient	0.472
COAL Tested	3.600"
Speer Part No.	1628

7mm Spitzer SP Hot-Cor®	
Ballistic Coefficient	0.416
COAL Tested	3.600"
Speer Part No.	1629

7mm Grand Slam® SP	
Ballistic Coefficient	0.353
COAL Tested	3.550"
Speer Part No.	1632

			Starting Charge		Maximum Charge	
Propellant	Case	Primer	Weight (grains)	Muzzle Velocity (feet/sec)	Weight (grains)	Muzzle Velocity (feet/sec)
Vihtavuori N560	Remington	Federal 215	89.0	3280	93.0	3422
Accurate 8700	Remington	Federal 215	102.0	3068	106.0	3305
Hodgdon US 869	Remington	Federal 215	103.0	3165	107.0	3305
Hodgdon Retumbo	Remington	Federal 215	92.0	3095	96.0	3261
IMR 7828	Remington	Federal 215	85.0	3150	89.0	3259
Alliant Reloder 25	Remington	Federal 215	88.0	3089	92.0	3251
Alliant Reloder 22	Remington	Federal 215	84.0	3101	88.0	3250
Ramshot Magnum	Remington	Federal 215	89.0	3107	93.0	3236
Alliant Reloder 19	Remington	Federal 215	81.0	3058	85.0	3200

WARNING! Maximum loads should be used with CAUTION • C = Compressed Load

160 GRAINS

DIAMETER	SECTIONAL DENSITY
.284"	0.283

7mm Spitzer BTSP
Ballistic Coefficient	0.519
COAL Tested	3.600"
Speer Part No.	1634

7mm Spitzer SP Hot-Cor®
Ballistic Coefficient	0.504
COAL Tested	3.600"
Speer Part No.	1635

7mm Grand Slam® SP
Ballistic Coefficient	0.389
COAL Tested	3.580"
Speer Part No.	1638

Propellant	Case	Primer	Starting Charge		Maximum Charge	
			Weight (grains)	Muzzle Velocity (feet/sec)	Weight (grains)	Muzzle Velocity (feet/sec)
Vihtavuori N560	Remington	Federal 215	87.0	3145	91.0	3311
Hodgdon US 869	Remington	Federal 215	101.0	3075	105.0	3237
Hodgdon Retumbo	Remington	Federal 215	91.0	3031	95.0	3219
Accurate 8700	Remington	Federal 215	99.0	3054	103.0	3198
Alliant Reloder 22	Remington	Federal 215	83.0	3014	87.0	3177
Alliant Reloder 25	Remington	Federal 215	87.0	3005	91.0	3174
Ramshot Magnum	Remington	Federal 215	88.0	3016	92.0	3169
IMR 7828	Remington	Federal 215	83.0	2984	87.0	3149
Alliant Reloder 19	Remington	Federal 215	81.0	2928	85.0	3132

WARNING! Maximum loads should be used with *CAUTION* • C = Compressed Load

175 GRAINS

DIAMETER	SECTIONAL DENSITY
.284"	0.310

7mm Grand Slam® SP

Ballistic Coefficient	0.436
COAL Tested	3.570"
Speer Part No.	1643

			Starting Charge		Maximum Charge	
Propellant	Case	Primer	Weight (grains)	Muzzle Velocity (feet/sec)	Weight (grains)	Muzzle Velocity (feet/sec)
Hodgdon US 869	Remington	Federal 215	98.0	2936	102.0	3106
Hodgdon Retumbo	Remington	Federal 215	89.0	2889	93.0	3081
Accurate 8700	Remington	Federal 215	97.0	2908	101.0	3073
Alliant Reloder 25	Remington	Federal 215	86.0	2896	90.0	3059
IMR 7828	Remington	Federal 215	82.0	2873	86.0	3045
Vihtavuori N560	Remington	Federal 215	81.0	2855	85.0	3031
Hodgdon H1000	Remington	Federal 215	86.0	2865	90.0	3017
Ramshot Magnum	Remington	Federal 215	85.0	2868	89.0	3009
Alliant Reloder 22	Remington	Federal 215	81.0	2871	85.0	2974

WARNING! *Maximum loads should be used with CAUTION • C = Compressed Load*

30 CARBINE

Alternate Names:	7.62x33mm, 30 M1 Carbine
Parent Cartridge:	32 Winchester Self-Loading
Country of Origin:	USA
Year of Introduction:	1941
Designer(s):	Marshall Williams and Winchester
Governing Body:	SAAMI/CIP

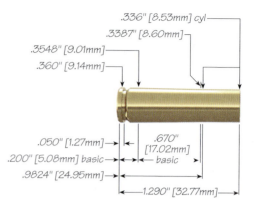

CARTRIDGE CASE DATA	
Case Type:	Rimless, tapered
Average Case Capacity:	21.0 grains H_2O
Max. Cartridge OAL	1.680 inch
Max. Case Length:	1.290 inch
Primer:	Small rifle
Case Trim to Length:	1.285 inch
RCBS Shell holder:	# 17
Current Manufacturers:	Federal, Remington, Winchester, Hornady, PMC, Sellier & Bellot, Aguila, Armscor, Wolf, Prvi Partizan, IMI, Magtech, PMP

BALLISTIC DATA			
Max. Average Pressure (MAP):	40,000 psi, 40,000 CUP - SAAMI	Test Barrel Length:	20 inch
Rifling Twist Rate:	1 turn in 20 inch		
Muzzle velocities of factory loaded ammunition		Bullet Wgt.	Muzzle velocity
		110-grain	1,990 fps

Muzzle velocity will decrease approximately 5 fps per inch for barrels less than 20 inches.

HISTORICAL NOTES

- Shortly before the United States entered World War II in 1941, the U.S. Army developed a compact, lightweight, semi-automatic carbine intended to replace the 45 caliber M1911A1 pistol for specialist troops such as artillery, signal corps, transport personnel, and infantry officers.

- For the new carbine, Winchester developed a small, low pressure, rimless cartridge based on the obsolete 32 Winchester Self-Loading cartridge of 1906.

- By any measure, ballistics of the new M1 Carbine cartridge were anemic, with limited lethality and a maximum effective range under combat conditions of approximately 100 yards.

- Despite these shortcomings, the short, lightweight M1 Carbine with its low recoil quickly became a popular weapon with U.S. soldiers, sailors, and airmen, mostly because both gun and ammunition were lighter than the M1 Garand.
- In 1957, the M1 carbine and its ammunition were declared obsolete by the U.S. military services.
- Beginning in the early 1950s, thousands of surplus M1 Carbines and millions of rounds of 30 M1 Carbine ammunition were sold to U.S. civilian shooters through the Civilian Marksmanship Program.
- With so many M1 Carbines in civilian hands, demand for 30 M1 Carbine ammunition grew exponentially.
- By the mid-1960s, the U.S. military's stocks of 30 Carbine ammunition were exhausted. The ongoing civil demand was then met by domestic and foreign commercial manufacturers, some of whom had military equipment and tooling on hand for this caliber.
- As many M1 carbines have fallen into disuse or become collector's items, current demand for 30 M1 Carbine ammunition has declined precipitously.
- The 30 Carbine cartridge's role as the go-to low cost military cartridge for instruction, training, and informal target shooting has been replaced by the 5.56x45mm NATO cartridge.

Interesting Fact

In the early 1950s, the U.S. Army briefly experimented with a 30 M1 Carbine cartridge case necked down to 22-caliber as a possible way of increasing maximum range and lethality. Results were disappointing and the program was terminated. At that time Melvin M. Johnson, a noted gun designer, introduced a similar cartridge called the 5.7mm MMJ Spitfire on the commercial market. Following limited interest in the concept, the 5.7mm MMJ Spitfire entered the history books. Since then, interest in the 5.7mm MMJ cartridge has waxed and waned several times, most recently in the late 1990s when a manufacturer of 30 M1 carbines in Texas offered M1 carbines and ammunition in 5.7mm Spitfire caliber.

BALLISTIC NOTES

- The anemic ballistics of the 30 M1 Carbine cartridge make it completely unsuitable for any type of hunting. In fact, it is illegal to hunt deer with this cartridge in many states.
- That said, the 30 M1 Carbine cartridge is a very good choice for personal defense. For example, the 110-grain bullet of the 30 Carbine retains 865 ft-lbs of striking energy at 25 yards while the 158-grain bullet of the 357 Magnum retains 495 ft-lbs of energy at the same distance. That is a 75% increase.
- Muzzle velocity of commercially made 30 Carbine ammunition varies from 1,960 fps to 2,025 fps. U.S. military specifications for 30 Carbine Ball ammunition call for a velocity of 1,900 fps +/- 30 fps.
- Bullet weight of both military and civil 30 M1 Carbine factory ammunition is a 110-grain FMJ round nose. In addition, most commercial manufacturers of this cartridge offer a round nose soft point of the same weight.
- Maximum effective range of the 30 M1 Carbine cartridge is approximately 100 yards.

TECHNICAL NOTES

- The M1 Carbine's short-stroke gas operating system is designed specifically for the low MAP levels and 110-grain bullet weight of the 30 Carbine cartridge, thus reducing the possibility of improving ballistics by raising MAP levels or loading different bullet weights.

- While it may appear to be straight sided, the 30 M1 Carbine cartridge case is tapered slightly to assist in extraction.

- The case head and rim dimensions are unique and shared with no other current cartridge.

HANDLOADING NOTES

- In addition to the manufacturers of loaded ammunition listed above, new, empty, unprimed brass in 30 M1 Carbine caliber is available from most mainstream domestic ammunition manufacturers and some foreign ones.

- Follow all loading data for the 30 M1 Carbine cartridge exactly as specified. Remember, this cartridge is not a hunting or target cartridge, nor can the muzzle velocity be significantly increased over factory levels.

- The low MAP level and small case capacity of the 30 Carbine cartridge dictates the use of fast burning propellants.

- As M1 carbines are semi-automatic, you must full-length resize all fired M1 Carbine cartridge cases with a small base die. Carbide sizing dies in this caliber are an option that will speed up this process. The M1 Carbine can be very hard on fired brass. Expect to discard a high number of fired cases damaged during ejection.

- Some foreign M1 Carbine ammunition was manufactured with Berdan primers. Carefully sort your fired brass to remove and destroy these. Failure to do so can result in broken decapping pins and /or cases stuck on punches or in dies.

- Russian-made 30 M1 Carbine ammunition using steel cartridge cases is currently being sold on the North American market. Do not attempt to reload steel cases. Sort them out with a magnet and destroy them.

SAFETY NOTES

SPEER 110-grain TMJ® RN @ a muzzle velocity of 1,969 fps:

- Maximum vertical altitude @ 90° elevation is 4,446 feet.

- Maximum horizontal distance to first impact with ground @ 31° elevation is 1,995 yards.

100 GRAINS

DIAMETER	SECTIONAL DENSITY
.308"	0.151

30 SPRN Plinker®

Ballistic Coefficient	0.144
COAL Tested	1.625"
Speer Part No.	1805

			Starting Charge		Maximum Charge	
Propellant	Case	Primer	Weight (grains)	Muzzle Velocity (feet/sec)	Weight (grains)	Muzzle Velocity (feet/sec)
Accurate No. 9	IMI	CCI 400	12.3	1930	14.3	2232
Winchester 296	IMI	CCI 450	13.5	1765	15.5	2041
Hodgdon H110	IMI	CCI 450	12.5	1680	14.5	1977
IMR 4227	IMI	CCI 400	13.5	1697	15.5	1971
Vihtavuori N110	IMI	CCI 400	11.0	1700	13.0 C	1964
Alliant 2400	IMI	CCI 400	10.5	1516	12.5	1831
IMR 4198	IMI	CCI 400	13.5	1444	15.5	1688
Accurate 1680	IMI	CCI 400	14.0	1451	16.0 C	1679

110 GRAINS

DIAMETER	SECTIONAL DENSITY
.308"	0.166

30 Varminter HP

Ballistic Coefficient	0.128
COAL Tested	1.635"
Speer Part No.	1835

30 Carbine TMJ® RN

Ballistic Coefficient	0.179
COAL Tested	1.680"
Speer Part No.	1846

			Starting Charge		Maximum Charge	
Propellant	Case	Primer	Weight (grains)	Muzzle Velocity (feet/sec)	Weight (grains)	Muzzle Velocity (feet/sec)
Winchester 296	IMI	CCI 450	13.0	1808	15.0	2010
Accurate No. 9	IMI	CCI 400	11.4	1747	13.4	1976
Hodgdon H110	IMI	CCI 450	12.0	1607	14.0	1905
IMR 4227	IMI	CCI 400	13.0	1625	15.0	1903
Vihtavuori N110	IMI	CCI 400	10.5	1560	12.5 C	1837
Alliant 2400	IMI	CCI 400	10.0	1455	12.0	1753
IMR SR 4759	IMI	CCI 400	10.0	1485	12.0	1680
Accurate 1680	IMI	CCI 400	14.0	1454	16.0 C	1676
IMR 4198	IMI	CCI 400	13.0	1411	15.0	1630

WARNING! Maximum loads should be used with CAUTION • C = Compressed Load

30-30 WINCHESTER

Alternate Names:	30 Winchester Center Fire (30 WCF), 7.8x51mm R
Parent Cartridge:	38-55 Winchester
Country of Origin:	USA
Year of Introduction:	1895
Designer(s):	Winchester
Governing Body:	SAAMI/CIP

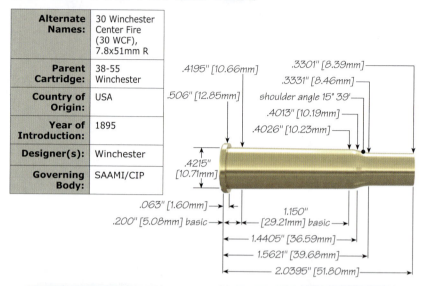

CARTRIDGE CASE DATA

Case Type:	Rimmed, bottleneck
Average Case Capacity:	45 grains H₂O
Max. Cartridge OAL	2.550 inch
Max. Case Length:	2.039 inch
Primer:	Large Rifle
Case Trim to Length:	2.030 inch
RCBS Shell holder:	# 2
Current Manufacturers:	Winchester, Federal, Remington, Hornady, PMC, Nosler, Sellier & Bellot

BALLISTIC DATA

Max. Average Pressure (MAP):	42,000 psi, 38,000 CUP - SAAMI
Test Barrel Length:	24 inch
Rifling Twist Rate:	1 turn in 12 inch

Muzzle velocities of factory loaded ammunition	Bullet Wgt.	Muzzle velocity
	150-grain	2,390 fps
	170-grain	2,200 fps

Muzzle velocity will decrease approximately 10 fps per inch for barrels less than 24 inches.

HISTORICAL NOTES

- If we judged rifle cartridges by their ballistics alone, the 30-30 Winchester would be a distant memory. By any measure, the ballistics of the 30-30 Win. are mediocre at best.
- If ballistics has not kept this cartridge at the apex of the top ten most popular rifle cartridges in North America for decades, then what has?

- The 30-30 Winchester cartridge owes its enduring popularity to a combination of mild recoil and American hunters' affection for lightweight, lever-action carbines. Some observers have called this: "The Old West in the American psyche".
- Availability is another reason for its enduring popularity. Nearly all major ammunition manufacturers, foreign and domestic, list the 30-30 Winchester cartridge in their catalog.
- Winchester, Marlin, and Henry Arms offer lever-action rifles in this caliber and millions of serviceable lever-guns remain in shooters' hands.
- Essentially, the 30-30 Winchester cartridge is an American thing we instinctively understand. On the other hand, European shooters just do not get it.
- Some observers have predicted the imminent demise of the 30-30 Winchester. They do not get it either.

Interesting Fact

The 30-30 Winchester cartridge was the first sporting cartridge on the American market designed for and loaded with smokeless propellant. Despite its black powder designation system, the 30-30 Winchester was never loaded with black powder.

BALLISTIC NOTES

- The 30-30 Winchester cartridge is limited to low MAP levels due to its intended use in lever-action rifles with weak actions.
- For this reason, muzzle velocity and energy levels of the 30-30 Win. are modest when compared to the high MAP cartridges designed for bolt-action rifles.
- Factory product lines for the 30-30 Winchester are simple, basic and easy to comprehend: there are two bullet weights, 150 and 170 grains. Both of these flat nose, soft point bullets have about the same ballistic coefficient as a brick. The lighter bullet accounts for 80% of sales. There are no +P loads, high velocity loads or boat tail bullets.

TECHNICAL NOTES

- The ballistic sweet spot for the 30-30 Winchester cartridge is the 150-grain flat nose bullet at a muzzle velocity of approximately 2,400 fps. This load is accurate, and the iron sights on most lever-action rifles are calibrated to the ballistics of this bullet weight.
- Some bolt-action and single-shot rifles have been chambered in 30-30 Winchester. To improve down range ballistic performance in these rifles, spitzer bullets weighing a maximum of 150 grains can be loaded.

HANDLOADING NOTES

- All 30-30 Win. bullets must be crimped securely to prevent the bullet being pulled from the case mouth by recoil or pushed into the case by the magazine spring and cartridges in the magazine tube.
- Speer offers four flat nose soft point bullets with a crimping cannelure especially designed for use with the 30-30 Win. cartridge. Weights include: 110-grain Varminter HP, 130-grain SPFN Hot-Cor®, 150-grain SPFN, and 170-grain SPFN.
- Medium burning rate propellants work best for the 30-30 Win. cartridge.

SAFETY NOTES

SPEER 170-grain SPFN @ a muzzle velocity of 2,118 fps:
- Maximum vertical altitude @ 90° elevation is 7,552 feet.
- Maximum horizontal distance to first impact with ground @ 36° elevation is 3,614 yards.
- Do not fire 30-30 Win. ammunition loaded with spitzer bullets in lever-action rifles with tubular magazines as doing so may result in a magazine tube explosion.

100 GRAINS

DIAMETER	SECTIONAL DENSITY
.308"	0.151

30 Plinker® SPRN

Ballistic Coefficient	0.144
COAL Tested	2.345"
Speer Part No.	1805

			Starting Charge		Maximum Charge	
Propellant	Case	Primer	Weight (grains)	Muzzle Velocity (feet/sec)	Weight (grains)	Muzzle Velocity (feet/sec)
Accurate 2200	Federal	Federal 210	32.9	2760	35.7	2921
Accurate Lt-32	Federal	Federal 210	32.7	2663	35.7	2873
Alliant Reloder 7	Winchester	CCI 200	31.0	2506	35.0	2865
Hodgdon H322	Winchester	CCI 200	33.0	2419	37.0	2798
Alliant Power Pro 1200-R	Federal	Federal 210	29.5	2642	32.1	2788
Alliant Reloder 10X	Federal	Federal 210	31.2	2641	33.6	2775
Accurate 2015	Winchester	CCI 200	31.0	2409	35.0	2721
IMR 4064	Winchester	CCI 200	33.5	2204	37.5 C	2581
Hodgdon BL-C(2)	Winchester	CCI 250	34.0	2203	38.0	2549
Winchester 748	Winchester	CCI 250	36.0	2138	40.0 C	2534
Vihtavuori N133	Winchester	CCI 200	28.0	2169	32.0	2451
Hodgdon H4895	Winchester	CCI 200	31.0	2077	35.0	2433
Hodgdon H380	Winchester	CCI 250	36.0	1989	40.0 C	2359

WARNING! *Maximum loads should be used with CAUTION • C = Compressed Load*

110 GRAINS

DIAMETER	SECTIONAL DENSITY
.308"	0.166

30 Varminter HP

Ballistic Coefficient	0.128
COAL Tested	2.415"
Speer Part No.	1835

Propellant	Case	Primer	Starting Charge		Maximum Charge	
			Weight (grains)	Muzzle Velocity (feet/sec)	Weight (grains)	Muzzle Velocity (feet/sec)
Alliant Reloder 7	Winchester	CCI 200	30.0	2341	34.0	2775
Hodgdon H322	Winchester	CCI 200	31.0	2264	35.0	2652
Accurate 2015	Winchester	CCI 200	30.0	2290	34.0	2649
Winchester 748	Winchester	CCI 250	36.0	2292	40.0 C	2621
IMR 4064	Winchester	CCI 200	33.0	2117	37.0 C	2509
Hodgdon BL-C(2)	Winchester	CCI 250	33.0	2116	37.0	2477
IMR 4895	Winchester	CCI 200	31.0	2127	35.0	2461
Vihtavuori N133	Winchester	CCI 200	27.0	1950	31.0	2405
Hodgdon H4895	Winchester	CCI 200	30.0	1972	34.0 C	2339
IMR 4350	Winchester	CCI 200	36.0	1995	40.0 C	2337
Accurate 2230	Winchester	CCI 200	27.0	2018	31.0	2335
Accurate 2460	Winchester	CCI 250	28.0	2007	32.0	2295

WARNING! Maximum loads should be used with CAUTION • C = Compressed Load

130 GRAINS

DIAMETER	SECTIONAL DENSITY
.308"	0.196

30 SPFN Hot-Cor®

Ballistic Coefficient	0.213
COAL Tested	2.550"
Speer Part No.	2007

			Starting Charge		Maximum Charge	
Propellant	Case	Primer	Weight (grains)	Muzzle Velocity (feet/sec)	Weight (grains)	Muzzle Velocity (feet/sec)
Hodgdon CFE 223	Federal	Federal 210	38.1	2428	42.0 C	2643
Alliant AR-Comp	Federal	Federal 210	32.5	2365	36.1 C	2601
Alliant Power Pro Varmint	Federal	Federal 210	32.9	2364	35.7	2516
Accurate 2520	Winchester	CCI 250	31.0	2092	35.0 C	2481
Accurate 2460	Winchester	CCI 250	30.0	2111	34.0	2472
Alliant Reloder 7	Winchester	CCI 200	27.0	2133	31.0	2438
Hodgdon H322	Winchester	CCI 200	29.0	2058	33.0	2410
Hodgdon Varget	Winchester	CCI 200	31.0	2006	35.0	2332
Alliant Reloder 10X	Winchester	CCI 200	26.5	2061	30.5	2310
Alliant Reloder 15	Winchester	CCI 200	32.0	1960	36.0 C	2295
Vihtavuori N140	Winchester	CCI 200	31.0	1982	35.0 C	2293
Winchester 748	Winchester	CCI 250	31.2	1878	35.5	2255
IMR 4895	Winchester	CCI 200	28.0	1869	32.0	2162
IMR 4064	Winchester	CCI 200	29.0	1763	33.0	2091

WARNING! *Maximum loads should be used with CAUTION • C = Compressed Load*

150 GRAINS

DIAMETER	SECTIONAL DENSITY
.308"	0.226

30 SPFN Hot-Cor®

Ballistic Coefficient	0.255
COAL Tested	2.550"
Speer Part No.	2011

			Starting Charge		Maximum Charge	
Propellant	Case	Primer	Weight (grains)	Muzzle Velocity (feet/sec)	Weight (grains)	Muzzle Velocity (feet/sec)
Alliant Power Pro 2000-MR	Federal	Federal 210	37.2	2321	41.0 C	2539
Hodgdon LEVERevolution	Federal	Federal 210	35.2	2332	38.2 C	2516
Hodgdon CFE 223	Federal	Federal 210	36.3	2318	39.9 C	2511
Alliant AR-Comp	Federal	Federal 210	31.2	2266	33.8	2425
Alliant Power Pro Varmint	Federal	Federal 210	30.2	2168	33.4	2355
Winchester 748	Winchester	CCI 250	33.0	1941	37.0 C	2273
Hodgdon H322	Winchester	CCI 200	27.0	1899	31.0	2253
Accurate 2520	Winchester	CCI 250	28.0	1875	32.0	2224
Alliant Reloder 7	Winchester	CCI 200	25.0	1895	29.0	2220
Alliant Reloder 15	Winchester	CCI 200	30.0	1833	34.0 C	2201
Vihtavuori N140	Winchester	CCI 200	30.0	1866	34.0	2186
Hodgdon Varget	Winchester	CCI 200	29.0	1835	33.0	2168
Alliant Reloder 10X	Winchester	CCI 200	24.0	1850	28.0	2144
Hodgdon H335	Winchester	CCI 250	28.0	1736	32.0	2138
Hodgdon H414	Winchester	CCI 250	34.0	1729	38.0 C	2103
IMR 4320	Winchester	CCI 200	29.0	1702	33.0	2070
Hodgdon H4895	Winchester	CCI 200	27.0	1675	31.0	2064
IMR 4895	Winchester	CCI 200	27.0	1701	31.0	2039
IMR 4350	Winchester	CCI 200	32.0	1692	36.0 C	2033

WARNING! Maximum loads should be used with CAUTION • C = Compressed Load

170 GRAINS

DIAMETER	SECTIONAL DENSITY
.308"	0.256

30 SPFN
Ballistic Coefficient	0.298
COAL Tested	2.550"
Speer Part No.	2041

			Starting Charge		Maximum Charge	
Propellant	Case	Primer	Weight (grains)	Muzzle Velocity (feet/sec)	Weight (grains)	Muzzle Velocity (feet/sec)
Alliant Power Pro 2000-MR	Federal	Federal 210	34.1	2133	37.5	2318
Hodgdon LEVERevolution	Federal	Federal 210	32.4	2111	35.6	2297
Hodgdon CFE 223	Federal	Federal 210	32.9	2102	36.2	2290
Alliant AR-Comp	Federal	Federal 210	27.5	1982	30.4	2166
Winchester 748	Winchester	CCI 250	30.0	1843	34.0	2145
Alliant Power Pro Varmint	Federal	Federal 210	28.5	2020	30.7	2143
Alliant Reloder 15	Federal	Federal 210	28.5	1875	31.7	2122
Hodgdon Varget	Winchester	CCI 200	27.0	1625	31.0	2027
Hodgdon H322	Winchester	CCI 200	25.0	1686	29.0	2025
Hodgdon H335	Winchester	CCI 250	27.0	1670	31.0	2007
Vihtavuori N140	Winchester	CCI 200	27.0	1643	31.0	2002
IMR 3031	Winchester	CCI 200	25.5	1702	29.5	1994
Alliant Reloder 10X	Winchester	CCI 200	22.5	1646	26.5	1990
IMR 4064	Winchester	CCI 200	27.0	1654	31.0	1982
Winchester 760	Winchester	CCI 250	31.0	1634	35.0	1963
Hodgdon H414	Winchester	CCI 250	31.0	1596	35.0	1942
IMR 4350	Winchester	CCI 200	30.5	1566	34.5	1930
IMR 4895	Winchester	CCI 200	25.0	1614	29.0	1892
Accurate 2460	Winchester	CCI 250	24.0	1587	28.0	1884

WARNING! Maximum loads should be used with CAUTION • C = Compressed Load

300 AAC BLACKOUT

Alternate Names:	300 AAC, 300 Blackout, 7.62x35mm
Parent Cartridge:	221 Remington Fireball
Country of Origin:	USA
Year of Introduction:	2011
Designer(s):	Robert Silvers of A.A.C. & Remington Defense, (J.D. Jones - 300 Whisper)
Governing Body:	SAAMI

CARTRIDGE CASE DATA

Case Type:	Rimless, bottleneck		
Average Case Capacity:	26.5 grains H$_2$O	**Max. Cartridge OAL**	2.260 inch
Max. Case Length:	1.368 inch	**Primer:**	Small Rifle
Case Trim to Length:	1.358 inch	**RCBS Shell holder:**	# 10
Current Manufacturers:	A.A.C. (Advanced Armament Corporation), Federal, Nosler, Hornady, Winchester, Aguila, Magtech, Starline, Black Hills, Fiocchi, Remington		

BALLISTIC DATA

Max. Average Pressure (MAP):	55,000 psi, CUP not established for this cartridge – SAAMI; 62,366 psi - CIP	**Test Barrel Length:**	16 inch
Rifling Twist Rate:	1 turn in 8 inch		
Muzzle velocities of factory loaded ammunition	**Bullet Wgt.**		**Muzzle velocity**
	90-grain		2,550 fps
	115-grain		2,270 fps
	120-grain		2,100 fps
	123-grain		2,080 fps
	125-grain		2,215 fps
	220-grain		1,010 fps
	Muzzle velocity will decrease approximately 10 fps per inch for barrels less than 16 inches.		

HISTORICAL NOTES

- As the popularity of suppressors for Modern Sporting Rifles or MSRs (read AR15) and others has grown exponentially among U.S. sportsmen, the need for a deer hunting cartridge designed especially for this purpose became evident.
- The new cartridge had to meet three requirements:
  - It must feed and function in modified MSR rifles with or without suppressors.
  - It must be capable of being loaded to sub-sonic or supersonic muzzle velocities.
  - Terminal ballistic performance must be equal to or better than the 7.62x39mm Soviet cartridge with equivalent bullet weights.
- In answer to this need, a development team from A.A.C. and Remington set to work designing such a cartridge. The result was the 300 AAC Blackout.
- SAAMI standardized the new 300 Blackout in 2011 after which it was introduced by domestic and foreign ammunition manufacturers.

Interesting Fact

The 300 Blackout is the first sporting cartridge designed especially for use with a suppressor that has been standardized by SAAMI.

BALLISTIC NOTES

- A suppressor is designed to do two things:
  - Reduce muzzle flash.
  - Reduce muzzle blast (noise).
- While a well-designed suppressor will significantly reduce both signatures, it will not totally eliminate them.
- A suppressor accomplishes its tasks by means of a tube affixed to the muzzle of a rifle barrel. Inside the tube are a series of baffles and expansion chambers intended to cool and dissipate unburned powder particles (flash) and reduce the velocity of the high pressure gas column behind the bullet (muzzle blast).
- A well designed suppressor will work with supersonic ammunition (muzzle velocity above about 1,120 fps). However, it will show much better results with subsonic ammunition (muzzle velocity below 1,120 fps).
- As a supersonic bullet travels down range, it creates a load crack or snapping noise. A subsonic bullet does not create such a noise.
- Launching a lightweight bullet at subsonic velocities is counter-productive as the low muzzle velocity and light weight bullet combine to limit maximum effective range.
- To overcome this handicap, a heavy bullet must be used loaded to just below 1,120 fps as it will hold its downrange velocity better due to its shape.
- Bullets weighing from 90 to 220 grains are available as factory loaded ammunition for the 300 Blackout. Note that only the 200 and 220-grain bullets are subsonic.
- The 300 Blackout is suitable for medium game animals such as deer, but bullet selection is critical for the size of the game and the range it is used at.

TECHNICAL NOTES

- The 300 Blackout is built on the earlier design work of J.D. Jones for his 300 Whisper cartridge. In fact the case dimensions of the two are similar save for a

- longer .015 inch leade in the Whisper's throat.
- The 300 Blackout is recognized by SAAMI whereas the 300 Whisper is not.
- Essentially, the 300 Blackout is a 221 Fireball cartridge case necked up to accept bullets of .308 inches in diameter.
- Overall loaded length of 2.260 inches is the same as the 223 Remington in order to fit in AR15 rifle platforms.
- At 55,000 psi, the MAP level of the 300 Blackout is the same as the 221 Fireball and 223 Remington.
- The rifling twist rate of 1 turn in 8 inches is necessary to stabilize long heavy, 30 caliber bullets at subsonic velocities.
- The case capacity of the 300 Blackout (26.5 grains of H_2O) is slightly higher than the 221 Fireball (24.5 grains of H_2O) but well below the 222 Remington (29.5 grains of H_2O) and the 223 Remington (31.9 grains of H_2O). As a result, the 300 Blackout is a very efficient design.
- Handloaders have a much broader choice of bullet weights and types than factory loaded ammunition in this caliber.
- Note that loading bullets from 110-grains to 180-grains at subsonic levels is not recommended as the bullets may not stabilize.

HANDLOADING NOTES

- Loading dies for the 300 Blackout and the 300 Whisper are identical.
- 300 Blackout ammunition fired in semi-automatic rifles such as the AR15 will require full length resizing with a small base die. You can reduce sizing effort by thoroughly cleaning and lubricating your cases before sizing.
- Neck sizing can be used for cartridges fired in bolt-action rifles.
- Be aware that many of the bullets listed here for the 300 Blackout were developed to expand and hold together in much faster cartridges. As such, they may not expand reliably at the lower velocities posted here.
- Never load less than the minimum charges shown in the loading data as the small charge of propellant may not be sufficient to push the bullet completely down the barrel.
- Faster burning rifle propellants are required for the 300 Blackout due to its limited case capacity.

SAFETY NOTES

SUBSONIC

SPEER 200-grain Spitzer SP bullet @ a muzzle velocity of 1,060 fps:
- Maximum vertical altitude @90° elevation is 10,656 feet.
- Maximum horizontal distance to first impact with ground @ 39° elevation is 3,940 yards.

SUPERSONIC

SPEER 180-grain BTSP bullet @ a muzzle velocity of 1,500 fps:
- Maximum vertical altitude @90° elevation is 11,928 feet.
- Maximum horizontal distance to first impact with ground @ 39° elevation is 6,079 yards.

110 GRAINS

DIAMETER	SECTIONAL DENSITY
.308"	0.166

30 Varminter HP

Ballistic Coefficient	0.128
COAL Tested	1.780"
Speer Part No.	1835

			Starting Charge		Maximum Charge	
Propellant	Case	Primer	Weight (grains)	Muzzle Velocity (feet/sec)	Weight (grains)	Muzzle Velocity (feet/sec)
Alliant Power Pro 300-MP	Federal	Federal 205	19.4	2142	21.2	2370
Winchester 296	Federal	Federal 205	18.9	2185	20.3	2330
Ramshot Enforcer	Federal	Federal 205	17.0	2103	19.0	2307
Alliant 2400	Federal	Federal 205	16.0	2058	17.6	2208
Accurate No. 9	Federal	Federal 205	14.1	1987	15.7	2148

125/130 GRAINS

DIAMETER	SECTIONAL DENSITY
.308"	0.196

30 HP

Ballistic Coefficient	0.244
COAL Tested	2.060"
Speer Part No.	2005

30 TNT® HP

Ballistic Coefficient	0.341
COAL Tested	2.060"
Speer Part No.	1986

			Starting Charge		Maximum Charge	
Propellant	Case	Primer	Weight (grains)	Muzzle Velocity (feet/sec)	Weight (grains)	Muzzle Velocity (feet/sec)
Alliant Power Pro 300-MP	Federal	Federal 205	18.7	2002	20.5	2175
Ramshot Enforcer	Federal	Federal 205	16.4	1977	18.2	2132
Vihtavuori N110	Federal	Federal 205	16.1	1955	17.9 C	2113
Accurate 5744	Federal	Federal 205	18.0	1851	19.7 C	2105
IMR 4227	Federal	Federal 205	17.3	1859	19.0 C	2029
Accurate No. 9	Federal	Federal 205	13.2	1810	14.6	1944

WARNING! Maximum loads should be used with CAUTION • C = Compressed Load

150 GRAINS

DIAMETER	SECTIONAL DENSITY
.308"	0.226

30 SPFN Hot-Cor®
Ballistic Coefficient	0.255
COAL Tested	2.190"
Speer Part No.	2011

30 Spitzer BTSP
Ballistic Coefficient	0.417
COAL Tested	2.190"
Speer Part No.	2022

30 Spitzer SP Hot-Cor®
Ballistic Coefficient	0.377
COAL Tested	2.190"
Speer Part No.	2023

30 Grand Slam® SP
Ballistic Coefficient	0.295
COAL Tested	2.190"
Speer Part No.	2026

Propellant	Case	Primer	Starting Charge Weight (grains)	Starting Charge Muzzle Velocity (feet/sec)	Maximum Charge Weight (grains)	Maximum Charge Muzzle Velocity (feet/sec)
Hodgdon Lil'Gun	Federal	Federal 205	18.2	2013	20.0 C	2157
Alliant Power Pro 300-MP	Federal	Federal 205	17.1	1866	19.2	2068
Winchester 296	Federal	Federal 205	16.7	1894	18.4	2049
Ramshot Enforcer	Federal	Federal 205	15.4	1839	17.2	1999
IMR 4227	Federal	Federal 205	16.7	1823	18.5 C	1991
Accurate 5744	Federal	Federal 205	17.5	1829	18.7 C	1967
Vihtavuori N110	Federal	Federal 205	15.0	1830	16.5 C	1955
Vihtavuori N120	Federal	Federal 205	18.1 C	1860	19.0 C	1947
Accurate No. 9	Federal	Federal 205	13.0	1763	14.0	1845

WARNING! *Maximum loads should be used with CAUTION • C = Compressed Load*

GOLD DOT RIFLE

150 GRAINS	DIAMETER	SECTIONAL DENSITY
	.308"	0.226

30 GD	
Ballistic Coefficient	0.463
COAL Tested	2.180"
Speer Part No.	308150BLKGDB

			Starting Charge		Maximum Charge	
Propellant	Case	Primer	Weight (grains)	Muzzle Velocity (feet/sec)	Weight (grains)	Muzzle Velocity (feet/sec)
Hodgdon Lil' Gun	Federal	Federal 205	20.0	2057	21.0 C	2154
Accurate 5744	Federal	Federal 205	17.6	1787	20.1 C	2041
Vihtavuori N110	Federal	Federal 205	15.1	1805	16.8 C	1961
Alliant Power Pro 300-MP	Federal	Federal 205	17.2	1786	19.0	1960
Accurate 1680	Federal	Federal 205	20.5	1785	22.0 C	1934
Ramshot Enforcer	Federal	Federal 205	15.5	1792	17.1	1932
IMR 4227	Federal	Federal 205	17.2	1746	18.8 C	1922
Hodgdon H110	Federal	Federal 205	15.7	1747	17.8	1915
Vihtavuori N120	Federal	Federal 205	18.0	1737	19.5 C	1894
Accurate No 9	Federal	Federal 205	12.7	1671	14.1	1818

WARNING! *Maximum loads should be used with CAUTION • C = Compressed Load*

165 GRAINS

DIAMETER	SECTIONAL DENSITY
.308"	0.248

30 Spitzer BTSP
Ballistic Coefficient	0.520
COAL Tested	2.250"
Speer Part No.	2034

30 Spitzer SP Hot-Cor®
Ballistic Coefficient	0.444
COAL Tested	2.250"
Speer Part No.	2035

30 Grand Slam® SP
Ballistic Coefficient	0.354
COAL Tested	2.250"
Speer Part No.	2038

			Starting Charge		Maximum Charge	
Propellant	Case	Primer	Weight (grains)	Muzzle Velocity (feet/sec)	Weight (grains)	Muzzle Velocity (feet/sec)
Hodgdon Lil'Gun	Federal	Federal 205	18.0	1928	19.5 C	2051
Accurate 5744	Federal	Federal 205	16.9	1732	18.8 C	1912
Alliant Power Pro 300-MP	Federal	Federal 205	16.4	1719	18.3	1891
Vihtavuori N120	Federal	Federal 205	17.5 C	1736	18.7 C	1848
IMR 4227	Federal	Federal 205	15.9	1678	17.4 C	1827
Vihtavuori N110	Federal	Federal 205	13.8	1684	15.4	1815
Winchester 296	Federal	Federal 205	15.1	1705	16.4	1805
Accurate No. 9	Federal	Federal 205	12.1	1622	13.3	1739
Alliant 2400	Federal	Federal 205	12.3	1583	13.2	1686

WARNING! Maximum loads should be used with CAUTION • C = Compressed Load

180 GRAINS

DIAMETER	SECTIONAL DENSITY
.308"	0.271

30 Spitzer BTSP
Ballistic Coefficient	0.545
COAL Tested	2.170"
Speer Part No.	2052

30 Spitzer SP Hot-Cor®
Ballistic Coefficient	0.441
COAL Tested	2.170"
Speer Part No.	2053

30 Grand Slam® SP
Ballistic Coefficient	0.374
COAL Tested	2.170"
Speer Part No.	2063

			Starting Charge		Maximum Charge	
Propellant	Case	Primer	Weight (grains)	Muzzle Velocity (feet/sec)	Weight (grains)	Muzzle Velocity (feet/sec)
Accurate 5744	Federal	Federal 205	15.5	1514	17.0 C	1693
Alliant Power Pro 300-MP	Federal	Federal 205	14.2	1510	15.5	1617
Vihtavuori N110	Federal	Federal 205	12.7	1488	14.1 C	1608
Ramshot Enforcer	Federal	Federal 205	12.6	1513	13.7	1604
IMR 4227	Federal	Federal 205	14.3	1463	15.8 C	1599
IMR 4198	Federal	Federal 205	15.5 C	1439	16.4 C	1563
Accurate No. 9	Federal	Federal 205	11.0	1397	12.3	1528

WARNING! *Maximum loads should be used with CAUTION • C = Compressed Load*

200 GRAINS

DIAMETER	SECTIONAL DENSITY
.308"	0.301

30 Spitzer SP Hot-Cor®

Ballistic Coefficient	0.478
COAL Tested	2.160"
Speer Part No.	2211

			Starting Charge		Maximum Charge	
Propellant	Case	Primer	Weight (grains)	Muzzle Velocity (feet/sec)	Weight (grains)	Muzzle Velocity (feet/sec)
Accurate 1680	Federal	Federal 205	11.9	934	13.4	1111
Accurate 5744	Federal	Federal 205	10.8	958	12.1	1110
Alliant Power Pro 1200-R	Federal	Federal 205	12.1	947	13.7 C	1109
Alliant Reloder 10X	Federal	Federal 205	12.7	960	13.9 C	1101
Vihtavuori N120	Federal	Federal 205	11.0	993	11.8	1096
Accurate LT-30	Federal	Federal 205	12.3	941	13.5 C	1091
IMR 4227	Federal	Federal 205	10.2	952	11.0	1088
Alliant Reloder 7	Federal	Federal 205	12.1	940	12.9	1088
IMR 4198	Federal	Federal 205	11.4	942	12.3	1080

WARNING! *Maximum loads should be used with* CAUTION • C = Compressed Load

300 SAVAGE

Parent Cartridge:	30-06 Springfield
Country of Origin:	USA
Year of Introduction:	1920
Designer(s):	Savage
Governing Body:	SAAMI/CIP

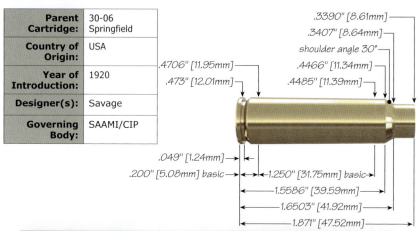

CARTRIDGE CASE DATA

Case Type:	Rimless, bottleneck		
Average Case Capacity:	52.0 grain H₂O	Max. Cartridge OAL	2.600 inch
Max. Case Length:	1.871 inch	Primer:	Large Rifle
Case Trim to Length:	1.861 inch	RCBS Shell holder:	# 3
Current Manufacturers:	Federal, Remington, Hornady, Winchester		

BALLISTIC DATA

Max. Average Pressure (MAP):	47,000 psi, 46,000 CUP - SAAMI	Test Barrel Length:	24 inch
Rifling Twist Rate:	1 turn in 12 inch		

Muzzle velocities of factory loaded ammunition	Bullet Wgt.	Muzzle velocity
	150-grain	2,630 fps
	180-grain	2,350 fps

Muzzle velocity will decrease approximately 10 fps per inch for barrels less than 24 inches.

HISTORICAL NOTES

- Savage designed the 300 Savage cartridge in 1920 specifically for the short action of their Model 99 lever-action rifle.
- A key goal of the new, rimless cartridge was to deliver ballistic performance superior in every way to the rimmed 30-30 Winchester cartridge. In this, Savage succeeded.
- The new cartridge owed most if its ballistic superiority to a 21% higher MAP and the use of spitzer bullets allowed by the rotary magazine of the Savage Model 99 rifle.

- In addition to the Savage Model 99 lever-action, the 300 Savage has been offered in many bolt-action rifles with short actions.
- Today, the 300 Savage has been eclipsed by the 308 Winchester. As a result, very few new rifles are being offered in 300 Savage caliber.
- Although ammunition in 300 Savage is still made by Remington, Winchester, and Federal, only Federal still lists both the 150-grain and 180-grain loads in their catalog.

Interesting Fact

When it was introduced, the 300 Savage was one of the first modern, high-pressure sporting cartridges designed for short-action rifles. It occupied this position for 32 years until the introduction of the 308 Winchester cartridge in 1952.

BALLISTIC NOTES

- Muzzle velocity of the 300 Savage with the 150-grain bullet is 240 fps higher than the 30-30 Winchester with a bullet of the same weight.
- Even though it weighs more, the 180-grain bullet of the 300 Savage offers 150 fps higher muzzle velocity than the 170-grain bullet of the 30-30 Winchester.
- In addition, the spitzer bullets used in the 300 Savage far outperform the down range ballistics of the flat nose bullets needed in the 30-30 Winchester.
- Due to its relatively limited case capacity and 1 in 12 inch rifling twist rate, the ballistic sweet spot for the 300 Savage stands with the 150-grain bullet at a muzzle velocity of 2,630 fps which is a fine combination for deer hunters. The relatively slow twist rate also works well with lighter bullets.

HANDLOADING NOTES

- As most 300 Savage ammunition will be fired from lever-action rifles, full length resizing of cases will be necessary. We recommend using a small base die to prevent feeding problems.
- The 300 Savage is very flexible when it comes to bullet weights. As factory ammunition options shrink, handloaders can take full advantage of this capability to match the bullet to the game type and range.
- Lighter weight bullets such as the Speer 110-grain Varminter HP and 125-grain TNT® HP work well for large varmints and predators at short ranges.
- For small deer at close ranges, try the Speer 130-grain SPFN Hot-Cor® bullet.
- Handloaders can duplicate factory loads with the Speer 150-grain bullets. We recommend the Spitzer SP Hot-Cor for this purpose.
- Bullets from 180-grain to 200-grain elevate the 300 Savage into the big game category, albeit at short ranges.
- The 300 Savage cartridge works best with slow burning powders.

SAFETY NOTES

SPEER 180-grain Spitzer BTSP @ a muzzle velocity of 2,469 fps:
- Maximum vertical altitude @ 90° elevation is 15,546 feet.
- Maximum horizontal distance to first impact with ground @ 39° elevation is 7,442 yards.

100 GRAINS

DIAMETER	SECTIONAL DENSITY
.308"	0.151

30 Plinker® SPRN

Ballistic Coefficient	0.144
COAL Tested	2.475"
Speer Part No.	1805

			Starting Charge		Maximum Charge	
Propellant	Case	Primer	Weight (grains)	Muzzle Velocity (feet/sec)	Weight (grains)	Muzzle Velocity (feet/sec)
Winchester 748	Federal	CCI 250	44.0	2901	48.0 C	3192
Alliant Reloder 7	Federal	CCI 200	36.0	2795	40.0	3154
Accurate 2230	Federal	CCI 250	41.0	2771	45.0	3096
IMR 4064	Federal	CCI 200	42.0	2791	46.0 C	3091
IMR 3031	Federal	CCI 200	39.0	2778	43.0 C	3091
IMR 4895	Federal	CCI 200	41.0	2777	45.0 C	3053
Vihtavuori N130	Federal	CCI 200	36.0	3032	40.0	3032
IMR 4320	Federal	CCI 200	41.0	2678	45.0 C	2924
IMR 4350	Federal	CCI 200	42.0	2345	46.0 C	2593
IMR SR 4759 (reduced load)	Federal	CCI 200	16.0	1676	18.0	1911

WARNING! Maximum loads should be used with CAUTION • C = Compressed Load

110 GRAINS

DIAMETER	SECTIONAL DENSITY
.308"	0.166

30 Varminter HP
Ballistic Coefficient	0.128
COAL Tested	2.255"
Speer Part No.	1835

30 Carbine TMJ® RN
Ballistic Coefficient	0.179
COAL Tested	2.330"
Speer Part No.	1846

			Starting Charge		Maximum Charge	
Propellant	Case	Primer	Weight (grains)	Muzzle Velocity (feet/sec)	Weight (grains)	Muzzle Velocity (feet/sec)
Accurate 2230	Federal	CCI 250	41.0	2776	45.0	3096
Hodgdon H322	Federal	CCI 200	40.0	2899	44.0	3070
Vihtavuori N130	Federal	CCI 200	36.0	2738	40.0	3032
Winchester 748	Federal	CCI 250	43.0	2749	47.0 C	3025
IMR 3031	Federal	CCI 200	38.0	2671	42.0 C	2953
IMR 4064	Federal	CCI 200	41.0	2644	45.0 C	2926
IMR 4895	Federal	CCI 200	40.0	2641	44.0 C	2909
IMR 4198	Federal	CCI 200	31.0	2552	35.0	2895
Alliant Reloder 7	Federal	CCI 200	34.0	2549	38.0	2885
Hodgdon H380	Federal	CCI 250	44.0	2500	48.0 C	2750
IMR 4350	Federal	CCI 200	42.0	2309	46.0 C	2559
IMR SR 4759 (reduced load)	Federal	CCI 200	15.0	1525	19.0	1939

WARNING! Maximum loads should be used with CAUTION • C = Compressed Load

125 GRAINS

DIAMETER	SECTIONAL DENSITY
.308"	0.188

30 TNT® HP

Ballistic Coefficient	0.341
COAL Tested	2.580"
Speer Part No.	1986

			Starting Charge		Maximum Charge	
Propellant	Case	Primer	Weight (grains)	Muzzle Velocity (feet/sec)	Weight (grains)	Muzzle Velocity (feet/sec)
Accurate 2460	Federal	CCI 250	40.0	2644	44.0 C	2987
Vihtavuori N140	Federal	CCI 200	42.0	2624	46.0 C	2946
IMR 4895	Federal	CCI 200	40.0	2601	44.0 C	2887
Hodgdon BL-C(2)	Federal	CCI 250	36.0	2583	40.0 C	2884
Winchester 748	Federal	CCI 250	43.0	2545	47.0 C	2858
IMR 4320	Federal	CCI 200	41.0	2490	45.0 C	2829
IMR 3031	Federal	CCI 200	38.0	2548	42.0 C	2796
IMR 4064	Federal	CCI 200	39.0	2453	43.0 C	2707
Hodgdon H380	Federal	CCI 250	44.0	2324	48.0 C	2626
Hodgdon H414	Federal	CCI 250	43.0	2272	47.0 C	2537
IMR 4350	Federal	CCI 200	41.0	2201	45.0 C	2443

WARNING! Maximum loads should be used with CAUTION • C = Compressed Load

130 GRAINS

DIAMETER	SECTIONAL DENSITY
.308"	0.196

30 HP
Ballistic Coefficient	0.244
COAL Tested	2.520"
Speer Part No.	2005

30 SPFN Hot-Cor®
Ballistic Coefficient	0.213
COAL Tested	2.375"
Speer Part No.	2007

			Starting Charge		Maximum Charge	
Propellant	Case	Primer	Weight (grains)	Muzzle Velocity (feet/sec)	Weight (grains)	Muzzle Velocity (feet/sec)
Vihtavuori N140	Federal	CCI 200	41.0	2608	45.0 C	2868
Accurate 2460	Federal	CCI 250	39.0	2579	43.0	2867
Hodgdon H322	Federal	CCI 200	38.0	2544	42.0	2839
IMR 4064	Federal	CCI 200	39.0	2507	43.0	2784
Winchester 748	Federal	CCI 250	40.0	2477	44.0	2753
IMR 4895	Federal	CCI 200	38.0	2462	42.0	2723
IMR 3031	Federal	CCI 200	36.0	2423	40.0	2693
Hodgdon H380	Federal	CCI 250	43.0	2427	47.0 C	2656
IMR 4320	Federal	CCI 200	38.0	2285	42.0	2559
IMR 4350	Federal	CCI 200	41.0	2260	45.0 C	2481

WARNING! Maximum loads should be used with CAUTION • C = Compressed Load

150 GRAINS

DIAMETER	SECTIONAL DENSITY
.308"	0.226

30 SPFN Hot-Cor®

Ballistic Coefficient	0.255
COAL Tested	2.375"
Speer Part No.	2011

30 Spitzer BTSP

Ballistic Coefficient	0.417
COAL Tested	2.550"
Speer Part No.	2022

30 Spitzer SP Hot-Cor®

Ballistic Coefficient	0.377
COAL Tested	2.550"
Speer Part No.	2023

30 Grand Slam® SP

Ballistic Coefficient	0.295
COAL Tested	2.535"
Speer Part No.	2026

			Starting Charge		Maximum Charge	
Propellant	Case	Primer	Weight (grains)	Muzzle Velocity (feet/sec)	Weight (grains)	Muzzle Velocity (feet/sec)
Vihtavuori N140	Federal	CCI 200	40.0	2451	44.0 C	2726
Accurate 2460	Federal	CCI 250	38.0	2461	42.0	2723
IMR 4064	Federal	CCI 200	37.5	2375	41.5	2648
Hodgdon H322	Federal	CCI 200	36.0	2347	40.0	2630
Hodgdon H380	Federal	CCI 250	42.0	2327	46.0 C	2566
IMR 4895	Federal	CCI 200	37.0	2286	41.0	2559
Winchester 748	Federal	CCI 250	38.0	2296	42.0	2539
IMR 3031	Federal	CCI 200	34.5	2262	38.5	2525
IMR 4320	Federal	CCI 200	37.5	2241	41.5	2493
IMR SR 4759 (reduced load)	Federal	CCI 200	17.0	1516	21.0	1886

WARNING! Maximum loads should be used with CAUTION • C = Compressed Load

165 GRAINS

DIAMETER	SECTIONAL DENSITY
.308"	0.248

30 Spitzer BTSP
Ballistic Coefficient	0.520
COAL Tested	2.550"
Speer Part No.	2034

30 Spitzer SP Hot-Cor®
Ballistic Coefficient	0.444
COAL Tested	2.550"
Speer Part No.	2035

30 Grand Slam® SP
Ballistic Coefficient	0.354
COAL Tested	2.540"
Speer Part No.	2038

			Starting Charge		Maximum Charge	
Propellant	Case	Primer	Weight (grains)	Muzzle Velocity (feet/sec)	Weight (grains)	Muzzle Velocity (feet/sec)
Alliant Reloder 15	Federal	CCI 200	40.0	2392	44.0 C	2674
Vihtavuori N140	Federal	CCI 200	39.0	2368	43.0 C	2647
Hodgdon H322	Federal	CCI 200	35.0	2238	39.0	2519
IMR 4064	Federal	CCI 200	36.0	2229	40.0	2493
Hodgdon H380	Federal	CCI 250	41.0	2254	45.0 C	2474
Winchester 748	Federal	CCI 250	37.0	2224	41.0	2468
IMR 4895	Federal	CCI 200	35.0	2169	39.0	2443
Accurate 2700	Federal	CCI 250	40.0	2207	44.0 C	2434
IMR 4350	Federal	CCI 200	41.0	2180	45.0 C	2425
IMR 4320	Federal	CCI 200	36.0	2120	40.0	2384
IMR SR 4759 (reduced load)	Federal	CCI 200	19.0	1594	21.0	1783

WARNING! Maximum loads should be used with CAUTION • C = Compressed Load

180 GRAINS

DIAMETER	SECTIONAL DENSITY
.308"	0.271

30 Spitzer BTSP
Ballistic Coefficient	0.545
COAL Tested	2.550"
Speer Part No.	2052

30 Spitzer SP Hot-Cor®
Ballistic Coefficient	0.441
COAL Tested	2.550"
Speer Part No.	2053

30 Grand Slam® SP
Ballistic Coefficient	0.374
COAL Tested	2.535"
Speer Part No.	2063

			Starting Charge		Maximum Charge	
Propellant	Case	Primer	Weight (grains)	Muzzle Velocity (feet/sec)	Weight (grains)	Muzzle Velocity (feet/sec)
Alliant Reloder 15	Federal	CCI 200	39.0	2314	43.0 C	2519
Vihtavuori N140	Federal	CCI 200	38.0	2262	42.0 C	2512
IMR 4350	Federal	CCI 200	41.0	2175	45.0 C	2413
Hodgdon H414	Federal	CCI 250	41.0	2164	45.0 C	2412
Winchester 760	Federal	CCI 250	40.5	2152	44.5 C	2395
Hodgdon H380	Federal	CCI 250	40.0	2156	44.0 C	2389
Winchester 748	Federal	CCI 250	36.0	2115	40.0	2372
IMR 4895	Federal	CCI 200	34.0	2103	38.0	2367
IMR 4064	Federal	CCI 200	35.0	2120	39.0	2355
Accurate 2700	Federal	CCI 250	38.0	2056	42.0 C	2278
IMR 4198 (reduced load)	Federal	CCI 200	20.0	1585	24.0	1747

WARNING! Maximum loads should be used with CAUTION • C = Compressed Load

200 GRAINS

DIAMETER	SECTIONAL DENSITY
.308"	0.301

30 Spitzer SP Hot-Cor®

Ballistic Coefficient	0.478
COAL Tested	2.550"
Speer Part No.	2211

			Starting Charge		Maximum Charge	
Propellant	Case	Primer	Weight (grains)	Muzzle Velocity (feet/sec)	Weight (grains)	Muzzle Velocity (feet/sec)
Alliant Reloder 15	Federal	CCI 200	38.0	2042	42.0 C	2423
Vihtavuori N140	Federal	CCI 200	36.0	2017	40.0 C	2301
Hodgdon H414	Federal	CCI 250	41.0	2049	45.0 C	2285
IMR 4350	Federal	CCI 200	39.0	2031	43.0 C	2245
IMR 4064	Federal	CCI 200	32.0	1913	36.0	2166
Hodgdon H380	Federal	CCI 250	37.0	1914	41.0 C	2156
Winchester 760	Federal	CCI 250	37.0	1931	41.0 C	2156
Winchester 748	Federal	CCI 250	33.0	1902	37.0	2151
Accurate 2700	Federal	CCI 250	36.0	1929	40.0 C	2130
IMR 4895	Federal	CCI 200	31.0	1874	35.0	2118
IMR 4198 (reduced load)	Federal	CCI 200	22.0	1585	24.0	1747

WARNING! *Maximum loads should be used with CAUTION • C = Compressed Load*

300 RUGER COMPACT MAGNUM

Alternate Names:	300 RCM
Parent Cartridge:	375 Ruger
Country of Origin:	USA
Year of Introduction:	2008
Designer(s):	Ruger & Hornady
Governing Body:	SAAMI

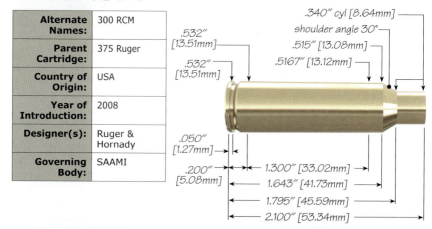

.340" cyl [8.64mm]
shoulder angle 30°
.515" [13.08mm]
.5167" [13.12mm]
.532" [13.51mm]
.532" [13.51mm]
.050" [1.27mm]
.200" [5.08mm]
1.300" [33.02mm]
1.643" [41.73mm]
1.795" [45.59mm]
2.100" [53.34mm]

CARTRIDGE CASE DATA

Case Type:	Rimless, bottleneck		
Average Case Capacity:	77.1 grains H₂O	Max. Cartridge OAL	2.840 inch
Max. Case Length:	2.100 inch	Primer:	Large Rifle
Case Trim to Length:	2.090 inch	RCBS Shell holder:	# 4
Current Manufacturers:	Hornady		

BALLISTIC DATA

Max. Average Pressure (MAP):	65,000 psi, CUP not established for this cartridge - SAAMI	Test Barrel Length:	24 inch
Rifling Twist Rate:	1 turn in 10 inch		
Muzzle velocities of factory loaded ammunition	Bullet Wgt.		Muzzle velocity
	150-grain		3,265 fps
	165-grain		3,185 fps
	178-grain		2,900 fps
	180-grain		3,040 fps

Muzzle velocity will decrease approximately 30 fps per inch for barrels less than 24 inches.

HISTORICAL NOTES

- In 2001, Winchester introduced their new 300 Winchester Short Magnum (WSM) cartridge--the first in the company's series of short, beltless magnum cartridges designed for use in short-action rifles.

- This started a wave of compact magnum cartridges of similar concept including the 300 Remington Short Action Ultra Magnum (RSAUM) introduced in 2002 and the 300 Ruger Compact Magnum (RCM) in 2008.
- Although none of these are interchangeable, they share many physical characteristics, market goals and ballistic capabilities.
- Remington and Winchester promoted their versions of this concept while Hornady added the 300 RCM to their product line.
- In Europe, no market for Short/Compact Magnum cartridges has developed.

BALLISTIC NOTES

- The short, fat, beltless case configuration of these new short magnums such as the 300 RCM are claimed to deliver equivalent muzzle velocities to the "standard" magnum cartridges while burning 10-15% less propellant.
- In theory, the efficiency of the compact case design is due to its low length-to-diameter ratio that allows a smaller amount of unburned propellant to follow the bullet up the barrel thus conserving energy.
- To emphasize the multi-purpose market ambitions of the 300 RCM cartridge, Hornady offers bullet weights of 150, 165, and 180 grains. This mirrors the product lines of the 300 WSM and 300 RSAUM.
- Muzzle velocities and muzzle energies of all three are comparable with a slight edge for the 300 WSM.
- While the 300 RCM is certainly capable of firing lightweight bullets, ammunition makers do not offer such a loading. Hint: you can handload these.

TECHNICAL NOTES

- All Compact/Short Magnum cartridges including the 300 RCM share certain design specifics:
  - They have a beltless, necked case design with a 30-35° shoulder angle.
  - Rim diameter is .534-.535 inches.
  - Case length is between 2.01 to 2.10 inches.
  - OAL is between 2.825 and 2.860 inches.
  - MAP level is 65,000 psi.
  - Rifling twist rate is 1 turn in 10 inches.

HANDLOADING NOTES

- Hornady is the sole source of new, empty brass in 300 RCM.
- Speer offers eleven different bullets for handloading the 300 RCM:
  - A 130-grain Hollow Point for hunting predators and small deer
  - Three 150-grain bullets for hunting deer and medium game
    1. Spitzer Soft Point (basic)
    2. Soft Point Boat tail (long range)
    3. Grand Slam Soft Point (premium)
  - Three 165-grain bullets for hunting big game
    1. Spitzer Soft Point (basic)
    2. Soft Point Boat tail (long range)
    3. Grand Slam Soft Point (premium)

- Three 180-grain bullets for hunting big game
  1. Spitzer Soft Point (basic)
  2. Soft Point Boat tail (long range)
  3. Grand Slam Soft Point (premium)
- A 200-grain Spitzer Soft Point for large heavy game
- The heavy construction of the 300 RCM cartridge case can cause problems with full length resizing. For this reason, we recommend thoroughly cleaning and neck sizing your brass before reloading as most rifles in 300 RCM are bolt-action type.
- The 300 RCM cartridge prefers slow burning propellants.

SAFETY NOTES

SPEER 180-grain Soft Point Boat tail bullet @ a muzzle velocity of 2,850 fps:
- Maximum vertical altitude @ 90° elevation is 16,905 feet.
- Maximum horizontal distance to first impact with ground @ 38° elevation is 7,927 yards.

130 GRAINS

DIAMETER	SECTIONAL DENSITY
.308"	0.196

30 HP

Ballistic Coefficient	0.244
COAL Tested	2.780"
Speer Part No.	2005

			Starting Charge		Maximum Charge	
Propellant	Case	Primer	Weight (grains)	Muzzle Velocity (feet/sec)	Weight (grains)	Muzzle Velocity (feet/sec)
Alliant Reloder 16	Hornady	CCI 250	60.5	3006	67.0 C	3304
Alliant Power Pro 2000-MR	Hornady	CCI 250	57.5	3036	63.5	3303
Alliant Reloder 17	Hornady	CCI 250	58.2	2969	64.5	3295
Hodgdon H414	Hornady	CCI 250	58.0	2971	64.1	3261
Accurate 4350	Hornady	CCI 250	61.4	2931	68.0 C	3259
Alliant Reloder 15	Hornady	CCI 250	54.2	2961	60.2	3256
Vihtavuori N550	Hornady	CCI 250	56.2	2930	62.4	3254
Hodgdon Varget	Hornady	CCI 250	52.9	3028	58.0	3218
IMR 4451	Hornady	CCI 250	58.4	2889	64.8	3195

WARNING! Maximum loads should be used with CAUTION • C = Compressed Load

150 GRAINS

DIAMETER	SECTIONAL DENSITY
.308"	0.226

30 Spitzer BTSP
Ballistic Coefficient	0.417
COAL Tested	2.840"
Speer Part No.	2022

30 Spitzer SP Hot-Cor®
Ballistic Coefficient	0.377
COAL Tested	2.840"
Speer Part No.	2023

30 Grand Slam® SP
Ballistic Coefficient	0.295
COAL Tested	2.820"
Speer Part No.	2026

			Starting Charge		Maximum Charge	
Propellant	Case	Primer	Weight (grains)	Muzzle Velocity (feet/sec)	Weight (grains)	Muzzle Velocity (feet/sec)
Alliant Reloder 16	Hornady	CCI 250	59.2	2878	65.5 C	3168
Accurate 4350	Hornady	CCI 250	61.0	2874	67.5 C	3163
Alliant Power Pro 2000-MR	Hornady	CCI 250	56.9	2914	62.9	3157
Alliant Reloder 17	Hornady	CCI 250	56.5	2801	62.5	3121
Hodgdon H414	Hornady	CCI 250	56.7	2836	63.0	3116
Hodgdon Hybrid 100V	Hornady	CCI 250	56.7	2842	62.7	3100
Ramshot Big Game	Hornady	CCI 250	56.5	2828	62.5	3094
Vihtavuori N550	Hornady	CCI 250	54.7	2803	60.6	3094
Alliant Reloder 15	Hornady	CCI 250	52.8	2835	58.7	3085
IMR 4451	Hornady	CCI 250	56.6	2745	62.6	3024

WARNING! Maximum loads should be used with CAUTION • C = Compressed Load

165 GRAINS

DIAMETER	SECTIONAL DENSITY
.308"	0.248

30 Spitzer BTSP
Ballistic Coefficient	0.520
COAL Tested	2.840"
Speer Part No.	2034

30 Spitzer SP Hot-Cor®
Ballistic Coefficient	0.444
COAL Tested	2.840"
Speer Part No.	2035

30 Grand Slam® SP
Ballistic Coefficient	0.354
COAL Tested	2.820"
Speer Part No.	2038

Propellant	Case	Primer	Starting Charge Weight (grains)	Starting Charge Muzzle Velocity (feet/sec)	Maximum Charge Weight (grains)	Maximum Charge Muzzle Velocity (feet/sec)
Hodgdon SUPERFORMANCE	Hornady	CCI 250	60.5	2790	66.9	3047
Alliant Power Pro 4000-MR	Hornady	CCI 250	60.2	2787	66.6 C	3035
Alliant Reloder 19	Hornady	CCI 250	62.3	2724	69.2 C	3027
Ramshot Hunter	Hornady	CCI 250	62.0	2840	66.8	3021
Alliant Reloder 16	Hornady	CCI 250	57.0	2715	63.2 C	3008
Alliant Reloder 17	Hornady	CCI 250	54.5	2671	60.5	2969
Hodgdon Hybrid 100V	Hornady	CCI 250	55.3	2726	61.3	2968
Vihtavuori N550	Hornady	CCI 250	53.3	2666	59.3	2952
Winchester 760	Hornady	CCI 250	54.8	2683	61.0	2948
IMR 4831	Hornady	CCI 250	58.2	2605	64.6	2896

WARNING! Maximum loads should be used with CAUTION • C = Compressed Load

180 GRAINS

DIAMETER	SECTIONAL DENSITY
.308"	0.271

30 Spitzer BTSP
Ballistic Coefficient	0.545
COAL Tested	2.820"
Speer Part No.	2052

30 Spitzer SP Hot-Cor®
Ballistic Coefficient	0.441
COAL Tested	2.820"
Speer Part No.	2053

30 Grand Slam® SP
Ballistic Coefficient	0.374
COAL Tested	2.820"
Speer Part No.	2063

			Starting Charge		Maximum Charge	
Propellant	Case	Primer	Weight (grains)	Muzzle Velocity (feet/sec)	Weight (grains)	Muzzle Velocity (feet/sec)
Hodgdon SUPERFORMANCE	Hornady	CCI 250	57.9	2629	64.0	2874
Alliant Power Pro 4000-MR	Hornady	CCI 250	56.9	2602	63.0	2863
Alliant Reloder 19	Hornady	CCI 250	59.4	2569	66.0 C	2853
Alliant Reloder 16	Hornady	CCI 250	54.8	2605	60.7	2848
Ramshot Hunter	Hornady	CCI 250	59.0	2680	63.0	2839
Alliant Reloder 17	Hornady	CCI 250	52.8	2581	58.4	2822
Vihtavuori N550	Hornady	CCI 250	51.2	2532	56.6	2783
Hodgdon Hybrid 100V	Hornady	CCI 250	52.3	2574	57.9	2781
Winchester 760	Hornady	CCI 250	51.8	2535	57.5	2760
IMR 4831	Hornady	CCI 250	55.8	2483	61.8	2736

WARNING! Maximum loads should be used with CAUTION • C = Compressed Load

200 GRAINS

DIAMETER	SECTIONAL DENSITY
.308"	0.301

30 Spitzer SP Hot-Cor®

Ballistic Coefficient	0.478
COAL Tested	2.830"
Speer Part No.	2211

			Starting Charge		Maximum Charge	
Propellant	Case	Primer	Weight (grains)	Muzzle Velocity (feet/sec)	Weight (grains)	Muzzle Velocity (feet/sec)
Hodgdon SUPERFORMANCE	Hornady	CCI 250	54.2	2477	60.2	2706
Alliant Power Pro 4000-MR	Hornady	CCI 250	53.7	2430	59.6	2695
Alliant Reloder 19	Hornady	CCI 250	55.4	2413	61.6 C	2685
Alliant Reloder 16	Hornady	CCI 250	50.9	2441	56.6	2661
Alliant Reloder 17	Hornady	CCI 250	52.5	2545	55.1	2651
Ramshot Hunter	Hornady	CCI 250	53.7	2424	59.4	2650
Hodgdon Hybrid 100V	Hornady	CCI 250	50.4	2468	54.4	2609
Winchester 760	Hornady	CCI 250	48.2	2364	53.5	2564
IMR 4831	Hornady	CCI 250	52.0	2315	57.8	2558
Vihtavuori N550	Hornady	CCI 250	47.1	2329	52.3	2549

WARNING! *Maximum loads should be used with CAUTION • C = Compressed Load*

308 WINCHESTER

Alternate Names:	7.62x51mm
Parent Cartridge:	30-06 Springfield
Country of Origin:	USA
Year of Introduction:	1952
Designer(s):	Winchester
Governing Body:	SAAMI/CIP

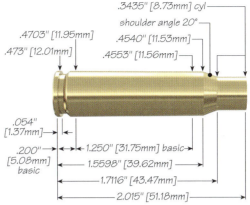

CARTRIDGE CASE DATA

Case Type:	Rimless, bottleneck		
Average Case Capacity:	56.0 grains H_2O	Max. Cartridge OAL	2.810 inch
Max. Case Length:	2.015 inch	Primer:	Large Rifle
Case Trim to Length:	2.005 inch	RCBS Shell holder:	# 3
Current Manufacturers:	Winchester, Federal, Remington, Hornady, Black Hills, Cor-Bon, PMC, Prvi Partizan, IMI, PMP, Wolf, MEN, RUAG (RWS), Nosler		

BALLISTIC DATA

Max. Average Pressure (MAP):	62,000 psi, 52,000 CUP – SAAMI; 60,191 psi - CIP	Test Barrel Length:	24 inch
Rifling Twist Rate:	1 turn in 12 inch		
Muzzle velocities of factory loaded ammunition	Bullet Wgt.		Muzzle velocity
	120-grain		2,850 fps
	150-grain		2,810 fps
	165-grain		2,700 fps
	168-grain		2,670 fps
Muzzle velocity will decrease approximately 20 fps per inch for barrels less than 24 inches.			

HISTORICAL NOTES

- In 1954, the U.S. Army adopted a new 7.62x51mm service cartridge to replace the aging 30-06 Springfield in U.S. military service. A modified M1 Garand rifle, the M14, was developed and adopted for the new cartridge at the same time. After all, why reinvent the wheel?

- Essentially, the new cartridge was a shorter, lighter and more efficient 30-06 Springfield cartridge case optimized for a 144-150-grain FMJBT Military Ball bullet at a muzzle velocity of 2,750 fps.

- Following its adoption by the U.S. military, the new U.S. service cartridge was shoved down the unwilling throats of NATO members after which it became, in military parlance, "Cartridge, Caliber 7.62mm NATO" a designation that it carries forward to this day.

- The 7.62mm NATO cartridge continues in the military service of all NATO countries, typically for use in machine guns and a shrinking number of service rifles.

- The U.S. developed 5.56x45mm NATO cartridge arrived a decade later after years of further wrangling by NATO members. This cartridge has taken the place of the 7.62x51mm cartridge in the service rifles and carbines of most NATO member countries.

- Recognizing that military cartridges usually enjoy success as a commercial cartridge, Winchester introduced their 308 Winchester cartridge two years before the U.S. government announced the adoption of the 7.62x51mm cartridge!

- As a commercial cartridge, the 308 Winchester was not as versatile as the familiar 30-06 Springfield. Hunters found that while the power of the 308 Winchester cartridge with a 150-grain bullet could match the ballistics of the 30-06 Springfield, it could not handle bullets heavier than 190-grains due its limited case capacity and slow 1 turn in 12 inch rifling twist rate.

- However, as the main game animal sought by 308 Winchester hunters were deer, such ballistics were perfectly acceptable. Hunters also liked that the compact 308 Winchester cartridge would fit in short-action rifles which reduced weight.

- The 7.62mm M852 match cartridge loaded at Lake City Army Ammunition Plant (LCAAP) with a Sierra 168-grain bullet has dominated National Match competition for many years now. Commercial manufacturers offer match ammunition in this cartridge as well.

- It is for these reasons the 308 Winchester cartridge has remained on the sporting ammunition best seller list for over 65 years, a position that it shows no sign of losing.

- Today, the 308 Winchester cartridge is a staple item that forms the core of all commercial ammunition manufacturers.

- Even European hunters have come to appreciate the ballistic capabilities of the 308 Winchester!

Interesting Fact

The 7.62x51mm NATO cartridge was the first U.S. service cartridge to use a metric designation.

BALLISTIC NOTES

- The 308 Winchester cartridge case is approximately .500 inch shorter than the 30-06 Springfield allowing it to comfortably fit in short-action rifles, a feature most hunters appreciate. However, some manufacturers have offered the 308 Winchester in standard (long) length action rifles. The resulting short cartridge in a long action has an odd appearance.

- Many hunters prefer to use an all-purpose bullet for most types of hunting. For this application, we recommend the Speer 165-grain Grand Slam SP loaded to a muzzle velocity of approximately 2,950 fps.

- For all types of rifle competition or for hunters who want to check the accuracy of their hunting rifle, the Speer 168-grain Match BTHP loaded to a muzzle velocity of approximately 2,900 fps is a great choice.

TECHNICAL NOTES

- Despite its short case length and small case capacity, the efficiency of the 308 Winchester's compact design has made it an inviting candidate for a number of wildcat cartridges. Few have made the transition to commercial production with the notable exceptions of the 243 Winchester, 7mm-08 Remington, and 30 Thompson-Center.

- Although the 308 Winchester and 7.62x51mm NATO cartridges differ in minor ways they are basically interchangeable with some exceptions.

- Military 7.62x51mm cartridge cases generally have less case capacity than commercial brass in 308 Winchester. For this reason, we recommend reducing maximum charges of propellant at least 10% when reloading military 7.62x51mm cartridge cases. Note: for some propellants, we used IMI military cases for load development so powder charge reduction is not necessary.

- Military 7.62x51mm NATO and commercial 308 Winchester ammunition has always been loaded with non-corrosive primers. For this reason, there is no need to clean the bore with hot, soapy water to remove corrosive salt deposits.

HANDLOADING NOTES

- 308 Winchester and 7.62x51mm NATO cartridges fired in bolt-action rifles can be neck sized to maximize case life. However, 308 Winchester ammunition fired in semi-automatic rifles such as the Springfield M1A will require full length resizing with a small base die. You can reduce sizing effort by thoroughly cleaning and lubricating your cases before sizing. Reduce neck sizing ball effort caused by the thick military case necks by polishing the necks inside with a bore brush held in an electric drill.

- Military cartridge cases in this caliber have primers that are crimped in place. Decapping these cases requires additional force which may result in broken decapping pins. The smart reloader keeps a stock of extra decapping pins on hand for such eventualities. Be sure to remove the crimp on the primer pocket before inserting a fresh primer. RCBS makes a Primer Pocket Swaging Die for this purpose.

- Despite its relatively limited case capacity, the 308 Winchester cartridge prefers slow burning propellants.

- Some Russian-made 308 Winchester ammunition is loaded with steel cartridge cases. We recommend that you do not attempt to reload such cartridge cases.

SAFETY NOTES

SPEER 180-grain Spitzer BTSP @ a muzzle velocity of 2,613 fps:
- Maximum vertical altitude @ 90° elevation is 16,059 feet.
- Maximum horizontal distance to first impact with ground @ 38° elevation is 7,627 yards.
- Military 7.62x51mm NATO ammunition can be fired safely in commercial rifles chambered for the 308 Winchester. However, commercial 308 Winchester factory loaded ammunition should not be fired in semi-automatic military rifles chambered for the 7.62x51mm NATO cartridge as these may not have a firing pin retraction system which can lead to out-of-battery firing when feeding a cartridge. Special military primers such as the CCI Large Rifle No. 34 that will prevent this problem are available to handloaders.

100 GRAINS

DIAMETER	SECTIONAL DENSITY
.308"	0.151

30 Plinker® SPRN

Ballistic Coefficient	0.144
COAL Tested	2.360"
Speer Part No.	1805

			Starting Charge		Maximum Charge	
Propellant	Case	Primer	Weight (grains)	Muzzle Velocity (feet/sec)	Weight (grains)	Muzzle Velocity (feet/sec)
Accurate 2460	IMI Commercial	CCI 250	47.0	3090	51.0 C	3403
Hodgdon H322	IMI Commercial	CCI 200	44.0	3011	48.0	3315
Vihtavuori N120	IMI Commercial	CCI 200	35.0	2867	39.0	3193
Hodgdon H4895	IMI Commercial	CCI 200	44.0	2806	48.0 C	3160
Winchester 748	IMI Commercial	CCI 250	48.0	2860	52.0 C	3116
IMR 4064	IMI Commercial	CCI 200	45.0	2853	49.0 C	3107
Alliant Reloder 7	IMI Commercial	CCI 200	37.0	2736	41.0	3047
IMR SR 4759 (reduced load)	IMI Commercial	CCI 200	16.0	1569	20.0	1949

WARNING! Maximum loads should be used with CAUTION • C = Compressed Load

110 GRAINS

DIAMETER	SECTIONAL DENSITY
.308"	0.166

30 Varminter HP	
Ballistic Coefficient	0.128
COAL Tested	2.405"
Speer Part No.	1835

Propellant	Case	Primer	Starting Charge		Maximum Charge	
			Weight (grains)	Muzzle Velocity (feet/sec)	Weight (grains)	Muzzle Velocity (feet/sec)
IMR 4895	IMI Commercial	CCI 200	39.0	2642	43.0	2908
IMR 4064	IMI Commercial	CCI 200	41.5	2644	45.5	2899
Hodgdon H380	IMI Commercial	CCI 250	47.0	2670	51.0 C	2894
IMR 3031	IMI Commercial	CCI 200	38.5	2619	42.5	2893
Winchester 748	IMI Commercial	CCI 250	42.0	2639	46.0	2887
IMR 4198	IMI Commercial	CCI 200	32.0	2561	36.0	2875
Hodgdon H322	IMI Commercial	CCI 200	37.0	2521	41.0	2830
Alliant Reloder 7	IMI Commercial	CCI 200	33.0	2481	37.0	2823
IMR 4227	IMI Commercial	CCI 200	25.0	2135	29.0	2494
IMR 4350	Federal	CCI 200	41.0	2260	45.0 C	2481

NOTE: *These loads held to under 2,900 fps due to bullet construction.*

WARNING! *Maximum loads should be used with CAUTION • C = Compressed Load*

110 GRAINS

DIAMETER	SECTIONAL DENSITY
.308"	0.166

30 Carbine TMJ® RN

Ballistic Coefficient	0.179
COAL Tested	2.490"
Speer Part No.	1846

			Starting Charge		Maximum Charge	
Propellant	Case	Primer	Weight (grains)	Muzzle Velocity (feet/sec)	Weight (grains)	Muzzle Velocity (feet/sec)
Accurate 2460	IMI Commercial	CCI 250	46.0	2870	50.0 C	3271
Hodgdon H322	IMI Commercial	CCI 200	42.0	2944	46.0	3206
Alliant Reloder 15	IMI Commercial	CCI 200	47.0	2868	51.0 C	3194
Accurate 2520	IMI Commercial	CCI 250	45.0	2899	49.0 C	3193
IMR 3031	IMI Commercial	CCI 200	44.0	2886	48.0 C	3179
IMR 4895	IMI Commercial	CCI 200	44.5	2848	48.5 C	3172
IMR 4320	IMI Commercial	CCI 200	47.0	2860	51.0 C	3115
Hodgdon Varget	IMI Commercial	CCI 200	46.0	2957	48.0 C	3108
Hodgdon H4895	IMI Commercial	CCI 200	43.0	2689	47.0 C	3064
Winchester 748	IMI Commercial	CCI 250	47.0	2682	51.0	3058
Vihtavuori N120	IMI Commercial	CCI 200	34.0	2708	38.0	3051
IMR 4064	IMI Commercial	CCI 200	44.5	2708	48.5 C	3051
IMR 4198 (reduced load)	IMI Commercial	CCI 200	26.0	1935	30.0	2286

WARNING! Maximum loads should be used with CAUTION • C = Compressed Load

125 GRAINS

DIAMETER	SECTIONAL DENSITY
.308"	0.188

30 TNT® HP	
Ballistic Coefficient	0.341
COAL Tested	2.635"
Speer Part No.	1986

Propellant	Case	Primer	Starting Charge Weight (grains)	Starting Charge Muzzle Velocity (feet/sec)	Maximum Charge Weight (grains)	Maximum Charge Muzzle Velocity (feet/sec)
Alliant AR-Comp	Federal	Federal 210	44.2	2995	49.0 C	3231
Alliant Power Pro Varmint	Federal	Federal 210	43.9	2912	48.8	3196
Alliant Power Pro 1200-R	Federal	Federal 210	38.6	2918	42.9	3128
Alliant Reloder 10X	IMI Commercial	CCI 200	38.0	2845	42.0	3120
Alliant Reloder 15	IMI Commercial	CCI 200	46.0	2791	50.0 C	3108
Accurate 2460	IMI Commercial	CCI 250	44.0	2727	48.0 C	3107
IMR 4320	IMI Commercial	CCI 200	46.0	2695	50.0 C	3036
Accurate 2230	IMI Commercial	CCI 250	42.0	2654	46.0 C	3025
Winchester 748	IMI Commercial	CCI 250	46.0	2760	50.0 C	3006
Accurate 2520	IMI Commercial	CCI 250	44.0	2714	48.0 C	2989
Hodgdon H322	IMI Commercial	CCI 200	40.0	2669	44.0	2972
Vihtavuori N135	IMI Commercial	CCI 200	42.0	2661	46.0 C	2963
IMR 4895	IMI Commercial	CCI 200	42.0	2685	46.0 C	2957
Hodgdon Varget	IMI Commercial	CCI 200	45.0	2820	47.0 C	2954
IMR 4064	IMI Commercial	CCI 200	44.0	2643	48.0 C	2943
IMR 3031	IMI Commercial	CCI 200	41.0	2702	48.0 C	2942
IMR 4198 (reduced load)	IMI Commercial	CCI 200	25.0	1978	29.0	2201

WARNING! *Maximum loads should be used with CAUTION • C = Compressed Load*

130 GRAINS

DIAMETER	SECTIONAL DENSITY
.308"	0.196

30 HP
Ballistic Coefficient	0.244
COAL Tested	2.615"
Speer Part No.	2005

30 SPFN Hot-Cor®
Ballistic Coefficient	0.213
COAL Tested	2.530"
Speer Part No.	2007

			Starting Charge		Maximum Charge	
Propellant	Case	Primer	Weight (grains)	Muzzle Velocity (feet/sec)	Weight (grains)	Muzzle Velocity (feet/sec)
Alliant AR-Comp	Federal	Federal 210	43.3	2908	48.6 C	3178
Alliant Reloder 10X	IMI Commercial	CCI 200	38.0	2845	42.0	3120
Alliant Reloder 15	IMI Commercial	CCI 200	46.0	2791	50.0 C	3108
Alliant Power Pro Varmint	Federal	Federal 210	42.9	2823	47.7	3108
Accurate 2460	IMI Commercial	CCI 250	44.0	2727	48.0 C	3107
IMR 4320	IMI Commercial	CCI 200	46.0	2695	50.0 C	3036
Accurate 2230	IMI Commercial	CCI 250	42.0	2654	46.0 C	3025
Winchester 748	IMI Commercial	CCI 250	46.0	2760	50.0 C	3006
Accurate 2520	IMI Commercial	CCI 250	44.0	2714	48.0 C	2989
Hodgdon H322	IMI Commercial	CCI 200	40.0	2669	44.0	2972
Vihtavuori N135	IMI Commercial	CCI 200	42.0	2661	46.0 C	2963
IMR 4895	IMI Commercial	CCI 200	42.0	2685	46.0 C	2957
Hodgdon Varget	IMI Commercial	CCI 200	45.0	2820	47.0 C	2954
IMR 4064	IMI Commercial	CCI 200	44.0	2643	48.0 C	2943
IMR 3031	IMI Commercial	CCI 200	41.0	2702	48.0 C	2942
IMR 4198 (reduced load)	IMI Commercial	CCI 200	25.0	1978	29.0	2201

WARNING! Maximum loads should be used with CAUTION • C = Compressed Load

150 GRAINS

DIAMETER	SECTIONAL DENSITY
.308"	0.226

30 SPFN Hot-Cor®
Ballistic Coefficient	0.255
COAL Tested	2.530"
Speer Part No.	2011

30 Spitzer BTSP
Ballistic Coefficient	0.417
COAL Tested	2.700"
Speer Part No.	2022

30 Spitzer SP Hot-Cor®
Ballistic Coefficient	0.377
COAL Tested	2.700"
Speer Part No.	2023

30 Grand Slam® SP
Ballistic Coefficient	0.295
COAL Tested	2.680"
Speer Part No.	2026

			Starting Charge		Maximum Charge	
Propellant	Case	Primer	Weight (grains)	Muzzle Velocity (feet/sec)	Weight (grains)	Muzzle Velocity (feet/sec)
Alliant Power Pro 2000-MR	Federal	Federal 210	48.3	2823	52.8 C	3037
Alliant Reloder 15	IMI Commercial	CCI 200	45.0	2715	49.0 C	2960
Alliant Power Pro Varmint	Federal	Federal 210	42.3	2738	47.1	2959
Accurate 2520	IMI Commercial	CCI 250	44.0	2593	48.0 C	2956
Alliant AR-Comp	Federal	Federal 210	40.6	2718	45.2 C	2948
Hodgdon H335	IMI Commercial	CCI 250	43.0	2590	47.0	2919
Winchester 748	IMI Commercial	CCI 250	46.0	2684	50.0 C	2907
IMR 8208 XBR	Federal	Federal 210	39.5	2695	43.9	2907
Hodgdon Varget	IMI Commercial	CCI 200	43.0	2663	47.0 C	2895
Vihtavuori N140	Federal	Federal 210	41.9	2653	46.5 C	2892
Vihtavuori N135	IMI Commercial	CCI 200	42.0	2635	46.0 C	2859
IMR 4064	IMI Commercial	CCI 200	43.0	2560	47.0 C	2851
IMR 4320	IMI Commercial	CCI 200	44.0	2514	48.0 C	2831
IMR 4895	IMI Commercial	CCI 200	41.0	2582	45.0	2812
IMR 3031	IMI Commercial	CCI 200	40.0	2458	44.0	2797
Alliant Reloder 10X	IMI Commercial	CCI 200	35.5	2526	39.5	2790
Hodgdon H414	IMI Commercial	CCI 250	47.0	2345	51.0 C	2673
Hodgdon BL-C(2)	IMI Commercial	CCI 250	40.0	2394	44.0	2637
SR 4759 (reduced load)	IMI Commercial	CCI 200	21.0	1632	25.0	1933

WARNING! Maximum loads should be used with CAUTION • C = Compressed Load

GOLD DOT RIFLE

150 GRAINS	DIAMETER	SECTIONAL DENSITY
	.308"	0.226

30 GD	
Ballistic Coefficient	0.503
COAL Tested	2.800"
Speer Part No.	308150GDB

30 TMJ®	
Ballistic Coefficient	0.503
COAL Tested	2.800"
Speer Part No.	308150TMJ

			Starting Charge		Maximum Charge	
Propellant	Case	Primer	Weight (grains)	Muzzle Velocity (feet/sec)	Weight (grains)	Muzzle Velocity (feet/sec)
Alliant Power Pro 2000-MR	Federal	Federal 210	47.9	2729	53.1 C	3025
Accurate 2520	Federal	Federal 210	43.4	2740	47.9	2957
Hodgdon CFE 223	Federal	Federal 210	46.2	2681	51.2	2951
Alliant Power Pro Varmint	Federal	Federal 210	42.2	2643	46.7	2895
Alliant Reloder 15	Federal	Federal 210	43.2	2622	47.8	2890
Hodgdon Varget	Federal	Federal 210	42.1	2635	46.7 C	2873
IMR 4064	Federal	Federal 210	42.0	2606	46.6 C	2872
Alliant AR-Comp	Federal	Federal 210	40.8	2628	45.1	2868
IMR 4895	Federal	Federal 210	41.7	2588	46.2	2862
Accurate 4064	Federal	Federal 210	43.4	2586	48.0 C	2848
Hodgdon H335	Federal	Federal 210	40.5	2583	44.8	2832
Vihtavuori N135	Federal	Federal 210	39.3	2546	43.5	2809

WARNING! *Maximum loads should be used with CAUTION • C = Compressed Load*

165 GRAINS

DIAMETER	SECTIONAL DENSITY
.308"	0.248

30 Spitzer BTSP
Ballistic Coefficient	0.520
COAL Tested	2.800"
Speer Part No.	2034

30 Spitzer SP Hot-Cor®
Ballistic Coefficient	0.444
COAL Tested	2.800"
Speer Part No.	2035

30 Grand Slam® SP
Ballistic Coefficient	0.354
COAL Tested	2.685"
Speer Part No.	2038

			Starting Charge		Maximum Charge	
Propellant	Case	Primer	Weight (grains)	Muzzle Velocity (feet/sec)	Weight (grains)	Muzzle Velocity (feet/sec)
Alliant Power Pro 2000-MR	Federal	Federal 210	45.7	2646	50.3 C	2857
Alliant Reloder 15	IMI Commercial	CCI 200	43.0	2616	47.0 C	2849
Accurate 2520	IMI Commercial	CCI 250	41.0	2527	45.0	2783
Vihtavuori N140	IMI Commercial	CCI 200	42.0	2551	46.0 C	2779
Accurate 2460	IMI Commercial	CCI 250	40.0	2489	44.0	2772
Hodgdon CFE 223	Federal	Federal 210	41.8	2560	46.2	2768
IMR 4064	IMI Commercial	CCI 200	41.0	2507	45.0	2761
IMR 3031	IMI Commercial	CCI 200	39.0	2507	43.0	2759
Alliant AR-Comp	Federal	Federal 210	38.7	2518	43.0	2750
Winchester 748	IMI Commercial	CCI 250	42.0	2494	46.0	2746
Alliant Power Pro Varmint	Federal	Federal 210	39.8	2518	44.2	2744
IMR 4320	IMI Commercial	CCI 200	42.0	2457	46.0 C	2736
Hodgdon H414	IMI Commercial	CCI 250	47.0	2425	51.0 C	2732
Winchester 760	IMI Commercial	CCI 250	47.0	2379	51.0 C	2711
IMR 4895	IMI Commercial	CCI 200	39.0	2373	43.0	2705
IMR 4166	Federal	Federal 210	38.3	2431	42.1	2630
Alliant Reloder 10X	IMI Commercial	CCI 200	34.0	2365	38.0	2625
IMR 4350	IMI Commercial	CCI 200	45.0	2334	49.0 C	2600
IMR SR 4759 (reduced load)	IMI Commercial	CCI 200	22.0	1639	24.0	1809

WARNING! *Maximum loads should be used with CAUTION • C = Compressed Load*

168 GRAINS

DIAMETER	SECTIONAL DENSITY
.308"	0.253

30 Match BTHP

Ballistic Coefficient	0.534
COAL Tested	2.800"
Speer Part No.	2040

			Starting Charge		Maximum Charge	
Propellant	Case	Primer	Weight (grains)	Muzzle Velocity (feet/sec)	Weight (grains)	Muzzle Velocity (feet/sec)
Alliant Power Pro 2000-MR	Federal	Federal 210	45.7	2672	50.5 C	2889
†Alliant AR-Comp	Federal	Federal 210	39.2	2570	43.3 C	2782
†Hodgdon Varget	IMI Commercial	CCI 200	42.0	2566	46.0	2781
Vihtavuori N150	IMI Commercial	CCI 200	43.0	2433	47.0 C	2773
†IMR 4064	IMI Commercial	CCI 200	42.0	2504	46.0	2758
†Winchester 748	IMI Commercial	CCI 250	42.0	2472	46.0	2754
†Alliant Power Pro Varmint	Federal	Federal 210	39.6	2544	43.6	2753
†Alliant Reloder 15	IMI Commercial	CCI 200	41.0	2435	45.0	2743
†IMR 4320	IMI Commercial	CCI 200	42.0	2482	46.0	2733
†Accurate 2460	IMI Commercial	CCI 250	40.0	2391	44.0	2725
†Accurate 2520	IMI Commercial	CCI 250	40.0	2471	44.0	2692
†IMR 4895	IMI Commercial	CCI 200	40.0	2412	44.0	2687
†IMR 3031	IMI Commercial	CCI 200	39.0	2466	43.0	2685
†IMR 4166	Federal	Federal 210	38.3	2470	42.2 C	2670
Hodgdon H414	IMI Commercial	CCI 250	45.0	2338	49.0	2665
Winchester 760	IMI Commercial	CCI 250	45.0	2441	49.0	2660
†Hodgdon BL-C(2)	IMI Commercial	CCI 250	41.0	2357	45.0	2655
Hodgdon H380	IMI Commercial	CCI 250	45.0	2294	49.0 C	2584

†—denotes propellant suitable for gas-operated semi-auto match rifles

WARNING! Maximum loads should be used with CAUTION • C = Compressed Load

GOLD DOT RIFLE

168 GRAINS	DIAMETER	SECTIONAL DENSITY
	.308"	0.253

30 GD	
Ballistic Coefficient	0.572
COAL Tested	2.800"
Speer Part No.	308168GDB

			Starting Charge		Maximum Charge	
Propellant	Case	Primer	Weight (grains)	Muzzle Velocity (feet/sec)	Weight (grains)	Muzzle Velocity (feet/sec)
Alliant Power Pro 2000-MR	Federal	Federal 210	45.3	2564	50.2 C	2821
†Hodgdon CFE 223	Federal	Federal 210	43.2	2507	47.7	2729
†Accurate 2520	Federal	Federal 210	40.9	2500	45.3	2725
Alliant Power Pro Varmint	Federal	Federal 210	40.0	2466	44.4	2709
†Alliant Reloder 15	Federal	Federal 210	40.7	2455	45.2	2704
†Winchester 748	Federal	Federal 210	41.5	2436	46.1	2696
†Accurate 4064	Federal	Federal 210	41.0	2409	45.5 C	2665
†Hodgdon Varget	Federal	Federal 210	39.6	2402	43.9	2665
IMR 4895	Federal	Federal 210	39.0	2380	43.3	2661
†IMR 4064	Federal	Federal 210	39.5	2396	43.6 C	2660
Vihtavuori N540	Federal	Federal 210	41.0	2379	45.3	2660
†Alliant AR-Comp	Federal	Federal 210	38.0	2419	42.2	2640

†—denotes propellant suitable for gas-operated semi-auto match rifles

WARNING! *Maximum loads should be used with CAUTION • C = Compressed Load*

180 GRAINS

DIAMETER	SECTIONAL DENSITY
.308"	0.271

30 Spitzer BTSP
Ballistic Coefficient	0.545
COAL Tested	2.800"
Speer Part No.	2052

30 Spitzer SP Hot-Cor®
Ballistic Coefficient	0.441
COAL Tested	2.800"
Speer Part No.	2053

30 Grand Slam® SP
Ballistic Coefficient	0.374
COAL Tested	2.680"
Speer Part No.	2063

			Starting Charge		Maximum Charge	
Propellant	Case	Primer	Weight (grains)	Muzzle Velocity (feet/sec)	Weight (grains)	Muzzle Velocity (feet/sec)
Alliant Power Pro 2000-MR	Federal	Federal 210	43.6	2491	47.8	2692
Alliant Reloder 15	IMI Commercial	CCI 200	41.0	2318	45.0	2643
Accurate 2460	IMI Commercial	CCI 250	39.0	2337	43.0	2633
Hodgdon Varget	IMI Commercial	CCI 200	40.0	2425	44.0	2620
Vihtavuori N150	IMI Commercial	CCI 200	41.0	2336	45.0 C	2602
Alliant AR-Comp	Federal	Federal 210	37.8	2412	41.5	2597
Winchester 748	IMI Commercial	CCI 250	41.0	2317	45.0	2581
Alliant Power Pro Varmint	Federal	Federal 210	37.9	2379	41.9	2574
IMR 4064	IMI Commercial	CCI 200	39.0	2313	43.0 C	2548
Winchester 760	IMI Commercial	CCI 250	44.0	2320	48.0 C	2527
Hodgdon H414	IMI Commercial	CCI 250	44.0	2202	48.0 C	2510
IMR 4320	IMI Commercial	CCI 200	40.0	2274	44.0	2504
Hodgdon H335	IMI Commercial	CCI 250	38.0	2296	42.0	2500
IMR 4166	Federal	Federal 210	36.0	2276	40.0	2485
Accurate 2520	IMI Commercial	CCI 250	37.0	2273	41.0	2475
Hodgdon H380	IMI Commercial	CCI 250	44.0	2162	48.0 C	2464
IMR 4895	IMI Commercial	CCI 200	37.0	2191	41.0	2441
IMR 4350	IMI Commercial	CCI 200	44.0	2163	48.0 C	2437
IMR 4198 (reduced load)	IMI Commercial	CCI 200	24.0	1589	28.0	1860

WARNING! Maximum loads should be used with CAUTION • C = Compressed Load

200 GRAINS

DIAMETER	SECTIONAL DENSITY
.308"	0.301

30 Spitzer SP Hot-Cor®

Ballistic Coefficient	0.478
COAL Tested	2.800"
Speer Part No.	2211

			Starting Charge		Maximum Charge	
Propellant	Case	Primer	Weight (grains)	Muzzle Velocity (feet/sec)	Weight (grains)	Muzzle Velocity (feet/sec)
Alliant Reloder 15	IMI Commercial	CCI 200	38.0	2140	42.0	2439
Winchester 748	IMI Commercial	CCI 250	39.0	2240	43.0	2439
Accurate 2460	IMI Commercial	CCI 200	36.5	2215	40.5	2438
Hodgdon H414	IMI Commercial	CCI 250	42.0	2138	46.0 C	2437
Winchester 760	IMI Commercial	CCI 250	44.0	2215	48.0 C	2412
IMR 4350	IMI Commercial	CCI 200	43.0	2127	47.0 C	2396
IMR 4320	IMI Commercial	CCI 200	38.0	2171	42.0	2391
IMR 4895	IMI Commercial	CCI 200	36.0	2095	40.0	2388
Hodgdon H380	IMI Commercial	CCI 250	43.0	2141	47.0 C	2384
IMR 4831	IMI Commercial	CCI 200	43.0	2139	47.0 C	2382
Vihtavuori N140	IMI Commercial	CCI 200	37.0	2106	41.0	2373
Accurate 2520	IMI Commercial	CCI 250	36.0	2171	40.0	2365
IMR 4064	IMI Commercial	CCI 200	36.5	2060	40.5	2347
IMR 4198 (reduced load)	IMI Commercial	CCI 200	24.0	1510	28.0	1760

WARNING! *Maximum loads should be used with CAUTION • C = Compressed Load*

30-40 KRAG

Alternate Names:	30-40, 30 US ARMY, 30 U.S.
Country of Origin:	USA
Year of Introduction:	1892
Designer(s):	U.S. Army Frankford Arsenal & Springfield Armory
Governing Body:	SAAMI/CIP

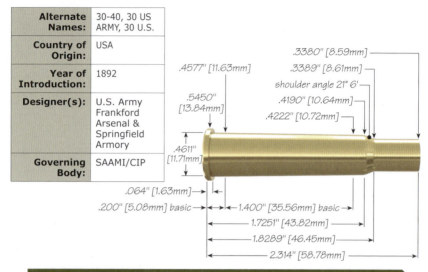

CARTRIDGE CASE DATA

Case Type:	Rimmed, bottleneck		
Average Case Capacity:	58.0 grains H$_2$O	**Max. Cartridge OAL**	3.089 inch
Max. Case Length:	2.314 inch	**Primer:**	Large Rifle
Case Trim to Length:	2.304 inch	**RCBS Shell holder:**	# 7
Current Manufacturers:	Remington, Winchester		

BALLISTIC DATA

Max. Average Pressure (MAP):	40,000 CUP, Piezo not established - SAAMI	**Test Barrel Length:**	24 inch
Rifling Twist Rate:	1 turn in 10 inch		
Muzzle velocities of factory loaded ammunition	**Bullet Wgt.**		**Muzzle velocity**
	180-grain		2,430 fps
	Muzzle velocity will decrease approximately 10 fps per inch for barrels less than 24 inches.		

HISTORICAL NOTES

- From 1892 to 1903, the 30-40 Krag was the official service cartridge of the U.S. Army. It replaced the 45-70 Government cartridge which had been in U.S. Army service since 1873.

- Initial production runs of 30-40 Krag military ammunition were loaded with black powder. This is why the black powder nomenclature system was used. Shortly after this, the popular name for the new cartridge unofficially became "30 Government".

- Following a quick transition to smokeless propellant in 1893, the 30-40 Krag became the first small bore U.S. military service cartridge standardized on smokeless powder and a jacketed bullet.
- After a relatively brief 11 year service life, the 30-40 Krag cartridge was replaced by the 30-06 Springfield cartridge in 1906.
- The 30-40 Krag cartridge quickly faded from U.S. military service only to be saved by its enduring popularity with civilian shooters.
- The rimmed case of the 30-40 Krag made it an ideal choice for single-shot rifles such as the Winchester Model 1885 and Ruger No. 3 as well as the Winchester Model 1895 lever-action rifle.
- Thousands of surplus Krag rifles and reloading components were sold to civilians through the Director of Civilian Marksmanship Program.
- Today, the 30-40 Krag cartridge soldiers on in the ammunition product lines of Remington and Winchester.
- Is retirement for the 30-40 Krag cartridge finally imminent? Don't bet on it!

Interesting Fact

Although the U.S. Army adopted the 30-40 Krag as its service cartridge in 1892, the U.S. Navy and U.S. Marine Corps most certainly did not follow suit! In 1895, the U.S. Sea Services adopted the innovative 236 U.S. Navy cartridge (aka the 6mm Lee Navy) which remained their service cartridge until 1901. The 6mm Lee Navy cartridge was used by the U.S. Marine Corps detachment in China to help break the Siege of the Legations in Peking during the Boxer Rebellion in 1899.

BALLISTIC NOTES

- As use of smokeless propellants in military cartridges spread in the 1880s, the militaries of major nations adopted new service cartridges loaded with long, heavy, jacketed round nose bullets.
- Adoption of the 30-40 Krag cartridge by the U.S. Army followed this trend. Muzzle velocity as adopted with the 220-grain FMJRN bullet was a leisurely 2,000 fps. In 1899, muzzle velocity was increased to 2,200 fps.
- Generations of hunters have found the 30-40 Krag loaded with a 180-grain round nose bullet to be the best combination for taking deer and other types of game.
- Maximum effective range of the 30-40 Krag cartridge loaded with 180-grain soft point round nose bullets is approximately 200 yards.

TECHNICAL NOTES

- The 30-40 Krag operates at MAP levels considerably lower than more modern 30 caliber cartridges such as the 30-06 Springfield. This should be kept in mind when reloading for Krag designed rifles.
- Chambers of 30-40 Krag military rifles have a long, generous throat in order to accommodate the long, heavy 220-grain service bullet. When loading lighter weight bullets, accuracy may suffer as a result.
- The 30-40 Krag rifle action and magazine are designed to feed round nose bullets. As a result, many Krag rifles will not reliably feed spitzer bullets (you can single load them).

- The industry specified groove diameter for 30-40 Krag barrels is .308 inches. As a result of manufacturing variations, some Krag military rifle barrels exceed this which may adversely affect accuracy.

HANDLOADING NOTES

- In addition to building loaded ammunition, new, empty, unprimed brass in 30-40 Krag caliber is available from Remington and Winchester.
- The low MAP level of the 30-40 Krag cartridge dictates the use of slow burning propellants.
- All 30-40 Krag military ammunition was loaded with corrosive primers. Do not attempt to fire or reload this ammunition. It should be destroyed.
- Neck sizing works very well with 30-40 Krag cartridges and prolongs their service life.

SAFETY NOTES

SPEER 180-grain Spitzer BTSP @ a muzzle velocity of 2,162 fps:
- Maximum vertical altitude @ 90° elevation is 14,445 feet.
- Maximum horizontal distance to first impact with ground @ 39° elevation is 7,037 yards.

100 GRAINS

DIAMETER	SECTIONAL DENSITY
.308"	0.151

30 Plinker® SPRN

Ballistic Coefficient	0.144
COAL Tested	2.610"
Speer Part No.	1805

			Starting Charge		Maximum Charge	
Propellant	Case	Primer	Weight (grains)	Muzzle Velocity (feet/sec)	Weight (grains)	Muzzle Velocity (feet/sec)
Hodgdon H322	Winchester	CCI 200	41.0	2795	45.0	3140
IMR 4320	Winchester	CCI 200	44.0	2765	48.0	3015
IMR 3031	Winchester	CCI 200	40.0	2604	44.0	2886
Hodgdon H380	Winchester	CCI 250	47.0	2653	51.0	2876
IMR 4064	Winchester	CCI 200	42.0	2593	46.0	2867
IMR 4895	Winchester	CCI 200	40.0	2511	44.0	2783
IMR 4350	Winchester	CCI 200	49.0	2465	53.0	2680
IMR SR 4759 (reduced load)	Winchester	CCI 200	16.0	1568	20.0	1953

WARNING! Maximum loads should be used with CAUTION • C = Compressed Load

110 GRAINS

DIAMETER	SECTIONAL DENSITY
.308"	0.166

30 Varminter HP	
Ballistic Coefficient	0.128
COAL Tested	2.760"
Speer Part No.	1835

30 Carbine TMJ® RN	
Ballistic Coefficient	0.179
COAL Tested	2.760"
Speer Part No.	1846

			Starting Charge		Maximum Charge	
Propellant	Case	Primer	Weight (grains)	Muzzle Velocity (feet/sec)	Weight (grains)	Muzzle Velocity (feet/sec)
IMR 4320	Winchester	CCI 200	43.0	2612	47.0	2873
IMR 3031	Winchester	CCI 200	39.0	2509	43.0	2783
Hodgdon H380	Winchester	CCI 250	46.0	2544	50.0	2760
IMR 4064	Winchester	CCI 200	41.0	2448	45.0	2715
IMR 4895	Winchester	CCI 200	39.0	2411	43.0	2671
Hodgdon H322	Winchester	CCI 200	38.0	2345	42.0	2656
IMR 4350	Winchester	CCI 200	48.0	2360	52.0	2579
IMR 4198 (reduced load)	Winchester	CCI 200	26.0	1979	30.0	2296

NOTE: The 110-grain Varminter HP bullet is not designed for velocities exceeding those listed here.

130 GRAINS

DIAMETER	SECTIONAL DENSITY
.308"	0.196

30 HP	
Ballistic Coefficient	0.244
COAL Tested	2.780"
Speer Part No.	2005

30 SPFN Hot-Cor®	
Ballistic Coefficient	0.213
COAL Tested	2.865"
Speer Part No.	2007

			Starting Charge		Maximum Charge	
Propellant	Case	Primer	Weight (grains)	Muzzle Velocity (feet/sec)	Weight (grains)	Muzzle Velocity (feet/sec)
IMR 4064	Winchester	CCI 200	42.0	2438	46.0	2694
IMR 4320	Winchester	CCI 200	42.0	2385	46.0	2632
Hodgdon H380	Winchester	CCI 250	44.0	2406	48.0	2622
IMR 3031	Winchester	CCI 200	39.0	2332	43.0	2611
Hodgdon H414	Winchester	CCI 250	47.0	2327	51.0	2582
IMR 4350	Winchester	CCI 200	48.0	2360	52.0	2571
Hodgdon H322	Winchester	CCI 200	33.0	2003	37.0	2253
IMR 4198 (reduced load)	Winchester	CCI 200	25.0	1983	29.0	2209

WARNING! Maximum loads should be used with CAUTION • C = Compressed Load

150 GRAINS

DIAMETER	SECTIONAL DENSITY
.308"	0.226

30 SPFN Hot-Cor®
Ballistic Coefficient	0.255
COAL Tested	3.089"
Speer Part No.	2011

30 Spitzer BTSP
Ballistic Coefficient	0.417
COAL Tested	3.089"
Speer Part No.	2022

30 Spitzer SP Hot-Cor®
Ballistic Coefficient	0.377
COAL Tested	3.089"
Speer Part No.	2023

30 Grand Slam® SP
Ballistic Coefficient	0.295
COAL Tested	3.089"
Speer Part No.	2026

Propellant	Case	Primer	Starting Charge Weight (grains)	Starting Charge Muzzle Velocity (feet/sec)	Maximum Charge Weight (grains)	Maximum Charge Muzzle Velocity (feet/sec)
IMR 4350	Winchester	CCI 200	46.0	2236	50.0	2494
IMR 3031	Winchester	CCI 200	37.0	2235	41.0	2491
IMR 4064	Winchester	CCI 200	38.0	2229	42.0	2489
Hodgdon H380	Winchester	CCI 250	43.0	2220	47.0	2480
Hodgdon H414	Winchester	CCI 250	45.0	2169	49.0	2416
IMR 4895	Winchester	CCI 200	35.0	2063	39.0	2356
Hodgdon H322	Winchester	CCI 200	31.0	1886	35.0	2173
IMR SR 4759 (reduced load)	Winchester	CCI 200	21.0	1631	25.0	1937

WARNING! Maximum loads should be used with CAUTION • C = Compressed Load

165 GRAINS

DIAMETER	SECTIONAL DENSITY
.308"	0.248

30 Spitzer BTSP	
Ballistic Coefficient	0.520
COAL Tested	3.089"
Speer Part No.	2034

30 Spitzer SP Hot-Cor®	
Ballistic Coefficient	0.444
COAL Tested	3.089"
Speer Part No.	2035

30 Grand Slam® SP	
Ballistic Coefficient	0.354
COAL Tested	3.089"
Speer Part No.	2038

			Starting Charge		Maximum Charge	
Propellant	Case	Primer	Weight (grains)	Muzzle Velocity (feet/sec)	Weight (grains)	Muzzle Velocity (feet/sec)
IMR 4064	Winchester	CCI 200	37.0	2098	41.0	2339
IMR 4831	Winchester	CCI 200	44.0	2115	48.0	2311
Hodgdon H380	Winchester	CCI 250	40.0	2032	44.0	2279
Hodgdon H414	Winchester	CCI 250	43.0	2044	47.0	2279
IMR 4350	Winchester	CCI 200	44.0	2057	48.0	2258
IMR 4895	Winchester	CCI 200	34.0	1946	38.0	2243
Hodgdon H322	Winchester	CCI 200	30.0	1818	34.0	2099
IMR SR 4759 (reduced load)	Winchester	CCI 200	22.0	1639	24.0	1812

WARNING! Maximum loads should be used with CAUTION • C = Compressed Load

180 GRAINS

DIAMETER	SECTIONAL DENSITY
.308"	0.271

30 Spitzer BTSP
Ballistic Coefficient	0.545
COAL Tested	3.089"
Speer Part No.	2052

30 Spitzer SP Hot-Cor®
Ballistic Coefficient	0.441
COAL Tested	3.089"
Speer Part No.	2053

30 Grand Slam® SP
Ballistic Coefficient	0.374
COAL Tested	3.089"
Speer Part No.	2063

			Starting Charge		Maximum Charge	
Propellant	Case	Primer	Weight (grains)	Muzzle Velocity (feet/sec)	Weight (grains)	Muzzle Velocity (feet/sec)
IMR 4831	Winchester	CCI 200	43.0	1997	47.0	2185
IMR 4350	Winchester	CCI 200	42.0	1960	46.0	2146
IMR 4895	Winchester	CCI 200	33.0	1841	37.0	2146
Winchester 760	Winchester	CCI 250	41.0	1914	45.0	2143
IMR 3031	Winchester	CCI 200	33.0	1876	37.0	2139
IMR 4064	Winchester	CCI 200	34.0	1872	38.0	2132
Hodgdon H414	Winchester	CCI 250	39.0	1855	43.0	2051
IMR 4198 (reduced load)	Winchester	CCI 200	24.0	1589	28.0	1863

WARNING! *Maximum loads should be used with CAUTION • C = Compressed Load*

200 GRAINS

DIAMETER	SECTIONAL DENSITY
.308"	0.301

30 Spitzer SP Hot-Cor®

Ballistic Coefficient	0.478
COAL Tested	3.089"
Speer Part No.	2211

			Starting Charge		Maximum Charge	
Propellant	Case	Primer	Weight (grains)	Muzzle Velocity (feet/sec)	Weight (grains)	Muzzle Velocity (feet/sec)
IMR 4350	Winchester	CCI 200	42.0	1926	44.0	2034
IMR 4831	Winchester	CCI 200	43.0	1909	45.0	2017
IMR 4895	Winchester	CCI 200	34.0	1857	36.0	1976
IMR 3031	Winchester	CCI 200	31.0	1715	35.0	1974
IMR 4064	Winchester	CCI 200	35.0	1837	37.0	1953
Winchester 760	Winchester	CCI 250	38.0	1714	42.0	1942
Hodgdon H414	Winchester	CCI 250	38.0	1742	40.0	1849
IMR 4198 (reduced load)	Winchester	CCI 200	24.0	1509	28.0	1762

WARNING! *Maximum loads should be used with CAUTION • C = Compressed Load*

30-06 SPRINGFIELD

Alternate Names:	7.62x63mm, 30 Government, 30 M1, 30 M2
Parent Cartridge:	30-03 Government
Country of Origin:	USA
Year of Introduction:	1906
Designer(s):	Springfield Armory
Governing Body:	SAAMI/CIP

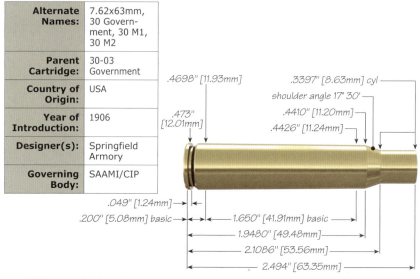

CARTRIDGE CASE DATA			
Case Type:	Rimmed, bottleneck		
Average Case Capacity:	68.0 grains H₂O	Max. Cartridge OAL	3.340 inch
Max. Case Length:	2.494 inch	Primer:	Large Rifle
Case Trim to Length:	2.484 inch	RCBS Shell holder:	# 3
Current Manufacturers:	Federal, Remington, Winchester, Hornady, Black Hills, PMC, IMI, PMP, Prvi Partizan, Sellier & Bellot, Wolf, RAUG, Norma, Nosler		

BALLISTIC DATA			
Max. Average Pressure (MAP):	60,000 psi, 50,000 CUP - SAAMI	Test Barrel Length:	24 inch
Rifling Twist Rate:	1 turn in 10 inch		
Muzzle velocities of factory loaded ammunition	Bullet Wgt.		Muzzle velocity
	147-grain		3,020 fps
	150-grain		2,910 fps
	165-grain		2,800 fps
	168-grain		2,700 fps
	180-grain		2,700 fps
	190-grain		2,750 fps
	200-grain		2,540 fps
	220-grain		2,400 fps

Muzzle velocity will decrease approximately 20 fps per inch for barrels less than 24 inches.

HISTORICAL NOTES

- In 1903, the U.S. Army adopted its first rimless, 30-caliber service cartridge, sometimes called the 30-03 Springfield.
- In step with other military service cartridges of that era, the 30-03 was loaded with the same 220-grain full metal jacket round nose bullet used in the 30-40 Krag, albeit at a higher muzzle velocity.
- As work progressed on the new 30-03 cartridge and rifle at Springfield Armory in Massachusetts, the premise on which the new 30-03 cartridge was based changed abruptly in 1905.
- In that year, the German Army adopted the new S Patrone, their 7.92x57mm JS (aka 8x57mm Mauser) military cartridge updated with a 154-grain full metal jacket pointed (*spitzer*) bullet at high velocity.
- This development turned military bullet technology on its ear. The new 30-03 cartridge with its lumbering 220-grain bullet was going to be obsolete even before its adoption was complete!
- In response, the U.S. military quickly initiated a revised program to develop a spitzer bullet for their new cartridge. The result was a 150-grain spitzer boat tail bullet with a cupro-nickel jacket which was, in fact, aerodynamically superior to the hollow base German bullet.
- At the same time, a sufficient number of improvements were made to the 30-03 cartridge case to create a new cartridge designated in military parlance as the "Ball Cartridge, Caliber 30, Model of 1906". This rather ponderous title was shortened to 30-06 Springfield for commercial use.
- After serving in two world wars and several lesser conflicts, the U.S. military declared the 30-06 Springfield cartridge obsolete in 1957; military production of 30-06 ammunition in the U.S. ended shortly thereafter.
- Most military cartridges have enjoyed success as a commercial cartridge and the 30-06 Springfield is a sterling example. Hunters found its power impressive and appreciated its ability to use a wide range of bullet weights and types. The 30-06 Springfield proved versatile and reliable enough to take every species of North American game and many types of African plains game as well.
- The 30-06 Springfield cartridge also enjoyed success in competition, winning numerous events and awards. Even today, some older competitors still prefer the 30-06.
- It is for these reasons that the 30-06 Springfield cartridge has remained at the top of the best seller list for over 112 years now, a position that it shows no sign of losing.
- Today, for all major and most minor ammunition makers, the 30-06 Springfield cartridge is a staple item that forms the core of their business.
- Even European hunters have come to appreciate the ballistic capabilities of the 30-06 Springfield!

Interesting Fact

One of the more arcane ballistic objectives in the development of the 30-03 and 30-06 military cartridges was that it had to be capable of killing a cavalry horse with one shot at 1,000 yards!

TECHNICAL NOTES

- The length, volume and construction of the 30-06 Springfield cartridge make it an inviting candidate for a bewildering number of wildcat designs. Several have made the transition to commercial production such as the 25-06 Remington, 270 Winchester, 280 Remington, and the 35 Whelen.
- In Europe the 30-06 Springfield is often called the 7.62x63mm Springfield.
- Military 30-06 Springfield cartridge cases are substantially heavier and have less case capacity than commercial brass in this caliber.
- Military surplus 30-06 ammunition made before 1952 was loaded with corrosive primers. After you fire this type of ammunition, clean the bore of your rifle thoroughly with hot, soapy water or a suitable cleaning agent to remove the corrosive salts. Never use a cleaner with ammonia as an ingredient!
- Empty cartridge cases fired with corrosive primers should be destroyed as the corrosive salts will attack and weaken brass.

HANDLOADING NOTES

- In addition to the manufacturers providing loaded ammunition listed above, Winchester, Remington, Federal, Norma, Hornady, Sako, Lapua, Sellier & Bellot, and Prvi Partizan offer new, empty, unprimed brass cartridge cases in 30-06 Springfield caliber for handloading.
- 30-06 Springfield ammunition fired in semi-automatic rifles such as the M1 Garand will require full length resizing with a small base die. You can reduce sizing effort by thoroughly cleaning and lubricating your cases before sizing. Reduce neck sizing ball effort caused by the thick military case necks by polishing the necks inside with a bore brush held in an electric drill.
- Military cartridge cases in this caliber have primers that are crimped in place. Decapping these cases requires additional force which may result in broken decapping pins. The smart reloader keeps a stock of extra decapping pins on hand for such eventualities. Be sure to remove the crimp on the primer pocket before inserting a fresh primer. RCBS makes a tool for this purpose.

SAFETY NOTES

SPEER 180-grain Spitzer BTSP @ a muzzle velocity of 2,756 fps:
- Maximum vertical altitude @ 90° elevation is 16,572 feet.
- Maximum horizontal distance to first impact with ground @ 38° elevation is 7,809 yards.
- Military 30-06 Springfield ammunition can be fired safely in commercial rifles chambered for this caliber. However, commercial ammunition is not recommended due to the potential for out-of-battery firings caused by floating firing pins which are found in most semi-automatic modern sporting rifles (MSRs). To prevent this problem, use CCI No. 34 Large Rifle primers which are designed especially for this application.

100 GRAINS

DIAMETER	SECTIONAL DENSITY
.308"	0.151

30 Plinker® SPRN

Ballistic Coefficient	0.144
COAL Tested	2.935"
Speer Part No.	1805

Propellant	Case	Primer	Starting Charge		Maximum Charge	
			Weight (grains)	Muzzle Velocity (feet/sec)	Weight (grains)	Muzzle Velocity (feet/sec)
IMR 3031	Winchester	CCI 200	53.0	3251	57.0	3510
IMR 4064	Winchester	CCI 200	55.0	3202	59.0	3450
Hodgdon H335	Winchester	CCI 250	54.0	3147	58.0	3383
Winchester 748	Winchester	CCI 250	56.0	3166	60.0	3369
IMR 4895	Winchester	CCI 200	51.0	3073	55.0	3323
IMR 4320	Winchester	CCI 200	54.0	3044	58.0	3289
Hodgdon H322	Winchester	CCI 200	48.0	2985	52.0	3268
Alliant Reloder 7	Winchester	CCI 200	43.0	2875	47.0	3239
IMR SR 4759 (reduced load)	Winchester	CCI 200	16.0	1545	20.0	1969

110 GRAINS

DIAMETER	SECTIONAL DENSITY
.308"	0.166

30 Varminter HP

Ballistic Coefficient	0.128
COAL Tested	2.870"
Speer Part No.	1835

This bullet is not designed for velocities exceeding those listed here.

Propellant	Case	Primer	Starting Charge		Maximum Charge	
			Weight (grains)	Muzzle Velocity (feet/sec)	Weight (grains)	Muzzle Velocity (feet/sec)
Winchester 760	Winchester	CCI 250	52.0	2682	56.0	2904
Winchester 748	Winchester	CCI 250	44.5	2631	48.5	2888
IMR 4350	Winchester	CCI 200	54.0	2651	58.0	2873
IMR 3031	Winchester	CCI 200	42.5	2601	46.5	2871
IMR 4895	Winchester	CCI 200	44.0	2588	48.0	2847
Alliant Reloder 7	Winchester	CCI 200	38.0	2541	42.0	2836
Hodgdon H322	Winchester	CCI 200	41.0	2530	45.0	2769
Hodgdon BL-C(2)	Winchester	CCI 250	48.0	2537	52.0	2766
IMR 4227 (reduced load)	Winchester	CCI 200	29.0	2316	31.0	2500

WARNING! Maximum loads should be used with CAUTION • C = Compressed Load

110 GRAINS

DIAMETER	SECTIONAL DENSITY
.308"	0.166

30 TMJ RN

Ballistic Coefficient	0.179
COAL Tested	2.915"
Speer Part No.	1846

			Starting Charge		Maximum Charge	
Propellant	Case	Primer	Weight (grains)	Muzzle Velocity (feet/sec)	Weight (grains)	Muzzle Velocity (feet/sec)
Winchester 748	Winchester	CCI 250	58.0	3201	62.0 C	3414
Alliant Reloder 15	Winchester	CCI 200	56.0	3124	60.0 C	3363
Accurate 2460	Winchester	CCI 250	51.0	3129	55.0	3349
Accurate 2520	Winchester	CCI 250	52.0	3144	56.0	3343
Hodgdon Varget	Winchester	CCI 200	55.0	3063	59.0 C	3312
IMR 4064	Winchester	CCI 200	54.0	2965	58.0	3264
Vihtavuori N135	Winchester	CCI 200	51.0	3047	55.0	3258
Accurate 2495	Winchester	CCI 200	51.0	2950	55.0	3218
IMR 4320	Winchester	CCI 200	53.0	2931	57.0	3135
IMR 4895	Winchester	CCI 200	50.5	2908	54.5	3127
Hodgdon H4895	Winchester	CCI 200	49.0	2855	53.0	3123
Hodgdon BL-C(2)	Winchester	CCI 250	51.0	2815	55.0	3096
Hodgdon H322	Winchester	CCI 200	46.0	2789	50.0	2941
Accurate 5744 (reduced load)	Winchester	CCI 200	26.0	1965	27.0	2044

WARNING! Maximum loads should be used with CAUTION • C = Compressed Load

125 GRAINS

DIAMETER	SECTIONAL DENSITY
.308"	0.188

30 TNT® HP

Ballistic Coefficient	0.341
COAL Tested	3.100"
Speer Part No.	1986

			Starting Charge		Maximum Charge	
Propellant	Case	Primer	Weight (grains)	Muzzle Velocity (feet/sec)	Weight (grains)	Muzzle Velocity (feet/sec)
Alliant AR-Comp	Federal	Federal 210	48.6	3037	53.7	3261
Alliant Power Pro Varmint	Federal	Federal 210	48.4	2964	53.6	3228
IMR 8208 XBR	Federal	Federal 210	48.4	3048	52.6	3222
Alliant Reloder 10X	Federal	Federal 210	46.3	2959	51.3	3210
Accurate 2460	Winchester	CCI 250	49.0	2974	53.0	3178
IMR 3031	Winchester	CCI 200	50.0	2862	54.0	3167
Vihtavuori N135	Winchester	CCI 200	49.0	2844	53.0	3116
Accurate 2015	Winchester	CCI 200	46.0	2905	50.0	3111
Hodgdon BL-C(2)	Winchester	CCI 250	51.0	2874	55.0	3106
Accurate 2495	Winchester	CCI 200	50.0	2876	54.0	3105
Accurate 2230	Winchester	CCI 200	47.0	2887	51.0	3103
Hodgdon H335	Winchester	CCI 250	51.0	2872	55.0	3093
Accurate 2520	Winchester	CCI 250	48.0	2867	52.0	3085
Hodgdon Varget	Winchester	CCI 200	51.5	2763	55.5	3037
Hodgdon H4895	Winchester	CCI 200	47.0	2741	51.0	3025
Alliant Power Pro 1200-R	Federal	Federal 210	38.5	2812	42.5	3025
IMR 4320	Winchester	CCI 200	51.0	2762	55.0	3011
IMR 4895	Winchester	CCI 200	48.0	2777	52.0	3002
Hodgdon H322	Winchester	CCI 200	44.0	2720	48.0	2916

WARNING! *Maximum loads should be used with* **CAUTION** *• C = Compressed Load*

130 GRAINS

DIAMETER	SECTIONAL DENSITY
.308"	0.196

30 HP	
Ballistic Coefficient	0.244
COAL Tested	3.060"
Speer Part No.	2005

30 SPFN Hot-Cor®	
Ballistic Coefficient	0.212
COAL Tested	2.984"
Speer Part No.	2007

Propellant	Case	Primer	Starting Charge Weight (grains)	Starting Charge Muzzle Velocity (feet/sec)	Maximum Charge Weight (grains)	Maximum Charge Muzzle Velocity (feet/sec)
Alliant Power Pro 2000-MR	Federal	Federal 210	51.2	2928	56.6	3192
Alliant Reloder 15	Federal	Federal 210	49.5	2862	54.7	3165
Alliant AR-Comp	Federal	Federal 210	46.5	2915	51.4	3149
IMR 8208 XBR	Federal	Federal 210	45.5	2905	50.6	3120
Alliant Power Pro Varmint	Federal	Federal 210	44.6	2841	49.3	3064
Accurate 2460	Winchester	CCI 250	47.5	2805	51.0	3031
IMR 4064	Winchester	CCI 200	51.0	2802	55.0	3022
Hodgdon H414	Winchester	CCI 250	56.0	2787	60.0	3012
Hodgdon Varget	Winchester	CCI 200	51.0	2771	55.0	3006
Accurate 2015	Winchester	CCI 200	45.0	2803	49.0	3004
IMR 3031	Winchester	CCI 200	48.5	2678	52.5	3003
Hodgdon H335	Winchester	CCI 250	50.0	2758	54.0	2979
IMR 4895	Winchester	CCI 200	47.5	2728	51.5	2937
Winchester 748	Winchester	CCI 250	51.0	2728	55.0	2910
Hodgdon BL-C(2)	Winchester	CCI 250	49.0	2699	53.0	2894
Vihtavuori N140	Winchester	CCI 200	48.0	2671	52.0	2868
Hodgdon H4895	Winchester	CCI 200	45.0	2654	49.0	2764
Hodgdon H322	Winchester	CCI 200	43.0	2546	47.0	2757
Accurate 5744 (reduced load)	Winchester	CCI 200	25.0	1819	27.0	1949

WARNING! Maximum loads should be used with CAUTION • C = Compressed Load

150 GRAINS

DIAMETER	SECTIONAL DENSITY
.308"	0.226

30 SPFN Hot-Cor®
Ballistic Coefficient	0.255
COAL Tested	2.984"
Speer Part No.	2011

30 Spitzer BTSP
Ballistic Coefficient	0.417
COAL Tested	3.250"
Speer Part No.	2022

30 Spitzer SP Hot-Cor®
Ballistic Coefficient	0.377
COAL Tested	3.250"
Speer Part No.	2023

30 Grand Slam® SP
Ballistic Coefficient	0.295
COAL Tested	3.160"
Speer Part No.	2026

Propellant	Case	Primer	Starting Charge Weight (grains)	Starting Charge Muzzle Velocity (feet/sec)	Maximum Charge Weight (grains)	Maximum Charge Muzzle Velocity (feet/sec)
Alliant Reloder 16	Federal	Federal 210	53.3	2754	59.0 C	3013
Alliant Reloder 17	Federal	Federal 210	51.7	2716	56.7	2958
IMR 4451	Federal	Federal 210	54.5	2700	60.4 C	2933
Alliant Power Pro 2000-MR	Federal	Federal 210	46.6	2685	51.4	2906
Hodgdon H380	Winchester	CCI 250	54.0	2690	58.0	2885
IMR 4350	Winchester	CCI 200	55.0	2620	59.0	2872
Vihtavuori N540	Winchester	CCI 200	45.0	2664	49.0	2867
Alliant AR-Comp	Federal	Federal 210	42.6	2656	47.1	2859
Hodgdon H414	Winchester	CCI 250	54.0	2633	58.0	2840
Hodgdon Varget	Winchester	CCI 200	49.0	2587	53.0	2817
Winchester 760	Winchester	CCI 250	53.0	2558	57.0	2814
Hodgdon H4350	Winchester	CCI 200	55.0	2541	59.0 C	2800
IMR 4064	Winchester	CCI 200	48.0	2547	52.0	2772
Alliant Reloder 15	Winchester	CCI 200	48.0	2550	52.0	2762
IMR 4895	Winchester	CCI 200	45.5	2543	49.5	2756
Alliant Reloder 19	Winchester	CCI 200	58.0	2548	62.0 C	2756
Accurate 2460	Winchester	CCI 250	44.0	2585	48.0	2750
Hodgdon H4895	Winchester	CCI 200	42.0	2451	46.0	2601
Accurate 5744 (reduced load)	Winchester	CCI 200	26.0	1941	28.0	2064

WARNING! Maximum loads should be used with CAUTION • C = Compressed Load

165 GRAINS

DIAMETER	SECTIONAL DENSITY
.308"	0.248

30 Spitzer BTSP
Ballistic Coefficient	0.520
COAL Tested	3.250"
Speer Part No.	2034

30 Spitzer SP Hot-Cor®
Ballistic Coefficient	0.444
COAL Tested	3.250"
Speer Part No.	2035

30 Grand Slam® SP
Ballistic Coefficient	0.354
COAL Tested	3.165"
Speer Part No.	2038

			Starting Charge		Maximum Charge	
Propellant	Case	Primer	Weight (grains)	Muzzle Velocity (feet/sec)	Weight (grains)	Muzzle Velocity (feet/sec)
Ramshot Hunter	Federal	Federal 210	57.4	2803	63.4 C	2974
Alliant Power Pro 4000-MR	Federal	Federal 210	54.8	2705	60.8 C	2943
Alliant Reloder 16	Federal	Federal 210	52.0	2733	57.0 C	2936
Alliant Reloder 17	Federal	Federal 210	51.9	2678	56.5	2879
Accurate 4350	Federal	Federal 210	53.6	2622	59.5 C	2870
Alliant Power Pro 2000-MR	Federal	Federal 210	47.2	2628	52.2	2851
Winchester 760	Winchester	CCI 250	53.0	2631	57.0	2840
Hodgdon H4831SC	Winchester	CCI 200	60.0	2534	62.0 C	2808
IMR 4350	Winchester	CCI 200	54.0	2501	58.0	2782
Vihtavuori N540	Winchester	CCI 200	43.0	2598	47.0	2774
Alliant Reloder 22	Winchester	CCI 200	58.0	2530	62.0 C	2759
Hodgdon H4350	Winchester	CCI 200	54.0	2489	58.0 C	2758
Hodgdon H414	Winchester	CCI 250	52.0	2520	56.0	2757
Hodgdon H380	Winchester	CCI 250	51.0	2544	55.0	2740
Hodgdon Varget	Winchester	CCI 200	46.0	2462	50.0	2703
IMR 4831	Winchester	CCI 200	55.0	2442	59.0	2702
Vihtavuori N140	Winchester	CCI 200	46.0	2490	50.0	2695
IMR 4064	Winchester	CCI 200	46.5	2433	50.5	2671
Alliant Reloder 19	Winchester	CCI 200	55.0	2372	59.0 C	2644
Accurate 2520	Winchester	CCI 250	42.0	2354	46.0	2624
IMR SR 4759 (reduced load)	Winchester	CCI 200	21.0	1615	25.0	1949

WARNING! Maximum loads should be used with CAUTION • C = Compressed Load

168 GRAINS

DIAMETER	SECTIONAL DENSITY
.308"	0.253

30 Match BTHP

Ballistic Coefficient	0.534
COAL Tested	3.295"
Speer Part No.	2040

			Starting Charge		Maximum Charge	
Propellant	Case	Primer	Weight (grains)	Muzzle Velocity (feet/sec)	Weight (grains)	Muzzle Velocity (feet/sec)
Alliant Reloder 16	Federal	Federal 210	52.9	2725	58.6 C	2952
Alliant Reloder 17	Federal	Federal 210	51.0	2626	56.7	2886
Vihtavuori N160	Winchester	CCI 200	57.0	2610	61.0	2863
IMR 4451	Federal	Federal 210	52.3	2633	58.1 C	2857
Hodgdon H4350	Winchester	CCI 200	56.0	2591	60.0 C	2831
IMR 4350	Winchester	CCI 200	55.0	2586	59.0	2818
Alliant AR-Comp	Federal	Federal 210	43.1	2590	47.7	2787
†Hodgdon H380	Winchester	CCI 250	51.0	2479	55.0	2770
IMR 7828	Winchester	CCI 250	58.0	2575	62.0	2739
Alliant Reloder 19	Winchester	CCI 200	57.0	2489	61.0 C	2730
Hodgdon H4831	Winchester	CCI 250	57.0	2450	61.0 C	2693
IMR 4831	Winchester	CCI 250	56.0	2398	60.0	2664
Hodgdon H414	Winchester	CCI 250	50.0	2453	54.0	2664
Winchester 760	Winchester	CCI 250	50.0	2411	54.0	2658
†IMR 4895	Winchester	CCI 200	44.0	2461	48.0	2635
†IMR 4064	Winchester	CCI 200	45.0	2389	49.0	2577

†—denotes propellant suitable for gas-operated semi-auto match rifles

WARNING! *Maximum loads should be used with* **CAUTION** • **C** = Compressed Load

180 GRAINS

DIAMETER	SECTIONAL DENSITY
.308"	0.271

30 Spitzer BTSP
Ballistic Coefficient	0.545
COAL Tested	3.250"
Speer Part No.	2052

30 Spitzer SP Hot-Cor®
Ballistic Coefficient	0.441
COAL Tested	3.160"
Speer Part No.	2053

30 Grand Slam® SP
Ballistic Coefficient	0.374
COAL Tested	3.160"
Speer Part No.	2063

			Starting Charge		Maximum Charge	
Propellant	Case	Primer	Weight (grains)	Muzzle Velocity (feet/sec)	Weight (grains)	Muzzle Velocity (feet/sec)
Ramshot Hunter	Federal	Federal 210	54.1	2592	59.2 C	2797
Hodgdon H4350	Winchester	CCI 200	54.0	2671	58.0 C	2791
IMR 4064	Winchester	CCI 200	46.0	2612	50.0	2791
Alliant Reloder 16	Federal	Federal 210	49.8	2545	55.2 C	2770
Alliant Reloder 23	Federal	Federal 210	53.2	2503	59.9 C	2769
Alliant Power Pro 4000-MR	Federal	Federal 210	51.4	2552	57.1 C	2764
Alliant Reloder 22	Winchester	CCI 200	58.0	2648	62.0 C	2755
Hodgdon H4831SC	Winchester	CCI 200	60.0	2610	62.0 C	2753
Alliant Reloder 17	Federal	Federal 210	49.0	2522	54.4	2732
IMR 4831	Winchester	CCI 200	55.0	2572	59.0 C	2716
Winchester 760	Winchester	CCI 250	51.0	2567	55.0	2709
Hodgdon H414	Winchester	CCI 250	51.0	2573	55.0	2705
Alliant Reloder 19	Winchester	CCI 200	55.0	2483	59.0 C	2671
IMR 4350	Winchester	CCI 200	52.0	2523	56.0 C	2670
Alliant Power Pro 2000-MR	Federal	Federal 210	45.0	2445	49.8	2666
Accurate 4350	Winchester	CCI 200	53.0	2469	57.0 C	2645
Vihtavuori N160	Winchester	CCI 200	52.0	2351	56.0	2584
Alliant Reloder 15	Winchester	CCI 200	45.0	2434	49.0	2579
IMR 4895	Winchester	CCI 200	43.0	2387	47.0	2564
IMR 4198 (reduced load)	Winchester	CCI 200	26.0	1725	30.0	2010

WARNING! Maximum loads should be used with CAUTION • C = Compressed Load

200 GRAINS

DIAMETER	SECTIONAL DENSITY
.308"	0.301

30 Spitzer SP Hot-Cor®
Ballistic Coefficient	0.478
COAL Tested	3.295"
Speer Part No.	2211

			Starting Charge		Maximum Charge	
Propellant	Case	Primer	Weight (grains)	Muzzle Velocity (feet/sec)	Weight (grains)	Muzzle Velocity (feet/sec)
Alliant Reloder 26	Federal	Federal 210	52.2	2408	57.8 C	2667
Alliant Reloder 23	Federal	Federal 210	49.6	2357	54.8 C	2580
Alliant Reloder 16	Federal	Federal 210	46.7	2354	51.7	2578
Alliant Power Pro 4000-MR	Federal	Federal 210	48.1	2370	53.2	2575
Alliant Reloder 17	Federal	Federal 210	45.4	2324	50.4	2561
IMR 7977	Federal	Federal 210	53.9	2303	59.7 C	2546
Hodgdon H4350	Federal	Federal 210	45.8	2322	50.8	2528
Alliant Reloder 22	Winchester	CCI 200	54.0	2281	58.0 C	2525
Alliant Reloder 25	Winchester	CCI 200	58.0	2378	60.0 C	2506
Hodgdon H414	Winchester	CCI 250	49.0	2339	53.0	2477
IMR 4350	Winchester	CCI 200	50.0	2265	54.0	2473
Hodgdon H4831SC	Winchester	CCI 200	53.0	2236	57.0 C	2471
IMR 4831	Winchester	CCI 200	52.0	2302	56.0 C	2453
Vihtavuori N160	Winchester	CCI 200	50.0	2214	54.0	2408
Alliant Reloder 15	Winchester	CCI 200	43.0	2219	47.0	2393
Hodgdon H1000	Winchester	CCI 200	57.0	2167	61.0 C	2393
Hodgdon H380	Winchester	CCI 250	46.0	2177	50.0	2382
Winchester 760	Winchester	CCI 250	47.0	2258	51.0	2369
Alliant Reloder 19	Winchester	CCI 200	51.0	2173	55.0	2356
IMR 4064	Winchester	CCI 200	42.0	2161	46.0	2332
IMR 4198 (reduced load)	Winchester	CCI 200	27.0	1723	31.0	1998

WARNING! Maximum loads should be used with CAUTION • C = Compressed Load

300 REMINGTON SHORT ACTION ULTRA MAGNUM

Alternate Names:	300 RSAUM
Parent Cartridge:	300 Remington Ultra Magnum
Country of Origin:	USA
Year of Introduction:	2002
Designer(s):	Remington
Governing Body:	SAAMI

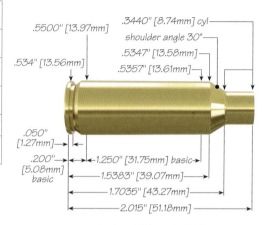

CARTRIDGE CASE DATA

Case Type:	Rimmed, bottleneck		
Average Case Capacity:	75.8 grains H$_2$O	**Max. Cartridge OAL**	2.825 inch
Max. Case Length:	2.015 inch	**Primer:**	Large Rifle
Case Trim to Length:	2.005 inch	**RCBS Shell holder:**	# 38
Current Manufacturers:	Remington		

BALLISTIC DATA

Max. Average Pressure (MAP):	65,000 psi, CUP not established for this cartridge - SAAMI	**Test Barrel Length:**	24 inch
Rifling Twist Rate:	1 turn in 10 inch		

Muzzle velocities of factory loaded ammunition	Bullet Wgt.	Muzzle velocity
	150-grain	3,200 fps
	165-grain	3,075 fps
	180-grain	3,250 fps

Muzzle velocity will decrease approximately 30 fps per inch for barrels less than 24 inches.

HISTORICAL NOTES

- In 2002, Remington matched Winchester's new 300 WSM cartridge with a new short magnum cartridge of their own—the 300 Remington Short Action Ultra Magnum (RSAUM).
- The 7mm RSAUM had been introduced the previous year.

- When developing their new SAUM cartridges, Remington did not try to match short action magnum calibers with rival Winchester. For example, there is no 270 RSAUM or 325 RSAUM.
- Introduction dates, calibers, bullet weights, and case dimensions indicate that the RSAUM cartridges were not developed in response to the WSM cartridges. Rather, they were a parallel development of their own.
- Remington and Winchester marketing strategies for their short magnum cartridges also differ. While Winchester aimed at a dual purpose deer/big game market for their WSM cartridges, Remington proposed their RSAUM cartridges squarely for big game hunting.
- The difference in marketing concepts is highlighted by the number of line items on offer for 300 Short Magnums (Winchester=12, Remington=2) and the bullet weights offered (Winchester= 150, 180, and 190-grain; Remington= 165 and 180-grain).
- As Remington also manufactured firearms, the company was able to simultaneously introduce the new 300 RSAUM cartridge along with rifles chambered for it.
- Rival firearms manufacturers have tended toward chambering Winchester's WSM cartridges in their product lines.
- The concept of a short magnum rifle cartridge in any caliber has not been accepted by European sportsmen.
- While the marketing battle of the short magnum cartridges continues to develop, it is too early to predict winners or losers.

Interesting Fact

In the present market, Remington's 300 RSAUM cartridge is up against a dense field of 13 different 300 magnum cartridges spread over 125 line items from domestic and foreign ammunition manufacturers. This raises the question: "How many 300 magnum cartridges are enough?"

BALLISTIC NOTES

- Despite its smaller size, the efficient design of the 300 RSAUM cartridge allows it to match the muzzle velocities of the same bullet weights in the 300 WSM cartridge.
- Both the 300 RSAUM and the 300 WSM cartridges are capable of nearly matching ballistics with the venerable 300 Winchester Magnum using lower powder charges.
- With its one turn in 10 inch rifling twist rate, the 300 RSAUM will stabilize long heavy bullets up to 190 grains as well as lighter weight bullets.
- While the 300 RSAUM cartridge is certainly capable of firing lightweight bullets, ammunition makers do not offer such loadings. Hint: you can handload these.

HANDLOADING NOTES

- In addition to building loaded ammunition, Remington offers new, empty, unprimed 300 RSAUM brass cartridge cases for reloading.
- The heavy construction of the 300 RSAUM cartridge case can cause problems with full length resizing. Since most rifles are bolt-action we recommend neck sizing for most uses, save hunting loads. Do not use bullets weighing less than 130 grains for hunting deer.
- The 300 RSAUM cartridge prefers slow burning propellants.

- Long, heavy bullets weighing much over 180 grains will take up too much volume inside the 300 RSAUM case to build a successful load.

SAFETY NOTES

SPEER 180-grain Spitzer BTSP @ a muzzle velocity of 2,921 fps:
- Maximum vertical altitude @ 90° elevation is 17,358 feet.
- Maximum horizontal distance to first impact with ground @ 38° elevation is 8,086 yards.

130 GRAINS

DIAMETER	SECTIONAL DENSITY
.308"	0.196

30 HP

Ballistic Coefficient	0.244
COAL Tested	2.625"
Speer Part No.	2005

			Starting Charge		Maximum Charge	
Propellant	Case	Primer	Weight (grains)	Muzzle Velocity (feet/sec)	Weight (grains)	Muzzle Velocity (feet/sec)
Winchester 760	Remington	CCI 250	66.0	3189	70.0 C	3381
IMR 4064	Remington	CCI 200	57.0	3127	61.0	3370
Vihtavuori N540	Remington	CCI 200	58.0	3089	62.0	3366
Hodgdon H414	Remington	CCI 250	65.0	3170	69.0 C	3366
Alliant Reloder 15	Remington	CCI 200	58.0	3063	62.0	3332
Hodgdon H380	Remington	CCI 250	62.0	3110	66.0	3313
Ramshot Big Game	Remington	CCI 250	62.0	3125	66.0	3306
IMR 4350	Remington	CCI 200	65.0C	3128	69.0 C	3293
Hodgdon Varget	Remington	CCI 200	56.0	3064	60.0	3277
Accurate 5744 (reduced load)	Remington	CCI 200	27.0	1977	29.0	2104

WARNING! Maximum loads should be used with CAUTION • C = Compressed Load

150 GRAINS

DIAMETER	SECTIONAL DENSITY
.308"	0.226

30 SPFN Hot-Cor®
Ballistic Coefficient	0.255
COAL Tested	2.680"
Speer Part No.	2011

30 Spitzer BTSP
Ballistic Coefficient	0.417
COAL Tested	2.800"
Speer Part No.	2022

30 Spitzer SP Hot-Cor®
Ballistic Coefficient	0.377
COAL Tested	2.800"
Speer Part No.	2023

30 Grand Slam® SP
Ballistic Coefficient	0.295
COAL Tested	2.680"
Speer Part No.	2026

			Starting Charge		Maximum Charge	
Propellant	Case	Primer	Weight (grains)	Muzzle Velocity (feet/sec)	Weight (grains)	Muzzle Velocity (feet/sec)
Vihtavuori N560	Remington	CCI 200	69.0	3030	73.0 C	3210
Winchester 760	Remington	CCI 250	64.0	3041	68.0	3194
Accurate 4350	Remington	CCI 200	64.0	2974	68.0 C	3173
IMR 4831	Remington	CCI 200	65.0	2963	69.0 C	3158
Hodgdon H414	Remington	CCI 250	62.0	3004	66.0	3158
Hodgdon H4350	Remington	CCI 200	62.0	2969	66.0	3152
IMR 4350	Remington	CCI 200	63.0	2981	67.0	3150
Alliant Reloder 19	Remington	CCI 200	67.0	2969	71.0 C	3150
Accurate 2700	Remington	CCI 250	60.0	2963	64.0	3106
Hodgdon Varget	Remington	CCI 200	54.0	2913	58.0	3088
Hodgdon H4831SC	Remington	CCI 200	67.0	2910	71.0 C	3072
Accurate 5744 (reduced load)	Remington	CCI 200	28.0	1922	30.0	2039

WARNING! *Maximum loads should be used with CAUTION • C = Compressed Load*

165 GRAINS

DIAMETER	SECTIONAL DENSITY
.308"	0.248

30 Spitzer BTSP

Ballistic Coefficient	0.520
COAL Tested	2.800"
Speer Part No.	2034

30 Spitzer SP Hot-Cor®

Ballistic Coefficient	0.444
COAL Tested	2.800"
Speer Part No.	2035

30 Grand Slam® SP

Ballistic Coefficient	0.354
COAL Tested	2.685"
Speer Part No.	2038

			Starting Charge		Maximum Charge	
Propellant	Case	Primer	Weight (grains)	Muzzle Velocity (feet/sec)	Weight (grains)	Muzzle Velocity (feet/sec)
Vihtavuori N560	Remington	CCI 200	67.0	2886	71.0 C	3063
Winchester 760	Remington	CCI 250	62.0	2860	66.0	3035
IMR 4831	Remington	CCI 200	63.0	2808	67.0 C	3011
Alliant Reloder 22	Remington	CCI 200	66.0	2839	70.0 C	3006
Alliant Reloder 19	Remington	CCI 200	65.0	2807	69.0 C	2999
Hodgdon H4350	Remington	CCI 200	60.0	2809	64.0	2983
IMR 4350	Remington	CCI 200	60.5	2784	64.5	2978
IMR 7828	Remington	CCI 200	67.0	2834	69.0 C	2928

WARNING! Maximum loads should be used with CAUTION • C = Compressed Load

180 GRAINS

DIAMETER	SECTIONAL DENSITY
.308"	0.271

30 Spitzer BTSP
Ballistic Coefficient	0.545
COAL Tested	2.800"
Speer Part No.	2052

30 Spitzer SP Hot-Cor®
Ballistic Coefficient	0.441
COAL Tested	2.800"
Speer Part No.	2053

30 Grand Slam® SP
Ballistic Coefficient	0.374
COAL Tested	2.680"
Speer Part No.	2063

			Starting Charge		Maximum Charge	
Propellant	Case	Primer	Weight (grains)	Muzzle Velocity (feet/sec)	Weight (grains)	Muzzle Velocity (feet/sec)
IMR 4831	Remington	CCI 200	61.0	2731	65.0 C	2921
Alliant Reloder 19	Remington	CCI 200	63.0	2727	67.0 C	2896
Alliant Reloder 22	Remington	CCI 200	63.0	2736	67.0 C	2896
IMR 7828	Remington	CCI 200	64.0	2722	68.0 C	2892
IMR 4350	Remington	CCI 200	58.0	2703	62.0	2880
Hodgdon H414	Remington	CCI 250	57.0	2726	61.0	2877
Winchester 760	Remington	CCI 250	57.0	2700	61.0	2854
Hodgdon H4350	Remington	CCI 200	57.0	2700	61.0	2853

WARNING! *Maximum loads should be used with CAUTION • C = Compressed Load*

300 WINCHESTER SHORT MAGNUM

Alternate Names:	300 WSM
Parent Cartridge:	404 Jeffery
Country of Origin:	USA
Year of Introduction:	2001
Designer(s):	Winchester
Governing Body:	SAAMI/CIP

Case diagram dimensions:
- .3440" [8.738mm] cyl
- shoulder angle 35°
- .5550" [14.10mm]
- .5381" [13.69mm]
- .535" [13.59mm]
- .5400" [13.72mm]
- .054" [1.37mm]
- .200" [5.08mm] basic
- 1.300" [33.02mm] basic
- 1.664" [42.25mm]
- 1.8021" [45.77mm]
- 2.100" [53.34mm]

CARTRIDGE CASE DATA

Case Type:	Rimmed, bottleneck		
Average Case Capacity:	79.0 grains H₂O	Max. Cartridge OAL:	2.860 inch
Max. Case Length:	2.100 inch	Primer:	Large Rifle
Case Trim to Length:	2.090 inch	RCBS Shell holder:	# 43
Current Manufacturers:	Winchester, Federal, Hornady, Black Hills, Remington		

BALLISTIC DATA

Max. Average Pressure (MAP):	65,000 psi, CUP not established for this cartridge – SAAMI; 63,817 psi - CIP	Test Barrel Length:	24 inch
Rifling Twist Rate:	1 turn in 10 inch		
Muzzle velocities of factory loaded ammunition	Bullet Wgt.		Muzzle velocity
	150-grain		3,300 fps
	180-grain		3,010 fps
	190-grain		2,875 fps

Muzzle velocity will decrease approximately 30 fps per inch for barrels less than 24 inches.

HISTORICAL NOTES

- In 2001, Winchester introduced the new 300 Winchester Short Magnum (WSM) cartridge—the first in the company's series of short, beltless magnum cartridges designed for use in short-action rifles.

- The 270 WSM and the 7mm WSM followed in 2002 and the 325 WSM completed the series in 2004.
- Remington introduced their own, competing line of "Short Action Ultra Magnum" cartridges in 2002.
- Not wanting to be left behind in developing a trend, competing domestic and foreign ammunition manufacturers have added some of these new Winchester Short Magnum cartridges to their product lines. Copying is a compliment and availability is a key component of success in the marketplace.
- Eager to ride a developing new market, many firearm manufacturers have introduced some WSM calibers to existing models of their short-action rifles.
- Certainly, Winchester seeks to duplicate the ongoing market success of their 300 Winchester Magnum cartridge with the new 300 WSM.
- While the marketing battle of the short magnum cartridges continues to develop, it is too early to predict winners or losers.

Interesting Fact

The field of 300 magnum cartridges is fast becoming a crowded one! Currently, there are over 13 cartridges of this type on offer from domestic and foreign ammunition manufacturers spread over an estimated 125 line items.

BALLISTIC NOTES

- To emphasize the dual purpose market ambitions of the new cartridge for both deer and big game applications, Winchester has gone "all in" with 12 different 300 WSM factory loadings spread over three bullet weights: 150, 180, and 190-grains.
- Despite its smaller size, the efficiency of the 300 WSM design allows it to match or slightly exceed the muzzle velocities of the same bullet weights loaded in the 300 Winchester Magnum cartridge.

TECHNICAL NOTES

- All Winchester Short Magnum cartridges share the same 2.100 inch case length, .555 inch beltless head diameter and 35° shoulder angle in order to fit in short rifle actions.
- Case capacity and volume of the 300 WSM is about 5% greater than the 300 Remington Short Action Ultra Magnum, 14% less than the 300 Win. Mag.
- MAP levels similar to many of the larger magnums, combined with a more efficient case design, allow the 300 WSM cartridge to compete with them on equal terms.
- With its one turn in 10 inch rifling twist rate, the 300 WSM will stabilize long heavy bullets up to 190 grains as well as lighter weight bullets.

HANDLOADING NOTES

- The heavy construction of the 300 WSM cartridge case can cause problems with full length resizing. For this reason neck sizing is recommended for practice and sight-in as most rifles in 300 WSM are bolt-action types. Hunters should consider full length sizing.
- Do not use bullets weighing less than 130 grains for hunting deer.
- The 300 WSM cartridge prefers slow burning propellants.

- Long, heavy bullets weighing over 180 grains will take up too much volume inside the 300 WSM case to build a successful load.

SAFETY NOTES

SPEER 180-grain Spitzer BTSP @ a muzzle velocity of 2,978 fps:
- Maximum vertical altitude @ 90° elevation is 17,358 feet.
- Maximum horizontal distance to first impact with ground @ 38° elevation is 8,086 yards.

130 GRAINS

DIAMETER	SECTIONAL DENSITY
.308"	0.196

30 HP

Ballistic Coefficient	0.244
COAL Tested	2.730"
Speer Part No.	2005

			Starting Charge		Maximum Charge	
Propellant	Case	Primer	Weight (grains)	Muzzle Velocity (feet/sec)	Weight (grains)	Muzzle Velocity (feet/sec)
Alliant Reloder 16	Federal	Federal 215	66.0	3205	73.2 C	3548
Winchester 760	Winchester	CCI 250	72.0	3353	76.0	3533
Hodgdon H414	Winchester	CCI 250	70.0	3345	74.0	3523
IMR 4064	Winchester	CCI 200	63.0	3325	67.0	3505
Vihtavuori N540	Winchester	CCI 200	64.0	3314	68.0	3498
Alliant Reloder 17	Federal	Federal 215	64.7	3134	71.6	3489
IMR 4350	Winchester	CCI 200	71.0	3277	75.0 C	3476
Hodgdon Varget	Winchester	CCI 200	64.0	3269	68.0	3468
Hodgdon 4350	Federal	Federal 215	66.5	3189	73.7	3466
Alliant Reloder 15	Winchester	CCI 200	63.0	3285	67.0	3459
Accurate 4350	Federal	Federal 215	68.0	3127	74.7 C	3457
Alliant Power Pro 2000-MR	Federal	Federal 215	62.2	3177	67.9	3439
Hodgdon H380	Winchester	CCI 250	68.0	3272	72.0	3437
Accurate 5744 (reduced load)	Winchester	CCI 200	29.0	2113	31.0	2227

WARNING! Maximum loads should be used with CAUTION • C = Compressed Load

150 GRAINS

DIAMETER	SECTIONAL DENSITY
.308"	0.226

30 SPFN Hot-Cor®
Ballistic Coefficient	0.255
COAL Tested	2.620"
Speer Part No.	2011

30 Spitzer BTSP
Ballistic Coefficient	0.417
COAL Tested	2.810"
Speer Part No.	2022

30 Spitzer SP Hot-Cor®
Ballistic Coefficient	0.377
COAL Tested	2.810"
Speer Part No.	2023

30 Grand Slam® SP
Ballistic Coefficient	0.295
COAL Tested	2.780"
Speer Part No.	2026

			Starting Charge		Maximum Charge	
Propellant	Case	Primer	Weight (grains)	Muzzle Velocity (feet/sec)	Weight (grains)	Muzzle Velocity (feet/sec)
Alliant Reloder 26	Federal	Federal 215	67.2	3017	74.6 C	3342
Alliant Power Pro 4000-MR	Federal	Federal 215	64.6	3002	71.4	3289
Alliant Reloder 16	Federal	Federal 215	61.7	3006	68.5	3284
Alliant Reloder 23	Federal	Federal 215	66.2	2989	73.4 C	3275
Alliant Reloder 17	Federal	Federal 215	61.4	2989	68.0	3274
Alliant Reloder 22	Federal	Federal 215	64.4	2974	71.6	3272
Accurate 4350	Winchester	CCI 200	67.0	3115	71.0 C	3269
Vihtavuori N560	Winchester	CCI 200	71.5	3098	75.5 C	3265
IMR 4831	Winchester	CCI 200	67.0	3101	71.0	3256
Hodgdon H4350	Winchester	CCI 200	64.0	3086	68.0	3256
Hodgdon H414	Winchester	CCI 250	64.0	3109	68.0	3255
IMR 4350	Winchester	CCI 200	65.0	3043	69.0	3245
Alliant Reloder 19	Winchester	CCI 200	69.5	3049	73.5	3244
Winchester 760	Winchester	CCI 250	64.5	3085	68.5	3238
Accurate 2700	Winchester	CCI 250	61.0	3069	65.0	3197
Hodgdon H4831SC	Winchester	CCI 200	69.0	3040	73.0	3177
Hodgdon Varget	Winchester	CCI 200	55.0	2972	59.0	3154
Hodgdon H380	Winchester	CCI 250	61.0	2994	65.0	3150
Winchester 748	Winchester	CCI 250	55.0	2966	59.0	3112
Vihtavuori N140	Winchester	CCI 200	52.0	2880	56.0	3024
Accurate 5744 (reduced load)	Winchester	CCI 200	29.0	2035	33.0	2259

WARNING! Maximum loads should be used with CAUTION • C = Compressed Load

165 GRAINS

DIAMETER	SECTIONAL DENSITY
.308"	0.248

30 Spitzer BTSP
Ballistic Coefficient	0.520
COAL Tested	2.810"
Speer Part No.	2034

30 Spitzer SP Hot-Cor®
Ballistic Coefficient	0.444
COAL Tested	2.810"
Speer Part No.	2035

30 Grand Slam® SP
Ballistic Coefficient	0.354
COAL Tested	2.780"
Speer Part No.	2038

			Starting Charge		Maximum Charge	
Propellant	Case	Primer	Weight (grains)	Muzzle Velocity (feet/sec)	Weight (grains)	Muzzle Velocity (feet/sec)
Alliant Reloder 26	Federal	Federal 215	65.5	2875	72.6 C	3191
IMR 7828	Winchester	CCI 200	71.0 C	3019	75.0 C	3167
Vihtavuori N560	Winchester	CCI 200	70.0	3012	74.0 C	3151
Accurate 4350	Winchester	CCI 200	66.0	2968	70.0 C	3138
Alliant Reloder 19	Winchester	CCI 200	69.0	2983	73.0 C	3135
Alliant Power Pro 4000-MR	Federal	Federal 215	62.1	2852	68.7	3133
IMR 4831	Winchester	CCI 200	66.5	2984	70.5 C	3131
Alliant Reloder 22	Winchester	CCI 200	69.0	2978	73.0 C	3126
Alliant Reloder 23	Federal	Federal 215	64.2	2860	71.2 C	3124
Alliant Reloder 17	Federal	Federal 215	59.3	2845	65.5	3115
Alliant Reloder 16	Federal	Federal 215	59.8	2870	66.1	3114
IMR 4350	Winchester	CCI 200	64.5	2932	68.5	3103
Hodgdon H414	Winchester	CCI 250	63.5	2961	67.5 C	3099
Winchester 760	Winchester	CCI 250	64.0	2968	68.0	3097
Accurate 3100	Winchester	CCI 200	71.0	2979	73.0 C	3075
Hodgdon H4350	Winchester	CCI 200	61.0	2944	65.0	3073
Hodgdon H4831SC	Winchester	CCI 200	68.5	2925	72.5 C	3062

WARNING! *Maximum loads should be used with CAUTION • C = Compressed Load*

180 GRAINS

DIAMETER	SECTIONAL DENSITY
.308"	0.271

30 Spitzer BTSP
Ballistic Coefficient	0.545
COAL Tested	2.800"
Speer Part No.	2052

30 Spitzer SP Hot-Cor®
Ballistic Coefficient	0.441
COAL Tested	2.780"
Speer Part No.	2053

30 Grand Slam® SP
Ballistic Coefficient	0.374
COAL Tested	2.760"
Speer Part No.	2063

			Starting Charge		Maximum Charge	
Propellant	Case	Primer	Weight (grains)	Muzzle Velocity (feet/sec)	Weight (grains)	Muzzle Velocity (feet/sec)
Alliant Reloder 26	Federal	Federal 215	61.8	2757	68.3 C	3022
Alliant Reloder 19	Winchester	CCI 200	64.5	2819	68.5 C	2978
IMR 4831	Winchester	CCI 200	63.0	2820	67.0 C	2970
Alliant Reloder 22	Winchester	CCI 200	64.5	2797	68.5 C	2958
Alliant Power Pro 4000-MR	Federal	Federal 215	57.5	2661	63.8	2948
IMR 7828	Winchester	CCI 200	66.0	2805	70.0 C	2947
IMR 4350	Winchester	CCI 200	61.0	2782	65.0	2946
Alliant Reloder 23	Federal	Federal 215	59.5	2694	65.9 C	2945
Winchester 760	Winchester	CCI 250	61.0	2786	65.0	2941
Hodgdon H414	Winchester	CCI 250	60.0	2786	64.0	2939
Alliant Reloder 17	Federal	Federal 215	55.5	2697	61.7	2934
Hodgdon H4350	Winchester	CCI 200	59.5	2745	63.5	2920
Alliant Reloder 16	Federal	Federal 215	55.5	2689	61.6 C	2913
Hodgdon H4831SC	Winchester	CCI 200	65.0	2780	69.0 C	2906
Accurate 2700	Winchester	CCI 250	58.0	2750	62.0	2896
Vihtavuori N160	Winchester	CCI 200	61.0	2732	65.0	2867
Hodgdon H380	Winchester	CCI 250	58.0	2705	62.0	2843

WARNING! *Maximum loads should be used with CAUTION • C = Compressed Load*

300 HOLLAND & HOLLAND MAGNUM

Alternate Names:	Super 30, 300 H&H
Parent Cartridge:	375 H&H Magnum
Country of Origin:	England
Year of Introduction:	1925
Designer(s):	Holland & Holland
Governing Body:	SAAMI/CIP

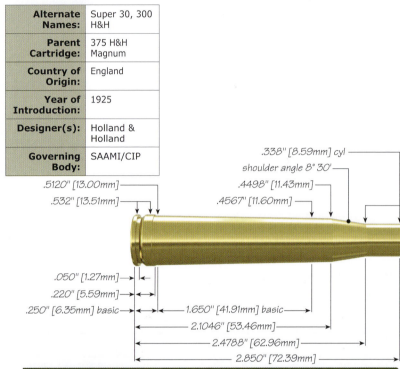

CARTRIDGE CASE DATA

Case Type:	Belted, rimless, bottlenecked		
Average Case Capacity:	86.0 grains H₂O	Max. Cartridge OAL	3.600 inch
Max. Case Length:	2.850 inch	Primer:	Large Rifle
Case Trim to Length:	2.840 inch	RCBS Shell holder:	# 4
Current Manufacturers:	Hornady, Norma, Nosler		

BALLISTIC DATA

Max. Average Pressure (MAP):	58,000 psi, 54,000 CUP - SAAMI	Test Barrel Length:	24 inch
Rifling Twist Rate:	1 turn in 10 inch		
Muzzle velocities of factory loaded ammunition		Bullet Wgt.	Muzzle velocity
		150-grain	3,190 fps
		180-grain	2,880 fps
		220-grain	2,620 fps
	Muzzle velocity will decrease approximately 30 fps per inch for barrels less than 24 inches.		

HISTORICAL NOTES

- Holland & Holland introduced their new "Holland's Super 30" cartridge (called the 300 H&H Magnum in the U.S.) in 1925 to great acclaim.
- As a junior relative of the highly respected 375 H&H Magnum introduced in 1912, the 300 H&H Magnum cartridge quickly became a popular choice for hunting African plains game.
- Unexpectedly, the 300 H&H Magnum developed a following among target shooters after Ben Comfort's victory in the 1935 Wimbledon Cup event at the National Matches shooting a 300 H&H Magnum.
- Prior to the introduction of the 300 Winchester Magnum in 1963, the 300 H&H Magnum had little competition in the field of 30 caliber magnum cartridges for nearly 43 years. It was the super cartridge of the era.
- It was the 375 & 300 H&H Magnum that established the concept that a magnum cartridge had to have a belt.
- The introduction of a wide range of new magnum cartridges in the late 1990s sealed the fate of the 300 H&H Magnum. Today, the popularity of the 300 H&H Magnum has declined to the point that only Nosler and Hornady offer ammunition in this caliber. Norma offers unprimed, empty brass in this caliber for handloading, but no longer loads ammunition in 300 H&H Magnum caliber.
- It seems only a matter of time before the 300 H&H Magnum cartridge slips into the pages of history.

Interesting Fact

Holland & Holland pioneered the belted case head design with their 400/375 Belted Nitro Express cartridge in 1905. Their new design provided an integral, raised belt of metal on the case head just ahead of the extraction groove which provided reliable headspace control on cases without an adequate shoulder. Introduced in 1925, the 300 H&H Magnum (in British parlance Holland's Super 30) was the father of all belted 300 magnum cartridges.

BALLISTIC NOTES

- In its heyday, factory loaded ammunition in 300 H&H Magnum was offered with 150-grain, 180-grain and 220-grain bullet weights.
- Today, only the 180-grain bullet survives in the Hornady product line. However in the Nosler product line bullet weights of 150, 165, 180, and 200-grains are listed.
- That said, the handloader can recreate and/or develop entirely new loads for the 300 H&H Magnum using any of a number of Speer bullets for the purpose.
- In the field, the slightly greater case capacity of the 300 Winchester Magnum gave it a slim 100-150 fps edge in muzzle velocity over the 300 H&H Magnum. A rather dubious advantage at best.

TECHNICAL NOTES

- With its long, tapered case, shallow 8° shoulder angle and long neck, the 300 H&H Magnum is one of the most efficient of magnum cartridges.
- The 300 H&H Magnum remains one of the few belted magnum cartridges that still headspaces on its belt. Many modern magnums can be headspaced on the shoulder though factory ammunition may start from the belt depending on your chamber dimensions.

- The enduring qualities of the 300 H&H Magnum case design can be gauged by the bewildering number of wildcat and commercial variations based on it.
- The 300 H&H Magnum shares head, belt, and rim dimensions with the 300 Winchester Magnum and the 308 Norma Magnum.
- Because of its 3.600 inch overall loaded length (identical to the modern 300 Remington Ultra Magnum), the 300 H&H Magnum will not fit in some long action rifles.

HANDLOADING NOTES

- As most 300 H&H Magnum ammunition will be fired from bolt-action rifles, we recommend neck sizing to reduce sizing and trimming chores and to extend case life, for all but hunting applications.
- Belted magnums that headspace on their belt have a tendency to stretch at the head just in front of the belt. After five or six reloads, it is not uncommon to experience head separations with such cases.
- Handloaders can take full advantage of the 300 H&H Magnum cartridge's flexibility with bullet weights using any of the large number of Speer bullets of .308 inch diameter.
- Speer Grand Slam® soft point bullets are an outstanding choice for the 300 H&H Magnum. We recommend the 150-grain Grand Slam SP or the 165-grain Grand Slam SP for deer and antelope. For moving up to the big game level, we recommend the 180-grain Grand Slam SP.
- For general purpose, handloaders can duplicate factory loads using the Speer 180-grain Spitzer SP Hot-Cor®.
- The 300 H&H cartridge works best with slow burning powders.

SAFETY NOTES

SPEER 180-grain Spitzer BTSP @ a muzzle velocity of 3,039 fps:
- Maximum vertical altitude @ 90° elevation is 17,739 feet.
- Maximum horizontal distance to first impact with ground @ 38° elevation is 8,219 yards.

100 GRAINS

DIAMETER	SECTIONAL DENSITY
.308"	0.151

30 Plinker® RNSP	
Ballistic Coefficient	0.144
COAL Tested	3.260"
Speer Part No.	1805

			Starting Charge		Maximum Charge	
Propellant	Case	Primer	Weight (grains)	Muzzle Velocity (feet/sec)	Weight (grains)	Muzzle Velocity (feet/sec)
Alliant Reloder 15	Federal	Federal 215	66.6	3463	73.8	3757
Alliant AR-Comp	Federal	Federal 215	60.9	3323	67.5	3691
IMR 4166	Federal	Federal 215	57.0	3170	63.1	3514
Alliant Reloder 10X	Federal	Federal 215	52.2	3349	55.7	3485
IMR 4895	Winchester	CCI 200	54.0	3098	58.0	3308
IMR 4064	Winchester	CCI 200	52.0	2930	56.0	3143
IMR 4320	Winchester	CCI 200	52.0	2716	56.0	2994
Hodgdon H380	Winchester	CCI 250	54.0	2776	58.0	2985
IMR 3031	Winchester	CCI 200	47.0	2723	51.0	2933
IMR 4198	Winchester	CCI 200	39.0	2562	43.0	2866
Winchester 748	Winchester	CCI 250	51.0	2624	55.0	2861
IMR 4350	Winchester	CCI 200	54.0	2574	58.0	2772
IMR SR 4759 (reduced load)	Winchester	CCI 200	21.0	1670	23.0	1839

The 100-grain Plinker RNSP may require single feeding into the chamber due to the very short COAL.

WARNING! Maximum loads should be used with CAUTION • C = Compressed Load

130 GRAINS

DIAMETER	SECTIONAL DENSITY
.308"	0.196

30 HP

Ballistic Coefficient	0.244
COAL Tested	3.440"
Speer Part No.	2005

			Starting Charge		Maximum Charge	
Propellant	Case	Primer	Weight (grains)	Muzzle Velocity (feet/sec)	Weight (grains)	Muzzle Velocity (feet/sec)
Alliant Reloder 16	Federal	Federal 215	67.2	3100	74.4	3433
Alliant Power Pro 4000-MR	Federal	Federal 215	68.4	3090	75.5	3417
IMR 4831	Winchester	CCI 200	70.0	3145	74.0 C	3330
IMR 4350	Winchester	CCI 200	68.0	3080	72.0 C	3316
IMR 3031	Winchester	CCI 200	55.0	3046	59.0	3255
Accurate 4350	Winchester	CCI 250	70.0	3014	74.0	3245
Alliant Reloder 19	Winchester	CCI 250	71.0	3050	75.0	3244
Accurate 3100	Winchester	CCI 250	74.0	3055	78.0 C	3236
IMR 4064	Winchester	CCI 200	58.0	2967	62.0	3205
Vihtavuori N160	Winchester	CCI 250	66.0	2941	70.0	3174
Winchester 760	Winchester	CCI 250	65.0	2910	69.0	3143
IMR 4895	Winchester	CCI 200	55.0	2939	59.0	3116
Hodgdon H380	Winchester	CCI 250	58.0	2730	62.0	2976
IMR SR 4759 (reduced load)	Winchester	CCI 200	22.0	1735	24.0	1894

WARNING! Maximum loads should be used with CAUTION • C = Compressed Load

150 GRAINS

DIAMETER	SECTIONAL DENSITY
.308"	0.226

30 SPFN Hot-Cor®
Ballistic Coefficient	0.255
COAL Tested	3.365"
Speer Part No.	2011

30 Spitzer BTSP
Ballistic Coefficient	0.417
COAL Tested	3.500"
Speer Part No.	2022

30 Spitzer SP Hot-Cor®
Ballistic Coefficient	0.377
COAL Tested	3.500"
Speer Part No.	2023

30 Grand Slam® SP
Ballistic Coefficient	0.295
COAL Tested	3.515"
Speer Part No.	2026

			Starting Charge		Maximum Charge	
Propellant	Case	Primer	Weight (grains)	Muzzle Velocity (feet/sec)	Weight (grains)	Muzzle Velocity (feet/sec)
Alliant Reloder 26	Federal	Federal 215	70.3	2954	77.9	3276
IMR 4831	Winchester	CCI 200	69.0	3084	73.0	3265
IMR 4350	Winchester	CCI 200	66.0	3051	70.0	3239
Alliant Power Pro 4000-MR	Federal	Federal 215	65.8	2947	72.8	3218
Alliant Reloder 16	Federal	Federal 215	63.2	2900	70.1	3208
Alliant Reloder 23	Federal	Federal 215	67.5	2921	74.7	3203
Alliant Reloder 17	Federal	Federal 215	61.7	2968	68.4	3194
Alliant Reloder 19	Winchester	CCI 250	68.0	2960	72.0	3170
Vihtavuori N165	Winchester	CCI 250	69.0	2941	73.0	3127
IMR 4064	Winchester	CCI 200	57.0	2902	61.0	3109
Accurate 3100	Winchester	CCI 250	68.0	2920	72.0	3092
Accurate 4350	Winchester	CCI 250	64.0	2886	68.0	3065
IMR 3031	Winchester	CCI 200	52.0	2926	56.0	3054
IMR 4895	Winchester	CCI 200	53.0	2703	57.0	2949
IMR 4320	Winchester	CCI 200	52.0	2642	56.0	2877
Hodgdon H380	Winchester	CCI 250	57.0	2620	61.0	2873
IMR SR 4759 (reduced load)	Winchester	CCI 200	25.0	1791	27.0	1934

WARNING! Maximum loads should be used with CAUTION • C = Compressed Load

165 GRAINS

DIAMETER	SECTIONAL DENSITY
.308"	0.248

30 Spitzer BTSP
Ballistic Coefficient	0.520
COAL Tested	3.500"
Speer Part No.	2034

30 Spitzer SP Hot-Cor®
Ballistic Coefficient	0.444
COAL Tested	3.500"
Speer Part No.	2035

30 Grand Slam® SP
Ballistic Coefficient	0.354
COAL Tested	3.355"
Speer Part No.	2038

			Starting Charge		Maximum Charge	
Propellant	Case	Primer	Weight (grains)	Muzzle Velocity (feet/sec)	Weight (grains)	Muzzle Velocity (feet/sec)
Alliant Reloder 26	Federal	Federal 215	67.0	2807	74.0	3136
IMR 4831	Winchester	CCI 200	67.0	2952	71.0	3134
IMR 4350	Winchester	CCI 200	65.0	2947	69.0	3134
Alliant Reloder 23	Federal	Federal 215	65.9	2811	72.8	3077
Alliant Power Pro 4000-MR	Federal	Federal 215	63.2	2796	70.1	3074
Alliant Reloder 17	Federal	Federal 215	60.2	2830	66.2	3053
Alliant Reloder 16	Federal	Federal 215	60.2	2787	66.4	3048
Alliant Reloder 19	Winchester	CCI 200	63.0	2835	67.0	3002
IMR 4064	Winchester	CCI 200	56.0	2799	60.0	2990
Winchester 760	Winchester	CCI 250	63.0	2741	67.0	2979
Accurate 4350	Winchester	CCI 250	61.0	2731	65.0	2898
Vihtavuori N165	Winchester	CCI 200	63.0	2714	67.0	2881
Accurate 3100	Winchester	CCI 250	64.0	2694	68.0	2869
IMR 4895	Winchester	CCI 200	52.0	3550	56.0	2841
IMR 3031	Winchester	CCI 200	52.0	2598	56.0	2833
Accurate 2700	Winchester	CCI 250	54.0	2628	58.0	2778
IMR 4320	Winchester	CCI 200	51.0	2518	55.0	2759
IMR SR 4759 (reduced load)	Winchester	CCI 200	24.0	1642	28.0	1901

WARNING! Maximum loads should be used with CAUTION • C = Compressed Load

180 GRAINS

DIAMETER	SECTIONAL DENSITY
.308"	0.271

30 Spitzer BTSP
Ballistic Coefficient	0.545
COAL Tested	3.500"
Speer Part No.	2052

30 Spitzer SP Hot-Cor®
Ballistic Coefficient	0.441
COAL Tested	3.500"
Speer Part No.	2053

30 Grand Slam® SP
Ballistic Coefficient	0.374
COAL Tested	3.515"
Speer Part No.	2063

			Starting Charge		Maximum Charge	
Propellant	Case	Primer	Weight (grains)	Muzzle Velocity (feet/sec)	Weight (grains)	Muzzle Velocity (feet/sec)
IMR 4350	Winchester	CCI 200	64.0	2857	68.0	3039
Alliant Reloder 26	Federal	Federal 215	66.5	2702	73.5	2998
IMR 4831	Winchester	CCI 200	66.0	2814	70.0	2993
Alliant Reloder 22	Winchester	CCI 250	66.0	2775	70.0	2952
Alliant Reloder 23	Federal	Federal 215	64.5	2695	71.3 C	2936
Alliant Power Pro 4000-MR	Federal	Federal 215	62.0	2692	68.6	2933
Alliant Reloder 17	Federal	Federal 215	62.5	2814	65.8	2922
Alliant Reloder 16	Federal	Federal 215	60.1	2661	66.7	2920
Winchester 760	Winchester	CCI 250	61.0	2655	65.0	2880
Hodgdon H414	Winchester	CCI 250	59.0	2621	63.0	2852
Vihtavuori N165	Winchester	CCI 250	63.5	2698	67.5	2851
IMR 4064	Winchester	CCI 200	54.0	2589	58.0	2829
Accurate 3100	Winchester	CCI 250	65.0	2650	69.0	2812
Accurate 4350	Winchester	CCI 250	60.0	2644	64.0	2794
IMR 4198 (reduced load)	Winchester	CCI 200	31.0	1836	35.0	2075

WARNING! Maximum loads should be used with CAUTION • C = Compressed Load

200 GRAINS

DIAMETER	SECTIONAL DENSITY
.308"	0.301

30 Spitzer SP Hot-Cor®

Ballistic Coefficient	0.478
COAL Tested	3.500"
Speer Part No.	2211

Propellant	Case	Primer	Starting Charge		Maximum Charge	
			Weight (grains)	Muzzle Velocity (feet/sec)	Weight (grains)	Muzzle Velocity (feet/sec)
IMR 4350	Winchester	CCI 200	62.0	2626	66.0	2839
IMR 4831	Winchester	CCI 200	63.0	2628	67.0	2806
Alliant Reloder 26	Federal	Federal 215	62.9	2534	68.9	2780
Alliant Reloder 23	Federal	Federal 215	60.7	2530	67.4 C	2763
Alliant Power Pro 4000-MR	Federal	Federal 215	58.0	2531	64.4	2755
Alliant Reloder 17	Federal	Federal 215	56.3	2570	61.6	2742
Alliant Reloder 22	Winchester	CCI 250	61.0	2575	65.0	2738
Hodgdon H414	Winchester	CCI 250	58.0	2512	62.0	2732
Alliant Reloder 16	Federal	Federal 215	55.9	2492	62.1	2719
Accurate 4350	Winchester	CCI 250	57.0	2487	61.0	2672
Vihtavuori N165	Winchester	CCI 250	59.0	2444	63.0	2654
Accurate 3100	Winchester	CCI 250	59.0	2458	63.0	2598
IMR 4198 (reduced load)	Winchester	CCI 200	32.0	1813	36.0	2021

WARNING! *Maximum loads should be used with CAUTION • C = Compressed Load*

308 NORMA MAGNUM

Alternate Names:	7.62x65mm
Parent Cartridge:	300 H&H Magnum
Country of Origin:	Sweden
Year of Introduction:	1960
Designer(s):	A.B. Norma Projektilfabrik
Governing Body:	CIP

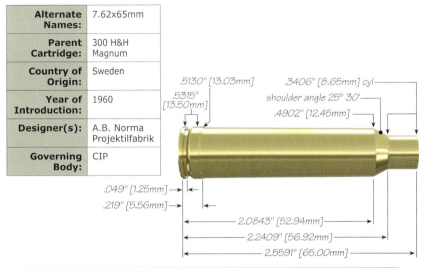

CARTRIDGE CASE DATA

Case Type:	Belted, rimless, bottleneck		
Average Case Capacity:	89.5 grains H$_2$O	Max. Cartridge OAL	3.346 inch
Max. Case Length:	2.559 inch	Primer:	Large Rifle
Case Trim to Length:	2.549 inch	RCBS Shell holder:	# 4
Current Manufacturers:	Norma		

BALLISTIC DATA

Max. Average Pressure (MAP):	55,100 psi - CIP	Test Barrel Length:	24 inch
Rifling Twist Rate:	1 turn in 10 inch		
Muzzle velocities of factory loaded ammunition		Bullet Wgt.	Muzzle velocity
		180-grain	2,953 fps
	Muzzle velocity will decrease approximately 20 fps per inch for barrels less than 24 inches.		

HISTORICAL NOTES

- When Norma announced their new 308 Norma Magnum cartridge in 1960, they followed an unconventional path of introduction.
- First, they offered unprimed, empty cases and handloading data for their new cartridge. No loaded ammunition in the new caliber was listed in the Norma catalog and no firearms makers offered guns in 308 Norma Magnum.
- As rifles in the new caliber would have to be made by custom gun makers, Norma instituted a program for "loaner" chambering reamers and headspace gauges to ensure uniformity of dimension.

- In 1962, Norma added 308 Norma Magnum loaded ammunition to their catalog and some European gun makers added the new caliber to their product line.
- The system worked, more or less. However, sales of 308 Norma Magnum ammunition never reached critical mass in the North American market. Why?
- In 1963, Winchester released their new 300 Winchester Magnum cartridge to critical acclaim.
- The 300 Winchester Magnum was the ballistic equal of the 308 Norma Magnum at a substantially lower price. For these reasons, the 300 Winchester Magnum went on to become the new icon of 300 Magnum cartridges, while the 308 Norma Magnum was relegated to semi-obscurity, but lives on in the Norma ammunition catalog.

TECHNICAL NOTES

- The 308 Norma Magnum is a belted magnum case short enough to fit in a 30-06 Springfield length rifle action, as is the 300 Winchester Magnum.
- Both magnums share very similar (but not identical) rim, belt and head dimensions. Case length is similar (but not identical) and shoulder angle is 25°30' on the Norma Magnum and 25° on the Winchester Magnum.
- A major difference between the two is the 300 Norma Magnum case has a noticeably longer neck than the 300 Winchester Magnum.
- The short case neck of the 300 Winchester Magnum allows a case capacity approximately 4% greater than the 308 Norma Magnum.
- Although the 308 Norma Magnum has been standardized in the CIP, it has not been listed by SAAMI.

HANDLOADING NOTES

- If need be, 308 Norma Magnum brass can be formed from 338 Winchester Magnum cases by necking them down in the 308 Norma Magnum sizing die, then trimming them to the correct length. Annealing the case necks afterward will extend case life.
- As do all big magnum cartridges, the 308 Norma Magnum works best with slow burning propellants.
- As most 308 Norma Magnum will be fired from bolt-action rifles, we recommend neck sizing to extend case life and full length sizing for hunting applications.

SAFETY NOTES

SPEER 180-grain Spitzer BTSP @ a muzzle velocity of 3,039 fps:
- Maximum vertical altitude @ 90° elevation is 17,475 feet.
- Maximum horizontal distance to first impact with ground @ 37° elevation is 8,127 yards.
- **Be careful not to confuse the 308 Norma Magnum data shown here with the recently introduced 300 Norma Magnum.**

100 GRAINS

DIAMETER	SECTIONAL DENSITY
.308"	0.151

30 Plinker® SPRN

Ballistic Coefficient	0.144
COAL Tested	2.870"
Speer Part No.	1805

			Starting Charge		Maximum Charge	
Propellant	Case	Primer	Weight (grains)	Muzzle Velocity (feet/sec)	Weight (grains)	Muzzle Velocity (feet/sec)
Hodgdon H414	Norma	CCI 250	73.0	3396	77.0	3645
Hodgdon H380	Norma	CCI 250	66.0	2383	70.0	3481
IMR 3031	Norma	CCI 250	57.0	3218	61.0	3433
IMR 4895	Norma	CCI 250	59.0	3196	63.0	3407
IMR 4064	Norma	CCI 250	62.0	3166	66.0	3373
IMR 4320	Norma	CCI 250	62.0	3146	66.0	3352
IMR 4198	Norma	CCI 250	46.0	2966	50.0	3207
IMR SR 4759 (reduced load)	Norma	CCI 250	20.0	1738	22.0	1906

130 GRAINS

DIAMETER	SECTIONAL DENSITY
.308"	0.196

30 HP

Ballistic Coefficient	0.244
COAL Tested	3.185"
Speer Part No.	2005

			Starting Charge		Maximum Charge	
Propellant	Case	Primer	Weight (grains)	Muzzle Velocity (feet/sec)	Weight (grains)	Muzzle Velocity (feet/sec)
IMR 4350	Norma	CCI 250	71.0	3137	75.0	3367
H380	Norma	CCI 250	66.0	3115	70.0	3362
IMR 4831	Norma	CCI 250	72.0	3097	76.0	3336
IMR 4064	Norma	CCI 250	60.0	3050	64.0	3304
Winchester 760	Norma	CCI 250	70.0	3038	74.0	3281
IMR 4320	Norma	CCI 250	60.0	2992	64.0	3257
Hodgdon H414	Norma	CCI 250	68.0	3006	72.0	3256
IMR 4895	Norma	CCI 250	58.0	2878	62.0	3122

WARNING! Maximum loads should be used with CAUTION • C = Compressed Load

150 GRAINS

DIAMETER	SECTIONAL DENSITY
.308"	0.226

30 Spitzer BTSP

Ballistic Coefficient	0.417
COAL Tested	3.300"
Speer Part No.	2022

30 Spitzer SP Hot-Cor®

Ballistic Coefficient	0.377
COAL Tested	3.300"
Speer Part No.	2023

30 Grand Slam® SP

Ballistic Coefficient	0.295
COAL Tested	3.220"
Speer Part No.	2026

			Starting Charge		Maximum Charge	
Propellant	Case	Primer	Weight (grains)	Muzzle Velocity (feet/sec)	Weight (grains)	Muzzle Velocity (feet/sec)
IMR 4350	Norma	CCI 250	70.0	2975	74.0	3213
Hodgdon H380	Norma	CCI 250	64.0	2966	68.0	3209
Hodgdon H4831SC	Norma	CCI 250	71.0	2950	75.0	3175
IMR 4064	Norma	CCI 250	58.0	2910	62.0	3133
IMR 4895	Norma	CCI 250	58.0	2882	62.0	3125
IMR 4320	Norma	CCI 250	59.0	2859	63.0	3099
Hodgdon H414	Norma	CCI 250	62.0	2742	66.0	2984
Winchester 760	Norma	CCI 250	63.0	2753	67.0	2975

WARNING! Maximum loads should be used with CAUTION • C = Compressed Load

165 GRAINS

DIAMETER	SECTIONAL DENSITY
.308"	0.248

30 Spitzer BTSP
Ballistic Coefficient	0.520
COAL Tested	3.400"
Speer Part No.	2034

30 Spitzer SP Hot-Cor®
Ballistic Coefficient	0.444
COAL Tested	3.400"
Speer Part No.	2035

30 Grand Slam® SP
Ballistic Coefficient	0.354
COAL Tested	3.230"
Speer Part No.	2038

			Starting Charge		Maximum Charge	
Propellant	Case	Primer	Weight (grains)	Muzzle Velocity (feet/sec)	Weight (grains)	Muzzle Velocity (feet/sec)
IMR 4831	Norma	CCI 250	70.0	2951	74.0	3192
IMR 4350	Norma	CCI 250	69.0	2931	73.0	3169
Hodgdon H380	Norma	CCI 250	63.0	2852	67.0	3095
IMR 4064	Norma	CCI 250	57.0	2755	61.0	3016
IMR 4895	Norma	CCI 250	55.5	2708	59.5	2967
Accurate 3100	Norma	CCI 250	67.0	2805	71.0	2962
IMR 4320	Norma	CCI 250	57.0	2719	61.0	2962
Winchester 760	Norma	CCI 250	61.0	2575	65.0	2799

WARNING! Maximum loads should be used with CAUTION • C = Compressed Load

168 GRAINS

DIAMETER	SECTIONAL DENSITY
.308"	0.253

30 Match BTHP

Ballistic Coefficient	0.534
COAL Tested	3.345"
Speer Part No.	2040

Propellant	Case	Primer	Starting Charge		Maximum Charge	
			Weight (grains)	Muzzle Velocity (feet/sec)	Weight (grains)	Muzzle Velocity (feet/sec)
Accurate 3100	Norma	CCI 250	67.0	2907	71.0	3090
IMR 4831	Norma	CCI 250	68.0	2861	72.0	3037
IMR 4350	Norma	CCI 250	65.0	2704	69.0	3035
IMR 7828	Norma	CCI 250	74.0	2833	78.0	3003
IMR 4320	Norma	CCI 250	55.0	2701	59.0	2923
Winchester 760	Norma	CCI 250	61.0	2710	65.0	2899
IMR 4064	Norma	CCI 250	56.0	2694	60.0	2893
Accurate 8700	Norma	CCI 250	80.0	2658	84.0	2804

WARNING! *Maximum loads should be used with CAUTION • C = Compressed Load*

180 GRAINS

DIAMETER	SECTIONAL DENSITY
.308"	0.271

30 Spitzer BTSP
Ballistic Coefficient	0.545
COAL Tested	3.345"
Speer Part No.	2052

30 Spitzer SP Hot-Cor®
Ballistic Coefficient	0.441
COAL Tested	3.345"
Speer Part No.	2053

30 Grand Slam® SP
Ballistic Coefficient	0.374
COAL Tested	3.225"
Speer Part No.	2063

			Starting Charge		Maximum Charge	
Propellant	Case	Primer	Weight (grains)	Muzzle Velocity (feet/sec)	Weight (grains)	Muzzle Velocity (feet/sec)
IMR 4831	Norma	CCI 250	67.0	2763	71.0	3000
Hodgdon H380	Norma	CCI 250	59.0	2644	63.0	2888
Accurate 3100	Norma	CCI 250	63.0	2645	67.0	2847
IMR 7828	Norma	CCI 250	68.0	2666	72.0	2830
IMR 4064	Norma	CCI 250	54.0	2560	58.0	2805
IMR 4320	Norma	CCI 250	55.0	2562	59.0	2797
Winchester 760	Norma	CCI 250	59.0	2512	63.0	2728
IMR 4198 (reduced load)	Norma	CCI 250	29.0	1798	31.0	1916

WARNING! Maximum loads should be used with CAUTION • C = Compressed Load

200 GRAINS

DIAMETER	SECTIONAL DENSITY
.308"	0.301

30 Spitzer SP Hot-Cor®

Ballistic Coefficient	0.478
COAL Tested	3.345"
Speer Part No.	2211

			Starting Charge		Maximum Charge	
Propellant	Case	Primer	Weight (grains)	Muzzle Velocity (feet/sec)	Weight (grains)	Muzzle Velocity (feet/sec)
IMR 4831	Norma	CCI 250	66.0	2771	70.0	2931
IMR 4350	Norma	CCI 250	65.0	2724	69.0	2906
Hodgdon H380	Norma	CCI 250	56.5	2491	60.5	2709
Accurate 3100	Norma	CCI 250	63.0	2545	67.0	2704
IMR 4064	Norma	CCI 250	52.0	2408	56.0	2635
Winchester 760	Norma	CCI 250	57.0	2395	61.0	2609
Hodgdon H870	Norma	CCI 250	75.0	2386	79.0	2562
IMR 4198 (reduced load)	Norma	CCI 250	30.0	1767	32.0	1880

WARNING! *Maximum loads should be used with CAUTION • C = Compressed Load*

300 WINCHESTER MAGNUM

Parent Cartridge:	300WM, 7.62x67mm
Country of Origin:	USA
Year of Introduction:	1963
Designer(s):	Winchester
Governing Body:	SAAMI/CIP

CARTRIDGE CASE DATA

Case Type:	Belted, rimless, bottleneck
Average Case Capacity:	90.4 grains H₂O
Max. Cartridge OAL:	3.340 inch
Max. Case Length:	2.620 inch
Primer:	Large Rifle
Case Trim to Length:	2.610 inch
RCBS Shell holder:	# 4
Current Manufacturers:	Winchester, Federal, Hornady, Nosler, Prvi Partizan, Black Hills, Sellier & Bellot, Fiocchi, Remington, Norma, RUAG

BALLISTIC DATA

Max. Average Pressure (MAP):	64,000 psi, 54,000 CUP - SAAMI.; 62,366 psi - CIP
Test Barrel Length:	24 inch
Rifling Twist Rate:	1 turn in 10 inch

Muzzle velocities of factory loaded ammunition

Bullet Wgt.	Muzzle velocity
150-grain	3,260 fps
165-grain	3,100 fps
180-grain	2,960 fps
190-grain	2,900 fps
200-grain	2,800 fps

Muzzle velocity will decrease approximately 25 fps per inch for barrels less than 24 inches.

HISTORICAL NOTES

- In 1963, Winchester released their new 300 Winchester Magnum cartridge to critical acclaim. Domestic gun makers hastened to add the new caliber to their product lines, quickly pushing sales of the new cartridge to a dominant level among magnum rifle cartridges.

- Winchester's new 300 Magnum was designed as a long range, big game cartridge that could be chambered in standard 30-06 Springfield length rifle actions.

- In other words, 300 Winchester Magnum was a "short magnum" which meant it was based on a 300 H&H Magnum case shortened to a length approximately that of a 30-06 Springfield. Today, the term "short magnum" means something quite different!

- The 300 Winchester Magnum was the fourth and final entry in Winchester's short (standard-length) magnum product line beginning with the 458 Winchester Magnum in 1956, followed by the 338 Winchester Magnum and the 264 Winchester Magnum in 1958.

- The advent of the 300 Winchester Magnum prompted most rifle makers to drop the venerable 300 H&H Magnum, pushing that cartridge to near extinction.

- Hunters found the 300 Winchester Magnum's muzzle velocity fully equal to advertised levels with remarkable accuracy over a wide range of bullet weights at a more competitive price than other 30-caliber magnum cartridges.

- In other words, the 300 Winchester Magnum was a game changer. Sales soon reached a dominant market position where it remains to this day.

- Surprisingly, long range competitors found the 300 Winchester Magnum a very good choice for 1,000 yard rifle competition, making the new magnum a game changer there as well.

- Today, the 300 Winchester Magnum has become the magnum cartridge by which all other 30-caliber magnum are measured. Nearly every ammunition and rifle maker offers it and there are few shooters who have not heard of it.

- Will the new, beltless magnums dethrone the king? A doubtful prospect any time soon.

Interesting Fact

To increase maximum effective range of their sniper rifles, in 2017 the U.S. Army recently began a program to rework their 7.62x51mm NATO caliber sniper rifles to 300 Winchester Magnum. The king has now gone to war.

BALLISTIC NOTES

- The 300 Winchester Magnum meets its factory loaded ballistic obligations with both 150-grain and 180-grain bullets. These are the foundation the 300 Winchester Magnum's reputation is built on.

- In ballistic terms, the muzzle velocity of factory loaded 300 Winchester Magnum occupies a position approximately mid-way between the 300 H&H Magnum on the low end and the 300 Weatherby Magnum on the high end.

- Of late, ammunition manufacturers have added 165 and 200-grain bullets to their 300 Winchester Magnum product lines. The 165-grain bullet weight has become very popular as a good general purpose weight suitable for most types of North American game.

- While the 300 Winchester Magnum is quite capable of firing a 220-grain bullet to a muzzle velocity of 2,665 fps, bullets of this weight have fallen from favor and are no longer offered by the large ammunition manufacturers.

- Factory loaded 300 Winchester Magnum ammunition with a 200-grain bullet is offered by a few manufacturers, but accounts for a small part of total sales volume.

TECHNICAL NOTES

- Basically, the 300 Winchester Magnum is based on a shortened 300 H&H Magnum case with less body taper to increase case capacity. This is a tried and true process to build a short magnum.
- In technical terms, there is no secret to the design of the 300 Winchester Magnum, so much as it is a combination of proven features. Below is a partial list of The King's assets:
  - It is a belted case, but in many rifles it can be reloaded to headspace on its shoulder (much better).
  - It has a very conservative 25° shoulder angle and neck length to ease manufacture and reduce trimming chores.
  - With a case capacity that is approximately 11% less than the 300 Weatherby Magnum, the 300 Winchester Magnum burns less powder.
  - Length-to-diameter ratio is 5.111, no short magnum efficiency to claim here.
  - MAP levels are similar to and competitive with other 30-caliber magnums.
  - The 1 turn in 10 inch rifling twist will stabilize a wide range of bullet weights including long boat tail bullets.
  - With a maximum overall loaded length (OAL) of 3.340 inches, the 300 Winchester Magnum will fit in standard 30-06 Springfield actions.
  - Factory loaded ammunition in 300 Winchester Magnum caliber is offered by all major domestic and foreign ammunition makers for world-wide availability.
  - The 300 Winchester Magnum ammunition and brass is substantially cheaper than many other 30-caliber magnum cartridges.

HANDLOADING NOTES

- Speer offers a wide variety of .308 inch diameter bullets suitable for use in the 300 Winchester Magnum.
- The Speer Grand Slam® SP premium-grade bullets in 150, 165, and 180-grain are designed with a protected tip and internal flutes in the jacket to assure consistent, reliable expansion so that hunters can take maximum advantage of the ballistics the 300 Winchester Magnum offers for big game.
- Just want to duplicate factory ballistics? Speer has you covered with Spitzer SP Hot-Cor® bullets in 150, 165, 180, and 200-grain weights.
- For competition or just checking the accuracy of your hunting rifle, the Speer BTHP 168-grain match bullet is a solid choice. This is not a bullet suited to hunting.
- As do all big magnum cartridges, the 300 Winchester Magnum works best with slow burning propellants.
- As most 300 Winchester Magnum cartridges will be fired from bolt-action rifles, we strongly recommend neck sizing to extend case life for practice and sight-in. Hunt with full length sized rounds.

SAFETY NOTES

SPEER 180-grain Spitzer BTSP @ a muzzle velocity of 3,055 fps:
- Maximum vertical altitude @ 90° elevation is 18,567 feet.
- Maximum horizontal distance to first impact with ground @ 38° elevation is 8,186 yards.

100 GRAINS

DIAMETER	SECTIONAL DENSITY
.308"	0.151

30 Plinker® SPRN

Ballistic Coefficient	0.144
COAL Tested	2.960"
Speer Part No.	1805

			Starting Charge		Maximum Charge	
Propellant	Case	Primer	Weight (grains)	Muzzle Velocity (feet/sec)	Weight (grains)	Muzzle Velocity (feet/sec)
Alliant Reloder 15	Winchester	CCI 250	68.0	3352	72.0	3604
Hodgdon H322	Winchester	CCI 250	61.0	3339	65.0	3552
Vihtavuori N135	Winchester	CCI 250	65.0	3330	69.0	3543
Accurate 2520	Winchester	CCI 250	64.0	3253	68.0	3479
IMR 4064	Winchester	CCI 250	65.0	3233	69.0	3421
Hodgdon H380	Winchester	CCI 250	70.0	3095	74.0	3396
IMR 4895	Winchester	CCI 250	62.0	3161	66.0	3381
IMR 4320	Winchester	CCI 250	64.0	3095	68.0	3258
IMR SR 4759 (reduced load)	Winchester	CCI 250	21.0	1801	23.0	1975

WARNING! *Maximum loads should be used with CAUTION • C = Compressed Load*

130 GRAINS

DIAMETER	SECTIONAL DENSITY
.308"	0.196

30 HP
Ballistic Coefficient	0.244
COAL Tested	3.260"
Speer Part No.	2005

Propellant	Case	Primer	Starting Charge Weight (grains)	Starting Charge Muzzle Velocity (feet/sec)	Maximum Charge Weight (grains)	Maximum Charge Muzzle Velocity (feet/sec)
Alliant Reloder 26	Federal	Federal 215	74.6	3035	82.8	3478
Vihtavuori N160	Winchester	CCI 250	76.0	3222	80.0	3465
Alliant Reloder 16	Federal	Federal 215	69.2	3144	76.6	3445
Alliant Reloder 23	Federal	Federal 215	73.2	3104	81.4 C	3428
Alliant Power Pro 4000-MR	Federal	Federal 215	68.2	3044	75.5	3400
Alliant Reloder 17	Federal	Federal 215	66.8	3164	71.9	3387
Hodgdon H4350	Winchester	CCI 250	74.0	3165	78.0 C	3385
IMR 4831	Winchester	CCI 250	76.0	3193	80.0	3379
Accurate 3100	Winchester	CCI 250	78.0	3161	82.0 C	3363
IMR 4350	Winchester	CCI 250	73.0	3175	77.0	3342
Hodgdon H4831SC	Winchester	CCI 250	78.0	3110	82.0 C	3291
IMR 7977	Federal	Federal 215	76.4	2928	84.8 C	3254
Alliant Reloder 15	Winchester	CCI 250	63.0	3016	67.0	3243
Hodgdon H380	Winchester	CCI 250	68.0	3052	72.0	3213
IMR 4064	Winchester	CCI 250	62.0	2984	66.0	3174
IMR 3031	Winchester	CCI 250	57.0	2882	61.0	3050
IMR 4320	Winchester	CCI 250	53.0	2574	57.0	2738

WARNING! Maximum loads should be used with CAUTION • C = Compressed Load

150 GRAINS

DIAMETER	SECTIONAL DENSITY
.308"	0.226

30 SPFN Hot-Cor®
Ballistic Coefficient	0.255
COAL Tested	3.330"
Speer Part No.	2011

30 Spitzer BTSP
Ballistic Coefficient	0.417
COAL Tested	3.330"
Speer Part No.	2022

30 Spitzer SP Hot-Cor®
Ballistic Coefficient	0.377
COAL Tested	3.330"
Speer Part No.	2023

30 Grand Slam® SP
Ballistic Coefficient	0.295
COAL Tested	3.285"
Speer Part No.	2026

			Starting Charge		Maximum Charge	
Propellant	Case	Primer	Weight (grains)	Muzzle Velocity (feet/sec)	Weight (grains)	Muzzle Velocity (feet/sec)
Alliant Reloder 26	Federal	Federal 215	75.1	3059	83.0 C	3395
Alliant Power Pro 4000-MR	Federal	Federal 215	70.4	3033	78.1	3328
Alliant Reloder 16	Federal	Federal 215	67.7	3032	75.2	3318
Alliant Reloder 17	Federal	Federal 215	67.7	3046	74.9	3308
Alliant Reloder 19	Winchester	CCI 250	74.0	3086	78.0 C	3301
Alliant Reloder 23	Federal	Federal 215	71.5	2934	79.0 C	3228
Alliant Reloder 22	Winchester	CCI 250	76.0	3001	80.0 C	3227
Accurate 3100	Winchester	CCI 250	76.0	3064	80.0 C	3225
Hodgdon H4350	Winchester	CCI 250	72.0	3026	76.0 C	3219
Vihtavuori N160	Winchester	CCI 250	72.0	2975	76.0	3199
Hodgdon H4831SC	Winchester	CCI 250	76.0	2982	80.0 C	3156
IMR 4831	Winchester	CCI 250	72.0	2915	76.0	3118
IMR 4350	Winchester	CCI 250	69.0	2918	73.0	3091
Winchester 760	Winchester	CCI 250	64.0	2932	68.0	3086
Hodgdon H414	Winchester	CCI 250	65.0	2902	69.0	3071
Hodgdon H380	Winchester	CCI 250	65.0	2855	69.0	3070
Accurate 2700	Winchester	CCI 250	65.0	2881	69.0	3065
Hodgdon H1000	Winchester	CCI 250	80.0	2910	84.0 C	3063
Alliant Reloder 15	Winchester	CCI 250	60.0	3058	64.0	3058
IMR SR 4759 (reduced load)	Winchester	CCI 250	26.0	1884	28.0	2028

WARNING! Maximum loads should be used with CAUTION • C = Compressed Load

165 GRAINS

DIAMETER	SECTIONAL DENSITY
.308"	0.248

30 Spitzer BTSP
Ballistic Coefficient	0.520
COAL Tested	3.340"
Speer Part No.	2034

30 Spitzer SP Hot-Cor®
Ballistic Coefficient	0.444
COAL Tested	3.340"
Speer Part No.	2035

30 Grand Slam® SP
Ballistic Coefficient	0.354
COAL Tested	3.290"
Speer Part No.	2038

			Starting Charge		Maximum Charge	
Propellant	Case	Primer	Weight (grains)	Muzzle Velocity (feet/sec)	Weight (grains)	Muzzle Velocity (feet/sec)
IMR 7828	Winchester	CCI 250	79.0	3116	83.0	3280
Alliant Reloder 26	Federal	Federal 215	71.9	2906	79.8 C	3233
Alliant Power Pro 4000-MR	Federal	Federal 215	67.2	2882	74.4	3165
Alliant Reloder 16	Federal	Federal 215	65.1	2885	72.4	3149
Alliant Reloder 17	Federal	Federal 215	64.3	2883	71.2	3145
Alliant Reloder 23	Federal	Federal 215	70.8	2859	78.0 C	3137
Alliant Reloder 22	Winchester	CCI 250	73.0	2886	77.0	3103
Hodgdon H4831SC	Winchester	CCI 250	73.0	2868	77.0	3087
IMR 4350	Winchester	CCI 250	70.0	2865	74.0	3064
Accurate 3100	Winchester	CCI 250	72.0	2882	76.0	3050
Alliant Reloder 19	Winchester	CCI 250	71.0	2802	75.0	2997
Accurate 4350	Winchester	CCI 250	69.0	2844	73.0	2994
Vihtavuori N160	Winchester	CCI 250	68.0	2785	72.0	2979
IMR 4831	Winchester	CCI 250	69.0	2742	73.0	2948
Hodgdon H414	Winchester	CCI 250	63.0	2726	67.0	2900
IMR 4064	Winchester	CCI 250	58.0	2735	62.0	2894
Hodgdon H1000	Winchester	CCI 250	78.0	2710	81.0	2883
Winchester 760	Winchester	CCI 250	60.0	2701	64.0	2873
Alliant Reloder 15	Winchester	CCI 250	56.0	2655	60.0	2809
IMR SR 4759 (reduced load)	Winchester	CCI 250	25.0	1763	29.0	2000

WARNING! Maximum loads should be used with CAUTION • C = Compressed Load

168 GRAINS

DIAMETER	SECTIONAL DENSITY
.308"	0.253

30 Match BTHP	
Ballistic Coefficient	0.534
COAL Tested	3.340"
Speer Part No.	2040

			Starting Charge		Maximum Charge	
Propellant	Case	Primer	Weight (grains)	Muzzle Velocity (feet/sec)	Weight (grains)	Muzzle Velocity (feet/sec)
Alliant Reloder 26	Federal	Federal 215	73.0	2914	80.0 C	3220
Alliant Reloder 22	Winchester	CCI 250	75.0	2983	79.0 C	3190
Hodgdon H4350	Winchester	CCI 250	71.0	2984	75.0	3174
IMR 4831	Winchester	CCI 250	72.0	2951	76.0 C	3139
Alliant Reloder 19	Winchester	CCI 250	73.0	2919	77.0	3138
Vihtavuori N160	Winchester	CCI 250	71.0	2965	75.0	3138
IMR 7828	Winchester	CCI 250	76.0	2927	80.0 C	3131
Alliant Reloder 16	Federal	Federal 215	64.5	2851	71.7	3130
Accurate 3100	Winchester	CCI 250	73.0	2926	77.0 C	3080
IMR 4350	Winchester	CCI 250	70.0	2895	74.0	3063
Hodgdon H4831SC	Winchester	CCI 250	73.0	2795	77.0 C	3005
Hodgdon H380	Winchester	CCI 250	63.0	2750	67.0	2926
Alliant Reloder 15	Winchester	CCI 250	59.0	2722	63.0	2911
Hodgdon H870	Winchester	CCI 250	83.0	2724	87.0 C	2867
Hodgdon H1000	Winchester	CCI 250	77.0	2699	81.0 C	2856

WARNING! Maximum loads should be used with CAUTION • C = Compressed Load

GOLD DOT RIFLE

300 WINCHESTER MAGNUM

168 GRAINS

DIAMETER	SECTIONAL DENSITY
.308"	0.253

30 GD	
Ballistic Coefficient	0.572
COAL Tested	3.340"
Speer Part No.	308168GDB

			Starting Charge		Maximum Charge	
Propellant	Case	Primer	Weight (grains)	Muzzle Velocity (feet/sec)	Weight (grains)	Muzzle Velocity (feet/sec)
Alliant Reloder 26	Federal	Federal 215	70.5	2806	78.1	3167
Alliant Reloder 19	Federal	Federal 215	70.4	2771	78.0 C	3132
Alliant Power Pro 4000-MR	Federal	Federal 215	66.1	2847	73.5	3123
Alliant Reloder 22	Federal	Federal 215	68.7	2808	76.1	3115
Vihtavuori N560	Federal	Federal 215	70.2	2797	77.6	3114
IMR 7828	Federal	Federal 215	70.4	2781	78.2 C	3109
Alliant Reloder 23	Federal	Federal 215	68.6	2813	76.1 C	3103
Alliant Reloder 16	Federal	Federal 215	63.7	2815	70.9	3101
Accurate 4350	Federal	Federal 215	66.5	2774	73.8	3095
Alliant Reloder 17	Federal	Federal 215	60.9	2836	67.5	3076
Hodgdon H1000	Federal	Federal 215	74.1	2819	82.0 C	3066
Hodgdon H4831SC	Federal	Federal 215	67.1	2830	74.3	3050
Hodgdon H4350	Federal	Federal 215	61.2	2827	68.0	3038
Ramshot Hunter	Federal	Federal 215	63.8	2779	70.8	3038

WARNING! Maximum loads should be used with CAUTION • C = Compressed Load

180 GRAINS

DIAMETER	SECTIONAL DENSITY
.308"	0.271

30 Spitzer BTSP
Ballistic Coefficient	0.545
COAL Tested	3.340"
Speer Part No.	2052

30 Spitzer SP Hot-Cor®
Ballistic Coefficient	0.441
COAL Tested	3.340"
Speer Part No.	2053

30 Grand Slam® SP
Ballistic Coefficient	0.374
COAL Tested	3.285"
Speer Part No.	2063

			Starting Charge		Maximum Charge	
Propellant	Case	Primer	Weight (grains)	Muzzle Velocity (feet/sec)	Weight (grains)	Muzzle Velocity (feet/sec)
Alliant Reloder 26	Federal	Federal 215	70.1	2763	77.8 C	3084
Alliant Reloder 19	Winchester	CCI 250	72.0	2845	76.0	3059
Alliant Reloder 22	Winchester	CCI 250	73	2844	77.0 C	3055
Alliant Reloder 25	Winchester	CCI 250	75.5	2893	79.5 C	3050
Alliant Reloder 23	Federal	Federal 215	69.8	2767	76.8 C	3041
Alliant Power Pro 4000-MR	Federal	Federal 215	66.9	2762	74.0	3033
Alliant Reloder 17	Federal	Federal 215	63.6	2780	70.5	3007
IMR 7828	Winchester	CCI 250	74.0	2818	78.0 C	2990
IMR 4350	Winchester	CCI 250	68.0	2802	72.0	2988
Alliant Reloder 16	Federal	Federal 215	63.4	2738	70.3	2987
IMR 4831	Winchester	CCI 250	69.0	2789	73.0 C	2951
Hodgdon H4831SC	Winchester	CCI 250	71.0	2816	75.0	2950
Hodgdon H1000	Winchester	CCI 250	77.0	2781	81.0 C	2943
Hodgdon H4350	Winchester	CCI 250	67.0	2762	71.0	2938
Accurate 3100	Winchester	CCI 250	71.0	2762	75.0 C	2937
Vihtavuori N160	Winchester	CCI 250	68.0	2754	72.0	2925
Winchester 760	Winchester	CCI 250	61.0	2670	65.0	2811
Hodgdon H414	Winchester	CCI 250	60.0	2647	64.0	2786
Accurate 8700	Winchester	CCI 250	82.0	2526	86.0 C	2716
IMR 4198 (reduced load)	Winchester	CCI 250	31.0	1879	33.0	1998

WARNING! Maximum loads should be used with CAUTION • C = Compressed Load

200 GRAINS

DIAMETER	SECTIONAL DENSITY
.308"	0.301

30 Spitzer SP Hot-Cor®

Ballistic Coefficient	0.478
COAL Tested	3.340"
Speer Part No.	2211

			Starting Charge		Maximum Charge	
Propellant	Case	Primer	Weight (grains)	Muzzle Velocity (feet/sec)	Weight (grains)	Muzzle Velocity (feet/sec)
Alliant Reloder 26	Federal	Federal 215	67.2	2619	74.0 C	2884
Alliant Reloder 25	Winchester	CCI 250	71.0	2735	75.0 C	2857
IMR 7828	Winchester	CCI 250	71.0	2656	75.0 C	2856
Alliant Reloder 23	Federal	Federal 215	66.8	2599	74.0 C	2855
Alliant Reloder 22	Winchester	CCI 250	69.0	2652	73.0 C	2852
IMR 4350	Winchester	CCI 250	65.0	2672	69.0	2843
Alliant Reloder 17	Federal	Federal 215	61.3	2606	68.1	2826
Alliant Power Pro 4000-MR	Federal	Federal 215	63.3	2548	70.1	2817
Hodgdon H1000	Winchester	CCI 250	73.0	2629	77.0 C	2797
Hodgdon H4350	Winchester	CCI 250	65.0	2637	69.0	2776
Hodgdon H4831SC	Winchester	CCI 250	67.0	2653	71.0	2770
Vihtavuori N165	Winchester	CCI 250	68.0	2601	72.0	2767
Alliant Reloder 19	Winchester	CCI 250	67.0	2582	71.0	2761
Hodgdon H870	Winchester	CCI 250	81.0	2579	85.0 C	2758
Winchester 760	Winchester	CCI 250	60.0	2605	64.0	2742
Hodgdon H414	Winchester	CCI 250	60.0	2597	64.0	2741
Accurate 4350	Winchester	CCI 250	63.0	2544	67.0	2735
Accurate 3100	Winchester	CCI 250	69.0	2496	73.0 C	2641
IMR 4198 (reduced load)	Winchester	CCI 250	31.0	1812	35.0	2036

WARNING! Maximum loads should be used with CAUTION • C = Compressed Load

300 WEATHERBY MAGNUM

Parent Cartridge:	375 H&H Magnum
Country of Origin:	USA
Year of Introduction:	1945
Designer(s):	Roy Weatherby
Governing Body:	SAAMI/ CIP

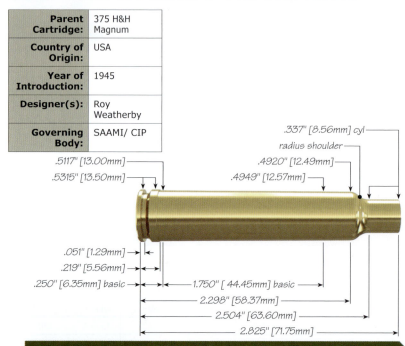

.337" [8.56mm] cyl radius shoulder
.5117" [13.00mm]
.5315" [13.50mm]
.4920" [12.49mm]
.4949" [12.57mm]
.051" [1.29mm]
.219" [5.56mm]
.250" [6.35mm] basic
1.750" [44.45mm] basic
2.298" [58.37mm]
2.504" [63.60mm]
2.825" [71.75mm]

CARTRIDGE CASE DATA

Case Type:	Rimless, Belted, double radius shoulder, bottleneck		
Average Case Capacity:	100.4 grains H$_2$O	Max. Cartridge OAL	3.560 inch
Max. Case Length:	2.825 inch	Primer:	Large Rifle
Case Trim to Length:	2.815 inch	RCBS Shell holder:	# 4
Current Manufacturers:	Weatherby, Norma, Hornady, Nosler		

BALLISTIC DATA

Max. Average Pressure (MAP):	65,000 psi, CUP not established - SAAMI	Test Barrel Length:	24 inch
Rifling Twist Rate:	1 turn in 10 inch		
Weatherby factory muzzle velocities are quoted from 26 inch barrels			

Muzzle velocities of factory loaded ammunition	Bullet Wgt.	Muzzle velocity
	150-grain	3,540 fps
	165-grain	3,390 fps
	180-grain	3,250 fps
	200-grain	3,060 fps
	220-grain	2,845 fps
	Muzzle velocity will decrease approximately 30 fps per inch for barrels less than 26 inches.	

HISTORICAL NOTES

- In 1945, Roy Weatherby introduced his new 300 Weatherby Magnum cartridge. It offered groundbreaking ballistic performance, but there was a war on and few people noticed.
- With the end of World War II, interest in Weatherby cartridges grew to the point that Weatherby added factory loaded ammunition in 300 Weatherby Magnum caliber to his product line in 1948.
- The 300 Weatherby Magnum and its two brethren, the 270 Weatherby Magnum and the 7mm Weatherby Magnum cartridges, formed the foundation of a new dynasty of Weatherby Magnum hunting cartridges capable of unheard of ballistic performance.
- All Weatherby cartridges incorporated Roy Weatherby's concept of the terminal ballistic effectiveness of hydraulic shock caused by a bullet entering a target at high velocity.
- Endorsements from the rich and famous combined with a dose of ballistic hyperbole helped spread the Weatherby message.
- Although Weatherby has continued to expand their proprietary cartridge product line (at recent count to 14 different calibers), 300 Weatherby Magnum has remained the lynchpin of the Weatherby Magnum cartridge product line.
- By the early 1990s, Weatherby had become the victim of his own success. In that year, mainstream domestic ammunition manufacturers began adding selected Weatherby Magnum cartridges including the 300 Weatherby Magnum to their own product lines. A relatively small market was divided among too many players. After a brief interval, Remington and Winchester moved on to their own short and long magnum cartridge designs, dropping most of the Weatherby calibers in the process.
- Today, the 300 Weatherby Magnum has become more mainstream, still sustained by its reputation.
- It is safe to say that the 300 Weatherby Magnum cartridge will remain with us for a few decades yet.

BALLISTIC NOTES

- The 300 Weatherby Magnum's reputation was built on 150-grain and 180-grain bullet weights. In recent years, a 165-grain bullet has been added.
- For most North American medium game the very high 3,540 fps muzzle velocity of the 150-grain bullet results in excessive destruction of freezer-bound meat.
- The 300 Weatherby Magnum offers its best balance of striking velocity and energy for hunting big game with 180-grain bullets. With boat tail bullets in this weight, maximum effective range can be extended if your marksmanship skills are up to the task.
- Many hunters now favor the 165-grain boat tail bullet as an excellent all-around choice for the 300 Weatherby Magnum. This load combines high striking velocity and energy, flatter trajectory, and less wind drift than flat base bullets at all ranges. For large, trophy size game at longer ranges, the 300 Weatherby Magnum is quite capable of firing a 200-grain bullet to a muzzle velocity of 2,977 fps.

TECHNICAL NOTES

- Like many cartridge designers before and after him, Roy Weatherby's masterpiece cartridge was formed by the tried and true process of blowing out a full length 300 H&H Magnum case to reduce body taper and increase case capacity. Roy was one of the first to do it and then offer it as a factory loaded cartridge. (As you know, many "high profile" hunters do not need or want to reload!)
- The 300 Weatherby Magnum produces prodigious muzzle velocities and it consumes a bunch of powder to do it. The astute reader will note that is completely the opposite of modern practices with the new "efficient" short magnums. Perhaps there is something to the brute force school of internal ballistics after all.
- There are two secrets to the ballistic performance of 300 Weatherby Magnum cartridges:
  - The first is that the chamber throats of Weatherby cartridges are free-bored for a considerable distance to reduce MAP levels.
  - Second, Weatherby muzzle velocities are taken from a 26 inch test barrel; the standard industry test barrel is 24 inches.
- In technical terms, there is no secret to the design of the 300 Weatherby Magnum:
  - It is a belted case that headspaces on its belt (as all proper magnums should according to Holland & Holland).
  - Case capacity is larger than all other 300 Magnum cartridges save the new 300 Remington Ultra Magnum and the chart topping 30-378 Weatherby.
  - The 1 in 10 inch rifling twist of the 300 Weatherby Magnum will stabilize a wide range of bullet weights including long boat tail bullets.
  - With a Maximum Overall Loaded length of 3.600 inches, the 300 Weatherby Magnum will not fit in standard length 30-06 Springfield actions.
  - As 300 Weatherby Magnum ammunition and brass are considered premium products, they are marketed and priced accordingly.

HANDLOADING NOTES

- Speer offers a wide variety of .308 inch diameter bullets suitable for use in the 300 Weatherby Magnum.
- The Grand Slam® SP bullets are in 150, 165, and 180-grain weights. These premium-grade bullets are designed with a protected tip and internal flutes in the jacket to assure consistent, reliable expansion so that magnum hunters can take maximum advantage of the ballistics the 300 Weatherby Magnum offers for big game.
- Every hunter wants a ballistic edge for those long range shots under difficult conditions. Speer boat tail soft point bullets give hunters using the 300 Weatherby Magnum that extra edge with higher striking velocity and energy, flatter trajectory, and less wind drift than flat base bullets at all ranges. They are available in 150, 165, and 180-grain weights which are an exact match for factory bullet weights.
- Just want to duplicate factory ballistics? Speer has you covered with flat base soft point bullets in 150, 165, 180, and 200-grain weights.
- As do all big magnum cartridges, the 300 Weatherby Magnum works best with slow burning propellants.

- As most 300 Weatherby Magnum cartridges will be fired from bolt-action rifles, we recommend neck sizing to extend case life for practice and sight-in. Full length size your hunting rounds.

SAFETY NOTES

SPEER 180-grain Spitzer BTSP @ a muzzle velocity of 3,109 fps:
- Maximum vertical altitude @ 90° elevation is 17,820 feet.
- Maximum horizontal distance to first impact with ground @ 38° elevation is 8,247 yards.

130 GRAINS

DIAMETER	SECTIONAL DENSITY
.308"	0.196

30 HP

Ballistic Coefficient	0.244
COAL Tested	3.530"
Speer Part No.	2005

			Starting Charge		Maximum Charge	
Propellant	Case	Primer	Weight (grains)	Muzzle Velocity (feet/sec)	Weight (grains)	Muzzle Velocity (feet/sec)
Alliant Reloder 26	Federal	Federal 215	82.4	3236	91.6	3674
Alliant Reloder 23	Federal	Federal 215	80.0	3246	88.5 C	3600
Alliant Power Pro 4000-MR	Federal	Federal 215	75.6	3229	83.6	3586
Alliant Reloder 22	Federal	Federal 215	78.3	3169	86.3	3576
Vihtavuori N560	Federal	Federal 215	79.9	3099	88.7	3534
IMR 7977	Federal	Federal 215	83.7	3152	93.0 C	3513
Alliant Reloder 19	Remington	CCI 250	82.0	3190	86.0	3432
Hodgdon H4350	Remington	CCI 250	77.5	3148	81.5	3404
Accurate 3100	Remington	CCI 250	81.0	3169	85.0 C	3368
IMR 7828	Remington	CCI 250	84.0	3168	88.0 C	3361
IMR 4831	Remington	CCI 250	79.0	3089	83.0	3344
Hodgdon H4831SC	Remington	CCI 250	82.0	3151	86.0 C	3327
IMR 4350	Remington	CCI 250	77.0	3061	81.0	3291
Accurate 4350	Remington	CCI 250	75.0	3050	79.0	3289
Hodgdon H4895	Remington	CCI 250	66.0	3080	70.0	3248

WARNING! *Maximum loads should be used with CAUTION • C = Compressed Load*

300 WEATHERBY MAGNUM — 150 GRAINS

DIAMETER	SECTIONAL DENSITY
.308"	0.226

30 SPFN Hot-Cor®
Ballistic Coefficient	0.255
COAL Tested	3.335"
Speer Part No.	2011

30 Spitzer BTSP
Ballistic Coefficient	0.417
COAL Tested	3.560"
Speer Part No.	2022

30 Spitzer SP Hot-Cor®
Ballistic Coefficient	0.377
COAL Tested	3.560"
Speer Part No.	2023

30 Grand Slam® SP
Ballistic Coefficient	0.295
COAL Tested	3.490"
Speer Part No.	2026

			Starting Charge		Maximum Charge	
Propellant	Case	Primer	Weight (grains)	Muzzle Velocity (feet/sec)	Weight (grains)	Muzzle Velocity (feet/sec)
Alliant Reloder 26	Federal	Federal 215	77.3	2994	85.8	3390
Alliant Power Pro 4000-MR	Federal	Federal 215	71.9	3058	79.6	3337
Alliant Reloder 23	Federal	Federal 215	74.6	3016	82.9	3334
Hodgdon H1000	Remington	CCI 250	87.0	3153	91.0 C	3321
Alliant Reloder 22	Remington	CCI 250	82.0	3140	86.0	3305
Vihtavuori N165	Remington	CCI 250	85.0	3089	89.0 C	3299
IMR 7977	Federal	Federal 215	79.7	2954	88.2 C	3291
Hodgdon H414	Remington	CCI 250	73.0	3040	77.0	3262
IMR 7828	Remington	CCI 250	81.0	3048	85.0	3243
Alliant Reloder 19	Remington	CCI 250	79.0	3017	83.0	3227
Accurate 3100	Remington	CCI 250	78.0	3013	82.0	3211
Vihtavuori N160	Remington	CCI 250	76.0	3039	80.0	3196
Hodgdon H4831SC	Remington	CCI 250	79.5	2985	83.5	3192
Hodgdon H4350	Remington	CCI 250	74.0	2927	78.0	3191
IMR 4831	Remington	CCI 250	76.0	2968	80.0	3169
Accurate 4350	Remington	CCI 250	72.5	2938	76.5	3169
Alliant Reloder 33	Federal	Federal 215	91.6 C	2965	96.0 C	3145
Winchester 760	Remington	CCI 250	73.0	2985	77.0	3067
IMR 4350	Remington	CCI 250	73.0	2911	77.0	3052

WARNING! Maximum loads should be used with CAUTION • C = Compressed Load

165 GRAINS

DIAMETER	SECTIONAL DENSITY
.308"	0.248

30 Spitzer BTSP
Ballistic Coefficient	0.520
COAL Tested	3.560"
Speer Part No.	2034

30 Spitzer SP Hot-Cor®
Ballistic Coefficient	0.444
COAL Tested	3.560"
Speer Part No.	2035

30 Grand Slam® SP
Ballistic Coefficient	0.354
COAL Tested	3.495"
Speer Part No.	2038

			Starting Charge		Maximum Charge	
Propellant	Case	Primer	Weight (grains)	Muzzle Velocity (feet/sec)	Weight (grains)	Muzzle Velocity (feet/sec)
Alliant Reloder 26	Federal	Federal 215	75.1	2868	83.4	3256
Alliant Power Pro 4000-MR	Federal	Federal 215	71.0	2942	78.5	3206
Alliant Reloder 25	Remington	CCI 250	85.0	3054	89.0 C	3204
Alliant Reloder 23	Federal	Federal 215	72.9	2891	81.1	3202
Hodgdon H1000	Remington	CCI 250	84.0	3007	88.0	3184
IMR 7977	Federal	Federal 215	78.5	2856	86.3 C	3163
Vihtavuori N165	Remington	CCI 250	82.0	2921	86.0	3160
Alliant Reloder 22	Remington	CCI 250	79.0	2964	83.0	3119
Accurate 3100	Remington	CCI 250	76.0	2923	80.0	3112
Hodgdon H4831SC	Remington	CCI 250	78.0	2939	82.0	3110
Alliant Reloder 19	Remington	CCI 250	76.0	2898	80.0	3105
IMR 4831	Remington	CCI 250	74.0	2914	78.0	3092
Alliant Reloder 33	Federal	Federal 215	86.7	2799	93.0 C	3081
IMR 7828	Remington	CCI 250	78.0	2844	82.0	3050
Hodgdon H414	Remington	CCI 250	70.0	2905	74.0	3042
Hodgdon H4350	Remington	CCI 250	71.0	2799	75.0	3011
Accurate 4350	Remington	CCI 250	70.0	2767	74.0	2982
Winchester 760	Remington	CCI 250	70.0	2819	74.0	2946
IMR 4350	Remington	CCI 250	70.0	2726	74.0	2941

WARNING! *Maximum loads should be used with CAUTION • C = Compressed Load*

300 WEATHERBY MAGNUM

168 GRAINS

DIAMETER	SECTIONAL DENSITY
.308"	0.253

30 Match BTHP

Ballistic Coefficient	0.534
COAL Tested	3.560"
Speer Part No.	2040

			Starting Charge		Maximum Charge	
Propellant	Case	Primer	Weight (grains)	Muzzle Velocity (feet/sec)	Weight (grains)	Muzzle Velocity (feet/sec)
Alliant Reloder 26	Federal	Federal 215	75.1	2868	83.4	3256
Alliant Power Pro 4000-MR	Federal	Federal 215	71.0	2942	78.5	3206
Alliant Reloder 25	Remington	CCI 250	85.0	3054	89.0 C	3204
Alliant Reloder 23	Federal	Federal 215	72.9	2891	81.1	3202
Hodgdon H1000	Remington	CCI 250	84.0	3007	88.0	3184
IMR 7977	Federal	Federal 215	78.5	2856	86.3 C	3163
Vihtavuori N165	Remington	CCI 250	82.0	2921	86.0	3160
Alliant Reloder 22	Remington	CCI 250	79.0	2964	83.0	3119
Accurate 3100	Remington	CCI 250	76.0	2923	80.0	3112
Hodgdon H4831SC	Remington	CCI 250	78.0	2939	82.0	3110
Alliant Reloder 19	Remington	CCI 250	76.0	2898	80.0	3105
IMR 4831	Remington	CCI 250	74.0	2914	78.0	3092
Alliant Reloder 33	Federal	Federal 215	86.7	2799	93.0 C	3081
IMR 7828	Remington	CCI 250	78.0	2844	82.0	3050
Hodgdon H414	Remington	CCI 250	70.0	2905	74.0	3042
Hodgdon H4350	Remington	CCI 250	71.0	2799	75.0	3011
Accurate 4350	Remington	CCI 250	70.0	2767	74.0	2982
Winchester 760	Remington	CCI 250	70.0	2819	74.0	2946
IMR 4350	Remington	CCI 250	70.0	2726	74.0	2941

WARNING! Maximum loads should be used with CAUTION • C = Compressed Load

180 GRAINS

DIAMETER	SECTIONAL DENSITY
.308"	0.271

30 Spitzer BTSP
Ballistic Coefficient	0.545
COAL Tested	3.560"
Speer Part No.	2052

30 Spitzer SP Hot-Cor®
Ballistic Coefficient	0.441
COAL Tested	3.560"
Speer Part No.	2053

30 Grand Slam® SP
Ballistic Coefficient	0.374
COAL Tested	3.450"
Speer Part No.	2063

			Starting Charge		Maximum Charge	
Propellant	Case	Primer	Weight (grains)	Muzzle Velocity (feet/sec)	Weight (grains)	Muzzle Velocity (feet/sec)
Alliant Reloder 26	Federal	Federal 215	72.7	2737	80.5	3122
Hodgdon Retumbo	Federal	Federal 215	79.5	2838	88.0 C	3114
Alliant Reloder 33	Federal	Federal 215	84.9	2726	94.0 C	3113
Alliant Reloder 23	Federal	Federal 215	70.9	2812	78.4	3089
Alliant Power Pro 4000-MR	Federal	Federal 215	68.0	2803	75.3	3066
Alliant Reloder 25	Remington	CCI 250	83.0	2876	87.0	3061
Vihtavuori N165	Remington	CCI 250	80.0	2827	84.0	3054
Vihtavuori N560	Remington	CCI 250	76.0	2860	80.0	3053
IMR 7977	Federal	Federal 215	75.6	2696	83.6 C	3045
Hodgdon H1000	Remington	CCI 250	81.5	2901	85.5	3037
Alliant Reloder 22	Remington	CCI 250	78.0	2844	82.0	3030
Hodgdon H4831SC	Remington	CCI 250	77.0	2821	81.0	3004
Accurate 3100	Remington	CCI 250	75.0	2763	79.0	2967
IMR 7828	Remington	CCI 250	76.0	2760	80.0	2957
Alliant Reloder 19	Remington	CCI 250	74.0	2769	78.0	2946
Winchester 760	Remington	CCI 250	69.0	2665	73.0	2941
IMR 4831	Remington	CCI 250	72.0	2753	76.0	2911
Hodgdon H414	Remington	CCI 250	68.5	2653	72.5	2907
Accurate 4350	Remington	CCI 250	68.0	2635	72.0	2828
IMR 4350	Remington	CCI 250	68.0	2597	72.0	2785

WARNING! Maximum loads should be used with CAUTION • C = Compressed Load

200 GRAINS

DIAMETER	SECTIONAL DENSITY
.308"	0.301

30 Spitzer SP Hot-Cor®

Ballistic Coefficient	0.478
COAL Tested	3.560"
Speer Part No.	2211

			Starting Charge		Maximum Charge	
Propellant	Case	Primer	Weight (grains)	Muzzle Velocity (feet/sec)	Weight (grains)	Muzzle Velocity (feet/sec)
Alliant Reloder 25	Remington	CCI 250	81.0	2801	85.0 C	2977
Alliant Reloder 26	Federal	Federal 215	72.4	2609	80.2	2950
Hodgdon Retumbo	Federal	Federal 215	77.5	2655	85.3 C	2915
Alliant Reloder 23	Federal	Federal 215	70.4	2657	77.4	2895
IMR 7977	Federal	Federal 215	74.9	2529	83.1 C	2883
Hodgdon H1000	Remington	CCI 250	78.0	2712	82.0	2867
Alliant Reloder 22	Remington	CCI 250	74.5	2684	78.5	2841
Alliant Reloder 19	Remington	CCI 250	73.0	2701	77.0	2839
Accurate 8700	Remington	CCI 250	92.0	2785	94.0 C	2819
IMR 7828	Remington	CCI 250	73.0	2591	77.0	2803
Hodgdon H4831SC	Remington	CCI 250	72.5	2624	76.5	2801
Accurate 3100	Remington	CCI 250	71.0	2602	75.0	2786
IMR 4831	Remington	CCI 250	69.0	2598	73.0	2743
Accurate 4350	Remington	CCI 250	66.0	2445	70.0	2689
IMR 4350	Remington	CCI 250	65.0	2440	69.0	2648
Hodgdon H414	Remington	CCI 250	64.0	2484	68.0	2629
Hodgdon H4350	Remington	CCI 250	65.0	2454	69.0	2618

300 REMINGTON ULTRA MAGNUM

Alternate Names:	300 RUM
Parent Cartridge:	404 Jeffery
Country of Origin:	USA
Year of Introduction:	1999
Designer(s):	Remington
Governing Body:	SAAMI

Dimensions:
- .5500" [13.97mm]
- .5340" [13.65mm]
- .3440" [8.74mm] cyl
- shoulder angle 30°
- .5250" [13.34mm]
- .5300" [13.46mm]
- .050" [1.27mm]
- .200" [5.08mm] basic
- 1.750" [44.45mm] basic
- 2.3873" [60.64mm]
- 2.5440" [64.62mm]
- 2.8500" [72.39mm]

CARTRIDGE CASE DATA

Case Type:	Rimless, bottleneck, rebated rim		
Average Case Capacity:	114.2 grains H₂O	Max. Cartridge OAL	3.600 inch
Max. Case Length:	2.850 inch	Primer:	Large Rifle
Case Trim to Length:	2.840 inch	RCBS Shell holder:	# 38
Current Manufacturers:	Federal, Remington		

BALLISTIC DATA

Max. Average Pressure (MAP):	CUP not established, 65,000 psi – SAAMI	Test Barrel Length:	24 inch
Rifling Twist Rate:	1 turn in 10 inch		

Muzzle velocities of factory loaded ammunition	Bullet Wgt.	Muzzle velocity
	150-grain	3,450 fps
	165-grain	3,350 fps
	180-grain	3,250 fps
	200-grain	3,025 fps
	220-grain	2,910 fps

Muzzle velocity will decrease approximately 30 fps per inch for barrels less than 24 inches.

HISTORICAL NOTES

- In 1999, the magnum rifle cartridge market was turned upside down when Remington introduced the new 300 Remington Ultra Magnum (RUM) cartridge.
- For the first time in over 55 years, a mainstream ammunition maker offered a magnum cartridge that could compete with the legendary 300 Weatherby Magnum on its own terms.
- And, the new 300 RUM cartridge shattered tradition in another way—it did not have the belted case head of other magnum rifle cartridges! Inspiration courtesy of the fatherly 404 Jeffrey cartridge.
- The 300 Remington Ultra Magnum was part of a trio of new cartridges introduced at the same time which included the 338 and 375 Remington Ultra Magnums, creating a sensation in these calibers as well.
- The 7mm Remington Ultra Magnum completed the series in 2001.
- With the 300 Remington Ultra Magnum cartridge, Remington also introduced the concept of "Power Levels." For example, both the 150 and 180-grain bullets are offered with a choice of two muzzle velocity levels allowing the hunter to more closely match ballistic performance to the type of game hunted.
- As Remington also manufactured rifles, introduction of the new cartridge trio gained momentum when the company simultaneously introduced rifles chambered for the new cartridges.
- Remington Ultra Magnum cartridges firmly established the concept of beltless magnum cartridges in the world of modern sporting ammunition.

BALLISTIC NOTES

- Remington covered all the ballistic bases with the 300 RUM cartridge. Bullet weights of 150, 165, 180, and 200-grain are listed in the current Remington ammunition catalog. All of these factory loads can be duplicated using Speer bullets.
- With its one in 10 inch rifling twist rate and case capacity, the 300 RUM will stabilize long heavy bullets up to 250 grains. This combination will stabilize boat tail bullets for those long range shots.

- While the 300 RUM cartridge is certainly capable of firing bullets weighing less than 150 grains, ammunition makers do not offer such loadings for a good reason—this is not a varmint cartridge.

TECHNICAL NOTES

- The 300 RUM case is slightly longer with a significantly larger head diameter than the 300 Weatherby Magnum. As a result, case capacity of the 300 RUM cartridge is about 15% larger than its Weatherby rival.
- Shoulder angle of both the 7mm and the 300 RUM is 30°. By contrast, the shoulder angle of the 300 Weatherby Magnum is a double radius.
- The 300 RUM cartridge has a 2.850 inch maximum case length and an overall loaded length of 3.600 inch making it suitable only for repeating rifles having long actions.
- The 300 RUM cartridge achieves exceptional muzzle velocities the old fashioned way—it burns heavy propellant charges. None of the short, efficient design concept here!

HANDLOADING NOTES

- Federal, Remington, Hornady, and Nosler offer new, unprimed brass for handloading the 300 RUM.
- The heavy construction of the 300 RUM cartridge case can cause problems with full length resizing such as excessive effort, case stretching, brass hardening, and head separations, all leading to short case life. For this reason, neck sizing only is recommended for load development and sight-in as most rifles in 300 RUM caliber are bolt-action types. Full length sizing will assist in trouble free hunting loads.
- Do not use bullets weighing less than 150 grains for hunting deer with the 300 RUM. At 300 RUM muzzle velocities, even bullets of this weight result in overkill and will leave you with lips, hooves, and tail for the freezer. With this cartridge, we recommend the 165-grain bullets for deer as a good balance of ballistics and recoil.
- The ballistic sweet spot for reloading the 300 RUM cartridge is a 180-grain bullet driven at 3,150 fps muzzle velocity using slow burning propellants.

SAFETY NOTES

SPEER 180-grain Spitzer BTSP @ a muzzle velocity of 3,209 fps:
- Maximum vertical altitude @ 90° elevation is 17,952 feet.
- Maximum horizontal distance to first impact with ground @ 37° elevation is 8,292 yards.

150 GRAINS

DIAMETER	SECTIONAL DENSITY
.308"	0.226

30 Spitzer BTSP
Ballistic Coefficient	0.417
COAL Tested	3.495"
Speer Part No.	2022

30 Spitzer SP Hot-Cor®
Ballistic Coefficient	0.377
COAL Tested	3.495"
Speer Part No.	2023

30 Grand Slam® SP
Ballistic Coefficient	0.295
COAL Tested	3.460"
Speer Part No.	2026

			Starting Charge		Maximum Charge	
Propellant	Case	Primer	Weight (grains)	Muzzle Velocity (feet/sec)	Weight (grains)	Muzzle Velocity (feet/sec)
Vihtavuori N560	Federal	Federal 215	93.0	3308	97.0	3442
Alliant Reloder 22	Federal	Federal 215	93.0	3283	97.0	3437
Alliant Reloder 33	Federal	Federal 215	97.5	3078	108.3 C	3437
Ramshot Magnum	Federal	Federal 215	100.0	3293	104.0	3425
IMR 7828	Federal	Federal 215	93.0	3246	97.0	3419
Alliant Reloder 26	Federal	Federal 215	83.4	3102	92.4	3417
Alliant Power Pro 4000-MR	Federal	Federal 215	79.0	3093	87.5	3404
IMR 7977	Federal	Federal 215	90.0	3031	99.2	3402
Alliant Reloder 19	Federal	Federal 215	90.0	3261	94.0	3401
Accurate 3100	Federal	Federal 215	90.0	3257	94.0	3388
Alliant Reloder 23	Federal	Federal 215	81.7	3059	90.4	3383
IMR 4831	Federal	Federal 215	87.0	3217	91.0	3372
Hodgdon H4831SC	Federal	Federal 215	92.0	3205	96.0	3335

WARNING! Maximum loads should be used with CAUTION • C = Compressed Load

165 GRAINS

DIAMETER	SECTIONAL DENSITY
.308"	0.248

30 Spitzer BTSP	
Ballistic Coefficient	0.520
COAL Tested	3.600"
Speer Part No.	2034

30 Spitzer SP Hot-Cor®	
Ballistic Coefficient	0.444
COAL Tested	3.600"
Speer Part No.	2035

30 Grand Slam® SP	
Ballistic Coefficient	0.354
COAL Tested	3.460"
Speer Part No.	2038

			Starting Charge		Maximum Charge	
Propellant	Case	Primer	Weight (grains)	Muzzle Velocity (feet/sec)	Weight (grains)	Muzzle Velocity (feet/sec)
Alliant Reloder 33	Federal	Federal 215	95.0	3016	105.0	3306
Hodgdon Retumbo	Federal	Federal 215	97.0	3146	101.0	3281
Alliant Reloder 25	Federal	Federal 215	93.0	3140	97.0	3279
Alliant Reloder 26	Federal	Federal 215	80.7	2960	89.7	3279
Ramshot Magnum	Federal	Federal 215	97.0	3148	101.0	3270
Alliant Reloder 22	Federal	Federal 215	89.0	3128	93.0	3268
Alliant Reloder 19	Federal	Federal 215	87.0	3140	91.0	3263
Accurate 3100	Federal	Federal 215	87.0	3154	91.0	3261
IMR 7977	Federal	Federal 215	85.8	2924	95.2	3247
Vihtavuori N560	Federal	Federal 215	88.0	3137	92.0	3245
IMR 7828	Federal	Federal 215	89.0	3103	93.0	3244
Alliant Reloder 23	Federal	Federal 215	78.0	2974	86.5	3221
Accurate MagPro	Federal	Federal 215	92.0	3103	96.0	3219
Hodgdon H4831SC	Federal	Federal 215	88.0	3080	92.0	3203
Alliant Power Pro 4000-MR	Federal	Federal 215	74.6	2926	82.5	3199

WARNING! Maximum loads should be used with CAUTION • C = Compressed Load

168 GRAINS

DIAMETER	SECTIONAL DENSITY
.308"	0.253

30 Match BTHP

Ballistic Coefficient	0.534
COAL Tested	3.600"
Speer Part No.	2040

Propellant	Case	Primer	Starting Charge		Maximum Charge	
			Weight (grains)	Muzzle Velocity (feet/sec)	Weight (grains)	Muzzle Velocity (feet/sec)
Alliant Reloder 33	Federal	Federal 215	95.0	3016	105.0	3306
Hodgdon Retumbo	Federal	Federal 215	97.0	3146	101.0	3281
Alliant Reloder 25	Federal	Federal 215	93.0	3140	97.0	3279
Alliant Reloder 26	Federal	Federal 215	80.7	2960	89.7	3279
Ramshot Magnum	Federal	Federal 215	97.0	3148	101.0	3270
Alliant Reloder 22	Federal	Federal 215	89.0	3128	93.0	3268
Alliant Reloder 19	Federal	Federal 215	87.0	3140	91.0	3263
Accurate 3100	Federal	Federal 215	87.0	3154	91.0	3261
IMR 7977	Federal	Federal 215	85.8	2924	95.2	3247
Vihtavuori N560	Federal	Federal 215	88.0	3137	92.0	3245
IMR 7828	Federal	Federal 215	89.0	3103	93.0	3244
Alliant Reloder 23	Federal	Federal 215	78.0	2974	86.5	3221
Accurate MagPro	Federal	Federal 215	92.0	3103	96.0	3219
Hodgdon H4831SC	Federal	Federal 215	88.0	3080	92.0	3203
Alliant Power Pro 4000-MR	Federal	Federal 215	74.6	2926	82.5	3199

WARNING! Maximum loads should be used with CAUTION • C = Compressed Load

180 GRAINS

DIAMETER	SECTIONAL DENSITY
.308"	0.271

30 Spitzer BTSP
Ballistic Coefficient	0.545
COAL Tested	3.600"
Speer Part No.	2052

30 Spitzer SP Hot-Cor®
Ballistic Coefficient	0.441
COAL Tested	3.600"
Speer Part No.	2053

30 Grand Slam® SP
Ballistic Coefficient	0.374
COAL Tested	3.460"
Speer Part No.	2063

Propellant	Case	Primer	Starting Charge		Maximum Charge	
			Weight (grains)	Muzzle Velocity (feet/sec)	Weight (grains)	Muzzle Velocity (feet/sec)
Alliant Reloder 33	Federal	Federal 215	93.4	2863	103.4	3209
Alliant Reloder 26	Federal	Federal 215	79.5	2849	88.3	3168
Alliant Reloder 25	Federal	Federal 215	90.0	3021	94.0	3146
IMR 7977	Federal	Federal 215	83.9	2847	93.2	3144
Alliant Reloder 23	Federal	Federal 215	77.3	2861	85.8	3128
Ramshot Magnum	Federal	Federal 215	93.0	3001	97.0	3119
Alliant Reloder 22	Federal	Federal 215	86.0	2997	90.0	3118
Hodgdon Retumbo	Federal	Federal 215	90.0	2981	94.0	3099
IMR 7828	Federal	Federal 215	85.0	2961	89.0	3095
Vihtavuori N560	Federal	Federal 215	82.0	2961	86.0	3077
Accurate 3100	Federal	Federal 215	81.0	2931	85.0	3047
Hodgdon H1000	Federal	Federal 215	90.0	2937	94.0	3043
Accurate MagPro	Federal	Federal 215	84.0	2896	88.0	2996

WARNING! Maximum loads should be used with CAUTION • C = Compressed Load

200 GRAINS

DIAMETER	SECTIONAL DENSITY
.308"	0.301

30 Spitzer SP Hot-Cor®

Ballistic Coefficient	0.478
COAL Tested	3.600"
Speer Part No.	2211

			Starting Charge		Maximum Charge	
Propellant	Case	Primer	Weight (grains)	Muzzle Velocity (feet/sec)	Weight (grains)	Muzzle Velocity (feet/sec)
Hodgdon US 869	Federal	Federal 215	100.0	2889	104.0	3000
Alliant Reloder 33	Federal	Federal 215	83.9	2736	92.9	2998
Alliant Reloder 50	Federal	Federal 215	86.8	2733	95.6	2983
Accurate 8700	Federal	Federal 215	100.0	2896	104.0 C	2962
Hodgdon Retumbo	Federal	Federal 215	86.0	2842	90.0	2949
Alliant Reloder 25	Federal	Federal 215	84.0	2837	88.0	2942
Alliant Reloder 26	Federal	Federal 215	72.9	2727	80.2	2939
Alliant Reloder 22	Federal	Federal 215	82.0	2829	86.0	2936
Ramshot Magnum	Federal	Federal 215	88.0	2825	92.0	2933
IMR 7828	Federal	Federal 215	81.0	2781	85.0	2915
Vihtavuori N560	Federal	Federal 215	78.0	2789	82.0	2903
IMR 7977	Federal	Federal 215	76.3	2652	84.7	2900
Alliant Reloder 23	Federal	Federal 215	69.7	2672	76.3	2863
Accurate MagPro	Federal	Federal 215	79.0	2714	83.0	2821

WARNING! Maximum loads should be used with CAUTION • C = Compressed Load

30-378 WEATHERBY MAGNUM

Parent Cartridge:	378 Weatherby Magnum
Country of Origin:	USA
Year of Introduction:	1959
Designer(s):	Roy Weatherby
Governing Body:	CIP

Dimensions:
- .5817" [14.76mm]
- .6035" [15.33mm]
- .579" [14.71mm]
- .3372" [8.56mm] cyl
- radius shoulder
- .5610" [14.25mm]
- .5642" [14.33mm]
- .063" [1.60mm]
- .252" [6.40mm]
- .280" [7.11mm] basic
- 1.750" [44.45mm] basic
- 2.345" [59.56mm]
- 2.5690" [65.25mm]
- 2.913" [73.99mm]

CARTRIDGE CASE DATA

Case Type:	Rimless, Belted, double radius bottleneck			
Average Case Capacity:	130 grains H$_2$O	Max. Cartridge OAL	3.648 inch	
Max. Case Length:	2.913 inch	Primer:	Large Rifle	
Case Trim to Length:	2.903 inch	RCBS Shell holder:	# 14	
Current Manufacturers:	Weatherby, Norma			

BALLISTIC DATA

Max. Average Pressure (MAP):	63,817 psi – CIP; SAAMI data is not available	Test Barrel Length:	26 inch	
Rifling Twist Rate:	1 turn in 10 inch			
Muzzle velocities of factory loaded ammunition	Bullet Wgt.		Muzzle velocity	
	165-grain		3,500 fps	
	180-grain		3,420 fps	
	200-grain		3,160 fps	
	Muzzle velocity will decrease approximately 30 fps per inch for barrels less than 24 inches.			

HISTORICAL NOTES

- When first considering the 30-378 Weatherby Magnum cartridge, two immediate impressions emerge:
  - This is a big cartridge. In fact, it is a REALLY big cartridge!
  - Weatherby calls it a "magnum"; it is a "super magnum" by any other name.
- Unlike other Weatherby Magnum cartridges that were based on established hunting cartridges, the 30-378 Weatherby Magnum is based on the 30-378 wildcat target cartridge developed for 1,000 yard competition.
- The 30-378 Weatherby Magnum is marketed as the ultimate, high performance cartridge for hunting big game at long ranges.
- To do this, it must be capable of sending heavy bullets down range at very high velocities, which it DOES!
- The development process was uncomplicated. To obtain the massive powder capacity needed to reach the high muzzle velocity levels, the mighty 378 Weatherby Magnum was necked down to 30-caliber.
- To date, rival ammunition manufacturers have not included the 30-378 Weatherby Magnum cartridge in their product lines and no firearms manufacturer other than Weatherby offers rifles in this caliber.

Interesting Fact

What characteristics must a cartridge have to be classed as a magnum? The answer is none. Whether or not a cartridge is a magnum depends entirely on how the designer wishes to describe it.

BALLISTIC NOTES

- The 30-378 Weatherby Magnum generates its astounding muzzle velocities the old-fashioned way—it burns powder, and lots of it.
- To obtain the very high muzzle velocities required, the 30-378 Weatherby Magnum must operate very close to the point of diminishing returns on the pressure-time curve. In practice, this means that increasing the weight of the powder charge may no longer increase (and may even DECREASE) muzzle velocity.
- In layman's terms, more energy is wasted accelerating the massive unburned portion of the powder charge down the barrel than is consumed accelerating the bullet to higher muzzle velocities.
- This situation is a classic case of overbore capacity.
- Avoiding overbore problems requires carefully matching a propellant with the right burning rate to a compatible charge weight. This is often a delicate balance indeed.
- With its one turn in 10 inch rifling twist rate, massive case capacity, and adequate neck length, the 30-378 Weatherby Magnum is optimized to stabilize long heavy bullets up to 220 grains.
- This combination is ideal to stabilize boat tail bullets for very long range shots.

HANDLOADING NOTES

- The 30-378 Weatherby Magnum is not a cartridge for novice handloaders. This is a highly specialized cartridge requiring experience and skill well beyond the entry level. As a result, this cartridge is best left to experienced handloaders.

- Factory loaded 30-378 Weatherby Magnum ammunition is not offered with bullets lighter than 165 grains. However, we have boldly gone where few have gone before to offer handloading data for 150-grain bullets in this caliber, through careful powder selection.
- Speer offers a wide variety of .308 diameter bullets suitable for use in the 30-378 Weatherby Magnum.
- The Speer Grand Slam®SP premium grade bullets in 165 and 180-grain are designed with a protected tip and internal flutes in the jacket to assure consistent, reliable expansion so that hunters can take maximum advantage of the ballistics the 30-378 Weatherby offers for big game.
- Just want to duplicate factory ballistics? Speer has you covered with flat base soft point bullets in 165, 180, and 200-grain weights.
- As do all big magnum cartridges, the 30-378 Weatherby Magnum works best with slow burning propellants.
- The heavy construction of the 30-378 Weatherby Magnum cartridge case can cause problems with full length resizing, such as excessive effort, case stretching, brass hardening and head separations, all leading to short case life. For this reason, neck sizing only is recommended for practice and sight-in since all rifles in 30-378 Weatherby Magnum caliber are bolt-action types.

SAFETY NOTES

SPEER 180-grain Spitzer BTSP @ a muzzle velocity of 3,249 fps:
- Maximum vertical altitude @ 90° elevation is 18,315 feet.
- Maximum horizontal distance to first impact with ground @ 38° elevation is 8,419 yards.

150 GRAINS

DIAMETER	SECTIONAL DENSITY
.308"	0.226

30 Spitzer BTSP

Ballistic Coefficient	0.417
COAL Tested	3.600"
Speer Part No.	2022

30 Spitzer SP Hot-Cor®

Ballistic Coefficient	0.377
COAL Tested	3.600"
Speer Part No.	2023

30 Grand Slam® SP

Ballistic Coefficient	0.295
COAL Tested	3.645"
Speer Part No.	2026

Propellant	Case	Primer	Starting Charge Weight (grains)	Starting Charge Muzzle Velocity (feet/sec)	Maximum Charge Weight (grains)	Maximum Charge Muzzle Velocity (feet/sec)
Alliant Reloder 26	Weatherby	CCI 250	107.5	3348	113.5	3608
IMR 7977	Weatherby	CCI 250	111.5	3323	118.1	3569
Accurate 3100	Weatherby	CCI 250	100.0	3269	104.0	3414
IMR 4831	Weatherby	CCI 250	96.0	3279	100.0	3406
Accurate 4350	Weatherby	CCI 250	97.0	3272	101.0	3405
Alliant Reloder 19	Weatherby	CCI 250	101.0	3308	105.0	3404
IMR 4350	Weatherby	CCI 250	93.0	3248	97.0	3385
Hodgdon H1000	Weatherby	CCI 250	108.0	3236	112.0	3364
Hodgdon H4350	Weatherby	CCI 250	90.0	3187	94.0	3317
Hodgdon H4831SC	Weatherby	CCI 250	97.0	3185	101.0	3305

WARNING! Maximum loads should be used with CAUTION • C = Compressed Load

165 GRAINS

DIAMETER	SECTIONAL DENSITY
.308"	0.248

30 Spitzer BTSP	
Ballistic Coefficient	0.520
COAL Tested	3.645"
Speer Part No.	2034

30 Spitzer SP Hot-Cor®	
Ballistic Coefficient	0.444
COAL Tested	3.645"
Speer Part No.	2035

30 Grand Slam® SP	
Ballistic Coefficient	0.354
COAL Tested	3.645"
Speer Part No.	2038

			Starting Charge		Maximum Charge	
Propellant	Case	Primer	Weight (grains)	Muzzle Velocity (feet/sec)	Weight (grains)	Muzzle Velocity (feet/sec)
Alliant Reloder 26	Weatherby	CCI 250	104.0	3162	110.5	3435
IMR 7977	Weatherby	CCI 250	108.0	3186	114.6	3430
Alliant Reloder 19	Weatherby	CCI 250	99.0	3185	103.0	3285
IMR 4831	Weatherby	CCI 250	94.0	3162	98.0	3284
Accurate 3100	Weatherby	CCI 250	97.0	3129	101.0	3268
IMR 7828	Weatherby	CCI 250	104.0	3200	106.0	3267
Hodgdon H1000	Weatherby	CCI 250	103.0	3125	109.0	3249
IMR 4350	Weatherby	CCI 250	92.0	3093	96.0	3223
Hodgdon H4831SC	Weatherby	CCI 250	95.0	3071	99.0	3187

WARNING! Maximum loads should be used with CAUTION • C = Compressed Load

168 GRAINS

DIAMETER	SECTIONAL DENSITY
.308"	0.253

30 Match BTHP

Ballistic Coefficient	0.534
COAL Tested	3.645"
Speer Part No.	2040

			Starting Charge		Maximum Charge	
Propellant	Case	Primer	Weight (grains)	Muzzle Velocity (feet/sec)	Weight (grains)	Muzzle Velocity (feet/sec)
Alliant Reloder 26	Weatherby	CCI 250	104.0	3162	110.5	3435
IMR 7977	Weatherby	CCI 250	108.0	3186	114.6	3430
Alliant Reloder 19	Weatherby	CCI 250	99.0	3185	103.0	3285
IMR 4831	Weatherby	CCI 250	94.0	3162	98.0	3284
Accurate 3100	Weatherby	CCI 250	97.0	3129	101.0	3268
IMR 7828	Weatherby	CCI 250	104.0	3200	106.0	3267
Hodgdon H1000	Weatherby	CCI 250	103.0	3125	109.0	3249
IMR 4350	Weatherby	CCI 250	92.0	3093	96.0	3223
Hodgdon H4831SC	Weatherby	CCI 250	95.0	3071	99.0	3187

WARNING! Maximum loads should be used with CAUTION • C = Compressed Load

180 GRAINS

DIAMETER	SECTIONAL DENSITY
.308"	0.271

30 Spitzer BTSP
Ballistic Coefficient	0.545
COAL Tested	3.645"
Speer Part No.	2052

30 Spitzer SP Hot-Cor®
Ballistic Coefficient	0.441
COAL Tested	3.645"
Speer Part No.	2053

30 Grand Slam® SP
Ballistic Coefficient	0.374
COAL Tested	3.645"
Speer Part No.	2063

			Starting Charge		Maximum Charge	
Propellant	Case	Primer	Weight (grains)	Muzzle Velocity (feet/sec)	Weight (grains)	Muzzle Velocity (feet/sec)
IMR 7977	Weatherby	CCI 250	106.5	3067	113.7	3334
Hodgdon H870	Weatherby	CCI 250	119.0	3147	123.0 C	3249
Accurate 8700	Weatherby	CCI 250	115.0	3080	119.0	3206
Alliant Reloder 26	Weatherby	CCI 250	99.5	2968	105.0	3190
IMR 7828	Weatherby	CCI 250	96.0	3062	100.0	3189
IMR 4831	Weatherby	CCI 250	91.0	3041	95.0	3161
Hodgdon H50BMG	Weatherby	CCI 250	114.0	3019	118.0 C	3137
Hodgdon H1000	Weatherby	CCI 250	102.0	3029	106.0	3134
Accurate 3100	Weatherby	CCI 250	94.0	2996	98.0	3121
Hodgdon H4831SC	Weatherby	CCI 250	92.0	2945	96.0	3069
Vihtavuori N170	Weatherby	CCI 250	93.0	2957	97.0	3057

WARNING! Maximum loads should be used with CAUTION • C = Compressed Load

200 GRAINS

DIAMETER	SECTIONAL DENSITY
.308"	0.301

30 Spitzer SP Hot-Cor®

Ballistic Coefficient	0.478
COAL Tested	3.645 "
Speer Part No.	2211

			Starting Charge		Maximum Charge	
Propellant	Case	Primer	Weight (grains)	Muzzle Velocity (feet/sec)	Weight (grains)	Muzzle Velocity (feet/sec)
Hodgdon H870	Weatherby	CCI 250	114.0	2973	118.0 C	3088
Accurate 8700	Weatherby	CCI 250	112.0	2952	116.0 C	3074
Alliant Reloder 26	Weatherby	CCI 250	96.0	2852	103.0	3073
IMR 7977	Weatherby	CCI 250	100.0	2803	106.0	3049
Hodgdon H50BMG	Weatherby	CCI 250	112.0	2930	116.0 C	3036
Accurate 3100	Weatherby	CCI 250	92.0	2889	96.0	3012
IMR 7828	Weatherby	CCI 250	93.0	2941	95.0	3002
Hodgdon H1000	Weatherby	CCI 250	99.0	2884	103.0	2994

WARNING! *Maximum loads should be used with CAUTION • C = Compressed Load*

7.62x39

Alternate Names:	7.62x39mm Russian, 7.62x39mm Soviet, 7.62mm Type 56, 7.62x39mm M43 & M67
Country of Origin:	Soviet Union
Year of Introduction:	1943
Designer(s):	N.M. Elizarov and B.V. Semin
Governing Body:	SAAMI/CIP

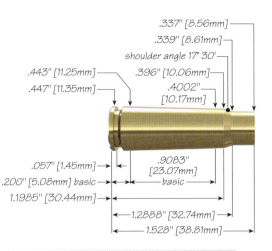

CARTRIDGE CASE DATA

Case Type:	Rimless, bottleneck		
Average Case Capacity:	35.8 grains H$_2$O	Max. Cartridge OAL	2.200 inch
Max. Case Length:	1.528 inch	Primer:	Large or Small Rifle depending on case manufacturer
Case Trim to Length:	1.518 inch	RCBS Shell holder:	# 32
Current Manufacturers:	Federal, Hornady, Remington, Winchester, Sellier & Bellot, Norinco, PMC, Prvi Partizan, NAMMO, IMI, Barnaul, Wolf		

BALLISTIC DATA

Max. Average Pressure (MAP):	50,000 CUP, 45,000 psi – SAAMI; 51,490 psi - CIP	Test Barrel Length:	20 inch
Rifling Twist Rate:	1 turn in 9.45 inch		
Muzzle velocities of factory loaded ammunition	Bullet Wgt.		Muzzle velocity
	123-grain		2,330 fps
	Muzzle velocity will decrease approximately 10 fps per inch for barrels less than 20 inches.		

HISTORICAL NOTES

- During World War II on the eastern front, the Russian Army encountered the German Stg. 44 assault rifle firing the compact German 7.9x33mm Infanterie Kurz Patrone.

- The assault rifle concept with its compact cartridge greatly impressed the Russians who quickly decided to copy it.

- The new Russian 7.62x39mm cartridge was initially introduced into Soviet military service in 1943 along with the SKS carbine and four years later in the AK-47.

- The 7.62x39mm M43 cartridge was adopted by all Warsaw Pact countries as well as China, North Korea, North Vietnam, Iraq, Indonesia, and many African countries.

- In the 1980s, surplus military SKS carbines and civilian variants of the AK-47 rifle began entering the U.S. market, creating a demand for ammunition in this caliber.

- Low cost, surplus military ammunition from Russia, China, and many other countries were imported to meet the demand.

- The SKS carbines and civil AK rifles became a popular choice for practice, training, and informal target shooting.

- Today, low cost surplus and newly manufactured military ammunition continues to be imported from Russia, Serbia, Hungary, and several other countries. Chinese-made ammunition can no longer be imported.

- Most large ammunition manufacturers now offer sporting loads in 7.62x39mm caliber.

Interesting Fact

Dr. Mikhail Kalashnikov, father of the AK-47, did not design the 7.62x39mm cartridge. As he was working on his AK-47 one day in 1945, he was handed a sample of the new 7.62x39mm cartridge and abruptly told to "make it shoot that". He had never seen the cartridge before.

BALLISTIC NOTES

- Here, it must be kept in mind that the 7.62x39mm cartridge was designed for the battlefield, not the hunting field. The SKS and the AK-47 are not known for their accuracy.

- As such, the 7.62x39mm cartridge is designed along a narrow set of ballistic requirements for a bullet weighing 122-125 grains at a muzzle velocity of 2,300 to 2,400 fps. Moving outside these parameters may result in poor operational reliability, excessive wear, inaccuracy, and iron sight adjustments that do not match the exterior ballistics.

- Low MAP levels, small case capacity, lightweight bullets, and modest muzzle velocity handicaps the 7.62x39mm cartridge for hunting anything but small deer and predators at a short range.

- At this point, it seems appropriate to point out that the striking energy of the 123-grain spitzer bullet of the 7.62x39mm cartridge remains slightly inferior to the 150-grain flat nose bullet of the 30-30 Winchester to a distance of 150 yards. Hardly inspiring.

TECHNICAL NOTES

- Military 7.62x39mm ammunition is often loaded in steel cartridge cases with corrosive, Berdan primers.

- As steel cases must be clad with copper, nickel, zinc, lacquer or polymer to prevent corrosion, they may not appear to be of steel construction. If in doubt, use a magnet to make your determination.

- Berdan primed steel cases cannot be reloaded and should be destroyed.

- Some ammunition manufacturers offer 7.62x39mm ammunition with brass cartridge cases and non-corrosive Boxer primers. Expect to pay more for these.

Technical Question
Should steel cartridge cases be reloaded?
Answer: definitely not.

- There are several reasons for this:
  - Military steel cartridge cases are designed for one-time use only.
  - When a steel cartridge case is fired, the corrosion-resistant coating on its inner and outer surfaces is compromised by scratches, dents, and nicks which allow corrosion to proceed rapidly.
  - Corrosion will quickly weaken a steel case making it unsafe to fire. The corrosion may be entirely internal and not evident from the outside.
  - Resizing steel cartridge cases also causes scratches and nicks that compromise the protective coatings of steel cases.
  - As steel case 7.62x39mm ammunition is normally fired in semi-automatic firearms, they must be resized in a small base die. This is a very difficult process with steel cases.
  - The corrosive primers used in some steel case military ammunition will accelerate the internal corrosion process dramatically.
  - Berdan primers in steel cases cannot be decapped easily.
- Sound advice; never attempt to reload "pick up" steel cartridge cases from outdoor ranges!

HANDLOADING NOTES

- As most 7.62x39mm ammunition is fired in semi-automatic firearms, empty cartridge cases must be full-length resized using a small base die set.
- Slam fires may occur when 7.62x39mm reloaded ammunition assembled with commercial primers is fired from semi-automatic rifles. For this reason, we recommend that you use CCI No. 34 Arsenal Large Rifle primers for semi-auto 7.62x39mm reloading activities — seat the primers .003 to .005 inches below flush and reduce powder charges one full grain.
- Note that the correct bullet diameter for the 7.62x39mm cartridge is .310 inch.
- Medium burning speed powders are best for loading this cartridge as it is important to maintain sufficient gas port pressure for reliable functioning.

SAFETY NOTES

A 123-grain GD bullet @ a muzzle velocity of 2,585 fps:
- Maximum vertical altitude @ 90° elevation is 7,980 feet.
- Maximum horizontal distance to first impact with ground @ 34° elevation is 3,654 yards.

GOLD DOT RIFLE

123 GRAINS

DIAMETER	SECTIONAL DENSITY
.310"	0.183

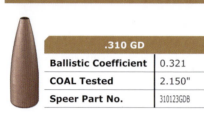

.310 GD

Ballistic Coefficient	0.321
COAL Tested	2.150"
Speer Part No.	310123GDB

			Starting Charge		Maximum Charge	
Propellant	Case	Primer	Weight (grains)	Muzzle Velocity (feet/sec)	Weight (grains)	Muzzle Velocity (feet/sec)
Accurate 2200	Federal	Federal 210	29.5	2378	32.9 C	2585
Alliant Power Pro 1200-R	Federal	Federal 210	28.2	2303	31.3 C	2488
Accurate 1680	Federal	Federal 210	25.4	2224	28.2	2455
Hodgdon H335	Federal	Federal 210	31.0	2228	34.4 C	2451
Accurate LT-32	Federal	Federal 210	27.8	2238	30.8 C	2448
Alliant Reloder 10X	Federal	Federal 210	27.3	2257	30.1 C	2438
Alliant Reloder 7	Federal	Federal 210	25.8	2248	28.5 C	2435
IMR 4198	Federal	Federal 210	23.6	2197	26.2 C	2400
Vihtavuori N120	Federal	Federal 210	22.9	2226	25.3	2397
Accurate 2015	Federal	Federal 210	27.8	2186	30.8 C	2389
Hodgdon BENCHMARK	Federal	Federal 210	28.7	2156	31.9 C	2363

WARNING! Maximum loads should be used with CAUTION • C = Compressed Load

303 BRITISH

Alternate Names:	7.7x56mmR, 303 Lee-Metford, 303 Vickers, 303 Lee Enfield
Parent Cartridge:	Original
Country of Origin:	Britain
Year of Introduction:	1888
Designer(s):	British military
Governing Body:	SAAMI/CIP

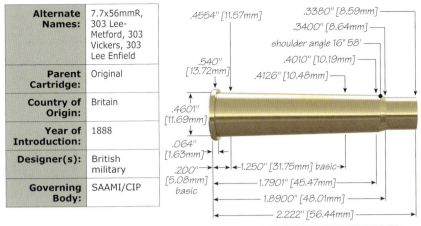

CARTRIDGE CASE DATA

Case Type:	Rimmed, bottleneck		
Average Case Capacity:	57.0 grains H_2O	Max. Cartridge OAL	3.075 inch
Max. Case Length:	2.222 inch	Primer:	Large Rifle
Case Trim to Length:	2.212 inch	RCBS Shell holder:	# 7
Current Manufacturers:	Federal, Hornady, Remington, Winchester, NAMMO, PMP, Prvi Partizan		

BALLISTIC DATA

Max. Average Pressure (MAP):	45,000 CUP, 49,000 psi – SAAMI; 52,939 psi - CIP	Test Barrel Length:	24 inch
Rifling Twist Rate:	1 turn in 8 inch, 1 turn in 10		
Muzzle velocities of factory loaded ammunition	Bullet Wgt.	Muzzle velocity	
	150-grain	2,690 fps	
	180-grain	2,460 fps	
	Muzzle velocity will decrease approximately 10 fps per inch for barrels less than 24 inches.		

HISTORICAL NOTES

- Few military cartridges can match the history of the 303 British. During nearly three quarters of a century of military service, it saw combat in all parts of the world putting down rebellions, breaking sieges, conducting punitive expeditions and fighting two world wars as well as numerous smaller ones.

- The 303 British cartridge was adopted by the British Army on February 20, 1889 to replace the 577/450 Martini-Henry black powder cartridge.

- Other members of the Commonwealth followed suit including the armies of India, Australia, New Zealand, Canada, Rhodesia and South Africa.

- The 303 British cartridge began its service life loaded with a 215-grain Mk 2 full metal jacket round nose bullet and a 71-grain charge of compressed black powder. Muzzle velocity was 1,970 fps.
- Cordite smokeless propellant quickly replaced the black powder making the 303 British cartridge the first to be loaded with the new propellant.

Interesting Fact
Origin of the Dum Dum Bullet

When the terminal ballistic performance of the 303 FMJ-RN Mark II bullets were found to be unsatisfactory against the Pathan tribesmen along the border with Afghanistan (some things never change!), the superintendent of the arsenal at Dum Dum, India developed a series of hollow and soft point designs that expanded on impact which significantly increased their terminal ballistic performance. The Mark II, IV and V "Dum Dum" bullets were adopted briefly for military service, then dropped when they were found to be unacceptable under international law.

Postscript: The superintendent of the Dum Dum Arsenal was Capt. Bertie Clay, a member of the British royal family who went on to serve with distinction in the Boer War.

- In 1910, the 174-grain Mark VII bullet was adopted. With its charge of Cordite smokeless propellant, muzzle velocity was increased to 2,440 fps. This load remained in front line British military service until the 303 British cartridge was replaced by the 7.62x51mm NATO cartridge in 1957.
- Epitaph: The sun never set on the British Empire and the 303 British cartridge kept it that way for nearly a century.

BALLISTIC NOTES

- The 30-40 Krag cartridge shares ballistic credentials with the 303 British.
- At one time or another, the 303 British cartridge has been used to take nearly every type of game in the world, often because it was the only cartridge that was available.
- That said, the 303 British cartridge is not suitable for hunting large, heavy, African plains game or dangerous game.
- The 303 British is fully capable of taking most North American game.

TECHNICAL NOTES

- When the rimmed 303 British cartridge was adopted for military service in 1889, it was already recognized as a semi-obsolescent design that would have to be replaced by a more modern, rimless cartridge after the turn of the century. Wars, politics and budgets prevented this from happening for another 50 years.
- The 303 British cartridge case suffered from a number of faults that effectively prevented making any improvements. Chief among them were:
  - The rimmed case design made feeding from box magazines difficult.
  - The shoulder and case length were too short, reducing case capacity.
  - A low MAP level handicapped needed improvements to ballistics.
  - A lightweight case that was not designed for modern high pressure loads.
- In addition, the SMLE service rifle was not designed for high MAP.

HANDLOADING NOTES

- The bolt of SMLE rifles locks at the rear which allows a considerable amount of springiness in the action when fired. This can cause case head separations after several reloads. As a result, we recommend that you carefully inspect your brass for cracks or stretch marks before reloading them. Don't be a cheapskate! Do not try to get just one more reload from a case with signs of head separation.
- Note that the 303 British cartridge uses a bullet diameter of .310 to .312 inch.
- Use slow burning propellants to reload the 303 British in order to keep MAP levels within limits.

SAFETY NOTES

SPEER 150-grain Spitzer SP Hot-Cor @ a muzzle velocity of 2,781 fps:
- Maximum vertical altitude @ 90° elevation is 9,531 feet.
- Maximum horizontal distance to first impact with ground @ 35° elevation is 4,381 yards.

150 GRAINS

DIAMETER	SECTIONAL DENSITY
.311"	0.222

303 Spitzer SP Hot-Cor®	
Ballistic Coefficient	0.351
COAL Tested	3.040"
Speer Part No.	2217

Propellant	Case	Primer	Starting Charge Weight (grains)	Starting Charge Muzzle Velocity (feet/sec)	Maximum Charge Weight (grains)	Maximum Charge Muzzle Velocity (feet/sec)
Ramshot Big Game	Federal	Federal 215	46.0	2637	50.0	2781
Winchester 760	Federal	Federal 215	47.0	2595	51.0	2763
Alliant Reloder 15	Federal	Federal 210	41.0	2511	45.0	2746
Hodgdon Varget	Federal	Federal 210	41.0	2501	45.0	2724
Vihtavuori N540	Federal	Federal 210	41.5	2459	45.5	2701
IMR 4895	Federal	Federal 210	40.0	2473	44.0	2695
Accurate 4064	Federal	Federal 210	38.5	2402	42.5	2611
Alliant Reloder 10X	Federal	Federal 210	33.5	2416	37.5	2606
Hodgdon H322	Federal	Federal 210	33.5	2341	37.5	2580
IMR 4350	Federal	Federal 210	44.0	2344	48.0 C	2516
Accurate 5744 (reduced load)	Federal	Federal 210	25.0	1966	27.0	2078

WARNING! *Maximum loads should be used with CAUTION • C = Compressed Load*

180 GRAINS

DIAMETER	SECTIONAL DENSITY
.311"	0.266

303 SPRN Hot-Cor®

Ballistic Coefficient	0.299
COAL Tested	3.075"
Speer Part No.	2223

			Starting Charge		Maximum Charge	
Propellant	Case	Primer	Weight (grains)	Muzzle Velocity (feet/sec)	Weight (grains)	Muzzle Velocity (feet/sec)
Winchester 760	Federal	Federal 215	44.0	2351	48.0	2514
Vihtavuori N540	Federal	Federal 210	40.0	2303	44.0	2497
Alliant Reloder 15	Federal	Federal 210	38.0	2274	42.0	2479
Ramshot Big Game	Federal	Federal 215	41.0	2316	45.0	2471
IMR 4895	Federal	Federal 210	37.0	2212	41.0	2420
Hodgdon Varget	Federal	Federal 210	37.0	2238	41.0	2408
IMR 4350	Federal	Federal 210	43.0	2181	47.0 C	2389
Accurate XMR 4064	Federal	Federal 210	35.0	2128	39.0	2339
Alliant Reloder 10X	Federal	Federal 210	30.5	2125	34.5	2324
Hodgdon H322	Federal	Federal 210	31.5	2122	35.5	2320
Accurate 5744 (reduced load)	Federal	Federal 210	27.0	1956	29.0	2076

WARNING! *Maximum loads should be used with CAUTION • C = Compressed Load*

32 WINCHESTER SPECIAL

Parent Cartridge:	30-30 Winchester
Country of Origin:	USA
Year of Introduction:	1902
Designer(s):	Winchester
Governing Body:	SAAMI

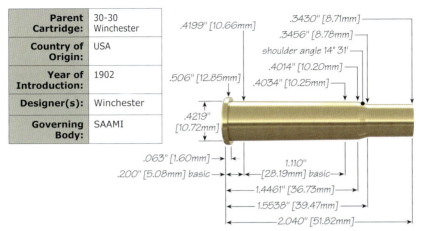

CARTRIDGE CASE DATA

Case Type:	Rimmed, bottleneck		
Average Case Capacity:	41.0 grains H$_2$O	Max. Cartridge OAL	2.565 inch
Max. Case Length:	2.040 inch	Primer:	Large Rifle
Case Trim to Length:	2.030 inch	RCBS Shell holder:	# 2
Current Manufacturers:	Federal, Hornady, Remington, Winchester		

BALLISTIC DATA

Max. Average Pressure (MAP):	42,000 psi, 38,000 CUP - SAAMI	Test Barrel Length:	24 inch
Rifling Twist Rate:	1 turn in 16 inch		

Muzzle velocities of factory loaded ammunition	Bullet Wgt.	Muzzle velocity
	170-grain	2,250 fps

Muzzle velocity will decrease approximately 10 fps per inch for barrels less than 24 inches.

HISTORICAL NOTES

- The 32 Winchester Special cartridge was introduced in 1902—seven years after its older brother, the 30-30 Winchester.

- Winchester and Marlin added the new caliber to their lever-action rifle product lines.

- The Winchester ammunition catalog of 1902 describes the purpose of the 32 Winchester Special as being "… to meet the demand from many sportsmen, for a smokeless powder cartridge of larger caliber than the 30 Winchester [ed., the 30-30 Winchester] and not yet so powerful as the 30 U.S. Army [ed., the 30-40 Krag], which could be reloaded with black powder and give satisfactory results."

- Today, this seems a rather narrow market segment on which to base a new cartridge. Here it is important to note that in 1902, the muzzle energy of the 32 Winchester Special was a significant 22% higher than that of the 30-30 Winchester. Today, the difference is less than 5%. The 32 Winchester Special has lost its ballistic advantage and market.
- Winchester, Remington, and Federal still offer loaded 32 Winchester Special in their ammunition catalogs. However, new rifles in this caliber have not been made in many years.
- Repeated forecasts of the imminent retirement of the 32 Winchester Special cartridge have proven in error. Why? The pundits have forgotten that the fun factor in handloading and shooting an old classic like the 32 Winchester Special keep cartridges such as this alive and well.

Interesting Fact

Throughout its life, the 32 Winchester Special cartridge has been plagued by an unjustified reputation for poor accuracy. This was due to the undersized, .318 inch diameter bullets used by Winchester for many years to load this cartridge rather than to any inherent firearm/cartridge design flaws.

Factory loaded 32 Winchester Special ammunition of today is assembled with bullets of the correct .321 inch diameter and suffers from no accuracy problems.

BALLISTIC NOTES

- In 2017 ammunition catalogs:
  - The 30-30 Winchester with a 170-grain bullet is listed with a muzzle velocity of 2,200 fps and a muzzle energy of 1,827 ft-lbs.
  - The 32 Winchester Special with a 170-grain bullet is listed with a muzzle velocity of 2,250 fps and a muzzle energy of 1,911 ft-lbs.
- However, let us consider the ballistics of the two cartridges in the real world at 100 yards.
  - The 30-30 Winchester 170-grain bullet retains 1,332 ft-lbs of striking energy.
  - The 32 Winchester Special retains 1,320 ft-lbs of energy at the same distance.
- Any energy advantage the 32 Winchester Special may have had at the muzzle has been completely erased by its larger diameter bullet at 100 yards.
- For North American hunting, the 32 Winchester Special is fully capable of reliably harvesting deer of all sizes at ranges of 100 yards or less.

TECHNICAL NOTES

- The 32 Winchester Special is essentially a 30-30 Winchester case necked up to accept .321 inch bullets.
- Bullets of the same weight are used in both cartridges.
- MAP levels of the 32 Winchester Special and 30-30 Winchester are the same.

HANDLOADING NOTES

- The ballistic coefficient (.283) of the Speer 170-grain SPFN Hot-Cor® is higher than factory bullets (.205). This offers handloaders the opportunity to increase the striking energy at 100 yards, to a level approximately 5-10% higher than factory loads depending on the muzzle velocity.

- To avoid magazine tube initiations in lever-action rifles, the 32 Winchester Special cartridge *must* be loaded with flat nose bullets.
- These bullets should be crimped securely in the case to prevent the bullet being pulled from the case mouth by recoil or pushed into the case by the magazine spring and cartridges in the magazine tube.

SAFETY NOTES

SPEER 170-grain SPFN Hot-Cor @ a muzzle velocity of 2,407 fps:
- Maximum vertical altitude @ 90° elevation is 7,596 feet.
- Maximum horizontal distance to first impact with ground @ 35° elevation is 3,520 yards.

170 GRAINS

DIAMETER	SECTIONAL DENSITY
.321"	0.236

32 SPFN Hot-Cor®

Ballistic Coefficient	0.283
COAL Tested	2.560"
Speer Part No.	2259

Propellant	Case	Primer	Starting Charge Weight (grains)	Starting Charge Muzzle Velocity (feet/sec)	Maximum Charge Weight (grains)	Maximum Charge Muzzle Velocity (feet/sec)
Alliant Power Pro 2000-MR	Federal	Federal 210	37.8	2205	42.0 C	2407
Alliant AR-Comp	Federal	Federal 210	31.0	2109	34.2 C	2305
Hodgdon CFE 223	Federal	Federal 210	36.0	2104	39.5 C	2301
IMR 4895	Winchester	CCI 200	33.0	2091	35.0	2238
IMR 3031	Winchester	CCI 200	32.0	2082	34.0	2234
Winchester 748	Winchester	CCI 250	34.0	2086	36.0	2229
Alliant Power Pro Varmint	Federal	Federal 210	31.5	2097	34.2	2229
Alliant Reloder 15	Federal	Federal 210	31.9	2025	35.0	2215
IMR 4064	Winchester	CCI 200	34.0	2060	36.0	2203
Hodgdon BL-C(2)	Winchester	CCI 250	31.0	2040	33.0	2196
IMR 4166	Federal	Federal 210	29.1	1933	32.1	2097
IMR 4320	Winchester	CCI 200	33.5	1958	35.5	2094
IMR 4198	Winchester	CCI 200	23.5	1921	25.5	2086
IMR 4350	Winchester	CCI 200	35.0	1839	37.0	1961
IMR SR 4759 (reduced load)	Winchester	CCI 200	16.0	1523	18.0	1713

WARNING! *Maximum loads should be used with CAUTION* • *C = Compressed Load*

8mm MAUSER

Alternate Names:	7.92x57mm Mauser, 8x57mm Mauser, 8mm JS Mauser, 8x57mm JS
Parent Cartridge:	7.92x57mmJ Mauser
Country of Origin:	Germany
Year of Introduction:	1888 (J Patrone), 1905 (JS Patrone)
Designer(s):	German Military Commission
Governing Body:	SAAMI/CIP

WARNING! *The reloading data presented here exceeds SAAMI MAP limits for the 8mm Mauser. It should be used in modern firearms (Model 98 Mausers of military or commercial manufacture) with a bore diameter of .323" or larger.*

Dimensions:
- .3493" [8.87mm]
- .3507" [8.91mm]
- .473" [12.01mm]
- .4698" [11.93mm]
- shoulder angle 20° 48'
- .4310" [10.95mm]
- .4340" [11.02mm]
- .049" [1.24mm]
- .200" [5.08mm] basic
- 1.500" [38.10mm] basic
- 1.8273" [46.41mm]
- 1.933" [49.10mm]
- 2.240" [56.90mm]

CARTRIDGE CASE DATA

Case Type:	Rimless, bottleneck		
Average Case Capacity:	62.5 grains H₂O	Max. Cartridge OAL	3.250 inch
Max. Case Length:	2.240 inch	Primer:	Large Rifle
Case Trim to Length:	2.230 inch	RCBS Shell holder:	# 3
Current Manufacturers:	Federal, Hornady, Remington, Winchester, Prvi Partizan, RUAG (RWS), NAMMO, Sellier & Bellot, Norma, Nosler		

BALLISTIC DATA

Max. Average Pressure (MAP):	35,000 psi, 37,000 CUP – SAAMI; 56,560 psi CIP	Test Barrel Length:	24 inch
Rifling Twist Rate:	1 turn in 9.5 inch		

Muzzle velocities of factory loaded ammunition	Bullet Wgt.	Muzzle velocity
	170-grain	2,250 fps

Muzzle velocity will decrease approximately 10 fps per inch for barrels less than 24 inches.

HISTORICAL NOTES

- In 1888, the German Army adopted a new M88 7.9x57mm J Patrone service cartridge designed especially for the smokeless propellants and new bolt-action rifles.

- The groundbreaking new cartridge was a rimless design with an undercut extractor groove in the head. Overnight, the new German cartridge made rimmed military cartridges obsolete.
- It was loaded with a .318 inch diameter 227-grain FMJ RN bullet at a muzzle velocity of 2,067 fps. This bullet was similar in design and concept to those used in military services of many other countries at the time—including the U.S.
- In 1905, the German Army created a second major earthquake in ammunition design by adopting a lightweight, 154-grain Spitzer (pointed) bullet at a muzzle velocity of over 2,891 fps in the new Model 98 rifles. Diameter of the new bullet was .323 inch to prevent it from being fired in the old M88 rifles with .318 inch bores.
- The new 8x57mm Mauser cartridge was designated the "S Patrone" today called the 8x57mm JS in Europe.
- The designers could not know the profound effect these two changes would have on ammunition design that continues to this day.
- It is for these reasons that many consider the 8x57mm cartridge one of the most influential in history.
- The 8x57mm JS Mauser cartridge remained in German Army service from 1905 to 1945. It was also the military service cartridge of many other countries such as Poland, Czechoslovakia, China, Iran, Turkey, and Yugoslavia.
- When American sportsmen refer to the 8mm Mauser cartridge, they are speaking of the 8x57mm JS Mauser.
- American sportsmen own a large number of ex-military German rifles in 8x57mm JS caliber although few use this caliber for hunting today.

BALLISTIC NOTES

- The 8x57mm Mauser cartridge is fully capable of taking all species of big game in North America (with European ammunition).
- European ammunition manufacturers load the 8x57mm JS cartridge to 22% higher MAP levels than domestic manufacturers as most European hunters are well aware of the dangers of firing the 8x57mm JS cartridge loaded with .323 inch bullets in old M88 rifles with .318 inch bores.
- The situation is different in the U.S. where the differences between the 8x57mm J and 8x57mm JS cartridges and their different bullet diameters are less well known.
- For this reason, as a safety precaution, domestic manufacturers load the 8x57mm JS to significantly lower MAP levels with lighter weight bullets than European ammunition makers. **The loads shown here are loaded to European guidelines and are above SAAMI pressures. They are safe in good quality commercial actions.**
- As a result, the ballistics of American-made 8x57mm JS ammunition can be compared to the 30-30 Winchester rather than European 8x57mm JS ammunition.
- European hunters prefer heavy bullets for the 8x57mm JS ranging from 180-grain to 220-grain with the 196-grain bullet being the most popular.
- With such bullets, European hunters have found the 8x57mm more than adequate for all species of European game as well as African plains game.
- American-made 8mm Mauser factory ammunition is suitable only for deer and predator hunting due to its lighter bullet and lower velocity.
- That said, handloaders have the opportunity to load the 8x57mm JS Mauser

cartridge with bullet weights and muzzle velocities more suitable to North American game and hunting conditions.

- The Speer 150-grain Spitzer SP Hot-Cor® can be handloaded to a muzzle velocity of 2,915 fps in the 8x57mm JS making it a ballistic equivalent to the 30-06 Springfield with a similar bullet weight.

- The Speer 170-grain Semi-Spitzer SP Hot-Cor can be used to duplicate domestic factory loads (2,360 fps), but this makes no sense when you can duplicate European loads (muzzle velocity 2,690 fps) with this same bullet.

- European hunters prefer the 196-grain bullet in the 8x57mm JS for big game hunting. The Speer 200-grain Spitzer SP Hot-Cor handloaded to a muzzle velocity of 2,469 fps will provide broadly equivalent performance.

- The one turn in 9.5 inch rifling twist of the 8x57mm JS Mauser will easily stabilize a wide range of bullets from 150 grains up to 220 grains.

TECHNICAL NOTES

- The German Army used 8x57mm Mauser ammunition loaded with steel cases during World Wars I and II. Consequently, most surplus military 8x57mm JS Mauser ammunition is loaded in steel cartridge cases with corrosive, Berdan primers.

- As steel cases must be clad with copper, nickel, zinc, lacquer or polymer to prevent corrosion, surplus 8x57mm ammunition may not appear to be of steel construction. If in doubt, use a magnet to make your determination. Do not attempt to reload steel cartridge cases of World War II manufacture! Destroy them.

HANDLOADING NOTES

- In addition to the manufacturers of loaded ammunition listed above, RUAG, Winchester, Remington, Norma, Hornady, Sako, Lapua and Sellier & Bellot offer new, empty, unprimed brass cartridge cases in 8x57mm JS caliber for reloading.

- 8x57mm JS Mauser cartridges fired in bolt-action rifles can be neck sized to maximize case life and reduce trimming chores.

- 8x57mm JS Mauser ammunition fired in semi-automatic rifles such as the G43 will require full length resizing with a small base die. You can reduce sizing effort by thoroughly cleaning and lubricating your cases before sizing. If you are unsure if the brass was fired in a semi-automatic, full length resize with a small base die.

- We recommend medium burning rate propellants for reloading the 8x57mm JS Mauser cartridge.

SAFETY NOTES

SPEER 200-grain Spitzer SP Hot-Cor @ a muzzle velocity of 2,469 fps:
- Maximum vertical altitude @ 90° elevation is 10,545 feet.
- Maximum horizontal distance to first impact with ground @ 38° elevation is 4,962 yards.
- There are a number of 8x57mm cartridge iterations, be sure the one you intend to shoot is for the chamber of the gun you have.
- Do not attempt to fire or salvage surplus military 8x57mm Mauser ammunition. Do not attempt to reload 8x57mm Mauser fired steel cases.
- Never attempt to fire 8x57mm JS Mauser ammunition with .323 inch diameter bullets in old Mauser Model 88 rifles with .318 inch diameter barrels!

150 GRAINS

DIAMETER	SECTIONAL DENSITY
.323"	0.205

8mm Spitzer SP Hot-Cor®

Ballistic Coefficient	0.343
COAL Tested	2.890"
Speer Part No.	2277

			Starting Charge		Maximum Charge	
Propellant	Case	Primer	Weight (grains)	Muzzle Velocity (feet/sec)	Weight (grains)	Muzzle Velocity (feet/sec)
IMR 4064	Remington	CCI 200	47.0	2695	51.0	2915
Hodgdon H335	Remington	CCI 250	46.0	2513	50.0	2771
IMR 3031	Remington	CCI 200	45.0	2488	49.0	2757
Alliant Reloder 15	Remington	CCI 200	47.0	2439	51.0	2726
Hodgdon H322	Remington	CCI 200	44.0	2433	48.0	2699
Vihtavuori N140	Remington	CCI 200	46.0	2436	50.0	2695
IMR 4895	Remington	CCI 200	44.0	2428	48.0	2675
IMR 4350	Remington	CCI 200	51.0	2458	55.0	2660
Accurate 2700	Remington	CCI 250	46.0	2358	50.0	2580
Hodgdon BL-C(2)	Remington	CCI 250	40.0	2324	44.0	2544
Accurate 4350	Remington	CCI 200	52.0	2317	56.0 C	2507
Hodgdon H414	Remington	CCI 250	51.0	2281	55.0	2506
IMR 4198 (reduced load)	Remington	CCI 200	24.0	1809	26.0	1955

WARNING! *Maximum loads should be used with CAUTION • C = Compressed Load*

170 GRAINS

DIAMETER	SECTIONAL DENSITY
.323"	0.233

8mm Semi-Spitzer SP Hot-Cor®

Ballistic Coefficient	0.311
COAL Tested	2.890"
Speer Part No.	2283

			Starting Charge		Maximum Charge	
Propellant	Case	Primer	Weight (grains)	Muzzle Velocity (feet/sec)	Weight (grains)	Muzzle Velocity (feet/sec)
IMR 4064	Remington	CCI 200	45.0	2509	49.0	2723
Winchester 748	Remington	CCI 250	50.0	2451	54.0	2716
IMR 4895	Remington	CCI 200	42.0	2401	46.0	2640
Alliant Reloder 15	Remington	CCI 200	45.0	2425	49.0	2632
IMR 4350	Remington	CCI 200	54.0	2429	55.0 C	2632
IMR 3031	Remington	CCI 200	40.0	2356	44.0	2600
Hodgdon H380	Remington	CCI 250	50.0	2359	54.0	2588
Vihtavuori N140	Remington	CCI 200	44.0	2378	48.0	2574
Hodgdon H335	Remington	CCI 250	42.0	2262	46.0	2525
Accurate 2700	Remington	CCI 250	45.0	2266	49.0	2486
Accurate 4350	Remington	CCI 200	49.0	2185	53.0 C	2368
Hodgdon H322	Remington	CCI 200	38.0	2049	42.0	2324
IMR 4198 (reduced load)	Remington	CCI 200	25.0	1778	27.0	1914

WARNING! *Maximum loads should be used with CAUTION • C = Compressed Load*

200 GRAINS

DIAMETER	SECTIONAL DENSITY
.323"	0.274

8mm Spitzer SP Hot-Cor®

Ballistic Coefficient	0.440
COAL Tested	3.200"
Speer Part No.	2285

			Starting Charge		Maximum Charge	
Propellant	Case	Primer	Weight (grains)	Muzzle Velocity (feet/sec)	Weight (grains)	Muzzle Velocity (feet/sec)
Hodgdon H380	Remington	CCI 250	48.0	2242	52.0	2469
IMR 4064	Remington	CCI 200	42.0	2196	46.0	2434
IMR 4350	Remington	CCI 200	49.0	2208	53.0 C	2432
IMR 4831	Remington	CCI 200	50.0	2213	54.0	2395
Winchester 760	Remington	CCI 250	48.0	2171	52.0	2392
Accurate 2700	Remington	CCI 250	44.0	2110	48.0 C	2324
Hodgdon H335	Remington	CCI 250	38.0	2066	42.0	2322
Alliant Reloder 15	Remington	CCI 200	40.0	2051	44.0	2267
Vihtavuori N140	Remington	CCI 200	39.0	2040	43.0	2242
Accurate 4350	Remington	CCI 200	46.0	2022	50.0 C	2149

WARNING! *Maximum loads should be used with CAUTION • C = Compressed Load*

325 WINCHESTER SHORT MAGNUM

Alternate Names:	325 WSM
Parent Cartridge:	300 WSM
Country of Origin:	USA
Year of Introduction:	2004
Designer(s):	Winchester
Governing Body:	SAAMI

CARTRIDGE CASE DATA

Case Type:	Rimless, bottle neck, rebated		
Average Case Capacity:	72.5 grains H_2O	Max. Cartridge OAL	2.860 inch
Max. Case Length:	2.100 inch	Primer:	Large Rifle
Case Trim to Length:	2.090 inch	RCBS Shell holder:	# 43
Current Manufacturers:	Winchester		

BALLISTIC DATA

Max. Average Pressure (MAP):	65,000 psi, CUP not established for this cartridge - SAAMI	Test Barrel Length:	24 inch
Rifling Twist Rate:	1 turn in 10 inch		
Muzzle velocities of factory loaded ammunition	Bullet Wgt.		Muzzle velocity
	180-grain		3,060 fps
	200-grain		2,950 fps
	220-grain		2,840 fps
	Muzzle velocity will decrease approximately 20 fps per inch for barrels less than 24 inches.		

HISTORICAL NOTES

- In 2005, Winchester introduced the new 325 Winchester Short Magnum (WSM) cartridge, the last in the company's series of short, beltless magnum cartridges designed for use in short-action rifles.

- The 325 WSM is the only purely American, 8mm, factory cartridge since the introduction of the 8mm Remington Magnum in 1977.
- Ballistic capabilities of the 325 WSM are roughly equal to the longer and larger 8mm Remington Magnum with the advantages of a beltless case that will fit in a short-action rifle. (The 8mm Remington Magnum requires a magnum-length action).
- Although Remington introduced their own line of "Short Action Ultra Magnum" cartridges in 2002, an 8mm variant was not included leaving the 325 WSM the sole occupant of this market niche.
- Certainly, Winchester seeks to build on the market success of their Short Magnum product line with the 325 WSM.
- Historically, the domestic market for American 8mm cartridges has been limited.

BALLISTIC NOTES

- Winchester markets the 325 WSM as a versatile big game cartridge suitable for all North American game and most African plains game.
- For this reason, factory loaded ammunition in this caliber includes a variety of heavy weight bullets, including 180, 200, and 220-grains.
- By comparison, the 8mm Remington Magnum is offered with just one bullet weight, a 200-grain.
- Despite its smaller size, the interior ballistic efficiency of the 325 WSM design allows it to nearly match muzzle velocities of the same 200-grain loaded in the 8mm Remington Magnum cartridge.
- While the 325 WSM is certainly capable of firing lightweight bullets, ammunition makers do not offer such a loading. Hint: you can handload these.

TECHNICAL NOTES

- All Winchester Short Magnum cartridges share the same 2.100 inch case length, .535 inch beltless head diameter and 35° shoulder angle in order to fit in short rifle actions.
- With its one turn in 10 inch rifling twist rate, the 325 WSM will stabilize long heavy bullets up to 220 grains.

HANDLOADING NOTES

- The heavy construction of the 325 WSM cartridge case can cause problems with full length resizing, which should be done for hunting loads. For this reason neck sizing is recommended for target and sight-in as rifles in 325 WSM caliber are bolt-action types.
- Long, heavy bullets weighing over 220 grains will take up too much volume inside the 325 WSM case to build a successful load.
- When handloaded with the Speer 150-grain Spitzer SP Hot-Cor® bullet, the 325 WSM becomes a very effective cartridge for deer hunting. The factory does not offer such a flat shooting load.
- The Speer 170-grain Semi-Spitzer SP Hot-Cor was designed especially for 8mm cartridges. With this bullet, the handloader can build effective loads for North American game equal to or better than factory loads with heavier bullets.
- Using the Speer 200-grain Spitzer SP Hot-Cor bullet, handloaders can build a load especially effective for heavy, North American game.

SAFETY NOTES

SPEER 200-grain Spitzer SP Hot-Cor @ a muzzle velocity of 2,837 fps:
- Maximum vertical altitude @ 90° elevation is 11,178 feet.
- Maximum horizontal distance to first impact with ground @ 36° elevation is 5,185 yards.

150 GRAINS

DIAMETER	SECTIONAL DENSITY
.323"	0.205

8mm Spitzer SP Hot-Cor®

Ballistic Coefficient	0.343
COAL Tested	2.850"
Speer Part No.	2277

			Starting Charge		Maximum Charge	
Propellant	Case	Primer	Weight (grains)	Muzzle Velocity (feet/sec)	Weight (grains)	Muzzle Velocity (feet/sec)
Winchester 760	Winchester	Federal 215	70.0	3134	74.0	3303
Hodgdon H414	Winchester	Federal 215	67.0	3103	71.0	3263
Ramshot Big Game	Winchester	Federal 215	68.0	3121	72.0	3260
Vihtavuori N540	Winchester	Federal 210	63.0	3060	67.0	3257
Alliant Reloder 15	Winchester	Federal 210	61.0	3090	65.0	3245
IMR 4895	Winchester	Federal 210	61.0	3047	65.0	3232
Hodgdon Varget	Winchester	Federal 210	61.0	3076	65.0	3222
IMR 3031	Winchester	Federal 210	57.0	3022	61.0	3207
Accurate 4064	Winchester	Federal 210	60.0	2986	64.0	3147
Alliant Reloder 16	Winchester	Federal 215	66.9	2610	74.0 C	2856
Alliant Reloder 17	Winchester	Federal 215	67.4	2623	72.5	2824
Alliant Power Pro 2000-MR	Winchester	Federal 215	62.8	2585	69.6	2822
Hodgdon H4350	Winchester	Federal 215	67.2	2588	74.6 C	2821
Vihtavuori N550	Winchester	Federal 215	62.1	2545	69.0	2812
Accurate 5744 (reduced load)	Winchester	Federal 210	30.0	1985	32.0	2097

WARNING! *Maximum loads should be used with CAUTION • C = Compressed Load*

170 GRAINS

DIAMETER	SECTIONAL DENSITY
.323"	0.233

8mm Semi-Spitzer SP Hot-Cor®

Ballistic Coefficient	0.311
COAL Tested	2.790"
Speer Part No.	2283

			Starting Charge		Maximum Charge	
Propellant	Case	Primer	Weight (grains)	Muzzle Velocity (feet/sec)	Weight (grains)	Muzzle Velocity (feet/sec)
Winchester 760	Winchester	Federal 215	66.0	2910	70.0	3074
Alliant Reloder 19	Winchester	Federal 210	70.0	2874	74.0 C	3064
Vihtavuori N540	Winchester	Federal 210	60.0	2879	64.0	3063
Hodgdon H414	Winchester	Federal 215	64.0	2878	68.0	3045
Ramshot Big Game	Winchester	Federal 215	64.0	2905	68.0	3044
Alliant Reloder 15	Winchester	Federal 210	58.0	2878	62.0	3038
IMR 4350	Winchester	Federal 210	65.0	2839	69.0	3027
Hodgdon Varget	Winchester	Federal 210	58.0	2865	62.0	3023
IMR 4895	Winchester	Federal 210	58.0	2852	62.0	3018
Accurate 4064	Winchester	Federal 210	56.0	2746	60.0	2906
Alliant Power Pro 4000-MR	Winchester	Federal 215	67.8	2501	73.8 C	2697
Alliant Reloder 16	Winchester	Federal 215	63.8	2452	70.6 C	2685
Alliant Reloder 17	Winchester	Federal 215	63.1	2415	69.9	2672
Hodgdon H4350	Winchester	Federal 215	63.7	2424	70.5	2638
Alliant Power Pro 2000-MR	Winchester	Federal 215	59.4	2429	65.8	2624

WARNING! Maximum loads should be used with CAUTION • C = Compressed Load

200 GRAINS

DIAMETER	SECTIONAL DENSITY
.323"	0.274

8mm Spitzer SP Hot-Cor®

Ballistic Coefficient	0.440
COAL Tested	2.840"
Speer Part No.	2285

Propellant	Case	Primer	Starting Charge Weight (grains)	Starting Charge Muzzle Velocity (feet/sec)	Maximum Charge Weight (grains)	Maximum Charge Muzzle Velocity (feet/sec)
Alliant Reloder 19	Winchester	Federal 210	65.0	2671	69.0	2837
IMR 4350	Winchester	Federal 210	61.0	2638	65.0	2802
Hodgdon H414	Winchester	Federal 215	60.0	2650	64.0	2791
Ramshot Big Game	Winchester	Federal 215	60.0	2654	64.0	2789
Winchester 760	Winchester	Federal 215	60.0	2614	64.0	2775
Accurate 4350	Winchester	Federal 210	62.0	2602	66.0	2766
Alliant Reloder 15	Winchester	Federal 210	53.0	2592	57.0	2742
Vihtavuori N540	Winchester	Federal 210	54.0	2559	58.0	2729
Alliant Reloder 26	Winchester	Federal 215	67.1	2347	72.0 C	2503
Alliant Reloder 23	Winchester	Federal 215	63.7	2240	70.5 C	2446
Alliant Power Pro 4000-MR	Winchester	Federal 215	61.1	2217	67.8	2442
Alliant Reloder 17	Winchester	Federal 215	59.1	2230	65.4	2435
IMR 4831	Winchester	Federal 215	61.2	2223	67.9 C	2430
Alliant Reloder 16	Winchester	Federal 215	58.8	2240	65.1	2418

WARNING! Maximum loads should be used with CAUTION • C = Compressed Load

8mm REMINGTON MAGNUM

Parent Cartridge:	300 H&H Magnum
Country of Origin:	USA
Year of Introduction:	1978
Designer(s):	Remington
Governing Body:	SAAMI/CIP

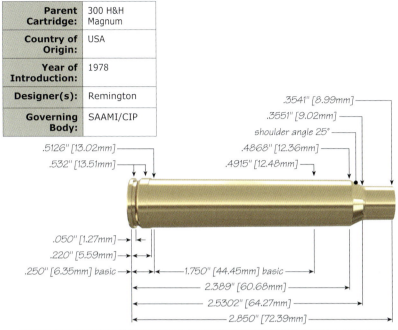

CARTRIDGE CASE DATA

Case Type:	Rimless, Belted, bottleneck		
Average Case Capacity:	98.0 grains H$_2$O	Max. Cartridge OAL	3.600 inch
Max. Case Length:	2.850 inch	Primer:	Large Rifle
Case Trim to Length:	2.840 inch	RCBS Shell holder:	# 4
Current Manufacturers:	Remington		

BALLISTIC DATA

Max. Average Pressure (MAP):	65,000 psi, 54,000 CUP – SAAMI; 63,817 psi - CIP	Test Barrel Length:	24 inch
Rifling Twist Rate:	1 turn in 10 inch		
Muzzle velocities of factory loaded ammunition	Bullet Wgt.		Muzzle velocity
	200-grain		2,900 fps
	Muzzle velocity will decrease approximately 20 fps per inch for barrels less than 24 inches.		

HISTORICAL NOTES

- When Remington introduced the 8mm Remington Magnum cartridge in 1978, they described their ballistic objectives for the new cartridge were to provide "…

optimum characteristics of flat shooting and high energy without developing excessively uncomfortable recoil."

- Inspiring though the hazy ballistic hyperbole may be, the recoil bit goes against the laws of physics.
  - The 8mm Remington Magnum became notable for its heavy recoil.
  - The part about high energy was true—too true. The 8mm Remington Magnum is too powerful for most North American game.
- The new 8mm Remington Magnum broke with convention in two ways:
  - At a time when short 30-06 Springfield length magnums were the hot tickets in the ammunition industry, the 8mm Remington Magnum was based on a full length 300 H&H Magnum case.
  - Its caliber was metric, but metric cartridges have never been popular with American sportsmen (with the exception of 6mm and 7mm).
- It will come as no surprise then, that sales of the 8mm Remington Magnum cartridge never reached critical mass. Remington is the sole manufacturer of this cartridge and they no longer produce rifles in this caliber.
- Today the 8mm Remington Magnum appears to be an orphan on life support. When will Remington pull the plug?

BALLISTIC NOTES

- The current Remington ammunition catalog lists only one loading for the 8mm Remington Magnum—a 200-grain Spitzer SP bullet loaded to a muzzle velocity of 2,900 fps.
- That said, the 8mm Remington Magnum can be handloaded with a variety of additional bullet weights.
- The Speer Semi-Spitzer SP Hot-Cor 170-grain can be handloaded to a maximum muzzle velocity of 3,172 fps in this cartridge. This bullet would be a good candidate for a general purpose load by dropping the muzzle velocity to about 2,800 fps.
- You can duplicate the 8mm Rem. Mag. factory load using the Speer 200-grain Spitzer SP Hot-Cor or, you can rev up the factory load muzzle velocity by nearly 100 fps.

TECHNICAL NOTES

- The 8mm Remington Magnum cartridge shares its rim, belt, and head dimensions as well as a 25° shoulder angle with the shorter 7mm Remington Magnum cartridge. However, the longer case length limits the 8mm Remington Magnum to rifles having long action lengths.
- Case capacity of the 8mm Rem. Mag. is virtually identical to the 340 Weatherby Magnum and 10% less than the 338 Remington Ultra Magnum.
- The 8mm Remington Magnum cartridge achieves its exceptional muzzle velocities the traditional way— by burning heavy powder charges and then adds a large dose of shoulder punishing recoil.
- MAP level of the 8mm Remington Magnum is equivalent to the 338 RUM.

HANDLOADING NOTES

- Remington is the sole source of new, empty, unprimed 8mm Remington Magnum brass cases for handloading.

- We recommend that you set your sizing dies to headspace the cartridge case on the shoulder instead of the belt.

SAFETY NOTES

SPEER 200-grain Spitzer SP Hot-Cor @ a muzzle velocity of 2,996 fps:
- Maximum vertical altitude @ 90° elevation is 11,433 feet.
- Maximum horizontal distance to first impact with ground @ 38° elevation is 5,275 yards.

150 GRAINS

DIAMETER	SECTIONAL DENSITY
.323"	0.205

8mm Spitzer SP Hot-Cor®

Ballistic Coefficient	0.343
COAL Tested	3.575"
Speer Part No.	2277

			Starting Charge		Maximum Charge	
Propellant	Case	Primer	Weight (grains)	Muzzle Velocity (feet/sec)	Weight (grains)	Muzzle Velocity (feet/sec)
IMR 4831	Remington	CCI 250	80.0	3194	86.0 C	3436
IMR 4350	Remington	CCI 250	77.0	3158	81.0	3322
Winchester 760	Remington	CCI 250	76.0	3076	80.0	3225
Hodgdon H380	Remington	CCI 250	72.0	3038	76.0	3214
Hodgdon H414	Remington	CCI 250	74.0	3025	78.0	3191
IMR 3031	Remington	CCI 250	63.0	2969	67.0	3149
IMR 4895	Remington	CCI 250	62.0	2955	66.0	3134

WARNING! *Maximum loads should be used with CAUTION • C = Compressed Load*

170 GRAINS

DIAMETER	SECTIONAL DENSITY
.323"	0.233

8mm Semi-Spitzer SP Hot-Cor®

Ballistic Coefficient	0.311
COAL Tested	3.575"
Speer Part No.	2283

			Starting Charge		Maximum Charge	
Propellant	Case	Primer	Weight (grains)	Muzzle Velocity (feet/sec)	Weight (grains)	Muzzle Velocity (feet/sec)
Alliant Reloder 17	Remington	CCI 250	72.0	2995	76.8	3172
Alliant Reloder 16	Remington	CCI 250	73.0	3007	77.4	3159
IMR 4831	Remington	CCI 250	74.0	2865	80.0	3114
IMR 4350	Remington	CCI 250	73.0	2902	77.0	3078
Hodgdon H380	Remington	CCI 250	67.0	2828	71.0	3000
Hodgdon H414	Remington	CCI 250	69.0	2817	73.0	2970
Winchester 760	Remington	CCI 250	70.0	2795	74.0	2965
IMR 4064	Remington	CCI 250	62.0	2761	66.0	2940
IMR 4895	Remington	CCI 250	59.0	2740	63.0	2919

WARNING! *Maximum loads should be used with CAUTION • C = Compressed Load*

200 GRAINS

DIAMETER	SECTIONAL DENSITY
.323"	0.274

8mm Spitzer SP Hot-Cor®

Ballistic Coefficient	0.440
COAL Tested	3.575"
Speer Part No.	2285

			Starting Charge		Maximum Charge	
Propellant	Case	Primer	Weight (grains)	Muzzle Velocity (feet/sec)	Weight (grains)	Muzzle Velocity (feet/sec)
IMR 4831	Remington	CCI 250	72.0	2763	78.0	2996
Alliant Power Pro 4000-MR	Remington	CCI 250	75.0	2870	78.6	2993
Alliant Reloder 17	Remington	CCI 250	69.5	2831	74.5	2985
IMR 7828	Remington	CCI 250	79.0	2712	83.0 C	2938
IMR 4350	Remington	CCI 250	70.0	2770	74.0	2936
Alliant Reloder 16	Remington	CCI 250	70.0	2813	73.0	2911
IMR 4064	Remington	CCI 250	60.0	2638	64.0	2803
IMR 4895	Remington	CCI 250	57.0	2564	61.0	2736
IMR 3031	Remington	CCI 250	57.0	2561	61.0	2732
IMR 4320	Remington	CCI 250	58.0	2544	62.0	2717

WARNING! *Maximum loads should be used with CAUTION • C = Compressed Load*

338 FEDERAL

Parent Cartridge:	308 Winchester
Country of Origin:	USA
Year of Introduction:	2005
Designer(s):	Federal
Governing Body:	SAAMI

CARTRIDGE CASE DATA

Case Type:	Rimless, bottleneck		
Average Case Capacity:	56.7 grains H$_2$O	Max. Cartridge OAL	2.820 inch
Max. Case Length:	2.015 inch	Primer:	Large Rifle
Case Trim to Length:	2.005 inch	RCBS Shell holder:	# 3
Current Manufacturers:	Federal		

BALLISTIC DATA

Max. Average Pressure (MAP):	62,000 psi, CUP not established for this round - SAAMI	Test Barrel Length:	24 inch
Rifling Twist Rate:	1 turn in 10 inch		
Muzzle velocities of factory loaded ammunition	Bullet Wgt.		Muzzle velocity
	185-grain		2,680 fps
	200-grain		2,700 fps
	Muzzle velocity will decrease approximately 20 fps per inch for barrels less than 24 inches.		

HISTORICAL NOTES

- Winchester created the market for .338 inch cartridges in 1958 with the introduction of their 338 Winchester Magnum. The popularity of Winchester's new cartridge spawned several competitors—both belted and beltless designs.

- Federal wanted to develop a cartridge with the company name on it. But, where to begin? Few gaps existed in the ballistic spectrum.

- One of the few gaps was the lack of a 338 caliber non-magnum woods cartridge for light rifles with short actions. The wildcat 338-08 cartridge looked promising, but needed changes to make the transition to commercial production.

- The changes were made and the new cartridge was standardized by SAAMI as the 338 Federal. Thus a new woods cartridge was born.
- Kimber, Sako, Steyr, Thompson-Center, and Savage offer rifles in the new caliber.
- The jury remains out on whether or not the 338 Federal has found a solid market niche. Old habits and old calibers die very hard indeed.
- Federal is the only manufacturer of this cartridge.

Interesting Fact

The 338 Federal was not the first new cartridge with the company's name on it. That honor goes to the 9mm Federal, a rimmed version of the 9mm Luger cartridge developed for law enforcement revolvers in 1989. The 338 Federal is the first rifle cartridge to carry the company name.

BALLISTIC NOTES

- The high ballistic coefficient (BC) of the bullets used in the 338 Federal offers a major advantage as a woods cartridge over its 35 caliber predecessors.
- This translates into greater striking velocity and energy, a flatter trajectory and increased maximum effective range over the 35 caliber "pumpkin rollers."
- Hunters have discovered that the high sectional density of the 338 caliber bullets enables them to buck brush as well as or better than 35 caliber bullets.
- Comparing down range ballistics of the 338 Federal with the 356 Winchester highlights the advantage of the former. At 200 yards the 200-grain bullet of the 338 Federal retains 2,241 fps of striking velocity and 2,231 ft-lbs of energy. The 200-grain bullet of the 356 Winchester retains 1,797 fps of striking velocity and 1,434 ft-lbs of energy at the same distance. Given a 100 yard zero, the trajectory of the 338 Federal bullet drops 4.5 inches while the 356 Winchester's bullet drops about 7 inches in 200 yards.
- To build a handload that approximates the ballistics of the 338 Federal factory load, we recommend the Speer 200-grain Spitzer SP Hot-Cor® bullet handloaded to a muzzle velocity of 2,598 fps.
- To take maximum advantage of the ballistic potential of the 338 Federal, we recommend the Speer 225-grain Spitzer BTSP bullet handloaded to a muzzle velocity of 2,440 fps. This boat tail bullet will provide the maximum possible striking velocity and energy at all ranges.

TECHNICAL NOTES

- Basically, the 338 Federal is a 308 Winchester cartridge necked up to accept .338 inch diameter bullets.
- Case head dimensions, rim, and case length are similar to the 308 Winchester as is the 20° shoulder angle.
- Maximum overall length of a loaded 338 Federal is slightly longer than the 308 Winchester.
- MAP levels remain the same as the 308 Winchester.

HANDLOADING NOTES

- If 338 Federal ammunition will be fired in bolt-action rifles, we recommend neck sizing to extend case life and reduce trimming chores for practice and sighting in,

and full length resizing for hunting loads and guns like the Savage MSR10.
- Fast burning propellants are the best choice for reloading the 338 Federal.

SAFETY NOTES

SPEER 225-grain Spitzer BTSP @ a muzzle velocity of 2,440 fps:
- Maximum vertical altitude @ 90° elevation is 14,598 ft.
- Maximum horizontal distance to first impact with ground @ 38° elevation is 6,958 yards.

200 GRAINS

DIAMETER	SECTIONAL DENSITY
.338"	0.250

338 Spitzer SP Hot-Cor®

Ballistic Coefficient	0.426
COAL Tested	2.820"
Speer Part No.	2405

Propellant	Case	Primer	Starting Charge		Maximum Charge	
			Weight (grains)	Muzzle Velocity (feet/sec)	Weight (grains)	Muzzle Velocity (feet/sec)
Alliant Power Pro Varmint	Federal	Federal 210	44.6	2499	49.6	2708
Hodgdon CFE 223	Federal	Federal 210	46.1	2478	51.0 C	2682
Alliant AR-Comp	Federal	Federal 210	41.8	2458	46.3	2655
IMR 8208 XBR	Federal	Federal 210	41.8	2417	46.3	2625
Alliant Reloder 15	Federal	Federal 210	44.0	2508	46.0 C	2598
Alliant Power Pro 1200-R	Federal	Federal 210	38.0	2393	42.2	2579
Hodgdon Varget	Federal	Federal 210	45.0	2485	47.0 C	2571
Winchester 748	Federal	Federal 210	45.5	2504	47.5	2570
Accurate LT-32	Federal	Federal 210	38.2	2342	42.2	2528
Ramshot TAC	Federal	Federal 210	42.0	2421	44.0	2504
Hodgdon H322	Federal	Federal 210	38.0	2303	40.0	2451
Alliant Reloder 10X	Federal	Federal 210	36.5	2345	38.5	2444
Accurate 2015	Federal	Federal 210	38.0	2303	40.0	2404
Alliant Reloder 7	Federal	Federal 210	34.5	2306	36.5	2403
IMR 4198	Federal	Federal 210	33.5	2268	35.5	2368

225 GRAINS

DIAMETER	SECTIONAL DENSITY
.338"	0.281

338 Spitzer BTSP

Ballistic Coefficient	0.497
COAL Tested	2.820"
Speer Part No.	2406

			Starting Charge		Maximum Charge	
Propellant	Case	Primer	Weight (grains)	Muzzle Velocity (feet/sec)	Weight (grains)	Muzzle Velocity (feet/sec)
Alliant Power Pro 2000-MR	Federal	Federal 210	45.4	2337	50.5 C	2551
Alliant Power Pro Varmint	Federal	Federal 210	42.5	2350	47.0 C	2545
Hodgdon CFE 223	Federal	Federal 210	44.1	2357	48.6 C	2544
Alliant AR-Comp	Federal	Federal 210	39.6	2305	43.9 C	2491
IMR 8208 XBR	Federal	Federal 210	39.8	2280	43.9 C	2462
Alliant Reloder 15	Federal	Federal 210	42.0	2350	44.0 C	2440
Hodgdon Varget	Federal	Federal 210	42.5	2326	44.5	2408
Winchester 748	Federal	Federal 210	42.5	2309	44.5	2392
Ramshot TAC	Federal	Federal 210	40.0	2277	42.0	2368
Accurate LT-32	Federal	Federal 210	35.8	2176	39.8 C	2361
IMR 3031	Federal	Federal 210	37.0	2204	39.0	2323
Alliant Reloder 10X	Federal	Federal 210	35.0	2207	37.0	2299
Hodgdon H322	Federal	Federal 210	35.5	2174	37.5	2276
Alliant Reloder 7	Federal	Federal 210	33.0	2161	35.0	2256
Accurate 2015	Federal	Federal 210	35.5	2139	37.5	2237

WARNING! Maximum loads should be used with CAUTION • C = Compressed Load

338 RUGER COMPACT MAGNUM

Alternate Names:	338 RCM
Parent Cartridge:	375 Ruger
Country of Origin:	USA
Year of Introduction:	2008
Designer(s):	Sturm Ruger & Hornady
Governing Body:	SAAMI/CIP

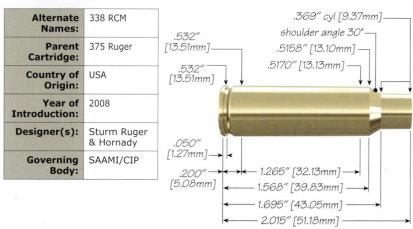

CARTRIDGE CASE DATA

Case Type:	Rimless, bottleneck		
Average Case Capacity:	75.0 grains H_2O	Max. Cartridge OAL	2.840 inch
Max. Case Length:	2.015 inch	Primer:	Large Rifle
Case Trim to Length:	2.005 inch	RCBS Shell holder:	# 4
Current Manufacturers:	Hornady		

BALLISTIC DATA

Max. Average Pressure (MAP):	65,000 psi, CUP not established for this cartridge - SAAMI	Test Barrel Length:	24 inch
Rifling Twist Rate:	1 turn in 10 inch		
Muzzle velocities of factory loaded ammunition	Bullet Wgt.		Muzzle velocity
	200-grain		2,950 fps
	225-grain		2,750 fps

Muzzle velocity will decrease approximately 20 fps per inch for barrels less than 24 inches.

HISTORICAL NOTES

- Prior to 2006, a market for 338 caliber, short/compact magnum cartridges did not exist.
- Ammunition makers saw the market for 338 cartridges to be in the big magnums such as the 338 Winchester Magnum and 338 Lapua Magnum.
- Thinking outside the box, Federal recognized a niche market for a short,

compact 338 non-magnum cartridge that would fit in a short action bolt rifles. Accordingly, Federal developed their 338 Federal cartridge to these parameters.

- Ruger followed suit in 2008 with their 338 Ruger Compact Magnum. Ruger's new cartridge was indeed a magnum while the 338 Federal was not.
- Today, the 338 Ruger Compact Magnum is offered by Hornady while Federal offers their 338 Federal cartridge. Other ammunition makers have not reacted to the new market.
- The jury is still out on whether or not a real market exists for a compact 338 caliber magnum cartridge.
- In Europe, no market for 338 Short/Compact Magnum cartridges has developed.

BALLISTIC NOTES

- Comparing the ballistics of the 338 RCM and the 338 Federal, it becomes apparent that these two cartridges are aimed at different markets. Both are factory-loaded with a 200-grain bullet. Muzzle velocity of this bullet from the 338 RCM is 2,950 fps; muzzle velocity of this same bullet from the 338 Federal is 2,630 fps.
- The muzzle velocity of the 338 RCM cartridge is fully comparable to the 338 Winchester Magnum with equivalent bullet weights.
- According to Ruger, the compact case configuration of the 338 RCM is the reason it can deliver equivalent muzzle velocities to the big 338 Winchester Magnum cartridge while burning 10-15% less propellant.
- In theory, the efficiency of the compact case design is due to its low length-to-diameter ratio that allows a smaller amount of unburned propellant to follow the bullet up the barrel thus conserving energy.
- The 338 RCM ballistic performance is built on the 200-grain bullet. Long, heavy bullets weighing over 250-grains take up too much volume inside the 338 RCM case to build a successful load.
- That said, standard magnum cartridges are more flexible in that they can be loaded with a greater variety of bullet weights.
- The 338 RCM is intended for medium and large game.

TECHNICAL NOTES

- The 338 RCM is derived from the ubiquitous 300 & 375 H&H Magnum cases, a family trait it shares with its smaller brother, the 300 RCM.
- By using very little case taper and a sharp shoulder, the 338 RCM cartridge offers a very respectable case capacity of 75 grains of H_2O.
- The 338 RCM cartridge case is quite capable of containing the high MAP levels of the new compact magnum cartridges.
- 338 RCM cases can be made by necking up 300 RCM brass or necking down 375 Ruger cases.

HANDLOADING NOTES

- As recoil of the 338 RCM in a short action rifle is substantial, the bullets of all handloaded 338 RCM cartridges should be securely crimped to prevent bullet set-back in the magazine.

- Speer offers three bullets for handloading the 338 RCM:
  - The 200-grain Spitzer Soft Point Hot-Cor is an all-purpose bullet that can be handloaded to a muzzle velocity of 2,900 fps to duplicate the ballistics of factory ammunition.
  - The 225-grain Soft Point Boat Tail (BTSP) bullet is the best choice for hunting at longer ranges loaded to a muzzle velocity of approximately 2,700 fps.
  - The ammunition makers do not offer a 250-grain bullet in 338 RCM caliber. However, you can one-up the factory by handloading this bullet to a muzzle velocity of approximately 2,600 fps. Makes for a very effective big game load.
- The 338 RCM cartridge prefers slow burning propellants.

SAFETY NOTES

SPEER 225-grain BTSP bullet @ a muzzle velocity of 2,750 fps:
- Maximum vertical altitude @ 90° elevation is 15,594 feet.
- Maximum horizontal distance to first impact with the ground @ 38° elevation is 7,315 yards.

200 GRAINS

DIAMETER	SECTIONAL DENSITY
.338"	0.250

338 Spitzer SP Hot-Cor®

Ballistic Coefficient	0.426
COAL Tested	2.820"
Speer Part No.	2405

			Starting Charge		Maximum Charge	
Propellant	Case	Primer	Weight (grains)	Muzzle Velocity (feet/sec)	Weight (grains)	Muzzle Velocity (feet/sec)
Alliant Reloder 16	Hornady	CCI 250	58.1	2638	64.5 C	2898
Accurate 2700	Hornady	CCI 250	57.9	2663	64.1	2897
Alliant Power Pro 2000-MR	Hornady	CCI 250	55.6	2652	61.5	2889
Ramshot Big Game	Hornady	CCI 250	56.4	2643	62.8	2865
Winchester 760	Hornady	CCI 250	57.3	2632	63.5	2863
Hodgdon 4350	Hornady	CCI 250	58.5	2632	64.7 C	2858
Alliant Reloder 17	Hornady	CCI 250	55.3	2551	61.2	2835
Hodgdon CFE 223	Hornady	CCI 250	52.9	2658	58.5	2827
Alliant Reloder 15	Hornady	CCI 250	52.1	2591	57.7	2826
Vihtavuori N550	Hornady	CCI 250	54.1	2561	59.9	2813
Alliant Power Pro Varmint	Hornady	CCI 250	50.2	2582	55.8	2811
Hodgdon Varget	Hornady	CCI 250	49.9	2593	55.4	2785
IMR 4064	Hornady	CCI 250	50.0	2537	55.5	2782
IMR 4451	Hornady	CCI 250	56.0	2515	62.1 C	2766

WARNING! Maximum loads should be used with CAUTION • C = Compressed Load

225 GRAINS

DIAMETER	SECTIONAL DENSITY
.338"	0.281

338 Spitzer BTSP

Ballistic Coefficient	0.497
COAL Tested	2.840"
Speer Part No.	2406

			Starting Charge		Maximum Charge	
Propellant	Case	Primer	Weight (grains)	Muzzle Velocity (feet/sec)	Weight (grains)	Muzzle Velocity (feet/sec)
Alliant Reloder 16	Hornady	CCI 250	53.6	2474	59.6 C	2716
Alliant Power Pro 2000-MR	Hornady	CCI 250	52.1	2484	57.5	2710
Accurate 2700	Hornady	CCI 250	53.6	2476	59.4	2700
Ramshot Big Game	Hornady	CCI 250	52.8	2435	58.6	2676
Hodgdon 4350	Hornady	CCI 250	54.1	2469	59.9 C	2671
Winchester 760	Hornady	CCI 250	52.4	2434	58.0	2664
Alliant Reloder 17	Hornady	CCI 250	51.1	2402	56.8	2661
Alliant Reloder 15	Hornady	CCI 250	48.8	2437	54.2	2659
Alliant Power Pro Varmint	Hornady	CCI 250	47.1	2420	52.2	2630
Vihtavuori N550	Hornady	CCI 250	50.2	2373	55.5	2628
IMR 4064	Hornady	CCI 250	47.2	2422	52.4	2623
Hodgdon CFE 223	Hornady	CCI 250	48.6	2403	53.9	2621
Hodgdon Varget	Hornady	CCI 250	47.0	2438	52.0	2609
IMR 4451	Hornady	CCI 250	52.5	2359	58.1 C	2578

WARNING! Maximum loads should be used with CAUTION • C = Compressed Load

250 GRAINS

DIAMETER	SECTIONAL DENSITY
.338"	0.313

338 Grand Slam® SP

Ballistic Coefficient	0.436
COAL Tested	2.800"
Speer Part No.	2408

			Starting Charge		Maximum Charge	
Propellant	Case	Primer	Weight (grains)	Muzzle Velocity (feet/sec)	Weight (grains)	Muzzle Velocity (feet/sec)
Alliant Reloder 19	Hornady	CCI 250	57.3	2375	63.9 C	2602
Alliant Reloder 16	Hornady	CCI 250	53.7	2384	59.3 C	2588
Alliant Power Pro 4000-MR	Hornady	CCI 250	55.8	2383	61.8 C	2570
Alliant Power Pro 2000-MR	Hornady	CCI 250	50.7	2315	56.2	2560
Accurate 2700	Hornady	CCI 250	52.4	2342	58.0 C	2551
Ramshot Big Game	Hornady	CCI 250	51.6	2333	57.4	2540
Alliant Reloder 17	Hornady	CCI 250	50.2	2271	55.8 C	2528
Hodgdon 4350	Hornady	CCI 250	52.9	2324	58.5 C	2527
Winchester 760	Hornady	CCI 250	51.1	2312	56.4	2514
Alliant Reloder 15	Hornady	CCI 250	47.1	2282	52.3	2495
Vihtavuori N550	Hornady	CCI 250	49.1	2237	54.3	2465
Hodgdon CFE 223	Hornady	CCI 250	49.0	2281	53.1	2456
IMR 4451	Hornady	CCI 250	51.3	2231	57.0	2449
Alliant Power Pro Varmint	Hornady	CCI 250	45.3	2237	50.3	2447

WARNING! Maximum loads should be used with CAUTION • C = Compressed Load

338 WINCHESTER MAGNUM

Parent Cartridge:	375 H&H Magnum
Country of Origin:	USA
Year of Introduction:	1958
Designer(s):	Winchester
Governing Body:	SAAMI/CIP

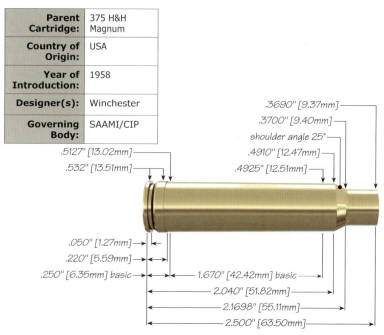

CARTRIDGE CASE DATA

Case Type:	Rimless, belted, bottleneck
Average Case Capacity:	86.0 grains H_2O
Max. Cartridge OAL:	3.340 inch
Max. Case Length:	2.500 inch
Primer:	Large Rifle
Case Trim to Length:	2.490 inch
RCBS Shell holder:	# 4
Current Manufacturers:	Winchester, Federal, Remington, Hornady, Norma, Nosler

BALLISTIC DATA

Max. Average Pressure (MAP):	64,000 psi, 54,000 CUP – SAAMI; 62,000 CIP
Test Barrel Length:	24 inch
Rifling Twist Rate:	1 turn in 10 inch

Muzzle velocities of factory loaded ammunition		
	Bullet Wgt.	Muzzle velocity
	180-grain	3,100 fps
	200-grain	2,960 fps
	225-grain	2,800 fps
	250-grain	2,650 fps

Muzzle velocity will decrease approximately 20 fps per inch for barrels less than 24 inches.

HISTORICAL NOTES

- In 1958, Winchester released their new 338 Winchester Magnum cartridge to critical acclaim. The caliber quickly became and has remained a popular choice in the North American market for hunting big game of all types including large bear. Experience soon proved it was an excellent choice for African plains game as well.

- The short case length of the new 338 Winchester Magnum cartridge allowed it to fit in standard, 30-06 Springfield length rifle actions.

- In other words, 338 Winchester Magnum was a "short magnum" which meant it was based on a 300 H&H Magnum case shortened to a length approximately that of a 30-06 Springfield. Today, the term "short magnum" means something quite different!

- The 338 Winchester Magnum was the second entry in Winchester's short magnum product line beginning with the 458 Winchester Magnum in 1956 followed by the 264 Winchester Magnum in 1958 and the 300 Winchester Magnum in 1963.

- The 338 Winchester Magnum cartridge was a game changer that created a whole new market for 338 caliber cartridges where none had existed before.

- Prior to 1958, in the minds of big game hunters, the choice of caliber went directly from 30 to 375. Anything in between was an oddity.

- The reputation of the new cartridge grew as hunters reported outstanding results on heavy North American game.

- The foundation of the 338 Winchester Magnum's reputation rests firmly in North America. This cartridge has not gained popularity among African hunters who feel it is too light for their game (many African professional hunters feel the minimum cartridge for African hunting is 375 H&H Magnum).

- European hunters have largely ignored the 338 Winchester Magnum as it has no practical application for their type of game.

- In marketing terms, the 338 Winchester Magnum has filled its short magnum slot so well, no competitors have emerged to challenge it.

BALLISTIC NOTES

- The 338 Winchester Magnum's ballistic reputation rests on two popular bullet weights: 200 and 225 grains.

- Winchester favors the lighter bullet in their product line while Remington prefers the heavier item. Likely, this is due to an effort in marketing differentiation efforts rather than ballistic ones.

- Of late, 180-grain and 250-grain bullets have been added to some factory product lines in this caliber.

- Duplicating factory load ballistic performance is easy with the Speer 200-grain Spitzer SP Hot-Cor®.

- Magnum cartridges need a premium bullet to take maximum advantage of their ballistic potential. For this reason, we recommend the Speer Grand Slam® SP premium 250-grain bullet for the 338 Winchester Magnum.

TECHNICAL NOTES

- Basically, the 338 Winchester Magnum is based on a shortened 300 H&H Magnum case with less body taper to increase case capacity.
- In technical terms, the 338 Winchester Magnum harbors no ballistic secrets, so much as a combination of proven features.
  - It is a belted case, but can be loaded so as to headspace on its shoulder (much better).
  - It has a very conservative 25° shoulder angle and an adequate neck length to ease manufacture and reduce trimming chores.
  - Case capacity of the 338 Win. Mag. is approximately 15% less than the 340 Weatherby Magnum and 50% less than the 338 RUM cartridge.
  - MAP levels are similar to and competitive with other 338 Magnums at 64,000 psi.
  - The 1 turn in 10 inch rifling twist will stabilize a wide range of bullet weights.
  - With a Maximum Overall Loaded length of 3.340 inches, the 338 Winchester Magnum will fit in standard 30-06 Springfield actions.
  - Factory loaded ammunition in 338 Winchester Magnum caliber is offered by all major domestic ammunition makers, but few foreign makers except Norma.

SAFETY NOTES

SPEER 225-grain Spitzer BTSP @ a muzzle velocity of 2,944 fps:
- Maximum vertical altitude @ 90° elevation is 16,380 feet.
- Maximum horizontal distance to first impact with ground @ 38° elevation is 7,534 yards.

200 GRAINS

DIAMETER	SECTIONAL DENSITY
.338"	0.250

338 Spitzer SP Hot-Cor®

Ballistic Coefficient	0.426
COAL Tested	3.300"
Speer Part No.	2405

Propellant	Case	Primer	Starting Charge Weight (grains)	Starting Charge Muzzle Velocity (feet/sec)	Maximum Charge Weight (grains)	Maximum Charge Muzzle Velocity (feet/sec)
Alliant Power Pro 4000-MR	Federal	Federal 215	70.9	2808	78.8 C	3059
Alliant Reloder 16	Federal	Federal 215	67.1	2799	74.3 C	3041
Alliant Reloder 17	Federal	Federal 215	66.7	2751	74.0	3009
IMR 4451	Federal	Federal 215	67.7	2696	75.7 C	2966
IMR 4350	Winchester	CCI 250	69.5	2791	73.5	2959
IMR 4831	Winchester	CCI 250	70.5	2782	74.5	2956
Hodgdon H4350	Winchester	CCI 250	71.0	2697	75.0 C	2932
Hodgdon H414	Winchester	CCI 250	66.0	2793	70.0	2905
Hodgdon H4831SC	Winchester	CCI 250	74.0	2781	78.0 C	2887
IMR 7828	Winchester	CCI 250	77.0	2682	81.0 C	2882
Vihtavuori N150	Winchester	CCI 250	61.0	2598	65.0	2824
Accurate 3100	Winchester	CCI 250	73.0	2654	77.0 C	2823
Winchester 760	Winchester	CCI 250	66.0	2604	70.0	2816
Alliant Reloder 19	Winchester	CCI 250	72.0	2596	76.0 C	2806
Accurate 2700	Winchester	CCI 250	65.0	2550	69.0	2757
IMR 3031	Winchester	CCI 250	55.0	2469	59.0	2627
IMR 4064	Winchester	CCI 250	57.0	2440	61.0	2610

WARNING! Maximum loads should be used with CAUTION • C = Compressed Load

225 GRAINS

DIAMETER	SECTIONAL DENSITY
.338"	0.281

338 Spitzer BTSP	
Ballistic Coefficient	0.497
COAL Tested	3.340"
Speer Part No.	2406

			Starting Charge		Maximum Charge	
Propellant	Case	Primer	Weight (grains)	Muzzle Velocity (feet/sec)	Weight (grains)	Muzzle Velocity (feet/sec)
Alliant Reloder 19	Winchester	CCI 250	74.0	2791	78.0 C	2944
Alliant Reloder 26	Federal	Federal 215	71.0	2669	78.3 C	2933
Hodgdon H4350	Winchester	CCI 250	71.0	2739	75.0 C	2898
Alliant Power Pro 4000-MR	Federal	Federal 215	65.6	2636	72.6 C	2862
Accurate 2700	Winchester	CCI 250	68.0	2700	72.0	2855
Alliant Reloder 16	Federal	Federal 215	63.8	2627	70.6 C	2854
Alliant Reloder 17	Federal	Federal 215	62.2	2584	69.1	2829
IMR 4350	Winchester	CCI 250	65.0	2644	69.0	2819
IMR 4831	Winchester	CCI 250	66.0	2655	70.0	2811
Accurate 3100	Winchester	CCI 250	73.0	2653	77.0 C	2807
Hodgdon H4831SC	Winchester	CCI 250	69.0	2611	73.0	2761
Alliant Reloder 23	Federal	Federal 215	69.5	2648	72.5 C	2739
IMR 4064	Winchester	CCI 250	56.0	2585	60.0	2721
Vihtavuori N165	Winchester	CCI 250	70.0	2496	74.0 C	2670

WARNING! Maximum loads should be used with CAUTION • C = Compressed Load

250 GRAINS

DIAMETER	SECTIONAL DENSITY
.338"	0.313

338 Grand Slam® SP

Ballistic Coefficient	0.436
COAL Tested	3.300"
Speer Part No.	2408

			Starting Charge		Maximum Charge	
Propellant	Case	Primer	Weight (grains)	Muzzle Velocity (feet/sec)	Weight (grains)	Muzzle Velocity (feet/sec)
Alliant Reloder 26	Federal	Federal 215	69.0	2506	76.6 C	2764
Alliant Power Pro 4000-MR	Federal	Federal 215	64.7	2467	71.9 C	2693
Alliant Reloder 17	Federal	Federal 215	61.9	2437	68.7 C	2665
Alliant Reloder 19	Winchester	CCI 250	68.0	2478	72.0 C	2664
IMR 4350	Winchester	CCI 250	65.0	2509	69.0	2655
Alliant Reloder 16	Federal	Federal 215	62.7	2465	68.3 C	2655
Alliant Reloder 22	Winchester	CCI 250	69.0	2441	73.0 C	2653
IMR 7828	Winchester	CCI 250	71.0	2480	75.0	2652
Alliant Reloder 23	Federal	Federal 215	66.1	2444	72.4 C	2644
Vihtavuori N165	Winchester	CCI 250	70.0	2439	74.0 C	2637
IMR 4831	Winchester	CCI 250	65.0	2451	69.0	2620
Accurate 3100	Winchester	CCI 250	69.0	2472	73.0 C	2616
Hodgdon H4831SC	Winchester	CCI 250	67.0	2492	71.0 C	2616
Hodgdon H4350	Winchester	CCI 250	64.0	2387	68.0 C	2581
Hodgdon H414	Winchester	CCI 250	62.0	2357	66.0	2548
Hodgdon H1000	Winchester	CCI 250	73.0	2380	77.0 C	2545
Accurate 2700	Winchester	CCI 250	61.0	2394	65.0	2526

WARNING! Maximum loads should be used with CAUTION • C = Compressed Load

340 WEATHERBY MAGNUM

Parent Cartridge:	375 H&H Magnum
Country of Origin:	USA
Year of Introduction:	1962
Designer(s):	Roy Weatherby
Governing Body:	SAAMI/CIP

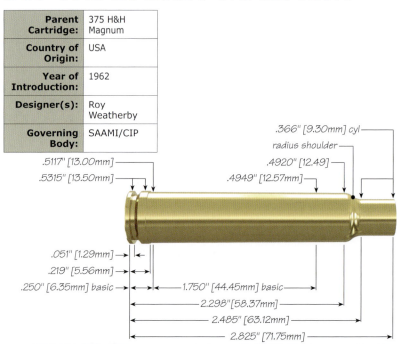

CARTRIDGE CASE DATA

Case Type:	Belted, rimless, double radius shoulder		
Average Case Capacity:	98.0 grains H₂O	Max. Cartridge OAL	3.675 inch
Max. Case Length:	2.825 inch	Primer:	Large Rifle
Case Trim to Length:	2.815 inch	RCBS Shell holder:	# 4
Current Manufacturers:	Weatherby, Norma		

BALLISTIC DATA

Max. Average Pressure (MAP):	62,500 psi, 53,500 CUP - SAAMI	Test Barrel Length:	24 inch
Rifling Twist Rate:	1 turn in 10 inch		
Muzzle velocities of factory loaded ammunition	Bullet Wgt.		Muzzle velocity
	225-grain		3,066 fps
	250-grain		2,963 fps
Muzzle velocity will decrease approximately 25 fps per inch for barrels less than 24 inches.			

HISTORICAL NOTES

- Weatherby introduced the 340 Weatherby Magnum in 1962 to fill a gap in their product line between the 300 Weatherby Magnum and the 378 Weatherby Magnum.

- Undoubtedly, this was in reaction to the success of the 338 Winchester Magnum introduced a few years earlier that established a market for 338 cartridges.

- The 340 Weatherby Magnum is the largest caliber Weatherby offers that is based on the full length "founding father" 300 Weatherby Magnum case.

- Introduction of the 338 Remington Ultra Magnum in 1999 threatened the position of the 340 Weatherby Magnum by offering near-equivalent ballistic numbers determined by the shooter's preference of rifle manufacturer (when the muzzle velocity from the Remington's 24 inch barrel vs. the muzzle velocity of Weatherby's 26 inch barrel are taken into account).

- However, never a company to be "out magnumized", Weatherby reset the 338 caliber ballistic bar with the 338-378 Weatherby Magnum.

BALLISTIC NOTES

- The 340 Weatherby Magnum's reputation is built on 225 and 250-grain bullet weights.

- By any measure, the 338 Winchester Magnum is not in the same ballistic class as the 340 Weatherby Magnum.

- For most North American medium game the 340 Weatherby Magnum suffers from a wretched excess of striking energy due to its high muzzle velocity and heavy, 250-grain bullet. The lighter 225-grain bullet at a higher muzzle velocity does not help matters much.

- Basically, the 340 Weatherby Magnum is a cartridge for large heavy game. It is also an excellent choice for African plains game, but too light for dangerous game.

- Many hunters who favor the 340 Weatherby Magnum feel the 250-grain bullet is the best all-around choice for this caliber. If you agree, then the premium Speer 250-grain Grand Slam® SP is a reliable choice for this cartridge.

- The factory does not offer a 340 Weatherby Magnum load with a 200-grain Spitzer soft point bullet. However, as a handloader you can "go where the factories do not" with the Speer 200-grain Spitzer SP Hot-Cor®. This lighter bullet can be driven at muzzle velocities approaching 3,100 fps which will provide a flat trajectory and excellent terminal performance.

TECHNICAL NOTES

- The 340 Weatherby Magnum follows the tried and true Weatherby process of blowing out a full length 375 H&H Magnum case to reduce body taper and increase case capacity. Its 3.675 inch overall loaded length requires a magnum length action.

- The 340 Weatherby Magnum produces prodigious muzzle velocities the old fashioned way—it burns large amounts of powder regardless of the efficiency of the process. The astute reader will note that it is completely the opposite of modern practices with the new "efficient" short magnums. Perhaps there is something to the brute force school of internal ballistics after all.

- There are two secrets to the ballistic performance of Weatherby Magnum cartridges:
  - The first is that the chamber throats of Weatherby cartridges are free-bored for a considerable distance to reduce MAP levels.
  - Second, Weatherby muzzle velocities are taken from a 26 inch test barrel; the standard industry test barrel is 24 inches in length.
- In technical terms, there is no secret to the design of the 340 Weatherby Magnum:
  - It is a belted case that headspaces on its belt (as all proper magnums should according to Holland & Holland).
  - It has double radii shoulder angle, very little body taper and a one caliber neck length to maximize case capacity.
  - Case capacity is larger than all other 338 Magnum cartridges save the new 338 Remington Ultra Magnum and the chart topping 338-378 Weatherby Magnum.
  - The 1 turn in 10 inch rifling twist of the 340 Weatherby Magnum will stabilize a wide range of bullet weights including long boat tail bullets.

HANDLOADING NOTES

- If need be, 340 Weatherby Magnum brass can be formed by necking up unfired 300 Weatherby Magnum or 300 H&H Magnum cases, fire forming them, then trimming them to length. An alternate choice is to begin with unfired 375 H&H Magnum brass, neck them down, fire form them, then trim to length. Annealing the case necks afterward will extend case life.
- As most 340 Weatherby Magnum cartridges will be fired from bolt-action rifles, we strongly recommend neck sizing to extend case life. Hunting with full length sized cases is recommended.
- As do all big magnum cartridges, the 340 Weatherby Magnum works best with slow burning propellants.

SAFETY NOTES

SPEER 225-grain Spitzer BTSP @ a muzzle velocity of 2,924 fps:
- Maximum vertical altitude @ 90° elevation is 16,152 feet.
- Maximum horizontal distance to first impact with ground @ 38° elevation is 7,511 yards.

200 GRAINS

DIAMETER	SECTIONAL DENSITY
.338"	0.250

338 Spitzer SP Hot-Cor®

Ballistic Coefficient	0.426
COAL Tested	3.560"
Speer Part No.	2405

			Starting Charge		Maximum Charge	
Propellant	Case	Primer	Weight (grains)	Muzzle Velocity (feet/sec)	Weight (grains)	Muzzle Velocity (feet/sec)
Alliant Reloder 17	Federal	Federal 215	70.9	2838	78.7	3104
IMR 4831	Federal	Federal 215	81.0	2923	85.0 C	3073
IMR 4350	Federal	Federal 215	79.0	2907	83.0 C	3058
Alliant Reloder 19	Federal	Federal 215	83.0	2899	87.0 C	3032
Winchester 760	Federal	Federal 215	76.0	2879	80.0	3012
Vihtavuori N540	Federal	Federal 215	71.0	2872	75.0	3006
Hodgdon H4350	Federal	Federal 215	77.0	2854	81.0	3004
Hodgdon H4831SC	Federal	Federal 215	85.0	2881	89.0 C	2989
Alliant Reloder 15	Federal	Federal 215	69.0	2796	73.0	2973
Accurate 4350	Federal	Federal 215	80.0	2821	84.0 C	2962
Ramshot Big Game	Federal	Federal 215	71.0	2776	75.0	2945

WARNING! *Maximum loads should be used with CAUTION • C = Compressed Load*

225 GRAINS

DIAMETER	SECTIONAL DENSITY
.338"	0.281

338 Spitzer BTSP	
Ballistic Coefficient	0.497
COAL Tested	3.670"
Speer Part No.	2406

Propellant	Case	Primer	Starting Charge Weight (grains)	Starting Charge Muzzle Velocity (feet/sec)	Maximum Charge Weight (grains)	Maximum Charge Muzzle Velocity (feet/sec)
Alliant Reloder 26	Federal	Federal 215	78.0	2709	86.3	3018
Alliant Power Pro 4000-MR	Federal	Federal 215	73.1	2703	81.1	2959
Alliant Reloder 23	Federal	Federal 215	75.5	2690	83.8 C	2951
Alliant Reloder 19	Federal	Federal 215	81.0	2776	85.0 C	2924
IMR 4831	Federal	Federal 215	78.0	2765	82.0	2911
Alliant Reloder 17	Federal	Federal 215	66.9	2664	74.1	2905
Alliant Reloder 22	Federal	Federal 215	83.0	2799	87.0 C	2901
Hodgdon H4350	Federal	Federal 215	75.0	2742	79.0	2892
IMR 4350	Federal	Federal 215	76.0	2738	80.0	2886
Hodgdon H4831SC	Federal	Federal 215	82.0	2755	86.0	2882
Accurate 4350	Federal	Federal 215	77.0	2697	81.0	2864
Winchester 760	Federal	Federal 215	73.0	2728	77.0	2854
Vihtavuori N540	Federal	Federal 215	68.0	2686	72.0	2822
Alliant Reloder 15	Federal	Federal 215	66.0	2653	70.0	2799
Ramshot Big Game	Federal	Federal 215	67.0	2611	71.0	2751

WARNING! Maximum loads should be used with CAUTION • C = Compressed Load

250 GRAINS

DIAMETER	SECTIONAL DENSITY
.338"	0.313

338 Grand Slam® SP

Ballistic Coefficient	0.436
COAL Tested	3.610"
Speer Part No.	2408

			Starting Charge		Maximum Charge	
Propellant	Case	Primer	Weight (grains)	Muzzle Velocity (feet/sec)	Weight (grains)	Muzzle Velocity (feet/sec)
Alliant Reloder 26	Federal	Federal 215	76.2	2541	84.6 C	2865
IMR 7977	Federal	Federal 215	81.1	2504	90.2 C	2807
Vihtavuori N560	Federal	Federal 215	81.0	2668	85.0 C	2802
Alliant Reloder 23	Federal	Federal 215	74.4	2546	82.4 C	2797
Accurate MagPro	Federal	Federal 215	84.0	2669	88.0 C	2789
Alliant Reloder 19	Federal	Federal 215	79.0	2644	83.0	2788
Alliant Reloder 22	Federal	Federal 215	81.0	2634	85.0	2781
IMR 7828	Federal	Federal 215	81.0	2613	85.0 C	2747
IMR 4831	Federal	Federal 215	75.0	2607	79.0	2746
Hodgdon H4350	Federal	Federal 215	73.0	2608	77.0	2733
IMR 4350	Federal	Federal 215	73.0	2596	77.0	2731
Accurate 4350	Federal	Federal 215	75.0	2574	79.0 C	2720
Ramshot Magnum	Federal	Federal 215	86.0	2623	90.0 C	2711

WARNING! Maximum loads should be used with CAUTION • C = Compressed Load

338 REMINGTON ULTRA MAGNUM

Alternate Names:	338 RUM
Parent Cartridge:	300 Remington Ultra Magnum
Country of Origin:	USA
Year of Introduction:	1999
Designer(s):	Remington
Governing Body:	SAAMI

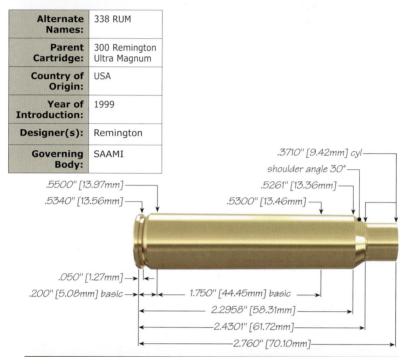

CARTRIDGE CASE DATA	
Case Type:	Beltless, rebated rim, bottleneck
Average Case Capacity:	134 grains H_2O
Max. Cartridge OAL	3.600 inch
Max. Case Length:	2.760 inch
Primer:	Large Rifle
Case Trim to Length:	2.750 inch
RCBS Shell holder:	# 38
Current Manufacturers:	Remington, Nosler

BALLISTIC DATA

Max. Average Pressure (MAP):	65,000 psi, CUP not established for this cartridge - SAAMI	Test Barrel Length:	24 inch
Rifling Twist Rate:	1 turn in 10 inch		

Muzzle velocities of factory loaded ammunition	Bullet Wgt.	Muzzle velocity
	180-grain	3,280 fps
	210-grain	3,030 fps
	225-grain	3,020 fps
	250-grain	2,860 fps
	300-grain	2,600 fps

Muzzle velocity will decrease approximately 25 fps per inch for barrels less than 24 inches.

HISTORICAL NOTES

- Introduced in 1999, the 338 Remington Ultra Magnum (RUM) was a member of Remington's new trio of long case length, magnum cartridges that turned the magnum cartridge market upside down.

- For the first time in over 40 years, a mainstream ammunition manufacturer offered a magnum rifle cartridge that could compete with the legendary 338 Winchester Magnum on its own terms.

- And, the new 338 RUM cartridge shattered magnum tradition in another way—it did not have a belted head! Inspiration courtesy of the fatherly 404 Jeffrey cartridge.

- As Remington also manufactured rifles, introduction of the new caliber trio gained a boost when the company simultaneously introduced rifles chambered for the new cartridges.

- Remington Ultra Magnum cartridges firmly established the concept of beltless magnum cartridges in the world of modern sporting ammunition.

- To date, except Nosler, rival ammunition manufacturers have not included any of the Remington Ultra Magnum cartridges in their product lines.

BALLISTIC NOTES

- The 338 Remington Ultra Magnum is fully capable of taking any North American game and most species of African plains game as well. It cannot be recommended for large, heavy African game or for dangerous game.

- Remington's 338 RUM cartridge is capable of providing an increase of up to 300 fps in muzzle velocity over the 338 Winchester Magnum. With a 225-grain bullet, that adds nearly 882 ft-lbs of energy. Of course recoil is increased as well.

- In their 338 RUM product line, Remington offers only the 250-grain bullet at a muzzle velocity of 2,869 fps and a muzzle energy of 4,540 ft-lbs.

- In a textbook example of the versatility of handloading, the Speer Grand Slam® SP 250-grain bullet can be loaded to a muzzle velocity of 2,936 fps which ices the muzzle velocity of the factory load by 67 fps and muzzle energy by 345 ft-lbs!

- The 338 RUM can also be loaded with lighter bullets of 200 and 225 grains that offer outstanding performance options.
- The Speer 225-grain Spitzer BTSP provides handloaders the opportunity to take the ballistics of the 338 RUM to an entirely new level of retained velocity and energy, flatter trajectory and less wind drift at all ranges.

TECHNICAL NOTES

- The 338 RUM case is slightly shorter with a significantly larger head diameter than the 340 Weatherby Magnum; the rim of the 338 RUM case is slightly rebated.
- Case capacity of the 338 RUM cartridge is 18% larger than its 340 Weatherby rival.
- The 338 RUM cartridge shares its overall loaded length with its brethren 7mm RUM and 300 RUM cartridges, making it suitable only for repeating rifles having long actions.
- All Remington Ultra Magnum cartridges achieve their exceptional muzzle velocities the old fashioned way—they burn heavy propellant charges. None of the short, efficient design concept here!

HANDLOADING NOTES

- Remington and Nosler are the sources of new, empty, unprimed 338 RUM brass cartridge cases for handloading.

SAFETY NOTES

SPEER 225-grain Spitzer BTSP @ a muzzle velocity of 3,103 fps:
- Maximum vertical altitude @ 90° elevation is 16,722 feet.
- Maximum horizontal distance to first impact with ground @ 38° elevation is 7,710 yards.

200 GRAINS

DIAMETER	SECTIONAL DENSITY
.338"	0.250

338 Spitzer SP Hot-Cor®

Ballistic Coefficient	0.426
COAL Tested	3.500"
Speer Part No.	2405

			Starting Charge		Maximum Charge	
Propellant	Case	Primer	Weight (grains)	Muzzle Velocity (feet/sec)	Weight (grains)	Muzzle Velocity (feet/sec)
Alliant Reloder 22	Federal	Federal 215	94.0	3105	98.0	3255
Vihtavuori N560	Federal	Federal 215	93.0	3062	97.0	3223
Alliant Reloder 19	Federal	Federal 215	91.0	3085	95.0	3216
Alliant Reloder 25	Federal	Federal 215	97.0	3060	101.0 C	3193
Hodgdon H4350	Federal	Federal 215	85.0	3043	89.0	3180
IMR 7828	Federal	Federal 215	92.0	3015	96.0	3179
Ramshot Magnum	Federal	Federal 215	101.0	3078	105.0 C	3168
Accurate MagPro	Federal	Federal 215	96.0	2985	100.0	3167
IMR 4350	Federal	Federal 215	84.0	2981	88.0	3151

WARNING! *Maximum loads should be used with CAUTION • C = Compressed Load*

225 GRAINS

DIAMETER	SECTIONAL DENSITY
.338"	0.281

338 Spitzer BTSP	
Ballistic Coefficient	0.497
COAL Tested	3.600"
Speer Part No.	2406

			Starting Charge		Maximum Charge	
Propellant	Case	Primer	Weight (grains)	Muzzle Velocity (feet/sec)	Weight (grains)	Muzzle Velocity (feet/sec)
Alliant Reloder 25	Federal	Federal 215	95.0	2965	99.0 C	3103
Ramshot Magnum	Federal	Federal 215	98.0	2953	102.0 C	3062
Vihtavuori N560	Federal	Federal 215	89.0	2911	93.0	3045
Alliant Reloder 22	Federal	Federal 215	89.0	2891	93.0	3029
Alliant Reloder 19	Federal	Federal 215	87.0	2884	91.0	3028
Hodgdon Retumbo	Federal	Federal 215	97.0	2913	101.0 C	3015
Accurate MagPro	Federal	Federal 215	92.0	2922	96.0	3007
IMR 7828	Federal	Federal 215	88.0	2840	92.0	2998
IMR 4831	Federal	Federal 215	83.0	2839	87.0	2997
Hodgdon H4831SC	Federal	Federal 215	88.0	2833	92.0	2965

WARNING! Maximum loads should be used with CAUTION • C = Compressed Load

250 GRAINS

DIAMETER	SECTIONAL DENSITY
.338"	0.313

338 Grand Slam® SP

Ballistic Coefficient	0.436
COAL Tested	3.550"
Speer Part No.	2408

			Starting Charge		Maximum Charge	
Propellant	Case	Primer	Weight (grains)	Muzzle Velocity (feet/sec)	Weight (grains)	Muzzle Velocity (feet/sec)
Ramshot Magnum	Federal	Federal 215	96.0	2839	100.0	2936
Alliant Reloder 25	Federal	Federal 215	91.0	2803	95.0	2915
Hodgdon Retumbo	Federal	Federal 215	94.0	2790	98.0	2907
Alliant Reloder 22	Federal	Federal 215	87.0	2779	91.0	2895
Vihtavuori N560	Federal	Federal 215	85.0	2733	89.0	2877
IMR 7828	Federal	Federal 215	87.0	2763	91.0	2871
Accurate MagPro	Federal	Federal 215	89.0	2742	93.0	2862
Alliant Reloder 19	Federal	Federal 215	83.0	2712	87.0	2849
Hodgdon H4831SC	Federal	Federal 215	85.0	2687	89.0	2817

WARNING! *Maximum loads should be used with* **CAUTION** • *C = Compressed Load*

338 LAPUA MAGNUM

Alternate Names:	8.58x70mm, 8.6x70mm
Parent Cartridge:	416 Rigby
Country of Origin:	USA & Finland
Year of Introduction:	1983
Designer(s):	1983 - Research Armament Industries, 1984 – Sako, Accuracy International & Lapua
Governing Body:	SAAMI/CIP

.371" cyl [9.42mm]
shoulder angle 20°
.5441" [13.82mm]
.5454" [13.85mm]
.5854" [14.87mm]
.588" [14.94mm]
.060" [1.52mm]
.200" [5.08mm]
1.900" [48.26mm]
2.1614" [54.90mm]
2.3972" [60.89mm]
2.724" [69.19mm]

CARTRIDGE CASE DATA			
Case Type:	Rimless, bottleneck		
Average Case Capacity:	115.0 grains H$_2$O	Max. Cartridge OAL	3.681 inch
Max. Case Length:	2.724 inch	Primer:	Large Rifle
Case Trim to Length:	2.714 inch	RCBS Shell holder:	# 48
Current Manufacturers:	Lapua, Norma, Federal, Remington, Prvi Partizan, RUAG, Winchester		

BALLISTIC DATA

Max. Average Pressure (MAP):	65,000 psi, CUP not established for this cartridge – SAAMI; 60,916 psi - CIP	Test Barrel Length:	24 inch
Rifling Twist Rate:	1 turn in 10 inch		

Muzzle velocities of factory loaded ammunition	Bullet Wgt.	Muzzle velocity
	225-grains	3,000 fps
	250-grains	2,995 fps
	300-grains	2,760 fps

Muzzle velocity will decrease approximately 20 fps per inch for barrels less than 24 inches.

HISTORICAL NOTES

- In 1983, Resource Armament Industries (RAI) in the U.S. responded to a U.S. Army request for proposals for a new, intermediate range sniper cartridge.
- At that time, U.S. Army tactical doctrine divided sniper cartridges into two calibers depending on their approximate maximum effective range:
  - The M852 7.62x51mm NATO Match cartridge to 1,000 yards.
  - The M33 50 caliber Browning Machine Gun cartridge to 2,200+ yards.
- Clearly, an intermediate cartridge was needed to bridge the gap.
- RAI selected a .338 inch diameter bullet loaded in a modified 416 Rigby cartridge case.
- At trials, problems emerged with case failures as the 416 Rigby case was not designed for the high MAP levels needed.
- RAI then partnered with SAKO (rifles) of Finland and Accuracy International (AI) in the UK for further development efforts. However, financial problems forced RAI to drop out.
- SAKO and AI then partnered with Lapua of Finland to design a stronger cartridge case to withstand the high MAP levels necessary to fire a 250-grain bullet at a muzzle velocity of 3,000 fps.
- When these efforts were successful, Lapua, Sako (ammunition), RUAG, Sellier & Bellot and PPU added 338 Lapua Magnum ammunition to their catalogs and Norma began making new, empty brass. Many major domestic ammunition manufacturers added this cartridge as well.
- Subsequently, a number of European military forces took the 338 Lapua Magnum cartridge into military service for sniper use.
- In 2016, experience in the field caused the U.S. Army to again revise their requirements for sniper cartridges:
  - The 7.62x51mm NATO cartridge was dropped altogether and replaced by the 300 Winchester Magnum. Expected maximum range is approximately 1,200 yards.

- The 338 Lapua Magnum is the new, intermediate range sniper cartridge. Expected maximum effective range is approximately 2,000+ yards.
- The 50 BMG cartridge remains the long range sniper cartridge with a maximum effective range of 3,000 yards.

Interesting Fact

A British soldier serving in Afghanistan recently scored a record kill at 2,707 yards with a 338 Lapua Magnum. Put in more prosaic terms, that is 27 football fields away or 1.538 miles! It is estimated that the time of flight of the bullet was 4.72 seconds. Striking velocity is estimated at 1,070 fps.

BALLISTIC NOTES

- The commercial 338 Lapua cartridge was standardized by CIP in 1989.
- Initially, the MAP level was established at 68,168 psi, however this was reduced to the current MAP level of 60,916 psi in 2007.
- For sporting use, the 338 Lapua Magnum is an excellent choice for long range hunting for North American big game and African plains game.
- Here it must be noted that hunting at very long ranges is a difficult challenge that requires the multiple skill set of an experienced shooter. It is not for the novice.
- Most bullets used to load this cartridge are spitzer boat tail types to maximize long range performance.

TECHNICAL NOTES

- Although the 416 Rigby case has plenty of capacity, it was not designed for the high MAP levels of the 338 Lapua Magnum. As a result, 338 Lapua Magnum cases cannot be made by necking down 416 Rigby brass.
- Case capacity of the 338 Lapua Magnum is about 1% higher than the 338 Remington Ultra Magnum and 12% greater than the 340 Weatherby Magnum.
- However, the 348-grain weight of the 338 Lapua Magnum cartridge case gives some idea of its strength. In contrast, the 338 RUM case weighs 270 grains and the 340 Weatherby Mag. case weighs 246 grains.
- MAP levels of all three of these cartridges are broadly comparable.
- Surprisingly, the 338 Lapua Magnum does not have the longest case length—this honor goes to the 340 Weatherby Mag. at 3.825 inches.
- However, the 338 Lapua Magnum does have the longest OAL at 3.681 inches. Because of this, the 338 Lapua Magnum requires a magnum length rifle action.

HANDLOADING NOTES

- For maximum loads, we recommend using once-fired or new brass only.
- To extend case life, we recommend neck sizing for handloading practice and training ammunition. This can be accomplished using a standard sizing die.
- We recommend full length resizing for operational ammunition.
- Use slow burning powders for big magnums such as this.
- Handloading ammunition for very long range shooting requires extra attention to details. For this reason, we recommend:
    1. Thoroughly cleaning your brass before reloading it.
    2. Check the length of every case before you reload it.

3. Weigh every powder charge.
4. Pay special attention to case neck runout.
5. Use a micrometer seating die.
6. Use magnum match primers.

SAFETY NOTES

SPEER 225-grain BTSP bullet @ a muzzle velocity of 3,100 fps:
- Maximum vertical altitude @ 90° elevation is 16,710 feet.
- Maximum horizontal distance to first impact with ground @ 38° elevation is 7,707 yards.

200 GRAINS

DIAMETER	SECTIONAL DENSITY
.338"	0.250

338 Spitzer SP Hot-Cor®

Ballistic Coefficient	0.426
COAL Tested	3.530"
Speer Part No.	2405

			Starting Charge		Maximum Charge	
Propellant	Case	Primer	Weight (grains)	Muzzle Velocity (feet/sec)	Weight (grains)	Muzzle Velocity (feet/sec)
Alliant Reloder 33	Lapua	Federal 215	101.0	2936	111.5 C	3225
Ramshot Hunter	Lapua	Federal 215	95.0	2943	105.2	3223
Alliant Reloder 26	Lapua	Federal 215	85.2	2951	94.4	3197
Hodgdon Retumbo	Lapua	Federal 215	93.1	2930	103.3 C	3195
IMR 7828	Lapua	Federal 215	85.0	2873	94.8	3165
Alliant Reloder 25	Lapua	Federal 215	87.7	2899	97.3	3156
Alliant Reloder 23	Lapua	Federal 215	83.8	2889	92.8	3152
Hodgdon H1000	Lapua	Federal 215	90.5	2895	100.7	3151
Vihtavuori N560	Lapua	Federal 215	82.7	2903	92.0	3144
Alliant Reloder 22	Lapua	Federal 215	80.1	2902	88.9	3131
IMR 7977	Lapua	Federal 215	90.0	2803	99.7	3117

WARNING! Maximum loads should be used with CAUTION • C = Compressed Load

225 GRAINS

DIAMETER	SECTIONAL DENSITY
.338"	0.281

338 Spitzer BTSP

Ballistic Coefficient	0.497
COAL Tested	3.530"
Speer Part No.	2406

			Starting Charge		Maximum Charge	
Propellant	Case	Primer	Weight (grains)	Muzzle Velocity (feet/sec)	Weight (grains)	Muzzle Velocity (feet/sec)
Hodgdon Retumbo	Lapua	Federal 215	92.0	2838	101.6	3093
Ramshot Magnum	Lapua	Federal 215	92.0	2804	101.0	3084
Alliant Reloder 26	Lapua	Federal 215	84.0	2833	92.0	3061
Alliant Reloder 25	Lapua	Federal 215	87.0	2820	95.5	3054
Hodgdon H1000	Lapua	Federal 215	89.0	2821	98.0	3048
IMR 7828	Lapua	Federal 215	80.0	2794	88.0	3018
Alliant Reloder 22	Lapua	Federal 215	80.0	2792	87.5	3007

WARNING! Maximum loads should be used with CAUTION • C = Compressed Load

250 GRAINS

DIAMETER	SECTIONAL DENSITY
.338"	0.313

338 Grand Slam® SP	
Ballistic Coefficient	0.436
COAL Tested	3.510"
Speer Part No.	2408

			Starting Charge		Maximum Charge	
Propellant	Case	Primer	Weight (grains)	Muzzle Velocity (feet/sec)	Weight (grains)	Muzzle Velocity (feet/sec)
Alliant Reloder 33	Lapua	Federal 215	93.6	2726	102.7 C	2926
Ramshot Magnum	Lapua	Federal 215	89.2	2643	98.2	2888
Hodgdon Retumbo	Lapua	Federal 215	87.0	2664	95.0	2877
Alliant Reloder 26	Lapua	Federal 215	81.0	2673	88.5	2876
Alliant Reloder 25	Lapua	Federal 215	82.0	2660	90.4	2847
Hodgdon H1000	Lapua	Federal 215	85.0	2627	93.5	2841
Alliant Reloder 22	Lapua	Federal 215	77.4	2641	84.0	2811
IMR 7828	Lapua	Federal 215	78.2	2628	85.0	2811
Alliant Reloder 23	Lapua	Federal 215	78.0	2606	85.5	2809

WARNING! *Maximum loads should be used with* CAUTION • *C = Compressed Load*

357 MAGNUM (RIFLE)

Alternate Names:	357 S&W Magnum
Parent Cartridge:	38 Special
Country of Origin:	USA
Year of Introduction:	1935
Designer(s):	Smith & Wesson
Governing Body:	SAAMI/CIP

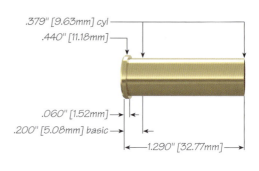

CARTRIDGE CASE DATA	
Case Type:	Rimmed, straight
Average Case Capacity:	26.2 grains H_2O
Max. Cartridge OAL:	1.590 inch
Max. Case Length:	1.290 inch
Primer:	Small Pistol
Case Trim to Length:	1.280 inch
RCBS Shell holder:	# 6
Current Manufacturers:	Speer, Federal, Remington, Hornady, Winchester, Cor-Bon, Black Hills, Lapua, PMC, Magtech, Aguila, Fiocchi, IMI, Prvi Partizan

BALLISTIC DATA			
Max. Average Pressure (MAP):	35,000 psi, 45,000 CUP	Test Barrel Length:	18.0 inch
Rifling Twist Rate:	1 turn in 16 inch (rifle); 1:18.75 (handgun)		
Muzzle velocities of factory loaded ammunition	Bullet Wgt.		Muzzle velocity
	158-grain		1,830 fps
Muzzle velocity will decrease approximately 5 fps per inch for barrels less than 18 inches.			

HISTORICAL NOTES

- In the Old West, a popular practice was to carry a carbine and a revolver of the same chambering to eliminate having to carry two different types of ammunition.
- This practice remains popular today for Cowboy Action Competition and for personal defense and varmint hunting (some would say the last two are the same).

BALLISTIC NOTES

- When a 357 Magnum cartridge is fired from an 18 inch length carbine barrel rather than from a handgun barrel, muzzle velocity is increased substantially. Typically the increase is approximately 150%. For example:

Bullet Wgt. Grains	Muzzle Velocity 18 inch bbl. Feet per second	Muzzle Velocity 4 inch bbl. Feet per second	Variance +/- %
110	2,467	1,295	+190%
125	2,125	1,450	+147%
140	1,934	1,290	+150%
158	1,738	1,235	+141%
170	1,684	1,145	+147%

- Speer offers a comprehensive line of GDHP, DCSP as well as other JHP and/or JSP bullets in each of these weights. See loading data for more information.
- We recommend using these loads only for hunting varmints, pests, and predators. They should not be used on deer or larger game.

TECHNICAL NOTES

- Many 357 Magnum cartridge cases are nickel-plated to assist extraction from revolvers. The nickel-plating process may cause hydrogen embrittlement of the case mouths. After four to six reloads, expect case mouth splits. When this occurs, avoid the temptation to try to get one more loading out of such cases. Destroy them immediately.
- Aluminum cases in 357 Magnum are not reloadable.
- Carbine loads must be loaded to the same industry standard 35,000 psi MAP levels as used for 357 Magnum handgun ammunition. Do not attempt to develop special carbine loads that depart from the MAP limits or loading data.

HANDLOADING NOTES

- As these cartridges will be fired in lever-action rifles with tubular magazines, use only flat nose soft point or hollow point bullets to prevent magazine tube explosions.
- Bullets should be crimped firmly in the case mouth to prevent elongation from recoil or being pushed down inside the case by the magazine spring and remaining cartridges.
- Never load Total Metal Jacket (TMJ) or pointed bullets for this application.
- Never load unjacketed lead bullets for this application. The high muzzle velocities will rapidly cause the buildup of lead deposits in the bore.
- Never load less than the minimum charges shown in the loading data as the small charge of propellant may not be sufficient to push the bullet completely down the barrel.
- We recommend using only new or once-fired cases for maximum loads.

SAFETY NOTES

SPEER 158-grain JSP @ a muzzle velocity of 1,738 fps:
- Maximum vertical altitude @ 90° elevation is 4,911 feet.
- Maximum horizontal distance to first impact with ground @ 32° elevation is 2,241 yards.
- Do not fire handloads with CCI plastic shot capsules from carbine barrels.

110 GRAINS

DIAMETER	SECTIONAL DENSITY
.357"	0.123

38 UCHP

Ballistic Coefficient	0.113
COAL Tested	1.575"
Speer Part No.	4007

NOTE: *Do not use the 110-grain Gold Dot Short Barrel bullet (#4009). It is not intended for 357 Magnum pressures.*

			Starting Charge		Maximum Charge	
Propellant	Case	Primer	Weight (grains)	Muzzle Velocity (feet/sec)	Weight (grains)	Muzzle Velocity (feet/sec)
Vihtavuori N110	Speer	CCI 500	19.5	2392	21.5 C	2542
Hodgdon H110	Speer	CCI 550	21.0	2268	23.0 C	2416
Winchester 296	Speer	CCI 550	21.0	2173	23.0 C	2381
Alliant 2400	Speer	CCI 500	17.5	2104	19.5	2348

125 GRAINS

DIAMETER	SECTIONAL DENSITY
.357"	0.140

38 GDHP

Ballistic Coefficient	0.140
COAL Tested	1.580"
Speer Part No.	4012

38 JHP

Ballistic Coefficient	0.129
COAL Tested	1.575"
Speer Part No.	4013

NOTE: *125-grain TMJ # 4015 is not suitable for use in tubular magazines.*

			Starting Charge		Maximum Charge	
Propellant	Case	Primer	Weight (grains)	Muzzle Velocity (feet/sec)	Weight (grains)	Muzzle Velocity (feet/sec)
Hodgdon H110	Speer	CCI 550	18.0	1946	20.0 C	2167
Winchester 296	Speer	CCI 550	18.3	1963	20.3 C	2167
Vihtavuori N110	Speer	CCI 500	16.8	1967	17.8	2076
Alliant 2400	Speer	CCI 500	16.5	1868	17.5	2051
Accurate No. 7	Speer	CCI 500	12.0	1583	13.5	1780

WARNING! *Maximum loads should be used with CAUTION • C = Compressed Load*

158 GRAINS

DIAMETER	SECTIONAL DENSITY
.357"	0.177

38 JHP
Ballistic Coefficient	0.163
COAL Tested	1.570"
Speer Part No.	4211

38 DCHP
Ballistic Coefficient	0.168
COAL Tested	1.575"
Speer Part No.	4215

38 JSP
Ballistic Coefficient	0.164
COAL Tested	1.570"
Speer Part No.	4217

NOTE: #4207 158-grain TMJ, not suitable for tubular magazines

			Starting Charge		Maximum Charge	
Propellant	Case	Primer	Weight (grains)	Muzzle Velocity (feet/sec)	Weight (grains)	Muzzle Velocity (feet/sec)
Vihtavuori N110	Speer	CCI 500	13.5	1557	15.0	1745
Hodgdon H110	Speer	CCI 550	13.9	1459	15.5	1648
Alliant 2400	Speer	CCI 500	13.8	1517	14.8	1626
IMR 4227	Speer	CCI 500	15.0	1377	17.0 C	1583
Winchester 296	Speer	CCI 550	13.2	1317	14.7	1557
Accurate No. 9	Speer	CCI 500	12.3	1330	13.7	1543

170 GRAINS

DIAMETER	SECTIONAL DENSITY
.357"	0.191

38 DCSP
Ballistic Coefficient	0.185
COAL Tested	1.590"
Speer Part No.	4230

			Starting Charge		Maximum Charge	
Propellant	Case	Primer	Weight (grains)	Muzzle Velocity (feet/sec)	Weight (grains)	Muzzle Velocity (feet/sec)
Hodgdon Lil' Gun	Speer	CCI 550	14.8	1635	15.4	1687
Hodgdon H110	Speer	CCI 550	14.4	1541	15.2	1620
Alliant 2400	Speer	CCI 500	13.9	1530	14.5	1613
Vihtavuori N110	Speer	CCI 500	13.2	1480	13.8	1573
IMR 4227	Speer	CCI 500	16.1	1457	16.7	1531
Accurate No. 9	Speer	CCI 550	11.0	1203	11.7	1321

WARNING! Maximum loads should be used with CAUTION • C = Compressed Load

35 REMINGTON

Parent Cartridge:	None
Country of Origin:	USA
Year of Introduction:	1908
Designer(s):	Remington
Governing Body:	SAAMI

CARTRIDGE CASE DATA

Case Type:	Rimless, bottleneck
Average Case Capacity:	51.0 grains H$_2$O
Max. Cartridge OAL	2.525 inch
Max. Case Length:	1.920 inch
Primer:	Large Rifle
Case Trim to Length:	1.910 inch
RCBS Shell holder:	# 9
Current Manufacturers:	Remington, Federal, Hornady, Winchester

BALLISTIC DATA

Max. Average Pressure (MAP):	33,500 psi, 35,000 CUP - SAAMI
Test Barrel Length:	24 inch
Rifling Twist Rate:	1 turn in 16 inch

Muzzle velocities of factory loaded ammunition

Bullet Wgt.	Muzzle velocity
150-grain	2,300 fps
200-grain	2,080 fps

Muzzle velocity will decrease approximately 10 fps per inch for barrels less than 24 inches.

HISTORICAL NOTES

- Remington introduced the 35 Remington cartridge in 1908 as a member of a new line of rimless cartridges designed for lever-action, slide-action and semi-automatic rifles.
- The 35 Remington was the largest of the group and the only one that remains in production today.
- What is the secret of its longevity? This is undoubtedly due to its reputation as a good brush buster and excellent short range woods cartridge for deer and bear.

- As this old favorite has declined in popularity in recent years, very few new guns are being chambered in this cartridge.
- However, due to the large number of 35 Remington rifles remaining in service, the 35 Remington cartridge looks to remain around for a good while yet.
- For this reason, Remington, Federal and Winchester continue to offer ammunition in this caliber.
- European hunters continue to be baffled by the continuing popularity of the 35 caliber among American sportsmen.

BALLISTIC NOTES

- By modern standards, factory ballistics of the 35 Remington are from another era. These include a very low MAP level (33,500 psi) and a heavy, 200-grain bullet launched at the modest muzzle velocity of 2,080 fps.
- As generations of American sportsmen have found, the combination of a large caliber, heavy bullet at a moderate muzzle velocity works very well for close range woods hunting. This explains the enduring popularity of the 35 Remington.
- Bullets weighing less than 200 grains have a reputation for poor accuracy and lack the deep penetration of the heavier bullet.
- To approximate the factory load, we recommend the Speer 220-grain SPFN Hot-Cor®, which can be handloaded to a muzzle velocity of 1,901 fps.
- Handloading the Speer 180-grain SPFN Hot-Cor, opens a wide vista of potential performance levels ranging from 2,224 fps to a reduced load at a muzzle velocity of 1,499 fps to keep recoil at bay.
- For plinking or dispatching varmints, pests, or predators at close ranges, you can load Speer 158-grain JHP or JSP revolver bullets. Note that due to the short COAL, single loading into the chamber is suggested.

TECHNICAL NOTES

- The 35 Remington cartridge has a non-standard, .457 inch head diameter which is smaller than the common .470 inch head diameter of the 30-06 Springfield et al.
- MAP levels of the 35 Remington are less than half that of most contemporary cartridges such as the 308 Winchester. Consequently, case capacity is lower and the 35 Remington's cartridge case is more lightly constructed.

HANDLOADING NOTES

- In addition to the manufacturers of loaded ammunition listed above, new, empty, unprimed 35 Remington brass for reloading is available from most domestic ammunition manufacturers such as Remington and Winchester.
- To avoid magazine tube explosions in lever-action and slide-action rifles, the 35 Remington cartridge must be loaded with flat nose, soft point bullets.
- These bullets *must* be crimped securely in the case mouth to prevent the bullet being pulled from the case mouth by recoil or pushed into the case by the magazine spring and cartridges in the magazine tube. Speer bullets in this caliber have a cannelure ring on their jacket for this purpose.
- Note that the correct bullet diameter for the 35 Remington cartridge is .358 inch.
- To avoid chambering problems in lever-action, slide-action, and semi-automatic rifles, we recommend full length resizing all 35 Remington brass with small base dies. Neck sizing can be used for bolt-action rifles.

- Fast burning propellants are the best choice for reloading the 35 Remington.

SAFETY NOTES

SPEER 220-grain SPFN Hot-Cor @ a muzzle velocity of 1,901 fps:
- Maximum vertical altitude @ 90° elevation is 7,443 feet.
- Maximum horizontal distance to first impact with ground @ 35° elevation is 3,498 yards.
- The 35 Remington must be handloaded with flat nose, soft point or hollow point bullets.

158 GRAINS

DIAMETER	SECTIONAL DENSITY
.357"	0.177

38 JHP
Ballistic Coefficient	0.163
COAL Tested	2.220"
Speer Part No.	4211

38 JSP
Ballistic Coefficient	0.164
COAL Tested	2.220"
Speer Part No.	4217

NOTE: Short COAL may require single-loading

			Starting Charge		Maximum Charge	
Propellant	Case	Primer	Weight (grains)	Muzzle Velocity (feet/sec)	Weight (grains)	Muzzle Velocity (feet/sec)
Alliant Reloder 7	Winchester	CCI 200	33.0	2117	37.0	2400
IMR 4895	Winchester	CCI 200	35.0	1948	39.0	2217
IMR 3031	Winchester	CCI 200	33.0	1910	37.0	2170

WARNING! Maximum loads should be used with CAUTION • C = Compressed Load

180 GRAINS

DIAMETER	SECTIONAL DENSITY
.358"	0.201

35 SPFN Hot-Cor®

Ballistic Coefficient	0.236
COAL Tested	2.470"
Speer Part No.	2435

Propellant	Case	Primer	Starting Charge Weight (grains)	Starting Charge Muzzle Velocity (feet/sec)	Maximum Charge Weight (grains)	Maximum Charge Muzzle Velocity (feet/sec)
Hodgdon H335	Winchester	CCI 250	34.0	1971	38.0	2258
Alliant AR-Comp	Federal	Federal 210	33.6	2058	36.7	2211
Accurate 2015	Winchester	CCI 200	32.0	1953	36.0	2167
Alliant Power Pro Varmint	Federal	Federal 210	35.1	2026	37.9	2153
Hodgdon BL-C(2)	Winchester	CCI 250	31.0	1841	35.0	2123
Winchester 748	Winchester	CCI 250	38.0	1870	42.0	2097
Alliant Power Pro 1200-R	Federal	Federal 210	28.5	1973	30.7	2092
IMR 4895	Winchester	CCI 200	34.0	1820	38.0	2078
Vihtavuori N133	Winchester	CCI 200	31.0	1863	35.0	2077
Accurate LT-32	Federal	Federal 210	28.5	1946	30.8	2066
Hodgdon H414	Winchester	CCI 250	43.0	1858	47.0	2064
Hodgdon H380	Winchester	CCI 250	40.0	1816	44.0	2045
Alliant Reloder 10X	Federal	Federal 210	28.5	1968	30.0	2028
IMR 4320	Winchester	CCI 200	32.0	1733	36.0	2002
Alliant Reloder 7	Winchester	CCI 200	26.0	1681	30.0	1985
IMR SR 4759 (reduced load)	Winchester	CCI 200	18.0	1491	20.0	1653

WARNING! Maximum loads should be used with CAUTION • C = Compressed Load

220 GRAINS

DIAMETER	SECTIONAL DENSITY
.358"	0.245

35 SPFN Hot-Cor®

Ballistic Coefficient	0.286
COAL Tested	2.470"
Speer Part No.	2439

			Starting Charge		Maximum Charge	
Propellant	Case	Primer	Weight (grains)	Muzzle Velocity (feet/sec)	Weight (grains)	Muzzle Velocity (feet/sec)
Alliant Power Pro 2000-MR	Federal	Federal 210	38.0	1920	41.2 C	2031
Alliant AR-Comp	Federal	Federal 210	30.2	1780	33.0	1925
Accurate 2015	Winchester	CCI 200	29.0	1666	33.0	1915
Hodgdon CFE 223	Federal	Federal 210	32.9	1797	35.3	1901
IMR 4064	Winchester	CCI 200	32.0	1641	36.0	1851
Hodgdon H414	Winchester	CCI 250	36.0	1656	40.0	1841
Winchester 748	Winchester	CCI 250	31.0	1675	35.0	1840
IMR 8208 XBR	Federal	Federal 210	29.0	1647	32.1	1840
Alliant Reloder 15	Federal	Federal 210	31.4	1643	34.9	1824
Alliant Power Pro Varmint	Federal	Federal 210	29.7	1650	32.6	1822
Vihtavuori N133	Winchester	CCI 200	27.0	1591	31.0	1816
Hodgdon BL-C(2)	Winchester	CCI 250	31.0	1552	35.0	1802
IMR 4895	Winchester	CCI 200	31.5	1640	35.5	1797
Hodgdon H335	Winchester	CCI 250	28.0	1467	32.0	1792
IMR 3031	Winchester	CCI 200	29.5	1525	33.5	1788
IMR 4320	Winchester	CCI 200	29.0	1494	33.0	1694
Alliant Reloder 7	Winchester	CCI 200	20.5	1149	24.5	1530

WARNING! Maximum loads should be used with CAUTION • C = Compressed Load

350 REMINGTON MAGNUM

Parent Cartridge:	300 H&H Magnum
Country of Origin:	USA
Year of Introduction:	1965
Designer(s):	Remington
Governing Body:	SAAMI

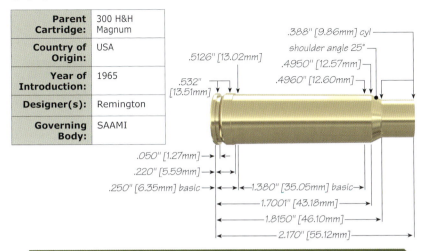

CARTRIDGE CASE DATA

Case Type:	Belted, rimless, bottleneck		
Average Case Capacity:	73.7 grains H$_2$O	Max. Cartridge OAL	2.800 inch
Max. Case Length:	2.170 inch	Primer:	Large Rifle
Case Trim to Length:	2.160 inch	RCBS Shell holder:	# 4
Current Manufacturers:	None		

BALLISTIC DATA

Max. Average Pressure (MAP):	Piezo pressure not established, 53,000 CUP - SAAMI	Test Barrel Length:	24 inch
Rifling Twist Rate:	1 turn in 16 inch		
Muzzle velocities of factory loaded ammunition	Bullet Wgt.		Muzzle velocity
	200-grain		2,710 fps
	Muzzle velocity will decrease approximately 20 fps per inch for barrels less than 24 inches.		

HISTORICAL NOTES

- In the mid-1960s, Remington introduced the 6.5mm Remington Magnum and the 350 Remington Magnum cartridges for their short-action length Model 600 and later the 660 carbine.

- Remington made an unfortunate error in selecting two calibers that have never appealed to American sportsman. As a result, sales of the two new cartridges were low, prompting Remington to retire the 350 Remington Magnum a few years later.

- Remington overlooked the major reason for the demise of their 350 Remington Magnum—recoil in the lightweight Model 600 carbine in this caliber can only be described as "brutal."
- In European markets, the 350 Remington Magnum remains virtually unknown (European shooters have never taken to 35-caliber cartridges).

BALLISTIC NOTES

- Remington saw the 350 Remington Magnum as a compact magnum cartridge capable of firing a heavy bullet to anchor big game at ranges of 200 yards or less.
- When Remington offered this cartridge as a factory load, they used a 200-grain spitzer soft point bullet at a muzzle velocity of 2,710 fps. This was undoubtedly to reduce recoil which can quickly become untenable using heavier bullets.
- To approximate the factory load, we recommend the Speer 220-grain SPFN Hot-Cor® which can be handloaded to a muzzle velocity of 2,676 fps.
- Fortunately, the 350 Remington Magnum chamber has a generous throat making it possible to handload both lighter and heavier bullets which adds versatility to this cartridge.
- A magnum cartridge such as the 350 Remington Magnum deserves a suitable heavy bullet for close range power. Speer offers one such pointed bullet in 250-grain weight: a Spitzer SP Hot-Cor. If you are a hunter that laughs in the face of heavy recoil, this bullet can be handloaded to a muzzle velocity of 2,484 fps. For us lesser mortals, this bullet can be handloaded to lower, but still effective levels.

TECHNICAL NOTES

- The 350 Remington Magnum cartridge case shares its rim, belt, and head dimensions with its parent 300 H&H Magnum as well as the 7mm Remington Magnum.
- In order to fit a loaded 350 Remington Magnum cartridge in a short action, the maximum overall loaded length must not exceed 2.800 inches. This limits case length of the 350 Remington Magnum to 2.170 inches.
- In concert with its relative short magnum cartridges, the 350 Remington Magnum achieves its muzzle velocities the modern way—it burns smaller propellant charges more efficiently.

HANDLOADING NOTES

- Unprimed 350 Remington Magnum brass cartridge cases for reloading are no longer available from Remington. However, they are available from Quality Cartridge at www.qual-cart.com.
- The heavy construction of the 350 Remington Magnum cartridge case can cause problems with full length resizing such as excessive effort, case stretching, brass hardening and head separations, all leading to short case life.
- For this reason, neck sizing only is recommended as most rifles in 350 Remington Magnum caliber are bolt-action types.

SAFETY NOTES

SPEER 250-grain Spitzer SP Hot-Cor @ a muzzle velocity of 2,484 fps:
- Maximum vertical altitude @ 90° elevation is 10,290 feet.
- Maximum horizontal distance to first impact with ground @ 36° elevation is 4,829 yards.

158 GRAINS

DIAMETER	SECTIONAL DENSITY
.357"	0.177

38 JHP	
Ballistic Coefficient	0.163
COAL Tested	2.470"
Speer Part No.	4211

38 JSP	
Ballistic Coefficient	0.164
COAL Tested	2.470"
Speer Part No.	4217

NOTE: Short COAL may require single-loading

			Starting Charge		Maximum Charge	
Propellant	Case	Primer	Weight (grains)	Muzzle Velocity (feet/sec)	Weight (grains)	Muzzle Velocity (feet/sec)
Alliant Reloder 7	Remington	CCI 200	51.0	2687	55.0	2941
IMR 3031	Remington	CCI 200	54.0	2487	58.0	2904
IMR 4064	Remington	CCI 200	58.0	2479	62.0	2879

WARNING! Maximum loads should be used with CAUTION • C = Compressed Load

180 GRAINS

DIAMETER	SECTIONAL DENSITY
.358"	0.201

35 SPFN Hot-Cor®

Ballistic Coefficient	0.236
COAL Tested	2.800"
Speer Part No.	2435

Propellant	Case	Primer	Starting Charge Weight (grains)	Starting Charge Muzzle Velocity (feet/sec)	Maximum Charge Weight (grains)	Maximum Charge Muzzle Velocity (feet/sec)
Hodgdon BL-C(2)	Remington	CCI 250	56.0	2729	60.0	2984
IMR 4064	Remington	CCI 200	58.0	2754	62.0 C	2955
IMR 4895	Remington	CCI 200	56.0	2732	60.0	2940
IMR 4320	Remington	CCI 200	57.0	2630	61.0 C	2822
Winchester 748	Remington	CCI 250	58.0	2486	62.0	2711
Hodgdon H380	Remington	CCI 250	58.0	2486	62.0 C	2666
Alliant Reloder 7	Remington	CCI 200	47.0	2349	51.0	2603
Winchester 760	Remington	CCI 250	61.0	2222	65.0 C	2445
IMR SR 4759 (reduced load)	Remington	CCI 200	26.0	1788	28.0	1934

WARNING! *Maximum loads should be used with CAUTION • C = Compressed Load*

220 GRAINS

DIAMETER	SECTIONAL DENSITY
.358"	0.245

35 SPFN Hot-Cor®

Ballistic Coefficient	0.286
COAL Tested	2.740"
Speer Part No.	2439

Propellant	Case	Primer	Starting Charge		Maximum Charge	
			Weight (grains)	Muzzle Velocity (feet/sec)	Weight (grains)	Muzzle Velocity (feet/sec)
Hodgdon BL-C(2)	Remington	CCI 250	56.0	2522	60.0	2708
Winchester 748	Remington	CCI 250	58.0	2515	62.0	2696
IMR 4895	Remington	CCI 200	56.0	2552	60.0	2686
IMR 3031	Remington	CCI 200	55.0	2475	59.0	2673
IMR 4320	Remington	CCI 200	56.0	2471	60.0 C	2660
Hodgdon H322	Remington	CCI 200	51.0	2452	55.0 C	2591
Hodgdon H380	Remington	CCI 250	58.0	2430	62.0 C	2522
Winchester 760	Remington	CCI 250	61.0	2320	65.0 C	2496
Alliant Reloder 7	Remington	CCI 200	45.5	2258	49.5	2450

WARNING! Maximum loads should be used with CAUTION • C = Compressed Load

250 GRAINS

DIAMETER	SECTIONAL DENSITY
.358"	0.279

35 Spitzer SP Hot-Cor®

Ballistic Coefficient	0.422
COAL Tested	2.800"
Speer Part No.	2453

Propellant	Case	Primer	Starting Charge Weight (grains)	Starting Charge Muzzle Velocity (feet/sec)	Maximum Charge Weight (grains)	Maximum Charge Muzzle Velocity (feet/sec)
Winchester 748	Remington	CCI 250	53.0	2284	57.0 C	2510
IMR 3031	Remington	CCI 200	48.0	2204	52.0 C	2404
IMR 4895	Remington	CCI 200	49.0	2174	53.0 C	2374
IMR 4064	Remington	CCI 200	51.0	2185	55.0 C	2369
Winchester 760	Remington	CCI 250	54.0	2130	58.0 C	2313
Hodgdon BL-C(2)	Remington	CCI 250	48.0	2085	52.0	2275
IMR 4320	Remington	CCI 200	50.0	2065	54.0 C	2236
Hodgdon H380	Remington	CCI 250	54.0	2029	58.0 C	2185
IMR SR 4759 (reduced load)	Remington	CCI 200	28.0	1681	30.0	1804

WARNING! Maximum loads should be used with CAUTION • C = Compressed Load

356 WINCHESTER

Parent Cartridge:	308 Winchester
Country of Origin:	USA
Year of Introduction:	1983
Designer(s):	Winchester
Governing Body:	SAAMI

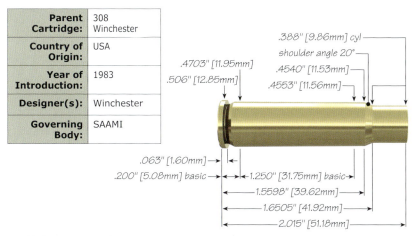

CARTRIDGE CASE DATA

Case Type:	Rimmed, bottleneck		
Average Case Capacity:	57.0 grains H₂O	Max. Cartridge OAL	2.560 inch
Max. Case Length:	2.015 inch	Primer:	Large Rifle
Case Trim to Length:	2.005 inch	RCBS Shell holder:	# 2
Current Manufacturers:	Winchester		

BALLISTIC DATA

Max. Average Pressure (MAP):	Piezo not established for this cartridge, 52,000 CUP - SAAMI	Test Barrel Length:	24 inch
Rifling Twist Rate:	1 turn in 12 inch		
Muzzle velocities of factory loaded ammunition	Bullet Wgt.		Muzzle velocity
	200-grain		2,460 fps
	250-grain		2,160 fps
	Muzzle velocity will decrease approximately 10 fps per inch for barrels less than 24 inches.		

HISTORICAL NOTES

- In the early 1980s, U.S. Repeating Arms developed a stronger version of their lever-action Model 94 rifle capable of firing modern, high pressure cartridges.

- For the new rifle, Winchester decided it was time (again) to replace the tired old 348 Winchester, 35 Remington, and more recent 358 Winchester brush busters with a more modern design; this time with a rim to make it compatible with the new Model 94 rifles.

- Winchester's record in such previous endeavors did not meet with success. In 1936 Winchester introduced the 348 Winchester cartridge for lever-action rifles to an indifferent market, then again in 1955 with the 358 Winchester to an indifferent market. With the new 356 Winchester cartridge, the third time might be the charm.
- To reduce design chores for the 356 Winchester to a minimum, Winchester selected a rimmed version of the 308 Winchester cartridge.
- The new cartridge offered several advantages:
  - The 356 Winchester would be compatible with U.S. Repeating Arms new, stronger Model 94 lever-action rifles, increasing the potential market sales base.
  - With a MAP level similar to its parent 308 Winchester cartridge, the 356 Winchester had real potential for improving ballistic performance.
  - Tooling costs were minimal; development times would be short.
- Following introduction of the new 356 Winchester cartridge in 1983, the market yawned (again), leaving the 356 Winchester (and its 307 Winchester companion) to putter along with its antecedents.
- Both are still listed in the current Winchester ammunition catalog—along with the 348 Winchester, 358 Winchester, and 35 Remington.
- Old cartridges never die. Just when you think you are finally rid of one, it returns to haunt you.

BALLISTIC NOTES

- Winchester factory-loads the 356 Winchester cartridge with a 200-grain bullet to a muzzle velocity of 2,460 fps. To build a handload that approximates the ballistics of the factory load, we recommend the Speer 220-grain SPFN Hot-Cor® handloaded to a muzzle velocity of 2,400 fps. The heavier bullet more than compensates for the lower muzzle velocity.
- Handloading the Speer 180-grain SPFN Hot-Cor opens a window of potential performance levels ranging from high velocity 2,700 fps to reduced recoil loads at 2,369 fps.
- For plinking or surprising varmints, pests, or predators at close ranges, try handloading the Speer 158-grain JHP or JSP revolver bullets at muzzle velocities of 2,600 fps (photo-grade expansion) to 2,200 fps.
- Regardless of the bullet weight used, the 356 Winchester cartridge is a short range proposition.

TECHNICAL NOTES

- Basically, the 356 Winchester is a 308 Winchester cartridge necked up to accept .358 inch diameter bullets.
- Case head diameter and case length are similar to the 308 Winchester, as is the 20° shoulder angle. However the similarity ends there.
- A larger rim diameter (.506 inch) creates a rimmed case. The rim of the 308 Winchester case is .473 inch diameter. In addition, the extractor groove typical of a rimless case has been eliminated and the length of the case head undercut increased. This creates a unique, hybrid case head configuration.
- Maximum overall length of a loaded 356 Winchester cartridge is 2.560 inches, in order for it to fit in short actions.
- MAP levels of the 356 Winchester cartridge remain the same as the 308 Win.

HANDLOADING NOTES

- In addition to building loaded ammunition, Winchester still offers new, empty, unprimed brass in 356 Winchester caliber.
- To avoid chambering problems in lever-action rifles, we recommend full length resizing all 356 Winchester fired brass.
- Medium burn rate propellants are the best choice for reloading the 356 Winchester.

SAFETY NOTES

SPEER 220-grain SPFN Hot-Cor @ a muzzle velocity of 2,344 fps:
- Maximum vertical altitude @ 90° elevation is 7,989 feet.
- Maximum horizontal distance to first impact with ground @ 35° elevation is 3,694 yards.

158 GRAINS

DIAMETER	SECTIONAL DENSITY
.357"	0.177

38 JHP

Ballistic Coefficient	0.163
COAL Tested	2.315"
Speer Part No.	4211

38 JSP

Ballistic Coefficient	0.164
COAL Tested	2.315"
Speer Part No.	4217

NOTE: Short COAL may require single-loading into chamber.

			Starting Charge		Maximum Charge	
Propellant	Case	Primer	Weight (grains)	Muzzle Velocity (feet/sec)	Weight (grains)	Muzzle Velocity (feet/sec)
Hodgdon H322	Winchester	CCI 200	45.0	2483	49.0	2631
IMR 3031	Winchester	CCI 200	45.0	2205	49.0	2556
Alliant Reloder 7	Winchester	CCI 200	36.0	2159	40.0	2370

WARNING! Maximum loads should be used with CAUTION • C = Compressed Load

180 GRAINS

DIAMETER	SECTIONAL DENSITY
.358"	0.201

35 SPFN Hot-Cor®

Ballistic Coefficient	0.236
COAL Tested	2.550"
Speer Part No.	2435

Propellant	Case	Primer	Starting Charge Weight (grains)	Starting Charge Muzzle Velocity (feet/sec)	Maximum Charge Weight (grains)	Maximum Charge Muzzle Velocity (feet/sec)
Accurate 2015	Winchester	CCI 200	43.0	2361	47.0 C	2717
IMR 8208 XBR	Winchester	CCI 200	44.5	2445	48.5	2644
Vihtavuori N133	Winchester	CCI 200	42.0	2396	46.0 C	2634
Hodgdon H322	Winchester	CCI 200	44.0	2350	48.0	2626
Hodgdon H335	Winchester	CCI 250	44.0	2322	48.0	2554
IMR 4064	Winchester	CCI 200	46.0	2358	50.0	2520
Hodgdon BL-C(2)	Winchester	CCI 250	47.0	2304	51.0 C	2516
IMR 4166	Winchester	CCI 200	43.5	2322	47.9	2509
IMR 4895	Winchester	CCI 200	45.0	2200	49.0	2449
IMR 3031	Winchester	CCI 200	42.0	2179	46.0	2440
Alliant Reloder 7	Winchester	CCI 200	36.0	2121	40.0	2401
Winchester 748	Winchester	CCI 250	47.0	2206	51.0	2393
IMR 4320	Winchester	CCI 200	43.0	2211	47.0	2369

WARNING! *Maximum loads should be used with CAUTION • C = Compressed Load*

220 GRAINS

DIAMETER	SECTIONAL DENSITY
.358"	0.245

35 SPFN Hot-Cor®	
Ballistic Coefficient	0.286
COAL Tested	2.550"
Speer Part No.	2439

			Starting Charge		Maximum Charge	
Propellant	Case	Primer	Weight (grains)	Muzzle Velocity (feet/sec)	Weight (grains)	Muzzle Velocity (feet/sec)
Alliant AR-Comp	Winchester	CCI 200	39.0	2173	44.0	2389
Accurate 2015	Winchester	CCI 200	38.0	2141	42.0 C	2386
Alliant Power Pro Varmint	Winchester	CCI 200	42.5	2234	46.4	2381
Winchester 748	Winchester	CCI 250	45.5	2172	49.5	2369
Vihtavuori N135	Winchester	CCI 200	41.0	2156	45.0 C	2345
IMR 4064	Winchester	CCI 200	42.0	2046	46.0	2340
IMR 4166	Winchester	CCI 200	40.5	2193	43.8	2339
Hodgdon H322	Winchester	CCI 200	39.0	2144	43.0	2323
IMR 4320	Winchester	CCI 200	42.0	2125	46.0	2310
Hodgdon H335	Winchester	CCI 250	39.0	2063	43.0	2294
IMR 4895	Winchester	CCI 200	42.0	2006	46.0	2278
Hodgdon BL-C(2)	Winchester	CCI 250	42.0	2054	46.0 C	2277
Hodgdon H380	Winchester	CCI 250	46.0	1992	50.0 C	2143
Alliant Reloder 7	Winchester	CCI 200	31.0	1877	35.0	2116

WARNING! *Maximum loads should be used with* CAUTION • C = Compressed Load

358 WINCHESTER

Alternate Names:	8.8x51mm
Parent Cartridge:	308 Winchester
Country of Origin:	USA
Year of Introduction:	1955
Designer(s):	Winchester
Governing Body:	SAAMI

CARTRIDGE CASE DATA

Case Type:	Rimless, bottleneck		
Average Case Capacity:	57.0 grains H$_2$O	**Max. Cartridge OAL**	2.780 inch
Max. Case Length:	2.015 inch	**Primer:**	Large Rifle
Case Trim to Length:	2.005 inch	**RCBS Shell holder:**	# 3
Current Manufacturers:	Winchester		

BALLISTIC DATA

Max. Average Pressure (MAP):	Piezo not established for this cartridge, 52,000 CUP - SAAMI	**Test Barrel Length:**	24 inch
Rifling Twist Rate:	1 turn in 12 inch		
Muzzle velocities of factory loaded ammunition	**Bullet Wgt.**		**Muzzle velocity**
	200-grain		2,490 fps
	Muzzle velocity will decrease approximately 10 fps per inch for barrels less than 24 inches.		

HISTORICAL NOTES

- By 1955, Winchester decided it was time to replace the tired old 348 Winchester and 35 Remington brush busters with a more modern, more powerful design. They designed the 358 Winchester cartridge for just this purpose.

- To reduce design chores to a minimum, Winchester simply necked up the 308 Winchester to accept .358 inch diameter bullets.

- The new cartridge offered several advantages:
  - Unlike the rimmed 348 Winchester, the new rimless cartridge would feed smoothly through bolt-action rifle magazines, increasing the potential market base.
  - With a MAP level similar to its 308 Winchester parent, it offered real potential for improving ballistic performance over the old cartridges.
  - It would be a good match for Winchester's new Model 88 lever-action rifle (that had a detachable box magazine, not a tubular one).
  - Tooling costs were minimal.
- The market yawned, leaving the 358 Winchester for dead along with its antecedents.
- Rather than push another 35-caliber dead duck uphill, Winchester quietly dropped the 358 Winchester in 1998.
- However, Winchester forgot that old cartridges never die. Just when you think you are finally rid of an old clunker, it returns to haunt you. Winchester returned the 358 Winchester cartridge to their product line in 2006. It is still listed—along with the 348 Winchester and 35 Remington!

BALLISTIC NOTES

- Winchester factory-loads this cartridge with a 200-grain bullet at a muzzle velocity of 2,490 fps, a ballistic performance that fully meets its original performance objectives.
- To build a handload that approximates the ballistics of the factory load, we recommend the Speer 220-grain SPFN Hot-Cor® handloaded to a muzzle velocity of 2,481 fps.
- If "brush busting" power is important and recoil levels not so much, we recommend for your consideration the Speer 250-grain Spitzer SP Hot-Cor loaded to a muzzle velocity of 2,333 fps. Handloading the Speer 180-grain SPFN Hot-Cor opens a wide window of potential performance levels ranging from 2,732 fps to a reduced load at a muzzle velocity of 2,420 fps to keep recoil at bay.
- For plinking or dispatching varmints, pests or predators at close ranges, you can load Speer 158-grain JHP or JSP revolver bullets at muzzle velocities of 2,850 fps (photo-grade expansion) to 2,496 fps (merely impressive expansion on impact).
- Savage Arms chambered their Model 99 lever action rifle in 358 Winchester. With their rotary magazine, handloading rounds with spitzer bullets can be safely loaded for flatter trajectory.

TECHNICAL NOTES

- Basically, the 358 Winchester is a 308 Winchester cartridge necked up to accept .358 inch diameter bullets.
- Case head dimensions, rim, and case length are similar as is the 20° shoulder angle.
- Maximum overall length of a loaded 358 Winchester cartridge is slightly shorter than the 308 Winchester to assure feeding with the blunt bullets.
- MAP levels remain the same as the 308 Winchester.

HANDLOADING NOTES

- To avoid chambering problems in lever-action rifles, we recommend full length resizing all 358 Winchester fired brass.
- Neck sizing can be used for bolt-action rifles.
- Fast burning propellants are the best choice for reloading the 358 Winchester.

SAFETY NOTES

SPEER 250-grain Spitzer SP Hot-Cor @ a muzzle velocity of 2,333 fps:
- Maximum vertical altitude @ 90° elevation is 10,035 feet.
- Maximum horizontal distance to first impact with ground @ 37° elevation is 4,737 yards.

158 GRAINS

DIAMETER	SECTIONAL DENSITY
.357"	0.177

38 JHP	
Ballistic Coefficient	0.163
COAL Tested	2.315"
Speer Part No.	4211

38 JSP	
Ballistic Coefficient	0.164
COAL Tested	2.315"
Speer Part No.	4217

			Starting Charge		Maximum Charge	
Propellant	Case	Primer	Weight (grains)	Muzzle Velocity (feet/sec)	Weight (grains)	Muzzle Velocity (feet/sec)
Alliant Reloder 7	Winchester	CCI 200	44.0	2538	48.0	2888
Hodgdon H322	Winchester	CCI 200	48.0	2562	52.0	2818
IMR 4064	Winchester	CCI 200	48.0	2522	52.0	2764

WARNING! *Maximum loads should be used with* CAUTION • C = Compressed Load

180 GRAINS

DIAMETER	SECTIONAL DENSITY
.358"	0.201

35 SPFN Hot-Cor®	
Ballistic Coefficient	0.236
COAL Tested	2.680"
Speer Part No.	2435

			Starting Charge		Maximum Charge	
Propellant	Case	Primer	Weight (grains)	Muzzle Velocity (feet/sec)	Weight (grains)	Muzzle Velocity (feet/sec)
Hodgdon H335	Winchester	CCI 250	48.0	2537	52.0	2766
Alliant Reloder 7	Winchester	CCI 200	41.0	2481	45.0	2762
IMR 3031	Winchester	CCI 200	47.0	2506	51.0	2755
IMR 4895	Winchester	CCI 200	47.0	2492	51.0	2734
Hodgdon H322	Winchester	CCI 200	46.0	2492	50.0	2713
IMR 4198	Winchester	CCI 200	38.0	2401	42.0	2706
Vihtavuori N133	Winchester	CCI 200	44.0	2494	48.0 C	2700
Accurate 2015	Winchester	CCI 200	43.0	2424	47.0 C	2658
Hodgdon BL-C(2)	Winchester	CCI 250	49.0	2439	53.0 C	2619
Winchester 748	Winchester	CCI 250	49.0	2360	53.0	2593
IMR 4320	Winchester	CCI 200	47.0	2443	51.0	2593

WARNING! Maximum loads should be used with CAUTION • C = Compressed Load

220 GRAINS

DIAMETER	SECTIONAL DENSITY
.358"	0.245

35 SPFN Hot-Cor®

Ballistic Coefficient	0.286
COAL Tested	2.565"
Speer Part No.	2439

			Starting Charge		Maximum Charge	
Propellant	Case	Primer	Weight (grains)	Muzzle Velocity (feet/sec)	Weight (grains)	Muzzle Velocity (feet/sec)
Winchester 748	Winchester	CCI 250	48.0	2348	52.0	2506
Vihtavuori N135	Winchester	CCI 200	44.0	2309	48.0 C	2476
IMR 3031	Winchester	CCI 200	43.0	2232	47.0	2474
Alliant Power Pro Varmint	Hornady	CCI 200	47.0	2342	50.6	2473
Accurate 2520	Winchester	CCI 250	44.0	2287	48.0 C	2455
Hodgdon H322	Winchester	CCI 200	41.0	2070	45.0	2434
Hodgdon H335	Winchester	CCI 250	43.5	2244	47.5	2428
IMR 4064	Winchester	CCI 200	44.0	2280	48.0	2427
IMR 4320	Winchester	CCI 200	43.5	2213	47.5	2393
IMR 8208 XBR	Hornady	CCI 200	43.0	2262	46.3	2392
Accurate 2015	Winchester	CCI 200	39.0	2202	43.0	2390
Hodgdon BLC-(2)	Winchester	CCI 250	46.0	2207	50.0 C	2388
IMR 4166	Hornady	CCI 200	42.5	2147	45.8	2285
Hodgdon H380	Winchester	CCI 250	46.0	2002	50.0 C	2231
Alliant Reloder 7	Winchester	CCI 200	34.0	2089	38.0	2209

WARNING! Maximum loads should be used with CAUTION • C = Compressed Load

250 GRAINS

DIAMETER	SECTIONAL DENSITY
.358"	0.279

35 Spitzer SP Hot-Cor®
Ballistic Coefficient	0.422
COAL Tested	2.775"
Speer Part No.	2453

			Starting Charge		Maximum Charge	
Propellant	Case	Primer	Weight (grains)	Muzzle Velocity (feet/sec)	Weight (grains)	Muzzle Velocity (feet/sec)
Hodgdon H335	Winchester	CCI 250	41.0	2133	45.0	2354
Accurate 2015	Winchester	CCI 200	39.0	2155	43.0	2334
Vihtavuori N135	Winchester	CCI 200	42.0	2141	46.0 C	2321
Hodgdon H322	Winchester	CCI 200	39.0	2065	43.0	2308
Alliant Power Pro Varmint	Hornady	CCI 200	42.0	2120	46.4	2298
IMR 4064	Winchester	CCI 200	40.0	2050	44.0	2282
Hodgdon BL-C(2)	Winchester	CCI 250	43.0	2081	47.0 C	2279
Winchester 748	Winchester	CCI 250	43.0	2042	47.0	2273
IMR 4320	Winchester	CCI 200	40.0	2017	44.0	2259
IMR 3031	Winchester	CCI 200	38.0	2021	42.0	2258
Hodgdon Benchmark	Hornady	CCI 200	40.0	2118	43.3	2242
IMR 8208 XBR	Hornady	CCI 200	40.0	2063	43.6	2240
Alliant Reloder 7	Winchester	CCI 200	33.0	1927	37.0	2184

WARNING! *Maximum loads should be used with* CAUTION • C = Compressed Load

35 WHELEN

Parent Cartridge:	30-06 Springfield
Country of Origin:	USA
Year of Introduction:	1987
Designer(s):	James Howe, Frankford Arsenal (1922). Reintroduced by Remington
Governing Body:	SAAMI

Case dimensions:
- .4698" [11.93mm]
- .473" [12.01mm]
- .3880" [9.86mm] cyl
- shoulder angle 17° 30'
- .4410" [11.20mm]
- .4426" [11.24mm]
- .049" [1.24mm]
- .200" [5.08mm] basic
- 1.650" [41.91mm] basic
- 1.9480" [49.48mm]
- 2.0320" [51.61mm]
- 2.494" [63.35mm]

CARTRIDGE CASE DATA

Case Type:	Rimless, bottleneck		
Average Case Capacity:	72.6 grains H$_2$O	Max. Cartridge OAL	3.340 inch
Max. Case Length:	2.494 inch	Primer:	Large Rifle
Case Trim to Length:	2.484 inch	RCBS Shell holder:	# 3
Current Manufacturers:	Remington, Hornady, Federal, Winchester, Nosler		

BALLISTIC DATA

Max. Average Pressure (MAP):	62,000 psi, 52,000 CUP - SAAMI	Test Barrel Length:	24 inch
Rifling Twist Rate:	1 turn in 16 inch		
Muzzle velocities of factory loaded ammunition	Bullet Wgt.	Muzzle velocity	
	200-grain	2,675 fps	
	250-grain	2,400 fps	

Muzzle velocity will decrease approximately 20 fps per inch for barrels less than 24 inches.

HISTORICAL NOTES

- The 35 Whelen is an example of a wildcat cartridge good enough to be standardized for commercial production by a major domestic ammunition manufacturer.
- It is also an example of a uniquely American sporting cartridge developed for American hunting tastes and conditions.
- Developed by gunsmith James Howe and named after Col. Townsend Whelen, the 35 Whelen was introduced by Remington in 1987.
- Howe saw his creation as a ballistic bridge between the 30-06 Springfield and the 375 H&H Magnum cartridge. From a purely marketing perspective, this was a narrow niche indeed.
- Time marches on and tastes change. To magnum-minded 21st century hunters, the 35 Whelen seems a relic from a past age. As a result, the 35 Whelen is slowly fading away.
- Remington is the only ammunition manufacturer that has undertaken production of this cartridge.

BALLISTIC NOTES

- Here it is important to note that as the 35 Whelen will not be used in rifles with tubular magazines, pointed bullets can be used.
- Although the 35 Whelen is not considered a magnum, it is capable of taking any species of North American big game.
- To approximate the 200-grain bullet factory load, we recommend the Speer 220-grain SPFN Hot-Cor® which can be handloaded to a muzzle velocity of 2,600 fps. This load generates 3,301 ft-lbs of muzzle energy. Also, this bullet can be downloaded to a muzzle velocity of 2,210 fps to reduce recoil while maintaining a respectable level of muzzle energy more suitable for deer hunting.
- For shooters who prefer an equivalent to the factory 250-grain bullet load, Speer offers the 250-grain Spitzer SP Hot-Cor. Remington's catalog lists no factory load with a lightweight bullet for deer hunting. To remedy this shortcoming, we propose the Speer 180-grain SPFN Hot-Cor handloaded to a muzzle velocity as high as 2,900 fps.

TECHNICAL NOTES

- Basically, the 35 Whelen cartridge is a 30-06 Springfield cartridge case necked up to accept .358 inch diameter bullets.
- Case head dimensions, case length, and overall loaded length of the two cartridges are similar. The shoulder length of the 35 Whelen is approximately half that of the 30-06 Springfield.
- MAP levels of the 35 Whelen are also comparable to the 30-06 Springfield.

HANDLOADING NOTES

- Note that the correct bullet diameter for the 35 Whelen cartridge is .358 inch.
- As most 35 Whelen ammunition will be fired in bolt-action rifles, we recommend neck sizing to extend the reloading life of your brass and reduce trimming chores for practice and sight-in. Hunt with full length resized cases.
- Slow burning propellants are the best choice for reloading the 35 Whelen.

SAFETY NOTES

SPEER 250-grain Spitzer SP Hot-Cor @ a muzzle velocity of 2,386 fps:
- Maximum vertical altitude @ 90° elevation is 10,128 feet.
- Maximum horizontal distance to first impact with ground @ 36° elevation is 4,770 yards.

158 GRAINS

DIAMETER	SECTIONAL DENSITY
.357"	0.177

38 JHP

Ballistic Coefficient	0.163
COAL Tested	2.800"
Speer Part No.	4211

38 JSP

Ballistic Coefficient	0.164
COAL Tested	2.800"
Speer Part No.	4217

NOTE: *COAL is less than minimum; may require single loading.*

			Starting Charge		Maximum Charge	
Propellant	Case	Primer	Weight (grains)	Muzzle Velocity (feet/sec)	Weight (grains)	Muzzle Velocity (feet/sec)
Alliant Reloder 7	Remington	CCI 200	DNR	—	42.0	2209
Accurate 2015	Remington	CCI 200	DNR	—	40.0	2139
IMR 4895	Remington	CCI 200	DNR	—	45.0	1988

DNR—Do not reduce

WARNING! Maximum loads should be used with CAUTION • C = Compressed Load

180 GRAINS

DIAMETER	SECTIONAL DENSITY
.358"	0.201

35 SPFN Hot-Cor®

Ballistic Coefficient	0.236
COAL Tested	3.030"
Speer Part No.	2435

Propellant	Case	Primer	Starting Charge		Maximum Charge	
			Weight (grains)	Muzzle Velocity (feet/sec)	Weight (grains)	Muzzle Velocity (feet/sec)
Alliant Power Pro Varmint	Federal	Federal 210	63.0	2911	70.0 C	3172
IMR 8208 XBR	Federal	Federal 210	59.6	2918	63.8 C	3080
Alliant Power Pro 1200-R	Federal	Federal 210	51.2	2793	56.1	2984
Alliant AR-Comp	Federal	Federal 210	57.6	2713	63.0 C	2950
Hodgdon H335	Remington	CCI 250	61.0	2841	65.0 C	2931
Hodgdon CFE 223	Federal	Federal 210	65.7	2775	69.0 C	2904
Accurate 2460	Remington	CCI 250	56.0	2291	60.0 C	2899
Accurate 2230	Remington	CCI 200	54.0	2703	58.0 C	2891
Hodgdon BL-C(2)	Remington	CCI 250	60.0	2719	64.0	2863
Accurate 2015	Remington	CCI 200	50.0	2591	54.0	2834
Hodgdon H322	Remington	CCI 200	54.0	2676	58.0 C	2834
Hodgdon H4895	Remington	CCI 200	54.0	2623	58.0 C	2818
Vihtavuori N140	Remington	CCI 200	58.0	2667	62.0 C	2807
IMR 4895	Remington	CCI 200	53.0	2538	57.0 C	2797
IMR 3031	Remington	CCI 200	53.0	2497	57.0 C	2775
IMR 4064	Remington	CCI 200	56.0	2536	60.0 C	2765
Alliant Reloder 15	Remington	CCI 200	56.0	2511	60.0 C	2710

WARNING! Maximum loads should be used with CAUTION • C = Compressed Load

220 GRAINS

DIAMETER	SECTIONAL DENSITY
.358"	0.245

35 SPFN Hot-Cor®

Ballistic Coefficient	0.286
COAL Tested	3.230"
Speer Part No.	2439

			Starting Charge		Maximum Charge	
Propellant	Case	Primer	Weight (grains)	Muzzle Velocity (feet/sec)	Weight (grains)	Muzzle Velocity (feet/sec)
Alliant Power Pro Varmint	Federal	Federal 210	57.8	2615	63.8 C	2826
Hodgdon CFE 223	Federal	Federal 210	61.0	2536	67.0 C	2788
Alliant Power Pro 2000-MR	Federal	Federal 210	62.2	2546	68.5 C	2786
Alliant AR-Comp	Federal	Federal 210	55.1	2557	61.0 C	2777
IMR 8208 XBR	Federal	Federal 210	52.8	2522	58.6	2741
Alliant Reloder 15	Remington	CCI 200	56.0	2445	60.0 C	2628
Winchester 748	Remington	CCI 250	59.0	2542	63.0 C	2588
Hodgdon H335	Remington	CCI 250	52.0	2312	56.0	2586
Accurate 2460	Remington	CCI 250	50.0	2390	54.0	2520
Vihtavuori N140	Remington	CCI 200	54.0	2330	58.0 C	2505
IMR 4451	Federal	Federal 210	57.1	2258	63.0 C	2504
IMR 3031	Remington	CCI 200	51.0	2294	55.0 C	2503
Hodgdon BL-C(2)	Remington	CCI 250	53.0	2371	57.0	2481
IMR 4064	Remington	CCI 200	52.0	2260	56.0 C	2468
Hodgdon H380	Remington	CCI 250	57.0	2300	61.0 C	2445
Accurate 2015	Remington	CCI 200	45.0	2252	49.0	2438
IMR 4895	Remington	CCI 200	49.0	2332	53.0	2400
Hodgdon H322	Remington	CCI 200	45.0	2236	49.0	2397
IMR 4320	Remington	CCI 200	50.0	2113	54.0	2298

WARNING! Maximum loads should be used with CAUTION • C = Compressed Load

250 GRAINS

DIAMETER	SECTIONAL DENSITY
.358"	0.279

35 Spitzer SP Hot-Cor®

Ballistic Coefficient	0.422
COAL Tested	3.340"
Speer Part No.	2453

Propellant	Case	Primer	Starting Charge Weight (grains)	Starting Charge Muzzle Velocity (feet/sec)	Maximum Charge Weight (grains)	Maximum Charge Muzzle Velocity (feet/sec)
Alliant Power Pro 2000-MR	Federal	Federal 210	60.0	2505	66.2 C	2709
Hodgdon CFE 223	Federal	Federal 210	57.9	2451	64.1	2664
Alliant Power Pro Varmint	Federal	Federal 210	53.5	2429	59.1	2617
Alliant AR-Comp	Federal	Federal 210	50.7	2379	56.1	2555
IMR 8208 XBR	Federal	Federal 210	50.0	2402	53.8	2525
IMR 4451	Federal	Federal 210	56.3	2236	62.1 C	2453
Hodgdon H335	Remington	CCI 250	49.0	2220	53.0	2408
Winchester 748	Remington	CCI 250	53.0	2296	57.0	2371
Accurate 2460	Remington	CCI 250	48.0	2209	52.0	2355
Hodgdon BL-C(2)	Remington	CCI 250	50.0	2178	54.0	2334
IMR 4064	Remington	CCI 200	49.0	2062	53.0	2331
Vihtavuori N140	Remington	CCI 200	50.0	2144	54.0	2318
Hodgdon H380	Remington	CCI 250	55.0	2157	59.0 C	2306
Alliant Reloder 15	Remington	CCI 200	50.0	2148	54.0	2303
Accurate 2015	Remington	CCI 200	43.0	2174	47.0	2262
IMR 3031	Remington	CCI 200	47.0	2072	51.0	2262
Hodgdon H322	Remington	CCI 200	44.0	2134	48.0	2197
IMR 4895	Remington	CCI 200	45.0	2097	49.0	2156

WARNING! Maximum loads should be used with CAUTION • C = Compressed Load

358 NORMA MAGNUM

Alternate Names:	9.1x64mmBR
Parent Cartridge:	375 H&H Magnum
Country of Origin:	Sweden
Year of Introduction:	1959
Designer(s):	Nils Kvale, Norma
Governing Body:	CIP

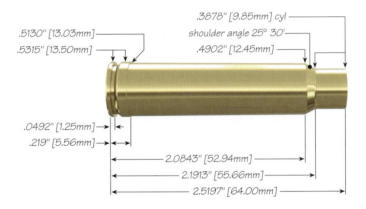

CARTRIDGE CASE DATA			
Case Type:	Belted, rimless, bottleneck		
Average Case Capacity:	88.0 grains H_2O	Max. Cartridge OAL	3.346 inch
Max. Case Length:	2.520 inch	Primer:	Large Rifle
Case Trim to Length:	2.510 inch	RCBS Shell holder:	# 4
Current Manufacturers:	Norma		

BALLISTIC DATA			
Max. Average Pressure (MAP):	63,817 psi - CIP	Test Barrel Length:	24 inch
Rifling Twist Rate:	1 turn in 12 inch		
Muzzle velocities of factory loaded ammunition		Bullet Wgt.	Muzzle velocity
		250-grain	2,790 fps
	Muzzle velocity will decrease approximately 20 fps per inch for barrels less than 24 inches.		

HISTORICAL NOTES

- When Norma announced their new 358 Norma Magnum cartridge in 1959, they followed an unconventional path of introduction in much the same fashion as their 308 Norma Magnum introduced earlier.
- First, they offered unprimed, empty cases and reloading data for their new cartridge. No loaded ammunition in the new cartridge was listed in the Norma catalog and no firearms makers offered guns in 358 Norma Magnum.
- As rifles in the new caliber would have to be made by custom gun makers, Norma instituted a program for "loaner" chambering reamers and headspace gauges to ensure uniformity of dimension.
- In 1962, Norma added 358 Norma Magnum loaded ammunition to their catalog. Some European gun makers added the new caliber to their product lines, however it was ignored by domestic firearms makers.
- The system worked, more or less. However, sales of 358 Norma Magnum ammunition never reached critical mass in the North American market. Why?
- North American hunters have never really taken to 35 caliber rifle cartridges. The 358 Norma Magnum might have changed this, however Norma did not have the marketing power then to create a North American demand for their new cartridge.
- The 358 Norma Magnum more than proved its capabilities on moose in Scandinavia and on plains game in Africa, but has remained something of a specialty item in the North American market.
- Today, the 358 Norma Magnum is alive and well in the Norma ammunition catalog. Both loaded ammunition and new, unprimed brass remains available to North American handloaders.

BALLISTIC NOTES

- While the 358 Norma Magnum has been standardized in the European CIP, it has not been standardized by SAAMI. As a result, there is no SAAMI MAP standard for the 358 Norma Mag.
- Norma loads the 358 Norma Magnums only with a 250-grain bullet at a muzzle velocity of 2,756 fps. Clearly, Norma considers their 358 Magnum a cartridge suitable for very large game.
- Fortunately, North American handloaders have the option of loading a 180-grain bullet such as the Speer SPFN Hot-Cor® at muzzle velocities perfectly suitable for hunting deer of all sizes.
- Should you wish to duplicate Norma factory load ballistics, a 250-grain bullet with a slightly higher ballistic coefficient, we can suggest the Speer Spitzer SP Hot-Cor.

TECHNICAL NOTES

- In much the same fashion as its junior sibling, the 358 Norma Magnum is a belted magnum case having an overall loaded length short enough to fit in a 30-06 Springfield length rifle action.
- The 358 Norma Magnum shares very similar (but not identical) rim, belt, and head dimensions with 338 Winchester Magnum cartridge. Case length is similar (but not identical) and shoulder angle is 25.5° on the Norma Magnum and 25° on the Winchester Magnum.

- Case capacity of the 358 Norma Magnum is on par with the 338 Winchester Magnum and about 20% greater than the 350 Remington Magnum.

HANDLOADING NOTES

- If need be, 358 Norma Magnum brass can be formed from 338 Winchester Magnum cases by necking them up in a 358 Norma Magnum sizing die, fire forming them, then trimming them to the correct length. Annealing the case necks afterward will extend case life.
- As most 358 Norma Magnum cartridges will be fired from bolt-action rifles, we strongly recommend neck sizing for practice and sight-in to extend case life, reduce trimming chores and cut down the number of head separations. Full length size for hunting loads.
- As do all big magnum cartridges, the 358 Norma Magnum works best with slow burning propellants.

SAFETY NOTES

SPEER 250-grain Spitzer SP Hot-Cor @ a muzzle velocity of 2,732 fps:
- Maximum vertical altitude @ 90° elevation is 10,701 feet.
- Maximum horizontal distance to first impact with ground @ 36° elevation is 4,973 yards.

180 GRAINS

DIAMETER	SECTIONAL DENSITY
.358"	0.201

35 SPFN Hot-Cor®

Ballistic Coefficient	0.236
COAL Tested	3.340"
Speer Part No.	2435

			Starting Charge		Maximum Charge	
Propellant	Case	Primer	Weight (grains)	Muzzle Velocity (feet/sec)	Weight (grains)	Muzzle Velocity (feet/sec)
IMR 4895	Norma	CCI 250	65.0	2943	69.0	3133
IMR 4320	Norma	CCI 250	68.0	2945	72.0	3132
IMR 4064	Norma	CCI 250	67.0	2933	71.0	3124
Hodgdon H380	Norma	CCI 250	68.0	2910	72.0	3075
IMR 4350	Norma	CCI 250	74.0	2778	78.0	2948
Hodgdon H414	Norma	CCI 250	73.0	2652	77.0	2836
IMR SR 4759 (reduced load)	Norma	CCI 250	30.0	1893	32.0	2013

WARNING! *Maximum loads should be used with* **CAUTION** *• C = Compressed Load*

250 GRAINS

DIAMETER	SECTIONAL DENSITY
.358"	0.279

35 Spitzer SP Hot-Cor®
Ballistic Coefficient	0.422
COAL Tested	3.340"
Speer Part No.	2453

			Starting Charge		Maximum Charge	
Propellant	Case	Primer	Weight (grains)	Muzzle Velocity (feet/sec)	Weight (grains)	Muzzle Velocity (feet/sec)
IMR 4350	Norma	CCI 250	72.0	2581	76.0	2732
IMR 4320	Norma	CCI 250	63.0	2483	67.0	2644
IMR 4064	Norma	CCI 250	61.0	2458	65.0	2638
IMR 4895	Norma	CCI 250	59.0	2414	63.0	2584
Hodgdon H380	Norma	CCI 250	63.0	2429	67.0	2579
IMR SR 4759 (reduced load)	Norma	CCI 250	30.0	1705	32.0	1821

WARNING! Maximum loads should be used with *CAUTION* • C = Compressed Load

9.3x62

Alternate Names:	9.3x62mm Mauser
Parent Cartridge:	8x57mm
Country of Origin:	Germany
Year of Introduction:	1905
Designer(s):	Otto Bock
Governing Body:	CIP

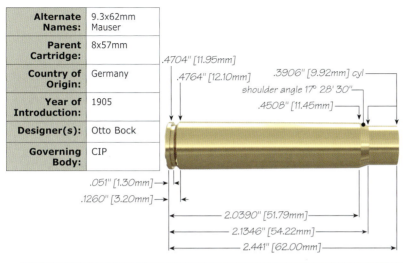

CARTRIDGE CASE DATA

Case Type:	Rimless, bottleneck
Average Case Capacity:	77.0 grains H_2O
Max. Cartridge OAL:	3.291 inch
Max. Case Length:	2.441 inch
Primer:	Large Rifle
Case Trim to Length:	2.431 inch
RCBS Shell holder:	# 3
Current Manufacturers:	Lapua, Norma, RUAG (RWS), Prvi Partizan, Nosler, Hornady

BALLISTIC DATA

Max. Average Pressure (MAP):	56,565 psi - CIP
Test Barrel Length:	24 inch
Rifling Twist Rate:	1 turn in 14 inch

Muzzle velocities of factory loaded ammunition

Bullet Wgt.	Muzzle velocity
231-grain	2,625 fps
256-grain	2,560 fps
286-grain	2,360 fps
293-grain	2,430 fps

Muzzle velocity will decrease approximately 20 fps per inch for barrels less than 24 inches.

HISTORICAL NOTES

- The 9.3x62 cartridge is another European cartridge that few American sportsmen have ever heard of or seen. It was designed for use in bolt-action magazine rifles with standard length actions.

- Developed in Germany and introduced in 1905, this caliber has become a world-wide favorite often found in former Dutch or German colonial countries where it is used as a working ranch rifle.

- Of all the German cartridges developed in the era before World War I, the 9.3x62 is one of the very few remaining in production.

- Several European manufacturers offer 9.3x62 ammunition.

Interesting Fact

Many countries ban possession of rifles in military calibers. However, ownership of rifles in non-military, sporting calibers is allowed. The criteria for determining a sporting cartridge from a military one is if the cartridge in question was ever used as a military service cartridge by any country. The 9.3x62 meets all requirements as a sporting cartridge.

BALLISTIC NOTES

- The 9.3x62 is broadly similar to the 35 Whelen in concept and dimension.

- Ballistics of the 9.3x62 fills the ballistic gap between the 8mm cartridges and the 375 H&H Magnum.

- That said, exterior ballistics of the 9.3x62 show it a bit more powerful than the 35 Whelen.

- The 9.3x62 cartridge is capable of taking all species of North American game and most African plains game. It is not powerful enough for use on dangerous game.

- Speer offers a .366 inch diameter 270-grain Semi-Spitzer SP Hot-Cor® designed specifically for the 9.3x62 cartridge. This compromise weight provides a better balance of muzzle velocity, striking energy and recoil for North American hunting conditions than some of the European loads. For example, when handloaded to a muzzle velocity of 2,583 fps, this bullet offers 4,000 ft-lbs of muzzle energy.

- Or, it can be loaded down to 2,253 fps with a muzzle energy of 3,043 ft-lbs for hunting lighter game and reducing recoil.

- Of course the 9.3x62 cartridge has been listed by CIP for decades. SAAMI has followed suit.

- Both Hornady and Nosler have added this caliber to their ammunition product lines.

HANDLOADING NOTES

- In addition to the manufacturers of loaded ammunition listed above, currently Hornady and Norma/RUAG offer new, empty, unprimed brass in 9.3x62 for handloading.

- The 9.3mm (.366 inch) diameter bullet for this cartridge will be unfamiliar to most American handloaders and shooters as there is no American equivalent. As a result, bullets for handloading the 9.3x62 have been difficult to find. Fortunately, Speer makes a suitable bullet for both the 9.3x62 and the 9.3x74R.

- As most 9.3x62 ammunition will be fired in bolt-action rifles, we recommend neck sizing to extend case reloading life and reduce trimming chores.

- Slower burning propellants work very well in the 9.3x62 cartridge.

SAFETY NOTES

SPEER 270-grain Semi-Spitzer SP Hot-Cor @ a muzzle velocity of 2,523 fps:
- Maximum vertical altitude @ 90° elevation is 9,438 feet.
- Maximum horizontal distance to first impact with ground @ 35° elevation is 4,375 yards.

270 GRAINS

DIAMETER	SECTIONAL DENSITY
.366"	0.288

9.3mm Semi-Spitzer SP Hot-Cor®

Ballistic Coefficient	0.361
COAL Tested	3.280"
Speer Part No.	2459

			Starting Charge		Maximum Charge	
Propellant	Case	Primer	Weight (grains)	Muzzle Velocity (feet/sec)	Weight (grains)	Muzzle Velocity (feet/sec)
Alliant Reloder 16	Federal	Federal 210	57.6	2318	63.9 C	2523
Alliant Reloder 17	Federal	Federal 210	55.5	2249	61.5	2482
Hodgdon H414	Federal	Federal 210	59.0	2352	62.4	2473
IMR 4831	Federal	Federal 210	58.6	2241	64.8 C	2461
IMR 4350	Federal	Federal 210	55.5	2237	61.7 C	2459
Winchester 760	Federal	Federal 210	55.7	2226	61.8	2454
Alliant Power Pro 2000-MR	Federal	Federal 210	56.0	2333	59.3	2439
Alliant Reloder 15	Federal	Federal 210	51.5	2243	57.1	2438
Hodgdon H380	Federal	Federal 210	54.2	2210	60.1	2425
Winchester 748	Federal	Federal 210	53.6	2267	58.0	2419
IMR 4451	Federal	Federal 210	56.7	2205	61.8	2378
IMR 4895	Federal	Federal 210	46.8	2180	51.9	2333

WARNING! Maximum loads should be used with CAUTION • C = Compressed Load

9.3x74R

Parent Cartridge:	9.3x72mm
Country of Origin:	Germany
Year of Introduction:	1900
Designer(s):	N/A
Governing Body:	CIP

Case dimensions:
- .5256" [13.35mm]
- .4685" [11.90mm]
- .055" [1.40mm]
- .3906" [9.92mm] cyl
- shoulder angle 5° 29'
- .40945" [10.40mm]
- 2.322" [59.00mm]
- 2.4213" [61.50mm]
- 2.941" [74.70mm]

CARTRIDGE CASE DATA

Case Type:	Rimmed, tapered, slight neck
Average Case Capacity:	82.0 grains H₂O
Max. Cartridge OAL:	3.720 inch
Max. Case Length:	2.941 inch
Primer:	Large Rifle
Case Trim to Length:	2.931 inch
RCBS Shell holder:	# 4
Current Manufacturers:	Hornady, Norma, Federal, Sako, RWS, RUAG, Sellier & Bellot

BALLISTIC DATA

Max. Average Pressure (MAP):	49,313 psi - CIP
Test Barrel Length:	24 inch
Rifling Twist Rate:	1 turn in 14 inch

Muzzle velocities of factory loaded ammunition

Bullet Wgt.	Muzzle velocity
232-grain	2,630 fps
258-grain	2,460 fps
285-grain	2,280 fps
296-grain	2,360 fps

Muzzle velocity will decrease approximately 15 fps per inch for barrels less than 24 inches.

HISTORICAL NOTES

- The 9.3x74R was Germany's answer to the English 400/360 Nitro Express.
- It is chambered in Germanic Drillings, Cape Rifles, single and double barreled rifles.

- The 9.3x74R ballistically compares to the 35 Whelen, 350 Remington Magnum and the 375 Flanged Magnum (Rimmed 375 H&H Magnum).
- This round is intended for medium and heavy game animals.

HANDLOADING NOTES

- In addition to the manufacturers of loaded ammunition listed above, cases are available from Hornady, Norma, RUAG (RWS), Nosler, SAKO, and Sellier & Bellot.
- Powders with a medium burn rate are recommended for use in this round for best velocity and accuracy.
- Be sure of adequate neck tension. We recommend taking the time to setup a firm, smooth taper crimp for optimum ignition and velocity.

SAFETY NOTES

SPEER 270-grain Soft Point Hot-Cor @ a muzzle velocity of 2,403 fps:
- Maximum vertical altitude @ 90° elevation is 9,183 feet.
- Maximum horizontal distance to first impact with ground @ 36° elevation is 4,285 yards.

270 GRAINS

DIAMETER	SECTIONAL DENSITY
.366"	0.288

9.3mm Semi-Spitzer SP Hot-Cor®

Ballistic Coefficient	0.361
COAL Tested	3.665"
Speer Part No.	2459

			Starting Charge		Maximum Charge	
Propellant	Case	Primer	Weight (grains)	Muzzle Velocity (feet/sec)	Weight (grains)	Muzzle Velocity (feet/sec)
Alliant Reloder 16	Norma	Federal 210	58.7	2238	64.4 C	2403
Winchester 760	Norma	Federal 210	58.7	2170	65.0	2382
IMR 4350	Norma	Federal 210	55.8	2149	61.8	2340
Alliant Reloder 15	Norma	Federal 210	51.0	2142	56.0	2322
IMR 4895	RWS	CCI 200	51.0	2097	55.0	2288
Hodgdon H380	Norma	Federal 210	53.4	2113	58.5	2281
IMR 4064	RWS	CCI 200	54.0	2157	58.0	2279
IMR 4451	Norma	Federal 210	55.5	2129	61.2	2272
IMR 4831	Norma	Federal 210	57.2	2070	63.2	2243
Winchester 748	RWS	CCI 200	56.0	2108	60.0	2235
Accurate 3100	RWS	CCI 200	60.0	1898	64.0 C	2086

WARNING! *Maximum loads should be used with CAUTION • C = Compressed Load*

375 HOLLAND & HOLLAND MAGNUM

Alternate Names:	9.5x72mm, 375 H&H MAGNUM
Parent Cartridge:	Original
Country of Origin:	Britain
Year of Introduction:	1912
Designer(s):	Holland & Holland
Governing Body:	SAAMI/CIP

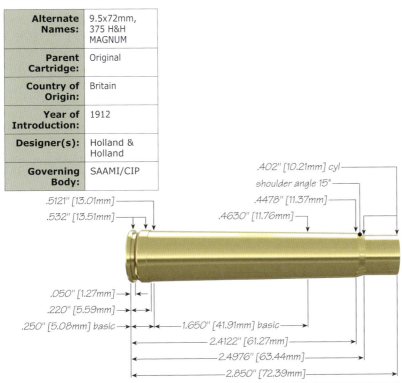

CARTRIDGE CASE DATA

Case Type:	Belted, tapered bottleneck		
Average Case Capacity:	95.0 grains H$_2$O	Max. Cartridge OAL	3.600 inch
Max. Case Length:	2.850 inch	Primer:	Large Rifle
Case Trim to Length:	2.840 inch	RCBS Shell holder:	# 4
Current Manufacturers:	Federal, Hornady, Remington, Winchester, Nosler, RUAG, Norma		

BALLISTIC DATA

Max. Average Pressure (MAP):	62,000 psi, 53,000 CUP - SAAMI	Test Barrel Length:	24 inch
Rifling Twist Rate:	1 turn in 12 inch		
Muzzle velocities of factory loaded ammunition	Bullet Wgt.		Muzzle velocity
	270-grain		2,690 fps
	300-grain		2,530 fps
	Muzzle velocity will decrease approximately 20 fps per inch for barrels less than 24 inches.		

HISTORICAL NOTES

- Holland & Holland (H&H) introduced their new 375 H&H Magnum cartridge in 1912 to general acclaim.
- A key feature of the new cartridge was its belted case developed by H&H. The belted case concept was to become the hallmark of future magnum cartridges.
- Holland & Holland's 375 H&H Magnum cartridge quickly became THE cartridge of choice for hunting all species of African game with magazine rifles. It retains this position today.
- A major reason for the popularity of the 375 H&H Magnum was its ability to take all species of African game, including dangerous game, with one caliber of cartridge.
- A second reason was the moderate recoil, described as a big push on your shoulder rather than a sharp blow.
- Beginning in the late 1980s, the introduction of several new 375 Magnum cartridges launched rumors of the impending retirement of the 375 H&H Magnum.
- Not so. The popularity of the 375 H&H Magnum remains as strong as ever.
- What is the secret of the 375 H&H? Many hunters feel it is the superior balance between power, weight, recoil and caliber.

Interesting Fact

In many African countries the 375 H&H Magnum is the *minimum* caliber that can be used on dangerous game.

BALLISTIC NOTES

- Although Holland & Holland designed their 375 H&H Magnum for hunting African game, it is versatile enough for North American game with the right bullet.
- The most common bullet weights for the 375 H&H Magnum are the 270-grain and the 300-grain. These bullets are designed for African hunting.
- Bullets as light as 235 grains are offered by some bullet manufacturers for lighter game.
- The 1 turn in 12 inch rifling twist rate of the 375 H&H Magnum will stabilize bullets up to 300 grains.

TECHNICAL NOTES

- With its belted head, long, tapered case, shallow 15° shoulder angle, and large caliber bullet, the 375 H&H Magnum looks like the quintessential magnum rifle cartridge—large, powerful, and deadly (visual cues are a neglected field of cartridge design).
- In similar manner to other belted magnum cartridges, the 375 H&H Magnum headspaces on the belt, just like a proper Holland & Holland magnum jolly well should!
- The enduring qualities of the 375 H&H Magnum case design can be gauged by the bewildering number of wildcat and commercial variations based on it.
- MAP level of the 375 H&H Magnum is competitive with its 375 RUM, 375 Ruger and 378 Weatherby Magnum rivals.

- Although case capacity of the 375 H&H Magnum is smaller than its modern rivals, arguably it strikes a better balance. Perhaps the rivals are too focused on high velocity and the large charges of propellant required to reach such levels. A wretched excess of striking energy may have its limits.
- Because of its 3.600 inch maximum overall loaded length (identical to the modern 300 Remington Ultra Magnum), the 375 H&H Magnum needs long action rifles.

HANDLOADING NOTES

- In addition to the manufacturers of loaded ammunition listed above, new, empty brass for reloading the 375 H&H Magnum is offered by most major ammunition manufacturers.
- Belted magnums that headspace on their belt have a tendency to stretch at the head just in front of the belt. After five or six reloads, it is not uncommon to experience head separations with such cases.
- For North American game, the Speer 235-grain Semi-Spitzer SP Hot-Cor® has proven very effective on larger species. Should you have African hunting conditions that require a heavier bullet, our recommendation is the Speer 285-grain Grand Slam® SP. This is an excellent general purpose bullet.
- The 375 H&H Magnum normally is not considered a long range cartridge. Handloaders have the option to change this with the Speer 270-grain Spitzer BTSP. The boat tail design of this bullet offers higher striking velocity and energy, flatter trajectory, and less wind drift at all ranges than flat base bullets. This is a perfect combination for long shots in open country.
- The 375 H&H cartridge works best with slow burning powders.

SAFETY NOTES

SPEER 270-grain Spitzer BTSP @ a muzzle velocity of 2,797 fps:
- Maximum vertical altitude @ 90° elevation is 17,730 feet.
- Maximum horizontal distance to first impact with ground @ 35° elevation is 5,473 yards.

235 GRAINS

DIAMETER	SECTIONAL DENSITY
.375"	0.239

375 Semi-Spitzer SP Hot-Cor®

Ballistic Coefficient	0.301
COAL Tested	3.600"
Speer Part No.	2471

Propellant	Case	Primer	Starting Charge Weight (grains)	Starting Charge Muzzle Velocity (feet/sec)	Maximum Charge Weight (grains)	Maximum Charge Muzzle Velocity (feet/sec)
Hodgdon CFE 223	Federal	CCI 250	71.0	2797	78.7	2969
Vihtavuori N540	Winchester	CCI 250	70.0	2835	74.0	2948
Hodgdon H380	Winchester	CCI 250	80.0	2826	84.0	2930
Alliant Reloder 15	Winchester	CCI 250	74.0	2828	78.0	2920
IMR 8208 XBR	Federal	CCI 250	67.0	2755	72.0	2901
IMR 4166	Federal	CCI 250	65.5	2707	72.0	2882
Accurate 4350	Winchester	CCI 250	81.0	2738	85.0 C	2877
Vihtavuori N140	Winchester	CCI 250	71.0	2766	75.0	2873
IMR 4064	Winchester	CCI 250	70.0	2707	74.0	2854
IMR 4350	Winchester	CCI 250	81.0	2672	85.0 C	2840
Hodgdon H414	Winchester	CCI 250	84.0	2736	86.0 C	2808
Hodgdon Varget	Winchester	CCI 250	70.0	2686	74.0	2803
Hodgdon H4350	Winchester	CCI 250	78.0	2715	82.0 C	2799
Accurate 2700	Winchester	CCI 250	74.0	2647	78.0	2778
IMR 3031	Winchester	CCI 250	63.0	2478	67.0	2702
IMR 4895	Winchester	CCI 250	64.0	2420	68.0	2591
IMR SR 4759 (reduced load)	Winchester	CCI 250	28.0	1610	30.0	1701

WARNING! Maximum loads should be used with CAUTION • C = Compressed Load

270 GRAINS

DIAMETER	SECTIONAL DENSITY
.375"	0.274

375 Spitzer BTSP

Ballistic Coefficient	0.478
COAL Tested	3.600"
Speer Part No.	2472

			Starting Charge		Maximum Charge	
Propellant	Case	Primer	Weight (grains)	Muzzle Velocity (feet/sec)	Weight (grains)	Muzzle Velocity (feet/sec)
Hodgdon CFE 223	Federal	CCI 250	75.0	2672	80.5	2822
Alliant Reloder 17	Federal	CCI 250	75.0	2682	79.0	2822
Accurate 4350	Winchester	CCI 250	79.0	2667	83.0 C	2797
IMR 4451	Federal	CCI 250	75.5	2615	81.5	2756
Hodgdon H4350	Winchester	CCI 250	76.0	2611	80.0 C	2731
Hodgdon H414	Winchester	CCI 250	80.0	2655	82.0 C	2708
Alliant AR-Comp	Federal	CCI 250	65.5	2596	69.1	2703
Alliant Reloder 15	Winchester	CCI 250	67.0	2527	71.0	2675
Vihtavuori N140	Winchester	CCI 250	66.0	2541	70.0	2665
IMR 4350	Winchester	CCI 250	76.0	2557	80.0 C	2655
IMR 4831	Winchester	CCI 250	80.0	2579	82.0 C	2643
Vihtavuori N160	Winchester	CCI 250	78.0	2562	80.0 C	2622
Accurate 2700	Winchester	CCI 250	70.0	2472	74.0	2621
Alliant Reloder 19	Winchester	CCI 250	81.0	2530	83.0 C	2589
Winchester 760	Winchester	CCI 250	80.0	2525	82.0 C	2564
Hodgdon Varget	Winchester	CCI 250	63.0	2363	67.0	2549

WARNING! Maximum loads should be used with CAUTION • C = Compressed Load

285 GRAINS

DIAMETER	SECTIONAL DENSITY
.375"	0.290

375 Grand Slam® SP

Ballistic Coefficient	0.354
COAL Tested	3.560"
Speer Part No.	2473

			Starting Charge		Maximum Charge	
Propellant	Case	Primer	Weight (grains)	Muzzle Velocity (feet/sec)	Weight (grains)	Muzzle Velocity (feet/sec)
Alliant Reloder 17	Federal	CCI 250	75.0	2606	79.0	2732
Hodgdon H414	Winchester	CCI 250	82.0	2645	84.0 C	2697
Accurate 4350	Winchester	CCI 250	77.0	2562	81.0 C	2694
Winchester 760	Winchester	CCI 250	83.0	2617	85.0 C	2658
IMR 4831	Winchester	CCI 250	79.0	2504	83.0 C	2649
IMR 4451	Federal	CCI 250	74.0	2503	79.0	2644
Hodgdon H4350	Winchester	CCI 250	75.0	2519	79.0 C	2615
IMR 4350	Winchester	CCI 250	75.0	2462	79.0 C	2575
Vihtavuori N160	Winchester	CCI 250	78.0	2531	80.0 C	2570
Hodgdon H4831SC	Winchester	CCI 250	82.0	2465	86.0 C	2561
IMR 4064	Winchester	CCI 250	64.0	2405	68.0	2552
Alliant Reloder 15	Winchester	CCI 250	65.0	2410	69.0	2533
Alliant AR-Comp	Federal	CCI 250	58.5	2391	64.0	2528
Accurate2700	Winchester	CCI 250	69.0	2392	73.0	2523
Hodgdon Varget	Winchester	CCI 250	64.0	2363	68.0	2510
Alliant Reloder 19	Winchester	CCI 250	78.0	2413	80.0 C	2456
IMR 4895	Winchester	CCI 250	60.0	2231	64.0	2400

WARNING! *Maximum loads should be used with CAUTION • C = Compressed Load*

375 RUGER

Alternate Names:	9.5x65.5mm
Parent Cartridge:	Unique
Country of Origin:	USA
Year of Introduction:	2007
Designer(s):	Ruger & Hornady
Governing Body:	SAAMI

CARTRIDGE CASE DATA

Case Type:	Rimless, bottleneck		
Average Case Capacity:	99.0 grains H$_2$O	Max. Cartridge OAL	3.340 inch
Max. Case Length:	2.580 inch	Primer:	Large Rifle
Case Trim to Length:	2.570 inch	RCBS Shell holder:	# 4
Current Manufacturers:	Hornady		

BALLISTIC DATA

Max. Average Pressure (MAP):	62,000 psi, CUP not established for this cartridge - SAAMI	Test Barrel Length:	24 inch
Rifling Twist Rate:	1 turn in 12 inch		

Muzzle velocities of factory loaded ammunition	Bullet Wgt.	Muzzle velocity
	250-grain	2,890 fps
	270-grain	2,840 fps
	300-grain	2,660 fps
	Muzzle velocity will decrease approximately 20 fps per inch for barrels less than 24 inches.	

HISTORICAL NOTES

- Introduced in 2007, the 375 Ruger cartridge was developed in cooperation with Hornady.
- The 375 Ruger is the second rifle cartridge to carry the Ruger name (the first was the 204 Ruger introduced in 2004).

- As Ruger also manufactures rifles, introduction of the new caliber gained a boost when the company simultaneously introduced rifles chambered for the new cartridges.
- To date, Hornady is the only ammunition manufacturer that has included the 375 Ruger cartridge in their product line.

Interesting Fact

The 375 Ruger shares many features and dimensions with its two brethren, the 300 Ruger Compact Magnum and the 338 Ruger Compact Magnum. Both of the latter are called magnums and offer magnum-level performance. The 375 Ruger also offers magnum performance, but is not called a magnum.

BALLISTIC NOTES

- The 375 Ruger is an unabashed big game cartridge designed to fit in standard length actions.
- It is fully capable of taking any species of North American or African plains game and some species of dangerous game as well.
- Speer offers three bullet weights for the handloader:
  - A 270-grain: muzzle velocity 3,005 fps.
  - A 285-grain: muzzle velocity 2,946 fps.
- With this level of ballistic performance, the 375 Ruger is a direct competitor to the 375 RUM.
- For North American big game, the premium Speer 285-grain Grand Slam® SP with its controlled expansion and reliable penetration is a good general purpose choice.

HANDLOADING NOTES

- Hornady is the sole source of new, empty, unprimed 375 Ruger brass cartridge cases for handloading.
- We do not recommend using the 375 Ruger cartridge for hunting deer of any size. At 375 Ruger muzzle velocities, lightweight bullets will likely result in excessive meat damage.
- However, the 375 Ruger with the 285 Grand Slam bullet it is a good choice for large, heavy North American game as well as African plains game.
- As do most magnum cartridges, the 375 Ruger prefers slow burning propellants.

SAFETY NOTES

SPEER 270-grain Spitzer BTSP @ a muzzle velocity of 2,870 fps:
- Maximum vertical altitude @ 90° elevation is 11,862 feet.
- Maximum horizontal distance to first impact with ground @ 37° elevation is 5,519 yards.

270 GRAINS

DIAMETER	SECTIONAL DENSITY
.375"	0.274

375 Spitzer BTSP

Ballistic Coefficient	0.478
COAL Tested	3.320"
Speer Part No.	2472

			Starting Charge		Maximum Charge	
Propellant	Case	Primer	Weight (grains)	Muzzle Velocity (feet/sec)	Weight (grains)	Muzzle Velocity (feet/sec)
Alliant Reloder 16	Hornady	CCI 250	78.8	2752	86.8 C	3005
Hodgdon H4350	Hornady	CCI 250	78.8	2714	87.3 C	2966
Alliant Reloder 17	Hornady	CCI 250	74.6	2665	82.9 C	2965
Ramshot Big Game	Hornady	CCI 250	75.8	2745	84.1	2944
Alliant Power Pro 2000-MR	Hornady	CCI 250	73.8	2695	81.5	2933
Alliant Power Pro 4000-MR	Hornady	CCI 250	79.3	2692	88.0 C	2927
Winchester 760	Hornady	CCI 250	73.4	2631	81.4	2893
Alliant Reloder 15	Hornady	CCI 250	69.4	2632	76.9	2886
IMR 4451	Hornady	CCI 250	77.3	2637	85.3 C	2885
Hodgdon Varget	Hornady	CCI 250	68.7	2659	76.0	2870
Alliant Power Pro Varmint	Hornady	CCI 250	66.6	2610	73.8	2836

WARNING! *Maximum loads should be used with CAUTION • C = Compressed Load*

285 GRAINS

DIAMETER	SECTIONAL DENSITY
.375"	0.290

375 Grand Slam® SP

Ballistic Coefficient	0.354
COAL Tested	3.320"
Speer Part No.	2473

			Starting Charge		Maximum Charge	
Propellant	Case	Primer	Weight (grains)	Muzzle Velocity (feet/sec)	Weight (grains)	Muzzle Velocity (feet/sec)
Alliant Reloder 19	Hornady	CCI 250	82.2	2700	91.0 C	2946
Alliant Reloder 16	Hornady	CCI 250	77.1	2685	85.5 C	2916
Alliant Reloder 17	Hornady	CCI 250	76.0	2746	82.0 C	2893
Alliant Power Pro 4000-MR	Hornady	CCI 250	79.3	2664	88.0 C	2883
Hodgdon H4350	Hornady	CCI 250	77.8	2665	86.0 C	2881
Ramshot Big Game	Hornady	CCI 250	74.0	2648	82.2	2850
Alliant Power Pro 2000-MR	Hornady	CCI 250	69.5	2628	76.8	2817
Vihtavuori N160	Hornady	CCI 250	76.2	2588	84.6 C	2816
IMR 4451	Hornady	CCI 250	75.0	2558	83.2 C	2812
Alliant Reloder 15	Hornady	CCI 250	68.5	2575	76.0	2811
Winchester 760	Hornady	CCI 250	71.9	2611	79.6	2807
Alliant Power Pro Varmint	Hornady	CCI 250	65.6	2556	72.6	2754

WARNING! *Maximum loads should be used with CAUTION • C = Compressed Load*

375 REMINGTON ULTRA MAGNUM

Alternate Names:	375 RUM
Parent Cartridge:	300 Remington Ultra Magnum
Country of Origin:	USA
Year of Introduction:	2000
Designer(s):	Remington
Governing Body:	SAAMI/CIP

.405" cyl [10.29mm]
shoulder angle 30°
.525" [13.34mm]
.530" [13.46mm]
.550" [13.97mm]
.534" [13.56mm]
.050" [1.27mm]
.200" [5.08mm]
1.750" [44.47mm]
2.387" [60.63mm]
2.491" [63.27mm]
2.850" [72.39mm]

CARTRIDGE CASE DATA			
Case Type:	Rimless, bottleneck, rebated		
Average Case Capacity:	118.7 grains H$_2$O	Max. Cartridge OAL	3.600 inch
Max. Case Length:	2.850 inch	Primer:	Large Rifle
Case Trim to Length:	2.840 inch	RCBS Shell holder:	# 38
Current Manufacturers:	Remington, Nosler, Doubletap Ammunition		

BALLISTIC DATA

Max. Average Pressure (MAP):	65,000 psi, CUP not established for this cartridge - SAAMI	Test Barrel Length:	24 inch
Rifling Twist Rate:	1 turn in 12 inch		

Muzzle velocities of factory loaded ammunition	Bullet Wgt.	Muzzle velocity
	260-grain	2,950 fps
	270-grain	2,900 fps
	300-grain	2,750 fps

Muzzle velocity will decrease approximately 20 fps per inch for barrels less than 24 inches.

HISTORICAL NOTES

- Introduced in 2000, the 375 Remington Ultra Magnum (RUM) was the last and largest caliber member of Remington's new quartet of long case length, magnum cartridges that turned the magnum cartridge market upside down.

- For the first time in over 90 years, a mainstream ammunition manufacturer offered a magnum rifle cartridge that could compete with the legendary 375 H&H Magnum on its own terms.

- And, the new 375 RUM cartridge shattered magnum tradition in another way—it did not have a belted case head! Inspiration courtesy of the fatherly 404 Jeffrey cartridge.

- As Remington also manufactured rifles, introduction of the new cartridge gained a boost when the company simultaneously introduced rifles chambered for the new cartridges.

- Remington Ultra Magnum cartridges firmly established the concept of beltless magnum cartridges in the world of modern sporting ammunition.

- To date, rival ammunition manufacturers have not included any of the Remington Ultra Magnum cartridges in their product lines.

Interesting Fact

The 375 RUM is the largest and most powerful member of Remington's series of beltless magnum rifle cartridges. Its ballistics bridge the gap between the 375 H&H Magnum and the 378 Weatherby Magnum.

BALLISTIC NOTES

- The 375 Remington Ultra Magnum is a big game cartridge fully capable of taking any species of North American or African plains game. It can be recommended for large, heavy African game and for some species of dangerous game as well.

- In striking energy, the 375 RUM cartridge stands between the 375 H&H Magnum and the 378 Weatherby Magnum.

- Remington's 375 RUM cartridge is capable of providing an increase of up to 200 fps in muzzle velocity over the 375 H&H Magnum. With a 270-grain bullet, that increases muzzle energy by nearly 700 ft-lbs.

- For North American big game, we recommend the Speer 285-grain Grand Slam® SP for its controlled expansion and reliable penetration.
- The Speer 270-grain Spitzer BTSP provides handloaders with the opportunity to take the down range ballistics of the 375 RUM to an entirely new level with higher striking velocity and energy, flatter trajectory, and less wind drift at all ranges and at factory bullet muzzle velocity levels.

TECHNICAL NOTES

- The Remington 375 RUM shares its overall loaded length with its 7mm RUM, 300 RUM and 338 RUM brethren making it suitable only for repeating rifles having long actions.
- The rim of the 375 RUM case is slightly rebated.
- Case capacity of the 375 RUM cartridge is approximately 21% greater than the 375 H&H Magnum, but 14% less than the 378 Weatherby Magnum placing it between the two.
- All Remington Ultra Magnum cartridges achieve their exceptional muzzle velocities the old fashioned way—they burn heavy propellant charges.

HANDLOADING NOTES

- Although the manufacturers listed above offer loaded ammunition, Remington is the sole source of new, empty, unprimed 375 RUM brass cartridge cases for handloading.
- The heavy construction of the 375 RUM cartridge case can cause problems with full length resizing such as excessive effort, case stretching, brass hardening and head separations, all leading to short case life. For this reason, neck sizing only is recommended for target/sight-in rounds as most rifles in 375 RUM are bolt-action types. Full length resize for hunting rounds.
- At 375 RUM muzzle velocities, even bullets weighing 270 grains may result in overkill on small deer. However, the 375 RUM is a good choice for large heavy North American game such as moose and large bears.
- The ballistic sweet spot for reloading the 375 RUM cartridge is a 270-grain bullet driven at 2,900 fps muzzle velocity using slow burning propellants.
- We recommend the 285-grain Grand Slam bullet be reserved for large North American and African game.
- The Speer 235-grain Semi-Spitzer SP Hot-Cor did not meet our level of performance criteria for this cartridge and therefore no data is shown.

SAFETY NOTES

SPEER 270-grain Spitzer BTSP @ a muzzle velocity of 2,900 fps:
- Maximum vertical altitude @ 90° elevation is 12,006 feet.
- Maximum horizontal distance to first impact with ground @ 37° elevation is 5,538 yards.

270 GRAINS

DIAMETER	SECTIONAL DENSITY
.375"	0.274

375 Spitzer BTSP

Ballistic Coefficient	0.478
COAL Tested	3.600"
Speer Part No.	2472

			Starting Charge		Maximum Charge	
Propellant	Case	Primer	Weight (grains)	Muzzle Velocity (feet/sec)	Weight (grains)	Muzzle Velocity (feet/sec)
Alliant Reloder 19	Remington	CCI 250	93.4	2782	103.7 C	3078
Vihtavuori N560	Remington	CCI 250	93.7	2754	103.7 C	3054
Alliant Reloder 22	Remington	CCI 250	89.9	2721	99.9	3047
IMR 7828	Remington	CCI 250	94.0	2748	104.4 C	3041
Alliant Power Pro 4000-MR	Remington	CCI 250	88.0	2781	97.9	3038
Alliant Reloder 23	Remington	CCI 250	91.4	2789	101.3 C	3034
Alliant Reloder 16	Remington	CCI 250	85.1	2751	94.6	3024
Accurate 4350	Remington	CCI 250	87.3	2721	96.6	3018
Alliant Reloder 17	Remington	CCI 250	82.4	2704	91.6	3008
Ramshot Hunter	Remington	CCI 250	87.5	2770	97.8	3002
Hodgdon H4350	Remington	CCI 250	85.1	2723	94.6	2989
Hodgdon H4831	Remington	CCI 250	91.7	2717	101.7	2985

WARNING! Maximum loads should be used with CAUTION • C = Compressed Load

285 GRAINS

DIAMETER	SECTIONAL DENSITY
.375"	0.290

375 Grand Slam® SP

Ballistic Coefficient	0.354
COAL Tested	3.580"
Speer Part No.	2473

			Starting Charge		Maximum Charge	
Propellant	Case	Primer	Weight (grains)	Muzzle Velocity (feet/sec)	Weight (grains)	Muzzle Velocity (feet/sec)
Alliant Reloder 26	Remington	CCI 250	94.1	2731	104.0 C	3028
Alliant Reloder 19	Remington	CCI 250	94.1	2726	104.1 C	2996
IMR 7828	Remington	CCI 250	93.6	2677	103.7 C	2963
Alliant Reloder 23	Remington	CCI 250	91.4	2699	101.6 C	2961
Vihtavuori N560	Remington	CCI 250	91.7	2662	101.7	2953
Alliant Power Pro 4000-MR	Remington	CCI 250	86.9	2694	96.2	2949
Alliant Reloder 16	Remington	CCI 250	84.2	2673	93.5	2926
Hodgdon H4831	Remington	CCI 250	90.7	2656	100.4	2909
Alliant Reloder 17	Remington	CCI 250	80.7	2620	89.8	2909
Accurate 4350	Remington	CCI 250	85.6	2636	95.1	2909
Hodgdon H4350	Remington	CCI 250	83.7	2629	92.7	2884
Ramshot Hunter	Remington	CCI 250	83.2	2608	92.5	2862

WARNING! *Maximum loads should be used with CAUTION • C = Compressed Load*

378 WEATHERBY MAGNUM

Parent Cartridge:	416 Rigby
Country of Origin:	USA
Year of Introduction:	1953
Designer(s):	Roy Weatherby
Governing Body:	SAAMI/CIP

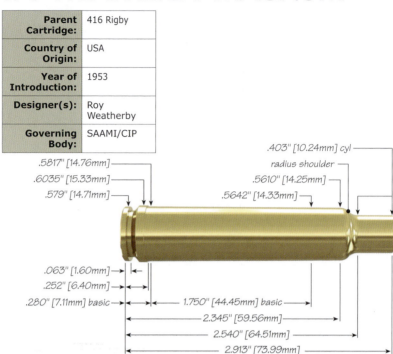

CARTRIDGE CASE DATA

Case Type:	Belted, double radius bottleneck
Average Case Capacity:	136.0 grains H_2O
Max. Cartridge OAL:	3.655 inch
Max. Case Length:	2.913 inch
Primer:	Large Rifle
Case Trim to Length:	2.903 inch
RCBS Shell holder:	# 14
Current Manufacturers:	Weatherby, Norma

BALLISTIC DATA

Max. Average Pressure (MAP):	63,817 psi CIP
Test Barrel Length:	24 inch
Rifling Twist Rate:	1 turn in 12 inch

Muzzle velocities of factory loaded ammunition	
Bullet Wgt.	Muzzle velocity
270-grain	3,180 fps
300-grain	2,925 fps

Muzzle velocity will decrease approximately 30 fps per inch for barrels less than 24 inches.

HISTORICAL NOTES

- The 378 Weatherby Magnum was the first of Roy Weatherby's "Mega-Magnums".
- Previous Weatherby Magnum cartridges were based on a modified 300 H&H Magnum case; the new mega-magnums were based on a case 13% larger in body diameter and longer than the 375 H&H Magnum case.
- Introduced in 1953, the 378 Weatherby Magnum was designed to significantly exceed the ballistic performance of the venerable 375 H&H Magnum for hunting dangerous game.
- The new mega-magnum was set to replace the earlier 375 Weatherby Magnum cartridge based on the 300 Weatherby Magnum case.
- The new 378 Weatherby Magnum was a success, but the old 375 Weatherby Magnum refused to pass quietly away and was reintroduced later. Both remain in the Weatherby product line today.

BALLISTIC NOTES

- By any measure, the 378 Weatherby Magnum resets the performance bar for 375 caliber dangerous game cartridges to a level which is not likely to be surpassed any time soon.
- The 378 Weatherby Magnum is much too powerful for North American game with the possible exception of large bear and moose.
- As a general purpose bullet for plains game, we suggest the Speer 285-grain Grand Slam® SP for its controlled expansion and high retained weight.
- Big game hunters who have field experience with the 378 Weatherby Magnum as well as the various larger caliber African calibers, all agree on two things.
    1. The 378 Weatherby Magnum wins the award for the cartridge with the most abusive recoil.
    2. When you fire at a dangerous animal in the field, you won't notice the recoil at all.

TECHNICAL NOTES

- The 378 Weatherby Magnum case — from the large head to the long length — was made to hold huge amounts of powder. It's a cross between the 375 H&H and the 416 Rigby. Interior ballistics came directly from the school of brute force, burn enough powder to get the velocity you want regardless of the efficiency of the process.
- The astute reader will note that this is diametrically opposed to modern practices with the new "efficient" short magnums. However, there is something to be said for the brute force school of internal ballistics after all.
- The 378 Weatherby Magnum cartridge did incorporate four concessions to interior ballistic sophistication perfected in previous Weatherby cartridges:
    - The shoulder angle exhibits the double-radius instead of sharp edges to smooth the flow of hot powder gasses.
    - The chamber throat was free-bored for a considerable distance to reduce MAP levels.
    - Muzzle velocities are taken from a 26 inch test barrel; the standard industry test barrel is 24 inches in length.

- And, the 378 Weatherby Magnum cartridge case incorporates a belt as all proper magnums should according to Holland & Holland.
- The 378 Weatherby Magnum has very little body taper and a one caliber length neck length to maximize case capacity.
  - Case capacity is substantially larger than all other 375 magnum rifle cartridges.
  - Length-to-diameter ratio of the 378 Weatherby Magnum is 5.00 in keeping with other Weatherby magnum calibers.
  - The 1 turn in 12 inch rifling twist of the 378 Weatherby Magnum will stabilize a wide range of bullet weights including long boat tail bullets.

HANDLOADING NOTES

- Norma is the sole source of new, empty, unprimed brass in 378 Weatherby Magnum caliber.
- Full length size the 378 Weatherby Magnum when hunting dangerous game. Due to the heavy recoil, it is very important to crimp the bullets securely in the case mouth. Use the cannelure on the bullet body for this purpose.
- When loading 378 Weatherby Magnum cases, be sure to allow time for the very heavy powder charges (well over 100 grains!) to flow into the case. You may have to drop some of the charges in two equal stages or use a long drop tube.
- Most powder charges for the 378 Weatherby Magnum will fill the massive case. This is because in such large cases, full charges are the most consistent.
- As do all big magnum cartridges, the 378 Weatherby Magnum works best with slow burning propellants.
- Postscript: Yes, components for loading the 378 Weatherby Magnum are expensive. For example, with a 100-grain propellant charge, you get only 70 loads from a one pound can of powder. But, do not let that get you down. The recent suggested retail price of a 20 round box of factory-loaded 378 Weatherby Magnum ammunition is $153.00. If that sounds cheap, you don't need to reload!

SAFETY NOTES

SPEER 285-grain Soft Point Grand Slam @ a muzzle velocity of 3,128 fps:
- Maximum vertical altitude @ 90° elevation is 10,026 feet.
- Maximum horizontal distance to first impact with ground @ 35° elevation is 4,562 yards.
- The Speer 235-grain Semi-Spitzer SP Hot-Cor® and the 270-grain Spitzer BTSP did not meet our level of performance criteria in the 378 Weatherby Magnum and therefore no data is shown.

285 GRAINS

DIAMETER	SECTIONAL DENSITY
.375"	0.290

375 Grand Slam® SP

Ballistic Coefficient	0.354
COAL Tested	3.640"
Speer Part No.	2473

			Starting Charge		Maximum Charge	
Propellant	Case	Primer	Weight (grains)	Muzzle Velocity (feet/sec)	Weight (grains)	Muzzle Velocity (feet/sec)
Alliant Power Pro 4000-MR	Norma	CCI 250	108.0	3024	112.4	3128
Hodgdon SUPERFORMANCE	Norma	CCI 250	112.5	3025	116.5	3128
Alliant Reloder 23	Norma	CCI 250	108.0	2971	113.0 C	3101
IMR 7828	Norma	CCI 250	109.0	2812	115.0	2996
IMR 4831	Norma	CCI 250	103.0	2823	109.0	2989
Alliant Reloder 25	Norma	CCI 250	113.0	2848	117.0 C	2974
Alliant Reloder 22	Norma	CCI 250	106.0	2788	112.0	2971
Alliant Reloder 19	Norma	CCI 250	105.0	2796	111.0	2967
IMR 4350	Norma	CCI 250	99.0	2862	105.0	2948
Accurate 4350	Norma	CCI 250	100.0	2732	108.0	2918
Hodgdon H4350	Norma	CCI 250	97.0	2746	103.0	2912
IMR 4955	Norma	CCI 250	100.0	2763	103.6	2879

WARNING! *Maximum loads should be used with CAUTION • C = Compressed Load*

416 RUGER

Parent Cartridge:	375 Ruger
Country of Origin:	USA
Year of Introduction:	2008
Designer(s):	Ruger & Hornady
Governing Body:	SAAMI/CIP

CARTRIDGE CASE DATA

Case Type:	Rimless, bottleneck		
Average Case Capacity:	100.0 grains H₂O	Max. Cartridge OAL	3.340 inch
Max. Case Length:	2.580 inch	Primer:	Large Rifle
Case Trim to Length:	2.572 inch	RCBS Shell holder:	# 4
Current Manufacturers:	Hornady		

BALLISTIC DATA

Max. Average Pressure (MAP):	62,000 psi, CUP not established for this cartridge - SAAMI	Test Barrel Length:	24 inch
Rifling Twist Rate:	1 turn in 14 inch		
Muzzle velocities of factory loaded ammunition	Bullet Wgt.		Muzzle velocity
	350-grain		2,730 fps
	Muzzle velocity will decrease approximately 10 fps per inch for barrels less than 24 inches.		

HISTORICAL NOTES

- The 416 Ruger cartridge was developed in cooperation with Hornady. It is the largest caliber member of the Ruger cartridge product line.
- Undoubtedly, this was an attempt by Ruger to join the parade of new, beltless, 416 caliber cartridges.
- As Ruger also manufactures rifles, introduction of the new caliber gained a boost when the company simultaneously introduced rifles chambered for the new cartridges.

- To date, Hornady is the only ammunition manufacturer that has included the 416 Ruger cartridge in their product line.

Interesting Fact

The 416 Ruger shares many features and dimensions with its brother the 375 Ruger cartridge. Neither are called magnums, but both offer magnum-level performance.

BALLISTIC NOTES

- The 416 Ruger is an unabashed big game cartridge designed to fit in standard length rifle actions.
- It is fully capable of taking any species of North American or African plains game and some species of dangerous game as well.
- In similar manner to other 416 caliber cartridges, Hornady offers the tried and true combination of a 400-grain bullet at a muzzle velocity of 2,400 fps.
- This places the 416 Ruger in direct competition with the 416 Rigby and 416 Remington Magnum. However, with all of these offering identical ballistics, how to choose?
- In any case, the Ruger fits in standard length actions while the Rigby requires a magnum length action. Cost will be a major consideration here.
- Handloaders can duplicate the factory ballistics of the 416 Ruger using the Speer 350-grain Mag-Tip® SP Hot-Cor loaded to a muzzle velocity of around 2,600 fps with 5,160 ft-lbs of muzzle energy. This load may require adjustments to metal express sights.

TECHNICAL NOTES

- In much the same fashion as the 416 Remington Magnum, the 416 Ruger has a beltless, rimless case, a 30° shoulder angle, and comparable MAP levels. Both cartridges use bullets of the same caliber and weight, however, the similarities end there.
- In order to fit in a standard length action, the 416 Ruger case is significantly shorter as is its overall loaded length.
- Case capacity of the 416 Ruger cartridge is virtually the same as the 416 Remington Magnum, but approximately 22% less than the 416 Rigby.
- MAP level of the 416 Rigby is approximately 30% lower than the 416 Ruger.
- The 416 Ruger case is very much a design unto its own, related directly only to the 300 Ruger Compact Magnum, the 338 Ruger Compact Magnum and the 375 Ruger with which it shares its beltless, rimless design as well as head and rim dimensions.

HANDLOADING NOTES

- Hornady is the sole source of new, empty, unprimed 416 Ruger brass cartridge cases for handloading.
- The heavy construction of the 416 Ruger cartridge case can cause problems with full length resizing such as excessive effort, case stretching, brass hardening and head separations, all leading to short case life. For this reason, neck sizing only is recommended as most rifles in 416 Ruger are bolt-action types. Save the full length resizing for your hunting rounds.

- All bullets loaded in the 416 Ruger should be firmly crimped in the case mouth using the cannelure on the bullet to prevent elongation in the magazine from recoil.
- As do most magnum cartridges, the 416 Ruger prefers slow burning propellants.

SAFETY NOTES

SPEER 350-grain Mag-Tip SP Hot-Cor @ a muzzle velocity of 2,577 fps:
- Maximum vertical altitude @ 90° elevation is 8,919 feet.
- Maximum horizontal distance to first impact with ground @ 35° elevation is 4,118 yards.

350 GRAINS

DIAMETER	SECTIONAL DENSITY
.416"	0.289

416 Mag-Tip SP Hot-Cor®

Ballistic Coefficient	0.332
COAL Tested	3.330"
Speer Part No.	2477

			Starting Charge		Maximum Charge	
Propellant	Case	Primer	Weight (grains)	Muzzle Velocity (feet/sec)	Weight (grains)	Muzzle Velocity (feet/sec)
Alliant Power Pro 2000-MR	Hornady	CCI 250	82.6	2503	91.4 C	2731
Winchester 760	Hornady	CCI 250	83.8	2504	93.1 C	2708
Alliant Reloder 17	Hornady	CCI 250	79.9	2438	88.5 C	2679
Hodgdon CFE 223	Hornady	CCI 250	80.6	2480	89.2	2669
Ramshot Big Game	Hornady	CCI 250	79.8	2479	87.4 C	2653
Accurate 2520	Hornady	CCI 250	73.6	2416	81.4	2642
Alliant Reloder 15	Hornady	CCI 250	73.8	2415	82.2	2619
Alliant Power Pro Varmint	Hornady	CCI 250	72.6	2390	80.6	2610
Vihtavuori N540	Hornady	CCI 250	74.0	2408	81.6	2596
Hodgdon Varget	Hornady	CCI 250	72.3	2393	79.9	2593
Alliant AR-Comp	Hornady	CCI 250	71.5	2368	79.6	2577
Hodgdon H335	Hornady	CCI 250	70.7	2366	78.5	2563

WARNING! Maximum loads should be used with CAUTION • C = Compressed Load

416 REMINGTON MAGNUM

Parent Cartridge:	375 H&H Magnum
Country of Origin:	USA
Year of Introduction:	1989
Designer(s):	Remington
Governing Body:	SAAMI/CIP

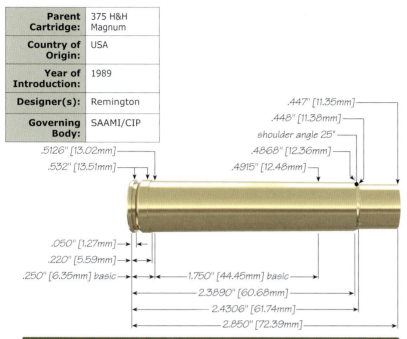

CARTRIDGE CASE DATA

Case Type:	Belted, rimless, bottleneck
Average Case Capacity:	107.0 grains H_2O
Max. Cartridge OAL:	3.600 inch
Max. Case Length:	2.850 inch
Primer:	Large Rifle
Case Trim to Length:	2.840 inch
RCBS Shell holder:	# 4
Current Manufacturers:	Remington

BALLISTIC DATA

Max. Average Pressure (MAP):	65,000 psi, 54,000 CUP - SAAMI
Test Barrel Length:	24 inch
Rifling Twist Rate:	1 turn in 14 inch

Muzzle velocities of factory loaded ammunition	Bullet Wgt.	Muzzle velocity
	400-grain	2,400 fps

Muzzle velocity will decrease approximately 10 fps per inch for barrels less than 24 inches.

HISTORICAL NOTES

- In the late 1980s, there was a flurry of interest in heavy caliber cartridges—in particular the 416 caliber.

- The ruling monarch of the 416 caliber was the 416 Rigby cartridge introduced by John Rigby & Son in 1911 and hoary with age. Its capabilities in taking every species of African game including the dangerous ones were legendary.

- However, the difficulty and expense of obtaining rifles and ammunition in 416 Rigby limited its success in the North American market. After Federal introduced 416 Rigby to their Premium ammunition product line, interest in the 416 caliber began to build.

- American ammunition manufacturers sensed a ballistic gap in their product lines between the 458 cartridges and the various 375 Magnum calibers. An intermediate caliber was needed to fill this gap and the 416 was the right choice for the job.

- Remington introduced their 416 Remington Magnum cartridge in 1989 chambered in their Model 700 Safari rifle with an action length for belted magnum cartridges.

- The 416 Remington Magnum offered the ballistics of the classic 416 Rigby in a slightly shorter, belted case.

- The new Remington Magnum incorporated several of the visual cues of the 416 Rigby: a long case with minimal taper, a large head diameter. Then there was the blunt heavy bullet in the case mouth.

- Of course there were other new 416 cartridges to contend with such as the 416 Weatherby Magnum and the 416 Ruger. On the plus side, all this activity in what was heretofore an obscure caliber in the U.S. spurred bullet makers to add 416 caliber bullets to their product lines.

- Despite all this activity and competition, the popularity of the 416 Rigby went on serenely as if nothing had happened.

Interesting Fact

Although the 416 Remington Magnum operates at higher MAP levels than the 416 Rigby, muzzle velocities of the two cartridges are near identical. To find out why, read below in the Ballistic Notes section.

BALLISTIC NOTES

- The 416 Remington Magnum is designed for hunting all species of large, dangerous African game. As factories load this cartridge, it is much too powerful for North American game.

- This narrow focus can be seen from the simple ballistic parameters of nearly all factory loaded 416 caliber cartridges; a 400-grain bullet at a muzzle velocity of 2,400 fps. Regardless of the cartridge used, these are the ballistics.

- Why? Surely the new magnums could be loaded to higher velocity and energy levels? Of course they can, however the 416 Rigby was not designed in a vacuum. Rather its ballistics were determined from a mixture of field experience, ballistics and tradition. Put another way, experience has shown this combination of factors is nearly ideal for the intended purpose. A change is definitely not needed.

- That is unless you have a different set of parameters in mind. Contrary to conventional wisdom, with the right bullet, the 416 Remington Magnum can play an active role in hunting North American big game.

- Handloaders have this option which is not available in factory ammunition. The Speer 350-grain Mag-Tip® SP Hot-Cor can be handloaded down to a muzzle velocity of 2,326 fps with 4,204 ft-lbs of muzzle energy. This load virtually duplicates the muzzle energy of the 300 RUM, 338 RUM, and 375 H&H Magnum.
- This load is an excellent top end choice for North American big game. Shooters who are adverse to heavy recoil should avoid the 416 Remington Magnum or handload this cartridge to lower muzzle velocities.

TECHNICAL NOTES

- Basically, the 416 Remington Magnum is an 8mm Remington Magnum cartridge case necked up to 416 caliber. Both cartridges share rim, belt, and head dimensions as well as a 25° shoulder angle, overall case length, overall loaded length, and have comparable MAP levels.
- Obviously, Remington did not attempt to reinvent the wheel when designing the 416 Rem. Mag. cartridge. However, one must consider its plight should the 8mm Rem. Mag., never a best-seller, be retired.
- The 416 Remington Magnum cartridge is definitely not one of the compact, modern, efficient magnum designs. Muzzle velocities are gained the traditional way— by burning heavy charges of slow burning powder.
- MAP levels of the 416 Rem. Magnum are equivalent to the 416 Ruger, but substantially higher than the 416 Rigby.

HANDLOADING NOTES

- In addition to the manufacturers of loaded ammunition listed above, Remington, Captech International (Jamison Brass), and Quality Cartridge are sources of new, empty, unprimed 416 Remington Magnum brass cases for handloading.
- The heavy construction of the 416 Rem. Magnum cartridge case can cause problems with full length resizing such as excessive effort, case stretching, brass hardening and head separations, all leading to short case life. Full-length resize when in pursuit of dangerous game.
- We recommend that you set your sizing dies to headspace this cartridge case on the shoulder instead of the belt.
- All bullets must be securely crimped in the case mouth to prevent elongation when the rifle is fired.

SAFETY NOTES

SPEER 350-grain Mag-Tip SP Hot-Cor @ a muzzle velocity of 2,636 fps:
- Maximum vertical altitude @ 90° elevation is 8,997 feet.
- Maximum horizontal distance to first impact with ground @ 35° elevation is 4,144 yards.

350 GRAINS

DIAMETER	SECTIONAL DENSITY
.416"	0.289

416 Mag-Tip SP Hot-Cor®

Ballistic Coefficient	0.332
COAL Tested	3.580"
Speer Part No.	2477

Propellant	Case	Primer	Starting Charge		Maximum Charge	
			Weight (grains)	Muzzle Velocity (feet/sec)	Weight (grains)	Muzzle Velocity (feet/sec)
Alliant Power Pro 2000-MR	Federal	Federal 215	87.8	2574	97.3	2811
Alliant Reloder 17	Federal	Federal 215	84.9	2478	93.9	2733
Alliant Power Pro Varmint	Federal	Federal 215	77.0	2484	85.4	2683
Alliant AR-Comp	Federal	Federal 215	75.6	2426	83.9	2652
Vihtavuori N540	Remington	CCI 250	78.0	2553	82.0	2636
Alliant Reloder 15	Remington	CCI 250	81.0	2541	85.0	2629
Hodgdon BL-C(2)	Remington	CCI 250	83.0	2496	87.0	2586
IMR 4064	Remington	CCI 250	77.0	2468	81.0	2565
IMR 4451	Federal	Federal 215	81.0	2343	90.0 C	2563
Vihtavuori N140	Remington	CCI 250	76.0	2410	80.0	2512
Accurate 2520	Remington	CCI 250	71.0	2364	75.0	2465
IMR 3031	Remington	CCI 250	69.0	2375	73.0	2456
IMR 4895	Remington	CCI 250	70.0	2326	74.0	2420

WARNING! *Maximum loads should be used with CAUTION • C = Compressed Load*

416 RIGBY

Alternate Names:	10.6x74mm
Country of Origin:	Britain
Year of Introduction:	1911
Designer(s):	John Rigby
Governing Body:	SAAMI/CIP

Case dimensions:
- .5812" [14.76mm]
- .5949" [15.11mm]
- .5902" [14.99mm]
- .446" [11.33mm]
- .4468" [11.35mm]
- shoulder angle 45°
- .5401" [13.72mm]
- .5480" [13.92mm]
- .065" [1.65mm]
- .500" [12.70mm] basic
- 1.500" [38.10] basic
- 2.3557" [59.84mm]
- 2.4024" [61.02mm]
- 2.900" [73.66mm]

CARTRIDGE CASE DATA

Case Type:	Rimless, bottleneck		
Average Case Capacity:	135.6 grains H$_2$O	**Max. Cartridge OAL**	3.750 inch
Max. Case Length:	2.900 inch	**Primer:**	Large Rifle
Case Trim to Length:	2.890 inch	**RCBS Shell holder:**	# 37
Current Manufacturers:	Federal, Hornady, Nosler, Norma, Kynamco (KYNOCH)		

BALLISTIC DATA

Max. Average Pressure (MAP):	52,000 psi, CUP not established for this cartridge – SAAMI 47,137 psi - CIP	**Test Barrel Length:**	24 inch
Rifling Twist Rate:	1 turn in 16.535 inch		
Muzzle velocities of factory loaded ammunition	**Bullet Wgt.**		**Muzzle velocity**
	410-grain		2,370 fps
	Muzzle velocity will decrease approximately 10 fps per inch for barrels less than 24 inches.		

HISTORICAL NOTES

- Few hunting cartridges can match the traditions associated with the 416 Rigby cartridge.
- Introduced in 1911 by John Rigby & Son of London, the new 416 cartridge was designed for hunting all species of dangerous game anywhere in the world using magazine rifles.
- The design of the new cartridge was a careful balance of field experience, ballistics and tradition.
- Of course, Rigby made bespoke rifles in this caliber to customer specification.
- The 416 Rigby cartridge soon became a popular choice for African and Asian safari hunting, expeditions, surveyors, game wardens and landowners.
- As the decades passed, the capabilities of the 416 Rigby cartridge became legendary; indeed the benchmark against which other dangerous game cartridges were measured.
- However, the difficulty and expense of obtaining rifles and ammunition in 416 Rigby limited its success in the North American market.
- After Federal introduced 416 Rigby to their Premium ammunition product line, interest in the 416 Rigby began to build.
- The market segment was getting crowded, however the 416 Rigby serenely went on as if nothing had happened. It is hard to beat a legend.

TECHNICAL NOTES

- The 416 Rigby cartridge is a rimless, beltless design with a noticeably short shoulder with a sharp 45° angle on which the cartridge headspaces. The case neck is 1.19 calibers in length to hold the heavy bullet securely in place.
- Although the 416 Rigby cartridge case is quite large and heavy, the MAP level is approximately 26% lower than the modern 416 Ruger and 29% lower than the 416 Remington Magnum. A low MAP level was standard procedure for safari caliber cartridges in 1911 to prevent excessive pressure from developing in the extreme heat conditions often found in Africa and Asia.
- The 416 Rigby cartridge is definitely not one of the compact, modern, efficient magnum designs. Muzzle velocities are produced in a thoroughly proper manner appropriate to a dangerous game cartridge— by burning heavy charges of slow burning powder at low MAP levels.
- This creates a problem for the modern handloader who must use a powder charge that fills the case, but not create excess MAP levels. The number of modern propellants that will do this is limited.

HANDLOADING NOTES

- In addition to the manufacturers of loaded ammunition listed above, Nosler, Hornady, Norma, Captech International (Jamison Brass), and Quality Cartridge offer new, empty, unprimed 416 Rigby brass cases for reloading.
- The heavy construction of the 416 Rigby cartridge case can cause problems with full length resizing such as excessive effort, case stretching, brass hardening and head separations, all leading to short case life. We recommend full length resizing when loading for hunting dangerous game.

- The Speer 350-grain bullet listed in the loading data is designed for North American game and the handloading data presented has been developed for that application.

SAFETY NOTES

SPEER 350-grain Mag-Tip SP Hot-Cor bullet @ a muzzle velocity of 2,747 fps:
- Maximum vertical altitude @ 90° elevation is 9,141 feet.
- Maximum horizontal distance to first impact with ground @ 35° elevation is 4,193 yards.

350 GRAINS

DIAMETER	SECTIONAL DENSITY
.416"	0.289

416 Mag-Tip SP Hot-Cor®

Ballistic Coefficient	0.332
COAL Tested	3.630"
Speer Part No.	2477

			Starting Charge		Maximum Charge	
Propellant	Case	Primer	Weight (grains)	Muzzle Velocity (feet/sec)	Weight (grains)	Muzzle Velocity (feet/sec)
Alliant Reloder 26	Federal	Federal 215	98.3	2434	108.8	2747
Alliant Reloder 16	Federal	Federal 215	89.9	2475	98.9	2711
Alliant Power Pro 4000-MR	Federal	Federal 215	91.9	2484	101.2	2698
Alliant Reloder 23	Federal	Federal 215	95.1	2430	105.1 C	2687
Alliant Reloder 17	Federal	Federal 215	85.8	2479	95.0	2681
IMR 7977	Federal	Federal 215	100.4	2369	111.0 C	2631
IMR 4831	Federal	CCI 250	98.0	2441	102.0	2577
IMR 4350	Federal	CCI 250	95.0	2424	99.0	2560
Alliant Reloder 19	Federal	CCI 250	101.0	2438	105.0	2560
Hodgdon H4831SC	Federal	CCI 250	103.0	2457	107.0	2555
Accurate 3100	Federal	CCI 250	101.0	2395	105.0	2524
IMR 7828	Federal	CCI 250	101.0	2379	105.0	2510

WARNING! *Maximum loads should be used with* CAUTION • C = Compressed Load

44 REMINGTON MAGNUM (RIFLE)

Alternate Names:	44 Mag.
Parent Cartridge:	44 S&W Special
Country of Origin:	USA
Year of Introduction:	1955
Designer(s):	Smith & Wesson and Remington
Governing Body:	SAAMI/CIP

CARTRIDGE CASE DATA

Case Type:	Rimmed, slightly tapered case		
Average Case Capacity:	39.0 grains H_2O	Max. Cartridge OAL	1.610 inch
Max. Case Length:	1.285 inch	Primer:	Large Pistol
Case Trim to Length:	1.275 inch	RCBS Shell holder:	# 18
Current Manufacturers:	Remington, Hornady, Federal, Winchester, Cor-Bon, Black Hills, PMC, Magtech, Fiocchi, Prvi Partizan, RUAG		

BALLISTIC DATA

Max. Average Pressure (MAP):	36,000 psi, 40,000 CUP - SAAMI	Test Barrel Length:	20 inch
Rifling Twist Rate:	1 turn in 38 inch older guns, 1:20 inch in newer guns		
Muzzle velocities of factory loaded ammunition		**Bullet Wgt.**	**Muzzle velocity**
		200-grain	2,100 fps
		210-grain	2,100 fps
		240-grain	1,760 fps
		270-grain	1,575 fps
	Muzzle velocity will decrease approximately 5 fps per inch for barrels less than 20 inches.		

HISTORICAL NOTES

- Elmer Keith was instrumental in the development of the 44 Magnum.
- This cartridge is actually a 43-caliber round but called a 44-caliber because previous related rounds were loaded with heeled bullets in which the bearing surface of the bullet is the same diameter as the case, in much the same fashion as the 22 Long Rifle rimfire cartridge.

- In the Old West, a popular practice was to carry a carbine and a revolver of the same chambering to eliminate having to carry two different types of ammunition.
- This practice remains popular today for Cowboy Action Competition and for personal defense and hunting.
- For these reasons, the 44 Remington Magnum cartridge, while introduced as a handgun round, has also become popular in carbines.

TECHNICAL NOTES

- The 44 Remington Magnum case length is .125 inches longer than the 44 S&W Special, however the Max COAL of the 44 S&W Special is longer than that of the 44 Remington Magnum. For this reason, do not attempt to fire 44 Special ammunition in carbines chambered for the 44 Magnum.
- Deer hunting with the 44 Magnum handloads listed in the data should be limited to 100 yards or less.

HANDLOADING NOTES

- As handloads in this caliber may be fired in lever-action rifles with tubular magazines, use only flat nose soft point or hollow point bullets to prevent magazine tube explosions.
- Bullets should be firmly roll crimped in the case mouth using the cannelure on the bullet's surface to prevent elongation from recoil or being pushed down inside the case by the magazine spring and remaining cartridges.
- Never fire handloads with Total Metal Jacket (TMJ), half-jacket, or lead bullets in a carbine.
- Never load less than the minimum charges shown in the loading data as the small charge of propellant may not be sufficient to push the bullet completely down the barrel.
- We recommend using only new or once-fired cases for maximum loads.
- Do not attempt to fire Speer Shot Capsules in a carbine.

SAFETY NOTES

- The 44 Remington Magnum is loaded to more than twice the pressure of earlier 44 cartridges (44 American, 44 Russian, and the 44 S&W Special) and should never be used in place of these rounds.

SPEER 270-grain DeepCurl Soft Point bullet @ a muzzle velocity of 1,569 fps:
- Maximum vertical altitude @ 90° elevation is 5,325 feet.
- Maximum horizontal distance to first impact with ground @ 33° elevation is 2,470 yards.

GOLD DOT

210 GRAINS

DIAMETER	SECTIONAL DENSITY
.429"	0.163

44 GDHP	
Ballistic Coefficient	0.154
COAL Tested	1.600"
Speer Part No.	4428

			Starting Charge		Maximum Charge	
Propellant	Case	Primer	Weight (grains)	Muzzle Velocity (feet/sec)	Weight (grains)	Muzzle Velocity (feet/sec)
Hodgdon Lil' Gun	Winchester	CCI 350	26.5	2067	28.5	2128
Hodgdon H110	Winchester	CCI 350	25.5	1892	27.5	2036
Winchester 296	Winchester	CCI 350	25.5	1907	27.5	2030
Ramshot Enforcer	Winchester	CCI 350	23.0	1857	25.0	1972
Vihtavuori N110	Winchester	CCI 300	21.0	1740	23.0	1927
Alliant 2400	Winchester	CCI 300	21.5	1739	23.5	1898
Accurate No. 9	Winchester	CCI 300	21.0	1775	23.0	1891
Alliant Power Pistol	Winchester	CCI 300	12.5	1515	14.5	1725
Alliant Unique	Winchester	CCI 300	10.5	1301	12.5	1513
Hodgdon H. Universal	Winchester	CCI 300	9.0	1155	11.0	1395

WARNING! *Maximum loads should be used with CAUTION • C = Compressed Load*

240 GRAINS

DIAMETER	SECTIONAL DENSITY
.429"	0.186

44 DCHP	
Ballistic Coefficient	0.175
COAL Tested	1.590"
Speer Part No.	4455

44 DCSP	
Ballistic Coefficient	0.175
COAL Tested	1.595"
Speer Part No.	4456

Propellant	Case	Primer	Starting Charge Weight (grains)	Starting Charge Muzzle Velocity (feet/sec)	Maximum Charge Weight (grains)	Maximum Charge Muzzle Velocity (feet/sec)
Hodgdon H110	Winchester	CCI 350	22.0	1675	24.0	1796
Hodgdon Lil' Gun	Winchester	CCI 350	21.0	1664	23.0	1787
Winchester 296	Winchester	CCI 350	22.0	1624	24.0	1739
Alliant 2400	Winchester	CCI 300	19.0	1514	21.0	1701
Vihtavuori N110	Winchester	CCI 300	18.0	1540	20.0	1647
IMR 4227	Winchester	CCI 350	21.4	1495	23.4	1628
Accurate No. 9	Winchester	CCI 300	18.0	1474	20.0	1623
Ramshot Enforcer	Winchester	CCI 350	18.5	1477	20.5	1614
Accurate No. 7	Winchester	CCI 300	15.5	1354	17.5	1532
H. Universal	Winchester	CCI 300	8.8	1091	9.6	1216

WARNING! *Maximum loads should be used with CAUTION • C = Compressed Load*

270 GRAINS

DIAMETER	SECTIONAL DENSITY
.429"	0.210

44 DCSP	
Ballistic Coefficient	0.193
COAL Tested	1.595"
Speer Part No.	4461

			Starting Charge		Maximum Charge	
Propellant	Case	Primer	Weight (grains)	Muzzle Velocity (feet/sec)	Weight (grains)	Muzzle Velocity (feet/sec)
Hodgdon H110	Winchester	CCI 350	19.0	1458	21.0	1569
Hodgdon Lil' Gun	Winchester	CCI 350	17.5	1445	19.5	1552
Winchester 296	Winchester	CCI 350	18.5	1406	20.5	1546
Ramshot Enforcer	Winchester	CCI 350	17.0	1338	19.0	1512
Vihtavuori N110	Winchester	CCI 300	16.0	1348	18.0	1463
Accurate 1680	Winchester	CCI 350	22.5	1272	24.5 C	1375
Accurate No. 9	Winchester	CCI 300	14.0	1159	16.0	1359
Alliant 2400	Winchester	CCI 300	15.5	1211	17.5	1352
IMR 4227	Winchester	CCI 300	18.5	1231	20.5	1350

WARNING! Maximum loads should be used with CAUTION • C = Compressed Load

444 MARLIN

Alternate Names:	10.9x57mm
Parent Cartridge:	44 Magnum
Country of Origin:	USA
Year of Introduction:	1964
Designer(s):	Remington & Marlin
Governing Body:	SAAMI/CIP

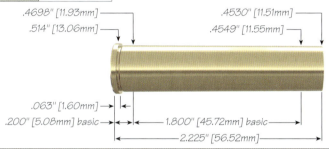

CARTRIDGE CASE DATA

Case Type:	Rimmed, slight taper		
Average Case Capacity:	69.0 grains H$_2$O	Max. Cartridge OAL	2.570 inch
Max. Case Length:	2.225 inch	Primer:	Large Rifle
Case Trim to Length:	2.215 inch	RCBS Shell holder:	# 28
Current Manufacturers:	Hornady, Remington		

BALLISTIC DATA

Max. Average Pressure (MAP):	42,000 psi, 44,000 CUP - SAAMI	Test Barrel Length:	24 inch
Rifling Twist Rate:	1 turn in 38 inches (12-groove), more recent: 1 turn in 20 inches (6-groove)		
Muzzle velocities of factory loaded ammunition	Bullet Wgt.		Muzzle velocity
	240-grain		2,350 fps
	Muzzle velocity will decrease approximately 10 fps per inch for barrels less than 24 inches.		

HISTORICAL NOTES

- The 444 Marlin cartridge was yet another effort to develop a modern, rimmed, big bore cartridge for lever-action rifles.

- It was developed by a technical team composed of personnel from Remington and Marlin.
- The 444 Marlin filled the big bore void in lever-action rifles when these rifles were no longer being chambered for the 45-70 Government.
- When Browning and Marlin resumed production of rifles in 45-70 Government, the 444 Marlin began dying a slow death.

BALLISTIC NOTES

- The 444 Marlin cartridge (42,000 psi) develops 50% higher MAP levels than the 45-70 Gov't (28,000 psi).
- The higher pressure combined with a lighter bullet, are the major reasons for the 444 Marlin's higher muzzle velocities and energies.
- Today, Remington lists only one load in their product catalog and Hornady two.
- Speer makes three bullets for handloading the 444 Marlin cartridge:
  - Two 240-grain bullets:
    1. A DeepCurl® Soft Point (DCSP) for hunting deer.
    2. A DeepCurl Hollow Point (DCHP) for hunting predators and pests.
  - One 270-grain DeepCurl Soft Point (DCSP) for hunting medium game such as deer.

TECHNICAL NOTES

- Essentially, the 444 Marlin cartridge case is a standard 44 Remington Magnum case lengthened by .940 inches.
- The correct bullet diameter for the 444 Marlin is .429 inches which is the same as the 44 Remington Magnum.

HANDLOADING NOTES

- The 444 Marlin should be loaded with bullets of stronger construction than pistol bullets for hunting purposes due to the higher velocities in rifles and carbines.
- Flat nosed bullets must be used to prevent magazine tube explosions.
- All bullets must be roll crimped securely in place using the cannelure on the bullets surface to prevent bullet set-back or elongation in tubular magazines.
- Do not use lighter propellant charges than those listed in the data as the bullet may fail to clear the barrel.

SAFETY NOTES

SPEER 270-grain DCSP bullet @ a muzzle velocity of 2,256 fps:
- Maximum vertical altitude @ 90° elevation is 5,907 feet.
- Maximum horizontal distance to first impact with ground @ 33° elevation is 2,675 yards.

240 GRAINS

DIAMETER	SECTIONAL DENSITY
.429"	0.186

44 DCHP

Ballistic Coefficient	0.175
COAL Tested	2.540"
Speer Part No.	4455

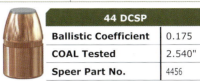

44 DCSP

Ballistic Coefficient	0.175
COAL Tested	2.540"
Speer Part No.	4456

			Starting Charge		Maximum Charge	
Propellant	Case	Primer	Weight (grains)	Muzzle Velocity (feet/sec)	Weight (grains)	Muzzle Velocity (feet/sec)
Alliant Reloder 7	Remington	CCI 200	46.0	2184	50.0	2354
Alliant Reloder 10X	Remington	CCI 200	49.0	2152	53.0	2348
Vihtavuori N133	Remington	CCI 200	54.0	2184	56.0 C	2319
IMR 8208 XBR	Hornady	CCI 200	54.5	2185	57.5 C	2313
Hodgdon H322	Remington	CCI 200	50.0	2107	54.0 C	2307
Hodgdon BENCHMARK	Remington	CCI 200	50.0	2065	54.0 C	2267
IMR 4198	Remington	CCI 200	40.0	2079	44.0	2245
Accurate 2015	Remington	CCI 200	50.0	2048	54.0	2240
Ramshot X-Terminator	Remington	CCI 250	49.0	2021	53.0	2165
Accurate 5744 (reduced load)	Remington	CCI 200	33.0	1833	37.0	2032

WARNING! *Maximum loads should be used with* CAUTION • C = Compressed Load

270 GRAINS

DIAMETER	SECTIONAL DENSITY
.429"	0.210

44 DCSP

Ballistic Coefficient	0.193
COAL Tested	2.530"
Speer Part No.	4461

			Starting Charge		Maximum Charge	
Propellant	Case	Primer	Weight (grains)	Muzzle Velocity (feet/sec)	Weight (grains)	Muzzle Velocity (feet/sec)
Vihtavuori N133	Remington	CCI 200	50.0	2089	54.0 C	2256
Alliant Reloder 7	Remington	CCI 200	43.0	2034	47.0	2216
Alliant Reloder 10X	Remington	CCI 200	46.0	2042	50.0	2212
IMR 8208 XBR	Hornady	CCI 200	51.0	2041	53.6	2155
Hodgdon H322	Remington	CCI 200	46.0	1961	50.0	2148
Hodgdon BENCHMARK	Remington	CCI 200	47.0	1969	51.0	2134
Accurate 2015	Remington	CCI 200	47.0	1948	51.0	2114
IMR 4895	Remington	CCI 200	50.0	1904	54.0 C	2062
IMR 4198	Remington	CCI 200	36.0	1882	40.0	2052
Ramshot X-Terminator	Remington	CCI 250	46.0	1883	50.0	2028

WARNING! Maximum loads should be used with CAUTION • C = Compressed Load

45-70 GOVERNMENT

Alternate Names:	45-70-405, 45-70-500, 45 U.S. Army, 45 Trapdoor
Parent Cartridge:	Originated from 1872 Ordnance Trials
Country of Origin:	USA
Year of Introduction:	1873
Designer(s):	Springfield Armory
Governing Body:	SAAMI/CIP

.608" [15.44mm]
.5039" [12.80mm]
.4800" [12.19mm]
.4813" [12.23mm]
.5055" [12.84mm]
.070" [1.78mm]
.200" [5.08mm] basic
1.800" [45.72mm] basic
2.105" [53.47mm]

CARTRIDGE CASE DATA

Case Type:	Rimmed, slight taper		
Average Case Capacity:	79.0 grains H₂O	Max. Cartridge OAL	2.550 inch
Max. Case Length:	2.105 inch	Primer:	Large Rifle
Case Trim to Length:	2.095 inch	RCBS Shell holder:	# 14
Current Manufacturers:	Federal, Remington, Winchester, Black Hills, Cor-Bon, Hornady		

BALLISTIC DATA

Max. Average Pressure (MAP):	28,000 psi, 28,000 CUP - SAAMI	Test Barrel Length:	24 inch
Rifling Twist Rate:	1 turn in 20 inches. Some rifles with "slow twist" 1:38 inches.		
Muzzle velocities of factory loaded ammunition	**Bullet Wgt.**	**Muzzle velocity**	
	300-grain	1,880 fps	
	350-grain	1,800 fps	
	405-grain	1,330 fps	
	Muzzle velocity will decrease approximately 5 fps per inch for barrels less than 24 inches.		

HISTORICAL NOTES

- When the 45-70 Government cartridge was taken into military service by the U.S. Army in 1873, the Civil War had been over for just eight years and was still fresh in the memory of most Americans.
- The 45-70 Gov't was standard issue for the U.S. Army during the taming of the Western Frontier and conflicts with Native Americans throughout the late 1800s.
- Loaded with a 405-grain lead bullet, it was carried by the 7th Cavalry troopers under General Custer at the Battle of The Little Big Horn.
- After it was replaced in U.S. military service by the 30-40 Krag cartridge in 1892, the 45-70 was relegated to the Army Reserves and National Guard.
- During the Spanish-American War in 1898, many of the Army Reserve and National Guard troops called up for service carried their 45-70 Trap Door Springfield rifles into combat in Cuba.
- Today, the 45-70 Government is the oldest military cartridge still in production, albeit for sporting use.
- What is the secret of the 45-70 cartridge's longevity? It continues as a favorite for hunting North American game at close range and in brush. Perhaps more important, it serves as a direct link with the Old West that you can hold in your hand.
- Despite its age (144 years and counting), the 45-70 Gov't cartridge refuses to die.

BALLISTIC NOTES

- The 45-70 Government was loaded initially with 70 grains of black powder under a 500-grain lead, flat nose bullet with a muzzle velocity of 1,100 fps. This load was designed to be fired in the Model 1873 Springfield "trap door" *rifle*.
- Later, the weight of the bullet was reduced to 405 grains in order to reduce recoil in cavalry and artillery *carbines*.
- Modern factory ammunition in this caliber is loaded to low MAP levels due to the age and weakness of the old "trap door" Model 1873 Springfield actions.
- The 500 grain lead bullet is no longer loaded by ammunition makers. The heaviest bullet loaded in factory ammunition today is 405 grains.
- Modern factory ammunition in 45-70 Government is loaded with jacketed bullets, except for rounds built especially for cowboy action shooting which requires lead projectiles.
- Sportsmen have always adapted military cartridges for hunting and the 45-70 Gov't is no exception. In the early 1900s, hunters found the expanding 300 and 330-grain hollow point lead bullets significantly improved muzzle velocity and striking energy.

TECHNICAL NOTES

- The 45-70 Government cartridge made the transition to smokeless propellants at the beginning of the 20th century.
- That said, the excess capacity of the 45-70 blackpowder cartridge case has always been a problem for the relatively small volume that smokeless propellants occupy. This requires the use of bulky propellants to partially compensate for this in order to prevent excessive velocity variations.

- Outside case dimensions of some factory loaded 45-70 ammunition is not sized to the exact dimensions on the case drawing. Rather, the outer dimensions of the loaded cartridge case body consists of a progressive series of slightly decreasing tapers rather than a constant taper in order to assure smooth feeding into the chambers of old rifles.

HANDLOADING NOTES

- **Handloading data is presented in three sections: Trap-Door Actions, Lever-Actions and Strong Actions. Make certain to use the correct load data for the strength of your action.**
- The 45-70 can have a very short leade in the chamber. Make sure your rounds chamber as intended and the overall cartridge length is not too long to feed or extract a loaded round from the action. Some bullets may not be suitable for use in lever-action rifles.
- Bullets should be crimped, especially when used in tubular magazines to prevent bullet set-back; thereby increasing pressure.
- Note: the 350-grain Speer SPFN Hot-Cor® is designed to expand at an impact velocity of 1,900 fps at the target; if you do not load to that velocity, expect little expansion.

SAFETY NOTES

400-grain Soft Point Flat Nose (SPFN) bullet @ a muzzle velocity of 1,799 fps:
- Maximum vertical altitude @ 90° elevation is 8,460 feet.
- Maximum horizontal distance to first impact with ground @ 34° elevation is 3,231 yards.

45-70 GOVERNMENT (TRAP-DOOR ACTIONS)

Maximum of 21,000 CUP

300 GRAINS

DIAMETER	SECTIONAL DENSITY
.458"	0.204

45 JHP

Ballistic Coefficient	0.206
COAL Tested	2.530"
Speer Part No.	2482

			Starting Charge		Maximum Charge	
Propellant	Case	Primer	Weight (grains)	Muzzle Velocity (feet/sec)	Weight (grains)	Muzzle Velocity (feet/sec)
Alliant Reloder 7	Winchester	CCI 200	38.0	1667	42.0	1771
Vihtavuori N133	Winchester	CCI 200	47.0	1623	49.0	1742
IMR 4198	Winchester	CCI 200	36.0	1530	38.0	1731
Hodgdon H4895	Winchester	CCI 200	52.0	1490	56.0	1711
Accurate 2015	Winchester	CCI 200	45.0	1587	49.0	1685
Alliant Reloder 10X	Winchester	CCI 200	40.0	1555	44.0	1678
IMR 3031	Winchester	CCI 200	50.0	1470	54.0	1677
IMR 4064	Winchester	CCI 200	53.0	1577	55.0	1668
Hodgdon Varget	Winchester	CCI 200	51.0	1503	55.0	1662
IMR 4895	Winchester	CCI 200	50.0	1463	54.0	1649
Hodgdon BENCHMARK	Winchester	CCI 200	49.0	1575	51.0	1648
Hodgdon H322	Winchester	CCI 200	49.0	1520	51.0	1571
IMR 4227	Winchester	CCI 200	30.0	1456	32.0	1543
Accurate 5744	Winchester	CCI 200	30.0	1367	34.0	1534
IMR SR 4759	Winchester	CCI 200	26.0	1361	28.0	1486

WARNING! Maximum loads should be used with CAUTION • C = Compressed Load

350 GRAINS

DIAMETER	SECTIONAL DENSITY
.458"	0.238

45 FNSP Hot-Cor®

Ballistic Coefficient	0.218
COAL Tested	2.715"
Speer Part No.	2478

			Starting Charge		Maximum Charge	
Propellant	Case	Primer	Weight (grains)	Muzzle Velocity (feet/sec)	Weight (grains)	Muzzle Velocity (feet/sec)
Accurate 2015	Winchester	CCI 200	46.0	1520	50.0	1713
Hodgdon BENCHMARK	Winchester	CCI 200	47.0	1551	51.0	1699
Vihtavuori N133	Winchester	CCI 200	44.0	1479	48.0	1699
IMR 8208	Winchester	CCI 200	47.0	1555	50.9	1697
IMR 4064	Winchester	CCI 200	51.0	1516	55.0	1633
Hodgdon H4895	Winchester	CCI 200	48.0	1464	52.0	1626
IMR 4198	Winchester	CCI 200	32.0	1427	36.0	1609
IMR 3031	Winchester	CCI 200	48.0	1397	52.0	1587
IMR 4166	Winchester	CCI 200	41.0	1402	45.0	1528
Alliant Reloder 10X	Winchester	CCI 200	32.0	1355	36.0	1485
IMR SR 4759	Winchester	CCI 200	26.0	1381	30.0	1468
Alliant Reloder 7	Winchester	CCI 200	31.0	1303	35.0	1463

WARNING! Maximum loads should be used with CAUTION • C = Compressed Load

400 GRAINS

DIAMETER	SECTIONAL DENSITY
.458"	0.272

45 FNSP

Ballistic Coefficient	0.259
COAL Tested	2.540"
Speer Part No.	2479

Propellant	Case	Primer	Starting Charge		Maximum Charge	
			Weight (grains)	Muzzle Velocity (feet/sec)	Weight (grains)	Muzzle Velocity (feet/sec)
Winchester 748	Winchester	CCI 250	55.0	1667	59.0 C	1795
Vihtavuori N133	Winchester	CCI 200	43.0	1521	47.0	1747
Alliant AR-Comp	Winchester	CCI 200	47.5	1565	51.0	1720
Hodgdon H4895	Winchester	CCI 200	49.0	1539	53.0 C	1709
Alliant Power Pro Varmint	Winchester	CCI 200	48.0	1554	52.8	1682
Accurate 2015	Winchester	CCI 200	42.0	1438	46.0	1621
IMR 8208	Winchester	CCI 200	46.0	1466	50.0	1599
IMR 3031	Winchester	CCI 200	45.0	1396	49.0	1586
Hodgdon BENCHMARK	Winchester	CCI 200	44.5	1427	48.4	1580
IMR 4064	Winchester	CCI 200	47.0	1398	51.0	1506
Alliant Reloder 10X	Winchester	CCI 200	35.0	1318	39.0	1469
IMR 4166	Winchester	CCI 200	37.0	1202	41.4	1379
IMR 4198	Winchester	CCI 200	30.0	1206	34.0	1360
Hodgdon H322	Winchester	CCI 200	37.0	1100	41.0	1294

WARNING! Maximum loads should be used with CAUTION • C = Compressed Load

45-70 GOVERNMENT (LEVER-ACTIONS)

Maximum of 28,000 CUP

300 GRAINS	DIAMETER	SECTIONAL DENSITY
	.458"	0.204

45 JHP	
Ballistic Coefficient	0.206
COAL Tested	2.530"
Speer Part No.	2482

			Starting Charge		Maximum Charge	
Propellant	Case	Primer	Weight (grains)	Muzzle Velocity (feet/sec)	Weight (grains)	Muzzle Velocity (feet/sec)
IMR 8208	Winchester	CCI 200	59.5	1927	63.4	2115
Hodgdon BENCHMARK	Winchester	CCI 200	58.0	1915	62.4	2114
Alliant Reloder 7	Winchester	CCI 200	43.0	1852	47.0	2011
Hodgdon H4895	Winchester	CCI 200	58.0	1739	62.0	1987
IMR 4166	Winchester	CCI 200	53.0	1783	59.0	1982
Hodgdon Varget	Winchester	CCI 200	57.0	1794	61.0	1976
Alliant Reloder 10X	Winchester	CCI 200	48.0	1837	52.0	1973
Hodgdon H322	Winchester	CCI 200	52.0	1675	56.0	1951
IMR 4895	Winchester	CCI 200	57.0	1723	61.0	1924
IMR 3031	Winchester	CCI 200	55.0	1690	59.0	1918
Vihtavuori N133	Winchester	CCI 200	50.0	1692	54.0	1915
IMR 4064	Winchester	CCI 200	57.0	1733	61.0	1908
XMR 2015	Winchester	CCI 200	51.0	1706	55.0	1878
IMR 4320	Winchester	CCI 200	55.0	1581	59.0	1827
IMR 4198	Winchester	CCI 200	39.0	1609	43.0	1765
Accurate 5744	Winchester	CCI 200	36.0	1559	40.0	1745
IMR SR 4759	Winchester	CCI 200	29.0	1481	31.0	1603

WARNING! Maximum loads should be used with CAUTION • C = Compressed Load

400 GRAINS

DIAMETER	SECTIONAL DENSITY
.458"	0.272

45 FNSP

Ballistic Coefficient	0.259
COAL Tested	2.540"
Speer Part No.	2479

			Starting Charge		Maximum Charge	
Propellant	Case	Primer	Weight (grains)	Muzzle Velocity (feet/sec)	Weight (grains)	Muzzle Velocity (feet/sec)
Alliant AR-Comp	Winchester	CCI 200	53.0	1803	56.0	1933
Hodgdon H335	Winchester	CCI 250	54.0	1724	58.0	1876
Accurate 2015	Winchester	CCI 200	48.0	1685	52.0	1871
Alliant Power Pro Varmint	Winchester	CCI 200	55.0	1733	59.0	1868
Vihtavuori N133	Winchester	CCI 200	47.0	1672	51.0	1847
Winchester 748	Winchester	CCI 250	58.0	1679	62.0 C	1839
Hodgdon H4895	Winchester	CCI 200	52.0	1669	56.0 C	1829
IMR 8208	Winchester	CCI 200	50.5	1610	54.5	1791
Hodgdon BENCHMARK	Winchester	CCI 200	49.5	1604	53.5	1785
IMR 4064	Winchester	CCI 200	51.0	1550	55.0	1720
IMR 3031	Winchester	CCI 200	49.0	1538	53.0	1706
Hodgdon H322	Winchester	CCI 200	45.0	1431	49.0	1652
Alliant Reloder 10X	Winchester	CCI 200	40.0	1483	44.0	1641
IMR 4320	Winchester	CCI 200	49.0	1442	53.0	1615
IMR 4166	Winchester	CCI 200	43.5	1443	47.8	1601
IMR 4198	Winchester	CCI 200	36.0	1361	40.0	1595
IMR SR 4759 (reduced load)	Winchester	CCI 200	26.0	1172	30.0	1343

WARNING! Maximum loads should be used with CAUTION • C = Compressed Load

45-70 GOVERNMENT (STRONG ACTIONS)

Maximum of 35,000 CUP

300 GRAINS	DIAMETER	SECTIONAL DENSITY
	.458"	0.204

45 JHP	
Ballistic Coefficient	0.206
COAL Tested	2.530"
Speer Part No.	2482

			Starting Charge		Maximum Charge	
Propellant	Case	Primer	Weight (grains)	Muzzle Velocity (feet/sec)	Weight (grains)	Muzzle Velocity (feet/sec)
Vihtavuori N133	Winchester	CCI 200	56.0	1982	60.0	2202
Alliant Reloder 10X	Winchester	CCI 200	53.0	2015	57.0	2167
Hodgdon H322	Winchester	CCI 200	57.0	1929	61.0 C	2145
Hodgdon BENCHMARK	Winchester	CCI 200	57.0	1912	61.0	2139
Accurate 2015	Winchester	CCI 200	57.0	1930	61.0	2120
Hodgdon H4895	Winchester	CCI 200	62.0	2006	64.0 C	2115
Hodgdon Varget	Winchester	CCI 200	63.0	2018	65.0 C	2087
IMR 4895	Winchester	CCI 200	62.0	1961	64.0 C	2060
Alliant Reloder 7	Winchester	CCI 200	50.0	1873	54.0	2050
IMR 4320	Winchester	CCI 200	61.0	1909	65.0 C	2048
IMR 4198	Winchester	CCI 200	44.0	1817	48.0	2037
IMR 3031	Winchester	CCI 200	59.0	1929	61.0 C	2023
IMR 4064	Winchester	CCI 200	61.0	1891	63.0 C	2002

WARNING! Maximum loads should be used with CAUTION • C = Compressed Load

350 GRAINS

DIAMETER	SECTIONAL DENSITY
.458"	0.238

45 SPFN Hot-Cor®

Ballistic Coefficient	0.218
COAL Tested	2.710"
Speer Part No.	2478

Propellant	Case	Primer	Starting Charge Weight (grains)	Starting Charge Muzzle Velocity (feet/sec)	Maximum Charge Weight (grains)	Maximum Charge Muzzle Velocity (feet/sec)
Accurate 2015	Winchester	CCI 200	54.0	1926	60.0	2146
Vihtavuori N133	Winchester	CCI 200	56.0	1943	60.0 C	2117
IMR 4198	Winchester	CCI 200	46.5	1941	51.5	2061
Hodgdon H4895	Winchester	CCI 200	57.0	1774	63.0 C	2030
IMR 3031	Winchester	CCI 200	55.0	1823	61.0 C	2027
Hodgdon H322	Winchester	CCI 200	54.0	1879	60.0	2027
IMR 4895	Winchester	CCI 200	55.0	1839	61.0 C	2027
Alliant Reloder 10X	Winchester	CCI 200	46.0	1893	50.0	1993
IMR 4064	Winchester	CCI 200	56.0	1675	62.0 C	1917
IMR 4320	Winchester	CCI 200	58.0	1751	62.0 C	1888
IMR SR 4759 (reduced load)	Winchester	CCI 200	28.0	1346	32.0	1503

WARNING! Maximum loads should be used with CAUTION • C = Compressed Load

400 GRAINS

DIAMETER	SECTIONAL DENSITY
.458"	0.272

45 FNSP	
Ballistic Coefficient	0.259
COAL Tested	2.540"
Speer Part No.	2479

			Starting Charge		Maximum Charge	
Propellant	Case	Primer	Weight (grains)	Muzzle Velocity (feet/sec)	Weight (grains)	Muzzle Velocity (feet/sec)
IMR 8208	Winchester	CCI 200	58.0	1961	62.0	2107
Hodgdon BENCHMARK	Winchester	CCI 200	57.0	1969	61.0	2102
Accurate 2015	Winchester	CCI 200	52.0	1857	56.0 C	2029
Hodgdon H4895	Winchester	CCI 200	56.0	1836	60.0 C	2007
Vihtavuori N133	Winchester	CCI 200	51.0	1837	55.0	2005
Hodgdon H335	Winchester	CCI 250	58.0	1844	62.0 C	1964
IMR 4166	Winchester	CCI 200	54.0	1813	58.2	1951
Hodgdon H322	Winchester	CCI 200	51.0	1724	55.0	1935
Alliant Reloder 10X	Winchester	CCI 200	47.0	1774	51.0	1929
IMR 4198	Winchester	CCI 200	42.0	1631	46.0	1819
IMR 3031	Winchester	CCI 200	50.0	1565	54.0 C	1790
IMR 4064	Winchester	CCI 200	52.0	1601	56.0 C	1764
IMR 4320	Winchester	CCI 200	53.0	1615	57.0	1761
IMR SR 4759 (reduced load)	Winchester	CCI 200	28.0	1349	32.0	1533

WARNING! Maximum loads should be used with CAUTION • C = Compressed Load

450 MARLIN

Parent Cartridge:	375 H&H Magnum, 458 Win. Mag.
Country of Origin:	USA
Year of Introduction:	2000
Designer(s):	Marlin & Hornady
Governing Body:	SAAMI/CIP

CARTRIDGE CASE DATA

Case Type:	Belted, rimless, slight taper		
Average Case Capacity:	74.0 grains H_2O	Max. Cartridge OAL	2.550 inch
Max. Case Length:	2.100 inch	Primer:	Large Rifle
Case Trim to Length:	2.090 inch	RCBS Shell holder:	# 4
Current Manufacturers:	Hornady, Buffalo Bore		

BALLISTIC DATA

Max. Average Pressure (MAP):	43,500 psi, CUP not established for this cartridge - SAAMI	Test Barrel Length:	24 inch
Rifling Twist Rate:	1 turn in 20 inch		
Muzzle velocities of factory loaded ammunition	Bullet Wgt.	Muzzle velocity	
	300-grain	1,880 fps	
	405-grain	1,330 fps	
Muzzle velocity will decrease approximately 5 fps per inch for barrels less than 24 inches.			

HISTORICAL NOTES

- Marlin has long been known for its large caliber, lever-action rifles in 444 Marlin and 45-70 Government.
- When sportsmen urged Marlin to develop a new, more powerful, large caliber cartridge, they listened—and acted.

- The solution required a new, high pressure rifle cartridge compatible with existing Marlin actions.
- Marlin formed a new product development team with Hornady to design and prove out the new cartridge which was introduced in 2000.
- Their goals for the new cartridge were to exceed the ballistic performance of both the 444 Marlin and the 45-70 Government.
- To reach this goal, the new cartridge had to be able to withstand higher MAP levels than either of the old cartridges.
- But there was a limit—lever-action rifles cannot withstand the same pressures as bolt-action rifles. Consequently, MAP levels for the 450 Marlin are limited to 43,500 psi which is quite low by modern standards, making ballistic development challenging.

BALLISTIC NOTES

- The sole manufacturer of factory ammunition in 450 Marlin is Hornady who offers but a single load—a 325-grain bullet at a muzzle velocity of 2,225 fps.
- This ballistic performance is significantly better than the 444 Marlin and 45-70 Gov't
- Speer offers two bullets for handloading the 450 Marlin cartridge:
  - The Speer 300-grain Jacketed Hollow Point (JHP) which is a great choice for general purpose hunting for all North American big game.
  - The Speer 400-grain Soft Point Flat Nose (SPFN). This is a "classic" bullet weight for hunting North American game with large caliber cartridges. If many years of experience and tradition are any indication, this bullet weight is your best choice.

TECHNICAL NOTES

- The parent cartridge of the 450 Marlin (and 458 Winchester Magnum) is the classic 375 H&H magnum. This is something of a departure from tradition as the 375 H&H Magnum case is a rimmed, belted, necked design which was new to lever-action rifle cartridges.
- One major difference between the 375 H&H Magnum cartridge and the 450 Marlin is that the belt of the 450 Marlin is .032 inches longer so as to make it impossible to chamber a 450 Marlin cartridge in another belted magnum chamber.
- The heavy sidewalls of the belted 450 Marlin case will easily withstand the higher pressures and the case body is tapered to ease extraction forces.
- Case capacity of the 450 Marlin is 74.0-grains of H_2O which is approximately 20% less than the 458 Win. Mag.
- MAP levels are very different: that of the 450 Marlin being 43,500 psi compared to the 458 Win. Mag. at 60,000 psi.
- The correct bullet diameter for the 450 Marlin is .458 inches.

HANDLOADING NOTES

- To avoid magazine tube explosions in lever-action rifles, the 450 Marlin cartridge must be loaded with flat nose bullets.
- These bullets must be roll crimped securely in the cannelure on the bullet jacket to prevent the bullet being pulled from the case mouth by recoil or pushed into the case by the magazine spring and cartridges in the magazine tube.
- When reloading the 450 Marlin, we recommend that all cases be thoroughly cleaned and full length resized to assure smooth feeding.
- Watch carefully for signs of stretching or cracking on the case head in front of the belt. These are signs of incipient case head separations. Discard and destroy all cases with such indicators.

SAFETY NOTES

SPEER 400-grain Soft Point Flat Nose (SPFN) bullet @ a muzzle velocity of 1,990 fps:
- Maximum vertical altitude @ 90° elevation is 6,933 feet.
- Maximum horizontal distance to first impact with ground @ 34° elevation is 3,220 yards.

300 GRAINS

DIAMETER	SECTIONAL DENSITY
.458"	0.204

45 JHP

Ballistic Coefficient	0.206
COAL Tested	2.525"
Speer Part No.	2482

			Starting Charge		Maximum Charge	
Propellant	Case	Primer	Weight (grains)	Muzzle Velocity (feet/sec)	Weight (grains)	Muzzle Velocity (feet/sec)
Alliant Power Pro 1200-R	Hornady	CCI 200	59.5	2391	63.5 C	2547
Hodgdon H322	Hornady	CCI 200	57.0	2228	61.0 C	2405
Alliant Reloder 7	Hornady	CCI 200	52.0	2220	56.0 C	2392
Vihtavuori N133	Hornady	CCI 200	55.0	2206	59.0 C	2366
Hodgdon BENCHMARK	Hornady	CCI 200	58.0	2229	62.0 C	2364
Vihtavuori N120	Hornady	CCI 200	49.0	2182	53.0	2359
IMR 4198	Hornady	CCI 200	46.0	2177	50.0	2353
Accurate 2230	Hornady	CCI 250	55.0	2234	59.0	2333
Accurate 2015	Hornady	CCI 200	56.0	2132	60.0 C	2303
Hodgdon H4227	Hornady	CCI 200	40.0	2017	44.0	2184
IMR 4895	Hornady	CCI 200	60.0C	2093	62.0 C	2184
Accurate 5744 (reduced load)	Hornady	CCI 200	36.0	1808	40.0	1996

WARNING! *Maximum loads should be used with CAUTION • C = Compressed Load*

400 GRAINS

DIAMETER	SECTIONAL DENSITY
.458"	0.272

45 FNSP

Ballistic Coefficient	0.259
COAL Tested	2.525"
Speer Part No.	2479

			Starting Charge		Maximum Charge	
Propellant	Case	Primer	Weight (grains)	Muzzle Velocity (feet/sec)	Weight (grains)	Muzzle Velocity (feet/sec)
Alliant AR-Comp	Hornady	CCI 200	52.0	1977	56.0 C	2133
Alliant Power Pro 1200-R	Hornady	CCI 200	50.0	1990	53.6	2130
Hodgdon BENCHMARK	Hornady	CCI 200	52.0	1949	56.0 C	2106
Alliant Power Pro Varmint	Hornady	CCI 200	56.0	1947	59.0 C	2057
Hodgdon H322	Hornady	CCI 200	47.5	1781	51.5 C	1990
Accurate 2230	Hornady	CCI 250	47.0	1852	51.0	1978
Vihtavuori N133	Hornady	CCI 200	46.0	1765	50.0 C	1964
Alliant Reloder 7	Hornady	CCI 200	43.0	1819	47.0	1963
Hodgdon Varget	Hornady	CCI 200	53.0	1821	57.0 C	1962
IMR 4198	Hornady	CCI 200	39.0	1780	43.0	1930
Accurate 2015	Hornady	CCI 200	47.0	1735	51.0 C	1914
Vihtavuori N120	Hornady	CCI 200	40.0	1766	44.0	1905
Winchester 748	Hornady	CCI 250	54.0	1745	56.0 C	1817
IMR 3031	Hornady	CCI 200	48.0C	1661	50.0 C	1783
Hodgdon H4227	Hornady	CCI 200	32.0	1563	36.0	1724

WARNING! Maximum loads should be used with CAUTION • C = Compressed Load

458 WINCHESTER MAGNUM

Parent Cartridge:	375 H&H Magnum
Country of Origin:	USA
Year of Introduction:	1956
Designer(s):	Winchester
Governing Body:	SAAMI/CIP

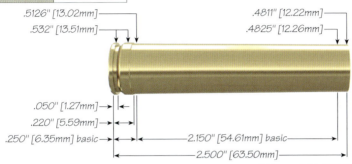

CARTRIDGE CASE DATA

Case Type:	Belted, rimless, slight taper		
Average Case Capacity:	95.6 grains H$_2$O	Max. Cartridge OAL	3.340 inch
Max. Case Length:	2.500 inch	Primer:	Large Rifle
Case Trim to Length:	2.490 inch	RCBS Shell holder:	# 4
Current Manufacturers:	Nosler, Federal, Hornady, Winchester, Norma, Swift		

BALLISTIC DATA

Max. Average Pressure (MAP):	60,000 psi, 53,000 CUP - SAAMI	Test Barrel Length:	24 inch
Rifling Twist Rate:	1 turn in 14 inch		
Muzzle velocities of factory loaded ammunition	Bullet Wgt.	Muzzle velocity	
	400-grain	2,250 fps	
	500-grain	2,100 fps	
	Muzzle velocity will decrease approximately 10 fps per inch for barrels less than 24 inches.		

HISTORICAL NOTES

- When Winchester introduced their new 458 Winchester Magnum cartridge in 1956, it was the first large-bore, American cartridge designed for hunting dangerous African game.

- Unlike the large British African cartridges that required a magnum-length bolt action, the 458 Win. Magnum was designed to fit in standard 30-06 Springfield actions.
- The 458 Win. Mag. became the first and most powerful in a series of Winchester, belted magnum, rifle cartridges which included the 300 Winchester Magnum and 338 Winchester Magnum among others.
- An immediate sales success, the 458 Winchester Magnum quickly surpassed the big British African cartridges in popularity. In the process, the 458 Win. Mag. became something of a legend in its own right. It remains so to this day.
- Many North American and European rifle makers now offer models in this caliber.
- Today, ammunition in this caliber is available from a number of American ammunition makers including Winchester, Federal, Hornady, and Nosler. Brass is available from Norma.

BALLISTIC NOTES

- Although the 458 Winchester Magnum has a smaller case capacity than its large-bore British counterparts, it partially makes up for that by loading to higher MAP levels suitable for modern bolt-action rifles.
- However, the case capacity does limit the muzzle velocity to 2,100 fps with a 500-grain bullet with 4,972 ft-lbs of energy. Any possible improvements are minimal.
- While this is certainly adequate for most African hunting, it remains less powerful than many of the British cartridges. Recently, more powerful cartridges such as the 458 Lott and the 416 Remington Magnum have been introduced that more effectively compete with the old British calibers.
- The 458 Win. Magnum's reputation rests on its 500-grain FMJ or JSP bullet. This bullet is designed for African hunting conditions and game, and is far too much power for most North American game.
- As most owners of 458 Winchester Magnum rifles hunt in Africa infrequently, we have developed loads for the 458 with lighter weight bullets. With these loads, the 458 Winchester Magnum can be used successfully on North American game.
- Ammunition makers do not offer such loads.
- For handloaders who own 458 caliber rifles we offer two Speer bullets for North American hunting conditions:
  - The Speer 350-grain Soft Point Hot-Cor (FNSP) bullet which can be handloaded to two different muzzle velocity levels according to game size. This bullet has a thick jacket to assure deep penetration and is suitable for all North American big game.
    - For lighter game this bullet can be loaded down to approximately 2,200 fps which offers ballistic performance comparable to the 338 Win. Magnum.
    - For large heavy game, we recommend a muzzle velocity of 2,250-2,350 fps for ballistic performance comparable to the 375 H&H Magnum.
  - The Speer 400-grain Soft Point Flat Nose (FNSP) bullet is more lightly constructed despite its heavier weight. It is suitable for all large North American game.
    - Handloaders can also prepare a low velocity, low recoil "punkin roller" load with the Speer 400-grain bullet at a muzzle velocity of 1,445 fps.

TECHNICAL NOTES

- Basically, the 458 Winchester Magnum is based on a 375 H&H Magnum case shortened .35 inches without a neck and less body taper to increase case capacity.
- The 458 Win. Magnum headspaces on the belt.
- In technical terms, the 458 Winchester Magnum harbors no ballistic secrets, so much as a combination of proven features.
  - The 1 turn in 14 inches rifling twist will stabilize a wide range of bullet weights from 300 to 500-grains.
  - With a Maximum Overall Loaded length of 3.340 inches, the 458 Winchester Magnum will fit in standard 30-06 length actions.
  - Factory loaded ammunition in 458 Win. Magnum caliber is offered by most, but not all, major domestic ammunition makers. However, few foreign manufacturers offer this caliber.

HANDLOADING NOTES

- We recommend using only new, empty brass for reloading maximum loads.
- All bullets loaded in 458 Winchester Magnum ammunition must be crimped securely using the cannelure on the bullet jacket to prevent the bullet being pulled from the case mouth or pushed into the case by recoil.
- We recommend thoroughly cleaning and full length resizing all cases to assure reliable feeding and chambering.
- Watch carefully for signs of stretching or cracking on the case head in front of the belt. These are signs of incipient case head separations. Discard and destroy all cases with such indicators.
- Like many big magnum cartridges, the 458 Winchester Magnum works best with slower burning rifle propellants.

SAFETY NOTES

Speer 400-grain FNSP bullet @ a muzzle velocity of 2,429 fps:
- Maximum vertical altitude @ 90° elevation is 7,392 feet.
- Maximum horizontal distance to first impact with ground @ 38° elevation is 3,384 yards.

350 GRAINS

DIAMETER	SECTIONAL DENSITY
.458"	0.238

45 FNSP Hot-Cor®	
Ballistic Coefficient	0.218
COAL Tested	3.105"
Speer Part No.	2478

			Starting Charge		Maximum Charge	
Propellant	Case	Primer	Weight (grains)	Muzzle Velocity (feet/sec)	Weight (grains)	Muzzle Velocity (feet/sec)
Accurate 2230	Winchester	CCI 250	82.0	2499	86.0 C	2593
Accurate 2015	Winchester	CCI 250	73.0	2419	77.0 C	2560
Hodgdon H322	Winchester	CCI 250	78.0	2399	82.0 C	2524
IMR 4198	Winchester	CCI 250	67.0	2399	71.0 C	2505
Vihtavuori N133	Winchester	CCI 250	72.0	2233	76.0 C	2471
IMR 4895	Winchester	CCI 250	76.0	2331	80.0 C	2467
IMR 4166	Federal	CCI 250	78.5	2376	80.9 C	2445
Hodgdon H335	Winchester	CCI 250	81.0	2227	85.0 C	2418
Accurate 2460	Winchester	CCI 250	75.0	2261	79.0 C	2371
Hodgdon BL-C(2)	Winchester	CCI 250	80.0	2204	84.0 C	2343
Alliant Reloder 7	Winchester	CCI 250	69.0	2186	73.0 C	2335
IMR 3031	Winchester	CCI 250	71.0	2165	75.0 C	2314

WARNING! *Maximum loads should be used with CAUTION • C = Compressed Load*

400 GRAINS

DIAMETER	SECTIONAL DENSITY
.458"	0.272

45 FNSP	
Ballistic Coefficient	0.259
COAL Tested	3.125"
Speer Part No.	2479

			Starting Charge		Maximum Charge	
Propellant	Case	Primer	Weight (grains)	Muzzle Velocity (feet/sec)	Weight (grains)	Muzzle Velocity (feet/sec)
Accurate 2230	Winchester	CCI 250	78.0	2290	82.0 C	2429
Hodgdon BL-C(2)	Winchester	CCI 250	75.0	2269	79.0 C	2410
IMR 8208 XBR	Federal	CCI 250	76.0	2300	80.2 C	2410
Hodgdon BENCHMARK	Federal	CCI 250	75.0	2283	79.4 C	2402
Accurate 2015 BR	Winchester	CCI 250	70.0	2269	74.0 C	2386
Alliant Power Pro 1200-R	Federal	CCI 250	70.5	2270	74.1	2381
Alliant Reloder 7	Winchester	CCI 250	70.0	2190	74.0	2316
Vihtavuori N133	Winchester	CCI 250	70.0	2174	74.0 C	2305
Hodgdon H4198	Winchester	CCI 250	60.0	2107	64.0	2231
IMR 3031	Winchester	CCI 250	67.0	2055	71.0 C	2169
IMR SR 4759 (reduced load)	Winchester	CCI 250	26.0	1262	30.0	1445

WARNING! Maximum loads should be used with CAUTION • C = Compressed Load

458 LOTT

Parent Cartridge:	375 H&H Magnum
Country of Origin:	USA
Year of Introduction:	1971
Designer(s):	Jack Lott
Governing Body:	SAAMI/CIP

CARTRIDGE CASE DATA

Case Type:	Belted, rimless, slight taper		
Average Case Capacity:	108.7 grains H$_2$O	Max. Cartridge OAL	3.600 inch
Max. Case Length:	2.800 inch	Primer:	Large Rifle
Case Trim to Length:	2.790 inch	RCBS Shell holder:	# 4
Current Manufacturers:	Federal, Winchester, Hornady, Nosler, Norma, Kynoch		

BALLISTIC DATA

Max. Average Pressure (MAP):	62,500 psi, CUP not established for this cartridge - SAAMI	Test Barrel Length:	24 inch
Rifling Twist Rate:	1 turn in 10 inch		
Muzzle velocities of factory loaded ammunition	Bullet Wgt.		Muzzle velocity
	500-grain		2,300 fps
	550-grain		2,100 fps

Muzzle velocity will decrease approximately 10 fps per inch for barrels less than 24 inches.

HISTORICAL NOTES

- Although the 458 Winchester Magnum is a popular cartridge for hunting African game, muzzle velocity is limited to about 2,400 fps due to case capacity. Many experienced African hunters felt that an additional 200-300 fps muzzle velocity would increase the striking energy of the bullet to a more advantageous level for dangerous game.
- Jack Lott, an experienced African hunter, was determined to improve the 458 Winchester Magnum cartridge by lengthening the cartridge case to 2.800 inches to allow case capacity to be increased approximately 13% in order to provide the additional muzzle velocity required.
- The added length meant the 458 Lott would require a magnum length action.
- After years of experimentation, the popularity of the 458 Lott gradually increased.
- The 458 Lott was standardized by SAAMI in 1998. Today, it has become a standard item in the product lines of Federal, Norma, Hornady and Nosler.
- Many North American and European rifle makers now offer models in this caliber.

BALLISTIC NOTES

- The large case capacity of the 458 Lott allows it to combine a heavy powder charge with the high MAP level (62,500 psi) of a modern cartridge.
- With a 500-grain bullet, factory loaded ammunition offers a muzzle velocity of 2,300 fps. This is an impressive 26% increase over the muzzle energy of the 458 Win. Magnum and comparable to the 500 Nitro Express.
- As most owners of 458 Lott rifles will attest, full power, factory loads with a 500-grain bullet are far too powerful for North American game. However, a lighter weight bullet for some types of African plains game would be welcome.
- For this application, we have developed an "African plains game" load using the Speer 350-grain Soft Point Hot-Cor® bullet.
- This bullet can be handloaded to a muzzle velocity of 2,868 fps with muzzle energy of 6,392 ft-lbs.
- For North American game, lighter loads are listed.
- Oh, and a word about recoil. The 458 Lott has enough recoil to allow your chiropractor to take the vacation he has dreamed of. It is not a caliber for the novice.

TECHNICAL NOTES

- Basically, the 458 Lott is based on a full length 375 H&H Magnum case without a neck and less body taper to increase case capacity.
- The 458 Lott headspaces on the belt.
- In technical terms, the 458 Lott harbors no ballistic secrets, so much as a combination of proven features.
  - A 1 turn in 10 inches rifling twist to stabilize a wide range of bullet weights from 350 to 500-grains.
  - With a Maximum Overall Loaded length of 3.600 inches, the 458 Lott requires a long length action.
  - Modern MAP levels allow high velocity and muzzle energy.

HANDLOADING NOTES

- We recommend using only new, empty brass for reloading maximum charges.
- All bullets loaded in 458 Lott ammunition must be crimped securely in the cannelure on the bullet jacket to prevent the bullet being pulled from the case mouth or pushed into the case by recoil.
- We recommend thoroughly cleaning and full length resizing all cases to assure reliable feeding and chambering.
- Watch carefully for signs of stretching or cracking on the case head in front of the belt. These are signs of incipient case head separations. Discard and destroy all cases with such indicators.
- The 458 Lott works best with slow burning rifle propellants.

SAFETY NOTES

SPEER 350-grain Soft Point Flat Nose Hot-Cor® bullet @ a muzzle velocity of 2,868 fps:

- Maximum vertical altitude @ 90° elevation is 9,285 feet.
- Maximum horizontal distance to first impact with ground @ 35° elevation is 4,244 yards.

350 GRAINS

DIAMETER	SECTIONAL DENSITY
.458"	0.238

45 FNSP Hot-Cor®

Ballistic Coefficient	0.218
COAL Tested	3.400"
Speer Part No.	2478

			Starting Charge		Maximum Charge	
Propellant	Case	Primer	Weight (grains)	Muzzle Velocity (feet/sec)	Weight (grains)	Muzzle Velocity (feet/sec)
Alliant Power Pro Varmint	Norma	Federal 215	96.0	2765	102.0 C	2868
Accurate 2460	Norma	Federal 215	88.5	2674	98.0 C	2865
Accurate LT-32	Norma	Federal 215	82.5	2580	90.0 C	2768
Hodgdon H322	Norma	Federal 215	86.0	2708	88.0 C	2749
Vihtavuori N130	Norma	Federal 215	77.7	2566	85.7 C	2739
Alliant Power Pro 1200-R	Norma	Federal 215	73.5	2552	81.5	2728
Ramshot TAC	Hornady	Federal 215	91.0	2676	93.0 C	2715
Hodgdon BENCHMARK	Hornady	Federal 215	87.0	2672	89.0 C	2714
Alliant Reloder 10X	Hornady	Federal 215	82.0	2662	84.0 C	2712
Alliant Reloder 7	Hornady	Federal 215	79.0	2650	81.0	2699
IMR 4198	Hornady	Federal 215	78.0	2645	80.0 C	2693
Accurate 2015	Hornady	Federal 215	83.0	2562	85.0 C	2603
Vihtavuori N133	Hornady	Federal 215	83.0	2534	85.0 C	2588

WARNING! *Maximum loads should be used with CAUTION • C = Compressed Load*

CHAPTER 12

A RELOADER'S JOURNEY; FROM JUNIOR SHOOTER TO CHAMPION

Julie Golob
Professional Sport Shooting Markswoman

I learned the value of brass at a young age. I was Dad's little helper on the range and collected his cases that were specially marked with a magic marker so that he could take them home and reload them into ammo for another day. In those early years I remember hearing the tap, tap, tap sound of my dad hammering open a mold when he made his own perfectly shaped lead bullets. I remember watching him work through the steps of making his own ammo with a single-stage press before I got bored and ran off to play with my siblings.

As I got older I became more interested and by the time I was a teenager, I wasn't just helping my father pick up brass, I was loading my own. My dad's ritual of manufacturing each round, one by one, could no longer be a meticulously slow process. Our ammo loading had to keep up with the demands of a father/daughter shooting team who traveled all over New York state on the weekends and throughout the northeast in the summer as we competed in United States Practical Shooting events whenever and however we could.

My father and I volunteered as range officers at many shooting competitions. Not only did that mean a free entry into the match, another perk was how we were often able to collect loads of brass left on the range. At these events we scrounged for every fired case we could find even if it wasn't in the caliber we shot. Why? Because we knew it would be valuable to someone along the way and that it might result in a trade or sale that would ultimately help feed our progressive loader set up in the basement.

Conversations on the range didn't just evolve around shooting performances or stage planning for the fast-paced practical shooting matches. It also centered around all things shooting, including finding the ideal ammo load for accuracy, reliability, power factor and, of course, cost. At the time I was shooting in the Open Division and my competition firearm was a double-stack 1911 style handgun chambered in 38 Super with a compensator, porting and a red dot optic. No two guns in this division were identical. Dad and I tackled loading ammo as a team. Collecting brass, cleaning it, loading, checking and inspecting every round became part of a weekly ritual, but we also had to develop our own unique ammo recipes.

It all started with brass. New or once-fired brass was like liquid gold, reserved for only major shooting competitions. The rest of the brass we collected was left for practice and local matches. We tumbled it all with corn cob media and a cleaner. Then we ran it through a sieve to ensure every bit of media was out of each case and inspected it for cracks and stress marks. Brass can only be reloaded so many times. Worn, split or bulged cases could result in a malfunction. In a sport with no alibis, an ammo issue would most definitely affect our match standings.

The next critical component was primers. If brass was like liquid gold, primers were like precious gems and consistent ignition was critical. No gun shop in our area carried the quantity or quality primers we needed to support our shooting habit so we'd often set up a group order with fellow shooting friends to save on costs, especially shipping. Primers were always in high demand so we had to plan well ahead to make sure we had enough for the shooting season.

Factory ammo wasn't an option for us based on cost alone, but even when reloading our ammunition, we tried to save money whenever we could. We used cast lead bullets for practice and local matches. Jacketed projectiles were reserved for zeroing our guns, the last practice before a major and for the "big matches." In the winter we'd experiment with different bullet weights and profiles in hopes of making the coveted match load a little more accurate or softer shooting.

Gunpowder selection was the most significant component to finding the perfect load. Typical reloading manuals didn't list data for ported and compensated handguns trying to reach an ideal bullet velocity. The starting point for load data was often too low. That meant we needed to handload small batches, increasing powder in tiny increments, placing those batches in small baggies and labeling them before taking them to the range to shoot over a chronograph.

Chronographs measure how fast bullets are flying out of the barrel. I remember spending a good amount of time setting up our chrono on a table with ideal lighting conditions in order to get accurate readings. Once we had a consistent average of the loads we wanted to test, we would determine the power factor of our ammo. To do this we simply multiplied the average velocity reading from the chrono by the bullet weight. That number divided by 1000 determined the power factor of our loads. The sport listed a specific minimum power factor for maximum scoring. If the minimum was 175, we loaded to 181-182 to give just the right amount of cushion. Ammo loaded too hot could affect how fast I could recover from the recoil of each shot. Ammo that didn't make power factor could result in lower points awarded on the stage or even a match disqualification.

Brass, primers, powder and projectiles were the fundamental components, but we also had to take into account other measurements like the overall length of our ammunition and how tightly we crimped the brass to hold the bullet in-place. I remember running my fingers over every primer of my match ammo to make sure they were seated deep enough into the pockets of each case to ensure proper ignition. We also dropped each round into a chamber gauge to simulate the chamber in our firearms. If it didn't drop in and out of the chamber gauge with ease, it could cause a malfunction. Making ammo was a tedious process and a labor of love.

Fast forwarding to today, many things have changed and yet some haven't. The shooting sports have evolved to feature factory firearms. There's still an Open Division, but because of its ease of entry, stock gun competition is globally booming. Factory ammunition, once something I couldn't really use in my race gun, is now an excellent option for many shooters who don't have the patience or time to reload their own ammunition. There are also so many more component options at different price points. Between bullet weight, projectile shape and bullet materials, you can choose a load that's ideal for your needs, whether it's competition, personal protection or plinking.

Even with the improvements to factory ammo, reloading is still a highly preferred and economical option for many shooters. There's also that added bonus of the personal satisfaction you get after creating that perfect load for you and your firearm. I compare it to buying a cake at the grocery store vs. baking one from scratch at home. Both are tasty, but when you reload your own ammo, there's a touch of pride that goes along with it that makes the experience all the more special.

Reloading is a lot like baking. Ingredients must be measured and added in order. Unlike baking however, you can break up the steps. No matter how you load, you'll want to set aside ample time to help ensure you don't make any mistakes. Reloading is not something you should do when you're tired or feel rushed. Specific steps must be followed for the end result to be desirable, and for the ammo to be safe. In fact, it's a good idea to keep notes or even a dedicated reloading notebook. Make a list of each step in the reloading process. Include specific information like load data regarding powder amounts, bullet type and weight as well as the desired overall length of each round. By creating and writing down a reloading plan, you'll avoid forgetting important steps and/or make ammunition that you ultimately can't use. List a few helpful reminders in your plan, things like verify primers are seated properly, check each case for powder, and caliper test for overall length and appropriate bullet depth. You can even make notes on when to take short breaks so that you can stay focused on the task at hand. Finally, your reloading space should be well lit, organized, and free from distractions or disruptors.

Even though I now rely on factory ammo for much of my shooting needs, I have a couple of loaders ready to manufacture my own ammunition. For example, when I need a special load for a specific firearm, like my highly customized competition NRA action pistol, reloading ammo gives me a competitive edge. As a busy mom and professional shooter, I have to make sure I plan my time accordingly. Prepping brass for the tumbler isn't unlike dumping a load of laundry in the washing machine but, when I need to sit down at the loading press, I make sure it has my undivided attention and I prefer to work in small batches to ensure I have the best results.

Reloading my own ammo over the years has taught me a lot about shooting and ammunition performance. Visually inspecting ammo before I feed it into my firearm is still the routine. Even when I grab a fresh box of American Eagle 147-grain 9mm, my go-to factory load for many competitions, I find myself running my fingers over the primers as a quick, one last check for a high primer. Old (and good) habits die hard.

CHAPTER 13

SPEER HANDGUN BULLETS

DEEPCURL®
Handgun Hunting Bullets

Hunting or field backup with a handgun requires a tough bullet with a core bonded to the jacket. This prevents core-jacket separation to assure deep penetration and maximum weight retention. Speer DeepCurl handgun bullets have been designed to meet this challenging set of requirements using heavy, electroplated jackets with pre-formed petals for controlled expansion.

GOLD DOT®
Jacketed Hollow Point Bullets for Personal Defense

There is a reason why Speer Gold Dot handgun bullets are the preferred choice of all types of shooters for their personal defense: true bonded core construction combined with carefully engineered cavity and jacket design to provide consistent, reliable bullet expansion and penetration. Repeated tests by law enforcement agencies, instructors, trainers, and individual shooters have confirmed Gold Dot bullets are the best, most reliable handgun bullets you can buy for personal defense.

Gold Dot Construction Process

GOLD DOT® SHORT BARREL®
Jacketed Hollow Point Bullets for Personal Defense

Many CCW holders prefer a compact handgun for concealed carry purposes. However, the short barrel of such guns substantially reduces the muzzle velocity which in turn reduces the bullet's terminal ballistic effectiveness. The Speer Gold Dot Short Barrel bullet line has been specifically designed to improve terminal ballistic performance from such compact handguns while retaining all the benefits that make Gold Dot effective.

TMJ®
Totally Encapsulated Lead Core

Unlike other so-called full metal jacket bullets that leave the lead core exposed at the base, Speer's Total Metal Jacket (TMJ) pistol bullets completely enclose the lead core in a copper jacket. TMJs are an excellent choice for handguns with ported compensators, suppressors and muzzle brakes because the closed base design prevents lead from fouling the ports. TMJ bullets are especially designed to feed exceptionally well in semi-automatic handguns, and they are available in most pistol calibers.

LEAD
Traditional Wadcutter, Semi-Wadcutter and Round Nose Handgun Bullets

For decades, Speer swaged lead handgun bullets have provided low cost training, practice, and informal target shooting (aka "plinking") to generations of shooters. Speer lead bullets are swaged to the correct size from lead alloy, then coated with a multi-layer lubrication system to minimize leading in your barrel.

PLASTIC TRAINING AMMUNITION
For Indoor Practice

You have always wanted to practice shooting your handgun in your basement, right? We all have. However, noise, smoke, and bullet containment are major obstacles. Speer offers an easy, low cost solution to this dilemma. Speer plastic bullets and cartridge cases use primers to propel the bullet accurately at short range without the loud noise, smoke, and bullet containment problems. Both the cartridge cases and the bullets are reusable! Available in 38/357, 44Spl/44, and 45 Auto.

PLASTIC SHOT CAPSULES
For Dispatching Pests and Rodents at Close Range

No doubt that you have seen Speer handgun caliber shot cartridges on dealer shelves. They seemed an ideal solution to dispatch pests and rodents around the house or workplace. As a handloader, you have undoubtedly considered shot capsules with shot sizes not offered by the factory. Consider no more. Speer shot capsules are offered as components in three popular handgun calibers (38, 44, 45).

CHAPTER 14

RELOADING HANDGUN CARTRIDGES
A Step-by-Step Guide

Economics often plays a major role in choosing to reload for handguns because shooters generally fire more handgun ammo in a session than rifle rounds. Because of the sheer volume of ammunition required, handgun shooters need a cost-effective yet reliable source of ammunition.

There are other reasons to load handgun cartridges. Cartridges like the 44 Magnum produce heavy recoil with factory ammunition but can be safely handloaded with lighter bullets and powder charges for practice. The handloader has access to a variety of bullet weights and designs that may not be available in over-the-counter ammunition.

Another factor is improved ballistic performance. Some cartridges developed decades ago for weaker firearms are now chambered in modern versions that can withstand substantially higher pressures. Where improved performance is possible, we have noted it in the cartridge introduction or provided a separate section for the high-performance loads.

Most handgun cases are straight-wall designs and loading them is very similar to a rifle case of the same design. Please read Chapter 6 of this manual first because there are more similarities than differences between rifle and handgun reloading.

The case must be inspected and then resized (to allow proper chambering) and deprimed. Straight-wall cases are neck-expanded and flared in another operation. Next, the case is primed and then charged with propellant. Bullet seating and crimping followed by final inspection completes the reloading operation.

Like their rifle counterparts, straight-wall handgun cases require three reloading dies.

Bottleneck handgun cartridges like the 22 Hornet and the 221 Remington Fireball are loaded like bottleneck rifle cartridges using a two-die set.

Many high-volume handgun shooters now choose to load on progressive or semi-automated equipment. With this sophisticated reloading equipment, a handloader can safely produce several hundred rounds per hour. The quality of the ammunition is just as good as that loaded on single-stage equipment. However, the greater complexity of the progressive press requires special attention and experience on the part of the operator. Before using progressive equipment, please read Chapter 8, "Automating the Loading Process."

Step 1—Know Your Firearm and Reloading Equipment

Read the equipment instructions and load data manuals carefully and completely. It is important to understand how your hardware works. Time invested in study now will help avoid headaches and safety hazards later. If you do not understand the instructions, GET HELP. Most equipment manufacturers have toll-free phone numbers or useful tutorials on their websites. RCBS® Tech Support is at (800) 379-1732 and on the internet at www.rcbs.com. Use these resources to ensure that you fully understand your equipment before attempting to load.

Understanding your firearm is as critical as understanding the reloading equipment, components, and processes. It is your responsibility, and yours alone, to know your firearm and its characteristics. It is vitally important to know what is "normal" based on firing factory ammunition in order to recognize something abnormal that may indicate a problem with your handloads.

Step 2—Case Cleaning (optional)

See Chapter 6 for full information on cleaning your cases.

Step 3—Case Inspection

As with rifle cartridges, handgun cases should be inspected for defects before loading. This operation is easier if the cases are clean. Potential defects are similar to those listed in the section on rifle reloading. Case splits in handgun ammunition are usually seen at the case mouth and seldom are longer than 1/8-inch. Even though this is not a safety hazard, these cases should be discarded because they will not allow consistent crimping and bullet pull.

Cases for semi-automatic pistols (especially the 45 Auto) may have bent case mouths from striking the slide during ejection. These cases can be reloaded, but the dent should be ironed out with a tapered plug or wooden dowel before sizing. If not removed, the sizing die will turn the dent into a sharp fold and ruin the case. Look for deformed rims in semi-auto cases. These will make inserting the case in the shell holder difficult and could cause a malfunction when fired. Cases with badly deformed rims should be discarded; however, minor burrs caused by the extractor and ejector during previous firings can be quickly removed with a small, fine-cut file.

Step Four—Case Sizing

There are two types of sizing dies for straight-wall cases: steel and carbide. The two types have different adjustment requirements and usage instructions.

Steel Sizing Dies

Standard steel dies are similar to rifle dies because lubricating the cases is required before resizing. Lubricant is applied with a case lube pad in the same manner as for rifle cases. Just as with rifle dies, the sizer die is screwed into the press until it touches the raised shell holder. After the cases are sized, you must be sure to remove all lubricant.

Most sizer dies for handgun cartridges incorporate the decapping pin, although in older die sets the decapping pin may be part of the expander die. In either instance, the pin should protrude about a quarter-inch below the bottom of the die for proper decapping.

Carbide Sizing Dies

For high-volume reloaders or those of us who don't relish the extra effort of applying and removing case lubricant, carbide dies are a must for sizing straight-wall handgun cartridges. The carbide insert in the steel die body is *tungsten carbide* and is the only portion of the die that touches the case.

Carbide inserts are hard, dense, and highly polished. They reduce sizing friction to such low levels that the need to lubricate the cases is virtually eliminated and produce a smooth, burnished finish. Years ago, carbide dies were practically handmade and quite expensive. Demand for these premium dies drove manufacturing improvements that reduced production costs. Today, there is little reason to forgo the benefits of carbide sizing. The modest additional cost of the carbide sizer is quickly offset by longer case/die life and convenience.

Adjusting the carbide die is accomplished differently from steel dies. Although very hard, carbide is also brittle. If the shell holder strikes the carbide insert, the insert may chip or shatter. To prevent damage to the insert, the die should be installed so that it clears the shell holder by about 1/32-inch (about the thickness of a matchbook cover). You should see a sliver of daylight between the shell holder and the carbide die with the ram fully raised. This small clearance will insure that the die will not be damaged. A carbide die may leave a slight ring just ahead of the case rim and could lead to problems chambering if the head is not properly resized. In some case, this effect is only cosmetic but you should work to reduce it by backing the die out a little until the ring is reduced. The case body will still be resized enough to permit normal chambering.

Cartridges that routinely operate at high-pressure, e.g., the 460 Smith and Wessons and the 44 Remington Magnums, stress the case more than cartridges producing modest pressures. Under these conditions, resizing will often cause a ring regardless of die position. Be sure to size the case far enough back to allow normal chambering. Many reloaders use only new or once-fired brass for maximum loads and afterward set the cases aside to use for lighter loads.

Step Five—Case Mouth Expanding and Flaring (Straight-wall cases)

The second die in a three-die pistol die set is a combination neck expander and flaring tool. The main body of the expander plug should be at least .001-inch smaller in diameter than the bullet. For heavy-recoil cartridges, the expander may be as much as .003-inch under bullet diameter to ensure the case walls firmly grip a jacketed bullet. Some reloaders keep two expander plugs for a given cartridge—one for lead bullets that is .001-inch undersize and another for jacketed bullets about .002 to .003-inch undersize.

Flaring the case mouth allows you to easily start the bullet into the case. This step is recommended for all straight-wall cases regardless of bullet type and is mandatory when loading lead bullets. A case with little or no flare will cut into the soft alloy of a lead bullet and destroy accuracy. Excessive flare will shorten case life by causing premature mouth splits. RCBS pistol expanders today feature an "M" style expander. These have a short, increased diameter step between the main body and the flare to enhance bullet alignment as it starts into the case mouth. The most effective flare is achieved using cases that are trimmed to uniform length. A "short" case (relative to the die setting) will not receive enough flare while a "long" case may be flared too much.

To test for the correct amount of flare, lightly press the bullet you plan to load into the case with your fingers and slowly invert the case. If the bullet enters about 1/32-inch and stays in place, the flare is sufficient.

Step Six—Priming

Priming handgun cases is no different than when reloading rifle ammunition. Therefore, you should review the priming section in Chapter 6 to refresh your memory.

CCI® and Federal® handgun primers give optimum sensitivity when seated .003 to .005-inch below flush. Failure to follow this simple guideline can result in misfires. Most handguns do not have the firing pin energy available in rifles, so anything in the reloading process that optimizes sensitivity will result in more reliable ammunition.

Primers must be seated so that the legs of the anvil seat firmly against the bottom of the primer pocket.

High primers can be hazardous in either semi-automatic pistols or revolvers. In semi-autos, a high primer can cause a slam-fire—the primer is activated by the slide slamming home. Ignition can occur before the action is fully locked resulting in hot, high-pressure gases being released from the action. Slam-fires may also cause the firearm to "double," firing more than once when the trigger is pulled. Either situation is dangerous.

High primers in revolvers will often cause the cylinder to bind. A revolver jammed with live ammo requires great care to disassemble and usually ends the shooting session. When you are priming, run your finger across the cartridge base to check for high primers. If detected at this stage (before charging), they can be safely reseated. If you detect a high primer in a loaded round, do not attempt to reseat it without first pulling the bullet and removing the powder.

Handgun shooters seldom worry about cases with crimped primer pockets; however, they do exist. Most U.S. 45 Auto military brass has a light primer crimp that may go unnoticed. Some 38 Special military cases made in Canada (IVI headstamp) have heavily crimped primers and military surplus 9mm brass is also crimped. For safety's sake, all military 45 Auto, 38 Special and 9mm cases should be processed through the RCBS® Primer Pocket Swager before loading.

Because most handguns have less firing pin energy than do rifles, primers for handgun cartridges may have thinner cups. Using a rifle primer in handgun ammo may cause misfires. In addition, rifle primers typically have more priming mix than handgun primers and, if substituted, can cause higher (and potentially dangerous) pressures. However, rifle primers are used for cartridges originally designed for rifles but later adapted to handguns like the 223 Remington, or for certain high-pressure handgun cartridges. In addition, a large rifle primer is taller than a large pistol primer; unless the case is designed for the large rifle primer, a high-primer condition will occur and you can't correct it. Follow the recommendations of the loading data.

CCI® and Federal® Magnum primers are recommended for charges of slow-burning propellants in large cases. Loads using propellants such as Winchester 296 and Hodgdon H110 were developed with magnum primers as indicated in the data. The magnum primer's increased energy output ensures complete ignition, especially in low temperatures.

Because of the volume nature of handgun reloading, accessories like the RCBS APS® Priming Tool, the Automatic Priming Tool, and Hand Priming Tool are popular options. In addition to speeding the loading operation, these tools allow the reloader to keep primers free of contamination. For a review of priming tool types, see the section on priming in Chapter 6.

Step Seven—Powder Selection and Charging

There are many different handgun propellants, so you need to carefully consider how you plan to use your handloads before choosing a powder. For light target loads, the "faster" propellants are the best choice to achieve uniform velocities, top accuracy and clean burning. Alliant Powder® Bullseye® is a popular and economical propellant that can be used in most target loads. Other powders such as Winchester 231, Accurate Arms No. 2, and Hodgdon TiteGroup are in this class.

Mid-power loads call for propellants with a "medium" burning rate. There are a number of shotgun propellants that function very well in these loads, including Unique® and Hodgdon Universal Clays, and handgun propellants like Alliant Power Pistol® and Accurate Arms No. 5. For the heaviest loads and top velocities where the cartridge and gun design permits such power, the slow burning propellants like Winchester 296, Hodgdon H110, Alliant 2400®, VihtaVuori N110, IMR 4227, Ramshot Enforcer and Accurate No. 9 are excellent candidates. Relatively heavy charges of these powders generate the large volume of gas needed to accelerate the bullet to top speed while staying within safe pressure limits.

Slow burning propellants should not be used for light loads, particularly in large cases. These powders operate most efficiently at relatively high pressures. At lower pressures or when significant air space remains in the case, the charge may fail to ignite completely causing the bullet to stick in the bore. If another bullet is fired into the obstructed barrel, it may damage the firearm, and can cause personal injury.

An experienced handgun reloader never starts with a maximum load. Begin with the published starting load and work up incrementally as test firing indicates each increment is safe. If you detect any pressure signs, STOP! You have reached the maximum for your firearm. In revolvers, one warning of excessive pressure is "sticky" extraction of the case from a revolver's cylinder. Other factors such as soft cases or rough chambers can cause poor extraction with otherwise safe ammo. This combined with badly flattened or loose primers, excessive recoil compared to "normal" or extreme "flyers" on the target probably indicates that you have passed the "safety zone" for your revolver.

It is likewise imprudent to load less than the published starting load. We selected our start loads to remain within the useful pressure range for each cartridge. Overly light loads can lead to bore obstructions, excessive leading, and poor accuracy.

Warning! Never exceed the maximum loads shown!

When loading small charges of quick-burning powders, you must be careful to avoid overcharging a case. Small charges occupy very little space, so it's possible to get two or more in a case. Reloading rifle ammo seldom poses this hazard because the powders are fairly bulky and a double charge would normally (but not always) overflow the case.

A "squib load" is one in which there is a light or missing powder charge, or when an otherwise normal charge fails to burn completely. A squib load may drive the bullet just far enough into the rifling to cause a bore obstruction. This condition can also occur when a light target load is fired in a revolver with an excessive barrel-cylinder gap. Too much gas is lost through the oversized gap and the next bullet fired can drive into the stuck bullet causing damage to the firearm. Jacketed bullets should not be used in very light loads—especially in revolver cartridges—except as noted in the data. The additional friction against the bore can cause the bullet to stick or to cause the lead core to separate from the jacket. In either circumstance, a dangerous bore obstruction occurs. Any bore obstruction is a hazardous condition.

Normally, the shooter should detect the greatly reduced report and light recoil of a squib load. If this occurs, stop shooting and clear any remaining ammunition from the firearm before removing the obstruction. However, during rapid-fire shooting or when shooting on a busy range, you may not notice the squib.

Prevention of squib loads and the double charge *must occur at the loading bench*—not the range. Careful and consistent loading techniques are the best insurance against gun damage or personal injury.

A good technique for preventing charging problems is using two loading blocks. Place one on each side of the powder scale or measure. Primed, empty cases are placed mouth down in one block. With the cases inverted, any debris that may have found its way into the case can fall out. Pick up a case, charge it with powder and put it in the block on the opposite side. After all are charged, pick up the block and visually check each case under a strong light to make certain that it contains ONLY ONE powder charge before seating any bullets.

Because of the high volume of handgun cartridges often loaded at one time, the powder measure is a real time saver for the reloader. If your adjustable powder measure has interchangeable drums, select the smaller size for more accurate metering of small charges. Remember—you must verify that the measure is throwing the correct charge weight by checking it with an accurate handloading scale.

It is common practice when using a powder measure to pass the entire loading block full of primed cases under the mouth of the measure, charging each case in turn. If you use this method, develop a uniform pattern of motion both for moving the block and operating the measure handle. Failure to cycle the measure handle uniformly can result in variations in charge weights that affect the quality of your handloads. Be careful not to miss or double-charge a row of cases.

Again, you must visually inspect every case. Inspecting large cases that contain only a small powder charge requires a strong light source and more attention. With either charging method, do not seat bullets until all cases have been charged and visually inspected—twice, if you are prudent.

Current RCBS Uniflow® powder measures come with a special metering screw shaped to accommodate small as well as large charges so no changeover is required. Because many handgun reloaders develop and stick to one basic load, say 2.8 grains of Bullseye for a 38 Special target load, a fixed-cavity measure like the RCBS Little Dandy™ is often used. Twenty-eight different rotors, each calibrated for specific charges of the popular pistol powders, are available for the Little Dandy.

Powder charging should be done at a leisurely pace with frequent inspection to ensure reloading safe ammunition.

Step Eight—Bullet Seating and Crimping

Seating bullets and crimping (as required) completes the loading process. Bullet seating depth is fairly critical to proper function in handguns. In revolvers, the cylinder will not rotate if the bullet is seated so long that it protrudes from the cylinder. In semi-auto pistols, feeding will be unreliable if the cartridge is too short yet an overly long cartridge may not fit the magazine or wedge in the rifling. In small capacity, high-pressure cases like the 9mm Luger, excessively deep-seated bullets will raise pressures to potentially unsafe levels. The cartridge overall length that Speer technicians used for load development is shown for each loaded bullet.

If you are loading a bullet with a crimping cannelure, the proper seating length will be achieved by seating to this point. Ammunition for revolvers is typically roll-crimped into the crimping cannelure. Ammunition for semi-automatic pistols is either taper crimped or requires no crimp at all. Crimping a revolver cartridge is important for proper performance. An uncrimped bullet can unseat due to recoil when other cartridges in the cylinder are fired. If the bullet moves enough, it can tie up the cylinder or its ballistic performance will change. Certain bullets like the Speer 45-caliber 300-grain DCHP have two cannelures. Refer to the loading data to determine the correct loading length.

Adjustment for Seating and Roll Crimping

The seater die consists of a die body and a bullet seater plug. Each has a lock ring to preserve its setting. The crimping shoulder is machined into the die body. The position of the seater plug relative to the shell holder determines the bullet seating depth. The position of the die body relative to the shell holder determines the amount of crimp, if any.

To set the proper seating depth for a revolver bullet, raise the ram to its highest position and screw the seater die into the loading press until the die body is about a quarter-inch above the shell holder. Screw the lock ring on the die body down against the press but do not tighten the lock screw. Lower the ram, put a bullet on the mouth of a charged case and place it in the shell holder. Raise the ram so the bullet and case enter the die. Continue raising it until you feel a slight resistance. The bullet is now starting into the case.

Lower the ram and check how far the bullet has been seated. The bullet needs to be seated so that almost all of the crimping cannelure is covered by the case mouth. If the bullet needs to be seated deeper, adjust the seater plug in (down) and raise the ram. Check the depth again and repeat the process until the bullet is properly positioned.

To set the crimp, loosen the die body lock ring, screw the seating plug almost all the way out (up) or until it cannot contact the bullet. Raise the ram to its highest point with the cartridge in the shell holder. Slowly screw the die into the press until you feel a slight resistance. The crimp shoulder is now just touching the case mouth. Lower the ram slightly and screw the body in about a quarter turn. Raise the ram fully and check the crimp. Continue until you achieve the desired crimp and then tighten the lock ring on the die body against the press. With the ram at its highest point and the cartridge fully in the die, screw the seater plug into the die body until you feel it touch the seated bullet. Tighten the seater plug lock nut and the die is now set for simultaneous seating and crimping. Check the seating and crimping of the next bullet. Sometimes a slight adjustment is needed to fine-tune the depth and crimp.

This setting procedure works for all RCBS® handgun dies and those of similar design. If you have dies of a different brand, read the instructions from the die manufacturer for proper bullet seating and crimping.

How much crimp is enough? Several factors are involved. When using slow burning propellants, a heavy crimp helps ensure that the propellant ignites completely achieving higher velocities and cleaner burning. Light target loads need not be heavily crimped so lightly crimping the case mouth is adequate to prevent bullet jump and gives a "finished" edge for easier chambering. The exception is light loads in large cases. We recommend a heavy crimp to minimize the chances of a squib.

You can have too much crimp. If the crimping operation budges the case, the cartridge may not chamber. Trimming cases to a uniform length is the key to consistent crimping.

More Effective Crimping for the "Big Bruisers"

The extra-wide crimping cannelure featured on all Gold Dot® and DeepCurl® revolver bullets allows a more robust crimping style known as the neckdown crimp. No special or extra equipment is required if you use Gold Dot bullets. Rather than rolling the case mouth into the groove, neckdown crimping irons a step at the case mouth that nearly fills the cannelure. To produce this crimp, set the seating dies as described in previous paragraphs, leaving only a hairline of the cannelure visible above the case mouth. Seat all the bullets—you will be crimping in a separate operation.

Raise the bullet seating stem to the top of the die. Adjust the die body for crimping, incrementally checking your progress at each step. Continue turning the die in (down) until you produce a step that begins slightly above where the bottom of the groove should be. Once you've achieved the desired amount of neckdown, tighten the lock ring and crimp the remaining cases.

If you've never done neckdown crimping before, practice on inert rounds until you develop a feel for it. Keeping the revolver cylinder at hand to check for proper chambering helps avoid over-crimping that can bulge cases. You can produce a neckdown crimp with any RCBS seating die made since 1984, but you must be using a Gold Dot or DeepCurl revolver bullet or one with a cannelure at least .060 inches wide and preferably square-bottomed (as opposed to the beveled crimp groove on most cast bullets). This crimp is best used when loading high-recoil revolver cartridges with slow-burning propellants and heavy bullets.

Seating and Taper Crimping for Semi-Autos

Most ammunition for semi-automatic pistols headspaces on the case mouth. If roll crimped, the cartridge may not be firmly supported against the blow of the firing pin and misfires or poor accuracy may occur. Instead, taper crimping is required for cartridges that headspace on the case mouth.

Taper crimping lightly swages the case mouth and part of the case body into the bullet to provide a tighter grip yet still leaves enough of the case mouth edge exposed to permit proper headspacing. Instead of the sharp crimp shoulder found in roll crimp dies, the taper crimp die has a shallow-angle shoulder that performs the necessary forming.

Bullets intended for semi-automatic pistols typically do not have a crimping cannelure. Proper seating depth depends on the individual firearm and its magazine. However, industry standards for maximum and minimum cartridge dimensions take gun variations into consideration. Unless otherwise noted, the data in this manual was developed at cartridge lengths within industry specifications.

Setting the seating depth and taper crimp for a semi-auto pistol cartridge is accomplished by adjusting the seating die like the method for revolver cartridges. Because there is usually no crimping cannelure on the bullet, the length must be carefully checked with a caliper or, more accurately, a micrometer. Measure at the case mouth and lower down on the case where the base of the bullet is located. The case mouth should be about .001 inches smaller in diameter than the measurement near the bullet's base, hence the term "taper crimp". Once the bullet is seated to the proper depth, setting the taper crimp is accomplished in a manner similar to setting the roll crimp for revolver cartridges except that you will not need to screw in the die body as far. Taper crimping will remove the flare from the case mouth for more reliable feeding. Excessive taper crimping can actually resize the bullet and cause poor accuracy. A light touch is best.

Use the barrel as a gauge to verify that handloads for a semi-auto pistol have the proper taper crimp and seating depth. Unload the pistol, disassemble it and remove the barrel. Clean it and remove any oil. Follow these steps:

- Drop a factory cartridge in the chamber and note the position where the cartridge stops.
- Remove the factory cartridge and drop in a handload. Does it stop where the factory cartridge did?
- Apply thumb pressure to the case head and turn the barrel muzzle-up. Does the handload fall free or does it stick? If it sticks, note the position.

A cartridge that protrudes from the chamber more than the factory cartridge means the case mouth has too much flare or the bullet is seated too long and is jammed in the rifling. A cartridge that sticks in the chamber and is deeper than the factory cartridge has too much crimp. A cartridge that enters the chamber deeper than the factory cartridge but does not stick probably has a short case.

Either extreme is unsatisfactory. Too long means the cartridge may jam or fire at unsafe pressures; too short means it may misfire or be inaccurate. Bullet seating and crimping handloads for semi-auto pistols must be done correctly for reliable and safe performance.

In cartridges that headspace on the case mouth, the case can shorten after many firings. This is due to the blow of the firing pin pushing the case into the chamber shoulder and peening the case mouth. Normally this shortening is not a problem. For critical target work, cases should be of uniform length within industry specifications.

When seating Speer 45 Auto bullets such as the 200-grain lead semi-wadcutter (SWC), the 230-grain lead round nose, and the 185 and 200-grain Uni-Cor TMJ® semi-wadcutters, leave the shoulder of the bullet exposed about 1/32-inch. This seating position provides improved function, particularly with the lead SWC bullet.

There is a wide variation in handgun bullet profiles. Using a seater punch that's the wrong shape can deform the bullet nose. RCBS die sets for revolver cartridges include seater plugs for wadcutter, semi-wadcutter and round nose bullets. Die sets for semi-auto cartridges have seater plugs for semi-wadcutter and round nose bullets. If none of these plugs fit the profile of the bullet you plan to load, RCBS will make modifications as part of their custom program if you send them the plug with five sample bullets. If you are using a different brand of die, contact the manufacturer for assistance.

Tech Tip: When seating lead bullets, lubricant can build up on the seater plug causing successive bullets to seat deeper. Check the seating depth every 20 cartridges to see if the depth is changing. If so, remove the die from the press and clean the plug. A very thin film of light oil or release compound in the seater die and on the plug will help slow the buildup. Don't over-lubricate!

Step Nine—Final Inspection and Identification

The big commercial makers carefully inspect their ammo—you should also.

Before boxing, lay the cartridges on a light-colored cloth and roll them around, carefully examining each one. Look for bulged, dented or split cases, damaged bullets, varying seating depths, irregular crimps or missing primers. As you box the ammo, check once more for high primers by running your finger over the case head. However, *never reseat a high primer in a loaded cartridge*! Set aside any cartridges with high primers for later disassembly and rework.

Cartridges loaded with lead bullets may have excess bullet lubricant on the outside that should be wiped off before boxing. If not removed, the lubricant on the case can cause extra strain on the firearm because the case won't adhere to the chamber walls properly during firing and will thrust harder against the breech.

Rifles Chambered for Handgun Cartridges

The concept of having a handgun and a rifle or carbine that fire the same ammunition dates to the earliest days of cartridge firearms. A rancher in 1880 commonly owned a Colt revolver, and a Winchester rifle chambered for the same cartridge. He only needed one type of ammo to fire either firearm. Modern rifles chambered for handgun cartridges fall into two categories:

- **Category 1**: repeating rifles and carbines chambered for powerful revolver cartridges.
- **Category 2**: semi-automatic carbines chambered for compact semi-auto pistol cartridges.

Category One: This includes common lever-action rifles and Ruger gas-operated 44 Magnum semi-autos. The industry pressure limit for a cartridge is the same whether it is to be fired in a rifle or a handgun. A 44 Magnum rifle will use the same loading data as a 44 Magnum revolver. However, there are some considerations the prudent handloader will note:

Bullet shape: A revolver's feed mechanism is the shooters hand—a remarkably adaptive and useful gadget. The feed mechanism in a repeating rifle is a mechanical device that must be carefully fabricated, adjusted and timed to position the cartridge for jam-free feeding. The limitation of this purely mechanical system means that some bullets with sharp shoulders like semi-wadcutters (that easily hand-feed into revolver cylinders) can jam when feeding in a repeating rifle. Cartridges that are considerably shorter or longer than factory ammo may not feed.

Bullet type: Unjacketed lead bullets are not suitable for gas-operated semi-automatic rifles. Lead shavings and bullet lubricant can foul the gas system and cause malfunctions. Jacketed bullets are the best choice for these rifles.

Propellant type and charge weight: The handloader must remember that the longer rifle barrel will require more gas to expel a bullet than a short handgun barrel. Although pressure is limited by industry standards, the handloader can control the volume of gas through propellant selection. The gas volume produced at firing is proportional to the amount of propellant used. Even though 14.8 grains of Alliant 2400® powder or 7.7 grains of Alliant Unique® under a 158-grain 357 Magnum bullet produce approximately the same peak pressure, the load of Alliant 2400 will generate nearly twice the volume of gas and is the better choice when loading for a 357 Magnum rifle.

Category Two: When preparing ammo for a semi-auto carbine chambered for

9mm Luger, 40 S&W and 45 Auto cartridges, the handloader must pay attention to a couple of facts: 1) the cartridges have relatively small cases that limit the amount of propellant, and 2) practically all the carbines are blowback designs, that is, the bolt is not locked. Its mass and a spring or two are all that resist the rearward thrust of firing.

Blowback actions can malfunction or rupture cases with large charges of slow-burning propellants even though the charge weight produces safe pressures. Low-velocity target loads that function fine in a 4-inch handgun barrel may not generate enough gas volume to push the bullet down a barrel that's four times longer.

For these specialized firearms, use load data yielding maximum velocities close to that of factory ammo with the same bullet weight. The 9mm Luger cartridge needs special consideration when you handload for a carbine. 147-grain loads are intended for barrels under 10 inches long. The low propellant weights dictated by the heavier bullet produce relatively low carbine velocities compared to 115 and 124-grain bullets. The risk of a bullet lodging in a carbine bore increases with heavy bullets. You will get the best performance with the lighter 9mm bullets. For the same reason, limit the maximum bullet weight for 40 S&W and 45 Auto carbines to 180 and 230 grains, respectively.

Be sure to test all handloads in your carbine before loading a large number. Load a small test batch first. Watch for feeding or ejection problems and unusual sounds. Be sure to check for bullets lodged in the bore—every pull of the trigger must make a hole in the target. Avoiding very light loads is the best insurance.

Special Considerations for Semi-auto Pistols

The semi-automatic pistol uses the energy from the fired cartridge to operate the action. Ammunition that closely matches the velocities of factory ammunition usually functions best. Very light loads may cause feeding and/or ejection problems because there is not enough energy to operate the mechanism. Heavy loads may accelerate wear or even damage your pistol.

A major factor in pistol wear is slide velocity. The speed at which the slide moves rearward when the pistol fires is proportional to bullet velocity, not pressure. Even though a load produces normal pressures, bullet velocity that is significantly higher than similar factory ammunition increases slide velocity. If the slide velocity exceeds the gun's design limits, battering of the pistol's frame can occur. It is best to keep velocities within the range of factory ammunition.

Low-velocity target loads usually function best with faster-burning propellants. The sharper impulse of these propellants allows the action to operate normally with relatively light charges. Because every firearm is different, you may find that the lighter loads listed may not cycle your pistol. Increasing the powder charge gradually toward the maximum will eventually result in a load which functions reliably.

Taper crimping is best for any cartridge fired in semi-auto pistols. Some cases like the 38 Super Auto are semi-rimmed and, in theory, headspace on the rim. However, this rim is small, and there is some variation in dimensions among different brands of cases. Thus, the rim may not control headspace properly. Taper crimping ensures positive headspace control.

Cartridges for semi-automatic pistols must resist shoving the bullet into the case during feeding. A bullet that telescopes deep into the case will produce excessive pressure. Normally, a properly sized expander plug and a firm taper crimp will provide adequate bullet grip. Test the cartridge by pushing the tip into the edge of a wooden bench. If the bullet moves, you must correct the situation before loading any more cartridges. Case wall thickness often varies considerably. If you are sure that your expander is the correct size, but bullets are still loose, try cases of a different brand to see if the setback problem can be eliminated.

9mm Luger Suggestions

Here are some suggestions for better 9mm handloads:

- Cases: the 9mm case is rather small compared to other high-performance pistol cartridges. Propellant space is limited and any variation in capacity among brands may create wide variations in pressure, velocity and reliability. Before reloading, sort your cases by headstamp in addition to brand. Even within one brand, there can be variations; however, cases with the same style of headstamp are normally uniform. Mixed cases cause ballistic variations and reloading problems. Neck expansion, bullet seating and crimping operations can all be adversely affected by mixing cases. We strongly recommend you use commercial cases—not military surplus—when reloading the 9mm.

- Bullets: While the industry maximum bullet diameter is .3555-inch, the groove diameter of 9mm pistol barrels varies from .354 inches to .357 inches; the majority of pistols are closer to the larger diameter. The accuracy potential of your pistol depends on how well bullets match the bore diameter. Speer 9mm jacketed bullets are built to the top of the industry diameter specification and are quite accurate in pistols.
  Short .355-inch diameter bullets intended for the 380 Auto may not feed in some pistols even with the bullet seated as far out as practical and we did not develop 9mm Luger loads for these bullets for that reason. The best feeding comes with bullets with longer nose sections that were designed for the 9mm Luger. 147-grain bullets are best loaded with a powder having a medium burning rate, such as Alliant Unique®, HS-6 and AA No. 7. They generally give better accuracy with heavy bullets than faster powders.

- Cartridge Length: in the loading data, the cartridge overall length we used for each type of bullet is listed. You must not seat bullets deeper than this without reducing the powder charge. The limited case capacity of the 9mm means that a deep-seated bullet will increase pressures dramatically.

At the Range

Now it's time to test your reloads to see how they shoot. Remember, small groups are more important than the point of impact at this point. Because many handguns have fixed sights or sights that are adjustable for windage only, finding an accurate load that hits close to point-of-aim may require more load development. Here are some suggestions for effective range testing of handgun ammo:

- *Safety First!* Remember to protect your eyes and ears. Handguns blow unburned powder from the barrel/cylinder gap in revolvers and from the ejection port in semi-autos. Well-designed eye protection keeps this residue out of your eyes. Handguns are quite noisy and continued shooting without proper ear protection can cause immediate and permanent hearing damage. Make certain that the backstop is appropriate and there is an adequate safety zone beyond. A 9mm Luger bullet can travel up to a mile.

- Testing is more meaningful if you use a rest and shoot from a bench. Sandbags may also be used. When testing any of the powerful magnum revolvers, be aware that the high-velocity jet of gas from the barrel/cylinder gap can cut through fabric-covered bags and blow sand in your face. When shooting high-pressure revolvers over fabric bags, protect the bags with a layer of heavy leather.
- Grip the handgun consistently for each shot. Changing your hand position or grip pressure between shots will change the point of impact and affect the group size. These effects are most apparent when shooting handguns with heavy recoil.

Tech Tip: When accuracy testing a revolver in single-action mode, you can maintain a constant grip by cocking the hammer for each shot with your non-shooting hand. This helps maintain a consistent grip because it minimizes the need to reposition the revolver for each shot.

- Extended shooting sessions with heavy caliber handguns are more enjoyable if you wear a padded shooting glove. It will distribute recoil and prevent chafing from checkered grips. They are available through several shooting accessory companies.
- Firing either two 5-shot groups or one 7-shot group for each load gives an excellent snapshot of the accuracy your ammunition can give. Most handgun accuracy testing is done at 25 yards. However, hunting handguns should be tested at a minimum of 50 yards and even farther if you plan to take longer shots. The bottom line—match your accuracy test distance to the kind of shooting you plan to do.
- Relax and take your time when testing loads. Pace your shots and your breathing. Don't try to make a judgment on accuracy based on a group that you shot rapid-fire after jogging back from the 50-yard target holder!

What Kind of Accuracy Should You Expect?

This is a difficult question to answer. The industry accuracy specification for most sporting handgun ammunition is three-inch groups at 25 yards fired from a fixed barrel. A production pistol or revolver of decent quality will generally shoot this well or better if you do your part. Groups under two inches at 25 yards are great in anyone's book from the typical sporting revolver or semi-auto pistol.

However, there are handguns that will routinely shoot well under one inch at this distance. Target handguns for bullseye competition may need to shoot less than two inches at 50 yards. Some rifles can't do that well. Heavy, single-shot pistols like the T/C Contender and the Remington XP-100 are closer to rifles when it comes to accuracy. It is very possible to shoot 50-yard groups of well under one inch with either gun.

Regardless of what you do as a handloader, each individual firearm will have some finite limit for tightest group size. A good rule of thumb is that the average handgun will shoot better than its owner (many shooters are distressed to discover this). However, wear, damage or mistreatment can cause even the best-quality handgun to shoot poorly.

Try to be realistic with your expectations. If you are looking for plinking loads, be happy with three-inch groups at 25 yards. However, if you are like most handloaders, knowing that you can adjust loads to give better performance will probably have you back at the bench, looking for just a bit more accuracy.

CHAPTER 15

SPEER® SHOTSHELL CAPSULES

(See the Handgun cartridge data for charge weight information on specific cartridges)

Speer component shot capsules have been a popular item for decades for close-range pest and rodent control. When first introduced they answered a long-standing problem for handgun reloaders: "How can I build good, handgun shotshells?"

Historically, making handgun shotshells for close-range pest control was usually more trouble than it was worth. Loading the various components was tedious, and the resulting ammo usually performed poorly.

Speer shot capsules are a two-part system that allows you to choose a shot size (you supply the shot) and assemble an easily handled package for loading. We make three diameters so you can load shotshell ammunition for 38 Special and 357 Magnum, 44 Special and Magnum, and 45 Colt. Each capsule has a semi-transparent, rigid plastic body and a soft plastic base wad. You fill the capsule body with shot, snap in the base wad, and it's ready to load.

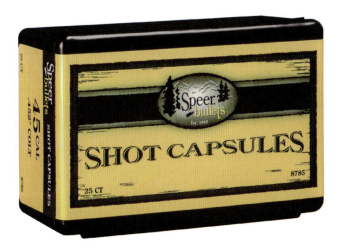

The rigid plastic body is designed to break on contact with the revolver's rifling yet protect the bore from excessive fouling. The flexible base wad is shaped to effectively seal the gas behind the capsule for ballistic efficiency. Standard cleaning methods are usually sufficient to remove any firing residue.

The best way to fill the capsules with shot is to pour a few ounces of pellets into a shallow container. Scoop the capsule through the shot to fill it just below level then tap it lightly several times to settle the pellets. You need to leave a little room for the wad to fit. Experiment with a few capsules to find the correct level for the shot size you are using. Overfilling can cause the capsule to break when the wad is inserted. Avoid "loose" loading as well; partially filled capsules will yield inconsistent ballistic performance and poor patterns.

SHOTSHELL PELLET COUNTS

Caliber	Payload Weight (grains)	Pellet Size	Pellet Diameter (in.)	Pellets per oz.	Pellets Capsule
38	109	9	0.08	576	143
		8 1/2	0.085	480	120
		8	0.09	404	101
		7 1/2	0.095	344	86
		6	0.11	221	55
		4	0.13	134	33
44	140	9	0.08	576	184
		8 1/2	0.085	480	154
		8	0.09	404	129
		7 1/2	0.095	344	110
		6	0.11	221	71
		4	0.13	134	43
45	150	9	0.08	576	211
		8 1/2	0.085	480	176
		8	0.09	404	148
		7 1/2	0.095	344	126
		6	0.11	221	81
		4	0.13	134	49

NOTE: *Speer shot capsules are designed for lead shot only. Steel or other lead-free shot can cause bore damage.*

You have control over shot size, but keep a few things in mind. These capsules hold small pellet charges compared to a standard shotgun shell, so pattern density is much more important. Smaller shot sizes like #8 and #9 will yield denser patterns perfect for pest control. If you use large shot like #4, expect more open patterns.

Once assembled, Speer shot capsules load almost like any standard bullet, with a few minor differences:

- Stick to the recommended propellants. Slower-burning propellants give poor results with such light projectiles.
- Seat capsules slowly and with minimum force to avoid breaking them.
- A flat-faced bullet seater plug works best, although a wadcutter-style plug works nearly as well. A deeply cupped punch for seating semi-wadcutter or round nose bullets can break the capsule.
- Crimp lightly, separate from the seating step, to avoid breakage.
- We show recommended seating depths in the data section of this manual and you should follow those guidelines. If you seat too long, the blast from one cartridge may break the capsule in an adjacent chamber and spill the payload.
- We urge 357 Magnum shooters to load their shotshells in 38 Special cases.
- The heavier walls of many magnum cases can present seating problems. There is no

real performance advantage to assembling shotshells in the larger case because extra velocity only degrades patterns.

Note that charge weights for shot capsules are relatively light. We limited muzzle velocity to maintain reasonable patterns. When fired from a rifled gun barrel, the shot charge spins and the pattern diameter increases rapidly. The loads we show gave decent patterns in our test firearms. Increasing the velocity will only make the pattern expand faster, reducing its effectiveness. On the other hand, slight charge reductions may improve patterning in your revolver.

Even with careful loading, handgun shotshells are short-range tools when fired from a rifled barrel. Depending on the shot size and the velocity, pattern density thins beyond 15 to 20 feet to the point of being ineffective. Although pattern size will vary with individual firearms and loading practices, we can give you a rough "rule of thumb" for figuring pattern size. Assume one inch of spread for each foot of distance. If you are shooting at ten feet, expect a pattern about ten inches in diameter.

Ported Barrel Advisory

Never fire any shot capsule regardless of make or type in a firearm with a ported barrel, compensator, or suppressor. Slivers of shot or pieces of the capsule can exit the ports at high velocity and in unpredictable directions, causing injury.

Shotshell Capsule Safety

- Show shotshell cartridges the same respect you show any other ammunition product.
- Always be sure of your target and what is beyond. Pellets fired from handgun shotshells can kill at very close range and injure at greater ranges. Pellets may travel up to 200 yards under the right conditions.
- Use only lead shot to fill capsules.
- Avoid shooting at hard surfaces that may cause pellets to ricochet back at the shooter or observers. Although a ricocheting pellet will likely cause only a minor injury to skin, it can cause serious injury to unprotected eyes. Always wear safety glasses when shooting any ammunition.
- Rifle chambers have rifling lands that start very close to the case mouth. They will break the capsule during loading.
- NEVER fire any shot cartridge in a handgun fitted with a ported recoil compensator.
- NEVER fire any shot cartridge from a carbine with a tubular magazine.

CHAPTER 16

SPEER® PLASTIC TRAINING AMMUNITION
EFFECTIVE, LOW-COST TRAINING

For years, shooters have sought ways to load accurate, low velocity practice ammunition. Speer® plastic training ammunition is a practical solution to this problem.

Speer's training ammunition is a complete system consisting of a reusable plastic bullet that seats in a reloadable plastic case of special design. The only power required is a large pistol primer; no propellant powder is ever used. You can assemble Speer T-Ammo with a minimum of equipment.

Speer T-Ammo bullets and cases are sold separately because T-cases last a long time but some T-bullets may be damaged or lost. T-bullets and T-cases are sold separately so that you can easily replace only those that become unserviceable.

Loading is quite simple. Cases come unprimed, so you need to insert primers. The CCI® primers tend to allow longer case life. Yes, we make and test those primers, but they do help the cases last longer.

You use a standard priming tool:
- Install the proper shell holder and a large priming punch in the priming tool.
- Place a large pistol primer on the punch and a T-case in the shell holder.
- Seat the primer, using a minimum of force to avoid damaging the plastic rim. The primer should be flush with the case head.
- Seat a T-bullet into the case with finger pressure. The shoulder on the bullet should contact the case.

When fired T-cases are ready for reloading, use a Universal Decapping Die to remove the spent primers. If you do not have a Universal Decapping Die, use a small punch to press out the spent primer. The decapping force required is very low compared to a brass case.

We recommend CCI® 350 Magnum pistol primers for highest velocity. However, misfires may occur in some revolvers due to the thicker primer cup or the cushioning effect of the plastic case. If you get misfires and are certain that the primers were properly seated, try CCI 300 Pistol primers. They are slightly more sensitive than magnum primers in firearms with marginal mainsprings.

Important! *Never use any propellant powder with Speer T-Ammo. Even a small propellant charge could rupture the plastic and vent hot gas into the firearm or onto the shooter.*

T-Ammo with a CCI Magnum pistol primer can post velocities up to 400 fps in some revolvers, and one-inch groups are possible at twenty feet. However, some makes and models of firearms may not shoot T-Ammo as well as others. T-bullets are designed to ride on the top of the rifling instead of engaging it like a standard bullet. If the bore dimensions of a particular revolver are on the large size, the plastic bullets may not be accurate. If too small, bullets could stick.

A simple test can tell you if your barrel is compatible with Speer T-bullets. Clean and dry the bore and then press a new T-bullet into the muzzle. The bullet should slide in with light finger pressure, but not fall out when the barrel is turned muzzle-down.

T-bullets can be reused if they are fired into a bullet trap that cushions the impact. A wooden or cardboard box with strips of carpet or rubber inner tube hung over the open end and padded with carpet at the back will stop the bullets without deforming them. With care, T-bullets can be used twenty times or more.

The Target-45 system is slightly different from the 38 and 44 versions. T-45 bullets are loaded in standard brass 45 Auto cases. Bullets are pressed into a primed, resized case with finger pressure until they stop. If primer setback occurs, open the flash hole in the case with a 7/64-inch drill. Do not use these modified cases for conventional loading. Mark them with a bright, permanent color or notch the rims with a file to clearly identify them as practice cases.

The resulting T-45 ammo will often feed from a M1911 magazine if cycled manually. However, the cartridges do not generate enough energy to operate the action, so you need to manually rack the slide between shots.

Because they produce little or no recoil, T-bullets will usually strike the target below the point of aim used with conventional ammunition. If you don't care to alter your sight settings, paste an auxiliary aiming point on the target to compensate for the lack of recoil.

T-45 bullets perform best when you sort cases by make. Mixed cases can cause variations in seating depth that can degrade accuracy.

When using T-Ammunitions, keep the barrel and chambers clean. Primers fired without powder leave residue that must be removed regularly to maintain accuracy and reliability. We recommend dry brushing the bore and chambers after every 12 to 20 shots. Clean the firearm thoroughly at the end of each shooting session.

Safety with Speer T-Ammo

- Speer T-Ammo is not a toy! It will injure skin and unprotected eyes. Show it the same respect you show any other ammunition.
- **Do not attempt to load T-45 bullets in the 45 Colt cartridge case.** The bullet may not seat close enough to the primer pocket, resulting in excessive air space that can cause a bullet to stick in the bore. T-45 bullets are dimensioned for the 45 Auto case only.
- Wear eye and ear protection. Primers alone make a loud noise, and repeated exposure can damage hearing. All ammunition emits tiny particles of residue; wear approved safety/shooting glasses while loading and shooting T-Ammo. Provide eye and ear protection to anyone in the area while you are shooting.
- All component primers emit lead residue. We recommend that Speer T-Ammo be used in a well-ventilated area with a smooth, easily cleaned floor such as a garage. If your garage door is used as a backstop, pad it generously as the bullets will make thin metal doors look like a sack of marbles. Never fire them in a carpeted area. It is nearly impossible to completely remove particulate lead residue from carpeting. Wash your hands thoroughly after shooting. See Chapter 5, "Safety" for additional information on minimizing lead exposure while reloading and shooting.
- Always use Speer T-Ammo in accordance with applicable local ordinances.
- Do not use T-Ammunition for hunting or personal defense.
- Do not fire T-bullets at glass or other fragile objects.
- Do not fire T-bullets at hard surfaces as the bullets may ricochet.

INTRODUCTION TO HANDGUN DATA

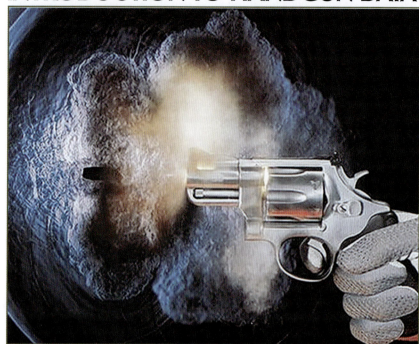

This section contains handloading data for use with Speer® bullets in today's popular handgun calibers and for many legacy cartridges that are still widely handloaded. We do not guess at these numbers. Charge weights and velocities published here are the result of thousands of ballistician-hours spent in loading, experimenting, collecting and vetting data. Speer's load recommendations are more robust than any in the industry and one of the most comprehensive that have been developed. All charge weights and velocities derive from meticulously collected laboratory pressure correlations using state-of-the-art equipment and techniques. While there may be subjectivity in the 'stopping power' of a given bullet design or the effective range of your two inch ankle gun, when it comes to the handloading data presented here, this is the best ballistic science on the market.

You will notice some differences in how the numbers are presented compared to previous load manuals. The number of propellants available to the handloader grows each year. Many of these are formulated for specific case volumes and operating pressures with their sweet spot in only a small family of cartridge designs. Finding charge recommendations for new propellants (and for new bullets using old propellants) is a continual process and you will see some cartridges have well over a dozen offerings. Classic loads in legacy cartridges are presented along with the latest and greatest. We think you will find the comparisons interesting. Many of the older propellants still rank in the top five highest posted velocities.

The newest powders, in most cases however, are phenomenal products. We are proud to collaborate with our sister company, Alliant Powder®.

Using many of their current selection, these cutting edge propellants are two steps ahead of the double-based propellants from decades past. They are much cleaner burning, with wide-ranging temperature stability, de-coppering agents, and low flash – all while generating some of the highest velocities at safe pressure. Our competitors are producing some top-notch offerings as well and we don't discriminate when it comes to powders used in loading data collection.

Powders are listed in descending order by maximum charge velocity. Charge weights are determined with the specific components listed for each data set. This does not mean that you will get the same velocity even if you use all of the same components shown. There is inherent variation in case volume, primer and powder chemistry, and barrel geometries. That said, you will get much closer to our results than you will by substituting components. Regardless of whose components you load with, it's important to begin with the start charge anytime you make a change and work up from there.

Contrary to popular Internet 'wisdom', we do not drastically limit maximum charge weights and pressures but rather apply the same industry-accepted practices that are used to produce high-performance factory ammunition. Our goal is to help handloaders duplicate that same top performance while keeping loads safe. Remember, maximum charges put you near the upper limit of acceptable pressures established by the industry and it will not benefit you or your handgun to exceed them. Starting charges on newly acquired data generally fall between 70 and 90 percent of the maximum pressure allowed for the cartridge. They are reduced enough to allow for component variation. In cases where unsafe conditions could result from too low of a charge weight, we have indicated "DNR" – Do Not Reduce. Bullet in bore, delayed ignition, and other phenomena can cause high pressure events with too little powder in these rare cases.

The muzzle velocities listed for handgun data are shown as tested through actual firearms rather than universal test barrels. For rifle data, the test barrels compare very closely with actual bolt guns of the same barrel length and velocity changes are reasonably predictable as that barrel length changes. In the case of handguns, the majority are either auto-loading or revolver design. Both types have additional velocity losses due to gas venting as compared to a closed bolt chamber. We have, therefore, shown the test firearm we used in the introduction preceding each cartridge dataset. Again, this is just for reference and, if you are measuring your own velocities, you should not expect them to align perfectly.

Cartridge overall lengths used in testing are shown for each bullet as has been standard in previous Speer load manuals. Note that these are provided only as a guideline. For many handgun bullets, COAL is determined by a crimping feature. In those instances, it will be necessary to adjust for your specific case length to ensure a good crimp and smooth chambering. For compressed charges (denoted with the letter "C" following the charge weight), the tested COAL shown gave us 'substantial' compression. We didn't list this just because the bullet heel may have touched the top of the powder charge. Consequently, variations in case volume between manufacturers and your charging technique may prevent you from putting this much powder in the case. Some Speer handgun bullets have two crimp grooves. These are designed to accommodate different handguns. The load data will instruct you which is intended to be used under those circumstances.

SAFETY INFORMATION

All reloading data contained herein is intended for use only by persons familiar with handloading practices and procedures, their own firearms, and reloading equipment. Before using this data to assemble any ammunition, you must read and understand the reloading safety guidelines in Chapter 5 and all safety related cautions in the individual cartridge sections. We strongly urge new reloaders to read and understand the text of this manual. It has been written to give clear instruction in the principles and processes of reloading. Use the most current data. Components and cartridge standards change over time and these changes will affect load recommendations in the Speer Manual. It is fruitless to compare modern data to that published decades ago. Using old data with current components can create unsafe ammunition. If you are uncertain of the operation of your reloading equipment or the properties of any components, contact the manufacturer for additional assistance. Never be afraid to ask for help.

DISCLAIMER

These loads are for Speer bullets. Bullets of other makes will not produce the same pressures and velocities and can create an unsafe condition if used with loads shown here. Because Vista Outdoor has no control over individual loading practices or the quality of the firearms in which the resulting ammunition may be used, we assume no liability—either expressed or implied—for the use of this load data information and instructional materials. The data contained herein replaces, supersedes and obsoletes all data previously published by Speer, Omark Industries, Blount International, Inc., and ATK.

22 HORNET

Alternate Names:	5.6x35mmR
Parent Cartridge:	22 WCF
Country of Origin:	USA
Year of Introduction:	1930
Designer(s):	G.L. Wotkyns, Townsend Whelen, G.A. Woody & A.L. Woodworth
Governing Body:	SAAMI/CIP

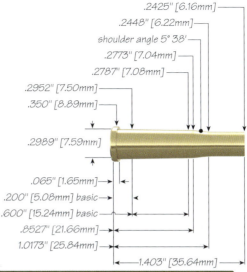

CARTRIDGE CASE DATA

Case Type:	Rimmed, necked
Average Case Capacity:	14.0 grains H_2O
Max. Cartridge OAL:	1.723 inch
Max. Case Length:	1.403 inch
Primer:	Small Pistol
Case Trim to Length:	1.393 inch
RCBS Shell holder:	# 12
Current Manufacturers:	Hornady, Remington, Nosler, Winchester, Sellier & Bellot, Prvi Partizan

BALLISTIC DATA

Max. Average Pressure (MAP):	49,000 psi, 43,000 CUP - SAAMI
Test Barrel Length:	24 inch - SAAMI recognizes 22 Hornet as a rifle cartridge and lists test barrel length as 24 inch only.
Rifling Twist Rate:	1 turn in 14, 1/16 inch in older rifles and SAAMI test barrels

Muzzle velocities of handloaded ammunition in 10 inch pistols:	Bullet Wgt.	Muzzle velocity
	33-grain	2,700 fps
	45-grain	2,320 fps
	50-grain	2,250 fps
	52-grain	2,125 fps

BALLISTIC NOTES

- Although originally designed as a rifle cartridge, the 22 Hornet works very well in single-shot handguns such as the Thompson/Center Contender.

- While the shorter handgun barrels do give up some muzzle velocity, the 22 Hornet's maximum effective range of 100 yards from a handgun will be adequate for most hunters.
- Unlike hunting with a rifle, when fired from a handgun the ballistic capabilities of the bullet used becomes far more important. Accordingly, we recommend the following Speer bullets in the T/C Contender:
  - For rodents, pests, and varmints, the Speer 33-grain HP
  - For pests, varmints, and small game, the Speer 40-grain Spire SP
  - For large varmints and small game, the Speer 45-grain Spitzer SP
  - For predators and large varmints, the Speer 50-grain TNT® HP or the Speer 52-grain HP

TECHNICAL NOTES

- The one turn in 14 inch rifling twist rate will not stabilize bullets over 52 grains.
- The TNT bullet will expand at the low impact velocities at 100 yards but must be loaded to maximum velocities at the muzzle in order to properly stabilize.

HANDLOADING NOTES

- As 22 Hornet cases are thin, we recommend neck sizing only for maximum case life.
- Even so, expect loading life to be three or four loadings before incipient head separations occur and the cases must be discarded. For this reason, it is very important to carefully inspect your cases before reloading them.
- The 22 Hornet cartridge case is designed for Small Rifle primers. However, note that we used Small Pistol primers for all loads listed here. This is important as substituting Small Rifle primers may cause excessive pressures. Do not use Small Pistol Magnum primers unless so specified by the loading data.

SAFETY NOTES

SPEER 50-grain TNT SP @ a muzzle velocity of 2,251 fps:
- Maximum vertical altitude @ 90° elevation is 6,615 feet.
- Maximum horizontal distance to first impact with ground @ 32° elevation is 3,025 yards.

33 GRAINS

DIAMETER	SECTIONAL DENSITY
0.224"	0.094

22 HP

Ballistic Coefficient	0.080
COAL Tested	1.680"
Speer Part No.	1014

			Starting Charge		Maximum Charge	
Propellant	Case	Primer	Weight (grains)	Muzzle Velocity (feet/sec)	Weight (grains)	Muzzle Velocity (feet/sec)
Winchester 296	Winchester	CCI 500	12.4	2556	12.8	2703
Accurate No. 9	Winchester	CCI 500	10.2	2526	10.8	2674
Hodgdon H110	Winchester	CCI 500	12.4	2473	12.8	2600
Vihtavuori N110	Winchester	CCI 500	10.0	2492	10.6 C	2580
Alliant 2400	Winchester	CCI 500	11.0	2519	11.5 C	2554
Hodgdon Lil' Gun	Winchester	CCI 500	13.5 C	2342	14.0 C	2451

40 GRAINS

DIAMETER	SECTIONAL DENSITY
0.224"	0.114

22 Spire SP

Ballistic Coefficient	0.144
COAL Tested	1.723"
Speer Part No.	1017

			Starting Charge		Maximum Charge	
Propellant	Case	Primer	Weight (grains)	Muzzle Velocity (feet/sec)	Weight (grains)	Muzzle Velocity (feet/sec)
Hodgdon H110	Winchester	CCI 500	9.2	2317	10.2	2400
Winchester 296	Winchester	CCI 500	9.2	2297	10.2	2375
Hodgdon Lil' Gun	Winchester	CCI 500	12.0	2276	13.0 C	2344
Vihtavuori N110	Winchester	CCI 500	8.1	2136	9.1	2338
Alliant 2400	Winchester	CCI 500	8.1	2125	9.1	2306
Accurate 1680	Winchester	CCI 500	12.4	2177	13.4 C	2258
IMR 4227	Winchester	CCI 500	10.5	2126	11.3 C	2238

WARNING! Maximum loads should be used with CAUTION • C = Compressed Load

22 HORNET

45 GRAINS

DIAMETER	SECTIONAL DENSITY
0.224"	0.128

22 Spitzer SP	
Ballistic Coefficient	0.143
COAL Tested	1.723"
Speer Part No.	1023

			Starting Charge		Maximum Charge	
Propellant	Case	Primer	Weight (grains)	Muzzle Velocity (feet/sec)	Weight (grains)	Muzzle Velocity (feet/sec)
Hodgdon Lil' Gun	Winchester	CCI 500	12.0	2225	13.0 C	2318
Winchester 296	Winchester	CCI 500	9.0	2145	10.0	2267
Hodgdon H110	Winchester	CCI 500	9.0	2083	10.0	2225
Accurate 1680	Winchester	CCI 500	12.0	2043	13.0 C	2194
Alliant 2400	Winchester	CCI 500	8.0	2003	9.0	2190
Vihtavuori N110	Winchester	CCI 500	8.2	2116	9.0	2188
IMR 4227	Winchester	CCI 500	10.1	2083	11.1	2183

50 GRAINS

DIAMETER	SECTIONAL DENSITY
0.224"	0.142

22 Spitzer SP	
Ballistic Coefficient	0.207
COAL Tested	1.723"
Speer Part No.	1029

22 TNT® HP	
Ballistic Coefficient	0.228
COAL Tested	1.850"†
Speer Part No.	1030

			Starting Charge		Maximum Charge	
Propellant	Case	Primer	Weight (grains)	Muzzle Velocity (feet/sec)	Weight (grains)	Muzzle Velocity (feet/sec)
Hodgdon Lil' Gun	Winchester	CCI 500	11.0 C	2114	12.0 C	2251
Winchester 296	Winchester	CCI 500	9.0	2141	9.7	2250
Hodgdon H110	Winchester	CCI 500	9.0	2186	9.6	2240
Vihtavuori N110	Winchester	CCI 500	7.9	2027	8.6	2099
Accurate 1680	Winchester	CCI 500	10.9	1941	11.8	2068
Accurate 2015	Winchester	CCI 500	11.5 C	1732	12.0 C	1860

† — COAL exceeds industry standards; for long-throated single-shots only

WARNING! Maximum loads should be used with CAUTION • C = Compressed Load

52 GRAINS

DIAMETER	SECTIONAL DENSITY
0.224"	0.148

22 HP
Ballistic Coefficient	0.168
COAL Tested	1.723"
Speer Part No.	1035

22 Match BTHP
Ballistic Coefficient	0.230
COAL Tested	1.723"
Speer Part No.	1036

Propellant	Case	Primer	Starting Charge Weight (grains)	Starting Charge Muzzle Velocity (feet/sec)	Maximum Charge Weight (grains)	Maximum Charge Muzzle Velocity (feet/sec)
Hodgdon H110	Winchester	CCI 500	7.9	1935	8.9	2125
Winchester 296	Winchester	CCI 500	7.9	2011	8.9	2091
Vihtavuori N110	Winchester	CCI 500	7.4	1899	8.0	2002
Hodgdon Lil' Gun	Winchester	CCI 500	9.0	1852	9.7	1986
IMR 4227	Winchester	CCI 500	8.6	1817	9.6	183
IMR 4198	Winchester	CCI 500	9.7 C	1822	10.5 C	1969
Alliant 2400	Winchester	CCI 500	6.7	1821	7.7	1946
Accurate 1680	Winchester	CCI 500	10.1	1833	10.8	1904

WARNING! *Maximum loads should be used with* CAUTION • *C = Compressed Load*

221 REMINGTON FIREBALL

Parent Cartridge:	222 Remington
Country of Origin:	USA
Year of Introduction:	1963
Designer(s):	Remington
Governing Body:	SAAMI

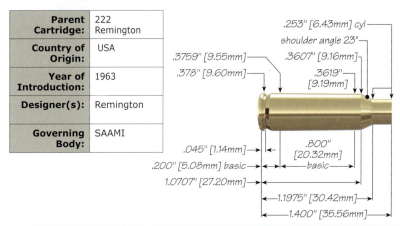

CARTRIDGE CASE DATA

Case Type:	Rimless, bottleneck		
Average Case Capacity:	21.0 grains H$_2$O	Max. Cartridge OAL	1.830 inch
Max. Case Length:	1.400 inch	Primer:	Small Rifle
Case Trim to Length:	1.390 inch	RCBS Shell holder:	# 10
Current Manufacturers:	Nosler, Remington		

BALLISTIC DATA

Max. Average Pressure (MAP):	60,000 psi, 52,000 CUP - SAAMI	Test Barrel Length:	10.75 inch
Rifling Twist Rate:	1 turn in 12 inch		
Muzzle velocities of factory loaded ammunition in pistols		Bullet Wgt.	Muzzle velocity
		45-grain	2,760 fps
		50-grain	2,690 fps

HISTORICAL NOTES

- When the 221 Fireball cartridge was introduced by Remington in 1963, a new concept in pistols was announced at the same time.
- At the heart of Remington's new XP100 single-shot pistol was a short-length, bolt-action rifle receiver capable of operating safely at the high MAP levels of rifles.
- The Remington XP100 pistol and its 221 Fireball cartridge were very much a specialized product aimed at a narrow market segment.
- Although the XP100 pistol is no longer being made, Remington offers the 221 Fireball in a bolt-action carbine and Thompson/Center offers their Contender pistol in that chambering.

BALLISTIC NOTES

- The rifling twist rate of one turn in 12 inches will stabilize bullets weighing from 40 to 55 grains.
- Unlike hunting with a rifle, when fired from a handgun the ballistic capabilities of the bullet used becomes far more important. Accordingly, we recommend the following Speer bullets in the XP-100 and Thompson/Center Contender:
- Handloaders can duplicate the factory load using the Speer 50-grain TNT® HP at a muzzle velocity of 2,693 fps from a 10 inch barrel.
- If more muzzle velocity is required to make short work of varmints and pests, the Speer 45-grain Spitzer SP can be handloaded to a muzzle velocity of 2,775 fps.
- To build an accuracy load, we suggest the Speer 52-grain Match BTHP loaded to a muzzle velocity of 2,607 fps. Expect minimal expansion from this bullet.

TECHNICAL NOTES

- The 221 Fireball cartridge is based on a shortened 222 Remington case with similar rim, head, and shoulder dimensions.
- The strength of the 221 Fireball case therefore allows the 221 to take full advantage of rifle MAP levels.
- The one in 12 inch rifling twist rate will not stabilize the longer bullets over 55 grains. Recoil is mild, but muzzle blast is loud.

HANDLOADING NOTES

- We recommend neck sizing only for maximum case life.
- Even so, expect loading life to be three or four loadings before incipient head separations occur and the cases must be discarded. For this reason, it is very important to carefully inspect your cases before reloading them.
- The 221 Fireball is a rifle case designed for Small Rifle Primers. Do not use Small Pistol primers to load this cartridge.

SAFETY NOTES

SPEER 50-grain TNT HP @ a muzzle velocity of 2,693 fps:
- Maximum vertical altitude @ 90° elevation is 7,005 feet.
- Maximum horizontal distance to first impact with ground @ 33° elevation is 3,160 yards.
- These loads are intended for use in XP-100 and Thompson/Center Contender pistols ONLY. Do not use these loads in any other firearms.

45 GRAINS

DIAMETER	SECTIONAL DENSITY
0.224"	0.128

22 Spitzer SP	
Ballistic Coefficient	0.143
COAL Tested	1.830"
Speer Part No.	1023

			Starting Charge		Maximum Charge	
Propellant	Case	Primer	Weight (grains)	Muzzle Velocity (feet/sec)	Weight (grains)	Muzzle Velocity (feet/sec)
Alliant Reloder 7	Remington	CCI 400	17.3	2603	18.3	2775
Alliant 2400	Remington	CCI 400	14.0	2599	15.0	2762
Hodgdon H110	Remington	CCI 450	13.0	2555	14.0	2757
IMR 4198	Remington	CCI 400	16.8	2556	17.8 C	2731
IMR 4227	Remington	CCI 400	15.2	2571	16.2	2727

50 GRAINS

DIAMETER	SECTIONAL DENSITY
0.224"	0.142

22 Spitzer SP	
Ballistic Coefficient	0.207
COAL Tested	1.830"
Speer Part No.	1029

22 TNT® HP	
Ballistic Coefficient	0.228
COAL Tested	1.830"
Speer Part No.	1030

			Starting Charge		Maximum Charge	
Propellant	Case	Primer	Weight (grains)	Muzzle Velocity (feet/sec)	Weight (grains)	Muzzle Velocity (feet/sec)
Alliant 2400	Remington	CCI 400	13.5	2521	14.5	2693
IMR 4198	Remington	CCI 400	16.5	2503	17.5 C	2664
Alliant Reloder 7	Remington	CCI 400	16.9	2497	17.9	2638
IMR 4227	Remington	CCI 400	14.9	1490	15.9	2634
Hodgdon H110	Remington	CCI 450	12.5	2429	13.5	2625

WARNING! Maximum loads should be used with CAUTION • C = Compressed Load

52 GRAINS

DIAMETER	SECTIONAL DENSITY
0.224"	0.148

22 HP

Ballistic Coefficient	0.168
COAL Tested	1.830"
Speer Part No.	1035

22 Match BTHP

Ballistic Coefficient	0.230
COAL Tested	1.830"
Speer Part No.	1036

Propellant	Case	Primer	Starting Charge		Maximum Charge	
			Weight (grains)	Muzzle Velocity (feet/sec)	Weight (grains)	Muzzle Velocity (feet/sec)
Alliant 2400	Remington	CCI 400	13.3	2411	14.3	2607
Alliant Reloder 7	Remington	CCI 400	16.7	2441	17.7	2606
IMR 4227	Remington	CCI 400	14.7	2404	15.7	2585
IMR 4198	Remington	CCI 400	16.0	2330	17.0	2527
Hodgdon H110	Remington	CCI 450	12.2	2268	13.2	2465

55 GRAINS

DIAMETER	SECTIONAL DENSITY
0.224"	0.157

22 Spitzer SP

Ballistic Coefficient	0.212
COAL Tested	1.830"
Speer Part No.	1047

22 TNT® HP

Ballistic Coefficient	0.233
COAL Tested	1.830"
Speer Part No.	1032

Propellant	Case	Primer	Starting Charge		Maximum Charge	
			Weight (grains)	Muzzle Velocity (feet/sec)	Weight (grains)	Muzzle Velocity (feet/sec)
IMR 4227	Remington	CCI 400	14.5	2419	15.4	2562
IMR 4198	Remington	CCI 400	15.5	2317	16.7	2502
Alliant Reloder 7	Remington	CCI 400	16.4	2348	17.4	2501
Alliant 2400	Remington	CCI 400	12.5	2267	13.5	2477
Hodgdon H110	Remington	CCI 450	12.0	2250	13.0	2432

WARNING! *Maximum loads should be used with CAUTION • C = Compressed Load*

223 REMINGTON

Alternate Names:	5.56x45mm
Parent Cartridge:	222 Remington
Country of Origin:	USA
Year of Introduction:	1963
Designer(s):	Remington & U.S. Military
Governing Body:	SAAMI/CIP

Dimensions: .253" [6.43mm] cyl; shoulder angle 23°; .3759" [9.55mm]; .3542" [9.00mm]; .378" [9.60mm]; .3584" [9.10mm]; .045" [1.14mm]; 1.000" [25.40mm] basic; .200" [5.08mm] basic; 1.4381" [36.53mm]; 1.5573" [39.56mm]; 1.760" [44.70mm]

CARTRIDGE CASE DATA

Case Type:	Rimless, bottleneck		
Average Case Capacity:	31.0 grains H$_2$O	Max. Cartridge OAL	2.260 inch
Max. Case Length:	1.760 inch	Primer:	Small Rifle
Case Trim to Length:	1.750 inch	RCBS Shell holder:	# 10
Current Manufacturers:	Remington, Federal, Hornady, Winchester, Black Hills, IMI, Prvi Partizan, Fiocchi, PMC, PMP, MEN, Sellier & Bellot, Lapua, Wolf		

BALLISTIC DATA

Max. Average Pressure (MAP):	55,000 psi, 52,000 CUP - SAAMI	Test Barrel Length:	14 inch
Rifling Twist Rate:	1 turn in 12 inch		
Muzzle velocities of handloaded pistol ammunition	Bullet Wgt.		Muzzle velocity
	45-grain		3,120 fps
	50-grain		3,070 fps
	52-grain		3,080 fps
	55-grain		3,010 fps

HISTORICAL NOTES

- Following its introduction in 1963, the popularity of the new 223 Remington cartridge grew rapidly.
- It was just a matter of time before someone chambered it in a single-shot pistol. After all, if the concept worked for the 221 Fireball in the XP-100 pistol, why would it not work for the 223 Remington? If a little is good, more must be better.
- Both Thompson/Center and Remington stepped up to the plate with pistols in 223 Remington. The concept proved to be a success.

- A frequently missed aspect of the concept was: "a long gun and a handgun in the same cartridge." Just like the good old days, a shooter could have one caliber of cartridge to shoot in both a handgun and a rifle, but now for reasons of convenience rather than necessity.
- From a ballistic point of view, the 223 Remington cartridge does surprisingly well from a 14 inch pistol barrel with some loads within 90% of rifle muzzle velocities.
- Here one must note that the military M4 carbine has a 14 inch barrel as well.
- One annoying detail will catch your eye when you fire the 223 Remington from a pistol—a dazzling muzzle flash.
- Of course, 223 Remington pistols are very much a specialized product aimed at a narrow market segment.
- For shooters considering a 223 Remington pistol, we feel it's necessary to point out that shooting such a handgun accurately places a premium on a correct and consistent shooting technique. But, of course that is no problem is it?

BALLISTIC NOTES

- From a pistol, the 223 Remington cartridge must be viewed as suitable mainly for varmints, pests, rodents, and small game. It is not suitable for deer or other medium game.
- Bullets heavier than 55 grains will not stabilize at 223 Remington pistol barrel velocities and the 1 turn in 12 inch rifling twist in commercial firearms.
- For this reason, we recommend 45 to 50-grain bullets for general purpose use in 223 Rem. pistols.
- For your consideration, we suggest the Speer 50-grain TNT® HP for its dramatic expansion at pistol velocities. The Speer 45-grain Spitzer SP is another very good choice for this application.
- In this same category are the Speer 52-grain HP bullets which can be driven at muzzle velocities in the order of 3,083 fps. You will find the No. 1036 bullet will not expand as readily, as the No. 1035, if at all.
- Should you wish to duplicate the factory load, the Speer 55-grain Spitzer SP is the ideal choice.
- Unlike hunting with a rifle, in a handgun the ballistic capability of the bullet used becomes far more important.

TECHNICAL NOTES

- The rimless 223 Remington case headspaces on its case shoulder.
- The strength of the 223 Remington case allows a pistol to take full advantage of rifle MAP levels.
- Note that commercial 223 Remington brass and military 5.56x45mm brass may have different case capacities which can adversely affect MAP levels and muzzle velocity.
- For this reason, we strongly recommend that you sort your cases into military and commercial types, then use the commercial brass for your pistol.
- Recoil is mild, but muzzle blast is loud. Did we mention muzzle flash?

HANDLOADING NOTES

- Fired brass from a semi-automatic rifle must be resized with a full-length, small base die before it can be fired in a pistol. Check length too, they will often be too long.
- After your cases have been fired in the pistol, neck sizing will extend the life of your cases and reduce head separations. Even so, expect loading life to be three or four loadings before incipient head separations occur and the cases must be discarded. For this reason, it is very important to carefully inspect your cases before reloading them.
- Remember, now you will find both commercial and military cases have crimped primers. Remove the crimp prior to reloading.
- Do no use CCI No. 41 primers for this application.

SAFETY NOTES

SPEER 50-grain TNT HP @ a muzzle velocity of 3,068 fps:
- Maximum vertical altitude @ 90° elevation is 7,311 feet.
- Maximum horizontal distance to first impact with ground @ 33° elevation is 3,265 yards.
- These loads are intended for use in Thompson/Center Contender and XP-100 pistols ONLY. Do not use these loads in any other firearms.

45 GRAINS

DIAMETER	SECTIONAL DENSITY
0.224"	0.128

22 Spitzer SP	
Ballistic Coefficient	0.143
COAL Tested	2.155"
Speer Part No.	1023

			Starting Charge		Maximum Charge	
Propellant	Case	Primer	Weight (grains)	Muzzle Velocity (feet/sec)	Weight (grains)	Muzzle Velocity (feet/sec)
IMR 3031	IMI	CCI 400	25.0	2712	27.0 C	3121
Winchester 748	IMI	CCI 450	26.5	2858	28.5 C	3097
Vihtavuori N133	IMI	CCI 400	22.5	2789	24.5	3065
IMR 4198	IMI	CCI 400	21.0	2782	23.0	3061
Hodgdon H322	IMI	CCI 400	24.0	2713	26.0	3029
IMR 4895	IMI	CCI 400	25.0	2701	27.0 C	3022
Accurate 2015	IMI	CCI 400	23.0	2760	25.0	3010
Accurate 2460	IMI	CCI 450	24.0	2683	26.0	2967
Alliant Reloder 7	IMI	CCI 400	18.0	2564	20.0	2636

WARNING! *Maximum loads should be used with CAUTION • C = Compressed Load*

50 GRAINS

DIAMETER	SECTIONAL DENSITY
0.224"	0.142

22 Spitzer SP	
Ballistic Coefficient	0.207
COAL Tested	2.185"
Speer Part No.	1029

22 TNT® HP	
Ballistic Coefficient	0.228
COAL Tested	2.250"
Speer Part No.	1030

Propellant	Case	Primer	Starting Charge		Maximum Charge	
			Weight (grains)	Muzzle Velocity (feet/sec)	Weight (grains)	Muzzle Velocity (feet/sec)
Hodgdon H322	IMI	CCI 400	24.0	2749	26.0	3068
IMR 4895	IMI	CCI 400	25.0	2714	27.0 C	3037
Accurate 2520	IMI	CCI 450	26.0	2848	28.0 C	3030
IMR 3031	IMI	CCI 400	24.0	2571	26.0 C	2960
Winchester 748	IMI	CCI 450	26.0	2728	28.0	2954
Hodgdon H4895	IMI	CCI 400	23.5	2537	25.5 C	2917
Vihtavuori N133	IMI	CCI 400	22.0	2638	24.0	2900
Accurate 2015	IMI	CCI 400	22.5	2651	24.5	2890
IMR 4198	IMI	CCI 400	20.0	2608	22.0	2870

WARNING! Maximum loads should be used with CAUTION • C = Compressed Load

52 GRAINS

DIAMETER	SECTIONAL DENSITY
0.224"	0.148

22 HP	
Ballistic Coefficient	0.168
COAL Tested	2.185"
Speer Part No.	1035

22 MATCH BTHP	
Ballistic Coefficient	0.230
COAL Tested	2.250"
Speer Part No.	1036

			Starting Charge		Maximum Charge	
Propellant	Case	Primer	Weight (grains)	Muzzle Velocity (feet/sec)	Weight (grains)	Muzzle Velocity (feet/sec)
Winchester 748	IMI	CCI 450	26.0	2846	28.0	3083
Accurate 2520	IMI	CCI 400	25.5	2892	27.5 C	3077
IMR 3031	IMI	CCI 400	24.0	2630	26.0 C	3027
IMR 4895	IMI	CCI 400	24.5	2680	26.5 C	2998
Hodgdon H4895	IMI	CCI 400	23.5	2600	25.5 C	2989
Vihtavuori N133	IMI	CCI 400	22.0	2684	24.0	2950
Accurate 2015	IMI	CCI 400	22.0	2662	24.0	2903
IMR 4198	IMI	CCI 400	20.0	2598	22.0	2858
Hodgdon H322	IMI	CCI 400	22.5	2550	24.5	2846

WARNING! *Maximum loads should be used with CAUTION • C = Compressed Load*

55 GRAINS

DIAMETER	SECTIONAL DENSITY
0.224"	0.157

22 Spitzer SP
Ballistic Coefficient	0.212
COAL Tested	2.175"
Speer Part No.	1047

22 TNT® HP
Ballistic Coefficient	0.233
COAL Tested	2.175"
Speer Part No.	1032

			Starting Charge		Maximum Charge	
Propellant	Case	Primer	Weight (grains)	Muzzle Velocity (feet/sec)	Weight (grains)	Muzzle Velocity (feet/sec)
Accurate 2520	IMI	CCI 450	25.0	2827	27.0	3008
Hodgdon H4895	IMI	CCI 400	23.5	2595	25.5	2983
Winchester 748	IMI	CCI 450	26.0	2735	28.0	2964
IMR 3031	IMI	CCI 400	24.0	2574	26.0	2962
IMR 4895	IMI	CCI 400	24.5	2621	26.5	2932
Vihtavuori N133	IMI	CCI 400	21.5	2593	23.5	2849
Hodgdon H322	IMI	CCI 400	22.5	2501	24.5	2792
Accurate 2015	IMI	CCI 400	21.5	2535	23.5	2765
IMR 4198	IMI	CCI 400	19.0	2473	21.0	2721

WARNING! Maximum loads should be used with CAUTION • C = Compressed Load

25 AUTOMATIC

Alternate Names:	25 ACP, 6.35mm ACP, 6.35mm Browning, 6.35x15.5mmSR
Parent Cartridge:	Original
Country of Origin:	Belgium
Year of Introduction:	1905
Designer(s):	John Browning
Governing Body:	SAAMI/CIP

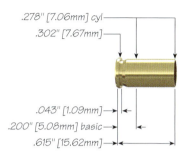

CARTRIDGE CASE DATA			
Case Type:	Semi rimmed, straight		
Average Case Capacity:	5.8 grains H$_2$O	Max. Cartridge OAL	.910 inch
Max. Case Length:	.615 inch	Primer:	Small Pistol
Case Trim to Length:	N/A	RCBS Shell holder:	# 29
Current Manufacturers:	CCI/Speer, Federal, Hornady, Remington, Winchester, Cor-Bon, Magtech, Fiocchi, Sellier & Bellot, Aguila		

BALLISTIC DATA			
Max. Average Pressure (MAP):	25,000 psi, 18,000 CUP - SAAMI	Test Barrel Length:	2 inch
Rifling Twist Rate:	1 turn in 16 inch		
Muzzle velocities of factory loaded ammunition	Bullet Wgt.		Muzzle velocity
	35-grain		900 fps
	45-grain		815 fps
	50-grain		760 fps

HISTORICAL NOTES

- In the late 1800s, small, cheap revolvers and derringers firing low-powered cartridges with lead bullets were the norm for personal defense.
- Ballistic performance was not important as these guns were intended to dissuade more than incapacitate. However, they could be lethal at close range.
- By the early 1900s, improved metallurgy and smokeless propellants made semi-automatic guns for this purpose feasible.

- John Browning stepped into this mix with a diminutive semi-auto pistol chambered for this new cartridge. Colt licensed the gun in 1908 and dubbed Browning's new 25 caliber cartridge the 25 ACP or 25 Automatic Colt Pistol.
- Today, the name of the cartridge has been shortened to 25 Automatic in the U.S. In Europe, it is called the 6.35mm Browning.
- Dozens of small pistols designed for this caliber have been made in the succeeding 110 years. The 25 Auto remains popular today for much the same purpose.
- Most 25 Auto pistols are blowback operated.
- Today, most domestic and many foreign ammunition manufacturers offer 25 Auto ammunition.

Interesting Fact

The quality of 25 Auto pistols runs the entire gamut from high quality to throw away.

The best of these small pistols are made with forged steel or aluminum frames and steel slides. Cheap pistols in this caliber have cast aluminum or zinc frames and slides with many small parts made from soft zinc alloy. We recommend against purchasing or firing the latter type of pistol.

BALLISTIC NOTES

- Despite its popularity for personal defense, the 25 Auto cartridge has always been considered a marginal choice for that purpose. However, crime statistics show a significant number of persons killed every year with this cartridge, highlighting its potential lethality.
- Ballistics of 25 Auto factory ammunition with the 50-grain FMJ bullet are truly depressing. Muzzle velocity is 760 fps with a muzzle energy of 64 ft-lbs. (For comparison, the 22 Long Rifle High Velocity hollow point fired from a handgun carries 106 ft-lbs of muzzle energy!)
- In the late 1980s, ammunition manufacturers made an effort to improve the ballistics of the 25 Auto cartridge by replacing the 50 grain FMJ bullet with a lighter, jacketed hollow point design that would allow higher muzzle velocity. These efforts quickly ran up against the limited case volume and modest MAP level of the 25 Auto. The lighter bullets did not result in a significantly higher muzzle velocity (only about 7%) and muzzle energy stayed essentially the same.
- Although the 25,000 psi MAP level of the 25 Auto cartridge may seem contemporary enough, the limited capacity of the small cartridge case and the very short barrel of most pistols in this caliber limit muzzle velocities to low levels.
- The 25 Auto is unique in another way. The primer not only serves to ignite the small propellant charge, it also contributes a substantial part of the energy used to accelerate the bullet down the barrel. In many blowback pistols, the energy from the primer alone is sufficient to push the bullet out of the barrel (albeit at very low velocity).
- Extractors frequently break on cheap 25 Auto pistols. However, many shooters do not notice this as the residual chamber pressure of the blowback operation is usually enough to push the empty case from the chamber and out of the gun!
- So, why does the 25 Auto remain so popular? The answer is that the compact size, light weight, and mild recoil of these small pistols are the main reasons people

buy them. The dismal ballistics of the cartridge is not a major factor in such a decision. Put another way, concealability is more important than lethality.

- Recently, many handgun manufacturers have introduced small pistols chambered for more powerful cartridges such as the 9mm Luger, 40 S&W and even the 45 Auto. However, the weight, heavy recoil and difficult operation of such handguns will never match those of the 25 Auto.

TECHNICAL NOTES

- John Browning designed his 25 Auto cartridge with a semi-rimmed case which allows the 25 Auto cartridge to headspace on its rim (rimless pistol cartridges without a neck headspace on the case mouth).
- The 25 Auto cartridge case is too small to fit in most factory centerfire loading machines. As a result, most ammunition makers must plate-load this caliber in similar manner to rimfire ammunition.
- The Speer 35-grain Gold Dot® Hollow Point can be handloaded to slightly improve the ballistics of the 25 Auto for personal defense. However, do not expect miracles.

HANDLOADING NOTES

- Why bother to handload the 25 Auto at all? Is such an effort not more difficult than it is worth?
- The answer is hobbyists handload the 25 Auto cartridge because they can. While it may not seem like it, handloading the 25 Auto is an exacting and difficult task due to its small size. It's a challenge, and handloaders like a challenge.
- Another reason to handload the 25 Auto is the "shock" factor (the mental shock, not the ballistic) when your shooting associates say: "You handload the what???" followed by "You must be kidding!" It can be fun to be the first one at the gun club to handload the 25 Auto!
- The Speer 35-grain Gold Dot JHP bullet can be safely handloaded to a muzzle velocity considerably higher than 25 Auto factory loaded ammunition. Here is a comparison:
    - Factory load 45-grain JHP bullet: Muzzle Velocity: 815 fps Muzzle Energy: 66 ft-lbs.
    - Handload 35-grain GDHP bullet Muzzle Velocity: 1,040 fps Muzzle Energy: 84 ft-lbs.
- OK, so the increase is not huge, but it is a 27% increase in muzzle energy over the factory loading.
- As most powder measures will not reliably drop such small powder charges, you will have to weigh each charge.
- Never load less than the charges shown in the loading data. All of the data is shown with a single powder charge and a comment "DNR=Do Not Reduce." For those of you considering the 25 Auto for Centerfire Pistol Competition, forget it. This was tried once, the offender got disqualified and the rules changed.

SAFETY NOTES

SPEER 35-grain Gold Dot HP @ a muzzle velocity of 1,040 fps:
- Maximum vertical altitude @90° elevation is 2,856 feet.
- Maximum horizontal distance to first impact with ground @ 31° elevation is 1,292 yards.

35 GRAINS

DIAMETER	SECTIONAL DENSITY
.251"	0.079

25 GDHP

Ballistic Coefficient	0.091
COAL Tested	0.870"
Speer Part No.	3985

Propellant	Case	Primer	Starting Charge		Maximum Charge	
			Weight (grains)	Muzzle Velocity (feet/sec)	Weight (grains)	Muzzle Velocity (feet/sec)
Alliant Bullseye	Speer	CCI 500	DNR	—	1.7	1040
Hodgdon TITEGROUP	Speer	CCI 500	DNR	—	1.7	1008
Accurate No. 2 Improved	Speer	CCI 500	DNR	—	1.8	1004
Hodgdon Hi-Skor 700-X	Speer	CCI 500	DNR	—	1.7	971
Alliant Red Dot	Speer	CCI 500	DNR	—	1.5	966
Winchester 231	Speer	CCI 500	DNR	—	1.7	937

DNR — do not reduce

WARNING! *Maximum loads should be used with CAUTION • C = Compressed Load*

7-30 WATERS

Parent Cartridge:	30-30 Winchester
Country of Origin:	USA
Year of Introduction:	1984
Designer(s):	Ken Waters
Governing Body:	SAAMI

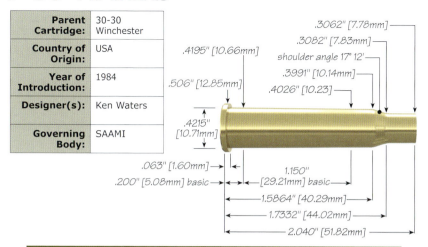

CARTRIDGE CASE DATA

Case Type:	Rimless, bottleneck		
Average Case Capacity:	45.0 grains H₂O	Max. Cartridge OAL:	2.550 inch
Max. Case Length:	2.040 inch	Primer:	Large Rifle
Case Trim to Length:	2.030 inch	RCBS Shell holder:	# 2
Current Manufacturers:	Federal		

BALLISTIC DATA

Max. Average Pressure (MAP):	45,000 psi, 40,000 CUP - SAAMI	Test Barrel Length:	14 inch
Rifling Twist Rate:	1 turn in 9.5 inch		

Muzzle velocities of loaded pistol ammunition	Bullet Wgt.	Muzzle velocity
	110-grain	2,460 fps
	130-grain	2,325 fps
	145-grain	2,295 fps

HISTORICAL NOTES

- In 1976, experimenter and writer Ken Waters began working on a new, flatter shooting cartridge for lever-action rifles such as the Winchester Model 94.

- Waters' concept was to neck down the venerable 30-30 Winchester cartridge to 7mm which would allow the use of smaller diameter, lighter bullets at higher muzzle velocities without exceeding existing MAP levels of the parent cartridge.

- Waters did not expect his new cartridge to become one of the best calibers for the Thompson/Center Contender pistol.

- The rimmed, necked case was ideal for a single-shot pistol, and pointed bullets could be used instead of the flat nose bullets required in lever-action rifles.
- The 7-30 Waters concept did not catch on with lever-action rifle shooters. However, it did with Contender shooters. This saved the 7-30 Waters cartridge from extinction.
- Federal lists loaded ammunition in 7-30 Waters in their current catalog.

BALLISTIC NOTES

- From a 14 inch Contender barrel, the 7-30 Waters cartridge is quite capable of achieving muzzle velocities of 2,330 fps with the Speer 130-grain Spitzer SP Hot-Cor® or Spitzer BTSP. This load works very well for small deer and predators.
- A muzzle velocity of 2,294 fps can be reached by handloading a 145-grain bullet.
- Such ballistic capabilities make the Contender and 7-30 Waters a very good choice for hunting deer at close ranges.
- The Speer 110-grain TNT® HP does a fine job of anchoring varmints, pests, and predators out to approximately 100 yards.

TECHNICAL NOTES

- The rimmed case of the 7-30 Waters makes extraction and setting headspace easy.
- The lightweight 7mm spitzer bullets strike an excellent balance with the case capacity of the 7-30 Waters cartridge while the 1 in 9.5 inch rifling twist rate will stabilize the heavier bullets.
- We recommend that bullets be crimped lightly in the case mouth to assure consistent ignition, especially given the short barrel length.
- Do not attempt to fire bullets heavier than those listed in the loading tables as they will not stabilize properly.

SAFETY NOTES

SPEER 145-grain Grand Slam® SP @ a muzzle velocity of 2,294 fps:
- Maximum vertical altitude @ 90° elevation is 10,692 feet.
- Maximum horizontal distance to first impact with ground @ 37° elevation is 5,088 yards.

110 GRAINS

DIAMETER	SECTIONAL DENSITY
.284"	0.195

7mm TNT® HP	
Ballistic Coefficient	0.384
COAL Tested	2.550"
Speer Part No.	1616

			Starting Charge		Maximum Charge	
Propellant	Case	Primer	Weight (grains)	Muzzle Velocity (feet/sec)	Weight (grains)	Muzzle Velocity (feet/sec)
Winchester 748	Federal	CCI 250	35.0	2191	39.0	2463
Vihtavuori N135	Federal	CCI 200	31.0	2092	35.0	2462
Accurate 2015	Federal	CCI 200	29.0	2253	33.0	2451
Hodgdon H4895	Federal	CCI 200	32.0	2147	36.0	2449
Hodgdon H335	Federal	CCI 250	32.0	2216	36.0	2422
Alliant Reloder 15	Federal	CCI 200	33.0	2079	37.0	2421
IMR 3031	Federal	CCI 200	30.0	2124	34.0	2376
Accurate 2230	Federal	CCI 250	27.5	2163	31.5	2376
IMR 4895	Federal	CCI 200	30.5	2155	34.5	2375

WARNING! *Maximum loads should be used with* CAUTION • C = Compressed Load

130 GRAINS

DIAMETER	SECTIONAL DENSITY
.284"	0.230

7mm Spitzer SP Hot-Cor®	
Ballistic Coefficient	0.368
COAL Tested	2.550"
Speer Part No.	1623

7mm Spitzer BTSP	
Ballistic Coefficient	0.424
COAL Tested	2.550"
Speer Part No.	1624

Propellant	Case	Primer	Starting Charge Weight (grains)	Starting Charge Muzzle Velocity (feet/sec)	Maximum Charge Weight (grains)	Maximum Charge Muzzle Velocity (feet/sec)
Alliant Reloder 15	Federal	CCI 200	31.5	2037	35.5	2327
Winchester 748	Federal	CCI 250	31.0	2005	35.0	2304
Hodgdon H4895	Federal	CCI 200	30.0	2022	34.0	2294
IMR 3031	Federal	CCI 200	29.0	1967	33.0	2264
Vihtavuori N135	Federal	CCI 200	28.5	1969	32.5	2260
Hodgdon H335	Federal	CCI 250	29.0	1996	33.0	2212
Accurate 2015	Federal	CCI 200	26.0	1976	30.0	2208
Accurate 2230	Federal	CCI 250	26.0	1951	30.0	2188
Alliant Reloder 7	Federal	CCI 200	23.0	1914	27.0	2137

WARNING! Maximum loads should be used with CAUTION • C = Compressed Load

145 GRAINS

DIAMETER	SECTIONAL DENSITY
.284"	0.257

7mm Spitzer BTSP	
Ballistic Coefficient	0.472
COAL Tested	2.550"
Speer Part No.	1628

7mm Spitzer SP Hot-Cor®	
Ballistic Coefficient	0.416
COAL Tested	2.550"
Speer Part No.	1629

7mm Grand Slam® SP	
Ballistic Coefficient	0.353
COAL Tested	2.550"
Speer Part No.	1632

			Starting Charge		Maximum Charge	
Propellant	Case	Primer	Weight (grains)	Muzzle Velocity (feet/sec)	Weight (grains)	Muzzle Velocity (feet/sec)
Alliant Reloder 15	Federal	CCI 200	31.0	2006	35.0	2294
IMR 4895	Federal	CCI 200	29.5	1964	33.5	2237
Vihtavuori N135	Federal	CCI 200	29.0	2002	33.0	2225
Hodgdon H4895	Federal	CCI 200	29.0	1947	33.0	2202
Accurate 2015	Federal	CCI 200	26.0	1908	30.0	2185
Hodgdon H335	Federal	CCI 250	28.0	1920	32.0	2094
IMR 3031	Federal	CCI 200	27.0	1808	31.0	2092
Winchester 748	Federal	CCI 250	30.0	1937	34.0	2066
Accurate 2230	Federal	CCI 250	24.0	1740	28.0	2034
Alliant Reloder 7	Federal	CCI 200	21.0	1726	25.0	1967

WARNING! *Maximum loads should be used with* **CAUTION** • *C = Compressed Load*

30 CARBINE

Alternate Names:	7.62x33mm, 30 M1 Carbine
Parent Cartridge:	32 WSL
Country of Origin:	USA
Year of Introduction:	1941
Designer(s):	Winchester & U.S. Army Ordnance
Governing Body:	SAAMI/CIP

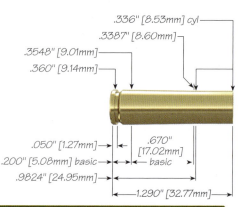

CARTRIDGE CASE DATA

Case Type:	Rimless, slight taper		
Average Case Capacity:	21.0 grains H_2O	Max. Cartridge OAL	1.680 inch
Max. Case Length:	1.290 inch	Primer:	Small rifle
Case Trim to Length:	1.280 inch	RCBS Shell holder:	# 17
Current Manufacturers:	Federal, Hornady, Remington, Winchester, Sellier & Bellot, Aguila, Armscor, Prvi Partizan, Magtech, Wolf, PMC, IMI, PMP		

BALLISTIC DATA

Max. Average Pressure (MAP):	40,000 psi, 40,000 CUP - SAAMI	Test Barrel Length:	7.5 inch
Rifling Twist Rate:	1 turn in 20 inch		
Muzzle velocities are from handloaded pistol ammunition		Bullet Wgt.	Muzzle velocity
		100-grain	1,590 fps
		110-grain	1,420 fps

HISTORICAL NOTES

- Beginning in the early 1950s, thousands of surplus M1 carbines and millions of rounds of 30 M1 Carbine ammunition were sold to U.S. civilian shooters through the Civilian Marksmanship Program.

- With so many M1 carbines in civilian hands, many owners sought to use the 30 Carbine for hunting with no success. The cartridge lacked the range and accuracy for hunting varmints or small game, and did not have sufficient power at any range for hunting deer or other medium game.

- Still, the ammunition manufacturers offered a 110-grain round nose soft point bullet in their catalogs (and still do). Go figure on this one.

- Surprisingly, the 30 Carbine has proven to be a very good cartridge for hunting small game and varmints with handguns.

Interesting Fact

Many people consider the 30 Carbine cartridge useless for anything but plinking. However, these same people consider the 357 Magnum as a powerful choice for personal defense. These folks would be correct: at least in handgun length barrels. The 30 Carbine with a 110-grain bullet tops out around 480 ft-lbs of muzzle energy while the same bullet from a 357 Mag is pushing 700 ft-lbs.

BALLISTIC NOTES

- We recommend that the 30 Carbine be used only for hunting varmints, pests, and small game with the Speer 100-grain Plinker®, or the Speer 110-grain Varminter.
- From a 7.5 inch Ruger Blackhawk revolver barrel, the 30 Carbine is quite capable of a muzzle velocity of 1,589 fps with the Speer 100-grain Plinker SPRN bullet.
- From the same barrel, the Speer 110-grain bullets are capable of 1,418 fps.
- Do not use the 30 Carbine for hunting deer. Not only are the ballistics totally unsuited for such game, doing so is illegal in many states!
- The 30 Carbine fired in a handgun is well-known for the strength of its muzzle blast. Accordingly, we take this opportunity to remind you to wear hearing and eye protection when firing the 30 Carbine cartridge from handguns. If you forget, you will do so only once!

HANDLOADING NOTES

- All traces of lube/oil must be removed from the cartridge case and revolver's chambers before firing. Failure to do so will result in the case sliding back and wedging the case head firmly against the recoil plate in the frame, locking up the cylinder.
- To eliminate this problem, many handloaders use a carbide sizing die which eliminates the need for lubricating cases before resizing.
- The 30 Carbine headspaces on the case mouth.
- Imported 30 Carbine ammunition with a steel case is available on the market. Do not attempt to reload these cases. Sort with a magnet and destroy them.
- All 30 Carbine cartridge cases must be full length resized before reloading them.
- We recommend a taper crimp on all bullets to prevent misfires and bullet elongation problems as the headspace is from the case mouth.
- Keep your 30 Carbine cases trimmed to the correct length to avoid headspace problems.
- Make certain to maintain the correct overall loaded length to prevent cylinder hang ups due to overly long seated bullets.
- Additional information on the 30 Carbine cartridge will be found in the Rifle Data Section.

SAFETY NOTES

SPEER 100-grain Plinker SPRN @ a muzzle velocity of 1,589 fps:
- Maximum vertical altitude @ 90° elevation is 4,386 feet.
- Maximum horizontal distance to first impact with ground @ 32° elevation is 1,999 yards.

100 GRAINS

DIAMETER	SECTIONAL DENSITY
.308"	0.151

30 Plinker® SPRN

Ballistic Coefficient	0.144
COAL Tested	1.620"
Speer Part No.	1805

Propellant	Case	Primer	Starting Charge		Maximum Charge	
			Weight (grains)	Muzzle Velocity (feet/sec)	Weight (grains)	Muzzle Velocity (feet/sec)
Hodgdon H110	IMI Commercial	CCI 450	14.5	1475	15.5	1589
Winchester 296	IMI Commercial	CCI 450	14.5	1415	15.5	1527
Alliant 2400	IMI Commercial	CCI 400	11.7	1385	12.7	1476
IMR 4227	IMI Commercial	CCI 400	13.5	1312	14.5	1417
Vihtavuori N110	IMI Commercial	CCI 400	12.0	1306	13.0 C	1394
IMR 4198	IMI Commercial	CCI 400	14.5	1116	15.5 C	1201
Alliant Unique	IMI Commercial	CCI 400	4.5	938	5.5	1142
Accurate 1680	IMI Commercial	CCI 400	15.0	1077	16.0 C	1126

WARNING! *Maximum loads should be used with* CAUTION • C = Compressed Load

110 GRAINS

DIAMETER	SECTIONAL DENSITY
.308"	0.166

30 Varminter HP
Ballistic Coefficient	0.128
COAL Tested	1.675"
Speer Part No.	1835

30 Carbine TMJ® RN
Ballistic Coefficient	0.179
COAL Tested	1.675"
Speer Part No.	1846

			Starting Charge		Maximum Charge	
Propellant	Case	Primer	Weight (grains)	Muzzle Velocity (feet/sec)	Weight (grains)	Muzzle Velocity (feet/sec)
Hodgdon H110	IMI Commercial	CCI 450	13.7	1315	14.7	1418
IMR 4227	IMI Commercial	CCI 400	13.5	1281	14.5	1387
Winchester 296	IMI Commercial	CCI 450	14.0	1259	15.0	1363
Alliant 2400	IMI Commercial	CCI 400	10.2	1132	11.2	1261
Vihtavuori N110	IMI Commercial	CCI 400	11.5	1164	12.5	1253
IMR 4198	IMI Commercial	CCI 400	14.0	967	15.0	1046
Accurate 1680	IMI Commercial	CCI 400	15.0	973	16.0	1040
Alliant Unique	IMI Commercial	CCI 400	4.5	779	5.5	945

WARNING! *Maximum loads should be used with CAUTION • C = Compressed Load*

30-30 WINCHESTER

Alternate Names:	30-30 Winchester Center Fire (30 WCF), 7.62X51mm R
Parent Cartridge:	38-55 Winchester
Country of Origin:	USA
Year of Introduction:	1895
Designer(s):	Winchester
Governing Body:	SAAMI/CIP

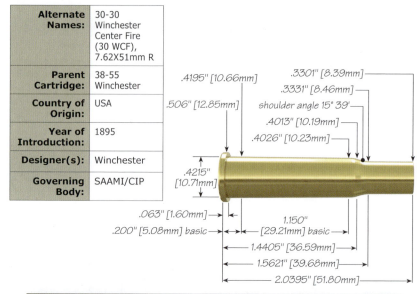

CARTRIDGE CASE DATA

Case Type:	Rimmed, bottleneck
Average Case Capacity:	45.0 grains H_2O
Max. Cartridge OAL	2.550 inch Exceeds Industry Max COAL, due to firearm.
Max. Case Length:	2.0395 inch
Primer:	Large Rifle
Case Trim to Length:	2.030 inch
RCBS Shell holder:	# 2
Current Manufacturers:	Winchester, Federal, Remington, Hornady, Prvi Partizan, Sellier & Bellot

BALLISTIC DATA

Max. Average Pressure (MAP):	42,000 psi, 38,000 CUP - SAAMI
Test Barrel Length:	24 inch
Rifling Twist Rate:	1 turn in 12 inch

Muzzle velocities of factory loaded ammunition	Bullet Wgt.	Muzzle velocity
	150-grain	2,390 fps
	170-grain	2,200 fps

HISTORICAL NOTES

- Surely when Winchester introduced their 30-30 Winchester cartridge in 1895, never in their wildest dreams did they consider it a handgun cartridge!
- In fact, the 30-30 Winchester does make a pretty good handgun cartridge.
- However, it took nearly one hundred years for American sportsmen to discover this, with a little help from Thompson/Center and their Contender pistol.

- If we judged rifle cartridges by their ballistics alone, the 30-30 Winchester would be a distant memory. However, not so in a handgun.
- The rimmed, necked case is ideal for a single-shot handgun, and pointed bullets can be used instead of the flat nose bullets required in lever-action rifles.
- Availability is another good reason for using the "Thutty Thutty" in a handgun. Nearly all domestic ammunition manufacturers list the 30-30 Winchester cartridge in their catalog and all major component bullet makers offer a wide variety of suitable bullets.
- Essentially, the 30-30 Winchester cartridge is an American thing we instinctively understand. For American sportsmen, a 30-30 Winchester pistol makes perfect sense.
- On the other hand, European shooters just do not get it.
- Some observers have predicted the imminent demise of the 30-30 Winchester. They do not get it either.

Interesting Fact

The 30-30 Winchester cartridge was the first sporting cartridge on the American market designed for, and always loaded with, smokeless propellant. Winchester used the old black powder nomenclature system to name their new 30-30 Win. cartridge, although it was never loaded with 30 grains of black powder (or 30 grains of smokeless powder either).

When the 30-30 Winchester was introduced in 1895, the black powder nomenclature system was on the way out, but most shooters were used to it. To avoid confusion, Winchester used the old system to name their new cartridge; the "30" indicated the muzzle velocity in terms of an equivalent amount of black powder. The sportsmen of that day understood, the name stuck and we still use it today.

BALLISTIC NOTES

- Factory loaded 30-30 Winchester ammunition is offered in two bullet weights, 150 and 170-grain. Both of these flat nose soft point bullets have about the same ballistic coefficient as a brick; the 150-grain is the more popular of the two bricks.
- The 30-30 Winchester cartridge is limited to 42,000 psi MAP levels due to its intended use in lever-action rifles with weak actions.
- Although MAP levels are modest by rifle standards, they are higher than most handgun cartridges, and velocity loss from a shorter barrel is not severe.
- The loading data listed was taken from a 14 inch handgun barrel. If you are using a 10 inch barrel you should expect lower muzzle velocities than listed.
- Maximum effective range of the 30-30 Winchester with any bullet weight is approximately 100 yards.

TECHNICAL NOTES

- When loaded for a handgun, the 30-30 Winchester offers several advantages:
  - The case headspaces on the rim making it easy to set and maintain headspace.
  - Case capacity is considerably greater than handgun cartridges.

- A wide variety of pointed bullets can be used instead of the flat nose bullets required in lever-action rifles.
- More bullet weights are available.
- Brass is readily available, inexpensive, and requires no alteration.
- Cases can be neck sized to increase case life.

HANDLOADING NOTES

- The ballistic sweet spot for handgun hunting with the 30-30 Winchester cartridge is the Speer 150-grain Spitzer SP Hot-Cor® handloaded to a muzzle velocity of approximately 2,170 fps. This load is capable of taking most deer at a range of approximately 100 yards.
- Speer bullets of similar weight in flat and round nose configurations can be used for shorter range hunting.
- The Speer 150-grain SPFN can be used to approximate the factory load in handguns.
- We do not recommend handloading bullets heavier than 150 grains as they will not stabilize properly from handguns.
- Do not fire 30-30 Winchester ammunition loaded with Spitzer bullets from a lever-action rifle as doing so may result in a magazine tube explosion
- It is not necessary to heavily crimp bullets for 30-30 Winchester ammunition to be fired from handguns. However, we recommend a light crimp for consistent ignition.
- We suggest neck sizing for 30-30 Win. handloads to be fired from a handgun. Doing so will increase case life, reduce head separations and minimize trimming chores.
- For this reason, we recommend segregating your handgun brass from your rifle brass.
- For handgun barrels shorter than 14 inches, we recommend 130 and 150-grain SPFN bullets.
- Faster burning rate propellants work best for the 30-30 Win. cartridge when fired in a handgun.

SAFETY NOTES

SPEER 150-grain Spitzer SP Hot-Cor @ a muzzle velocity of 2,171 fps:
- Maximum vertical altitude @ 90° elevation is 9,090 feet.
- Maximum horizontal distance to first impact with ground @ 36° elevation is 4,290 yards.

110 GRAINS

DIAMETER	SECTIONAL DENSITY
.308"	0.166

30 Varminter HP

Ballistic Coefficient	0.128
COAL Tested	2.415"
Speer Part No.	1835

			Starting Charge		Maximum Charge	
Propellant	Case	Primer	Weight (grains)	Muzzle Velocity (feet/sec)	Weight (grains)	Muzzle Velocity (feet/sec)
Alliant Reloder 7	Winchester	CCI 200	30.0	2356	34.0	2618
Hodgdon H322	Winchester	CCI 200	31.0	2003	35.0	2373
Winchester 748	Winchester	CCI 250	36.0	2111	40.0 C	2343
Accurate 2015	Winchester	CCI 200	30.0	1974	34.0	2340
IMR 4064	Winchester	CCI 200	33.0	1912	37.0 C	2266
IMR 4895	Winchester	CCI 200	31.0	1884	35.0	2206
Hodgdon H4895	Winchester	CCI 200	30.0	1853	34.0	2165
Vihtavuori N133	Winchester	CCI 200	27.0	1817	31.0	2153

WARNING! *Maximum loads should be used with CAUTION • C = Compressed Load*

125 GRAINS

DIAMETER	SECTIONAL DENSITY
.308"	0.188

30 TNT® HP

Ballistic Coefficient	0.341
COAL Tested	2.740"
Speer Part No.	1986

			Starting Charge		Maximum Charge	
Propellant	Case	Primer	Weight (grains)	Muzzle Velocity (feet/sec)	Weight (grains)	Muzzle Velocity (feet/sec)
Alliant Reloder 7	Winchester	CCI 200	27.0	2095	31.0	2328
Accurate 2460	Winchester	CCI 250	30.0	2037	34.0	2313
Accurate 2520	Winchester	CCI 250	31.0	2060	35.0	2296
Hodgdon H322	Winchester	CCI 200	29.0	1908	33.0	2260
Alliant Reloder 10X	Winchester	CCI 200	26.5	1938	30.5	2131
Hodgdon Varget	Winchester	CCI 200	31.0	1871	35.0	2106
Vihtavuori N140	Winchester	CCI 200	31.0	1868	35.0	2101
Winchester 748	Winchester	CCI 250	31.5	1889	35.5	2096
IMR 4895	Winchester	CCI 200	28.0	1686	32.0	1975
IMR 4064	Winchester	CCI 200	29.0	1634	33.0	1937

WARNING! Maximum loads should be used with CAUTION • C = Compressed Load

130 GRAINS

DIAMETER	SECTIONAL DENSITY
.308"	0.196

30 HP	
Ballistic Coefficient	0.244
COAL Tested	2.730"
Speer Part No.	2005

30 SPFN Hot-Cor®	
Ballistic Coefficient	0.213
COAL Tested	2.550"
Speer Part No.	2007

			Starting Charge		Maximum Charge	
Propellant	Case	Primer	Weight (grains)	Muzzle Velocity (feet/sec)	Weight (grains)	Muzzle Velocity (feet/sec)
Alliant Reloder 7	Winchester	CCI 200	27.0	2095	31.0	2328
Accurate 2460	Winchester	CCI 250	30.0	2037	34.0	2313
Accurate 2520	Winchester	CCI 250	31.0	2060	35.0	2296
Hodgdon H322	Winchester	CCI 200	29.0	1908	33.0	2260
Alliant Reloder 10X	Winchester	CCI 200	26.5	1938	30.5	2131
Hodgdon Varget	Winchester	CCI 200	31.0	1871	35.0	2106
Vihtavuori N140	Winchester	CCI 200	31.0	1868	35.0	2101
Winchester 748	Winchester	CCI 250	31.5	1889	35.5	2096
IMR 4895	Winchester	CCI 200	28.0	1686	32.0	1975
IMR 4064	Winchester	CCI 200	29.0	1634	33.0	1937

WARNING! *Maximum loads should be used with CAUTION • C = Compressed Load*

150 GRAINS

DIAMETER	SECTIONAL DENSITY
.308"	0.226

30 SPFN Hot-Cor®
Ballistic Coefficient	0.255
COAL Tested	2.550"
Speer Part No.	2011

30 Spitzer BTSP
Ballistic Coefficient	0.417
COAL Tested	2.700"
Speer Part No.	2022

30 Spitzer SP Hot-Cor
Ballistic Coefficient	0.377
COAL Tested	2.700"
Speer Part No.	2023

30 Grand Slam SP
Ballistic Coefficient	0.295
COAL Tested	2.700"
Speer Part No.	2026

			Starting Charge		Maximum Charge	
Propellant	Case	Primer	Weight (grains)	Muzzle Velocity (feet/sec)	Weight (grains)	Muzzle Velocity (feet/sec)
Winchester 748	Winchester	CCI 250	33.0	1956	37.0	2171
Alliant Reloder 7	Winchester	CCI 200	25.0	1931	29.0	2144
Hodgdon H322	Winchester	CCI 200	27.0	1780	31.0	2110
Vihtavuori N140	Winchester	CCI 200	30.0	1847	34.0	2078
Accurate 2520	Winchester	CCI 250	31.0	1853	35.0	2066
Hodgdon H335	Winchester	CCI 250	28.0	1841	32.0	2024
Hodgdon Varget	Winchester	CCI 200	29.0	1776	33.0	2009
Alliant Reloder 10X	Winchester	CCI 200	24.0	1732	28.0	1960
IMR 4895	Winchester	CCI 200	27.0	1669	31.0	1955
IMR 4198	Winchester	CCI 200	24.0	1287	26.0	1458

WARNING! Maximum loads should be used with CAUTION • C = Compressed Load

32 SMITH & WESSON LONG

Alternate Names	32 Colt New Police
Parent Cartridge:	32 S&W
Country of Origin:	USA
Year of Introduction:	1902
Designer(s):	Smith & Wesson
Governing Body:	SAAMI/CIP

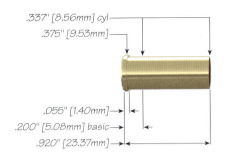

CARTRIDGE CASE DATA

Case Type:	Rimmed, straight		
Average Case Capacity:	14.4 grains H$_2$O	Max. Cartridge OAL	1.280 inch
Max. Case Length:	.920 inch	Primer:	Small Pistol
Case Trim to Length:	.910 inch	RCBS Shell holder:	# 23
Current Manufacturers:	Remington, Winchester, Fiocchi, Sellier & Bellot, Magtech, Aguila, PMC, RUAG		

BALLISTIC DATA

Max. Average Pressure (MAP):	15,000 psi, 12,000 CUP - SAAMI	Test Barrel Length:	5.320 inch unvented, 5.311 inch vented
Rifling Twist Rate:	1 turn in 18.75 inch		
Muzzle velocities of factory loaded ammunition	Bullet Wgt.		Muzzle velocity
	60-grain		970 fps
	98-grain		775 fps

HISTORICAL NOTES

- In the late 1800s, small cheap 32 caliber revolvers chambered for a wide variety of low powered cartridges were a common choice for personal defense. One of the more popular cartridges for this purpose was the 32 S&W Short introduced in 1875 and still in production today (an 85-grain LRN bullet at a muzzle velocity of 680 fps with 87 ft-lbs of energy).
- Ballistic performance obviously was not a consideration in those days.
- Introduction of the more powerful 32 S&W Long in 1902 changed this. The 32 S&W Long became a popular choice for small snub-nosed revolvers, a position it held until the late 1980s.
- Not to be outdone by their rival, in 1903 Colt introduced their 32 Colt New Police cartridge which is identical to the 32 S&W Long. Today, Colt's effort to

steal the thunder of the S&W Long cartridge is long forgotten as is the 32 Colt New Police name.

- In Europe, the 32 S&W Long loaded with a wadcutter bullet became the caliber of choice for International Shooting Union (ISU) rapid fire competition on turning targets.
- In North America, the 32 S&W Long has found a second life as a caliber for Cowboy Action Shooting competition.
- In 1983, Federal teamed with Harrington & Richardson to introduce the new, 32 H&R Magnum cartridge which began to replace the 32 S&W Long for personal defense applications. Federal followed this with the 327 Federal Magnum in 2007.
- Despite the onslaught of 32 magnums, the 32 S&W Long is far from obsolete.
- Today, most domestic and many foreign ammunition manufacturers offer 32 S&W Long ammunition and brass.

Interesting Fact

The term "Saturday Night Special" has long been used as a derogatory term for small, cheap revolvers carried for personal defense. The 38 S&W Short cartridge (NOT the 32 S&W Long) was one of the popular calibers for such guns which explains the anemic ballistics for that cartridge.

BALLISTIC NOTES

- Despite its long popularity for personal defense, the 32 S&W Long cartridge has always been considered a marginal choice for that purpose.
- Factory ammunition is loaded with a 98-grain lead, round nose bullet at a muzzle velocity of 705 fps with a muzzle energy of 108 ft-lbs. (For comparison, the 22 Long Rifle High Velocity hollow point fired from a handgun offers 106 ft-lbs of energy!)
- The 15,000 psi MAP level of the 32 S&W Long was established over 110 years ago when cheap revolvers in this caliber were common. This severely limits the muzzle velocity levels when used in strong, modern revolvers.
- Compare MAP levels of the 32 H&R Long with the MAP levels of the contemporary 32 H&R Magnum (21,000 CUP) and the 327 Federal Magnum (45,000 psi) and you can understand why.
- We recommend using the 32 S&W Long only for plinking, informal target shooting, or for pest elimination.

TECHNICAL NOTES

- The correct bullet diameter for the 32 S&W Long is .314 inch which causes a problem for jacketed bullets which are .312 inch in diameter.
    - Jacketed bullets in .312 inch diameter were designed for the 32-20 WCF, 32 magnum cartridges such as the 32 H&R Magnum, and the 327 Federal Magnum. They were not intended for use in the 32 S&W Long caliber.
    - Being undersized, jacketed bullets are difficult to crimp securely in the 32 S&W Long cartridge (a very important factor for any revolver cartridge).
    - Undersized jacketed bullets will not engrave evenly in the rifling of 32 S&W Long barrels due to the low MAP levels.

- The 32 S&W Long can be safely fired in revolvers chambered for the 32 H&R Magnum and the 327 Federal Magnum.
- The Speer 98-grain Lead Hollow Base Wadcutter is a very good general purpose bullet for the 32 S&W Long. Accuracy from a target gun is excellent.
- In addition, the flat nose of the wadcutter bullet is superior to the lead round nose bullet for energy transfer in dispatching pests and rodents.

HANDLOADING NOTES

- The Speer 98-grain Hollow Base WC must be crimped lightly in the case mouth which will prevent elongation from recoil.
- The muzzle velocity using this bullet can safely be loaded to 777 fps with 131 ft-lbs of muzzle energy which is a 21% increase over the factory LRN bullet loading.
- If necessary, the wadcutter bullet can be loaded with the hollow base forward to improve energy transfer.
- Never load less than the minimum charges shown in the loading data as the small charge of propellant may not be sufficient to push the bullet completely down the barrel.

SAFETY NOTES

SPEER 98-grain HBWC @ a muzzle velocity of 777 fps:
- Maximum vertical altitude @ 90° elevation is 1,476 feet.
- Maximum horizontal distance to first impact with ground @ 29° elevation is 654 yards.

98 GRAINS

DIAMETER	SECTIONAL DENSITY
0.314"	0.142

32 HBWC
Ballistic Coefficient	0.044
COAL Tested	0.920"
Speer Part No.	4600

NOTE: Test Firearm - Walther GSP 4"

			Starting Charge		Maximum Charge	
Propellant	Case	Primer	Weight (grains)	Muzzle Velocity (feet/sec)	Weight (grains)	Muzzle Velocity (feet/sec)
Alliant Bullseye	Remington	CCI 500	1.6	674	1.8	777
Alliant Red Dot	Remington	CCI 500	1.6	703	1.8	771
Hodgdon HP-38	Remington	CCI 500	1.7	689	1.9	765
Alliant Herco	Remington	CCI 500	2.0	700	2.2	758
Accurate No. 5	Remington	CCI 500	2.5	701	2.7	756
Winchester 231	Remington	CCI 500	1.7	672	1.9	739
IMR PB	Remington	CCI 500	1.5	649	1.7	735
Alliant Unique	Remington	CCI 500	1.8	663	2.0	733
Hodgdon Hi-Skor 700-X	Remington	CCI 500	1.5	720	1.7	733

WARNING! Maximum loads should be used with CAUTION • C = Compressed Load

32 H&R MAGNUM

Parent Cartridge:	32 S&W Long
Country of Origin:	USA
Year of Introduction:	1983
Designer(s):	Harrington & Richardson and Federal Cartridge
Governing Body:	SAAMI

CARTRIDGE CASE DATA

Case Type:	Rimmed, straight		
Average Case Capacity:	17.2 grains H_2O	Max. Cartridge OAL	1.350 inch
Max. Case Length:	1.075 inch	Primer:	Small Pistol
Case Trim to Length:	1.065 inch	RCBS Shell holder:	# 23
Current Manufacturers:	Federal, Hornady		

BALLISTIC DATA

Max. Average Pressure (MAP):	21,000 CUP, Piezo not established - SAAMI	Test Barrel Length:	5.500 inch
Rifling Twist Rate:	1 turn in 16 inch		

Muzzle velocities of factory loaded ammunition	Bullet Wgt.	Muzzle velocity
	85-grain	1,120 fps
	95-grain	1,020 fps

HISTORICAL NOTES

- For decades, the 32 S&W Long was tolerated as the minimum caliber for personal defense simply because there was nothing else to replace it.
- This changed in 1983 when Federal teamed with Harrington & Richardson to introduce the new 32 H&R Magnum cartridge.
- Overnight, the anemic ballistics of the 32 S&W Long became obsolete.
- Manufacturers of revolvers scrambled to develop new and stronger guns to take advantage of the new cartridges' ballistics.
- Despite the success of the new cartridge, Remington, Winchester, and other major ammunition makers have ignored the 32 H&R Magnum cartridge in favor of sticking to the old 32 S&W Short and Long cartridges.

- Today, Federal, and Hornady remain the sole manufacturers of this caliber. The cartridge remains a non-event in the European market.

Interesting Fact

The 32 H&R Magnum was the first 32-caliber magnum handgun cartridge to be offered on the commercial ammunition market. It was a game changer.

BALLISTIC NOTES

- Despite its long popularity, the 32 S&W Long cartridge had always been considered a marginal choice for personal defense.

- The 32 H&R Magnum changed that by using a longer and stronger cartridge case with a MAP level of 21,000 CUP which was a 43% increase over that of the 32 S&W Long.

- The longer cartridge case of the 32 H&R Magnum prevented it from being chambered in 32 S&W Long revolvers, however 32 S&W Long ammunition could be fired safely in revolvers chambered for the 32 H&R Magnum for practice and training.

TECHNICAL NOTES

- The correct bullet diameter for the 32 H&R Magnum is .312 inches which makes it suitable for jacketed bullets as well as .314 inch diameter lead bullets.

- The Speer 98-grain lead hollow base wadcutter is a very good general purpose bullet for plinking and informal target shooting with the 32 H&R Magnum. Accuracy potential is excellent, noise level is low and recoil is mild.

- However, attempting to increase the muzzle velocity of this bullet over the maximum 843 fps listed in the data will result in severe leading in the bore.

HANDLOADING NOTES

- The Speer 98-grain wadcutter bullet must be crimped firmly in the case mouth to prevent elongation from recoil.

- This bullet can safely be loaded to a muzzle velocity of 843 fps with 155 ft-lbs of muzzle energy.

- If necessary, the wadcutter bullet can be loaded with the hollow base forward to improve energy transfer.

- Never load less than the minimum charges shown in the loading data as the small charge of propellant may not be sufficient to push the bullet completely down the barrel.

SAFETY NOTES

SPEER 98-grain HBWC @ a muzzle velocity of 843 fps:
- Maximum vertical altitude @ 90° elevation is 1,551 feet.
- Maximum horizontal distance to first impact with ground @ 29° elevation is 682 yards.

98 GRAINS

DIAMETER	SECTIONAL DENSITY
.314"	0.142

32 HBWC	
Ballistic Coefficient	0.044
COAL Tested	1.075"
Speer Part No.	4600

			Starting Charge		Maximum Charge	
Propellant	Case	Primer	Weight (grains)	Muzzle Velocity (feet/sec)	Weight (grains)	Muzzle Velocity (feet/sec)
Accurate No. 5	Federal	CCI 500	3.2	783	3.4	843
Alliant Unique	Federal	CCI 500	2.8	770	3.0	814
IMR PB	Federal	CCI 500	2.2	760	2.4	812
Alliant Bullseye	Federal	CCI 500	2.1	752	2.3	810
Alliant Red Dot	Federal	CCI 500	2.1	735	2.3	805
Hodgdon HP-38	Federal	CCI 500	2.3	740	2.5	801
Hodgdon Hi-Skor 700-X	Federal	CCI 500	2.0	735	2.2	792
Alliant Green Dot	Federal	CCI 500	2.3	751	2.5	791
Winchester 231	Federal	CCI 500	2.2	742	2.4	778

WARNING! Maximum loads should be used with CAUTION • C = Compressed Load

327 FEDERAL MAGNUM

Parent Cartridge:	32 H&R Magnum
Country of Origin:	USA
Year of Introduction:	2007
Designer(s):	Federal Cartridge Co.
Governing Body:	SAAMI

.337" [8.56mm] cyl
.375" [9.53mm]
.055" [1.40mm]
.200" [5.08mm] basic
1.200" [30.48mm]

CARTRIDGE CASE DATA

Case Type:	Rimmed, Straight		
Average Case Capacity:	19.6 grains H₂O	Max. Cartridge OAL	1.475 inch
Max. Case Length:	1.200 inch	Primer:	Small Magnum Pistol
Case Trim to Length:	1.190 inch	RCBS Shell holder:	# 23
Current Manufacturers:	Federal, Buffalo Bore, Starline		

BALLISTIC DATA

Max. Average Pressure (MAP):	45,000 psi, CUP is not established - SAAMI	Test Barrel Length:	5 inch unvented, 5.591 inch vented
Rifling Twist Rate:	1 turn in 16 inch		

Muzzle velocity of factory loaded ammunition	Bullet Wgt.	Muzzle velocity
	85-grain	1,400 fps
	100-grain	1,500 fps

HISTORICAL NOTES

- In 1878, the 32 Smith & Wesson cartridge was introduced. By the standards of that era, ballistics of the 32 S&W were contemporary. By today's standards, they were pathetic (see chart in Ballistics Notes). However, ballistic performance in those days was not so important.

- Smith & Wesson introduced the 32 S&W Long cartridge in 1902. Ballistic improvement was marginal at best. Today, we wonder why S&W bothered, but minor improvements were acceptable then.

- And there they stayed for the next 81 years until the 32 H&R Magnum was introduced in 1983. The new cartridge offered ballistic performance a quantum level above the 32 S&W Long (rather easily done), however it still lacked power for personal defense.

- Federal realized that plenty of ballistic potential remained in 32 caliber cartridges. Accordingly, the 327 Federal Magnum cartridge was developed to take maximum advantage of it.
- For the first time, a 32 caliber revolver cartridge existed that could offer serious ballistic performance for personal defense.

Interesting Fact

The 327 Federal Magnum is the *second* handgun cartridge with the Federal name. Pop quiz: Name the first. (See below for answer).

BALLISTIC NOTES

- Here is a brief summary of factory loaded 32 revolver cartridge ballistics all taken from a 4 inch revolver barrel:

Caliber	Bullet Wt. (grs.)	Muzzle Velocity (fps)	Muzzle Energy (ft-lbs)
32 S&W (Short)	85 LRN	680	89
32 S&W Long	98 LRN	705	08
32 H&R Magnum	85 JHP	1,120	235
327 Federal Mag.	85 JHP	1,400	370
327 Federal Mag.	100 JSP	1,500	500

- Note that the 327 Federal Magnum 85-grain bullet has a muzzle energy equal to or greater than the 9mm Luger, 38 Special+P, and 45 Colt.
- The 327 Federal Magnum 100-grain bullet has more muzzle energy than the 9mm Luger, 38 Special+P, 40 S&W, 10mm Auto, 45 Auto, and 45 Colt!

HANDLOADING NOTES

- The longer cartridge case of the 327 Federal Magnum prevents it from being chambered in 32 H&R Magnum and 32 S&W Long caliber revolvers.
- However, 32 S&W Long and 32 H&R Magnum ammunition can be fired safely in revolvers chambered for the 327 Federal Magnum.
- Never load less than the minimum charges shown in the loading data as the small charge of propellant may not be sufficient to push the bullet completely down the barrel.

Answer to pop quiz question: The first handgun cartridge to carry the Federal name was the 9mm Federal. It was a revolver cartridge developed for the City Police of Quebec. This cartridge is now obsolete.

SAFETY NOTES

SPEER 100-grain Gold Dot ®HP @ a muzzle velocity of 1,500 fps:
- Maximum vertical altitude @ 90° elevation is 4,779 feet.
- Maximum horizontal distance to first impact with ground @ 33° elevation is 2,203 yards.

GOLD DOT

100 GRAINS

DIAMETER	SECTIONAL DENSITY
.312"	0.147

32 GDHP

Ballistic Coefficient	0.137
COAL Tested	1.465"
Speer Part No.	3990

			Starting Charge		Maximum Charge	
Propellant	Case	Primer	Weight (grains)	Muzzle Velocity (feet/sec)	Weight (grains)	Muzzle Velocity (feet/sec)
Ramshot Enforcer	Federal	Federal 200	12.5	1429	13.5 C	1547
Accurate No. 9	Federal	Federal 200	11.0	1406	13.0	1545
Alliant 2400	Federal	Federal 200	10.5	1333	12.5 C	1533
Winchester 296	Federal	Federal 200	13.5	1412	14.5 C	1524
Hodgdon H110	Federal	Federal 200	13.0	1377	14.0 C	1502
Alliant Power Pistol	Federal	Federal 200	6.5	1300	8.0	1468
Vihtavuori N110	Federal	Federal 200	11.0 C	1357	12.0 C	1465
Hodgdon LONGSHOT	Federal	Federal 200	6.0	1221	7.0	1360

WARNING! *Maximum loads should be used with CAUTION • C = Compressed Load*

32-20 WINCHESTER (CONTENDER ONLY)

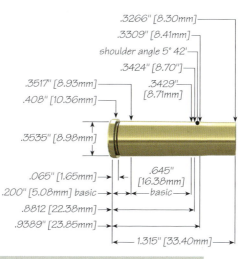

Alternate Names:	32 Winchester Center Fire, 32 WCF, 308-20 Contender
Parent Cartridge:	Original design
Country of Origin:	USA
Year of Introduction:	1882
Designer(s):	Winchester
Governing Body:	SAAMI/CIP

This data is applicable to the Thompson/Center Contender Only.

The bore diameter of the T/C Contender is .308, not standard for the 32-20 Winchester. These loads are at pressures far exceeding those for the caliber, read on for more information.

CARTRIDGE CASE DATA

Case Type:	Rimmed, bottleneck		
Average Case Capacity:	22.0 grains H_2O	Max. Cartridge OAL	1.592 inch for standard loads, exceeded for this data
Max. Case Length:	1.315 inch	Primer:	Small Pistol used in this load data
Case Trim to Length:	1.305 inch	RCBS Shell holder:	# 1
Current Manufacturers:	Winchester, Remington		

BALLISTIC DATA

Max. Average Pressure (MAP):	16,000 CUP, Exceeded in the data reported here. Piezo not established for this cartridge - SAAMI	Test Barrel Length:	10 inch
Rifling Twist Rate:	1 turn in 20 inch		
Muzzle velocities of factory loaded ammunition	Bullet Wgt.		Muzzle velocity
	100-grain		1,200 fps (20 inch barrel)

HISTORICAL NOTES

- By the late 1970s, the 32-20 Winchester cartridge was near death.
- Then, the metallic silhouette competitors discovered it was a good choice for the Field Pistol class events using Thompson/Center Contender pistols.
- Still, it may come as a surprise that the 32-20 Winchester cartridge remains in the current product lines of both Remington and Winchester. Factory loads are not recommended for use in the T/C.
- It seems the 135-year old 32-20 Winchester cartridge has beat the odds again as it looks to remain in production well into the 21st century.

BALLISTIC NOTES

- Before the 32-20 Winchester could be used for metallic silhouette competition, several major problems had to be solved.
  - The 32-20 Winchester cartridge was designed for .312 inch diameter lead bullets.
  - Metallic silhouette shooters needed to use .308 inch diameter jacketed bullets, so they resized the 32-20 Winchester case neck down to accept .308 inch diameter jacketed bullets.
  - Thompson/Center made their Contender barrels with a .308 inch bore diameter and chambered for the modified 32-20 cartridge case.
  - The strength of the modern Contender pistol allowed the 16,000 CUP MAP level to be increased to obtain higher muzzle velocity.
- With these changes, the 32-20 Winchester silhouette cartridge was born. It proved very effective on 100 yard silhouettes.

TECHNICAL NOTES

- The 32-20 Winchester cartridge is a rimmed design with a short, shallow, 5° shoulder angle and a 1.2 caliber neck length. This configuration serves perfectly well for a silhouette cartridge in the Contender pistol.
- The modified "308-20 Contender" cartridge works very well with Speer 110-grain bullets such as the Varminter HP.

HANDLOADING NOTES

- All new 32-20 cases will need to be neck sized to .307 inches using a small diameter expander ball prior to loading.
- We recommend neck sizing the modified 32-20 Winchester cases to extend case life and reduce trimming chores.
- Do not substitute lead bullets for the jacketed bullet loads listed for this cartridge.

SAFETY NOTES

SPEER 110-grain Spire SP bullet @ a muzzle velocity of 1,813 fps:

- Maximum vertical altitude @ 90° elevation is 6,492 feet.
- Maximum horizontal distance to first impact with ground @ 34° elevation is 3,027 yards.
- These loads are intended for use in Thompson/Center Contender pistols ONLY. Do not use these loads in any other firearm.

100 GRAINS

DIAMETER	SECTIONAL DENSITY
.308"	0.151

30 Plinker® SPRN

Ballistic Coefficient	0.144
COAL Tested	1.710"
Speer Part No.	1805

			Starting Charge		Maximum Charge	
Propellant	Case	Primer	Weight (grains)	Muzzle Velocity (feet/sec)	Weight (grains)	Muzzle Velocity (feet/sec)
Hodgdon H110	Winchester	CCI 500	16.0	1734	17.0	1908
Winchester 296	Winchester	CCI 500	15.5	1646	16.5	1897
Accurate No. 9	Winchester	CCI 500	13.0	1666	14.0	1833
IMR 4227	Winchester	CCI 500	15.5	1637	16.5 C	1831
Alliant 2400	Winchester	CCI 500	12.0	1595	13.0	1793
Hodgdon HS-6	Winchester	CCI 500	9.1	1606	10.1	1713
Alliant Herco	Winchester	CCI 500	8.1	1587	9.1	1712
IMR 4198	Winchester	CCI 500	17.0	1527	18.0 C	1683
IMR SR 4759	Winchester	CCI 500	12.0	1326	13.0 C	1582

WARNING! *Maximum loads should be used with* **CAUTION** • *C = Compressed Load*

110 GRAINS

DIAMETER	SECTIONAL DENSITY
.308"	0.166

30 Varminter HP
Ballistic Coefficient	0.128
COAL Tested	1.710"
Speer Part No.	1835

30 Carbine TMJ® RN
Ballistic Coefficient	0.179
COAL Tested	1.710"
Speer Part No.	1846

			Starting Charge		Maximum Charge	
Propellant	Case	Primer	Weight (grains)	Muzzle Velocity (feet/sec)	Weight (grains)	Muzzle Velocity (feet/sec)
Hodgdon H110	Winchester	CCI 500	15.0	1598	16.0	1813
Winchester 296	Winchester	CCI 500	14.5	1610	15.5	1765
Accurate No. 9	Winchester	CCI 500	12.5	1579	13.5	1739
IMR 4227	Winchester	CCI 500	15.0	1540	16.0	1730
Alliant 2400	Winchester	CCI 500	11.0	1371	12.0	1594
IMR 4198	Winchester	CCI 500	16.0	1375	17.0 C	1576
IMR SR 4759	Winchester	CCI 500	12.0	1279	13.0 C	1566
Alliant Herco	Winchester	CCI 500	7.4	1472	8.4	1552
Hodgdon HS-6	Winchester	CCI 500	8.1	1484	9.1	1539

WARNING! *Maximum loads should be used with CAUTION • C = Compressed Load*

130 GRAINS

DIAMETER	SECTIONAL DENSITY
.308"	0.196

30 HP	
Ballistic Coefficient	0.244
COAL Tested	1.910"
Speer Part No.	2005

30 SPFN Hot-Cor®	
Ballistic Coefficient	0.213
COAL Tested	1.865"
Speer Part No.	2007

			Starting Charge		Maximum Charge	
Propellant	Case	Primer	Weight (grains)	Muzzle Velocity (feet/sec)	Weight (grains)	Muzzle Velocity (feet/sec)
Hodgdon H110	Winchester	CCI 500	14.0	1479	15.0	1664
IMR 4227	Winchester	CCI 500	14.5	1479	15.5 C	1645
Accurate No. 9	Winchester	CCI 500	12.0	1476	13.0	1632
Winchester 296	Winchester	CCI 500	13.5	1443	14.5	1602
IMR SR 4759	Winchester	CCI 500	12.0	1256	13.0	1489
Alliant 2400	Winchester	CCI 500	10.5	1234	11.5	1488
IMR 4198	Winchester	CCI 500	15.0	1339	16.0 C	1453
Alliant Herco	Winchester	CCI 500	6.8	1270	7.8	1387
Hodgdon HS-6	Winchester	CCI 500	7.6	1246	8.6	1340

WARNING! *Maximum loads should be used with CAUTION • C = Compressed Load*

380 AUTOMATIC

Alternate Names:	9mm Browning Short/Court/Corto/Kurz, 9x17mm
Parent Cartridge:	Original design
Country of Origin:	Belgium
Year of Introduction:	1908
Designer(s):	John Browning
Governing Body:	SAAMI/CIP

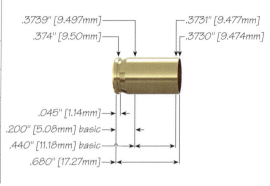

CARTRIDGE CASE DATA			
Case Type:	Rimless, straight		
Average Case Capacity:	12.6 grains H$_2$O	Max. Cartridge OAL	.984 inch
Max. Case Length:	.680 inch	Primer:	Small Pistol
Case Trim to Length:	.670 inch	RCBS Shell holder:	# 10
Current Manufacturers:	CCI/Speer, Federal, Remington, Winchester, Cor-Bon, Fiocchi, Magtech, Aguila, Prvi Partizan, Sellier & Bellot, Armscor, PMC		

BALLISTIC DATA			
Max. Average Pressure (MAP):	21,500 psi, 17,000 CUP - SAAMI	Test Barrel Length:	3.750 inch
Rifling Twist Rate:	1 turn in 16 inch		
Muzzle velocities of factory loaded ammunition	Bullet Wgt.		Muzzle velocity
	85 to 90-grain		1,000 fps
	95-grain		955 fps

HISTORICAL NOTES

- In 1908, most gun owners considered a 32 caliber pistol a "big gun."
- Consequently, when John Browning's Pocket Pistol in 380 Auto was introduced in that year, it created quite a stir.
- Most pistols designed for the 32 Auto cartridge could be adapted easily for the new 380 Auto cartridge which encouraged other handgun manufacturers such as Mauser, Walther, Beretta, Remington, and Savage to introduce pistols in the new caliber.
- In Europe, the 380 Auto is called the 9mm Kurz/Corto/Court/ or 9x17mm.

Interesting Fact

While the 9x17mm Short was never taken into military service by any European country, it did enter U.S. military service during World War II in the form of a special 380 caliber pistol for general officers. Of course, ammunition had to be made available for these guns, so it was procured from commercial sources under military contract. A 95-grain FMJ RN bullet was used.

BALLISTIC NOTES

- Compared to the anemic ballistics of the 32 Auto cartridge, the 380 Auto is a quantum level improvement. Muzzle energy levels of the 9mm Short are 47% higher than the 32 Auto.

- Despite this, most European law enforcement agencies were not interested in handgun stopping power and so they stuck to the familiar 32 Auto or the (7.65mm Browning as it is called in Europe). As a result, the popularity of the 9mm Short in Europe grew slowly.

- However, U.S. shooters and police officers have always been more concerned with the stopping power of a cartridge. After a slow start in the U.S. market, by the 1970s the 380 Auto had become a popular choice for a backup gun by many police officers and for home defense.

- At that time, American manufacturers offered only one loading in 380 Auto—a 95-grain full metal jacket round nose bullet at a muzzle velocity of 950-960 fps. Muzzle energy was approximately 190 ft-lbs.

- In the mid-1970s, Federal introduced a 90-grain JHP bullet with a muzzle velocity of 1,000 fps. This load substantially upgraded the ballistic performance of the 380 Auto, although it did not feed reliably from some pistols.

- Today, the 380 Auto is offered by nearly every major ammunition maker. Most manufacturers of handguns offer several models of pistol in this caliber.

- The 380 Auto is a fine choice for personal defense.

TECHNICAL NOTES

- The 380 Auto cartridge does not share the semi-rimmed case design favored by John Browning for his 25 Auto and 32 Auto pistol cartridges. Rather, it is a rimless, straight sided case that looks, at first glance, very much like a short 9mm Luger cartridge case.

- For this reason, many people consider the 380 Auto cartridge case to be a short 9mm Luger. This is not correct as the rim, head, and interior taper of the 380 Auto case differs substantially from those of the 9mm Luger.

- Ammunition in 380 Auto should not be fired from a 9mm Luger pistol.

HANDLOADING NOTES

- Bullet weights for the 380 Auto range from 80 to 100 grains with 90 and 95 grains being the most common.

- Speer offers two bullets that have been designed specifically for the 380 Auto cartridge: a 90-grain Gold Dot HP and a 95-grain TMJ.

- Although 380 Auto and 9mm Luger bullets share a common diameter, the two are not interchangeable. The heavy bullets for the 9mm Luger are too long for the short 380 Auto cartridge case, while the light 380 Auto bullets will not operate 9mm pistols.

- Most pistols in 380 Auto are blowback operated (unlocked breech). Fired cases from such guns are frequently damaged by the violent extraction or ejection forces. For this reason, we recommend that you carefully inspect all fired cases before reloading them. Discard any that are dented, split, scratched, cracked or have damaged rims.
- Finish your reloads with a light taper crimp on the case mouth to hold the bullet securely, and to improve shot start and feeding reliability.
- Do not seat bullets deeper than listed in the reloading data. Do not seat bullets out beyond maximum overall loaded length.
- Do not attempt to reload 380 Auto empty cartridge cases with Berdan primers. Destroy them.
- Some 380 Auto pistols may experience problems feeding hollow point bullets. Should that occur, we recommend adjusting the overall loaded length slightly to compensate. If that fails to solve the problem, try another bullet type or weight.
- Never load less than the minimum charges shown in the loading data as the small charge of propellant may not be sufficient to push the bullet completely down the barrel.

SAFETY NOTES

SPEER 95-grain TMJ® RN @ a muzzle velocity of 1,027 fps:
- Maximum vertical altitude @ 90° elevation is 3,621 feet.
- Maximum horizontal distance to first impact with ground @ 33° elevation is 2,066 yards.

GOLD DOT

90 GRAINS	DIAMETER	SECTIONAL DENSITY
	.355"	0.102

380 GDHP	
Ballistic Coefficient	0.101
COAL Tested	0.970"
Speer Part No.	3992

			Starting Charge		Maximum Charge	
Propellant	Case	Primer	Weight (grains)	Muzzle Velocity (feet/sec)	Weight (grains)	Muzzle Velocity (feet/sec)
Accurate No. 2 Improved	Winchester	CCI 500	3.5	982	3.9	1056
Accurate No. 7	Winchester	CCI 500	6.3	941	7.0 C	1050
Vihtavuori N320	Winchester	CCI 500	3.1	953	3.4	1044
Alliant Unique	Winchester	CCI 500	4.1	877	4.6 C	1034
Winchester 231	Winchester	CCI 500	3.6	978	4.0	1031
Alliant Power Pistol	Winchester	CCI 500	4.4	944	4.8 C	1020
Hodgdon H. Universal	Winchester	CCI 500	3.8	821	4.3	994
Hodgdon Hi-Skor 700-X	Winchester	CCI 500	3.2	812	3.6	988
Accurate No. 5	Winchester	CCI 500	4.8	845	5.4	984
Alliant Bullseye	Winchester	CCI 500	3.0	885	3.4	981
Hodgdon TITEGROUP	Winchester	CCI 500	2.8	885	3.2	976
Winchester WSL	Winchester	CCI 500	3.2	825	3.6	972
Alliant BE 86	Federal	Federal 100	3.2	804	3.9	963
Alliant American Select	Winchester	CCI 500	2.8	841	3.3	955
Winchester AutoComp	Federal	Federal 100	3.5	863	3.9	954
Hodgdon CFE Pistol	Federal	Federal 100	3.4	861	3.8	948
Alliant Sport Pistol	Federal	Federal 100	2.4	773	2.9	914

WARNING! *Maximum loads should be used with CAUTION • C = Compressed Load*

95 GRAINS

DIAMETER	SECTIONAL DENSITY
.355"	0.108

380 Auto TMJ® RN

Ballistic Coefficient	0.131
COAL Tested	0.970"
Speer Part No.	4001

Propellant	Case	Primer	Starting Charge Weight (grains)	Starting Charge Muzzle Velocity (feet/sec)	Maximum Charge Weight (grains)	Maximum Charge Muzzle Velocity (feet/sec)
Winchester 231	Winchester	CCI 500	3.6	945	4.0	1027
Accurate No. 7	Winchester	CCI 500	5.9	971	6.5	1019
Hodgdon Hi-Skor 700-X	Winchester	CCI 500	3.1	912	3.4	1012
Alliant Unique	Winchester	CCI 500	3.8	918	4.2	1006
Vihtavuori N320	Winchester	CCI 500	3.0	893	3.4	998
Alliant Bullseye	Winchester	CCI 500	3.0	874	3.3	990
Hodgdon H. Universal	Winchester	CCI 500	3.6	854	4.1	979
Alliant Power Pistol	Winchester	CCI 500	4.2	883	4.7	974
Alliant BE 86	Federal	Federal 100	3.5	870	4.0	970
Accurate No. 2	Winchester	CCI 500	3.3	887	3.7	965
Winchester WSL	Winchester	CCI 500	3.1	849	3.5	960
Winchester AutoComp	Federal	Federal 100	3.5	852	4.0	960
Accurate No. 5	Winchester	CCI 500	4.6	871	5.0	949
Hodgdon CFE Pistol	Federal	Federal 100	3.5	856	3.9	943
Alliant American Select	Winchester	CCI 500	2.8	824	3.3	935
Hodgdon TITEGROUP	Winchester	CCI 500	2.7	851	3.1	930
Alliant Sport Pistol	Federal	Federal 100	2.5	799	3.0	928

WARNING: Maximum loads should be used with CAUTION • C = Compressed Load

9mm LUGER

Alternate Names:	9x19mm Luger, 9x19mm Parabellum, 9x19mm P08, 9 Para
Parent Cartridge:	7.65mm Luger
Country of Origin:	Germany
Year of Introduction:	1902
Designer(s):	DWM
Governing Body:	SAAMI/CIP

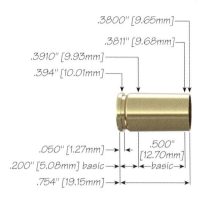

CARTRIDGE CASE DATA

Case Type:	Rimless, slight taper		
Average Case Capacity:	14.5 grains H$_2$O	Max. Cartridge OAL	1.169 inch
Max. Case Length:	.754 inch	Primer:	Small Pistol
Case Trim to Length:	.744 inch	RCBS Shell holder:	# 16
Current Manufacturers:	CCI/Speer, Federal, Remington, Winchester, Hornady, Fiocchi, Magtech, Sellier & Bellot, Lapua, Prvi Partizan, Cor-Bon, PMC, IMI, RUAG		

BALLISTIC DATA

Max. Average Pressure (MAP):	35,000 psi, 33,000 CUP - SAAMI	Test Barrel Length:	4.000 inch
Rifling Twist Rate:	1 turn in 10 inch		

Muzzle velocities of factory loaded ammunition	Bullet Wgt.	Muzzle velocity
	115-grain	1,190 fps
	124-grain	1,140 fps
	135-grain	1,010 fps
	147-grain	990 fps

HISTORICAL NOTES

- The 9mm Luger or 9x19mm Parabellum cartridge can trace its history back to 1902 when Georg Luger redesigned his 7.65mm Luger cartridge case to accept a 9mm bullet.
- The new 9x19mm cartridge and Luger pistol were adopted by the German Navy in 1904.

- The German Army followed suit in 1908.
- The 9mm Luger served the German military forces well through two World Wars in both pistols and submachine guns.
- When NATO was formed in the early 1950s, the 9mm Luger cartridge was adopted as the standard pistol cartridge for all NATO military services. The U.S. military deferred, preferring to stick with the 45 Auto cartridge until 1985 when the 9mm cartridge was finally adopted along with the Beretta M9 pistol.
- Prior to that time, the 9mm Luger was mostly ignored by American sportsmen. With the exception of some souvenir Lugers and P38 pistols from World War II, there were relatively few pistols in 9mm caliber in the U.S. Few of the domestic handgun manufacturers made guns in this chambering.
- This changed overnight with the U.S. military adoption of the 9mm cartridge. Handgun makers rushed to bring out 9mm caliber pistols, ammunition makers beefed up their 9mm product lines and American law enforcement agencies adopted it in droves.
- Today, the 9mm Luger cartridge is by far the most popular pistol cartridge in the world. Every major ammunition manufacturer and most military arsenals make it. Indeed, it is hard to find a major military organization or law enforcement agency that does not use it.
- How about Russia? In the early 2000s, the Russian military made a momentous decision; the 9mm Luger cartridge was taken into Russian military service along with the new "Grach" (crow) pistol for it.
- In the U.S., this cartridge is called the 9mm Luger. In Europe (and in military service) it is called the 9x19mm Luger or 9x19 Parabellum.

What Is The Meaning of "Parabellum"?

The German firm of Deutsche Waffen und Munition Fabrik (DWM) was one of the first companies to manufacture the new 9x19mm cartridge. The company telegraphic address was "Parabellum" which is Latin meaning "for war." The surname stuck to the cartridge until recently.

Interesting Fact

When the Russian military took the 9mm Luger cartridge into military service in the early 2000s, it was the first time the Russian military adopted a cartridge that was not designed for and unique to the Russian military.

BALLISTIC NOTES

- There are three "standard" loads for the 9mm Luger cartridge:
  - A 115-grain bullet at a muzzle velocity of approximately 1,190 fps.
  - A 124-grain bullet at a muzzle velocity of approximately 1,150 fps.
  - A 147-grain bullet at a muzzle velocity of 990 fps (subsonic).
- Bullets may be full metal jacket (FMJ) designs with a round nose (RN), semi-round nose (SRN) or flat nose (FN) ogive. Jacketed hollow point (JHP) and jacketed soft point (JSP) designs are popular as well.
- The 9mm NATO military load consists of a 124-grain FMJ RN bullet at a muzzle velocity of 1,250 fps.
- 9mm Luger +P ammunition with similar ballistics to the 9mm NATO cartridge have been developed for law enforcement use. These loads offer

- a 10% improvement in muzzle energy over the standard load at the cost of increased wear on the handguns.
- Many military pistols and submachine guns in 9mm Luger are not designed to feed or function with JHP or JSP bullets. In addition, such guns may not cycle reliably with mild loads.
- Speer offers two outstanding 115-grain bullets for the 9mm Luger cartridge:
  - A Total Metal Jacket Round Nose (TMJ® RN) which is a great choice for duplicating the factory load.
  - A Gold Dot Hollow Point (GDHP) which is an unbeatable choice for personal defense.
- For shooters who prefer a heavier bullet (many 9mm Luger caliber guns function better with this bullet weight), Speer has you covered with two 124-grain 9mm choices:
  - A Total Metal Jacket (TMJ)
  - A Gold Dot Hollow Point (GDHP)
- When 9mm Luger 124-grain ammunition is fired from a carbine or submachine gun with a barrel 10 inches or more in length, muzzle velocities can be expected to increase by approximately 15-20% over those from handguns. MAP will not increase.
- The recent surge in ownership of suppressors by sportsmen has created a need for subsonic ammunition in 9mm Luger. Speer has you covered here as well with two 147-grain bullets to choose from that are designed for subsonic loads:
  - A Gold Dot Hollow Point (GDHP)
  - A Total Metal Jacket Flat Nose (TMJ FN)
  - Use of the 147-grain bullets in barrels exceeding 10 inches is not recommended because of the long bearing surface and possibility of a bullet-in-bore.

TECHNICAL NOTES

- The 9mm Luger cartridge case is a rimless, tapered body design that headspaces on the case mouth.
- The 9mm Luger cartridge case is a limited capacity design that requires fast burning propellants as there is insufficient space for slower burning propellants. The good news is that it is virtually impossible to double charge a 9mm Luger case.
- Most 9mm Luger caliber pistols are recoil operated. The 9mm Luger cartridge is too powerful for straight blowback operation in a handgun. An exception is the roller-delayed blowback operated pistols from H&K. On the other hand, most 9mm Luger carbines and submachine guns are blowback operated.
- Most 9mm Luger caliber carbines and submachine guns work best with 124-grain full metal jacket bullets loaded to maximum muzzle velocity.
- The correct bullet diameter for the 9mm Luger is .355 inch. Note that this is the same diameter of bullet for the 380 Auto. However, the lightweight 90 to 95-grain bullets for the 380 Auto will not reliably feed or function in the 9mm Luger.
- Old 9mm Luger wartime German military ammunition is Berdan primed with a corrosive priming compound. We do not recommend attempting to fire or salvage such old ammunition.

HANDLOADING NOTES

- Recently, 9mm Luger ammunition with steel cartridge cases has been imported from Russia. We strongly recommend against attempting to reload these cases even though they may have Boxer primers.

- Some cartridge cases may be nickel-plated to assist extraction. The nickel-plating process may cause hydrogen embrittlement of the case mouths. After four to six reloads, expect case mouth splits. When this occurs, avoid the temptation to try to get one more loading out of such cases. Destroy them immediately.

- Ex-military 9mm Luger cartridge cases may have crimped primers. As these cases are hard to deprime, decapping pins may break with depressing regularity. For this reason, we recommend that you keep a supply of these inexpensive parts on hand as replacements.

- You may encounter seating difficulties when loading long, heavy 9mm bullets. The inside taper of some brands of 9mm Luger cases may not allow seating of such bullets to a depth that will meet the overall loaded length dimension. In such instances, switching case brands may solve this problem as the inside taper of 9mm cases varies from one brand to the next.

- Never load less than the minimum charges shown in the loading data as the small charge of propellant may not be sufficient to push the bullet completely down the barrel.

SAFETY NOTES

SPEER 124-grain TMJ RN @ a muzzle velocity of 1,238 fps:

- Maximum vertical altitude @ 90° elevation is 4,398 feet.

- Maximum horizontal distance to first impact with ground @ 33° elevation is 2,043 yards.

- These loads were developed and tested for safe use in HANDGUNS. Not all loads may be suitable for use in carbines or rifles chambered for this cartridge. When loading for carbine or rifle, choose the loads that developed the highest velocity in a handgun, load a few for test, ensuring bullet exit from the barrel. Pulling bullets is one of the least rewarding experiences in handloading.

115 GRAINS

DIAMETER	SECTIONAL DENSITY
.355"	0.130

9mm GDHP
Ballistic Coefficient	0.125
COAL Tested	1.125"
Speer Part No.	3994

9mm TMJ® RN
Ballistic Coefficient	0.151
COAL Tested	1.135"
Speer Part No.	3995

			Starting Charge		Maximum Charge	
Propellant	Case	Primer	Weight (grains)	Muzzle Velocity (feet/sec)	Weight (grains)	Muzzle Velocity (feet/sec)
Alliant Blue Dot	Speer	CCI 500	7.7	1161	8.5	1258
Alliant Unique	Speer	CCI 500	5.6	1166	6.3	1244
Alliant BE 86	Federal	Federal 100	5.4	1136	6.2	1241
Vihtavuori 3N37	Speer	CCI 500	6.0	1128	6.7	1225
Accurate No. 7	Speer	CCI 500	8.6	1158	9.6 C	1220
Alliant Power Pistol	Speer	CCI 500	6.2	1122	6.7	1212
Vihtavuori N350	Speer	CCI 500	5.8	1109	6.5	1210
Winchester AutoComp	Federal	Federal 100	5.2	1091	5.8	1196
Hodgdon CFE Pistol	Federal	Federal 100	5.1	1094	5.7	1188
Hodgdon HS-6	Speer	CCI 500	6.6	1048	7.4	1178
Hodgdon H. Universal	Speer	CCI 500	4.7	1046	5.3	1172
Winchester WSF	Speer	CCI 500	5.0	1041	5.6	1156
Alliant Bullseye	Speer	CCI 500	4.2	1037	4.7	1144
Winchester 231	Speer	CCI 500	4.4	1026	4.9	1133
Hodgdon TITEGROUP	Speer	CCI 500	4.1	1061	4.5	1121
Alliant Sport Pistol	Federal	Federal 100	4.0	1029	4.5	1115
Accurate No. 5	Speer	CCI 500	6.0	1003	6.7	1102
Alliant American Select	Speer	CCI 500	4.8	1067	5.4	1102
Hodgdon Hi-Skor 700-X	Speer	CCI 500	4.0	1007	4.4	1101

WARNING! *Maximum loads should be used with CAUTION • C = Compressed Load*

124 GRAINS

DIAMETER	SECTIONAL DENSITY
.355"	0.141

9mm TMJ® RN
Ballistic Coefficient	0.159
COAL Tested	1.135"
Speer Part No.	3993

9mm GDHP
Ballistic Coefficient	0.134
COAL Tested	1.120"
Speer Part No.	3998

Propellant	Case	Primer	Starting Charge Weight (grains)	Starting Charge Muzzle Velocity (feet/sec)	Maximum Charge Weight (grains)	Maximum Charge Muzzle Velocity (feet/sec)
Alliant Blue Dot	Speer	CCI 500	7.1	1121	7.9	1238
Alliant BE 86	Federal	Federal 100	5.4	1124	6.0	1199
Accurate No. 9	Speer	CCI 500	9.4	1061	10.5 C	1185
Alliant Unique	Speer	CCI 500	5.2	1080	5.8	1180
Accurate No. 7	Speer	CCI 500	8.1	1077	9.0	1180
Vihtavuori 3N37	Speer	CCI 500	5.7	1063	6.4	1179
Alliant Power Pistol	Speer	CCI 500	5.6	1033	6.4	1157
Winchester AutoComp	Federal	Federal 100	5.1	1075	5.6	1156
Hodgdon CFE Pistol	Federal	Federal 100	4.7	1024	5.3	1127
Hodgdon TITEGROUP	Speer	CCI 500	4.0	1020	4.4	1095
Hodgdon H. Universal	Speer	CCI 500	4.5	993	5.0	1089
Accurate No. 5	Speer	CCI 500	5.7	963	6.4	1069
Hodgdon Hi-Skor 700-X	Speer	CCI 500	3.9	989	4.3	1067
Alliant Sport Pistol	Federal	Federal 100	3.8	984	4.3	1067
Alliant Bullseye	Speer	CCI 500	3.9	966	4.4	1059
Hodgdon HS-6	Speer	CCI 500	6.0	951	6.7	1059
Alliant American Select	Speer	CCI 500	4.5	994	5.0	1053
Winchester 231	Speer	CCI 500	4.0	887	4.5	998

WARNING! *Maximum loads should be used with CAUTION • C = Compressed Load*

125 GRAINS

DIAMETER	SECTIONAL DENSITY
.356"	0.142

9mm Lead-RN

Ballistic Coefficient	0.155
COAL Tested	1.130"
Speer Part No.	4602

			Starting Charge		Maximum Charge	
Propellant	Case	Primer	Weight (grains)	Muzzle Velocity (feet/sec)	Weight (grains)	Muzzle Velocity (feet/sec)
Winchester WAP	Speer	CCI 500	4.2	921	4.6	1012
Alliant Unique	Speer	CCI 500	4.1	911	4.5	1007
Alliant Red Dot	Speer	CCI 500	3.3	888	3.6	1004
Hodgdon HP38	Speer	CCI 500	3.9	917	4.2	995
Hodgdon HS-6	Speer	CCI 500	5.1	913	5.5	993
Hodgdon H. Universal	Speer	CCI 500	3.9	899	4.3	991
Winchester 231	Speer	CCI 500	3.8	911	4.1	982
Hodgdon Hi-Skor 700-X	Speer	CCI 500	3.2	920	3.4	977
Alliant Bullseye	Speer	CCI 500	3.5	929	3.8	962

WARNING! Maximum loads should be used with CAUTION • C = Compressed Load

147 GRAINS

DIAMETER	SECTIONAL DENSITY
.355"	0.167

9mm GDHP	
Ballistic Coefficient	0.164
COAL Tested	1.130"
Speer Part No.	4002

9mm TMJ® FN	
Ballistic Coefficient	0.188
COAL Tested	1.130"
Speer Part No.	4006

NOTES: 147-grain bullets not recommended for barrels longer than 10 inches.

			Starting Charge		Maximum Charge	
Propellant	Case	Primer	Weight (grains)	Muzzle Velocity (feet/sec)	Weight (grains)	Muzzle Velocity (feet/sec)
Alliant BE 86	Federal	Federal 100	4.5	936	5.1	1027
Alliant Blue Dot	Speer	CCI 500	5.1	900	5.8	1001
Winchester AutoComp	Federal	Federal 100	4.3	906	4.8	993
Hodgdon CFE Pistol	Federal	Federal 100	4.1	897	4.6	980
Alliant Power Pistol	Speer	CCI 500	4.5	872	5.0	975
Vihtavuori 3N37	Speer	CCI 500	4.4	886	4.9	969
Accurate No. 7	Speer	CCI 500	6.1	867	6.8	961
IMR SR 4756	Speer	CCI 500	4.2	841	4.6	957
Hodgdon HS-6	Speer	CCI 500	5.0	845	5.5	956
Alliant Unique	Speer	CCI 500	3.8	852	4.3	954
Winchester WSF	Speer	CCI 500	3.6	840	4.1	931
Accurate No. 5	Speer	CCI 500	4.5	821	5.1	931
Alliant Sport Pistol	Federal	Federal 100	3.2	820	3.6	890

WARNING! Maximum loads should be used with CAUTION • C = Compressed Load

9mm LARGO

Alternate Names:	9mm Bergmann-Bayard, 9mm Bergmann 1910/21, 9mm Bayard Long, 9mm Astra M21, 9mm Star S.P., 9x23mm Largo
Country of Origin:	Belgium
Year of Introduction:	1903
Designer(s):	Theodor Bergmann
Governing Body:	CIP

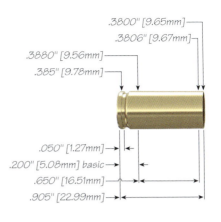

CARTRIDGE CASE DATA

Case Type:	Rimless, slight taper
Average Case Capacity:	18.2 grains H$_2$O
Max. Cartridge OAL	1.300 inch
Max. Case Length:	.905 inch
Primer:	Small Pistol
Case Trim to Length:	.900 inch
RCBS Shell holder:	# 16
Current Manufacturers:	None

BALLISTIC DATA

Max. Average Pressure (MAP):	Set at 30,000 psi for this manual
Test Barrel Length:	5.25 inch
Rifling Twist Rate:	1 turn in 10 inch

Muzzle velocities of factory loaded ammunition	Bullet Wgt.	Muzzle velocity
	124-grain	1,120 fps

HISTORICAL NOTES

- The 9mm Largo cartridge can trace its history back to 1903 when T. Bergmann designed the cartridge for his new Bergmann-Bayard semi-automatic pistol.

- Bergmann's new cartridge was one of the many "long 9" pistol cartridges introduced after 1900. It predated the classic 9mm Luger by at least three years and the 45 Auto by eight years.

- The Spanish Army took the cartridge into military service in 1913 where it remained until the mid-1950s.

- The 9mm Bergmann cartridge case is .905 inch in length (the 9mm Luger case length is .754 inch). In order to distinguish the Bergmann cartridge from the Luger, the Spanish military called their cartridge the 9mm Largo (long is "Largo" in Spanish).
- During the 42 year period it remained in Spanish military service, Spanish ammunition manufacturers were the sole source of 9mm Largo ammunition.
- The 9mm Largo remained something of a curiosity in the U.S. until the early 1990s when surplus Spanish Star and Astra pistols began arriving. However, 9mm Largo ammunition was scarce.
- The increasing demand prompted CCI® to add 9mm Largo to their "Blazer®" aluminum case product line. As demand dropped off, CCI dropped the 9mm Largo in 2004. No other domestic ammunition manufacturer has offered 9mm Largo ammunition.
- Surplus Spanish 9mm Largo ammunition is Berdan primed, often corrosive, old and not reloadable.

Interesting Fact

Many shooters believe that 9mm Largo is the Spanish name for the 38 Super Auto +P. In addition, the two cartridges look very much alike, so they must be interchangeable. **THIS IS NOT TRUE!** While the two cartridges do look somewhat alike, they are not the same and are not interchangeable. Dimensions and design of the two cartridge cases differ in several major ways and the MAP levels of the 38 Super Auto +P are substantially higher. Attempting to fire 38 Super Auto +P ammunition in Spanish pistols chambered for 9mm Largo can result in serious personal injury and damage to the pistol. Don't do it!

BALLISTIC NOTES

- Despite its larger case capacity, the muzzle velocity of the 9mm Largo cartridge is comparable to the much smaller 9mm Luger.
- In preparing this loading data, we have erred on the side of safety by recommending only loads with a MAP level of 30,000 psi. In our tests, these loads functioned in pistols reliably and were clean burning.
- You can duplicate the 9mm Largo Spanish factory load with either of two Speer 124-grain bullets:
  - The Total Metal Jacket (TMJ®) RN (closest to the factory bullet profile).
  - The Gold Dot® Hollow Point (GDHP).
- As Spanish pistols were not designed to feed hollow point or soft point bullets, the TMJ bullet will be the most reliable.
- Although Spanish 9mm Largo ammunition was not factory loaded with 115-grain bullets, we found two Speer bullets in this weight that functioned 9mm Largo pistols reliably:
  - The Total Metal Jacket (TMJ) RN.
  - The Gold Dot Hollow Point (GDHP).
- Due to the worn condition of many surplus Spanish pistols in 9mm Largo, we cannot recommend this caliber for personal defense.

TECHNICAL NOTES

- The correct bullet diameter for the 9mm Largo is .355 inches.

- The 9mm Largo cartridge headspaces on the case mouth.
- There is considerable variation in the type, strength and quality of surplus Spanish handguns in 9mm Largo caliber.
- At the top of the list are the locked breech Star Model A pistols marked "super" which are equipped with inertial firing pins. Star Model A pistols not marked "super" do not have inertial firing pins. The former are more desirable and safer, however the latter are acceptable if you remember never to carry it with the hammer down on a loaded chamber.
- Most Astra pistols are blowback operated (unlocked breech). Many of these can develop cracked slides after heavy use. Before firing one of these, we recommend you have it checked by a qualified gunsmith.
- Pistols marked "9mm/38" are chambered for 9mm Largo. Those marked "9mm/08" or "9mm/P08" are chambered for 9mm Luger.

HANDLOADING NOTES

- Handloading the 9mm Largo cartridge does not present any major problems provided you have suitable cartridge cases (See: Starlinebrass.com).
- As many Spanish pistols in 9mm Largo caliber are blowback operated, fired cases from such handguns must be carefully inspected for cracks, stretch marks, incipient head separations and damage from ejection.
- Never load less than the minimum charges shown in the loading data as the small charge of propellant may not be sufficient to push the bullet completely down the barrel.

SAFETY NOTES

SPEER 124-grain TMJ RN @ a muzzle velocity of 1,107 fps:
- Maximum vertical altitude @ 90° elevation is 4,230 feet.
- Maximum horizontal distance to first impact with ground @ 33° elevation is 1,978 yards.

115 GRAINS

DIAMETER	SECTIONAL DENSITY
.355"	0.130

9mm GDHP

Ballistic Coefficient	0.125
COAL Tested	1.260"
Speer Part No.	3994

9mm TMJ® RN

Ballistic Coefficient	0.151
COAL Tested	1.290"
Speer Part No.	3995

Propellant	Case	Primer	Starting Charge Weight (grains)	Starting Charge Muzzle Velocity (feet/sec)	Maximum Charge Weight (grains)	Maximum Charge Muzzle Velocity (feet/sec)
Alliant Power Pistol	Starline	CCI 500	6.0	1063	6.8	1207
Hodgdon HS-6	Starline	CCI 500	6.5	1031	7.5	1186
Accurate No. 5	Starline	CCI 500	6.4	1009	7.1	1138
Vihtavuori 3N37	Starline	CCI 500	5.6	1051	6.4	1137
Hodgdon Hi-Skor 700-X	Starline	CCI 500	4.1	967	4.7	1110
Hodgdon H. Universal	Starline	CCI 500	4.8	1006	5.2	1099
Alliant Bullseye	Starline	CCI 500	4.4	979	5.1	1093
Winchester 231	Starline	CCI 500	4.8	990	5.3	1082

WARNING! Maximum loads should be used with CAUTION • C = Compressed Load

124 GRAINS

DIAMETER	SECTIONAL DENSITY
.355"	0.141

9mm TMJ® RN	
Ballistic Coefficient	0.159
COAL Tested	1.290"
Speer Part No.	3993

9mm GDHP	
Ballistic Coefficient	0.139
COAL Tested	1.260"
Speer Part No.	3998

Propellant	Case	Primer	Starting Charge		Maximum Charge	
			Weight (grains)	Muzzle Velocity (feet/sec)	Weight (grains)	Muzzle Velocity (feet/sec)
Alliant Power Pistol	Starline	CCI 500	5.6	1040	6.1	1107
Hodgdon H. Universal	Starline	CCI 500	4.3	885	4.9	1095
Accurate No. 7	Starline	CCI 500	7.5	989	8.3	1085
Accurate No. 5	Starline	CCI 500	6.0	939	6.7	1069
Hodgdon HS-6	Starline	CCI 500	6.4	965	6.9	1065
Alliant Unique	Starline	CCI 500	4.5	951	5.0	1053
Vihtavuori 3N37	Starline	CCI 500	5.2	849	5.8	1037
Winchester 231	Starline	CCI 500	4.3	951	4.7	1013
IMR PB	Starline	CCI 500	4.2	882	4.6	990

WARNING! *Maximum loads should be used with CAUTION • C = Compressed Load*

357 SIG

Parent Cartridge:	10mm Auto/40 S&W
Country of Origin:	USA
Year of Introduction:	1994
Designer(s):	Sig Sauer & Federal
Governing Body:	SAAMI/CIP

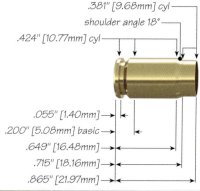

.381" [9.68mm] cyl
shoulder angle 18°
.424" [10.77mm] cyl
.055" [1.40mm]
.200" [5.08mm] basic
.649" [16.48mm]
.715" [18.16mm]
.865" [21.97mm]

CARTRIDGE CASE DATA

Case Type:	Rimless, bottleneck		
Average Case Capacity:	20.2 grains H₂O	Max. Cartridge OAL	1.140 inch
Max. Case Length:	.865 inch	Primer:	Small Pistol
Case Trim to Length:	.860 inch	RCBS Shell holder:	# 27
Current Manufacturers:	Speer, Federal, Hornady, Remington, Winchester, Black Hills, Cor-Bon, Fiocchi and Sellier & Bellot		

BALLISTIC DATA

Max. Average Pressure (MAP):	40,000 psi, CUP not established for this cartridge -SAAMI	Test Barrel Length:	4.000 inch
Rifling Twist Rate:	1 turn in 16 inch		
Muzzle velocities of factory loaded ammunition	Bullet Wgt.		Muzzle velocity
	115-grain		1,425 fps
	125-grain		1,350 fps
	147-grain		1,225 fps

HISTORICAL NOTES

- The 357 SIG cartridge was developed in 1994 by Federal Cartridge and SIG Arms in response to a requirement from a U.S. government law enforcement agency for a 9mm pistol cartridge with a higher muzzle velocity than the 9mm Luger.

- As the required muzzle velocity could not be reached with the limited case capacity of the 9mm Luger, the 40 &W was necked down to accept a .355 inch diameter bullet.

- The 357 SIG cartridge has remained something of a law enforcement specialty and is not particularly popular among sportsmen.

Interesting Fact

The 357 SIG is unique in that it is the only law enforcement pistol cartridge with a necked cartridge case.

BALLISTIC NOTES

- Factory 357 SIG ammunition has a nominal muzzle velocity of 1,350 fps with a 125-grain bullet. This is about 20% higher than the 9mm Luger with near the same weight bullet.
- Muzzle energy of the 357 SIG is 40% higher than the 9mm Luger with nearly the same weight bullet.
- Due to the restriction in overall loaded length, some standard 9mm bullets are too long for the 357 SIG (the case neck will not hold the bullet securely at the maximum OAL). Speer has designed bullets specifically for the 357 SIG.
- You can, of course, experiment to find a suitable bullet. But, why bother when Speer offers two bullets *expressly designed* for the 357 SIG cartridge? You can duplicate the factory load with either of these bullets.
    - A 125-grain SIG-GDHP (Gold Dot® Hollow Point)
    - A 125-grain SIG-TMJ® FN (Total Metal Jacket Flat Nose)
- Factories do not offer the 357 SIG loaded with a 147-grain bullet. However, handloaders have the option of two; a GDHP and a TMJ FN.
- The 357 SIG is a fine choice for personal defense as well as hunting pests, varmints, and small game.

TECHNICAL NOTES

- Despite its nomenclature, the correct bullet diameter for the 357 SIG cartridge is .355 inch which is the same as the 9mm Luger.
- The 357 SIG cartridge is unusual in that it is one of the very few necked sporting/law enforcement pistol cartridges. Most previous necked pistol cartridges have been military.
- This design approach allows increased case capacity without increasing overall loaded length. For this reason, the 357 SIG cartridge will fit in most 9mm Luger or 40 S&W caliber pistols with barrel and chamber modifications.
- The bottleneck case design also contributes to very reliable feeding and chambering.
- Unlike other necked cartridges, the 357 SIG headspaces on the case mouth and not on the shoulder.
- MAP levels of the 357 SIG are higher than those of the 9mm Luger cartridge.

HANDLOADING NOTES

- You will need to full length resize all fired 357 SIG cases before reloading them.
- Case length increases can be a problem as the 357 SIG headspaces on the case mouth. For this reason, we recommend carefully inspecting resized cases for proper length before reloading them. Trim any cases that exceed the maximum allowable length.
- Some 357 SIG cases have a reduced size flash hole. It is suggested that a small diameter decapping pin be used, and RCBS® can supply.

- Never load less than the minimum charges shown in the loading data as the small charge of propellant may not be sufficient to push the bullet completely down the barrel.

SAFETY NOTES

SPEER 125-grain TMJ FN @ a muzzle velocity of 1,350 fps:
- Maximum vertical altitude @ 90° elevation is 4,266 feet.
- Maximum horizontal distance to first impact with ground @ 33° elevation is 1,963 yards.

125 GRAINS

DIAMETER	SECTIONAL DENSITY
.355"	0.142

357 SIG/38 Super GDHP	
Ballistic Coefficient	0.141
COAL Tested	1.135"
Speer Part No.	4360

357 SIG/38 Super TMJ® FN	
Ballistic Coefficient	0.147
COAL Tested	1.135"
Speer Part No.	4362

			Starting Charge		Maximum Charge	
Propellant	Case	Primer	Weight (grains)	Muzzle Velocity (feet/sec)	Weight (grains)	Muzzle Velocity (feet/sec)
Accurate No. 9	Speer	CCI 500	13.1	1287	14.6	1437
Alliant Blue Dot	Speer	CCI 500	9.9	1293	11.0 C	1416
Accurate No. 7	Speer	CCI 500	11.1	1264	12.3	1403
Vihtavuori N105	Speer	CCI 500	10.1	1257	11.2 C	1400
Vihtavuori N350	Speer	CCI 500	7.6	1242	8.5	1350
Alliant Unique	Speer	CCI 500	7.2	1231	8.0	1344
Hodgdon HS-6	Speer	CCI 500	8.6	1199	9.6	1335
Vihtavuori 3N37	Speer	CCI 500	7.6	1200	8.5	1301
Alliant Herco	Speer	CCI 500	7.3	1172	8.1	1277

WARNING! Maximum loads should be used with CAUTION • C = Compressed Load

147 GRAINS

DIAMETER	SECTIONAL DENSITY
.355"	0.167

9mm GDHP
Ballistic Coefficient	0.164
COAL Tested	1.135"
Speer Part No.	4002

9mm TMJ® FN
Ballistic Coefficient	0.188
COAL Tested	1.135"
Speer Part No.	4006

			Starting Charge		Maximum Charge	
Propellant	Case	Primer	Weight (grains)	Muzzle Velocity (feet/sec)	Weight (grains)	Muzzle Velocity (feet/sec)
Alliant Blue Dot	Speer	CCI 500	7.9	1130	8.8	1218
Vihtavuori N105	Speer	CCI 500	8.2	1100	9.0	1207
Accurate No. 9	Speer	CCI 500	11.0	1094	12.0	1204
Hodgdon HS-6	Speer	CCI 500	7.5	1075	8.3	1170
Accurate No. 7	Speer	CCI 500	9.0	1069	10.0	1169
Alliant Power Pistol	Speer	CCI 500	6.7	1065	7.5	1152
Vihtavuori N350	Speer	CCI 500	6.2	1040	6.8	1111
Alliant Unique	Speer	CCI 500	5.8	1008	6.6	1101

WARNING! *Maximum loads should be used with* **CAUTION** • C = Compressed Load

38 SUPER AUTOMATIC +P

Alternate Names:	38 Super +P, 38 Auto Colt +P
Parent Cartridge:	38 Automatic
Country of Origin:	USA
Year of Introduction:	1900 - 38 ACP, 1929 - 38 Super Auto, 1974 - 38 Super Auto +P
Designer(s):	Colt
Governing Body:	SAAMI/CIP

CARTRIDGE CASE DATA			
Case Type:	Semi-Rimmed, straight		
Average Case Capacity:	18.0 grains H$_2$O	Max. Cartridge OAL	1.280 inch
Max. Case Length:	.900 inch	Primer:	Small Pistol
Case Trim to Length:	.890 inch	RCBS Shell holder:	# 39
Current Manufacturers:	Federal, Remington, Winchester, Aguila		

BALLISTIC DATA			
Max. Average Pressure (MAP):	36,500 psi, 33,000 CUP – SAAMI 38 Super +P	Test Barrel Length:	5.00 inch
Rifling Twist Rate:	1 turn in 16 inch		
Muzzle velocities of factory loaded ammunition	Bullet Wgt.		Muzzle velocity
	115-grain		1,130 fps
	124-grain		1,240 fps
	130-grain		1,215 fps

HISTORICAL NOTES

- When the 38 Automatic cartridge was introduced in 1900, it was one of the first commercially successful semi-auto pistol cartridges. It predated the classic 9mm Luger by at least 3 years.

- Designed by John Browning, the 38 Automatic cartridge and the Browning semi-automatic pistol to fire it, were licensed by Colt.

- By 1929, the 38 Automatic cartridge was in bad need of a ballistic update, however the Browning pistol was not capable of handling higher MAP levels.

- As a result, Colt switched to the M1911 pistol platform which enabled them to increase the MAP level resulting in the 38 Super Auto cartridge.
- However, living in the commercial shadow of the 45 Auto cartridge, the 38 Super Auto did not prove to be a sales success.
- Then a new market opened in countries where handguns in any military caliber were banned. As the 38 Super Auto was not a military caliber, it was allowed. Mexico became an especially good market for handguns in 38 Super Auto caliber.
- When countries rescinded such laws, the 38 Super Auto became an orphan once again.
- It was then that the combat pistol shooters discovered the 38 Super Auto was the ideal caliber for their type of competition. Once again, the 38 Super Auto was saved from the scrap heap of cartridge history.
- In 1974, SAAMI members adopted the +P designator to the 38 Super Auto as another indicator of the difference between it and the old 38 Automatic.
- Today, the 38 Super Auto+P is an integral part of most major domestic manufacturer's line of ammunition. Several manufacturers have updated the 38 Super Auto +P with JHP bullets as well as FMJ types.
- Still, the 38 Super Auto +P remains on the edge of obsolescence, subject at any time to the cost accountant's pencil.

Interesting Fact

Recently, manufacturers have increased the suggested retail price of the 38 Super Auto +P ammunition substantially. Is this an effort to price it out of the market or simply to increase profits on a slow moving product? Good question.

BALLISTIC NOTES

- The 38 Super Auto +P cartridge case is unusual in that it is a semi-rimmed design in similar fashion to the Browning designed 25 Auto and 32 Auto cartridges.
- Despite the larger case capacity of the 38 Super Auto +P, the MAP level is similar to the much smaller 9mm Luger case.
- These numbers show the 38 Super Auto +P muzzle energy is approximately 20% that of the 9mm Luger with a 124-grain bullet.
- You can duplicate the 115-grain bullet factory load with one of two 115-grain Speer bullets; the Gold Dot® Hollow Point (GDHP) or the TMJ® RN. We recommend the former for personal defense.
- To duplicate the 124-grain bullet factory loads, Speer has two excellent bullets to choose from: the TMJ RN and the Gold Dot Hollow Point. Practice with the TMJ and carry the Gold Dot HP- it's the best you can get for outstanding performance.
- The factories do not offer a 147-grain bullet in the 38 Super Auto +P. However, you can handload either the 147-grain Speer TMJ FN, or the GDHP.
- The 38 Super Auto +P is a fine choice for personal defense as well as combat pistol competition.

TECHNICAL NOTES

- John Browning designed his 38 Auto (and indirectly the 38 Super Auto +P) cartridge with a semi-rimmed case which allows the 38 Super Auto +P cartridge to headspace on its rim.
- The 38 Super Auto +P cartridge is too long to fit in pistols designed for the 9mm Luger cartridge. For this reason, the 38 Super Auto +P must be made on 45 Auto frames and slides.

HANDLOADING NOTES

- With the rapidly increasing cost of 38 Super Auto +P factory ammunition, reloading this caliber makes more economic sense every day.
- Some 38 Super Auto +P pistols may experience problems feeding one or more of the bullets above. Should that occur, we recommend switching to Speer 125-grain SIG GDHP or SIG TMJ FN.
- Never load less than the minimum charges shown in the loading data as the small charge of propellant may not be sufficient to push the bullet completely down the barrel.
- Use fast burning pistol powders for loading the 38 Super Auto +P.

SAFETY NOTES

SPEER 124-grain TMJ RN @ a muzzle velocity of 1,312 fps:

- Maximum vertical altitude @ 90° elevation is 4,454 feet.
- Maximum horizontal distance to first impact with ground @ 33° elevation is 2,066 yards.

115 GRAINS

DIAMETER	SECTIONAL DENSITY
.355"	0.130

9mm GDHP
Ballistic Coefficient	0.125
COAL Tested	1.260"
Speer Part No.	3994

9mm TMJ® RN
Ballistic Coefficient	0.151
COAL Tested	1.270"
Speer Part No.	3995

			Starting Charge		Maximum Charge	
Propellant	Case	Primer	Weight (grains)	Muzzle Velocity (feet/sec)	Weight (grains)	Muzzle Velocity (feet/sec)
Alliant Blue Dot	Winchester	CCI 500	9.0	1265	10.0 C	1362
Accurate No. 7	Winchester	CCI 500	9.5	1219	10.5	1328
Accurate No. 5	Winchester	CCI 500	7.8	1229	8.6	1326
Accurate No. 9	Winchester	CCI 500	11.7	1222	12.7 C	1324
Vihtavuori 3N37	Winchester	CCI 500	7.0	1188	7.7	1323
Winchester WSF	Winchester	CCI 500	6.2	1164	6.8	1282
Hodgdon H. Universal	Winchester	CCI 500	5.7	1145	6.3	1278
Alliant Herco	Winchester	CCI 500	7.0	1232	7.8 C	1276
Hodgdon HS-6	Winchester	CCI 500	8.0	1177	8.8	1253

WARNING! *Maximum loads should be used with CAUTION • C = Compressed Load*

124 GRAINS

DIAMETER	SECTIONAL DENSITY
.355"	0.141

9mm TMJ® RN
Ballistic Coefficient	0.159
COAL Tested	1.280"
Speer Part No.	3993

9mm GDHP
Ballistic Coefficient	0.134
COAL Tested	1.260"
Speer Part No.	3998

			Starting Charge		Maximum Charge	
Propellant	Case	Primer	Weight (grains)	Muzzle Velocity (feet/sec)	Weight (grains)	Muzzle Velocity (feet/sec)
Alliant Blue Dot	Winchester	CCI 500	8.3	1182	9.2	1312
Alliant Herco	Winchester	CCI 500	6.7	1176	7.3	1272
Accurate No. 9	Winchester	CCI 500	11.0	1187	12.0 C	1267
Hodgdon HS-6	Winchester	CCI 500	7.5	1134	8.3	1245
Accurate No. 5	Winchester	CCI 500	7.2	1102	8.0	1213
Alliant Unique	Winchester	CCI 500	5.6	1127	6.2	1208
Hodgdon H. Universal	Winchester	CCI 500	5.3	1078	5.9	1202
Vihtavuori 3N37	Winchester	CCI 500	6.4	1092	7.1	1198
Winchester WSF	Winchester	CCI 500	5.6	1057	6.1	1184
Accurate No. 7	Winchester	CCI 500	9.0	1058	9.9	1169
Alliant Bullseye	Winchester	CCI 500	4.7	1073	5.2	1158
Accurate No. 2 Improved	Winchester	CCI 500	5.3	1079	5.8	1135
Hodgdon Hi-Skor 700-X	Winchester	CCI 500	4.5	1050	5.0	1132
Alliant Green Dot	Winchester	CCI 500	4.8	1051	5.3	1125
Winchester 231	Winchester	CCI 500	4.8	1021	5.3	1117
Alliant Red Dot	Winchester	CCI 500	4.3	1027	4.8	1086

WARNING! *Maximum loads should be used with CAUTION • C = Compressed Load*

125 GRAINS

DIAMETER	SECTIONAL DENSITY
.355"	0.142

9mm GDHP
Ballistic Coefficient	0.141
COAL Tested	1.260"
Speer Part No.	4360

9mm TMJ® FN
Ballistic Coefficient	0.147
COAL Tested	1.260"
Speer Part No.	4362

Propellant	Case	Primer	Starting Charge Weight (grains)	Starting Charge Muzzle Velocity (feet/sec)	Maximum Charge Weight (grains)	Maximum Charge Muzzle Velocity (feet/sec)
Alliant Blue Dot	Winchester	CCI 500	8.3	1182	9.2	1312
Alliant Herco	Winchester	CCI 500	6.7	1176	7.3	1272
Accurate No. 9	Winchester	CCI 500	11.0	1187	12.0 C	1267
Hodgdon HS-6	Winchester	CCI 500	7.5	1134	8.3	1245
Accurate No. 5	Winchester	CCI 500	7.2	1102	8.0	1213
Alliant Unique	Winchester	CCI 500	5.6	1127	6.2	1208
Hodgdon H. Universal	Winchester	CCI 500	5.3	1078	5.9	1202
Vihtavuori 3N37	Winchester	CCI 500	6.4	1092	7.1	1198
Winchester WSF	Winchester	CCI 500	5.6	1057	6.1	1184
Accurate No. 7	Winchester	CCI 500	9.0	1058	9.9	1169
Alliant Bullseye	Winchester	CCI 500	4.7	1073	5.2	1158
Accurate No. 2 Improved	Winchester	CCI 500	5.3	1079	5.8	1135
Hodgdon Hi-Skor 700-X	Winchester	CCI 500	4.5	1050	5.0	1132
Alliant Green Dot	Winchester	CCI 500	4.8	1051	5.3	1125
Winchester 231	Winchester	CCI 500	4.8	1021	5.3	1117
Alliant Red Dot	Winchester	CCI 500	4.3	1027	4.8	1086

WARNING! Maximum loads should be used with CAUTION • C = Compressed Load

147 GRAINS

DIAMETER	SECTIONAL DENSITY
.355"	0.167

9mm GDHP
Ballistic Coefficient	0.164
COAL Tested	1.275"
Speer Part No.	4002

9mm TMJ® FN
Ballistic Coefficient	0.188
COAL Tested	1.275"
Speer Part No.	4006

			Starting Charge		Maximum Charge	
Propellant	Case	Primer	Weight (grains)	Muzzle Velocity (feet/sec)	Weight (grains)	Muzzle Velocity (feet/sec)
Accurate No. 9	Winchester	CCI 500	9.5	1021	10.5	1122
Alliant 2400	Winchester	CCI 500	8.5	960	9.5	1099
Vihtavuori 3N37	Winchester	CCI 500	5.2	979	6.2	1081
Hodgdon H. Universal	Winchester	CCI 500	4.7	961	5.2	1065
Accurate No. 7	Winchester	CCI 500	7.4	914	8.2	1061
Hodgdon HS-6	Winchester	CCI 500	6.4	948	7.1	1048
Alliant Unique	Winchester	CCI 500	4.9	984	5.4	1043
Alliant Bullseye	Winchester	CCI 500	4.2	958	4.6	1041
Winchester WSF	Winchester	CCI 500	4.8	938	5.3	1029
Accurate No. 2 Improved	Winchester	CCI 500	4.6	941	5.1	1021
Winchester 231	Winchester	CCI 500	4.3	899	4.8	1008
Accurate No. 5	Winchester	CCI 500	5.8	910	6.4	1004
Hodgdon HP-38	Winchester	CCI 500	4.3	919	4.8	992

WARNING! *Maximum loads should be used with CAUTION • C = Compressed Load*

38 SPECIAL

Alternate Names:	38 S&W Special
Parent Cartridge:	38 Long Colt
Country of Origin:	USA
Year of Introduction:	1902
Designer(s):	Smith & Wesson
Governing Body:	SAAMI

CARTRIDGE CASE DATA

Case Type:	Rimmed, straight		
Average Case Capacity:	24.0 grains H_2O	Max. Cartridge OAL	1.550 inch
Max. Case Length:	1.155 inch	Primer:	Small Pistol
Case Trim to Length:	1.145 inch	RCBS Shell holder:	# 6
Current Manufacturers:	CCI/Speer, Federal, Remington, Winchester, Hornady, Cor-Bon, RUAG, Black Hills, Aguila, Fiocchi, Prvi Partizan		

BALLISTIC DATA

Max. Average Pressure (MAP):	17,000 psi, 20,000 CUP - SAAMI	Test Barrel Length:	7.710 inch (Unvented), 5.631 inch (Vented)
Rifling Twist Rate:	1 turn in 18.75 inch		

Muzzle velocities of factory loaded ammunition	Bullet Wgt.	Muzzle velocity
	90-grain	1,200 fps
	110-grain	980 fps
	125-grain	900 fps
	130-grain	900 fps
	158-grain	800 fps

HISTORICAL NOTES

- From 1892 until 1911, the 38 Long Colt was the official revolver cartridge of the U.S. Army.
- Like most other black powder revolver cartridges of that day, ballistic performance of the 38 Long Colt was anemic; a 150-grain lead, round nose bullet at a muzzle velocity of 770 fps.
- In 1900, domestic revolver and ammunition manufacturers began pitching the 38 Long Colt cartridge to U.S. law enforcement agencies.

- When these agencies objected to the black powder in the 38 Long Colt cartridge, Smith & Wesson developed a new cartridge for smokeless propellant with a MAP 30% higher than the 38 Long Colt. The new 38 S&W Special cartridge had a .120 inch longer case so as to prevent it from being fired in 38 Long Colt revolvers.
- Other than smokeless propellant, the new cartridge offered no ballistic improvement over that of the 38 Long Colt.
- Introduced in 1902, the new 38 Special cartridge quickly came to dominate U.S. law enforcement handgun and ammunition sales. This dominance continued until the 1990s when it was replaced by the 9mm Luger and 40 S&W cartridges.
- An additional 17.7% increase in MAP in the mid-1930s resulted in the 38 Special +P load.
- Lighter weight, jacketed bullets were introduced in the early 1970s.
- Today, the popularity of the 38 Special cartridge has declined as the popularity of the 9mm Luger and 40 S&W cartridge has increased.
- However, virtually every major manufacturer of ammunition offers factory loaded 38 Special ammunition in a wide variety of bullet weights and styles.
- Given the large number of 38 Special and 357 Magnum handguns owned by generations of American shooters, the 38 Special will continue in popularity for many years to come.

BALLISTIC NOTES

- The original factory load for the 38 Special consisted of a 158-grain lead, round nose bullet at a muzzle velocity of 755 to 800 fps. These loads are still in production today.
- For reloading the 38 Special, Speer offers a complete line of suitable bullets.
  - For practice, training, plinking or dispatching varmints and pests (in revolvers with barrels four inches or more in length only):
    - The Speer 158-grain Lead Round Nose (LRN).
    - The Speer 158-grain Lead Semi-Wadcutter (LSWC).
    - A 158-grain Lead Semi-Wadcutter Hollow Point (LSWC HP).
    - The 109-grain (filled w/shot) Plastic Shot Capsule (recommended muzzle velocity 1,000 fps) for rodents and pests at ranges of 15 feet or less.
  - For personal defense in revolvers with barrels four inches or more in length, Speer offers three jacketed bullets:
    - The 110-grain standard JHP.
    - The 125-grain premium Gold Dot® Hollow Point (GDHP).
    - The 125-grain Total Metal Jacket (TMJ® FN).
  - For personal defense in compact revolvers with barrels 2-3 inches in length:
    - The Speer 110-grain Gold Dot Hollow Point SB (GDHP SB). This is a bullet especially designed to work in short barrel revolvers.

TECHNICAL NOTES

- The 38 Special cartridge case is a classic revolver design with a rim and a straight sided case. Basically, it is a longer 38 Long Colt case.

- Most revolver bullets must be of a special, compact ogive design to maximize case capacity. All the bullets shown in the 38 Special load data are designed to these parameters.
- The correct bullet diameter for the 38 Special is .357 inch (jacketed) and .358 inch (lead).
- Ammunition in 38 Special may be safely fired in guns chambered for the 357 Magnum.

HANDLOADING NOTES

- The loading data in this section is for 38 Special ammunition only. It is NOT for 38 Special +P ammunition which is listed in a following section.
- It is important to keep in mind that the 38 Special cartridge is based on the 38 Long Colt black powder cartridge. As a result, the case capacity of the 38 Special is much larger than necessary for smokeless propellants.
- A maximum charge of smokeless propellant may take up very little space in a 38 Special cartridge case. For this reason, it is very important to guard against double charges.
- Light loads of smokeless propellants take up even less space than maximum loads. For this reason, light loads can be adversely affected by low temperatures (muzzle velocity can drop off quickly) as well as the position of the powder in the case at the time of ignition (forward behind the bullet or rearward at the primer can cause variations in muzzle velocity).
- To prevent bullet elongation in revolvers and magazine tube explosions in carbines and rifles, all bullets for the 38 Special cartridge must be roll crimped securely in the cannelure on the bullet's surface.
- We recommend loading lead bullets no faster than 1,050 fps to avoid leading the barrel.
- The 38 Special was designed to fire 158-grain lead bullets. We do not recommend firing 158-grain jacketed bullets in the 38 Special cartridge as they may not clear the barrel.
- Never load less than the minimum charges shown in the loading data as the small charge of propellant may not be sufficient to push the bullet completely down the barrel. This is especially true if used in a carbine or rifle.
- Use fast burning pistol powders for loading the 38 Special.

SAFETY NOTES

SPEER 158-grain Lead Round Nose (LRN) @ a muzzle velocity of 967 fps:
- Maximum vertical altitude @ 90° elevation is 4,089 feet.
- Maximum horizontal distance to first impact with ground @ 34° elevation is 1,940 yards.

109 GRAINS

DIAMETER	SECTIONAL DENSITY
.358"	N/A

38/357 Shot Capsule

Ballistic Coefficient	N/A
COAL Tested	1.500"
Speer Part No.	8780

NOTE: Shot capsules must not be used in firearms with ported recoil compensators.

Propellant	Case	Primer	Weight (grains)	Muzzle Velocity (feet/sec)
Alliant Unique	Speer	CCI 500	5.5	1111
Hodgdon Hi-Skor 700-X	Speer	CCI 500	4.5	1060
Hodgdon HP-38	Speer	CCI 500	4.5	1054
Alliant Bullseye	Speer	CCI 500	4.5	1021
Winchester 231	Speer	CCI 500	5.0	996

WARNING! Maximum loads should be used with CAUTION • C = Compressed Load

110 GRAINS

DIAMETER	SECTIONAL DENSITY
.357"	0.123

38 JHP
Ballistic Coefficient	0.113
COAL Tested	1.455"
Speer Part No.	4007

38 GDHP SB
Ballistic Coefficient	0.117
COAL Tested	1.455"
Speer Part No.	4009

Long barrel velocities (these from the 7.7 inch test barrel listed)

Propellant	Case	Primer	Starting Charge Weight (grains)	Starting Charge Muzzle Velocity (feet/sec)	Maximum Charge Weight (grains)	Maximum Charge Muzzle Velocity (feet/sec)
Alliant Power Pistol	Speer	CCI 500	6.2	1006	6.6	1074
Vihtavuori 3N37	Speer	CCI 500	6.5	990	6.9	1071
Alliant Unique	Speer	CCI 500	5.4	947	5.8	1065
Accurate No. 5	Speer	CCI 500	6.8	979	7.2	1043
Hodgdon TITEGROUP	Speer	CCI 500	4.1	890	4.5	1002
Hodgdon H. Universal	Speer	CCI 500	5.1	829	5.5	998
Hodgdon Hi-Skor 700-X	Speer	CCI 500	4.2	907	4.6	997
Alliant Bullseye	Speer	CCI 500	4.2	891	4.6	990
Winchester 231	Speer	CCI 500	4.6	871	5.0	971
Alliant American Select	Speer	CCI 500	DNR	—	4.3	887

DNR — do not reduce

WARNING! Maximum loads should be used with CAUTION • C = Compressed Load

110 GRAINS

DIAMETER	SECTIONAL DENSITY
.357"	0.123

38 JHP

Ballistic Coefficient	0.113
COAL Tested	1.455"
Speer Part No.	4007

38 GDHP SB

Ballistic Coefficient	0.117
COAL Tested	1.455"
Speer Part No.	4009

SHORT BARREL VELOCITIES
Test Firearm: S&W M15 2"

			Starting Charge		Maximum Charge	
Propellant	Case	Primer	Weight (grains)	Muzzle Velocity (feet/sec)	Weight (grains)	Muzzle Velocity (feet/sec)
Alliant Unique	Speer	CCI 500	5.4	806	5.8	936
Accurate No. 5	Speer	CCI 500	6.8	860	7.2	900
Vihtavuori 3N37	Speer	CCI 500	6.5	845	6.9	895
Hodgdon H. Universal	Speer	CCI 500	5.1	760	5.5	882
Alliant Power Pistol	Speer	CCI 500	6.2	823	6.6	880
Hodgdon Hi-Skor 700-X	Speer	CCI 500	4.2	784	4.6	879
Alliant Bullseye	Speer	CCI 500	4.2	791	4.6	852
Hodgdon TITEGROUP	Speer	CCI 500	4.1	782	4.5	850
Winchester 231	Speer	CCI 500	4.6	817	5.0	848
Alliant American Select	Speer	CCI 500	DNR	—	4.3	784

DNR — do not reduce

WARNING! Maximum loads should be used with CAUTION • C = Compressed Load

125 GRAINS

DIAMETER	SECTIONAL DENSITY
.357"	0.140

38 GDHP
Ballistic Coefficient	0.140
COAL Tested	1.440"
Speer Part No.	4012

38 JHP
Ballistic Coefficient	0.129
COAL Tested	1.435"
Speer Part No.	4013

38 TMJ® FN
Ballistic Coefficient	0.146
COAL Tested	1.435"
Speer Part No.	4015

			Starting Charge		Maximum Charge	
Propellant	Case	Primer	Weight (grains)	Muzzle Velocity (feet/sec)	Weight (grains)	Muzzle Velocity (feet/sec)
Vihtavuori 3N37	Speer	CCI 500	DNR	—	6.8	1037
Accurate No. 5	Speer	CCI 500	DNR	—	7.1	1011
Accurate No. 2 Improved	Speer	CCI 500	DNR	—	5.4	994
Alliant Power Pistol	Speer	CCI 500	DNR	—	6.1	986
Alliant Unique	Speer	CCI 500	DNR	—	5.7	980
Hodgdon H. Universal	Speer	CCI 500	DNR	—	5.5	966
Winchester WSF	Speer	CCI 500	DNR	—	5.3	934
Hodgdon TITEGROUP	Speer	CCI 500	DNR	—	4.4	933
IMR PB	Speer	CCI 500	DNR	—	4.9	927
Alliant Bullseye	Speer	CCI 500	DNR	—	4.5	914
Hodgdon Hi-Skor 700-X	Speer	CCI 500	DNR	—	4.6	905
Alliant American Select	Speer	CCI 500	DNR	—	4.1	839

DNR — do not reduce

WARNING! Maximum loads should be used with CAUTION • C = Compressed Load

158 GRAINS

DIAMETER	SECTIONAL DENSITY
.358"	0.176

38 LSWC
Ballistic Coefficient	0.123
COAL Tested	1.440"
Speer Part No.	4624

38 LSWC HP
Ballistic Coefficient	0.121
COAL Tested	1.455"
Speer Part No.	4628

38 LRN
Ballistic Coefficient	0.170
COAL Tested	1.510"
Speer Part No.	4648

			Starting Charge		Maximum Charge	
Propellant	Case	Primer	Weight (grains)	Muzzle Velocity (feet/sec)	Weight (grains)	Muzzle Velocity (feet/sec)
IMR SR 4756	Speer	CCI 500	5.0	844	5.6	967
Alliant Power Pistol	Speer	CCI 500	4.8	856	5.4	948
Accurate No. 5	Speer	CCI 500	5.8	874	6.2	922
Hodgdon H. Universal	Speer	CCI 500	4.2	827	4.6	902
Hodgdon Hi-Skor 700-X	Speer	CCI 500	3.2	774	3.8	877
Winchester 231	Speer	CCI 500	3.8	783	4.3	863
IMR PB	Speer	CCI 500	3.7	770	4.2	858
Hodgdon HP-38	Speer	CCI 500	3.6	756	4.1	855
Winchester WSF	Speer	CCI 500	3.8	738	4.3	830
Vihtavuori N350	Speer	CCI 500	4.5	717	5.0	818
Alliant Unique	Speer	CCI 500	4.0	740	4.7	815
Alliant Bullseye	Speer	CCI 500	3.1	752	3.5	814
Alliant Red Dot	Speer	CCI 500	3.0	727	3.4	793
Accurate No. 2	Speer	CCI 500	3.6	708	4.0	781

WARNING! Maximum loads should be used with CAUTION • C = Compressed Load

38 SPECIAL +P

Alternate Names:	38HV, 38HS, 38/44
Parent Cartridge:	38 Long Colt
Country of Origin:	USA
Year of Introduction:	late 1930s
Designer(s):	Smith & Wesson
Governing Body:	SAAMI/CIP

CARTRIDGE CASE DATA

Case Type:	Rimmed, straight		
Average Case Capacity:	24.0 grains H₂O	Max. Cartridge OAL:	1.550 inch
Max. Case Length:	1.155 inch	Primer:	Small Pistol
Case Trim to Length:	1.145 inch	RCBS Shell holder:	# 6
Current Manufacturers:	CCI/Speer, Federal, Hornady, Remington, Winchester, Cor-Bon, Black Hills, Magtech, Aguila, Fiocchi, Prvi Partizan, PMC		

BALLISTIC DATA

Max. Average Pressure (MAP):	20,000 psi, 20,000 CUP	Test Barrel Length:	7.710 inch (Unvented), 5.631 inch (Vented)
Rifling Twist Rate:	1 turn in 18.75 inch		

Muzzle velocities of factory loaded ammunition	Bullet Wgt.	Muzzle velocity
	110-grain	1,090 fps
	125-grain	945 fps
	130-grain	950 fps
	158-grain lead bullet	890 fps

HISTORICAL NOTES

- In the 1930s, an effort was made to improve the ballistics of the standard 38 Special cartridge by increasing the MAP level 18% from 17,000 psi to 20,000 psi.
- The new, higher pressure loads were intended for use in revolvers built on heavy, 44 Special frames.
- To differentiate the new high pressure loads from the older low pressure cartridges, cases were sometimes headstamped "38HV", "38HS", or "38/44."
- More often than not, the cases bore no special headstamp leaving the original box as the only means of identification.

- In 1974, the ammunition manufacturers agreed to identify the high pressure 38 Special cartridges with a "+P" headstamp and appropriate labels on the packaging.
- At the same time, firearms makers agreed to determine which of their guns were suitable for +P ammunition and make such information available to their customers.
- Boxes of 38 Special +P ammunition also carried the warning not to fire +P ammunition in older handguns unless recommended by the manufacturer for such loads.
- Today, nearly all newly manufactured 38 Special revolvers are approved for +P ammunition.

BALLISTIC NOTES

- The higher MAP level of the +P load allowed the muzzle velocity of the 158-grain lead bullet to be increased from 755 fps to 890 fps.
- With a lighter 125-grain bullet, muzzle velocity increased from 850 fps to 945 fps.
- All of these loads are still in production today.
- For reloading 38 Special +P ammunition, Speer offers a complete line of suitable bullets.
  - For practice, training, plinking, or dispatching varmints and pests in revolvers with barrels 4 inches or more in length:
    - The Speer 158-grain Lead Round Nose (LRN). This load will match the fixed sights on modern revolvers.
    - The Speer 158-grain Lead Semi-Wadcutter (LSWC).
    - A 158-grain Lead Semi-Wadcutter Hollow Point (LSWC HP). This bullet will expand at these velocities.
  - For personal defense in revolvers with barrels 4 inches or more in length, Speer offers five jacketed bullets:
    - The 110-grain premium Gold Dot® HP (GDHP SB)
    - The 110-grain standard JHP
    - The 125-grain Gold Dot HP (GDHP)
    - The 125-grain Total Metal Jacket (TMJ®FN)
    - The 135-grain Gold Dot HP (GDHP SB)
  - For personal defense in compact revolvers with barrels 2-3 inches in length:
    - The Speer 110-grain Gold Dot Hollow Point SB (GDHP SB). This is a bullet especially designed to work in short barrel revolvers.
    - The Speer 135-grain Gold Dot Hollow Point SB (GDHP SB). This bullet too was designed for use in short barrel revolvers.

TECHNICAL NOTES

- Case length of the 38 Special and the 38 Special +P, are identical as is case capacity.
- The MAP level of the 38 Special +P is 20,000 psi which is 18% higher than that of the 38 Special.
- All 38 Special +P ammunition has a "+P" on the headstamp.
- Most revolver bullets must be of a special, compact ogive design (flat nose)

to maximize case capacity. All Speer 38 caliber bullets are designed to these parameters.

- The correct bullet diameter for the 38 Special +P is .357 inch (jacketed) and .358 inch (lead).
- Ammunition marked 38 Special and 38 Special +P may be safely fired in guns chambered for the 357 Magnum.

HANDLOADING NOTES

- The loading data in this section is for 38 Special +P ammunition only.
- It is important to keep in mind that the case capacity of the 38 Special +P cartridge is much larger than necessary for smokeless propellants.
- A maximum charge of smokeless propellant may take up very little space in a 38 Special +P cartridge case. For this reason it is very important to guard against double charges.
- Light loads of smokeless propellants take up even less space. For this reason, light loads can be adversely affected by low temperatures (muzzle velocity can drop off quickly) as well as the position of the powder in the case at the time of ignition (forward behind the bullet or rearward at the primer can cause variations in muzzle velocity).
- To prevent bullet elongation in revolvers and OAL reduction in the magazine tube of carbines and rifles, all bullets for the 38 Special +P ammunition must be crimped securely in the cannelure on the bullet's surface.
- We recommend loading lead bullets no faster than 1,050 fps to avoid leading the barrel.
- The 38 Special was designed to fire 158-grain lead bullets. We do not recommend firing 158-grain jacketed bullets in the 38 Special +P cartridge as they may not clear the barrel with light loads.
- Never load less than the minimum charges shown in the loading data as the small charge of propellant may not be sufficient to push the bullet completely down the barrel.

SAFETY NOTES

SPEER 158-grain Lead, Round Nose (LRN) @ a muzzle velocity of 1,037 fps:
- Maximum vertical altitude @ 90° elevation is 4,293 feet.
- Maximum horizontal distance to first impact with ground @ 34° elevation is 2,027 yards.

110 GRAINS

DIAMETER	SECTIONAL DENSITY
.357"	0.123

38 JHP
Ballistic Coefficient	0.113
COAL Tested	1.455"
Speer Part No.	4007

38 GDHP SB
Ballistic Coefficient	0.117
COAL Tested	1.455"
Speer Part No.	4009

Long barrel velocities (these from the 7.7 inch test barrel listed).

Propellant	Case	Primer	Starting Charge Weight (grains)	Starting Charge Muzzle Velocity (feet/sec)	Maximum Charge Weight (grains)	Maximum Charge Muzzle Velocity (feet/sec)
Alliant Power Pistol	Speer	CCI 500	7.0	1123	7.4	1192
Vihtavuori 3N37	Speer	CCI 500	6.9	1071	7.3	1150
Accurate No. 5	Speer	CCI 500	7.5	1099	7.9	1143
Alliant Unique	Speer	CCI 500	5.9	1090	6.3	1117
Hodgdon H. Universal	Speer	CCI 500	5.7	1028	6.1	1100
Alliant Bullseye	Speer	CCI 500	4.8	1027	5.2	1098
Hodgdon Hi-Skor 700-X	Speer	CCI 500	4.7	1017	5.1	1085
Hodgdon TITEGROUP	Speer	CCI 500	4.7	1013	5.1	1082
Winchester 231	Speer	CCI 500	5.2	1008	5.6	1059
Alliant American Select	Speer	CCI 500	4.4	894	4.8	967

WARNING! *Maximum loads should be used with CAUTION • C = Compressed Load*

110 GRAINS

DIAMETER	SECTIONAL DENSITY
.357"	0.123

38 JHP	
Ballistic Coefficient	0.113
COAL Tested	1.455"
Speer Part No.	4007

38 GDHP SB	
Ballistic Coefficient	0.117
COAL Tested	1.455"
Speer Part No.	4009

SHORT BARREL VELOCITIES
Test Firearm: S&W M15 2"

			Starting Charge		Maximum Charge	
Propellant	Case	Primer	Weight (grains)	Muzzle Velocity (feet/sec)	Weight (grains)	Muzzle Velocity (feet/sec)
Alliant Unique	Speer	CCI 500	5.9	929	6.3	976
Hodgdon H. Universal	Speer	CCI 500	5.7	895	6.1	976
Accurate No. 5	Speer	CCI 500	7.5	915	7.9	969
Alliant Power Pistol	Speer	CCI 500	7.0	911	7.4	967
Vihtavuori 3N37	Speer	CCI 500	6.9	903	7.3	958
Hodgdon Hi-Skor 700-X	Speer	CCI 500	4.7	878	5.1	954
Hodgdon TITEGROUP	Speer	CCI 500	4.7	875	5.1	945
Winchester 231	Speer	CCI 500	5.2	884	5.6	944
Alliant Bullseye	Speer	CCI 500	4.8	873	5.2	941
Alliant American Select	Speer	CCI 500	DNR	—	4.8	879

DNR — do not reduce

WARNING! *Maximum loads should be used with* CAUTION • C = Compressed Load

125 GRAINS

DIAMETER	SECTIONAL DENSITY
.357"	0.140

38 GDHP
Ballistic Coefficient	0.140
COAL Tested	1.440"
Speer Part No.	4012

38 JHP
Ballistic Coefficient	0.129
COAL Tested	1.455"
Speer Part No.	4013

38 TMJ® FN
Ballistic Coefficient	0.146
COAL Tested	1.435"
Speer Part No.	4015

Propellant	Case	Primer	Starting Charge Weight (grains)	Starting Charge Muzzle Velocity (feet/sec)	Maximum Charge Weight (grains)	Maximum Charge Muzzle Velocity (feet/sec)
Vihtavuori 3N37	Speer	CCI 500	6.8	1037	7.2	1098
Alliant Unique	Speer	CCI 500	5.7	980	6.0	1082
Alliant Power Pistol	Speer	CCI 500	6.1	986	6.8	1082
Hodgdon H. Universal	Speer	CCI 500	5.6	976	5.9	1058
Accurate No. 5	Speer	CCI 500	7.5	927	7.8	1030
Alliant Bullseye	Speer	CCI 500	4.5	914	4.8	1021
IMR PB	Speer	CCI 500	4.9	927	5.4	1021
Winchester WSF	Speer	CCI 500	5.3	934	5.8	1021
Accurate No. 2 Improved	Speer	CCI 500	5.4	994	5.7	1014
Hodgdon Hi-Skor 700-X	Speer	CCI 500	4.6	905	4.9	1013
Hodgdon TITEGROUP	Speer	CCI 500	4.4	933	4.9	1012
Alliant American Select	Speer	CCI 500	DNR	—	4.7	931

DNR — do not reduce

WARNING! Maximum loads should be used with CAUTION • C = Compressed Load

135 GRAINS

DIAMETER	SECTIONAL DENSITY
.357"	0.151

38 GDHP SB	
Ballistic Coefficient	0.141
COAL Tested	1.450"
Speer Part No.	4014

Propellant	Case	Primer	Starting Charge Weight (grains)	Starting Charge Muzzle Velocity (feet/sec)	Maximum Charge Weight (grains)	Maximum Charge Muzzle Velocity (feet/sec)
Alliant Power Pistol	Speer	CCI 500	6.0	983	6.4	1065
Accurate No. 5	Speer	CCI 500	6.6	1000	7.0	1052
Accurate No. 7	Speer	CCI 500	7.8	964	8.2	1030
Hodgdon HS-6	Speer	CCI 500	6.8	944	7.2	1027
Vihtavuori 3N37	Speer	CCI 500	6.0	969	6.4	1007
Alliant Unique	Speer	CCI 500	4.8	867	5.2	988
Hodgdon H. Universal	Speer	CCI 500	5.0	937	5.2	977
IMR PB	Speer	CCI 500	DNR	—	4.7	936

DNR — do not reduce

WARNING! Maximum loads should be used with CAUTION • C = Compressed Load

135 GRAINS

DIAMETER	SECTIONAL DENSITY
.357"	0.151

38 GDHP SB

Ballistic Coefficient	0.141
COAL Tested	1.450"
Speer Part No.	4014

SHORT BARREL VELOCITIES
Test Firearm: S&W M15 2"

			Starting Charge		Maximum Charge	
Propellant	Case	Primer	Weight (grains)	Muzzle Velocity (feet/sec)	Weight (grains)	Muzzle Velocity (feet/sec)
Accurate No. 7	Speer	CCI 500	7.8	838	8.2	882
Accurate No. 5	Speer	CCI 500	6.6	819	7.0	878
Hodgdon HS-6	Speer	CCI 500	6.8	780	7.2	856
Alliant Power Pistol	Speer	CCI 500	6.0	797	6.4	845
Alliant Unique	Speer	CCI 500	4.8	768	5.2	834
Hodgdon H. Universal	Speer	CCI 500	5.0	785	5.2	825
Vihtavuori 3N37	Speer	CCI 500	6.0	760	6.4	823
IMR PB	Speer	CCI 500	DNR	—	4.7	788

DNR — do not reduce

WARNING! Maximum loads should be used with CAUTION • C = Compressed Load

158 GRAINS

DIAMETER	SECTIONAL DENSITY
.358"	0.176

35 LSWC	
Ballistic Coefficient	0.123
COAL Tested	1.440"
Speer Part No.	4624

35 LSWC HP	
Ballistic Coefficient	0.121
COAL Tested	1.455"
Speer Part No.	4628

35 LRN	
Ballistic Coefficient	0.170
COAL Tested	1.510"
Speer Part No.	4648

			Starting Charge		Maximum Charge	
Propellant	Case	Primer	Weight (grains)	Muzzle Velocity (feet/sec)	Weight (grains)	Muzzle Velocity (feet/sec)
Alliant Power Pistol	Speer	CCI 500	5.4	948	6.0	1037
Hodgdon Hi-Skor 700-X	Speer	CCI 500	3.8	877	4.4	980
Accurate No. 5	Speer	CCI 500	6.2	922	6.6	978
Hodgdon HS-6	Speer	CCI 500	6.3	914	6.7	971
Hodgdon H. Universal	Speer	CCI 500	4.6	902	5.0	971
IMR PB	Speer	CCI 500	4.2	858	4.6	962
Winchester 231	Speer	CCI 500	4.3	863	4.7	935
Alliant Unique	Speer	CCI 500	4.7	815	5.2	919
Hodgdon HP-38	Speer	CCI 500	4.1	855	4.5	918
Vihtavuori N350	Speer	CCI 500	5.0	818	5.4	901
Winchester WSF	Speer	CCI 500	4.3	830	4.7	892
Alliant Bullseye	Speer	CCI 500	3.5	814	3.9	874
Alliant Red Dot	Speer	CCI 500	3.4	793	3.8	846
Accurate No. 2 Improved	Speer	CCI 500	4.0	781	4.3	843

WARNING! Maximum loads should be used with CAUTION • C = Compressed Load

357 MAGNUM

Parent Cartridge:	38 Special
Country of Origin:	USA
Year of Introduction:	1935
Designer(s):	Smith & Wesson
Governing Body:	SAAMI/CIP

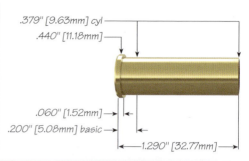

CARTRIDGE CASE DATA	
Case Type:	Rimmed, straight
Average Case Capacity:	26.2 grains H₂O
Max. Cartridge OAL:	1.590 inch
Max. Case Length:	1.290 inch
Primer:	Small Pistol
Case Trim to Length:	1.280 inch
RCBS Shell holder:	# 6
Current Manufacturers:	CCI/Speer, Federal, Hornady, Remington, Winchester, Cor-Bon, Black Hills, Lapua, Magtech, Aguila, Fiocchi, Prvi Partizan, PMC

BALLISTIC DATA	
Max. Average Pressure (MAP):	35,000 psi, 45,000 CUP - SAAMI
Test Barrel Length:	10.0 inch (Unvented), 5.643 inch (Vented)
Rifling Twist Rate:	1 turn in 18.75 inch

Muzzle velocities of factory loaded ammunition	
Bullet Wgt.	Muzzle velocity
110-grain	1,295 fps
125-grain	1,450 fps
135-grain	1,275 fps
140-grain	1,400 fps
158-grain	1,235 fps
180-grain	1,080 fps

HISTORICAL NOTES

- Until 1935, the muzzle velocity of most handgun cartridges was limited by low MAP levels required by weak gun designs and poor metallurgy.

- As a result, their terminal ballistic performance was based on heavy, blunt, lead bullets at low muzzle velocities. The larger the caliber, the better.

- In the early 1930s, noted gun writer and experimenter Elmer Keith felt that new propellants could dramatically increase the muzzle velocity and terminal ballistic effectiveness of revolver cartridges. (For additional information on Elmer Keith see the 44 Remington Magnum data).

- Keith focused on improving the 38 Special cartridge for hunting. His concept proved successful. In turn, this stimulated Smith & Wesson to commercialize the concept.
- The result was the new 357 S&W Magnum cartridge introduced in 1935, along with a suitably reinforced revolver to fire it.
- The MAP level of the 357 Magnum cartridge is more than twice that of the 38 Special. In order to prevent shooters from loading a 357 Magnum in a 38 Special revolver, the cartridge case of the 357 Magnum was increased by .135 inches.
- Although the ballistic capabilities of the new cartridge were a quantum level improvement, the expensive guns (during the Depression few people had money for such things) and the looming threat of another world war limited sales.
- The 357 Magnum did not become popular until the mid-1950s when economic prosperity returned and less expensive revolvers hit the market.
- A persistent problem was that the lead bullets used in factory loaded 357 Magnum ammunition caused barrel leading. This problem was not resolved until the introduction of jacketed bullets for the 357 Magnum in the late 1960s.
- Today, virtually every manufacturer of revolvers offers several models chambered for the 357 Magnum. Likewise, all domestic ammunition makers offer 357 Magnum factory loaded ammunition in a wide variety of bullet weights and styles.

Interesting Fact

During World War II, General George Patton became famous for carrying two ivory handled revolvers. One of them was in 357 Magnum.

BALLISTIC NOTES

- The original Remington factory load for the 357 Magnum was a 158-grain lead, semi-wadcutter bullet at a muzzle velocity of approximately 1,235 fps. This bullet remained the only factory load until the introduction of jacketed bullets. It is still listed by several manufacturers.
- For reloading the 357 Magnum, Speer offers a complete line of suitable bullets.
    - For practice, training, plinking, personal protection, and hunting small game:
        - A 158-grain Lead, Semi-wadcutter (LSWC)
        - A 158-grain Lead, Semi-wadcutter Hollow Point (LSWC HP)
    - For personal protection or hunting varmints, pests or rodents:
        - A 110-grain Jacketed Hollow Point (JHP)
        - A 125-grain Jacketed Hollow Point (JHP)
        - A 125-grain Gold Dot Hollow Point (GDHP)
        - A 125-grain Total Metal Jacket (TMJ FN)
        - A 135-grain Gold Dot Hollow Point-Short Barrel (GDHP SB)
    - To duplicate factory loads, for personal protection and for hunting predators, pests and deer:
        - A 158-grain Gold Dot Hollow Point (JHP) for personal defense
        - A 158-grain Total Metal Jacket Flat Nose (TMJ FN) for dispatching wounded game

- A 158-grain Jacketed DeepCurl Hollow Point (DCHP) for hunting deer
- A 158-grain Jacketed Soft Point (JSP) for hunting deer
- A 170-grain DeepCurl Soft Point (DCSP) has been designed especially for the 357 Magnum. It offers the deep penetration and controlled expansion necessary for hunting big game.

TECHNICAL NOTES

- The 357 Magnum cartridge case is a classic revolver design with a rim and a straight sided case. Basically, it is a longer 38 Special case.
- Case length of the 357 Magnum is .135 inches longer than the 38 Special in order to prevent chambering a 357 Magnum cartridge in 38 Special handguns.
- Case capacity of the 357 Magnum is approximately 10% more than the 38 Special.
- The MAP level of the 357 Magnum is 35,000 psi which is over twice that of the 38 Special and 175% higher than the 38 Special +P.
- Most revolver bullets must be of a special, compact ogive design (flat nose) to maximize case capacity. All Speer 357 Magnum bullets are designed to these parameters.
- Ammunition in 38 Special and 38 Special +P may be safely fired in guns chambered for the 357 Magnum.

HANDLOADING NOTES

- To prevent bullet elongation in revolvers, all bullets for the 357 Magnum cartridge must be crimped securely in the cannelure on the bullet's surface.
- We recommend loading lead bullets no faster than 1,034 fps to avoid leading the barrel.
- Never load less than the minimum charges shown in the loading data as the small charge of propellant may not be sufficient to push the bullet completely down the barrel.
- If you wish to load Speer Plastic Shot Capsules for pest and rodent control, we recommend that you load them in 38 Special cases for best patterning. Shot capsules loaded in 38 Special cases can be fired safely from 357 Magnum revolvers. Shot capsule loading data will be found in the 38 Special data section.

SAFETY NOTES

SPEER 170-grain DeepCurl Soft Point @ a muzzle velocity of 1,166 fps:
- Maximum vertical altitude @ 90° elevation is 4,743 feet.
- Maximum horizontal distance to first impact with ground @ 34° elevation is 2,234 yards.

110 GRAINS

DIAMETER	SECTIONAL DENSITY
.357"	0.123

38 JHP
Ballistic Coefficient	0.113
COAL Tested	1.575"
Speer Part No.	4007

NOTE: *Do not use the 110-grain Gold Dot SB HP (#4009) in the 357 Magnum.*

			Starting Charge		Maximum Charge	
Propellant	Case	Primer	Weight (grains)	Muzzle Velocity (feet/sec)	Weight (grains)	Muzzle Velocity (feet/sec)
Vihtavuori N110	Speer	CCI 500	19.0	1557	21.0 C	1693
Alliant 2400	Speer	CCI 500	17.5	1536	19.5	1670
Alliant Power Pistol	Speer	CCI 500	9.5	1326	10.5	1451
Alliant Unique	Speer	CCI 500	8.5	1284	9.7	1447
Vihtavuori 3N37	Speer	CCI 500	9.7	1305	10.8	1433
Alliant Bullseye	Speer	CCI 500	7.8	1246	8.7	1403
Hodgdon Hi-Skor 700-X	Speer	CCI 500	7.0	1208	8.0	1366
Hodgdon H. Universal	Speer	CCI 500	8.0	1264	9.0	1359
Accurate No. 5	Speer	CCI 500	10.8	1246	12.0	1330
Winchester 231	Speer	CCI 500	8.5	1231	9.5	1319

WARNING! *Maximum loads should be used with CAUTION • C = Compressed Load*

125 GRAINS

DIAMETER	SECTIONAL DENSITY
.357"	0.140

38 GDHP

Ballistic Coefficient	0.140
COAL Tested	1.580"
Speer Part No.	4012

38 JHP

Ballistic Coefficient	0.129
COAL Tested	1.575"
Speer Part No.	4013

38 TMJ® FN

Ballistic Coefficient	0.146
COAL Tested	1.575"
Speer Part No.	4015

			Starting Charge		Maximum Charge	
Propellant	Case	Primer	Weight (grains)	Muzzle Velocity (feet/sec)	Weight (grains)	Muzzle Velocity (feet/sec)
Vihtavuori N110	Speer	CCI 500	16.8	1410	17.8	1443
Alliant 2400	Speer	CCI 500	16.5	1335	17.5	1409
Alliant Power Pistol	Speer	CCI 500	9.5	1273	10.5	1345
Alliant Unique	Speer	CCI 500	8.6	1259	9.6	1343
Winchester 296	Speer	CCI 550	18.3	1188	20.3	1336
Hodgdon H110	Speer	CCI 550	18.0	1154	20.0	1282
Accurate No. 9	Speer	CCI 500	12.6	1119	14.6	1238
Vihtavuori N350	Speer	CCI 500	9.0	1097	10.0	1226
Hodgdon H. Universal	Speer	CCI 500	7.5	1148	8.2	1200
Vihtavuori 3N37	Speer	CCI 500	9.0	1035	10.2	1180
Winchester 231	Speer	CCI 500	7.6	1129	8.3	1168
Accurate No. 7	Speer	CCI 500	12.0	1045	13.5	1134
Hodgdon HS-6	Speer	CCI 550	10.0	1009	11.3	1124

WARNING! Maximum loads should be used with CAUTION • C = Compressed Load

135 GRAINS

DIAMETER	SECTIONAL DENSITY
.357"	0.151

38 GDHP SB	
Ballistic Coefficient	0.141
COAL Tested	1.590"
Speer Part No.	4014

NOTE: *Long barrel velocities (these from the 10 inch test barrel listed).*

			Starting Charge		Maximum Charge	
Propellant	Case	Primer	Weight (grains)	Muzzle Velocity (feet/sec)	Weight (grains)	Muzzle Velocity (feet/sec)
Hodgdon H110	Speer	CCI 550	17.5	1313	18.5	1387
Winchester 296	Speer	CCI 550	17.5	1264	18.5	1377
Alliant 2400	Speer	CCI 500	15.0	1219	16.0	1377
Accurate No. 9	Speer	CCI 500	14.5	1234	15.5	1345
Alliant Power Pistol	Speer	CCI 500	8.6	1192	9.6	1291
Vihtavuori 3N37	Speer	CCI 500	7.7	1093	8.7	1185
Alliant Unique	Speer	CCI 500	6.8	1082	7.8	1185

WARNING! *Maximum loads should be used with* **CAUTION** • *C = Compressed Load*

135 GRAINS

DIAMETER	SECTIONAL DENSITY
.357"	0.151

38 GDHP SB

Ballistic Coefficient	0.141
COAL Tested	1.590"
Speer Part No.	4014

SHORT BARREL VELOCITIES
Test Firearm: S&W Model 19 2.5"

Propellant	Case	Primer	Starting Charge		Maximum Charge	
			Weight (grains)	Muzzle Velocity (feet/sec)	Weight (grains)	Muzzle Velocity (feet/sec)
Accurate No. 9	Speer	CCI 500	14.5	1202	15.5	1258
Hodgdon H110	Speer	CCI 550	17.5	1128	18.5	1205
Alliant 2400	Speer	CCI 500	15.0	1124	16.0	1176
Alliant Power Pistol	Speer	CCI 500	8.6	1046	9.6	1137
Winchester 296	Speer	CCI 550	17.5	1105	18.5	1130
Alliant Unique	Speer	CCI 500	6.8	971	7.8	1109
Vihtavuori 3N37	Speer	CCI 500	7.7	874	8.7	1012

WARNING! *Maximum loads should be used with CAUTION • C = Compressed Load*

158 GRAINS

DIAMETER	SECTIONAL DENSITY
.357"	0.177

38 TMJ® FN
Ballistic Coefficient	0.173
COAL Tested	1.570"
Speer Part No.	4207

38 JHP
Ballistic Coefficient	0.163
COAL Tested	1.570"
Speer Part No.	4211

38 DCHP
Ballistic Coefficient	0.168
COAL Tested	1.575"
Speer Part No.	4215

38 JSP
Ballistic Coefficient	0.164
COAL Tested	1.570"
Speer Part No.	4217

			Starting Charge		Maximum Charge	
Propellant	Case	Primer	Weight (grains)	Muzzle Velocity (feet/sec)	Weight (grains)	Muzzle Velocity (feet/sec)
Alliant 2400	Speer	CCI 500	13.8	1128	14.8	1265
Vihtavuori N110	Speer	CCI 500	13.5	1102	15.0	1253
Hodgdon H110	Speer	CCI 550	13.9	1151	15.5	1217
Winchester 296	Speer	CCI 550	13.2	1089	14.7	1185
Accurate No. 5	Speer	CCI 500	9.0	1032	10.0	1152
Accurate No. 7	Speer	CCI 500	10.5	1015	11.7	1140
Accurate No. 9	Speer	CCI 500	12.3	1052	13.7	1136
IMR 4227	Speer	CCI 500	15.0	1003	17.0	1126
Alliant Power Pistol	Speer	CCI 500	7.5	963	8.5	1078
Vihtavuori N350	Speer	CCI 500	7.7	958	8.6	1072
Hodgdon HS-6	Speer	CCI 550	8.7	925	9.7	1040
Alliant Unique	Speer	CCI 500	6.9	978	7.7	1040
Hodgdon H. Universal	Speer	CCI 500	6.5	904	7.3	1015

WARNING! Maximum loads should be used with CAUTION • C = Compressed Load

170 GRAINS

DIAMETER	SECTIONAL DENSITY
.357"	0.191

357 DCSP

Ballistic Coefficient	0.185
COAL Tested	1.590"
Speer Part No.	4230

Propellant	Case	Primer	Starting Charge Weight (grains)	Starting Charge Muzzle Velocity (feet/sec)	Maximum Charge Weight (grains)	Maximum Charge Muzzle Velocity (feet/sec)
Alliant 2400	Speer	CCI 500	13.9	1100	14.5	1166
Vihtavuori N110	Speer	CCI 500	13.2	1046	13.8	1132
Hodgdon Lil' Gun	Speer	CCI 550	14.8	1100	15.4	1121
IMR 4227	Speer	CCI 500	16.1	1037	16.7	1084
Hodgdon H110	Speer	CCI 500	14.4	1024	15.2	1076
Accurate No. 9	Speer	CCI 550	11.0	1030	11.7	1071

WARNING! Maximum loads should be used with CAUTION • C = Compressed Load

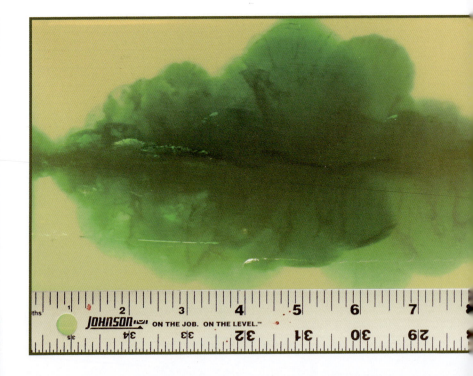

158 GRAINS

DIAMETER	SECTIONAL DENSITY
.358"	0.176

38 LSWC
Ballistic Coefficient	0.123
COAL Tested	1.570"
Speer Part No.	4624

38 LSWC HP
Ballistic Coefficient	0.121
COAL Tested	1.575"
Speer Part No.	4628

Propellant	Case	Primer	Starting Charge		Maximum Charge	
			Weight (grains)	Muzzle Velocity (feet/sec)	Weight (grains)	Muzzle Velocity (feet/sec)
Alliant Unique	Speer	CCI 500	5.5	970	6.0	1034
IMR SR 7625	Speer	CCI 500	4.8	926	5.3	1021
Hodgdon Hi-Skor 700-X	Speer	CCI 500	4.5	904	5.0	1002
Winchester 231	Speer	CCI 500	4.9	897	5.4	989
Alliant Bullseye	Speer	CCI 500	4.3	848	4.8	939
Hodgdon HP-38	Speer	CCI 500	4.5	839	5.0	932

WARNING! *Maximum loads should be used with CAUTION • C = Compressed Load*

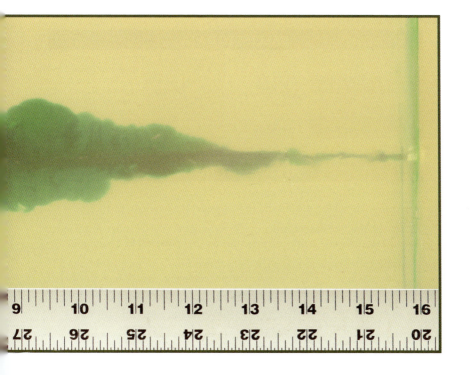

35 REMINGTON

Parent Cartridge:	Original design
Country of Origin:	USA
Year of Introduction:	1908
Designer(s):	Remington
Governing Body:	SAAMI

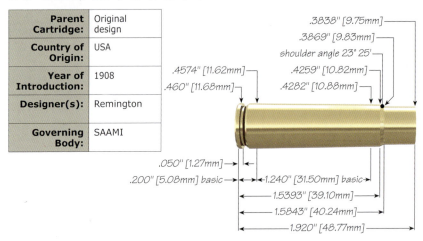

CARTRIDGE CASE DATA

Case Type:	Rimless, bottleneck		
Average Case Capacity:	51.0 grains H$_2$O	Max. Cartridge OAL	2.525 inch
Max. Case Length:	1.920 inch	Primer:	Large Rifle
Case Trim to Length:	1.910 inch	RCBS Shell holder:	# 9
Current Manufacturers:	Remington, Federal, Hornady, Winchester		

BALLISTIC DATA

Max. Average Pressure (MAP):	33,500 psi, 35,000 CUP – SAAMI	Test Barrel Length:	14 inch (SAAMI does not list a handgun length test barrel) was used for the data presented.
Rifling Twist Rate:	1 turn in 16 inch		

HISTORICAL NOTES

- Surely when Remington introduced their 35 Remington cartridge in 1908, never in their wildest dreams did they consider it a handgun cartridge!
- At first glance, the idea of firing the 35 Remington rifle cartridge in a handgun seems preposterous. A rifle cartridge this big and powerful in a handgun?
- Actually, the combination is a good one. Fired from a 14 inch barrel, the 35 Remington loses very little muzzle velocity compared to a 22 inch rifle barrel.
- Looked at from another perspective, the 35 Remington is capable of delivering an additional 200 fps more than the 357 Maximum handgun cartridge.
- This elevates the 35 Remington/handgun combination to a level suitable for hunting deer.

Interesting Fact

Is the recoil from the 35 Remington fired from a handgun heavy? Certainly. Unmanageable? No. The low MAP level of the 35 Remington results in a big push rather than a short, sharp hit. Most shooters find this is acceptable.

BALLISTIC NOTES

- Factory loaded 35 Remington ammunition is offered in two bullet weights:
  - A 150-grain SP at a muzzle velocity of 2,300 fps.
  - A 200-grain SPRN at a muzzle velocity of 2,080 fps.
- The 35 Remington cartridge is limited to 33,500 psi MAP levels due to its intended use in pump and lever-action rifles with weaker actions.
- Although MAP level is modest by rifle standards, they are in line with most magnum caliber handgun calibers.
- When loaded for a pistol, the 35 Remington offers several advantages:
  - Case capacity is considerably greater than standard handgun cartridges.
  - Brass is readily available, inexpensive, and requires no alteration.
  - Cases can be neck sized to increase case life.
- The ballistic sweet spot for handgun hunting with the 35 Remington cartridge is the Speer 180-grain SPFN Hot-Cor® handloaded to a muzzle velocity of approximately 2,000 fps. This load is capable of taking most deer at a range of approximately 100 yards.
- For short range in heavy brush, the Speer 220-grain SPFN Hot-Cor is a fine choice.
- We do not recommend handloading bullets heavier than 220 grains as they will not stabilize properly from handguns.
- The loading data listed was taken from a 14 inch pistol barrel. If you are using a 10 inch barrel expect lower muzzle velocities than listed.

TECHNICAL NOTES

- The 35 Remington cartridge is a rimless, necked design with a very short shoulder at a 23° angle.
- The 35 Remington headspaces on the narrow shoulder. Cases with a minimum shoulder may suffer from misfires as the impact of the firing pin is absorbed driving the case into the chamber. Cases fire-formed to the chamber dimensions will not have this problem and can be neck sized.
- Cases fired in another firearm will need to be full length resized. Use care not to set back the shoulder more than necessary when doing so.

HANDLOADING NOTES

- New, empty, unprimed brass for the 35 Remington is available from most domestic ammunition makers.
- We recommend crimping bullets in the case mouth of 35 Remington cartridges to be fired from handguns. However, the heavy crimp needed for use in rifles with tubular magazines is not necessary. Rather a light crimp in the bullet cannelure will suffice and may improve accuracy.

- We suggest neck sizing for 35 Remington handloads to be fired from a pistol, especially those that have been fired in the pistol. Doing so will increase case life, reduce head separations, and minimize trimming chores.
- The 35 Remington is designed for a Large Rifle primer. Do not use Large Pistol primers with this loading data.
- Slower burning rate propellants work best for the 35 Rem. when fired in a pistol.

SAFETY NOTES

SPEER 220-grain SPFN Hot-Cor @ a muzzle velocity of 1,638 fps:

- Maximum vertical altitude @ 90° elevation is 6,117 feet.
- Maximum horizontal distance to first impact with ground @ 35° elevation is 3,290 yards.

180 GRAINS

DIAMETER	SECTIONAL DENSITY
.358"	.201"

35 SPFN Hot-Cor®

Ballistic Coefficient	0.236
COAL Tested	2.315"
Speer Part No.	2435

			Starting Charge		Maximum Charge	
Propellant	Case	Primer	Weight (grains)	Muzzle Velocity (feet/sec)	Weight (grains)	Muzzle Velocity (feet/sec)
Hodgdon H335	Winchester	CCI 200	36.0	1871	38.0	2023
Hodgdon H322	Winchester	CCI 200	36.0	1825	38.0	1997
IMR 4895	Winchester	CCI 200	38.0	1786	40.0	1896
Hodgdon BL-C(2)	Winchester	CCI 250	33.0	1736	35.0	1885
Winchester 748	Winchester	CCI 250	40.0	1714	42.0	1879
IMR 3031	Winchester	CCI 200	36.0	1734	38.0	1837
IMR 4198	Winchester	CCI 200	28.0	1683	30.0	1806
Hodgdon H380	Winchester	CCI 250	42.0	1653	44.0	1782
Alliant Reloder 7	Winchester	CCI 200	28.0	2565	30.0	1739

220 GRAINS

DIAMETER	SECTIONAL DENSITY
.358"	0.245

35 SPFN Hot-Cor®

Ballistic Coefficient	0.286
COAL Tested	2.470"
Speer Part No.	2439

			Starting Charge		Maximum Charge	
Propellant	Case	Primer	Weight (grains)	Muzzle Velocity (feet/sec)	Weight (grains)	Muzzle Velocity (feet/sec)
IMR 4064	Winchester	CCI 200	34.0	1558	36.0	1638
Hodgdon H414	Winchester	CCI 250	38.0	1550	40.0	1626
IMR 4895	Winchester	CCI 200	33.5	1539	35.5	1620
IMR 3031	Winchester	CCI 200	31.5	1495	33.5	1611
Hodgdon H335	Winchester	CCI 200	30.0	1429	32.0	1567
Hodgdon BL-C(2)	Winchester	CCI 250	33.0	1460	35.0	1561
Winchester 748	Winchester	CCI 250	33.0	1438	35.0	1550
Alliant Reloder 7	Winchester	CCI 200	22.5	1243	24.5	1421

WARNING! *Maximum loads should be used with CAUTION • C = Compressed Load*

9x18 MAKAROV

Alternate Names:	9mm Makarov
Parent Cartridge:	Original design
Country of Origin:	USA
Year of Introduction:	1948
Designer(s):	Nikolai Makarov
Governing Body:	SAAMI/CIP

CARTRIDGE CASE DATA

Case Type:	Rimless, straight
Average Case Capacity:	14.2 grains H$_2$O
Max. Cartridge OAL:	.984 inch
Max. Case Length:	.713 inch
Primer:	Small Pistol
Case Trim to Length:	.703 inch
RCBS Shell holder:	# 16
Current Manufacturers:	Hornady, Winchester, Fiocchi, Prvi Partizan, Sellier & Bellot, Wolf, MFS

BALLISTIC DATA

Max. Average Pressure (MAP):	24,100 psi, CUP not established for this cartridge - SAAMI
Test Barrel Length:	3.625 inch
Rifling Twist Rate:	1 turn in 9.45 inch

Muzzle velocities of factory loaded ammunition	Bullet Wgt.	Muzzle velocity
	95-grain	1,000 fps

HISTORICAL NOTES

- The 9mm Makarov cartridge can trace its history back to 1936 when Carl Walther G.m.b.H. designed a new 9x18mm Ultra pistol cartridge for the German Luftwaffe. The new cartridge was not adopted, however, it set in motion the concept for a pistol cartridge midway in power between the 9x19mm Luger (9mm Luger) and the 9x17mm Kurz (380 Auto).

- Following the end of World War II in 1945, the Russian military needed a new pistol cartridge to replace the 7.62x25mm Tokarev. Undoubtedly, the previous German work on the 9x18mm Ultra was influential in their adoption of the 9x18mm Makarov cartridge.

- The 9x18mm "middle" power concept came up once again. In 1972, European law enforcement agencies sought to replace their 32 Auto pistols with

something more powerful than the 380 Auto but not as powerful as the 9mm Luger. After considerable study and prolonged testing, the new 9x18mm Police cartridge was put forward, but never adopted.
- Beginning in the 1980s, the Russian military saw a need to increase the power of the 9x18mm Makarov cartridge. Many different ideas were tried with limited success.
- Finally, in the early 2000s, the Russian military made a momentous decision; the 9mm Luger cartridge was taken into Russian military service. The Makarov was declared obsolete.

Interesting Fact

All Russian-made Makarov pistols were made at the Izhmekh (Baikal) factory in Izhevsk. Production for the Russian military services ended in the late 1990s. However, production for export and civilian sales continued for some years afterward. When the Russian military adopted the 9mm Luger cartridge, the new "Grach" (crow) pistol in this caliber entered production at the Baikal plant.

BALLISTIC NOTES

- Russian military 9mm Makarov ball ammunition is loaded with a 93 to 106-grain FMJRN bullet to a muzzle velocity of 1,020-1,115 fps.
- MAP levels of the 9mm Makarov are approximately 12% higher than the 380 Auto giving it an edge in muzzle velocity and muzzle energy. However, the 9mm Makarov is considerably less powerful than the 9mm Luger.
- Speer offers one bullet for handloading the 9mm Makarov cartridge:
  - A 95-grain TMJ® RN which can be used to duplicate the factory load.
- Makarov pistols were not designed to feed or chamber hollow point bullets. For this reason you may experience feeding problems with such bullets. These problems can usually be solved by adjusting the overall loaded length.
- Some Makarov pistols have been converted to fire 380 Auto ammunition and are so marked on the slide. Be certain to check this before firing your pistol.

TECHNICAL NOTES

- The correct bullet diameter for the 9mm Makarov is .364 inch. Note that this is larger in diameter from the .355 inch bullets for either the 380 Auto or 9mm.
- For this reason, bullets for the 380 Auto or 9mm cannot be used to load the 9mm Makarov cartridge.
- The case length of the 9mm Makarov is 18mm placing it in between the 380 Auto (9x17mm) and the 9mm Luger (9x19mm).
- The 9x18mm Makarov is not interchangeable with either of these cartridges.
- The 9mm Makarov cartridge head spaces on the case mouth.
- Most Russian 9mm Makarov ammunition is Berdan primed and cannot be reloaded easily.
- However, Boxer primed brass in this caliber is available from Starlinebrass.com.

HANDLOADING NOTES

- Makarov pistols are blowback operated (unlocked breech). Fired cases from such guns are frequently damaged by the violent extraction or ejection forces. For this reason, we recommend that you carefully inspect all fired cases before reloading them. Discard any that are dented, split, scratched, cracked, or have damaged rims.
- Do not attempt to reload 9mm Makarov empty cartridge cases with Berdan primers. Destroy them.
- Never load less than the minimum charges shown in the loading data as the small charge of propellant may not be sufficient to push the bullet completely down the barrel.

SAFETY NOTES

SPEER 95-grain TMJ RN @ a muzzle velocity of 1,068 fps:
- Maximum vertical altitude @ 90° elevation is 3,606 feet.
- Maximum horizontal distance to first impact with ground @ 32° elevation is 1,665 yards.

95 GRAINS

DIAMETER	SECTIONAL DENSITY
.364"	0.102

9mm Mak TMJ® RN

Ballistic Coefficient	0.127
COAL Tested	0.980"
Speer Part No.	4375

Propellant	Case	Primer	Starting Charge Weight (grains)	Starting Charge Muzzle Velocity (feet/sec)	Maximum Charge Weight (grains)	Maximum Charge Muzzle Velocity (feet/sec)
Accurate No. 5	Starline	CCI 500	5.6	891	6.3	1068
Accurate No. 2 Improved	Starline	CCI 500	3.9	936	4.4	1042
Accurate No. 7	Starline	CCI 500	7.0	912	7.8	1038
Winchester 231	Starline	CCI 500	3.9	911	4.4	1029
Hodgdon HS-6	Starline	CCI 500	5.6	828	6.3	1010
Alliant Bullseye	Starline	CCI 500	3.5	896	3.9	1010
Vihtavuori N330	Starline	CCI 500	4.0	841	4.5	966
Hodgdon H. Universal	Starline	CCI 500	4.0	774	4.5	965
Vihtavuori N320	Starline	CCI 500	3.3	832	3.7	963

WARNING! *Maximum loads should be used with CAUTION • C = Compressed Load*

40 SMITH & WESSON

Alternate Names:	40 S&W, 40 AUTO
Parent Cartridge:	10mm Automatic
Country of Origin:	USA
Year of Introduction:	1990
Designer(s):	Winchester and Smith & Wesson
Governing Body:	SAAMI/CIP

CARTRIDGE CASE DATA

Case Type:	Rimless, straight
Average Case Capacity:	21.0 grains H_2O
Max. Cartridge OAL	1.135 inch
Max. Case Length:	.850 inch
Primer:	Small Pistol
Case Trim to Length:	.840 inch
RCBS Shell holder:	# 27
Current Manufacturers:	CCI/Speer, Federal, Hornady, Remington, Winchester, Cor-Bon, Black Hills, Fiocchi, Sellier & Bellot, Magtech, Aguila, Armscor, PMC

BALLISTIC DATA

Max. Average Pressure (MAP):	35,000 psi, CUP not established for this cartridge - SAAMI
Test Barrel Length:	4.0 inch
Rifling Twist Rate:	1 turn in 16 inch

Muzzle velocities of factory loaded ammunition

Bullet Wgt.	Muzzle velocity
155-grain	1,205 fps
165-grain	1,050 fps
180-grain	1,045 fps
200-grain	1,000 fps

HISTORICAL NOTES

- Noted author and experienced shooting instructor Jeff Cooper observed that while the 45 Auto cartridge packed plenty of stopping power, its heavy recoil was more than novice shooters could handle without extensive instruction and practice.
- On the other hand, Cooper felt the 9mm Luger lacked stopping power, but its low recoil made instruction and training of novice shooters substantially easier.

- At this time, American law enforcement agencies found most of their new recruits had never fired a gun before which increased the amount of training required for them to qualify.
- After considering this dilemma, Cooper proposed a new, 40 caliber pistol cartridge with a balanced blend of effective stopping power and light recoil that would reduce the amount of training required for novice shooters. Such a cartridge would fit in 9mm Luger pistols with a minimum number of modifications in order to keep size and weight down.
- Ammunition manufacturers began experimenting with 10mm pistol cartridges. The first 10mm Auto cartridge was far too powerful and would not fit in pistols designed for the 9mm Luger. However, it created a market of its own and survives to this day.
- Winchester and Smith & Wesson developed a "10mm Short" cartridge that met all of Cooper's requirements. The new 40 S&W pistol cartridge was introduced in 1990 to great acclaim.
- Pistol manufacturers hastened to develop pistols in the new chambering, and ammunition makers added the 40 S&W to their product lines.
- By 2000, the 40 S&W had rivaled the 9mm Luger as the most popular cartridge of choice for American law enforcement agencies.
- However, the 40 S&W cartridge was not received as enthusiastically by sportsmen who did not have the same requirements for training, power and size.

BALLISTIC NOTES

- Winchester's interpretation of Cooper's ballistic balance of stopping power and manageable recoil for the 40 S&W consisted of a 180-grain bullet at a muzzle velocity of 980 fps (subsonic).
- However, law enforcement agencies soon began requesting lighter bullets at increased muzzle velocities.
- In response to this demand, ammunition manufacturers have added lighter bullets at supersonic muzzle velocities.
- Speer offers two outstanding bullet types and weights designed especially for the 40 S&W cartridge:
  - Total Metal Jacket Flat Nose (TMJ® FN) 40/10mm in 155, 165, and 180-grain. These bullets are the best choice for duplicating the factory loads for training, practice and qualification.
  - Gold Dot® Hollow Point (GDHP) 40/10mm in 155, 165, and 180-grain. Gold Dot bullets have a reputation for being the best JHP handgun bullets on the market for law enforcement and personal defense.

TECHNICAL NOTES

- The 40 S&W cartridge case is a rimless design that headspaces on the case mouth. Case capacity is 45% greater than the 9mm Luger, but 35% less than the 45 Auto.
- In most 9mm Luger pistol frames, the 40 S&W cartridge is a tight fit. As a result, bullets for the 40 S&W must be of a special, compact ogive design.
  - The maximum overall loaded length of a 40 S&W cartridge is 1.135 inches.
  - Maximum case length is .850 inch.

- This leaves just .285 inch for bullet protrusion. By comparison, the 9mm Luger cartridge allows for .415 inch of bullet protrusion.
- Speer 40/10mm bullets are designed to fit these parameters.
- MAP level for the 40 S&W is 35,000 psi which is comparable to the 9mm Luger, but substantially higher than the 45 Auto.
- Most 40 S&W caliber pistols are recoil operated. The 40 S&W cartridge is too powerful for straight blowback operation. An exception is the roller-delayed blowback operated pistols from H&K.

HANDLOADING NOTES

- Be certain to use .400-inch diameter bullets designed especially for the 40 S&W.
- Finish your reloads with a light taper crimp on the case mouth to hold the bullet securely, improve shot start, and enhance feeding reliability.
- Never load less than the minimum charges shown in the loading data as the small charge of propellant may not be sufficient to push the bullet completely down the barrel.
- The recent surge in ownership of suppressors by sportsmen has increased the demand for subsonic ammunition in 40 S&W caliber. Speer has you covered here with loading data for subsonic loads.

SAFETY NOTES

SPEER 40/10mm 180-grain TMJ FN, @ a muzzle velocity of 1,026 fps:
- Maximum vertical altitude @ 90° elevation is 3,834 feet.
- Maximum horizontal distance to first impact with ground @ 33° elevation is 1,788 yards.

155 GRAINS

DIAMETER	SECTIONAL DENSITY
.400"	0.138

40/10mm TMJ® FN
Ballistic Coefficient	0.125
COAL Tested	1.120"
Speer Part No.	4399

40/10mm GDHP
Ballistic Coefficient	0.123
COAL Tested	1.120"
Speer Part No.	4400

Propellant	Case	Primer	Starting Charge Weight (grains)	Starting Charge Muzzle Velocity (feet/sec)	Maximum Charge Weight (grains)	Maximum Charge Muzzle Velocity (feet/sec)
Alliant Blue Dot	Speer	CCI 500	10.0	1113	11.0	1221
Alliant Power Pistol	Speer	CCI 500	8.0	1112	9.0	1213
Alliant Unique	Speer	CCI 500	7.2	1048	8.0	1207
Hodgdon H. Universal	Speer	CCI 500	6.2	995	7.0	1159
Hodgdon TITEGROUP	Speer	CCI 500	5.4	1011	6.2	1144
Accurate No. 5	Speer	CCI 500	7.9	956	8.7	1116
Winchester WSF	Speer	CCI 500	6.7	981	7.5	1090
Accurate No. 7	Speer	CCI 500	10.0	984	11.0	1089
Vihtavuori N350	Speer	CCI 500	6.8	858	7.6	1061
Winchester 231	Speer	CCI 500	5.8	867	6.5	1038
Hodgdon HS-6	Speer	CCI 500	7.3	786	9.0	1033
Alliant Bullseye	Speer	CCI 500	5.4	905	6.0	1023
Alliant American Select	Speer	CCI 500	5.0	931	5.6	1001
Accurate No. 2 Improved	Speer	CCI 500	5.8	840	6.5	956

WARNING! *Maximum loads should be used with CAUTION • C = Compressed Load*

165 GRAINS

DIAMETER	SECTIONAL DENSITY
.400"	0.147

40/10mm TMJ® FN
Ballistic Coefficient	0.135
COAL Tested	1.120"
Speer Part No.	4410

40/10mm GDHP
Ballistic Coefficient	0.138
COAL Tested	1.120"
Speer Part No.	4397

Propellant	Case	Primer	Starting Charge Weight (grains)	Starting Charge Muzzle Velocity (feet/sec)	Maximum Charge Weight (grains)	Maximum Charge Muzzle Velocity (feet/sec)
Alliant BE 86	Federal	Federal 100	6.0	1034	6.8	1144
Winchester AutoComp	Federal	Federal 100	5.8	992	6.6	1107
Vihtavuori N350	Speer	CCI 500	6.7	989	7.5	1106
Hodgdon CFE Pistol	Federal	Federal 100	5.4	951	6.4	1103
Winchester WSF	Speer	CCI 500	6.2	1007	6.8	1082
Alliant Power Pistol	Speer	CCI 500	7.0	978	7.8	1081
Hodgdon H. Universal	Speer	CCI 500	5.7	999	6.2	1074
Accurate No. 5	Speer	CCI 500	7.6	916	8.5	1067
Alliant Unique	Speer	CCI 500	6.2	882	7.2	1064
Hodgdon HS-6	Speer	CCI 500	8.0	1012	8.5	1060
Accurate No. 7	Speer	CCI 500	9.6	951	10.5	1041
Hodgdon TITEGROUP	Speer	CCI 500	5.0	957	5.4	1035
Alliant Sport Pistol	Federal	Federal 100	4.1	888	5.1	1033
Winchester 231	Speer	CCI 500	5.8	955	6.3	1031
Alliant Bullseye	Speer	CCI 500	5.3	949	5.8	1022

WARNING! Maximum loads should be used with CAUTION • C = Compressed Load

180 GRAINS

DIAMETER	SECTIONAL DENSITY
.400"	0.161

40/10mm TMJ® FN
Ballistic Coefficient	0.143
COAL Tested	1.120"
Speer Part No.	4402

40/10mm GDHP
Ballistic Coefficient	0.143
COAL Tested	1.120"
Speer Part No.	4406

			Starting Charge		Maximum Charge	
Propellant	Case	Primer	Weight (grains)	Muzzle Velocity (feet/sec)	Weight (grains)	Muzzle Velocity (feet/sec)
Alliant BE 86	Federal	Federal 100	4.9	879	6.0	1026
Hodgdon Hi-Skor 700-X	Speer	CCI 500	5.0	953	5.5	1020
Alliant Blue Dot	Speer	CCI 500	8.0	922	8.9	1018
Alliant Power Pistol	Speer	CCI 500	6.2	890	7.2	1013
Winchester AutoComp	Federal	Federal 100	5.1	909	5.8	1011
Hornady CFE Pistol	Federal	Federal 100	5.0	911	5.7	1009
Alliant Unique	Speer	CCI 500	6.0	849	6.7	1000
Vihtavuori N350	Speer	CCI 500	6.2	804	6.9	987
IMR SR 7625	Speer	CCI 500	5.4	884	6.0	981
Accurate No. 7	Speer	CCI 500	8.7	895	9.7	972
Accurate No. 5	Speer	CCI 500	7.0	791	7.8	969
Vihtavuori 3N37	Speer	CCI 500	6.6	841	7.2	960
Hodgdon HS-6	Speer	CCI 500	7.3	786	8.2	942
Alliant Bullseye	Speer	CCI 500	4.9	783	5.5	929
Alliant Sport Pistol	Federal	Federal 100	3.8	829	4.4	919
Alliant TITEGROUP	Speer	CCI 500	4.0	793	4.7	917
Hodgdon H. Universal	Speer	CCI 500	5.3	802	5.9	904
Alliant American Select	Speer	CCI 500	4.3	770	5.1	865

WARNING! Maximum loads should be used with CAUTION • C = Compressed Load

10mm AUTOMATIC

Alternate Names:	Bren 10
Parent Cartridge:	Original design
Country of Origin:	USA
Year of Introduction:	1983
Designer(s):	Jeff Cooper and Norma
Governing Body:	SAAMI/CIP

CARTRIDGE CASE DATA	
Case Type:	Rimless, straight
Average Case Capacity:	25.7 grains H_2O
Max. Cartridge OAL	1.260 inch
Max. Case Length:	.992 inch
Primer:	Large Pistol
Case Trim to Length:	.982 inch
RCBS Shell holder:	# 27
Current Manufacturers:	Blazer, Federal, Hornady, Remington, Winchester, Cor-Bon, Magtech, Armscor, PMC

BALLISTIC DATA			
Max. Average Pressure (MAP):	37,500 psi, CUP not established for this cartridge - SAAMI	Test Barrel Length:	5 inch
Rifling Twist Rate:	1 turn in 16 inch		
Muzzle velocities of factory loaded ammunition	Bullet Wgt.		Muzzle velocity
	180-grain		1,200 fps

HISTORICAL NOTES

- In 1983, a small company in California named Dornaus & Dixon introduced their Bren Ten pistol chambered for a new, full-power 10mm Auto cartridge.

- At the same time, Norma of Sweden announced a new cartridge they had developed expressly for the Bren Ten pistol.

- As interest grew, in 1987 Colt began production of their 10mm Delta Elite pistol on a strengthened M1911 platform. Not to be outdone by Colt, other handgun makers and ammunition manufacturers introduced pistols and ammunition in the new cartridge.

- For a brief period, the FBI adopted the new cartridge (although not the Bren Ten pistol).

- Today, every major domestic ammunition manufacturer offers 10mm Auto ammunition.
- However, the market segment occupied by the 10mm Auto cartridge is a highly specialized one with small sales volume. As interest in and sales of the 10mm Auto cartridge wanes, some of the ammunition manufacturers will drop this caliber, placing more emphasis on handloading.
- Norma no longer manufactures pistol ammunition.
- In European markets, the 10mm Auto pistol is regarded as an overpowered, American specialty of limited interest.

BALLISTIC NOTES

- Norma's original 10mm Auto load consisted of a 200-grain bullet at a muzzle velocity of 1,200 fps. This was a heavy load with considerable recoil best left to experienced shooters.
- Today, the 200-grain bullet has been dropped in favor of 180-grain bullets at muzzle velocities of 1,030-1,275 fps. Both FMJ and JHP bullet designs are offered.
- Lighter weight bullets are offered by a limited number of manufacturers.
- Top of the line is Federal's 180-grain TBBC JHP bullet at a muzzle velocity of 1,275 fps with a muzzle energy of 650 ft-lbs. This one is best left to experienced handgunners!
- The ballistic potential and wide variety of 10mm component bullets make the 10mm Auto an ideal candidate for handloading.
    - Speer offers three bullet weights designed especially for the 10mm handloading:
    - Total Metal Jacket Flat Nose (TMJ® FN) bullets weighing 155, 165, and 180-grain. These bullets are a good choice for practice, training, and informal target shooting.
    - Gold Dot® Hollow Point (GDHP) bullets weighing 155, 165, and 180-grain are well-known as outstanding choices for personal defense.

TECHNICAL NOTES

- The 10mm Auto cartridge case is a rimless, tapered body design that headspaces on the case mouth.
- Case capacity of the 10mm Auto cartridge case is 22% greater than the 40 S&W, providing sufficient space for slower burning propellants.
- MAP level for 10mm Auto sporting ammunition is 37,500 psi which is 7% higher than MAP levels for 9mm Luger and 40 S&W.
- Most 10mm Auto pistols are recoil operated. The 10mm Auto cartridge is too powerful for straight blowback operation.
- The correct bullet diameter for the 10mm Auto is .400 inches. Note that this is the same diameter of bullet for the 40 S&W.

HANDLOADING NOTES

- Note that the 165-grain bullet can be handloaded to a higher muzzle velocity than the 155-grain.

- The ballistic sweet spot of the 10mm Auto is a 165-grain bullet at a muzzle velocity of approximately 1,350 fps.
- Finish your reloads with a light taper crimp on the case mouth to hold the bullet securely, and improve shot start and enhance feeding reliability.
- Never load less than the minimum charges shown in the loading data as the small charge of propellant may not be sufficient to push the bullet completely down the barrel.
- Use medium burning rate pistol powders for loading the 10mm Auto.

SAFETY NOTES

SPEER 180-grain TMJ FN 40/10mm @ a muzzle velocity of 1,295 fps:
- Maximum vertical altitude @ 90° elevation is 4,143 ft.
- Maximum horizontal distance to first impact with ground @ 32° elevation is 1,907 yards.

155 GRAINS

DIAMETER	SECTIONAL DENSITY
.400"	0.138

40/10mm TMJ® FN
Ballistic Coefficient	0.125
COAL Tested	1.250"
Speer Part No.	4399

40/10mm GDHP
Ballistic Coefficient	0.123
COAL Tested	1.250"
Speer Part No.	4400

			Starting Charge		Maximum Charge	
Propellant	Case	Primer	Weight (grains)	Muzzle Velocity (feet/sec)	Weight (grains)	Muzzle Velocity (feet/sec)
Accurate No. 7	Hornady	CCI 300	12.0	1187	13.0	1320
Alliant Blue Dot	Hornady	CCI 300	11.0	1164	12.0	1291
Alliant Unique	Hornady	CCI 300	7.5	1091	8.5	1246
Hodgdon HS-6	Hornady	CCI 350	9.5	1095	10.5	1223
Winchester 231	Hornady	CCI 300	7.0	1062	7.7	1183
Vihtavuori N340	Hornady	CCI 300	7.2	1034	8.0	1180
Accurate No. 5	Hornady	CCI 300	9.2	1004	10.2	1176
Winchester WSF	Hornady	CCI 300	7.6	1017	8.4	1162

WARNING! Maximum loads should be used with CAUTION • C = Compressed Load

165 GRAINS

DIAMETER	SECTIONAL DENSITY
.400"	0.147

40/10mm GDHP
Ballistic Coefficient	0.138
COAL Tested	1.255"
Speer Part No.	4397

40/10mm TMJ® FN
Ballistic Coefficient	0.135
COAL Tested	1.255"
Speer Part No.	4410

Propellant	Case	Primer	Starting Charge Weight (grains)	Starting Charge Muzzle Velocity (feet/sec)	Maximum Charge Weight (grains)	Maximum Charge Muzzle Velocity (feet/sec)
Accurate No. 9	Hornady	CCI 350	14.5	1277	15.5	1344
Alliant Power Pistol	Hornady	CCI 300	9.0	1204	10.0	1314
Accurate No. 7	Hornady	CCI 300	11.2	1177	12.2	1278
Alliant Blue Dot	Hornady	CCI 300	10.5	1181	11.5	1273
Alliant 2400	Hornady	CCI 300	13.8	1159	14.8	1234
Vihtavuori 3N37	Hornady	CCI 300	8.3	1091	9.2	1228
Hodgdon H. Universal	Hornady	CCI 300	6.8	1100	7.5	1205
Alliant Unique	Hornady	CCI 300	7.4	1126	8.3	1194
Hodgdon HS-6	Hornady	CCI 350	9.0	1071	10.0	1185
Winchester WSF	Hornady	CCI 300	7.2	1065	8.0	1177
Winchester 231	Hornady	CCI 300	6.3	1043	7.0	1143

WARNING! *Maximum loads should be used with* **CAUTION** • *C = Compressed Load*

180 GRAINS

DIAMETER	SECTIONAL DENSITY
.400"	0.161

40/10mm TMJ® FN
Ballistic Coefficient	0.143
COAL Tested	1.250"
Speer Part No.	4402

40/10mm GDHP
Ballistic Coefficient	0.143
COAL Tested	1.250"
Speer Part No.	4406

			Starting Charge		Maximum Charge	
Propellant	Case	Primer	Weight (grains)	Muzzle Velocity (feet/sec)	Weight (grains)	Muzzle Velocity (feet/sec)
Alliant Blue Dot	Hornady	CCI 300	10.0	1105	11.0	1295
Alliant 2400	Hornady	CCI 300	11.5	1051	12.8	1214
Accurate No. 7	Hornady	CCI 300	11.0	1065	12.0	1180
Vihtavuori N350	Hornady	CCI 300	8.9	1077	9.7	1152
Vihtavuori 3N37	Hornady	CCI 300	9.0	1027	10.0	1150
Alliant Unique	Hornady	CCI 300	7.2	1043	8.0	1138
Winchester WSF	Hornady	CCI 300	6.8	1001	7.5	1120
Accurate No. 5	Hornady	CCI 300	8.5	1015	9.5	1116
Hodgdon HS-6	Hornady	CCI 350	8.2	1001	9.1	1099

WARNING! *Maximum loads should be used with CAUTION • C = Compressed Load*

41 REMINGTON MAGNUM

Alternate Names:	41 S&W Magnum, 41 Magnum
Parent Cartridge:	Original design
Related Cartridges:	41 Long Colt
Country of Origin:	USA
Year of Introduction:	1964
Designer(s):	Remington and Smith & Wesson
Governing Body:	SAAMI/CIP

CARTRIDGE CASE DATA

Case Type:	Rimmed, straight
Average Case Capacity:	34.8 grains H$_2$O
Max. Cartridge OAL:	1.590 inch
Max. Case Length:	1.290 inch
Primer:	Large Pistol
Case Trim to Length:	1.280 inch
RCBS Shell holder:	# 30
Current Manufacturers:	Federal, Remington, Winchester, Cor-Bon, Starline

BALLISTIC DATA

Max. Average Pressure (MAP):	36,000 psi, 40,000 CUP - SAAMI
Test Barrel Length:	10.135 inch (Unvented), 5.788 inch (Vented)
Rifling Twist Rate:	1 turn in 18.75 inch

Muzzle velocities of factory loaded ammunition	Bullet Wgt.	Muzzle velocity
	210-grain	1,300 fps
	240-grain	1,180 fps

HISTORICAL NOTES

- In the early 1960s, many law enforcement agencies felt the need for a revolver cartridge offering more power than the 357 Magnum, but less than the 44 Magnum.
- Remington answered the call in 1964 with the 41 Remington Magnum in two power levels:
  - A law enforcement load with a 210-grain lead semi-wadcutter (LSWC) bullet at a muzzle velocity of 1,000 fps.
  - A hunting load with a 210-grain JSP bullet at a muzzle velocity of 1,350 fps.

- From the beginning, a number of problems emerged:
  - Recoil was too heavy for law enforcement use.
  - Both the JSP and LSWC bullets passed completely through a human target.
  - Many elected officials were opposed to law enforcement use of magnum cartridges.
  - No JHP bullet was offered.
  - The LSWC bullet frequently leaded the barrel.
- For these reasons, the law enforcement community never accepted the 41 Rem. Magnum.
- Some hunters found the 41 Remington Magnum effective for deer in areas where handgun hunting was allowed. However, more hunters preferred the 44 Magnum for that purpose.
- From a marketing standpoint, any perceived ballistic gap between the 357 Magnum and the 44 Magnum was simply too narrow on which to base a cartridge.
- As a result, sales of 41 Remington Magnum ammunition were never large.
- Currently, most domestic ammunition manufacturers offer only one load in 41 Rem. Magnum.
- Can the demise of the 41 Remington Magnum be far off?

Interesting Fact

The 41 Long Colt, located between the 45 Colt and the 38 Long Colt, introduced in the late 19th century was not a success either.

In the later 20th century, the 41 Action Express, located between the 45 Auto and 9mm Luger, also was not successful.

TECHNICAL NOTES

- The 41 Remington Magnum cartridge case is a classic revolver design with a rim and a straight sided case.
- Case length is similar to the 44 Magnum, but case capacity is approximately 12% less.
- Most 41 Magnum revolvers are built on 44 Magnum frames.
- Most revolver bullets must be of a special, compact ogive design (flat nose) to maximize case capacity. The Speer 210-grain DCHP bullet is designed to these parameters.
- MAP level for the 41 Remington Magnum is 36,000 psi which is comparable to the 44 Magnum.

HANDLOADING NOTES

- To prevent bullet elongation in revolvers, all bullets for the 41 Remington Magnum cartridge must be roll crimped securely in the cannelure on the bullet's surface
- Never load less than the minimum charges shown in the loading data as the small charge of propellant may not be sufficient to push the bullet completely down the barrel.
- Use fast burning pistol powders for loading the 41 Remington Magnum.

SAFETY NOTES

SPEER 210-grain DeepCurl Hollow Point @ a muzzle velocity of 1,295 fps:
- Maximum vertical altitude @ 90° elevation is 4,869 feet.
- Maximum horizontal distance to first impact with ground @ 34° elevation is 2,278 yards.

210 GRAINS

DIAMETER	SECTIONAL DENSITY
.410"	0.178

41 DCHP

Ballistic Coefficient	0.183
COAL Tested	1.575"
Speer Part No.	4430

			Starting Charge		Maximum Charge	
Propellant	Case	Primer	Weight (grains)	Muzzle Velocity (feet/sec)	Weight (grains)	Muzzle Velocity (feet/sec)
Alliant Power Pro 300-MP	Federal	CCI 350	21.2	1216	23.6	1369
Winchester 296	Winchester	CCI 350	20.5	1251	21.5	1295
Hodgdon H110	Winchester	CCI 350	20.5	1237	21.5	1265
Accurate No. 9	Winchester	CCI 300	17.0	1199	18.0	1265
Vihtavuori N110	Winchester	CCI 300	17.0	1136	18.0	1244
Alliant Power Pistol	Federal	CCI 350	10.8	1167	11.6	1228
Alliant 2400	Winchester	CCI 300	18.0	1176	19.0	1223
Alliant BE-86	Federal	CCI 350	10.1	1171	10.8	1221
IMR 4227	Winchester	CCI 300	21.0	1117	22.0	1203
Winchester AutoComp	Federal	CCI 350	9.2	1054	10.2	1158
Hodgdon CFE Pistol	Federal	CCI 350	9.0	1054	9.9	1155
Alliant Unique	Winchester	CCI 300	8.7	1034	9.7	1123
Vihtavuori N350	Winchester	CCI 300	9.8	1035	10.5	1110

WARNING! *Maximum loads should be used with CAUTION • C = Compressed Load*

44 S&W SPECIAL

Alternate Names:	44 Special
Parent Cartridge:	44 Russian
Country of Origin:	USA
Year of Introduction:	1907
Designer(s):	Smith & Wesson
Governing Body:	SAAMI/CIP

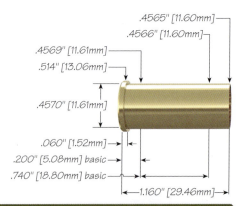

CARTRIDGE CASE DATA			
Case Type:	Rimmed, straight		
Average Case Capacity:	34.8 grains H_2O	Max. Cartridge OAL	1.615 inch
Max. Case Length:	1.160 inch	Primer:	Large Pistol
Case Trim to Length:	1.150 inch	RCBS Shell holder:	# 18
Current Manufacturers:	CCI/Speer, Federal, Hornady, Remington, Winchester, Black Hills, Cor-Bon, Magtech, Fiocchi, Prvi Partizan		

BALLISTIC DATA			
Max. Average Pressure (MAP):	15,500 psi, 14,000 CUP - SAAMI	Test Barrel Length:	8.150 inch (Unvented), 5.638 inch (Vented)
Rifling Twist Rate:	1 turn in 20 inch		
Muzzle velocities of factory loaded ammunition	Bullet Wgt.		Muzzle velocity
	200-grain		900 fps
	240-grain		750 fps
	246-grain		755 fps

HISTORICAL NOTES

- The 44 Special cartridge has a long and impeccable pedigree dating back to the dawn of the self-contained cartridge.

- Its grandfather, the 44 Russian, dates from 1870. Its contemporaries include the 44 Colt (1870), the 44 S&W American (1870), and the 44 Merwin & Hulbert (1882). All are mere historical curiosities today.

- Despite its black powder heritage, the 44 Special was designed for and always loaded with smokeless propellants. It was introduced by S&W in 1907.

- Why has the 44 Special survived for over 110 years? The answer may be divided into three eras.

- Era One: (1907 to 1957) The 44 Special was a popular caliber for target shooters who appreciated its accuracy, modest muzzle velocities, and mild recoil.
- In the early 1950s, noted gun writer Elmer Keith used the 44 Special cartridge as the basis for experiments in high velocity revolver cartridges with heavy bullets for hunting.
- Era Two: (1957 to 1987) Informed of Keith's results, in 1956 Remington introduced the new 44 Remington Magnum cartridge. S&W followed with their Model 29 revolver in the new caliber.
- The new 44 Magnum cartridge rapidly became popular and has remained so to this day.
- However, the rise of the 44 Magnum did not result in the death of the 44 S&W Special; it could be fired in 44 Magnum revolvers for low cost practice and informal target shooting where full power loads were not needed.
- Era Three: (1987-present) A new market for the 44 Special opened when revolver manufacturers introduced compact, 5-shot revolvers in this caliber.
- Ammunition makers updated their 44 Special product lines to include JHP bullets at muzzle velocities of about 900 fps which were better suited for personal defense.
- Today, nearly every domestic ammunition manufacturer offers 44 Special ammunition.

BALLISTIC NOTES

- The classic target load for the 44 Special is a 246-grain lead bullet at a leisurely 755 fps. This load is still offered by Winchester and Remington.
- For modern personal defense in compact revolvers, domestic ammunition makers have developed 200-grain hollow point bullets at muzzle velocities of 870-900 fps.
- For reloading the 44 Special, Speer offers a 200-grain Gold Dot® Hollow Point, which has been designed especially for the 44 Special. It can be handloaded to a wide range of muzzle velocities ranging from 788 fps to 976 fps.

TECHNICAL NOTES

- Case length is .125 inch shorter than the 44 Magnum and case capacity is approximately 12% less. Other dimensions are comparable to the 44 Magnum, with the exception of Max. COAL, where the 44 Special is longer by .005 inch.
- Most revolver bullets must be of a special, compact ogive design (flat nose) to maximize case capacity. The Speer 200-grain Gold Dot Hollow Point bullet is designed to these parameters.
- MAP level for the 44 Special is 15,500 psi which is 57% lower than the 44 Magnum.
- The correct jacketed bullet diameter for the 44 Special is .429 inch and .430 inches for lead bullets.

HANDLOADING NOTES

- To prevent bullet elongation in revolvers, all bullets for the 44 Special cartridge must be roll crimped securely in the cannelure on the bullet's surface.

- Never load less than the minimum charges shown in the loading data as the small charge of propellant may not be sufficient to push the bullet completely down the barrel.
- Use fast burning pistol powders for loading the 44 Special.

SAFETY NOTES

SPEER 200-grain Gold Dot Hollow Point @ a muzzle velocity of 976 fps:
- Maximum vertical altitude @ 90° elevation is 3,768 feet.
- Maximum horizontal distance to first impact with ground @ 33° elevation is 1,767 yards.

140 GRAINS

DIAMETER	SECTIONAL DENSITY
.430"	N/A

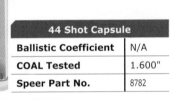

44 Shot Capsule

Ballistic Coefficient	N/A
COAL Tested	1.600"
Speer Part No.	8782

NOTE: Shot capsules must not be used in firearms with ported recoil compensators.

Propellant	Case	Primer	Weight (grains)	Muzzle Velocity (feet/sec)
Hodgdon HP-38	Remington	CCI 300	5.8	1055
Winchester 231	Remington	CCI 300	6.3	1045
Hodgdon HS-6	Remington	CCI 350	8.2	1029
Hodgdon Hi-Skor 700-X	Remington	CCI 300	5.3	1014
Alliant Unique	Remington	CCI 300	6.7	1005

Test firearm—S&W Model 29 4"

WARNING! Maximum loads should be used with CAUTION • C = Compressed Load

GOLD DOT

200 GRAINS

DIAMETER	SECTIONAL DENSITY
.429"	0.155

44 GDHP SB

Ballistic Coefficient	0.145
COAL Tested	1.490"
Speer Part No.	4427

Propellant	Case	Primer	Starting Charge		Maximum Charge	
			Weight (grains)	Muzzle Velocity (feet/sec)	Weight (grains)	Muzzle Velocity (feet/sec)
Alliant Power Pistol	Remington	CCI 300	7.6	872	8.6	976
Vihtavuori N350	Remington	CCI 300	8.0	823	8.8	952
Hodgdon H. Universal	Remington	CCI 300	7.0	842	7.6	950
Accurate No. 5	Remington	CCI 300	8.8	805	9.9	935
Hodgdon Hi-Skor 700-X	Remington	CCI 300	5.3	800	6.1	902
Hodgdon TITEGROUP	Remington	CCI 300	5.3	795	6.1	902
Winchester 231	Remington	CCI 300	6.0	730	6.9	886
Alliant Bullseye	Remington	CCI 300	5.1	766	5.9	884
Alliant Red Dot	Remington	CCI 300	5.4	801	5.9	868
Alliant Unique	Remington	CCI 300	7.0	788	7.8	855
Accurate No. 2 Improved	Remington	CCI 300	DNR	—	5.9	828
Alliant American Select	Remington	CCI 300	DNR	—	5.7	821

DNR — do not reduce

WARNING! *Maximum loads should be used with CAUTION • C = Compressed Load*

240 GRAINS

DIAMETER	SECTIONAL DENSITY
.430"	0.185

44 LSWC

Ballistic Coefficient	0.151
COAL Tested	1.475"
Speer Part No.	4661

NOTE: *Velocities determined using a Taurus revolver with 3" barrel.*

			Starting Charge		Maximum Charge	
Propellant	Case	Primer	Weight (grains)	Muzzle Velocity (feet/sec)	Weight (grains)	Muzzle Velocity (feet/sec)
Alliant Unique	Remington	CCI 300	5.7	746	6.3	820
Alliant Herco	Remington	CCI 300	5.8	730	6.4	816
Hodgdon HS-6	Remington	CCI 350	7.0	695	8.0	815
Winchester 231	Remington	CCI 300	5.2	701	5.7	796
Alliant Bullseye	Remington	CCI 300	4.7	691	5.2	793
Alliant Red Dot	Remington	CCI 300	4.5	658	5.0	750
Alliant Green Dot	Remington	CCI 300	5.2	672	5.7	749
Hodgdon Hi-Skor 700-X	Remington	CCI 300	4.1	640	4.6	734

WARNING! *Maximum loads should be used with CAUTION • C = Compressed Load*

44 REMINGTON MAGNUM

Alternate Names:	44 Magnum
Parent Cartridge:	44 S&W Special
Country of Origin:	USA
Year of Introduction:	1955
Designer(s):	Remington, Elmer Keith, Smith & Wesson
Governing Body:	SAAMI

CARTRIDGE CASE DATA

Case Type:	Rimmed, straight
Average Case Capacity:	39.0 grains H₂O
Max. Cartridge OAL	1.610 inch
Max. Case Length:	1.285 inch
Primer:	Large Pistol
Case Trim to Length:	1.275 inch
RCBS Shell holder:	# 18
Current Manufacturers:	From all major ammunition manufacturers

BALLISTIC DATA

Max. Average Pressure (MAP):	36,000 psi, 40,000 CUP - SAAMI
Test Barrel Length:	20 inch
Rifling Twist Rate:	1 turn in 20 inch

Muzzle velocities of factory ammunition: (Rifle)	Bullet Wgt.	Muzzle velocity
	200-grain	2,100 fps
	210-grain	2,100 fps
	240-grain	1,760 fps
	270-grain	1,575 fps

HISTORICAL NOTES

- The 44 Remington Magnum cartridge is based on the 44 S&W Special cartridge of 1907.

- In the early 1950s, noted gun writer Elmer Keith identified the need for a new magnum revolver cartridge that could be used to hunt big game.

- Keith began experimenting with heavy bullets at high velocities from the 44 Special cartridge and was successful in developing such loads. Essentially, Keith's idea was to substantially increase the MAP level of the 44 Special cartridge to increase muzzle velocity and energy.

- Keith explained his concept to his friends at Remington who immediately recognized its market potential.
- Remington and Smith & Wesson teamed up to develop the cartridge and revolver which were introduced in 1955.
- This proved a winning combination for Remington and S&W. Handgun hunters and shooters quickly accepted the new cartridge; sales increased rapidly.
- One of the reasons sales increased so rapidly was a movie called "Dirty Harry" starring Clint Eastwood. In the movie, Eastwood plays a detective named Harry Callahan who carries a 44 Magnum S&W Model 29 revolver.
- Several scenes in the movie dramatically focus the viewer's attention on the power of the cartridge and size of the revolver. The movie was a box office bonanza that carried sales of the 44 Magnum and Model 29 revolver to dizzying heights that persisted for years.
- Meanwhile, handgun hunters found the 44 Magnum was indeed an effective caliber for hunting big game, just as Elmer Keith predicted.
- Rifle manufacturers also found the 44 Magnum an excellent cartridge for short, light carbines.
- At the muzzle velocities the 44 Magnum cartridge was capable of, barrel leading was a problem. The solution was to use a jacketed bullet and Speer had been selling such bullets to handloaders for years.
- Using jacketed bullets, muzzle velocities unheard of with lead bullets became routine.
- Today, the 44 Magnum cartridge and the various revolvers and carbines chambered for it are considered staple items in the product lines of all major gun and ammunition manufacturers.

TECHNICAL NOTES

- The 44 Magnum cartridge case is a classic revolver design with a rim and a straight sided case. Basically, it is a longer 44 Special case.
- Case length is .125 inches longer than the 44 Special and case capacity is approximately 10% more. Other dimensions are comparable to the 44 Special.
- MAP level for the 44 Magnum is 36,000 psi which is more than double the 44 Special.
- The correct bullet diameter for the 44 Magnum is .429 inch (.430 for lead bullets).
- 44 Special ammunition may be safely fired in guns chambered for 44 Remington Magnum.

HANDLOADING NOTES

- To prevent reduction in COAL in carbine and rifle magazine tubes and elongation in revolvers cylinders, all bullets for the 44 Magnum cartridge must be crimped securely in the cannelure on the bullet's surface.
- Never load less than the minimum charges shown in the loading data as the small charge of propellant may not be sufficient to push the bullet completely down the barrel.

- Lead bullets should not be used in gas-operated, semi-automatic pistols such as the Desert Eagle as bullet lubricant and lead particles can foul the gas system.
- We recommend loading lead bullets no faster than 1,050 fps to avoid leading the barrel.

SAFETY NOTES

SPEER 270-grain DeepCurl Soft Point @ a muzzle velocity of 1,309 fps:
- Maximum vertical altitude @ 90° elevation is 5,052 feet.
- Maximum horizontal distance to first impact with ground @ 34° elevation is 2,371 yards.
- Do not feed 44 Magnum ammunition loaded with Speer Plastic Shot Capsules through tubular magazines in rifles or carbines as they may break open under recoil.

GOLD DOT

200 GRAINS	DIAMETER	SECTIONAL DENSITY
	.429"	0.115

44 Special GDHP SB	
Ballistic Coefficient	0.145
COAL Tested	1.610"
Speer Part No.	4427

SHORT BARREL VELOCITIES
Test Firearm: S&W M29 4"
Note: these loads do not produce maximum pressure.

			Starting Charge		Maximum Charge	
Propellant	Case	Primer	Weight (grains)	Muzzle Velocity (feet/sec)	Weight (grains)	Muzzle Velocity (feet/sec)
Alliant Unique	Remington	CCI 300	5.7	746	6.3	820
Alliant Herco	Remington	CCI 300	5.8	730	6.4	816
Hodgdon HS-6	Remington	CCI 350	7.0	695	8.0	815
Winchester 231	Remington	CCI 300	5.2	701	5.7	796
Alliant Bullseye	Remington	CCI 300	4.7	691	5.2	793
Alliant Red Dot	Remington	CCI 300	4.5	658	5.0	750
Alliant Green Dot	Remington	CCI 300	5.2	672	5.7	749
Hodgdon Hi-Skor 700-X	Remington	CCI 300	4.1	640	4.6	734

WARNING! Maximum loads should be used with CAUTION • C = Compressed Load

GOLD DOT

210 GRAINS

DIAMETER	SECTIONAL DENSITY
.429"	0.163

44 GDHP

Ballistic Coefficient	0.154
COAL Tested	1.600"
Speer Part No.	4428

			Starting Charge		Maximum Charge	
Propellant	Case	Primer	Weight (grains)	Muzzle Velocity (feet/sec)	Weight (grains)	Muzzle Velocity (feet/sec)
Alliant Unique	Remington	CCI 300	5.7	746	6.3	820
Alliant Herco	Remington	CCI 300	5.8	730	6.4	816
Hodgdon HS-6	Remington	CCI 350	7.0	695	8.0	815
Winchester 231	Remington	CCI 300	5.2	701	5.7	796
Alliant Bullseye	Remington	CCI 300	4.7	691	5.2	793
Alliant Red Dot	Remington	CCI 300	4.5	658	5.0	750
Alliant Green Dot	Remington	CCI 300	5.2	672	5.7	749
Hodgdon Hi-Skor 700-X	Remington	CCI 300	4.1	640	4.6	734

WARNING! *Maximum loads should be used with CAUTION • C = Compressed Load*

240 GRAINS

DIAMETER	SECTIONAL DENSITY
.429"	0.186

44 DCHP

Ballistic Coefficient	0.175
COAL Tested	1.575"
Speer Part No.	4455

44 DCSP

Ballistic Coefficient	0.175
COAL Tested	1.575"
Speer Part No.	4456

			Starting Charge		Maximum Charge	
Propellant	Case	Primer	Weight (grains)	Muzzle Velocity (feet/sec)	Weight (grains)	Muzzle Velocity (feet/sec)
Hodgdon H110	Speer	CCI 350	22.0	1362	24.0	1451
Alliant 2400	Speer	CCI 300	19.0	1269	21.0	1434
Winchester 296	Speer	CCI 350	22.0	1344	24.0	1420
Accurate No. 9	Speer	CCI 300	18.0	1222	20.0	1404
Hodgdon Lil' Gun	Speer	CCI 350	21.0	1325	23.0	1383
Vihtavuori N110	Speer	CCI 300	18.0	1307	20.0	1382
Ramshot Enforcer	Speer	CCI 350	18.5	1269	20.5	1344
IMR 4227	Speer	CCI 300	21.4	1252	23.4	1340
Accurate No. 7	Speer	CCI 300	15.5	1183	17.5	1319
Hodgdon HS-6	Speer	CCI 350	12.3	1172	13.7	1271
Vihtavuori N350	Speer	CCI 300	10.4	1155	11.6	1212
Alliant Unique	Speer	CCI 300	9.2	1077	10.3	1175

WARNING! Maximum loads should be used with CAUTION • C = Compressed Load

240 GRAINS

DIAMETER	SECTIONAL DENSITY
.430"	0.185

44 LSWC

Ballistic Coefficient	0.151
COAL Tested	1.605"
Speer Part No.	4661

			Starting Charge		Maximum Charge	
Propellant	Case	Primer	Weight (grains)	Muzzle Velocity (feet/sec)	Weight (grains)	Muzzle Velocity (feet/sec)
Hodgdon HS-6	Speer	CCI 300	8.5	822	9.5	947
IMR SR 4756	Speer	CCI 300	6.5	751	7.5	923
IMR SR 7625	Speer	CCI 300	6.0	834	7.0	912
Alliant Red Dot	Speer	CCI 300	6.0	871	6.5	905
Alliant Green Dot	Speer	CCI 300	6.0	804	7.0	901
Alliant Unique	Speer	CCI 300	6.5	720	7.0	899
Alliant Bullseye	Speer	CCI 300	5.5	828	6.0	894
Hodgdon Hi-Skor 700-X	Speer	CCI 300	5.5	836	6.0	871
Winchester 231	Speer	CCI 300	6.0	808	6.5	867

WARNING! *Maximum loads should be used with CAUTION • C = Compressed Load*

270 GRAINS

DIAMETER	SECTIONAL DENSITY
.429"	0.210

44 DCSP	
Ballistic Coefficient	0.193
COAL Tested	1.585"
Speer Part No.	4461

			Starting Charge		Maximum Charge	
Propellant	Case	Primer	Weight (grains)	Muzzle Velocity (feet/sec)	Weight (grains)	Muzzle Velocity (feet/sec)
Hodgdon H110	Speer	CCI 350	19.0	1205	21.0	1309
Winchester 296	Speer	CCI 350	18.5	1198	20.5	1283
Vihtavuori N110	Speer	CCI 300	16.0	1184	18.0	1265
Ramshot Enforcer	Speer	CCI 350	17.0	1166	19.0	1255
Hodgdon Lil' Gun	Speer	CCI 350	17.5	1178	19.5	1241
Alliant 2400	Speer	CCI 300	15.5	1083	17.5	1182
IMR 4227	Speer	CCI 300	18.5	1101	20.5	1182
Accurate 1680	Speer	CCI 350	22.5	1067	24.5 C	1176
Accurate No. 9	Speer	CCI 300	14.0	1026	16.0	1172

WARNING! *Maximum loads should be used with CAUTION • C = Compressed Load*

45 GLOCK AUTOMATIC PISTOL

Alternate Names:	45 GAP
Parent Cartridge:	45 Auto
Country of Origin:	USA & Austria
Year of Introduction:	2003
Designer(s):	CCI/Speer & Glock
Governing Body:	SAAMI/CIP

CARTRIDGE CASE DATA

Case Type:	Rimless, straight		
Average Case Capacity:	22.2 grains H_2O	Max. Cartridge OAL	1.137 inch
Max. Case Length:	.760 inch	Primer:	Small Pistol
Case Trim to Length:	.750 inch	RCBS Shell holder:	# 3
Current Manufacturers:	CCI/Speer, Federal, Remington, Winchester, Magtech, Starline		

BALLISTIC DATA

Max. Average Pressure (MAP):	23,000 psi, CUP not established for this cartridge - SAAMI	Test Barrel Length:	5 inch
Rifling Twist Rate:	1 turn in 16 inch		
Muzzle velocities of factory loaded ammunition	Bullet Wgt.	Muzzle velocity	
	185-grain	1,060 fps	
	200-grain	990 fps	

HISTORICAL NOTES

- The classic 45 Auto cartridge is too long to fit in small frame guns designed originally for the 9mm Luger. So, what can you do?
- You can design a shorter 45 Auto cartridge that will fit in a small frame pistol.
- That is exactly what the 45 Glock Automatic Pistol (GAP) cartridge is designed to do.
- Introduced in 2003, the 45 GAP cartridge is now offered by major domestic and foreign ammunition manufacturers.
- Although designed and named for the Glock pistol, other handgun makers have since added pistols in this chambering to their product lines.

- Ernest Durham, a development engineer with CCI/Speer, helped develop the new cartridge. Speer shipped the first factory loaded ammunition in this new caliber.

BALLISTIC NOTES

- The concept of the 45 GAP was to offer similar ballistic performance to the 45 Auto in a shorter cartridge with nearly the same OAL as the 40 S&W cartridge.
- The 45 GAP cartridge does this, and then some.

Cartridge	Bullet Weight (grs)	Muzzle velocity (fps)
45 Auto	185	1,060
45 GAP	185	1,060
45 Auto +P	185	1,140
45 GAP	200	990
45 Auto +P	200	1,080
45 Auto	230	830

- From a ballistic standpoint, the 45 GAP has more in common with the 45 Auto +P than with the 45 Auto.
- When the 45 GAP is fired from a small frame pistol, recoil is quite heavy which is not acceptable for many shooters.
- Small frame pistols chambered for 45 caliber cartridges such as the 45 GAP must use a very heavy recoil spring to compensate for the recoil making it difficult to pull back the slide.
- Still, in the opinion of many, the 45 GAP concept is a good idea. Others dismiss the concept as being hardly worth all the effort. Time will tell.
- Speer offers three outstanding bullets for the 45 GAP cartridge:
  - A 185-grain Total Metal Jacket Flat Nose (TMJ® FN).
    This bullet is an economical choice for duplicating the factory loads for training, practice and qualification.
  - A 185-grain Gold Dot® Hollow Point (GDHP).
  - A 200-grain Gold Dot Hollow Point (GDHP).
- Gold Dot bullets have a reputation for being the best JHP handgun bullets on the market for law enforcement and personal defense.

TECHNICAL NOTES

- Although the 45 GAP shares many dimensions with the 45 Auto, there are several major differences:
  - The case length and OAL of the 45 GAP is .138 inches shorter.
  - The rim of the 45 GAP is rebated slightly.
  - The extractor cut angle is different to allow for a thicker and stronger case head.
  - The inner contour of the 45 GAP cartridge case is different and stronger than 45 Auto.
  - MAP level of the 45 GAP is the same as the 45 Auto +P (23,000 psi).
- The 45 GAP cartridge case is a rimless design that headspaces on the case mouth.
- Case capacity is about 20% less than the 45 Auto.

- In most small pistol frames, the 45 GAP is a tight fit. As a result, bullets for the 45 GAP must have a compact ogive design.

HANDLOADING NOTES

- Be certain to use .451 inch bullets designed especially for the 45 Auto or 45 GAP.
- Finish your reloads with a light taper crimp on the case mouth to hold the bullet securely, and to improve ignition consistency and feeding reliability.
- Never load less than the minimum charges shown in the loading data as the small charge of propellant may not be sufficient to push the bullet completely down the barrel.
- We use fast burning pistol powders for loading the 45 GAP as case capacity is limited.
- Do not load lead bullets in the 45 GAP cartridge as the polygon rifling in many Glock, H&K, and other pistols will not stabilize such bullets and excessive barrel leading can occur.

SAFETY NOTES

SPEER 200-grain Gold Dot Hollow Point (GDHP) @ a muzzle velocity of 988 fps:
- Maximum vertical altitude @ 90° elevation is 3,675 feet.
- Maximum horizontal distance to first impact with ground @ 33° elevation is 1,716 yards.

185 GRAINS

DIAMETER	SECTIONAL DENSITY
.451"	0.130

45 TMJ® FN

Ballistic Coefficient	0.094
COAL Tested	1.070"
Speer Part No.	4476

Propellant	Case	Primer	Starting Charge Weight (grains)	Starting Charge Muzzle Velocity (feet/sec)	Maximum Charge Weight (grains)	Maximum Charge Muzzle Velocity (feet/sec)
Hodgdon H. Universal	Speer	CCI 500	6.7	1007	7.1	1089
Alliant Bullseye	Speer	CCI 500	5.7	981	6.4	1072
Alliant Power Pistol	Speer	CCI 500	7.9	994	8.5	1061
Alliant Unique	Speer	CCI 500	7.2	1002	7.7	1061
Hodgdon TITEGROUP	Speer	CCI 500	5.3	956	5.9	1041
Accurate No. 5	Speer	CCI 500	8.4	953	9.2	1035
Ramshot True Blue	Speer	CCI 500	7.8	940	8.6	1033
Vihtavuori 3N37	Speer	CCI 500	8.0	919	8.6	1011
Winchester 231	Speer	CCI 500	5.7	912	6.3	1001
Accurate No. 2 Improved	Speer	CCI 500	5.0	882	5.5	946

WARNING! *Maximum loads should be used with CAUTION • C = Compressed Load*

GOLD DOT

185 GRAINS	DIAMETER	SECTIONAL DENSITY
	.451"	0.130

45 GDHP	
Ballistic Coefficient	0.109
COAL Tested	1.070"
Speer Part No.	4470

			Starting Charge		Maximum Charge	
Propellant	Case	Primer	Weight (grains)	Muzzle Velocity (feet/sec)	Weight (grains)	Muzzle Velocity (feet/sec)
Hodgdon H. Universal	Speer	CCI 500	6.3	938	6.8	1044
Alliant Bullseye	Speer	CCI 500	5.5	950	6.1	1037
Vihtavuori 3N37	Speer	CCI 500	7.7	881	8.4	1018
Alliant Unique	Speer	CCI 500	7.1	984	7.7	1009
Ramshot True Blue	Speer	CCI 500	7.4	908	8.2	1005
Winchester 231	Speer	CCI 500	5.5	892	6.2	1000
Accurate No. 5	Speer	CCI 500	8.1	922	8.8	999
Hodgdon TITEGROUP	Speer	CCI 500	5.1	934	5.6	994
Alliant Power Pistol	Speer	CCI 500	7.2	927	7.8	993
Accurate No. 2 Improved	Speer	CCI 500	4.6	807	5.2	897

WARNING! Maximum loads should be used with CAUTION • C = Compressed Load

GOLD DOT

200 GRAINS

DIAMETER	SECTIONAL DENSITY
.451"	0.140

45 GDHP

Ballistic Coefficient	0.138
COAL Tested	1.070"
Speer Part No.	4478

			Starting Charge		Maximum Charge	
Propellant	Case	Primer	Weight (grains)	Muzzle Velocity (feet/sec)	Weight (grains)	Muzzle Velocity (feet/sec)
Alliant Unique	Speer	CCI 500	6.3	918	6.8	988
Hodgdon H. Universal	Speer	CCI 500	5.8	893	6.2	988
Alliant Power Pistol	Speer	CCI 500	6.9	903	7.6	977
Alliant Bullseye	Speer	CCI 500	4.9	859	5.4	943
Hodgdon TITEGROUP	Speer	CCI 500	4.6	865	5.1	940
Accurate No. 5	Speer	CCI 500	7.3	848	8.0	921
Ramshot True Blue	Speer	CCI 500	6.8	851	7.4	912
Winchester 231	Speer	CCI 500	5.0	840	5.5	900
Vihtavuori 3N37	Speer	CCI 500	6.8	811	7.2	863
Accurate No. 2 Improved	Speer	CCI 500	4.3	783	4.7	838

WARNING! *Maximum loads should be used with CAUTION • C = Compressed Load*

45 AUTOMATIC

Alternate Names:	45 ACP, 45 Ball M1911, 45 Colt Government
Parent Cartridge:	Original design
Country of Origin:	USA
Year of Introduction:	1911
Designer(s):	John Browning, U.S. Army Ordnance Board
Governing Body:	SAAMI/CIP

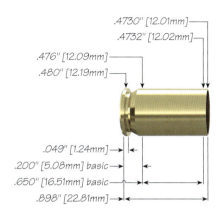

CARTRIDGE CASE DATA

Case Type:	Rimless, straight		
Average Case Capacity:	28.3 grains H$_2$O	Max. Cartridge OAL	1.275 inch
Max. Case Length:	.898 inch	Primer:	Large Pistol, Some Small Pistol
Case Trim to Length:	.888 inch	RCBS Shell holder:	# 3
Current Manufacturers:	CCI/Speer, Federal, Nosler, Hornady, Remington, Winchester, Black Hills, Cor-Bon, Prvi Partizan, Magtech, PMC, Armscor, Aguila		

BALLISTIC DATA

Max. Average Pressure (MAP):	21,000 psi, 18,000 CUP - SAAMI	Test Barrel Length:	5 inch
Rifling Twist Rate:	1 turn in 16 inch		
Muzzle velocities of factory loaded ammunition		Bullet Wgt.	Muzzle velocity
		200-grain	900 fps
		230-grain	835 fps

HISTORICAL NOTES

- Although the 9mm Luger (1908) and the 45 Auto (1911) cartridges are military contemporaries, they come from opposite sides of the ballistic debate on handgun incapacitation.
- Which is better: a small caliber, light bullet at high velocity or a large caliber, heavy bullet at low velocity?
- The debate was framed by different European and American historical experience.

- American opinion was based on experience in the American Indian Wars, taming the Old West, the Philippine Insurrection of 1899-1902 and Moro Rebellion from 1899-1913.
  - In these scenarios, handguns played an active role in law enforcement and military combat.
  - This meant that law enforcement and military officers were expected to become proficient with handguns.
  - The sum of these experiences clearly indicated that a handgun firing a large caliber, heavy bullet at low velocity was the best choice to immediately incapacitate an assailant.
  - British colonial experiences backed this up.
- On the other hand, European military and law enforcement experience led them to view handguns more as a badge of office rather than an actual combat weapon.
  - As military and law enforcement officers were not expected to engage in combat using their handguns, incapacitation of an assailant was not important.
  - As a badge of office, a low power handgun of modest ballistic performance was more than sufficient and lighter to carry.
- The 45 Auto cartridge continued to prove its incapacitation capabilities for 74 years through two World Wars, the Korean War, Vietnam, and several smaller conflicts.
- In 1985, the U.S. military adopted the 9mm Luger cartridge as part of a NATO interchangeability effort.
- In several military conflicts since then, the incapacitation ability of the 9mm Luger cartridge has again been found wanting which has ignited the debate yet again.
- In 2014, the U.S. Marine Corps readopted the 45 Auto cartridge and an updated M1911 pistol to fire it.
- Meanwhile many law enforcement SWAT teams have adopted the 45 Auto as well.
- And so the debate continues, at least in the U.S.

Interesting Fact

After U.S. soldiers in the Philippines complained their 38 Long Colt revolvers repeatedly failed to stop insurgents during the Philippine Insurrection (1899-1902) and Moro Rebellion (1899-1913), the U.S. War Department purchased 2,000 Luger 9mm pistols in 1910 and sent them to the U.S. Army units in the Philippines for testing. Reports from the field indicated that the 9mm cartridge was no better than the 38 Long Colt at incapacitating an insurgent. On the other hand, a few officers who carried their personal Colt Single-Action Army revolvers in 45 Colt reported a single body hit from the Colt 250-grain lead bullet was enough to put down an insurgent immediately.

BALLISTIC NOTES

- John Browning's original concept for his 45 Auto cartridge in 1905 was a 200-grain FMJ RN bullet at a muzzle velocity of about 900 fps. Winchester began commercial manufacture of this cartridge in 1906.
- When the 45 Auto cartridge was adopted by the U.S. Army in 1911, the standard military load was a 230-grain FMJ RN bullet at a velocity of 820 fps.
- Muzzle velocity of modern commercial 45 Auto ammunition loaded with a 230-grain bullet ranges from 780 fps (Match) to 835-890 fps (Ball) depending on the manufacturer.

- Jacketed hollow point bullets of 185-grain are loaded to muzzle velocities up to 1,172 fps.
- Speer offers a wide range of jacketed and lead bullets for handloading the 45 Auto cartridge:
  - Two 45 caliber lead bullets for low cost practice, training and plinking.
    - A 200-grain Lead Semi-Wadcutter (LSWC)
    - A 230-grain Lead Round Nose (LRN)
  - Two Total Metal Jacket (TMJ®) Match bullets for serious target competition.
    - A 185-grain Match TMJ SWC
    - A 200-grain Match TMJ SWC
  - Two Total Metal Jacket Ball (TMJ) bullets for general purpose use.
    - A 185-grain TMJ FN
    - A 230-grain TMJ RN, (recommended muzzle velocity 840 fps) to match GI Ball velocity
  - Four Gold Dot® Hollow Point (GDHP) bullets for personal defense.
    - A 185-grain GDHP
    - A 200-grain GDHP
    - A 230-grain GDHP Short Barrel (SB)
    - A 230-grain GDHP
- The famous Gold Dot bullets are a superior choice for personal defense.

TECHNICAL NOTES

- The 45 Auto cartridge case is a rimless design that headspaces on the case mouth.
- MAP level of the 45 Auto is 21,000 psi which is low by modern standards.
- There is an established industry MAP standard for 45 Auto +P ammunition, in two bullet weights, 185-grain and 230-grain of 23,000 psi. Some manufacturers offer such loads. They may be identified by the "+P" on the headstamp. Other than the headstamp, 45 Auto +P cases are similar to standard 45 Auto cases.
- Target pistols in 45 Auto are modified to shoot light loads. Do not attempt to fire full power ammunition in such guns as damage will result.
- Most 45 Auto pistols are designed to function with full metal jacket round nose bullets. As a result, some will not feed JHP bullets reliably without modification.
- Carbines and submachine guns in 45 Auto require full power loads with full metal jacket round nose bullets for reliable operation.

HANDLOADING NOTES

- Recently, 45 Auto ammunition with steel cartridge cases has been imported from Russia. We strongly recommend against reloading these cases even though they may have Boxer primers.
- Military 45 Auto cartridge cases may have crimped primers. As these cases are hard to deprime, decapping pins may break with depressing regularity. For this reason, we recommend that you keep a supply of these inexpensive parts on hand as replacements.
- The 45 Auto cartridge case was designed originally for Large Pistol primers such as the CCI No. 300 primer. For over 100 years, all 45 Auto cartridge cases were made for Large Pistol Boxer primers. Recently, some ammunition manufacturers have switched to using Small Pistol primers for 45 Auto cartridge cases. For this reason,

you may find 45 Auto cases for both sizes of primers mixed together. Be sure to inspect once fired brass and separate the two primer types during the case cleaning steps so that primer seating goes smoothly.

- Finish your reloads with a light taper crimp on the case mouth to hold the bullet securely, and to improve shot start and feeding reliability.
- Never load less than the minimum charges shown in the loading data as the small charge of propellant may not be sufficient to push the bullet completely down the barrel.
- Use fast burning pistol powders for loading the 45 Auto as case capacity is limited.
- Do not fire lead bullets in pistols with polygon rifling as this type of rifling will not stabilize such bullets and will cause severe leading.

SAFETY NOTES

SPEER 230-grain TMJ RN @ a muzzle velocity of 916 fps:
- Maximum vertical altitude @ 90° elevation is 3,741 feet.
- Maximum horizontal distance to first impact with ground @ 34° elevation is 1,776 yards.

185 GRAINS

DIAMETER	SECTIONAL DENSITY
.451"	0.130

45 TMJ® Match SWC

Ballistic Coefficient	.090
COAL Tested	1.275"
Speer Part No.	4473

NOTE: These loads are not necessarily at maximum pressure. They are held to velocities popular for target shooting.

Propellant	Case	Primer	Starting Charge Weight (grains)	Starting Charge Muzzle Velocity (feet/sec)	Maximum Charge Weight (grains)	Maximum Charge Muzzle Velocity (feet/sec)
Accurate No. 5	Speer	CCI 300	7.2	764	8.0	859
Alliant Red Dot	Speer	CCI 300	4.5	767	4.9	829
Alliant Unique	Speer	CCI 300	5.0	652	5.8	829
Alliant Bullseye	Speer	CCI 300	4.5	727	4.9	790
Hodgdon Hi-Skor 700-X	Speer	CCI 300	4.3	701	4.7	788
IMR PB	Speer	CCI 300	5.0	719	5.5	770
Hodgdon HP-38	Speer	CCI 300	4.9	668	5.4	759
Winchester 231	Speer	CCI 300	5.0	669	5.5	752
IMR SR 7625	Speer	CCI 300	5.1	615	5.6	717

Light target loads may not reliably function pistols set up for standard ammunition.

WARNING! Maximum loads should be used with CAUTION • C = Compressed Load

185 GRAINS

DIAMETER	SECTIONAL DENSITY
.451"	0.130

45 GDHP	
Ballistic Coefficient	0.109
COAL Tested	1.200"
Speer Part No.	4470

45 TMJ® FN	
Ballistic Coefficient	0.094
COAL Tested	1.200"
Speer Part No.	4476

Propellant	Case	Primer	Starting Charge		Maximum Charge	
			Weight (grains)	Muzzle Velocity (feet/sec)	Weight (grains)	Muzzle Velocity (feet/sec)
Alliant BE-86	Federal	Federal 150	6.9	944	8.9	1172
Accurate No. 5	Federal	Federal 150	9.5	1053	10.6	1169
Alliant Power Pistol	Federal	Federal 150	8.2	1016	9.5	1162
Hodgdon CFE Pistol	Federal	Federal 150	7.1	925	9.0	1157
Accurate No. 7	Federal	Federal 150	10.8	1022	12.0	1154
Alliant Unique	Federal	Federal 150	7.3	1058	8.2	1151
Winchester AutoComp	Federal	Federal 150	6.9	912	8.9	1145
Hodgdon H. Universal	Federal	Federal 150	6.9	998	7.7	1125
IMR SR 7625	Federal	Federal 150	7.0	979	7.8	1094
Hodgdon HS-6	Federal	Federal 150	8.9	966	9.9	1080
Hodgdon Hi-Skor 700-X	Federal	Federal 150	5.8	993	6.5	1079
Winchester WSF	Federal	Federal 150	6.9	951	7.7	1071
Winchester 231	Federal	Federal 150	6.6	995	7.4	1069
Alliant Sport Pistol	Federal	Federal 150	5.5	884	6.9	1069
Accurate No. 2	Federal	Federal 150	6.0	974	6.7	1043
Vihtavuori 3N37	Federal	Federal 150	8.1	913	9.0	1043
Alliant Bullseye	Federal	Federal 150	5.7	957	6.4	1039
Alliant American Select	Federal	Federal 150	5.5	902	6.2	984

WARNING! Maximum loads should be used with CAUTION • C = Compressed Load

200 GRAINS

DIAMETER	SECTIONAL DENSITY
.452"	0.140

45 LSWC

Ballistic Coefficient	0.078
COAL Tested	1.190"
Speer Part No.	4678

NOTE: *These loads are not necessarily at maximum pressure. They are held to velocities popular for target shooting.*

Propellant	Case	Primer	Starting Charge Weight (grains)	Starting Charge Muzzle Velocity (feet/sec)	Maximum Charge Weight (grains)	Maximum Charge Muzzle Velocity (feet/sec)
Alliant Red Dot	Speer	CCI 300	4.1	749	4.5	831
Alliant Herco	Speer	CCI 300	5.5	750	6.0	826
IMR SR 7625	Speer	CCI 300	4.7	726	5.2	811
Alliant Bullseye	Speer	CCI 300	4.2	744	4.6	807
Hodgdon H. Universal	Speer	CCI 300	4.9	710	5.4	804
Winchester 231	Speer	CCI 300	4.6	739	5.0	803
IMR SR 4756	Speer	CCI 300	5.3	728	5.8	800
Alliant Unique	Speer	CCI 300	4.9	716	5.4	790
Hodgdon Hi-Skor 700-X	Speer	CCI 300	3.8	715	4.2	790

WARNING! *Maximum loads should be used with CAUTION • C = Compressed Load*

200 GRAINS

DIAMETER	SECTIONAL DENSITY
.451"	0.140

45 TMJ® Match SWC
Ballistic Coefficient	0.128
COAL Tested	1.275"
Speer Part No.	4475

45 GDHP
Ballistic Coefficient	0.138
COAL Tested	1.200"
Speer Part No.	4478

Propellant	Case	Primer	Starting Charge Weight (grains)	Starting Charge Muzzle Velocity (feet/sec)	Maximum Charge Weight (grains)	Maximum Charge Muzzle Velocity (feet/sec)
Alliant BE-86	Federal	Federal 150	6.0	825	8.1	1083
Winchester AutoComp	Federal	Federal 150	6.2	834	8.1	1076
Hodgdon CFE Pistol	Federal	Federal 150	6.1	824	8.1	1067
Alliant Unique	Federal	Federal 150	6.5	927	7.3	1057
Hodgdon HS-6	Federal	Federal 150	8.5	944	9.5	1054
Alliant Blue Dot	Federal	Federal 150	9.4	917	10.5	1048
Accurate No. 7	Federal	Federal 150	9.9	912	11.0	1037
Alliant Power Pistol	Federal	Federal 150	7.0	874	8.3	1026
Hodgdon H. Universal	Federal	Federal 150	6.3	905	7.0	1018
Accurate No. 5	Federal	Federal 150	8.1	916	9.0	1013
Winchester WSF	Federal	Federal 150	6.4	894	7.2	1004
Alliant Sport Pistol	Federal	Federal 150	4.8	779	6.3	993
Alliant Bullseye	Federal	Federal 150	5.2	864	5.8	957
Vihtavuori N340	Federal	Federal 150	6.3	814	7.0	947
Vihtavuori 3N37	Federal	Federal 150	7.3	794	8.2	942
Winchester 231	Federal	Federal 150	5.6	826	6.3	931

WARNING! Maximum loads should be used with CAUTION • C = Compressed Load

230 GRAINS

DIAMETER	SECTIONAL DENSITY
.452"	0.161

45 LRN

Ballistic Coefficient	0.160
COAL Tested	1.240"
Speer Part No.	4691

			Starting Charge		Maximum Charge	
Propellant	Case	Primer	Weight (grains)	Muzzle Velocity (feet/sec)	Weight (grains)	Muzzle Velocity (feet/sec)
Hodgdon CFE Pistol	Federal	Federal 150	5.6	809	7.2	989
Winchester AutoComp	Federal	Federal 150	5.6	795	7.3	988
Alliant BE 86	Federal	Federal 150	5.8	850	7.2	986
Alliant Herco	Federal	Federal 150	5.9	884	6.4	931
Alliant Sport Pistol	Federal	Federal 150	4.4	777	5.6	919
Alliant Green Dot	Federal	Federal 150	4.8	847	5.3	908
Alliant Red Dot	Federal	Federal 150	4.7	856	5.1	899
Alliant Unique	Federal	Federal 150	5.3	837	5.8	895
Hodgdon Hi-Skor 700-X	Federal	Federal 150	4.3	839	4.7	890
Hodgdon H. Universal	Federal	Federal 150	5.2	818	5.5	867
Winchester 231	Federal	Federal 150	5.1	794	5.6	853
IMR SR 4756	Federal	Federal 150	6.0	739	6.5	816

WARNING! *Maximum loads should be used with CAUTION • C = Compressed Load*

230 GRAINS

DIAMETER	SECTIONAL DENSITY
.451"	0.162

45 TMJ® RN

Ballistic Coefficient	0.153
COAL Tested	1.260"
Speer Part No.	4480

SAFETY NOTICE: Do not use these loads with the 230-grain Gold Dot HP (#4483). Gold Dot loads are in the next data block.

Propellant	Case	Primer	Starting Charge		Maximum Charge	
			Weight (grains)	Muzzle Velocity (feet/sec)	Weight (grains)	Muzzle Velocity (feet/sec)
Alliant Power Pistol	Federal	Federal 150	7.0	882	8.1	1001
Alliant BE-86	Federal	Federal 150	5.9	810	7.5	988
Winchester AutoComp	Federal	Federal 150	6.0	785	7.6	978
Hodgdon CFE Pistol	Federal	Federal 150	6.0	793	7.5	973
Hodgdon HS-6	Federal	Federal 150	7.8	873	8.5	947
Alliant Unique	Federal	Federal 150	5.5	806	6.5	920
Alliant Bullseye	Federal	Federal 150	5.2	849	5.7	914
Hodgdon H. Universal	Federal	Federal 150	5.5	806	6.3	910
Winchester 231	Federal	Federal 150	5.6	833	6.2	903
Alliant Sport Pistol	Federal	Federal 150	4.8	761	5.8	895
Alliant Red Dot	Federal	Federal 150	4.8	827	5.3	892
Hodgdon Hi-Skor 700-X	Federal	Federal 150	4.6	815	5.1	880
Vihtavuori N340	Federal	Federal 150	5.5	750	6.3	876

WARNING! Maximum loads should be used with CAUTION • C = Compressed Load

GOLD DOT

230 GRAINS

DIAMETER	SECTIONAL DENSITY
.451"	0.162

45 GDHP SB
Ballistic Coefficient	0.148
COAL Tested	1.200"
Speer Part No.	4482

45 GDHP
Ballistic Coefficient	0.143
COAL Tested	1.200"
Speer Part No.	4483

			Starting Charge		Maximum Charge	
Propellant	Case	Primer	Weight (grains)	Muzzle Velocity (feet/sec)	Weight (grains)	Muzzle Velocity (feet/sec)
Alliant Blue Dot	Federal	Federal 150	8.1	822	9.0	957
Accurate No. 7	Federal	Federal 150	8.6	842	9.6	955
Hodgdon HS-6	Federal	Federal 150	7.2	816	8.0	945
Alliant Power Pistol	Federal	Federal 150	6.3	800	7.4	943
Hodgdon CFE Pistol	Federal	Federal 150	6.0	820	6.9	940
Vihtavuori N350	Federal	Federal 150	6.3	821	7.1	939
Winchester AutoComp	Federal	Federal 150	6.0	828	6.8	930
Alliant BE-86	Federal	Federal 150	5.6	787	6.7	923
Hodgdon H. Universal	Federal	Federal 150	5.4	823	6.0	917
Alliant Unique	Federal	Federal 150	5.4	835	6.0	912
Accurate No. 5	Federal	Federal 150	7.0	811	7.8	906
IMR SR 7625	Federal	Federal 150	5.4	810	6.0	888
Vihtavuori N340	Federal	Federal 150	5.4	754	6.1	870
Hodgdon Hi-Skor 700-X	Federal	Federal 150	4.5	786	5.0	860
Winchester 231	Federal	Federal 150	5.0	774	5.6	859
Alliant Sport Pistol	Federal	Federal 150	4.6	769	5.2	852
Alliant Bullseye	Federal	Federal 150	4.5	763	5.0	846

WARNING! *Maximum loads should be used with CAUTION • C = Compressed Load*

45 COLT

Alternate Names:	45 Long Colt, 45 Colt Army, 11.48x33R
Parent Cartridge:	Original design
Country of Origin:	USA
Year of Introduction:	1873
Designer(s):	Colt & Union Metallic Cartridge Company
Governing Body:	SAAMI/CIP

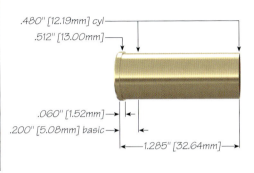

CARTRIDGE CASE DATA

Case Type:	Rimmed, straight
Average Case Capacity:	41.6 grains H₂O
Max. Cartridge OAL:	1.600 inch
Max. Case Length:	1.285 inch
Primer:	Large Pistol
Case Trim to Length:	1.275 inch
RCBS Shell holder:	# 20
Current Manufacturers:	CCI/Speer, Federal, Hornady, Remington, Winchester, Cor-Bon, Black Hills, Magtech

BALLISTIC DATA

Max. Average Pressure (MAP):	14,000 psi, 14,000 CUP - SAAMI
Test Barrel Length:	7.260 inch unvented, 5.673 inch vented
Rifling Twist Rate:	1 turn in 16 inch

Muzzle velocities of factory loaded ammunition

Bullet Wgt.	Muzzle velocity
185-grain	920 fps
225-grain	960 fps
250-grain	750 fps
255-grain	860 fps

Muzzle velocity will decrease approximately 5 fps per inch for barrels less than 7 inches.

HISTORICAL NOTES

- The 45 Colt cartridge has a long and colorful pedigree dating back to the dawn of the self-contained cartridge.
- In 1873, the U.S. Army adopted the Colt Single-Action Army revolver and the 45 Colt cartridge with it. Both remained in U.S. Army service until replaced by the 38 Long Colt in 1892.

Interesting Facts

In the Old West, the 45 Colt cartridge was preferred by men on both sides of the law. Famous outlaws such as Butch Cassidy, the Sundance kid, and a host of other ner'-do-wells preferred it as did stalwart lawmen such as "Bat" Masterson, Bill Tilghman, and Wyatt Earp. U.S. Cavalry troopers carried Single-Action Colt revolvers in 45 Colt during the conflicts with Native Americans including the Battle of the Little Big Horn. General George Patton carried a pair of Colt Single-Action Army pistols during his campaign in Mexico and was famously seen with them during World War II. In modern times, the 45 Colt was also the favorite of many celluloid cowboys such as John Wayne, Roy Rogers and James Arness—and a real cowboy, Elmer Keith.

- Why has the 45 Colt cartridge survived for over 142 years? The answer may be divided into two parts:
  - It works. Given a fair hit, most men are incapacitated when struck by a bullet from the 45 Colt.
  - Nostalgia. The legends of the Old West are part of the American psyche and the 45 Colt is an integral part of the Old West.
- Today, most domestic ammunition makers regard the 45 Colt as a staple item in their product line.
- The historically correct name for this cartridge is: 45 Colt. There was a 45 Short Colt cartridge and a 45 Colt cartridge. There never was a 45 Long Colt. However, in the popular lexicon, the 45 Long Colt and the 45 Colt are the same. So be it.

BALLISTIC NOTES

- The classic load for the 45 Colt consists of a 250-grain lead, conical flat nose bullet with 30 grains of black powder. Muzzle velocity was a leisurely 750 fps. This load is still offered by Winchester (albeit with smokeless propellant).
- The 45 Colt survived the transition to smokeless propellants, although its low MAP level of 14,000 psi remained a handicap.
- The transition to smokeless propellants allowed a modest increase in muzzle velocity from 750 fps to 860 fps.
- Do not let the 45 Colt fool you. Despite its age, it remains an effective caliber for personal defense. Until the introduction of the 357 Magnum in 1935, the 45 Colt produced more muzzle energy than any other handgun cartridge.
- The 45 Colt delivers its energy the old fashioned way: with a large diameter, and a heavy, lead bullet at relatively low muzzle velocities. The heavy weight of the bullet assures penetration while its diameter transfers energy inside the target.
- In the late 1970s, 45 Colt ammunition loaded with 225-grain lead, semi-wadcutter bullets at a muzzle velocity of approximately 920 fps was introduced.
- For reloading the 45 Colt, Speer offers a range of bullets in the correct styles and weights:
  - While hardly a "race horse" the 200-grain Lead Semi-Wadcutter can be loaded from the high-700's to a bit over 1,000 fps, has mild recoil and is economical which puts it in the "fun to shoot" category.
  - The 250-grain Lead, Semi-Wadcutter can be used to duplicate factory loads for economical practice, plinking, or dispatching pests and varmints. It can be handloaded to a wide range of muzzle velocities ranging from 780 fps to 1,000 fps.

- A 250-grain DeepCurl® Hollow Point (DCHP).
  - The DCHP bullet is an expanding design using Speer's Gold Dot® technology. It was designed specifically for the low MAP levels and muzzle velocities of the 45 Colt. The weight of the bullet allows fixed-sight revolvers to remain on target. It is the perfect choice for updating your 45 Colt with jacketed bullets.
- A 260-grain Jacketed Hollow Point.
  - This heavy bullet is designed to expand at the low muzzle velocities of the 45 Colt.
  - For rodents and pests at ranges of 15 ft. or less, we recommend the Speer 150-grain (filled w/shot) Plastic Shot Capsule.

TECHNICAL NOTES

- At first glance, the 45 Colt cartridge looks old fashioned. By modern standards, it looks too long and too big for its purpose, and the deeply seated bullet looks too blunt. Then there is the vestigial rim which gives the cartridge an unfinished look.
- Of course these features exist because the 45 Colt cartridge was designed for black powder. The large case capacity was required to hold the heavy charge of black powder and the blunt bullet was necessary to allow the cylinder to rotate.
- The low, 14,000 psi MAP level of the 45 Colt has always been a problem as it does not allow a sufficiently high pressure range for load development. Perhaps, this is part of the 45 Colt's attraction.
- Despite interest, no 45 Colt +P standards have been developed.
- Prior to 1945, most 45 Colt revolvers had a bore diameter of .454 inch. After that date, bore diameters were reduced to .451-.452 inch which is the same as the 45 Auto.
- Today, the correct bullet diameter for the 45 Colt is .451 inch for jacketed bullets and .452 inch for lead bullets.

HANDLOADING NOTES

- To prevent bullet elongation in revolvers, all bullets for the 45 Colt cartridge must be crimped securely in the cannelure on the bullet's surface and on the shoulder of lead, semi-wadcutter bullets.
- Never load less than the minimum charges shown in the loading data as the small charge of propellant may not be sufficient to push the bullet completely down the barrel.

SAFETY NOTES

SPEER 250-grain DeepCurl Hollow Point @ a muzzle velocity of 874 fps:
- Maximum vertical altitude @ 90° elevation is 3,783 feet.
- Maximum horizontal distance to first impact with ground @ 35° elevation is 1,816 yards.

150 GRAINS

DIAMETER	SECTIONAL DENSITY
.452"	N/A

45 Colt Shot Capsule	
Ballistic Coefficient	N/A
COAL Tested	1.575"
Speer Part No.	8785

NOTE: Shot capsules must not be used in firearms with ported recoil compensators.

Propellant	Case	Primer	Weight (grains)	Muzzle Velocity (feet/sec)
Alliant Unique	Winchester	CCI 300	7.5	975
Winchester 231	Winchester	CCI 300	6.0	925
Hodgdon TITEGROUP	Winchester	CCI 300	5.7	920
Hodgdon Hi-Skor 700-X	Winchester	CCI 300	5.5	915
Alliant Bullseye	Winchester	CCI 300	5.5	875

Test firearm—S&W Model 25-5 6"

WARNING! Maximum loads should be used with CAUTION • C = Compressed Load

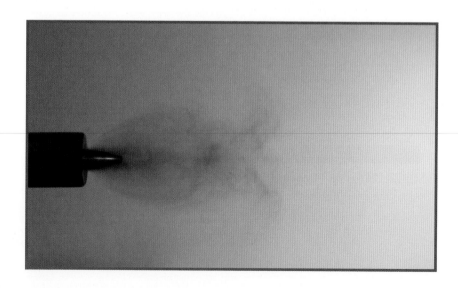

200 GRAINS

DIAMETER	SECTIONAL DENSITY
.452"	0.140

45 LSWC

Ballistic Coefficient	0.078
COAL Tested	1.515"
Speer Part No.	4678

NOTE: *Firmly roll-crimp over the bullet shoulder for reliable performance.*

			Starting Charge		Maximum Charge	
Propellant	Case	Primer	Weight (grains)	Muzzle Velocity (feet/sec)	Weight (grains)	Muzzle Velocity (feet/sec)
Alliant Unique	Winchester	CCI 300	8.0	896	9.5	1061
Hodgdon HS-6	Winchester	CCI 300	10.7	898	12.2	1036
Alliant Herco	Winchester	CCI 300	8.0	855	9.5	1021
Alliant Red Dot	Winchester	CCI 300	6.3	859	7.3	1001
Winchester 231	Winchester	CCI 300	7.3	854	8.3	998
Alliant Bullseye	Winchester	CCI 300	6.5	835	7.5	988
Alliant Green Dot	Winchester	CCI 300	7.3	834	8.3	980
IMR SR 7625	Winchester	CCI 300	7.1	860	8.1	959
Hodgdon Hi-Skor 700-X	Winchester	CCI 300	5.9	795	6.9	959

WARNING! *Maximum loads should be used with CAUTION • C = Compressed Load*

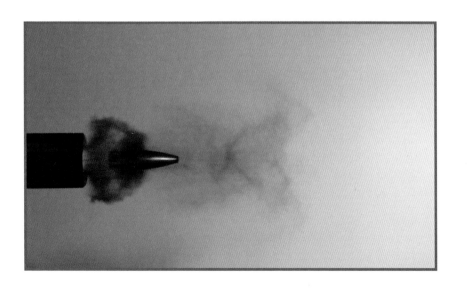

GOLD DOT

200 GRAINS	DIAMETER	SECTIONAL DENSITY
	.451"	0.140

45 GDHP SB	
Ballistic Coefficient	0.138
COAL Tested	1.555"
Speer Part No.	4478

			Starting Charge		Maximum Charge	
Propellant	Case	Primer	Weight (grains)	Muzzle Velocity (feet/sec)	Weight (grains)	Muzzle Velocity (feet/sec)
Hodgdon HS-6	Winchester	CCI 350	11.0	945	12.5	1081
Alliant Unique	Winchester	CCI 300	8.8	940	9.8	1048
Alliant Herco	Winchester	CCI 300	9.0	928	10.0	1032
IMR SR 7625	Winchester	CCI 300	7.7	880	8.7	1002
Alliant Bullseye	Winchester	CCI 300	7.4	920	7.9	994
Alliant Green Dot	Winchester	CCI 300	7.8	868	8.8	991
Hodgdon H. Universal	Winchester	CCI 300	8.4	892	9.2	985
Alliant Red Dot	Winchester	CCI 300	7.1	911	7.6	981
Hodgdon Hi-Skor 700-X	Winchester	CCI 300	6.1	852	7.1	921
Alliant Power Pistol	Winchester	CCI 300	8.6	829	9.2	885
Hodgdon TITEGROUP	Winchester	CCI 300	6.2	788	6.8	865

WARNING! Maximum loads should be used with CAUTION • C = Compressed Load

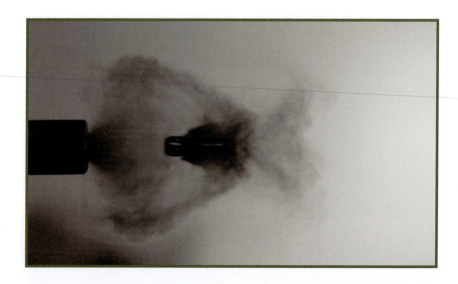

GOLD DOT

230 GRAINS

DIAMETER	SECTIONAL DENSITY
.451"	0.162

45 GDHP SB

Ballistic Coefficient	0.148
COAL Tested	1.600"
Speer Part No.	4482

45 GDHP

Ballistic Coefficient	0.143
COAL Tested	1.600"
Speer Part No.	4483

			Starting Charge		Maximum Charge	
Propellant	Case	Primer	Weight (grains)	Muzzle Velocity (feet/sec)	Weight (grains)	Muzzle Velocity (feet/sec)
Alliant Blue Dot	Winchester	CCI 300	12.0	967	13.0	1036
IMR SR 4756	Winchester	CCI 300	10.3	836	11.0	962
Vihtavuori N110	Winchester	CCI 300	16.0	778	18.0	946
Hodgdon HS-6	Winchester	CCI 350	10.8	876	11.8	936
Alliant Unique	Winchester	CCI 300	8.1	827	9.0	932
Alliant Herco	Winchester	CCI 300	8.4	839	9.4	918
Accurate No. 5	Winchester	CCI 300	10.8	840	11.8	912
Alliant Bullseye	Winchester	CCI 300	6.4	825	7.1	890
Alliant Power Pistol	Winchester	CCI 300	8.5	823	9.5	878
Hodgdon H. Universal	Winchester	CCI 300	8.2	819	9.0	873
Winchester 231	Winchester	CCI 300	7.5	804	8.3	870

WARNING! Maximum loads should be used with CAUTION • C = Compressed Load

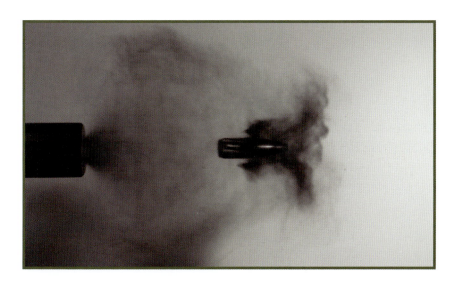

250 GRAINS

DIAMETER	SECTIONAL DENSITY
.452"	0.175

45 DCHP

Ballistic Coefficient	0.165
COAL Tested	1.600"
Speer Part No.	4484

Propellant	Case	Primer	Starting Charge Weight (grains)	Starting Charge Muzzle Velocity (feet/sec)	Maximum Charge Weight (grains)	Maximum Charge Muzzle Velocity (feet/sec)
Alliant Blue Dot	Winchester	CCI 300	11.9	912	12.9	1028
Vihtavuori 3N37	Winchester	CCI 300	10.5	889	11.5	1012
Alliant 2400	Winchester	CCI 300	13.4	838	15.4	972
Hodgdon HS-6	Winchester	CCI 350	11.0	917	12.0	945
Hodgdon H. Universal	Winchester	CCI 300	8.3	826	9.2	942
Alliant Unique	Winchester	CCI 300	8.6	891	9.5	941
Accurate No. 5	Winchester	CCI 300	10.6	840	11.6	927
IMR 4227	Winchester	CCI 300	17.0	775	19.0	904
Alliant Bullseye	Winchester	CCI 300	6.3	810	7.0	879
Winchester 231	Winchester	CCI 300	7.2	780	8.0	852

WARNING! Maximum loads should be used with CAUTION • C = Compressed Load

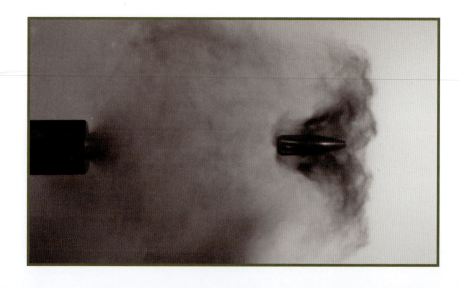

250 GRAINS

DIAMETER	SECTIONAL DENSITY
.452"	0.175

45 LSWC

Ballistic Coefficient	0.117
COAL Tested	1.600"
Speer Part No.	4684

			Starting Charge		Maximum Charge	
Propellant	Case	Primer	Weight (grains)	Muzzle Velocity (feet/sec)	Weight (grains)	Muzzle Velocity (feet/sec)
Alliant Blue Dot	Winchester	CCI 300	11.9	912	12.9	1028
Vihtavuori 3N37	Winchester	CCI 300	10.5	889	11.5	1012
Alliant 2400	Winchester	CCI 300	13.4	838	15.4	972
Hodgdon HS-6	Winchester	CCI 350	11.0	917	12.0	945
Hodgdon H. Universal	Winchester	CCI 300	8.3	826	9.2	942
Alliant Unique	Winchester	CCI 300	8.6	891	9.5	941
Accurate No. 5	Winchester	CCI 300	10.6	840	11.6	927
IMR 4227	Winchester	CCI 300	17.0	775	19.0	904
Alliant Bullseye	Winchester	CCI 300	6.3	810	7.0	879
Winchester 231	Winchester	CCI 300	7.2	780	8.0	852

WARNING! *Maximum loads should be used with CAUTION • C = Compressed Load*

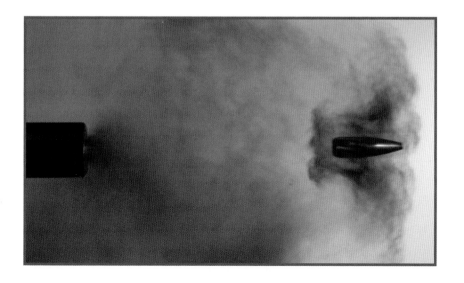

45 COLT (RUGER & CONTENDER ONLY)

Alternate Names:	45 Long Colt, 45 Colt Army, 11.48x33R
Parent Cartridge:	Original design
Country of Origin:	USA
Year of Introduction:	1873
Designer(s):	Colt & Union Metallic Cartridge Company
Governing Body:	SAAMI/CIP

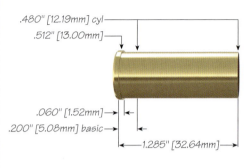

CARTRIDGE CASE DATA

Case Type:	Rimmed, straight		
Average Case Capacity:	41.6 grains H$_2$O	Max. Cartridge OAL	1.600 inch
Max. Case Length:	1.285 inch	Primer:	Large Pistol
Case Trim to Length:	1.275 inch	RCBS Shell holder:	# 20
Current Manufacturers:	CCI/Speer, Federal, Hornady, Remington, Winchester, Cor-Bon, Black Hills, Magtech, PMC		

BALLISTIC DATA

Chamber Pressure:	28,000 psi — exceeds SAAMI	Test Barrel Length:	7.260 inch unvented, 5.673 inch vented
Due to firearm design, Speer Data for these loads FAR EXCEEDS SAAMI MAP, shown above. Not intended for use in New (4/5ths size) Model Ruger Vaquero revolvers.			
Rifling Twist Rate:	1 turn in 16 inch		
Muzzle velocities of factory loaded ammunition		Bullet Wgt.	Muzzle velocity
		250-grain	750 fps
		255-grain	860 fps

HISTORICAL NOTES

- The modern Ruger Blackhawk and early Vaquero revolvers as well as the Thompson/Center Contender pistol are strong enough to handle higher MAP levels than traditional Colt Single-Action revolvers.
- Handloaders can use this to increase the muzzle velocity of the 45 Colt cartridge making it a more effective hunting caliber.

BALLISTIC NOTES

- For use in a Ruger Blackhawk, early model Vaquero, or T/C Contender, the Speer 250-grain DeepCurl® Hollow Point (DCHP) bullet can be handloaded to a recommended muzzle velocity of 1,200 fps and delivering 734 ft-lbs of energy. Now you can go hunting—but only for predators, pests, and small game. This Speer bullet was designed to expand at velocities of approximately 850 fps. Above 1,000 fps, this bullet will expand violently—just the ticket for predators and pests.

- If hunting deer or other medium game is your passion, we recommend the Speer 260-grain Jacketed Hollow Point at a muzzle velocity of 1,183 fps with 698 ft-lbs of muzzle energy.

- For big game, we recommend the Speer 300-grain Jacketed Soft Point. This heavy bullet can be driven to a recommended muzzle velocity of 1,100 fps and more for a muzzle energy of 805 ft-lbs. Expect less expansion from this bullet, but deep penetration. NOW you can go deer hunting!

TECHNICAL NOTES

- We recommend that these loads be used in new or once fired cases of recent manufacture as some old 45 Colt cases are not strong enough for these loads.

- Do not substitute unjacketed lead bullets with these loads as the increased velocity will quickly lead your barrel.

- The recommended muzzle velocity levels discussed above are a good balance between accuracy, muzzle velocity, and muzzle energy.

- Recoil from these loads will be heavy. If you are sensitive to recoil, we recommend against shooting these loads. Select lighter loads from the loading data instead, or the standard MAP pressure 45 Colt loads.

- The potential maximum effective range of these loads requires the skill of an experienced handgun shooter.

HANDLOADING NOTES

- To prevent bullet elongation in revolvers, all bullets for the 45 Colt cartridge must be crimped securely in the cannelure on the bullet's surface. Use a roll crimp for these bullets.

- Although they are the correct diameter, jacketed bullets designed for the 45 Auto do not have a cannelure so they cannot be securely held in place. For this reason, we recommend against loading 45 Auto bullets in the 45 Colt data shown on the following pages.

- Never load less than the minimum charges shown in the loading data as the small charge of propellant may not be sufficient to push the bullet completely down the barrel.

- Use fast burning pistol powders for loading the 45 Colt.

SAFETY NOTES

SPEER 300-grain Jacketed Soft Point (JSP) @ a muzzle velocity of 1,193 fps:
- Maximum vertical altitude @ 90° elevation is 5,001 feet.
- Maximum horizontal distance to first impact with ground @ 34° elevation is 2,366 yards.

IMPORTANT: *The cartridges made using the load data on this page to be used only in modern Ruger Blackhawk's, early (full size) Vaquero's, and T/C Contender's.*

250 GRAINS

DIAMETER	SECTIONAL DENSITY
.452"	0.175

45 DCHP	
Ballistic Coefficient	0.165
COAL Tested	1.600"
Speer Part No.	4484

			Starting Charge		Maximum Charge	
Propellant	Case	Primer	Weight (grains)	Muzzle Velocity (feet/sec)	Weight (grains)	Muzzle Velocity (feet/sec)
Winchester 296	Winchester	CCI 350	19.0	1118	21.0	1203
Hodgdon H110	Winchester	CCI 350	19.0	1091	21.0	1200
Accurate No. 9	Winchester	CCI 350	16.0	1052	18.0	1182
Vihtavuori N110	Winchester	CCI 300	18.0	1003	20.0	1148
Alliant 2400	Winchester	CCI 300	18.0	1058	20.0	1145
Alliant Power Pistol	Winchester	CCI 300	11.0	1039	12.0	1112
Vihtavuori N350	Winchester	CCI 300	11.0	973	12.0	1105
Alliant Unique	Winchester	CCI 300	9.8	995	10.8	1075

WARNING! *Maximum loads should be used with CAUTION • C = Compressed Load*

IMPORTANT: The cartridges made using the load data on this page to be used only in modern Ruger Blackhawk's, early (full size) Vaquero's, and T/C Contender's.

260 GRAINS

DIAMETER	SECTIONAL DENSITY
.452"	0.183

45 JHP

Ballistic Coefficient	0.183
COAL Tested	1.590"
Speer Part No.	4481

Propellant	Case	Primer	Starting Charge Weight (grains)	Starting Charge Muzzle Velocity (feet/sec)	Maximum Charge Weight (grains)	Maximum Charge Muzzle Velocity (feet/sec)
Winchester 296	Winchester	CCI 350	19.0	1096	20.5	1183
Alliant 2400	Winchester	CCI 350	16.0	1045	18.0	1180
Hodgdon H110	Winchester	CCI 350	18.5	1042	20.0	1151
Alliant Herco	Winchester	CCI 300	10.0	996	11.0	1082
Alliant Unique	Winchester	CCI 300	9.5	987	10.5	1079
Winchester 231	Winchester	CCI 300	9.2	987	10.2	1067
Alliant Bullseye	Winchester	CCI 300	8.5	1005	9.4	1064

300 GRAINS

DIAMETER	SECTIONAL DENSITY
.451"	0.211

45 JSP

Ballistic Coefficient	0.199
COAL Tested	1.640"
Speer Part No.	4485

NOTE: Seat bullet to REAR cannelure and use a neckdown crimp.

Propellant	Case	Primer	Starting Charge Weight (grains)	Starting Charge Muzzle Velocity (feet/sec)	Maximum Charge Weight (grains)	Maximum Charge Muzzle Velocity (feet/sec)
Winchester 296	Winchester	CCI 350	20.7	1084	23.0	1193
Hodgdon H110	Winchester	CCI 350	21.1	974	23.5	1156
Alliant 2400	Winchester	CCI 300	15.8	938	17.5	1048
Accurate No. 9	Winchester	CCI 350	15.0	959	15.5	1041
† IMR SR 4759	Winchester	CCI 300	20.3	825	22.5	1029

† DO NOT confuse this with SR4756 or excessive pressure will result.

WARNING! Maximum loads should be used with CAUTION • C = Compressed Load

454 CASULL

Parent Cartridge:	45 Colt
Country of Origin:	USA
Year of Introduction:	1998
Designer(s):	Dick Casull & Jack Fullmer
Governing Body:	SAAMI/CIP

.4775" [12.13mm] cyl
.512" [13.00mm]
.057" [1.45mm]
.200" [5.08mm] basic
1.383" [35.13mm]

CARTRIDGE CASE DATA

Case Type:	Rimmed, straight		
Average Case Capacity:	46.9 grains H$_2$O	Max. Cartridge OAL	1.765 inch
Max. Case Length:	1.383 inch	Primer:	Small Rifle
Case Trim to Length:	1.373 inch	RCBS Shell holder:	# 20
Current Manufacturers:	Federal, Doubletap, Hornady, Remington, Winchester		

BALLISTIC DATA

Max. Average Pressure (MAP):	65,000 psi, CUP not established for this cartridge - SAAMI	Test Barrel Length:	9.300 inch unvented, 7.500 inch vented
Rifling Twist Rate:	1 turn in 24 inch		

Muzzle velocities of factory loaded ammunition	Bullet Wgt.	Muzzle velocity
	240-grain	1,900 fps
	250-grain	1,300 fps
	260-grain	1,600 fps

HISTORICAL NOTES

- The 454 Casull cartridge began life as a proprietary handgun cartridge for Freedom Arms.
- Dick Casull, co-owner of Freedom Arms, saw the need for a 45 caliber super magnum revolver cartridge for hunting big game, and as a backup caliber for hunting dangerous game.
- Casull realized that in order to achieve this goal, two important things would be needed:
  - To reach the muzzle velocities required, MAP would have to reach unprecedented levels for a handgun cartridge. As no existing revolver could withstand such MAP levels, a completely new revolver designed specifically

for the new super magnum cartridge would be required.
- Casull introduced his 454 Casull as a proprietary cartridge in 1957. For the next 41 years, the 454 Casull cartridge was available only from Freedom Arms.
- Then, in 1998, the 454 Casull cartridge and Freedom Arms revolver finally reached critical mass.
- In that year, the 454 Casull cartridge was standardized by the industry, leading to commercial production by Remington, Winchester, Federal, Hornady and Starline (cases only).

BALLISTIC NOTES

- Winchester's 454 Casull factory load consists of a 260-grain bullet at a muzzle velocity of 1,800 fps and—wait for it—1,870 ft-lbs of muzzle energy!!!
- While this load may not kill the bear chewing on your left boot, it sure will get his attention. And, you will not feel the recoil—guaranteed.
- For the faint of heart and/or hunting varmints, pests and small game, there is a "light" 454 Casull factory load with a 250-grain JHP bullet at a muzzle velocity of only 1,300 fps and a measly 938 ft-lbs of muzzle energy.
- The 454 Casull delivers its performance the new fashioned way: with a large diameter, heavy weight bullet at very high muzzle velocities. The high velocity assures plenty of striking energy. The heavy weight of the bullet provides penetration. And, the thick bullet jacket controls energy transfer inside the target.
- Speer understands the demands such ballistic performance can place on a handgun bullet and applied their years of expertise to design suitable bullets and build loads for the 454 Casull.
  - The 454 Casull and the Speer 250-grain DeepCurl® HP were made for each other. This combination is perfect for deer and medium game hunting.
  - The Speer, 260-grain JHP and the 300-grain JSP have thinner jackets and are designed for reduced recoil loads. They have a velocity range of 1,074 fps to 1,572 fps.
  - The Speer 300-grain DeepCurl HP bullet has been especially designed for big game hunting and personal defense in the field with a 454 Casull.

TECHNICAL NOTES

- The 454 Casull is based on a 45 Colt cartridge case lengthened by .098 inch. This allows an OAL of 1.765 inch to prevent a 454 Casull cartridge from being chambered in a 45 Colt revolver.
- The 454 Casull case has approximately 10% more capacity than the 45 Colt.
- Case hardness becomes more important for high pressure cartridges such as the 454 Casull.
  - Hard cases have more "spring back" and will not stick to chamber walls, making them easier to extract. The down side is hard cases tend to split and will not last as long.
  - Soft cases have less spring back and tend to stick to the chamber walls, making them difficult to extract. On the plus side, soft cases tend to last longer.
- The hardness or softness of various brands and lots of 454 Casull brass will become evident during extraction.

- If you experience hard extraction, try reducing the powder charge one grain and/or using another brand of case.
- MAP level for the 454 Casull is 65,000 psi. By comparison, the MAP of the 45 Colt is 14,000 psi and that of the 44 Magnum is 36,000 psi.
- However, the 65,000 psi MAP of the 454 Casull is not a practical working pressure in the real world. For this reason, most factory 454 Casull ammunition is loaded to a more realistic MAP level of about 55,000 psi. Our loading data is within the 55,000 MAP level as well.

HANDLOADING NOTES

- We recommend using new cases for all maximum loads.
- To prevent bullet elongation in revolvers, all bullets loaded in the 454 Casull cartridge must be roll crimped securely in place using the cannelure on the bullet's surface.
- Bullets for maximum loads in the 454 Casull must have a thick jacket such as on the Speer 300-grain DCHP.
- Although 45 Auto bullets are the correct diameter, they are too lightly constructed for use in the 454 Casull and have no crimp cannelure to hold them in place.
- The 454 Casull cartridge case was designed for **Small Rifle** primers such as the CCI No. 400. **Do not use Small Pistol primers**.
- Use medium burning pistol powders for loading the 454 Casull. Do not use cases bearing the Freedom Arms headstamp (F-A) with the 300-grain DCHP data. However, they can be used with the Reduced Recoil Loads.

SAFETY NOTES

SPEER 300-grain DeepCurl HP @ a muzzle velocity of 1,587 fps:
- Maximum vertical altitude @ 90° elevation is 6,081ft/1,853 meters.
- Maximum horizontal distance to first impact with ground @ 34° elevation is 2,849yds./2,605 meters.

250 GRAINS

DIAMETER	SECTIONAL DENSITY
.452"	0.175

45 DCHP
Ballistic Coefficient	0.165
COAL Tested	1.670"
Speer Part No.	4484

			Starting Charge		Maximum Charge	
Propellant	Case	Primer	Weight (grains)	Muzzle Velocity (feet/sec)	Weight (grains)	Muzzle Velocity (feet/sec)
Alliant Power Pro 300-MP	Federal	Federal 205	29.0	1446	31.1	1572
Alliant 2400	Starline	CCI 400	24.0	1422	26.0	1531
Ramshot Enforcer	Federal	Federal 205	24.1	1328	27.2	1510
Vihtavuori N110	Starline	CCI 400	23.0	1381	25.0	1499
Alliant Power Pistol	Federal	Federal 205	13.4	1277	15.0	1402
IMR 4227	Starline	CCI 400	27.0	1248	29.0 C	1399
Accurate No. 9	Starline	CCI 400	23.0	1323	25.0	1375
Accurate 5744	Starline	CCI 400	26.0	1225	28.0	1341
Alliant BE-86	Federal	Federal 205	12.4	1259	13.9	1339
Ramshot True Blue	Starline	CCI 400	14.0	1164	16.0	1325
Vihtavuori N350	Starline	CCI 400	13.0	1129	15.0	1277
Hodgdon CFE Pistol	Federal	Federal 205	11.9	1188	13.2	1276

WARNING! Maximum loads should be used with CAUTION • C = Compressed Load

260 GRAINS

DIAMETER	SECTIONAL DENSITY
.452"	0.183

45 JHP

Ballistic Coefficient	0.183
COAL Tested	1.670"
Speer Part No.	4481

			Starting Charge		Maximum Charge	
Propellant	Case	Primer	Weight (grains)	Muzzle Velocity (feet/sec)	Weight (grains)	Muzzle Velocity (feet/sec)
Alliant Power Pro 300-MP	Federal	Federal 205	29.0	1446	31.1	1572
Alliant 2400	Starline	CCI 400	24.0	1422	26.0	1531
Ramshot Enforcer	Federal	Federal 205	24.1	1328	27.2	1510
Vihtavuori N110	Starline	CCI 400	23.0	1381	25.0	1499
Alliant Power Pistol	Federal	Federal 205	13.4	1277	15.0	1402
IMR 4227	Starline	CCI 400	27.0	1248	29.0 C	1399
Accurate No. 9	Starline	CCI 400	23.0	1323	25.0	1375
Accurate 5744	Starline	CCI 400	26.0	1225	28.0	1341
Alliant BE-86	Federal	Federal 205	12.4	1259	13.9	1339
Ramshot True Blue	Starline	CCI 400	14.0	1164	16.0	1325
Vihtavuori N350	Starline	CCI 400	13.0	1129	15.0	1277
Hodgdon CFE Pistol	Federal	Federal 205	11.9	1188	13.2	1276

WARNING! *Maximum loads should be used with CAUTION • C = Compressed Load*

300 GRAINS

DIAMETER	SECTIONAL DENSITY
.451"	0.211

45 JSP
Ballistic Coefficient	0.199
COAL Tested	1.760"
Speer Part No.	4485

REDUCED RECOIL LOADS

Propellant	Case	Primer	Starting Charge Weight (grains)	Starting Charge Muzzle Velocity (feet/sec)	Maximum Charge Weight (grains)	Maximum Charge Muzzle Velocity (feet/sec)
Alliant Power Pro 300-MP	Federal	Federal 205	28.0	1337	30.7	1479
Hodgdon H110	Winchester	CCI 400	26.5	1328	28.5	1452
Winchester 296	Winchester	CCI 400	26.0	1298	28.0	1426
Ramshot Enforcer	Federal	Federal 205	24.0	1269	26.5	1383
Accurate No. 9	Winchester	CCI 400	21.5	1218	23.5	1349
IMR 4227	Winchester	CCI 400	25.5	1142	27.5	1327
Alliant 2400	Winchester	CCI 400	22.0	1209	24.0	1325
Vihtavuori N110	Winchester	CCI 400	20.0	1220	22.0	1322
Alliant Power Pistol	Federal	Federal 205	12.5	1119	14.8	1262
Alliant BE-86	Federal	Federal 205	12.1	1127	13.6	1222
Hodgdon CFE Pistol	Federal	Federal 205	11.7	1074	13.0	1166

WARNING! *Maximum loads should be used with* CAUTION • C = Compressed Load

300 GRAINS

DIAMETER	SECTIONAL DENSITY
.452"	0.210

45 DCHP

Ballistic Coefficient	0.233
COAL Tested	1.750"
Speer Part No.	3974

FULL POWER LOADS

Propellant	Case	Primer	Starting Charge Weight (grains)	Starting Charge Muzzle Velocity (feet/sec)	Maximum Charge Weight (grains)	Maximum Charge Muzzle Velocity (feet/sec)
Winchester 296	Winchester	CCI 400	29.0	1475	31.0 C	1587
Vihtavuori N110	Winchester	CCI 400	25.5	1446	27.5	1549
Accurate No. 9	Winchester	CCI 400	24.5	1403	26.5	1535
Alliant 2400	Winchester	CCI 400	25.0	1379	27.0	1479
IMR 4227	Winchester	CCI 400	28.0	1320	30.0 C	1426

WARNING! *Maximum loads should be used with CAUTION • C = Compressed Load*

460 S&W MAGNUM

Parent Cartridge:	45 Colt
Country of Origin:	USA
Year of Introduction:	2005
Designer(s):	Smith & Wesson and Hornady
Governing Body:	SAAMI/CIP

.478" [12.14mm] cyl
.520" [13.21mm]
.455" [11.56mm]
.059" [1.50mm]
1.800" [45.72mm]

CARTRIDGE CASE DATA

Case Type:	Rimmed, straight
Average Case Capacity:	47.2 grains H₂O
Max. Cartridge OAL:	2.290 inch
Max. Case Length:	1.800 inch
Primer:	Large Rifle
Case Trim to Length:	1.790 inch
RCBS Shell holder:	# 4
Current Manufacturers:	Federal, Hornady, Remington, Winchester, Cor-Bon

BALLISTIC DATA

Max. Average Pressure (MAP):	65,000 psi, CUP not established for this cartridge - SAAMI
Test Barrel Length:	10.000 inch unvented, 10.746 inch vented
Rifling Twist Rate:	1 turn in 20 inch

Muzzle velocities of factory loaded ammunition	Bullet Wgt.	Muzzle velocity
	200-grain	2,200 fps
	250-grain	1,450 fps
	260-grain	1,600 fps
	275-grain	1,670 fps

HISTORICAL NOTES

- Smith & Wesson has a long and distinguished history of developing new cartridges, as well as the guns to fire them.
- The 460 S&W Magnum is one of the most recent of their developments. It is an integral participant in the recent trend toward very powerful, large caliber revolver cartridges for hunting big game.
- Of course this is a niche market that is still developing, so no one knows the depth or size of this market.

- However, these developments beg the question "How much power is enough?" Just when you think the limit has been reached, a new, more powerful revolver cartridge is introduced.
- These developments also raise two personal questions:
  - "How much power can you handle?" (Be honest—or optimistic)
  - "How much more power can you afford?" (Big magnums are expensive, but that is what credit cards are for).
- In the past, these questions were perfunctory, today they are serious.
- One could be forgiven for considering the 460 S&W Magnum as an effort by S&W to one up the 454 Casull. But, you would be wrong. S&W introduced their 500 S&W Magnum cartridge three years before the 460 S&W Magnum.
- Technically, that makes the 460 S&W Magnum cartridge a step down in power for the faint of heart who cannot handle a 500 S&W Magnum.
- After introduction of the 460 S&W Magnum, commercial production of ammunition was undertaken by Winchester, Federal, Hornady and Starline (cases only).

TECHNICAL NOTES

- The 460 S&W Magnum cartridge is a classic, rimmed, straight revolver cartridge that headspaces on the rim which has an undercut.
- Head diameter, rim thickness, and nominal rim diameter of the 460 S&W Magnum and 454 Casull cartridges are similar.
- The major difference between the two cartridges is case length and OAL:
  - Case length: 460 S&W Magnum 1.800 inch; 454 Casull 1.383 inch.
  - OAL: 460 S&W Magnum 2.290 inch; 454 Casull 1.765 inch.
- The OAL of the 460 S&W Magnum prevents it from being chambered in a 454 Casull revolver.
- The 460 S&W Magnum cartridge case has substantially more capacity than the 454 Casull.
- Case hardness becomes more important for high pressure cartridges such as the 460 S&W Magnum.
  - Hard cases have more "spring back" and will not stick to chamber walls, making them easier to extract. The down side is hard cases tend to split and will not last as long.
  - Soft cases have less spring back and tend to stick to the chamber walls, making them difficult to extract. On the plus side, soft cases tend to last longer.
- The hardness or softness of various brands and lots of 460 S&W Magnum brass will become evident during extraction.
- If you experience hard extraction, try reducing the powder charge one grain and/or using another brand of case.
- MAP level for the 460 S&W Magnum is 65,000 psi which is the same as the 454 Casull. By comparison, the MAP of the 45 Colt is 14,000 psi and that of the 44 Magnum is 36,000 psi.

- However, the 65,000 psi MAP of the 460 S&W Magnum is not a practical working pressure in the real world. For this reason, most factory 460 S&W Magnum ammunition is loaded to a more realistic MAP level of about 55,000 psi. Our loading data is within the 55,000 MAP level as well.

HANDLOADING NOTES

- We recommend using new cases for all maximum loads.
- To prevent bullet elongation in revolvers, all bullets loaded in the 460 S&W Magnum cartridge must be crimped securely in place using the cannelure on the bullet's surface.
- We recommend a neckdown crimp for DeepCurl® bullets and a roll crimp for all others.
- Bullets for maximum loads in the 460 S&W Magnum must have a thick jacket such as on the Speer 300-grain DCHP.
- Although 45 Auto bullets are the correct diameter, they are too lightly constructed for use in the 460 S&W Magnum and have no crimp cannelure to hold them in place.
- **Do not use Large Pistol primers** to reload the 460 S&W Magnum, it was designed for **Large Rifle primers**!
- Never load less than the minimum charges shown in the loading data as the small charge of propellant may not be sufficient to push the bullet completely down the barrel.
- Use medium burning pistol powders for loading the 460 S&W Magnum.

SAFETY NOTES

SPEER 300-grain DeepCurl® Hollow Point @ a muzzle velocity of 1,784 fps:
- Maximum vertical altitude @ 90° elevation is 6,255 feet.
- Maximum horizontal distance to first impact with ground @ 34° elevation is 2,909 yards.

250 GRAINS

DIAMETER	SECTIONAL DENSITY
.452"	0.175

45 DCHP

Ballistic Coefficient	0.165
COAL Tested	2.090"
Speer Part No.	4484

			Starting Charge		Maximum Charge	
Propellant	Case	Primer	Weight (grains)	Muzzle Velocity (feet/sec)	Weight (grains)	Muzzle Velocity (feet/sec)
Accurate No. 9	Hornady	Federal 210	28.0	1403	30.0	1591
Alliant 2400	Hornady	Federal 210	29.0	1499	31.0	1553
Vihtavuori N110	Hornady	Federal 210	29.0	1498	31.0	1551
Alliant Power Pistol	Hornady	Federal 210	19.0	1400	21.0	1514
Winchester 296	Hornady	Federal 210	26.0	1328	30.6	1497
Ramshot Enforcer	Hornady	Federal 210	25.8	1376	29.4	1481
Ramshot True Blue	Hornady	Federal 210	19.0	1332	21.0	1436
Alliant BE-86	Hornady	Federal 210	16.0	1268	18.4	1373
Accurate 5744	Hornady	Federal 210	33.0	1282	35.0	1366
Hodgdon CFE Pistol	Hornady	Federal 210	15.5	1236	17.5	1324

WARNING! *Maximum loads should be used with CAUTION • C = Compressed Load*

260 GRAINS

DIAMETER	SECTIONAL DENSITY
.452"	0.183

45 JHP	
Ballistic Coefficient	0.183
COAL Tested	2.090"
Speer Part No.	4481

			Starting Charge		Maximum Charge	
Propellant	Case	Primer	Weight (grains)	Muzzle Velocity (feet/sec)	Weight (grains)	Muzzle Velocity (feet/sec)
Accurate No. 9	Hornady	Federal 210	28.0	1403	30.0	1591
Alliant 2400	Hornady	Federal 210	29.0	1499	31.0	1553
Vihtavuori N110	Hornady	Federal 210	29.0	1498	31.0	1551
Alliant Power Pistol	Hornady	Federal 210	19.0	1400	21.0	1514
Winchester 296	Hornady	Federal 210	26.0	1328	30.6	1497
Ramshot Enforcer	Hornady	Federal 210	25.8	1376	29.4	1481
Ramshot True Blue	Hornady	Federal 210	19.0	1332	21.0	1436
Alliant BE-86	Hornady	Federal 210	16.0	1268	18.4	1373
Accurate 5744	Hornady	Federal 210	33.0	1282	35.0	1366
Hodgdon CFE Pistol	Hornady	Federal 210	15.5	1236	17.5	1324

WARNING! *Maximum loads should be used with CAUTION • C = Compressed Load*

300 GRAINS

DIAMETER	SECTIONAL DENSITY
.451"	0.211

45 JSP

Ballistic Coefficient	0.199
COAL Tested	2.170"
Speer Part No.	4485

REDUCED RECOIL LOADS

Propellant	Case	Primer	Starting Charge Weight (grains)	Starting Charge Muzzle Velocity (feet/sec)	Maximum Charge Weight (grains)	Maximum Charge Muzzle Velocity (feet/sec)
Accurate 1680	Hornady	Federal 210	42.0	1478	44.0	1591
Alliant 2400	Hornady	Federal 210	28.0	1392	30.0	1550
Hodgdon Lil' Gun	Hornady	Federal 210	29.0	1464	31.0	1544
Accurate No. 9	Hornady	Federal 210	25.0	1420	27.0	1527
Ramshot Enforcer	Hornady	Federal 210	30.0	1457	32.0	1515
Hodgdon H110	Hornady	Federal 210	29.0	1406	31.0	1475
IMR 4227	Hornady	Federal 210	33.0	1375	35.0	1471
Winchester 296	Hornady	Federal 210	32.0	1504	34.0	1469
Vihtavuori N110	Hornady	Federal 210	29.0	1394	31.0	1458
Alliant Power Pistol	Hornady	Federal 210	18.0	1292	20.0	1359
Alliant BE-86	Hornady	Federal 210	15.6	1102	17.7	1269
Hodgdon CFE Pistol	Hornady	Federal 210	15.1	1073	17.1	1184

WARNING! Maximum loads should be used with CAUTION • C = Compressed Load

300 GRAINS

DIAMETER	SECTIONAL DENSITY
.452"	0.210

45 DCHP	
Ballistic Coefficient	0.233
COAL Tested	2.150"
Speer Part No.	3974

FULL POWER LOADS

Propellant	Case	Primer	Starting Charge Weight (grains)	Starting Charge Muzzle Velocity (feet/sec)	Maximum Charge Weight (grains)	Maximum Charge Muzzle Velocity (feet/sec)
Accurate No. 9	Hornady	Federal 210	33.0	1669	35.0	1784
Alliant 2400	Hornady	Federal 210	34.0	1610	36.0	1782
Accurate 1680	Hornady	Federal 210	46.0	1614	48.0 C	1715
Hodgdon Lil' Gun	Hornady	Federal 210	34.0	1634	36.0	1703
Ramshot Enforcer	Hornady	Federal 210	34.0	1627	36.0	1677
IMR 4227	Hornady	Federal 210	38.0	1567	40.0 C	1656
Hodgdon H110	Hornady	Federal 210	34.0	1581	36.0	1645
Vihtavuori N110	Hornady	Federal 210	34.0	1563	36.0	1625
Winchester 296	Hornady	Federal 210	36.0	1635	38.0	1597
Alliant Power Pistol	Hornady	Federal 210	22.0	1457	24.0	1525

WARNING! *Maximum loads should be used with* CAUTION • C = Compressed Load

480 RUGER

Parent Cartridge:	475 Linebaugh
Country of Origin:	USA
Year of Introduction:	2003
Designer(s):	Sturm, Ruger & Co. and Hornady
Governing Body:	SAAMI/CIP

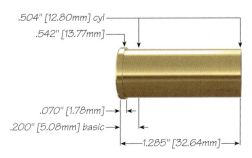

.504" [12.80mm] cyl
.542" [13.77mm]
.070" [1.78mm]
.200" [5.08mm] basic
1.285" [32.64mm]

CARTRIDGE CASE DATA

Case Type:	Rimmed, straight		
Average Case Capacity:	47.3 grains H₂O	Max. Cartridge OAL	1.650 inch
Max. Case Length:	1.285 inch	Primer:	Large Pistol
Case Trim to Length:	1.275 inch	RCBS Shell holder:	# 40
Current Manufacturers:	Hornady		

BALLISTIC DATA

Max. Average Pressure (MAP):	48,000 psi, CUP not established for this cartridge - SAAMI	Test Barrel Length:	7.5 inch unvented, 9.197 inch vented
Rifling Twist Rate:	1 turn in 18 inch		
Muzzle velocities of factory loaded ammunition		Bullet Wgt.	Muzzle velocity
		325-grain	1,350 fps

HISTORICAL NOTES

- The 480 Ruger is the first handgun cartridge to carry the Ruger name.
- It was introduced jointly by Ruger and Hornady in 2001. To date, Hornady remains the sole manufacturer of ammunition in 480 Ruger.
- In similar manner to other large caliber magnum handgun cartridges, the 480 Ruger is a specialty cartridge intended for big game hunting by experienced handgunners.
- Although Ruger and Hornady chose not to label the 480 Ruger a magnum, it is a magnum by any other name.

BALLISTIC NOTES

- Although it offers magnum performance, the 480 Ruger does not attempt to one-up other handgun magnum cartridges in muzzle velocity, energy or bullet weight.
- Rather, the 480 Ruger is designed to avoid being over-powered by striking a balance between power and controllability.
- The 480 Ruger accomplishes this by balancing five ballistic factors:
  - MAP level of 48,000 psi (lower than competitors).
  - A muzzle velocity of 1,350 fps (lower than competitors).
  - A muzzle energy of 1,315 ft-lbs (more than enough to hunt North American big game).
  - A bullet weighing 325 grains (lighter than competitors).
  - A .475 inch diameter bullet (greater diameter than competitors).
- Handloaders have the capability of shifting the ballistic balance point up or down depending on their specific requirements and personal preferences.
- Speer has developed two DeepCurl® premium bullets with extra thick jackets specifically for the 480 Ruger:
  - A 275-grain DeepCurl Hollow Point (DCHP)
    (A good choice for high velocity loads to 1,695 fps or for reduced power loads to 1,205 fps).
  - A 325-grain DeepCurl Soft Point (DCSP)
    (The "standard" bullet for the 480 Ruger; muzzle velocity range from a chart topping 1,492 fps to a mild and friendly 991 fps or duplicating the factory load in between).

TECHNICAL NOTES

- The 480 Ruger is essentially a 475 Linebaugh cartridge case shortened from 1.400 inch to 1.285 inch. All other dimensions are similar.
- OAL is adjusted downward accordingly to prevent a 475 Linebaugh cartridge from being chambered in a 480 Ruger revolver.
- However, 480 Ruger ammunition may be fired safely in revolvers chambered for the 475 Linebaugh.
- The 480 Ruger case has approximately 8% less capacity than the 475 Linebaugh.
- Case hardness becomes more important for high pressure handgun cartridges such as the 480 Ruger.
  - Hard cases have more "spring back" and will not stick to chamber walls, making them easier to extract. The down side is hard cases tend to split and will not last as long.
  - Soft cases have less spring back and tend to stick to the chamber walls, making them difficult to extract. On the plus side, soft cases tend to last longer.
- The hardness or softness of various brands and lots of 480 Ruger brass will become evident during extraction.
- If you experience hard extraction, try reducing the powder charge one grain and/or using another brand of case.

HANDLOADING NOTES

- We recommend using new cases for all maximum loads.
- To prevent bullet elongation in revolvers, all bullets loaded in the 480 Ruger cartridge must be crimped securely in place using the extra wide cannelure on the bullet's surface. We recommend a neckdown crimp.
- Bullets for maximum loads in the 480 Ruger must have an extra thick jacket such as the Speer 275-grain DCHP and the 325-grain DCSP.
- We used slow burning pistol powders for loading the 480 Ruger.

SAFETY NOTES

SPEER 325-grain DeepCurl Soft Point @ a muzzle velocity of 1,492 fps:
- Maximum vertical altitude @ 90° elevation is 5,217 feet.
- Maximum horizontal distance to first impact with ground @ 34° elevation is 2,424 yards.

275 GRAINS

DIAMETER	SECTIONAL DENSITY
.475"	0.174

475 DCHP

Ballistic Coefficient	0.162
COAL Tested	1.640"
Speer Part No.	3973

			Starting Charge		Maximum Charge	
Propellant	Case	Primer	Weight (grains)	Muzzle Velocity (feet/sec)	Weight (grains)	Muzzle Velocity (feet/sec)
Winchester 296	Hornady	CCI 350	32.0	1590	34.0	1695
Hodgdon H110	Hornady	CCI 350	32.0	1554	34.0	1663
Vihtavuori N110	Hornady	CCI 300	25.5	1461	27.5	1575
Accurate No. 9	Hornady	CCI 300	26.0	1474	28.0	1566
Alliant 2400	Hornady	CCI 300	27.0	1454	29.0	1560
IMR 4227	Hornady	CCI 300	31.0	1424	33.0	1523
Accurate No. 7	Hornady	CCI 300	20.0	1314	22.0	1493
Alliant Power Pistol	Hornady	CCI 300	15.5	1324	17.5	1465
Alliant Unique	Hornady	CCI 300	14.0	1275	16.0	1400
Vihtavuori N350	Hornady	CCI 300	14.0	1205	16.0	1341

WARNING! Maximum loads should be used with CAUTION • C = Compressed Load

325 GRAINS

DIAMETER	SECTIONAL DENSITY
.475"	0.206

475 DCSP	
Ballistic Coefficient	0.191
COAL Tested	1.650"
Speer Part No.	3978

			Starting Charge		Maximum Charge	
Propellant	Case	Primer	Weight (grains)	Muzzle Velocity (feet/sec)	Weight (grains)	Muzzle Velocity (feet/sec)
Hodgdon Lil' Gun	Hornady	CCI 350	26.0	1427	28.0	1492
Winchester 296	Hornady	CCI 350	26.0	1366	28.0	1464
Vihtavuori N110	Hornady	CCI 300	22.5	1349	24.5 C	1457
Hodgdon H110	Hornady	CCI 350	26.0	1368	28.0	1445
Accurate No. 9	Hornady	CCI 300	23.0	1360	25.0	1444
Alliant 2400	Hornady	CCI 300	23.0	1319	25.0	1435
IMR 4227	Hornady	CCI 300	27.0 C	1263	29.0 C	1389
Accurate 1680	Hornady	CCI 350	28.0	1138	30.0 C	1239
Alliant Unique	Hornady	CCI 300	10.0	991	13.0	1178

WARNING! *Maximum loads should be used with* CAUTION • C = Compressed Load

475 LINEBAUGH

Parent Cartridge:	45-70 Government
Country of Origin:	USA
Year of Introduction:	2000
Designer(s):	John Linebaugh
Governing Body:	SAAMI

Dimensions: .504" [12.80mm] cyl; .542" [13.77mm]; .070" [1.78mm]; .200" [5.08mm] basic; 1.400" [35.56mm]

CARTRIDGE CASE DATA	
Case Type:	Rimmed, straight
Average Case Capacity:	51.5 grains H₂O
Max. Cartridge OAL:	1.765 inch
Max. Case Length:	1.400 inch
Primer:	Large Pistol
Case Trim to Length:	1.390 inch
RCBS Shell holder:	# 40
Current Manufacturers:	Hornady and Buffalo Bore

BALLISTIC DATA	
Max. Average Pressure (MAP):	50,000 psi, CUP not established for this cartridge - SAAMI
Test Barrel Length:	7.500 inch unvented and vented
Rifling Twist Rate:	1 turn in 18 inch

Muzzle velocities of factory loaded ammunition	
Bullet Wgt.	Muzzle velocity
350-grain	1,500 fps
400-grain	1,300 fps

HISTORICAL NOTES

- Custom pistol smith John Linebaugh developed this powerful cartridge in the 1980s for hunting North American big game.

- Linebaugh based his cartridge on the massive 45-70 Government case shortened to 1.400 inches and straightened to accept a .475 inch diameter bullet.

- Subsequently, the rim diameter was reduced slightly and the case strengthened by Buffalo Bore when they initiated production of factory ammunition in this caliber.

- Currently, Buffalo Bore and Hornady are the only manufacturers of factory loaded 475 Linebaugh ammunition. Brass is available from both manufacturers as well as from Starline.

- Although it is not called a magnum, the 475 Linebaugh is a magnum by any other name.

Interesting Fact

The 475 Linebaugh was the first factory loaded handgun cartridge in .475 inch caliber since the 476 Enfield Mark III revolver cartridge entered British military service in 1881.

BALLISTIC NOTES

- On the muzzle energy chart, the 475 Linebaugh falls between the 454 Casull and the 480 Ruger making it on par with the 50 Action Express. However, the 475 Linebaugh and the 50 Action Express are not ballistic equals, nor are they designed for the same purpose.
- When it was introduced, the 475 Linebaugh was a trend setter in large caliber magnum handgun cartridges. Since then, it has been surpassed by the 460 S&W Magnum and 500 S&W Magnum in this regard.
- The 475 Linebaugh is an unabashed big game cartridge with enough recoil to impress even an experienced big game hunter. As such, it is a specialty caliber for a singular purpose. It cannot be recommended for novice shooters.
- Hornady offers a single factory load in 475 Linebaugh. It consists of a 400-grain JHP bullet at a muzzle velocity of 1,300 fps and a muzzle energy of 1,501 ft-lbs. Hornady does not offer this 400-grain bullet to handloaders.
- Buffalo Bore offers two full power factory loads in 475 Linebaugh:
  - A 400-grain JSP bullet at a muzzle velocity of 1,400 fps and a muzzle energy of 1,741 ft-lbs.
  - A 350-grain JSP bullet at a muzzle velocity of 1,500 fps and 1,748 ft-lbs of muzzle energy.
- Of course, handloaders have the capability of shifting all of these factors up or down depending on their specific requirements and personal preferences.
- Speer has developed a premium bullet with an extra thick jacket specifically for the 475 Linebaugh:
  - A 325-grain DeepCurl® Soft Point (DCSP).

TECHNICAL NOTES

- The 475 Linebaugh cartridge case length is 1.400 inch compared to 1.285 inch of the 480 Ruger.
- 480 Ruger ammunition can be fired safely from revolvers chambered for the 475 Linebaugh cartridge.
- The 475 Linebaugh case has approximately 8% more capacity than the 480 Ruger.
- Case hardness becomes more important for high pressure handgun cartridges such as the 475 Linebaugh.
  - Hard cases have more "spring back" and will not stick to chamber walls, making them easier to extract. The down side is hard cases tend to split and will not last as long.
  - Soft cases have less spring back and tend to stick to the chamber walls, making them difficult to extract. On the plus side, soft cases tend to last longer.
- The hardness or softness of various brands and lots of 475 Linebaugh brass will become evident during extraction.

- If you experience hard extraction, try reducing the powder charge one grain and/or using another brand of case.
- MAP level for the 475 Linebaugh cartridge is 50,000 psi. In comparison, the MAP level of the 480 Ruger is 48,000 psi, the 44 Magnum is 36,000 psi, and the 454 Casull is 65,000 psi.

HANDLOADING NOTES

- We recommend using new cases or once-fired brass for all maximum loads.
- To prevent bullet elongation in revolvers, all bullets loaded in the 475 Linebaugh cartridge must be crimped securely in place using the extra wide cannelure on the DCSP bullet's surface. We recommend a neckdown crimp.
- Bullets for maximum loads in the 475 Linebaugh must have an extra thick jacket such as the Speer 325-grain DCSP. Bullets with thin jackets should not be used for the 475 Linebaugh.
- We used slow burning pistol powders for loading the 475 Linebaugh.

SAFETY NOTES

SPEER 325-grain DeepCurl Soft Point @ a muzzle velocity of 1,429 fps:
- Maximum vertical altitude @ 90° elevation is 5,154 feet.
- Maximum horizontal distance to first impact with ground @ 34° elevation is 2,401 yards.

325 GRAINS

DIAMETER	SECTIONAL DENSITY
.475"	0.206

475 DCSP	
Ballistic Coefficient	0.191
COAL Tested	1.750"
Speer Part No.	3978

			Starting Charge		Maximum Charge	
Propellant	Case	Primer	Weight (grains)	Muzzle Velocity (feet/sec)	Weight (grains)	Muzzle Velocity (feet/sec)
Accurate No. 9	Buffalo Bore	CCI 350	26.0	1324	28.0	1429
Vihtavuori N110	Buffalo Bore	CCI 350	25.5	1308	27.5	1412
Alliant 2400	Buffalo Bore	CCI 350	25.0	1262	27.0	1371
Accurate No. 7	Buffalo Bore	CCI 350	19.0	1153	23.0	1363
Alliant Blue Dot	Buffalo Bore	CCI 350	18.0	1159	20.0	1324
Alliant Power Pistol	Buffalo Bore	CCI 350	15.5	1168	17.5	1302
Alliant Unique	Buffalo Bore	CCI 350	13.5	1107	15.5	1221
Vihtavuori N350	Buffalo Bore	CCI 350	14.5	1065	16.5	1220

WARNING! Maximum loads should be used with CAUTION • C = Compressed Load

50 ACTION EXPRESS

Alternate Names:	50 AE
Parent Cartridge:	Original design
Country of Origin:	USA & Israel
Year of Introduction:	1991
Designer(s):	Evan Whildin, IMI
Governing Body:	SAAMI

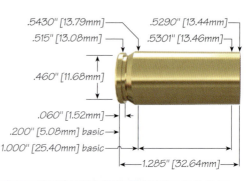

CARTRIDGE CASE DATA

Case Type:	Rebated, straight		
Average Case Capacity:	55.6 grains H$_2$O	Max. Cartridge OAL	1.595 inch
Max. Case Length:	1.285 inch	Primer:	Large Pistol
Case Trim to Length:	1.276 inch	RCBS Shell holder:	# 33
Current Manufacturers:	CCI/Speer, Federal, Hornady, Magnum Research, Starline		

BALLISTIC DATA

Max. Average Pressure (MAP):	35,000 psi, CUP not established for this cartridge - SAAMI	Test Barrel Length:	6 inch
Rifling Twist Rate:	1 turn in 20 inch		
Muzzle velocities of factory loaded ammunition	Bullet Wgt.		Muzzle velocity
	300-grain		1,550 fps
	325-grain		1,400 fps

HISTORICAL NOTES

- The 50 Action Express cartridge is in a class by itself. It is the largest and most powerful semi-automatic pistol cartridge on the market.
- The 50 Action Express (AE) cartridge was designed by Evan Whildin for Action Arms, Ltd.
- There was only one semi-automatic pistol that could be modified to fire the new cartridge—the massive, gas-operated, Desert Eagle pistol designed by Bernie White and made by Israel Military Industries (IMI) for Action Arms.
- The engineers at CCI/Speer worked with Whildin and IMI to commercialize the 50 AE cartridge.

- The 50 Action Express cartridge was introduced in 1991 along with a model of the Desert Eagle chambered for it.
- Subsequently, manufacture, sales and distribution of the Desert Eagle pistol were taken over by Magnum Research, now a division of Kahr Arms.
- Today, Federal Premium, Hornady, and Magnum Research are the principle sources for 50 AE ammunition, and Starline offers brass in this caliber.

Interesting Fact

Engineers working on the 50 AE Desert Eagle at the IMI Weapons Plant in Israel jokingly referred to it as "The Hammer" because of its size and weight. Other employees at IMI quipped: "Israel has developed the world's first crew-served pistol!"

- Power has it costs however:
  - Recoil of the 50 AE Desert Eagle pistol with full power loads is seriously heavy, although the gas-operation and grip design of the pistol presents the recoil to the shooter quite differently than a revolver.
  - As a specialty product in a niche market, 50 AE ammunition is expensive, offered by a limited number of manufacturers and stocked by few dealers, making it an economic imperative to handload.
  - Factory loaded 50 AE ammunition is designed for one purpose only—hunting North American big game. This cartridge has no other practical application.
- However, practicality has no influence on the most important reason to purchase a 50 AE caliber Desert Eagle — "Pride of Ownership".

BALLISTIC NOTES

- Factory ammunition ballistics place the 50 AE well below the 500 S&W Magnum, 460 S&W Magnum and 454 Casull, but on par with the 475 Linebaugh, and superior to the 44 Magnum and 480 Ruger.
- However, these raw numbers are not definitive as the bullets for the big, high pressure, magnum revolver calibers have thick jackets and hard lead cores to assure deep penetration and reliable energy transfer on tough big game.
- The bullets for the 50 AE have thinner jackets and a softer lead core, more suitable for hunting thin skinned big game.
- Accordingly, Speer offers three bullets designed specifically for handloading the 50 AE:
  - A 300-grain premium DeepCurl® Hollow Point (DCHP), which is the perfect choice for duplicating factory loads in this bullet weight.
  - A 300-grain Speer Total Metal Jacket Flat Nose (TMJ® FN), for general purpose use on tougher game where deeper penetration with no loss of weight is required; this bullet is not offered by factories.
  - A 325-grain Speer Jacketed Hollow Point (JHP), for heavy game that require reliable energy transfer with deeper penetration.
- To reduce recoil levels for practice and plinking, Speer 300-grain bullets can be loaded down to a muzzle velocity of 1,266 fps which will still function the Desert Eagle.
- To a bystander, even reduced 50 AE loads create impressive levels of muzzle blast, flash and muzzle flip. (No one will know you are shooting reduced loads—after all, you have an image to protect!)

TECHNICAL NOTES

- The 50 Action Express cartridge is designed to be fired in a 44 Magnum Desert Eagle pistol by changing only the barrel and magazine (a quick and easy task).

- To enable this, the rim of the 50 AE cartridge case is similar in diameter to the 44 Magnum. In order to fit in the frame of the Desert Eagle pistol, the rim of the 50 AE cartridge case is rebated with a rimless undercut extractor groove and a slightly tapered case body.

- Case dimensions, case capacity and case weight of the 50 AE are unique to this caliber, as are the bullets.

- Unlike the very high MAP levels of the big revolver magnum cartridges, MAP level for the 50 AE is 35,000 psi which is similar to that of the 9mm Luger, 357 Magnum, and 44 Magnum cartridges.

- Bullets designed for the 500 S&W Magnum must not be used in the 50 AE.

HANDLOADING NOTES

- Use new or once-fired cases for maximum loads.

- To reliably control headspace, we recommend taper crimping bullets in place after seating them in the 50 AE case, a two-step operation.

- Never load less than the minimum charges shown in the loading data as the small charge of propellant may not be sufficient to push the bullet completely down the barrel.

- Do not use unjacketed lead bullets in the 50 AE as lead particles and lubricant can clog the gas system.

- We used slow burning pistol powders for loading the 50 AE.

SAFETY NOTES

SPEER 325-grain Jacketed Hollow Point (JHP) @ a muzzle velocity of 1,437 fps:
- Maximum vertical altitude @ 90° elevation is 4,764 feet.
- Maximum horizontal distance to first impact with ground @ 33° elevation is 2,202 yards.

300 GRAINS

DIAMETER	SECTIONAL DENSITY
.500"	0.171

50 TMJ® FN
Ballistic Coefficient	0.157
COAL Tested	1.580"
Speer Part No.	4490

50 DCHP
Ballistic Coefficient	0.155
COAL Tested	1.580"
Speer Part No.	4493

			Starting Charge		Maximum Charge	
Propellant	Case	Primer	Weight (grains)	Muzzle Velocity (feet/sec)	Weight (grains)	Muzzle Velocity (feet/sec)
Winchester 296	Speer	CCI 350	33.5	1466	34.5	1567
Hodgdon H110	Speer	CCI 350	33.5	1482	34.5	1510
Vihtavuori N110	Speer	CCI 300	28.0	1418	29.0	1501
Alliant 2400	Speer	CCI 300	28.0	1368	29.0	1435
Accurate No. 9	Speer	CCI 350	25.0	1343	26.0	1380
IMR 4227	Speer	CCI 350	31.5	1266	32.5	1303

325 GRAINS

DIAMETER	SECTIONAL DENSITY
.500"	0.186

50 JHP
Ballistic Coefficient	0.169
COAL Tested	1.575"
Speer Part No.	4495

			Starting Charge		Maximum Charge	
Propellant	Case	Primer	Weight (grains)	Muzzle Velocity (feet/sec)	Weight (grains)	Muzzle Velocity (feet/sec)
Hodgdon H110	Speer	CCI 350	29.4	1298	32.6	1437
Winchester 296	Speer	CCI 350	29.5	1279	32.7	1409
Alliant 2400	Speer	CCI 300	26.0	1259	28.0	1377
Vihtavuori N110	Speer	CCI 300	25.0	1229	27.0	1376
Accurate 1680	Speer	CCI 350	34.0	1155	37.8 C	1305
IMR 4227	Speer	CCI 350	29.5	1224	31.1	1289
Accurate No. 9	Speer	CCI 350	22.6	1157	23.8	1247

WARNING! *Maximum loads should be used with CAUTION • C = Compressed Load*

300 GRAINS

DIAMETER	SECTIONAL DENSITY
.500"	0.171

50 TMJ® FN
Ballistic Coefficient	0.157
COAL Tested	1.580"
Speer Part No.	4490

50 AE DCHP
Ballistic Coefficient	0.155
COAL Tested	1.580"
Speer Part No.	4493

REVOLVER VELOCITIES Freedom Arms M555 7.5"

			Starting Charge		Maximum Charge	
Propellant	Case	Primer	Weight (grains)	Muzzle Velocity (feet/sec)	Weight (grains)	Muzzle Velocity (feet/sec)
Winchester 296	Speer	CCI 350	33.5	1465	34.5	1526
Vihtavuori N110	Speer	CCI 300	28.0	1445	29.0	1509
Hodgdon H110	Speer	CCI 350	33.5	1448	34.5	1505
Alliant 2400	Speer	CCI 300	28.0	1435	29.0	1483
Accurate No. 7	Speer	CCI 300	21.5	1282	23.5	1437
Accurate No. 9	Speer	CCI 350	25.0	1404	26.0	1426
IMR 4227	Speer	CCI 350	31.5	1284	32.5	1334

325 GRAINS

DIAMETER	SECTIONAL DENSITY
.500"	0.186

50 AE JHP
Ballistic Coefficient	0.169
COAL Tested	1.575"
Speer Part No.	4495

REVOLVER VELOCITIES Freedom Arms M555 7.5"

			Starting Charge		Maximum Charge	
Propellant	Case	Primer	Weight (grains)	Muzzle Velocity (feet/sec)	Weight (grains)	Muzzle Velocity (feet/sec)
Hodgdon H110	Speer	CCI 350	29.4	1324	32.6	1475
Winchester 296	Speer	CCI 350	29.5	1321	32.7	1461
Alliant 2400	Speer	CCI 300	26.0	1345	28.0	1461
Vihtavuori N110	Speer	CCI 300	25.0	1283	27.0	1444
Accurate 1680	Speer	CCI 350	34.0	1243	37.8 C	1374
IMR 4227	Speer	CCI 350	29.5	1256	31.1	1344
Accurate No. 9	Speer	CCI 350	22.6	1270	23.8	1318

WARNING! Maximum loads should be used with CAUTION • C = Compressed Load

500 S&W MAGNUM

Alternate Names:	12.7x41mmSR
Parent Cartridge:	Original design
Country of Origin:	USA
Year of Introduction:	2003
Designer(s):	Smith & Wesson
Governing Body:	SAAMI

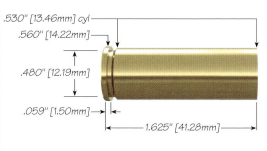

CARTRIDGE CASE DATA

Case Type:	Semi-rimmed, straight		
Average Case Capacity:	70.4 grains H_2O	**Max. Cartridge OAL**	2.250 inch
Max. Case Length:	1.625 inch	**Primer:**	Large Rifle
Case Trim to Length:	1.615 inch	**RCBS Shell holder:**	# 44
Current Manufacturers:	Federal, Hornady, Winchester, Cor-Bon		

BALLISTIC DATA

Max. Average Pressure (MAP):	60,000 psi, CUP Not available for this cartridge.	**Test Barrel Length:**	6 inch
Rifling Twist Rate:	10 inch unvented, 10.675 inch vented		

Muzzle velocities of factory loaded ammunition	Bullet Wgt.	Muzzle velocity
	300-grain	1,950 fps
	325-grain	1,800 fps
	350-grain	1,600 fps
	375-grain	1,725 fps
	385-grain	1,700 fps
	400-grain	1,675 fps
	500-grain	1,300 fps

HISTORICAL NOTES

- Smith & Wesson has a well-earned reputation for developing new handgun cartridges, as well as the guns to fire them.
- However, with the 500 S&W Magnum they have outdone themselves and established new benchmarks for factory loaded revolver cartridges that are unlikely to be bested--ever.

- Most powerful factory loaded handgun cartridge on the market: 300-grain bullet at a muzzle velocity of 1,950 fps with 2,533 ft-lbs of muzzle energy (Hornady).
- Heaviest factory loaded handgun bullet: 500 grains.
- Largest diameter of bullet allowed by law: .500 inch.
- An empty 500 S&W Magnum cartridge case is longer than a loaded 44 Magnum, 45 Colt, or 50 Action Express.

• Wretched excess has its costs however:
- Recoil of the 500 S&W Magnum with full power loads is seriously heavy.
- As a specialty product in a niche market, 500 S&W Magnum ammunition is expensive, hard to find, and offered by a limited number of manufacturers.
- S&W X-frame revolvers for the 500 S&W Magnum are massive and heavy, making them difficult to carry comfortably in the field.
- Factory loaded 500 S&W Magnum is mono-chromatic in that it is designed for one purpose only--big game hunting. This cartridge has no other practical application.
- Unless you live and work in a rural area where you must cohabitate with dangerous game, the 500 S&W Magnum is unlikely to see much use.

• However, all negatives fade into insignificance in the face of the single most important reason to purchase a 500 S&W Magnum-- "Pride of Ownership".

• Pride of Ownership does not ask the questions "How much power is enough?" or "How much power can you handle?"

• In the past, these questions were perfunctory; today the 500 S&W Magnum has made them serious.

• After introduction of the 500 S&W Magnum cartridge in 2003, commercial production of ammunition was undertaken by Winchester, Federal, Hornady and Starline (cases only).

BALLISTIC NOTES

• Winchester offers three 500 S&W Magnum factory loads:
- A full-on hunting load with a 400-grain bullet at a muzzle velocity of 1,675 fps and 2,491 ft-lbs of muzzle energy!!!
- A full-on hunting load with a 375-grain bullet at a muzzle velocity of 1,725 fps and 2,477 ft-lbs of muzzle energy.
- A "reduced" power hunting load with a 350-grain bullet at a muzzle velocity of 1,350 fps and 1,416 ft-lbs of muzzle energy.

• Hornady takes a dual approach to the 500 S&W Magnum:
- A high velocity load using a 300-grain bullet at a muzzle velocity of 1,950 fps and 2,533 ft-lbs of industry topping muzzle energy.
- A super heavy bullet load using a 500-grain bullet at a muzzle velocity of 1,300 fps and 1,876 ft-lbs of muzzle energy.

• Excessively light or heavy .500 inch diameter bullets are specialty items inside a narrow niche market.

• Speer understands the demands such ballistic performance can place on a handgun bullet and applied their years of expertise to design a suitable bullet and tested load data especially for the 500 S&W Magnum.

- For handloading the 500 S&W Magnum, Speer has the 350-grain DeepCurl® Soft Point (DCSP) for your consideration:
  - A full power load with this bullet provides a muzzle velocity of 1,739 fps and 2,350 ft-lbs of muzzle energy which is more than sufficient for hunting any big or dangerous game that walks, swims, or crawls in North America.
  - To reduce recoil, this bullet can be loaded down to a muzzle velocity of 1,446 fps and 1,614 ft-lbs of muzzle energy which is sufficient for most medium game in North America.
  - To a bystander, even reduced 500 S&W Magnum loads create impressive levels of muzzle blast, flash and muzzle flip. (So, no one will know you are shooting reduced loads!). Speer is happy to help you maintain your image in this manner.

TECHNICAL NOTES

- The 500 S&W Magnum cartridge is a semi-rimmed, straight revolver cartridge that headspaces on the rim.
- Head diameter, rim diameter case capacity and case weight of the 500 S&W Magnum are unique to this caliber as are the bullets.
- Case hardness becomes more important for high pressure cartridges such as the 500 S&W Magnum.
  - Hard cases have more "spring back" and will not stick to chamber walls, making them easier to extract. The down side is hard cases tend to split and will not last as long.
  - Soft cases have less spring back and tend to stick to the chamber walls, making them difficult to extract. On the plus side, soft cases tend to last longer.
- The hardness or softness of various brands and lots of 500 S&W Magnum brass will become evident during extraction.
- If you experience hard extraction, try reducing the powder charge one grain and/or using another brand of case.
- MAP level for the 500 S&W Magnum is 60,000 psi. By comparison, the MAP of the 45 Colt is 14,000 psi and that of the 44 Remington Magnum is 36,000 psi.
- However, this MAP level is not a practical working pressure in the real world. For this reason, most factory 500 S&W Magnum ammunition is loaded to a more realistic lower MAP level. Our loading data is well below the 60,000 psi MAP level as well.

HANDLOADING NOTES

- We recommend using new cases for all maximum loads.
- To prevent bullet elongation in revolvers, all bullets loaded in the 500 S&W Magnum cartridge must be crimped securely in place using the cannelure on the bullet's surface.
- We recommend a neckdown crimp for the Speer 350-grain DeepCurl Soft Point bullet.
- Bullets for maximum loads in the 500 S&W Magnum must have a thick jacket such as the Speer 350-grain DCSP bullet.
- Case capacity—too much of it—limits what can be done with light practice

- loads for the 500 S&W Magnum. As a result, we recommend using the starting loads listed in the data as light practice loads.
- Although 50 Action Express bullets are the correct diameter, they are too lightly constructed for use in the 500 S&W Magnum even with reduced loads. In addition, they have no crimp cannelure to hold them in place.
- The 500 S&W Magnum cartridge case was designed for **Large Rifle primers** such as the CCI No. 250 and Federal 215 Magnum primers. **Do not use Large Pistol primers.**
- Never load less than the minimum charges shown in the loading data as the small charge of propellant may not be sufficient to push the bullet completely down the barrel.
- Use slow burning pistol powders for loading the 500 S&W Magnum.

SAFETY NOTES

SPEER 350-grain DeepCurl Soft Point @ a muzzle velocity of 1,739 fps:

- Maximum vertical altitude @ 90° elevation is 5,193 feet.
- Maximum horizontal distance to first impact with ground @ 33° elevation is 2,381 yards.

350 GRAINS

DIAMETER	SECTIONAL DENSITY
.500"	0.200

500 DCSP	
Ballistic Coefficient	0.178
COAL Tested	2.070"
Speer Part No.	4491

			Starting Charge		Maximum Charge	
Propellant	Case	Primer	Weight (grains)	Muzzle Velocity (feet/sec)	Weight (grains)	Muzzle Velocity (feet/sec)
Hodgdon Lil' Gun	Starline	Federal 215	45.0	1667	49.0	1739
Ramshot Enforcer	Starline	Federal 215	40.0	1585	44.0	1673
Accurate 1680	Starline	Federal 215	49.0	1550	53.0 C	1667
Vihtavuori N110	Starline	Federal 215	36.0	1534	40.0	1649
Accurate No. 9	Starline	Federal 215	34.0	1441	38.0	1643
Alliant 2400	Starline	Federal 215	38.0	1565	42.0	1642
Winchester 296	Starline	Federal 215	44.0	1585	46.0	1639
Hodgdon H110	Starline	Federal 215	44.0	1598	46.0	1631
IMR 4227	Starline	Federal 215	43.0	1554	45.0 C	1608
Alliant Power Pistol	Starline	Federal 215	23.0	1446	27.0	1564

WARNING! *Maximum loads should be used with CAUTION • C = Compressed Load*

REFERENCE MATERIAL

QUICK REFERENCE VELOCITY/MACH NUMBER COMPARISON CHART †

(† Footnote: "At Standard Temperature and Pressure; Mach number is affected by atmospheric conditions")

FT/S	M/S	MPH	MACH	FT/S	M/S	MPH	MACH
100	30	68	0.09	2300	710	1568	2.06
200	61	136	0.18	2400	732	1636	2.15
300	91	205	0.27	2500	762	1705	2.24
400	122	273	0.36	2600	792	1773	2.33
500	152	341	0.45	2700	823	1841	2.42
600	183	409	0.54	2800	853	1909	2.51
700	213	477	0.63	2900	884	1977	2.60
800	244	545	0.72	3000	914	2045	2.69
900	274	614	0.81	3100	945	2114	2.78
1000	304	682	0.90	3200	975	2182	2.87
1100	335	750	0.99	3300	1006	2250	2.96
1100	341	762	1.00	3400	1036	2318	3.02
1200	366	818	1.08	3500	1067	2386	3.14
1300	396	886	1.16	3600	1097	2454	3.23
1400	427	955	1.25	3700	1128	2523	3.31
1500	457	1023	1.34	3800	1158	2591	3.40
1600	488	1091	1.43	3900	1189	2659	3.49
1700	518	1159	1.52	4000	1219	2727	3.58
1800	549	1227	1.61	4100	1250	2795	3.67
1900	579	1295	1.70	4200	1280	2864	3.76
2000	610	1364	1.79	4300	1311	2932	3.89
2100	640	1432	1.88	4400	1341	3000	3.94
2200	671	1500	1.97	4500	1372	3068	4.02

STANDARD CONDITIONS FOR TESTING SPORTING AMMUNITION

Altitude: sea level = 0 feet/meters

Air Temperature: 59° Fahrenheit/15° Centigrade

Air Density: .0751 lbs/ft^3

Relative humidity: 78%

Barometric pressure: 29.53 In./750.0 MM of Hg (Mercury)

Manufacturers of sporting ammunition use these standard conditions as a baseline for testing production lots of ammunition. In addition, most manufacturers also develop additional company standards for their ammunition, such as ballistics at very low and very high temperatures.

When necessary, samples of ammunition from production lots are "conditioned" under specific temperature and humidity conditions before testing.

For the handloader, the lesson here is to store your primers, propellants, and loaded ammunition in a cool, dry place.

APPROXIMATE CORRECTION FACTORS FOR AMBIENT AIR TEMPERATURE (SAAMI)

For every 1° F. below 59° F. at standard conditions, deduct 1.7 fps from muzzle velocity down to -40° F.

For every 1° F. above 59° F. at standard conditions, add 1.7 fps to muzzle velocity up to +160° F.

EXPECTED CHANGE IN MUZZLE VELOCITY IN FPS PER INCH OF RIFLE BARREL LENGTH

Muzzle Velocity +/-	Expected Change in Muzzle Velocity Per inch of Rifle Barrel Length
Less than 2,000 fps	5 fps
2,001 to 2,500 fps	10 fps
2,501 to 3,000 fps	20 fps
3,001 to 3,500 fps	30 fps
3,501 to 4,000 fps	40 fps
4,001 to 4,500 fps	50 fps

Test barrel length is listed for each cartridge. Most rifle test barrels are 24 inches in length.

INTERIOR BALLISTIC FORMULAS
RECOIL

Use these four steps to calculate the recoil energy of your gun and evaluate the results.

Step 1. Calculate the *Recoil Impulse* of Your Gun in Foot-Pounds

Formula:

$$RI = \frac{(W_B \times V_M + 1.75 \times V_M \times W_P)}{225,400}$$

Where:

RI = Recoil Impulse of the gun in foot-pounds.
W_B = Bullet weight in grains.
V_M = Velocity of bullet at the muzzle in feet per second.
W_P = Weight of powder charge in grains.

Step 2. Calculate the *Recoil Velocity* of Your Gun in Feet per Second
Formula:

$$RV = \frac{32.2 \times RI}{W_G}$$

RV = Recoil velocity of your gun in feet per second.
RI = Recoil impulse of your gun in foot-pounds (from Step 1).
W_G = Weight of gun in pounds (including all accessories such as scope, mounts, lasers, white lights, sling and a full magazine of ammunition).

Step 3. Calculate the Free Recoil Energy of Your Gun in Foot-Pounds
Formula:

$$FE = W_G \times RV^2 / 64.4$$

FE = Free recoil energy of gun in foot-pounds.
WG = Weight of gun in pounds (from Step 2).
RV = Recoil velocity of gun in feet per second (from Step 2).

Step. 4 Evaluate the Results

Of course recoil is perceived by each shooter differently. However, here is a general categorization to give you an idea. As a reference point: 224 Valkyrie produces about 5 ft-lbs of recoil, a 30-06 in the neighborhood of 25 ft-lbs, and a 470 Nitro Express comes in at a bruising 70 plus ft-lbs!

Perceived Recoil	Foot-Pounds of Recoil
Light	Less than 10 ft-lbs.
Mild	11 to 20 ft-lbs.
Moderate	21-30 ft-lbs.
Heavy	31-40 ft-lbs.
Very Heavy	41-50 ft-lbs.
Extremely Heavy	51 or more ft-lbs.

EXPANSION RATIO

This formula is used to evaluate the ratio of bore volume to cartridge case volume. Cartridge cases with excessive case capacity in relation to bore volume are said to be "over bore capacity" as they cannot efficiently burn all of the heavy powder charge in the available bore volume.

STEP 1. Calculate the Bore Volume of Your Gun in Cubic Inches

Formula:

$$V_B = L \times D_G \times .773$$

V_B = Bore volume in cubic inches.

L = Distance from the base of the seated bullet to the muzzle in inches.

Don't measure this with an assembled cartridge. The risk of accidental discharge is too great. Instead, on a closed and empty chamber, simply measure the distance from the muzzle to the bolt face with a cleaning rod. Then do a little arithmetic to subtract out the distance from the case head to the approximate location of the bullet heel when properly seated.

D_G = Groove diameter in inches.

STEP 2. Calculate the Expansion Ratio

Formula:

$$ER = \frac{V_B + V_C}{V_C}$$

ER = Expansion ratio.

V_B = Bore volume in cubic inches.

V_C = Chamber volume in cubic inches.

EFFICIENCY

Use this four step formula to calculate the efficiency of your handload in converting the potential chemical energy in your propellant into bullet kinetic energy.

STEP 1. Calculate *Muzzle Energy* in Foot-Pounds

Formula:

$$ME = \frac{W_B \times V_M^2}{450{,}400}$$

ME = Muzzle energy in foot-pounds.

W_B = Bullet weight in grains.

V_M = Muzzle velocity in feet per second.

STEP 2. Calculate *Potential* Energy

Formula:

$$PE = W_P \times AE$$

PE = Potential energy in ft-lbs

W_P = Powder weight in grains

AE ("Average Energy" is an estimate of energy contained in one grain of propellant) = 170 ft-lb/gr for single-base propellants, 200 ft-lb/gr for double-base propellants.

Step 3. Calculate Cartridge Load Efficiency in percent

Formula:

$$CE = \frac{ME}{PE}$$

CE = Efficiency percentage
ME = Muzzle energy in ft-lbs
PE = Potential energy in ft-lbs

STEP 4. Evaluate the Results

Cartridge Load Efficiency	Rating
50%	Excellent
36-49%	Above average
25-35%	Average
Less than 25%	Very common

GREENHILL'S FORMULA FOR THE RIFLING TWIST RATE

Every bullet has an optimum rifling twist rate. Over the years, this formula has proven useful to determine the approximate rifling twist rate for a specific bullet diameter and length. This has become more important today as many calibers are available in several different rifling twist rates depending on which bullet you plan to use. For example the 223 Rem/5.56 barrels are made with rifling twist rates of 1:14 in., 1:12 in., 1:10 in., 1:9 in., 1:8 in. and 1:7 in.

Greenhill's formula is quick and easy to use for "back of the napkin" type estimates. There are certainly more precise, and more cumbersome methods that can be used.

In general, a faster rifling twist rate is required to stabilize longer, heavier bullets in a given caliber. Lighter and shorter bullets in a given caliber are best served by a slower rifling twist rate.

Use the constant's value of "150" for bullets with a muzzle velocity below about 2,800 fps. Use a value of "180" for muzzle velocities greater than 2,800 fps. Also note that this simplified version of Greenhill's Formula assumes a traditional lead core and copper jacket bullet construction. Solid copper bullets, for instance, would predict a needed twist rate about 10% faster due to the lower specific gravity of the material. It should also be noted that Mr. Greenhill's math predicts a generally conservative number; meaning that many bullets can be spin-stabilized at somewhat slower rotational velocities.

Use this formula to estimate the approximate rifling twist rate for your handloads.

Formula:

$$TR = \frac{150 \times D_B^2}{L_B}$$

TR = Twist rate in inches per turn.
D_B = Bullet diameter in inches (squared).
L_B = Bullet length in inches.

EXTERIOR BALLISTIC FORMULAS
BULLET STRIKING ENERGY

This formula will allow you to calculate bullet striking energy at a given distance. In order to determine the best bullet and load combination for their requirements, many handloaders like to compare the striking energy and momentum of various bullets at different selected ranges. If such data is not at hand, you can calculate any bullet's striking energy and momentum using the formulas below.

Formula:

$$SE = \frac{W_B \times V_I^2}{450{,}400}$$

SE = Striking energy in foot-pounds.
W_B = Bullet weight in grains.
V_I = Impact velocity of bullet in feet per second at desired range.

BULLET STRIKING MOMENTUM

Using this formula, you can calculate the striking momentum of a bullet.

Formula:

$$SM = \frac{W_B \times V_I}{225{,}200}$$

SM = Striking momentum in *pound-seconds.*
W_B = Bullet weight in grains.
V_I = Striking velocity of bullet in feet per second at desired range.

BULLET MASS

Formula:

$$M_B = \frac{W_B \times 7000}{32.17}$$

M_B = Mass of bullet in pounds mass.
W_B = Weight of bullet in grains.

SECTIONAL DENSITY OF A BULLET

This formula is useful to calculate the sectional density of a bullet. A higher number can indicate increased stability.

Formula:

$$SD = \frac{W_B}{7000 \times D_B^2}$$

SD = Sectional density
W_B = Bullet weight in grains.
D_B^2 = Bullet diameter in inches squared.

BALLISTIC COEFFICIENT OF A BULLET

The ballistic coefficient of a bullet is a numerical expression of its ability to overcome air resistance in flight. A high ballistic coefficient is increasingly desirable as distance to the target increases. The form factor chart below will allow you to calculate an *approximate* ballistic coefficient. We also list a relative G1 ballistic coefficient of our bullets on the web.

While a ballistic coefficient is certainly better than nothing, it is worth noting that the BC of a given bullet varies substantially with velocity. It also varies to a lesser extent with atmospheric conditions and bullet stability.

The ballistic coefficient can be approximated using the following formula.

Formula:

$$BC = \frac{W_B}{7000 \times i \times D_B^2}$$

BC = Ballistic coefficient number.
W_B = Weight of bullet in grains.
D_B^2 = Bullet diameter in inches squared.
i = Form factor (see chart below).

Bullet Ogive Profile	Form Factor (i)
Very sharp	.60
Sharp (secant)	.70
Sharp (tangent)	.85
Semi-round nose	1.00
Round or flat nose	1.20
Boat tail base, subtract	.06
Very small meplat, subtract	.07

BULLET TIME OF FLIGHT IN AIR

Bullet time of flight is an important factor to reduce the effects of wind drift. A bullet with a high ballistic coefficient reduces flight time compared to those with low ballistic coefficients.

Formula:

$$T = \frac{2R}{MV + V_I}$$

T = Time of flight in seconds.
R = Range to target in feet.
MV = Muzzle velocity in feet per second.
V_I = Bullets impact velocity at target in feet per second.

BULLET TIME OF FLIGHT IN A VACUUM

You will need this to calculate wind drift (see below).

Formula:

$$T_V = \frac{R}{MV}$$

T_V = Time of flight in a vacuum in seconds.
R = Range to target *in feet*.
MV = Muzzle velocity in feet per second.

BULLET WIND DRIFT IN A 90° CROSSWIND

Wind drift is a factor shooters must always take into account. Bullets with high ballistic coefficients have less wind drift than bullets with low ballistic coefficients.

Formula:

$$D_W = V_W (T - T_V)$$

D_W = Wind deflection in feet.
V_W = Crosswind velocity in feet per second.
T = Bullet time of flight in air in seconds (see above).
T_V = Bullet time of flight in a vacuum in seconds (see above).

BULLET ROTATIONAL SPEED

This number can be used to compare twist rates at various muzzle velocities. Bullet rotational speed drops off very little in flight.

Formula:

$$V_R = \frac{MV \times 60 \times 12}{T}$$

V_R = Rotational velocity of bullet in revolutions per minute.
MV = Muzzle velocity in feet per second.
T = Rifling twist rate in inches per turn.

TERMINAL BALLISTIC FORMULAS

MEAN VERTICAL OR HORIZONTAL DEVIATION

$$D_A = \frac{\sum (DH \text{ or } DV)}{N}$$

D_A = Average distance of all shots from horizontal or vertical center.
DH = Horizontal distance of each shot from center of group.
DV = Vertical distance of each shot from center of group.
$\sum$ = Sum of all horizontal or vertical shots from center of group.
N = Number of shots in group.

MEAN RADIUS OF SHOTS

$$MR = \frac{\sum (DC)}{N}$$

MR = Mean radius of shots (average distance from center of group).
DC = Distance of each shot from center of group.
$\sum$ = Sum of the distances of each shot from center of group.
N = Number of shots in group.

HATCHER'S FORMULA FOR RELATIVE STOPPING POWER OF HANDGUN BULLETS

This formula was developed by General Julian Hatcher in 1935. While it lacks in many technical aspects, it is of historical interest, if not practical use.

Formula:

$$M_B \times S_B \times A = RSP$$

RSP = Relative stopping power number.
M_B = Momentum of bullet.
S_B = Multiplier for shape of bullet (from chart below).
A = Cross sectional area of bullet (see chart below).

S_B Multipliers

Bullet Construction/Shape	Multiplier
Jacketed round nose	.90
Jacketed flat nose	1.00
Lead round nose	1.00
Lead blunt round nose	1.05
Lead flat nose	1.10
Lead wadcutter	1.25

Caliber	Cross Sectional Area in Sq. Inches
22	.039
25	.049
30	.075
32	.077
9mm	.098
357/38	.101
41	.129
44	.144
45	.159
50	.196

POWER FACTOR (NRA)

This number is used to determine the classification of various handgun calibers and loads for NRA combat pistol competition.

Formula:

$$NPF = V_B \times W_B$$

NPF = NRA power factor (must be 120,000 or more).
V_B = Muzzle velocity of bullet in feet per second.
W_B = Bullet weight in grains.

POWER FACTOR (IPSC)

This number is used to determine the classification of various handgun calibers and loads for IPSC combat pistol competition.

Formula

$$IPF = \frac{W_B \times V_B^2}{1000}$$

IPF = IPSC power factor (must be 160 or more to make major caliber classification).
W_B = Bullet weight in grains.
V_B^2 = Muzzle velocity in feet per second squared.

COMMON HEADSTAMPS

Here is an abbreviated list of common manufacturer's headstamps found on centerfire rifle and handgun ammunition you can use as a reference when sorting and identifying fired brass.

HEADSTAMP	MANUFACTURER	COUNTRY
ADI	Australian Defense Industries	Australia
AGUILA	Industrias Technos S.A.	Mexico
ARMSCOR, AP	Armscor U.S.A.	U.S.
BHA	Black Hills Ammunition	U.S.
CBC	Comphania Brasilia de Cartuchos	Brazil
CCI	CCI/Speer	U.S.
COR-BON	Cor Bon	U.S.
F C	Federal Premium Ammunition	U.S.
GFL	Fiocchi Munizioni S.p.A.	Italy
HORNADY	Hornady Manufacturing Co.	U.S.
IMI	Israel Military Industries, Ltd.	Israel
JAG	Jagemann Sporting Group	U.S.
LAPUA	NAMMO Lapua Oy	Finland
LAZZERONI	Lazzeroni Arms Co.	U.S.
LC	Lake City Army Ammunition Plant	U.S.
LFB	Luft fur Ballistik	Germany
MEN	Metallwerk Elisenhutte GmbH	Germany
MESKO	MESKO Spolka Akcyjna	Poland
MFS	MFS 2000 Inc. (div. of RUAG)	Hungary
MKE	Makina ve Kimya Endustrisi	Turkey
NORMA	Norma AB (div. of RUAG)	Sweden
NOS	Nosler, Inc.	U.S.
PETERSON	Peterson Cartridge	U.S.
PMC	Poongsan Metals Corp.	South Korea
PMP	Pretoria Metal Pressings (DENEL)	South Africa
PPU	Prvi Partizan Uzice	Serbia
REM, R-P	Remington Arms Co.	U.S.
RUAG	RUAG Ammotec	Germany, Switzerland
SAKO	Sako, Ltd. (div. of Beretta)	Finland
SAX	Sax Munitions GmbH	Germany
SBR	Southern Ballistic Research	U.S.
S&B	Sellier & Bellot	Czech Republic
SHM	Suddeutsche Hulsenmanufactur	Germany
SIG	SIG Sauer, Inc.	U.S.
SPEER	CCI/Speer	U.S.
SWIFT	Swift Bullets	U.S.
TW	Twin Cities Army Ammunition Plant	U.S.
WEATHERBY	Weatherby, Inc. (made by Norma)	U.S.
WIN, W-W	Winchester Ammunition	U.S.
X-treme	Howell Munitions	U.S.
2nd AMEND	2nd Amendment Ammunition	U.S.

GLOSSARY

ACCURACY: A numerical measurement of the distance a bullet strikes from its intended target, the ability of a firearm and/or shooter to hit an aiming point on a target; not to be confused with precision. (See also: PRECISION)

ACCURACY LIFE: An estimated, or empirically determined, number of rounds that can be fired through a rifle or handgun barrel before it loses the ability to produce an acceptable level of dispersion. (See also: DISPERSION)

ACTION: In a firearm, an assembly consisting of the receiver or frame, locking system, and fire control system by which a firearm is loaded, locked, fired, unlocked and unloaded; the barrel, stock, sights, and external magazines are not considered part of the action.

AERODYNAMIC LIFT: The force perpendicular to the bullet's trajectory tending to pull the bullet in the direction the ogive is pointed.

AERODYNAMIC STABILITY: The stability of a bullet in flight due to its velocity, spin rate, shape, and how that shape assists or disrupts the airflow over the ogive, bearing surface, heel, and base.

AIMING POINT: The point on the target on which the sights of the firearm are aligned.

AIR RESISTANCE: The resistance of air to the passage of the bullet in flight. (See also: BALLISTIC COEFFICIENT)

AIR SPACE: The volume inside a cartridge not occupied by the propellant powder and bullet. (See also: LOAD DENSITY)

AMMUNITION: One or more loaded cartridge. (See also: BULLET and CARTRIDGE)

ANGLE OF DEPARTURE: The angle formed between a line extending to the target and the center line of the bore at the moment the projectile leaves the muzzle of the gun.

ANGLE OF IMPACT OR ARRIVAL: The angle formed by the intersection of a straight line tangent to the bullet's descending flight path, *and the ground* at the bullet's first impact point.

ANNEALING: The process of softening the mouth of brass cartridge cases using carefully controlled exposure to heat. The production steps used to manufacture, reform, or repeatedly reload brass cartridge cases work-hardens the neck making it brittle and prone to cracking or splitting. Annealing the neck reduces the internal stresses that cause this. (See also: HARDNESS GRADIENT; IRIS)

ANTIMONY: A metallic element used to alloy lead to increase hardness. Symbol Sb.

ANVIL: An internal, metallic component that is a key part of a percussion priming system; the impact of the firing pin crushes the explosive primer pellet in the cup against the anvil to initiate the ignition process; Boxer primer anvils may have either two - or three legs; in Berdan primers, the anvil is an integral part of the cartridge case primer pocket.

ASCENDING BRANCH: A bullet's trajectory from the muzzle to the highest point on its path of travel to the target.

AUTOMATIC: A fully automatic firearm that starts firing when the trigger is pulled and continues until the trigger is released or ammunition is exhausted. The term should not be used in conjunction with semi-automatic firearms. Also, a name used in abbreviated form in the nomenclature of some pistol cartridges, e.g. 25 Auto, 32 Auto, 380 Auto, 38 Super Auto, 10mm Auto, and 45 Auto; this term is not used in the nomenclature of rifle cartridges.

BACK STOP: A structure, material(s), or device designed to safely stop a bullet on impact.

BALL:
1). A round lead ball for a muzzle loading rifle or handgun.
2). A full metal jacket military bullet.

BALL AMMUNITION: A descriptive term for military cartridges loaded with full metal jacket (FMJ) bullets.

BALL (SPHERICAL) POWDER: Ball Powder is a registered trademark of General Dynamics Ordnance and Tactical Systems. It is a double-base, smokeless propellant having grains of spherical or flattened spherical shape; a popular type of propellant for reloading.

BALLISTICS: The scientific study of projectiles in motion; the study of ballistics is divided into three parts according to the time frame in which they occur:
1). Interior ballistics – the time interval between the start of primer ignition and the bullet's exit from the muzzle of the gun barrel.
2). Exterior ballistics – the time interval between the bullet's exit from the barrel to its initial contact with the target.
3). Terminal ballistics – the time interval between the bullet's initial contact with the target until it stops inside the target or exits.

BALLISTIC COEFFICIENT (BC): An index of the deceleration of a specific bullet in free flight; the higher the BC number, the more aerodynamically efficient the bullet. (See also: P. 910)

BALLISTIC TABLE: A numerical summary in tabular form of a given bullet's exterior ballistic performance. A ballistic table may include some or all of the following data at different ranges: muzzle velocity, striking velocity, striking energy, wind drift, time of flight, bullet path above or below line of sight, bullet drop, mid-range trajectory, point blank range, bullet spin drift, etc. A ballistic table is an excellent reference source for shooters to determine their requirements for various types of hunting, competition, and personal defense.

BARREL-CYLINDER GAP: The gap or open space between the back end of the barrel and the front face of the cylinder of a revolver.

BARREL EROSION: The physical deterioration of bore and throat of a barrel caused by the hot, expanding powder gases behind the bullet.

BARREL FOULING: Propellant residue, plastic, or metals (such as lead, copper or nickel) deposited in the bore during firing; barrel fouling should be removed frequently to maintain accuracy.

BARREL LENGTH: The length of a barrel as measured through the bore from the muzzle to the breech face; note that barrel length does include the chamber; the barrel length of a revolver *does not* include the cylinder.

BARREL LIFE: The number of rounds which can be fired through a barrel until it becomes unserviceable.

BEARING SURFACE: That portion of the outside surface of a bullet that contacts the bore and is engraved by the lands and grooves of the rifling.

BELL: A reloading operation to slightly expand the front portion of the case mouth in order to seat a bullet more easily. Also called flare.

BELTED CARTRIDGE CASE: A type of metallic, centerfire rifle cartridge case having a belt or raised band at the junction of the case body and extractor groove. This type of case configuration is often used for magnum rifle cartridges. This design was originally intended to headspace cartridges with an insufficient shoulder angle.

BENCHREST:
1). A type of rifle competition fired at one hundred and two hundred yards from a solid rest.
2). A table specifically designed to eliminate as much human error as possible by supporting a rifle for competitive shooting or sighting-in purposes.

BERDAN PRIMER: A type of centerfire primer with no integral anvil. A Berdan primer is a three-piece assembly consisting of the metal cup, primer pellet and foil cover over the pellet. The anvil is not a part of the primer and is formed in the primer pocket of the cartridge case. Once very popular, particularly for military ammunition, Berdan primers are being rapidly replaced by Boxer primers for all ammunition. Berdan primers carry the name of its inventor, Gen. Hiram Berdan U.S.A. of Civil War fame.

BIG BORE: A non-technical term for a rifle cartridge having a bore diameter of .300 inches or greater. This mostly applies to benchrest rifle competition categories, not military terminology.

BLACK POWDER: The earliest form of propellant, reputed to have been made by the Chinese or Hindus before the remote beginnings of history. First used for guns in the 13th century. It is a mechanical mixture of potassium or sodium nitrate ("saltpeter"), charcoal, and sulfur.

BLANK AMMUNITION: Specialized cartridges assembled with selected components to produce a flash, noise, or both, or to propel an object other than a bullet. Blanks are used to start races, make movies, fire salutes at military funerals, reenactments, line-throwing, grenade launching, and driving studs in construction; NEVER try to reload blank cartridge cases!

BLOWBACK: A leakage of propellant gas rearward between the cartridge case and chamber wall. Do not attempt to reload cartridge cases that have experienced blowback.

BLOWBACK ACTION: A type of unlocked operating system used in many semi-automatic or fully automatic guns that uses the expanding propellant gases to push a heavy bolt or breechblock rearward using the inertia of the bolt and recoil spring pressure to keep the action closed until the bullet has exited the muzzle and the chamber pressure has decreased to a safe level. Blowback operated firearms are very hard on brass; expect a large percentage of cases fired in such guns to have excess head expansion requiring a small base resizing die and/or large dents rendering them useless.

BLOWN PRIMER: A primer that is separated completely from the cartridge or shotshell after firing due to severe expansion of the primer pocket and head.

BOAT TAIL: A bullet with a tapering slope from the full-caliber bearing surface on the body to a smaller diameter at the base. A boat tail significantly reduces drag.

BODY: That part of a cartridge case between the head and the point where the shoulder begins to taper toward the neck.

BODY SPLIT: A lengthwise crack or split in a cartridge case sidewall. (See also: RUPTURE)

BOLT: The locking and cartridge head supporting mechanism of a firearm that operates in line with the axis of the bore.

BOLT THRUST: The pressure exerted on the breech or bolt face of the firearm by the head of the cartridge case when it is fired.

BORE: The interior surface of the barrel forward of the chamber between the throat and the muzzle.

BORE AXIS: An imaginary straight line through the center of the bore.

BORE DIAMETER: The distance across the top of the lands in a rifle barrel measured in inches or millimeters; the distance across the grooves of a rifle barrel is the caliber.

BORE GUIDE: A device used during barrel cleaning that keeps the cleaning rod centered in the bore to prevent damage to the throat, leade, and muzzle crown. A bore guide designed for bolt-action rifles replaces the bolt when cleaning.

BORE SCOPE: A small optical device that can be inserted in a barrel to allow the shooter to visually inspect the surfaces of the bore, leade, and throat by means of a small mirror and light.

BORE SIGHT: The process of aligning the sights of the firearm with the axis of the bore; normally, this is performed with an optical or laser device designed for this purpose. This process may reduce the time and number of shots needed for zeroing in.

BOXER PRIMER: This is by far the most common type of centerfire rifle and pistol primer in the world today; this design is a four-piece assembly consisting of a metal cup, primer pellet, anvil, and in most cases a foil disc. This primer is named after the inventor of the type, Col. Edward Boxer of the British Army.

BRASS: This popular term is often used to describe centerfire rifle or pistol cartridge cases, individually or in bulk, either fired or unfired; this description is derived from the brass alloy used to manufacture cartridge cases consisting of approximately 70% copper and 30% zinc.

BREECH: The rear end of the barrel where the chamber is located.

BREECH PRESSURE: The pressure exerted in an axial direction by the case head against the breech of the firearm when a cartridge is fired.

BRISANCE: A measure of the shattering power of a high explosive; the burning speed at which a high explosive material reaches maximum pressure; priming compound is a high explosive mixture.

BROACHED RIFLING: A method of rifling barrels using a progressive cutter to create the rifling grooves by removing metal from the bore surface with one pass of the broach. Today this method is used only to rifle handgun barrels.

BROWN POWDER: A physical mixture of the same ingredients as black powder, namely potassium nitrate (saltpeter), straw charcoal, and sulfur. However, brown powder uses just enough sulfur to assure reliable ignition (2-3% compared to the normal 10% for black powder). So named because of its color, brown powder has been obsolete since the late 1880s.

BUCKSHOT: Round lead or steel balls with a diameter between .20 inches and .36 inches for loading into a shotshell.

BULLET: That part of a loaded cartridge which is accelerated down the gun barrel by the propellant gases. Once in motion, a bullet is referred to as a "projectile"; note that a bullet is a component part of a cartridge, however, a cartridge is not a bullet.

BULLET CORE: The interior part of a jacketed bullet, usually made of lead or a lead alloy, steel, bismuth, tin, aluminum, or a combination of these metals. Cores made of composites containing polymer and powdered metals such as copper and/or iron will be found also. Note that solid lead, copper, or zinc homogenous bullets and molded frangible bullets do not have a separate core.

BULLET DROP: The vertical distance a bullet will fall below the bore line at a given point along its trajectory with the bore line held perpendicular to the ground.

BULLET JACKET: The outer casing around the core of a rifle or handgun bullet. Most bullet jackets are drawn from 90/10 (commercial bronze) or 95/5 (gilding metal) copper alloys, but examples of other metal and polymer jackets will be found also.

BULLET JUMP: The distance the bullet must travel from its seated position in the chambered cartridge case to the first point at which it starts to be engraved by the rifling.

BULLET OGIVE: The radius on the curved, pointed, or tapered nose of a bullet from the bearing surface to the meplat (tip).

BULLET PULL: The amount of force, measured in pounds, needed to pull a seated bullet from a loaded cartridge.

BULLET PULLER: A special tool for extracting bullets from loaded cartridges; inertial and collet types are most common.

BULLET PUSH: The amount of force, measured in pounds, needed to push a seated bullet inside a loaded cartridge.

BULLET SLIP: The failure of a bullet to fully engrave in the rifling as it travels down the bore, often resulting in an unstable bullet.

BULLET STRIPPING: An internal ballistic problem caused by jacket failure which allows jacket metal to be stripped off the bullet as it travels down the barrel.

BULLET TIPPING: The corkscrew-like trajectory of an unstable bullet that yaws uncontrollably and does not travel point first.

BULLET TRAP: A device or structure designed to safely decelerate and stop bullets while preventing ricochets and back splatter of bullet fragments.

BULLET UPSET:
1). The expansion of a bullet inside a target.
2). The seating of a bullet in the barrel as it is engraved by the rifling.

BULLET WOBBLE: The yaw or side-to-side motion of an unbalanced bullet in flight caused by manufacturing defects, poor design, damage, or a rifling twist rate that is too slow.

BURN RATE: The rate at which a given propellant burns under confinement in relation to other propellants.

BUTTON RIFLING: A popular method of rifling gun barrels using a slightly oversized carbide button having reverse lands and grooves on its body; as the button is pushed or pulled through the bore, it displaces metal on the bore surface to create the lands and grooves in a single pass.

CALIBER: An alpha-numeric expression or name used to describe a specific cartridge such as 30-06 Springfield, 8x57mm Mauser, 22-250 Remington, 5.56x45mm NATO. The approximate land diameter of a barrel (ex: 22-caliber, 30-caliber, 8mm-caliber, 9mm-caliber, 45-caliber).

CANNELURE: A circumferential groove or grooves cut or impressed on the bearing surface of a bullet. Used to provide a crimping location and to control seating depth, bullet pull, and bullet push. May also be used as a design feature to control expansion.

CANISTER POWDER: A propellant powder sold to handloaders in containers suitable for consumer use. Canister powders are carefully standardized for consistency.

CAP: A percussion device used for igniting black powder firearms.

CARTRIDGE: A complete round of self-contained ammunition consisting of a primer, propellant powder, bullet, and cartridge case. "Bullets" are the projectile and a component of the cartridge.

CARTRIDGE CASE: The body of a self-contained cartridge that holds the other components and serves as a gas seal when fired. Cartridge cases may be formed from many different materials.

CARTRIDGE OVERALL LENGTH: The overall length of a loaded round of ammunition as measured from its base to the tip of the bullet; also called OAL or COAL.

CASE CAPACITY: The volume inside a cartridge case, normally expressed in either grains of water or cubic centimeters (cc) of water.

CASE LIFE: The number of times a cartridge case can be safely reloaded and fired before becoming unserviceable.

CASE NECK BRUSH: A brush used to clean and lubricate the inside neck of a cartridge case before reloading.

CASE NECK SIZING DIE: A metal die used for resizing the neck only of a fired cartridge case.

CASE SEPARATION: The partial or complete failure of a cartridge case forward of the head when fired. A special tool could be required to remove it from the chamber.

CASE SPLITS: Splits or cracks that appear on a cartridge case before or after it is fired. Cases with splits or cracks are unserviceable and must be discarded.

CASE STRETCHING: The elongation of a cartridge case caused by firing or firearm problem. Cartridge cases which exceed Max. Case Length must be trimmed.

CASE TRIMMER: A small, lathe-like device with a multi-cutter head used for trimming the length of fired cartridge cases back to specification.

CASE TRIMMER PILOT: A caliber-specific metal guide on the cutter head of a case trimmer that fits inside the case mouth to hold the cutter head and cartridge case on center.

CAST BULLET: An elongated, unjacketed bullet for handguns or rifles made by pouring molten lead or lead alloy into a mold, allowing it to harden, then removing it.

CENTER OF IMPACT: The center of a group of shots on a target.

CENTERFIRE AMMUNITION: Self-contained, metallic, centerfire rifle or handgun cartridges with a primer in the center of the case head.

CHAMBER: The breech end of the barrel that holds and supports the cartridge when it is fired. In a revolver, the chambers are located in the cylinder.

CHAMBER CAST: A casting made with low melting point metal that is poured into the chamber and allowed to cool. After cooling it facilitates chamber/throat measurement.

CHAMBER PRESSURE: The pressure exerted against the chamber walls by the expanding powder gases. (See also: BREECH PRESSURE)

CHAMFER: The process of removing small amounts of metal from the edges of the case mouth, flash hole, or primer pocket to remove burrs and sharp edges.

CHARGE: The weight of propellant powder loaded into a cartridge case; normally expressed in grains or grams.

CHRONOGRAPH: An electronic or mechanical instrument for measuring the elapsed time required for a projectile to travel over a fixed length course between two measured points. The distance traveled in feet divided by the time of flight in seconds determines the velocity of the projectile at the midpoint in feet per second (fps).

CLIP: A semi-disposable device which holds cartridges for loading into a magazine or gun; there are two types of clips: "stripper clips" which are an accessory to aid filling a separate or integral magazine, then discarded (ex. M1903-A3 Springfield and M16/AR15). The "charger or en-bloc clips" type which are inserted in the gun where they remain as an essential part of its operation, and when empty, they are ejected and discarded (ex. M1 Garand); both types may be refilled and reused if necessary. A clip is not a magazine.

COEFFICIENT OF FORM: A numerical term indicating the general profile of a projectile. Used to calculate the ballistic coefficient of a bullet.

COLLIMATOR: An optical or laser device used to align telescopic rifle or handgun sights with the bore axis. Used as a rough method of sighting-in, reducing the number of rounds needed for that purpose.

COMBUSTION: Deflagration, the chemical process in which oxygen, nitrogen, and other substances in gunpowder rapidly oxidize to produce energy in the form of flame and hot, rapidly expanding gases.

COMPENSATOR: Slots, vents, or ports in a gun barrel or muzzle device designed to divert rapidly expanding propellant gases upward to reduce muzzle rise, reduce perceived recoil and speed recovery. (See also: MUZZLE BRAKE and SUPPRESSOR)

COMPONENTS: For a centerfire cartridge it is the four individual parts of its construction. They are the cartridge case, propellant powder, primer, and bullet; all four are needed in order to reload a cartridge.

COMPRESSED CHARGE: A charge of propellant powder occupying a volume that exceeds the useable volume of the cartridge case when the bullet is seated. Noted by a "C" in load data.

COPPER CRUSHER: A copper alloy cylinder of precise dimensions, hardness, and density used to measure the chamber pressure developed by a cartridge. (See also: COPPER UNITS OF PRESSURE)

COPPER FOULING: Deposits of copper jacket material in a rifle or handgun barrel. Remove these deposits as they are normally detrimental to accuracy. (See also: FOULING)

COPPER UNITS OF PRESSURE (CUP): The chamber pressure of a cartridge as measured using a copper alloy crusher system. A copper alloy cylinder of precise dimensions, hardness, and density is subjected to the chamber pressure when the cartridge is fired. The change in the crusher's length is measured and compared to a tarage table to determine the pressure. This system of measurement is being phased out in favor of piezoelectric transducers which are easier to use, more accurate, and provide more data. (See also: COPPER CRUSHER)

CORDITE: The trade name for an extruded, double-base, smokeless propellant patented by Fredrick Abel in England in 1889. The name is derived from its long, spaghetti-like strands or cords that were often as long as the cartridge case body. Cordite was the basis for many of our modern extruded propellants and was widely used in British military ammunition until the early 1990s. Cordite is now obsolete.

CORIOLIS EFFECT: As a bullet travels downrange, the earth moves beneath it; this movement is called the Coriolis Effect and can amount to as much as one inch at 1,000 yds.; north of the equator, bullets will drift to the right, south of the equator, to the left.

CORROSION: A chemical reaction that breaks down a material.

CORROSIVE PRIMER: A primer containing potassium chlorate, mercury or both; when fired, such primers deposit hygroscopic salts and acids in the bore that react with moisture in the air causing rust or etching. All U.S. military ammunition and modern American and European sporting primers have been non-corrosive for decades.

C-PRESS: A popular design of metallic cartridge reloading press so named for the shape of its frame.

CRATERED PRIMER: A fired primer with a small ridge of primer cup metal surrounding the firing pin indentation. Can be an indication of high chamber pressures.

CRIMP: A method of controlling bullet pull and push in loaded ammunition. The process consists of turning in or pressing the case mouth of a loaded cartridge into a cannelure (if present) on the bullet's surface to increase the grip on the bullet. A vital part of loading revolver cartridges, rifle ammunition for use in tubular magazines and large bore cartridges with heavy recoil. It is also common on military rifle ammunition which may be used in machine guns.

CRIMPED PRIMER (also Staked Primer): A primer which has been secured in its pocket by pressing, crimping, staking, or stabbing part of the case head over the primer cup. Common on military ammunition which may be fired in machine guns. Removal is required prior to seating a new primer.

CROWN: The point of the bore at the muzzle where the rifling terminates. There are many crown designs used to protect the end of the bore.

CUP: (See: COPPER UNITS OF PRESSURE)

CUPRO-NICKEL JACKET: A bullet made of copper-plated steel with a soft nickel plating on the outer surface. The nickel and copper plating are thick enough to engrave the rifling while preventing the steel from contacting the bore. Both the "silverish color" and being attracted to a magnet make identification easy.

DEBURR: To remove the sharp edges on the mouth of a cartridge case or primer pocket. (See also: CHAMFER)

DEBURRING TOOL: A hand tool designed to remove burrs on the edges of the case mouth, flash hole, or primer pocket.

DECAP/DEPRIME: To remove a spent primer from its pocket in the head of a cartridge case in preparation for reloading. (See also: DECAPPING PIN)

DECAPPING PIN: A steel pin inside a sizing die that pushes the spent primer from its pocket in the case head.

DEFLAGRATION: A rapid, exothermic reaction propagated at subsonic velocity by heat transfer through the reactants in a propellant powder. The reactants, flame, and hot gases, flow in the opposite direction of the propagation. (See also: DETONATION)

DEFLECTION: The lateral distance a bullet diverges from its intended flight path due primarily to crosswinds.

DESCENDING BRANCH: The trajectory of a projectile in flight from its <u>highest</u> point (apogee) of travel to its impact point on the target.

DETERRENT COATING: A coating applied to the outer surface of propellant powder granules to control the burning rate.

DETONATION: An extremely rapid exothermic reaction propagated through the reactants of an explosive substance at <u>supersonic</u> velocities. The reactants flow in the <u>same</u> direction as the propagation. (See also: DEFLAGRATION)

DEVIATION: The angular or linear distance between the point of aim and the point of impact of a bullet on a target.

DIE: In manufacturing, a metal alloy tool for extruding lead or copper wire, swaging bullet cores, or drawing cartridge cases and bullet jackets. In reloading, a metal alloy tool for resizing or reforming cartridge cases, or seating and crimping bullets.

DIE SET: In reloading, a set of dies for reloading a specific cartridge.

DISCHARGE: The firing of a gun.

DISPERSION: The distribution of hits on a target. The greatest distance between any two bullet holes (most often center-to-center) on both the horizontal or vertical axis of a target; normally expressed in inches or millimeters. (See also: HORIZONTAL DISPERSION and VERTICAL DISPERSION)

DOUBLE-BASE POWDER: A single-base smokeless propellant enhanced with more chemical energy by the addition of up to 49% nitroglycerine.

DRAG: The resistance a bullet encounters as it flies through the air.

DRAM: An archaic English measure of weight equal to 1/16 of an ounce or 27.3 grains; for many years, drams were the standard unit of measure used for loading shotshells with black powder; today, the dram as a unit of measure is obsolete.

DRAM EQUIVALENT: An archaic, confusing and semi-obsolete method of indicating the muzzle velocity of a shotshell loaded with *smokeless* powder as compared to a similar one loaded with *black powder*; for example, if a 12-ga. 2 ¾ inch shotshell loaded with 3 drams of black powder and 1 1/8 oz. of lead shot produces a muzzle velocity of 1,200 fps, a 12-ga. smokeless powder shotshell with a similar shot charge weight, and muzzle velocity would be a "3 dram equivalent load". A 3 ¼ dram equivalent load with the same amount of shot would have a higher muzzle velocity and a 2 ¾ dram equivalent load a lower muzzle velocity.

DROP: The vertical distance between the bullet and its line of departure at a given range. Usually expressed in inches or millimeters; drop is caused by the downward pull of gravity on a projectile in flight.

DUMMY CARTRIDGE: A dimensionally correct cartridge often with a simulated weight of inert filler replacing the propellant, an actual or replica bullet and an inert primer; such cartridges are used for training and testing feed systems.

DUPLEX LOAD: A propellant charge consisting of two different powders with different burning rates; also a cartridge loaded with two bullets. Speer does not recommend such loads and does not provide data for either definition.

DYNAMIC BALANCE: The condition when a bullet's axis of form (centerline) is coincident with the axis of rotation.

EFFECTIVE RANGE: The maximum range at which a bullet retains effective exterior and terminal ballistic performance. (See also: POINT BLANK RANGE)

EFFICIENCY: A measure of how efficiently the stored chemical energy in the propellant powder is converted to kinetic energy for a given load and cartridge. Normally expressed as a percentage with very few cartridges more than 35% efficient, and many are substantially lower.

EJECTA: The total weight of the bullet, hot gases, and unburned powder from the propellant and primer that exit the muzzle when a firearm is discharged.

EJECTION: That part of a firearm's operating cycle in which the spent cartridge case or unfired cartridge is thrown from the gun. (See also: EXTRACTION)

EJECTOR: The part of a firearm that throws the fired cartridge case from the gun after it has been extracted from the chamber. Usually located on the bolt face or on the receiver and may be spring-loaded or fixed, internal or external.

ELEVATION:
1). The amount of vertical sight adjustment required to raise or lower the bullet's point of impact on the target; normally expressed in inches or millimeters.
2). The altitude of the shooter above sea level expressed in feet or meters.

ENGRAVING:
1). The cuts or marks left on a bullet's bearing surface by the lands and grooves in a rifled barrel.
2). Decorative embellishments on a firearm's outer surface.

ENGRAVING FORCE: The amount of force needed to completely seat or engrave a bullet in the origin of the rifling in a gun barrel.

EROSION: The physical deterioration of the bore and throat of a rifled barrel caused by friction and hot powder gases. Visually, erosion appears as worn, rough, and/or discolored areas in the bore.

EXPANDER BALL or BUTTON: The steel ball or tapered plug on the decapping pin inside a sizing die. The expander ball passes through the case mouth resetting it to the correct diameter needed to hold the bullet firmly.

EXPANDING BULLET: Bullets designed to expand or mushroom upon impact with the target.

EXPLOSION: An exothermic chemical reaction that propagates at *supersonic* speeds; a detonation; propellants that propagate at *subsonic* speeds are deflagrations. (See also: DEFLAGRATION)

EXTRACTION: That part of the operating cycle of a firearm in which the fired cartridge case is pulled from the chamber by the extractor.

EXTRACTOR: That part of a firearm that pulls the fired cartridge case from the chamber. (See also: EJECTOR)

EXTRACTOR GROOVE: A circumferential groove or recess cut into the outer surface of a centerfire cartridge case head. The extractor groove allows the extractor to grip and control the cartridge case.

EXTREME SPREAD: The maximum distance between the *centers* of the two furthest apart bullet holes in a group. A popular method of measuring dispersion.

EXTRUDED POWDER: A smokeless propellant extruded in the form of spaghetti-like tubular strands that are then cut into smaller lengths. The tubes may or may not have perforations.

FAR ZERO: The *second* point at which the flight path of the bullet crosses the line of sight. The point where the point of aim and the point of impact coincide. Commonly called the "zero" point.

FIREFORM: A method of changing the shape and dimensions of a cartridge case by firing it a chamber of larger dimensions to increase case volume. A process often used to form wildcat or "Improved" cartridges. (See also: WILDCAT CARTRIDGE and IMPROVED CARTRIDGE)

FIRING PIN: That part of a firearm mechanism which strikes the primer cup or rim of rimfire cartridges to initiate ignition in order to fire the cartridge.

FLAKE POWDER: An extruded, smokeless propellant in which the strands are cut into thin flakes of various shapes and sizes.

FLASH: A chemical reaction at the muzzle of a gun caused when the hot hydrogen and carbon monoxide propellant gases mix with the oxygen in the air.

FLASH HOLE: A small hole or holes located in the case web in the front of the primer pocket designed to channel the flame and hot primer gases to ignite the propellant charge.

FLASH INHIBITOR: A chemical compound added in very small amounts to smokeless propellants to reduce muzzle flash.

FLASH SUPPRESSANT: (See: FLASH INHIBITOR)

FLASH SUPPRESSOR: A muzzle attachment designed to reduce muzzle flash.

FLAT NOSE/FLAT POINT: A lead or jacketed bullet with a profile having an ogive with a flat surface at the tip of less than bore diameter. In revolvers they reduce the overall loaded length of the cartridge. In rifles with tubular magazines they prevent magazine detonation.

FLATTENED PRIMER: A fired primer in which the rounded edge of the primer cup has been displaced into the gap between it and the primer pocket giving it an "ironed" or flat appearance. An indication of high pressure or excessive headspace. (See also: CRATERED PRIMER)

FLECHETTE: A sub-caliber, fin-stabilized, metal dart designed to be fired from a gun barrel at very high velocity using a discarding sabot as a carrier. Used in some types of military ammunition, they have no sporting applications.

FLYER: A bullet which strikes the target markedly outside the previously fired group of shots.

FOOT-POUNDS: An English unit of work indicating the amount of kinetic energy of a bullet in flight at a given distance. Technically, one foot-pound is the energy required to lift one pound a distance of one foot.

FORM FACTOR: A correction factor or multiplier used to calculate the ballistic coefficient of a bullet as it relates to a "standard" projectile shown on a ballistic table such as the Ingalls Tables.

FOULING: Metal, polymer, or propellant residue deposited in the bore during firing, often in layers. Such residues may adversely affect accuracy and should be removed promptly.

FORCING CONE:
1). The tapered bore surface at the breech end of a revolver barrel just in front of the cylinder.
2). The tapered cone in the front of a shotgun chamber.

FRANGIBLE BULLET: A monolithic bullet made from molded, compressed, and/or sintered powdered metal, possibly using a polymer or another powdered metal as a binder. Designed to break up on steel targets into fragments small enough to not cause injury to the shooter or others. Frangible bullets will not break up on soft targets.

FREE BORE: The transitional zone in the bore forward of the chamber to the origin of the rifling that guides the bullet as it is engraved. Some guns have no free bore; however, a long free bore is common in many magnum calibers. (See also: LEADE and THROAT)

FREE RECOIL ENERGY: A numerical measure of the recoil energy of a given gun determined by multiplying the weight of the gun in pounds by the recoil velocity of the gun squared, then dividing the result by 64.4. The product given in units of foot-pounds.

FRONTAL IGNITION: A cartridge case design in which the flame and hot gases from the primer are directed forward through a metal tube so as to ignite the front of the propellant charge for a more efficient burn. While it works, the gains are not worth the added complexity in small caliber ammunition.

FULL METAL JACKET: A bullet having a gilding metal (copper alloy) or clad steel jacket over its outer surface, except for the base. Most military bullets are of full metal jacket configuration.

GAIN TWIST RIFLING: A type of rifling having an increasing rate of rotation from leade to muzzle. Also called progressive rifling. Seldom seen now in most small caliber firearms. It does have some application in artillery barrels to reduce torque on firing.

GALLING: Metal deposits and/or surface roughness resulting from friction between two metal surfaces.

GANG MOLD: A multiple cavity mold which speeds casting of more than one projectile from each pour.

GAS: The hot, rapidly expanding vapor in a gun barrel from the rapid burn of the primer and combustion of the propellant powder.

GAS CHECK: A shallow, protective cup crimped on the base of an unjacketed lead bullet. Designed to reduce deformation of the bullet's base and protect it from the hot propellant gases. Used to reduce leading in the bore.

GAS CUTTING:
   1). Erosion of the throat and bore of a gun barrel from the flame and hot propellant gases.
   2). Erosion of jacket material on a bullet by hot propellant gases.
   3). Erosion of the top strap through the barrel-cylinder gap on revolvers.

GAS-OPERATED: A popular type of locked breech firearm operating system used in many semi-automatic rifles. As the bullet travels down the barrel a small portion of the gas is bled into a port to power the operation cycle of the firearm.

GAS PORT: A small hole in a gun barrel that bleeds off a sufficient amount of the propellant gases to power the gas system's operational components.

GAUGE: A traditional English method of measuring and expressing the bore diameter of a shotgun barrel. The gauge number is determined by the number of bore diameter pure lead balls of equal weight in one pound. A 12-gauge has 12, a 20-gauge 20, and so on. The .410 bore is an exception in that it is a caliber, not a gauge.

GILDING METAL: A common metal alloy used for bullet jackets consisting of 95% copper and 5% zinc (95/5). Conversely, Commercial Bronze is composed of 90% copper and 10% zinc (90/10).

GO, NO-GO GAUGE: A caliber-specific set of precision measuring tools used to check the headspace in a firearm. Headspace gauges are in sets of three: Go, No Go, and Field, and are cartridge specific.

GRAIN: An Avoirdupois unit of weight measurement commonly used to express powder charge and bullet weights. There are 7,000 grains in one pound and 437.5 grains in one ounce.

GRAM: A measurement of weight used in countries that use the Metric system to express powder charge and bullet weights. There are 15.432 grains in one gram, 28.35 grams in one ounce, and 453.6 grams in one pound.

GRANULATION: The grain size and shape of black or smokeless propellants; one of the factors used to control burning rate.

GRANULE: A single particle or grain of black or smokeless propellant.

GREASE GROOVE: A circumferential groove in a lead bullet's outer surface designed to hold a solid lubricant.

GREENHILL'S FORMULA: Developed by Sir Alfred Greenhill, a mathematic method to determine the rifling twist rate necessary to stabilize a bullet. The formula is: the twist required (in calibers) = 150 divided by the length of the bullet in calibers. (See also: CALIBER and RIFLING)

GROOVES: Spiral depressions cut, swaged, hammered, broached, or etched in the bore of a gun barrel to form the rifling.

GROOVE DIAMETER: The diameter of a major circle circumscribed by the bottom of the grooves. (See also: LAND DIAMETER)

GROUP: A given number of consecutive shots fired at the same aiming point on a target.

GUN COTTON: Chemical name is nitrocellulose, made from cotton linters, wood pulp or a combination of the two.

GUN POWDER: A popular, generic term for propellants of all types.

GYROSCOPIC STABILITY: Bullet stability in flight due to rotation along its long axis as caused by the rifling.

HALF-JACKET: A jacketed bullet in which the jacket covers the base and bearing surface of the bullet, but leaves the ogive and meplat uncovered.

HAMMER FORGED RIFLING: A method of rifling a gun barrel using a machine with a series of hammers to physically compress the barrel around a mandrel (a metal rod with a reverse of the lands and grooves). The hammers compress the barrel walls around the mandrel, eliminating voids, improving grain structure, and strength.

HANDGUN: A short, compact firearm designed to be fired with one hand. The three common types of handguns: semi-automatic, revolver, and single-shot.

HANDLOADING: The manual process of assembling loaded ammunition for personal use (not resale) using new or previously fired cartridge cases. (See also: RELOADING)

HANG FIRE: A delay in primer detonation after it has been struck by the firing pin or striker. A distinctive, noticeable pause between the impact of the firing pin on the primer cup and primer detonation. This condition is sometimes referred to as a "click—bang."

HARDBALL: A popular slang term for a Full Metal Jacket (FMJ/TMJ) rifle or handgun bullet, or ammunition loaded with such bullets. (See also: FULL METAL JACKET, BALL AMMUNITION)

HARDNESS GRADIENT: The intentional differences in grain structure and degree of hardness of a brass cartridge case as it transitions from the head (very hard) to the neck (soft).

HEAD: The base of a cartridge case including the primer pocket, rim, extractor groove (or undercut), and web.

HEAD SEPARATION: A condition where the head of a cartridge case breaks off or separates leaving the case body in the chamber of the gun.

HEAD SPACE: The distance from the face of the closed breech of a firearm to the surface in the chamber on which the cartridge case seats. (See also: HEAD SPACE GAUGE)
  1). BELT: A type of chamber design in which the cartridge seats in the chamber on an enlarged band ahead of the extractor groove of the cartridge body.
  2). MOUTH: A type of chamber design in which the cartridge seats in the chamber on the mouth of the cartridge case.
  3). RIMLESS: A type of chamber design in which the cartridge seats in the chamber on the shoulder of the cartridge case.
  4). RIMMED: A type of chamber design in which the cartridge seats in the chamber on the rim or flange of the cartridge case.

HEAD SPACE GAUGE: (See Go, No Go Gauge)

HEADSTAMP: A combination of numbers, letters, or symbols stamped into the base of a cartridge case around the primer, which may denote information such as: the caliber of the cartridge, manufacturer, date of manufacture, other data or be absent entirely.

HEEL: The edge of a bullet's base. The lower part of a bullet's bearing surface where it transitions to the base; a boat tail bullet is sometimes described as having a tapered heel.

HIGH PRIMER: A primer that protrudes above the head of a cartridge case because it is not properly seated in the primer pocket. To check for this condition stand the case upright on a flat surface; a high primer will cause the case to wobble.

HOLD-OFF: A method of visually compensating for the effects of wind and other sources of deflection by intentionally holding the point of aim off the target by an estimated amount; commonly called "Kentucky Windage."

HOLD OVER/UNDER: The amount necessary to aim above or below a target in order to hit it when the zero range and target's range are different; you must aim high for targets at longer range, and low for targets at shorter range; also, the amount needed to aim below a target for shots uphill or downhill.

HOLLOW POINT: A cavity or opening in the nose of a bullet designed to cause expansion on impact to improve energy transfer and/or control penetration inside the target. In match rifle bullets, the hollow point [Open Tip Match (OTM)] moves the center of gravity rearward for greater accuracy; hollow point match rifle bullets are not designed for reliable penetration and should not be used for hunting.

HORIZONTAL DISPERSION: The maximum horizontal distance across a target between two vertical parallel lines through the farthest left and right holes in a group. (See also: VERTICAL DISPERSION)

HULL: A popular term for the body of a shotshell. Normally, this term is not used in reference to metallic cartridge cases.

HYGROSCOPIC (PROPELLANTS): Smokeless propellants that readily absorb moisture; black powder is very hygroscopic.

HYDROSTATIC SHOCK: A destructive shock wave or pressure wave propagated through tissue caused by the passage of a bullet.

IGNITION: The initiation of propellant deflagration (burning) by the flame and hot gases from the primer.

IGNITION TIME: The elapsed time between the impact of the firing pin on the primer and the rise in chamber pressure.

IMPROVED CARTRIDGE: A standard cartridge that has been altered by fire forming to increase its powder capacity by using a sharper shoulder angle, less case body taper, or both.

INGALLS TABLES: A set of ballistic tables computed by Col. James Ingalls U.S.A. derived by combining a number of sources. By using the coefficient of form for a given bullet shape, calculations are used to determine the Ballistic Coefficient. (See also: BALLISTIC COEFFICIENT)

INSIDE LUBRICATED: A type of lead bullet with a bearing surface that is completely covered by the case sidewalls when the bullet is fully seated. This prevents the bullet lubricant from being worn off. (See also: OUTSIDE LUBRICATED)

INTERNAL BALLISTICS: (Interior Ballistics) The study of projectiles in motion while inside a firearm.

INTERNAL VOLUME: The capacity of a cartridge case to hold propellant powder, generally expressed in cubic centimeters (cc) of water.

INSTRUMENTAL VELOCITY: The velocity of a bullet taken at a given distance from the muzzle, then is used with a correction factor in a formula to calculate the muzzle velocity.

IRIS: The blue/black discoloration found on the case mouth and neck of brass-case military rifle ammunition, intentionally left to indicate the annealing of the case has been accomplished. Most often removed from sporting ammunition.

JACKET: A covering or skin on a bullet that partially or fully covers its core. The covering can be of several substances and in varying amounts of coverage on the bullet.

JACKETED HOLLOW POINT (JHP): A jacketed rifle or handgun bullet with a cavity or opening at the tip designed to cause expansion or mushrooming as it penetrates.

JACKETED SOFT POINT (JSP): A jacketed rifle or handgun bullet open at the tip to expose the lead core.

KERNEL: A single particle or granule of propellant powder.

KEYHOLE: An oval or oblong hole in a paper target made by the impact of an unstable bullet. A "keyhole" in the target indicates unstable flight.

KINETIC ENERGY: The energy associated with the motion of a projectile in flight at a given distance; normally expressed in foot-pounds, joules, or kilogram-meters. A function of the projectile's mass and the square of its velocity at any point in the flight path.

LANDS: The raised, uncut portion of the bore that forms the rifling after the grooves have been cut or formed in the bore surface. Rotation of the bullet is a result of its engagement with the lands in the barrel. (See also: GROOVES)

LAND DIAMETER: The diameter of a major circle circumscribing the tops of the lands; the top surface of each land is convex.

LEAD CRUSHER: Obsolete pressure measurement system, much like CUP pressure method, but using a lead cylinder. Primary use was in shotshell pressure measurement. (See also: LEAD UNITS OF PRESSURE)

LEAD FURNACE: A metal container used to melt lead for casting bullets or round balls; also called a Melting Pot.

LEAD UNITS OF PRESSURE (LUP): An obsolete system of determining the chamber pressure of low-pressure metallic cartridges and shotshells in similar manner to the copper crusher system using lead crushers instead of copper. (See also: LEAD CRUSHER)

LEADE: That section of the bore of a rifled gun barrel located immediately ahead of the chamber in which the rifling is conically removed to provide clearance for the seated bullet. (See also: THROAT and FREE BORE)

LEADING: A form of metal fouling deposited in the bore of a rifle, handgun, or shotgun caused by the friction of lead rubbing against the bore surfaces or from gas cutting, or both. May adversely affect accuracy and should be removed promptly.

LEVEL POINT: The point on the *descending* curve of the bullet's trajectory where it crosses the same level as the muzzle; also called the Point of Fall or Line of Fall.

LINE OF THE BORE: (See: BORE AXIS)

LINE OF DEPARTURE: The imaginary projection of the bore axis to infinity as a straight line at the exact moment a bullet leaves the muzzle. Bullet drop is measured from this line.

LINE OF FALL: (See: LEVEL POINT)

LINE OF FIRE: An imaginary, horizontal straight line extending from the muzzle in the direction of the projectile's path of travel.

LINE OF SIGHT: An imaginary straight line to infinity passing through the sights of a gun and coincident with the point of aim.

LIVE AMMUNITION: Loaded, self-contained metallic cartridges or shotshells.

LOAD:
1). The specific combination of components used to assemble a self-contained cartridge or shotshell.
2). The procedure for inserting live ammunition into the feeding system of a gun.

LOAD DENSITY: The ratio of the case volume occupied by the propellant charge after the bullet is seated to the total available volume in an empty case, expressed as a percentage.

OVERALL LOADED LENGTH: The overall loaded length (OAL) of a cartridge as measured from the base of the case to the tip of the bullet. The OAL must not be more than the maximum specification for each cartridge as listed in the loading data.

LOADING BLOCK: An accessory for reloading with rows of holes to hold and orient a number of cartridge cases. They are made in different sizes to match specific groups of calibers.

LOCK TIME: The elapsed time between the release of the trigger sear and the firing pin striking the primer.

LOCKING LUGS: One or more projections on a bolt which fit into mating recesses in the receiver or barrel extension, securely holding the bolt during firing.

LUBRICATION PAD: A pad holding a liquid lubricant on which cartridge cases are rolled before sizing.

LUBRICANT: A liquid or solid compound used to reduce friction between two or more surfaces.

LUBRICATOR/LUBE-SIZER: A device used for simultaneously lubricating and sizing cast or swaged lead bullets.

MACHINE GUN: A fully automatic firearm that will keep firing until the ammunition supply is exhausted or the shooter takes their finger off the trigger. Technically, a machine gun fires *rifle caliber* ammunition while a submachine gun fires *pistol caliber* ammunition. (See also: AUTOMATIC and SEMI-AUTOMATIC)

MAGAZINE: A detachable or integral container holding a number of cartridges to be fed into the operating system of a firearm. In the simplest terms, magazines are refilled and used again, clips are intended for single use. Magazines take many forms, such as box, drum, rotary, tubular, or removable. (See also: CLIP)

MAGNUM: A term used to describe a high performance, purposely-designed cartridge or shotshell having a larger capacity case, higher muzzle velocity, and higher maximum average pressure than standard cartridges of similar caliber or gauge. The term "magnum" was first used by Holland & Holland in 1912 to describe their new 375 H&H Magnum cartridge, reportedly, inspired by a magnum bottle of champagne.

MANDREL: A tapered or cylindrical metal bar that serves as a core around which a material may be cast, molded, forged, bent or otherwise shaped; in reloading, a mandrel is used to true and size case necks.

MATCH AMMUNITION: Centerfire or rimfire ammunition loaded to higher standards of consistency and precision.

MAXIMUM AVERAGE PRESSURE (MAP): The maximum average pressure as set by SAAMI for loaded ammunition. Normally expressed in pounds per square inch (psi) or Copper Units of Pressure (CUP).

MAXIMUM CHARGE: The heaviest charge, in grains, of a given propellant that may be safely loaded into a specific caliber cartridge without exceeding the maximum average pressure (MAP) limit.

MAXIMUM HORIZONTAL RANGE: The farthest horizontal distance a bullet may travel to the point of first impact with the ground with the muzzle elevated at the optimum angle, normally expressed in yards or meters. An important consideration for range safety.

MAXIMUM ORDINATE: The vertical distance between a horizontal straight line from the muzzle to the target and the highest point on the trajectory curve of the bullet's flight path; normally expressed in inches.

MAXIMUM VERTICAL RANGE: The highest altitude a bullet will reach when fired vertically; usually expressed in feet; an important safety consideration.

MEAN RADIUS: A method for measuring the precision of ammunition. The arithmetic mean of distances between centers of each shot hole from the calculated group center.

MEPLAT: The diameter of the flat surface on the tip of a bullet, specifically the tip's diameter.

MERCURIC PRIMER: A type of primer having a primary explosive initiator pellet containing fulminate of mercury. The corrosive residue from firing attacks brass cases; reloading of these cartridge cases is not recommended.

METAL FOULING: Lead, copper, nickel, or other metal deposits left in the bore after firing. Metal fouling should be removed as it can adversely affect accuracy.

METALLIC AMMUNITION: Self-contained centerfire or rimfire ammunition with cartridge cases made of a metal alloy. While most often brass or steel, there are other materials such as aluminum, polymers, stainless steel, and hybrids containing two or more materials.

MICROMETER: A handheld precision measuring instrument. The preferred tool to measure dimensions smaller than 1/1000 of an inch, such as bullet diameter and case head expansion.

MID-RANGE TRAJECTORY: The distance the bullet's flight path rises above the line of sight halfway between the muzzle and the target; usually expressed in inches; also called Mid-Range Trajectory Height.

MIL: The angle subtended by one unit at 1000 units. A measure commonly used by military artillery or rifle scope reticles, a MIL is not the same as a minute-of-angle (MOA).

MILITARY AMMUNITION: Centerfire rifle, centerfire handgun, and shotshell ammunition manufactured under government contract to military specifications by government arsenals or commercial manufacturers.

MINIMUM CALIBER: A statutory, regulatory, or administrative limit on the smallest caliber of cartridge that may be used for hunting specified types of game animals. The limits are based on one or more of the following criteria: bullet diameter, bullet weight, bullet type, muzzle velocity, muzzle energy, case dimensions, or overall cartridge characteristics. These requirements are established by the political entity having control over hunting.

MINUTE OF ANGLE (MOA): A unit of measure commonly used by shooters; $1/60^{th}$ of a degree, subtending 1.047 inches at 100 yards.; normally taken as 1.00 inch at 100 yards.; a minute of angle is not a MIL. (See also: MIL)

MIRAGE: The shimmering effect caused by heated air refracting light. Rising air currents and crosswinds affecting mirage cause the target to appear to move.

MISFIRE: Failure of a primer to initiate after being struck a normal blow by the firing pin or striker, or failure of a properly initiated primer to ignite the propellant powder.

MOLD BLOCKS: Two-piece, hinged metal blocks having one or more projectile-shaped cavities which can be filled with molten lead to cast bullets.

MONOLITHIC BULLET: A cast, swaged, molded, sintered, extruded, or turned bullet made from a single material such as copper, gilding metal, lead, zinc, or frangible composite. Monolithic bullets have no jacket although they may be coated with another material.

MOUTH: The open front end of a cartridge case that holds the bullet.

MULTI-STAGE RELOADING PRESS: A type of automatic or semi-automatic progressive reloading press that performs several operations on each stroke; designed for high output.

MUSHROOM: A commonly used, non-technical term that describes the post-impact appearance of a bullet designed to expand upon striking a target.

MUZZLE: The front end of a gun barrel where the bullet exits.

MUZZLE BLAST: The compression wave caused by the release of high-pressure propellant gases jetting from the muzzle following the bullet's exit. Always wear hearing protection.

MUZZLE BRAKE: A muzzle device (permanent or removable) designed to reduce recoil by redirecting high-pressure propellant gases to the side. These devices can reduce recoil by as much as 25%, but not eliminate it.

MUZZLE ENERGY: A numerical expression of the kinetic energy of a bullet at the muzzle; normally expressed in foot-pounds or joules. (See also: KINETIC ENERGY and FOOT-POUNDS)

MUZZLE FLASH: The brief burst of light at the muzzle caused by burning particles of propellant and hot gases ejected from the muzzle as they mix with the oxygen in the air. Flash suppressing additives in propellants can significantly reduce muzzle flash. (See also: FLASH SUPPRESSOR)

MUZZLE JUMP: The horizontal, vertical, and rotating motion of a firearm when it is fired.

MUZZLE PRESSURE: The remaining pressure of the expanding propellant gases at the muzzle immediately before the bullet exits, normally expressed in pounds per square inch; muzzle pressure is lower than port pressure or chamber pressure.

MUZZLE VELOCITY: The velocity of a bullet at the muzzle; normally expressed in feet per second or meters per second. (See also: REMAINING VELOCITY)

NECK: The straight-sided, cylindrical part of a cartridge case located between the mouth and the end of the shoulder, which holds the bullet. Straight walled cartridge cases do not have a neck. (See also: MOUTH and SHOULDER)

NECK RADIUS: The small curvature at the junction of the case neck and shoulder.

NECK REAM: The process of removing material from the inside of the case neck. Commonly done when forming a shorter case from a longer one. (See also: NECK TURN)

NECK SIZE: The procedure of resizing all or part of the case neck back to its original dimensions, leaving the case body unchanged. This method of sizing increases case life and reduces work hardening of the brass.

NECK SPLIT: A longitudinal crack in the neck portion of a cartridge. Not suitable for reloading.

NECK TENSION: The force exerted by the sidewalls of the case neck on the bearing surface of the bullet. This interference fit of the neck interior and the bullet diameter holds the bullet in place. (See also: BULLET PULL and BULLET PUSH)

NECK TURN: The process of removing material from the outside of the case neck in order to improve the concentricity of the bullet when seated. (See also: NECK REAM)

NECK UP OR NECK DOWN: The process of increasing or decreasing the neck diameter of a cartridge case to accept a bullet of a different diameter; a popular procedure for creating wildcat cartridges.

NITROCELLULOSE: Nitrated wood or cotton cellulose used to make smokeless propellants.

NITROGLYCERINE: Glyceryl nitrate or nitric ester of glycerin is a very energetic liquid explosive, used to increase the energy content of propellants. A propellant with nitroglycerine as a component is called a double-base propellant.

NON-CORROSIVE: A term describing priming compounds that do not leave corrosive residues in gun barrels when fired. For a half-century, sporting primers and most military small arms primers have been non-corrosive. (See also: CORROSIVE PRIMER)

NON-HYGROSCOPIC: A term describing some smokeless propellants that will absorb very little or no moisture. Some smokeless propellants are hygroscopic, as are all black powder propellants. Too much moisture can cause erratic ballistic performance.

NOSE: The part of a bullet from the forward end of its bearing surface, including the ogive, to its tip.

OBTURATION: The expansion of the cartridge case body against the chamber walls which acts as a seal to prevent a rearward flow of hot, high-pressure propellant gases.

OGIVE: The curved portion of a bullet forward of its bearing surface. Often expressed in calibers. (See also: SECANT OGIVE and TANGENT OGIVE)

OUTSIDE LUBRICATED: A cast or swaged lead bullet having a lubricated bearing surface that is the same diameter as the *outside or OD* of the case neck. A smaller diameter heel on the bullet's base holds it in the case mouth leaving the bearing surface exposed. Most 22 LR/L/S bullets are outside lubricated.

OVERALL LENGTH: The length of a loaded cartridge as measured from its base to the meplat on the tip of the bullet. Normally expressed in inches, it can prove critical for reliable feeding and chambering.

OIL DENT: A depression in the neck or shoulder of a bottleneck cartridge case caused by excess lubricant. Three most common causes: in manufacturing, during resizing, or in the chamber during firing. Cases with oil dents should be discarded.

OUT OF BATTERY FIRING: The condition of the breeching mechanism of a firearm being improperly positioned for firing.

PARALLAX: A condition in a telescopic gun sight that exists when the reticle (cross hairs) does not lie precisely in the image plane. Excessive parallax can cause inaccuracy as the point of aim wanders in the image according to the shooter's eye position. With parallax corrected, the reticle remains stationary in the image plane regardless of the shooter's eye position; scopes under 9X normally have fixed parallax set at 100-150 yds. Many scopes over 10X have an adjustable objective lens for correcting parallax at all ranges.

PAPER PATCHED BULLET: A cast lead rifle bullet in which the bearing surface of the bullet is wrapped in paper to increase its diameter to groove depth. The paper wrap engages the rifling, acts as a gas seal, reduces leading, and then falls away cleanly after the bullet clears the muzzle. A practice popular in the 1870s and 1880s for long-range target shooting and still used today.

PEAK PRESSURE: The maximum chamber pressure of an individual cartridge when fired. (See also: MAXIMUM AVERAGE PRESSURE)

PIERCED PRIMER: A fired primer in which the primer cup has been pierced by the tip of the striker (firing pin). A pierced primer may leak hot, high-pressure gas rearward which can damage the tip of the striker.

PISTOL: A semi-automatic handgun or a handgun in which the chamber and the barrel in a fixed position relative to one another. Often heard but incorrect term used to describe all handguns. (See also: REVOLVER)

PLINKING: The uniquely American past-time of informal target shooting on inanimate targets of opportunity. Normally not done on a formal shooting range, with the 22 rimfire as the cartridge of choice, but other calibers can be used.

PLUS P (+P) AMMUNITION: Handgun or rifle ammunition loaded to a higher maximum average pressure than standard ammunition in that caliber. Some examples include: 38 Super Auto +P, 9mm Luger +P, 45 Auto +P, and 257 Roberts +P; ammunition loaded to +P levels can be identified by the +P labeling on the boxes and the headstamp.

POINT BLANK RANGE: A method of sighting-in a hunting rifle so that the farthest distance at which the rise and drop of the bullet path do not exceed the vital zone of the target. Within this range bracket the hunter does not have to adjust his aim.

POINT OF AIM: The aiming point on the target on which the gun sights are aligned.

POINT OF IMPACT: The location or point where a bullet first strikes the target or the ground.

PORT PRESSURE: The propellant gas pressure as measured at a barrel's gas port. This opening in the barrel allows hot gas to bleed-off which is used to cycle a gas-operated firearm. Port pressure can be controlled by port diameter, port location, and powder selection.

POUNDS PER SQUARE INCH (psi): A measure of pressure in English units commonly used to indicate chamber, breech, or port pressure in a firearm.

POWDER: Smokeless or black powder propellants that, when ignited, deflagrate rapidly into large amounts of hot, expanding gas which is used to accelerate a bullet down the barrel of a firearm. A firearm is technically a heat engine and gunpowder is its fuel.

POWDER BRIDGING: A blockage that may occur in a powder measure, a drop tube or funnel caused when powder granules interlock to create a logjam. Bridging is most common with long stick powders.

POWDER BURNING RATE: The speed at which a given propellant deflagrates in comparison to other propellants.

POWDER CHARGE: The amount of propellant loaded into a firearm (case or muzzle loader). Usually expressed as weight in grains or grams.

POWDER DETERIORATION: The partial or full decomposition of smokeless powder which is normally due to adverse storage conditions, contamination, or age. An acidic acrid smell is typically the first indicator. Do not attempt to use powder that has deteriorated.

POWDER FOULING: A solid residue of burnt propellant that remains in the barrel after a cartridge has been fired. Unburned or partially burned granules of powder should be removed promptly after shooting.

POWDER FUNNEL: A tapered plastic or metal reloading accessory used to facilitate transfer of propellant from a scale or powder measure into the mouth of a cartridge case.

POWDER MEASURE: An adjustable, volumetric measuring device used to accurately meter powder charges. Today both manual and electric are found in use.

POWDER SCALE: A mechanical or electronic device used to accurately weigh reloading components such as powder charges, bullets, and other items.

POWDER TRICKLER: A mechanical or electronic device used to drop small quantities of propellant on a scale for precision weighing.

PRECISION: A measure of the ability to cluster all shots into a small group on a target regardless of where the center of impact is located; ultimate precision would be all shots striking in one hole; the difficulty of achieving precision increases exponentially with the number of shots in the group; for example a tight ten shot group is more difficult to achieve than a five shot group. (See also: EXTREME SPREAD)

PRESSURE: The force per unit area exerted by the hot, expanding powder gases on the component parts of the firearm and cartridge case. Normally expressed as pressure in pounds per square inch (psi) or copper units of pressure (CUP). (See also: MAXIMUM AVERAGE PRESSURE and COPPER UNITS OF PRESSURE)

PRESSURE CURVE: A graphical presentation of the relationship of chamber pressure to elapsed time when a cartridge is fired using piezoelectric transducers. Normally displayed as a curve showing rise, dwell, and decline of pressure levels over time.

PRESSURE GAUGE: The electronic or mechanical device for measuring the chamber or port pressure in a firearm. Electronic devices use a piezoelectric transducer to measure in pounds per square inch (psi). Because piezoelectric transducers are more accurate and easier to use, they are widely used in ammunition manufacturing facilities. The copper units of pressure (CUP) measuring system is semi-obsolete and used only for limited runs of the older classic caliber cartridges.

PRESSURE GUN: A laboratory fixture (Universal Receiver) used for measuring the chamber pressure of ammunition. A typical pressure gun is a falling block, single-shot design made of steel and is designed to allow barrels of various calibers to be quickly mounted or dismounted as required.

PRESSURE TESTING BARREL: A special test barrel configured for use in a pressure gun with provision for mounting piezoelectric transducers, a copper crusher fixture or both.

PRIMER: A percussion initiated device designed to ignite the propellant of a cartridge. The impact of the striker or firing pin on the primer cup causes the primer pellet to initiate, sending flame and high-temperature gases into the propellant powder causing deflagration to begin. Modern primers may be of the Boxer, Berdan, battery cup (No. 209 shotshell), or rimfire type.

PRIMER CUP: The small, metallic cup of a centerfire or shotshell primer that holds the explosive priming compound and is the target of the striker or firing pin.

PRIMER DROP TEST: A test of primer sensitivity using a measuring device to drop a steel ball of a given weight from calibrated heights onto a primer housed in a fixture.

PRIMER FLIPPER: A two-piece plastic tray used to orient and turn primers to facilitate filling primer feed tubes.

PRIMER INDENT:
1). The small depression made in the cup of a centerfire or shotshell primer by the impact of the striker or firing pin.
2). The indent made by the firing pin on a copper crusher which can be used to determine whether the striker's impact energy meets industry standards.

PRIMER LEAK: The unintended leakage of primer gases around the primer pocket annulus or firing pin indent. Primer leakage may be a sign of excessive chamber pressure. Leakage in the firing pin indent may also be a sign of a damaged firing pin tip.

PRIMER MIX: An impact sensitive, rapid burn, chemical compound used to ignite propellants. When initiated it generates a hot flame and burning particles that ignite the propellant powder.

PRIMER POCKET: The round, central cavity in the head of centerfire cartridge case that holds and supports the primer. Primer pockets vary in dimension according to the primer size.

PRIMER POCKET REAMER: A steel or carbide cutting tool used to ream out and/or re-profile the crimp and the bottom radius of the primer pocket, mostly on military cartridge cases. (See also: PRIMER POCKET SWAGING).

PRIMER POCKET SWAGING: The process of cold-reforming the outer rim of the primer pocket of a fired military cartridge case to remove the crimp. While slower, removing the crimp may be accomplished also by reaming. (See also: PRIMER POCKET REAMER)

PRIMER PUNCH: The metal punch in a primer seating tool that pushes the primer in the primer pocket of a cartridge case. (See also: DECAPPING PIN)

PRIMER SENSITIVITY: A statistical measure of the average impact force of the firing pin or striker required for reliable primer ignition as compared to industry standards. (See also: PRIMER DROP TEST and PRIMER INDENT)

PRIMING TOOL: A hand-held or freestanding accessory tool for priming unprimed cartridge cases.

PROGRESSIVE BURNING POWDER: A characteristic of smokeless propellants that describes how they deflagrate. As the bullet travels down the barrel, volume increases causing pressures to drop. The burning rate of progressive burning smokeless propellants *increases* with time in order to compensate for the increasing volume and extend the high-pressure levels for a longer period of time.

PROGRESSIVE RELOADING PRESS: A type of automated or semi-automated reloading press designed to perform several operations at once to increase production rates.

PROGRESSIVE RIFLING: Rifling with an increasing rate to twist from the leade to the muzzle, also called gain twist rifling.

PROJECTILE: A bullet or other object propelled into motion by the application of force and continuing in motion by its own inertia.

PROOF: The process of confirming the strength of a firearm or barrel by firing one or more rounds of high-pressure test or proof ammunition in same. European countries have proof testing mandated by law and is conducted in government proof houses. Proof testing is voluntary in the U.S., it is conducted independently by the gun manufacturers. (See also: PROOF AMMUNITION)

PROOF AMMUNITION: Rimfire, centerfire rifle, handgun, or shotshell ammunition loaded between 130% and 140% over the maximum probable lot mean (MPLM) of standard cartridges. MPLM is two standard errors higher in pressure than the maximum average pressure (MAP). This ammunition is used for confirming the strength of new or repaired firearms or barrels. This ammunition is specially marked and packed in specially labelled boxes. Distribution is strictly controlled and not available to the public.

PROPELLANT: A physical mixture or chemical compound with high energy content that serves as both the fuel and oxidizer for a heat engine such as a firearm. When ignited and confined, it deflagrates, releasing its energy in the form of flame and hot, rapidly expanding gases used to accelerate a bullet down a gun barrel.

PROPRIETARY CARTRIDGE: A non-standard cartridge or line of cartridges designed and distributed solely by a company or person under their own brand name. The seller may or may not manufacture the cartridges.

PROTRUDING PRIMER: A primer that partially backs out of the primer pocket so as to protrude above the surface of the case head, normally as a result of low pressure or excess head space.

RAM: The reciprocating vertical shaft most often in the center of a reloading press used to move cases to/through the reloading process.

RANGE:
 1). The horizontal distance in a straight line from the muzzle to the intended target; normally expressed in yards or meters.
 2). A place for shooting.

RATE OF SPIN: A bullet's rate of rotation in flight after it exits the muzzle of a rifled barrel, usually expressed as revolutions per minute (RPM). Rotational rates can be very high; for example the rate of spin for a 150 gr. bullet at a muzzle velocity of 2,910 fps from a 1:10 twist barrel is 209,520 RPM!

RATE OF TWIST: The distance in which the rifling makes one complete revolution, normally expressed as one turn in a specific number of inches or millimeters.

REAM: The process of removing material from a hole, cavity, or chamber.

REAMER: A rotary cutting tool with one or more blades used to remove material from a hole, cavity, or chamber. (See also: REAM)

REBATED RIM: A centerfire cartridge case with the rim diameter smaller in diameter than its body. Examples include 284 Win. and 50 AE. (See also: SEMI-RIMMED CASE)

RECEIVER: The main structural part of a firearm that holds the barrel, locking system, and fire control system in place; the receiver may be stressed (load bearing) or unstressed (non-load bearing).

RECOIL: The practical effect of Newton's Third Law of Motion: for each action, there is an equal and opposite reaction. The rearward motion of a firearm in reaction to the bullet or shot charge being accelerated down and out the barrel, often called "kick."

RECOIL BUFFER: An energy absorbing device designed to cushion the impact of the bolt assembly on the receiver at the end of its rearward travel. Commonly found in semi-automatic rifles.

REFERENCE AMMUNITION: Specially made factory ammunition tested and certified by participating SAAMI companies used to calibrate chronographs and pressure measuring equipment. Also called SAAMI Reference Ammunition. Reference Ammunition is not available to the public.

REFORMING: The process of changing the dimensions of a cartridge case in order to change its caliber, shoulder angle, overall length, interior volume, or a combination of these.

RELOADING: The manual process of assembling loaded ammunition for personal use (not resale) using spent cartridge cases and new components. (See also: HANDLOADING)

RELOADING PRESS: A force-multiplying device that uses mechanical advantage to preform multiple procedures to reload centerfire ammunition or shotshells.

REMAINING ENERGY: The residual or downrange energy of a bullet at a given distance from the muzzle; normally expressed in foot-pounds (ft-lbs) or Joules.

REMAINING VELOCITY: The residual or downrange velocity of a bullet at a given distance from the muzzle; normally expressed in feet per second (FPS) or meters per second (MS).

RESIDUAL PRESSURE: The pressure remaining in the chamber and barrel the instant the bullet exits the muzzle. This residual pressure produces the jet of hot gas at the muzzle that causes muzzle blast and flash.

RESIZING DIE: A reloading die that reforms a fired centerfire rifle or handgun cartridge case; a resizing die may be neck only, full length or small base. An integral decapping pin may remove the spent primer.

RETICLE: The adjustable aiming indicator marks in the image of a telescopic sight the shooter aligns on the target. These marks may consist of straight or tapered crosshairs, dots, posts, or combinations of the same; some reticles have range estimating marks. Indicator marks may be located on the first or second focal plane of a scope.

REVOLVER: A type of manually operated handgun having a frame holding a fixed barrel with a revolving cylinder inside the frame; the cylinder holds a number of cartridges in chambers that align in-turn with the barrel for firing.

RICOCHET: A bullet that strikes a surface without penetrating, and is deflected on a new, but erratic, trajectory.

RIFLED SLUG: A conical, lead shotgun projectile having a number of angled grooves cut or swaged into its outer surface. The grooves cause a slow rotation which is insufficient to stabilize the slug; stabilization occurs because the center of gravity is in front of the center of pressure. Sometimes called a "Foster" named after its American inventor Carl Foster.

RIFLING: Spiral grooves cut, impressed, broached, hammered, or etched in the bore of a gun barrel which causes the bullet to spin in flight to provide gyroscopic stability. The rate of twist, number of grooves, and land configuration varies.

RIFLING PITCH: (See RATE OF TWIST)

RIM: A flange at the base of a cartridge case which provides a gripping surface for the extractor to remove an unfired cartridge or fired cartridge case from the chamber. The rim of a cartridge may take one of several different configurations such as: rimmed, rimless, rebated, or semi-rimmed.

RIMFIRE AMMUNITION: A self-contained, metallic cartridge in which the priming mixture is held inside the hollow rim of the case head. Rimfire ammunition is the oldest type of self-contained, metallic ammunition still in production.

RIMFIRE PRIMER: (See: RIMFIRE AMMUNITION)

RIMLESS: A common type of case head on metallic centerfire rifle or pistol cartridge cases in which the base flange is the same diameter as the case head. Rimless cartridge cases normally headspace on either the shoulder (if present) or case mouth; the designation is a misnomer as a rimless case does have a rim.

RIMMED: A common type of case head on metallic rifle and revolver cartridge cases and shotshells in which the base flange is of larger diameter than the case. Rimmed cartridge cases have an undercut forward of the rim, but do not have an extractor groove; rimmed cases normally headspace on their rim.

ROUND: A vernacular term meaning a loaded, self-contained cartridge; a loaded cartridge having a case, bullet (or shot charge), primer, and propellant powder.

ROUND NOSE (RN): A particular shape of bullet ogive which is hemispherical or semi-hemispherical; a type of heavy weight bullet often selected for hunting heavy game at close ranges.

RUPTURE: A failure or break in the wall of a cartridge case that allows high-pressure propellant gases to escape rearward. (See also: CASE SEPARATION)

SABOT: (pronounced sa'bo or 'sabo) A lightweight, groove diameter carrier holding a sub-caliber bullet that is fired in a larger caliber barrel. Sabot's are generally of the discarding type that fall away from the bullet at the muzzle. Most modern sabots are made of polymer while older versions were made of wood, paper, or leather. The word "sabot" is derived from the French word for "shoe," actually referring to the wooden shoes common in the 19th and 20th centuries.

SEASON CRACKING: Fine cracks in brass cartridge case necks, sidewalls or heads due to age, hardness, defective brass, or chemical action. Also called age cracking or stress cracking, do not reload cartridge cases with stress cracks—discard them.

SEATING DEPTH: A dual use term.
1). The depth the base of the bullet is seated in the mouth of a loaded rifle or handgun cartridge case establishing the overall length (OAL) of the loaded cartridge.
2). The depth of an unfired primer as seated in the primer pocket of a loaded centerfire cartridge. (See also: OVERALL LENGTH)

SEATING DIE: A reloading die used to insert a bullet into the case mouth of a centerfire rifle or handgun cartridge. Most have the ability to crimp the bullet in the case.

SECANT OGIVE: A bullet having an ogive slope *not tangent* to its bearing surface; the radius of the ogive is normally expressed in calibers. Secant ogive bullets often have a more pointed tip. (See also: TANGENT OGIVE)

SECTIONAL DENSITY: The ratio of a bullet's weight in pounds to the square of its diameter in inches.

SELECTIVE FIRE: A fire control system in a firearm that allows the shooter to select either semi-automatic, burst (designated number of rounds fired) or fully automatic fire.

SEMI-AUTOMATIC: A firearm that fires with each pull of the trigger and without having to manually cycle the gun.

SEMI-RIMMED CASE: A centerfire rifle or pistol cartridge case having a rim that is larger in diameter than the case head and also has an extractor groove.

SEMI-WADCUTTER: A jacketed or lead handgun bullet having a truncated cone ogive; may be solid or hollow point.

SHANK: That part of a bullet with parallel surfaces between the ogive and the base that is engraved by the rifling. Also called the bearing surface.

SHELL HOLDER: An interchangeable, rim diameter-specific part of a reloading press that controls the cartridge case by its rim.

SHOCK: The physical effects caused by the rapid transfer of kinetic energy into living tissue as a bullet penetrates.

SHOCKING POWER: A popular, non-technical term used to loosely describe the ability of a bullet to transfer kinetic energy.

SHOCK WAVE: Compression waves formed in the air by a bullet at supersonic velocities that creates disturbances in the air flow around the ogive, bearing surface and base. This compression wave creates a distinctive noise or "crack" as the bullet passes through the air.

SHOT: Small spherical lead alloy, steel, composite, or polymer pellets for use in shotshells.

SHOT SIZE: The diameter of lead alloy, steel or composite shot pellets according to the industry standard listing 16 different sizes ranging from .050 inches to .36 inches in diameter and designed by numbers from 1 to 12 or a series of letters including B, T, F, or O.

SHOTSHELL: A complete round of loaded ammunition designed to fire a charge of shot pellets or a slug; an assembly consisting of a polymer or paper case, rimmed metal head of brass, aluminum or steel, a No. 209 battery cup primer, propellant, and a paper or plastic wad column, and a folded or rolled crimp closure on the case mouth; shotshells with all-metal hulls and centerfire primer pockets will also be found.

SHOULDER: The sloping portion of a metallic cartridge case between the case body and the neck; slope angles may be as much as 40°.

SHOULDER RADIUS: The small curvature at the junction of the shoulder and the body of a cartridge case.

SIGHT ELEVATION: Movement of an adjustable metallic or optical sight up or down to compensate for the vertical displacement of bullet impact points from the aiming point.

SIGHT RADIUS: The distance between front and rear metallic sights; normally expressed in inches or millimeters.

SIGHTING-IN: The process of firing a rifle or handgun at a specific range to determine the bullet's point of impact, then adjusting the sights so that the bullet's point of impact has the desired correlation to the point of aim.

SILENCER: (See: SUPPRESSOR)

SINGLE-BASE POWDER: A smokeless, nitrocellulose propellant made without the addition of any other highly nitrated chemical boosters such as nitroglycerine. (See also: DOUBLE-BASE POWDER)

SINGLE STAGE PRESS: A reloading press capable of holding only one die at a time.

SIZING:

1). The process of reducing the dimensions of a fired cartridge case to allow it to be chambered in a firearm of the appropriate caliber; sizing may be full length small base, full length, partial, or neck only.

2). Lead bullets may also be sized by passing them through a die designed for the purpose; also called resizing.

SLAM FIRE: An accidental discharge of a firearm during feeding and chambering in which the primer detonates before the operating system is fully locked. Slam fires are commonly caused by a free-floating firing pin, improper headspace, cartridges with a high primer, or a combination of both. A very dangerous condition frequently associated with semi-auto service rifles.

SLUG: A single projectile, normally swaged of lead alloy, used in shotguns. Some have angled, pre-cut grooves, in its outer surface it is called a rifled slug; also, a vernacular term for a bullet.

SMALL ARMS AMMUNITION: A military classification for all ammunition made to military specification for weapons having a bore diameter of .510 inches or less; this includes service rifles, pistols, shotguns, machine guns, and submachine guns; ammunition for weapons with a bore diameter greater than .510 inches are designated as cannon.

SMALL BASE DIE: A full length resizing die that reduces the body diameter of rifle cartridge case closer to the head than a standard die. Often necessary to reload cases fired in semi-automatic or pump-action rifles.

SMALL BORE CARTRIDGE: A colloquial term for a rimfire cartridge.

SMOKELESS POWDER: A progressive burning propellant made from a chemical mixture of nitrocellulose with a variety of additives such as stabilizers, coatings, and energy boosters. May be designated single-base, double-base, or triple-base.

SOFT POINT (SP): A jacketed rifle or handgun bullet having an open front end exposing the core which causes the bullet to mushroom as it penetrates to deposit some or all of its kinetic energy inside the target. Popular choice of bullet for hunting, which may have a protected point, spitzer, flat nose, semi-round nose, or round nose design.

SOLID HEAD CASE: A common metallic, centerfire cartridge case design combining the rim, head, primer pocket, web, and body drawn from a single material. Developed by Col. Hiram Berdan who also designed the Berdan primer.

SPENT: A vernacular shooting term describing a cartridge that has been fired.

SPHERICAL POWDER: A popular type of double-base propellant having round or semi-round granules the size and mixture of which control the burning rate. Also called Ball Powder.

SPIN: The stabilizing rotation of a bullet in flight about its longitudinal axis created by the rifling in the barrel. The twist rate of the rifling determines the RPM of the bullet in flight. (See also: RATE OF SPIN)

SPIN DAMPING MOMENT: The force which opposes and reduces a bullet's rate of spin as it flies through the air.

SPIN DRIFT: The lateral movement of a projectile in flight due to gyroscopic precession.

SPITZER BULLET: A general term describing a pointed bullet with most having tangent or secant ogives. The word "spitzer" comes from the German word for pointed. (See also: SECANT OGIVE and TANGENT OGIVE)

SPIRE POINT BULLET: A pointed bullet with a conical nose section. The line from the shank to the point is nearly straight.

STABILITY: A bullet's resistance to change, diversion, or dislodgement. This is a result of many factors including velocity, length, weight, rate of rotation, and ogive profile among others.

STABILIZED BULLET: A properly designed bullet in-flight with a sufficient rate of spin and velocity to maintain it in a point-first attitude along its trajectory. (See also: STABILITY, AERODYNAMIC STABILITY and GYROSCOPIC STABILITY, and RATE OF SPIN)

STABILIZER: A chemical compound added to smokeless propellants to prevent deterioration.

STANDARD CONDITIONS: Ammunition manufacturers test sporting ammunition interior and exterior ballistics using a set of standard atmospheric conditions; includes Altitude: sea level (0 feet), Temperature: 59°F./15°C., Humidity: 78%, Barometric pressure: 29.53 in. of Hg (Mercury).

STRIKER: A type of firing pin in a rifle, handgun, or shotgun powered only by the tension of a concentric coil spring which travels in a linear path to strike the primer.

STRIKING ENERGY: The remaining kinetic energy of a bullet when it first impacts the target, expressed in ft.-lbs.

STRIPPING:
1). The act of disassembling a firearm.
2). The act of transferring cartridges from a loading clip to the magazine.
3). An internal ballistic problem in which jacket metal is removed as the bullet travels down the barrel.

STUCK CASE REMOVER: An accessory device for removing cartridge cases stuck in a sizing die.

SUBMACHINE GUN: A compact, selective-fire or automatic-only firearm chambered for a pistol cartridge.

SUBSONIC AMMUNITION: Ammunition loaded to muzzle velocities below the speed of sound; the nominal speed of sound is approximately 1,117 fps at standard conditions. (See also: STANDARD CONDITIONS)

SUPPRESSOR: A detachable muzzle device for a firearm that significantly reduces, but does not eliminate, muzzle flash and muzzle blast. It does not quiet the sounds generated by the firearm's moving parts or the sound of a supersonic bullet in flight.

SWAGING: The process of forming metal by forcing it into a closed die.

TANGENT OGIVE: A bullet having an ogive slope *tangent* to the bearing surface. The radius of the ogive is normally expressed in calibers. (See also: SECANT OGIVE)

TARAGE TABLE: A table of numerical values used to quantify the relationship between the compressed length of a copper or lead crusher and peak chamber pressure. (See also: COPPER CRUSHER and PRESSURE TESTING BARREL)

TEMPERATURE EFFECT: The increase or decrease in muzzle velocity due to an increase or decrease in propellant temperature.

TEMPERATURE OF IGNITION: The lowest temperature to which the surface of a material (propellant) must be raised to initiate self-sustaining deflagration.

TERMINAL BALLISTICS: The study of the effects of projectiles at or inside the target.

TERMINAL VELOCITY: The remaining velocity often expressed in feet per second (FPS) or meters per second (M/S) of a bullet at the point of maximum range.

THROAT: (See LEADE)

TIME OF FLIGHT (TOF): The elapsed time in milliseconds of a bullet's flight from the muzzle to a given range.

TITANIUM NITRIDE: A hard, gold-colored coating with a low coefficient of friction sometimes applied to metal surfaces to reduce wear and corrosion and to eliminate the need for lubrication; commonly found on sizing dies and some firearm parts.

TRACER: A type of specialized military bullet that emits a colored flame from its base as it flies toward its target. Used in machine guns to allow the gunner to adjust their fire onto the target. Do not attempt to reload tracer bullets pulled from military ammunition.

TRAJECTORY: The curved flight path of the bullet from muzzle to target relative to the line of sight.

TRAJECTORY TABLE: A numerical table of data calculated or measured, showing various aspects of the downrange flight path of a projectile. (See also: BALLISTIC TABLE)

TRANSDUCER: A piezoelectric sensing device mounted in the chamber wall of a test barrel that measures a voltage directly proportional to the amount of pressure applied over an elapsed period of time. Using this data, a pressure-time curve can be calculated to determine the interior ballistic performance of a given load in great detail.

TRIPLE-BASE PROPELLANT: A double-base propellant whose energy content is further enhanced by the addition of nitroguanadine.

TUMBLING BULLET: The end-over-end rotation of an unstable projectile in flight.

TUBULAR POWDER: A smokeless propellant with elongated cylindrical granules which may have one or more longitudinal holes through them.

TUNGSTEN CARBIDE: A metal alloy of tungsten and cobalt known for its hardness and resistance to wear. Used as an insert in some handgun caliber resizing dies.

TURNED BULLET: A bullet made by turning copper or gilding metal alloy bar stock on a lathe or Swiss screw machine. They are homogenous or monolithic and contain no separate core. (See also: SWAGING)

TURRET TOOL: A type of manually operated reloading press having a turret holding several dies that can be rotated conveniently into position as needed.

TWIST RATE: The rate of turn or the pitch of the rifling in the barrel measured in the number of inches or millimeters required to rotate a bullet one complete turn.

UNIVERSAL RECEIVER: (See: PRESSURE GUN)

VELOCITY: Projectile speed at a given point along its trajectory.

VERNIER CALIPER: A precision measuring tool having sliding jaws and a graduated numerical readout in inches or millimeters.

VERTICAL DISPERSION: The maximum vertical distance in inches or millimeters on a target between two parallel *horizontal* lines: one through the uppermost bullet hole and the other through the lowermost bullet hole. (See also: DISPERSION and HORIZONTAL DISPERSION)

WADCUTTER: A type of flat nose, lead revolver bullet designed to cut a clean hole in a paper target for competition.

WEB: The integral part of a metallic, centerfire cartridge case between the bottom of the primer pocket and the interior of the case body.

WILDCAT CARTRIDGE: An experimental or non-standard cartridge.

WINDAGE: The amount of sight correction, left or right, needed to compensate for the horizontal defection of a projectile in flight caused by cross winds, sighting errors or other effects.

WIND DRIFT: The lateral deflection of a projectile in flight due to the effects of crosswinds.

WORK HARDENING: The change in grain structure and metal hardness caused by repeated flexing or stress.

WORKING-UP: Load development process used by experienced handloaders to develop safe, accurate loads.

X-RING: The small "X" or inner ring inside the bullseye or 10 ring of a paper target.

YAW: A condition in which a bullet in flight rotates around its axis at a small angle not coincident with the line of flight.

ZERO: The procedure of adjusting a firearm's sights so that the aim point coincides with the bullet's point of impact. (See also: SIGHTING-IN).

ZERO RANGE: A bullet in flight has two zero ranges: the first near the muzzle as the bullet's path *ascends* through the line of sight, and the second downrange where the bullet's path *descends* through the line of sight.

Thanks to Brett Olin for helping us gather images of his collection of past Speer Manuals; the first printing of volume one hit the presses December 1954.